Find out how Gillette builds a global management team with training in three international centers—Boston, Singapore, and London. See Chapter 5.

What happened to Mark Jorgensen when he acted ethically and reported corporate fraud? See Chapter 13.

How did the San Diego Zoo use self-managed work teams to improve coordination and customer service? See the *You Be the Manager* feature in Chapter 8.

Learn about succession planning and career development at Australia's Westpac Bank in Chapter 18.

ORGANIZATIONAL BEHAVIOR

FOURTH EDITION

ORGANIZATIONAL BEHAVIOR

UNDERSTANDING AND MANAGING LIFE AT WORK

GARY JOHNS

CONCORDIA UNIVERSITY

HarperCollinsCollegePublishers

For my parents, Bill and Jean

Acquisitions Editor: *Mike Roche*
Developmental Editors: *Vicki Cohen* and *Mimi Melek*
Supplements Editor: *Julie Zasloff*
Project Coordination and Text Design: *Thompson Steele Production Services*
Cover Design: *Judi Arisman*
Cover Illustration: *Piero Dorazio*
Photo Researcher: *Diane Kraut*
Electronic Production Manager: *Eric Jorgensen*
Manufacturing Manager: *Hilda Koparanian*
Electronic Page Makeup: *Thompson Steele Production Services*
Printer and Binder: *RR Donnelley & Sons Company*
Cover Printer: *New England Book Components, Inc.*

Organizational Behavior: Understanding and Managing Life at Work, Fourth Edition

Library of Congress Cataloging-in-Publication Data

Johns, Gary, 1946–
Organizational behavior : understanding and managing life at work
/ Gary Johns.—4th ed.
p.   cm.
Includes bibliographical references and index.
ISBN 0-673-99562-3
1. Organizational behavior. 2. Organization. 3. Management.
I. Title.
HD58.7.J6 1996
658.3—dc20   95-562
      CIP

96 97 98 9 8 7 6 5 4 3 2

BRIEF CONTENTS

CONTENTS

◆ IN FOCUS:
*Writing Style Causes
Conflict* 9

◆ YOU BE THE
MANAGER:
*Service Excellence at
Marriott International,
Inc.* 12

◆ IN FOCUS:
Becoming a Manager
19

◆ THE MANAGER'S
NOTEBOOK:
*Service Excellence at
Marriott International,
Inc.* 24

◆ IN FOCUS:
E-Mail Overload 386

◆ IN FOCUS:
*Group Decision
Making Damages TV
Quality 396*

◆ THE MANAGER'S
NOTEBOOK:
*Reframing Pizza Hut's
Problem 404*

◆ IN FOCUS:
*Empowerment at
FedEx, Rules at UPS
420*

◆ YOU BE THE
MANAGER:
*Power and Politics at
Honda 433*

PREFACE

In writing this book I have been guided by two goals. First, I wish to convey the genuine excitement inherent in the subject of organizational behavior. Second, I want the presentation of the material to have both academic and practical integrity, acknowledging the debt of the field to both behavioral science research and organizational practice. To put this another way, I wanted to develop a book that would be useful, as well as enjoyable to read, without oversimplifying key subjects on the premise that this somehow makes them easier to understand.

GENERAL CONTENT AND WRITING STYLE

Organizational Behavior, Fourth Edition, is comprehensive; the material included is authoritative and up-to-date, reflecting current research and practical concerns. Both traditional subjects (such as expectancy theory) and newer topics (such as diversity, reengineering, and total quality management) are addressed. Balanced treatment is provided to micro topics (covered in the earlier chapters) and macro topics (covered in the later chapters).

Although *Organizational Behavior* is comprehensive, I have avoided the temptation to include too many concepts, theories, and ideas. Rather than comprising a long laundry list of marginally related concepts, each chapter is organized in interlocked topics. The topics are actively interrelated and are treated in enough detail to ensure understanding. Special attention has been devoted to the flow and sequencing of the topics.

The writing style is personal and conversational. Excessive use of jargon is avoided, and important ideas are well defined and illustrated. Special attention has been paid to consistency of terminology throughout the book.

I've tried to foster critical thinking about the concepts under discussion by using devices such as asking the reader questions in the body of the text.

Believing that a well-tailored example can illuminate the most complex concept, I have used examples liberally throughout the text to clarify the points under consideration. The reader is not left wondering how a key idea applies to the world of organizations. The book is illustrated with exhibits, cartoons, and excerpts from the business press, such as *Fortune* and the *Wall Street Journal*, to enhance the flow of the material and reinforce the relevance of the examples for the student.

I have treated the subject matter generically, recognizing that organizational behavior occurs in *all* organizations. The reader will find examples, cases, "In Focus" selections, and "You Be the Manager" features drawn from a variety of settings, including large and small businesses, high technology firms, hospitals, schools, and the military. In addition, care has been taken to demonstrate that the material covered is relevant to various levels and jobs within these organizations.

ORGANIZATION

Organizational Behavior is organized in a simple but effective building-block manner. **Part One,** An Introduction, defines organizational behavior, discusses the nature of organizations, introduces the concept of management, and explains how we acquire knowledge about organizational behavior. **Part Two,** Individual Behavior, covers the topics of learning, personality, perception, attribution, diversity, attitudes, job satisfaction, and motivation. **Part Three,** Social Behavior and Organizational Processes, discusses groups, teamwork, socialization, culture, leadership, communication, decision making, power, politics, ethics, conflict, negotiation, and stress. **Part Four,** The Total Organization, considers organizational structure, environment, strategy, technology, change, innovation, and careers.

Some instructors may prefer to revise the order in which their students read particular chapters, and they can accomplish this easily. However, Chapter 6, Theories of Work Motivation, should be read before Chapter 7, Motivation in Practice. Also, Chapter 15, Organizational Structure, should be read before Chapter 16, Environment, Strategy, and Technology. The book has been designed to be used in either a quarter or semester course.

MAJOR THEMES AND NEW CONTENT

In preparing the fourth edition of *Organizational Behavior,* I concentrated on developing several themes that are current in contemporary organizational life. This development included adding new content, expanding previous coverage, and addressing the themes throughout the text to enhance integration.

The **global aspects of organizational life** have received expanded treatment in this edition to enable students to become more comfortable and more competent in dealing with people from other cultures. Major sections on this theme appear in Chapters 5, 6, and 11, which deal respectively with values, motivation, and communication. New content includes expanded coverage of implications of cultural variation for importing and exporting organizational behavior theories, appreciating global customers, and developing global employees (Chapter 5). New content is also seen in the introduction of cultural context and advice for communicating across cultures (Chapter 11). Pedagogical support for the global theme includes a number of boxed "Global Focus" features (e.g., Chapters 2, 4, 11, 16) and a "You Be the Manager" feature (Chapter 5). It also includes three experiential exercises (Chapters 5, 6, and 11) and a case study (Chapter 11).

The changing nature of workplace demographics and a need to provide a welcoming work environment for all organizational members has led to explicit coverage of **workforce diversity**. The major treatment of this topic occurs in Chapter 4 in the context of interpersonal perception and attribution. Additional treatment occurs in the context of motivation (Chapter 6), groups (Chapter 8), and careers (Chapter 18). Pedagogical support for the diversity theme can be found in "You Be the Manager" features (Chapters 1, 4, 14, and 17). We also see it in the "In Focus" selections (e.g., Chapter 14), a chapter-opening vignette (Chapter 4), an exercise (Chapter 4), and case studies (Chapters 4 and 18).

Contemporary organizations are focusing more and more on **teamwork.**
This has led to new coverage of using pay to motivate teamwork (Chapter 7)
and expanded coverage of self-managed teams and new coverage of cross-
functional teams (Chapter 8). Also, material on team building has been
updated and expanded (Chapter 17). Pedagogical backup for the teamwork
theme includes "You Be the Manager" features (Chapters 6 and 8) as well as
chapter opening vignettes (Chapters 8 and 11), an "In Focus" selection
(Chapter 8), and a case study (Chapter 8). In addition, three experiential exercises (Chapters 8, 9, and 12) discuss aspects of teamwork.

Many organizations are **reengineering,** exploiting **advanced technology,**
and experimenting with **total quality management** programs. These interrelated topics, all involving organizational change, are the focus of another
theme highlighted in this edition. New coverage of reengineering can be found
in Chapter 17 with related new coverage of downsizing in Chapter 16. Total
quality management is covered in some detail in Chapters 7 and 17. Although
principal coverage of advanced technology is seen in Chapter 16, the role of
technology in communication and decision making can also be found in
Chapters 11 and 12, where groupware, e-mail, electronic groups, electronic
brainstorming, telecommuting, and company television networks are covered
in the text or as part of various pedagogical features. Case studies focusing on
changing structure, technology, and supporting management systems are
included in Chapters 7, 15, 16, and 17.

Finally, the fourth edition of Organizational Behavior reflects the continuing role of **ethics** in organizational decision making. The major formal coverage of ethics is now included in Chapter 13 with power and politics. The
material has been expanded to cover additional causes of unethical behavior. In
addition, ethics in organizational research is discussed in Chapter 2.
Pedagogical support for the ethics theme can be found in several chapter-
opening vignettes (Chapters 1, 12, and 13), a number of "Ethical Focus" features (Chapters 6, 9, 11, 13, and 14), and an experiential exercise (Chapter 13).
Case studies are particularly good vehicles for examining the complexity surrounding ethical issues, and the cases for Chapters 1, 5, 6, 9, 13, and 18 concern explicit ethical dilemmas.

In addition to the above themes which are interwoven throughout the
book, major new coverage is included in specific locations. In Chapter 1, I present an historical overview of management, discuss what managers do, and
introduce some areas of current concern to managers. The role of personality
and disposition is covered in Chapter 3 as a prelude to additional coverage at
later points in the text. Phases of group development, including the punctuated
equilibrium model, are now found in Chapter 8. Major new coverage of conflict and negotiation is located in Chapter 14. In addition, I have included new
material on empowerment, social loafing, organizational commitment, 360
degree feedback, communication skills, cognitive biases in decision making,
network organizations, and developing a resilient career.

PEDAGOGICAL FEATURES

The fourth edition's pedagogical features are designed to complement, supplement, and reinforce the textual material. More specifically, they are designed

to promote self-awareness, critical thinking, and an appreciation of how the subject matter applies in actual organizations.

- Each chapter begins with several **Learning Objectives** to help focus the student's attention on the chapter's subject matter. This feature is new to the fourth edition.

- All chapters begin with a short **Opening Vignette** chosen to stimulate interest in the chapter's subject matter. Except for the quiz that begins Chapter 2, all of these vignettes concern real people in real organizations. Each vignette is carefully analyzed at several points in the chapter to illustrate the ideas under consideration. For example, Chapter 9 begins with a discussion of the corporate culture at the Walt Disney Company. This vignette is then used as an example at nine other points in the chapter, at pages 274, 281, 283, 284, 286, 288, 294, 296, and 297.

- In each chapter, students encounter a **"You Be the Manager"** feature that invites them to stop and reflect on the relevance of the material they are studying to a real problem in a real organization. Venues range from the San Diego Zoo (Chapter 8) to Sun Microsystems (Chapter 18). Problems range from improving customer service (Chapters 1 and 16) to fostering cultural change (Chapter 9). At the end of each chapter, **"The Manager's Notebook"** offers some observations about the problem and reveals what the organization actually did.

- All chapters contain **"In Focus," "Global Focus,"** or **"Ethical Focus"** selections that illustrate or supplement the textual material with material from the practicing management literature (e.g., *Fortune*, the *Wall Street Journal*), the research literature (e.g., the *Academy of Management Journal*), and the popular press (e.g., *Los Angeles Times*). They are chosen to exemplify real-world problems and practices as they relate to organizational behavior.

- Each chapter includes an **Experiential Exercise.** These exercises span individual self-assessment, role plays, and group activities. To increase confidence in the feedback students receive, the self-assessments generally have a research base.

- A **Case Study** is found in each chapter. The cases are of medium length, allowing great flexibility in tailoring the use of them to one's personal instructional style. I have selected cases that require active analysis and decision making, not simply passive description. Cases span important topics in contemporary organizations such as acting ethically (Chapter 1), managing diversity (Chapter 4), doing global business (Chapter 11), and introducing technological change (Chapter 16).

- Each chapter concludes with an **Executive Summary, Key Concepts,** and **Discussion Questions.** Key concepts are set in boldface type when they are discussed in the body of the text. They are also defined in the margin in a **Running Glossary** that is new to this edition.

SUPPLEMENTS FOR THE INSTRUCTOR

Instructor's Resource Book.   Written by the text author to ensure close coordination with the book, this extensive manual includes an introduction to the supplements, suggested course syllabi, and audiovisual references. It also includes chapter objectives, a chapter outline, answers to all of the text questions and cases, supplemental lecture material, video case teaching notes, and teaching notes for each chapter. In addition, material for using the experiential exercises from the Study Guide is included. New to this edition are over 300 transparency masters that are keyed to the lecture outlines, teaching notes, and case solutions.

Test Bank. Also written by the text author, this test bank includes about 1,700 questions, including a mix of factual and application questions. Multiple choice, true-false, and short answer formats are provided.

TestMaster. This computer program allows instructors to assemble their own customized tests from the items included in the test bank. If desired, the test items can be viewed on screen, edited, saved, and printed. In addition you can add questions to any test or item bank. A real time-saver, the TestMaster is available for IBM-PC and compatible personal computers.

Videos. A series of eighteen videos is available to qualified adopters of Organizational Behavior.

Electronic Transparencies. All 300 transparency masters are available in electronic form for use with IBM-PC and compatible projection systems.

Transparency Acetates. A set of 100 acetates reproducing major exhibits and original complementary material is available to qualified adopters. The set of acetates is coordinated with the transparency masters that are found in the Instructor's Resource Book.

Grades Free. Available to qualified adopters, this computerized grade-keeping and classroom management package for use on IBM-PC or compatibles maintains data for up to 200 students.

Quizmaster. This is a program for IBM-PC or compatibles that coordinates with the TestMaster test generator program. Quizmaster allows students to take timed or untimed tests created with TestMaster at the computer. Upon completing a test, a student can see his or her test score and view or print a diagnostic report that lists the topics or objectives that have been mastered or that need to be restudied. When Quizmaster is installed on a network, student scores are saved on a disk and instructors can use the Quizmaster utility program to view records and print reports for individual students, class sections, and entire courses.

SUPPLEMENTS FOR THE STUDENT

Study Guide. Written by John Usher of Memorial University, this manual contains for each chapter a self-test section with approximately 75 multiple choice, true-false, and essay questions, an expanded outline, and additional experiential exercises and cases.

Study Guide with Canadian Cases and Applications. Written by John Usher of Memorial University, this manual contains for each chapter a self-test section with approximately 75 multiple choice, true-false, and essay questions, an expanded outline, and additional experiential exercises and cases specifically designed for use with Canadian students.

The Manager's Workshop. Written by Randy Dunham of the University of Wisconsin-Madison, this widely acclaimed interactive computer simulation is the ideal supplement to a course that is using *Organizational Behavior: Understanding and Managing Life at Work*. Contact a local HarperCollins sales representative for more information regarding pricing and packaging options.

ACKNOWLEDGMENTS

Books are not written in a vacuum. In writing *Organizational Behavior, Fourth Edition*, I have profited from the advice and support of a number of individuals. This is my chance to say thank you.

First, I am grateful to my Concordia University Management Department colleagues for their interest, support, and ideas. Additionally, I would like to thank my students over the years. In one way or another, many of their questions, comments, challenges, and suggestions are reflected in the book.

In preparing for this edition, an extensive survey of the market was undertaken to determine the needs of both teachers and students in an organizational behavior course. I received extensive information through mail surveys and follow-up phone interviews that proved invaluable in crafting my ideas for this edition. I would especially like to thank the following colleagues who provided in-depth feedback on their and their students' needs:

Timothy Baldwin
Indiana University
Regina Bento
University of Baltimore
Richard Blackburn
*University of North Carolina
at Chapel Hill*
Art Brief
Tulane University
John Close
University of Wisconsin-Eau Claire
Bruce J. Eberhardt
University of North Dakota
Todd Hostager
University of Wisconsin-Eau Claire
Donald Hovey
Youngstown State University
Worth Hadley
Langston University
James L. Hall
Santa Clara University

Edyth Hargis
University of South Florida
Robert Harp
Miami University of Ohio
Thomas Head
DePaul University
Debra Hulse
University of Texas at Tyler
John M. Jermier
University of South Florida
Pamela Johnson
Miami University of Ohio
Kathy Jones
University of North Dakota
Ken Jones
Aurora University
Jeanne King
*California State University at
San Bernardino*
Wesley C. King
Miami University of Ohio

Brad Kirkman
University of North Carolina at Chapel Hill
Jacki Landau
Suffolk University
Steven M. Levy
California State University at San Bernadino
Rodney Lim
Tulane University
Kay Lovelace
University of North Carolina at Chapel Hill
Terry Lukas
Southern College of Technology
Lynne K. Madden
Aurora University
Edwin Makamson
Hampton University
Edward K. Marlow
Eastern Illinois University
Steven B. Moser
University of North Dakota
Anthony Novallie
Southern Vermont College
Preston Probasco

San Jose State University
Michelle Rabouin
Community College of Denver
Ernesto Reza
California State University at San Bernardino
Benson Rosen
University of North Carolina at Chapel Hill
Debra Shapiro
University of North Carolina at Chapel Hill
Sue Somers
Quincy College
Dana L. Stover
University of Idaho
Lee Sutherland
Suffolk University
Ted Valvoda
Lakeland Community College
Robert Vaughn
Lakeland Community College
Mark Andrew Wesolowski
Miami University of Ohio
William B. Zachary
San Jose State University

A number of colleagues in the field provided informative, thoughtful suggestions for the revision. They include:

Reviewers of *Organizational Behavior 4e*
Timothy Baldwin
Indiana University
Robert A. Beaudry
Hesser College
Hrach Bedrosian
New York University
Regina Bento
University of Baltimore
Regina Eisenbach
California State University, San Marcos
Mitch Fields
University of Windsor
Joan Finegan
University of Western Ontario
Edyth Hargis
University of South Florida

Marilyn E. Harris
Central Michigan University
Thomas Head
Tennessee State University
James K. Henderson
Kingwood College
Jeffrey S. Hornsby
Ball State University
Deborah Baker Hulse
University of Texas, Tyler
Daniel F. Jennings
Baylor University
Bradley Lane Kirkman
University of North Carolina at Chapel Hill
Ronald A. Klocke
Mankato State University
Debbie Laxer
Concordia University

Craig C. Lundberg
Cornell University
Edward K. Marlow
Eastern Illinois University
Christine McBrien
Hesser College
Jeff Mello
Golden Gate University
David T. Morgan
St. Ambrose University
C. Glenn Pearce
Virginia Commonwealth University
Karen J. Pike
Hesser College
Barbara M. Pitts
McMaster University
Marc Siegall
California State University, San Marcos

Cynthia A.M. Simerly
Lakeland Community College
Randall G. Sleeth
Virginia Commonwealth University
B. Kay Snavely
Miami University
William E. Stratton
Idaho State University
Kathleen Watson
California State University, San Marcos
Mark A. Wesolowski
Miami University
Stephen L. West
Coconino Community College
Brenda White
Saint Mary's University
Michael A. Yahr
Robert Morris College

I would also like to thank the reviewers of the previous three editions of *Organizational Behavior*:

Richard Blackburn; Allen Bluedorn; David Cherrington; Sharon Clinebell; Patricia A. Fitzgerald; Jeffrey Goldstein; David B. Greenberger; Royston Greenwood; Steven Grover; W. Clay Hamner; Eugene H. Hunt; Linda Jewell; Martha G. Juckett; Alvin M. Kelly; Ron Klocke; James McFillen; Lissa McRae; John W. Medcof; Steven B. Moser; Richard Mowday; Gerald Parselay; Lyman Porter; Raymond Read; Ben Rosen; Elizabeth Ryland; Allen J. Schuh; Yaghoub Shafi; Jonathan E. Smith; Irwin N. Talbot; Marlene Turner; Jack W. Wimer; Jeffrey D. Young.

Also, thanks to all my colleagues who have taken time to suggest ideas for the book when we have met at professional conferences. Special thanks to Lyman Porter for his ongoing advice and support.

The people at HarperCollins have provided great support for this project. In particular, I thank Michael Roche for keeping the project on track and Vicki Cohen and Jennifer Suitor for knowing when and how to do what. Also, thanks to Diane Kraut for photo research assistance and Elinor Stapleton for production assistance. In Montreal, special thanks to Sylvie Gauthier for providing order to chaos.

Gary Johns

ORGANIZATIONAL BEHAVIOR
UNDERSTANDING AND MANAGING LIFE AT WORK
FOURTH EDITION

Gary Johns
Concordia University, Montreal

ISBN 0-673-99562-3

This major revision has been made even more accessible and current by careful updating, streamlining of discussions, and reorganization of some topics for greater clarity. Furthermore, five themes—globalization, diversity, organizational change, teamwork, and ethics—are integrated throughout to better reflect the recent curriculum changes in business education and today's real business environment. *Organizational Behavior* offers a perfect balance of research, management examples, and pedagogical apparatus, making it suitable for a variety of courses and approaches. For example, boxed features that exemplify real-world problems and practices are excerpted from popular and professional publications, while various pedagogical features make the material even more approachable to students. The well-received "You Be the Manager" and "The Manager's Notebook" sections are also featured again in this edition and continue to reflect the real-world focus of the text.

The next few pages offer you a sampling of the cutting-edge coverage and pedagogical features of this exciting new edition.

ORGANIZATIONAL BEHAVIOR

UNDERSTANDING AND MANAGING LIFE AT WORK / *FOURTH EDITION*

Gary Johns

As business has become more international in scope, globalization and organizations have become more important. Globalization is one of the five central themes of this text and is demonstrated within the textual discussions as well as through *Global Focus* boxes which highlight international themes.

GLOBAL FOCUS   Human Resources Practices Need Cultural Awakening

Nancy Adler and Susan Bartholomew surveyed 50 U.S. and Canadian firms that do extensive global business. The firms' human resources practices were less than global in thrust.

In selecting future senior managers, the 50 firms ranked an outstanding overall track record as the most important criterion, with foreign business experience, demonstrated cultural sensitivity and adaptability, and a track record for outstanding performance outside the home country ranked as somewhat, but not highly, important. Moreover, foreign language skills were not considered at all important. Similarly, while considering three out of four transnational scope and process skills to be somewhat important for promotion to senior management (understanding world issues and trends; working effectively with clients and colleagues from other countries; and, demonstrating cultural sensitivity), none was considered highly important. Once again, foreign language skills were not considered important for promotion.

Fewer than one in four of the firms reported that the content of their training programs was global in focus, that they had representatives of many nations attending each program, or that their programs were designed or delivered by multinational training teams. Only four percent reported that cross-cultural training was offered to all managers.

In reviewing foreign assignments, the 50 firms report using expatriates primarily to "get the job done abroad," not to develop the organization, nor to develop the individual manager's career. Given their emphasis on getting the immediate job done, it is not surprising that they did not report

consistently selecting the "stars" (either high potential junior managers or very senior, top-performing executives) for expatriate positions. To increase globalization in their development programs, the surveyed executives strongly recommended "transferring different nationalities to different countries several times in their career" and "making it clear to these employees that international assignments are important to career

Many organizations are involved in the modification and management of attitudes. Dow Chemical, for example, offers diversity and family issues training programs to reinforce positive attitudes.

development." However, to date, the majority of the surveyed firms do not have such recommended programs in place.

Source: Excerpted from Adler, N.J., & Bartholomew, S. (1992, August). Managing globally competent people. *Academy of Management Executive*, 52–65.

As you proceed through the text, you will encounter further discussion about the impact of cultural values on organizational behavior. Now, let's examine attitudes and see how they are related to values.

WHAT ARE ATTITUDES?

An **attitude** is a fairly stable emotional tendency to respond consistently to some specific object, situation, person, or category of people. First, notice that _____ ns directed toward *specific* targets. If I inquire about _____ boss, you will probably tell me something about _____. This illustrates the emotional aspect of attitudes. _____ ore specific than values, which dictate only broad

Attitude. A fairly stable emotional tendency to respond consistently to some specific object, situation, person, or category of people.

Diversity—Local and Global

The demographics of the North American work force are changing. Contributing to this is the increased movement of women into paid employment as well as immigration patterns. In the past decade, the minority population in California grew by 61 percent. In Canada, visible minorities are the fastest growing segment of the population. Native-born Caucasian North Americans frequently find themselves working with people whose ethnic backgrounds are very different from their own.

Diversity of age is also having an impact in organizations. As a simple example, perhaps you have observed people of various ages working in fast food restaurants that were at one time staffed solely by young people. Both the re-entry of retired people into the workforce and the trend to remove vertical layers in organizations have contributed to much more intergenerational contact in the workplace than was common in the past. So has the rapid promotion of young technical experts in jobs where knowledge is more critical than long experience.

Diversity is also coming to the fore as many organizations realize that they have not treated certain segments of the population, including women, gays, and the disabled, fairly in many aspects of employment and that organizations have to be able to get the best from everyone in order to be truly competitive. Although legal pressures (such as the Americans with Disabilities Act and the Family Leave Act) have contributed to this awareness, general social pressure, especially from customers and clients, has also done so.

Finally, diversity issues are having increased impact as organizations go global. Multinational expansion, strategic alliances, and joint ventures increasingly require employees and managers to come into contact with their counterparts from other cultures. Although many of these people have an

International managers must adapt to cross-cultural differences to successfully interact with potential clients and overseas affiliates.

Another of Johns' five themes is diversity in the workplace and how to manage it. The theme is woven throughout the fourth edition to explain the changing nature of workplace demographics and a need to provide a welcoming work environment for all organizational members.

Downsizing

A reduction in work force size, popularly called downsizing, has been an organizational trend of the 1980s and 1990s. During this period, millions of jobs have disappeared as organizations seek to bolster efficiency and cut costs in an era of global competition, government deregulation, corporate raiding, changing consumer preferences, and advancing technologies.[42] We have discussed this topic in passing earlier in the book. For example, the "In Focus: Does Downsizing Decrease Motivation?" (Chapter 6) considered how poorly executed downsizing can damage employee motivation. Here, I want to concentrate on some structural aspects of downsizing.

Downsizing and Structure.   Downsizing might be formally defined as the intentional reduction in workforce size with the goal of improving organizational efficiency or effectiveness.[43] Notice that this definition does not imply that the organization's fortunes are necessarily in decline, although a shrinking market could motivate downsizing. In fact, Compaq Computer announced substantial downsizing during a year of record revenues and shipments in anticipation of the need to be more competitive in the future.[44]

How should downsizing affect organizational structure? It is tempting to "work backwards" through Exhibit 15–11 and simply say that as size decreases the firm should reduce its complexity, centralize, and become less formalized. In the case of a very simple downsizing, this logic might work.

...zing became a popular way of trying to reduce ...mproving organizational efficiency. IBM ...team to achieve these effects.

DESIGNING EFFECTIVE WORK TEAMS

The double-edged nature of group cohesiveness suggests that a delicate balance of factors dictates whether a workgroup is effective or ineffective. In turn, this raises the idea that organizations should pay considerable attention to how workgroups are designed and managed. At first, the notion of designing a workgroup might seem strange. After all, don't workgroups just "happen" in response to the demands of the organization's goals or technology? While these factors surely set some limits on how groups are organized and managed, organizations are finding that there is still plenty of scope for creativity in workgroup design.

A good model for thinking about the design of effective workgroups is to consider a successful sports team, whether professional or amateur. In most cases, such teams are small groups made up of highly skilled individuals who are able to meld these skills into a cohesive effort. The task they are performing is intrinsically motivating and provides very direct feedback. If there are status differences on the team, the basis for these differences is contribution to the team, not some extraneous factor. The team shows an obsessive concern with obtaining the right personnel, relying on tryouts or player drafts, and the team is "coached" not supervised. With this informal model in mind, let's examine the concept of group effectiveness more closely.

J. Richard Hackman of Harvard University (co-developer of the Job Characteristics Model, Chapter 7) has written extensively about workgroup effectiveness.[49] According to Hackman, a workgroup is effective when (1) its physical or intellectual output is acceptable to management and to the other parts of the organization that use this output, (2) group members' needs are satisfied rather than frustrated by the group, and (3) the group experience enables members to continue to work together.

What leads to group effectiveness? In colloquial language, we might say "sweat, smarts, and style." More formally, Hackman notes that group effectiveness occurs when high effort is directed toward the group's task, when great knowledge and skill are directed toward the task, and when the group adopts sensible strategies for accomplishing its goals. And just how does an organization achieve this? As with XEL Communications, there is growing awareness in many organizations that the answer is **self-managed work teams.** Although the exact details vary tremendously, such teams generally provide their members with the opportunity to do challenging work under reduced supervision. Other labels that we often apply to such groups are autonomous, semiautonomous, and self-regulated. The general idea, which is more important than the label, is that the groups tend to regulate much of their own members' behavior.

Critical to the success of self-managed teams are the nature of the task, the composition of the group, and various support mechanisms.[50] Notice that many of the suggestions that follow should improve coordination and discourage social loafing.

Self-managed work teams. Work groups that have the opportunity to do challenging work under reduces supervision.

Tasks for Self-Managed Teams

Experts agree that tasks assigned to self-managed work teams should be complex and challenging, requiring high interdependence among team members for accomplishment. In general, these tasks should have the qualities of

---

ETHICAL FOCUS BOXES

The fifth integrated theme is the role of ethics in making organizational decisions, including the additional causes of unethical behavior as well as ethics in organizational research. This important topic is integrated within the textual discussion as well as highlighted in *Ethical Focus* boxes which provide real-world examples.

ETHICAL FOCUS   Is Integrity Testing Ethical?

How would you like to apply for a job and be asked to take a written test that purported to measure your honesty? This is a more and more common occurrence in North American organizations. Estimates suggest that there are somewhere around 5 million integrity tests administered in the U.S. each year. This testing stems directly from an increasing concern about employee theft and fraud and indirectly from the passage of the Employee Polygraph Protection Act. This act, which effectively prohibits the use of electronic "lie detectors" for selection, prompted increased research into the use of written integrity tests. These tests, much cheaper to administer, have been embraced by many more businesses. There are two basic kinds of integrity tests. Some are straightforward measures of attitudes toward dishonesty that may also ask about past dishonest acts. Surprisingly, faking of responses does not seem to be a serious problem. Other integrity tests are less overt in purpose, because they measure personality characteristics such as conscientiousness and reliability. A careful and comprehensive review by Deniz Ones, Chockalingam Viswesvaran, and Frank Schmidt concludes that integrity tests are valid predictors of work behavior. Although relationships with theft per se are small, the tests do a pretty good job of predicting a broader class of counterproductive behaviors that includes theft, absenteeism, substance abuse, property damage, and so on. But are such tests ethical? Some observers have criticized the tests on the grounds of invasion of privacy. However, Dan Dalton and Michael Metzger take a different viewpoint. They argue that such tests are ethically questionable because they generate many "false positives," labeling people dishonest who are not dishonest. All tests make such classification errors, but they contend that integrity tests are especially prone because true dishonesty is fairly uncommon, and rare events are hard to predict. They further argue that the unfairly rejected applicant is unlikely to be told the true reason due to fear of legal problems.

What do you think about the ethics of integrity testing? Remember, they do predict counterproductive behavior despite the classification errors.

Sources: Ones, D. S., Viswesvaran, C., & Schmidt, F. L. (1993). Comprehensive meta-analysis of integrity test validities: Findings and implications for personnel selection and theories of job performance. Journal of Applied Psychology, 78, 679-703; Dalton, D. R., & Metzger, M. B. (1992). "Integrity testing" for personnel selection: An unsparing perspective. Journal of Business Ethics, 12, 147-156.

CHAPTER 5

VALUES, ATTITUDES, AND JOB SATISFACTION

...ZATIONS

...son & Johnson subsidiary that was responsible for ...vely withdrew the product from the market after ...it were discovered. Subsequent to this, Copley ...ed for acting slowly to recall tainted drugs, and ...oth charged with obscuring negative side effects in ... How can we account for the apparent difference ...cisions that underpinned these actions?

...cs can be defined as systematic thinking about the ...sions. Moral consequences can be framed in terms ...o any stakeholders in the decision. Stakeholders are ...side of the organization who have a potential to be ...is could range from the decision makers themselves ...' Ethics is a major branch of philosophy, and no ...describe the various schools of ethical thought. ...he kinds of ethical issues that organizational deci-...of the factors that stimulate unethical decisions.

Armed with a $5 correspondence course in ice cream making obtained from Penn State, Ben Cohen and Jerry Greenfield opened their ice cream shop in a former gas station in Burlington, Vermont, in 1978. By 1981, a Time cover story decreed Ben & Jerry's the best ice cream in the world. Ben & Jerry's Homemade Inc. is now headquartered in Waterbury, Vermont, and employs around 400 people. It is one of the state's most popular tourist attractions.

BEN & JERRY'S HOMEMADE INC.

CHAPTER-OPENING VIGNETTES

Real-world *chapter-opening vignettes* stimulate interest in the chapter's subject matter and bring concepts to life by applying them to actual situations in real companies. Each vignette is then used as an example throughout the chapter.

LEARNING OBJECTIVES

AFTER READING CHAPTER 5 YOU SHOULD BE ABLE TO:

◆ DEFINE VALUES AND DISCUSS THE IMPLICATIONS OF CROSS-CULTURAL VARIATION IN VALUES FOR ORGANIZATIONAL BEHAVIOR.

◆ DEFINE ATTITUDES AND EXPLAIN HOW PEOPLE DEVELOP AND CHANGE ATTITUDES.

◆ EXPLAIN THE CONCEPT OF JOB SATISFACTION AND DISCUSS SOME OF ITS KEY CONTRIBUTORS.

◆ DISCUSS THE ROLES OF DISCREPANCY, FAIRNESS, AND DISPOSITION IN PROMOTING JOB SATISFACTION.

◆ OUTLINE THE VARIOUS CONSEQUENCES OF JOB SATISFACTION AND EXPLAIN THE RELATIONSHIP BETWEEN JOB SATISFACTION AND MENTAL HEALTH, ABSENTEEISM, TURNOVER, PERFORMANCE, AND ORGANIZATIONAL CITIZENSHIP BEHAVIOR.

LEARNING OBJECTIVES

New to this edition are chapter-opening *Learning Objectives* which direct students to the central concepts to be covered in the chapter. These objectives are revisited in the Executive Summary at the end of the chapter.

THE WEYERHAEUSER TRUCK

YOU BE THE Manager

Drivers Weyerhaeuser Company is a large forest products firm headquartered in Tacoma, Washington. Weyerhaeuser faced a problem that commonly crops up in production operations: the underutilization of expensive resources. The problem centered on truck drivers who hauled logs from the forest to a company sawmill. The drivers, who also loaded the trucks, were unionized and paid on an hourly basis. Management determined that the trucks were averaging only about 60 percent of their legal weight capacity. This extreme underloading was very undesirable, because extra trucks, extra drivers, and extra diesel fuel were necessary to transport a given amount of timber. Management was convinced that it could improve the situation if drivers could be motivated to pay more attention to their loading procedures. Because logs differ in diameter and length, a full load could vary between 60 and 120 logs. Thus, drivers had to exercise judgment in the loading process. Although a scale was available at the loading point, drivers didn't seem to be making good use of it.

> MAGAGEMENT AND DRIVERS AT THE WEYERHAEUSER COMPANY HAD TO WORK TOGETHER TO SOLVE AN EXPENSIVE PROBLEM: THE UNDER-UTILIZATION OF RESOURCES.

1. As a manager, what would you do to improve truck utilization? Remember, you don't want to encourage loading over the legal limit. What are the pros and cons of using a monetary incentive to improve the loading process?

2. What are the pros and cons of using goal setting to improve the loading process?

To find out what Weyerhaeuser did, see The Manager's Notebook at the end of the chapter.

Source: Adapted from Latham, G. P., & Locke, E. (1979, Autumn). Goal setting a motivational technique that works. Organizational Dynamics, 68-80; Latham, G. P., & Baldes, J. J. (1975). The practical significance of Locke's theory of goal setting. Journal of Applied Psychology, 60, 122-124. Photo 7.6]

YOU BE THE MANAGER BOXES

You Be the Manager boxes invite students to solve a problem based on events in an actual organization, providing them with "hands-on" experience from the business world.

The Manager's Notebook — The Weyerhaeuser Truck Drivers

In theory, a monetary incentive could certainly get the drivers' attention and motivate them to haul heavier loads. In practice, however, unions have not shown great enthusiasm for such incentives (especially when they are given individually), and management might balk at paying drivers extra for what they should already be doing. Also, a financial incentive could encourage overloading, and it will require an expensive system to record weights and calculate bonuses.

Weyerhaeuser chose goal setting. With the union's cooperation, drivers were assigned a specific, challenging performance goal of loading their trucks to 94 percent of legal weight capacity.

Before setting this goal, management simply asked drivers to do their best to maximize their weight. The results? Over the first several weeks, load capacity gradually increased to over 90 percent and remained at this high level for seven years! In the first nine months alone, company accountants conservatively estimated the savings at $250,000. These results were achieved without driver participation in setting the goal and without monetary incentives for goal accomplishment. Drivers evidently found the 94 percent goal motivating in and of itself; they frequently recorded their weights in informal competition with other drivers.

THE MANAGER'S NOTEBOOK FEATURES

The decisions of the organizations' real managers are then provided for comparison in *The Manager's Notebook* section at the end of each chapter.

THE CONCEPT OF ORGANIZATIONAL CHANGE

Common experience indicates that organizations are far from static. Our favorite small restaurant experiences success and expands. We return for a visit to our alma mater and observe a variety of new programs and new buildings. The local Chevy dealer also begins to sell Geos. As consumers, we are aware that such changes may have a profound impact on our satisfaction with the product or service offered. By extension, we can also imagine that these changes have a strong impact on the people who work at the restaurant, university, or car dealership. In and of themselves, such changes are neither good nor bad. Rather, it is the way in which the changes are implemented and managed that is crucial to both customers and members. This is the focus of the present chapter.

Why Organizations Must Change

All organizations face two basic sources of pressure to change—external sources and internal sources.

In Chapter 16 it was pointed out that organizations are open systems that take inputs from the environment, transform some of these inputs, and send them back into the environment as outputs. Most organizations work hard to stabilize their inputs and outputs. For example, a manufacturing firm might use a variety of suppliers to avoid a shortage or raw materials and attempt to turn out quality products to ensure demand. However, there are limits on the extent to which such control over the environment can occur. In this case, environmental changes must be matched by organizational changes if the organization is to remain effective. For example, consider the successful producer of record turntables in 1970. In only a few years, the turntable market virtually disappeared with the advent of reasonably priced cassette and CD

IN FOCUS BOXES

Chosen to exemplify real-world problems and practices as they relate to organizational behavior, *In Focus* boxes illustrate or supplement textual discussion with practicing-management literature (i.e., *Fortune, The Wall Street Journal*) current research literature (i.e., the *Academy of Management Journal*), and the popular press (i.e., *Los Angeles Times*).

 IN FOCUS   Organizational Learning

Dr. Matthew J. Kiernan, chairman of the Innovest Group International describes the concept of organizational learning: In the twenty first century, the case for the "learning organization," with knowledge creation as its primary strategic task, will be overwhelming. Organizational learning will replace control as the dominant responsibility and test of senior management and leadership. It requires, first of all, an organizational culture which exalts above all else continuous improvement and innovation from everybody, and which embraces change rather than fearing and seeking to minimize it.

Successful firms of the next century (and, increasingly, even of this one) will also have to have feedback and data-gathering instruments, such as MIS and performance measurement systems, which are capable of delivering strategically relevant information—ie, qualitative as well as quantitative—to the right people, and in real time. Performance measurement is absolutely fundamental to organizational learning. If one has little or no idea how successful one's last marketplace intervention has been, or why, the prospects for learning very much of use to the next project are slim indeed.

One important technique for maximizing organizational learning from the business environment is bench marking best practices; not only those of direct competitors but of anyone from whom something useful can be learned or adapted. Yet another potentially useful but grossly under used instrument for gathering strategic intelligence is the training and deployment of the firm's "front-line troops" (delivery, sales, repair, and secretarial staff, bank tellers and the like) as incredibly fertile sources of customer feedback and market information. A third tech-

nique is the strategic use of temporary personnel assignments and rotations—not only between departments but even with suppliers, customers, and strategic alliance partners.

Organizational learning also has major implications for strategic human resource management. For starters, the company's attitude to training needs to change substantially to embrace life-long learning for everyone, and to stress group rather than individual learning experiences. The content of the training programs has to change too, placing far greater emphasis on the "soft" process skills of managing change, innovation and learning, and less on seeking to implant hard "factual" knowledge, which has an increasingly short half-life.

Perhaps most difficult of all, organizational learning also means surfacing and re-examining all of those inarticulate assumptions about the firm and its business environment which, while never explicitly scrutinized or even acknowledged, drive much of what the firm actually does. Thus, organizational learning is about more than simply acquiring new knowledge and insights; it is also crucial (and arguably more difficult) to un-learn the old ones when they have outlived their relevance. Rigorously rooting out these obsolescent assumptions and challenging them can expose critical discrepancies between external reality and the firm's internal mental models, and it is these gaps which provide much of the creative tension and dynamic energy which drives organizational learning.

Source: Excerpted from Kiernan, M. J. (1993, February). The new strategic architecture: Learning to compete in the twenty-first century. Academy of Management Executive, 7-21, pp. 9, 10.

EXECUTIVE SUMMARY

◆ Perception involves interpreting the input from our senses to provide meaning to our environment, and any instance of perception involves a perceiver, a target, and a situational context. The experience, needs, and emotions of the perceiver affect perception, as does the ambiguity of the target.

Bruner's model of the perceptual process suggests that we are very receptive to cues provided by the target and the situation when we encounter an unfamiliar target. However, as we discover familiar cues, we quickly categorize the target and process other cues to maintain a consistent and constant picture of the target. When the target is a person, this drive for constancy and consistency is revealed in a number of specific perceptual biases, including primacy, recency, implicit personality theory, reliance on central traits, projection, and stereotyping. Gender, age, race, and ethnic stereotypes are especially problematic for organizations.

◆ Attribution is the process of assigning causes or motives to people's behavior. The observer is often interested in determining whether the behavior is due to dispositional (internal) or situational (external) causes. Behavior is likely to be attributed to the dis-

position of the actor when the behavior (1) is performed consistently, (2) differs from that exhibited by other people, and (3) occurs in a variety of situations or environments. An opposite set of cues will prompt a situational attribution. Observers are biased toward making dispositional attributions, while actors are more likely to explain their own behavior in situational terms, especially when its outcomes are unfavorable.

◆ The changing nature of the workplace has highlighted the advantages of valuing and managing employee diversity. Organizations can use a number of tactics, including training, to combat stereotypes that threaten diversity efforts.

◆ Judging the suitability of job applicants in an interview and appraising job performance are especially difficult perceptual tasks, in part because the target is motivated to convey a good impression. In addition, interviewers and performance raters exhibit a number of perceptual tendencies that are reflected in inaccurate judgments, including contrast effects, leniency, harshness, central tendency, halo, and similar-to-me effects.

KEY CONCEPTS

Perception
Perceptual defense
Primacy effect
Recency effect
Central trait
Implicit personality theory
Projection
Stereotyping
Attribution
Dispositional attributions
Situational attributions
Consistency cues

Consensus cues
Distinctiveness cues
Fundamental attribution error
Actor-observer effect
Self-serving bias
Workforce diversity
Contrast effects
Leniency
Harshness
Central tendency
Halo effect
Similar-to-me effect

DISCUSSION QUESTIONS

1. Discuss how differences in the experiences of students and professors might affect their perceptions of students' written work and class comments.

2. Discuss the occupational stereotypes that you hold of computer programmers, the clergy, truck drivers, bartenders, and bankers. How do you think

---

END-OF-CHAPTER MATERIAL

Each chapter concludes with an *Executive Summary, Key Concepts,* and *Discussion Questions.* The *Executive Summary* is directly linked to the Learning Objectives and provides answers to the questions posed there. *Key Concepts* alert students to the more important topics in the chapter and discussion questions stimulate the students' critical-thinking ability.

END-OF-CHAPTER CASES

These medium-length cases allow great flexibility in tailoring their use to the instructor's personal teaching style. These selected cases require students to actively analyze and apply their decision-making skills by spanning important, high-interest topics in contemporary organizations, such as acting ethically, managing diversity, conducting global business, and introducing technological change.

CASE STUDY
ACCOUNTING FOR FAILURE

It had been a long two years, but Nancy Koharski had at last gained some peace of mind. She was struck with the irony of how the same company that acted as a consultant to help other firms increase productivity and employee morale could be so blind to its own problems.

COMPANY BACKGROUND

Berry, Hepworth & Associates (BH&A) is a large regional accounting firm headquartered in Calgary. Over 125 professionals work at the Calgary office, and additional branch offices are located in Edmonton, Red Deer, and Regina. BH&A is the dominant audit firm in the region, and has earned a solid reputation in bank auditing and management information systems. The company was founded in the 1940s, and has experienced tremendous growth in recent years.

BH&A is divided into four departments: Commercial Audit, Healthcare, Financial Institutions Audit Group (FIAG), and the Management Information Systems Group. The latter is composed mainly of computer programmers, but incudes two psychologists who consult with clients on organizational behavior issues. Among the audit staff it is informally recognized that Commercial Audit is the best department in terms of clientele and working conditions, but opportunities are limited due to a large number of staff. The bank audits performed by FIAG are widely seen as boring and therefore undesirable, and the FIAG staff are quietly referred to as "nerds" and "brown-nosers." However, it is acknowledged that FIAG does offer a good career path, as banks constitute a significant portion of BH&A's business. In fact, because they are so terribly overworked, FIAG actively recruits (in effect, forces) BH&A people into the department.

All new staff persons are first assigned to Commercial Audit; the "choice" to specialize is made after a year or so of experience. There is no direct supervisor responsible for any particular person's training and development. Instead, the manager or "in-charge" on a particular assignment is responsible for helping the new "junior" on the job. While the in-charge is required to provide a verbal review after each assignment, focusing on areas for improvement, these are seldom provided. Every six months, a formal performance appraisal is held. In preparation, review forms are completed anonymously by everyone in the firm. Each junior can review in-charges and managers, who in turn evaluate the juniors.

Scheduling for jobs is, according to company policy, unbiased: juniors are to be assigned to upcoming jobs purely on a rotational basis. No in-charge can request that a particular junior be placed or withheld from a job.

THE WORKING ENVIRONMENT

BH&A is a very conservative firm. Most of the partners come from small towns or rural environments. Among the entire professional staff at Calgary, there is only one divorcee, fewer than 10 smokers, and one "possible" homosexual. The older members of the firm believe that while the firm has grown, it has not sacrificed the positive qualities it enjoyed as a smaller firm, including company loyalty and pride.

Chartered accounting at BH&A is structured to be competitive. More staff are hired each year than is necessary. It is commonly understood that one must outperform one's peers to survive. The six-month review is especially dreaded because BH&A tends to fire the two lowest ranked juniors – despite assurances that the firm will retain newcomers at least until they have met the two-year requirement for the Chartered Accountant license. Juniors are apprehensive about the anonymous comments because they figure prominently in the review process, and yet juniors are unable to defend themselves against unknown sources. Numerous juniors reported being afraid to open a small envelope that appeared unexpectedly during review time: the envelopes in fact contained the employee's income tax statement. Much gallows humor can be heard around review time, and juniors tend to develop a real sense of comradeship.

The high performance expectations of BH&A appear to have given rise to a "martyr complex," a curious blend of masochism and machoism. Ulcers and other stress-related illnesses are seen as evidence of hard work and status symbols. Numerous complaints are made about long working hours, but in reality these are boasts about how hard one is working. Overtime statistics are kept informally and compared among co-workers as if they were baseball statistics. FIAGs are particularly notorious for this sort of behavior. Calling in sick is not acceptable as it is seen as a sign of weakness and lack of dedication. One manager was in a car accident and taken to the hospital with a concussion. He returned to work that afternoon wearing the hospital bandage around his head.

It is understood that people must prove their loyalty by working very hard for years on end. The ultimate payoff is elevation to partnership. Currently, there are only 35 partners dividing the profits of one of the top accounting firms in the region. The monetary reward should be great indeed for those who survive.

EXPERIENTIAL EXERCISE
WOMEN IN BUSINESS

The following items are an attempt to assess the attitudes people have about women in business. The statements cover many different and opposing points of view; you may find yourself agreeing strongly with some of the statements, disagreeing just as strongly with others, and perhaps uncertain about others.

Using the numbers from 1 to 7 on the rating scale, mark your personal opinion about each statement in the blank that immediately precedes it. Remember, give your personal opinion according to how much you agree or disagree with each item.

```
1 = Strongly Disagree      5 = Slightly Agree
2 = Disagree               6 = Agree
3 = Slightly Disagree      7 = Strongly Agree
4 = Neither Disagree nor Agree
```

1. _____ It is less desirable for women than men to have a job that requires responsibility.

2. _____ Women have the objectivity required to evaluate business situations properly.

3. _____ Challenging work is more important to men than it is to women.

4. _____ Men and women should be given equal opportunity for participation in management training programs.

5. _____ Women have the capability to acquire the necessary skills to be successful managers.

6. _____ On the average, women managers are less capable of contributing to an organization's overall goals than are men.

7. _____ It is not acceptable for women to assume leadership roles as often as men.

8. _____ The business community should someday accept women in key managerial positions.

9. _____ Society should regard work by female managers as valuable as work by male managers.

10. _____ It is acceptable for women to compete with men for top executive positions.

11. _____ The possibility of pregnancy does not make women less desirable employees than men.

12. _____ Women would no more allow their emotions to influence their managerial behavior than would men.

13. _____ Problems associated with menstruation should not make women less desirable than men as employees.

14. _____ To be a successful executive, a woman does not have to sacrifice some of her femininity.

15. _____ On the average, a woman who stays at home all the time with her children is a better mother than a woman who works outside the home at least half time.

16. _____ Women are less capable of learning mathematical and mechanical skills than are men.

17. _____ Women are not ambitious enough to be successful in the business world.

18. _____ Women cannot be assertive in business situations that demand it.

19. _____ Women possess the self-confidence required of a good leader.

20. _____ Women are not competitive enough to be successful in the business world.

21. _____ Women cannot be aggressive in business situations that demand it.

The scale you have just completed is the Women as Managers Scale (WAMS). It measures your attitudes toward women assuming managerial roles. To score your WAMS, subtract your responses to each of the following items from 8: 1, 3, 6, 7, 15, 16, 17, 18, 20, 21. For example, if you put 3 for item 1, give yourself a 5 (8 minus 3). Then, simply add up your resulting responses to all 21 items. Your score should fall somewhere between 21 and 147. The higher the score, the more favorable are your attitudes toward women as managers.

One study of 1,014 university business students and 602 managers reported the following WAMS averages: Male managers = 111; female managers = 128; male students = 103; female students = 130.[58] A more recent study showed that experienced human resources managers had a much more favorable attitude toward women as managers than university students did. The managers scored around 130, while the students scored around 79.[59] In a third study, conducted in an electronics manufacturing company, women managers scored an average of 128 while men scored 106. In this study, those who had more favorable attitudes toward women as managers also had more favorable attitudes toward blacks as managers.[60]

To facilitate discussion, the instructor might have students write their WAMS score and their sex on pieces of paper. Working in groups and using calculators, the class can compute the class average, the male average, and the female average.

END-OF-CHAPTER EXPERIENTIAL EXERCISES

Developed to improve students' self-understanding, interpersonal skills, and group work, these exercises include individual self-assessments, role plays, and group activities.

AN INTRODUCTION

AFTER READING CHAPTER 1 YOU SHOULD BE ABLE TO:

1 DEFINE ORGANIZATIONS AND DESCRIBE THEIR BASIC CHARACTERISTICS.

2 EXPLAIN THE CONCEPT OF ORGANIZATIONAL BEHAVIOR AND DESCRIBE THE GOALS OF THE FIELD.

3 CONTRAST THE CLASSICAL VIEWPOINT OF MANAGEMENT WITH THAT WHICH THE HUMAN RELATIONS MOVEMENT ADVOCATED.

4 DESCRIBE THE CONTEMPORARY CONTINGENCY APPROACH TO MANAGEMENT.

5 EXPLAIN WHAT MANAGERS DO—THEIR ROLES, ACTIVITIES, AGENDAS FOR ACTION, AND THOUGHT PROCESSES.

6 DESCRIBE THE SOCIETAL AND GLOBAL TRENDS THAT ARE SHAPING CONTEMPORARY MANAGEMENT CONCERNS.

A CLIP FROM THE NBC SEGMENT "WAITING TO EXPLODE" SHOWS A GM PICKUP TRUCK EXPLODING INTO FLAMES. WHAT MOTIVATED NBC TO RIG THE EXPLOSION?

ORGANIZATIONAL BEHAVIOR AND MANAGEMENT

DETROIT *In an unprecedented and meticulously detailed attack, General Motors Corp. sued NBC charging defamation, and publicly accused the network of rigging a test crash of GM pickup trucks on its Dateline news program. The announcement of the lawsuit, General Motors' (GM) first defamation suit ever, was the first public action in what The Wall Street Journal described as "the most humiliating episode of crow-eating in the nearly four-decade history of NBC News." The suit stemmed from an episode of the NBC television news program Dateline. That episode showed a car ramming a full-sized GM pickup truck in its side, causing the truck to explode in a ball of flames. NBC staged the crash to illustrate an alleged consumer*

GM TRUCK
EXPLODES,
NBC NEWS
BADLY
INJURED

safety defect in the older GM pickup trucks—gas tanks that were vulnerable to side impact collisions. The story was entitled "Waiting to Explode."

TV producers often simulate or recreate events to obtain footage when film of actual events is unavailable. However, sharp-eyed observers, including GM officials, noted something unusual about the staged accident. There were small flashes of fire below the pickup *before* the car hit it. General Motors launched an investigation that subsequently resulted in the lawsuit for defamation. It charged that NBC News had rigged the demonstration by setting off a series of toy model rocket engines just before the collision, thus ensuring an explosion and fire upon impact. Who could imagine that toys would cause so much trouble for NBC?

The publicly announced lawsuit shocked NBC executives. It was accompanied by a GM boycott on advertising on NBC News. Prior to the announcement, GM had sent letters to NBC, but NBC News President Michael Gartner was not informed of the problem until it was near full crisis. Gartner, a former newspaper editor and columnist, had presided over radical cost-cutting measures at NBC News, measures that along with the success of shows such as *Dateline*, finally made the news division profitable. NBC personnel variously described Gartner's management style as frosty, aloof, and prickly.

When NBC top managers saw the evidence, they knew they had to act. Three months after "Waiting to Explode" was shown, *Dateline* hosts Jane Pauley and Stone Phillips apologized on *Dateline* to GM and to viewers for the rocket fiasco, although NBC stood by the rest of the story. NBC also agreed to reimburse GM $2 million in investigation costs. In turn, GM dropped the lawsuit and reinstituted its advertising.

About three weeks later, Michael Gartner resigned from NBC. Two weeks after this, following an independent investigation that Gartner initiated, three top executives involved with the truck incident were fired—Jeff Diamond, executive producer of *Dateline*; David Rummel, senior producer; and Robert Read, producer of the GM episode. Diamond and Read were veteran TV newspeople previously recruited from ABC's *20/20*.

In the aftermath of the events, there was much discussion about the erosion of journalistic values in the face of stiff competition among seven prime time newsmagazines. Some observers alleged that the quest for ratings was resulting in "tabloid television." Even the journalistic establishment, which often closes ranks in the face of threat, found nothing to defend in this incident.[1]

■

What we have here is a slice of worklife—just what this book is about. Admittedly, this slice of worklife is more dramatic than most in that it concerns questions of judgment, leadership, and ethics. Still, the question remains: How could so many talented people have made such a big mistake? This book will help you uncover answers to this question.

In this chapter we will define organizations and organizational behavior and examine its relationship to management. We'll explore historical and contemporary approaches to management and consider what managers do and how they think. The chapter concludes with some issues of concern to contemporary managers.

WHAT ARE ORGANIZATIONS?

This book is about what happens in organizations. **Organizations** are social inventions for accomplishing common goals through group effort. General Motors and NBC News are obviously organizations, but so are the Chicago Bulls, the Sierra Club, Pearl Jam, and a college sorority or fraternity.

Organizations. Social inventions for accomplishing common goals through group effort.

Social Inventions

When we say that organizations are social inventions we mean that their essential characteristic is the coordinated presence of *people*, not necessarily things. General Motors owns a lot of things, such as factories, equipment, and offices. However, you are probably aware that through advanced information technology and contracting out work some contemporary organizations make and sell computers or clothes without owning much of anything. Also, many service organizations, such as consulting firms, have little physical capital. Still, these organizations have people, people who present both opportunities and challenges. *The field of organizational behavior is about understanding people and managing them to work effectively.*

Goal Accomplishment

Individuals are assembled into organizations for a reason. The organizations mentioned above have the very basic goals of selling cars, delivering news, and winning basketball games. Nonprofit organizations have goals such as saving souls, promoting the arts, helping the needy, or educating people. Virtually all

There are a variety of different organizations in which individuals work together to accomplish goals through group effort. Though the motivation of Greenpeace may differ from that of ACT UP, both groups strive for survival and goal accomplishment.

A football team is an organization that accomplishes common goals through team effort.

organizations have *survival* as a goal. Despite this, consider the list of organizations that have failed to survive: Eastern Airlines, Gimbel's, Child World, and a ton of U.S. savings and loan companies. *The field of organizational behavior is concerned with how organizations can survive and adapt to change.* Certain behaviors are necessary for survival and adaptation. People have to

- be motivated to join and remain in the organization;
- carry out their basic work reliably, in terms of productivity, quality, and service;
- be flexible and innovative.[2]

The field of organizational behavior is concerned with all of these basic activities. Innovation and flexibility, which provide for adaptation to change, are especially important for contemporary organizations. Management guru Tom Peters has gone so far as to advise firms to "Get Innovative or Get Dead."[3] General Motors has explored new forms of manufacturing and management in its Saturn organization. Under Michael Gartner, NBC News developed an innovative 24-hour-a-day news feed for affiliated stations.

Group Effort

The final component of our definition of organizations is that they are based on group effort. At its most general level, this means that organizations depend on interaction and coordination among people to accomplish their goals. Much of the intellectual and physical work done in organizations is quite literally performed by groups, whether they are permanent work teams or short-term project teams, such as the one that produced the NBC segment "Waiting to Explode." Also, informal grouping occurs in all organizations, because friendships develop and individuals form informal alliances to accomplish work. The quality of this informal contact in terms of communication and morale can have a strong impact on goal achievement. For all of these reasons, *the field of organizational behavior is concerned with how to get people to practice effective teamwork.*

Now that we've reviewed the basic characteristics of organizations, let's look more directly at the meaning and scope of organizational behavior.

WHAT IS ORGANIZATIONAL BEHAVIOR?

Organizational behavior. The attitudes and behaviors of individuals and groups in organizations.

Organizational behavior refers to the attitudes and behaviors of individuals and groups in organizations. The discipline of organizational behavior systematically studies these attitudes and behaviors and provides insight about effectively managing and changing them. It also studies how organizations can be structured more effectively and how events in their external environments affect organizations. Those who study organizational behavior are interested in attitudes—how satisfied people are with their jobs, how committed they feel to the goals of the organization, or how supportive they are of promoting of women or minorities into management positions. Behaviors like cooperation, conflict, innovation, resignation, or ethical lapses are important areas of study in the field of organizational behavior.

Using an organizational behavior perspective reconsider the GM/NBC vignette that opened the chapter. The immediate question is: *Why did these events happen?* Although we won't answer this question directly, we can pose some subsidiary questions highlighting some of the topics that the field of organizational behavior covers and that we will explore in later chapters.

- Why didn't NBC anticipate GM's aggressive response to the *Dateline* segment? People selectively perceive information when they deal with threatening events. Chapter 4 will explore the perceptual process.

- What motivated the *Dateline* NBC story team to rig the truck with the rockets? Motivation is a key concept in organizational behavior, and it will be covered extensively in Chapters 6 and 7.

- Why didn't someone inside NBC "blow the whistle" on the truck-rigging incident before GM protested? Cohesive groups are able to exact a high degree of conformity from their members. This process will be covered in Chapters 8 and 9.

- Who was in charge at NBC News? Was there a leadership problem? As you will learn in Chapter 10, the field of organizational behavior has a longstanding interest in leadership.

- Why wasn't Michael Gartner informed about the GM correspondence until it was too late? This is a problem in upward communication, and communication will be the focus of Chapter 11.

- Many people were involved in making the decision to rig the truck. How did so many people manage to make a questionable decision? Sometimes people in groups make successful decisions and sometimes they make costly mistakes. Chapter 12 will explore the dynamics of group decision making.

- Was rigging the truck unethical behavior? Why and how ethical lapses occur in organizations is something we consider throughout the text; however we put particular emphasis on it in Chapter 13.

- How did the highly competitive TV ratings environment contribute to the events in the case? How the external environment affects what happens in organizations is the focus in Chapter 16.

These questions provide a good overview of some issues those in the field of organizational behavior study. Accurate answers to these questions would go a long way toward explaining why the events in the vignette transpired and suggesting a future course of management action. Analysis followed by action is what organizational behavior is all about.

WHY STUDY ORGANIZATIONAL BEHAVIOR?

Why should you attempt to read and understand the material in *Organizational Behavior*?

Organizational Behavior Is Interesting

At its core, organizational behavior is interesting because it is about people and human nature. How could so many experienced, capable people have made the mistakes that contributed to the *Dateline* fiasco? This question is interesting—even if you don't care about pickup trucks or network TV—because these people apparently acted against their own best self-interest. This seems counterintuitive. We'll try to understand other examples of counterintuitive behavior throughout the text. For example, why do organizations often commit more and more resources to failing products or strategies?

Organizational behavior includes interesting examples of success as well as failure. Later in the text, we will study a company that has to bar employees from starting work too early (Lincoln Electric), a company with a committee dedicated to fun in the workplace (Ben & Jerry's Homemade Ice Cream), and a company that fought its way back from the edge of extinction (Harley-Davidson). All of these companies are extremely successful, and organizational behavior helps explain why.

Organizational behavior doesn't have to be exotic to be interesting. Anyone who has negotiated with a recalcitrant bureaucrat or had a really excellent boss has probably wondered what made them behave the way they did. Organizational behavior provides the tools to find out why.

For an interesting example of organizational behavior, see the "In Focus: *Writing Style Causes Conflict*."

Organizational Behavior Is Important

Looking through the lens of other disciplines, it would be possible to frame the GM/NBC case as a problem in law, marketing, public relations, or media studies. Notice, however, that underlying all of these perspectives, it was *still* a problem in organizational behavior. What happens in organizations often has a profound impact on people. At NBC news, four talented managers lost their jobs and two prominent media people had to apologize for something that they didn't personally do. It's clear that the impact of organizational behavior doesn't stop at the walls of the organization. The consumers of an organization's products and services are also affected, as were the viewers of *Dateline* who were exposed to the dubious crash video. Thus, organizational behavior is important to managers, employees, and consumers; and understanding it can make us more effective managers, employees, or consumers.

We sometimes fail to appreciate that there is tremendous variation in organizational behavior. For example, skilled salespeople in insurance or real estate make many, many more sales than some of their peers. Similarly, for every Green Peace or Sierra Club, there are dozens of failed organizations that were dedicated to saving the environment. The field of organizational behavior is concerned with explaining these differences and using the explanations to improve organizational effectiveness and efficiency.

Finally, there is growing awareness that "people problems" and opportunities are at the core of organizational failure and success, and students need to be better prepared in this domain. An influential study by the American Assembly of Collegiate Schools of Business concluded:

> Corporate respondents showed an overwhelming preponderance of opinion that behaviorally oriented subject matter should receive more attention in the curriculum. Deans and faculty members themselves perceive a gap between how much "soft" skills and personal characteristics are currently emphasized in the curriculum versus how much they "should be." Also, and perhaps most important, the corporate sector gives business school graduates relatively low ratings in terms of the strength (or lack thereof) of their leadership and interpersonal skills.[4]

IN FOCUS   Writing Style Causes Conflict

DEARBORN, Mich. A police corporal was suspended and ordered to undergo psychiatric evaluation because he writes the number seven with a line through the down stroke.

Brian Yinger said he tried to break the habit when he was ordered to six months ago but was brought before a department disciplinary board when he forgot while writing some reports.

"The way he was writing them was confusing for the typist," said Police Chief Robert Deziel. "He defied the order to stop. He was told he would face disciplinary action."

The board suspended Yinger without pay for three days. He was also ordered by Deziel to undergo psychiatric evaluation to determine whether the old sevens are out of his system.

"I've been making these sevens for 30 years," said Yinger, who returned to work Thursday after his suspension. "I've never had a problem before."

He said he fears the incident might hurt his career and cost him a promotion to sergeant, and he is considering a lawsuit.

The dispute could end up costing the city nearly $4,000 in transcripts, arbitration fees and back pay, union and police officials estimated.

Deziel said the matter "will be time-consuming for the city . . . but it's worth it."

Sgt. Gary Pushee, president of the Police Officers Association of Dearborn, called it "the weirdest case I've ever seen."

Who is correct in this situation, Corporal Yinger or Chief Deziel? How do incidents such as this influence organizational effectiveness?

Source: *The Gazette* (Montreal) November 7, 1992, p. A12. (Associated Press).

GOALS OF THE FIELD

Like any discipline, the field of organizational behavior has a number of commonly agreed upon goals. Chief among these are effectively predicting, explaining, and managing behavior that occurs in organizations. For example, in Chapter 7 we'll discuss the factors that predict which reward systems are most effective in motivating employees. Then, we will explain the reasons for this effectiveness and describe how managers can implement effective reward systems.

Predicting Organizational Behavior

Predicting the behavior of others is an essential requirement for everyday life, both inside and outside of organizations. Our lives are made considerably easier by the ability to anticipate when our friends will get angry, when our professors will respond favorably to a completed assignment, and when salespeople and politicians are telling us the truth about a new product or the state of the nation. In organizations, there is considerable interest in predicting when people will make ethical decisions, create innovative products, or engage in sexual harassment.

The very regularity of behavior in organizations permits the prediction of its future occurrence. However, as we'll see in the next chapter, untutored predictions of organizational behavior are not always as accurate. Through systematic study, the field of organizational behavior provides a scientific foundation that helps improve predictions of organizational events.

Reconsider the opening vignette on the GM truck explosion. What factors might have predicted the ethically questionable rigging of the truck explosion? As Chapter 13 will illustrate, intense competition among organizations is one factor that predicts unethical behavior, and the oversupply of newsmagazine shows and the TV ratings race are good examples of this. But why did this happen at NBC and not at other networks? For a more specific prediction, we would have to look at factors in addition to extreme competition that are associated with ethical lapses.

Had NBC been able to predict the *Dateline* fiasco, it would have been better equipped to deal with the crisis. As it was, even GM's tough response was unexpected. With planning, it might have been possible to prevent the whole event if one knew the conditions under which it might happen. Of course, being able to predict organizational behavior does not guarantee that we can explain the reason for the behavior and develop an effective strategy to manage it. This brings us to the second goal of the field.

Explaining Organizational Behavior

Another goal of organization behavior is explanation of events in organizations—why do they occur? Prediction and explanation are not synonymous. Ancient societies were capable of predicting the regular setting of the sun but were unable to explain where it went or why it went there. In general, accurate prediction precedes explanation. Thus, the very regularity of the sun's disappearance gave some clues about why it was disappearing.

Organizational behavior is especially interested in determining why people are more or less motivated, satisfied, or prone to resign. Explaining events is more complicated than predicting them. For one thing, a particular behavior could have multiple causes. People may resign their jobs because they are dissatisfied with their pay, because they are discriminated against, or because they have failed to respond appropriately to an organizational crisis. Obviously, the last reason is the most likely explanation for Michael Gartner's resignation from NBC. An organization that finds itself with a "turnover problem" is going to have to find out why this is happening before it can put an effective correction into place. This behavior could have many different causes, each of which would require a specific solution. Furthermore, explanation is also complicated by the fact that the underlying causes of some event or behavior can change over time. For example, the reasons people quit may vary greatly depending upon the overall economy and whether there is high or low unemployment in the field in question.

In the next chapter we will discuss some factors that interfere with accurately explaining organizational behavior. Throughout the book, we'll consider material that should improve your grasp of organizational behavior. The ability to understand behavior is a necessary prerequisite for effectively managing it.

Managing Organizational Behavior

Management. The art of getting things accomplished in organizations through others.

Management is defined as the art of getting things accomplished in organizations. Managers acquire, allocate, and utilize physical and human resources to accomplish goals.[5] The definition doesn't include a prescription about how to get things accomplished. As we proceed through the text, you will learn that a variety of management styles might be effective depending on the situation at hand. Despite his "prickly" and "frosty" style, Michael Gartner moved NBC News from red ink to profitability. It is likely, though, that this style inhibited subordinates from letting him know sooner about the brewing crisis with GM.

If behavior can be predicted and explained, it can often be controlled or managed. That is, if we truly understand the reasons for high quality service, ethical behavior, or anything else, we can often take sensible action to manage it effectively. If prediction and explanation constitute analysis, then management constitutes action. Unfortunately, we see all too many cases in which managers act without analysis, looking for a quick fix to problems. The result is often disaster. The point isn't to overanalyze a problem. Rather, it is to approach a problem with a systematic understanding of behavioral science.

Now that we've covered predicting, explaining, and managing organizational behavior, let's apply this knowledge. Read the case about Marriott International in the *You Be the Manager* feature and answer the questions. At the end of the chapter, find out what Marriott did in *The Manager's Notebook*. This is not a test, but rather an exercise to improve critical thinking, analytical skills, and management skills. Pause and reflect on these application features as you encounter them in each chapter.

EARLY PRESCRIPTIONS CONCERNING MANAGEMENT

For many years, experts interested in organizations were concerned with prescribing the "correct" way to manage an organization to achieve its goals. There were two basic phases to this prescription, which experts often call the classical view and the human relations view. A summary of these viewpoints will illustrate how the history of management thought and organizational behavior developed.

The Classical View and Bureaucracy

Most of the major advocates of the classical viewpoint were experienced managers or consultants who took the time to write down their thoughts on organizing. For the most part, this activity occurred in the early 1900s. The classical writers acquired their experience in military settings, mining operations, and factories that produced everything from cars to candy. Prominent names include Henri Fayol, General Motors executive James D. Mooney, and consultant Lyndall Urwick.[6] Although exceptions existed, the **classical viewpoint** tended to advocate a very high degree of specialization of labor and a very high degree of coordination. Each department was to tend to its own affairs, with centralized decision making from upper management providing coordination. To maintain control, the classical view suggested that managers have fairly few subordinates, except for lower-level jobs, where machine pacing might substitute for close supervision.

Frederick Taylor (1856–1915), the father of Scientific Management, was also a contributor to the classical school, although he was mainly concerned with job design and the structure of work on the shop floor.[7] Rather than

Classical viewpoint. An early prescription on management that advocated high specialization of labor, intensive coordination, and centralized decision making.

Marriott International is a successful service organization specializing in lodging and food service. Its empire includes accommodations that suit various budgets and tastes (Marriott Hotels, Resorts, and Suites, Courtyard, Residence Inn, Fairfield Inn) and institutional food services (in schools, hospitals, and businesses). Industry analysts often point to Marriott's financial skills and savvy strategic marketing as keys to its success. However, people management skills are equally important, especially in its hotel operations. Marriott management set an extremely ambitious strategic goal for its hotel operations—to be the provider of choice—in other words, the hotel people think of when they are traveling for business or pleasure. Management realized that only employees with a true commitment to customer service could enable Marriott to reach this goal. This meant hiring and retaining the very best personnel. At the same time, the company was aware that its traditional hiring pool of 18- to 25-year-olds was shrinking in size, while an older and more culturally diverse work force offered some excellent opportunities for recruiting. To compete with other firms for the very best personnel, Marriott also set a goal to become the employer of choice—that is, the place the best people want to work. But how can it do this? *You* be the manager.

> MARRIOT KNOWS THAT SUCCESS IN THE HOSPITALITY INDUSTRY DEPENDS UPON ITS EMPLOYEES AND THEIR COMMITMENT TO CUSTOMER SERVICE.

1. What predictions has Marriott made and what explanations are required to decide on a course of action?

2. What are some management actions that might enable Marriott to become an employer of choice?

To find out what Marriott did, see *The Manager's Notebook* at the end of the chapter.

Source: Adapted from Ulrich, D., & Lake. D. (1991, February). Organizational capability: Creating competitive advantage. *Academy of Management Executive*, 77–92.

Scientific Management. Frederick Taylor's system for using research to determine the optimum degree of specialization and standardization of work tasks.

informal "rules of thumb" for job design, Taylor's **Scientific Management** advocated the use of careful research to determine the optimum degree of specialization and standardization. Also, he supported the development of written instructions that clearly defined work procedures, and he encouraged supervisors to standardize workers' movements and breaks for maximum efficiency. Taylor even extended Scientific Management to the supervisor's job, advocating "functional foremanship," whereby supervisors would specialize in particular functions. For example, one might become a specialist in training workers, while another might fulfill the role of a disciplinarian.

The practicing managers and consultants had an academic ally in Max Weber (1864–1920), the distinguished German social theorist. Weber made the term bureaucracy famous by advocating it as a means of rationally managing complex organizations. During Weber's lifetime, managers were certainly in need of advice. In this time of industrial growth and development, most management was by intuition, and nepotism and favoritism were rampant. According to Weber, a **bureaucracy** has the following qualities:

Bureaucracy. Max Weber's ideal type of organization that included a strict chain of command, detailed rules, high specialization, centralized power, and selection and promotion based on technical competence.

- A strict chain of command in which each member reports to only a single superior.
- Criteria for selection and promotion based on impersonal technical skills rather than nepotism or favoritism.
- A set of detailed rules, regulations, and procedures ensuring that the job gets done regardless of who the specific worker is.
- The use of strict specialization to match duties with technical competence.
- The centralization of power at the top of the organization.[8]

Weber saw bureaucracy as an "ideal type" or theoretical model that would standardize behavior in organizations and provide workers with security and a sense of purpose. Jobs would be performed as intended rather than following the whims of the specific role occupant; in exchange for this conformity, workers would have a fair chance of being promoted and rising in the power structure. Rules, regulations, and a clear-cut chain of command that further clarified required behavior provided the workers' sense of security.

Even during this period, some observers, such as the "business philosopher" Mary Parker Follett (1868–1933), noted that the classical view of management seemed to take for granted an essential conflict of interest between managers and employees.[9] This sentiment found expression in the human relations movement.

The Human Relations Movement and a Critique of Bureaucracy

The human relations movement generally began with the famous **Hawthorne studies** of the 1920s and 1930s.[10] These studies, conducted at the Hawthorne plant of Western Electric near Chicago, began in the strict tradition of industrial engineering. They were concerned with the impact of fatigue, rest pauses, and lighting on productivity. However, during the course of the studies, the researchers (among others, Harvard University's Elton Mayo and Fritz Roethlisberger and Hawthorne's William J. Dickson) began to notice the effects of psychological and social processes on productivity and work adjustment. This impact suggested that there could be dysfunctional aspects to how work was organized. One obvious sign was resistance to management through strong informal group mechanisms like norms that limited productivity to less than management wanted.

After World War II, a number of theorists and researchers, who were mostly academics, took up the theme begun at Hawthorne. Prominent names included Chris Argyris, Alvin Gouldner, and Rensis Likert. The **human relations movement** called attention to certain dysfunctional aspects of classical management and bureaucracy and advocated more people-oriented styles of management that catered more to the social and psychological needs of employees. This critique of bureaucracy addressed several specific problems:

- Strict specialization is incompatible with human needs for growth and achievement.[11] This can lead to employee alienation from the organization and its clients.
- Strong centralization and reliance upon formal authority often fail to take advantage of the creative ideas and knowledge of lower-level members, who are often closer to the customer.[12] As a result, the organization

Hawthorne studies. Research conducted at the Hawthorne plant of Western Electric in the 1920s and 1930s that illustrated how psychological and social processes affect productivity and work adjustment.

Human relations movement. A critique of classical management and bureaucracy that advocated management styles that were more participative and oriented toward employee needs.

will fail to learn from its mistakes, which threatens innovation and adaptation. Resistance to change will occur as a matter of course.

- Strict, impersonal rules lead members to adopt the minimum acceptable level of performance that the rules specify.[13] If a rule states that employees must process at least eight claims a day, eight claims will become the norm, even though higher performance levels are possible.

- Strong specialization causes employees to lose sight of the overall goals of the organization.[14] Forms, procedures, and required signatures become ends in themselves, divorced from the true needs of customers, clients, and other departments in the organization. This is the "red-tape mentality" that we sometimes observe in bureaucracies.

Obviously, not all bureaucratic organizations have these problems. However, they were common enough that human relations advocates and others began to call for the adoption of more flexible systems of management and the design of more interesting jobs. They also advocated open communication, more employee participation in decision making, and less rigid, more decentralized forms of control.

CONTEMPORARY MANAGEMENT—THE CONTINGENCY APPROACH

How has the apparent tension between the classical approach and the human relations approach been resolved? First, contemporary scholars and managers recognize the merits of both approaches. The classical advocates pointed out the critical role of control and coordination in getting organizations to achieve their goals. The human relationists pointed out the dangers of certain forms of control and coordination and addressed the need for flexibility and adaptability. Second, as we will study in later chapters, contemporary scholars have learned that management approaches need to be tailored to fit the situation. For example, we would generally manage a payroll department more bureaucratically than a research and development department. Getting out a payroll every week is a routine task with no margin for error. Research requires creativity that is fostered by a more flexible work environment.

Reconsider the eight questions we posed earlier about the NBC/GM incident. Answering these questions is not an easy task, partly because human nature is so complex. This complexity means that an organizational behavior text can't be a "cookbook." In what follows, you will not find formulas to improve job satisfaction or service quality with one cup of leadership style and two cups of group dynamics. We have not discovered a simple set of laws of organizational behavior that you can memorize and then retrieve when necessary to solve any organizational problem. It is this "quick fix" mentality that produces simplistic and costly management fads and fashions.[15]

There is a growing body of research and management experience to help sort out the complexities of what happens in organizations. However, the general answer to many of the questions we will pose in the following chapters is: "It depends." Which leadership style is most effective? This depends on the characteristics of the leader, those of the people being led, and what the leader is trying to achieve. Will an increase in pay lead to an increase in performance? This depends on who is getting the increase and the exact reason for the increase. These dependencies are called contingencies. The **contingency approach** to man-

Contingency approach. An approach to management that recognizes that there is no one best way to manage, and that an appropriate management style depends on the demands of the situation.

agement recognizes that there is no one best way to manage; rather, an appropriate style depends on the demands of the situation. Thus, the effectiveness of a leadership style is contingent on the abilities of followers and the consequence of a pay increase is partly contingent on the need for money. Contingencies illustrate the complexity of organizational behavior and show why we should study it systematically. Throughout the text we will discuss organizational behavior with a contingency approach in mind.

WHAT DO MANAGERS DO?

Organizational behavior isn't just for managers or aspiring managers. As we noted earlier, a good understanding of the field can be useful for consumers or anyone else who has to interact with organizations or get things done through them. Nevertheless, many readers of this text have an interest in management as a potential career. Managers can have a strong impact on what happens in and to organizations. They both influence and are influenced by organizational behavior, and the net result can have important consequences for organizational effectiveness.

There is no shortage of texts and popular press books oriented toward what managers *should* do. However, the field of organizational behavior is also concerned with what really happens in organizations. Let's look at several research studies that explore what managers *do* do. This provides a context for appreciating the usefulness of understanding organizational behavior.

Managerial Roles

Canadian management theorist Henry Mintzberg conducted an in-depth study of the behavior of several managers.[16] The study earned him a Ph.D. from MIT in 1968. In Chapter 2 we will discuss how he conducted the study and some of its more basic findings. Here, however, we're concerned with Mintzberg's discovery of a rather complex set of roles played by the managers: figurehead, leader, liaison, monitor, disseminator, spokesperson, entrepreneur, disturbance handler, resource allocator, negotiator. These roles are summarized in Exhibit 1.1.

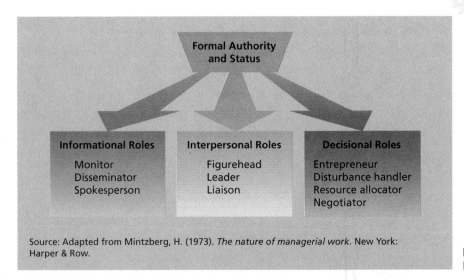

Source: Adapted from Mintzberg, H. (1973). *The nature of managerial work*. New York: Harper & Row.

EXHIBIT 1.1
Mintzberg's managerial roles.

Interpersonal Roles.   Interpersonal roles are expected behaviors that have to do with establishing and maintaining interpersonal relations. In the *figurehead role*, the manager serves as a symbol of his or her organization rather than an active decision maker. Examples of the figurehead role are making a speech to a trade group, entertaining clients, or signing legal documents. In the *leadership role*, the manager selects, mentors, rewards, and disciplines subordinates. In the *liaison role*, the manager maintains horizontal contacts inside or outside the organization. This might include discussing a project with a colleague in another department or touching base with an embassy delegate of a country where one hopes to do future business.

Informational Roles.   These roles are concerned with various ways the manager receives and transmits information. In the *monitor role* the manager scans the internal and external environments of the firm to follow current performance and keep informed of new ideas and trends. For example, the head of Research and Development might attend a professional engineering conference. In the *disseminator role*, managers send information on both facts and preferences to others. For example, the R&D head might summarize what she learned at the conference in an electronic mail message for subordinates. The *spokesperson role* concerns mainly sending messages into the organization's external environment, for example, drafting an annual report to stockholders or giving an interview to the press.

Decisional Roles.   The final set of managerial roles Mintzberg discussed deals with decision making. In the *entrepreneur role* the manager turns problems and opportunities into plans for improved changes. This might include suggesting a new product or service that will please customers. In the *disturbance handler role* the manager deals with problems stemming from subordinate conflict and addresses threats to resources and turf. In the story that began the chapter, NBC News management did not handle this role very effectively. In their *resource allocation roles*, managers decide how to deploy time, money, personnel, and other critical resources. Finally, in their *negotiator roles*, managers conduct major negotiations with other organizations or individuals. The agreement hammered out between GM and NBC about the apology and dropping the lawsuit is a good example of management's negotiation role.

Of course, the relative importance of these roles will vary with management level and organizational technology.[17] First level supervisors do more disturbance handling and less figureheading. Still, Mintzberg's major contribution to organizational behavior is to highlight the *complexity* of the roles managers are required to play and the variety of skills they require for effectiveness, including leadership, communication, and negotiation. His work also illustrates the complex balancing act managers face when they must play different roles for different audiences. A good grasp of organizational behavior is at the heart of acquiring these skills and performing this balancing act.

Managerial Activities

Fred Luthans, Richard Hodgetts, and Stuart Rosenkrantz studied the behavior of a large number of managers in a variety of different kinds of organizations.[18] They determined that the managers engaged in four basic types of activities:

- *Routine communication.* This includes the formal sending and receiving of information (as in meetings) and handling paperwork.
- *Traditional management.* Planning, decision making, and controlling are the primary types of traditional management.
- *Networking.* Networking consists of interacting with people outside of the organization and informal socializing and politicking with insiders.
- *Human resource management.* This includes motivating and reinforcing, disciplining and punishing, managing conflict, staffing, and training and developing subordinates.

Exhibit 1.2 summarizes these managerial activities and shows how a sample of 248 managers divided their time and effort, as determined by research observers (discipline and punishment were done in private and were not open to observation). Perhaps the most striking observation about this figure is how all of these managerial activities involve dealing with people.

One of Luthans' and colleagues' most fascinating findings is how emphasis on these various activities correlated with managerial success. If we define success as moving up the ranks of the organization quickly, networking proved to be critical. The people who were promoted quickly tended to do more networking (politicking, socializing, and making contacts) and less human resource management than the averages in Exhibit 1.2. If we define success in terms of unit effectiveness and subordinate satisfaction and commitment, the more successful managers were those who devoted more time and effort to human resource management and less to networking than the averages in the exhibit. A good understanding of organizational behavior should help you to manage this tradeoff more effectively, reconciling the realities of organizational politics with the demands of accomplishing things through others.

Note: Figures do not total 100% due to rounding.

Source: Adapted from Luthans, F., Hodgetts, R.M., & Rosenkrantz, S.A. (1988). *Real managers.* Cambridge, MA: Ballinger.

EXHIBIT 1.2
Summary of managerial activities.

Managerial Agendas

John Kotter studied the behavior patterns of a number of successful general managers.[19] Although he found some differences among them, he also found a strong pattern of similarities that he grouped into the categories of agenda setting, networking, and agenda implementation.

Agenda Setting.   Kotter's managers all gradually developed agendas of what, given their positions, they wanted to accomplish for the organization. Many began these agendas even before they assumed their positions. These agendas were almost always informal and unwritten, and they were much more concerned with "people issues" and less numerical than most formal strategic plans. The managers based their agendas on wide ranging informal discussions with a wide variety of people.

Networking.   Kotter's managers established a wide formal and informal network of key people both inside and outside of their organizations. Insiders included peers, subordinates, and bosses, but they also extended to these people's subordinates and bosses. Outsiders included customers, suppliers, competitors, government officials, and the press. This network provided managers with information and established cooperative relationships relevant to their agendas. Formal hiring, firing, and reassigning shaped the network, but so did informal liaisons in which they created dependencies by doing favors for others.

Agenda Implementation.   The managers used networks to implement the agendas. They would go *anywhere* in the network for help—up or down, in or out of the organization. In addition, they employed a wide range of influence tactics, from direct orders to subtle language and stories that conveyed their message indirectly.

John Kotter's research of successful business managers showed that exemplary managers practice agenda setting, networking, and agenda implementation. Michael Dell, of Dell Computers, is an example of such a manager.

IN FOCUS   Becoming a Manager

What is the process of becoming a manager? Harvard Business School professor Linda Hill conducted an in-depth, year-long study of 19 new managers who had been promoted from sales and customer accounts positions. Although Hill determined most had made a successful transition, these individuals nevertheless found the year filled with ambiguity, conflict, and inconsistency. The new managers' initial expectations emphasized the rights and privileges of the job—power, control, and accountability. What they really hadn't anticipated were the "people management" demands involved in supervising and coordinating others. Hill notes ironically that because these people received promotions as a result of their own high motivation and technical skills, they sometimes had trouble dealing with less-talented subordinates. The problem was magnified because people skills were not often criteria for promotion. Most of the new managers found the transition from doer to manager difficult and could not resist the temptation to revert to a subordinate role. For example, they would continue to go on sales calls with their people. The new managers viewed building good subordinate relationships as their most difficult task. A critical factor was how the managers reacted to mistakes; an unduly critical reaction was sure to lead subordinates to mistrust the manager. The new managers also had to learn the difference between being liked by subordinates and being respected. They found that making exceptions for individuals to gain their favor usually backfired. Over time, the managers' strategies shifted from gaining control over subordinates to gaining their commitment. This was necessary as they recognized the real limits on their own power and authority.

Source: Adapted from Hill, L. A. (1992). *Becoming a manager: Mastery of a new identity.* Boston: Harvard Business School Press.

The theme that runs through Kotters's findings is the high degree of informal interaction and concern with people issues that were necessary for the managers to achieve their agendas. To be sure, the managers used their formal organizational power, but they often found themselves dependent upon people over whom they wielded no power. An understanding of organizational behavior helps to recognize and manage these realities.

Both Mintzberg and Kotter studied experienced managers. For a look at the trials of becoming a new manager, see Linda Hill's findings in the "In Focus: *Becoming a Manager.*"

Managerial Minds

In contrast to how managers act, the focus of the previous section, Herbert Simon and Daniel Isenberg have both explored how managers think.[20] Although they offer a wealth of observations, we will concentrate here on a specific issue that each examined in independent research—managerial intuition.

Some people think that organizational behavior and its implications for management are just common sense. Obviously, however, this doesn't account for incidents such as the apparent failure of common sense exhibited by the NBC executives in the truck fiasco. The next chapter will demonstrate that organizational behavior isn't just common sense. Nevertheless, careful observers of successful managers have often noted that intuition seems to guide many of their actions. Isenberg's research suggests that experienced managers use intuition in several ways:

- to sense that a problem exists;
- to perform well-learned mental tasks rapidly (e.g., sizing up a written contract);

- to synthesize isolated pieces of information and data;

- to doublecheck more formal or mechanical analyses ("Do these projections look correct?").

Does the use of intuition mean that managerial thinking is random, irrational, or undisciplined? Both Simon and Isenberg say no. In fact, both strongly dispute the idea that intuition is the opposite of rationality or that intuitive means unanalytical. Rather, good **intuition** is problem identification and problem solving based on a long history of systematic education and experience that enables the manager to locate problems within a network of previously acquired information. The theories, research, and management practices that we cover in organizational behavior will contribute to your own information net and give you better managerial intuition about problems like the reaction of General Motors to the disclosure of the rigged crash test.

Intuition. Problem identification and solving based on systematic education and experiences that locate problems within a network of previously acquired information.

International Managers

The research we discussed above describes how managers act and think in North America. Would managers in other global locations act and think the same way? Up to a point, the answer is probably yes. After all, we are dealing here with some very basic managerial behaviors and thought processes. However, the style with which managers do what they do and the emphasis given to various activities will vary greatly across cultures because of cross-cultural variations in values that affect both managers' and subordinates' expectations about interpersonal interaction. Thus, in Chapter 6 we will study cross-cultural differences in motivation and in Chapter 11 we will explore how communication varies across cultures.

Geert Hofstede has done pioneering work on cross-cultural differences in values that we will study in Chapter 5. Hofstede provides some interesting observations about how these value differences promote contrasts in the general role that managers play across cultures.[21] He asserts that managers are

International managers must adapt to cross-cultural differences to successfully interact with potential clients and overseas affiliates.

cultural heroes and even a distinct social class in North America, where individualism is treasured. In contrast, Germany tends to worship engineers and have fewer managerial types. In Japan, managers are required to pay obsessive attention to group solidarity rather than star subordinates. In the Netherlands, managers are supposed to exhibit modesty and strive for consensus. In the family-run businesses of Taiwan and Singapore, "professional" management, North American-style, is greatly downplayed.

The contrasts that Hofstede raises are fascinating because the technical requirements for accomplishing goals are actually the same across cultures. It is only the *behavioral* requirements that differ. Thus, national culture is one of the most important contingency variables in organizational behavior. The appropriateness of various leadership styles, motivation techniques, and communication methods depends on where one is in the world.

SOME CONTEMPORARY MANAGEMENT CONCERNS

To conclude the chapter, we will examine briefly a few issues with which managers are currently concerned. As with previous sections, our goal is to illustrate how the field of organizational behavior can help you understand and manage these issues.

Diversity—Local and Global

The demographics of the North American work force are changing. Contributing to this is the increased movement of women into paid employment, as well as immigration patterns. In the past decade, the minority population in California grew by 61 percent.[22] In Canada, visible minorities are the fastest growing segment of the population.[23] Native-born Caucasian North Americans frequently find themselves working with people whose ethnic backgrounds are very different from their own.

Diversity of age is also having an impact in organizations. As a simple example, perhaps you have observed people of various ages working in fast food restaurants that were at one time staffed solely by young people. Both the re-entry of retired people into the workforce and the trend to remove vertical layers in organizations have contributed to much more intergenerational contact in the workplace than was common in the past. So has the rapid promotion of young technical experts in jobs where knowledge is more critical than long experience.[24]

Diversity is also coming to the fore as many organizations realize that they have not treated certain segments of the population, such as women, gays, and the disabled, fairly in many aspects of employment and that organizations have to be able to get the best from *everyone* in order to be truly competitive. Although legal pressures (such as the Americans with Disabilities Act and the Family Leave Act) have contributed to this awareness, general social pressure, especially from customers and clients, has also done so.

Finally, diversity issues are having increased impact as organizations "go global." Multinational expansion, strategic alliances, and joint ventures increasingly require employees and managers to come into contact with their counterparts from other cultures. Although many of these people have an interest in North American consumer goods and entertainment, it is naive to assume that business values are rapidly converging on some North American model.

What does diversity have to do with organizational behavior? The field has long been concerned with stereotypes, conflict, cooperation, and teamwork. These are just some of the factors that managers must manage effectively for organizations to benefit from the considerable opportunities that a diverse workforce affords.

Morale Crisis?

Downsizing, restructuring, and reengineering have had a profound effect on North American and European organizations in the past ten years or so. Companies such as General Motors, Mercedes Benz, IBM, and Digital Equipment each have laid off thousands of workers. These companies have eliminated high paying manufacturing jobs and once-secure middle management jobs because of increased global competition and advanced technology.

Surveys suggest that the consequence of these events has been decreased morale and shifting loyalties among the survivors. While people remain attached to the work they do, they are much less attached to their employers. A survey by the Families and Work Institute found that 57 percent of respondents strongly agreed that they always tried to do their jobs well, but only 28 percent strongly agreed that they would work harder to help their employer succeed.[25] Other results from this survey are shown in Exhibit 1.3. As you can see, open communication and impact on family life have become critical factors in job choice, much more important than salary or company size. Another survey by Hay Research for Management found a marked decrease in the attitudes of middle managers toward their employing firms.[26]

The field of organizational behavior offers many potential solutions to such morale problems. To take just one example, research shows that a remarkable number of organizations failed to adequately communicate their plans to either the victims or the survivors of restructuring.[27] Communication is an important topic in organizational behavior, and we'll study it.

Most observers feel that the forces that led to restructuring have ended the days of joining an organization in one's 20s and staying there until retirement.

EXHIBIT 1.3
Factors that influence job choice.

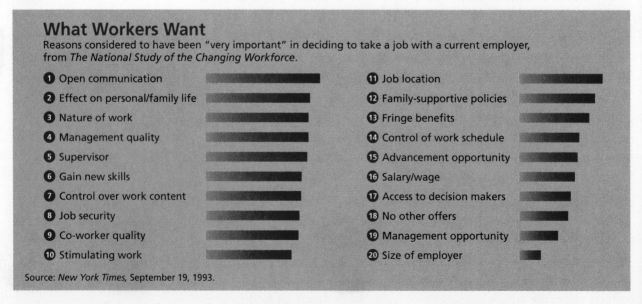

What Workers Want

Reasons considered to have been "very important" in deciding to take a job with a current employer, from *The National Study of the Changing Workforce*.

1. Open communication
2. Effect on personal/family life
3. Nature of work
4. Management quality
5. Supervisor
6. Gain new skills
7. Control over work content
8. Job security
9. Co-worker quality
10. Stimulating work
11. Job location
12. Family-supportive policies
13. Fringe benefits
14. Control of work schedule
15. Advancement opportunity
16. Salary/wage
17. Access to decision makers
18. No other offers
19. Management opportunity
20. Size of employer

Source: *New York Times*, September 19, 1993.

A succession of jobs with a succession of employers, going where one's skills are needed, is an increasingly common scenario. This means that people will have to look out for their own careers and be able to adapt to a larger variety of people and larger mix of corporate cultures. A good grasp of organizational behavior can help prepare you for that challenge.

A Focus on Quality and Speed

Intense competition for customers, both locally and globally, has given rise to a strong emphasis on quality, both for products and services. Correctly identifying customer needs and satisfying them before, during, and after the sale (whether the consumer purchased a car or health care) are now seen as key competitive advantages. To achieve these advantages, many organizations have begun to pursue **total quality management (TQM)**, a systematic attempt to achieve continuous improvement in the quality of an organization's products and/or services.

> **Total quality management (TQM).** A systematic attempt to achieve continuous improvement in the quality of an organization's products and/or services.

Quality can be very generally defined as everything from speedy delivery to producing goods or services in an environmentally friendly manner. For example, AT&T used its TQM program to radically reduce paper pollution in its operations. Other firms with notable TQM efforts include Cadillac, Xerox, FedEx, and Motorola.[28] TQM tactics include extensive training, frequent measurement of quality indicators, meticulous attention to work processes, and an emphasis on preventing (rather than correcting) service or production errors. Maine's L.L. Bean mail order clothing and camping operation claims to have shipped 500,000 orders without an error over a period of several months.

Closely allied with quality is speed. Lenscrafters makes glasses "in about an hour," and Dominos became famous for speedy pizza delivery. Local car dealers now do on-the-spot oil changes. Previously, you had to make an appointment days in advance. Perhaps even more important than this external manifestation of speed is the behind-the-scene speed that has reduced the cycle time for getting new products to market. Firms such as Benetton and The Limited can move new fashions into stores in a couple of months instead of a couple of years, the former norm. Chrysler and Ford are beginning to approach the Japanese standards for getting a new car design in the showroom in three years instead of five. Such speed can prove to be a real competitive advantage. Sega successfully challenged Nintendo in the video game market by being the first to launch a 16-bit system.

What does the passion for quality and speed have to do with organizational behavior? For one thing, both require a high degree of employee *involvement* and *commitment*. Often, this means that management must give employees the power to make on-the-spot decisions that were previously reserved for managers. In addition, quality and speed both require a high degree of *teamwork* between both individuals and groups who might have some natural tendency to be uncooperative (such as the engineers and accountants involved in car design). The field of organizational behavior is deeply concerned with such issues.

I hope this brief discussion of several issues that are of concern to managers has reinforced your awareness of using organizational behavior to better understand and manage life at work. These concerns permeate today's workplace and we will cover them in more detail throughout the book.

The Manager's Notebook   Service Excellence at Marriott International Inc.

1. Marriott predicted that becoming the employer of choice will help it to become the hotel provider of choice for customers. It accepted the idea that customer-oriented employee behavior predicts customer satisfaction. It also used demographic trends to predict increased difficulties in attracting excellent candidates from its traditional labor pool of young people, since that labor pool was shrinking in size. What the firm needs now is some explanation of the factors that will both attract and retain excellent personnel. To find this out, the company used extensive employee surveys (it was already experienced in surveying customers). The surveys revealed that training, career opportunities, and interesting work were some critical factors to attract and retain the kind of service-oriented employees they wanted.

2. In terms of management actions, Marriott began to provide more extensive training and career opportunities, including internships with high schools and colleges. It also redesigned work to provide for more teamwork and responsibility and began to provide managers with second language training (e.g., Spanish) where appropriate. Second language facility among managers obviously makes Marriott an attractive employer for entry level people whose first language is not English. The company also enlarged its recruiting pool by targeting retired people who wanted part-time work and by seeing itself as competing with the military for entry-level hiring. Accommodating diversity provided the company with more excellent job candidates from which to choose.

EXECUTIVE SUMMARY

◆ Organizations are social inventions for accomplishing common goals through group effort.

◆ Organizational behavior refers to the attitudes and behaviors of individuals and groups in an organizational context. The field of organizational behavior systematically studies these attitudes and behaviors and provides advice about how organizations can manage them effectively. Goals of the field include the prediction, explanation, and management of organizational behavior.

◆ Management is the art of getting things accomplished in organizations through others. It consists of acquiring, allocating, and utilizing physical and human resources to accomplish goals.

◆ The classical view of management advocated a high degree of employee specialization and a high degree of coordination of this labor from the top of the organization. Taylor's Scientific Management and Weber's views on bureaucracy are in line with the classical position.

◆ The human relations movement pointed out the "people problems" that the classical management style sometimes provoked and advocated more interesting job design, more employee participation in decisions, and less centralized control.

◆ The contemporary contingency approach to management suggests that the most effective management styles and organizational designs are dependent upon the demands of the situation.

◆ Research on what managers do shows that they fulfill interpersonal, informational, and decisional roles. Important activities include routine communication, traditional management, networking, and human resource management. Managers pursue agendas through networking, and use intuition to guide decision making. The demands on managers vary across cultures. A good grasp of organizational behavior is essential for effective management.

KEY CONCEPTS

Organizations

Organizational behavior

Management

Classical viewpoint

Scientific Management

Bureaucracy

Hawthorne studies

Human relations movement

Contingency approach

Intuition

Total quality management (TQM)

DISCUSSION QUESTIONS

1. What are your goals in studying organizational behavior? What practical advantages might this study have for you?

2. Consider absence from work as an example of organizational behavior. What are some of the factors that might *predict* who will tend to be absent from work? How might you *explain* absence from work? What are some techniques that organizations use to *manage* absence?

3. To demonstrate that you grasp the idea of contingencies in organizational behavior, consider how closely managers should supervise the work of their subordinates. What are some factors upon which closeness of supervision might be contingent?

4. Management is the art of getting things accomplished in organizations through others. Given this definition, what are some factors that make management a difficult, or at least a challenging, occupation?

5. Use the contingency approach to describe a work task or an organizational department where a more classical management style might be effective. Then, do the same for a task or department where the human relations style would be effective.

6. Give an example of a managerial *figurehead* role, *negotiator* role, and *disseminator* role.

7. Why do studies of managerial behavior reveal the importance of networking?

8. What are some of the demands that increased workforce diversity and increased global operations make on managers? What are some of the opportunities that these trends offer to managers?

The purpose of this exercise is to help you get acquainted with some of your classmates by learning something about their experiences with work and organizations. To do this, we will focus on an important and traditional topic in organizational behavior—what makes people satisfied or dissatisfied with their jobs (a topic that we will cover formally in Chapter 5).

1. Students should break into learning groups of four to six people. Each group should choose a recording secretary.
2. In each group, members should take turns introducing themselves and then describing to the others either the best job or the worst job that they have ever had. Take particular care to explain why this particular job was either satisfying or dissatisfying. For example, did factors such as pay, co-workers, your boss, or the work itself affect you level of satisfaction? The recording secretary should make a list of the jobs group members held, noting which were good and which were bad. (15 minutes)
3. Using the information from Step 2, each group should develop a profile of four or five characteristics that seem to contribute to a dissatisfying job and four or five that contribute to a satisfying job. In other words, are there some common experiences among the group members? (10 minutes)
4. Each group should write its "good job" and "bad job" characteristics on the board. (3 minutes)
5. The class should reconvene, and each group's recording secretary should report on the specific jobs the group considered good and bad. The instructor will discuss the profiles on the board, noting similarities and differences. Other issues worth probing are behavioral consequences of job attitudes (e.g., quitting) and differences of opinion within the groups (e.g., one person's bad job might have seemed attractive to someone else). (15 minutes)

CASE STUDY
CAUGHT IN A BIND

Like most people, Nora Pollard knows the difference between right and wrong. But what happens when what is ethically right is wrong from a business standpoint? If doing the right thing puts you out of business, is doing the wrong thing justifiable? Pollard, president of Phoenix Industries Ltd., of Saskatoon, Canada, is wrestling with these questions now as she tries to pull her company from the brink of bankruptcy.

Phoenix, a family business owned by Pollard and her two sisters, began operations in 1964 as a manufacturer of plastic garden hoses for the consumer market. These products are sold through garden centers, hardware stores, and mass merchandisers.

Although Phoenix got started as a maker of plastic hoses for householders, this side of the business accounted for only 20 percent of total sales by 1984. The rest of the company's sales were generated by its industrial water irrigation products division. This division was the result of a chance meeting with an engineer when Pollard was vacationing in Mexico in 1970. The engineer was installing an irrigation system for a large area of farmland. Pollard concluded a deal with him on the spot to provide some plastic hoses and pipes for the project.

Phoenix built new production facilities to fill the order. This expansion of the company's product line resulted in a rapid growth in sales. From $200,000 in 1964, sales grew to $1 million in 1973 and reached $2 million in 1982.

Some 90 percent of the revenues of the irrigation products division now come from exports. Markets include Mexico, Brazil, Argentina, Greece, Italy, France, Japan, and Australia. No one country represents more than 29 percent of the company's total exports. This is the result of a deliberate decision by Pollard, who wants to avoid excessive reliance on one country, fearing that political or other problems there could cause serious problems for Phoenix.

In 1983, Pollard expanded her production facilities to meet anticipated contracts for the next three years. However, her estimates for this period proved to be overly optimistic, and so far Phoenix hasn't been able to use its increased capacity. Now, in 1986, the company is just marginally profitable.

In order to respond to Phoenix's poor financial condition, Nora Pollard overrode her own policy of avoiding excessive reliance on any one customer and signed a $500,000 contract—exceptionally large by Phoenix's standards—to supply industrial irrigation products to a firm in Brazil. Because of the size of the contract, she bypassed her Brazilian distributor and made the deal directly with the customer.

Everything went smoothly until hours before the order was to be shipped, when Pollard's inspectors discovered defects in the product. While the problems were not evident to the eye—and wouldn't become evident until after the order had been received and paid for—they would cause difficulties for the customer in the field and would require repairs. However, if Pollard delayed shipment or informed the customer of the problem, Phoenix might lose the order. And if that were to happen, the company could be forced into bankruptcy.

Pollard has only a few hours to come up with a solution to her dilemma, and none of the alternatives she is considering is totally satisfactory. She believes she has four from which to choose:

• Not ship the order and not tell the customer the reason, which would place Phoenix Industries in voluntary bankruptcy.
• Inform the customer of the quality problem, not ship the products and declare voluntary bankruptcy.
• Ship the order and inform the customer of the defects after receiving payment.
• Ship the order and say nothing to the customer (Pollard doubts that the Brazilian firm could obtain any legal judgment against her in this event.)

Source: Disguised case prepared by Stephen Tax under the direction of Professor Walter Good, University of Manitoba. From Stoffman, D. (1987, November). Caught in a bind. *Canadian Business*, 173–174.

1. Assess the merits of each of the four alternatives that Nora Polland is considering.
2. Can you think of any other courses of managerial action besides those Nora is contemplating?
3. What are the factors that might *predict* which course of action Nora Polland will take?
4. Which of Mintzberg's managerial roles is Nora exhibiting?
5. What should Nora do, and why?

AFTER READING CHAPTER 2 YOU SHOULD BE ABLE TO:

1 EXPLAIN THE DIFFICULTIES OF RELYING TOTALLY ON COMMON SENSE TO UNDERSTAND ORGANIZATIONAL BEHAVIOR.

2 EXPLAIN WHAT A HYPOTHESIS IS AND DIFFERENTIATE RELIABILITY FROM VALIDITY.

3 UNDERSTAND OBSERVATIONAL RESEARCH AND DISTINGUISH BETWEEN PARTICIPANT AND DIRECT OBSERVATION.

4 DESCRIBE CORRELATIONAL RESEARCH AND EXPLAIN WHY CAUSATION CANNOT BE INFERRED FROM CORRELATION.

5 EXPLAIN EXPERIMENTAL RESEARCH AND DISTINGUISH BETWEEN INDEPENDENT AND DEPENDENT VARIABLES.

6 DISCUSS THE RELATIVE ADVANTAGES AND DISADVANTAGES OF VARIOUS RESEARCH TECHNIQUES.

7 EXPLAIN THE HAWTHORNE EFFECT.

8 STATE THE BASIC ETHICAL CONCERNS TO WHICH RESEARCHERS MUST ATTEND.

ALTHOUGH EMPLOYEES MAY FEEL PERSONALLY SATISFIED WHEN THEY DEVELOP SOCIAL CONTACTS IN THE WORKPLACE, STUDIES SHOW THAT THESE RELATIONSHIPS OFTEN IMPAIR PRODUCTIVITY.

CHAPTER 2

FINDING OUT ABOUT ORGANIZATIONAL BEHAVIOR

Although this is probably your first formal course in organizational behavior, you already have a number of opinions about the subject. To illustrate this, let's begin this chapter with a short quiz. Are the following statements true or false? Please jot down a one-sentence rationale for your answer. There are no tricks involved!

1. *Workers who are more satisfied with their jobs tend to be much more productive than those who are less satisfied.*
2. *Effective organizational leaders tend to possess identical personality traits.*
3. *Nearly all workers prefer stimulating, challenging jobs.*
4. *Managers have a very accurate idea about how much their peers and superiors are paid.*

Now that you have answered the questions, do one more thing. Assume that the correct answer is opposite to the one you have given. That is, if you answered true to a statement, assume that it is actually false, and vice versa. Now, give a one-sentence rationale why this opposite answer could also be correct.

Each of these statements concerns the behavior of people in organizations. Furthermore, each statement has important implications for the functioning of organizations. If satisfied workers are indeed more productive, organizations might sensibly invest considerable time, energy, and money in fostering satisfaction. Similarly, if most employees prefer stimulating jobs, there are many jobs that could benefit from upgrading. In this book we will investigate the extent to which statements such as these are true or false and why they are true or false. The answers to our brief quiz will be presented shortly.

In this chapter we will examine some of the factors that contribute to our commonsense understanding of organizational behavior and challenge the notion that common sense is the best source of knowledge about organizational behavior. Then, we will examine some research techniques that contribute more accurate knowledge about what happens in organizations.

HOW MUCH DO YOU KNOW ABOUT ORGANIZATIONAL BEHAVIOR?

Let's now return to our quiz. If this were an introductory course in accounting, statistics, computer science, or art appreciation, the reader would likely cry "Foul!" upon encountering such a test. How could the instructor expect you to know that the standard deviation equals the square root of the variance or that Picasso painted his final cubist work in 1921? While we will readily concede ignorance when approaching subjects such as these, our direct and indirect experiences have enabled us to "know" a fair amount about organizational behavior in advance of its formal study. Thus, it is likely that you easily and willingly completed the quiz.

The answers to this quiz may be surprising. Substantial research indicates that each of the statements in the quiz is essentially false. Of course, there are exceptions, but in general, researchers have found that satisfied workers are not more productive, the personalities of effective leaders vary a fair amount, many people prefer routine jobs, and managers are not well informed about the pay of their peers and superiors. However, you should not jump to unwarranted conclusions based on the inaccuracy of these statements until we determine *why* they tend to be incorrect. There are good reasons for an organization to attempt to satisfy its employees. Also we can predict who might prefer challenging jobs. We will discuss these issues in more detail in later chapters.

Experience indicates that people are amazingly good at giving sensible reasons as to why the same statement is either true or false. Thus, satisfied workers are productive because they identify with their work, or because they are repaying the organization for satisfactory employment conditions. Conversely, workers are satisfied because they have developed rewarding social contacts in the workplace, but these relationships interfere with productivity. The ease with which people can generate such contradictory responses suggests that "common sense" develops through unsystematic and incomplete experiences with organizational behavior.

COMMON SENSE AND ORGANIZATIONAL BEHAVIOR

There is a tendency for beginning students of organizational behavior to assume that the statements included in the quiz are true. "After all, it's only common sense. . . ." Where does this common sense come from? By the time we reach adulthood we have acquired considerable *direct experience* with human behavior, organizations, and behavior in organizations. Since birth we have been "behaving" in the informal organization of the family and in formal organizations such as schools, colleges, and workplaces. Most of us have had reasonable success in negotiating the challenges these organizations have presented to us. Furthermore, as consumers of the products and services created by organizations, we have had the opportunity to observe those behaviors that seem to lead to efficient performance (e.g., the typical McDonald's restaurant) or inefficient performance (e.g., the typical college course change system). Finally, *indirect experience* powerfully shapes our views on the nature of work and organizations. When a friend says, "You wouldn't believe what happened to me at work today," or informs us that her bank credit card limit was raised on the same day her loan application was refused, we form implicit assumptions about the nature of behavior in organizations. Similarly, when we follow the progress of a political campaign, a strike, or a military action on *60 Minutes* or in *Newsweek,* we add to our arsenal of knowledge about organizational behavior. Just how systematic this study has been is debatable.

Although people rely on common sense every day, common sense can result in curious contradictions. For example, consider the following "wisdom of the ages":

- Look before you leap BUT He who hesitates is lost.
- Better safe than sorry BUT Nothing ventured, nothing gained.
- Absence makes the heart grow fonder BUT Out of sight, out of mind.
- Many hands make light work BUT Too many cooks spoil the broth.
- Two heads are better than one BUT If you want something done, do it yourself.

The common sense these old sayings provide is certainly common, but is it sensible? These sayings are so abstract that it is impossible to deduce when they are applicable. The last two pairs of sayings have some clear relevance to the design of work groups and to decision making in organizations, but it's hard to determine when to implement which advice. The failure of general common sense to provide us with truly useful information suggests that we should carefully differentiate opinions about organizational behavior from actual behavior that occurs in organizations.

WHAT CREATES INACCURATE OPINIONS?

There are several reasons for developing inaccurate opinions about organizational behavior. These reasons stem from the nature and quality of direct and indirect experiences with organizations. They include overgeneralization, organizational practice, media attention, and value judgments.

Overgeneralization

Individuals have a tendency to assume that their personal experience with a particular organization is typical of other people's. Thus, the student politician who has acquired considerable expertise in furthering the goals of his or her constituency in a university setting might find it difficult to translate this expertise to a management trainee job with a bank after graduation. Although both the university and the bank are organizations, and "people are people," the knowledge acquired in one setting might not apply directly to the other. Additionally, people often assume that their own experiences in organizations are shared by other people. Thus, workers who are both satisfied with their jobs and productive assume that other satisfied workers will also be productive.

Organizational Practice and Media Attention

Some ideas about behavior in organizations may be generally accepted simply because they are visible. This visibility may stem from actual organizational practices or from the exploration of an issue by the media.

Many people think that standard reference checks must be an effective hiring tool because employers use them so frequently in screening job applicants: "If organizations use them, then they must work." Likewise, people often assume that pay and fringe benefit increases must be an attempt to bolster productivity through increased satisfaction. However, such assumptions do not take into account nonrational actions of organizations, which are more frequent than you might expect. In fact, organizations have exhibited excessive faddishness and a tendency to follow the leader in areas such as the design of pay systems and management training and development. For example, the "In Focus: *Outdoor Training: Revolution or Fad?*" describes how many organizations have adopted outdoor training programs in spite of the fact that there is little systematic evidence about their effectiveness.

Media attention can also provide us with oversimplified or inaccurate ideas about the relationships between people and organizations. Magazine and television portrayals of high-profile organizational people and events (Silicon Valley computer whiz kids, thirty-year-old Wall Street millionaires, Japanese management, and lusty corporate takeovers) surely shape our views about work. However, the critical observer must wonder whether the issue deserves attention or the attention creates the issue.

In recent years there has been a phenomenal upsurge of popular books about business and management. Titles such as *In Search of Excellence, Reengineering the Corporation, Iacocca,* and *The One Minute Manager* have dominated the best seller lists, reaching a much larger audience than the typical college textbook. Although such books vary tremendously in quality, some do contain valuable insights about organizational behavior. However, it would

IN FOCUS   Outdoor Training: Revolution or Fad?

More and more organizations are investigating out-door training programs for individual managers, management teams, and work groups.

More than 100 training organizations currently offer some type of outdoor training, also known as adventure or experiential learning. Such programs are designed to develop leadership and teamwork skills through structured outdoor activities.

Participants include such varied groups as *Fortune* 100 executives, nurses, and civic group volunteers. Several organizations, such as the Norton Company and the Naval Weapons Support Center, have even developed their own outdoor training programs. Indiana and Xavier universities, among others, are sending people "into the woods" as part of their traditional executive education programs.

But is outdoor training a revolution or a fad? At one time or another, American organizations have tried virtually everything in pursuit of more effective managers and teams. The most intriguing aspect of the outdoor training movement is the intensity of the debate regarding its usefulness as a training strategy.

Much anecdotal evidence supports the effectiveness of outdoor training programs. One need not look far to find former participants who rave about the benefits of their outdoor training experiences.

Even top executives are among the converts. Nelson Farris, a vice-president at Nike Corporation, spoke about outdoor training on a *MacNeil-Lehrer* news broadcast. "I think every one of our employees should go through it, not just some people," he said. "We are looking for ways to get people to open their minds and deal with the process of change—this program will help our company."

But outdoor training has also evoked fervent opposition. Skeptics contend that such programs are at best a waste of time and at worst harmful to managerial effectiveness.

More than a decade ago, Ron Zemke suggested in a *Training* article, "outdoor programming is nothing more than an opportunity for organiza-

While outdoor training programs have been criticized by some as being a waste of time, others believe they are productive and adventurous ways to develop leadership and teamwork skills.

tions to pack whole management teams off to risk life and limb together." More recently, Jack Falvey argued in the *Wall Street Journal* that "building outdoor party games and simulations when the real work to be done is all around, should be grounds for managerial malpractice indictments."

Source: Excerpted from Wagner, R. J., Baldwin, T. T., & Roland, C. C. (1991, March). Outdoor training: Revolution or fad? *Training and Development Journal*, 50–57.

---

be a mistake to assume that all popular books contain wisdom because they are popular. Frequently, popularity stems from catering to what the reader wishes were true rather than what is true. Avid readers of such books might be excused for thinking that phenomenal advances in organizational behavior research and management practice have occurred just recently! In fact, research evidence and practical management experience usually accumulate gradually, by trial and error.

Value Judgments

Our values—our feelings about what is good or bad and right or wrong—often influence our views about what happens or should happen in organizations. These values often differ according to our background and position in the social structure. Thus, it is unlikely that managers and unionists would have similar views about the nature of blue-collar work. The values of society and its subgroups also change over time, and this change is reflected in thinking about organizational behavior. For example, the current emphasis on organizational diversity and teamwork reflects changes in the larger society.

The point, however, is that such value orientations often influence our views about behavior in organizations in spite of the actual consequences of these values. We favor what we perceive as "good," even if this goodness is unsupported by evidence or is contrary to the values of others. If we see stimulating, challenging work in a positive light, we expect to encounter such work in organizations.

Our common sense is frequently a product of overgeneralization, media attention, and value judgments. However, this does not mean that opinions derived from these sources are unimportant. On the contrary, they frequently influence our expectations and our behavior. The manager who assumes that people prefer stimulating, challenging work might design subordinates' jobs very differently from one who assumes the contrary. The organization whose president thinks that money is an important motivator of productivity might distribute wages and salaries very differently from one whose president does not. Opinions about organizational behavior do affect management practice. However, such practice should be based upon informed opinion and systematic study.

RESEARCH IN ORGANIZATIONAL BEHAVIOR

Research is a way of finding out about the world through objective and systematic information gathering. The key words here are *objective* and *systematic,* and it is these characteristics that separate the outcomes of the careful study of organizational behavior from opinion and common sense.

Understanding how researchers conduct their research is important to the study of organizational behavior for several reasons. First of all, you should be aware of how the information presented in this book was collected. This should increase your confidence in the advantages of systematic study over common sense. Second, you will likely encounter reports in management periodicals and the popular press of interventions to improve organizational behavior, such as job redesign or employee development programs. A critical perspective is necessary to differentiate those interventions that are carefully designed and evaluated from useless or even damaging ones. Those backed by good research deserve the greatest confidence. Occasionally, a manager may have to evaluate a research proposal or consultant's intervention to be carried out in his or her own organization. A brief introduction to research methodology should enable you to ask some intelligent questions about such plans.

Trained behavioral scientists who have backgrounds in management, applied psychology, or applied sociology carry out research in organizational behavior. While this introduction will not make you a trained behavioral scientist, it should provide an appreciation of the work that goes into generating accurate knowledge about organizational behavior.

The Basics of Organizational Behavior Research

All research in organizational behavior begins with a question about work or organizations. Sometimes, this question might stem from a formal theory in the field. For example, in Chapter 6 we will study a motivation theory called equity theory that is concerned with peoples' reactions to fairness or lack of it. Equity theory suggests the following research question: What do people do when they perceive their pay to be too low in comparison to other people? Other times, a research question might stem from an immediate organizational problem. For example, a human resources manager might ask herself: How can we reduce absenteeism among our customer service personnel?

Often, research questions are expressed as hypotheses. A **hypothesis** is a formal statement of the expected relationship between two variables. Variables are simply measures that can take on two or more values. Temperature is a variable, but so are pay, fairness, and absenteeism. A formal hypothesis stemming from equity theory might be: The less fair people perceive their pay to be, the more likely they will be to resign their jobs. Here, a variable that can take on many values, perceived fairness, is linked to a variable made up of two values, staying or leaving. The human resources manager might develop this hypothesis: The introduction of a small attendance bonus will reduce absenteeism. Here, a variable with two values, bonus versus no bonus, is related to one that can take on many values, days of absenteeism.

Good researchers carefully measure the variables they choose. For one thing, a measure should exhibit high reliability. **Reliability** is an index of the consistency of a research subject's responses. For example, if we ask someone several questions about how fair his or her pay is, the person should respond roughly the same way to each question. Similarly, the person should respond roughly the same way to the same questions next week or next month if there has been no change in pay.

Measures should also exhibit high validity. **Validity** is an index of the extent to which a measure truly reflects what it is supposed to measure. For instance, a good measure of perceived pay fairness should not be influenced by employees' feelings of fairness about other workplace factors such as supervision. Also, a researcher would expect people who are objectively underpaid to report high pay unfairness and for them to report increased fairness if their pay were increased. Researchers are often able to choose measures with a known history of reliability and validity.

There are three basic kinds of research techniques—observation, correlation, and experimentation. As you will see, each begins with a research question or questions. Correlation and experimentation are most likely to test specific hypotheses and devote explicit attention to measurement quality.

Observational Techniques

Observational research techniques are the most straightforward ways of finding out about behavior in organizations and thus come closest to the ways in which we develop commonsense views about such behavior. In this case,

Hypothesis. A formal statement of the expected relationship between two variables.

Reliability. An index of the consistency of a research subject's responses.

Validity. An index of the extent to which a measure truly reflects what it is supposed to measure.

Observational research. Research that examines the natural activities of people in an organizational setting by listening to what they say and watching what they do.

observation means just what it implies—the researcher proceeds to examine the natural activities of people in an organizational setting by listening to what they say and watching what they do. The difference between our everyday observations and the formal observations of the trained behavioral scientist is expressed by those key words *systematic* and *objective*.

First, the researcher approaches the organizational setting with extensive training concerning the nature of human behavior and a particular set of questions that the observation is designed to answer. These factors provide a systematic framework for the business of observing. Second, the behavioral scientist attempts to keep a careful ongoing record of the events that he or she observes, either as they occur or as soon as possible afterward. Thus, excessive reliance upon memory, which may lead to inaccuracies, is unnecessary. Finally, the behavioral scientist is well-informed of the dangers of influencing the behavior of those whom he or she is observing and is trained to draw reasonable conclusions from his or her observations. These factors help ensure objectivity.

The outcomes of observational research are summarized in a narrative form, sometimes called a *case study*. This narrative specifies the nature of the organization, people, and events studied, the particular role of and techniques used by the observer, the research questions, and the events observed.

Participant observation.
Observational research in which the researcher becomes a functioning member of the organizational unit being studied.

Participant Observation. One obvious way for a researcher to find out about organizational behavior is to actively participate in this behavior. In **participant observation** the researcher becomes a functioning member of the organizational unit he or she is studying in order to conduct the research. At this point you may wonder, "Wait a minute. What about objectivity? What about influencing the behavior of those being studied?" These are clearly legitimate questions, and they might be answered in the following way: In adopting participant observation the researcher is making a conscious bet that the advantages of participation outweigh these problems. It is doubtless true in some cases that "there is no substitute for experience." For example, researcher Robert Sutton wanted to find out how employees cope with jobs that require them to express negative emotions.[1] To do this, he trained and then worked as a bill collector. This is obviously a more personal experience than simply interviewing bill collectors.

Another advantage to participant observation is its potential for secrecy—the subjects need not know that they are being observed. This potential for secrecy does raise some ethical issues, however. Sociologist Tom Lupton served as an industrial worker in two plants in England to study the factors that influenced productivity.[2] Although he could have acted in secrecy, he was required to inform management and union officials of his presence to secure records and documents, and he thus felt it unfair not to inform his workmates of his purpose. It should be stressed that his goals were academic, and he was *not* working for the managements of the companies involved. Sometimes, however, secrecy seems necessary to accomplish a research goal, as the following study of "illegal" industrial behavior shows.

Joseph Bensman and Israel Gerver investigated an important organizational problem: What happens when the activities that appear to be required to get a job done conflict with official organizational policy?[3] Examples of such conflicts include the punch press operator who must remove the safety guard from his machine to meet productivity standards, the executive who must deliver corporate money to a political slush fund, or the police officer who can't find time to complete an eight-page report to justify having drawn her revolver on a night patrol.

The behavior of interest to Bensman and Gerver was the unauthorized use of taps by aircraft plant workers. A tap is a hard steel hand tool used to cut threads into metal. The possession of this device by aircraft assemblers was strictly forbidden because the workers could use it to correct sloppy or difficult work such as the misalignment of bolt holes in two pieces of aircraft skin or stripped lock nuts; both of these problems could lead to potential structural weaknesses or maintenance problems.

Possession of a tap was a strict violation of company policy, and a worker could be fired on the spot for it. On the other hand, since supervisors were under extreme pressure to maintain a high quota of completed work, the occasional use of a tap to correct a problem could save hours of disassembly and realignment time. How was this conflict resolved? The answer was provided by one of the authors, who served as a participant observer while functioning as an assembler. Put simply, the supervisors and inspectors worked together to encourage the cautious and appropriate use of taps. New workers were gradually introduced to the mysteries of tapping by experienced workers, and the supervisors provided refinement of skills and signals as to when a tap might be used. Taps were not to be used in front of inspectors or to correct chronic sloppy work. If "caught," promiscuous tappers were expected to act truly penitent in response to a chewing out by the supervisors, even if the supervisors themselves had suggested the use of the tap. In short, a *social ritual* was developed to teach and control the use of the tap to facilitate getting the work out without endangering the continued presence of the crucial tool. Clearly, this is the kind of information about organizational behavior that would be extremely difficult to obtain except by participant observation.

Direct Observation.   In **direct observation** the researcher observes organizational behavior without participation in the activity being observed. There are a number of reasons why one might choose direct observation over participant observation. First, there are many situations in which the introduction of a new person into an existing work setting would severely disrupt and change the nature of the activities in that setting. These are cases in which the "influence" criticism of participant observation is especially true. Second, there are many job tasks that a trained behavioral scientist could not be expected to learn for research purposes. For example, it seems unreasonable to expect a researcher to spend years acquiring the skills of a pilot or banker in order to be able to investigate what happens in the cockpit of an airliner or in a boardroom. Finally, participant observation places rather severe limitations upon the observers' opportunity to record information. Existence of these conditions suggests the use of direct observation. In theory, the researcher could carry out such observation covertly, but there are few studies of organizational behavior in which the presence of the direct observer was not known and explained to those being observed.

Henry Mintzberg's study of the work performed by chief executives of two manufacturing companies, a hospital, a school system, and a consulting firm provides an excellent example of the use of direct observation.[4] At first glance,

Direct observation. Observational research in which the researcher observes organizational behavior without taking part in the studied activity.

this might appear to be an inane thing to investigate. After all, everybody knows that managers plan, organize, lead, and control, or some similar combination of words. In fact, Mintzberg argues that we actually know very little about the routine, everyday behavior managers use to achieve these vague goals. Furthermore, if we ask managers what they do (in an interview or questionnaire), they usually respond with a variation of the plan-organize-lead-control theme.

Mintzberg spent a week with each of his five executives, watching them at their desks, attending meetings with them, listening to their phone calls, and inspecting their mail. He kept detailed records of these activities and gradually developed a classification scheme to make sense of them. What Mintzberg found counters the commonsense view that some hold of managers—sitting behind a large desk, reflecting on their organization's performance, and affixing their signatures to impressive documents all day. In fact, Mintzberg found that his managers actually performed a terrific amount of work and had little time for reflection. On an average day they examined 36 pieces of mail, engaged in five telephone conversations, attended eight meetings, and made one tour of their facilities. Work-related reading encroached upon home lives. These activities were varied, unpatterned, and of short duration. Half of the activities lasted less than nine minutes, and 90 percent less than one hour. Furthermore, these activities tended to be directed toward current, specific issues rather than past, general issues. Finally, the managers revealed a clear preference for verbal communications, by either telephone or unscheduled face-to-face meetings; in fact, two-thirds of their contacts were of this nature. In contrast, they generated an average of only one piece of mail a day.

In summary, both participant and direct observation capture the depth, breadth, richness, spontaneity, and realism of organizational behavior. However, they also share some weaknesses. One of these weaknesses is a lack of control over the environment in which the study is being conducted. Thus, Mintzberg could not ensure that unusual events would not affect the executives' behavior. Also, the small number of observers and situations in the typical observational study is problematic. With only one observer there is a strong potential for selective perceptions and interpretations of observed events. Since only a few situations are analyzed, the extent to which the observed behaviors can be generalized to other settings is limited. (Do most executives behave like the five Mintzberg studied?) It is probably safe to say that observational techniques are best used to make an initial examination of some organizational event on which little information is available and to generate ideas for further investigation with more refined techniques.

Correlational Techniques

Correlational research.
Research that attempts to measure variables precisely and examine relationships among these variables without introducing change into the research setting.

Correlational research attempts to measure variables precisely and examine relationships among these variables without introducing change into the research setting. Correlational research sacrifices some of the breadth and richness of the observational techniques for more precision of measurement and greater control. It necessarily involves some abstraction of the real event that is the focus of observation in order to accomplish this precision and control. More specifically, correlational approaches differ from observational approaches in terms of the nature of the data researchers collect and the issues they investigate.

The data of observational studies are most frequently observer notes. We hope that these data exhibit reliability and validity. Unfortunately, because observations are generally the products of a single individual viewing a unique event, we have very little basis on which to judge their reliability and validity.

The data of correlational studies involve interviews and questionnaires as well as existing data. Existing data come from organizational records and include productivity, absence, and demographic information (age, gender, etc.). Variables often measured by questionnaires and interviews include:

- subordinates' perceptions of how their managers behave on the job,
- the extent to which employees are satisfied with their jobs,
- employees' reports about how much autonomy they have on their jobs.

It is possible to determine in advance of doing research the extent to which such measures are reliable and valid. Thus, when constructing a questionnaire to measure job satisfaction, the researcher can check its reliability by repeatedly administering it to a group of workers over a period of time. If individual responses remain fairly stable, there is evidence of reliability. Evidence of the validity of a questionnaire might come from its ability to predict which employees would quit the organization for work elsewhere. It seems reasonable that dissatisfied employees would be more likely to quit, and such an effect is partial evidence of the validity of a satisfaction measure.

In addition to the nature of the data collected, it was pointed out above that correlational studies differ from observational studies in terms of the kinds of events they investigate. Although the questions investigated by observational research appear fairly specific (What maintains an "illegal" behavior such as tapping? What do executives do?), virtually any event relevant to the question is fair game for observation. Thus, such studies are extremely broad based. Correlational research sacrifices this broadness to investigate the relationship (correlation) between specific, well-defined variables. The relationship between the variables of interest is usually stated as a hypothesis. Using the variables mentioned above, we can construct three sample hypotheses and describe how they would be tested:

- Employees who are satisfied with their jobs will tend to be more productive than those who are less satisfied. To test this, a researcher might administer a reliable, valid questionnaire concerning satisfaction and obtain production data from company records.

- Employees who perceive their supervisor as friendly and considerate will be more satisfied with their jobs than those who do not. To test this, a researcher might use reliable, valid questionnaires or interview measures of both variables.

- Older employees will be absent less than younger employees. To test this, a researcher might obtain data concerning the age of employees and their absenteeism from organizational personnel records.

In each case, the researcher is interested in a very specific set of variables, and he or she devotes effort to measuring them precisely.

A good example of a correlational study is that of Belle Rose Ragins and John Cotton, who studied employees' willingness to serve as mentors to newer organizational members.[5] Mentorship was defined as helping a junior person with career support and upward mobility. The major focus of the study was the relationship between gender and willingness to mentor. The authors reviewed literature that hypothesizes that women may face more barriers to becoming mentors than men, because they are in a minority in many employment settings. The authors were also interested in the relationships between age, organizational rank, length of employment, and prior mentorship experience and willingness to mentor.

These variables were measured with questionnaires completed by over 500 employees in three research and development organizations. The researchers found that men and women were equally willing to serve as mentors, although the women perceived more barriers (e.g., lack of qualifications and time) to being a mentor. They also found that higher rank and prior experience as a mentor or a protégé were associated with greater willingness to mentor. Notice that a study such as this could also incorporate existing data from records. For example, we might hypothesize that those with better performance evaluations would be more confident about serving as mentors.

Correlation and Causation.   A final important point should be made about correlational studies. Consider a hypothesis that friendly, considerate supervisors will have more productive subordinates than unfriendly, inconsiderate supervisors. In this case, a researcher might have some subordinates describe the friendliness of their supervisors on a reliable, valid questionnaire designed to measure this variable and obtain subordinates' productivity levels from company records. The results of this hypothetical study are plotted in Exhibit 2.1, where each dot represents a subordinate's response to the questionnaire in con-

Belle Rose Ragins and John Cotton conducted a correlational study investigating employees' willingness to serve as mentors to newer organizational members. They found that higher rank was associated with an increased willingness to mentor.

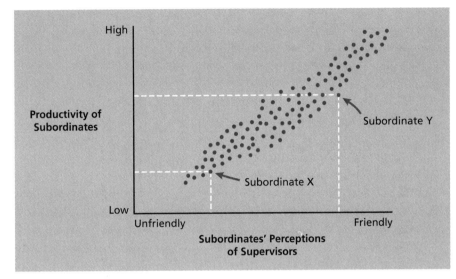

EXHIBIT 2.1
Hypothetical data from a correlational study of the relationship between supervisory friendliness and subordinate productivity.

junction with his or her productivity. In general, it would appear that the hypothesis is confirmed—that is, subordinates who describe their supervisor as friendly tend to be more productive than those who describe him or her as unfriendly. As a result of this study, should an organization attempt to select friendly supervisors or even train existing supervisors to be more friendly to obtain higher productivity? The answer is *no*. The training and selection proposal assumes that friendly supervisors *cause* their subordinates to be productive, and this might not be the case. Put simply, supervisors might be friendly *if* their subordinates are productive. This is a possible interpretation of the data, and it does not suggest that selection or training to make supervisors friendly will achieve higher productivity. This line of argument should not be unfamiliar to you. Heavy smokers and cigarette company lobbyists like to claim that smoking is related to the incidence of lung cancer because cancer proneness prompts smoking, rather than vice versa. The point here is that *correlation does not imply causation*. How can we find out which factors cause certain organizational behaviors? The answer is to perform an experiment.

Experimental Techniques

If observational research involves observing nature, and correlational research involves measuring nature, **experimental research** manipulates nature. In an experiment, a variable is manipulated or changed under controlled conditions, and the consequence of this manipulation for some other variable is measured. If all other conditions are truly controlled, and a change in the second variable follows the change that was introduced in the first variable, we can infer that the first change has caused the second change.

In experimental language the variable that the researcher manipulates or changes is called the **independent variable**. The variable that the independent variable is expected to affect is called the **dependent variable**. Consider the following hypothesis: The introduction of recorded music into the work setting will lead to increased productivity. In this hypothesis, the independent variable is music, which is expected to affect productivity, the dependent variable.

Experimental research. Research which changes or manipulates a variable under controlled conditions and examines the consequences of this manipulation for some other variable.

Independent variable. The variable that is manipulated or changed in an experiment.

Dependent variable. In an experiment, the variable that is expected to vary as a result of the manipulation of the independent variable.

Consider another hypothesis: Stimulating, challenging jobs will increase the satisfaction of the work force. Here, the design of the job is the independent variable and satisfaction is the dependent variable.

Let's return to our hypothesis that friendly, considerate supervisors will tend to have more productive subordinates. If we wish to determine whether friendly supervision contributes to subordinate productivity, the style of supervision becomes the independent variable, and productivity becomes the dependent variable. This means that the researcher must manipulate or change the friendliness of some supervisors and observe what happens to the productivity of their subordinates. In practice, this would probably be accomplished by exposing the bosses to some form of human relations training designed to teach them to be more considerate and personable toward their workers.

Exhibit 2.2 shows the results of this hypothetical experiment. The line on the graph represents the average productivity of a number of subordinates whose supervisors have received our training. We see that this productivity increased and remained higher following the introduction of the training. Does this mean that friendliness indeed increases productivity and that we should proceed to train all of our supervisors in this manner? The answer is again no. We cannot be sure that *something else* didn't occur at the time of the training to influence productivity, such as a change in equipment or job insecurity prompted by rumored layoffs. To control this possibility, we need a control group of supervisors who are not exposed to the training, and we need productivity data for their subordinates. A **control group** is a group of research subjects who have not been exposed to the experimental treatment, in this case not exposed to the training (see the cartoon). Ideally, these supervisors should be as similar as possible in experience and background to those who receive the training, and their subordinates should be performing at the same level. The results of our improved experiment are shown in Exhibit 2.3. Here, we see that the productivity of the subordinates whose supervisors were trained increases following training, while that of the control supervisors remains con-

Control group. A group of research subjects who have not been exposed to the experimental treatment

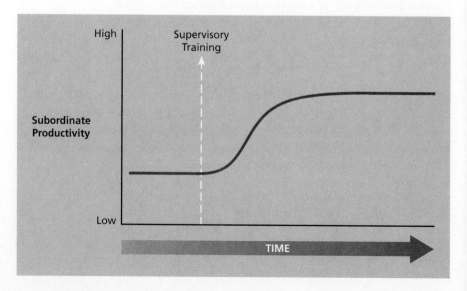

EXHIBIT 2.2
Hypothetical data from an experiment concerning human relations training.

CONTROL GROUP   OUT OF CONTROL GROUP.

stant. We can thus infer that the human relations training affected subordinate productivity.

John Ivancevich and Herbert Lyon conducted an interesting experiment that examined the effects of a shortened workweek on the employees of a company that manufactures food-packaging equipment.[6] The independent variable was the length of the workweek (4 days, 40 hours versus 5 days, 40 hours). Two of the company's divisions were converted to a 4–40 week from a 5–40 week. A third division, remaining on the 5–40 schedule, served as a control group. Workers in the control division were similar to those in the other divisions in terms of age, seniority, education, and salary. The dependent variables (measured one month before the conversion and several times after) included the workers' responses to a questionnaire concerning job satisfaction and

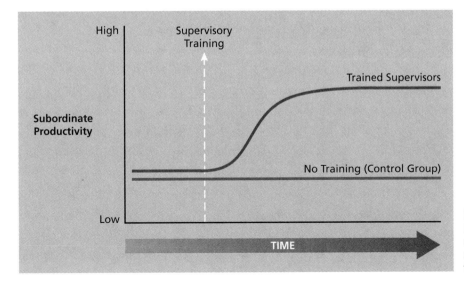

EXHIBIT 2.3
Hypothetical data from an improved experiment concerning human relations training.

stress, absence data from company records, and performance appraisals conducted by supervisors. After twelve months, several aspects of satisfaction and performance showed a marked improvement for the 4–40 workers when compared with the 5–40 workers. However, at 25 months this edge existed for only one aspect of satisfaction, satisfaction with personal worth. The authors concluded that benefits that had been proposed for the 4–40 workweek were of short-term duration.

A Continuum of Research Techniques

You might reasonably wonder which of the research techniques just discussed is most effective. As shown in Exhibit 2.4, these methods can be placed on a continuum ranging from rich, broad based, and loosely controlled (observation) to specific, precise, and rigorous (experimentation). The method that researchers use to investigate organizational behavior is dictated by the nature of the problem that interests us. In the writing of this section of the chapter, special pains were taken to choose examples of problems that were well suited to the research techniques employed to investigate them. Bensman and Gerver, as well as Mintzberg, were interested in variables that were not well defined. The variables were thus not easy to isolate and measure precisely, and observation was the appropriate technique. Furthermore, "tapping" was a controversial issue, and the researchers would have had to develop considerable trust to investigate it with questionnaires or formal interviews. Similarly, Mintzberg insists that questionnaires and interviews have failed to tell us what executives actually do. Ragins and Cotton, who studied mentoring, were interested in specific variables that were relatively easily measured. On the other hand, they were not in a position to manipulate the causes of intention to mentor. Ivancevich and Lyon were also interested in a specific set of variables, and they conducted their research on the short workweek in a situation where it was both possible and ethical to manipulate the workweek. In all of these cases, the research technique the researchers chose was substantially better than dependence on common sense or opinion.

Now that we have compared the various research techniques, why not try out your knowledge on an actual management problem? Please consult *You Be the Manager*.

Combining Research Techniques

Robert Sutton and Anat Rafaeli tested what might seem to be an obvious hypothesis—that friendly, pleasant behavior on the part of sales clerks would be positively associated with store sales.[7] As obvious as this might seem, it

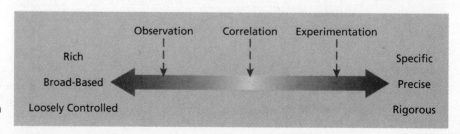

EXHIBIT 2.4
Continuum of research techniques.

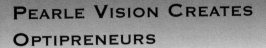

PEARLE VISION CREATES OPTIPRENEURS

YOU BE THE Manager

Dallas-based Pearle Vision has over 1,000 retail stores in 46 states and 10 countries. The firm specializes in eye-wear services and products, such as glasses and contact lenses. About half of the Pearle outlets are franchises owned by individual entrepreneurs, while the other half are corporately owned. Senior management had determined that the franchises were rather consistently more profitable than the corporately controlled stores. Management felt this difference in performance resulted from the considerably greater entrepreneurial freedom accorded to the franchisees to tailor their operations to local conditions and customer needs. In the franchises, employee salaries were paid out of store sales rather than corporate coffers, motivating their managers to control expenses and generate higher sales. In the corporate stores, managers received fixed-cap bonuses if they met a budget dictated from Dallas, regardless of the outlet's actual potential for greater performance. Greater

> PEARLE VISION RETAIL OUTLETS ARE OWNED EITHER PRIVATELY OR CORPORATELY. A RECENT TASKFORCE DETERMINED THAT THE PRIVATELY OWNED FRANCHISES WERE SIGNIFICANTLY MORE PROFITABLE.

freedom and a more enticing reward structure among franchisees stimulated innovation and risk taking that resulted in higher profits than those in the rigidly controlled corporate stores.

A Human Resources task force felt that the corporate stores' performance could improve if their managers were given entrepreneurial training, more freedom over local operations, and an incentive for higher performance. However, some senior managers were skeptical about the rather strong change in corporate culture the plan suggested. Would it really work? *You* be the manager.

1. What research technique should Pearle Vision use to examine the proposed changes in its corporate stores?

2. Which stores should participate in the research?

To find out what the firm did, see *The Manager's Notebook* at the end of the chapter.

Source: Adapted from Laabs, J. J. (1993,.January). Pearle Vision's managers think like entrepreneurs. *Personnel Journal*, 38–46.

would be a good idea to confirm it before spending thousands of dollars on human relations training for clerks. The study combined correlational and observational methods. In the quantitative correlational part of the study, teams of researchers entered a large North American chain's 576 convenience stores and, posing as shoppers, evaluated the friendliness of the sales clerks on rating scales. They also recorded other factors, such as the length of the line at the register. Existing data from company records provided the total annual sales each store recorded. When the researchers analyzed the data, the results were surprising—the "unfriendly" stores tended to chalk up higher sales!

To understand this unexpected result, the authors resorted to qualitative, observational research techniques. Specifically, each author spent extensive time in many of the convenience stores directly observing transactions between customers and clerks. In addition, each spent time as a participant-observer,

Stores with clerks who did not engage in "friendly behavior" often yielded higher sales than their more personable counterparts, mainly because they were so busy and didn't have time to chat with customers.

actually doing the sales clerk job. This observation resolved the mystery. The researchers found that when the stores were busy, the sales clerks tended to stop the small talk, concentrate on their work, and process customers as quickly as possible. This behavior corresponded to customers' expectations for fast service in a convenience store. When business was slow, clerks tended to be friendly and engage in small talk to relieve boredom. Since the busier stores generated higher sales, it is not surprising that their clerks were less friendly. In fact, further analysis of the correlational data showed that clerks were less friendly when the lines were longer.

This study illustrates how two research techniques can complement each other. It also shows that correlation does not imply causation. Although sales were negatively correlated with friendliness, volume of sales affected the expression of friendliness, not the other way around. Of course, these results would probably not generalize to sales settings in which customers expect more personal attention.

Issues and Concerns in Organizational Research

As in every field of study, particular issues confront researchers in organizational behavior. Three of these issues include sampling, Hawthorne effects, and ethical concerns.

Sampling.   Researchers who wish to generalize the results of their research beyond the particular setting they are studying can have the greatest confidence in results that are based on large, random samples. Large samples ensure that the results they obtain are truly representative of the individuals, groups, or organizations being studied and not merely the product of an extreme case or two. Similarly, random samples that ensure that all relevant individuals, groups, or organizations have an equal probability of being studied also give confidence in the generalizability of findings. As was noted earlier, observational studies usually involve small samples, and they are seldom randomized. Thus, generalizing from such studies is a problem. However, a well-designed observational study that answers important questions is surely superior to a large-sample, randomized correlational study that enables one to generalize about a trivial hypothesis.

In experimental research, randomization means randomly assigning subjects to experimental and control conditions. To illustrate the importance of this, we can reconsider the hypothetical study on human relations training. Suppose that, instead of randomly assigning supervisors to the experimental and control groups, managers nominate supervisors for training. Suppose further that to "reward" them for their long service, more-experienced supervisors are nominated for the training. This results in an experimental group containing more-experienced supervisors and a control group containing less-experienced supervisors. If supervisory experience promotes subordinate productivity, we might erroneously conclude that it was the *human relations training* that led to any improved results and that our hypothesis is confirmed. Poor sampling due to a lack of randomization has biased the results in favor of our hypothesis. To achieve randomization, it would be a good idea to ascertain that the subordinates of the experimental and control supervisors were equally productive *before* the training began.

Hawthorne Effects.   The Hawthorne effect was discovered as a result of a series of studies conducted at the Hawthorne plant of the Western Electric Company near Chicago many years ago. As explained in Chapter 1, these studies examined the effects of independent variables such as rest pauses, lighting intensity, and pay incentives on the productivity of assemblers of electrical components.[8] In a couple of these loosely controlled experiments, unusual results occurred (see the "In Focus: *The Hawthorne Effect*"). In the illumination study, both experimental and control workers improved their productivity. In another study, productivity increased and remained high despite the introduction and withdrawal of factors such as rest pauses, shortened workdays, and so on. These results gave rise to the **Hawthorne effect,** which might be defined as a favorable response of subjects in an organizational experiment to a factor other than the independent variable that is formally being manipulated. Researchers have concluded that this "other factor" is psychological in nature, although it is not well understood.[9] Likely candidates include subjects' reactions to special attention, including feelings of prestige, and heightened morale, and so on. The point is that researchers might misinterpret the true reason for any observed change in behavior because research subjects can have unmeasured feelings about their role in the research.

Hawthorne effect. A favorable response by subjects in an organizational experiment that is the result of a factor other than the independent variable that is formally being manipulated.

To return to the human relations training experiment, a Hawthorne effect might occur if the experimental subjects are grateful to management for selecting them for this special training and resolve to work harder back on the job. The supervisors might put in longer hours thinking up ways to improve productivity that have nothing to do with the training they received. However,

IN FOCUS The Hawthorne Effect

Placed in separate enclosures, control subjects received a constant illumination of 10 foot-candles while the illumination for experimental subjects, begun at this level, was decreased in 1 foot-candle steps in successive work periods. Throughout the experiment, both sets of subjects increased their performance, slowly but steadily. It was not until illumination in the experimental room reached 3 foot-candles that subjects started to complain that they could hardly see what they were doing, and productivity finally started to decline. Something other than level of illumination was affecting productivity.... In one instance the illumination was reduced to .06 of a foot-candle, the level of ordinary moonlight, and yet efficiency was maintained!

The Hawthorne effect probably owes its existence to a second experiment, called the Relay Assembly Test Room Study. Five female employees who spent each work day assembling relays, were separated from their large department and placed into a special test room where all relevant variables could be better controlled or evaluated. The study was designed to explore the optimal cycle of rest and work periods. However, to make the subjects independent of influences from their former department and sensitive to experimental manipulations, the investigators began by changing the method of determining wages. During the experiment the investigators also manipulated, on different occasions and sometimes concurrently, the length and timing of rest periods, the length of the work week, the length of the work day, and whether or not the company provided lunch and/or beverage. Productivity seemed to increase regardless of the manipulation introduced. Finally, well into the second year the investigators decided to discontinue all treatments and to return the workers to full work days and weeks without breaks or lunches. Unexpectedly, rather than dropping to preexperiment levels, productivity was maintained.

Before the experiment had begun, the investigators had feared that workers taken from their regular work to be placed in a test room would be negative and resistant to the experiment. To overcome this anticipated negative set supervision was removed, special privileges were allowed, and considerable interest and attention was expressed

The Hawthorne plant of the Western Electric Company served as a laboratory for examining influences on productivity.

toward the worker, all changes intended to provide for a controlled experiment. However, it was these unintentional manipulations, researchers were forced to conclude, that had caused the subjects to improve their overall productivity and that had given birth to the Hawthorne effect.

Source: Excerpted from Adair, J. G. (1984). The Hawthorne effect: A reconsideration of the methodological artifact. *Journal of Applied Psychology, 69,* 334–345, pp. 336–337.

the researcher could easily conclude that the human relations training itself had improved productivity.

It is very difficult to prevent Hawthorne effects. However, it is possible, if expensive, to see whether they have occurred. To do so, investigators establish a second experimental group that receives special treatment and attention but is not exposed to the key independent variable. In the human relations experiment, this could involve training that is not expected to increase productivity. If the productivity of the subjects' subordinates in both experimental groups increases equally, the Hawthorne effect is probably present. If productivity increases only in the human relations training condition, it is unlikely to be due to the Hawthorne effect.

Ethics. Researchers in organizational behavior, no matter who employs them, have an ethical obligation to do rigorous research and to report that research accurately[10]. In all cases, the psychological and physical well-being of the research subjects is of prime importance. In general, ethical researchers avoid unnecessary deception, inform participants about the general purpose of their research, and protect the anonymity of research subjects. For example, in a correlational study involving the use of questionnaires, investigators should explain the general reason for the research and afford potential subjects the opportunity to decline participation. If names or company identification numbers are required to match responses with data in personnel files (e.g., absenteeism or subsequent turnover), investigators must guarantee that they will not make individual responses public. In some observation studies and experiments, subjects may be unaware that their behavior is under formal study. In these cases, researchers have special obligations to prevent negative consequences for subjects. Ethical research has a practical side as well as a moral side. Good cooperation from research subjects is necessary to do good research. Such cooperation is easier to obtain when people are confident that ethical procedures are the rule, not the exception.

The Manager's Notebook   Pearle Vision Creates Optipreneurs

1. Pearle Vision used an experiment to evaluate its new training, incentive, and control program. This "Optipreneur" program was tried out in 14 locations for a period of seven months. The performance of these experimental stores was compared with that of control stores, including other local stores in the same city, the franchise stores, and other company stores. The independent variable is exposure to the program. The dependent variables included store sales and controllable profit. This is a sensible situation for an experiment—a specific intervention has been proposed, so why not test its effects?

2. Giving store managers increased autonomy and performance incentives was a radical change, so Pearle Vision tried it out in a few stores rather than changing all the stores at once. The company also wisely chose stores at several current performance levels, ranging from average to exceptional. Choosing only very bad or very good stores would not provide much information about how the majority of managers might respond to the program. The experiment did use volunteer managers, a factor that might have biased its success.

The Optipreneur experiment was considered a great success, as the 14 stores increased sales by 185 percent. Profits also improved. Subsequently, Pearle Vision extended the program to all corporate stores.

EXECUTIVE SUMMARY

◆ Common sense provides a somewhat limited basis for understanding organizational behavior. This is because knowledge derived from common sense is often a function of overgeneralization and value judgments. In addition, we frequently assume that actual organizational practices or media presentations of them yield correct pictures of organizational behavior.

◆ The systematic study of organizational behavior, using carefully designed research, represents a useful alternative to reliance only on common sense.

◆ All research in organizational behavior begins with a basic question about work or organizations. Frequently, researchers express the question as a hypothesis, a formal statement of the expected relationship between two variables.

◆ Careful measurement of variables is important in research. Reliability is an index of the consistency of a research subject's responses. Validity is an index of the extent to which a measure truly reflects what it is supposed to measure.

◆ In observational research, one or a few observers assess one or a few instances of organizational behavior in its natural setting. In participant observation the observer actually takes part in the activity being observed. In direct observation the assessment occurs without the active participation of the researcher.

◆ Compared with observation, correlational research techniques attempt to measure the variables in question more precisely by using questionnaires, interviews, and existing data. No change is introduced into the research setting. One problem with correlational research is its inability to reveal which variables cause other variables. Researchers use experiments to overcome this problem.

◆ In experimental research, the investigator actually changes or manipulates some factor in the organizational setting and measures the effect that this manipulation has on behavior. Causation can be inferred from a carefully designed experiment.

◆ Proper sampling, attention to Hawthorne effects, and ethical considerations are all components of good organizational research.

KEY CONCEPTS

Hypothesis
Reliability
Validity
Observational research
Participant observation
Direct observation

Correlational research
Experimental research
Independent variable
Dependent variable
Control group
Hawthorne effect

DISCUSSION QUESTIONS

1. Describe the assumptions about organizational behavior that are reflected in television shows such as situation comedies and police dramas. How accurate are these portrayals? Do they influence our thinking about what occurs in organizations?

2. Discuss an example in which an inaccurate assumption about organizational behavior caused you a problem.

3. State three very specific hypotheses about behavior in organizations and describe how you would test them.

4. Review the comparative strengths and weaknesses of experimental research, correlational research, and observational research.

5. A researcher finds that superior ratings of subordinate performance are reliable but not valid. What does this mean?

6. A company introduces a complicated new bonus plan for its factory workers. To explain how it works, it holds a number of meetings, puts up posters, and prepares a video information campaign. After introducing the bonus plan, productivity increases for a while and then reverts to preplan levels. Interpret what happened in terms of the Hawthorne effect.

7. In principle, an investigator could conduct a workplace experiment without the employees being aware that they were research subjects. Is this ethical? Why or why not?

EXPERIENTIAL EXERCISE
OB ON TV

In the first part of the chapter we examined various unsystematic sources of knowledge about organizational behavior. The purpose of this exercise is to explore in greater detail one of these sources—the portrayal of organizational behavior on television. Most experts on the function of TV as a communication medium agree on two points. First, although TV may present an inaccurate or distorted view of many specific events, the overall content of TV programming does accurately reflect the general values and concerns of society. Second, experts generally agree that TV has the power to shape the attitudes and expectations of viewers. If this is so, we should pay some attention to the portrayal of work and organizational behavior on TV.

Prepare this exercise before its assigned class:

1. Choose a prime time TV show that interests you. (This means a show that begins between 8 P.M. and 10 P.M. in your viewing area. If your schedule prohibits this, choose another time.) The show in question could be a comedy, a drama, or a documentary ranging from *Roseanne* to *NYPD Blue*. Your instructor may give you some more specific instructions about what to watch.
2. On a piece of paper, list the name of the program, its date, and time of broadcast. Write the answers to the following questions during or immediately following the broadcast:
   a. What industry is the primary focus of the program? Use the following list to categorize your answer: agriculture; mining; construction; manufacturing; transportation; communication; wholesale trade; retail trade; finance; service; public administration. (Examples of service industries include hotel, health, legal, education, newspaper, amusement, and private investigation. Examples of public administration include justice, police work, and national security.)
   b. What industries or occupations are of secondary focus in the program?
   c. What exact job categories or occupational roles do the main characters in the program play? Use this list to categorize your answers: managerial; clerical; professional; sales; service; craftsperson; machine operator; laborer; lawbreaker; military personnel; customer/patient/client; housework.
   d. Write several paragraphs describing how organizational life is portrayed in the program. For example, is it fun or boring? Does it involve conflict or cooperation? Are people treated fairly? Do they seem motivated? Is work life stressful?
   e. What aspects of the TV portrayal of organizational behavior do you think were realistic? Which were unrealistic?
3. Be prepared to discuss your findings in class. Your instructor will have some research information about how organizational life has actually been portrayed on TV over the years.

Source: Inspired by the research of Leah Vande Berg and Nick Trujillo as reported in Vande Berg, L., & Trujillo, N. (1989). *Organizational life on television.* Norwood, NJ: Ablex.

CASE STUDY
ELECTRIC CITY

Twenty-five years ago, Ollie Grayson had a good idea. Over the years the fruits of that idea provided him with a lot of personal satisfaction and made him a lot of money. At the time, Ollie owned a modest appliance store on the main street of a medium-sized southern city. Ollie's store prospered by selling stoves, refrigerators, washers, dryers, and televisions to the good citizens of that city. Ollie's main competitors were two large chain department stores located on the same street. However, a combination of lower overhead and more personalized selling techniques enabled Ollie's store to more than hold its own against the department stores.

During this period, Ollie accurately foresaw several trends that were to radically reshape American retailing. One of these was the rise in popularity of large suburban shopping malls located on relatively low-priced land outside of city centers. Another was a boom in the home appliance and consumer electronics market. Electric dishwashers and trash compactors were coming onto the market already, and Ollie knew that microwave ovens for home use were not far behind. And the home entertainment market had nowhere to go but up, as his increased sales of color televisions were already showing. Ollie was a great fan of classical music, and he had recently purchased a sophisticated, expensive component stereo system from a very small specialist music shop. His own store did not carry such equipment, only low-priced one-unit record player systems and overpriced (he thought) console versions of the same thing. But Ollie read all the electronics trade magazines, and he foresaw the day when most American homes would have component sound systems. And Ollie felt that when the market for such sound systems was saturated, new devices such as video recorders or even home computers might come along to take up the slack.

What Ollie saw was space in the marketplace for a new kind of store that wasn't a department store, a specialist shop, or even a traditional appliance store like his own. Rather, it was predicated on selling large volumes of appliances and electronic gear at very competitive prices—a "warehouse-type operation" Ollie called it at the time. Ollie predicted that when the big department stores moved to the malls, they would think twice about devoting much floor space to bulky, low-turnover items like appliances. And he felt that they would not attract the sales talent to do a good job of selling the more sophisticated electronic equipment. On the other hand, he felt that as the mystique disappeared from sound systems, price—not esoteric music knowledge—would be key to sales. This would make the small specialist shops less competitive.

When he heard rumors of a large mall development just outside of town, Ollie jumped into action. He took an option on a piece of property on the main road between the city and the proposed mall, and he began to turn his dream into a reality. Ollie named his new store Electric City, and it was immediately successful. As he says today, "I let the glitzy shopping mall attract the customers, and I peddled them low-cost appliances and electronics gear from my rather spartan premises."

Over the years, using basically the same tactics, Ollie repeated his success, gradually opening eighteen Electric City stores throughout the South. All the stores are profitable, although this varies according to store location. The average store employs 35 people, most of whom are sales personnel, and none of whom are unionized. Nowadays, Ollie spends most of his time touring his stores and "managing by walking around." He visits each store at least three times a year and is well-liked and respected by almost all personnel. For relaxation, Ollie listens to classical music on a top-of-the-line compact disc system that is readily available in any Electric City outlet.

In the late 1980s, Ollie became aware that the profitability of the Electric City chain was gradually leveling off. In response he called in a consulting firm that he had employed successfully in the past and asked them to do a thorough analysis of the situation. The consultants examined financial data, visited Electric City stores, talked to store managers and personnel, and visited competing electronics and appliance outlets. The partner who headed the consulting project summarized the results for Ollie:

"Mr. Grayson, you have prime store locations, a good selection of merchandise, a good pricing policy, and an efficient distribution system. What we think you need to do is pursue a more aggressive selling policy in the stores. Competition has increased tremendously in your market sector, and clinching sales on the premises seems to be the key to continued success. We recommend a two-part strategy. First, we think you need to institute a formal sales training program for your personnel. This may cover some product knowledge, but they seem pretty good there. What they need more is some advanced sales skills training. To reinforce your concern with sales, we also recommend that you replace your current hourly pay plan for sales personnel with a system based partly on hourly pay and partly on commission. Here, let me show you some projected figures. . . . "

Ollie Grayson pondered the consultant's recommendations. It was true that Electric City had never used formal sales training. Sales personnel had been viewed more as order takers in the warehouse-type operation. Sales training was expensive. Would it be effective? Ollie also debated the question of commissions. How would the sales staff react? How would the nonsales staff react? Electric City stores had always had good labor relations, and Ollie didn't want this to change. And how would customers react to all this? Would the sales staff become overly aggressive? Could training be used without the commission scheme, or vice versa? Ollie just wasn't sure.

1. Construct a research design to help Ollie Grayson solve his dilemmas. Justify the logic behind your choice of research techniques, and state the hypotheses you are testing.
2. Discuss the issue of measurement in your proposed research design. What should be measured, how should it be measured, and when should it be measured?
3. Discuss any problems that might occur in performing the research you propose.
4. Could the Hawthorne effect come into play in your research study?
5. What are the ethical concerns about the research you propose?

PART TWO

INDIVIDUAL
BEHAVIOR

LEARNING OBJECTIVES

AFTER READING CHAPTER 3 YOU SHOULD BE ABLE TO:

1 DEFINE LEARNING AND UNDERSTAND ITS GENERAL ROLE IN INFLUENCING ORGANIZATIONAL BEHAVIOR.

2 DIFFERENTIATE BETWEEN POSITIVE AND NEGATIVE REINFORCEMENT AND EXPLAIN HOW TO USE THEM EFFECTIVELY.

3 EXPLAIN WHEN TO USE IMMEDIATE VERSUS DELAYED REINFORCEMENT, WHEN TO USE CONTINUOUS VERSUS PARTIAL REINFORCEMENT, AND HOW TO SCHEDULE PARTIAL REINFORCEMENT.

4 DISCUSS ORGANIZATIONAL BEHAVIOR MODIFICATION.

5 EXPLAIN MODELING AND SELF-MANAGEMENT.

6 DISTINGUISH BETWEEN EXTINCTION AND PUNISHMENT AND EXPLAIN HOW TO PUNISH EFFECTIVELY.

7 DEFINE PERSONALITY AND DISCUSS ITS GENERAL ROLE IN INFLUENCING ORGANIZATIONAL BEHAVIOR.

8 DISCUSS THE "BIG FIVE" DIMENSIONS OF PERSONALITY.

9 DISCUSS THE ORGANIZATIONAL CONSEQUENCES OF DIFFERENCES IN LOCUS OF CONTROL, SELF-MONITORING, AND SELF-ESTEEM.

ROBERT CAMPEAU'S LEARNING HISTORY AND PERSONALITY LED TO HIS RISKY INVESTMENT STYLE, INCLUDING THE PURCHASE OF BLOOMINGDALE'S.

CHAPTER 3

LEARNING AND PERSONALITY

Robert Campeau and Paul Reichmann were two of North America's largest real estate developers. In 1988, The Campeau Corporation owned 1,500 department and specialty stores, including the jewel in the crown, the famed Bloomingdale's.

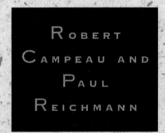

ROBERT
CAMPEAU AND
PAUL
REICHMANN

Through Olympia and York Development, Reichmann and his family controlled over 40 office buildings containing some 43 million square feet of rentable space. With 14 Manhattan skyscrapers, the Reichmanns were New York's biggest landlords.

If Canadians Campeau and Reichmann are both intelligent, ambitious, and successful, their similarities end there. Campeau grew up in a poor family, quit school at 14, and went to work as a laborer in a mining company. Today he is charming and outgoing, a lover of publicity and parties, a flamboyant dresser. Reichmann, in contrast, grew up in a prosperous family and attended an English college to "improve his mind." Reichmann is a contemplative, private, some even say secretive, man. A conservative dresser, his understated house stands in sharp contrast to Campeau's elaborate mansion.

Campeau built his success on hard work and a flair for promotion. His contagious enthusiasm was an attractive quality to others. Beginning with a small side-line construction company, he turned it into a $100 million business. In 1972, Campeau lost control of the company in a deal gone sour and entered a state of nervous depression, not the last time that this would happen. Gradually, he rebuilt his real estate empire, capped by the much-desired acquisition of Bloomingdale's. Reichmann built his success on a genius for financing and a reputation for ethical business behavior. What Reichmann touched in real estate turned to gold, and creditors accepted his obscurity and secrecy as a small price to pay for their return on investment.

By 1990, Campeau was in bad trouble. His obsessive pattern of acquisitions, funded with lusty borrowing, came to a crunch with the effects of the North American recession on real estate and retail buying. Both his Allied Stores, and Federal Department Stores, acquired just two years earlier for $6.6 billion to snare Bloomingdale's, filed for Chapter 11 protection. Observers said it was the largest retailing bankruptcy ever. By 1992, Paul Reichmann was also in trouble. His most ambitious project, London's $3 billion Canary Wharf business district, was beset by similar financing problems, and Olympia and York filed for protection from its creditors, who were now a lot more concerned about the exact details of Reichmann's money management.[1]

How could two people who are so different both gain such success? And how could they fail in spite of this earlier success? In this chapter we will concentrate on individual differences and their impact on organizational behavior. First, we'll consider the learning process and see how effective learning in organizations can be encouraged. Then, we'll study how individuals can "unlearn" ineffective behavior. Finally, we'll see how people's personalities influence what happens in organizations.

WHAT IS LEARNING?

Learning. A relatively permanent change in behavior potential that occurs due to practice or experience.

Learning occurs when practice or experience leads to a relatively permanent change in behavior potential. The words *practice* or *experience* rule out viewing behavioral changes caused by factors like drug intake or biological maturation as learning. One does not learn to be relaxed after taking a tranquilizer, and a boy does not suddenly learn to be a bass singer at the age of 14. The practice or experience that prompts learning stems from an environment that gives feedback concerning the consequences of behavior.

In the 1930s the psychologist B. F. Skinner investigated the behavior of rats confined in a box containing a lever that delivered food pellets when the rats pulled it. Initially, the rats ignored the lever, but at some point they would accidentally operate it and a pellet would appear. Over time, the rats gradually acquired the lever-pulling response as a means of obtaining food. In other words, they *learned* to pull the lever. The kind of learning Skinner studied is called *operant* learning because the subject learns to operate on the environment to achieve certain consequences. The rats learned to operate the lever to achieve food. Notice that operantly learned behavior is controlled by the consequences that follow it. These consequences usually depend upon the behavior, and this connection is what is learned. For example, salespeople learn effective sales techniques to achieve commissions and avoid criticism from their managers. The consequences of commissions and criticism depend upon which sales behaviors salespeople exhibit.

Besides directly experiencing consequences, humans can learn by observing the behavior of others. This form of learning is called *social* learning. Generally, social learning involves examining the behavior of others, seeing what consequences they experience, and thinking about what might happen if we act the same way. If we expect favorable consequences, we might imitate the behavior. In training, the rookie salesperson might be required to make calls with a seasoned sales veteran. By simply observing the veteran in action, the rookie will probably acquire considerable skill without yet having personally made a sale. Obviously, operant learning theory and social learning theory complement each other in explaining organizational behavior.[2]

INCREASING THE PROBABILITY OF BEHAVIOR

One of the most important consequences that promotes behavior is reinforcement. **Reinforcement** is the process by which stimuli strengthen behaviors. Thus, a *reinforcer* is a stimulus that follows some behavior and increases or maintains the probability of that behavior. The sales commissions and criticism mentioned above are reinforcers. In each case, reinforcement serves to strengthen behaviors such as proper sales techniques that fulfill organizational goals. In general, organizations are interested in maintaining or increasing the probability of behaviors such as correct performance, prompt attendance, and accurate decision making. As we shall see, positive reinforcers work by their application to a situation, while negative reinforcers work by their removal from a situation.

Reinforcement. The process by which stimuli strengthen behaviors.

Positive Reinforcement

Positive reinforcement increases or maintains the probability of some behavior by the *application* or *addition* of a stimulus to the situation in question. Such a stimulus is a positive reinforcer. In the basic Skinnerian learning situation described earlier, we can assume that reinforcement occurred because the probability of lever operation increased over time. We can further assume that the food pellets were positive reinforcers because they were introduced after the lever was pulled.

Positive reinforcement. The application or addition of a stimulus that increases or maintains the probability of some behavior.

Consider the experienced securities analyst who tends to read a particular set of financial newspapers regularly. If we had been able to observe the development of this reading habit, we might have found that it occurred as the result of a series of successful business decisions. That is, the analyst learns to scan those papers whose reading is positively reinforced by subsequent successful decisions. In this example, something is added to the situation (favorable decisions) that increases the probability of certain behavior (selective reading). Also, the appearance of the reinforcer is dependent or contingent upon the occurrence of that behavior.

In general, positive reinforcers tend to be pleasant things such as food, praise, money, or business success. However, the intrinsic character of stimuli do not determine whether they are positive reinforcers, and pleasant stimuli are not positive reinforcers when considered in the abstract. Whether or not something is a positive reinforcer depends only upon whether it increases or maintains the occurrence of some behavior by its application. Thus, it is improbable that the Christmas turkey employers give to all the employees of a manufacturing plant positively reinforces anything. The only behavior upon which receipt of the turkey is contingent is being employed by the company during the third week of December. It is unlikely that the turkey increases the probability that employees will remain for another year or work harder. On the other hand, stimuli that most of us find unpleasant might serve as positive reinforcers for the behavior of masochists, who seek pain. Reinforcers are designated by what they do and how they do it, not by their surface appearance.

In the vignette that opened the chapter, both Mr. Campeau and Mr. Reichmann had considerable early success that positively reinforced their interest in real estate acquisitions.

Negative Reinforcement

Negative reinforcement. The removal of a stimulus that in turn increases or maintains the probability of some behavior.

Negative reinforcement increases or maintains the probability of some behavior by the *removal* of a stimulus from the situation in question. Also, negative reinforcement occurs when a response *prevents* some event or stimulus from occurring. In each case, the removed or prevented stimulus is a *negative reinforcer*. Negative reinforcers are usually aversive or unpleasant stimuli, and it stands to reason that we will learn to repeat behaviors that remove or prevent these stimuli.

Let's repeat this point, because it frequently confuses students of organizational behavior: Negative reinforcers *increase* the probability of behavior. Suppose we rig a cage with an electrified floor so that it provides a mild shock to its inhabitant. In addition, we install a lever that will turn off the electricity. On the first few trials, a rat put in the cage will become very upset when shocked. Sooner or later, however, it will accidentally operate the lever and turn off the current. Gradually, the rat will learn to operate the lever as soon as it feels the shock. The shock serves as a negative reinforcer for the lever pulling, increasing the probability of the behavior by its removal.

Managers who continually nag their subordinates unless they work hard are attempting to use negative reinforcement. The only way subordinates can stop the aversive nagging is to work hard and be diligent. The nagging maintains the probability of productive responses by its removal. In this situation, subordinates often get pretty good at anticipating the onset of nagging by the look on the boss's face. This look serves as a signal that they can avoid nagging altogether if they work harder.

Rules and regulations with penalties attached are a common form of negative reinforcement. *Success* magazine instituted a system of fines for spelling and grammatical errors to encourage its writers to be more meticulous. The motive to avoid fines was expected to stimulate better writing.[3]

Negative reinforcers generally tend to be unpleasant things such as shock, nagging, or threat of fines. Again, however, negative reinforcers are defined only by what they do and how they work, not by their unpleasantness. Above, we indicated that nagging could serve as a negative reinforcer to increase the probability of productive responses. However, nagging could also serve as a positive reinforcer to increase the probability of unproductive responses if a subordinate has a need for attention and nagging is the only attention the manager provides. In the first case, nagging was a negative reinforcer—it was terminated following productive responses. In the second case, nagging was a positive reinforcer—it was applied following unproductive responses. In both cases, the responses increased in probability.

Organizational Errors Involving Reinforcement

Experience indicates that managers sometimes make errors in trying to use reinforcement. The most common errors are confusing rewards with reinforcers, neglecting diversity in preferences for reinforcers, and neglecting important sources of reinforcement.

Confusing Rewards With Reinforcers.　Organizations and individual managers frequently "reward" workers with things such as pay, promotions, fringe benefits, paid vacations, overtime work, and the opportunity to perform challenging tasks. Such rewards can fail to serve as reinforcers, however, because organizations don't make them contingent upon specific behaviors that are of interest to the organization, such as attendance, innovation, or productivity. For example, many organizations assign overtime work on the basis of seniority, rather than performance or good attendance, even when the union contract doesn't require it. Although the opportunity to earn extra money might have strong potential as a reinforcer, it is seldom made contingent upon some desired behavior.

For another example of a "lost" reinforcer, take an advertising manager whose graphic artist has trouble meeting deadlines for the completion of projects. When the artist completed his work on an especially crucial sales presentation well before the deadline, the manager waited until a slack period two weeks later to reward him with an afternoon off work. Not only did the manager fail to specify why she was granting the time off, but during the two-week interval the artist failed to complete two other projects on time! The long period of time between the good performance and the reward destroyed any contingent reinforcing effects, and one might suspect that, if anything, the tardy completions were more likely reinforced.

Neglecting Diversity in Preferences for Reinforcers.　Organizations often fail to appreciate individual differences in preferences for reinforcers. In this case, even if managers administer rewards after a desired behavior, they might fail to have a reinforcing effect. Intuitively, it seems questionable to reinforce a workaholic's extra effort with time off from work, yet such a strategy is fairly common. A more appropriate reinforcer might be the assignment of some challenging task, such as work on a very demanding key project. Some labor contracts include clauses that dictate that supervisors assign overtime to the workers who have the greatest seniority. Not surprisingly, high-seniority workers are often the best paid and the least in need of the extra pay available through overtime. Even if it is administered so that the best-performing high-seniority workers get the overtime, such a strategy might not prove reinforcing—the usual time off might be preferred over extra money.

Managers should carefully explore the possible range of stimuli under their control (such as task assignment and time off from work) for their applicability as reinforcers for particular subordinates. Furthermore, organizations should attempt to administer their formal rewards (such as pay and promotions) to capitalize upon their reinforcing effects for various individuals.

Neglecting Important Sources of Reinforcement.   There are many reinforcers of organizational behavior that are not especially obvious. While concentrating upon potential reinforcers of a formal nature, such as pay or promotions, organizations and their managers often neglect those which are administered by co-workers or intrinsic to the jobs being performed. Many managers cannot understand why a worker would persist in potentially dangerous horseplay despite threats of a pay penalty or dismissal. Frequently, such activity is positively reinforced by the attention provided by the joker's co-workers. In fact, on a particularly boring job, even such threats might act as positive reinforcers for horseplay by relieving the boredom, especially if the threats are never carried out. Consider the vignette that began the chapter. Money per se was probably not a reinforcer for millionaires Reichmann and Campeau. Rather, power, prestige and the thrill of the big deal probably were.

One very important source of reinforcement that managers often ignore is that which accompanies the successful performance of tasks. This reinforcement is available on jobs that provide *feedback* concerning the adequacy of performance. On some jobs, feedback contingent upon performance is readily available. Doctors can observe the success of their treatment by observing the progress of their patients' health, and mechanics can take the cars they repair for a test drive. In other cases, organizations must design some special feedback mechanism into the job.

Consultant Edward J. Feeney, former vice-president of Emery Air Freight, has described that company's experience in providing such a system. Emery's profits were highly dependent upon the use of large containers to forward smaller pieces of freight to a common destination. Costs soared when these containers were not fully utilized. For this reason, warehouse workers and their supervisors were carefully trained to use the containers when possible, and both parties felt that they were achieving around 90 percent utilization. In fact, a performance audit indicated a rate of 45 percent. The change in the job implemented by Feeney was very simple. Workers had to keep a checklist to provide themselves with feedback concerning container utilization. This feedback so reinforced correct performance that utilization jumped to 95 percent within a very short time. Emery estimated that this simple change saved $650,000 in one year.[4]

Before continuing, please consult *You Be the Manager.*

Reinforcement Strategies and Their Effects

What is the best way to administer reinforcers? Should we apply a reinforcer immediately after the behavior of interest occurs, or should we wait for some period of time? Should we reinforce every correct behavior, or should we reinforce only a portion of correct responses?

To obtain the *fast acquisition* of some response, continuous and immediate reinforcement should be used—that is, the reinforcer should be applied

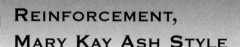

REINFORCEMENT, MARY KAY ASH STYLE

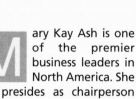

Mary Kay Ash is one of the premier business leaders in North America. She presides as chairperson emeritus over Mary Kay Cosmetics, a Dallas-based firm with 300,000 salespeople and $613 million in sales. The great majority of these salespeople ("beauty consultants") are women, who begin by purchasing a $100 makeup case and selling cosmetic products to friends, colleagues, and acquaintances at a markup. Home parties are a common selling technique. Salespeople who recruit others to the selling ranks can become managers and receive a share of their sales. Currently, about two-thirds of the sales staff hold full-time jobs over and above their Mary Kay work.

Things weren't always so easy for Mary Kay. Imagine the task facing her in 1963 when she founded the company. She had a product that she believed in but no way to get it to the public. Also, she had been discriminated against in business because of her gender, so she

> MARY KAY ASH IS ONE OF THE PREMIER BUSINESS FOUNDERS IN NORTH AMERICA. AN EARLY TASK WAS TO FIND REINFORCERS FOR HER SALES FORCE.

wanted to develop a company that would affirm the worth of women. Thus, she hit on the free-lance beauty consultant system. How could she motivate these people? Buying products direct from Dallas and marking them up pretty much took care of the money angle. Besides, Mary Kay didn't want to overrely on money, given her firm motto of "God first, family second, job third." What, besides money, might motivate a work force of independent operators, many of whom lacked much conventional employment experience? You be the manager.

1. What are some potential reinforcers that Mary Kay Ash might use given the nature of her sales force?

2. What are the special problems of trying to reinforce 300,000 salespeople scattered all over North America?

To find out what Ms. Ash did, see *The Manager's Notebook* at the end of the chapter.

Sources: Farnham, A. (1993, September 20). Mary Kay's lessons in leadership. *Fortune,* 68–77; Ash, M. K. (1984). *Mary Kay on people management.* New York: Warner.

---

every time the behavior of interest occurs, and it should be applied without delay after each occurrence. Many conditions exist in which the fast acquisition of responses is desirable. These include correcting the behavior of "problem" employees, training employees for emergency operations, and dealing with unsafe work behaviors. Consider the otherwise excellent performer who tends to be late for work. Under pressure to demote or fire this good worker, the boss might sensibly attempt to positively reinforce instances of prompt attendance with compliments and encouragement. To modify the subordinate's behavior as quickly as possible, the supervisor might station herself near the office door each morning to supply these reinforcers regularly and immediately.

You might wonder when one would not want to use a continuous, immediate reinforcement strategy to mold organizational behavior. Put simply, behavior that individuals learn under such conditions tends not to persist when reinforcement is made less frequent or stopped. Intuitively, this should not be surprising. For example, under normal conditions, operating the power switch on your stereo system is continuously and immediately reinforced by music. If the system develops a short circuit and fails to produce music, your switch-operating behavior will extinguish very quickly. In the example in the preceding paragraph, the need for fast learning justified the use of continuous, immediate reinforcement. Under more typical circumstances, we would hope that prompt attendance could occur without such close attention.

Behavior tends to be *persistent* when it is learned under conditions of partial and delayed reinforcement. That is, it will tend to persist under reduced or terminated reinforcement when not every instance of the behavior is reinforced during learning or when some time period elapses between its enactment and reinforcement. In most cases, the supervisor who wishes to reinforce prompt attendance knows that he will not be able to stand by the shop door every morning to compliment his crew's timely entry. Given this constraint, the supervisor should compliment prompt attendance occasionally, perhaps later in the day. This should increase the persistence of promptness and reduce the subordinates' reliance on the boss's monitoring.

To repeat, continuous, immediate reinforcement facilitates fast learning, and delayed, partial reinforcement facilitates persistent learning (Exhibit 3.1). Notice that it is impossible to maximize both speed and persistence with a single reinforcement strategy. Also, many responses in our everyday lives cannot be continuously and immediately reinforced, so in many cases it pays to sacrifice some speed in learning to prepare the learner for this fact of life. All of this suggests that managers have to tailor reinforcement strategies to the needs of the situation. Often, managers must alter the strategies over time to achieve effective learning and maintenance of behavior. For example, the manager training a new subordinate should probably use a reinforcement strategy that is fairly continuous and immediate (whatever the reinforcer). Looking over the subordinate's shoulder to obtain the fast acquisition of behavior is appropriate. Gradually, however, the supervisor should probably reduce the frequency of reinforcement and perhaps build some delay into its presentation to reduce the subordinate's dependency upon his or her attention.

Schedules of Partial Reinforcement

In this section we will consider the different ways partial reinforcement might be scheduled and the particular effects that these schedules have upon behavior. A consideration of reinforcement schedules enables us to explain

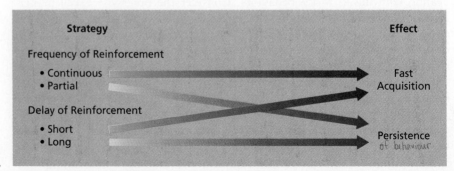

EXHIBIT 3.1
Summary of reinforcement strategies and their effects.

many natural variations in behavior that appear somewhat puzzling at first glance. Also, reinforcers are often expensive and time-consuming to administer, and we need to know which schedules will enable us to achieve most efficiently the behaviors we desire. We can divide reinforcement schedules into interval schedules and ratio schedules.

One kind of reinforcement schedule that we will consider is called an *interval schedule*. Under interval schedules, some *time period* must elapse after a reinforced response before another reinforcement is available. In this case, the number of responses following a reinforcement is irrelevant to how quickly the next reinforcement becomes available, since interval schedules are time-dependent. (Of course, responses must be made for reinforcement to occur.) The other kind of schedule we will examine is a *ratio schedule*. Under ratio schedules, some *number of responses* must occur after a reinforced response before another reinforcement is available. Here, the number of responses following a reinforcement determines how quickly the next reinforcement becomes available. In other words, "fast work equals more reinforcement" under ratio schedules, which are response-dependent.

Fixed Interval. Under a **fixed interval schedule,** some *fixed* time period occurs between a reinforced response and the availability of the next reinforcement. Under ideal conditions, mail is delivered according to this schedule—every 24 hours your mailbox-checking activity is reinforced by the mail carrier's visit. Similarly, if you have three equally spaced announced tests during the semester in your organizational behavior class, you can see a fixed interval schedule at work. Your studying behavior is reinforced by the opportunity to demonstrate your knowledge and receive a grade. Notice the kind of behavior that this schedule induces (Exhibit 3.2). The individual in question learns to anticipate when reinforcement is available and tends to respond more rapidly as this time approaches. After reinforcement, the behavior subsides because the individual has learned that no further reinforcement will occur for awhile. The fixed interval exam schedule often leads to "cramming" behavior on the part of students in advance of "E day," followed by a moratorium on studying until the next exam approaches.

Organizations abound with examples of fixed interval schedules. Companies arrange yearly performance reviews in this manner. On a certain date, or on an employee's anniversary date with the firm, his or her supervisor sits down and discusses the employee's performance during the previous year. In advance of this reinforcement, many managers have seen performance improve as the date for the review draws near. Also, records often reveal that the best attendance occurs on paydays.

Variable Interval. Under this schedule, some *variable* time period occurs between a reinforced response and the chance for the next reinforcement. In other words, reinforcement can occur at any time, unexpectedly. As shown in Exhibit 3.2, a **variable interval schedule** leads to a slow, steady rate of response, because the individual cannot anticipate when a reinforcement will occur and cannot influence its occurrence by responding faster. A random "pop quiz" system, in which the students do not know when they will have an exam during the semester, is an example of a variable interval schedule. Not surprisingly, such a system makes "cramming" impossible and tends to distribute study time more evenly over the semester. For obvious reasons, bank examiners tend to

> **Fixed interval schedule.** A partial reinforcement schedule in which some fixed time period occurs between a reinforced response and the availability of the next reinforcement.

> **Variable interval schedule.** A partial reinforcement schedule in which some variable time period occurs between a reinforced response and the chance for the next reinforcement.

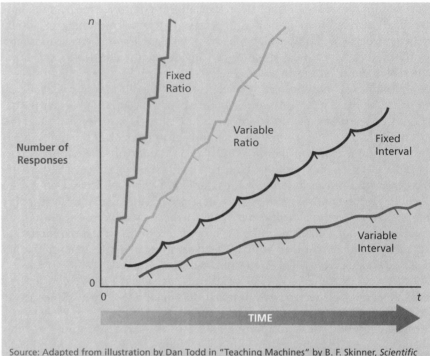

EXHIBIT 3.2
Idealized response curves for reinforcement schedules. The steeper the curve, the higher the rate of response. Reinforcements are indicated by short diagonal lines.

schedule their visits to banks according to a variable interval schedule, arranged around some average number of inspections per year. By the same token, some managers have learned to overcome the deficiencies of the formal yearly performance appraisal system by providing unannounced informal reviews during the year.

Fixed ratio schedule. A partial reinforcement schedule in which some fixed number of responses must be made between a reinforced response and the availability of the next reinforcement.

Fixed Ratio. Under a **fixed ratio schedule,** after a reinforced response, some *fixed* number of responses must be made before another reinforcement becomes available. Hand-operated water pumps work according to a fixed ratio schedule. A given number of pumping movements is necessary before the water flows. As shown in Exhibit 3.2, this schedule leads to a high rate of response followed by a short pause after reinforcement. The loading dock supervisor who permits his workers to take a rest break after they stack a hundred crates is implementing a fixed ratio schedule. He is assuming that the break will serve as a reinforcer for high performance when coupled with a specific, known performance goal of a hundred crates. The firm that gives its office employees an extra vacation day for every 40 working days they complete without being absent is applying a fixed ratio schedule to reinforce attendance.

Variable ratio schedule. A partial reinforcement schedule in which some variable number of responses must be made between a reinforced response and the availability of the next reinforcement.

Variable Ratio. With this schedule, some *variable* number of responses is necessary after a reinforcement before another reinforcement is offered. As shown in Exhibit 3.2, a **variable ratio schedule** typically leads to a very high response rate with little or no pause after reinforcement. Slot machines are programmed according to a variable ratio schedule, paying off after some variable number of attempts by the players. The ratio of payoffs to plays is designed around some average that nets the casino a handsome profit. Door-to-door salespeople are reinforced by sales according to a variable ratio schedule. The more houses they call on, the more likely they are to make a sale, but the number of houses called on between sales varies. Lower-level managers have their suggestions accepted by top management according to this schedule. The more suggestions the managers offer, the greater the chance top management will approve one, although the number of ideas managers generate between approvals varies.

Organizational Behavior Modification

Most reinforcement occurs naturally, rather than as the result of a conscious attempt to manage behavior. However, the description of the feedback procedure that Emery Air Freight instituted is an example of **organizational behavior modification,** or the systematic use of learning principles to influence organizational behavior. The results achieved at Emery have been essentially anecdotal. In this section we will describe researchers' attempts to scientifically monitor practical applications of organizational behavior modification. In each case, a firm attempted to positively reinforce employee behaviors that were of interest to the organization. In general, research supports the effectiveness of such programs.[5]

Organizational behavior modification. The systematic use of learning principles to influence organizational behavior.

Reinforcing Attendance. A manufacturing company was interested in improving the attendance of its employees. Workers in four sections served as control subjects, while those in another section were confronted with the following behavior modification plan:

> Each day an employee comes to work on time, he is allowed to choose a card from a deck of playing cards. At the end of the five-day week, he will have five cards or a normal poker hand. The highest hand wins $20. There will be eight winners, one for approximately each department.[6]

Supervisors were in charge of monitoring attendance, passing out the cards, and posting on a large chart the poker hands held by subordinates as the week progressed. Over four months, the attendance rate increased 18 percent for workers exposed to the behavior modification plan, while the attendance rate for control workers actually decreased somewhat. Notice that at least two reinforcers were probably responsible for this success. First, the $20 that could be won evidently worked according to a variable ratio schedule. That is, more instances of prompt attendance increased the probability of winning $20, but a certain level of attendance did not guarantee reinforcement in any given week. Second, the cards themselves and the attendant discussion concerning the progress of the week's hands as revealed on the chart probably acquired continuous and immediate reinforcing properties. These reinforcers were available even for those who did not win the $20.

Reinforcing Workplace Safety. A second example of the use of organizational behavior modification involves the reinforcement of safe working behavior in a food-manufacturing plant. At first glance, accidents appeared to be chance events or wholly under the control of factors such as equipment failures. However, the researchers felt that accidents could be reduced if specific safe working practices could be identified and reinforced. These practices were identified with the help of past accident reports and advice from supervisors. Systematic observation of working behavior indicated that employees followed safe practices only about 74 percent of the time. A brief slide show was prepared to illustrate safe versus unsafe job behaviors. Then, two reinforcers of safe practices were introduced into the workplace. The first consisted of a feedback chart that was conspicuously posted in the workplace to indicate the percentage of safe behaviors observers noted. This chart included the percentages achieved in observational sessions before the slide show, as well as those achieved every three days after the slide show. This approximated a fixed interval schedule of reinforcement. A second source of reinforcement was supervisors who were encouraged to praise instances of safe performance that they observed, approximating a variable interval schedule. These interventions were successful in raising the percentage of safe working practices to around 97 percent almost immediately. When the reinforcers were terminated, the percentage of safe practices quickly returned to the level before the reinforcement was introduced. (See Exhibit 3.3.)[7]

For a cross-cultural study of organizational behavior modification see "Global Focus: *OB Mod Da, Participation Nyet.*"

Modeling

Organizational behavior modification programs involve the conscious use of reinforcement to manage organizational behavior. However, it has perhaps occurred to you that much learning can occur in organizations without the conscious control of positive and negative reinforcers by managers. Often, behavior seems to occur "automatically," without the benefit of gradual shaping through trial and error and selective reinforcement. For instance, after

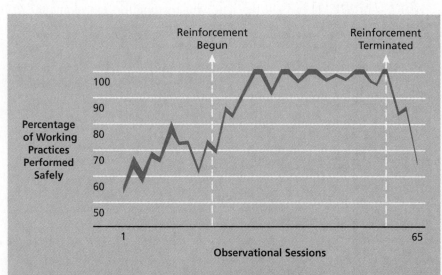

EXHIBIT 3.3
Percentage of safe working practices achieved with and without reinforcement.

Source: Adapted from Komaki, J., et al. (1978, August). A behavioral approach to occupational safety: Pinpointing and reinforcing safe performance in a food manufacturing plant. *Journal of Applied Psychology*, 63(4), 439. Copyright © 1978 by American Psychological Association. Adapted by permission.

GLOBAL FOCUS   OB Mod Da, Participation Nyet

Which Western management techniques might translate best to the newly developing economies of the former Soviet Union? This is the question that guided the research of Dianne Welsh, Fred Luthans, and Steve Sommer. They conducted research at the Kalinin Cotton Mill, the biggest textile mill in Russia. The research subjects were employees who set up and maintained the weaving machines and assisted the weavers with their work. Three different groups were exposed to three management techniques that have received some support in Western studies: organizational behavior modification, participative management, and productivity-based rewards. Under "OB Mod," the employees were informed of functional and dysfunctional work behaviors, and their supervisors were trained to give recognition and praise for functional behavior. Under participation, the employees were given the chance to suggest and implement changes that might improve weaving performance. Under rewards, employees were promised valued American consumer goods if productivity increased.

The researchers hypothesized that OB Mod and productivity-based rewards were compatible with Russian culture but that the participative approach was not, especially since it was implemented by outsiders. The hypotheses were confirmed. Both the OB Mod approach and the provision of contingent rewards led to an increase in the production of top-grade fabric. Participation actually resulted in

decreased production. The authors surmised that this resulted from past inaction on employee suggestions during the era of a centrally planned

In research performed at the Kalinin Cotton Mill, the largest textile mill in Russia, researchers found that organizational behavior modification and rewards stimulated productivity while worker participation in decisions did not.

economy. They concluded that care needs to be taken in translating management practices across cultures.

Source: Adapted from Welsh, D. H. B., Luthans, F., & Sommer, S. M. (1993). Managing Russian factory workers: The impact of U.S.-based behavioral and participative techniques. *Academy of Management Journal, 36,* 58–79.

experiencing just a couple of executive committee meetings, a newly promoted vice-president might look like an "old pro," bringing appropriate materials to the meeting, asking questions in an approved style, and so on.

How are we to account for such learning? One important factor is **modeling,** the process of imitating the behavior of others. With modeling, learning occurs by observing or imagining the behavior of others, rather than through direct personal experience.[8] Thus, the new vice-president doubtless modeled his or her behavior on that of the more experienced peers on the executive committee. But has reinforcement occurred here? It is *self-reinforcement* that occurs in the modeling process. For one thing, it is reinforcing to acquire an understanding of others who are viewed positively. In addition, we are able to imagine the reinforcers that the model experiences coming our way when we imitate his or her behavior. Surely this is why we imitate the behavior of sports heroes and entertainers, a fact that advertisers capitalize on when they choose them to endorse products. In any event, modeling is an aspect of what we earlier called social learning.

Modeling. The process of imitating the behavior of others.

What kinds of models are likely to provoke the greatest degree of imitation? In general, attractive, credible, competent, high-status people stand a good chance of being imitated. In addition, it is important that the model's behavior provoke consequences that are seen as positive and successful to the observer. Finally, it helps if the model's behavior is vivid and memorable—bores do not make good models.[9] In business schools, it is not unusual to find students who have developed philosophies or approaches that are modeled on credible, successful, high-profile business leaders. Current examples include Microsoft's Bill Gates and Disney's Michael Eisner, both of whom have been the object of extensive coverage in the business and popular press.

The extent of modeling as a means of learning in organizations suggests that managers should pay more attention to the process. For one thing, managers who operate on a principle of "do as I say, not as I do" will find that what they do is more likely to be imitated, including undesirable behaviors such as expense account abuse. Also, in the absence of credible management models, workers might imitate dysfunctional peer behavior if peers meet the criteria for strong models. On a more positive note, well-designed performance appraisal and reward systems permit organizations to publicize the kind of organizational behavior that should be imitated.

REDUCING THE PROBABILITY OF BEHAVIOR

Thus far in our discussion of learning, we have been interested in *increasing* the probability of various work behaviors, such as attendance or good performance. Both positive and negative reinforcement can accomplish this goal. However, in many cases we encounter learned behaviors that we wish to *stop* from occurring. Such behaviors are detrimental to the operation of the organization and could be detrimental to the health or safety of an individual employee.

There are two strategies that can reduce the probability of learned behavior: extinction and punishment.

Extinction

Extinction. The gradual dissipation of behavior following the termination of reinforcement.

Extinction simply involves terminating the reinforcement that is maintaining some unwanted behavior. If the behavior is not reinforced, it will gradually dissipate or be extinguished.

Consider the case of a bright, young marketing expert who was headed for the "fast track" in his organization. Although his boss, the vice-president of marketing, was considering him for promotion, the young expert had developed a very disruptive habit—the tendency to play comedian during department meetings. The vice-president observed that this wisecracking was reinforced by the appreciative laughs of two other department members. He proceeded to enlist their aid to extinguish the joking. After the vice-president explained the problem to them, they agreed to ignore the disruptive one-liners and puns. At the same time, the vice-president took special pains to positively reinforce constructive comments by the young marketer. Very quickly, joking was extinguished, and the young man's future with the company improved.[10]

This example illustrates that extinction works best when coupled with the reinforcement of some desired substitute behavior. Remember that behaviors that have been learned under delayed or partial reinforcement schedules are more difficult to extinguish than those learned under continuous, immediate reinforcement. Ironically, it would be harder to extinguish the joke-telling behavior of a partially successful committee member than of one who was always successful at getting a laugh.

Punishment

Punishment involves following an unwanted behavior with some unpleasant, aversive stimulus. In theory, this should reduce the probability of the response when the actor learns that the behavior leads to unwanted consequences. Notice the difference between punishment and negative reinforcement. In negative reinforcement a nasty stimulus is *removed* following some behavior, increasing the probability of that behavior. With punishment, a nasty stimulus is *applied* after some behavior, *decreasing* the probability of that behavior. If a boss criticizes her secretary after seeing the secretary use the office phone for personal calls, we expect to see less of this activity in the future. Exhibit 3.4 compares punishment with reinforcement and extinction.

Punishment. The application of an aversive stimulus following some behavior designed to decrease the probability of that behavior.

EXHIBIT 3.4
Summary of learning effects.

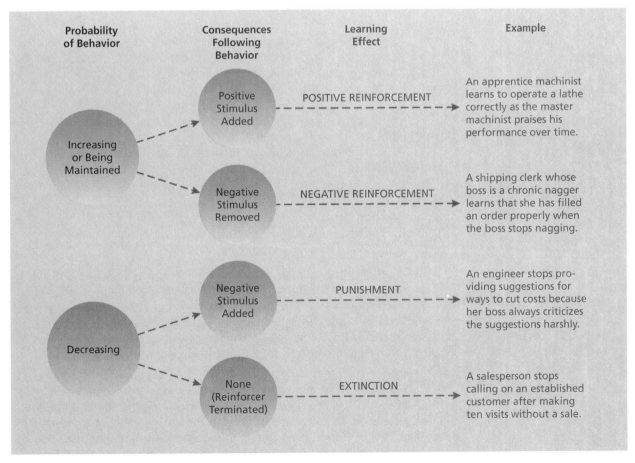

SUNTOON by Jim Phillips

FITCHLY... THAT PRODUCT YOU CAME UP WITH IS GREAT... UH... I GUESS NOW WE CAN LAY YOU OFF...

RESEARCH & DEVELOPMENT

Using Punishment Effectively

In theory, punishment should be useful for eliminating unwanted behavior. After all, it seems unreasonable to repeat actions that cause us trouble. Unfortunately, punishment has some unique characteristics that often limit its effectiveness in stopping unwanted activity. First of all, while punishment provides a clear signal as to which activities are inappropriate, it does not by itself demonstrate which activities should *replace* the punished response. Reconsider the executive who chastises her secretary for making personal calls at the office. If the secretary makes personal calls only when she has caught up on her work, she might legitimately wonder what she is supposed to be doing during her occasional free time. If the boss fails to provide substitute activities, the message contained in the punishment might be lost.

Both positive and negative reinforcers specify which behaviors are appropriate. Punishment indicates only what is not appropriate. Since no reinforced substitute behavior is provided, punishment only temporarily suppresses the unwanted response. When surveillance is removed, the response will tend to recur. Constant monitoring is very time-consuming, and individuals become amazingly adept at learning when they can get away with the forbidden activity. The secretary will soon learn when she can make personal calls without detection. The moral here is clear: *Provide an acceptable alternative for the punished response.*

A second difficulty with punishment is that it has a tendency to provoke a strong emotional reaction on the part of the punished individual.[11] This is especially likely when the punishment is delivered in anger or perceived to be unfair. Managers who try overly hard to be patient with subordinates and then finally blow up risk overemotional reactions. So do those who tolerate unwanted behavior on the part of their subordinates and then impulsively decide to make an example of one individual by punishing him or her. Managers should be sure that their own emotions are under control before punishing, and they should generally avoid punishment in front of observers.[12] Because of the emotional problems involved in the use of punishment, some organizations, such as Tampa Electric Company and Union Carbide, have downplayed its use in discipline systems. They give employees who have committed infractions *paid* time off to think about their problems.

In addition to providing correct alternative responses and limiting the emotions involved in punishment, there are several other principles that can increase the effectiveness of punishment.

- *Make sure the chosen punishment is truly aversive.* Organizations frequently "punish" chronically absent employees by making them take several days off work. Managers sometimes "punish" ineffective performers by requiring them to work overtime, which allows them to earn extra pay. In both cases, the presumed punishment might actually act as a positive reinforcer for the unwanted behavior.

- *Punish immediately.* Managers frequently overlook early instances of rules violations or ineffective performance, hoping that things will "work out."[13] This only allows these behaviors to gain strength through repetition. If immediate punishment is difficult to apply, the manager should delay action until a more appropriate time and then reinstate the circumstances surrounding the problem behavior. For example, the bank manager who observes her teller exhibiting inappropriate behaviors

IN FOCUS   No Flex at California's Department of Motor Vehicles

California's campaign to force state employers to be more flexible ends in a veto by Gov. Pete Wilson.

In the latest example of government involvement in workplace scheduling, the issue erupted into a legislative battle last spring after California's Department of Motor Vehicles imposed a punitive pay cut on employee Lesbhia Morones, an East Oakland mother of five, for repeated tardiness. Ms. Morones conceded that she was often late, usually by less than five minutes, partly because she didn't want to leave her children alone before school started at 8 A.M. Otherwise, she was a conscientious employee, the record showed.

An administrative law judge revoked the pay cut, but was overruled by the state's personnel board.

Amid a blitz of media attention to the plight of Ms. Morones, a deeply divided state Legislature passed a measure, backed by the 130,000-member state employees' union, requiring agencies to be flexible in accommodating workers with family duties. But Gov. Wilson disagreed, saying state law already provides ample protection for family needs.

The brouhaha is "a classic case" of how rigid policies can unfairly "catch in their net" and punish committed workers with family conflicts, says Fran Sussner Rodgers, chief executive of Work/Family Directions, a Boston consultant.

1. What does this story say about the difficulties of using punishment as a management tool?

2. To be effective, punishment must be perceived as fair. Who is most likely to view such a punitive pay cut as unfair?

Source: Shellengbarger, S. (1993, October 13). California stays rigid on scheduling. *The Wall Street Journal*, p. B1.

might ask this person to remain after work. She should then carry out punishment at the teller's window rather than in her office, perhaps demonstrating correct procedures and role-playing a customer to allow the subordinate to practice them.

- *Do not reward unwanted behaviors before or after punishment*. Many supervisors join in horseplay with their subordinates until they feel it's time to get some work done. Then, unexpectedly, they do an about-face and punish those who are "goofing around." Sometimes, managers feel guilty about punishing their subordinates for some rule infraction and then quickly attempt to make up with displays of good-natured sympathy or affection. For example, the boss who criticizes her secretary for personal calls might show up an hour later with a gift of flowers. Such actions present subordinates with extremely confusing signals about how they should behave, since the manager could be inadvertently reinforcing the very response that he or she wants to terminate.

- *Do not inadvertently punish desirable behavior*. This happens commonly in organizations (See the cartoon). Managers who do not use all of their capital budget for a given fiscal year might have their budget for the next year reduced, punishing their prudence. Government employees who "blow the whistle" on wasteful or inefficient practices might find themselves demoted.[14] University professors who are considered excellent teachers might be assigned to onerous, time-consuming duty on a curriculum committee, cutting into their class preparation time (see "In Focus: *No Flex at California's Department of Motor Vehicles*").

In summary, punishment can be an effective means of stopping undesirable behavior. However, managers must apply it very carefully and deliberately in order to achieve this effectiveness. In general, reinforcing correct behaviors and extinguishing unwanted responses are safer strategies for managers than the frequent use of punishment.

SELF-MANAGEMENT

In much of this chapter we have been concerned with how organizations and individual managers can use learning principles to manage the behavior of organizational members. However, employees can use learning principles to manage their *own* behavior, making external control less necessary. This process is called **self-management.**[15]

Self-management. The use of learning principles to manage one's own behavior.

How can self-management occur? You will recall that our discussion of social learning and modeling involved factors such as observation, imagination, imitation, and self-reinforcement. Individuals can use these and similar techniques in an intentional way to control their own behavior. The basic process involves observing one's own behavior, comparing the behavior with a standard, and rewarding oneself if the behavior meets the standard.[16]

To illustrate some specific self-management techniques, consider the executive who finds that he is taking too much work home to do in the evenings and over weekends. While his peers seem to have most evenings and weekends free, his own family is ready to disown him due to lack of attention! What can he do?[17]

- *Collect self-observation data.* This involves collecting objective data about one's own behavior. For example, the executive might keep a log of phone calls and other interruptions for a few days if he suspects that these contribute to his inefficiency.
- *Observe models.* The executive might examine the time-management skills of his peers to find someone successful to imitate.
- *Set goals.* The executive might set specific short-term goals to reduce telephone interruptions and unscheduled personal visits, enlisting the aid of his secretary and using self-observation data to monitor his progress. Longer-term goals might involve four free nights a week and no more than four hours of work on weekends.
- *Rehearse.* The executive might anticipate that he will have to educate his co-workers about his reduced availability. So as not to offend them, he might practice explaining the reason for his revised accessibility.
- *Reinforce oneself.* The executive might promise himself a weekend at the beach with his family the first time he gets his take-home workload down to his target level.

One western state used a self-management program to improve work attendance among unionized maintenance employees. Those who had used over half of their sick leave were invited by the personnel department to participate in an eight-week program with the following features:

- Discussion of general reasons for use of sick leave. High on the list were transportation problems, family difficulties, and problems with supervisors and co-workers.
- Self-assessment of personal reasons for absence and development of personal coping strategies.

- Goal setting to engage in behaviors that should improve attendance (short-term goals) and to improve attendance by a specific amount (long-term goal).

- Self-observation using charts and diaries. Employees recorded their own attendance, reasons for missing work, and steps they took to get to work.

- Identification of specific reinforcers and punishers to be self-administered for reaching or not reaching goals.

Compared to a control group, the employees who were exposed to the program achieved a significant improvement in attendance, and they also felt more confident that they would be able to come to work when confronted with various obstacles to attendance.[18] Self-management programs are frequently successful in positively changing work behavior.

In concluding this section on learning, you should understand that because of personality differences everyone does not react exactly the same way to reinforcement and punishment. On the other hand, learning experiences can actually shape one's personality. Let's examine the concept of personality.

WHAT IS PERSONALITY?

The notion of personality permeates thought and discussion in our culture. We are bombarded with information about "personalities" in the print and broadcast media. We are sometimes promised exciting introductions to people with "nice" personalities. We occasionally meet people who seem to have "no personality." But exactly what *is* personality?

Personality is the relatively stable set of psychological characteristics that influences the way an individual interacts with his or her environment. An individual's personality summarizes his or her personal style of dealing with the world. You have certainly noticed differences in personal style on the part of your parents, friends, professors, bosses, and subordinates. It is reflected in the distinctive way that they react to people, situations, and problems.

Where does personality come from? Personality consists of a number of dimensions and traits that are complexly determined by genetic predisposition and one's long-term learning history. Although personality is relatively stable, it is certainly susceptible to change through adult learning experience.

Personality. The relatively stable set of psychological characteristics that influences the way an individual interacts with his or her environment.

PERSONALITY AND ORGANIZATIONAL BEHAVIOR

Because of measurement problems, personality has a rather rocky history in organizational behavior. However, advances in measurement and trends in organizations have prompted renewed interest. For example, increased emphasis on service jobs with customer contact, concern about ethics and integrity, and contemporary interest in teamwork and cooperation all point to the potential contribution of personality.[19]

A few words of caution about personality. First, although we often use labels such as "high self-esteem" to describe people, we always should remember that people have a *variety* of personality characteristics. Excessive typing of people doesn't help us to appreciate their unique potential to contribute to an organization. Second, as we will see, some personality characteristics are useful in certain organizational situations. However, there is no one best personality, and managers need to appreciate the advantages of employee diversity. A key concept here is *fit*, putting the right person in the right job or exposing different employees to different management styles. Finally, we often tend to exaggerate the impact of personality on organizational behavior. Personality will have the most impact in "weak" situations. These are situations with loosely defined roles, few rules, and weak reinforcement and punishment contingencies. For example, consider a newly formed volunteer community organization. In "strong" situations with more defined roles, rules, and contingencies, personality should have less impact.[20] For example, consider routine military operations. In the vignette that began the chapter, neither the flamboyant Campeau nor the conservative Reichmann could overcome the strong situational realities of the recession and the depressed real estate market.

In what follows, we discuss five general personality dimensions. Then, we cover three personality characteristics with special relevance to organizational behavior. Later in the text, we will explore the impact of other personality characteristics on job satisfaction, motivation, ethics, organizational politics, stress, and career choice.

The "Big Five" Dimensions of Personality

People are unique, people are complex, and there are literally hundreds of adjectives that we can use to reflect this unique complexity. Yet, over the years, psychologists have discovered that there are about five basic but general dimensions that describe personality. These "big five" dimensions are summarized in Exhibit 3.5 along with some illustrative traits.[21] The dimensions are:

- *Extraversion*—this is the extent to which a person is outgoing versus shy. High extraverts enjoy social situations, while those low on this dimension (introverts) avoid them.

- *Emotional stability*—the degree to which a person has appropriate emotional control. People with high emotional stability are self-confident and have high self-esteem. Those with lower emotional stability tend toward self-doubt and depression.

- *Agreeableness*—the extent to which a person is friendly and approachable. More agreeable people are warm and considerate. Less agreeable people tend to be cold and aloof.

- *Conscientiousness*—the degree to which a person is responsible and achievement-oriented. More conscientious people are dependable and positively motivated. Less conscientious people are unreliable.

- *Openness to experience*—the extent to which a person thinks flexibly and is receptive to new ideas. More open people tend toward creativity and innovation. Less open people favor the status quo.

These dimensions are relatively independent. That is, you could be higher or lower in any combination of dimensions. Also, they tend to hold up well cross-culturally. Thus, people in different cultures use these same dimensions when describing the personalities of friends and acquaintances.

Extraversion	Emotional Stability	Agreeableness	Conscientiousness	Openness to Experience
Sociable, Talkative vs. Withdrawn, Shy	Stable, Confident vs. Depressed, Anxious	Tolerant, Cooperative vs. Cold, Rude	Dependable, Responsible vs. Careless, Impulsive	Curious, Original vs. Dull, Unimaginative

EXHIBIT 3.5
The "big five" personality dimensions.

Research has only recently begun to link these personality dimensions to organizational behavior. However, the results seem promising so far. First, there is evidence that each of the big five dimensions is related to job performance.[22] Generally, traits like those in the top half of Exhibit 3.5 lead to better job performance. One review found that high extraversion was important for managers and salespeople and that high conscientiousness facilitated performance for all occupations.[23] Another suggests that conscientiousness is an important antidote for counterproductive behaviors such as theft, absenteeism, and disciplinary problems.[24] Finally, as proof of our earlier discussion about situational constraints, one study showed that elevated conscientiousness and extraversion contributed more to managerial performance for managers who had more autonomy in the way they handled their jobs.[25]

In the story that began this chapter, Robert Campeau used his extraversion to promote his projects. He also exhibited some emotional instability. Paul Reichmann, an introvert, stayed behind the scenes and crafted financing packages.

As noted earlier, the "big five" personality dimensions are basic and general. We turn now to several more specific personality characteristics that influence organizational behavior.

Locus of Control

Consider the following comparison. Laurie and Stan are both management trainees in large banks. However, they have rather different expectations regarding their futures. Laurie has just enrolled in an evening Master of Business Administration program in a nearby university. Although some of her M.B.A. courses are not immediately applicable to her job, Laurie feels that she must be prepared for greater responsibility as she moves up in the bank hierarchy. Laurie is convinced that she will achieve promotions because she studies hard, works hard, and does her job properly. She feels that an individual makes her own way in the world and that she can control her own destiny. She is certain that she can someday be the president of the bank if she really wants to do so. Her personal motto is: "I can do it."

Stan, on the other hand, sees no use in pursuing additional education beyond his bachelor's degree. According to him, such activities just don't pay off. People who get promoted are just plain lucky or have special connections, and further academic preparation or hard work have nothing to do with it. Stan feels that it is impossible to predict his own future but knows that the world is pretty unfair.

Laurie and Stan differ on a personality dimension called **locus of control.** This variable refers to individuals' beliefs about the *location* of the factors that

Locus of control. A set of beliefs about whether one's behavior is controlled mainly by internal or external forces.

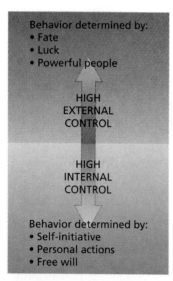

Behavior determined by:
• Fate
• Luck
• Powerful people

HIGH EXTERNAL CONTROL

HIGH INTERNAL CONTROL

Behavior determined by:
• Self-initiative
• Personal actions
• Free will

EXHIBIT 3.6
The internal/external locus of control continuum.

control their behavior. At one end of the continuum are high internals (like Laurie, Robert Campeau, and Paul Reichmann) who believe that the opportunity to control their own behavior rests within themselves. At the other end of the continuum are high externals (like Stan) who believe that external forces determine their behavior. Not surprisingly, compared with internals, externals see the world as an unpredictable, chancy place in which luck, fate, or powerful people control their destinies.[26] (See Exhibit 3.6)

Internals tend to see stronger links between the effort they put into their jobs and the performance level that they achieve. In addition, they perceive to a greater degree than externals that the organization will notice high performance and reward it.[27] Since internals believe that their work behavior will influence the rewards they achieve, they are more likely to be aware of and take advantage of information that will enable them to perform effectively.[28]

Research shows that locus of control influences organizational behavior in a variety of occupational settings. For example, in my own research with customer service representatives and teachers, I found that people who felt that they had internal control over their health were absent less than health externals. In another study, more internal CEOs engaged in greater business risk, pursued more product-market innovation, and led rather than followed competition.[29]

Evidently because they perceive themselves as able to control what happens to them, people who are high on internal control are more satisfied with their jobs, earn more money, and achieve higher organizational positions.[30] In addition, they seem to perceive less stress, to cope with stress better, and to engage in more careful career planning.[31]

How should people with various levels of locus of control be managed to enable them to excel? Tellingly, research shows that internals are not necessarily better performers than externals. Rather, internals seem to perform better on jobs that require initiative and innovation, while externals do better on more routine role assignments.[32] Thus, one might look for an internal to staff a startup operation and an external to fill a well-established post. Externals seem to prefer somewhat more directive supervision.[33] On the other hand, participation or self-management might be more appropriate for an internal subordinate.

Self-Monitoring

Self-monitoring. The extent to which people observe and regulate how they appear and behave in social settings and relationships.

I'm sure that you have known people who tend to "wear their hearts on their sleeves." These are people who act like they feel and say what they think in spite of their social surroundings. On the other hand, I'm also sure that you've known people who were a lot more sensitive to their social surroundings, a lot more likely to fit what they say and do to the nature of those surroundings, regardless of how they think or feel. What we have here is a contrast in **self-monitoring**, which is the extent to which people observe and regulate how they appear and behave in social settings and relationships.[34] The people who "wear their hearts on their sleeves" are low self-monitors. They aren't so concerned with scoping out and fitting in with those around them. Their opposites are high self-monitors who take great care to observe and control the images that they project. In this sense, high self-monitors behave somewhat like actors. In particular, high self-monitors tend to show concern for socially appropriate behavior, tune in to social cues, and regulate their behavior according to these cues.

How does self-monitoring affect organizational behavior?[35] For one thing, high self-monitors might tend to gravitate toward jobs that require by their nature a degree of role-playing. Sales, law, public relations, and politics are examples. In such jobs, ability to adapt to one's clients and contacts is critical; so are communication skills and persuasive abilities, characteristics that high self-monitors frequently exhibit. A couple of studies show that managers are inclined to be higher self-monitors than nonmanagers in the same organization. Promotion in the management ranks is often a function of subjective performance appraisals, and the ability to read and conform to the boss's expectations can be critical for advancement.

One interesting study found that field representatives for a prominent franchise organization were rated as higher performers if they were high self-monitors. This position required the reps to mediate among many competing interests, including those of the corporation, franchisees, and suppliers. Thus, the ability to adjust successfully to competing social demands, a strength of high self-monitors, came in very handy in this role.[36]

In social settings that require a lot of verbal interaction, high self-monitors tend to emerge as leaders. Furthermore, they seem to have the behavioral flexibility to adjust their leadership style to the demands of the situation (i.e., friendly versus directive).[37] Again, we see the ability to read and adapt to the social environment.

Are high self-monitors always at an organizational advantage? Not likely. They are unlikely to feel comfortable in ambiguous social settings where it is hard to determine exactly what behaviors are socially appropriate. Dealing with unfamiliar cultures (national or corporate) might provoke stress. Also, some roles require people to go against the grain or really stand up for what they truly believe. Thus, high self-monitoring types would seem to be weak innovators and would have difficulty resisting social pressure.

Self-Esteem

How well do you like yourself? This is the essence of the personality characteristic called self-esteem. More formally, **self-esteem** is the degree to which a person has a positive self-evaluation. People with high self-esteem have favorable self-images. People with low self-esteem have unfavorable self-images. They also tend to be uncertain about the correctness of their opinions, attitudes, and behaviors. In general, people tend to be highly motivated to protect themselves from threats to their self-esteem.

Self-esteem. The degree to which a person has a positive self-evaluation.

One of the most interesting differences between high and low self-esteem people has to do with the *plasticity* of their thoughts and behavior. People with low self-esteem tend to be more susceptible to external and social influences than those who are high in self-esteem. That is, they are more pliable. Thus, events and people in the organizational environment have more impact on the beliefs and actions of low self-esteem employees. This occurs because, being unsure of their own views and behavior, they are more likely to look to others for information and confirmation. In addition, people who have low self-esteem seek social approval from others, approval that they might gain from adopting others' views. Finally, people with low self-esteem are more likely than those with higher esteem to take negative feedback personally. This will induce change, but this change is not always for the better.[38]

Overall, there is not a consistent relationship between self-esteem and performance. However, low self-esteem employees tend to react badly to negative feedback—it lowers their subsequent performance.[39] In line with our previous discussion of learning, this means that managers should be especially cautious when using negative reinforcement and punishment with low self-esteem subordinates. If external causes are thought to be responsible for a performance problem, this should be made very clear. Also, managers should direct criticism at the performance difficulty and not at the person. As we will explain shortly, modeling the correct behavior should be especially effective with low self-esteem employees. Finally organizations should try to avoid assigning low self-esteem employees to jobs (such as life insurance sales) that inherently provide a lot of negative feedback.

People with low self-esteem do not react well to ambiguous and stressful situations. Being sensitive to their social environment, they tend to perceive more stress and to cope less well with it.[40] It is probably wise to avoid placing people with very low esteem in jobs with competing role demands. For example, first-level supervisors can face competing demands from above and below.

Can a person have too much self-esteem? Probably. Excessive concern for maintaining self-esteem can damage negotiating skills and inhibit people from seeking the help of others. Also, excessive self-confidence can lead people to avoid searching for information that is critical to the solution of a problem or avoid information that threatens their self-image.[41] A little more subtly, the increased plasticity that comes from depressed esteem can actually be beneficial when adaptability and openness to external information are useful. Also, those with lower self-esteem are quite willing to imitate credible models, and they respond well to mentoring.

Despite a possible downside to excessive esteem, organizations will generally benefit from a workforce with high self-esteem. Such people tend to make more fulfilling career decisions, they exhibit higher job satisfaction, and they are generally more resilient to the strains of everyday work life.[42] What can organizations do to bolster self-esteem? Opportunity for participation in decision making, autonomy, and interesting work have been fairly consistently found to be positively correlated with self-esteem.[43] Also, organizations should avoid creating a culture with excessive and petty work rules that signal employees that they are incompetent or untrustworthy.[44]

The Manager's Notebook   Reinforcement, Mary Kay Ash Style

The genius of Mary Kay Ash is that she doesn't confuse rewards with reinforcers and that she exploits a source of reinforcement that many, many organizations neglect—recognition as a form of feedback.

1. Mary Kay uses a variety of forms of recognition to reinforce performance in sales and recruiting. These include various pins, sashes, and badges, as well as pink Cadillacs and coveted five-star vacations with Mary Kay herself. Although some of these things have monetary value, it is their *symbolic* value in denoting various levels of achievement that is especially reinforcing. The company confers much of this recognition at a glitzy Dallas convention with over 30,000 in attendance. Good performers thus serve as models for others. Remember, this is a labor force that might not attain a lot of recognition in other life spheres.

2. One problem with trying to reinforce 300,000 people is figuring out what reinforcers they might prefer. To some extent, Mary Kay handles this by self-selection. That is, people who don't care for the kind of recognition the company offers would be unlikely to become and remain involved. The recognition system builds organizational commitment and gives a sense of corporate identity to people who are otherwise independent operators.

EXECUTIVE SUMMARY

◆ Learning occurs when practice or experience leads to a relatively permanent change in behavior potential. Operant learning occurs as a function of the consequences of behavior. Social learning occurs through observation of others' behavior.

◆ If some behavior is occurring regularly or increasing in probability, you can assume that it is being reinforced. The consequence that is maintaining the behavior is the reinforcer. If the reinforcer is added to the situation following the behavior, it is a positive reinforcer. These are usually pleasant consequences. If the reinforcer is removed from the situation following the behavior, it is a negative reinforcer. These are typically unpleasant stimuli.

◆ Behavior is learned quickly when it is reinforced immediately and continuously. Behavior tends to be persistent under reduced or terminated reinforcement when it is learned under conditions of delayed and/or partial reinforcement. Partial reinforcement can be administered under interval or ratio schedules. The former are time dependent, and the latter are response dependent. Ratio schedules usually lead to higher response rates, because the individual can increase the frequency of reinforcement by responding faster.

◆ Organizational behavior modification is the systematic use of learning principles to influence organizational behavior. Companies have successfully used it to improve employees' attendance and to reinforce workplace safety.

◆ Modeling, an example of social learning, is the process of imitating others. Models are most likely to be imitated when they are high in status, attractive, competent, credible, successful, and vivid.

◆ If some behavior decreases in probability, you can assume that it is being either extinguished or punished. If the behavior is followed by no observable consequence, it is being extinguished. That is, some reinforcer that was maintaining the behavior has been terminated. If the behavior is followed by the application of some unpleasant consequence, it is being punished.

◆ Self-management occurs when people use learning principles to manage their own behavior, thus reducing the need for external control. Aspects of self-management include collecting self-observation data, observing models, goal setting, rehearsing, and using self-reinforcement.

◆ Personality is the relatively stable set of psychological characteristics that influences the way that we interact with our environment. It has more impact on behavior in weak situations than in strong situations.

◆ Research reveals that there are five basic dimensions to personality—extraversion, emotional stability, agreeableness, conscientiousness, and openness to experience.

◆ Personality characteristics of particular importance for organizational behavior include locus of control, self-monitoring, and self-esteem. In general, managers should try to match their management styles and work assignments to the personalities of their staff.

KEY CONCEPTS

Learning
Reinforcement
Positive reinforcement
Negative reinforcement
Fixed interval schedule
Variable interval schedule
Fixed ratio schedule
Variable ratio schedule
Organizational behavior modification

Modeling
Extinction
Punishment
Self-management
Personality
Locus of control
Self-monitoring
Self-esteem

DISCUSSION QUESTIONS

1. Consider some examples of behavior that you repeat fairly regularly (such as studying or going to work every morning). What are the positive and negative reinforcers that maintain this behavior?

2. We pointed out that managers frequently resort to punishing ineffective behavior. What are some of the practical demands of the typical manager's job that lead to this state of affairs?

3. Discuss a situation that you have observed in which the use of punishment was ineffective in terminating some unwanted behavior. Why was punishment ineffective in this case?

4. Describe a situation in which you think an employer could use organizational behavior modification to improve or correct employee behavior. Can you anticipate any dangers in using this approach?

5. A supervisor in a textile factory observes that one of her subordinates is violating a safety rule that could result in severe injury. What combination of reinforcement, punishment, extinction, and modeling could she use to correct this behavior?

6. Contrast the reinforcement strategies that a supervisor might use to manage the work behavior of an experienced versus an inexperienced subordinate. Be sure to consider the issue of self-management.

7. Suppose that you are the manager of two subordinates, one of whom has an internal locus of control and one of whom has an external locus of control. Describe the leadership tactics that you would use with each subordinate.

8. Contrast the management styles that you would employ for subordinates with high versus low self-esteem.

EXPERIENTIAL EXERCISE
LOCUS OF CONTROL

Want to test your locus of control? Just answer the 16 questions below as frankly as possible using the following response scale:

1 = Disagree very much   4 = Agree slightly
2 = Disagree moderately   5 = Agree moderately
3 = Disagree slightly   6 = Agree very much

1. _____ A job is what you make of it.

2. _____ On most jobs, people can pretty much accomplish whatever they set out to accomplish.

3. _____ If you know what you want out of a job, you can find a job that gives it to you.

4. _____ If employees are unhappy with a decision made by their boss, they should do something about it.

5. _____ Getting the job you want is mostly a matter of luck.

6. _____ Making money is primarily a matter of good fortune.

7. _____ Most people are capable of doing their jobs well if they make the effort.

8. _____ In order to get a really good job you need to have family members or friends in high places.

9. _____ Promotions are usually a matter of good fortune.

10. _____ When it comes to landing a really good job, who you know is more important than what you know.

11. _____ Promotions are given to employees who perform well on the job.

12. _____ To make a lot of money you have to know the right people.

13. _____ It takes a lot of luck to be an outstanding employee on most jobs.

14. _____ People who perform their jobs well generally get rewarded for it.

15. _____ Most employees have more influence on their supervisors than they think they do.

16. _____ The main difference between people who make a lot of money and people who make a little money is luck.

SCORING AND INTERPRETATION

You have just completed the Work Locus of Control Scale developed by Paul Spector. To score your scale, first subtract your responses to questions 1, 2, 3, 4, 7, 11, 14, and 15 from seven. For example, if you gave a response of 3 to question 1, give yourself a 4 (7 minus 3). Then add up your resulting scores to all 16 items. Your total should be somewhere between 16 and 96. The lower your score the more *internal* you are—you see what happens to you to be a result of your own actions and initiative. The higher your score, the more *external* you are—you see what happens to you to be a result of luck, chance, or connections. The average score of 1165 people in a variety of occupations was 38. Thus, these people tended to see themselves as somewhat more internal than external. In this research, internals tended to report more job satisfaction, more influence at work, and less role stress.

_____

Source: Spector, P. (1988). Development of the Work Locus of Control Scale. *Journal of Occupational Psychology*, 61, 335–340.

CASE STUDY
TOO MANY PERSONAL CALLS

THE ORGANIZATION

John Dixon, vice president of operations for Consolidated Stores, Inc., is responsible for the Springdale region. Forty-four retail clothing stores and outlets in four midwestern states are in the region, which is divided into three districts. Each district is supervised by a district manager and an assistant district manager. Managerial, accounting, merchandising, and advertising activities serving the stores are carried out in the Springdale regional office. A common clerical group in the Springdale office serves all managers and supervisors and is located on the second and fourth floors of the company building. A spacious, well-appointed lounge, used by office personnel, is located on the third floor along with the cafeteria and restrooms.

At the time of this case, John Dixon had over thirty-five years of service with the company. During his five years as regional manager in Springdale, he had been very successful in meeting the problems created by shortages of facilities and by an increase of nearly 40 percent in store sales. Service and operating results for the region were above average for several years, and the current year had shown improvement over the corresponding months of the previous years.

In addition to the district managers and their assistants, a number of other managers and supervisors maintain offices in the Springdale building. A controller, a merchandise manager, and an advertising director each have private office space. Although a number of clerical employees work directly for the various managers and supervisors at

Springdale, many employees report directly to several office supervisors who in turn report to the office manager, Harriet Black.

Since more managers and supervisors travel frequently to the stores, all clerical employees are responsible to Ms. Black for office procedures, practices, and discipline. Harriet Black is an experienced manager who has been in the Springdale office for over fifteen years. She generally is recognized as being exceptionally capable, and other supervisors and managers often consult with her for help on various problems. All other office supervisors are former clerical employees who have been promoted and trained during the last five years.

THE PERSONAL CALLS PROBLEM

John Dixon devoted some time each week to operating and personnel problems within the Springdale office. Sometimes he observed various office activities jointly with one or more of the managers and supervisors, but he also made it a frequent practice to observe certain operations by himself.

Over a period of weeks, Dixon became increasingly aware that a number of personal telephone calls were being made by the office supervisors and certain clerical employees at their desks. He noticed that this was not peculiar to any one unit but seemed to be a general practice. On several occasions when he was in the various offices, he had to wait for supervisors to finish their personal calls before he could discuss business matters with them. One morning, as he was observing activities alone, he noted a supervisor's telephone was tied up for almost an hour with two successive calls that Dixon believed to be personal in nature. He was not always sure that he was able to distinguish a personal from a business call, but it was obvious that company telephones were often used for other than business communications.

Company policy was not to prohibit personal calls, but such calls were to be strictly limited so that the telephone lines would be available for calls from stores, suppliers, customers, and other business people needing to communicate with the regional office. Several complaints from store managers had been received by Dixon to the effect that it was difficult "to get through" to the regional office by telephone. Consequently, on two different occasions earlier in the year, Dixon had discussed the policy on personal calls in regular meetings with his management personnel, and he believed the policy was generally understood. Further, Dixon felt that the office supervisors and managers through their own observations could have been aware of the excessive number of personal calls currently being made by their people.

THE NEW POLICY

It seemed apparent to Dixon that the corrective action—if any—that had been taken by the managers and office supervisors had not been effective. He decided that prompt personal action on his part was needed.

To dispose quickly of the problem, as was his usual practice, Dixon issued the following memo, a copy of which was distributed to every person in the Springdale office: "To keep our telephones available for business calls, all personal calls by supervisors and employees should be made from the telephones that have been placed in the lounge." Dixon then arranged for four additional telephones to be connected in the lounge that same afternoon.

PROBLEMS

During his observations the following week, Dixon did not discern any personal calls. However, early one morning about two weeks after he had issued the directive regarding telephone calls, Dixon received a call from Janet Smythe, one of the most reliable people in the business communication center. He invited her to come right up to his office. Ms. Smythe had been a "Class 1" word processor for three years; she frequently was called on for special assignments because she was popular and well liked by everyone. As she walked into his office, Dixon noticed that she seemed to be quite upset.

Ms. Smythe, in her usual low voice, commenced by saying, "I would like to question the fairness of your ruling on personal telephone calls." She went on to cite her own experience on the day before. She had been informed of an overtime assignment by Ms. Black, late in the afternoon. Feeling obligated to let her family know that she would be late, she started for the lounge to call home, when Ms. Black questioned her as to why she would be leaving her desk since she had already taken her afternoon coffee break. After explaining her reason for leaving, she was told by Ms. Black that the only time personal calls were allowed was during a normal rest period.

Dixon promptly told Ms. Smythe that the directive had been issued for the purpose of stopping excessive calling from the supervisors' and employees' desks, and he had not intended it to be interpreted as it had been in her case. He told her that he would like to investigate this incident and that he would get in touch with her later.

Several days later Dixon discussed the situation at a regular meeting of his managers and supervisors. He found that the supervisors and managers were unanimous in disagreeing with his directive. They pointed out that the instructions permitted no flexibility and were too severe. Dixon apologized to the group for not discussing the problem with them prior to issuing the directive, and he asked for their suggestions.

A supervisor in accounting was emphatic and insisted that the directive should be rescinded in its entirety. She said, "Really, Mr. Dixon, if you expect an order like that to be enforced by us, you should have let us give the instructions to the people ourselves!" The advertising department director commented, "This whole matter is ridiculous; it's a waste of time! Why not let employees make personal calls? To stop excessive calls would cost more than they are worth!" One of the assistant managers suggested that employees should be allowed to make personal calls only with the approval of their supervisors. Several members of the group immediately disagreed with this suggestion, stating that the responsibility for policing telephone calls should not be placed on supervisors who are trying to motivate their people positively.

After a prolonged discussion of the telephone-call problem and other matters, Dixon adjourned the meeting stating that they would hear from him or the district managers at a later date about the problem of personal calls.

As he returned to his office, Dixon wondered what alternate procedures could be used to reduce successfully the time wasted and the expense of excessive personal telephone calls. In addition, he began to speculate on what method of communications or supervisory practices could be used to help him obtain a better reception of management policies and decisions.

_____

Source: Hilgert, R. L., Schoen, S. H., & Towle, J. W. (1982). *Cases & Experiential Exercises in Human Resources Management* (4th ed.). Boston: Houghton Mifflin, pp. 56–59.

1. Does Consolidated Stores, Inc., have a right to concern itself with the personal calls of its employees?
2. What is the precise behavioral problem that John Dixon detects at the beginning of the case? What reinforcers are responsible for this problem?
3. Discuss the roles that social learning and modeling play in the case.
4. In learning theory terms, describe precisely the system that Mr. Dixon implemented by putting the phones in the lounge. Use the concepts of reinforcement, punishment, and/or extinction.
5. Comment on the statement at the meeting "that the responsibility for policing personal telephone calls should not be placed on supervisors who are trying to motivate their people positively."
6. Broadly, the case has to do with rules, regulations, and their implementation. Speculate about how people with different personalities (locus of control, self-esteem) react to such matters.
7. Do you have any advice for John Dixon about his managerial style?
8. What should John Dixon do now?

LEARNING OBJECTIVES

AFTER READING CHAPTER 4 YOU SHOULD BE ABLE TO:

1 DEFINE PERCEPTION AND DISCUSS SOME OF THE GENERAL FACTORS THAT INFLUENCE PERCEPTION.

2 EXPLAIN SOME BASIC BIASES IN PERSON PERCEPTION.

3 DESCRIBE HOW PEOPLE FORM ATTRIBUTIONS ABOUT THE CAUSES OF BEHAVIOR.

4 DISCUSS VARIOUS BIASES IN ATTRIBUTION.

5 APPRECIATE THE CONCEPTS OF WORKFORCE DIVERSITY AND VALUING DIVERSITY.

6 DISCUSS HOW RACIAL, ETHNIC, GENDER, AND AGE STEREOTYPES AFFECT ORGANIZATIONAL BEHAVIOR.

7 DISCUSS HOW PERCEPTION AFFECTS THE OUTCOMES OF SELECTION INTERVIEWS AND PERFORMANCE APPRAISALS.

ANN HOPKINS FELL VICTIM TO GENDER STEREOTYPING WHEN SHE FAILED TO BE SELECTED FOR PARTNERSHIP STATUS WITH PRICE WATERHOUSE. ARE WOMEN STILL EXPECTED TO CONFORM TO A FEMININE STEREOTYPE?

CHAPTER 4

PERCEPTION, ATTRIBUTION, AND JUDGMENT OF OTHERS

PRICE WATERHOUSE AND ANN HOPKINS

Price Waterhouse is a large public accounting and management consulting firm with an international presence. Several years ago, Ann Hopkins took a job as a manager in the firm's management consulting operation. During the next five years she proceeded to bring in over $30 million in new business. Finally, she was nominated for partnership in the firm, along with 87 other employees, all of them men. Among the 88 nominees, Hopkins ranked number one in generating new business, and she had more billable hours than any of them in the previous fiscal year. This is one of the chief roles of a partner and a very important consideration for partnership in accounting and consulting firms. At the time of the Hopkins nomination, only seven of the 662 Price Waterhouse partners were women.

Especially in an accounting firm, Ann Hopkins' ability to generate revenue was hard to dispute. However, opposition to the Hopkins partnership soon surfaced. Thirty-two existing partners offered comments on the Hopkins nomination. Thirteen were supportive, eight claimed to have no informed opinion, and three suggested that she be put on hold. Eight partners felt that she should be denied partnership. Most of the opposition centered on her interpersonal skills, which, opponents said, were aggressive and abrasive. Some partners claimed that she was "too macho" and needed to enroll in a "charm school." Others complained about her swearing. Even one of her supporters advised her to walk, talk, and dress in a more feminine manner.

Half of the nominees achieved partnership status. Ann Hopkins was not among them. When she failed to be nominated the next year, she resigned. She subsequently filed a suit claiming sex discrimination under Title VII of the Civil Rights Act. A U.S. District Court ruled that Hopkins had been a victim of sex discrimination. In rendering its verdict, the court explicitly recognized that Hopkins had been the victim of a gender stereotype by failing to conform to stereotyped expectations of how a woman should act. The court ordered that she receive $371,000 in back pay, and, in a very unusual decision, ruled that Hopkins be admitted into partnership at Price Waterhouse.[1]

Why was Ann Hopkins denied partnership in spite of her financial performance? Why did Price Waterhouse have so few women partners? And what exactly is a gender stereotype? These are the kinds of questions that we will attempt to answer in this chapter. First, we will define perception and examine how various aspects of the perceiver, the object or person being perceived, and the situation influence perception. Following this, we will present a model of the perceptual process, and we will consider some of the perceptual tendencies that we employ in forming impressions of people and attributing causes to their behavior. Finally, we will examine the role of perception in achieving a diverse workforce, selection interviewing, and performance appraisal. In general, you will learn that perception and attribution influence who gets into organizations, how they are treated as members, and how they interpret this treatment.

WHAT IS PERCEPTION?

Perception. The process of interpreting our senses to provide order and meaning to the environment.

Perception is the process of interpreting the messages of our senses to provide order and meaning to the environment. Perception helps sort out and organize the complex and varied input received by our senses of sight, smell, touch, taste, and hearing. The key word in this definition is *interpreting*. People frequently base their actions on the interpretation of reality that their perceptual system provides, rather than reality itself. If you perceive your pay to be very low, you might seek employment in another firm. The reality—that you are the best-paid person in your department—will not matter if you are unaware of the fact. However, to go a step further, you might be aware that you are the best-paid person and *still* perceive your pay as low in comparison to that of the president of Apple Computer or your ostentatious next-door neighbor.

Some of the most important perceptions that influence organizational behavior are the perceptions that organizational members have of each other. Because of this, we will concentrate on person perception in this chapter.

COMPONENTS OF PERCEPTION

Perception has three components—a perceiver, a target that is being perceived, and some situational context in which the perception is occurring. Each of these components influences the perceiver's impression or interpretation of the target (Exhibit 4.1).

The Perceiver

The perceiver's experience, needs, and emotions can affect his or her perceptions of a target.

One of the most important characteristics of the perceiver that influences his or her impressions of a target is experience. Past experiences lead the perceiver to develop expectations, and these expectations affect current perceptions. An interesting example of the influence of experience on perception is shown in Exhibit 4.2. It illustrates the perceptions of 268 managerial personnel in a *Fortune* 500 company concerning the influence of race and gender on promotion opportunities. As you can see, white men were much less likely to perceive race or gender barriers to promotion than were white women, nonwhite men, and nonwhite women.[2] Remember, these people were ostensibly viewing the same "objective" promotion system.

Frequently, our needs unconsciously influence our perceptions by causing us to perceive what we wish to perceive. Research has demonstrated that perceivers who have been deprived of food will tend to "see" more edible things in ambiguous pictures than will well-fed observers. Similarly, lonely college students might misperceive the most innocent actions of members of the opposite sex as indicating interest in them.

Emotions such as anger, happiness, or fear can influence our perceptions. We have all had the experience of misperceiving the innocent comment of a friend or acquaintance when we were angry. For example, a worker who is upset about not getting a promotion might perceive the consolation provided by a co-worker as gloating condescension. On the other hand, consider the worker who does get a promotion. He is so happy that he fails to notice how upset his co-worker is because she wasn't the one promoted.

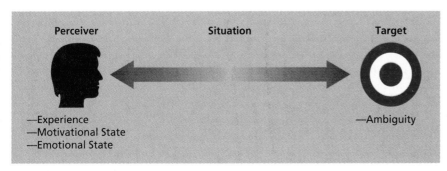

EXHIBIT 4.1
Factors that influence perception.

	White Men (N = 123)	White Women (N = 76)	Non-White Men (N = 52)	Non-White Women (N = 17)
Race	26	62	75	76
Gender	31	87	71	82

Note: Table values are the percentages saying that race or gender was important or very important. N = number of cases.

Source: Cox, T. Jr. (1993). *Cultural diversity in organizations: Theory, research, & practice.* San Francisco: Berrett-Koehler, p. 119.

EXHIBIT 4.2
Ratings of the perceived importance of race and gender for promotion opportunity in executive jobs.

Perceptual defense. The tendency for the perceptual system to defend the perceiver against unpleasant emotions.

In some cases, our perceptual system serves to defend us against unpleasant emotions. This phenomenon is **perceptual defense.** We have all experienced cases in which we "see what we want to see" or "hear what we want to hear." In many of these instances, our perceptual system is working to ensure that we don't see or hear things that are threatening. Consider several examples of "blind spots" in which industry executives have failed to perceive imminent competitive threats.[3]

- Prominent, well established newspapers such as the *New York Times,* *Los Angeles Times* and *Chicago Tribune* have been threatened by the emergence of specialized television cable services in news, sports, and home shopping.
- NBC, ABC, and CBS failed to anticipate the challenge that the Turner Broadcasting System and the Fox Network posed.
- Pharmaceutical executives did not adequately predict the entry of chemical firms into the drug and biotechnology fields.

In each of these cases, perceptual defense from the unpleasant competitive scenarios probably contributed to the blind spot.

The Target

Perception involves interpretation and the addition of meaning to the target, and ambiguous targets are especially susceptible to interpretation and addition. Perceivers have a need to resolve such ambiguities. You might be tempted to believe that providing more information about the target will necessarily improve perceptual accuracy. Unfortunately, this is not always the case. Writing clearer memos might not always get the message across. Similarly, assigning minority workers to a prejudiced manager will not always improve his or her perceptions of their true abilities. As we shall see shortly, the perceiver does not or cannot always use all of the information provided by the target. In these cases a reduction in ambiguity might not be accompanied by greater accuracy.

In the Price Waterhouse case, the billable hours Ann Hopkins achieved were unambiguous. Rather, the resistance to Hopkins centered around social skills, a performance dimension open to a lot more interpretation.

The Situation

Every instance of perception occurs in some situational context, and this context can affect what one perceives. The most important effect that the situation can have is to add information about the target. Imagine a casual critical comment about your performance from your boss the week before she is to decide whether or not you will be promoted. You will likely perceive this comment very differently than you would if you were not up for promotion. Also, a worker might perceive a racial joke overheard on the job very differently before and after racial strife has occurred in the plant. In both of these examples, the perceiver and the target are the same, but the perception of the target changes with the situation. To her detractors, Ann Hopkins' interpersonal style might have been acceptable in some other occupational role, such as a bartender or welder!

A MODEL OF THE PERCEPTUAL PROCESS

Exactly how does the perceiver go about putting together the information contained in the target and the situation to form a picture of the target? Respected psychologist Jerome Bruner has developed a model of the perceptual process that can provide a useful framework for this discussion.[4] According to Bruner, when the perceiver encounters an unfamiliar target, the perceiver is very open to the informational cues contained in the target and the situation surrounding it. In this unfamiliar state, the perceiver really needs information upon which to base perceptions of the target and will actively seek out cues to resolve this ambiguity. Gradually, the perceiver encounters some familiar cues (note the role of the perceiver's experience here) that enable her to make a crude categorization of the target. At this point, the cue search becomes less open and more selective. The perceiver begins to search out cues that confirm the categorization of the target. As this categorization becomes stronger, the perceiver actively ignores or even distorts cues that violate initial perceptions. (See the left side of Exhibit 4.3.) This does not mean an early categorization can't be changed. It does mean, however, that it will take a good many contradictory cues before one recategorizes the target, and that these cues will have to overcome the expectations that have been developed.

Let's clarify your understanding of Bruner's perceptual model with an example, shown on the right side of Exhibit 4.3. Imagine that a woman who works as an engineer for a large aircraft company is trying to size up a newly hired co-worker. Since he is an unfamiliar target, she will probably be especially open to any cues that might provide information about him. In the course of her cue search, she discovers that he has a Master's degree in aeronautical engineering from Stanford University and that he graduated with top grades. These are familiar cues because she knows that Stanford is a top school in the field, and she has worked with many excellent Stanford graduates. She then proceeds to categorize her new co-worker as a "good man" with "great potential." With these perceptions, she takes a special interest in observing his performance, which is good for several months. This increases the strength of her initial categorization. Gradually, however, the engineer's performance deteriorates for some reason, and his work becomes less and less satisfactory.

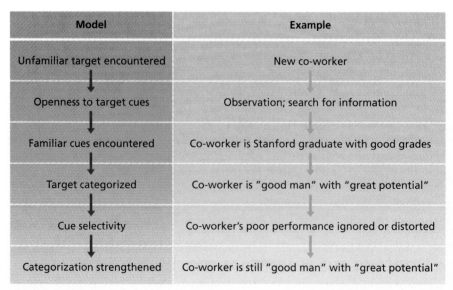

Model	Example
Unfamiliar target encountered	New co-worker
↓	↓
Openness to target cues	Observation; search for information
↓	↓
Familiar cues encountered	Co-worker is Stanford graduate with good grades
↓	↓
Target categorized	Co-worker is "good man" with "great potential"
↓	↓
Cue selectivity	Co-worker's poor performance ignored or distorted
↓	↓
Categorization strengthened	Co-worker is still "good man" with "great potential"

EXHIBIT 4.3
Bruner's model of the perceptual process and an example.

This is clear to everyone except the other engineer, who continues to see him as adequate and excuses his most obvious errors as stemming from external factors beyond his control.

Selectivity. Perception is selective. Perceivers don't use all the available cues, and those they use are thus given special emphasis. The established engineer was especially interested in the new recruit's academic credentials and his job performance. A different observer might be interested in different cues but would doubtless be just as selective in forming an impression of the target. This selectivity means that our perception is efficient, and this efficiency can both aid and hinder our perceptual accuracy. The interviewer screening applicants for a sales job will sensibly pay more attention to a candidate's social skills than whether the person is wearing designer clothes. Of course, the efficiency provided by selectivity can also hurt perceptual accuracy. The engineer in the above example, in concentrating upon her new co-worker's academic background, probably ignored other cues that might have predicted the subsequent performance problem.

Constancy. Bruner's model and the accompanying example also illustrate that our perceptual system works to paint a constant and consistent picture of the target. Perceptual *constancy* refers to the tendency for the target to be perceived in the same way over time or across situations. We have all had the experience of "getting off on the wrong foot" with a teacher or a boss and finding it difficult to change their constant perception of us. The engineer's image of the new co-worker's performance remained constant despite objective reality.

Consistency. Perceptual *consistency* refers to the tendency to select, ignore, and distort cues in such a manner that they fit together to form a homogeneous image of the target. We strive for consistency in our perception of people. We do not tend to see the same person as both good and bad or dependable and untrustworthy. For the engineer, consistency demanded that a Stanford graduate be a good performer. Often, we distort cues that are discrepant with our general image of a person to make the cues consistent with this image. An individual who has a generally good impression of an executive might perceive some of her actions as indicative of confidence. Another observer with an unfavorable image might see the same actions as evidence of conceit.

In the next section we consider some specific perceptual biases that contribute to selectivity, constancy, and consistency in our perception of people.

SOME BASIC BIASES IN PERSON PERCEPTION

For accuracy's sake, it would be convenient if we could encounter others under laboratory conditions, in a vacuum or a test tube, as it were. Because the real world lacks such ideal conditions, the impressions that we form of others are susceptible to a number of perceptual biases.

Primacy and Recency Effects

Given the examples of person perception that we have discussed thus far, you might gather that we form our impressions of others fairly quickly. One reason for this fast impression formation is our tendency to rely on the cues that we encounter early in a relationship. This reliance on early cues or first impressions is known as the **primacy effect.** Primacy often has a lasting impact. Thus, the worker who can favorably impress his or her boss in the first days on the job is in an advantageous position due to primacy. Similarly, the labor negotiator who comes across as "tough" on the first day of contract talks might find this image difficult to shake as the talks continue. Primacy is a form of selectivity, and its lasting effects illustrate the operation of constancy. Sometimes, a **recency effect** occurs in which people give the cues they encountered most recently undue weight. In other words, last impressions count most. Landing a big contract today might be perceived as excusing a whole year's bad sales performance.

Primacy effect. The tendency for a perceiver to rely on early cues or first impressions. first impressions

Recency effect. The tendency for a perceiver to rely on recent cues or last impressions.

Reliance on Central Traits

Even though perceivers tend to rely upon early information when developing their perceptions, these early cues do not receive equal weight. People tend to organize their perceptions around **central traits,** personal characteristics of the target that are of special interest to them. In developing her perceptions of her new co-worker, the experienced engineer seemed to organize her impressions around the trait intellectual capacity. The centrality of traits depends upon the perceiver's interests and the situation. Thus, not all engineers would organize their perceptions of the new worker around his intellectual abilities, and the established engineer might not use this trait as a central factor in forming impressions of the people she meets at a party.

Central traits often have a very powerful influence on our perceptions of others. Researchers presented groups of English university students with contrived newspaper stories about a soccer club manager and a local police officer. There were two forms of each story. In one form of the soccer story, the manager was described by the team captain as "warm-hearted." In the other, he

Central traits. Personal characteristics of a target person that are of particular interest to a perceiver.

was called "a cold fish at times." The officer was alternately described as "humane" and "ruthless." These traits were mixed with a number of others that remained constant across stories. Evidently, the varied traits were central to the impressions that the students formed of the manager and the officer because these traits strongly influenced students' descriptions of the targets on other dimensions. For example, the ruthless police officer was seen as more self-centered, blunt, irritable, and evasive than the humane officer.[5] Thus, central traits are a basis for the development of consistent perceptions.

Physical appearance is a common central trait in work settings. Research shows an overwhelming tendency for those who are "beautiful" to also be perceived as "good," especially when it comes to judgments about their social competence.[6] Ann Hopkins evidently paid the price here, since the partners associated her "unfeminine" appearance with negative opinions about her interpersonal skills. In general, research shows that conventionally attractive people are more likely than unattractive people to be hired, given good performance evaluations, and promoted.[7] (See the "In Focus: *Attractiveness Pays Off, But It Pays Off Better for Men.*")

Implicit Personality Theory

Implicit personality theories. Personal theories that people have about which personality characteristics go together.

In the previous example, how was it that the students also saw the ruthless police officer as blunt, irritable, and evasive when there was no information about these characteristics in the newspaper stories? Each of us has an implicit personal "theory" about which personality characteristics go together. These are called **implicit personality theories.** Thus, the students saw ruthlessness as indicative of other traits, even though they had no objective cues to this effect. Perhaps you expect hard-working people to also be honest. Perhaps you feel that people of average intelligence tend to be most friendly. To the extent that such implicit theories are inaccurate, they provide a basis for misunderstanding.[8] The employee who assumes that her very formal boss is also insensitive might be reluctant to discuss a work-related problem with him that could be solved fairly easily.

Projection

Projection. The tendency for perceivers to attribute their own thoughts and feelings to others.

In the absence of information to the contrary, and sometimes in spite of it, people often assume that others are like themselves. This tendency to attribute one's own thoughts and feelings to others is called **projection.** In some cases, projection is an efficient and sensible perceptual strategy. After all, people with similar backgrounds or interests often *do* think and feel similarly. Thus, it is not unreasonable for a capitalistic businessperson to assume that other businesspeople favor the free enterprise system and disapprove of government intervention in this system. However, projection can also lead to perceptual difficulties. The chairperson who feels that an issue has been resolved and perceives committee members to feel the same way might be very surprised when a vote is taken. The honest warehouse manager who perceives others as honest might find stock disappearing. In the case of threatening or undesirable characteristics, projection can serve as a form of perceptual defense. The dishonest worker might say, "Sure I steal from the company, but so does everyone else." Such perceptions can be used to justify the perceiver's thievery.

IN FOCUS   Attractiveness Pays Off, But It Pays Off Better for Men

Consistent with evidence that physical attractiveness is related to obtaining employment and promotion, more attractive employees also have been found to enjoy more economic success in their careers. The research so far suggests that attractiveness is more consistently related to economic success for men than for women. Roszell, Kennedy and Grabb (1989) examined the relationship of attractiveness to income attainment for over 1,000 Canadians. Attractive persons earned higher annual salaries than less attractive persons. With each increase in rated attractiveness on a five-point scale of attractiveness, the 1981 annual income of the respondent increased by $1,988. After controlling for respondent sex, the sex composition of the job, and 1979 salary, this figure dropped to $1,046 but was still statistically significant. This relationship was found for men, older employees, and those engaged in male dominated occupations, but not for women, younger employees, and those in female dominated occupations.

Two studies at the University of Pittsburgh have provided further evidence that good looks pay. In one study, Good, Olson, and Frieze (1986) used height, weight, and body mass (weight relative to height) as indicators of physical attractiveness. They surveyed over 2,000 MBA graduates of the University of Pittsburgh who graduated between 1973 and 1982. For men, weight but not height

was found to predict starting salary, and both height and weight predicted the current (1983) salary. However, neither of these variables predicted the starting and current salary of the women in the sample. For each one inch increase in height, salary of the men was $600 higher. Overweight men earned $4,000 less in salary than those of normal weight.

In a more recent study, Frieze, Olson, and Russell (1991) asked a group of people with corporate management experience to rate the physical attractiveness of 700 MBA graduates on a five-point scale. The starting salaries of male graduates receiving the highest attractiveness rating were approximately $5,000 a year more than those receiving the lowest attractiveness rating. After five years, those receiving the highest rating earned $10,000 more than those receiving the lowest rating. Attractiveness had no impact on starting salaries of women, but was related to later salaries, although not as strongly as for men. For each increment in attractiveness on the five-point scale, women earned $2,000 more in salary five years later.

Source: Excerpted from Stone, E. F., Stone D. L., &. Dipboye, R. L. (1992). Stigmas in Organizations: Race, Handicaps, and Physical Unattractiveness. In K. Kelley (Ed.), *Issues, Theory, and Research in Industrial/Organizational Psychology*. New York: Elsevier, pp. 419–420.

Stereotyping

One way to form a consistent impression of other people is simply to assume that they have certain characteristics by virtue of some category that they fall into. This perceptual tendency is known as **stereotyping,** or the tendency to generalize about people in a social category and ignore variation among them. Categories upon which people might base a stereotype include: race, age, gender, ethnic background, social class, occupation, and so on.[9] There are three specific aspects to stereotyping.[10]

Stereotyping. The tendency to generalize about people in a social category and ignore variation among them.

- We distinguish some category of people (college professors).
- We assume that the individuals in this category have certain traits (absent-minded, disorganized, ivory tower mentality).
- We perceive that everyone in this category possesses these traits ("All of my professors this year will be absent-minded, disorganized, and have an ivory tower mentality.")

People can evoke stereotypes with incredibly little information. In a "first impressions" study, the mere designation of a woman as preferring to be addressed as Ms. led to her being perceived as more masculine, more achievement oriented, and less likable than those who preferred the traditional titles Miss or Mrs.[11]

Not all stereotypes are unfavorable. You probably hold favorable stereotypes of the social categories of which you are a member, such as student. However, these stereotypes are often less well developed and less rigid than others you hold. Stereotypes help us develop impressions of ambiguous targets, and we are usually pretty familiar with the people in our own groups. In addition, this contact helps us appreciate individual differences among group members, and such differences work against the development of stereotypes.

Language can be easily twisted to turn neutral or even favorable information into a basis for unfavorable stereotypes. For example, if British people do tend to be reserved, it is fairly easy to interpret this reserve as snobbishness. Similarly, if women who achieve executive positions have had to be aggressive, it is easy to interpret this aggressiveness as pushiness.

Knowing a person's occupation or field of study, we often make assumptions about his or her behavior and personality. Accountants might be stereotyped as compulsive, precise, and one-dimensional, while engineers might be perceived as cold and calculating. Reflect on your own stereotypes of psychology or computer science students.

On the average, not all stereotypes are inaccurate. You probably hold fairly correct stereotypes about the educational level of the typical college professor and the on-the-job demeanor of the typical telephone operator. These accurate stereotypes ease the task of developing perceptions of others. However, it is probably safe to say that most stereotypes are inaccurate, especially when we use them to develop perceptions of specific individuals. This follows from the fact that stereotypes are most likely to develop when we don't have good information about a particular group.

This raises an interesting question: If many stereotypes are inaccurate, why do they persist?[12] After all, reliance upon inaccurate information to develop our perceptions would seem to be punishing in the long run. In fact, a couple of factors work to *reinforce* inaccurate stereotypes. For one thing, even incorrect stereotypes help us process information about others quickly and efficiently. Sometimes, it is easier for the perceiver to rely on an inaccurate stereotype than it is to discover the true nature of the target. The male manager who is required to recommend one of his 20 subordinates for a promotion might find it easier to automatically rule out promoting a woman than to carefully evaluate all of his subordinates, regardless of gender. Second, inaccurate stereotypes are often reinforced by selective perception and the selective application of language that was discussed above. The Hispanic worker who stereotypes all non-Hispanic managers as unfair might be on the lookout for behaviors to confirm these stereotypes and fail to notice examples of fair and friendly treatment. If such treatment *is* noticed, it might be perceived as patronizing rather than helpful.

Later, we'll cover gender, age, racial, and ethnic stereotypes at work. For now, consider *You Be the Manager*.

BANK OF MONTREAL TASK FORCE ON THE ADVANCEMENT OF WOMEN IN THE BANK

You Be The Manager

The Bank of Montreal is Canada's third largest bank, with branches across the country and global operations. Despite the bank's success, President and Chief Operating Officer F. Anthony Comper felt that it had a problem. Like many financial institutions, 75 percent of the bank's 28,000 employees were women. However, women held 91 percent of all nonmanagement jobs but only 9 percent of executive jobs. Even at the subexecutive senior management level, women held only 13 percent of the jobs. The bank established a Task Force on the Advancement of Women in the Bank to explore the underrepresentation of women at senior levels. In an initial series of interviews with employees, the task force found that both men and women had several commonly held perceptions about why women had not advanced.

• Women at the bank are either too young or too old to compete with men for promotions.

WHILE FEMALE EMPLOYEES COMPRISE ABOUT 75 PERCENT OF THE STAFF AT MOST FINANCIAL INSTITUTIONS, ONLY 9 PERCENT OF THESE WOMEN HOLD EXECUTIVE POSITIONS. THE BANK OF MONTREAL SET UP A SPECIAL TASK FORCE TO RESOLVE THIS DISCREPANCY.

• Women are less committed to their careers because they have babies and leave the bank while their children are young.
• More women need to be better educated to compete in significant numbers with men.
• Women don't have "the right stuff" to compete effectively with men for more senior jobs.
• Time will take care of women's advancement to senior levels of the bank.

The task force wasn't sure about the reality of these perceptions, but it knew that perceptions often guide behavior. Given this initial information, how would *you* proceed?

1. Is it important to explore the reality of the employees' perceptions about advancement? If so, how would you do it?
2. Are there any merits to formally surveying the entire work force about womens' advancement?

To find out what the Bank of Montreal did, consult *The Manager's Notebook* at the end of the chapter.

Source: Bank of Montreal Task Force on the Advancement of Women in the Bank. (1991, November). *Report to employees.*

ATTRIBUTION: PERCEIVING CAUSES AND MOTIVES

Thus far we have considered a general model of perception and discussed some specific perceptual tendencies that operate as we form impressions of others. We will now consider a further aspect of impression formation—how we perceive people's motives. **Attribution** is the process by which we assign causes or motives to explain people's behavior. The attribution process is important because many rewards and punishments in society are based upon judgments about what really caused a target person to behave in a certain way.

Attribution. The process by which causes or motives are assigned to explain peoples' behavior.

Unusual behaviors provide us with more information about a person's motives than do conforming behaviors.

Internal

Dispositional attributions.
Explanations for behavior
based on an actor's personality
or intellect.

External

Situational attributions.
Explanations for behavior based
on an actor's external situation
or environment.

Consistency cues. Attribution
cues that reflect how consistently a person engages in some
behavior over time.

Consensus cues. Attribution
cues that reflect how a person's
behavior compares with that
of others.

*extent,
# of times*

Distinctiveness cues.
Attribution cues that reflect
the extent to which a person
engages in some behavior
across a variety of situations.

In making attributions about behavior, an important goal is to determine whether the behavior is caused by dispositional or situational factors. **Dispositional attributions** suggest that some personality or intellectual characteristic unique to the person is responsible for the behavior, and that the behavior thus reflects the "true person." If we explain a behavior as a function of intelligence, greed, friendliness, or laziness we are making dispositional attributions. In general, the business press attributed the turnaround of the Chrysler Corporation to Lee Iacocca's leadership skills and market savvy, not to government loan guarantees or an improving economy.

Situational attributions suggest that the external situation or environment in which the target person exists was responsible for the behavior, and that the person might have had little control over the behavior. If we explain behavior as a function of bad weather, good luck, proper tools, or poor advice, we are making situational attributions.

Obviously, it would be nice to be able to read minds in order to understand people's motives. Since we can't do this, we are forced to rely on external cues and make inferences from these cues. Research indicates that as we gain experience with the behavior of a target person, three implicit questions guide our decisions as to whether we should attribute the behavior to dispositional or situational causes.[13]

- Does the person engage in the behavior regularly and consistently? (**Consistency cues**)
- Do most people engage in the behavior, or is it unique to this person? (**Consensus cues**)
- Does the person engage in the behavior in many situations, or is it distinctive to one situation? (**Distinctiveness cues**)

Let's examine consistency, consensus, and distinctiveness cues in more detail.

Consistency Cues

Unless we see clear evidence of external constraints that force a behavior to occur, we tend to perceive behavior that a person performs regularly as indicative of his or her true motives. In other words, high consistency leads to dispositional attributions. Thus, one might assume that the professor who has generous office hours and is always there for consultation really cares about students. Similarly, we are likely to make dispositional attributions about workers who are consistently good or poor performers, perhaps perceiving the former as "dedicated" and the latter as "lazy." When behavior occurs inconsistently, we begin to consider situational attributions. For example, if a person's performance cycles between mediocre and excellent, we might look to variations in workload to explain the cycles.

Consensus Cues

In general, acts that deviate from social expectations provide us with more information about the actor's motives than conforming behaviors do. Thus, unusual, low-consensus behavior leads to more dispositional attributions than typical, high-consensus behavior. The person who acts differently from the majority is seen as revealing more of his or her true motives. Ann Hopkins' detractors viewed her failure to act stereotypically feminine as a character flaw. The informational effects of low-consensus behavior are magnified when the actor is expected to suffer negative consequences because of the deviance. Consider the job applicant who makes favorable statements about the role of big business in society while being interviewed for a job at General Motors. Such statements are so predictable in this situation that the interviewer can place little confidence in what they really indicate about the candidate's true feelings and motives. On the other hand, imagine an applicant who makes critical comments about big business in the same situation. Such comments are hardly expected, and could clearly lead to rejection. In this case, the interviewer would be more confident about the applicant's true disposition regarding big business.

A corollary to this suggests that we place more emphasis upon people's private actions than their public actions when assessing their motives.[14] When our actions are not open to public scrutiny, we are more likely to act out our genuine motives and feelings. Thus, we place more emphasis upon a coworker's private statements about his boss than we do on his public relations with the boss.

Distinctiveness Cues

When a behavior occurs across a variety of situations, it lacks distinctiveness, and the observer is prone to provide a dispositional attribution about its cause. We reason that the behavior reflects a person's true motives if it "stands up" in a variety of environments. Thus, the professor who has generous office hours, stays after class to talk to students, and attends student functions is seen as truly student oriented. The worker whose performance was good in his first job as well as several subsequent jobs is perceived as having real ability. When a behavior is highly distinctive, in that it occurs in only one situation, we are likely to assume that some aspect of the situation caused the behavior. If the only student-oriented behavior that we observe is generous office hours, we assume that they are dictated by department policy. If a worker performed well on only one job, back in 1985, we suspect that his uncle owned the company!

Attribution in Action

Frequently, observers of real life behavior have information at hand about consistency, consensus, and distinctiveness. Let's take an example that shows how the observer puts such information together in forming attributions. At the same time, the example will serve to review the previous discussion. Imagine that Smith, Jones, and Kelley are employees who work in separate firms. Each is absent from work today, and a manager must develop an attribution about the cause in order to decide which personnel action is warranted.

- *Smith*—Smith is absent a lot, his peers are seldom absent, and he was absent a lot in his previous job.
- *Jones*—Jones is absent a lot, her peers are also absent a lot, but she was almost never absent in her previous job.
- *Kelley*—Kelley is seldom absent, his co-workers are seldom absent, and he was seldom absent in his previous job.

Just what kind of attributions are managers likely to make regarding the absences of Smith, Jones, and Kelley? Smith's absence is highly consistent, it is a low-consensus behavior, and it is not distinctive, since he was absent in his previous job. As shown in Exhibit 4.4, this combination of cues is very likely to prompt a dispositional explanation, perhaps that Smith is lazy or irresponsible. Jones is also absent consistently, but it is high-consensus behavior in that her peers also exhibit absence. In addition, the behavior is highly distinctive—she is absent only on this job. As indicated, this combination of cues will usually result in a situational attribution, perhaps that working conditions are terrible or that the boss is nasty. Finally, Kelley's absence is inconsistent. In addition, it is similar to that of co-workers and not distinctive, in that he was inconsistently absent on his previous job as well. As shown, this combination of cues suggests that some temporary, short-term situational factor causes his absence. It is possible that a sick child occasionally requires him to stay home.

Biases in Attribution

As the preceding section indicates, observers often operate in a rational, logical manner in forming attributions about behavior. The various cue combinations and the resulting attributions have a sensible appearance. This does not mean that such attributions are always correct, but that they do represent

	Consistency	Consensus	Distinctiveness	Likely Attribution
Smith	High	Low	Low	Disposition
Jones	High	High	High	Situation
Kelley	Low	High	Low	Temporary Situation

EXHIBIT 4.4
Cue combinations and resulting attributions.

good bets about why some behavior occurred. Having made this observation, it would be naive to assume that attributions are always free from bias or error. Earlier, we discussed a number of very basic perceptual biases, and it stands to reason that the complex task of attribution would also be open to bias. Let's consider the fundamental attribution error, actor-observer effect, and self-serving bias.[15]

Fundamental Attribution Error. Suppose you make a mistake in attributing a cause to someone else's behavior. Would you be likely to err on the side of a dispositional cause or a situational cause? Substantial evidence indicates that when we make judgments about the behavior of people other than ourselves, we tend to overemphasize dispositional explanations at the expense of situational explanations. This is called the **fundamental attribution error.**[16] For example, some Price Waterhouse partners evidently saw Ann Hopkins as having a flawed personality and discounted the situational impact of her minority status in the firm.

> **Fundamental attribution error.** The tendency to overemphasize dispositional explanations for behavior at the expense of situational explanations.

Why does the fundamental attribution error occur? For one thing, we often discount the strong effects that social roles can have on behavior. We might see bankers as truly conservative people because we ignore the fact that their occupational role and their employer dictate that they act conservatively. Second, many people whom we observe are seen in rather constrained, constant situations (at work, or at school) that reduce our appreciation of how their behavior can vary in other situations. Thus, we fail to realize that the observed behavior is distinctive to a particular situation. That conservative banker might actually be a weekend skydiver!

The fundamental attribution error can lead to problems for the managers of poorly performing subordinates. It suggests that dispositional explanations for the poor performance will sometimes be made even when situational factors are the true cause. Laziness or low aptitude might be cited, while poor training or a bad sales territory are ignored. However, this is less likely when the manager has had actual experience in performing the subordinate's job and is thus aware of situational roadblocks to good performance.[17]

Actor-Observer Effect. It is not surprising that actors and observers often view the causes for the actor's behavior very differently. This difference in attributional perspectives is called the **actor-observer effect.**[18] Specifically, while the observer might be busy committing the fundamental attribution error, the actor might be emphasizing the role of the situation in explaining his or her own behavior. Thus, as actors, we are often particularly sensitive to those environmental events that led us to be late or absent. As observers of the same behavior in others, we are more likely to invoke dispositional causes.

> **Actor-observer effect.** The propensity for actors and observers to view the causes of the actor's behavior differently.

We see some of the most striking examples of this effect in cases of illegal behavior such as price fixing and the bribery of government officials. The perpetrators and those close to them often cite stiff competition or management pressure as causes of their ethical lapses. Observers see the perpetrators as immoral or unintelligent.[19]

Why are actors prone to attribute much of their own behavior to situational causes? First, they might be more aware than observers of the constraints and advantages that the environment offered. At the same time they are aware of their private thoughts, feelings, and intentions regarding the behavior, all of which might be unknown to the observer. Thus, I might know that I sincerely wanted to get to the meeting on time, that I left home extra early, and that the accident that delayed me was truly unusual. My boss might be unaware of all of this information and figure that I'm unreliable.

Self-Serving Bias.   It has probably already occurred to you that certain forms of attributions have the capacity to make us feel good or bad about ourselves. In fact, people have a tendency to take credit and responsibility for successful outcomes of their behavior and to deny credit and responsibility for failures.[20] This tendency is called **self-serving bias,** and it is interesting because it suggests that people will explain the very same behavior differently on the basis of events that happened *after* the behavior occurred. If the vice-president of marketing champions a product that turns out to be a sales success, she might attribute this to her retailing savvy. If the very same marketing process leads to failure, she might attribute this to the poor performance of the marketing research firm that she used. Notice that the self-serving bias can overcome the tendency for actors to attribute their behavior to situational factors. In this example, the vice-president invokes a dispositional explanation ("I'm an intelligent, competent person") when the behavior is successful.

Self-serving bias can reflect intentional self-promotion or excuse making. However, again, it is possible that it reflects unique information on the part of the actor. Especially when behavior has negative consequences, the actor might scan the environment and find situational causes for the failure.[21]

To review the basics of attribution, people often use consistency, consensus, and distinctiveness cues in a sensible and rational manner when trying to explain some observed behavior. However, the fundamental attribution error suggests that observers are often overly ready to invoke dispositional explanations for the behavior of actors. The actor-observer effect suggests that the actor is more ready to attribute his or her own behavior to situational factors. Given the self-serving bias, this is especially likely if the behavior is unsuccessful.

PERSON PERCEPTION AND WORKFORCE DIVERSITY

The realities of workforce diversity have become an important factor for many organizations in recent years. **Workforce diversity** refers to differences among employees or potential recruits in characteristics such as gender, race, age, religion, cultural background, physical ability, and sexual orientation. The interest in diversity stems from at least two broad facts. First, the North American workforce is becoming more diverse. Second, there is growing recognition that many organizations have not successfully managed workforce diversity.

The Changing Workplace

As we mentioned in Chapter 1, the composition of the North American labor force is changing.[22] Thirty years ago, it was mainly white and mainly male. Now, changing immigration patterns, the aging of baby boomers, and the increasing movement of women into paid employment make for a lot more variety. People of Asian and Hispanic background have become a growing segment of the labor pool. Not only is the labor pool changing, but many orga-

---

Self-serving bias. The tendency to take credit for successful outcomes and to deny responsibility for failures.

Workforce diversity. Differences among recruits and employees in characteristics such as gender, race, age, religion, cultural background, physical ability, and sexual orientation.

nizations are seeking to recruit more representatively from this pool so that they employ people who reflect their customer base—to better mirror their markets. This is especially true in the growing service sector, where contact between organizational members and customers is very direct.

The changing employment pool isn't the only factor that has prompted interest in diversity issues. Globalization, mergers, and strategic alliances mean that many employees are required to interact with people from substantially different national or corporate cultures. Compounding all of this is an increased emphasis on teamwork as a means of job design and quality enhancement. How can a diverse group of individuals work well together?

Valuing Diversity

In the past, organizations were thought to be doing the right thing if they merely tolerated diversity, that is, if they engaged in fair hiring and employment practices with respect to women and minorities. Firms were considered to be doing especially well if they assisted these people to "fit into" the mainstream corporate culture by "fixing" what was different about them.[23] For example, women managers were sometimes given assertiveness training to enable them to be as hard-nosed and aggressive as their male counterparts!

Recently, some have argued that organizations should *value* diversity, not just tolerate it or try to blend everyone into a narrow mainstream. To be sure, a critical motive is the basic fairness of valuing diversity. However, there is increasing awareness that diversity and its proper management can yield strategic and competitive advantages. These advantages include the potential for improved problem solving and creativity when diverse perspectives are brought to bear on an organizational problem such as product or service quality. They also include improved recruiting and marketing when the firm's human resources profile matches that of the labor pool and customer base (see Exhibit 4.5).

Stereotypes and Workforce Diversity

If there is a single concept that serves as a barrier to valuing diversity it is the stereotype. Let's examine several workplace stereotypes and their consequences. Common workplace stereotypes are based on gender, age, race, and ethnicity.

Racial and Ethnic Stereotypes.   Racial and ethnic stereotypes are pervasive, persistent, frequently negative, and often self-contradictory. Most of us hold at least some stereotypical views of other races or cultures. Over the years, such stereotypes exhibit remarkable stability unless some major event, such as a war, intervenes to change them. Then, former allies can acquire negative attributes in short order.

Personal experience is unnecessary for such stereotype formation. In one study, people were asked to describe the traits of a number of ethnic groups, including several fictional ones. Although they had never met a Danerian, a Pirenian, or a Wallonian, this did not inhibit them from assigning traits, and those they assigned were usually unfavorable![24] Such stereotypes often contain contradictory elements. A common reaction is to describe a particular group as being too lazy while at the same time criticizing it for taking one's job opportunities away.

Beverly Harvard brought diversity to the police force and broke gender stereotypes by becoming Atlanta's first black woman police chief.

1. Cost Argument	As organizations become more diverse, the cost of a poor job in integrating workers will increase. Those who handle this well will thus create cost advantages over those who don't.
2. Resource-Acquisition Argument	Companies develop reputations on favorability as prospective employers for women and ethnic minorities. Those with the best reputations for managing diversity will win the competition for the best personnel. As the labor pool shrinks and changes composition, this edge will become increasingly important.
3. Marketing Argument	For multi-national organizations, the insight and cultural sensitivity that members with roots in other countries bring to the marketing effort should improve these efforts in important ways. The same rationale applies to marketing to subpopulations within domestic operations.
4. Creativity Argument	Diversity of perspectives and less emphasis on conformity to norms of the past (which characterize the modern approach to management of diversity) should improve the level of creativity.
5. Problem-Solving Argument	Heterogeneity in decision and problem solving groups potentially produces better decisions through a wider range of perspectives and more thorough critical analysis of issues.
6. System Flexibility Argument	An implication of the multicultural model for managing diversity is that the system will become less determinant, less standardized, and therefore more fluid. The increased fluidity should create greater flexibility to react to environmental changes (i.e., reactions should be faster and at less cost).

Source: Cox, T.H., & Blake, S. (1991, August). Managing cultural diversity: Implications for organizational competitiveness. *Academy of Management Executive*, 45–56, p. 47.

EXHIBIT 4.5
Competitive advantages to valuing and managing a diverse workforce.

There is a remarkable shortage of serious research into racial and ethnic matters in organizations.[25] Nevertheless, what follows is a sample of some typical findings. Just getting in the door can be a problem. For example:

> The Urban Institute sent out teams of black and white job applicants with equal credentials. The men applied for the same entry-level jobs in Chicago and Washington, D.C., within hours of each other. They were the same age and physical size, had identical education and work experience, and shared similar personalities. Yet in almost 20% of the 476 audits, whites advanced farther in the hiring process, researchers found.[26]

Even after getting in the door, career tracking based on racial or ethnic stereotypes is common. For instance, one study found that a stereotype that "blacks can't handle pressure" was partially responsible for a lack of acceptance of African Americans in managerial roles.[27] Many companies have promoted African American executives to positions having to do with affirmative action, diversity, or urban affairs in spite of their extensive credentials in other substantive areas of business. Similarly, the stereotype of Asian Americans as technical whizzes has interfered with their opportunity to ascend to high general management positions.[28]

Attributions can play an important role in determining how job performance is interpreted. For example, one study found that good performance on the part of African American managers was seen to be due to help from others (a situational attribution) while good performance by Caucasian managers was seen to be due to their effort and abilities (a dispositional attribution).[29]

Finally, racial and ethnic stereotypes are also important in the context of the increasing globalization of business. In one study, researchers asked American business students to describe Japanese and American managers along a number of dimensions. The students viewed Japanese managers as having more productive subordinates and being better overall managers. However, the students preferred to work for an American manager.[30] One can wonder how such students will respond to international assignments. Of course, all groups have stereotypes of each other. Japanese stereotypes of Americans probably contribute to Americans not being promoted above a certain level in Japanese firms.

Gender Stereotypes.   One of the most problematic stereotypes for organizations is the gender stereotype. Considering their numbers in the work force, women are severely underrepresented in managerial and administrative jobs. There is evidence that gender stereotypes are partially responsible for discouraging women from business careers and blocking their ascent to managerial positions. This underrepresentation of women managers and administrators happens because stereotypes of women do not correspond especially well with stereotypes of businesspeople or managers.

What is the nature of gender stereotypes? A series of studies has had managers describe men in general, women in general, and typical "successful middle managers." These studies have determined that successful middle managers are perceived as having traits and attitudes that are similar to those generally ascribed to men.[31] That is, successful managers are seen as more similar to men in qualities such as leadership ability, competitiveness, self-confidence, ambitiousness, and objectivity. Thus, stereotypes of successful middle managers do not correspond to stereotypes of women. The trend over time in the results of these studies contains some bad news and some good news. The bad news is that *male* managers today hold the same dysfunctional stereotypes about women and management that they held in the early 1970s when researchers conducted the first of these studies. At that time, women managers held the same stereotypes as the men. The good news is that the recent research shows a shift by the women—they now see successful middle managers as possessing attitudes and characteristics that describe *both* men and women in general.[32]

Granting that gender stereotypes exist, do they lead to biased personnel decisions? The answer would appear to be yes. In a typical study, researchers asked male bank supervisors to make hypothetical personnel decisions about workers who were described equivalently except for sex.[33] Women were discriminated against for promotion to a branch manager position. They were also discriminated against when they requested to attend a professional development conference. In addition, female supervisors were less likely than males to receive support for their request that a problem employee be fired. In one case, bias worked to *favor* women. The bank supervisors were more likely to approve a request for a leave of absence to care for one's children when it came from a female. This finding is similar to others that show gender stereotypes tend to favor women when they are being considered for "women's" jobs (such as secretary) or for "women's" tasks (such as supervising other women).[34]

In general, research suggests that the above findings are fairly typical. Women suffer from a stereotype that is detrimental to their hiring, development, promotion, and salaries. Women managers are also more likely than men managers to have to make off-the-job sacrifices and compromises in family life to maintain their careers.[35] However, there is growing evidence that the detrimental effects of such stereotypes are reduced or removed when decision makers have good information about the qualifications and performance of particular women and an accurate picture of the job that they are applying for or seeking promotion into.[36] In particular, several field studies reveal convincingly that women do not generally suffer from gender stereotypes in *performance evaluations* that their supervisors provide.[37] This is not altogether surprising. As we noted earlier, stereotypes help us process information in ambiguous situations. To the extent that we have good information upon which to base our perceptions of people, reliance on stereotypes is less necessary. Day-to-day performance is often fairly easy to observe, and gender stereotypes do not intrude on evaluations. On the other hand, hiring and promotion decisions might confront managers with ambiguous targets or situations and prompt them to resort to gender stereotypes in forming impressions.

What about Ann Hopkins? Was she simply an exception to the general rule that women don't suffer in performance appraisals? Probably not. When women make up a very *small* proportion of an employee group (15–20 percent) they tend to suffer a "tokenism" effect that exaggerates the effect of stereotypes.[38] You will recall that Price Waterhouse had only seven women out of 662 partners and that Ann Hopkins was the only woman out of 88 partner nominees. Under such circumstances, research shows that women's performance appraisals suffer.[39] Evidently people view token women as less capable of doing a "man's" job. Also, Ann Hopkins' nomination was not a routine performance appraisal but an evaluation for promotability as well. More subjective criteria and people who were not well acquainted with Hopkins were implicated in this decision.

Age Stereotypes.   Another kind of stereotype that presents problems for organizations is the age stereotype. Knowing that a person falls into a certain age range, we have a tendency to make certain assumptions about the person's physical, psychological, and intellectual capabilities.

What is the nature of work-related age stereotypes? Older workers are seen as having less *capacity for performance*. They tend to be viewed as less productive, creative, logical, and capable of performing under pressure than younger workers. In addition, older workers are seen as having less *potential for development*. Compared with younger workers, they are considered more rigid and dogmatic and less adaptable to new corporate cultures. Not all stereotypes of older workers are negative, however. They tend to be perceived as more honest, dependable, and trustworthy (in short, more *stable*). In general, these stereotypes are held by both younger and older individuals.[40] It is worth noting that these stereotypes are essentially inaccurate. For example, age seldom limits the capacity for development until post-employment years.[41] Also, research shows that age and performance are unrelated.[42]

Again, the relevant question arises: Do age stereotypes affect personnel decisions? It would appear that such stereotypes can affect decisions regarding hiring, promotion, and skills development. In one study, researchers had university students make hypothetical recommendations regarding younger and older male workers. An older man was less likely to be hired for a finance job that required rapid, high-risk decisions. An older man was considered less promotable for a marketing position that required creative solutions to difficult problems. Finally, an older worker was less likely to be permitted to attend a conference on advanced production systems.[43] These decisions reflect the stereotypes of the older worker depicted above, and they are doubtless indicative of the tendency for older employees to be laid off during corporate restructuring. Again, however, we should recognize that age stereotypes may have less impact upon personnel decisions when managers have good information about the capacities of the particular employee in question.

Managing Diversity with Stereotype Reduction

Given the prevalence of the stereotypes noted above, valuing diversity isn't something that occurs automatically. Rather, diversity needs to be *managed* to have a positive impact on work behavior. Management can use a number of strategies to help reduce the effects of workplace stereotypes.[44]

- Select enough minority members to get them beyond token status. When this happens, the majority starts to look at individual accomplishments, rather than group membership, because they can see variation in the behavior of the minority.
- Encourage teamwork that brings minority and majority members together.
- Ensure that those making career decisions about employees have accurate information about them rather than having to rely on hearsay and second-hand opinion.
- Train people to be aware of stereotypes.

Training is the most widely used tool for instituting the management of diversity (see "Global Focus: *Diversity Training Goes Global*"). Most training begins by illustrating the value of diversity and increasing the awareness of stereotypes.

Among the many companies who have made extensive use of such training are McDonnell Douglas, Hewlett-Packard, and Ortho Pharmaceuticals. McDonnell Douglas has a program ("Woman-Wise and Business Savvy") focusing on gender differences in work-related behaviors. It uses same-gender group meetings and mixed-gender role-plays. At its manufacturing plant in San Diego, Hewlett-Packard conducted training on cultural differences between American-Anglos and Mexican, Indochinese, and Filipinos. Much of the content focused on cultural differences in communication styles. In one of the most thorough training efforts to date, Ortho Pharmaceuticals started its three-day training with small groups (ten to twelve) of senior managers and eventually trained managers at every level of the company.[45]

GLOBAL FOCUS   Diversity Training Goes Global

Diversity management efforts have begun to acquire an international flavor in big American businesses.

Many major employers provide diversity training in the U.S. This training seeks to create workplaces conducive to retaining and promoting a diverse work force with many women and minority members. Some corporations even link executives' pay increases partly to achievement of diversity goals.

Now, a handful of companies—including Dow Chemical, Nynex, and Colgate-Palmolive—want to broaden their diversity push to include employees abroad. "Companies are starting to figure out what it might mean abroad and how you integrate the domestic program with the international perspective," says Bernardo Ferdman, assistant professor of psychology and Latin American and Caribbean studies at the Sate University of New York at Albany.

Nynex is typical. Though it employs 4,500 people abroad, the regional phone company gives its two-day diversity training program only to individuals based in the U.S. So, Joseph Anderson, director of managing diversity, will spend several months this year visiting Nynex operations in Hong Kong, Belgium and elsewhere to assess their need for diversity training.

"We are ready now to move diversity training overseas," a Nynex spokesman says. "It's the next step." In some cases, Mr. Anderson may offer informal training on the spot. He also will make sure female Nynex employees aren't discriminated against in countries "where women may not be treated equally" outside the office, the spokesman says.

Yet foreign employees may resent the imposition of an all-American concept, warns Judith Katz, vice

At Avon, diversity training highlights the value of diversity and makes employees more conscious of stereotypes.

president of Kaleel Jamison Consulting Group, a Cincinnati firm advising DuPont on this issue. Workforce diversity "is seen as a U.S. problem," she says, and in many ways, "as U.S. imperialism."

Source: Excerpted from Staff. (1993, March 12). Diversity training extends beyond U.S. *The Wall Street Journal*, p.B1.

Other firms with well-developed diversity training programs include Avon, G.E. Silicones, and U.S. West Telecommunications.

Asset Recognition Training is one form of training that goes beyond group differences and emphasizes individual uniqueness.[46] In this training, people record on worksheets their own personal knowledge, insights, and experiences. Then, in small groups, each person's unique assets and potential contributions to his or her work group and the organization are identified. Focusing on the individual and going beyond his or her current work role expertise fosters appreciation for diversity. Notice how this training counteracts the perceptual narrowing we described in Bruner's model.

There is as yet little hard research on the success of diversity training programs. However, there is some anecdotal evidence that these programs can actually cause disruption and bad feelings when all they do is get people to open up and generate stereotypes and then send them back to work.[47] Awareness training should be accompanied by skills training that is relevant to the particular needs of the organization. This might include training in resolving inter-cultural conflict, team building, handling a charge of sexual harassment, or learning a second language. Hewlett-Packard is a company that soon realized that awareness training wasn't enough. Such training now constitutes only one of nine diversity training modules of this type.[48]

Basic awareness and skills training are not the only components of managing diversity. Organizations must use a number of other tactics. In future chapters we'll consider the following:

- Comprehensive attitude change programs that focus on diversity (Chapter 5).
- Recognizing diversity in employee needs and motives (Chapter 6).
- Using alternative working schedules to offer employees flexibility (Chapter 7).
- Using employee surveys to foster better communication (Chapters 11 and 17).
- Providing mentors and other career guidance mechanisms that cater to diversity (Chapter 18).

To overcome stereotypes and achieve a diverse workforce we have to select people based on their talents and appraise their performance fairly. Let's look at the role of perception in these two tasks.

PERSON PERCEPTION IN THE SELECTION INTERVIEW

You have probably had the pleasure (or displeasure!) of sitting through one or more job interviews in your life. After all, the interview is one of the most common organizational selection devices, applied with equal opportunity to applicants for everything from the janitorial staff to the executive suite. With our futures on the line, we would like to think that the interview is a fair and accurate selection device, but is it? Research shows that the interview is a valid selection device, although it is far from perfectly accurate, especially when the interviewer conducts it in an unstructured, free-form format. Validity improves whenever interviewers use a guide to order and organize their questions and impressions.[49]

What factors threaten the validity of the interview? To consider the most obvious problem first, applicants are usually motivated to present an especially favorable impression of themselves. As our discussion of the perception of people implies, it is difficult enough to gain a clear picture of another individual without having to cope with active deception! A couple of the perceptual tendencies that we already discussed in this chapter can also operate in the interview. For one thing, there is evidence that interviewers compare applicants with a stereotype of the ideal applicant.[50] In and of itself, this is not a bad thing. However, this ideal stereotype must be accurate, and this requires a clear understanding of the nature of the job in question and the kind of person who can do well in this job. This is a tall order, especially for the interviewer who is hiring applicants for a wide variety of jobs. Second, interviewers have a tendency to exhibit primacy reactions.[51] Minimally, this means that information the interviewer acquired early in the interview will have an undue impact on the final decision. However, it also means that information the interviewer

The interview is a difficult setting in which to form accurate impressions about a candidate. Interview validity increases when interviews are more structured and interviewers ask a set of predetermined questions.

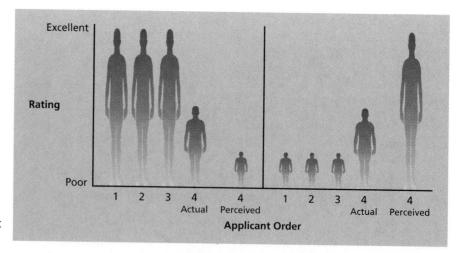

EXHIBIT 4.6
Two examples of contrast effects.

Contrast effects. Previously interviewed job applicants affect an interviewer's perception of a current applicant, leading to an exaggeration of differences between applicants.

obtained *before* the interview (for instance, by scanning an application form or résumé) can have exaggerated influence on the interview outcome.

A couple of perceptual tendencies that we haven't discussed are also at work in interviews. First, interviewers have a tendency to underweight positive information about the applicant.[52] This tendency means that negative information has undue impact on the decision.[53] It might occur because interviewers get more feedback about unsuccessful hiring than successful hiring ("Why did you send me that idiot?"). It might also happen because positive information isn't perceived as telling the interviewer much, since the candidate is motivated to put up a good front. In addition, **contrast effects** sometimes occur in the interview.[54] This means that the applicants who have been interviewed earlier affect the interviewer's perception of a current applicant, leading to an exaggeration of differences between applicants. For example, if the interviewer has seen two excellent candidates and then encounters an average candidate, she might rate this person lower than if he had been preceded by two average applicants. (See Exhibit 4.6.) This is an example of the impact of the situation upon perception.

It is clear that the interview constitutes a fairly difficult setting in which to form accurate impressions about others. It is of short duration, a lot of information is generated, and the applicant is motivated to present a favorable image. Thus, interviewers often adopt "perceptual crutches" that hinder accurate perception. Earlier, we noted that unstructured interviews are less valid than structured interviews where the interviewer scores the applicant's responses to a predetermined series of questions. This form of interview probably reduces information overload and ensures that applicants can be more easily compared, since they have all responded to an identical sequence of questions.[55]

PERSON PERCEPTION AND PERFORMANCE APPRAISAL

Once a person is hired, however imperfectly, further perceptual tasks confront organization members. Specifically, the organization will want some index of the person's job performance for decisions regarding pay raises, promotions, transfers, and training needs.

Objective and Subjective Measures

It is possible to find objective measures of performance for certain aspects of some jobs. These are measures that do not involve a substantial degree of human judgment. Ann Hopkins' billable hours are one such measure. In general, though, as we move up the organizational hierarchy, it becomes more difficult to find objective indicators of performance. Thus, it is often hard to find countable evidence of a manager's success or failure. When objective indicators of performance do exist, they are often contaminated by situational factors. For example, it might be very difficult to compare the dollar sales of a snowmobile salesperson whose territory covers Maryland and Virginia with one whose territory is northern Ontario. Also, while dollar sales might be a good indicator of current sales performance, it says little about a person's capacity for promotion to district sales manager.

Because of the difficulties that objective performance indicators present, organizations must often rely upon subjective measures of effectiveness, usually provided by managers. However, the manager is confronted by a number of perceptual roadblocks. He or she might not be in a position to observe many instances of effective and ineffective performance. This is especially likely when the subordinate's job activities cannot be monitored directly. For example, a police sergeant cannot ride around in six squad cars at the same time, and a telephone company supervisor cannot visit customers' homes or climb telephone poles with all of his or her installers. Such situations mean that the target (the subordinate's performance) is frequently ambiguous, and we have seen that the perceptual system resolves ambiguities in an efficient but often inaccurate manner. Even when performance is observable, employees often alter their behavior so that they look good when their manager is around.

Rater Errors

Subjective performance appraisal is susceptible to some of the perceptual biases we discussed earlier—primacy, recency, and stereotypes. In addition, a number of other perceptual tendencies occur in performance evaluation. They are often called rater errors. One interrelated set of these tendencies includes leniency, harshness, and central tendency (Exhibit 4.7). **Leniency** refers to the tendency to perceive the performance of one's ratees as especially good, while **harshness** is the tendency to see their performance as especially ineffective. Lenient raters tend to give "good" ratings, and harsh raters tend to give "bad" ratings. Professors with reputations as easy graders or tough graders exemplify these types of raters. **Central tendency** involves assigning most ratees to a middle-range performance category—the extremes of the rating categories are not used. The professor who assigns 80 percent of her students Cs is committing this error. Each of these three rating tendencies is probably partially a function of the rater's personal experiences. For example, the manager who has had an especially good group of subordinates might respond with special harshness when management transfers him to supervise a group of slightly less able workers. It is worth noting that not all instances of leniency, harshness, and central tendency necessarily represent perceptual errors. In some cases, raters intentionally commit these errors, even though they have accurate perceptions of workers' performance. For example, a manager might use leniency

Leniency. The tendency to perceive the job performance of ratees as especially good.

Harshness. The tendency to perceive the job performance of ratees as especially ineffective.

Central tendency. The tendency to assign most ratees to middle-range job performance categories.

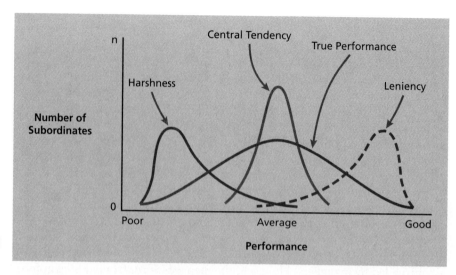

EXHIBIT 4.7
Leniency, harshness, and central tendency rater errors.

or central tendency in performance reviews so that his subordinates do not react negatively to his evaluation.

Another perceptual error that is frequently committed by performance raters is called the **halo effect**.[56] The halo effect occurs when the observer allows the rating of an individual on one trait or characteristic to color ratings on other traits or characteristics. For example, in a teacher evaluation system, a student might perceive his instructor as a nice person, and this might favorably influence his perception of the instructor's knowledge of the material and speed in returning exams and papers. Similarly, a manager might rate a subordinate as frequently late for work, and this might in turn lead her to devalue the subordinate's productivity and quality of work. As these examples illustrate, halo can work either for or against the ratee. In both cases, the rater fails to perceive differences *within* ratees. The halo effect tends to be organized around central traits that the rater considers important. The student feels that being nice is an especially important quality, while the manager places special emphasis upon promptness. Ratings on these characteristics then affect the rater's perceptions of other characteristics.

The **similar-to-me effect** is an additional rater error that may in part reflect perceptual bias. The rater tends to give more favorable evaluations to people who are similar to the rater in terms of background or attitudes. For example, the manager with an M.B.A. degree who comes from an upper middle class family might perceive a similar subordinate as a good performer even though the person is only average. Similarly, a rater might overestimate the performance of an individual who holds similar religious and political views. Such reactions probably stem from a tendency to view our own performance, attitudes, and background as "good." We then tend to generalize this evaluation to others who are to some degree similar to us. Ann Hopkins probably suffered from similar-to-me when she received negative evaluations from the Price Waterhouse partners. Raters with diverse subordinates should be especially wary of this error.

Given all of these problems, it should be clear that it is difficult to get good subjective evaluations of employee performance. Because of this, personnel specialists have explored various techniques for reducing perceptual errors and

Halo effect. The rating of an individual on one trait or characteristic tends to color ratings on other traits or characteristics.

Similar-to-me effect. A rater gives more favorable evaluations to people who are similar to the rater in terms of background or attitudes.

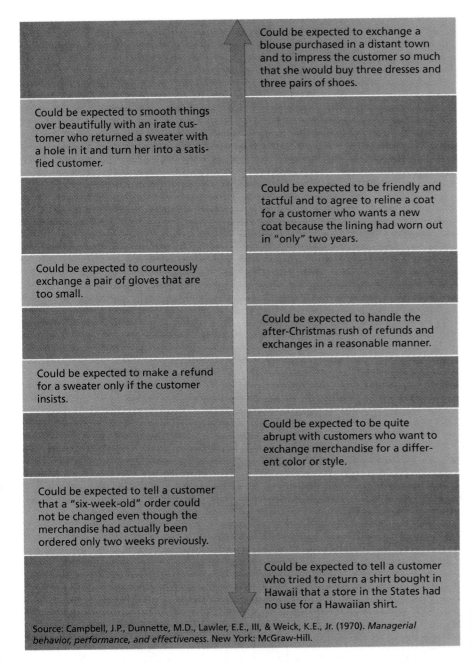

Could be expected to exchange a blouse purchased in a distant town and to impress the customer so much that she would buy three dresses and three pairs of shoes.

Could be expected to smooth things over beautifully with an irate customer who returned a sweater with a hole in it and turn her into a satisfied customer.

Could be expected to be friendly and tactful and to agree to reline a coat for a customer who wants a new coat because the lining had worn out in "only" two years.

Could be expected to courteously exchange a pair of gloves that are too small.

Could be expected to handle the after-Christmas rush of refunds and exchanges in a reasonable manner.

Could be expected to make a refund for a sweater only if the customer insists.

Could be expected to be quite abrupt with customers who want to exchange merchandise for a different color or style.

Could be expected to tell a customer that a "six-week-old" order could not be changed even though the merchandise had actually been ordered only two weeks previously.

Could be expected to tell a customer who tried to return a shirt bought in Hawaii that a store in the States had no use for a Hawaiian shirt.

Source: Campbell, J.P., Dunnette, M.D., Lawler, E.E., III, & Weick, K.E., Jr. (1970). *Managerial behavior, performance, and effectiveness*. New York: McGraw-Hill.

EXHIBIT 4.8
Behaviorally anchored scale for rating customer service.

biases. There has been a tendency to attempt to reduce rater errors by going to rating scales with more specific behavioral labels. The assumption here is that giving specific examples of effective and ineffective performance will facilitate the rater's perceptual processes and recall. Exhibit 4.8 shows a behaviorally anchored rating scale that gives very specific behavioral examples (from top to bottom) of good, average, and poor customer service. It was developed for the J.C. Penney Company. With such an aid, the rater might be less likely to succumb to perceptual errors when completing the rating task, although the evidence for this is mixed.[57]

Bank of Montreal Task Force on the Advancement of Women in the Bank

The Manager's Notebook

The task force commissioned the research activities described below. As a first step, the results of the research were provided to all bank employees to correct faulty stereotypes. The task force developed an action plan for advancement of women in the bank that included enhanced training, better posting of job vacancies, redesigned career development opportunities, and more flexible work schedules. Within only two years, there were substantial gains in the percentages of women at all management levels.

1. The task force used the bank's human resources information system to establish that employee perceptions about women's advancement were incorrect. 1) The age distribution of men and women in the bank was nearly equivalent. 2) At all levels except senior management, women had longer service records than men. 3) There were more women with degrees than men at the bank's lower ranks. 4) At all levels, larger percentages of women than men received top performance ratings. 5) Historical analysis showed that the movement of women into senior ranks had not improved much in recent years.

2. A formal survey has the advantage of giving everyone the opportunity to make his or her views known. It is also more anonymous than interviews. The task force survey found a rather wide discrepancy between men and women in terms of many perceptions about opportunity. It also asked employees to choose among options for promoting and developing women and for helping employees to balance work and family commitments. Their choices were the basis for some of the action plan features described above.

EXECUTIVE SUMMARY

◆ Perception involves interpreting the input from our senses to provide meaning to our environment, and any instance of perception involves a perceiver, a target, and a situational context. The experience, needs, and emotions of the perceiver affect perception, as does the ambiguity of the target.

◆ Bruner's model of the perceptual process suggests that we are very receptive to cues provided by the target and the situation when we encounter an unfamiliar target. However, as we discover familiar cues, we quickly categorize the target and process other cues to maintain a consistent and constant picture of the target. When the target is a person, this drive for constancy and consistency is revealed in a number of specific perceptual biases, including primacy, recency, implicit personality theory, reliance on central traits, projection, and stereotyping. Gender, age, race, and ethnic stereotypes are especially problematic for organizations.

◆ Attribution is the process of assigning causes or motives to people's behavior. The observer is often interested in determining whether the behavior is due to dispositional (internal) or situational (external) causes. Behavior is likely to be attributed to the disposition of the actor when the behavior (1) is performed consistently, (2) differs from that exhibited by other people, and (3) occurs in a variety of situations or environments. An opposite set of cues will prompt a situational attribution. Observers are biased toward making dispositional attributions, while actors are more likely to explain their own behavior in situational terms, especially when its outcomes are unfavorable.

◆ The changing nature of the workplace has highlighted the advantages of valuing and managing employee diversity. Organizations can use a number of tactics, including training, to combat stereotypes that threaten diversity efforts.

◆ Judging the suitability of job applicants in an interview and appraising job performance are especially difficult perceptual tasks, in part because the target is motivated to convey a good impression. In addition, interviewers and performance raters exhibit a number of perceptual tendencies that are reflected in inaccurate judgments, including contrast effects, leniency, harshness, central tendency, halo, and similar-to-me effects.

KEY CONCEPTS

Perception
Perceptual defense
Primacy effect
Recency effect
Central traits
Implicit personality theories
Projection
Stereotyping
Attribution
Dispositional attributions
Situational attributions
Consistency cues

Consensus cues
Distinctiveness cues
Fundamental attribution error
Actor-observer effect
Self-serving bias
Workforce diversity
Contrast effects
Leniency
Harshness
Central tendency
Halo effect
Similar-to-me effect

DISCUSSION QUESTIONS

1. Discuss how differences in the experiences of students and professors might affect their perceptions of students' written work and class comments.

2. Discuss the occupational stereotypes that you hold of computer programmers, the clergy, truck drivers, bartenders, and bankers. How do you think these stereotypes have developed? Has an occupational stereotype ever caused you to commit a socially embarrassing error when meeting someone for the first time?

3. Use Bruner's perceptual model (Exhibit 4.3) to explain why performance appraisals and interviewers' judgments are frequently inaccurate.

4. Discuss the assertion that "the perception of reality is more important than reality itself" in the context of organizations.

5. Suppose an employee does a particularly poor job on an assigned project. Discuss the attribution process that this person's manager will use to form judgments about this poor performance. Be sure to

discuss how the manager will use consistency, consensus, and distinctiveness cues.

6. A study of small business failures found that owners generally cited factors such as economic depression or strong competition as causes. However, creditors of these failed businesses were much more likely to cite ineffective management. What attribution bias is indicated by these findings? Why do you think the difference in attribution occurs?

7. Discuss the factors that make it difficult for employment interviewers to form accurate perceptions of interviewees.

8. Using the material in the chapter, explain why managers and subordinates often differ in their perceptions of subordinate performance.

9. List several advantages for an organization that hires and effectively manages a diverse workforce.

10. Explain why a gender or racial stereotype might be more likely to affect a hiring decision than a performance appraisal decision.

EXPERIENTIAL EXERCISE
WOMEN IN BUSINESS

The following items are an attempt to assess the attitudes people have about women in business. The statements cover many different and opposing points of view; you may find yourself agreeing strongly with some of the statements, disagreeing just as strongly with others, and perhaps uncertain about others.

Using the numbers from 1 to 7 on the rating scale, mark your personal opinion about each statement in the blank that immediately precedes it. Remember, give your personal opinion according to how much you agree or disagree with each item.

1 = Strongly Disagree	5 = Slightly Agree
2 = Disagree	6 = Agree
3 = Slightly Disagree	7 = Strongly Agree
4 = Neither Disagree nor Agree	

1. _____ It is less desirable for women than men to have a job that requires responsibility.

2. _____ Women have the objectivity required to evaluate business situations properly.

3. _____ Challenging work is more important to men than it is to women.

4. _____ Men and women should be given equal opportunity for participation in management training programs.

5. _____ Women have the capability to acquire the necessary skills to be successful managers.

6. _____ On the average, women managers are less capable of contributing to an organization's overall goals than are men.

7. _____ It is not acceptable for women to assume leadership roles as often as men.

8. _____ The business community should someday accept women in key managerial positions.

9. _____ Society should regard work by female managers as valuable as work by male managers.

10. _____ It is acceptable for women to compete with men for top executive positions.

11. _____ The possibility of pregnancy does not make women less desirable employees than men.

12. _____ Women would no more allow their emotions to influence their managerial behavior than would men.

13. _____ Problems associated with menstruation should not make women less desirable than men as employees.

14. _____ To be a successful executive, a woman does not have to sacrifice some of her femininity.

15. _____ On the average, a woman who stays at home all the time with her children is a better mother than a woman who works outside the home at least half time.

16. _____ Women are less capable of learning mathematical and mechanical skills than are men.

17. _____ Women are not ambitious enough to be successful in the business world.

18. _____ Women cannot be assertive in business situations that demand it.

19. _____ Women possess the self-confidence required of a good leader.

20. _____ Women are not competitive enough to be successful in the business world.

21. _____ Women cannot be aggressive in business situations that demand it.

SCORING AND INTERPRETATION

The scale you have just completed is the Women as Managers Scale (WAMS). It measures your attitudes toward women assuming managerial roles. To score your WAMS, subtract your responses to each of the following items from 8: 1, 3, 6, 7, 15, 16, 17, 18, 20, 21. For example, if you put 3 for item 1, give yourself a 5 (8 minus 3). Then, simply add up your resulting responses to all 21 items. Your score should fall somewhere between 21 and 147. The higher the score, the more favorable are your attitudes toward women as managers.

One study of 1,014 university business students and 602 managers reported the following WAMS averages: Male managers = 111; female managers = 128; male students = 103; female students = 130.[58] A more recent study showed that experienced human resources managers had a much more favorable attitude toward women as managers than university students did. The managers scored around 130, while the students scored around 79.[59] In a third study, conducted in an electronics manufacturing company, women managers scored an average of 128 while men scored 106. In this study, those who had more favorable attitudes toward women as managers also had more favorable attitudes toward blacks as managers.[60]

To facilitate discussion, the instructor might have students write their WAMS score and their sex on pieces of paper. Working in groups and using calculators, the class can compute the class average, the male average, and the female average. Also, a distribution of the scores might be posted on the board.

WAMS Source: Peters, L. H., Terborg, J. R., & Taynor, J. (1974). Women as managers scale (WAMS): A measure of attitudes toward women in management positions. *JSAS Catalog of Selected Documents in Psychology,* Ms. No. 585.

CASE STUDY
ACCOUNTING FOR FAILURE

It had been a long two years, but Nancy Koharski had at last gained some peace of mind. She was struck with the irony of how the same company that acted as a consultant to help other firms increase productivity and employee morale could be so blind to its own problems.

COMPANY BACKGROUND

Berry, Hepworth & Associates (BH&A) is a large regional accounting firm headquartered in Calgary. Over 125 professionals work at the Calgary office, and additional branch offices are located in Edmonton, Red Deer, and Regina. BH&A is the dominant audit firm in the region, and has earned a solid reputation in bank auditing and management information systems. The company was founded in the 1940s, and has experienced tremendous growth in recent years.

BH&A is divided into four departments: Commercial Audit, Healthcare, Financial Institutions Audit Group (FIAG), and the Management Information Systems Group. The latter is composed mainly of computer programmers, but incudes two psychologists who consult with clients on organizational behavior issues. Among the audit staff it is informally recognized that Commercial Audit is the best department in terms of clientele and working conditions, but opportunities are limited due to a large number of staff. The bank audits performed by FIAG are widely seen as boring and therefore undesirable, and the FIAG staff are quietly referred to as "nerds" and "brown-nosers." However, it is acknowledged that FIAG does offer a good career path, as banks constitute a significant portion of BH&A's business. In fact, because they are so terribly overworked, FIAG actively recruits (in effect, forces) BH&A people into the department.

All new staff persons are first assigned to Commercial Audit; the "choice" to specialize is made after a year or so of experience. There is no direct supervisor responsible for any particular person's training and development. Instead, the manager or "in-charge" on a particular assignment is responsible for helping the new "junior" on the job. While the in-charge is required to provide a verbal review after each assignment, focusing on areas for improvement, these are seldom provided. Every six months, a formal performance appraisal is held. In preparation, review forms are completed anonymously by everyone in the firm. Each junior can review in-charges and managers, who in turn evaluate the juniors.

Scheduling for jobs is, according to company policy, unbiased: juniors are to be assigned to upcoming jobs purely on a rotational basis. No in-charge can request that a particular junior be placed or withheld from a job.

THE WORKING ENVIRONMENT

BH&A is a very conservative firm. Most of the partners come from small towns or rural environments. Among the entire professional staff at Calgary, there is only one divorcee, fewer than 10 smokers, and one "possible" homosexual. The older members of the firm believe that while the firm has grown, it has not sacrificed the positive qualities it enjoyed as a smaller firm, including company loyalty and pride.

Chartered accounting at BH&A is structured to be competitive. More staff are hired each year than is necessary. It is commonly understood that one must outperform one's peers to survive. The six-month review is especially dreaded because BH&A tends to fire the two lowest ranked juniors—despite assurances that the firm will retain newcomers at least until they have met the two-year requirement for the Chartered Accountant license. Juniors are apprehensive about the anonymous comments because they figure prominently in the review process, and yet juniors are unable to defend themselves against unknown sources. Numerous juniors reported being afraid to open a small envelope that appeared unexpectedly during review time: the envelopes in fact contained the employee's income tax statement. Much gallows humor can be heard around review time, and juniors tend to develop a real sense of comradeship.

The high performance expectations of BH&A appear to have given rise to a "martyr complex," a curious blend of masochism and machoism. Ulcers and other stress-related illnesses are seen as evidence of hard work and status symbols. Numerous complaints are made about long working hours, but in reality these are boasts about how hard one is working. Overtime statistics are kept informally and compared among co-workers as if they were baseball statistics. FIAGs are particularly notorious for this sort of behavior. Calling in sick is not acceptable as it is seen as a sign of weakness and lack of dedication. One manager was in a car accident and taken to the hospital with a concussion. He returned to work that afternoon wearing the hospital bandage around his head.

It is understood that people must prove their loyalty by working very hard for years on end. The ultimate payoff is elevation to partnership. Currently, there are only 35 partners dividing the profits of one of the top accounting firms in the region. The monetary reward should be great indeed for those who survive.

GOLDEN BOYS AND AUDIT DRONES

The college recruiter who first interviewed Nancy Koharski spoke at length about the informal, family atmosphere at BH&A, and how Nancy would find greater personal attention and a more relaxed working environment than at a traditional accounting firm. BH&A, he had gone on to say, was proud of its success in attracting women to the firm. He noted that the first female professional had been hired in 1977, and related several humorous stories about the "early pioneers." One story concerned a female auditor who was not strong enough to carry the old-fashioned adding machines to clients. Rather than admit it, she kept "forgetting" to bring the machine. Nancy was impressed by the interview, and eventually accepted an offer from BH&A.

Nancy was determined to make partner, and to that end she threw herself into her new job with a vengeance. She took considerable pride in her hard work and initial accomplishments during her first few months. This pride, however, was tempered by a gnawing feeling that her efforts were not being noticed and that she was being passed over for more important assignments and being given more than her fair share of "grunt work." She noticed that, somehow, certain male juniors were always assigned to the prize jobs and clients, and worked repeatedly for the same managers. These "golden boys," as her colleagues sarcastically nicknamed them, also seemed to learn the office gossip and other information well before the women in the office. They seemed to enjoy excellent personal relationships with the managers, playing together on company sponsored sports teams and joking about incidents that happened while they roomed together while out of town.

In contrast, Nancy's female friends at the office referred to themselves and most other women at BH&A as "audit drones." Each staff member was required to complete time sheets which billed time to clients at quarter hour intervals. It was regarded as a major humiliation to write "unassigned," especially after having been at the firm for a while. It soon became apparent to Nancy that the audit drones were often left to fend for themselves over long periods, trying to scrounge up work. They were usually the last to be assigned to jobs, which tended to be the dreaded bank audits. When unassigned, they had little choice but to go door-to-door asking for any kind of menial work, while the golden boys worked over time on plum assignments. One of Nancy's female friends put the situation this way: "I'm not given the chance to develop. But what can I do? If I complain, I could be replaced by somebody fresh out of school who could do what I'm doing inside a week. And for less money." Another friend remarked that "The most a woman can hope for here is to avoid being fired."

Nancy also began to hear stories that were considerably more disturbing than the ones the interviewer had first told her. One story described the difficult transition period at BH&A when women first joined the company at the professional level. Apparently, some men openly blamed the women for upsetting what had been a comfortable work environment. A second story concerned the lone woman assigned to the Red Deer office. She was told by co-workers that the manager "hated to waste time developing women

who would eventually end up leaving the firm." She was assigned to Commercial Audit, but it became so obvious that she was not being scheduled for commercial jobs that her male co-workers commented on it to her. She spoke with the managing partner of the office and, after apparently receiving no help, felt compelled to join the FIAGs as the only way to work in the office. Another story concerned a pregnant manager who was said to have been relieved of her clients as soon as she began to "show," and was not allowed to work on engagements outside the office. Following her pregnancy, she was apparently told, she had lost her "special relationship" with clients. Further, her requests for occasional time off for child-care were denied.

Most disturbing of all were the statements of a number of male colleagues. Female staff members were told repeatedly and directly that "Women don't belong in public accounting" as it was "no place for a woman." Since the women would "obviously" marry and want children, it was inevitable that they would eventually leave the firm. These men pointed to the high turnover rate for female staff members as proof of the validity of their beliefs. They explained that because the work was so demanding and time-consuming, it would be "impossible" for women to combine a family life with an accounting career.

Nancy was startled to learn that these attitudes were espoused, not only by older men at the firm, but by a number of younger men as well. The more sympathetic men admitted that it was "unfair that they didn't have to make the same choice . . . " but they had wives at home or in less demanding jobs who could manage the family in their absence.

This belief in the unsuitability of women was never openly questioned by male staff members. If a woman countered with something like: "The job is only impossible for working mothers if the company chooses to make it impossible," she was apt to be met with blank stares. Working mothers were told that BH&A could not offer them special treatment, shorter hours, or less travel time because the men who had accepted these hardships would rebel. The more arguments and stories that Nancy heard with a similar ring, the more she began to resent the company and the golden boys.

THE DRAGON LADY

Several of the older women at BH&A struck Nancy as being rather cold and demanding. Indeed, the most loathed of these women was nicknamed "dragon lady." While they were always very professional in their dress and manner, they did not go out of their way to offer support or encouragement to the younger female staff members. Three of these women tended to fawn over two influential male partners. It was rumored that one of these women had supported the policy of selected firings as a "way to shake them up and make them work harder."

THE CONFRONTATION

Two women who had been at the firm for several years complained to the partners about the apparent bias in the scheduling of work assignments. They were told that they were "imagining things" because company policy was designed to prohibit such abuses. When pressed to explain why women were always the "extra junior" on bank jobs, the partners responded that this was because there were higher level women in FIAG with whom they could room while out of town, but none at Commercial Audit. The cost of an extra hotel room for a lone woman was not feasible, given the tight budgets. The women were also told that, while the men at the firm were liberal and had no problems working with women, many of the older clients could not accept dealing with a female authority figure. To avoid this problem, women were not assigned where it was felt they would not be accepted. Finally, it was explained that if any one woman had been neglected, it was a "regrettable oversight" in trying to assign so many employees. The meeting concluded with a promise to review the situation. Nothing more was heard.

THE DECISION

One by one, Nancy's more senior female friends quit the firm after they had "served time," that is, fulfilled the two-year licensing requirement. If they were mentioned in the company at all after they had left, it was along the lines of: "They obviously weren't Berry, Hepworth material," or "They couldn't hack life in Calgary."

After two years and six days with BH&A, Nancy, too, announced she was leaving. One colleague, the "dragon lady," urged her to voice her complaints about the treatment of women at the firm to the personnel partner during the exit interview. Nancy decided to do so, and received what she concluded was a fitting send-off: throughout the entire interview, the partner sat clipping his nails and declined to respond to a single issue she raised.

Source: Case prepared by Kathleen Solonika and Blake Ashforth. From Kelly, J., Prince, J. B., & Ashforth, B. (1991). *Organizational Behavior: Readings, Cases, and Exercises* (2nd ed.), Scarborough: Prentice-Hall Canada.

1. Discuss several examples of conflicting or contradictory perceptions at BH&A.
2. The chapter discusses how selection interviewers can make perceptual errors. What does the case say about perceptual errors on the part of job *applicants*?
3. Use the concepts of stereotyping and halo to explain the contrast between the golden boys and the audit drones.
4. Are there any aspects to the organization of work at BH&A that could lead to perceptual problems in performance appraisal?
5. Compare and contrast this case with the Ann Hopkins case that opened the chapter.
6. Suppose that you were appointed to a newly created position at BH&A, Manager of Diversity Assurance. What would you do to better manage diversity at the firm?

Learning Objectives

After reading Chapter 5 you should be able to:

1 Define values and discuss the implications of cross-cultural variation in values for organizational behavior.

2 Define attitudes and explain how people develop and change attitudes.

3 Explain the concept of job satisfaction and discuss some of its key contributors.

4 Discuss the roles of discrepancy, fairness, and disposition in promoting job satisfaction.

5 Outline the various consequences of job satisfaction and explain the relationship between job satisfaction and mental health, absenteeism, turnover, performance, and organizational citizenship behavior.

In its Russian joint venture, Ben & Jerry's has to appreciate cross-cultural differences in values.

CHAPTER 5

VALUES, ATTITUDES, AND JOB SATISFACTION

BEN &
JERRY'S
HOMEMADE
INC.

Armed with a $5 correspondence course in ice cream making obtained from Penn State, Ben Cohen and Jerry Greenfield opened their ice cream shop in a former gas station in Burlington, Vermont, in 1978. By 1981, a Time *cover story decreed Ben & Jerry's the best ice cream in the world. Ben & Jerry's Homemade Inc. is now headquartered in Waterbury, Vermont, and employs around 400 people. It is one of the state's most popular tourist attractions.*

If the quality of Ben & Jerry's gourmet-style ice cream is remarkable, the firm that produces it is equally so. For one thing, the company has a number of unusual personnel practices. Among these is a committee (a word too formal for this company) —the Joy Gang—that sponsors such events as National Clash-Dressing Day and Barry Manilow Appreciation Day to keep the troops amused. Such fun is taken seriously at

Ben & Jerry's, and the two founders are often part of the action. Dress is strictly casual at the company. The domestic partners of all employees (married, unmarried, gay, straight) receive company benefits such as health insurance. The company has a profit sharing plan indexed to how long one has been employed there.

The Waterbury firm takes communication seriously. The firm uses upward appraisals, with subordinates evaluating the boss's performance. In addition, the company conducts job satisfaction surveys and publishes the results in its annual report.

Under the guidance of its founders, Ben & Jerry's pursues a strong policy of social responsibility to the community and the environment. Thus, the firm donates 7.5 percent of pretax profits to worthy causes (that the employees help designate) through the Ben & Jerry's foundation. Employees can volunteer to do community work while receiving their normal salary. The company has used proceeds from its Rainforest Crunch to support a Brazilian nut producers' cooperative, purchased berries from Native American producers, and purchased brownies (for Chocolate Fudge Brownie) from a bakery staffed by the homeless.

Cohen and Greenfield received the Small Business Persons of the Year award from the Small Business Administration. Also, the company has received *Personnel Journal*'s Optimus Award for Quality of Life. Employee turnover is very low for a manufacturing operation. However, its unusual personnel policies have occasionally caused difficulties. For years, Ben & Jerry's had a firm policy that there could be no more than a 7:1 ratio between the highest paid and the lowest paid employee. This is a remarkably small difference by the standards of corporate America, and it caused considerable difficulty in recruiting talent for top positions because the pay offered was thousands of dollars below market value. When Ben Cohen announced that he was stepping down from his CEO position, the company decided to abandon the salary cap to enable it to attract the very best top executive talent.

If you happen to be in Petrozavodsk, Russia, up near the Arctic Circle, be sure to stop in for a cool Ben & Jerry's. This joint venture with local Russians is in perfect keeping with the firm's peace-oriented capitalism.[1]

Would you be happy working at Ben & Jerry's? Under the former 7:1 salary ratio, would you have sacrificed thousands of dollars to work at a company with a social conscience? This would probably be influenced by your values and attitudes, important topics that we will cover in this chapter. Our discussion of values will be particularly oriented towards cross-cultural variations in values and their implications for organizational behavior. Our discussion of attitudes will cover attitude formation and change. A critical attitude is job satisfaction. We'll consider its causes and consequences.

WHAT ARE VALUES?

Values. A broad tendency to prefer certain states of affairs over others.

We might define **values** as "a broad tendency to prefer certain states of affairs over others."[2] The *preference* aspect of this definition means that values have to do with feelings and emotions, with what we consider good and bad. The feelings or emotions inherent in values are motivational, since they signal the attractive aspects of our environment that we should seek and the unattractive aspects that we should avoid or change. The words *broad tendency* in this definition mean that values are very general emotional orientations, and that they don't predict behavior in specific situations very well. Knowing that a person generally embraces the values that support capitalism doesn't tell us much about how he or she will respond to a homeless person on the street this afternoon.

It is useful to classify values into several categories: intellectual, economic, aesthetic, social, political, and religious.[3] Not everyone holds the same values. Managers might value high productivity (an economic value), while union officials might be more concerned with enlightened supervision and full employment (social values). Ben and Jerry hold stronger social values and weaker economic values than the typical entrepreneur. Professors probably value clear, accurate writing (an intellectual value) more than illiterates do. We learn values through the reinforcement processes we discussed in Chapter 3. Most are socially reinforced by parents, teachers, and representatives of religions. In fact, our entire social system is designed to teach and reinforce the values deemed appropriate by our society.

To firm up your understanding of values and their impact on organizational behavior, let's examine some occupational differences in values and see how work values differ across cultures.

Occupational Differences in Values

Members of different occupational groups espouse different values. A research program showed that university professors, city police officers, oil company salespeople, and entrepreneurs had values that distinguished them as groups from the general population.[4] For example, the professors valued "equal opportunity for all" more highly than the average American. On the other hand, the salespeople and entrepreneurs ranked social values (peace, equality, freedom) lower than the average American. Value differences such as these might be partially responsible for the occupational stereotypes that we discussed in Chapter 4. Further, these differences can cause conflict between organizations and within organizations when members of different occupations are required to interact with each other. For instance, the evidence cited above indicates that police officers and professors differ rather radically in the value they place on equal opportunity. This suggests that the average professor who is asked to serve as a consultant in developing a community relations program for a police force might encounter a severe case of value conflict. The same kind of problem can exist within an organization. Doctors frequently report that their social values are at odds with the economic values of hospital administrators. In general, a good "fit" between the values of supervisors and subordinates promotes subordinate satisfaction and commitment.[5]

Do differences in occupational values develop after a person enters an occupation, or do such differences cause people to gravitate to certain occupations? Given the fact that values are relatively stable and that many values are acquired early in life, it would appear that people choose occupations that correspond to their values.[6]

Values Across Cultures

It is by now a cliché to observe that business has become global in its scope—Ben & Jerry's goes to Russia; Japanese cars dot American roads; Mickey Mouse invades Japan and France; McDonald's opens in Moscow; Europe reduces internal trade barriers. All of this activity obscures just how difficult it can be to forge business links across cultures. For example, research shows that anywhere from 16 to 40 percent of managers who receive foreign assignments terminate them early because they perform poorly or don't adjust to the culture.[7] Similarly, a lengthy history of failed business negotiations is attributable to a lack of understanding of cross-cultural differences. At the root of many of these problems might be a lack of appreciation of basic differences in work-related values across cultures. On the other hand, consider the opportunities for organizations that are globally adept (and for graduating students who are cross-culturally sensitive!).

Work Centrality.   Work itself is valued differently across cultures. One large-scale survey of over 8,000 individuals in several nations found marked cross-national differences in the extent to which people perceived work as a central life interest.[8] As shown in Exhibit 5.1, Japan topped the list, with very high work centrality. Belgians and Americans exhibited average work centrality; the British scored low.

One question in the survey asked respondents whether they would continue working if they won a large amount of money in a lottery. As you might imagine, those with more central interest in work were more likely to report that they would continue working despite new-found wealth.

The survey also found that people for whom work was a central life interest tended to work longer hours. This illustrates how cross-cultural differences in work centrality can lead to adjustment problems for foreign employees and managers. Imagine the unprepared British executive who is posted to Japan only to find that Japanese managers commonly work late and

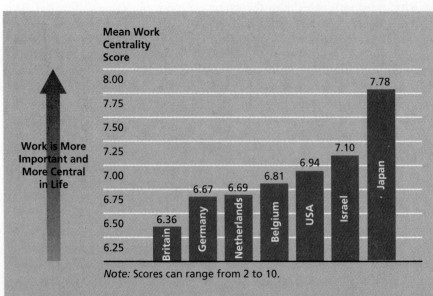

Note: Scores can range from 2 to 10.

EXHIBIT 5.1
Work centrality across cultures.

Source: MOW International Research Team (1987). *The Meaning of Work*. London: Academic Press, p. 83. Reprinted by permission of the publisher and Dr. P. J. D. Drenth.

In Japan, socializing with colleagues is often part of the job, reflecting the high centrality of work in Japanese values.

then socialize with co-workers or customers long into the night. In Japan, this is all part of the job, often to the chagrin of the lonely spouse. On the other hand, consider the Japanese executive posted to Britain who finds out that an evening at the pub is *not* viewed as an extension of the day at the office and not a place to continue talking business.

Hofstede's Study.   In one of the most ambitious survey programs ever, Dutch social scientist Geert Hofstede questioned over 116,000 IBM employees located in 40 countries about their work-related values.[9] (There were 20 different language versions of the questionnaire.) Virtually everyone in the corporation participated, from blue-collar workers to top executives. When Hofstede analyzed the results, he discovered four basic dimensions along which work-related values differed across cultures: power distance, uncertainty avoidance, masculinity/femininity, and individualism/collectivism. Subsequent work with Canadian Michael Bond that catered more to Eastern cultures resulted in a fifth dimension, the long-term/short-term orientation.[10]

- *Power distance.* **Power distance** refers to the extent to which society members accept an unequal distribution of power, including those who hold more power and those who hold less. In small power distance cultures, inequality is minimized, superiors are accessible, and power differences are downplayed. In large power distance societies, inequality is accepted as natural, superiors are inaccessible, and power differences are highlighted. Small power distance societies include Denmark, New Zealand, Israel, and Austria. Large power distance societies include the Philippines, Venezuela, and Mexico. Out of 40 societies, Canada and the United States rank 14 and 15, falling on the low power distance side of the average, which would be 20.

Power distance. The extent to which an unequal distribution of power is accepted by society members.

Uncertainty avoidance. The extent to which people are uncomfortable with uncertain and ambiguous situations.

- *Uncertainty avoidance.* **Uncertainty avoidance** refers to the extent to which people are uncomfortable with uncertain and ambiguous situations. Strong uncertainty avoidance cultures stress rules and regulations, hard work, conformity, and security. Cultures with weak uncertainty avoidance are less concerned with rules, conformity, and security, and hard work is not seen as a virtue. However, risk taking is valued. Strong uncertainty avoidance cultures include Japan, Greece, and Portugal. Weak uncertainty avoidance cultures include Singapore, Denmark, and Sweden. On uncertainty avoidance, the United States and Canada are well below average, ranking 9 and 10 out of 40.

- *Masculinity/feminity.* More masculine cultures clearly differentiate gender roles, support the dominance of men, and stress economic performance. More feminine cultures accept fluid gender roles, stress sexual equality, and stress quality of life. In Hofstede's research, Japan is the most masculine society, followed by Austria, Mexico, and Venezuela. The Scandinavian countries are the most feminine. Canada ranks about mid-pack, and the United States is fairly masculine, falling about halfway between Canada and Japan.

Individualistic vs. collective. Individualistic societies stress independence, individual initiative, and privacy. Collective cultures favor interdependence and loyalty to family or clan.

- *Individualism/collectivism.* More **individualistic** societies tend to stress independence, individual initiative, and privacy. More **collective** cultures favor interdependence and loyalty to one's family or clan. The United States, Australia, Great Britain, and Canada are among the most individualistic societies. Venezuela, Columbia, and Pakistan are among the most collective, with Japan falling about mid-pack.

- *Long-term/short-term orientation.* Cultures with a long-term orientation tend to stress persistence, perseverance, thrift, and close attention to status differences. Cultures with a short-term orientation stress personal steadiness and stability, face-saving, and social niceties. China, Hong Kong, Taiwan, Japan, and South Korea tend to be characterized by a

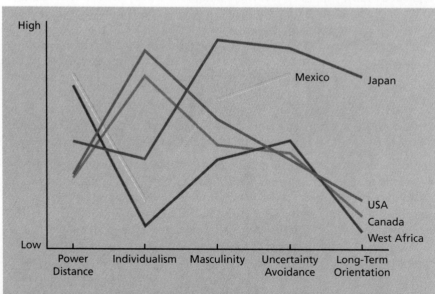

EXHIBIT 5.2
Cross-cultural value comparisons.

Source: Graph by author. Data from Hofsted, G. (1991). *Cultures and organizations: Software of the mind.* London: McGraw-Hill. (Time orientation data for Mexico unavailable.)

long-term orientation. The United States, Canada, Great Britain, Zimbabwe, and Nigeria are more short-term oriented. Hofstede and Bond argue that the long-term orientation in part explains prolific East Asian entrepreneurship.

Exhibit 5.2 compares the United States, Canada, Mexico, Japan, and West Africa on Hofstede's value dimensions. Note that the profiles for Canada and the United States are very similar, but they differ considerably from Mexico. You might want to consider the implications of this for enhanced free trade among the three countries.

Hofstede has produced a number of interesting "cultural maps" that show how countries and regions cluster together on pairs of cultural dimensions. The map in Exhibit 5.3 shows the relationship between power distance and degree of individualism. As you can see, these two values tend to be related. Cultures that are more individualistic tend to downplay power differences, while those that are more collectivistic tend to accentuate power differences.

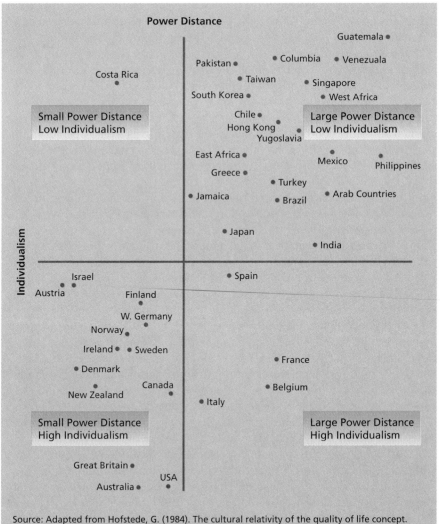

Source: Adapted from Hofstede, G. (1984). The cultural relativity of the quality of life concept. *Academy of Management Review*, 9, 389–398, p. 391. Reprinted by permission of the Academy of Management and the author.

EXHIBIT 5.3
Power distance and individualism values for various countries and regions.

Implications of Cultural Variation

Exporting OB Theories.   An important message from the cross-cultural study of values is that organizational behavior theories, research, and practices from North America might not translate well to other societies, even the one located just south of Texas.[11] The basic questions (How should I lead? How should we make this decision?) remain the same. It is just the *answers* that differ. For example, North American managers tend to encourage a moderate degree of participation in work decisions by subordinates. This corresponds to the fairly low degree of power distance valued here. Trying to translate this leadership style to cultures that value high power distance might prove unwise. In these cultures, people might be more comfortable deferring to the boss's decision. Thus, it is unlikely that Ben and Jerry could translate their low power distance style to all overseas locations. Similarly, in individualistic North America, calling attention to one's accomplishments is expected and often rewarded in organizations. In more collective Asian or South American cultures, individual success might be devalued and it might make sense to reward groups rather than individuals. Finally, in extremely masculine cultures, integrating women into management positions might require special sensitivity and timing.

Successful firms have learned to blend the values of their headquarters' corporate culture with those of the host nation in overseas operations. In other words, they export an overall philosophy while tailoring it to local customs and values. For example, U.S.-based National Semiconductor tends to stress very systematic technical decision making. The Israeli culture tends to be very informal and more collective than that in the States. In its Israeli operations, the firm has developed a decision-making process that is systematic but team-oriented and participative, meeting corporate needs but respecting local values.[12]

Importing OB Theories.   Not all theories and practices that concern organizational behavior are perfected in North America or even in the West. The most obvious examples are the "Japanese management" techniques such as quality circles, total quality management, and just-in-time production. Although there are success stories of importing these techniques from Japan to North America, there are also numerous examples of difficulties and failure, especially in manufacturing firms. Many of the problems seem to stem from basic value differences between Japan and North America.

Although they are generally successful operations, the pace of work required has led to employee complaints in the U.S. plants of Mazda, Nissan, and Honda. Similarly, the quest for continuous improvement and the heavy reliance on employee suggestions for improvement has had a mixed reaction.[13] Leading U.S. companies receive about two suggestions a year from each employee, while the Japanese operations of these auto makers receive between 39 (Nissan) and 127 (Mazda) per employee per year![14] In Japan, cultural values have traditionally dictated a fairly high degree of employment security. Thus, working at a fast pace and providing suggestions for improvement won't put one out of a job. American workers are uncertain about this.

Many of the Japanese-inspired means of organizing work are team-oriented. Since Japan has fairly collective cultural values, submerging one's own interests to those of the team is natural. Although employers have successfully used teams in North America, as you will see in Chapter 8, our more individualistic culture would suggest that more careful selection of team members is necessary.

Understanding cultural value differences can enable organizations to successfully import management practices by tailoring the practice to the home culture's concerns. For example, the innovative General Motors Saturn plant in Spring Hill, Tennessee, (discussed in detail in Chapter 16) effectively guarantees lifetime employment to 80 percent of the workforce to ensure that its Japanese-inspired practices are palatable to American employees.

Appreciating Global Customers.   An appreciation of cross-cultural differences in values is essential to understanding the needs and tastes of customers or clients around the world. Once relegated to the status of a marketing problem, it is now clear that such understanding fundamentally has to do with organizational behavior. Errors occur with regularity. For instance, the initial French response to the Euro Disney theme park was less enthusiastic than Disney management expected, probably due in part to a failure to truly appreciate French tastes in food, lifestyle, and organized entertainment. Samsung, South Korea's largest company, recalled a calendar featuring models displaying its products that was destined for overseas customers. Some Americans were offended at Miss July's see-through blouse.

Appreciating the values of global customers is also important when the customers enter your own culture. Many firms have profited from an understanding of the increasing ethnic diversity in the United States and Canada. In this regard, pause for a moment and consider the *You Be the Manager* feature.

Developing Global Employees.   Success in translating management practices to other cultures, importing practices developed elsewhere, and appreciating global customers aren't things that happen by accident. Rather, companies need to select, train, and develop employees to have a much better appreciation of differences in cultural values and the implications of these differences for behavior in organizations.

Gillette is recognized as having one of the best of such programs. The firm produces razor blades, pens (PaperMate), and electrical appliances (Braun) in 28 countries and markets them in more than 200. Over 25 years, it has built a global management team by using a variety of tactics. These include the following:

- Hiring local people as managers outside the United States;

- Finding key talent among overseas students studying in North American universities;

- Moving managers to posts in other countries to sharpen their international exposure;

- Rewarding managers with extensive international experience by putting them in charge of new international markets or joint ventures (such as one in China);

- Bringing groups of young international management trainees to one of three international headquarters (Boston, Singapore, or London) for 18 months of intensive development.[15]

WEST COAST BUILDERS AND REALTORS CATER TO ASIAN CULTURAL VALUES

M**YOU BE THE** anager

A mong the 19 Asian countries on the Pacific Rim, North America has been particularly enriched in recent years by newcomers from Hong Kong, Taiwan, Korea, the Philippines, Vietnam, and Japan. According to the Census Bureau, Asians comprise the fastest growing, best educated, and most affluent cultural group in the United States. Given its proximity and climate, the west coast of the United States and Canada has become an attractive location for immigrants from Asia. This influx has been especially advantageous to California's home builders and realtors, including Kathryn Thompson Development Company, Kaufman and Broad Home Corporation, and The William Lyon Company. In an era of recessionary sales, Asians and Asian Americans comprise 30 to 40 percent of California's home buyers.

In a fiercely competitive market, home builders and realtors gradually realized that they were uncertain about Asian cultural values. For

> WITH THE LARGE NUMBER OF ASIAN IMMIGRANTS RELOCATING TO NORTH AMERICA, COMPANIES HAVE HAD TO ADAPT CULTURAL STRATEGIES TO WIN IN THE FIERCELY COMPETITIVE MARKET.

example, they were not used to the involvement of older family members (such as grandparents) in the buying process and the predilection of some Asian cultures to avoid certain unlucky colors and numbers (e.g., street addresses). Furthermore, they didn't understand the Chinese concept of *feng shui* which dictates that a house design should follow certain principles to maintain harmony and good luck. Put yourself in the shoes of these builders and realtors. You realize that your construction firm can gain a competitive advantage by catering better to Asian clients. What would you do?

1. Design a plan to better inform your employees about Asian cultural values. Who should be involved?
2. What general lessons about the globalization of business are apparent from this case?

To find out what the California real estate firms did, see *The Manager's Notebook* at the end of the chapter.

Source: Adapted from Forsberg, M. (1993, May). Cultural training improves relations with Asian clients. *Personnel Journal*, 79–89.

Other firms use different techniques for developing an international perspective. To better get their designers to appreciate the values of the North American market, Japanese car makers, including Nissan and Toyota, have opened design studios in California. The top ranks of Detroit's Big Three automakers, once the bastion of mid-westerners, are now liberally filled with Europeans or those with European experience. This has led to improved overall performance and the development of cars that are more suitable for worldwide export. Korea's Samsung now sends about 400 of its most promising young employees overseas for a year to simply immerse themselves in the values of another culture (as one executive put it, "to goof off at the mall"). The company feels that this will pay long-term dividends in terms of international competition.[16] However, not all firms do so well in their international human resources practices. For details see "Global Focus: *Human Resources Practices Need Cultural Awakening.*"

GLOBAL FOCUS   Human Resources Practices Need Cultural Awakening

Nancy Adler and Susan Bartholomew surveyed 50 U.S. and Canadian firms that do extensive global business. The firms' human resources practices were less than global in thrust.

In selecting future senior managers, the 50 firms ranked an outstanding overall track record as the most important criterion, with foreign business experience, demonstrated cultural sensitivity and adaptability, and a track record for outstanding performance outside the home country ranked as somewhat, but not highly, important. Moreover, foreign language skills were not considered at all important. Similarly, while considering three out of four transnational scope and process skills to be somewhat important for promotion to senior management (understanding world issues and trends; working effectively with clients and colleagues from other countries; and, demonstrating cultural sensitivity), none was considered highly important. Once again, foreign language skills were not considered important for promotion.

Fewer than one in four of the firms reported that the content of their training programs was global in focus, that they had representatives of many nations attending each program, or that their programs were designed or delivered by multinational training teams. Only four percent reported that cross-cultural training was offered to all managers.

In reviewing foreign assignments, the 50 firms report using expatriates primarily to "get the job done abroad," not to develop the organization, nor to develop the individual manager's career. Given their emphasis on getting the immediate job done, it is not surprising that they did not report

consistently selecting the "stars" (either high potential junior managers or very senior, top-performing executives) for expatriate positions. To increase globalization in their development programs, the surveyed executives strongly recommended "transferring different nationalities to different countries several times in their career" and "making it clear to these employees that international assignments are important to career

Many organizations are involved in the modification and management of attitudes. Dow Chemical, for example, offers diversity and family issues training programs to reinforce positive attitudes.

development." However, to date, the majority of the surveyed firms do not have such recommended programs in place.

Source: Excerpted from Adler, N. J., & Bartholomew, S. (1992, August). Managing globally competent people. *Academy of Management Executive*, 52–65.

As you proceed through the text, you will encounter further discussion about the impact of cultural values on organizational behavior. Now, let's examine attitudes and see how they are related to values.

WHAT ARE ATTITUDES?

An **attitude** is a fairly stable emotional tendency to respond consistently to some specific object, situation, person, or category of people. First, notice that attitudes involve *emotions* directed toward *specific* targets. If I inquire about your attitude toward your boss, you will probably tell me something about how well you *like* him or her. This illustrates the emotional aspect of attitudes. Attitudes are also much more specific than values, which dictate only broad

Attitude. A fairly stable emotional tendency to respond consistently to some specific object, situation, person, or category of people.

preferences. For example, you could value working quite highly but still dislike your specific job.

The definition states that attitudes are *relatively stable*. Under normal circumstances, if you truly dislike Mexican food or your boss today, you will probably dislike them tomorrow. Of course, some attitudes are less strongly held than others and are thus more open to change. If your negative attitude toward Mexican cuisine stems only from a couple of fast food experiences, I might be able to improve it greatly by exposing you to a home-cooked Mexican meal. This provides you with some new information.

Our definition indicates that attitudes are *tendencies to respond* to the target of the attitude. Thus, attitudes often influence our behavior toward some object, situation, person, or group:

$$ATTITUDE \rightarrow BEHAVIOR$$

This is hardly surprising. If you truly dislike Mexican food, I would not expect to see you eating it. By the same token, if you like your boss, it would not be surprising to hear you speaking well of him:

$$DISLIKE\ MEXICAN\ FOOD \rightarrow DON'T\ EAT\ MEXICAN\ FOOD$$

$$LIKE\ BOSS \rightarrow PRAISE\ BOSS$$

Of course, not everyone who likes the boss goes around praising him in public for fear of being too political. Similarly, people who dislike the boss don't always engage in public criticism for fear of retaliation. These examples indicate that attitudes are not always consistent with behavior, and that attitudes provide useful information over and above the actions that we can observe.

ATTITUDE FORMATION

Where do attitudes come from? Put simply, attitudes are a function of what we think and what we feel. That is, attitudes are the product of a related belief and value. If you believe that your boss is consultative, and you value consultation, we can conclude that you might have a favorable attitude toward the boss. We can represent this relationship in the form of a simple syllogism.[17] For example:

If the boss is consultative, (Belief)

And consultation is good, (Value)

Then the boss is good. (Attitude)

Given this point of view, we can now expand the attitude model presented earlier to include the thinking and feeling aspects of attitudes represented by beliefs and values:

$$\begin{matrix} BELIEF \\ + \\ VALUE \end{matrix} \Rightarrow ATTITUDE \rightarrow BEHAVIOR$$

Thus, we can imagine the following sequence of ideas in the case of a person experiencing work-family conflict:

"My job is interfering with my family life." (Belief)

"I dislike anything that hurts my family." (Value)

"I dislike my job." (Attitude)

"I'll search for another job." (Behavior)

In attempting to understand attitudes, it is important to distinguish between their belief components and their value components. For example, consider the manager of a manufacturing plant that is plagued by low-quality production. Working backward through our attitude model, the manager might assume that low quality is caused by "poor attitudes" toward quality on the part of the workforce. Are such "poor attitudes" likely to stem from the employees' values or their beliefs about quality? Either might be true. First, the work force might *value* high quality but *believe* that it is impossible to achieve. Beliefs of this nature might include: "My performance depends on the performance of my work group. My equipment is unreliable." On the other hand, the work force might *believe* that it can turn out high quality work but not *value* high quality: "I value a lack of fatigue more than I value making a buck for the company. I value social interaction on the job more than I value attention to quality."

The kind of administrative action that might be necessary to change the workforce's attitudes toward quality depends upon the accurate assessment of these beliefs and values. For example, if the beliefs listed above appear to limit quality, management will have to carefully explore the basis for these beliefs (Is equipment really unreliable?). On the other hand, if values appear to be the problem, a different intervention might be called for, such as attempting to hire workers whose value systems correspond more closely to the desired corporate culture.

CHANGING ATTITUDES

In our everyday lives, we frequently try to change other people's attitudes. By presenting ourselves in a favorable light (putting our best foot forward), we attempt to get others to develop favorable attitudes toward us. By arguing the case for some attitude we hold, we attempt to get others to embrace this attitude. Thus, it should not surprise us that organizations are also involved in the modification and management of attitudes. Some examples of cases in which management might desire attitude change include the following:

- Attitudes toward workforce diversity;
- Attitudes toward ethical business practices;
- Attitudes toward anticipated changes, such as the introduction of new technology or total quality management;
- Attitudes toward safety practices and the use of safety equipment.

Most attempts at attitude change are initiated by a communicator who tries to use persuasion of some form to modify the beliefs or values of an audience that supports a currently held attitude. For example, management might hold a seminar to persuade managers to value workforce diversity, or it might develop a training program to change attitudes toward workplace safety. Persuasion that is designed to modify or emphasize values is usually emotionally oriented. A safety message that concentrates upon a dead worker's weeping, destitute family exemplifies this approach. Persuasion that is slanted toward modifying certain beliefs is usually rationally oriented. A safety message that tries to convince workers that hard-hats and safety glasses are not uncomfortable to wear reveals this angle. You have probably seen both of these approaches used in AIDS and antismoking campaigns.

What factors influence the extent to which persuasion will actually change attitudes? Some answers to these questions have been provided by a large number of experiments begun at Yale University.[18]

The Effective Communicator

Who would be most able to change the beliefs or values that support a currently held attitude? Research indicates that communicators who are perceived as *believable* are most effective at inducing attitude change. In general, we tend to perceive others as believable when they are seen as expert, unbiased, and likable.

Expertise.   To induce attitude change, experts must be perceived as having special skills and knowledge relevant to the *subject at hand*. Thus, an extremely successful salesperson might be an especially credible trainer in a program designed to change attitudes toward ethical sales practices. In fact, many organizations have begun to use such individuals to do such training exactly because outside experts often lack credibility as trainers. On the other hand, such a manager would probably not be perceived as an expert on work-force diversity and would be unlikely to induce much attitude change concerning this subject.

Lack of Bias.   Besides having expertise, the communicator who wishes to change attitudes must also be seen as unbiased. A safety campaign initiated by a union safety officer is probably more convincing than one initiated by the company's accident insurance carriers. The former will probably be seen as caring for the health and welfare of the workforce, while the latter might be seen as attempting to reduce claims costs. This might occur in spite of the fact that both parties are perceived as equally expert in matters of safety. By the same token, union support for a total quality program will probably induce more favorable attitudes than will exhortations from the company president, who might be perceived as seeing increased productivity as the main goal of the change.

Likability.   Finally, likeable communicators will usually be able to induce more attitude change than disliked individuals. It is easy to imagine the thoughts of an audience when a persuader they dislike confronts them "If a character like this supports total quality, there must be something wrong with the idea." Not surprisingly, clever managers often attempt to effect attitude changes among subordinates by converting a well-liked subordinate to their cause.

Proven Persuasion Techniques

Research has provided some sound advice about using persuasion to change attitudes.

Use Face-to-Face.   Face-to-face persuasion is more likely to change attitudes than indirect communication, i.e., memo, newsletter, or posters. This probably occurs because face-to-face persuasion is flexible, demands attention, and gives the audience the opportunity to be more certain about the credibility of the source. Written communications such as posters and newsletters cannot offer active counterarguments or demand attention, and they might be of ambiguous origin (who knows whether the union or the insurance company supplied that safety poster?).

Seek Moderate Change.   How much attitude change should the communicator try to induce? It is usually best to stick with arguments that are moderately discrepant with the audience's viewpoint. Positions that are especially "soft" or "hard" are less likely to induce change. For example, consider a seminar leader who is attempting to change the attitudes of salespeople in the direction of more ethical sales practices. Simply telling people to act more ethically probably won't have much impact on their behavior. On the other hand, basic moral values are a product of many years of personal experience and are highly resistant to change. The seminar leader will probably do well to seek moderate attitude change, perhaps illustrating how ethical practices can result in repeat sales and referrals to other customers.

Offer Both Sides or One?   Finally, should the communicator attempt to present the audience with both sides of the attitude change argument or just stick to the side in favor of change? Presenting only the case for change is effective if the audience is basically receptive and unlikely to generate counterarguments or hear them from others. However, when the audience is not especially receptive and knows (or will be exposed to) counterarguments against change, the communicator should present both points of view. For example, the seminar leader should raise and discuss arguments that safety equipment is cumbersome or uncomfortable. Similarly, the seminar leader might acknowledge that reasonable people can differ in their opinions about what constitutes ethical sales behavior.

Cognitive Dissonance Theory

When communicators are successful in changing attitudes, exactly why are they successful? The theory of cognitive dissonance provides an explanation for many instances of attitude changes.[19] Cognitions are simply thoughts or knowledge that people have about their own beliefs, values, attitudes, and behavior. **Cognitive dissonance** refers to a feeling of tension experienced when certain cognitions are contradictory or inconsistent with each other (i.e., dissonant). For example, knowing that you have spent a great deal of money on a car that has turned out to be a "lemon" involves inconsistent cognitions that should arouse dissonance.

> **Cognitive dissonance.** A feeling of tension experienced when certain cognitions are contradictory or inconsistent with each other.

There are several ways that people might reduce dissonance. One of them is to downplay the importance of the inconsistency ("I have more important things to worry about than my car"). Another is to marshal additional cognitions that can reduce the dissonance ("At least the car looks classy and prestigious—it impresses my friends"). For our purposes, however, the most interesting way to reduce dissonance is to *change* one of the dissonant cognitions to bring it in line with the other and reduce the tension-producing inconsistency ("My car really isn't so bad"). Notice that this example illustrates a *change in attitude* toward the car that now corresponds to the belief that one paid a lot for it. Communicators attempt to change attitudes by stressing beliefs and values that are inconsistent with attitudes that people currently hold with the hope that this will arouse dissonance. This dissonance will in turn be reduced by changing one's attitudes to correspond to the new cognitions.

Changing Behavior to Change Attitudes

In our discussion of using persuasion to change attitudes, we have been moving from left to right in our attitude model:

CHANGED BELIEFS AND/OR VALUES →

CHANGED ATTITUDES → CHANGED BEHAVIOR

Indeed, this is the traditional design of most organizational attitude change programs. However, our discussion of dissonance theory suggests an alternative approach. Specifically, would it be sensible to change a person's behavior *first*, with the assumption that the person would realign his or her attitudes to support this behavior? Dissonance theory suggests that engaging in behavior that is not supported by our attitudes might indeed lead us to change our attitudes to reduce the tension produced by inconsistency. Researchers have observed such effects in studies where people had to role-play behaviors that were inconsistent with their attitudes. For example, researchers had heavy smokers role-play lung cancer victims and had prejudiced Caucasians advocate pro-African American positions. Evidence indicated that attitude change in the expected direction followed the role-playing—the smokers smoked less and the Caucasians became less prejudiced toward African Americans.[20]

Arnold Goldstein and Melvin Sorcher argue that the traditional view of attitude change has not always proven effective in organizations (Exhibit 5.4).[21] They suggest that attempts to use persuasion to change beliefs and values often fail to lead to attitude change because the audience is unable to see how the new beliefs or values will be applicable to their on-the-job behavior. For example, trainees might learn that people with various ethnic backgrounds have different styles of communication but not understand how to apply this knowledge to dealing with these people on the job. To deal with this problem, Goldstein and Sorcher suggest that individuals should be taught specific *behaviors* they can apply on the job that correspond to the desired attitude change. When the trainees find these behaviors are successful in carrying out their daily activities, dissonance theory suggests that attitudes will change to correspond to the newly learned behaviors. To teach the new behaviors, Goldstein and Sorcher recommend three techniques:

- *Modeling of correct behaviors.* Videotape is usually employed for this purpose.

- *Role-playing of correct behaviors by trainees.* In this phase, trainees get a chance to actually *practice* the desired behaviors.

- *Social reinforcement of role-played behaviors.* Trainers and fellow trainees provide reinforcement (usually praise) for correct role-playing performance.

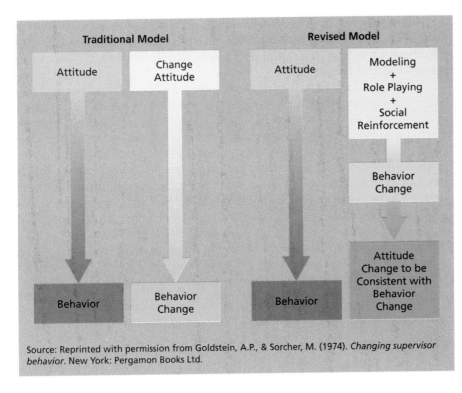

Source: Reprinted with permission from Goldstein, A.P., & Sorcher, M. (1974). *Changing supervisor behavior*. New York: Pergamon Books Ltd.

EXHIBIT 5.4
Models of attitude change.

The revised model of attitude change that Goldstein and Sorcher suggest is shown in the right portion of Exhibit 5.4. Organizations such as Agway, AT&T, IBM, and General Electric have applied these techniques with success. Experts recommend them highly for cross-cultural training programs because the trainees actually get a chance to practice social skills useful in other cultures.[22]

WHAT IS JOB SATISFACTION?

Job satisfaction refers to a collection of attitudes that workers have about their jobs. We can differentiate at least two aspects of satisfaction. The first of these is facet satisfaction, the tendency for an employee to be more or less satisfied with various facets of the job. The notion of facet satisfaction is especially obvious when we hear someone say, "I love my work but hate my boss" or "This place pays lousy, but the people I work with are great." Both of these statements represent different attitudes toward separate facets of the speakers' jobs. Research suggests that the most relevant attitudes toward jobs are contained in a rather small group of facets: the work itself, pay, promotions, recognition, benefits, working conditions, supervision, co-workers, and organizational policy.[23]

In addition to facet satisfaction, we can also conceive of overall satisfaction, an overall, or summary, indicator of a person's attitude toward his or her job that cuts across the various facets.[24] The statement, "On the whole, I really like my job, although a couple of aspects could stand some improvement," is indicative of the nature of overall satisfaction. In a sense, overall satisfaction

Job satisfaction. A collection of attitudes that workers have about their jobs.

is an average or total of the attitudes individuals hold toward various facets of the job. Thus, two workers might express the same level of overall satisfaction for different reasons. Specifically, they would have offsetting attitudes toward various facets of the job.

The most popular measure of job satisfaction is the *Job Descriptive Index* (JDI).[25] This questionnaire is designed around five facets of satisfaction. Employees are asked to respond "yes," "no," or "?" (can't decide) in describing whether a particular word or phrase is descriptive of particular facets of their jobs. Exhibit 5.5 shows some sample JDI items under each facet, scored in the "satisfied" direction. A scoring system is available to provide an index of satisfaction for each facet. In addition, an overall measure of satisfaction can be calculated by adding the separate facet indexes.

Another carefully constructed measure of satisfaction, using a somewhat different set of facets, is the *Minnesota Satisfaction Questionnaire* (MSQ).[26] On this measure, respondents indicate how happy they are with various aspects of their job on a scale ranging from "very satisfied" to "very dissatisfied." Sample items from the short form of the MSQ include:

- The competence of my supervisor in making decisions;
- The way my job provides for steady employment;
- The chance to do things for other people;
- My pay and the amount of work I do.

Scoring the responses to these items provides an index of overall satisfaction as well as satisfaction on the facets on which the MSQ is based.

A number of firms, including Sears, Marriott, and Maryland's Preston Trucking, make extensive use of employee attitude surveys (see the "In Focus: *Surveying Job Satisfaction at United Technologies*"). We will cover the details of such surveys in Chapter 11 when we explore communication and in Chapter 17 when we cover organizational change and development.

Work
N Routine
Y Creative
N Tiresome
Y Gives sense of accomplishment

People
Y Stimulating
Y Ambitious
N Talk too much
N Hard to meet

Promotions
Y Good opportunity for advancement
Y Promotion on ability
N Dead-end job
N Unfair promotion policy

Supervision
Y Asks my advice
Y Praises good work
N Doesn't supervise enough
Y Tells me where I stand

Pay
Y Income adequate for normal expenses
N Bad
N Less than I deserve
Y Highly paid

EXHIBIT 5.5
Sample items from the Job Descriptive Index with "satisfied" responses.

Source: The Job Descriptive Index, revised 1985, is copyrighted by Bowling Green State University. The complete forms, scoring key, instructions, and norms can be obtained from the Department of Psychology, Bowling Green State University, Bowling Green, Ohio, 43404. Reprinted with permission.

IN FOCUS   Surveying Job Satisfaction at United Technologies

Surveys that permit employees to respond anonymously are gaining in popularity in corporate America. The most enlightening polls, companies find, are those that ask the toughest questions. Five years ago United Technologies started trying to change its culture by empowering the lower echelons, cutting red tape, and continually improving quality. It has also eliminated 7,500 jobs. Now the company is asking employees to assess how much progress has been made. "No one person is smart enough to know what is going on in every part of a company this big," says Franklyn Caine, a senior vice president. "And a survey puts in front of people the fact that you really do want to change, and you're ready to do what that takes."

The questionnaire is one facet of a wholesale training effort aimed at altering employees' perceptions of the company, the job, and the market. The *Readiness-to-Compete Survey,* as it is called, went out in April of this year to 7,000 workers,

including some 500 middle managers who had been carefully briefed beforehand. Part of it asked respondents to rank, on a scale of 1 to 5, the seriousness of 10 obstacles to competitiveness. These include: "Management complacency; indifference; lack of urgency"; "Management not really committed to change"; "Reactionary management, not proactive"; and "Ineffective immediate supervisor." The quiz ends with plenty of space for further comments.

Says Caine: "We wish we'd done this five years ago so we'd have some basis for comparison after we analyze the answers." Now he's trying to persuade other technology outfits to ask their people the same questions, so each company could compare its findings with the industry aggregate.

Source: Excerpted from Fisher, A. B. (1991, November 18). Morale crisis. *Fortune,* 70–80.

WHAT DETERMINES JOB SATISFACTION?

When workers on a variety of jobs complete the JDI or the MSQ, we often find differences in the average scores across jobs. Of course, we could almost expect such differences. The various jobs might differ objectively in the facets that contribute to satisfaction. Thus, you would not be astonished to learn that a corporate vice-president was more satisfied with her job than a janitor in the same company. Of greater interest is the fact that we frequently find decided differences in job satisfaction expressed by individuals performing the same job in a given organization. For example, two nurses who work side by side might indicate radically different satisfaction in response to the MSQ item "The chance to do things for other people." How does this happen?

Discrepancy

You will recall that attitudes such as job satisfaction are the product of associated beliefs and values. It would appear that these two factors operate to cause differences in job satisfaction even when jobs are identical. First, workers might differ in their beliefs about the job in question. That is, they might differ in their *perceptions* concerning the actual nature of the job. For example, one of the nurses might perceive that most of her working time is devoted to direct patient care, while the other might perceive that most of her time is spent on administrative functions. To the extent that they both value patient care, the former nurse should be more satisfied with this aspect of the job than the latter nurse. Second, even if individuals perceive their jobs as equivalent, they might differ in what they *want* from the jobs. Such desires are

Discrepancy theory. A theory that job satisfaction stems from the discrepancy between the job outcomes wanted and the outcomes that are perceived to be obtained.

preferences that are dictated in part by the workers' value systems. Thus, if the two nurses perceive their opportunities to engage in direct patient care as high, the one who values this activity more will be more satisfied with the patient care aspect of work. The **discrepancy theory** of job satisfaction asserts that satisfaction is a function of the discrepancy between the job outcomes people want and the outcomes that they perceive they obtain[27]. The individual who desires a job entailing interaction with the public but who is required to sit alone in an office should be dissatisfied with this aspect of the job. In general, employees who have more of their job-related desires met will report more overall job satisfaction.

Fairness

In addition to the discrepancy between the outcomes people receive and those they desire, the other factor that determines job satisfaction is fairness. Issues of fairness affect both what people want from their jobs and how they react to the inevitable discrepancies of organizational life. As we will see, there are two basic kinds of fairness. Distributive fairness has to do with the outcomes we receive, and procedural fairness concerns the process that led to those outcomes.

Distributive fairness. Fairness that occurs when people receive what they think they deserve from their jobs.

Equity theory. A theory that job satisfaction stems from a comparison of the inputs one invests in a job and the outcomes one receives in comparison with the inputs and outcomes of another person or group.

Distributive Fairness.   **Distributive fairness** (often called distributive justice) occurs when people receive what they think they deserve from their jobs. That is, it involves the ultimate *distribution* of work rewards and resources. Above, we indicated that what people want from their jobs is a partial function of their value systems. In fact, however, there are practical limitations to this notion. You might value money and the luxurious lifestyle that it can buy very highly, but this does not suggest that you expect to receive a salary of $200,000 a year. In the case of many job facets, individuals want "what's fair." And how do we develop our conception of what is fair? **Equity theory** states that the inputs that people perceive themselves as investing in a job and the outcomes that the job provides are compared against the inputs and outcomes of some other relevant person or group.[28] Equity will be perceived when the following distribution ratios exist:

$$\frac{\text{My outcomes}}{\text{My inputs}} = \frac{\text{Other's outcomes}}{\text{Other's inputs}}$$

Inputs. Anything that people give up, offer, or trade to their organization in exchange for outcomes.

Outcomes. Factors that an organization distributes to employees in exchange for their inputs.

In these ratios, **inputs** consist of anything that individuals consider relevant to their exchange with the organization, anything that they give up, offer, or trade to their organization. These might include factors such as education, training, seniority, hard work, and high-quality work. **Outcomes** are those factors that the organization distributes to employees in return for their inputs. The most relevant outcomes are represented by the job facets we discussed earlier—pay, promotions, supervision, the nature of the work, and so on. The "other" in the ratio above might be a co-worker performing the same job, a number of co-workers, or even one's conception of all the individuals in one's occupation.[29] For example, the president of the Ford Motor Company probably compares his outcome/input ratio with those that he assumes exist for the presidents of General Motors and Chrysler. You probably compare your outcome/input ratio in your organizational behavior class with that of one or more fellow students.

Equity theory has important implications for job satisfaction. First, inequity itself is a dissatisfying state of affairs, especially when we ourselves are on the "short end of the stick." For example, suppose you see the hours spent studying as your main input to your organizational behavior class and the final grade as an important outcome. Imagine that a friend in the class is your comparison person. Under these conditions, the following situations appear equitable and should not provoke dissatisfaction on your part:

$$\frac{\textbf{You}}{\text{C grade}} \quad \frac{\textbf{Friend}}{\text{A grade}} \qquad \frac{\textbf{You}}{\text{A grade}} \quad \frac{\textbf{Friend}}{\text{C grade}}$$
$$\frac{\text{C grade}}{\text{50 hours}} = \frac{\text{A grade}}{\text{100 hours}} \quad or \quad \frac{\text{A grade}}{\text{60 hours}} = \frac{\text{C grade}}{\text{30 hours}}$$

In each of these cases, a "fair" relationship seems to exist between study time and grades distributed. Now consider the following relationships:

$$\frac{\textbf{You}}{\text{C grade}} \quad \frac{\textbf{Friend}}{\text{A grade}} \qquad \frac{\textbf{You}}{\text{A grade}} \quad \frac{\textbf{Friend}}{\text{C grade}}$$
$$\frac{\text{C grade}}{\text{100 hours}} \neq \frac{\text{A grade}}{\text{50 hours}} \quad or \quad \frac{\text{A grade}}{\text{30 hours}} \neq \frac{\text{C grade}}{\text{60 hours}}$$

In each of these situations, an unfair connection appears to exist between study time and grades received, and you should perceive inequity. However, the situation on the left, in which you put in more work for a lower grade, should be most likely to prompt dissatisfaction. This is a "short end of the stick" situation. Conditions such as this often lead to dissatisfaction in organizational life. For example, the employee who frequently remains on the job after regular hours (input) and receives no special praise or extra pay (outcome) might perceive inequity and feel dissatisfied. Similarly, the teacher who obtains a Master's degree (input) and receives no extra compensation (outcome) might react the same way if others have been rewarded for achieving extra education. Equity considerations also have an indirect effect on job satisfaction by influencing what people want from their jobs. If you study 100 hours while the rest of the students average 50 hours, you will expect a higher grade than the class average.

From the vignette that began the chapter, you will recall that Ben & Jerry's had problems recruiting for top executive positions when they enforced a 7:1 ratio between top and bottom salaries. Equity principles easily explain this difficulty. In comparing themselves to other qualified executives, the salary cap imposed by the company translated to radically reduced outcomes for applicants. Notice that they would likely compare themselves with other executives, not the line workers at Ben & Jerry's. The company removed the salary cap to allow for greater outcomes.

In summary, the equitable distribution of work outcomes contributes to job satisfaction by providing for feelings of distributive fairness. However, let's remember our earlier discussion of cross-cultural differences in values. The equity concept suggests that outcomes should be tied to individual contributions or inputs. This corresponds well with the individualistic North American culture. In more collective cultures, *equality* of outcomes might produce more feeling of distributive fairness. In more feminine cultures, allocating outcomes according to *need* (rather than performance) might provide for distributive fairness.

Procedural Fairness. **Procedural fairness** (often called procedural justice) occurs when individuals see the process used to determine outcomes as

Procedural fairness. Fairness that occurs when the process used to determine work outcomes is seen as reasonable.

reasonable. That is, rather than involving the actual distribution of resources or rewards, it is concerned with how these outcomes are decided and allocated. An example will illustrate the difference between distributive and procedural fairness. Out of the blue, Alan's boss tells him that she has completed his performance evaluation and that he will receive a healthy pay raise starting next month. Alan has been working very hard, and he is pleased with the pay raise (distributive fairness). However, he is vaguely unhappy about the fact that all of this occurred without his participation. Where he used to work, the subordinate and the boss would complete independent performance evaluation forms and then sit down and discuss their differences. This provided good feedback for the subordinate. Alan wonders how his peers who got less generous raises are reacting to the boss's style.

Procedural fairness is particularly relevant to outcomes such as performance evaluations, pay raises, promotions, layoffs, and work assignments. In allocating such outcomes, the following factors contribute to perceptions of procedural fairness.[30] The allocator

- gives adequate reasons for decisions she takes;
- follows consistent procedures over time and across people;
- uses accurate information and appears unbiased;
- allows two-way communication during the allocation process;
- welcomes appeals of the procedure or allocation.

As you might imagine, procedural fairness seems especially likely to provoke dissatisfaction when people also see distributive fairness as low.[31] One view notes that dissatisfaction will be "maximized when people believe that they *would* have obtained better outcomes if the decision maker had used other procedures that *should* have been implemented."[32] (Students who receive lower grades than their friends will recognize the wisdom of this observation!) Thus, Alan, mentioned above, will probably not react too badly to the lack of consultation, while his peers who didn't receive large raises might strongly resent the process that the boss used.

Disposition

Could your personality contribute to your feelings of job satisfaction? This is the essential question guiding recent research on the relationship between disposition and job satisfaction. Underlying the previous discussion is the obvious implication that job satisfaction can be increased by changing the work environment to increase fairness and decrease the discrepancy between what an individual wants and what the job offers. Underlying the dispositional view of job satisfaction is the idea that some people are *predisposed* by virtue of their personalities to be more or less satisfied despite changes in discrepancy or fairness.

Some of the research that suggests disposition contributes to job satisfaction is fascinating. Although each of these studies has some problems, as a group they point to a missing dispositional link.[33] For example:

- Identical twins raised apart from early childhood tend to have similar levels of job satisfaction.
- Job satisfaction tends to be fairly stable over time, even when changes in employer occur.

- Disposition measured early in adolescence is correlated with one's job satisfaction as a mature adult.

Taken together, these findings suggest that some personality characteristics originating in genetics or early learning contribute to adult job satisfaction.

Recent research on disposition and job satisfaction has centered around a couple of personality traits. One of these is the general tendency for a person to respond negatively or positively to the environment. The other concerns the dysfunctional thought process that characterizes depression—thoughts that one must be perfect and that one depends on others for feelings of self-worth. Research shows that negativity and such dysfunctional thought processes threaten people's feeling of well-being and provoke job dissatisfaction.[34] Optimists with more realistic thinking processes are more likely to be satisfied. Research also shows that people who are intrinsically more positive are better decision makers and have better interpersonal skills.[35]

Exhibit 5.6 summarizes what research has to say about the determinants of job satisfaction. To recapitulate, satisfaction is a function of certain dispositional factors and the discrepancy between the job outcomes a person wants and the outcomes that a person perceives she has received. More specifically, people experience greater satisfaction when they meet or exceed the job outcomes they want; perceive the job outcomes they receive as equitable compared to those others receive and believe that fair procedures determine job outcomes. The outcomes that people want from a job are a function of their personal value systems, moderated by equity considerations. The outcomes that people perceive themselves as receiving from the job represent their beliefs about the nature of that job. Again, we see that job satisfaction represents a set of attitudes about the job stemming from the beliefs and values of the person.

Key Contributors to Job Satisfaction

From what we've said thus far, you might expect that job satisfaction is a highly personal experience. While this is essentially true, we can make some general statements about the facets that seem to contribute the most to feelings of job satisfaction for most North American workers. These include mentally challenging work, high pay, promotions, and friendly or helpful colleagues.[36]

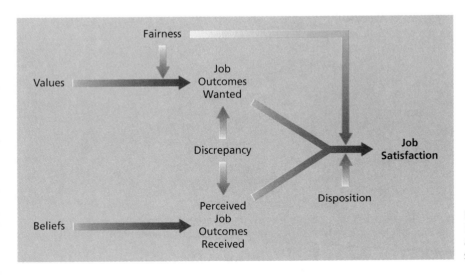

EXHIBIT 5.6
How discrepancy, fairness, and disposition affect job satisfaction.

Mentally Challenging Work. This is work that tests employees' skills and abilities and allows them to set their own working pace. Employees usually perceive such work as personally involving and important. It also provides the worker with clear feedback regarding performance. Of course, some types of work can be too challenging, and this can result in feelings of failure and reduced satisfaction. In addition, some employees seem to prefer repetitive, unchallenging work that makes few demands on them.

High Pay. It should not surprise you that pay and satisfaction are positively related. However, not everyone is equally desirous of money, and some people are certainly willing to accept less responsibility or fewer working hours for lower pay. In fact, Ben Cohen and Jerry Greenfield sacrificed personal income to foster their vision of a socially responsible organization. Individual differences in preferences for pay are especially obvious in the case of reactions to overtime work. In most companies, one finds a group of employees who are especially anxious to earn extra money through overtime and another group that actively avoids overtime work.

Promotions. The ready availability of promotions that management administers according to a fair system contributes to job satisfaction. Ample opportunity for promotion is an important contributor to job satisfaction because promotions contain a number of valued signals about a person's self-worth. Some of these signals may be material (such as an accompanying raise), while others are of a social nature (recognition within the organization and increased prestige in the community). Of course, there are cultural and individual

When one worker voluntarily helps out another it is an example of organizational citizenship which positively affects organizational effectiveness.

differences in what people see as constituting a fair promotion system. Some employees might prefer a strict seniority system, while others might wish for a system based strictly upon job performance. Many of today's flatter, "downsized" organizations no longer offer the promotion opportunities of the past. Well-run firms have offset this by designing lateral moves that provide for challenging work.

People.   It should not surprise you that friendly, considerate, good-natured superiors and co-workers contribute to job satisfaction. There is, however, another aspect to interpersonal relationships on the job that contributes to job satisfaction. Specifically, we tend to be satisfied in the presence of people who help us attain job outcomes that we value. Such outcomes might include doing our work better or more easily, obtaining a raise or promotion, or even staying alive. For example, a company of soldiers in battle might be less concerned with how friendly their commanding officer is than with how competently he is able to act to keep them from being overrun by the enemy. Similarly, an aggressive young executive might like a considerate boss but prefer even more a boss who can clarify her work objectives and reward her for attaining them. The friendliness aspect of interpersonal relationships seems most important in lower-level jobs with clear duties and various dead-end jobs. As jobs become more complex, pay is tied to performance, or promotion opportunities increase, the ability of others to help us do our work well contributes more to job satisfaction.

THE CONSEQUENCES OF JOB DISSATISFACTION

If you have to spend eight hours a day five days a week on the job, it would obviously be worthwhile for you to have favorable attitudes toward that job. Thus, job satisfaction is an attitude worthy of interest in and of itself. However, job satisfaction also has important personal and organizational consequences beyond mere happiness with the job. Xerox, Levi Strauss, and Michigan office equipment maker Steelcase are firms that have maintained a competitive advantage by paying particular attention to employee satisfaction.

Mental Health and Off-the-Job Satisfaction

Can your job drive you crazy? Phrased more formally, can job dissatisfaction promote psychological disturbance? It would appear that more satisfied workers do tend to be psychologically healthier.[37] In addition, positive attitudes toward one's job are often associated with positive attitudes toward one's life in general.[38] That is, satisfied workers tend to report satisfaction with various nonwork aspects of their lives. Of course, the actual causality in these findings can be ambiguous. For example, an individual could become psychologically disturbed because of off-the-job factors and *then* encounter problems on the job due to this disturbance, leading to dissatisfaction. However, to the extent that job satisfaction does contribute to mental health and general life satisfaction, this probably happens because of self-esteem. That is, people feel a sense of accomplishment and worth in performing a satisfying job, and this feeling spills over into their off-job life.

Absence from Work

Absenteeism is an expensive behavior in North America. One estimate pegs the annual U.S. cost up to $46 billion and the Canadian cost up to $10 billion.[39] Such costs are attributable to "sick" pay, lost productivity, and chronic overstaffing to compensate for absentees and so on. Many more days are lost to absenteeism than to strikes and other industrial disputes. Is some of this absenteeism the product of job dissatisfaction? The research literature is fairly firm.[40] From it we can draw the following conclusions.

- Speaking generally, the association between job satisfaction and absenteeism is fairly small.

- The satisfaction facet that is the best predictor of absenteeism is the content of the work itself.

- Job satisfaction is a better predictor of how *often* employees are absent rather than how many *days* they are absent. In other words, it is associated more with frequency of absenteeism than with time lost.

Why is the relationship between absenteeism and job satisfaction not stronger? Several factors probably constrain the ability of many people to convert their like or dislike of work into corresponding attendance patterns.

- Some absence is simply unavoidable because of illness, weather conditions, or day care problems. Thus, some very happy employees will occasionally be absent owing to circumstances beyond their control.

- Opportunities for off-the-job satisfaction on a missed day may vary. Thus, you might love your job but love skiing or sailing even more. In this case, you might skip work while a dissatisfied person who has nothing better to do shows up.

- Some organizations have attendance control policies that can influence absence more than satisfaction does. In a company that refuses to pay workers for missed days (typical of many hourly paid situations), absence may be more related to economic needs than to dissatisfaction. The unhappy worker who absolutely needs money will probably show up for work. By the same token, dissatisfied and satisfied workers might be equally responsive to threats of dismissal if they are absent.

- On many jobs, it might be unclear to employees how much absenteeism is reasonable or sensible. With a lack of company guidelines, workers might look to the behavior of their peers for a norm to guide their behavior. This norm and its corresponding "absence culture" might have a stronger effect than the individual employee's satisfaction with his or her job.[41]

Research regarding the connection between job satisfaction and absence has some interesting implications for managing absenteeism. For one thing, general increases in job satisfaction will probably have little effect on absence levels unless this satisfaction stems mainly from a revision in job content (a topic that we will consider in Chapter 7). In addition, a high frequency of short-term absence spells is probably a better indicator of an "attitude problem" than a few long spells of time lost. The latter pattern is more likely to reflect medical problems or family demands than job dissatisfaction.

Turnover

Turnover refers to resignation from an organization, and it can be incredibly expensive. For example, it costs several thousand dollars to replace a nurse or a bank teller who resigns. As we move up the organizational hierarchy, or into technologically complex jobs, such costs escalate dramatically. For example, it costs hundreds of thousands of dollars to hire and train a single military fighter pilot. Estimates of turnover costs usually include the price of hiring, training, and developing to proficiency a replacement employee. Such figures probably underestimate the true costs of turnover, however, because they do not include intangible costs such as work group disruption or the loss of employees who informally acquire special skills and knowledge over time on a job. All of this would not be so bad if turnover were concentrated among poorer performers. Unfortunately, this is not always the case. In one study, 23 percent of scientists and engineers who left an organization were among the top 10 percent of performers.[42]

What is the relationship between job satisfaction and turnover? Research indicates a moderately strong connection.[43] That is, less-satisfied workers are more likely to quit. Thus, Ben & Jerry's has a low turnover rate. However, the relationship between the attitude (job satisfaction) and the behavior in question (turnover) is far from perfect. This is because a number of steps intervene between being dissatisfied and actually leaving (Exhibit 5.7). At each of these steps, the dissatisfied individual might decide that it is too much trouble to proceed further or that resignation would be an unwise move. A few comments on some of the steps that we see in the model in Exhibit 5.7 are appropriate.[44]

Step 2: Certain individuals might be highly dissatisfied with their jobs but do not even think of quitting. Bad experiences with previous job searches or a poor self-image might not even permit *fantasies* about quitting.

Step 3: One key factor affecting this step is the labor market situation.[45] Under conditions of high unemployment, the dissatisfied worker might evaluate the chances of finding another decent job at nearly zero. The

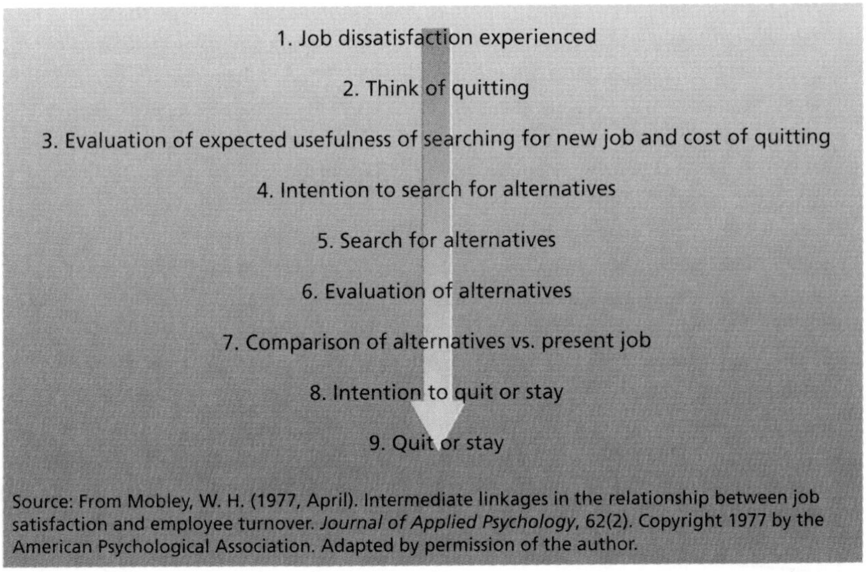

1. Job dissatisfaction experienced

2. Think of quitting

3. Evaluation of expected usefulness of searching for new job and cost of quitting

4. Intention to search for alternatives

5. Search for alternatives

6. Evaluation of alternatives

7. Comparison of alternatives vs. present job

8. Intention to quit or stay

9. Quit or stay

Source: From Mobley, W. H. (1977, April). Intermediate linkages in the relationship between job satisfaction and employee turnover. *Journal of Applied Psychology*, 62(2). Copyright 1977 by the American Psychological Association. Adapted by permission of the author.

EXHIBIT 5.7
Decision process between job dissatisfaction and turnover.

cost of quitting also receives serious consideration here. You might hate your job but have to remain in it because it provides excellent health benefits for your family.

Step 7: It is probably safe to assume that comparisons of alternative jobs with one's present job involve equity considerations. That is, the job seeker compares the inputs and outcomes of his or her present job with those that are anticipated on alternative jobs. If the comparison favors the alternative, the person will intend to resign.

Step 8: Substantial research indicates that stated intentions to quit are better predictors of turnover than is job satisfaction.[46] Intentions to quit are "closer" to an actual behavior—quitting—than is job satisfaction. Such intentions take into account a number of factors that do not influence satisfaction, and they represent very specific attitudes about *quitting* rather than more general attitudes about the job.

Performance

For many years, the literature targeted at practicing managers was filled with articles extolling the virtues of the human relations approach. In a nutshell, this approach suggested that considerate, humane supervision and expressing interest in the personal needs of employees were useful ways to manage. Such a management style was not advocated on sheerly humanitarian grounds, however. Each article usually indicated that such a style would pay off with increased performance on the part of the work force. Thus, good human relations were seen as a good motivational strategy:

GOOD HUMAN RELATIONS → JOB SATISFACTION → PERFORMANCE

That is, the literature assumed that good human relations would lead to job satisfaction and that satisfaction would in turn stimulate high performance. In discussing the causes of job satisfaction, we have pointed out that certain human relations practices do lead to increased satisfaction. But, does high satisfaction (however achieved) lead to high performance? Formally stated, this viewpoint is called the **"satisfaction causes performance" hypothesis.**

"Satisfaction causes performance" hypothesis. An assumption that high job satisfaction leads to high job performance.

From the quiz in Chapter 2, you will recall that satisfied workers are not generally much more productive than dissatisfied workers. In fact, a large body of research shows that the relationship between satisfaction and performance is positive but usually very low and often inconsistent.[47] Why is this correlation between job attitudes and job behavior so low? Intuition suggests that we might work harder to pay back the organization for a satisfying job. However, intuition also suggests that we might be so busy enjoying our satisfying job that we have little *time* to be productive. For example, satisfying co-workers and a pleasant superior might lead us to devote more time to social interactions than to work. These contradictory intuitions provoke suspicion that the "satisfaction causes performance" hypothesis might be incorrect.

"Performance causes satisfaction" hypothesis. An assumption that high job performance leads to high job satisfaction.

In recent years, the "satisfaction causes performance" hypothesis has been replaced by the so-called **"performance causes satisfaction" hypothesis,** which asserts that it is high performance that leads to high satisfaction.[48] On the face of it, this viewpoint seems rather curious. How does performance lead to satisfaction? Specifically, performance would seem to lead to satisfaction when the performance is *followed by rewards.* That is:

PERFORMANCE → REWARDS → JOB SATISFACTION

For example, if you study hard for a midterm exam and are rewarded with a good grade, you should be satisfied with at least some aspects of the course. In this case your performance would be related to your satisfaction because the performance was rewarded. Similarly, if a supermarket manager increases his store's sales by 30 percent (performance) and is then promoted to district manager (reward), this should increase his job satisfaction. Again, in cases like this, performance and satisfaction should be fairly closely related.

Now for a final crucial question: If performance does cause satisfaction, why do so many studies show a very low relationship between the two variables? Put very simply, many organizations do not do a very good job of tying rewards to performance. In many cases, especially high productivity is not followed by a promotion, extra pay, or assignment to a more interesting task. For example, you have probably experienced doing what you thought was a good job in a course only to receive a mediocre grade. It is doubtful that such an outcome will cause you to be happy with the course. In summary, simply increasing employees' satisfaction should not cause them to perform better.

Organizational Citizenship Behavior

Despite your author's best efforts in the previous section, you might well be saying to yourself, "Wait a minute. Somehow, some way, job satisfaction has to have some impact on the extent to which employees will 'go the extra mile' or the extent to which they'll cooperate to get the job done." In fact, you could be correct. Recent theory and research suggests that although job satisfaction is not closely related to formal performance measures, it is more strongly related to the informal "citizenship" aspects of organizational membership. **Organizational citizenship behavior** (OCB) is voluntary, informal behavior that contributes to organizational effectiveness.[49] In many cases, the formal performance evaluation system does not detect and reward it.

> **Organizational citizenship behavior.** Voluntary, informal behavior that contributes to organizational effectiveness.

An example of OCB should clarify the concept. You are struggling to master a particularly difficult piece of software and making the attendant noises of discouragement. A colleague at the next desk, busy on her own rush job, comes over and offers assistance. Irritated with the software, you aren't even very grateful at first, but within ten minutes you've solved the problem with her help. Notice the defining characteristics of this example of OCB:

- The behavior is voluntary. It is not included in her job description.
- The behavior is spontaneous. Someone didn't order or suggest it.
- The behavior contributes to organizational effectiveness. It extends beyond simply doing you a personal favor.
- The behavior is unlikely to be explicitly picked up and rewarded by the performance evaluation system, especially since it isn't part of the job description.

What are the various forms that OCB might take? As the software example indicates, one prominent form is *helping* behavior, offering assistance to others. Another might be *conscientiousness* to the details of work, including getting in on the snowiest day of the year and not wasting organizational resources. A third form of OCB involves being a *good sport* when the inevitable frustrations of organizational life crop up—not everyone can have the best office or the best parking spot. A final form of OCB is *courtesy and cooperation*.[50] Examples might include warning the photocopy unit about a big job that is on the way or delaying one's own work to assist a colleague on a rush job.

Just how does job satisfaction contribute to OCB? Fairness seems to be the key.[51] Although distributive fairness (especially in terms of pay) is important, procedural fairness on the part of one's boss seems especially critical.[52] If the boss strays from the prescriptions for procedural fairness we gave earlier, OCB can suffer. If one feels unfairly treated it might be difficult to lower formal performance for fear of dire consequences. It might be much easier to withdraw the less visible, informal activities that make up OCB. On the other hand, fair treatment and its resulting satisfaction might be reciprocated with OCB, a truly personalized input.

It is interesting that OCB is also influenced by employees' mood at work. People in a pleasant, relaxed, optimistic mood are more likely to provide special assistance to others.[53] Some of this research is based on studies with salespeople, and I'm sure it is obvious to you how OCB would make customer service more competitive. Given the pleasant atmosphere at Ben & Jerry's, we would expect much OCB in the firm.

The Manager's Notebook   West Coast Builders and Realtors Cater to Asian Cultural Values

1. Many firms have exposed their employees to training seminars in which consultants familiarize them with Asian cultural values and practices. Although the sales staff is the most obvious choice for training, some firms have trained senior managers, designers, and architects as well. Such training should cover value differences, but it should also use role-playing and other techniques to teach appropriate behavior, such as how to shake hands or exchange business cards. It should also teach participants to understand the cultural diversity that distinguishes the various Asian countries.

2. This case reminds us that the globalization of business doesn't just affect what goes on in or between global firms. It also affects the interface between the firm and its clients. Organizations often anticipate cultural differences when they go into another culture to do business. They are less sensitive to such differences when people from another culture come into the firm's traditional home markets. Training seminars can sensitize employees to the cultural distinctiveness of the firm's various clients.

EXECUTIVE SUMMARY

◆ Values are broad preferences for particular states of affairs. Values tend to differ across occupational groups and across cultures.

◆ Critical cross-cultural dimensions of values include power distance, uncertainty avoidance, masculinity/feminity, individualism/collectivism, and time orientation.

◆ Differences in values across cultures set constraints on the export and import of organizational behavior theories and management practices. They also have

implications for satisfying global customers and developing globally aware employees.

◆ Attitudes are a function of what we think about the world (our beliefs) and how we feel about the world (our values). Attitudes are important because they influence how we behave, although we have discussed several factors that reduce the correspondence between our attitudes and behaviors.

◆ One method of attitude change is to attempt to change individuals' beliefs and values through persuasion. In general, this procedure works best when a credible, believable communicator requests a moderate degree of change from an audience. Cognitive dissonance theory suggests that attitude change occurs in cases such as this because the newly learned cognitions are inconsistent with previously held attitudes. Dissonance theory also suggests that attitudes can be changed by getting people to enact desired behaviors that are incompatible with their attitudes.

◆ Job satisfaction is an especially important attitude for organizations. Satisfaction is a function of the discrepancy between what individuals want from their jobs and what they perceive that they obtain, taking into account distributive and procedural fairness. Dispositional factors also seem to influence job satisfaction. Factors such as challenging work, high pay, promotion opportunities, and friendly, helpful co-workers contribute to job satisfaction. Job satisfaction is important because it may promote mental health and reduce expensive turnover. Satisfied workers are not necessarily much better performers, since good performance might not lead to the acquisition of satisfying rewards. However, satisfied workers might be better organizational citizens.

KEY CONCEPTS

Values	Distributive fairness
Power distance	Equity theory
Uncertainty avoidance	Inputs
Individualistic vs. collective	Outcomes
Attitude	Procedural fairness
Cognitive dissonance	"Satisfaction causes performance" hypothesis
Job satisfaction	"Performance causes satisfaction" hypothesis
Discrepancy theory	Organizational citizenship behavior

DISCUSSION QUESTIONS

1. What are some of the conditions under which a person's attitudes might *not* predict his or her work behavior?

2. Many organizations use diversity training to promote favorable attitudes among employees who differ in gender, age, race, ethnicity, or sexual orientation. Given our discussion of attitude change, what factors would improve the success of such efforts at persuasion? Could behavior change foster attitude change?

3. Discuss the pros and cons of the argument, "Organizations should do everything they can to enhance the job satisfaction of their employees."

4. Using the model of the turnover process in Exhibit 5.7, explain why a very dissatisfied worker might not quit his or her job.

5. Use equity theory to explain why a dentist who earns $60,000 a year might be more dissatisfied with her job than a factory worker who earns $20,000.

6. Explain why workers who are very satisfied with their jobs might not be better performers than those who are less satisfied.

7. Mexico has a fairly high power distance culture, while the United States and Canada have lower power distance cultures. Discuss how effective management techniques might vary between Mexico and its neighbors to the north.

8. Describe some job aspects that might contribute to job satisfaction for a person in a more collective culture. Do the same for a person in a more individualistic culture.

9. Give an example of an employee who is experiencing distributive fairness but not procedural fairness. Give an example of an employee who is experiencing procedural fairness but not distributive fairness.

10. Give an example of value conflict between two occupations.

EXPERIENTIAL EXERCISE
YOUR INDIVIDUALISM-COLLECTIVISM ORIENTATION

Assume that you are in the United States or Canada and want to have a good career in an American or Canadian corporation. Please answer the following questions about your behavior in the workplace. Please use the following scale, placing the appropriate number in the blank before each question.

5	4	3	2	1
strongly agree	agree	not sure	disagree	strongly disagree

1. _____ I would offer my seat in a bus to my supervisor.

2. _____ I prefer to be direct and forthright when dealing with people.

3. _____ I enjoy developing long-term relationships among the people with whom I work.

4. _____ I am very modest when talking about my own accomplishments.

5. _____ When I give gifts to people whose cooperation I need in my work, I feel I am indulging in questionable behavior.

6. _____ If I want my subordinate to perform a task, I tell the person that my superiors want me to get that task done.

7. _____ I prefer to give opinions that will help people save face rather than give a statement of the truth.

8. _____ I say "No" directly when I have to.

9. _____ To increase sales, I would announce that the individual salesperson with the highest sales would be given the "Distinguished Salesperson" award.

10. _____ I enjoy being emotionally close to the people with whom I work.

11. _____ It is important to develop a network of people in my community who can help me when I have tasks to accomplish.

12. _____ I enjoy feeling that I am looked upon as equal in worth to my superiors.

13. _____ I have respect for the authority figures with whom I interact.

14. _____ If I want a person to perform a certain task I try to show how the task will benefit others in the person's group.

Now, imagine yourself working in one of the following countries. Choose the one about which you have the most knowledge because of actual overseas experience, reading, having friends from that country, classes that you have taken, and so forth.

Japan   Mexico   Brazil   Philippines   Hong Kong   Thailand
Taiwan   Peru   Venezuela   India   Argentina   Greece

If you do not have enough knowledge about any of these countries, imagine yourself working on a class project with three foreign students from any of these countries.

The next part of the exercise is to answer the same 14 questions, but to answer them while imagining that you are working in one of the countries listed above or working on a class project with three students from that country. Imagine that you will be living in that country for a long period of time and want to have a good career in a corporation there. Use the same scale and place the appropriate number (5 for strongly agree, 4 for agree, 3 for not sure, 2 for disagree, and 1 for strongly disagree)

1. _____	8. _____
2. _____	9. _____
3. _____	10. _____
4. _____	11. _____
5. _____	12. _____
6. _____	13. _____
7. _____	14. _____

The scoring of this exercise is different from most in that it involves comparison of the two sets of numbers, the one for imagining a career in the United States or Canada and the one for imagining a career in one of the other listed countries. Let's call the first time you answered the questions "the first pass" and the other time "the second pass." In scoring, give yourself 1 point according to the following guidelines.

Question 1: Give yourself a point if your number in the second pass is higher than in the first pass.
Question 2: Give yourself a point if your number in the first pass is higher than in the second pass.
Question 3: A point if number is higher in the second pass.
Question 4: A point if number is higher in the second pass.
Question 5: A point if number is higher in the first pass.
Question 6: A point if number is higher in the second pass.
Question 7: A point if number is higher in the second pass.
Question 8: A point if number is higher in the first pass.
Question 9: A point if number is higher in the first pass.
Question 10: A point if number is higher in the second pass.
Question 11: A point if number is higher in the first pass.
Question 12: A point if number is higher in the first pass.

Question 13: A point if number is higher in the
        second pass.

Question 14: A point if number is higher in the
        second pass.

If you scored 6 or more points, this means that you are sensitive to the cultural differences summarized by the concepts of *individualism* and *collectivism*. You are sensitive to the fact that different behaviors are likely to lead to the accomplishment of goals and to success in one's career depending on the emphasis on individualism or collectivism in the culture.

Source: Exercise developed by Richard W. Brislin. From Brislin, R. W., & Yoshida, T. (Eds.) (1994). *Improving intercultural interactions: Modules for cross-cultural training programs.* Thousand Oaks, CA: Sage.

CASE STUDY
THE WELL-PAID RECEPTIONIST

Harvey Finley did a quick double take when he caught a glimpse of the figure representing Ms. Brannen's salary on the year-end printout. A hurried call to payroll confirmed it. Yes, his receptionist had been paid $127,614.21 for her services last year. As he sat in stunned silence, he had the sudden realization that, since his firm was doing so well this year, she would earn at least 10 to 15 percent more money during the current fiscal year. This was a shock, indeed.

BACKGROUND

Harvey began his career as a service technician for a major manufacturer of copy machines. He received rather extensive technical training, but his duties were limited to performing routine, on-site maintenance and service for customers. After a year's experience as a service technician, he asked for and received a promotion to sales representative. In this capacity, he established many favorable contacts in the business community of Troupville and the surrounding towns. He began to think seriously about capitalizing on his success by opening his own business.

Then, seven years ago, he decided to take the plunge and start his own firm. He was tired of selling for someone else. When he mentioned his plan to his friends, they all expressed serious doubts; Troupville, a city of approximately 35,000 people located in the deep South, had just begun to recover from a severe recession. The painful memories of the layoffs, bankruptcies, and plummeting real estate values were too recent and vivid to be forgotten.

Undeterred by the sceptics, Harvey was optimistic that Troupville's slow recovery would soon become a boom. Even though his firm would certainly have to be started on a shoestring, Harvey thought his sales experience and technical competence would enable him to survive what was sure to be a difficult beginning. He was nervous but excited when he signed the lease on the first little building. A lifelong dream was either about to be realized or dashed forever. Troupville Business Systems was born.

While he had managed to borrow, rent, lease, or subcontract for almost everything that was absolutely necessary, he did need one employee immediately. Of course, he hoped the business would expand rapidly and that he would soon have a complete and competent staff. But until he could be sure that some revenue would be generated, he thought he could get by with one person who would be a combination receptionist/secretary and general assistant.

The typical salary for such a position in the area was about $14,000 per year; for Harvey, this was a major expense. Nevertheless, he placed what he thought was a well-worded ad in the "Help Wanted" section of the local newspaper. There were five applicants, four of whom just did not seem quite right for the position he envisioned. The fifth applicant, Ms. Cathy Brannen, was absolutely captivating.

Ms. Brannen was a twenty-seven-year-old divorcee with one small child. Her resume showed that she had graduated from a two-year office administration program at a state university. She had worked for only two employers following graduation, one for five years and the most recent for two years. Since returning to her hometown of Troupville two months ago, following her divorce, she had not been able to find suitable employment.

From the moment she sat down for the interview, Harvey and Ms. Brannen seemed to be on exactly the same wavelength. She was very articulate, obviously quite bright, and, most important, very enthusiastic about assisting with the start-up of the new venture. She seemed to be exactly the sort of person Harvey had envisioned when he first began to think seriously about taking the plunge. He resisted the temptation to offer her the job on the spot, but ended the hour-long interview by telling her that he would check her references and contact her again very soon.

Telephone calls to her two former employers convinced Harvey that he had actually underestimated Ms. Brannen's suitability for the position. Each one said without equivocation that she was the best employee he had ever had in any position. Both former employers concluded the conversation by saying they would rehire her in a minute if she were still available. The only bit of disturbing information gleaned from these two calls was the fact that her annual salary had risen to $15,900 in her last job. Although Harvey thought that the cost of living was probably a bit higher in Houston, where she had last worked, he wasn't sure she would react favorably to the $14,000 offer he was planning to make. However, he was determined that somehow, Cathy Brannen would be his first employee.

Ms. Brannen seemed quite pleased when Harvey telephoned her at home that same evening. She said she would be delighted to meet him at the office the next morning to discuss the position more fully.

Cathy Brannen was obviously very enthusiastic about the job as outlined in the meeting. She asked all of the right questions, responded quickly and articulately to every query posed to her, and seemed ready to accept the position even before the offer was extended. When Harvey finally got around to mentioning the salary, there was a slight change in Cathy's eager expression. She stiffened. Since Harvey realized that salary might be a problem, he decided to offer Cathy an incentive of sorts in addition to the $14,000 annual salary. He told her that he realized his salary offer was lower than the amount she had earned on her last job. And, he told her, he understood that a definite disadvantage of working for a new firm was the complete absence of financial security. Although he was extremely reluctant to guarantee a larger salary because of his own uncertainty regarding the future, he offered her a sales override in the amount of two percent of sales. He explained that she would largely determine the success or failure of the firm. She needed to represent the firm in the finest possible manner to potential customers who telephoned and to those who walked in the front door. For this reason, the sales override seemed to be an appropriate addition to her straight salary. It would provide her with incentive to take an active interest in the firm.

Cathy accepted the offer immediately. Even though she was expecting a salary offer of $16,000, she hoped the sales override might make up the difference. "Who knows," she thought, "two percent of sales may amount to big money someday." It did not, however, seem very likely at the time.

Troupville Business Systems began as a very small distributor of copy machines. The original business plan was just to sell copy machines and provide routine, on-site service. More extensive on-site service and repairs requiring that a machine be removed from a customer's premise were to be provided by a regional distributor located in a major city approximately 100 miles from Troupville.

Troupville Business Systems did well from the start. Several important changes were made in the services the firm offered during the first year. Harvey soon found that there was a greater demand for the leasing of copy machines, particularly the large expensive models which he originally planned to sell. He also soon discovered that his customers wanted to be able to contract directly with his firm for all of their service needs. Merely guaranteeing that he could get the machines serviced was not sufficient in the eyes of potential customers. In attempting to accommodate the market, he developed a complete service facility and began to offer leasing options on all models. These changes in the business all occurred during the first

year. Growth during that year was steady but not spectacular. While sales continued to grow steadily the second year, it was early in the third year that Harvey made what turned out to be his best decision. He entered the computer business.

Harvey had purchased a personal computer soon after Troupville Business Systems was founded. The machine and its capabilities fascinated him, although he knew virtually nothing about computers. He was soon a member of a local users club, was subscribing to all the magazines, and was taking evening computer courses at the local university—in short, he became a computer buff. Harvey recognized the business potential of the rapidly growing personal computer market, but he did not believe that his original business was sufficiently stable to introduce a new product line just yet.

During his third year of operations, he decided the time was right to enter the computer business. He added to his product line a number of personal computers popular with small businesses in the area. This key decision cause a virtual explosion in the growth of his firm. Several key positions were added, including that of a comptroller. By the fourth year of operations, computers produced by several other manufacturers had been added to Harvey's product line, and he had developed the capability of providing complete service for all products carried. His computer enterprise was not limited to business customers, because he quickly developed a significant walk-in retail trade. Rapid growth continued unabated.

During the first seven years of the company's existence, Cathy Brannen had proven truly indispensable. Her performance exceeded Harvey's highest expectations. Although her official position remained that of secretary/receptionist, she took it upon herself to learn about each new product or service. During the early years, Harvey often thought that she did a better job than he did whenever a potential customer called in his absence. Even after he acquired a qualified sales staff, Harvey had no concerns when Cathy had to field questions from a potential customer because a regular salesperson was not available. The customer never realized that the professional young lady capably handling all inquiries was "only" the receptionist.

Cathy began performing fewer sales functions because of the increased number of professional salespersons, but her secretarial duties expanded tremendously. She was still Harvey's secretary, and she continued to answer virtually every telephone call coming into the business. Since her office was in an open area, she still was the first to greet many visitors.

Cathy took a word processing course at a local business school shortly after joining the firm. As she began working with Harvey's first personal computer, she, too, developed into a computer aficionado and became the best computer operator in the firm.

THE CURRENT SITUATION

Harvey was shaken by the realization that Cathy Brannen had been paid over $127,000 last year. As he wondered what, if anything, should be done about her earnings, he began to reflect on the previous seven years.

Success had come almost overnight. It seemed as though Troupville Business Systems could do no wrong. The work force had grown at a rate of approximately 15 percent per year since the third year of operations. Seventeen people were now employed by the firm. While Harvey did acknowledge that some of this success was due to being in the right place at the right time, he also had reason to be proud of the choices he had made. Time had proven that all of his major decisions had been correct. He also could not overestimate Cathy's contribution to the success of the firm. Yes, certainly, one of the most important days in the life of the firm was the day when Cathy responded to his ad in the newspaper.

Success had brought with it the ever-increasing demands on his time. He had never worked so hard, but the rewards were certainly forthcoming. First there was the new Jaguar, then the new home on Country Club Drive, the vacation home on the coast, the European trips. . . . Yes, success was wonderful.

During these years Cathy, too, had prospered. Harvey had not thought much about it, but he did remember making a joking comment the first day she drove her new Mercedes to work. He also remembered commenting on her mink coat at the company banquet last December. Cathy had been dazzling.

Now that Harvey realized what he was paying Cathy, he was greatly disturbed. She was making over twice as much money as anyone else in the firm with the exception of himself. The best salesman had earned an amount in the low sixties last year. His top managers were paid salaries ranging from the high forties to the mid-fifties. The average salary in the area for executive secretaries was now probably between $22,000 and $25,000 per year. A good receptionist could be hired for under $20,000, and yet Cathy had been paid $127,614.21 last year. The sales override had certainly enabled Cathy to share in the firm's success. Yes, indeed.

As Harvey thought more and more about the situation, he kept returning to the same conclusion. He felt something had to be done about her compensation. It was just too far out of line with other salaries in the firm. Although Harvey was drawing over $200,000 per year in salary and had built an equity in the business of more than $1 million, these facts did not seem relevant as he pondered what to do. It seemed likely that a number of other employees did know about Cathy's compensation level. Harvey wondered why no one ever mentioned it. Even the comptroller never mentioned Cathy's compensation. This did seem quite odd to Harvey, as the comptroller, Frank Bain, knew that Harvey did not even attempt to keep up with the financial details. He relied on Frank to bring important matters to his attention.

With no idea of how to approach this problem, Harvey decided to begin by making a list of alternatives. He got out a piece of paper and, as he stared at the blank lines, overheard Cathy's cheerful exchange with a customer in the next room.

Source: Case prepared by Roland B. Cousins, LaGrange College. Management cooperated in the field research for this case, which was written solely for the purpose of stimulating student discussion. All individuals and incidents are real, but names and data have been disguised at the request of the organization. From the *Case Research Journal*, Spring 1992, pp. 74–79. Copyright the *Case Research Journal* and Roland B. Cousins.

1. Use the ideas of distributive fairness and equity theory to explain why Harvey Finley thinks he pays Cathy Brannen too much.
2. Use the ideas of distributive fairness and equity theory to explain why Cathy Brannen might feel that her pay is fair.
3. What are the likely consequences if Ms. Brannen's pay level is truly known to other organizational members? Use equity theory to support your answer.
4. Suppose that you had been in Mr. Finley's position at the time that he hired Ms. Brannen. What would you have done differently to avoid the current situation while still attracting her to join the fledgling firm?
5. What ethical or moral issue does this case raise?
6. What should Mr. Finley do now? Be sure to consider procedural fairness in framing your answer.

LEARNING OBJECTIVES

AFTER READING CHAPTER 6 YOU SHOULD BE ABLE TO:

1 DEFINE MOTIVATION, DISCUSS ITS BASIC PROPERTIES, AND DISTINGUISH IT FROM PERFORMANCE.

2 COMPARE AND CONTRAST INTRINSIC AND EXTRINSIC MOTIVATION.

3 EXPLAIN AND DISCUSS THE MANAGERIAL IMPLICATIONS OF NEED THEORIES OF MOTIVATION.

4 EXPLAIN AND DISCUSS THE MANAGERIAL IMPLICATIONS OF EXPECTANCY THEORY.

5 EXPLAIN AND DISCUSS THE MANAGERIAL IMPLICATIONS OF EQUITY THEORY.

6 DISCUSS THE CROSS-CULTURAL LIMITATIONS OF THEORIES OF MOTIVATION.

7 USE THE PORTER-LAWLER MODEL TO SUMMARIZE THE RELATIONSHIP AMONG THE VARIOUS THEORIES OF MOTIVATION, PERFORMANCE, AND JOB SATISFACTION.

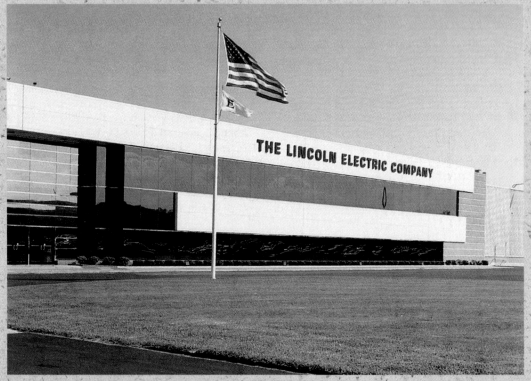

THE LINCOLN ELECTRIC COMPANY NEAR CLEVELAND, OHIO, IS EXEMPLARY IN EMPLOYEE MOTIVATION.

CHAPTER 6

THEORIES OF WORK MOTIVATION

LINCOLN
ELECTRIC
COMPANY

On the surface, the Lincoln Electric Company might look like a motivational disaster. The firm, located near Cleveland, Ohio, offers employees no paid sick days and no paid holidays. Lincoln employees have to pay their own health insurance, and overtime work and unexpected job reassignments are mandatory. If older workers lower their productivity they receive less pay. Management does not take seniority into account in promotions. Lincoln managers receive no executive "perks"—no cars, no executive dining room, no club memberships, no management seminars, and no reserved parking.

Despite these apparently draconian policies, Lincoln has become something of a mecca for visiting managers (from Ford, GM, TRW, 3M, Motorola, and McDonnell Douglas) who flock to Cleveland to learn something about motivation. Lincoln is the world's largest producer of arc welding equipment and it also makes electric motors. The firm has turned a handsome profit every quarter for over 50 years and hasn't laid anyone off for over 40 years. Employee turnover is extremely low, and Lincoln workers are estimated to be roughly twice as productive as other manufacturing workers. This productivity is an important key to Lincoln's success, because it is not dealing in high tech products, and it does not compete strongly on price.

What's the secret to Lincoln's motivational success? In a word, *money*. Lots of it. Lincoln Electric offers what some say are the best paid factory jobs in the country. At the core of the system is an intricate piecerate pay plan that rewards workers for what they produce and a merit-based profit sharing plan that provides a yearly bonus. This bonus, which can approach 100% of regular earnings, is also allocated on merit to managers and staff. The average production worker has earned $45,000 in recent years, with some earning well over $85,000! If workers think up a way to increase productivity, the company doesn't adjust the piecerate to cap potential wages. Also, they can't work themselves out of a job, since Lincoln has a no-layoff policy. Effectively, this amounts to lifetime employment. Employees are so keen to get working that the company enforces a policy prohibiting them from coming in too early.

Life at Lincoln isn't for everyone. Some managers would resent the lack of perks. Some new production workers can't take the fast pace and quit shortly after hiring. Many never even apply because of Lincoln's nonunion status.[1]

How would *you* like to work at Lincoln Electric? What underlying philosophy of motivation is Lincoln using? Who would be susceptible to this kind of motivation? These are some of the questions that this chapter will explore.

First, we will define motivation and distinguish it from performance. After this, we will describe several popular theories of work motivation and contrast them. Then we will present a model that links motivation, performance, and job satisfaction. Finally, we will briefly explore a controversy about the compatibility of various forms of motivation.

WHY STUDY MOTIVATION?

Why should you study motivation? Motivation is one of the most traditional topics in organizational behavior, and it has interested managers, researchers, teachers, and sports coaches for years. However, a good case can be made that motivation has become even more important in contemporary organizations. Much of this is a result of the need for increased productivity to be globally competitive (as at Lincoln Electric). It is also a result of the rapid changes that contemporary organizations are undergoing. Stable systems of rules, regulations, and procedures that once guided behavior are being replaced by requirements for flexibility and attention to customers that necessitate higher levels of initiative. This initiative depends on motivation.

What would a good motivation theory look like? In fact, as we shall see, there is no single all-purpose motivation theory. Rather, we will consider several theories that serve somewhat different purposes. In combination, though, a good set of theories should recognize human diversity and consider that the same conditions won't motivate everyone. Also, a good set of theories should be able to explain how it is that some people seem to be self-motivated, while others seem to require external motivation. Finally, a good set of theories should recognize the social aspect of human beings—people's motivation is often affected by how they see others are treated. Before getting to our theories, let's define motivation more precisely.

WHAT IS MOTIVATION?

The term motivation is not easy to define. However, from an organization's perspective, when we speak of a person as being motivated, we usually mean that the person works "hard," "keeps at" his or her work, and directs his or her behavior toward appropriate outcomes.

Basic Characteristics of Motivation

We can formally define **motivation** as the extent to which persistent effort is directed toward a goal.[2]

Motivation. The extent to which persistent effort is directed toward a goal.

Effort.   The first aspect of motivation is the strength of the person's work-related behavior or the amount of *effort* the person exhibits on the job. Clearly, this involves different kinds of activities on different kinds of jobs. A loading dock worker might exhibit greater effort by carrying heavier crates, while a researcher might reveal greater effort by searching out an article in some obscure foreign technical journal. Both are exerting effort in a manner appropriate to their jobs.

Persistence.   The second characteristic of motivation is the *persistence* that individuals exhibit in applying effort to their work tasks. The organization would not be likely to think of the loading dock worker who stacks the heaviest crates for two hours and then goofs off for six hours as especially highly motivated. Similarly, the researcher who makes an important discovery early in her career and then rests on her laurels for five years would not be considered especially highly motivated. In each case, workers have not been persistent in the application of their effort.

Direction.   Effort and persistence refer mainly to the quantity of work an individual produces. Of equal importance is the quality of a person's work. Thus, the third characteristic of motivation is the *direction* of the person's work-related behavior. In other words, do workers channel persistent effort in a direction that benefits the organization? Employers expect motivated stockbrokers to advise their clients of good investment opportunities and motivated software designers to design software, not play computer games. These correct decisions increase the probability that persistent effort is actually translated into accepted organizational outcomes. Thus, motivation means working smart as well as working hard.

Goals.   Ultimately, all motivated behavior has some goal or objective toward which it is directed. We have presented the preceding discussion from an organizational perspective, that is we assume that motivated people act to enhance organizational objectives. In this case, employee goals might include

IN FOCUS Does Downsizing Decrease Motivation?

Corporate downsizing, the elimination of existing jobs, has been ubiquitous since the late 1980s. As a cost-cutting response to recessionary economics and global competition, hundreds of firms have eliminated thousands of jobs. The list includes such prominent companies as IBM, Goodyear, Chevron, Exxon, and Black & Decker. General Motors eliminated almost *half* of its workforce in the U.S. and Canada (61,000 people) during this period. In the public sector, the reduction in the threat of nuclear war has led to substantial cuts in the Department of Defense, and advanced technology has done the same at the Postal Service and at Ontario Hydro.

Does downsizing increase or decrease the motivation of the lucky survivors who avoid the cuts? One theory holds that survivors might be grateful for being spared or fearful of being next on the list. Either of these reasons might provide an incentive for high motivation. On the other hand, much downsizing has occurred among the once-loyal management ranks, people whose disillusionment might prompt decreased motivation. Which view is correct?

Research supports the second theory. Reduced effort and decreased organizational commitment are common among survivors, especially those who were highly committed before the layoffs and viewed the layoff process as unfair. Perceived

unfairness is common because many layoffs are reactive and poorly planned. What employee motivation that remains is often directed toward self-preservation and risk avoidance.

What happens to motivation after downsizing?

Sources: Cascio, W. F. (1993, February). Downsizing: What do we know? What have we learned? *Academy of Management Executive*, 95–104; Adler, T. (1993, August). Layoffs just part of downsizing formula. *APA Monitor*, 23–24; Brockner, J., Tyler, T. R., & Cooper-Schneider, R. (1992). The influence of prior commitment to an institution on reactions to perceived unfairness. The higher they are the harder they fall. *Administrative Science Quarterly, 37*, 241–261.

high productivity, good attendance, or creative decisions. Of course, employees can also be motivated by goals that are contrary to the objectives of the organization, including absenteeism, sabotage, and embezzlement. In these cases, they are channeling their persistent efforts in directions that are dysfunctional for the organization (see the "In Focus: *Does Downsizing Decrease Motivation?*").

Extrinsic and Intrinsic Motivation

Some views hold that people are motivated by factors in the external environment (such as supervision or pay), while others hold that people can in some sense be self-motivated without the application of these external factors. You might have experienced this distinction. As a worker, you might recall tasks that you enthusiastically performed simply for the sake of doing them and others that you performed only to keep your job or placate your boss.

Experts in organizational behavior distinguish between intrinsic and extrinsic motivation. At the outset, we should emphasize that there is only weak consensus concerning the exact definitions of these concepts and even weaker agreement about whether we should label specific motivators as intrinsic or extrinsic.[3] However, the following definitions and examples seem to capture the distinction fairly well.

Intrinsic motivation stems from the direct relationship between the worker and the task and is usually self-applied. Feelings of achievement, accomplishment, challenge, and competence derived from performing one's job are examples of intrinsic motivators, as is sheer interest in the job itself. Off the job, avid participation in sports and hobbies is often intrinsically motivated.

Extrinsic motivation stems from the work environment external to the task and is usually applied by someone other than the person being motivated. Pay, fringe benefits, company policies, and various forms of supervision are examples of extrinsic motivators.

Obviously, employers can't package all conceivable motivators as neatly as these definitions suggest. For example, a promotion or a compliment might be applied by the boss but might also be a clear signal of achievement and competence. Thus, some potential motivators have both extrinsic and intrinsic qualities.

Despite the fact that the distinction between intrinsic and extrinsic motivation is fuzzy, many theories of motivation implicitly make the distinction.

Intrinsic motivation. Motivation that stems from the direct relationship between the worker and the task; it is usually self-applied.

Extrinsic motivation. Motivation that stems from the work environment external to the task; it is usually applied by others.

Motivation and Performance

At this point, you might well be saying, "Wait a minute, I know many people who are 'highly motivated' but just don't seem to perform well. They work long and hard, but they just don't measure up." This is certainly a sensible observation, and it points to the important distinction between motivation and performance. **Performance** can be defined as the extent to which an organizational member contributes to achieving the objectives of the organization.

Some of the factors that contribute to individual performance in organizations are shown in Exhibit 6.1.[4] While motivation clearly contributes to performance, the relationship is not one-to-one because a number of other factors intervene. Thus, it is certainly possible for performance to be low even when a person is highly motivated—low aptitude, weak skills, poor understanding of the task, or chance can damage the performance of the most highly motivated individual. Of course, an opposite effect is also conceivable. An individual with rather marginal motivation might understand the task so well that some compensation occurs—what little effort the individual makes is expended very efficiently in terms of goal accomplishment. Also, a person with weak motivation might perform well because of some luck or chance factor that boosts performance. Thus, it is no wonder that workers sometimes complain that they receive lower performance ratings than colleagues who "don't work as hard."

In this chapter we will concentrate on the motivational components of performance, rather than the other determinants in Exhibit 6.1. However, the moral here should be clear: We can't consider motivation in isolation; high motivation will not result in high performance if employees lack basic aptitudes and skills, don't understand their jobs, or encounter unavoidable obstacles over which they have no control. Contemporary management techniques such as total quality management simply won't *work* if employees are deficient in reading, math, and technical skills.[5]

Performance. The extent to which an organizational member contributes to achieving the objectives of the organization.

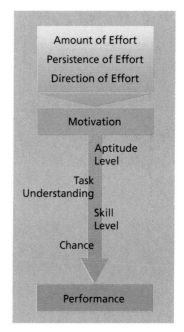

EXHIBIT 6.1
Factors contributing to individual job performance.

NEED THEORIES OF WORK MOTIVATION

Need theories. Motivation theories that specify the kinds of needs people have and the conditions under which they will be motivated to satisfy these needs in a way that contributes to performance.

The first three theories of motivation that we will consider are **need theories.** These theories attempt to specify the kinds of needs people have and the conditions under which they will be motivated to satisfy these needs in a way that contributes to performance. Needs are physiological and psychological wants or desires that individuals can satisfy by acquiring certain incentives or achieving particular goals. It is the behavior stimulated by this acquisition process that reveals the motivational character of needs:

$$\text{NEEDS} \rightarrow \text{BEHAVIOR} \rightarrow \text{INCENTIVES AND GOALS}$$

Notice that need theories are concerned with *what* motivates workers (needs and their associated incentives or goals). They can be contrasted with *process theories,* which are concerned with exactly *how* various factors motivate people. Need and process theories are complementary rather than contradictory. Thus, a need theory might contend that money can be an important motivator (what), and a process theory might explain the actual mechanics by which money motivates (how).[6] In this section we will examine three prominent need theories of motivation.

Maslow's Hierarchy of Needs

Abraham Maslow was a psychologist who, over a number of years, developed and refined a general theory of human motivation.[7] According to Maslow, humans have five sets of needs that are arranged in a hierarchy, beginning with the most basic and compelling needs (see the left side of Exhibit 6.2). These needs include:

1. *Physiological needs.* These include the needs that must be satisfied for the person to survive, such as food, water, oxygen, and shelter. Organizational factors that might satisfy these needs include the minimum pay necessary for survival and working conditions that promote existence.
2. *Safety needs.* These include needs for security, stability, freedom from anxiety, and a structured and ordered environment. Organizational conditions that might meet these needs include safe working conditions, fair and sensible rules and regulations, job security, a comfortable work environment, pension and insurance plans, pay above the minimum needed for survival, and freedom to unionize.
3. *Belongingness needs.* These include needs for social interaction, affection, love, companionship, and friendship. Organizational factors that might meet these needs include the opportunity to interact with others on the job, friendly and supportive supervision, opportunity for teamwork, and opportunity to develop new social relationships.
4. *Esteem needs.* These include needs for feelings of adequacy, competence, independence, strength, and confidence, and the appreciation and recognition of these characteristics by others. Organizational factors that might satisfy these needs include the opportunity to master tasks leading to feelings of achievement and responsibility. Also, awards, promotions, prestigious job titles, professional recognition, and the like might satisfy these needs when they are felt to be truly deserved.

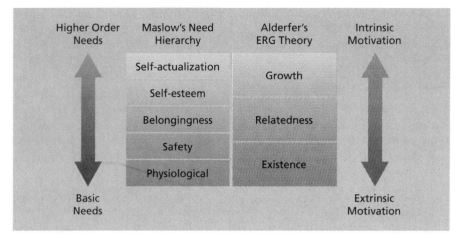

EXHIBIT 6.2
Relationship between Maslow and Alderfer need theories.

5. *Self-actualization needs*. These needs are the most difficult to define. They involve the desire to develop one's true potential as an individual to the fullest extent and to express one's skills, talents, and emotions in a manner that is most personally fulfilling. Maslow suggests that self-actualizing people have clear perceptions of reality, accept themselves and others, and are independent, creative, and appreciative of the world around them. Organizational conditions that might provide self-actualization include absorbing jobs with the potential for creativity and growth as well as a relaxation of structure to permit self-development and personal progression.

Given the fact that individuals may harbor these needs, in what sense do they form the basis of a theory of motivation? That is, what exactly is the motivational premise of **Maslow's hierarchy of needs**? Put simply, the lowest-level unsatisfied need category has the greatest motivating potential. Thus, none of the needs is a "best" motivator; motivation depends upon the person's position in the need hierarchy. According to Maslow, individuals are motivated to satisfy their physiological needs before they reveal an interest in safety needs, and safety must be satisfied before social needs become motivational, and so on. When a need is unsatisfied, it exerts a powerful effect on the individual's thinking and behavior, and this is the sense in which needs are motivational. However, when needs at a particular level of the hierarchy are satisfied, the individual turns his or her attention to the next higher level. Notice the clear implication here that a *satisfied need is no longer an effective motivator*. Once one has adequate physiological resources and feels safe and secure, one doesn't seek more of the factors that met these needs but looks elsewhere for gratification. According to Maslow, the single exception to this rule involves self-actualization needs. He felt that these were "growth" needs that become stronger as they are gratified.

Individuals who are in the lower-level need categories (physiological, safety, and belongingness) seem to be most susceptible to extrinsic motivation, its exact form corresponding to the need that is most pressing. Observe that money and money substitutes (e.g., insurance and pension plans) figure heavily here. However, as individuals progress up the hierarchy, and higher-order

Maslow's hierarchy of needs.
A five-level hierarchical need theory of motivation that specifies that the lowest-level unsatisfied need has the greatest motivating potential.

needs (esteem and self-actualization) become prominent, intrinsic motivation comes into play. Here, employers must design work to encourage people to "motivate themselves."

Alderfer's ERG Theory

ERG theory. A three-level hierarchical need theory of motivation (existence, related-ness, growth) that allows for movement up and down the hierarchy.

Clayton Alderfer developed another need-based theory, called **ERG theory**.[8] It streamlines Maslow's need classifications and makes some different assumptions about the relationship between needs and motivation. The name ERG stems from Alderfer's compression of Maslow's five-category need system into three categories—existence, relatedness, and growth needs:

1. *Existence needs.* These are needs that are satisfied by some material substance or condition. As such, they correspond closely to Maslow's physiological needs and to those safety needs that are satisfied by material conditions rather than interpersonal relations. These include the need for food, shelter, pay, and safe working conditions.
2. *Relatedness needs.* These are needs that are satisfied by open communication and the exchange of thoughts and feelings with other organizational members. They correspond fairly closely to Maslow's belongingness needs and to those esteem needs that involve feedback from others. However, Alderfer stresses that relatedness needs are satisfied by open, accurate, honest interaction rather than by uncritical pleasantness.
3. *Growth needs.* These are needs that are fulfilled by strong personal involvement in the work setting. They involve the full utilization of one's skills and abilities and the creative development of new skills and abilities. Growth needs correspond to Maslow's need for self-actualization and the aspects of his esteem needs that concern achievement and responsibility.

As you can see in Exhibit 6.2, Alderfer's need classification system does not represent a radical departure from that of Maslow. In addition, Alderfer agrees with Maslow that as lower-level needs are satisfied, the desire to have higher-level needs satisfied will increase. Thus, as existence needs are fulfilled, relatedness needs gain motivational power. Alderfer explains this by arguing that as more "concrete" needs are satisfied, energy can be directed toward satisfying less concrete needs. Finally, Alderfer agrees with Maslow that the least concrete needs—growth needs—become *more* compelling and *more* desired as they are fulfilled.

It is, of course, the differences between ERG theory and the need hierarchy that represent Alderfer's contribution to the understanding of motivation. First, unlike the need hierarchy, ERG theory does not assume that a lower-level need *must* be gratified before a less concrete need becomes operative. Thus, ERG theory does not propose a rigid hierarchy of needs, and some individuals, owing to background and experience, might seek relatedness or growth even though their existence needs are ungratified. Hence, ERG theory seems to account for a wide variety of individual differences in motive structure. Second, ERG theory assumes that if the higher-level needs are ungratified, individuals will increase their desire for the gratification of lower-level needs. Notice that this represents a *radical* departure from Maslow. According to Maslow, if esteem needs are strong but ungratified, a person will not revert to an interest in belongingness needs because these have necessarily already been gratified. (Remember, he argues that satisfied needs are not motivational.) According to Alderfer, however, the frustration of higher-order needs will lead workers to regress to a more concrete need category. For example, the software designer who is unable to establish rewarding social relationships with superiors or co-workers might increase his interest in fulfilling existence needs, perhaps by seeking a pay increase. Thus, according to Alderfer, an apparently satisfied need can act as a motivator by substituting for an unsatisfied need.

Given the preceding description of ERG theory, we can identify its two major motivational premises as follows: *The more lower-level needs are gratified, the more higher-level need satisfaction is desired; the less higher-level needs are gratified, the more lower-level need satisfaction is desired.*

ERG theory is particularly interesting in its implications for extrinsic and intrinsic motivation. Obviously, extrinsic motivators are especially likely to satisfy existence and relatedness needs, while intrinsic motivators are especially likely to satisfy growth needs. Notice, however, that Alderfer contends that all three need categories can be operative at the same time. Thus, the opportunity to satisfy growth needs through stimulating and challenging work might prove motivational even though existence needs are not fully gratified. Similarly, extrinsic motivators can sometimes serve as substitutes for intrinsic motivators. For example, the person who is denied a job that provides for the satisfaction of growth needs might respond to an open, trusting, helpful supervisor.

McClelland's Theory of Needs

Psychologist David McClelland has spent several decades studying the human need structure and its implications for motivation. According to **McClelland's theory of needs,** needs reflect relatively stable personality characteristics that one acquires through early life experiences and exposure to selected aspects of one's society. Unlike Maslow and Alderfer, McClelland has not been interested in specifying a hierarchical relationship among needs. Rather, he has been more concerned with the specific behavioral consequences of needs. In other words, under what conditions are certain needs likely to result in particular patterns of motivation? The three needs that McClelland studied most have special relevance for organizational behavior—needs for achievement, affiliation, and power.[9]

Individuals who are high in **need for achievement** (*n* Ach) have a strong desire to perform challenging tasks well. More specifically, they exhibit the following characteristics:

- *A preference for situations in which personal responsibility can be taken for outcomes.* Those high in *n* Ach do not prefer situations in which outcomes are determined by chance, because success in such situations does not provide an experience of achievement.

- *A tendency to set moderately difficult goals that provide for calculated risks.* Success with easy goals will provide little sense of achievement, while extremely difficult goals might never be reached. The calculation of successful risks is stimulating to the high *n* Ach person.

McClelland's theory of needs. A nonhierarchical need theory of motivation that outlines the conditions under which certain needs result in particular patterns of motivation.

Need for achievement. A strong desire to perform challenging tasks well.

- *A desire for performance feedback.* Such feedback permits individuals with high *n* Ach to modify their goal attainment strategies to ensure success and signals them when success has been reached.[10]

People who are high in *n* Ach are concerned with bettering their own performance or that of others. They are often concerned with innovation and long-term goal involvement. However, these things are not done to please others or to damage the interests of others. Rather, they are done because they are *intrinsically* satisfying. Thus, *n* Ach would appear to be an example of a growth or self-actualization need.

Need for affiliation. A strong desire to establish and maintain friendly, compatible interpersonal relationships.

People who are high in **need for affiliation** (*n* Aff) have a strong desire to establish and maintain friendly, compatible interpersonal relationships. In other words, they like to like others, and they want others to like them! More specifically, they have an ability to learn social networks quickly and a tendency to communicate frequently with others, either face-to-face, by telephone, or by letter. Also, they prefer to avoid conflict and competition with others, and they sometimes exhibit strong conformity to the wishes of their friends. The *n* Aff motive is obviously an example of a belongingness or relatedness need.

Need for power. A strong desire to influence others, making a significant impact or impression.

People who are high in **need for power** (*n* Pow) strongly desire to have influence over others (see the cartoon). In other words, they wish to make a significant impact or impression on them. People who are high in *n* Pow seek out social settings in which they can be influential. When in small groups, they act in a "high-profile," attention-getting manner. There is some tendency for those who are high in *n* Pow to advocate risky positions. Also, some people who are high in *n* Pow show a strong concern for personal prestige. The need for power is a complex need because power can be used in a variety of ways, some of which serve the power seeker and some of which serve other people or the organization. However, *n* Pow seems to correspond most closely to Maslow's self-esteem need.

McClelland predicts that people will be motivated to seek out and perform well in jobs that match their needs. Thus, people with high *n* Ach should be strongly motivated by sales jobs or entrepreneurial positions, such as running a small business. Such jobs offer the feedback, personal responsibility, and opportunity to set goals noted above. People who are high in *n* Aff will be motivated by jobs such as social work or customer relations because these jobs have as a primary task establishing good relations with others. Finally, high *n* Pow will result in high motivation on jobs that enable one to have a strong impact on others, jobs such as journalism and management. In fact, McClelland has found that the most effective managers have a low need for affiliation, a high need for power, and the ability to direct power toward organizational goals.[11] (We will study this further in Chapter 13.)

McClelland is careful to point out that there is not a one-to-one correspondence between a person's need structure and his or her behavior. Needs are only one determinant of behavior, and the person's values, habits, and skills, as well as environmental opportunities, are also influential. Thus, a person with high *n* Ach will not always exhibit higher motivation than a person with another need structure. For example, a person with high *n* Aff might perform better than a person with high *n* Ach on a work team in which high performance is the norm and friendship is contingent upon being a good team player. Here, the need achiever's desire to set individual goals and take personal responsibility is constrained by the demands of the task.

"It disturbs me that so many of today's young people go into medicine for the money—in my time, the chance to play God was enough."

Source: Current Contents, 1993, Institute for Scientific Information.

Individuals who seek jobs that offer them feedback, responsibility, and an opportunity to set goals are high in need for achievement. The young adults who founded Ghetto Gear had these motives when they started their own tee shirt business.

Research Support for Need Theories

Measuring peoples' needs and the extent to which they have these needs fulfilled has proven to be a difficult task. Thus, the need theories are not especially easy to test. Nevertheless, we can draw some conclusions about their usefulness.

Maslow's need hierarchy suggests two main hypotheses. First, specific needs should cluster into the five main need categories that Maslow proposes. Second, as the needs in a given category are satisfied, they should become less important, while the needs in the adjacent higher-need category should become more important. This second hypothesis captures the progressive, hierarchical aspect of the theory. In general, research support for both of these hypotheses is weak or negative. This is probably a function of the rigidity of the theory, which suggests that most people experience the same needs in the same hierarchical order. However, in this research, there is fair support for a simpler two-level need hierarchy comprising the needs toward the top and the bottom of Maslow's hierarchy.[12]

This latter finding provides some indirect encouragement for the compressed need hierarchy found in Alderfer's ERG theory. Several tests indicate fairly good support for many of the predictions generated by the theory, including expected changes in need strength. Particularly interesting is confirmation that the frustration of relatedness needs increases the strength of existence needs.[13] The simplicity and flexibility of ERG theory seem to capture the human need structure better than the greater complexity and rigidity of Maslow's theory.

McClelland's need theory has generated a wealth of predictions about many aspects of human motivation. Recently, researchers have tested more and more of these predictions in organizational settings, and the results are generally supportive of the idea that particular needs are motivational when the work setting permits the satisfaction of these needs.[14]

Managerial Implications of Need Theories

The need theories have some important things to say about managerial attempts to motivate employees.

Appreciate Diversity.   The lack of support for the fairly rigid need hierarchy suggests that managers must be adept at evaluating the needs of individual employees and offering incentives or goals that correspond to their own needs. Unfounded stereotypes about the needs of the "typical" employee and naive assumptions about the universality of need satisfaction are bound to reduce the effectiveness of chosen motivational strategies. The best salesperson might not make the best sales manager! The needs of a young recent college graduate probably differ from those of an older employee preparing for retirement.

Appreciate Intrinsic Motivation.   The need theories also serve the valuable function of alerting managers to the existence of higher-order needs (whatever specific label we apply to them). The recognition of these needs in many employees is important for two key reasons. One of the basic conditions for organizational survival is the expression of some creative and innovative behavior on the part of members. Such behavior seems most likely to occur during the pursuit of higher-order need fulfillment, and ignorance of this factor can cause the demotivation of the people who have the most to offer the organization. Second, observation and research evidence support Alderfer's idea that the frustration of higher-order needs prompts demands for greater satisfaction of lower-order needs. This can lead to a vicious motivational circle. That is, because the factors that gratify lower-level needs are fairly easy to administer (e.g., pay and fringe benefits), management has grown to rely on them to motivate employees. In turn, some employees, deprived of higher-order need gratification, come to expect more and more of these extrinsic factors in exchange for their services. Thus, a circle of deprivation, regression, and temporary gratification continues at great cost to the organization.[15]

How can organizations benefit from the intrinsic motivation that is inherent in strong higher-order needs? First, such needs will fail to develop for most employees unless lower-level needs are reasonably well gratified.[16] Thus, very poor pay, job insecurity, and unsafe working conditions will preoccupy most workers at the expense of higher-order outcomes. Second, if basic needs are met, jobs can be "enriched" to be more stimulating and challenging and to provide feelings of responsibility and achievement. We will discuss this process fully in the next chapter. Finally, organizations could pay more attention to designing career paths that enable interested workers to progress through a series of jobs that continue to challenge their higher-order needs. Individual managers could also assign tasks to subordinates with this goal in mind.

PROCESS THEORIES OF WORK MOTIVATION

In contrast to need theories of motivation, which concentrate upon *what* motivates people, **process theories** concentrate upon *how* motivation occurs. In this section we will examine two important process theories–expectancy theory and equity theory.

Process theories. Motivation theories that specify the details of how motivation occurs.

Expectancy Theory

The basic idea underlying **expectancy theory** is the belief that motivation is determined by the outcomes that people expect to occur as a result of their actions on the job. Psychologist Victor Vroom is usually credited with developing the first complete version of expectancy theory and applying it to the work setting.[17] The basic components of Vroom's theory are shown in Exhibit 6.3:

Expectancy theory. A process theory that states that motivation is determined by the outcomes that people expect to occur as a result of their actions on the job.

- **Outcomes** are the consequences that may follow certain work behaviors. First-level outcomes are of particular interest to the organization; for example, high productivity versus average productivity, illustrated in Exhibit 6.3, or good attendance versus poor attendance. Expectancy theory is concerned with specifying how an employee might attempt to choose one first-level outcome instead of another. Second-level outcomes are consequences that follow the attainment of a particular first-level outcome. Contrasted with first-level outcomes, second-level outcomes are most personally relevant to the individual worker and might involve amount of pay, sense of accomplishment, acceptance by peers, fatigue, and so on.

Outcomes. Consequences that follow work behavior.

- **Instrumentality** is the probability that a particular first-level outcome (such as high productivity) will be followed by a particular second-level outcome (such as pay). For example, a bank teller might figure that the odds are 50–50 (instrumentality = .5) that a good performance rating will result in a pay raise.

Instrumentality. The probability that a particular first-level outcome will be followed by a particular second-level outcome.

- **Valence** is the expected value of outcomes, the extent to which they are attractive or unattractive to the individual. Thus, good pay, peer acceptance, the chance of being fired, or any other second-level outcome might be more or less attractive to particular workers. According to Vroom, the valence of first-level outcomes is the sum of products of the associated second-level outcomes and their instrumentalities. That is, *the valence of a particular first-level outcome = $\sum$ instrumentalities $\times$ second-level valences*. In other words, the valence of a first-level outcome depends upon the extent to which it leads to favorable second-level outcomes.

Valence. The expected value of work outcomes; the extent to which they are attractive or unattractive.

- **Expectancy** is the probability that the worker can actually achieve a particular first-level outcome. For example, a machinist might be absolutely certain (expectancy = 1.0) that she can perform at an average level (producing 15 units a day) but less certain (expectancy = .6) that she can perform at a high level (producing 20 units a day).

Expectancy. The probability that a particular first-level outcome can be achieved.

- **Force** is the end product of the other components of the theory. It represents the relative degree of effort that will be directed toward various first-level outcomes. According to Vroom, the force directed

Force. The effort directed toward a first-level outcome.

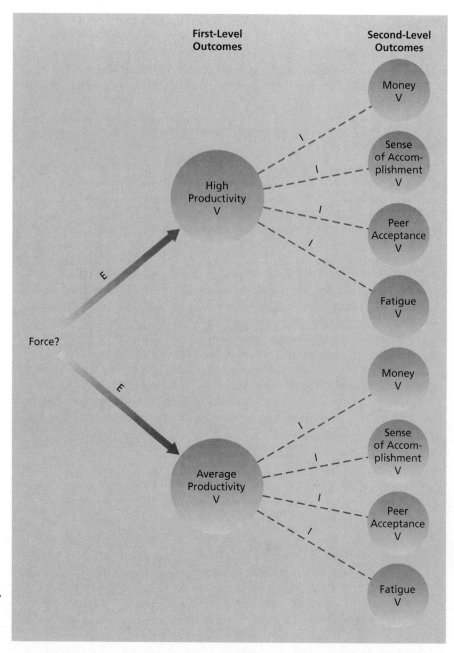

EXHIBIT 6.3
A hypothetical expectancy
model (E = Expectancy,
I = Instrumentality,
V = Valence).

toward a first-level outcome is a product of the valence of that outcome and the expectancy that it can be achieved. Thus, *force = first-level valence × expectancy*. We can expect an individual's effort to be directed toward the first-level outcome that has the largest force product. Notice that no matter how valent a particular first-level outcome might be, a person will not be motivated to achieve it if the expectancy of accomplishment approaches zero.

Believe it or not, the mechanics of expectancy theory can be distilled into a couple of simple sentences! In fact, these sentences nicely capture the premises of the theory: *People will be motivated to perform in those work activities that they find attractive and that they feel they can accomplish. The attractiveness of various work activities depends upon the extent to which they lead to favorable personal consequences.*

It is extremely important to understand that expectancy theory is based on the perceptions of the individual worker. Thus, expectancies, valences, instrumentalities, and relevant second-level outcomes depend upon the perceptual system of the person whose motivation we are analyzing. For example, two employees performing the same job might attach different valences to money, differ in their perceptions of the instrumentality of performance for obtaining high pay, and differ in their expectations of being able to perform at a high level. Therefore, they would likely exhibit different patterns of motivation.

Although expectancy theory does not concern itself directly with the distinction between extrinsic and intrinsic motivators, it can handle any form of second-level outcome that has relevance for the person in question. Thus, some people might find second-level outcomes of an intrinsic nature, such as feeling good about performing a task well, positively valent. Others might find extrinsic outcomes such as high pay positively valent.

To firm up your understanding of expectancy theory, consider Tony Angelas, a middle manager in a firm that operates a chain of retail stores (Exhibit 6.4). Second-level outcomes that are relevant to him include the opportunity to obtain a raise and the chance to receive a promotion. The promotion is more highly valent to Tony than the raise (7 versus 5 on a scale of 10) because the promotion means more money *and* increased prestige. Tony figures that if he can perform at a very high level in the next few months, the odds are six in ten that he will receive a raise. Thus, the instrumentality of high performance for obtaining a raise is .6. Promotions are harder to come by, and Tony figures the odds at .3 if he performs well. The instrumentality of average performance for achieving these favorable second-level outcomes is a good bit lower (.2 for the raise and only .1 for the promotion). Recall that the valence of a first-level outcome is the sum of the products of second-level outcomes and their instrumentalities. Thus, the valence of high performance for Tony is $(5 \times .6) + (7 \times .3) = 5.1$. Similarly, the valence of average performance is $(5 \times .2) + (7 \times .1) = 1.7$. We can conclude that high performance is more valent for Tony than average performance.

Does this mean that Tony will necessarily try to perform at a high level in the next few months? To determine this, we must take into account his expectancy that he can actually achieve the competing first-level outcomes. As shown in Exhibit 6.4, Tony is absolutely certain that he can perform at an average level (expectancy = 1.0) but much less certain (.3) that he can sustain high performance. Force is a product of these expectancies and the valence of their respective first-level outcomes. Thus, the force associated with high performance is $.3 \times 5.1 = 1.53$, while that associated with average performance is $1.0 \times 1.7 = 1.70$. As a result, although high performance is attractive to Tony, he will probably perform at an average level.

With all this complicated figuring, you might be thinking "Look, would Tony really do all this calculation to decide his motivational strategy? Do people actually think this way?" The answer to these questions is probably no. Rather, the argument is that people *implicitly* take expectancy, valence, and instrumentality into account as they go about their daily business of being motivated. If you reflect for a moment on your behavior at work or school,

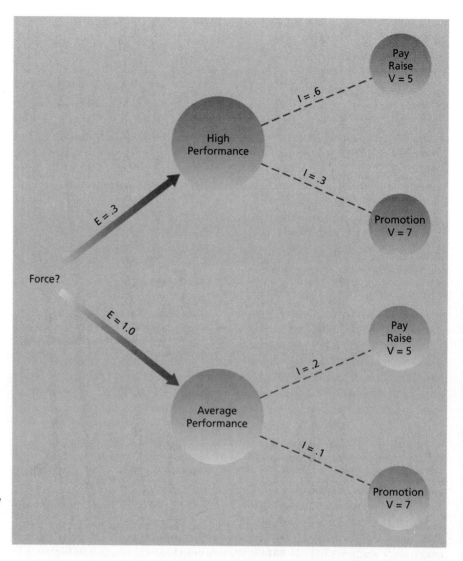

EXHIBIT 6.4
Expectancy model for Tony
Angelas (E = Expectancy,
I = Instrumentality,
V = Valence).

you will realize that you have certain expectancies about what you can accomplish, the chances that these accomplishments will lead to certain other outcomes, and the value of these outcomes for you.

Research Support for Expectancy Theory

Tests have provided moderately favorable support for expectancy theory.[18] In particular, there is especially good evidence that the valence of first-level outcomes depends upon the extent to which they lead to favorable second-level consequences. We must recognize, however, that the sheer complexity of expectancy theory makes it difficult to test. We have already suggested that people are not used to *thinking* in expectancy terminology. Thus, some research studies show that individuals have a difficult time discriminating between instrumentalities and second-level valences. Despite this and other technical problems, experts in motivation generally accept expectancy theory.

Managerial Implications of Expectancy Theory

The motivational practices suggested by expectancy theory involve "juggling the numbers" that individuals attach to expectancies, instrumentalities, and valences.

Boost Expectancies.   One of the most basic things managers can do is ensure that their subordinates *expect* to be able to achieve first-level outcomes that are of interest to the organization. No matter how positively valent high productivity or good attendance might be, the force equation suggests that workers will not pursue these goals if expectancy is low. Low expectancies can take many forms, but a few examples will suffice to make the point.

- Employees might feel that poor equipment, poor tools, or lazy co-workers impede their work progress.
- Employees might not understand what the organization considers to be good performance or see how they can achieve it.
- If performance is evaluated by a subjective supervisory rating, employees might see the process as capricious and arbitrary, not understanding how to obtain a good rating.

Although the specific solutions to these problems vary, expectancies can usually be enhanced by providing proper equipment and training, demonstrating correct work procedures, carefully explaining how performance is evaluated, and listening to employee performance problems. The point of all this is to clarify the path to beneficial first-level outcomes.

Clarify Reward Contingencies.   Managers should also attempt to ensure that the paths between first- and second-level outcomes are clear. Employees should be convinced that first-level outcomes desired by the organization are clearly *instrumental* to obtaining positive second-level outcomes and avoiding negative outcomes. If a manager has a policy of recommending good performers for promotion, she should spell out this policy. Similarly, if managers desire regular attendance, they should clarify the consequences of good and poor attendance. To ensure that instrumentalities are strongly established, they should be clearly stated and then acted upon by the manager. Managers should also attempt to provide stimulating, challenging tasks for workers who appear to be interested in such work. On such tasks, the instrumentality of good performance for feelings of achievement, accomplishment, and competence is almost necessarily high. The ready availability of intrinsic motivation reduces the need for the manager to constantly monitor and clarify instrumentalities.[19]

Appreciate Diverse Needs.   Obviously, it might be difficult for managers to change the valences that subordinates attach to second-level outcomes. Individual preferences for high pay, promotion, interesting work, and so on are the product of a long history of development and unlikely to change rapidly. However, managers would do well to analyze the diverse preferences of particular subordinates and attempt to design individualized "motivational packages" to meet their needs. Of course, all concerned must perceive such packages to be fair. Let's examine another process theory that is concerned specifically with the motivational consequences of fairness.

Equity Theory

Equity theory. A process theory that states that motivation stems from a comparison of the inputs one invests in a job and the outcomes one receives in comparison with the inputs and outcomes of another person or group.

In Chapter 5 we discussed the role of **equity theory** in explaining job satisfaction. To review, the theory asserts that workers compare the inputs that they invest in their jobs and the outcomes that they receive against the inputs and outcomes of some other relevant person or group. When these ratios are equal, the worker should feel that a fair and equitable exchange exists with the employing organization. Such fair exchange contributes to job satisfaction. When the ratios are unequal, workers perceive inequity exists, and they should experience job dissatisfaction, at least if the exchange puts the worker at a disadvantage vis-à-vis others.

But in what sense is equity theory a theory of motivation? Put simply, *individuals are motivated to maintain an equitable exchange relationship.* Inequity is unpleasant and tension producing, and people will devote considerable energy to reducing inequity and achieving equity. What tactics can do this? Psychologist J. Stacey Adams has suggested the following possibilities:

- Perceptually distort one's own inputs or outcomes.
- Perceptually distort the inputs or outcomes of the comparison person or of the group.
- Choose another comparison person or group.
- Alter one's inputs or alter one's outcomes.
- Leave the exchange relationship.[20]

Notice that the first three tactics for reducing inequity are essentially psychological, while the last two involve overt behavior.

To clarify the motivational implications of equity theory, consider Terry, a middle manager in a consumer products company. He has five years' work experience and an M.B.A. degree and considers himself a good performer. His salary is $45,000 a year. Terry finds out that Maxine, a co-worker with whom he identifies closely, makes the same salary he does. However, she has only a Bachelor's degree and one year of experience, and he sees her performance as average rather than good. Thus, from Terry's perspective, the following outcome/input ratios exist:

$$\frac{\text{TERRY } \$45,000}{\text{Good performance, M.B.A., 5 years}} \neq \frac{\text{MAXINE } \$45,000}{\text{Average performance, Bachelors, 1 year}}$$

In Terry's view, he is underpaid and should be experiencing inequity. What might he do to resolve this inequity? Psychologically, he might distort the outcomes that he is receiving, rationalizing that he is due for a certain promotion that will bring his pay into line with his inputs. Behaviorally, he might try to increase his outcomes (by seeking an immediate raise) or reduce his inputs. Input reduction could include a decrease in work effort or perhaps excessive absenteeism. Finally, Terry might resign from the organization to take what he perceives to be a more equitable job somewhere else.

Let's reverse the coin and assume that Maxine views the exchange relationship identically to Terry—same inputs, same outcomes. Notice that she too should be experiencing inequity, this time from relative overpayment. It doesn't take a genius to understand that Maxine would be unlikely to seek equity by marching into the boss's office and demanding a pay cut. However, she might well attempt to increase her inputs by working harder or enrolling in an M.B.A. program. Alternatively, she might distort her view of Terry's performance to make it seem closer to her own. As this example implies, equity theory is somewhat vague about just when individuals will employ various inequity reduction strategies.

Gender and Equity.   As an addendum to the previous example, it is extremely interesting to learn that both women and men have some tendency to choose same-sex comparison persons. That is, when judging the fairness of the outcomes that they receive, men tend to compare themselves with other men, and women tend to compare themselves with other women. This might provide a partial explanation for why women are paid less than men, even for the same job. If women restrict their equity comparisons to (lesser paid) women, they are less likely to be motivated to correct what we observers see as wage inequities.[21]

Research Support for Equity Theory.   Most research on equity theory has been restricted to economic outcomes and has concentrated on the alteration of inputs and outcomes as a means of reducing inequity. In general, this research is very supportive of the theory when inequity occurs because of *underpayment*.[22] For example, when workers are underpaid on an hourly basis, they tend to lower their inputs by producing less work. This brings inputs in line with (low) outcomes. Also, when workers are underpaid on a piecerate basis (e.g., paid $1 for each market research interview conducted), they tend to produce a high volume of low-quality work. This enables them to raise their outcomes to achieve equity. Finally, there is also evidence that underpayment inequity leads to resignation. Presumably, some underpaid workers thus seek equity in another organizational setting.

The theory's predictions regarding *overpayment* inequity have received less support.[23] The theory suggests that such inequity can be reduced behaviorally by increasing inputs or by reducing one's outcomes. The weak support for these strategies suggests either that people tolerate overpayment more than underpayment or that they use perceptual distortion to reduce overpayment inequity.

Managerial Implications of Equity Theory.   The most straightforward implication of equity theory is that perceived underpayment will have a variety of negative motivational consequences for the organization, including low productivity, low quality, theft, and/or turnover. (See the "Ethical Focus: *Inequity and Employee Theft*.") On the other hand, attempting to solve organizational problems through overpayment (disguised bribery) might not have the intended motivational effect. The trick here is to strike an equitable balance.

But how can such a balance be struck? Managers must understand that feelings about equity stem from a *perceptual* social comparison process in which the worker "controls the equation." That is, employees decide what are considered relevant inputs, outcomes, and comparison persons, and management must be sensitive to these decisions. For example, offering the outcome of more interesting work might not redress inequity if pay is considered a more relevant outcome. Similarly, basing pay only on performance might not be perceived as equitable if employees consider seniority an important job input.

ETHICAL FOCUS   Inequity and Employee Theft

In a survey conducted by the London House publishing firm and the Food Marketing Institute, supermarket employees admitted that they stole an average of $168 worth of merchandise a year. This figure was substantially higher than in previous years' surveys. The most popular products were meat, cheese, cigarettes, and beauty and health care items. Some of this theft is probably due to feelings of exploitation by employees. Equity theory predicts that underpayment inequity can be resolved by increasing one's outcomes. Theft could be an informal mechanism for doing this. As one survey respondent noted, "During the last couple of years, the company has kept raising the standards and cutting back on the hours allotted to keeping those standards up. If you don't work *off the clock* the job won't get done. Some people steal as a way to get even."

Psychologist Jerald Greenberg studied employee theft in manufacturing plants before, during, and after the imposition of a temporary 10-week pay cut that was necessitated by a loss of orders. In line with equity theory predictions, he found that theft increased greatly during the rollback and then returned to previous levels once normal pay levels were reinstituted. Greenberg also found that the increase in theft was less pronounced in a plant where management provided an honest and caring explanation for the pay cuts. Perceptions that management was trying to act ethically despite the need for the cuts reduced feelings of inequity.

Sources: London House/Food Marketing Institute (1992). *Third annual report on employee theft in the supermarket industry.* Rosemont, IL: London House; Greenberg, J. (1990). Employee theft as a reaction to underpayment inequity: The hidden cost of pay cuts. *Journal of Applied Psychology, 75,* 561–568.

Understanding the role of comparison people is especially crucial.[24] Even if the best engineer in the design department earns $2,000 more than anyone else in the department, she might still have feelings of inequity if she compares her salary with that of more prosperous colleagues in *other* companies. Similarly, blue-collar workers might experience inequity when they hear about the fantastic salaries companies pay those in exotic locations such as remote mining sites or oil fields. However, they often ignore the inputs that might be mandated to achieve these high outcomes, such as separation from the family or high expenses. Awareness of the comparison people chosen by workers might suggest strategies for reducing felt inequity. Perhaps the company will have to pay even more to retain its star engineer. Perhaps a detailed article in the company newsletter about remote employment will reduce felt inequity for the blue-collar workers.

Having covered the various motivation theories, let's use them to evaluate an actual motivation program. Please consult *You Be the Manager*.

APPLYING MOTIVATION AT LINCOLN ELECTRIC COMPANY

Let's use the material you have been studying to analyze the motivational philosophy at Lincoln Electric. The company tends to emphasize extrinsic rewards, notably money and job security. These rewards are located in the lower reaches of the Maslow and Alderfer hierarchies. The piecerate pay system ties pay directly to productivity. In expectancy theory terms, the instrumentality connection between productivity and pay is perfect. (We will have more to say about this pay system in the next chapter.) On the other hand, the

DOWNSIZING AND DUPONT'S ACHIEVEMENT SHARING PROGRAM

M YOU BE THE anager

Facing stiff domestic and global competition, DuPont's largest division, the fibers division, determined that a radical change in strategy and structure was necessary. They began reducing the work force from 27,000 to 20,000. In turn, as in many contemporary "downsized" organizations, employees were required to learn new skills and to employ these skills in self-directed teams.

Management was especially concerned with developing a new compensation system that would reinforce the team spirit and concentrate employee attention squarely on the business strategy of improved competitiveness. To this end, it developed the Achievement Sharing Program, a program that tied employee pay to the fibers division's profits and losses. A specific goal of four percent growth in profits each year was set. Gradually, through a reduction in regular raises, base pay in the division was to be reduced six percent compared to other DuPont divisions. If the profit goal was achieved, fibers employees would get back the six percent as

> DUPONT'S ACHIEVEMENT SHARING PROGRAM LINKED EMPLOYEES' PAY TO THEIR DIVISION'S PROFITS AND LOSSES.

a bonus. If 80 percent of the goal was achieved, they would get three percent; less than 80 percent would result in no bonus. On the other hand, 150 percent of the goal would result in a 12 percent bonus. A worker who had been earning $30,000 would now earn between $28,200 and $33,600, depending on the fibers division's yearly profit picture.

Use the questions below to frame *your* opinion about the motivational effectiveness of the Achievement Sharing Program.

1. Use expectancy theory to evaluate the strengths and weaknesses of the program.

2. How could equity considerations influence employee receptiveness to the program?

For some commentary on DuPont's program, see *The Manager's Notebook* at the end of the chapter.

Sources: Ost, E. J. (1990, Spring). Team-based pay: New wave strategic incentives. *Sloan Management Review,* 19–27; Hays, L. (1988, December 5). All eyes on DuPont's incentive-pay plan. *The Wall Street Journal,* p. B1; Santora, J. E. (1991, February). DuPont returns to the drawing board. *Personnel Journal,* 34–36.

yearly bonus, based on overall company profits, should motivate organizational citizenship behavior and cooperation among employees. It might also stimulate feelings of relatedness to others and promote morale. The no-layoff policy means that workers are not motivated to limit productivity to protect their jobs. They do not have to worry about producing too much for their own good.

What about equity in a system in which employees can earn such radically different amounts of money depending upon their individual productivity? And what about diversity of needs? Lincoln goes to great trouble to hire and retain high-need achievers who are well suited to its motivational strategy. Because it is considered an attractive place to work and has many job applicants, the firm can be very selective in hiring for its few open positions. Thus, it has been somewhat insulated from changes in the external labor market.

Cultures differ in how they define achievement. In collective societies where group solidarity is dominant, achievement may be more group oriented than in individualistic societies.

DO MOTIVATION THEORIES TRANSLATE ACROSS CULTURES?

Are the motivation theories that we have been considering in this chapter culture-bound? That is, do they apply only to North America, where they were developed? The answer to this question is important for North American organizations that must understand motivational patterns in their international operations. It is also important to foreign managers, who are often exposed to North American theory and practice as part of their training and development.

It is safe to assume that most theories that revolve around human needs will come up against cultural limitations to their generality. For example, both Maslow and Alderfer suggest that people pass through a social stage (belongingness, relatedness) on their way to a higher-level personal growth or self-actualization stage. However, as we discussed in the previous chapter, it is well established that there are international differences in the extent to which societies value a more collective or a more individualistic approach to life.[25] In individualistic societies (e.g., the United States, Canada, Great Britain, Australia), people tend to value individual initiative, privacy, and taking care of oneself. In more collective societies (e.g., Mexico, Singapore, Pakistan), more closely knit social bonds are observed in which members of one's in-group (family, clan, organization) are expected to take care of each other in exchange for strong loyalty to the in-group.[26] This suggests that there might be no superiority to self-actualization as a motive in more collective cultures. In some cases, for example, appealing to employee loyalty might prove more motivational than the opportunity for self-expression because it relates to strong belongingness needs that stem from cultural values. Also, cultures differ in the extent to which they value achievement as it is defined in North America, and conceptions of achievement might be more group-oriented in collective cultures than in individualistic North America. Similarly, the whole concept of intrinsic motivation might be more relevant to wealthy societies than to third-world societies.

Turning to equity theory, we noted that people should be appropriately motivated when outcomes received "match" job inputs. Thus, higher producers are likely to expect superior outcomes compared to lower producers. This is only one way to allocate rewards, however, and it is one that is most likely to be endorsed in individualistic cultures. In collective cultures there is a tendency to favor reward allocation based on equality rather than equity.[27] In other words, everyone should receive the same outcomes despite individual differences in productivity, and group solidarity is a dominant motive. Trying to motivate employees with a "fair" reward system might backfire if your definition of fairness is equity and theirs is equality.

Finally, because of its flexibility, expectancy theory is very effective when applied cross-culturally. The theory allows for the possibility that there may be cross-cultural differences in the expectancy that effort will result in high performance. It also allows for the fact that work outcomes (such as social acceptance versus individual recognition) may have different valences across cultures.[28]

International management expert Nancy Adler has exemplified how cultural blinders often lead to motivational errors:

> International management literature is replete with examples of over-generalization, due to the dominance of American reward structures.

For example, . . . raising the salaries of a particular group of Mexican workers motivated them to work *fewer,* not more, hours. As the Mexicans explained, "We can now make enough money to live and enjoy life [one of their primary values] in less time than previously. Now, we do not have to work so many hours." In another example, an expatriate manager in Japan decided to promote one of his Japanese sales representatives to manager (a status reward). To the surprise of the expatriate boss, the promotion diminished the new Japanese manager's performance. Why? Japanese have a high need for harmony—to fit in with their work colleagues. The promotion, an individualistic reward, separated the new manager from his colleagues, embarrassed him, and therefore diminished his motivation to work.[29]

A primary theme running through this discussion is that appreciating cultural diversity is critical in maximizing motivation.

PUTTING IT ALL TOGETHER: THE PORTER-LAWLER MODEL

In this chapter, we have presented several theories of work motivation and attempted to distinguish between motivation and performance. In Chapter 5 we discussed the relationship between job performance and job satisfaction. At this point, it seems appropriate to review just how all of these concepts fit together. Lyman Porter and Edward Lawler have devised an excellent model to portray these relationships (Exhibit 6.5).[30] Boxes 1 through 3 are simply a restatement of the expectancy theory of motivation. *Value of Reward* (Box 1) refers to the valence of second-level outcomes, while *Perceived Effort → Reward Probability* (Box 2) refers to perceptions of expectancy and instrumentality. Thus, an individual will exert effort on the job to the extent that this effort is expected to be followed by valued rewards.

Boxes 3 through 6 illustrate that high effort will be translated into good performance *if* the worker has traits and abilities relevant to the job and *if* the worker understands his or her role in the organization (especially with regard to what the organization considers good performance). If these conditions are not met, high effort will not result in good performance. For example, consider a hospital nurse who exhibits tremendous effort but lacks compassion, doesn't know how to use a syringe properly, and is confused about the respective responsibilities of nurses, doctors, and attendants. Clearly, such an individual will perform poorly in spite of high effort. It is at the link between effort and performance that observers frequently make judgments about the motivation of workers. Thus, the head nurse might judge the nurse as having "high" but "misdirected" motivation because the nurse is directing persistent effort in a way that doesn't help the hospital achieve its goals. This portion of the Porter-Lawler model is essentially a simplification of the relationships in Exhibit 6.1.

A particular level of performance (Box 6) will be followed by certain outcomes. To the extent that these are positively valent second-level outcomes, they can be considered *rewards* for good performance (Boxes 7A and 7B). In general, the connection between performance and the occurrence of *intrinsic* rewards should be strong and reliable because such rewards are self-administered. For example, the nurse who assists several very sick patients back to

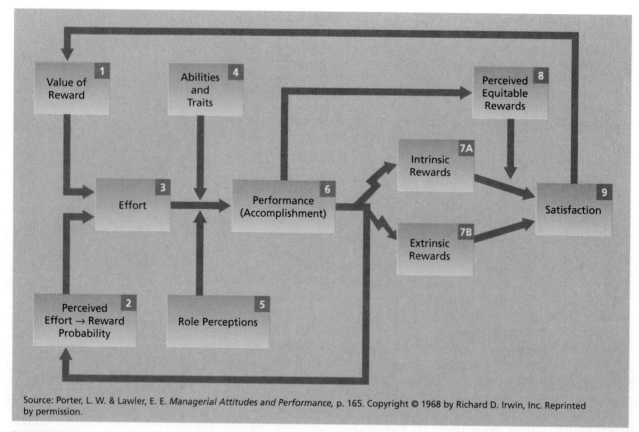

Source: Porter, L. W. & Lawler, E. E. *Managerial Attitudes and Performance*, p. 165. Copyright © 1968 by Richard D. Irwin, Inc. Reprinted by permission.

EXHIBIT 6.5
The Porter-Lawler model.

health is almost certain to feel a sense of competence and achievement because such feelings stem directly from the job. On the other hand, the connection between performance and *extrinsic* rewards might be much less reliable (note the wavy line in Exhibit 6.5) because the occurrence of such rewards depends on the actions of management. Thus, the head nurse might or might not recommend attendance at a nursing conference (an extrinsic fringe benefit) for the good performance.

The availability of intrinsic and extrinsic rewards affects job satisfaction (Box 9) to the extent that these rewards are seen as equitable (Box 8). You will recall that this relationship between job outcomes, equity, and job satisfaction was discussed in Chapter 5. Also recall that in Chapter 5 we emphasized that job satisfaction does not lead to good performance. Conversely, *good performance leads to job satisfaction if that performance is rewarded.*

The feedback loop in the lower portion of the model indicates that the worker's actual experience with the connection between performance and rewards influences *future* expectations of the probability that effort will lead to reward. Thus, the worker whose effort is eventually rewarded uses this information to guide future effort expenditure. The feedback loop in the upper portion of the model suggests that the satisfaction derived from job rewards can influence the valence (anticipated value) of these rewards in the future. Sometimes, satisfaction might decrease the valence of a reward. For example, the person who is highly paid, and thus financially satisfied, might not appreciate overtime pay as much as time off from work. On the other hand, satisfaction might increase the valence of some rewards. For example, Maslow argued that as the self-actualization need is satisfied, it should become more highly valent. Thus, people who experience challenging work may desire even more of it.

A FOOTNOTE: DO EXTRINSIC REWARDS DECREASE INTRINSIC MOTIVATION?

Frequently, when students are asked what kind of job they would like to achieve following graduation, they respond, "Give me an interesting job that pays well." Indeed, this might be the most commonly held stereotype of a good job, and people who desire such a job would probably report that they would be motivated to perform the job especially well. Notice that there is an implicit assumption operating here—intrinsic motivators (in this case, interesting work) and extrinsic motivators (in this case, pay) "add up" to enhance motivation. Thus, from a motivational standpoint, a "Superjob" would be one that is especially high on both intrinsic and extrinsic motivation. Thus far in the chapter, little has been said about the possible relationship between extrinsic and intrinsic motivation.

Some research studies have reached the conclusion that the availability of extrinsic motivators can reduce the intrinsic motivation stemming from the task itself.[31] At first, this might seem counterintuitive to you. However, many parents have observed that linking a monetary allowance to the completion of household chores leads their children to denigrate work that they once enthusiastically performed. Similarly, many professors have noticed that a strong emphasis on grades seems to reduce students' motivation to engage in learning for its own sake. The notion here, then, is that when extrinsic rewards depend upon performance, the valence of intrinsic rewards decreases. Proponents of this view have suggested that making extrinsic rewards contingent upon performance makes individuals feel less competent and less in control of their own behavior.[32] That is, they come to believe that their performance is controlled by the environment and that they perform well only because of the money. Thus, intrinsic motivation suffers.

Research tests of the effects of extrinsic rewards on intrinsic motivation have produced mixed results—sometimes intrinsic motivation is reduced, and sometimes it is not. Many of these tests have used students as subjects, and many have relied on rather artificial short-term tasks. Intrinsic motivation is likely to suffer under these highly restrictive conditions. However, in realistic settings in which individuals see extrinsic rewards as symbols of success and as signals of what to do to achieve future rewards, they increase their task performance.[33] Thus, it is safe to assume that both kinds of rewards are compatible in enhancing motivation in actual work settings.

This contrast between intrinsic and extrinsic motivation brings us to the topic of the next chapter—practical methods of motivation that apply the theories we have been studying in this chapter.

The Manager's Notebook   Downsizing and DuPont's Achievement Sharing Program

DuPont's Achievement Sharing Program was unusual in that it built a real element of risk into pay—employees could effectively *lose* money as well as *gain* it. The program was discontinued after two years in the face of two problems: Individual employees wanted to choose the amount of their pay that was put at risk (note how our need theories would explain this). Because of a provision of Securities Act of 1933, such variable compensation would have required the company to disclose detailed competitive financial information about the fibers division. Also, the company was not anywhere near achieving its profit goal for the second year.

Let's put the Achievement Sharing Program through a motivation theory audit:

1. In expectancy theory terms, the four percent division profit growth was a first-level outcome, and the bonus was a second-level outcome. The bonus was clearly large enough to get employees' attention (up to 12 percent of base pay), and it should thus have been highly valent. Also, the instrumen-

tality connection between profit and the bonus was clear and obvious, being spelled out by a formula. Potential problems centered on the *expectancy* that employees would be able to achieve the earnings goal. Outstanding management support would be necessary, as would true teamwork. Also, factors beyond the employees' control could adversely affect profit growth and thus damage expectancy. A weak economy did just that.

2. A couple of potential equity problems could have led to reduced motivation, and they center on comparison people. First, employees in the fibers division might have felt inequity in comparison to other DuPont employees. After all, they would have to contribute more inputs just to get back to par with the six percent base pay disadvantage. Also, feelings of inequity could have cropped up within the fibers division if some individuals or units felt that others had performed poorly and were threatening the bonus. Some conflict about this was reported.

EXECUTIVE SUMMARY

◆ Motivation is the extent to which persistent effort is directed toward a goal. Intrinsic motivation stems from the direct relationship between the worker and the task and is usually self-applied. Extrinsic motivation stems from the environment surrounding the task and is applied by others. Performance is the extent to which an organization member contributes to achieving the objectives of the organization. It is influenced by motivation but also by aptitudes, skills, task understanding, and chance factors.

◆ Need theories propose that motivation will occur when employee behavior can be directed toward goals or incentives that satisfy personal wants or desires. The three need theories discussed were Maslow's need hierarchy, Alderfer's ERG theory, and McClelland's theory of needs for achievement, affiliation, and power. Maslow and Alderfer have concentrated on the hierarchical arrangement of needs and the distinction between intrinsic and extrinsic

motivation. McClelland has focused on the conditions under which particular need patterns stimulate high motivation.

◆ Process theories attempt to explain how motivation occurs rather than what specific factors are motivational. Expectancy theory argues that people will be motivated to engage in work activities that they find attractive and that they feel they can accomplish. The attractiveness of these activities depends upon the extent to which they lead to favorable personal consequences. Equity theory states that workers compare the inputs that they apply to their jobs and the outcomes that they achieve from their jobs with the inputs and outcomes of others. When these outcome/input ratios are unequal, inequity exists, and workers will be motivated to restore equity. The Porter-Lawler model summarizes the relationships among the process theory variables and performance, rewards, and job satisfaction.

KEY CONCEPTS

Motivation
Intrinsic motivation
Extrinsic motivation
Performance
Need theories
Maslow's hierarchy of needs
ERG theory
McClelland's theory of needs
Need for achievement
Need for affiliation

Need for power
Process theories
Expectancy theory
Outcomes
Instrumentality
Valence
Expectancy
Force
Equity theory

DISCUSSION QUESTIONS

1. Many millionaires continue to work long, hard hours, sometimes even beyond the usual age of retirement. Use the ideas developed in the chapter to speculate about the reasons for this motivational pattern. Is the acquisition of wealth still a motivator for these individuals?

2. Discuss a time when you were highly motivated to perform well (at work, at school, in a sports contest) but performed poorly in spite of your high motivation. How do you know that your motivation was really high? What factors interfered with good performance? What did you learn from this experience?

3. Use Maslow's hierarchy of needs and Alderfer's ERG theory to explain why assembly line workers and executive vice-presidents might be susceptible to different forms of motivation.

4. Do you feel that unions are more concerned with obtaining extrinsic rewards or intrinsic rewards for their members? What does ERG theory say about this?

5. Describe in detail a specific job in which a person with high need for affiliation would be more motivated and perform better than a person with high need for achievement.

6. Colleen is high in need for achievement, Eugene is high in need for power, and Max is high in need

for affiliation. They are thinking about starting a business partnership. To maximize the motivation of each, what business should they go into, and who should assume which roles or jobs?

7. Reconsider the case of Tony Angelas, which was used to illustrate expectancy theory. Imagine that you are Tony's boss and you think that he can be motivated to perform at a high level. Suppose you cannot modify second-level outcomes or their valences, but you can affect expectancies and instrumentalities. What would you do to motivate Tony? Prove that you have succeeded by recalculating the force equations to demonstrate that Tony will now perform at a high level.

8. Feelings of inequity at work can obviously make people unhappy. But how can feelings of inequity act as a motivator?

9. More and more people are doing freelance contract work from their homes rather than being employed "permanently" by an organization. Speculate about the motivational dynamics of this.

10. Critique the following assertion: People are basically the same. Thus, the motivation theories discussed in the chapter apply equally around the globe.

EXPERIENTIAL EXERCISE
ATTITUDES TOWARD ACHIEVEMENT

The purpose of this exercise is to measure your attitudes toward the achievement of others. Using the following scale, place the number that best expresses your opinion in front of each of the twenty questions.

7 = I agree very much   3 = I disagree a little
6 = I agree on the whole   2 = I disagree on the whole
5 = I agree a little   1 = I disagree very much

1. _____ People who are very successful deserve all the rewards they get for their achievements.

2. _____ It's good to see very successful people fail occasionally

3. _____ Very successful people often get too big for their boots.

4. _____ People who are very successful in what they do are usually friendly and helpful to others.

5. _____ At school it's probably better for students to be near the middle of the class than the very top student.

6. _____ People shouldn't criticize or knock the very successful.

7. _____ Very successful people who fall from the top usually deserve their fall from grace.

8. _____ Those who are very successful ought to come down off their pedestals and be like other people.

9. _____ The very successful person should receive public recognition for his/her accomplishments.

10. _____ People who are "tall poppies" (very successful) should be cut down to size.

11. _____ One should always respect the person at the top.

12. _____ One ought to be sympathetic to very successful people when they experience failure and fall from their very high positions.

13. _____ Very successful people sometimes need to be brought back a peg or two, even if they have done nothing wrong.

14. _____ Society needs a lot of very high achievers.

15. _____ People who always do a lot better than others need to learn what it's like to fail.

16. _____ People who are right at the top usually deserve their high position.

17. _____ It's very important for society to support and encourage people who are very successful.

18. _____ People who are very successful get too full of their own importance.

19. _____ Very successful people usually succeed at the expense of other people.

20. _____ Very successful people who are at the top of their field are usually fun to be with.

SCORING AND INTERPRETATION

This questionnaire is called the Tall Poppy Scale. Professor Norman T. Feather of Flinders University in Australia developed it to measure attitudes toward the success and achievement of others. The term "tall poppy" is commonly used in Australia to describe a person who is conspicuously successful. Although Australians value achievement as much as North Americans, they are very ambivalent about its public expression, and they are known to take delight in seeing tall poppies cut down to size and lose status.

To score your Tall Poppy Scale, add your responses to the following ten items: 2, 3, 5, 7, 8, 10, 13, 15, 18, 19. The higher your score (which should range between 10 and 70), the more you favor seeing a tall poppy fall. Now add your responses to the remaining ten items. The higher your score (again, the range is 10 to 70), the more you favor the reward of tall poppies for their success. In a sample of Australian adults, the average fall score was 38, and the average reward score was 45. Speaking generally, those who were more favorably disposed toward tall poppies valued achievement more highly, had higher self-esteem, were more politically conservative, and held higher-status jobs.

Source: Tall Poppy Scale from Feather, N. T. (1989). Attitudes toward the high achiever: The fall of the tall poppy. *Australian Journal of Psychology, 41*, 239–267. Reprinted by permission of the author.

CASE STUDY
CHEMPLUS INC. (A)

Chemplus Inc. was a Canadian firm that provided sophisticated instrumentation and applications engineering assistance to research laboratories, chiefly in analytical chemistry and biology. The company, with annual sales of about $12 million in 1990, had its head office in Montreal and branch offices in Halifax, Ottawa-Hull, Toronto, Winnipeg, Edmonton, and Vancouver.

AN OVERVIEW OF CHEMPLUS

The head office took care of promotion, sales fulfilment, general administrative functions, and Montreal-region sales. The president, a sales force of two sales engineers, a repair department with a service manager and two technicians, and an administrative and warehouse staff of seven were located in a 600 square metre facility in a suburban industrial area. Except in Halifax, each branch office had two sales engineers (one of whom served as regional manager) and a secretarial staff of one. Toronto and Vancouver offices also had small repair departments, each staffed by one technician. The President, Harry Barlow, spent more than one-half of his time in direct sales activities with certain key accounts, which he alone served, and in supervising the two Montreal-based sales engineers.

The instrumentation that Chemplus sold was, for the most part, imported from foreign suppliers with which the firm had exclusive distribution arrangements for Canada. Most of the time, the equipment was simply shipped to the customer and set up in a researcher's laboratory by the responsible sales engineer. Occasionally, the technicians in the Montreal office would preassemble various pieces of equipment and perhaps add some part that they had fabricated in order to meet the customer's needs for instrumentation that was not available "off the shelf."

Virtually all the sales engineering staff had an educational background in science—usually in chemistry, physics, or in engineering itself. It was Harry Barlow's opinion that sales training could be learned, but that the technical education required to sell effectively in their market had to be of a level that would enable the sales engineer to converse intelligently with researchers about their work. In fact, two of the 13 sales engineers actually had doctorates. Service technicians, on the other hand were usually selected purely on their ability to repair diverse types of electronic equipment, and they had mixed formal qualifications—from a university degree to only completing high school and being self-taught beyond that. Although technicians and sales engineers were "laterally" related with no formal reporting relationship from one to the other, the sales engineers enjoyed greater respect, better compensation, and more pleasant working conditions.

When Harry Barlow began Chemplus in 1973, he had just left a laboratory where he had been a junior researcher. He began his entrepreneurial life as a sales engineer and hired the services of repair people as needed. He fondly remembered his days of traveling across Canada by car while his wife back in Montreal provided all the administrative support. Since the couple owned all the shares, profits had an immediate impact on their material well-being. Harry sometimes forgot that the incentive for his employees was not as strong. He paid salaries that were just within the top third of the industry and was reluctant to pay much higher, regardless of performance. Commission or bonuses for good sales performance was being talked about but was not yet implemented. Often, he was annoyed when he called a branch office at six P.M. and found that everyone had already left. He routinely put in 12-hour days and six and one-half-day weeks. If he had a philosophy of success, it was that hard work could make up for any minor lack of ability and work would always pay off. The existence of three other firms in Canada with similar product lines all competing for the same market strengthened his belief in these contentions. Although a pleasant person in personal relationships, it was often difficult to get him off the topic of business; and about business, he was always serious.

THE OTTAWA-HULL OFFICE

Located in Hull, because Harry Barlow thought that the rents would be cheaper there, this office was managed by Marie Benoit. She had a master's degree in Analytical Chemistry and had previously served as a sales engineer in the Montreal head office for two and one-half years. There, she had impressed the president with her dedication and very satisfactory sales levels. When a resignation opened up the regional manager's job in Ottawa-Hull, she was an easy choice. Her appointment raised eyebrows and some resentment among more experienced staff in other offices who would have liked the promotion. She was the first woman hired for a sales engineering position, and it was clear that some of her peers felt that just being hired in the first place was "good for a woman."

While Marie herself had no doubts about deserving the promotion, she did wonder about her ability to manage an office, even though the staff complement was only one other sales engineer and a secretary. It was just that she had no managerial experience or training. She voiced these fears to her friends who reassured her, but not within the company where it might comfort those who envied her.

THE ALEX CLINTON SITUATION

Only days after her arrival in the Ottawa area, she was confronted by the resignation of the other sales engineer in the office, Carl St. Pierre, whom she was to supervise. He stated, as reasons for leaving, an excellent offer from a competitor and the prospect of working in their Vancouver office. In order to discuss the situation and the plans for hiring a replacement, she drove down to Montreal on a Saturday morning to meet with the president. On her arrival, she found out that he thought he had already solved the problem.

"This may surprise you, Marie, but I'm sending you Alex Clinton."

"For the sales job? He's a technician. I mean he is a great technician—probably our best. But a sales engineer . . . ?"

"Well frankly, Marie, he's been bugging me for about 6 months now. He wants to get into sales. I'm afraid if I don't try him this time, he'll leave. And with his abilities, I know the competition would love to get their hands on him."

"Gee, I don't know, Harry," she said, "He's not even really fluent in French."

"I've already thought of that, you can give him only English speaking accounts. Anyway, in your territory there's many more of them. Look, its just something that we have to try. I'm only sorry that, with Carl quitting, there's no time to give him any sales training here at head office. You'll have to give him guidance on that. I know you can do it," Harry said, flashing a smile.

"Okay, I guess I'll have to make the best of it. But I'm going to be honest with you. I don't think it's a good idea. Alex is not really suitable. I've been with him on repair visits. The customers just love him because he can fix anything, and he just laps up the praise. It's not the same in sales. You've got to be tactful and empathetic. And you don't always get such a great reception when you arrive at the customer's office."

"Work on it with him, Marie. If anyone can turn him into a sales engineer, you can. By the way, he's arriving in ten days."

Marie drove back to Ottawa in a sombre mood. She understood Alex Clinton's desire to get out of the service shop. The service manager was a strict and humourless individual who felt superior to those he supervised because he had a university degree. Among repair personnel, only the technician in Vancouver shared that qualification. Alex himself actually had little formal postsecondary education, but had easily taught himself the repair of mechanical and electronic equipment. He had the reputation of being able to fix anything, an attribute that did not endear him to the service manager who preferred to take credit personally. And although repair competence did endear him to the sales staff, it would never earn him equal status.

Marie was also somewhat discomfited by the prospect of a supervisory relationship with someone who had kept calling her "dear" and had often winked at her conspiratorially when she had worked in Montreal. Well, she thought to herself, that would be the first thing to get squared away between them.

As it happened, that issue never arose. Alex was obviously as surprised as Marie had been that he had actually succeeded in getting the position. During the first two weeks, when Marie introduced him around to the customers and during their discussions in the office, he was the model of attentiveness and obviously had a serious intention not to blow this opportunity. Marie was almost beginning to feel relieved. It was during the third week that misgivings began to surface once more. It was Marie's plan to now let Alex do the sales presentations. She would observe and go over his performance with him later. Alex was obviously ill at ease in that role. In the past, customers had always been delighted to see him, because he was there to repair some equipment that they badly needed. Now they appeared impatient as he haltingly went through a sales presentation for products that they had no present intention to purchase. It seemed to Alex, that the customers were looking down upon him. Often, he would turn to Marie with a look of mild panic, and she would be forced to take over from him. Marie asked Alex in the office about these incidents. Away from the sales situation,

however, he seemed more poised and confident. He would quickly brush aside her comments and questions with a statement that suggested that Marie's impressions were totally wrong. She decided to inform Harry Barlow of this problem by telephone.

"Harry, I'm worried about Alex. He's not doing well talking to customers. He's stumbling over his words, and I keep having to help him out. He doesn't know how to get the customer interested. I try to give him some pointers, and he does okay in the office. But when we get out there, he seems like a different person."

"How long has he been with you now, Marie, a few weeks? You know, you've been doing this for a few years and its a lot easier for you. He's probably nervous about you being there watching him. Maybe its time to let him out on his own a bit. I'd like to come down and help, but I'm not sure I could do anything that you're not doing. Anyway, Mike (the Halifax Sales Engineer) is in the hospital for a couple weeks and I've got to get down there and fill in for him. The best advice you can give Alex is to work hard at it. He's sure to improve. I gather he's bought a house now in Kanata (a suburb of Ottawa). If he doesn't work out in your office, we'll definitely lose him. And with what he knows about the technical problems with some of our products. . . I don't want to think about the consequences. Give him some room to breathe, Marie. Take some of your lower priority accounts and work up a week's schedule for him. He'll solve his problem."

"I don't think he believes that he's got a problem, Harry. But I'll try what you suggested."

After a week of letting Alex go out on his own, it seemed that Harry Barlow's suggestion might be succeeding. Every evening, Marie discussed the day's sales activities with Alex and then went over his sales reports of visits with prospective customers. The initial discussions provided Marie with little useful information, but by the end of the week, the reports were showing that Alex was getting into more substantive product discussions. She decided to try another two weeks and gratefully began to concentrate more on her own sales responsibilities. During the second week, the reports continued to show evidence of improved sales presentations, and by the third week, definite expressions of interest in purchasing instrumentation began to appear. Alex's demeanor around the office seemed almost overly cheerful, but he still avoided any detailed discussion of his activities. Marie felt that it might take more time to develop a rapport between them and decided to let him plan the next couple of weeks for her approval.

At this time, a quarterly sales forecast was due and it was Marie's responsibility to submit it out for her region. Alex was asked to provide an estimate for the customers he had visited so far, which he completed. Due to his inexperience, however, Marie felt that she should corroborate his data by checking with some of his key customers for whom he reported good sales prospects. As she knew most of them herself, she began to make some phone calls. The first few, from sales reports dating back to the second week that Alex was on his own, drew a puzzled response. The prospective purchasers seemed not to recall expressing any purchasing intentions. A few indicated that Alex had only been in to see them very briefly in order to drop off some sales literature. The next group of customers she called was from the next week of his sales reports and Marie received much more startling responses to her inquiries. Alex had not been in to see them at all!

Source: Case prepared by Randy Hoffman. From Hoffman, R., & Ruemper, F. (1991). *Organizational behaviour: Canadian cases and exercises*. North York, Ontario: Captus Press.

1. Alex Clinton obviously chose to move from a job in which he was a good performer to one in which he is a poor performer. Use equity theory to explain his motives to seek out the sales job.
2. Speculate about Alex's need structure. Does the sales job suit this need structure?
3. Use expectancy theory to analyze Alex's motivational problem. Is there any case evidence that such problems are typical at Chemplus?
4. How do you account for Harry Barlow's failure to anticipate Alex's problem?
5. What should Marie Benoit do now?
6. What should Alex Clinton do now?
7. What does this case say about the distinction between motivation and performance?

LEARNING OBJECTIVES

AFTER READING CHAPTER 7 YOU SHOULD BE ABLE TO:

1 DISCUSS HOW TO TIE PAY TO PERFORMANCE ON PRODUCTION JOBS AND THE DIFFICULTIES OF WAGE INCENTIVE PLANS.

2 EXPLAIN HOW TO TIE PAY TO PERFORMANCE ON WHITE-COLLAR JOBS AND THE DIFFICULTIES OF MERIT PAY PLANS.

3 UNDERSTAND HOW TO USE PAY TO MOTIVATE TEAMWORK.

4 DESCRIBE THE DETAILS OF THE JOB CHARACTERISTIC MODEL.

5 DISCUSS THE MOTIVATIONAL PROPERTIES OF JOB ENRICHMENT.

6 UNDERSTAND THE CONNECTION BETWEEN GOAL SETTING AND MANAGEMENT BY OBJECTIVES.

7 EXPLAIN HOW ALTERNATIVE WORK SCHEDULES RESPECT EMPLOYEE DIVERSITY.

8 REVIEW THE MOTIVATIONAL ASPECTS OF TOTAL QUALITY MANAGEMENT.

AT QUAD/GRAPHICS, EMPLOYEES FEEL AND ACT LIKE OWNERS.

CHAPTER 7

MOTIVATION IN PRACTICE

QUAD/
GRAPHICS

Quad/Graphics is one of the largest magazine printers in the country. The company prints more than 100 magazines and catalogues, including Newsweek *and* Harper's. *Its president, Harry Quadracci, founded the company in 1972 with 10 others and a 20,000-square-foot plant with one press in Pewaukee, Wisconsin. It now boasts more than 3,700 employees, more than a million square feet in floor space, and operations in Wisconsin and on the East Coast. The company has maintained a compound sales growth rate of 30–40 percent a year, though the industry average is less than 10 percent. Quad/Graphics makes its own ink and has a self-supporting trucking fleet.*

Quad/Graphics' employees own 37 percent of the company through the Employee Stock Ownership Plan. But this is only the beginning of Quad/Graphics' efforts to make employees feel and act like owners. New workers have a mentor to school them in company culture. Performance is the key to success, they are told, and success is defined in terms of both job performance and personal satisfaction.

Each spring, Quadracci puts his managerial philosophy, his employees, and his company to the test. During the "Spring Fling," all managers take one day off for a special management retreat, leaving the company in the hands of the rank and file. Anything could go wrong, from a misplaced advertisement to a miscalculated ink hue on millions of magazine covers. The risk is worth it. "Responsibility should be shared," Quadracci says. "Our people shouldn't need me or anyone else to tell them what to do." This is "Theory Q"—management by walking away. Theory Q trains employees to be owners of the company.

Theory Q also trains managers to manage. Quadracci believes that the managerial function at any level is to coordinate, not control. Since Quadracci feels that "managers should be virtually indistinguishable from those they manage," Quad/Graphics has only three reporting levels.

The workweek at Quad/Graphics is short: just 36 hours in three days. Two shifts keep the presses going 24 hours a day. Institution of the three-day workweek increased productivity 20 percent and saved tremendous amounts in overtime pay.

These and other innovative management practices have earned Quad/Graphics numerous awards, including a spot in *The 100 Best Companies to Work for in America*. For Quad/Graphics' employee-partners, working at the company is its own reward, both financially and personally.[1]

Notice the motivational strategies that Quad/Graphics employs—an economic incentive through stock ownership, job design that provides considerable independence, and a very unusual work schedule. In this chapter we will discuss four motivational techniques—money, job enrichment, goal setting, and alternative working schedules. In each case, we will consider the practical problems that are involved in implementation. The chapter will conclude with a discussion of the role of motivation in total quality management.

MONEY AS A MOTIVATOR

The money that employees receive in exchange for organizational membership is in reality a package made up of pay and various fringe benefits that have dollar values, such as insurance plans, sick leave, and vacation time. Here, we shall be concerned with the motivational characteristics of pay itself.

According to Maslow and Alderfer, pay should prove especially motivational to people who have strong lower-level needs. For these people, pay can be exchanged for food, shelter, and other necessities of life. However, suppose you receive a healthy pay raise. Doubtless, this raise will enable you to purchase food and shelter, but it might also demonstrate that your boss cares about you, give you prestige among friends and family, and signal your competence as a worker. Thus, using need hierarchy terminology, pay can also function to satisfy social, esteem, and self-actualization needs. If pay has this capacity to fulfill a variety of needs, then it should have especially good potential as a motivator. How can this potential be realized? Expectancy theory provides the clearest answer to this question. According to expectancy theory, if pay can satisfy a variety of needs, it should be highly valent, and it should be a good motivator to the extent that *it is clearly tied to performance.*

Linking Pay to Performance on Production Jobs

The prototype of all schemes to link pay to performance on production jobs is piecerate. In its pure form, **piecerate** is set up so that individual workers are paid a certain sum of money for each unit of production they complete. For example, sewing machine operators might be paid two dollars for each dress stitched together, or punch press operators might be paid a few cents for each piece of metal fabricated. More common than pure piecerate is a system whereby workers are paid a basic hourly wage and paid a piecerate differential on top of this hourly wage. For example, a forge operator might be paid eight dollars an hour plus thirty cents for each unit he produces. In some cases, of course, it is very difficult to measure the productivity of an individual worker because of the nature of the production process. Under these circumstances, group incentives are sometimes employed. For example, workers in a steel mill might be paid an hourly wage and a monthly bonus for each ton of steel produced over some minimum quota. These various schemes to link pay to performance on production jobs are called **wage incentive plans**.

Compared with straight hourly pay, the introduction of wage incentives usually leads to substantial increases in productivity.[2] One review reports a median productivity improvement of 30 percent following the installation of piecerate pay, an increase not matched by goal setting or job enrichment.[3] Also, a study of 400 manufacturing companies found that those with wage incentive plans achieved 43 to 64 percent greater productivity than those

Piecerate. A pay system in which individual workers are paid a certain sum of money for each unit of production completed.

Wage incentive plans. Various systems that link pay to performance on production jobs.

Steelcase, Inc. uses wage incentives to motivate production employees.

without such plans.[4] Successful firms that make extensive use of wage incentives include Cleveland's Lincoln Electric Company (profiled in Chapter 6), Steelcase, the Michigan manufacturer of office furniture, and Nucor, a steel producer. In fact, however, not as many organizations use wage incentives as we might expect. What accounts for this relatively low utilization of a motivational system that has proven results?[5]

Potential Problems with Wage Incentives

Despite their theoretical and practical attractiveness, wage incentives have some potential problems when they are not managed with care.

Lowered Quality.   It is sometimes argued that wage incentives can increase productivity at the expense of quality. While this may be true in some cases, it does not require particular ingenuity to devise a system to monitor and maintain quality in manufacturing. However, the quality issue can be a problem when employers use incentives to motivate faster "people processing," such as conducting consumer interviews on the street or in stores. Here, quality control is more difficult.

Differential Opportunity.   A threat to the establishment of wage incentives exists when workers have differential opportunities to produce at a high level. If the supply of raw materials or the quality of production equipment varies from workplace to workplace, some workers will be at an unfair disadvantage under an incentive system. In expectancy theory terminology, workers will differ in the expectancy that they can produce at a high level.

Reduced Cooperation.   Wage incentives that reward individual productivity might decrease cooperation among workers. For example, to maintain a high wage rate, machinists might hoard raw materials or refuse to engage in peripheral tasks such as keeping the shop clean or unloading supplies. Consider what happened when Solar Press, an Illinois printing and packaging company, installed a team wage incentive.

> It wasn't long before both managers and employees began to spot problems. Because of the pressure to produce, teams didn't perform regular maintenance on the equipment, so machines broke down more often than before. When people found better or faster ways to do things, some hoarded them from fellow employees for fear of reducing the amount of their own payments. Others grumbled that work assignments weren't fairly distributed, that some jobs demanded more work than others. They did, but the system didn't take this into account.[6]

Incompatible Job Design.   In some cases, the way jobs are designed can make it very difficult to install wage incentives. On an assembly line, it is almost impossible to identify and reward individual contributions to productivity. As pointed out above, wage incentive systems can be designed to reward team productivity in such a circumstance. However, as the size of the team *increases,* the relationship between any individual's productivity and his or her pay *decreases.* For example, the impact of your productivity in a team of two is much greater than the impact of this productivity in a team of ten—as team size increases, the linkage between your performance and your pay is erased, removing the intended incentive effect.

Restriction of Productivity. A chief psychological impediment to the use of wage incentives is the tendency for workers to restrict productivity. This restriction is illustrated graphically in Exhibit 7.1. Under normal circumstances, without wage incentives, we can often expect productivity to be distributed in a "bell-shaped" manner—a few workers are especially low producers, a few are especially high producers, and most produce in the middle range. When wage incentives are introduced, however, workers sometimes come to an informal agreement about what constitutes a fair day's work and artificially limit their output accordingly. In many cases, this **restriction of productivity** can decrease the expected benefits of the incentive system, as in Exhibit 7.1.

Why does restriction often occur under wage incentive systems? Sometimes, it happens because workers feel that increased productivity due to the incentive will lead to reductions in the work force. More frequently, however, employees fear that if they produce at an especially high level, an employer will reduce the rate of payment to cut labor costs. In the early days of industrialization, when unions were nonexistent or weak, this happened. Engineers studied workers under normal circumstances, and management would set a payment rate for each unit of productivity. When management introduced the incentive system, workers employed legitimate shortcuts that they had learned on the job to produce at a higher rate than expected. In response to this, management simply changed the rate to require more output for a given amount of pay! Stories of such rate-cutting are often passed down from one generation of workers to another in support of restricting output under incentive systems. As you might expect, restriction seems less likely when a climate of trust and a history of good relations exist between employees and management.

> **Restriction of productivity.** The artificial limitation of work output that can occur under wage incentive plans.

Linking Pay to Performance on White-Collar Jobs

Compared with production jobs, white-collar jobs (including clerical, professional, and managerial) frequently offer fewer objective performance criteria to which pay can be tied. To be sure, company presidents are often paid annual

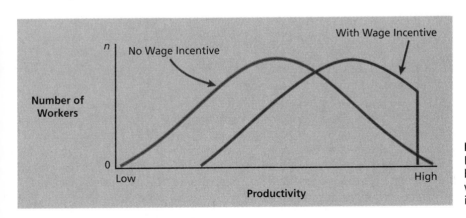

EXHIBIT 7.1
Hypothetical productivity distributions, with and without wage incentives, when incentives promote restriction.

Merit pay plans. Systems that attempt to link pay to performance on white-collar jobs.

bonuses that are tied to the profitability of the firm, and salespeople are frequently paid commissions on sales. However, trustworthy objective indicators of individual performance for the majority of white-collar jobs are often difficult to find. Thus, performance in many such jobs is evaluated by the subjective judgment of the performer's manager.

Attempts to link pay to performance on white-collar jobs are often called **merit pay plans.** Just as straight piecerate is the prototype for most wage incentive plans, there is also a prototype for most merit pay plans: Periodically (usually yearly), managers are required to evaluate the performance of subordinates on some form of rating scales or by means of a written description of performance. Using these evaluations, the managers then recommend that some amount of merit pay be awarded to individuals over and above their basic salaries. This pay is usually incorporated into the subsequent year's salary checks. Since the indicators of good performance can be unclear or highly subjective on some white-collar jobs (especially managerial jobs), merit pay can provide an especially tangible signal that the organization considers an employee's performance "on track."

Individuals who see a strong link between rewards and performance tend to perform better.[7] In addition, white-collar workers (especially managers) particularly support the notion that performance should be an important determinant of pay.[8] Thus, merit pay plans are employed with a much greater frequency than wage incentive plans. Despite the fact that merit pay can stimulate effective performance, that substantial support exists for the idea of merit pay, and that most organizations claim to provide merit pay, it appears that many of these systems now in use are *ineffective.* Many individuals who work under such plans do not perceive a link between their job performance and their pay. There is also evidence that pay is in fact *not* related to performance under some merit plans.[9] Adding more evidence of ineffectiveness are studies that track pay increases over time. For example, one study of managers showed that pay increases in a given year were often uncorrelated with pay increases in adjacent years.[10] From what we know about the consistency of human performance, such a result seems unlikely if organizations are truly tying pay to performance. In most organizations, seniority, number of subordinates, and job level account for more variation in pay than performance does. Of course, some organizations do hold the line. HBO, Inc., the entertainment company, is one firm that seriously tries to maintain the link between pay and performance. Even the U.S. health care system is starting to think about doing so (see the "In Focus: *Tying Doctors' Pay to Performance*").

Potential Problems with Merit Pay Plans

As with wage incentive plans, merit pay plans have several potential problems if employers don't manage them carefully.

Low Discrimination.   One reason that many merit pay plans fail to achieve their intended effect is that managers might be unable or unwilling to discriminate between good performers and poor performers. In Chapter 4 we pointed out that subjective evaluations of performance can be difficult to make and are often distorted by a number of perceptual errors. In the absence of performance rating systems designed to control these problems, managers might feel that the only fair response is to rate most employees as equal performers.

IN FOCUS　　Tying Doctors' Pay to Performance

FORT WASHINGTON, Pa. — Family physician David Badolato wins high marks from patients for being available in emergencies, explaining treatments clearly and caring about their needs.

He also qualified this month for a 19 percent pay bonus from U.S. Healthcare Inc., a major health-maintenance organization that provides him about half of his 2,300 patients. Each year, U.S. Healthcare surveys its members to see how they like their doctors. Dr. Badolato's incentive pay for 1992 was tied in part to his score on patients' questionnaires. His 19 percent bonus exceeded the 15 percent average for doctors in the U.S. Healthcare system

Incentive-pay systems for doctors are catching on, spurred by a belief that they may help upgrade the quality of medical care provided by HMOs and other managed-care programs. Other HMOs that have begun using them include FHP International Corp. in California, the managed-care units of Cigna Corp. and New York Life Insurance Co., and Florida-based Avmed-Santa Fe.

But paying bonuses to doctors raises hackles at a lot of other HMOs. Skeptics don't like the idea of basing incentives on patients' sense of "quality," arguing that patients rely too much on fringe issues such as a receptionist's demeanor or a doctor's punctuality.

The incentive systems are designed for physicians like Dr. Badolato who are in private practice but have a contract to treat patients who subscribe to an HMO. Typically, such doctors are paid a flat rate, such as $10 a month, for each patient they handle.

But flat-rate systems aren't always seen as being in patients' best interests. Because doctors don't get paid extra for handling complicated cases, critics contend that HMOs can amount to assembly-line medicine, in which doctors are judged mostly on their ability to process patients quickly and cheaply.

"We want to create an environment where we can empower the physician," says Bernard Mansheim, chief of medical services for Avmed-Santa Fe. His company pays doctors a quality-performance bonus of 5 percent to 15 percent of

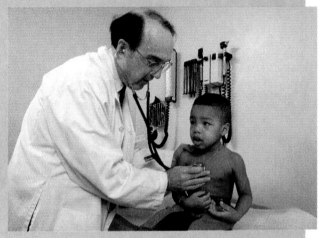

Managed health care systems use incentive pay to help upgrade the quality of medical care. Patients' views of the quality of a doctor's care help determine the amount of the incentive pay. Is this a fair acknowledgment of a physician's performance?

their base pay, depending on how they score on patient-satisfaction questionnaires and a review of their office records.

1. Do you think that merit pay can actually improve the performance of physicians, or are they more intrinsically motivated?

2. What are the ethical implications of merit pay for physicians?

Source: Excerpted from Anders, G. (1993, January 25). More managed health-care systems use incentive pay to reward 'best' doctors. *The Wall Street Journal*, pp. B1, B4.

Good rating systems are rarely employed. Surveys show consistent dissatisfaction with both giving and receiving performance evaluations.[11] Even when managers feel capable of clearly discriminating between good and poor performers, they might be reluctant to do so. If the performance evaluation system does not assist the manager in giving feedback about his or her decisions to subordinates, the equalization strategy might be employed to prevent conflicts with them or among them. If there are true performance differences among subordinates, equalization overrewards poorer performers and underrewards better performers.[12]

Small Increases. A second threat to the effectiveness of merit pay plans exists when merit increases are simply too small to be effective motivators. In this case, even if rewards are carefully tied to performance and managers do a good job of discriminating between more and less effective performers, the intended motivational effects of pay increases might not be realized. Ironically, some firms all but abandon merit when inflation soars or when they encounter economic difficulties. Just when high motivation is needed, the motivational impact of merit pay is removed. Sometimes, a reasonable amount of merit pay is provided, but its motivational impact is reduced because it is spread out over a year or because the organization fails to communicate how much of a raise is for merit and how much is for cost-of-living. To overcome this visibility problem, some firms have replaced conventional merit pay with a **lump sum bonus** that is paid out all at one time and not built into base pay. Such bonuses get people's attention!

Lump sum bonus. Merit pay that is awarded in a single payment and not built into base pay.

When merit pay makes up a substantial portion of the compensation package, management has to take extreme care to ensure that it ties the merit pay to performance criteria that truly benefit the organization. Otherwise, employees could be motivated to earn their yearly bonus at the expense of long-term organizational goals.

Pay Secrecy. A final threat to the effectiveness of merit pay plans is the extreme secrecy that surrounds salaries in most organizations. It has long been a principle of personnel management that salaries are confidential information, and management frequently implores employees who receive merit increases not to discuss these increases with their co-workers. Notice the implication of such secrecy for merit pay plans: Even if merit pay is administered fairly, contingent on performance, and generous, employees might remain ignorant of these facts because they have no way of comparing their own merit treatment with the treatment of others. In consequence, such secrecy might severely damage the motivational impact of a well-designed merit plan. Rather incredibly, many organizations fail to inform employees about the average raise received by those doing similar work.

Given this extreme secrecy, you might expect that employees would profess profound ignorance about the salaries of other organizational members. In fact, this isn't true—in the absence of better information, employees are inclined to "invent" salaries for other members. Unfortunately, this invention seems to reduce both satisfaction and motivation. Specifically, several studies have shown that managers have a tendency to overestimate the pay of their subordinates and their peers and underestimate the pay of their superiors (see Exhibit 7.2).[13] In general, these tendencies will reduce satisfaction with pay, damage perceptions of the linkage between performance and rewards, and reduce the valence of promotion to a higher level of management.

An interesting experiment examined the effects of pay disclosure on the performance and satisfaction of pharmaceutical salespeople who operated under a merit pay system.

> At the time of a regularly scheduled district sales meeting, each of the 14 managers in the experimental group presented to his subordinates the new open salary administration program. The salesmen were given the individual low, overall average, and individual high merit raise amounts for the previous year. The raises ranged from no raise to $75 a month, with a company average of $43. Raises were classi-

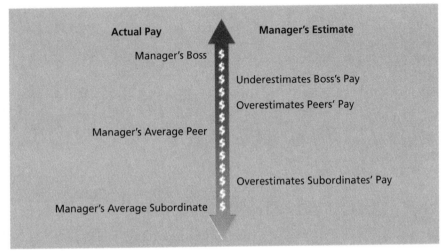

EXHIBIT 7.2
Managers' estimates of pay
earned by boss, peers, and
subordinates.

fied according to district, region, and company increases in pay. Likewise, salary levels (low, average, and high) were given for salesmen on the basis of their years with the company (1 to 5; 5 to 10; 10 to 20; and more than 20 years). Specific individual names and base salaries were not disclosed to the salesmen. However, this information could be obtained from the supervisor. Each salesman's performance evaluation was also made available by the district manager for review by his other salesmen.[14]

After the pay disclosure was implemented, salespeople in the experimental group revealed significant increases in performance and satisfaction with pay. However, since performance consisted of supervisory ratings, it is possible that supervisors felt pressured to give better ratings under the open pay system, in which their actions were open to scrutiny. This, of course, raises an important point. If performance evaluation systems are inadequate and poorly justified, a more open pay policy will simply expose the inadequacy of the merit system and lead managers to evaluate performance in a manner that reduces conflict. Unfortunately, this might be why most organizations maintain relative secrecy concerning pay. One exception is Steven Jobs's Next Computers, which has a completely open salary system. Although many public and civil service jobs have open pay systems, most make little pretense of paying for performance.

Using Pay to Motivate Teamwork

Some of the dysfunctional aspects of wage incentives and merit pay stem from their highly individual orientations. People sometimes end up pursuing their own agendas (and pay) at the expense of the goals of their work group, department, or organization. As a result, some firms have either replaced or supplemented individual incentive pay with plans designed to foster more cooperation and teamwork.[15] Notice that each of the plans we discuss below has a somewhat different motivational focus. Organizations have to choose pay plans that support their strategic needs.

Profit Sharing. Profit sharing is one of the most commonly used group-oriented incentive systems. In years in which the firm makes a profit, some of this is returned to employees in the form of a bonus, sometimes in cash and

Profit sharing. The return of some company profit to employees in the form of a cash bonus or a retirement supplement.

sometimes in a deferred retirement fund. Such money is surely welcome, and it might reinforce some identification with the organization. However, it is unlikely that profit sharing, as normally practiced, is highly motivational. Its greatest problem is that too many factors beyond the control of the workforce (such as the general economy) can affect profits no matter how well people perform their jobs. Also, in a large firm, it is difficult to see the impact of one's own actions on profits. For example, for two years after Chrysler Corporation's first profit sharing payment, the company made no payments. And with a work force of 63,000, one's impact on profits would be completely obscure.

Profit sharing seems to work best in smaller firms that regularly turn a handsome profit and then distribute this profit according to merit. Lincoln Electric, which we discussed in Chapter 6, uses this strategy.

Gainsharing.   **Gainsharing** plans are group incentive plans that are based on improved productivity or performance over which the workforce has some control.[16] This often includes reductions in the cost of labor, material, or supplies. When measured costs decrease, the company pays a monthly bonus according to a predetermined formula that shares this "gain" between employees and the firm. For example, a plan installed by Canadian pulp and paper producer Fraser, Inc. rewards employees for low scrap and low steam usage during production. The plan sidesteps the cost of steam generation and the international price for paper, things over which the workforce lacks control.[17]

Gainsharing plans have usually been installed using committees that include extensive workforce participation. This builds trust and commitment to the formulas that are used to convert gains into bonuses. Also, most plans include all members of the work unit, including production people, managers, and support staff.

The most common gainsharing plan is the Scanlon Plan, developed by union leader Joe Scanlon in the 1930s.[18] The plan stresses participatory management and joint problem solving between employees and managers, but it also stresses using the pay system to reward employees for this cooperative behavior. Thus, pay is used to align company and employee goals. The Scanlon Plan has been used successfully by many small family-owned manufacturing firms. Also, in recent years, many large corporations (e.g., General Electric, Motorola, Carrier, Dana) have installed Scanlon-like plans in some manufacturing plants.[19] The turnaround of the motorcycle producer Harley-Davidson is in part attributed to the institution of gainsharing. In general, productivity improvements following the introduction of Scanlon-type plans support the motivational impact of this group wage incentive.[20] However, perception that the plan is fair is critical.[21]

Skill Based Pay.   The idea behind **skill based pay** (also called pay for knowledge) is to motivate employees to learn a wide variety of work tasks, irrespective of the job that they might be doing at any given time. The more skills that are acquired, the higher the person's pay.[22] Companies use skill based pay to encourage employee flexibility in task assignments and to give them a broader picture of the work process. It is especially useful on self-managed teams (Chapter 8) in which employees divide up the work as they see fit. It is also useful in flexible manufacturing (Chapter 16) in which rapid changes in job

Gainsharing. A group pay incentive plan based on productivity or performance improvements over which the workforce has some control.

Skill based pay. A system in which people are paid according to the number of job skills they have acquired.

At Quebec's Bell Helicopter Textron plant, skill based pay encourages flexibility in the aircraft assemblers' work assignments and provides them with an overall picture of the work process.

demands can occur. Quebec's Bell Helicopter Textron plant uses skill based pay for its aircraft assemblers to enhance their flexibility.

Training costs can be high with a skill based pay system. Also, when the system is in place, it has to be used. Sometimes, managers want to keep employees on a task they are good at rather than letting them acquire new skills.

Exhibit 7.3 compares the various pay plans that organizations use to motivate teamwork.

JOB DESIGN AS A MOTIVATOR

If the use of money as a motivator is primarily an attempt to capitalize on extrinsic motivation, current approaches to using job design as a motivator represent an attempt to capitalize on intrinsic motivation. In essence, the current goal of job design is to identify the characteristics that make some tasks more motivating than others and to capture these characteristics in the design of jobs.

Traditional Views of Job Design

From the advent of the Industrial Revolution until the 1960s, the prevailing philosophy regarding the design of most nonmanagerial jobs was job simplification. The historical roots of job simplification are found in social, economic, and technological forces that existed even before the Industrial Revolution. This pre-industrial period was characterized by increasing urbanization and the growth of a free market economy, which prompted a demand for manufactured

PLAN TYPE	HOW IT WORKS	WHAT IT REQUIRES TO BE EFFECTIVE	ADVANTAGES	DISADVANTAGES
Profit sharing	Employees receive a varying annual bonus based on corporate profits. Payments can be made in cash or deferred into a retirement fund.	• Participating employees collectively must be able to influence profits. • Owners must value employees' contributions enough to be willing to share profits.	• The incentive formula is simple and easy to communicate. • The plan is guaranteed to be affordable: It pays only when the firm is sufficiently profitable. • It unites the financial interests of owners and employees.	• Annual payments may lead employers to ignore long-term performance. • Factors beyond the employee's control can influence profits. • The plan forces private companies to open their books.
Gain sharing	When a unit beats predetermined performance targets, all members get bonuses. Objectives often include better productivity, quality, and customer service.	• Objectives must be measurable. • Management must encourage employee involvement. • Employees must have a high degree of trust in management.	• The plan enhances coordination and teamwork. • Employees learn more about the business and focus on objectives. • Employees work harder and smarter.	• Plans that focus only on productivity may lead employees to ignore other important objectives, such as quality. • The company may have to pay bonuses even when unprofitable.
Skill based pay	An employee's salary or wage rises with the number of tasks he or she can do, regardless of the job performed.	• Skills must be identified and assigned a pay grade. • The company must have well-developed employee assessment and training procedures.	• By increasing flexibility, the plan lets the company operate with a leaner staff. • The plan gives workers a broader perspective, making them more adept at problem solving.	• Most employees will learn all applicable skills, raising labor costs. • Training costs are high.

Source: Perry, N.J. (1988, December 19). Here come richer, riskier pay plans. *Fortune*, 50–58, p. 52.

EXHIBIT 7.3
Characteristics of team-oriented incentive plans.

goods. Thus, a division of labor within society occurred, and specialized industrial concerns, using newly developed machinery, emerged to meet this demand. With complex machinery and an uneducated, untrained work force, these organizations recognized that *specialization* was the key to efficient productivity. If the production of an object could be broken down into very basic, simple steps, even an uneducated and minimally trained worker could contribute his or her share by mastering one of these steps.

The zenith of job simplification occurred in the early 1900s when industrial engineer Frederick Winslow Taylor presented the industrial community with his principles of Scientific Management.[23] From Chapter 1 you will recall that Taylor advocated extreme division of labor and specialization, even extending to the specialization of supervisors in roles such as trainer, disciplinarian, and so on. Also, he advocated careful standardization and regulation of work activities and rest pauses. Intuitively, jobs designed according to the principles of Scientific Management do not seem intrinsically motivating. The motivational strategies that management used during this period consisted of close supervision and the use of piecerate pay. It would be a historical disservice to conclude that job simplification was unwelcomed by workers, who were mostly nonunionized, uneducated, and fighting to fulfill their basic needs. Such simplification helped them to achieve a reasonable standard of living. However, in recent years, with a better-educated work force whose basic needs are fairly well met, behavioral scientists have begun to question the impact of job simplification on performance, customer satisfaction, and the quality of working life.

Job Scope and Motivation

Job scope can be defined as the breadth and depth of a job.[24] Breadth refers to the number of different activities performed on the job, while depth refers to the degree of discretion or control the worker has over how these tasks are performed. "Broad" jobs require workers to *do* a number of different tasks, while "deep" jobs emphasize freedom in *planning* how to do the work.

As shown in Exhibit 7.4, jobs that have great breadth and depth are called high-scope jobs. The professor's job is a good example of a high-scope job. It is broad because it involves the performance of a number of different tasks, such as teaching, grading, doing research, writing, and participating in committees. It is also deep because there is considerable discretion in how academics perform these tasks. In general, professors have a fair amount of freedom to choose a particular teaching style, grading format, and research area. Similarly, management jobs are high-scope jobs. Managers perform a wide variety of activities (supervision, training, performance evaluation, report writing) and have some discretion over how they accomplish these activities.

The classic example of a low-scope job is the traditional assembly line job. This job is both "shallow" and "narrow" in the sense that a single task (such as bolting on car wheels) is performed repetitively and ritually, with no discretion as to method. Traditional views of job design were attempts to construct low-scope jobs in which workers specialized in a single task.

Occasionally, we encounter jobs that have high breadth but little depth or vice versa. For motivational purposes, we can also consider these jobs relatively low in scope. For example, a utility worker on an assembly line fills in for absent workers on various parts of the line. While this job involves the performance of a number of tasks, it involves little discretion as to when or how the worker performs the tasks. On the other hand, some jobs involve a fair amount of discretion over a single, narrowly defined task. For example, quality control inspectors perform a single, repetitive task, but they might be required to exercise a fair degree of judgment in performing this task. Similarly, workers who monitor the performance of equipment (such as in a nuclear power plant) might perform a single task but again be required to exercise considerable discretion when a problem arises.

The motivational theories we discussed in the previous chapter suggest that high-scope jobs (*both* broad and deep) should provide more intrinsic motivation than low-scope jobs. Maslow's need hierarchy and the ERG theory both seem to indicate that people can fulfill higher-order needs by the opportunity to perform high-scope jobs. Expectancy theory suggests that high-scope jobs can provide intrinsic motivation if the outcomes derived from such jobs are attractive.

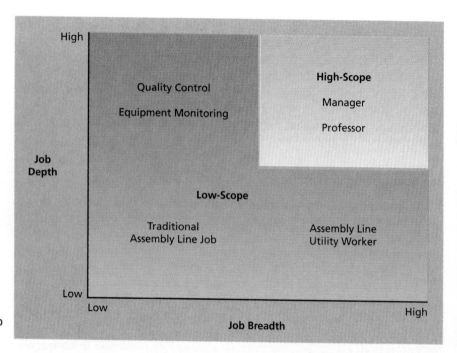

EXHIBIT 7.4
Job scope as a function of job depth and job breadth.

The Job Characteristics Model

The concept of job scope provides an easy-to-understand introduction to why some jobs seem more intrinsically motivating than others. However, we can find a more rigorous delineation of the motivational properties of jobs in the Job Characteristics Model that J. Richard Hackman and Greg Oldham developed (Exhibit 7.5).[25] As you can observe, the Job Characteristics Model proposes that there are several "core" job characteristics that have a certain psychological impact upon workers. In turn, the psychological states induced by the nature of the job lead to certain outcomes that are relevant to the worker and the organization. Finally, several other factors (moderators) influence the extent to which these relationships hold true.

Skill variety. The opportunity to do a variety of job activities using various skills and talents.

Autonomy. The freedom to schedule one's own work activities and decide work procedures.

Task significance. The impact that a job has on other people.

Task identity. The extent to which a job involves doing a complete piece of work, from beginning to end.

Feedback. Information about the effectiveness of one's work performance.

Core Job Characteristics. The Job Characteristics Model shows that there are five core job characteristics that have particularly strong potential to affect worker motivation: skill variety, task identity, task significance, autonomy, and job feedback. These characteristics are described in detail in Exhibit 7.6. In general, higher levels of these characteristics should lead to the favorable outcomes shown in Exhibit 7.5. Notice that **skill variety,** the opportunity to do a variety of job activities using various skills and talents, corresponds fairly closely to the notion of job breadth we discussed earlier. **Autonomy,** the freedom to schedule one's own work activities and decide work procedures, corresponds to job depth. However, Hackman and Oldham recognized that one could have a high degree of control over a variety of skills that were perceived as meaningless or fragmented. Thus, the concepts of task significance and task identity are introduced. **Task significance** is the impact that a job has on others. **Task identity** is the extent to which a job involves doing a complete piece of work, from beginning to end. In addition, they recognized that **feedback,** information about one's performance effectiveness, is also essential

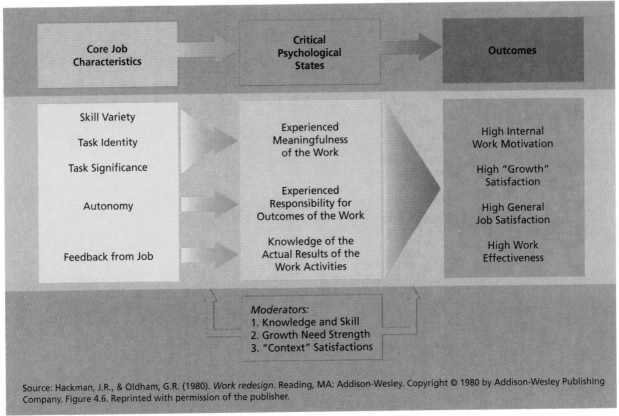

Source: Hackman, J.R., & Oldham, G.R. (1980). *Work redesign.* Reading, MA: Addison-Wesley. Copyright © 1980 by Addison-Wesley Publishing Company. Figure 4.6. Reprinted with permission of the publisher.

EXHIBIT 7.5
The Job Characteristics Model.

for high intrinsic motivation. People aren't motivated for long if they don't know how well they are doing.

Hackman and Oldham developed a questionnaire called the Job Diagnostic Survey (JDS) to measure the core characteristics of jobs. The JDS requires job holders to report the amount of the various core characteristics contained in their jobs. From these reports, we can construct profiles to compare the motivational properties of various jobs. For example, Exhibit 7.7 shows JDS profiles for lower-level managers in a utility company (collected by your author) and those for keypunchers in another firm (reported by Hackman and Oldham). While the managers perform a full range of managerial duties, the keypunchers perform a highly regulated job—anonymous work from various departments is assigned to them by a supervisor, and their output is verified for accuracy by others. Not surprisingly, the JDS profiles reveal that the managerial jobs are consistently higher on the core characteristics than are the keypunching jobs.

According to Hackman and Oldham, an overall measure of the motivating potential of a job can be calculated by the following formula:

$$\text{Motivating potential score} = \frac{\text{Skill variety} + \text{Task identity} + \text{Task significance}}{3} \times \text{Autonomy} \times \text{Job feedback}$$

Since the JDS measures the job characteristics on seven-point scales, a motivating potential score could theoretically range from 1 to 343. For example, the motivating potential score for the keypunchers' jobs shown in Exhibit 7.6 is 20,

1. Skill variety: The degree to which a job requires a variety of different activities in carrying out the work, involving the use of a number of different skills and talents of the person.
   High variety: The owner-operator of a garage who does electrical repair, rebuilds engines, does body work, and interacts with customers.
   Low variety: A body shop worker who sprays paint eight hours a day.

2. Task identity: The degree to which a job requires completion of a "whole" and identifiable piece of work, that is, doing a job from beginning to end with a visible outcome.
   High identity: A cabinet maker who designs a piece of furniture, selects the wood, builds the object, and finishes it to perfection.
   Low identity: A worker in a furniture factory who operates a lathe solely to make table legs.

3. Task significance: The degree to which a job has substantial impact on the lives of other people, whether those people are in the immediate organization or in the world at large.
   High significance: Nursing the sick in a hospital intensive care unit.
   Low significance: Sweeping hospital floors.

4. Autonomy: The degree to which the job provides substantial freedom, independence, and discretion to the individual in scheduling the work and determining the procedures to be used in carrying it out.
   High autonomy: A telephone installer who schedules his or her own work for the day, makes visits without supervision, and decides on the most effective techniques for a particular installation.
   Low autonomy: A telephone operator who must handle calls as they come according to a routine, highly specified procedure.

5. Job feedback: The degree to which carrying out the work activities required by the job provides the individual with direct and clear information about the effectiveness of his or her performance.
   High feedback: An electronics factory worker who assembles a radio and then tests it to determine if it operates properly.
   Low feedback: An electronics factory worker who assembles a radio and then routes it to a quality control inspector who tests it for proper operation and makes needed adjustments.

Source: Definitions from Hackman, J.R., & Oldham, G.R. (1980). The properties of motivating jobs. *Work redesign.* Reading, MA: Addison-Wesley. Copyright © 1980 by Addison-Wesley Publishing Company, Reading, Massachusetts. Reprinted by permission of the publisher. Examples by author.

EXHIBIT 7.6
Core job characteristics and example.

while that for the managers' jobs is 159. Thus, the managers are more likely than the keypunchers to be motivated by the job itself. The average motivating potential score for 6,930 employees on 876 jobs has been calculated at 128.[26]

Critical Psychological States. Why should jobs that are higher on the core characteristics be intrinsically motivating? What is their psychological impact? Hackman and Oldham argue that work will be intrinsically motivating when it is perceived as *meaningful,* when the worker feels *responsible* for the outcomes of the work, and when the worker has *knowledge* about his or her work progress. As shown in Exhibit 7.5, the Job Characteristics Model proposes that the core job characteristics affect meaningfulness, responsibility, and knowledge of results in a systematic manner. When an individual uses a variety of skills to do a "whole" job that is perceived as significant to others, he or she perceives the work as meaningful. When a person has autonomy to organize and perform the job as he or she sees fit, the person feels personally

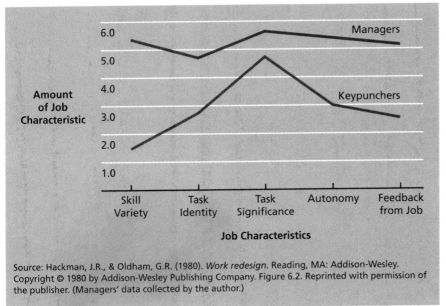

Source: Hackman, J.R., & Oldham, G.R. (1980). *Work redesign.* Reading, MA: Addison-Wesley. Copyright © 1980 by Addison-Wesley Publishing Company. Figure 6.2. Reprinted with permission of the publisher. (Managers' data collected by the author.)

EXHIBIT 7.7
Levels of core job characteristics for managers and keypunchers.

responsible for the outcome of the work. Finally, when the job provides feedback about performance, the worker will have knowledge of the results of this opportunity to exercise responsibility.

Outcomes. The presence of the critical psychological states leads to a number of outcomes that are relevant to both the individual and the organization. Chief among these is high intrinsic motivation. When the worker is truly in control of a challenging job that provides good feedback about performance, the key prerequisites for intrinsic motivation are present. The relationship between work and the worker is emphasized, and the worker is able to draw motivation from the job itself. This will result in high-quality productivity. By the same token, workers will report satisfaction with higher-order needs (growth needs) and general satisfaction with the job itself. This should lead to reduced absenteeism and turnover.

Moderators. Hackman and Oldham recognize that jobs that are high in motivating potential do not *always* lead to favorable outcomes. Thus, as shown in Exhibit 7.5, they propose certain moderator or contingency variables (Chapter 1) that intervene between job characteristics and outcomes. One of these is the job-relevant knowledge and skill of the worker. Put simply, workers with weak knowledge and skills should not respond favorably to jobs that are high in motivating potential, since such jobs will prove too demanding. Another proposed moderator is **growth need strength,** which refers to the extent to which people desire to achieve higher-order need satisfaction by performing their jobs. Hackman and Oldham argue that those with high growth needs should be most responsive to challenging work. Finally, they argue that workers who are dissatisfied with the context factors surrounding the job (such as pay, supervision, and company policy) will be less responsive to challenging work than those who are reasonably satisfied with context factors.

Growth need strength. The extent to which people desire to achieve higher-order need satisfaction by performing their jobs.

In tests of the Job Characteristics Model researchers usually require workers to describe their jobs by means of the Job Diagnostic Survey and then measure their reactions to these jobs. Although there is some discrepancy regarding the relative importance of the various core characteristics, these tests have generally been very supportive of the basic prediction of the model— workers tend to respond more favorably to jobs that are higher in motivating potential.[27] Where the model seems to falter is in its predictions about growth needs and context satisfaction. Evidence that these factors influence reactions to job design is weak or contradictory.[28]

Job Enrichment

Job enrichment. The design of jobs to enhance intrinsic motivation and the quality of working life.

Job enrichment is the design of jobs to enhance intrinsic motivation and the quality of working life. In general, enrichment involves increasing the motivating potential of jobs via the arrangement of their core characteristics. There are no hard and fast rules for the enrichment of jobs. Specific enrichment procedures depend upon a careful diagnosis of the work to be accomplished, the available technology, and the organizational context in which enrichment is to take place. However, many job enrichment schemes combine tasks, establish client relationships, reduce supervision, form teams, or make feedback more direct.[29]

- *Combining tasks.* This involves assigning tasks that might be performed by different workers to a single individual. For example, in a furniture factory a lathe operator, an assembler, a sander, and a stainer might become four "chair makers"; each worker would then do all four tasks. Such a strategy should increase the variety of skills employed and might contribute to task identity as each worker approaches doing a unified job from start to finish.

- *Establishing external client relationships.* This involves putting employees in touch with people outside the organization who depend upon their products or services. Such a strategy might involve the use of new (interpersonal) skills, increase the identity and significance of the job, and increase feedback about one's performance. Consider this example:

  At the Duncan Hines angel food cake factory in Jackson, Tennessee, the line workers are given letters from customers who have problems with the product. One factory hand called up a customer whose angel food cake didn't rise, and helped figure out why by asking such questions as "How long did you beat the mix?" and "At what temperature did you bake it?" Says [Procter & Gamble CEO]: "What we've said to the workers is, this is the only place we make angel food cake, and you're responsible for it, and if you want to talk to the consumer, we'd like you to talk to the consumer."[30]

- *Establishing internal client relationships.* This involves putting employees in touch with people who depend upon their products or services within the organization. For example, billers and expediters in a manufacturing firm might be assigned permanently to certain salespeople, rather than working on any salesperson's order as it comes in. The advantages are similar to those mentioned for establishing external client relationships.

- *Reducing supervision or reliance on others.* The goal here is to increase autonomy and control over one's own work. For example, management

IN FOCUS　　Job Enrichment at Carrier Corporation Plant Focuses on Flexibility, Autonomy

ARKADELPHIA, Ark. — On a pothole-filled road across from a big chicken processor in this remote town sits a Carrier Corp. plant that could be a blueprint for the future of U.S. manufacturing.

The Carrier plant, which produces compressors for air conditioners, operates in some unusual ways. What most distinguishes this plant, however, are its workers, a breed apart from yesterday's lunch-pail crowd. Hopeful job applicants must complete a grueling six-week course before being even considered for employment—a selection process that results in a job for only one of every 16 applicants and yields a top-quality work force. Once on the job, the workers have unusual authority. They can, for example, shut down production if they spot a problem, and, within limits, they can order their own supplies.

Women work beside men in every area and can handle every job. Carrier designed the plant so that no one has to lift anything heavier than 12 pounds repeatedly.

Flexibility is crucial, both among workers and in the design of the plant. Carrier teaches workers several jobs, so that if one is sick, another can fill in quickly. In addition, "the whole plant could probably be reconfigured in several weeks' time," Mr. Kassouf says.

The first workers hired suggested that they themselves install the machines. Management agreed, and several workers jetted off to machine-tool plants—some flying for the first time—where they learned how to assemble the equipment. That experience instilled a sense of ownership; many talk about "my machine." It also saved $1 million of installation costs.

When Gene Whitaker, a 24-year-old assembly worker, noticed the paint wasn't adhering well to the compressors, he decided the pretreatment process needed sodium ash to make the paint stick better. So he picked up a phone and placed a $5,000 order with a supplier. "I've never been stopped" when ordering supplies, he says.

Source: Excerpted from Norton, E. (1993, January 3). Small, flexible plants may play crucial role in U.S. manufacturing. *The Wall Street Journal*, pp. A1, A8.

---

might permit clerical employees to check their own work for errors instead of having someone else do it. Similarly, firms might allow workers to order needed supplies or contract for outside services up to some dollar amount without obtaining permission. (See the "In Focus: *Job Enrichment at Carrier Corporation Plant Focuses on Flexibility, Autonomy*.")

- *Forming work teams.* Management can use this format as an alternative to a sequence of "small" jobs that individual workers perform when a product or service is too large or complex for one person to complete alone. For example, social workers with particular skills might operate as a true team to assist a particular client, rather than passing the client from person to person. Similarly, stable teams can form to construct an entire product, such as a car or boat, in lieu of an assembly-line approach. Such approaches should lead to the formal and informal development of a variety of skills and increase the identity of the job.

- *Making feedback more direct.* This technique is usually used in conjunction with other job design aspects that permit workers to be identified with their "own" product or service. For example, an electronics firm might have assemblers "sign" their output on a tag that includes an address and toll-free phone number. If a customer encounters problems, he or she contacts the assembler directly. In Sweden, workers who build trucks by team assembly are responsible for service and warranty work on "their" trucks that are sold locally.

Job Enrichment at AT&T Enhances Quality

American Telephone and Telegraph and its former associated companies in the Bell System have been involved in an ongoing series of enrichment exercises.

The first job that the company enriched was that of stockholder correspondent in the AT&T Treasury Department. This job involves dealing with queries and complaints from AT&T stockholders by mail or telephone. Since many of these issues can be quite complex, the workforce consisted mostly of college graduates. Ironically, although interactions with stockholders are important and sensitive, the correspondent's job had been a glorified clerical job—after correspondents had researched the problem in question, they composed a form letter response, which their supervisors verified and signed. Job dissatisfaction was high among the correspondents, and this dissatisfaction was reflected in a high rate of costly turnover. In addition, quality measures indicated an unacceptable level of errors and delays in responses. Gradually, AT&T introduced a number of changes to the correspondent's job with the goal of enhancing its motivating potential. These changes included combining tasks, increasing teamwork, reducing supervision, and indirectly enhancing the external client relationship. AT&T's management

- appointed subject-matter experts within each unit for others to consult with before seeking supervisory help;
- told correspondents to sign their own names to letters from the very first day on the job after training;
- had supervisors examine the work of the more experienced correspondents less frequently, doing so at each correspondent's desk;
- discussed production, but only in general terms: "A full day's work is expected," for example;
- had outgoing work go directly to the mail room without crossing the supervisor's desk;
- told all correspondents they would be held fully accountable for work quality;
- encouraged correspondents to answer letters in a more personalized way, rather than using the form letter approach.[31]

In general, these changes would seem to affect each of the five core job characteristics, and the results were highly favorable. Compared with control groups, job satisfaction increased, while absence and turnover decreased.[32] In addition, the quality of performance rose, and there were more promotions made from among the correspondents whose jobs had been enriched. Presumably this success occurred because these correspondents were now better able to demonstrate their skills and responsibility to management.

AT&T and the former Bell System made other enrichment attempts on jobs as diverse as service representatives, toll and information operators, telephone installers, keypunchers, and equipment engineers. Most changes were considered successful.

Potential Problems with Job Enrichment

Despite the theoretical attractiveness of job enrichment as a motivational strategy, and despite the fact that many organizations have experimented with such programs, enrichment can encounter a number of challenging problems.

Poor Diagnosis. Problems with job enrichment can occur when it is instituted without a careful diagnosis of the needs of the organization and the particular jobs in question. Some enrichment attempts might be half-hearted tactical exercises that really don't increase the motivating potential of the job adequately. An especially likely error here is increasing job breadth (variety) while leaving the other crucial core characteristics unchanged. Thus, workers are simply given *more* boring, fragmented, routine tasks to do, such as bolting intake manifolds and water pumps onto engines. On the other side of the coin, in their zeal to use enrichment as a cure-all, organizations might attempt to enrich jobs that are already perceived as too rich by their incumbents. This has happened in some "downsized" firms in which the remaining managers have been assigned too many extra responsibilities.

Lack of Desire or Skill. Put simply, some workers do not *desire* enriched jobs. Almost by definition, enrichment places greater demands upon workers, and some might not relish this extra responsibility. Even when people have no basic objections to enrichment in theory, they might lack the skills and competence necessary to perform enriched jobs effectively. Thus, for some poorly educated or trained work forces, enrichment might entail substantial training costs. In addition, it might be difficult to train some workers in certain skills required by enriched jobs, such as social skills. For example, part of the job enrichment scheme at a Philips television manufacturing plant in Holland required TV assemblers to initiate contacts with high-status staff members in other departments when they encountered problems. This is an example of the establishment of an internal client relationship, and many workers found this job requirement threatening.[33]

Demand for Rewards. Occasionally, workers who experience job enrichment ask that greater extrinsic rewards, such as pay, accompany their redesigned jobs. Most frequently, this desire is probably prompted by the fact that such jobs require the development of new skills and entail greater responsibility. For example, one enrichment exercise for clerical jobs in a U.S. government agency encountered this reaction.[34] Sometimes, such requests are motivated by the wish to share in the financial benefits of a successful enrichment exercise. In one documented case, workers with radically enriched jobs in a General Foods dog food plant in Topeka sought a financial bonus based on the system's success.[35] Equity in action!

Union Resistance. Traditionally, North American unions have not been enthusiastic about job enrichment. In part, this is due to a historical focus on negotiating with management about easily quantified extrinsic motivators, such as money, rather than the soft stuff of job design. Also, unions have tended to equate the narrow division of labor with preserving jobs for their members. Faced with global competition, the need for flexibility, and the need for employee initiative to foster quality, companies and unions have begun to dismantle restrictive contract provisions regarding job design. Fewer job classifications mean more opportunities for flexibility by combining tasks and using team approaches.

Supervisory Resistance. Even when enrichment schemes are carefully implemented to truly enhance the motivating potential of deserving jobs, they might fail because of their unanticipated impact on other jobs or other parts of the organizational system. A key problem here concerns the supervisors of the workers whose jobs have been enriched. By definition, enrichment increases the autonomy of employees. Unfortunately, such a change might "disenrich" the boss's job, a consequence that will hardly facilitate the smooth implementation of the job redesign. Some organizations have responded to this problem by effectively doing away with direct supervision of workers performing enriched jobs. Others use the supervisor as a trainer and developer of individuals on enriched jobs. Enrichment can increase the need for this supervisory function.

GOAL SETTING AS A MOTIVATOR

One of the basic characteristics of all organizations is that they have goals. In Chapter 6, individual performance was defined as the extent to which a member contributes to the attainment of these goals or objectives. Thus, if employees are to achieve acceptable performance, some method of translating organizational goals into individual goals must be implemented.

Unfortunately, there is ample reason to believe that personal performance goals are vague or nonexistent for many organizational members. Employees frequently report that their role in the organization is unclear or that they don't really know what their boss expects of them. Even in cases in which performance goals would seem to be obvious because of the nature of the task (e.g., filling packing crates to the maximum to avoid excessive freight charges), employees might be ignorant of their current performance. This suggests that the implicit performance goals simply aren't making an impression.

The notion of **goal setting** as a motivator has been around for a long time. However, theoretical developments and some very practical research demonstrations have begun to suggest just when and how goal setting can be effective.[36]

Goal setting. A motivational technique that uses specific, challenging, and acceptable goals and provides feedback to enhance performance.

What Kinds of Goals are Motivational?

A large body of evidence suggests that goals are most motivational when they are *specific, challenging,* and *accepted* by organizational members. In addition, *feedback* about progress toward goal attainment should be provided.[37]

Goal Specificity. Specific goals are goals that specify an exact level of achievement for people to accomplish in a particular time frame. For example, "I will enroll in five courses next semester and achieve a *B* or better in each course" is a specific goal. Similarly, "I will increase my net sales by 20 percent in the coming business quarter" is a specific goal. On the other hand, "I will do my best" is not a specific goal, since level of achievement and time frame are both vague.

Goal Challenge. Obviously, specific goals will not motivate effective performance if the goals are especially easy to achieve. However, goal challenge is a much more personal matter than goal specificity, since it depends upon the experience and basic skills of the organizational member. One thing is certain, however—when goals become so difficult that they are perceived as *impossible* to achieve, the goals will lose their potential to motivate. Thus, goal challenge is best when it is pegged to the competence of individual workers and increased as the particular task is mastered. One practical way to do this is to base initial goals upon past performance. For example, an academic counselor might encourage a *D* student to set a goal of achieving *C*s in the coming semester and encourage a *C* student to set a goal of achieving *B*s. Similarly, a sales manager might ask a new salesperson to try to increase his sales by 5 percent in the next quarter and ask an experienced salesperson to try to increase her sales by 10 percent.

Goal Acceptance.   Specific, challenging goals must be accepted by the individual if the goals are to have effective motivational properties. In a sense, goals really aren't goals unless they are consciously accepted. In a following section we will discuss some factors that affect goal acceptance.

Goal Feedback.   Specific, challenging, accepted goals have the most beneficial effect when they are accompanied by ongoing feedback that enables the person to compare current performance with the goal. This is why a schedule of tasks to be completed often motivates goal accomplishment. Progress against the schedule provides feedback.

How Do Goals Motivate?

Just why should specific, challenging, accepted goals, in and of themselves, serve as effective motivators? First, in expectancy theory terms, goal specificity should strengthen both expectancy and instrumentality connections. The individual now has a clear picture of a first-level outcome to which her effort should be directed and greater certainty about the consequences of achieving this outcome.[38] Turning to goal challenge, the need theories of motivation suggest that feelings of achievement, competence, and esteem should accompany the mastery of a challenging goal. In addition, certain motivational side effects might accompany goal setting. For one thing, workers might compete with their own "best record" and set even higher goals. For example, the programmer who sets and achieves a goal of programming so many lines of code on Monday might set a higher goal for Tuesday. In addition, in some goal-setting situations, employees might informally compete among themselves to outdo each other. Again, this might stimulate individual workers to set more challenging personal goals.

Enhancing Goal Acceptance

It has probably not escaped you that the requirements for goal challenge and goal acceptance seem potentially incompatible. After all, you might be quite amenable to accepting an easy goal but balk at accepting a tough one. Thus, it is important to consider some of the factors that might affect the acceptance of challenging, specific goals, including participation, rewards, and management support.

Participation.   It seems reasonable that organizational members should be more accepting of goals that are set with their participation than of those simply handed down from their superior. Sensible as this sounds, the research evidence on the effects of participation is very mixed—sometimes participation in goal setting increases performance, and sometimes it doesn't.[39] If goal acceptance is a potential *problem,* participation might prove beneficial.[40]

When a climate of distrust between superiors and subordinates exists, or when participation provides information that assists in the establishment of fair, realistic goals, then it should facilitate performance. On the other hand, when subordinates trust their boss, and when the boss has a good understanding of the capability of the subordinates, participation might be quite unnecessary for acceptance.[41] It is interesting that research shows participation can increase performance by increasing the *difficulty* of the goals that employees adopt.[42] This might occur because participation induces competition or a feeling of team spirit among members of the work unit that leads them to exceed the goal expectations of the supervisor.

Rewards. Will the promise of extrinsic rewards (such as money) for goal accomplishment increase the acceptance of goals? Probably, but there is plenty of evidence that goal setting has led to performance increases *without* the introduction of monetary incentives for goal accomplishment. One reason for this might be that many ambitious goals involve no more than doing the job as it was designed to be done in the first place. For example, encouraging employees to pack crates or load trucks to within 5 percent of their maximum capacity doesn't really involve a greater expenditure of effort or more work. It simply requires more attention to detail. Goal setting should, however, be compatible with any system to tie pay to performance that already exists for the job in question, such as wage incentives, commissions, or merit pay.

Supportiveness. There is considerable agreement about one factor that will *reduce* the acceptance of specific, challenging performance goals. When supervisors behave in a coercive manner to encourage goal accomplishment, they can badly damage employee commitment to the goal. For goal setting to work properly, supervisors must demonstrate a desire to assist employees in goal accomplishment and behave supportively if failure occurs, even adjusting the goal downward if it proves to be unrealistically high. Threat and punishment in response to failure will be extremely counterproductive.[43]

Goal setting has led to increased performance on a wide variety of tasks, including servicing drink machines, entering data, selling, cutting trees, and typing text. Studies reveal that the positive results of goal setting are not short lived—they persist over a long enough time to have practical value.[44] However, the performance impact of goal setting is strongest for simpler jobs rather than more complex jobs, such as scientific and engineering work.[45]

Before continuing, let's apply what you've been reading by considering the *You Be the Manager* feature.

Management by Objectives

In the bare-bones form presented above, goal setting is just that—a specific, challenging goal is established to solve a particular performance problem. In this basic form, goal setting is rather lacking in the potential to assist in employee development over time. Usually, management makes no particular provisions for counseling employees in goal accomplishment or for changing goals in some systematic manner as the need arises. It might also occur to you that certain jobs require the simultaneous accomplishment of *several* goals and that superiors and subordinates might differ in the importance that they attach to these goals or disagree about how to evaluate goal accomplishment. This is particularly likely in the more complex jobs that exist at higher levels in the

THE WEYERHAEUSER TRUCK DRIVERS

M YOU BE THE anager

Weyerhaeuser Company is a large forest products firm headquartered in Tacoma, Washington. Weyerhaeuser faced a problem that commonly crops up in production operations—the underutilization of expensive resources. The problem centered on truck drivers who hauled logs from the forest to a company sawmill. The drivers, who also loaded the trucks, were unionized and paid on an hourly basis. Management determined that the trucks were averaging only about 60 percent of their legal weight capacity. This extreme underloading was very undesirable, because extra trucks, extra drivers, and extra diesel fuel were necessary to transport a given amount of timber.

Management was convinced that it could improve the situation if drivers could be motivated to pay more attention to their loading procedures. Because logs differ in diameter and length, a full

> MANAGEMENT AND DRIVERS AT THE WEYERHAEUSER COMPANY HAD TO WORK TOGETHER TO SOLVE AN EXPENSIVE PROBLEM: THE UNDERUTILIZATION OF RESOURCES.

load could vary between 60 and 120 logs. Thus, drivers had to exercise judgment in the loading process. Although a scale was available at the loading point, drivers didn't seem to be making good use of it.

As a manager, what would you do to improve truck utilization? Remember, you don't want to encourage loading *over* the legal limit.

1. What are the pros and cons of using a monetary incentive to improve the loading process?

2. What are the pros and cons of using goal setting to improve the loading process?

To find out what Weyerhaeuser did, see *The Manager's Notebook* at the end of the chapter.

Sources: Adapted from Latham, G. P., & Locke, E. (1979, Autumn). Goal setting—a motivational technique that works. *Organizational Dynamics*, 68–80; Latham, G. P., & Baldes, J. J. (1975). The "practical significance" of Locke's theory of goal setting. *Journal of Applied Psychology, 60,* 122–124.

---

organization, such as management jobs and staff jobs (e.g., the personnel department or the research and development department).

Management by Objectives (MBO) is an elaborate, systematic, ongoing management program to facilitate goal establishment, goal accomplishment, and employee development.[46] The concept was developed by management theorist Peter Drucker. The objectives in MBO are simply another label for goals. In a well-designed MBO program, objectives for the organization as a whole are developed by top management and diffused down through the organization through the MBO process. In this manner, organizational objectives are translated into specific behavioral objectives for individual members. Our primary focus here is with the nature of the interaction between superiors and individual subordinates in an MBO program. Although there are many variations on the MBO theme, most superior-subordinate interactions share the following similarities:

1. The superior meets with individual subordinates to develop and agree upon subordinate objectives for the coming months. These objectives usually involve both current job performance and personal

Management by Objectives (MBO). An elaborate, systematic, ongoing program designed to facilitate goal establishment, goal accomplishment, and employee development.

development that may prepare the subordinate to perform other tasks or seek promotion. The objectives are made as specific as possible and quantified, if feasible, to assist in subsequent evaluation of accomplishment. Time frames for accomplishment are specified, and the objectives may be given priority according to their agreed-upon importance. The methods to achieve the objectives might or might not be topics of discussion. Objectives, time frames, and priorities are put in writing.

2. There are periodic meetings to monitor subordinate progress in achieving objectives. During these meetings, people can modify objectives if new needs or problems are encountered.

3. An appraisal meeting is held to evaluate the extent to which the agreed-upon objectives have been achieved. Special emphasis is placed upon diagnosing the reasons for success or failure so that the meeting serves as a learning experience for both parties.

4. The MBO cycle is repeated.

An example of a simple MBO objectives form is shown in Exhibit 7.8. Plant manager John Atkins has met with company president Freda Cranford and agreed upon eight objectives for the coming months. Notice that these objectives are specific and in most cases quantified. Objectives 7 and 8 are personal development objectives, while the others are performance objectives. The objectives have been given "A" priority or "B" priority (column 2), and a specific deadline for accomplishment (column 3). In his own role as a manager, Atkins would probably use some of these objectives as a basis for establishing the objectives of his subordinates. Thus, objectives 1 through 6 would become the basis of even more specific goals for the production manager, the shipping manager, and the personnel manager who report to Atkins. Thus, the MBO program diffuses a goal orientation throughout the organization.

Over the years, a wide variety of organizations has implemented MBO, including Kodak Australasia, Paul Revere Life, the U.S. Air Force, and the Colorado State Patrol. Overall, the research evidence shows clear productivity gains.[47] However, a number of factors are associated with the failure of MBO programs. For one thing, MBO is an elaborate, difficult, time-consuming process, and its implementation must have the full commitment of top management. One careful review showed a 56 percent average gain in productivity for programs with high top management commitment and a 6 percent gain for those with low commitment.[48] If such commitment is absent, managers at lower levels simply go through the motions of practicing MBO. At the very least, this reaction will lead to the haphazard specification of objectives and thus subvert the very core of MBO, goal setting. A frequent symptom of this degeneration is the complaint that MBO is "just a bunch of paperwork."[49] Indeed, at this stage, it is!

Even with the best of intentions, setting specific, quantified objectives can be a difficult process. This might lead to an overemphasis on measurable objectives at the expense of more qualitative objectives. For example, it might be much easier to agree on production goals than on goals that involve subordinate development, although both might be equally important. Also, excessive short-term orientation can be a problem with MBO. Finally, even if reasonable objectives are established, MBO can still be subverted if the performance review becomes an exercise in browbeating or punishing subordinates for failure to achieve objectives.[50]

Statement of Objectives	Priority	Deadline	Outcomes or Results
1. To Increase Deliveries to 98% of All Scheduled Delivery Dates	A	6/31	
2. To Reduce Waste and Spoilage to 3% of All Raw Materials Used	A	6/31	
3. To Reduce Lost Time Due to Accidents to 100 Person-Days/Year	B	2/1	
4. To Reduce Operating Cost to 10% Below Budget	A	1/15	
5. To Install a Quality Control Radioisotope System at a Cost of Less Than $53,000	A	3/15	
6. To Improve Production Scheduling and Preventative Maintenance so as to Increase Machine Utilization Time to 95% of Capacity	B	10/1	
7. To Complete the UCLA Executive Program This Year	A	6/31	
8. To Teach a Production Management Course in University Extension	B	6/31	

Manager's job title

John Atkins — 7/2 — PLANT MANAGER
Prepared by the Manager — Date — Managerial Job Objectives

F. W. Cranford — 7/2 — PRESIDENT
Reviewed by Supervisor — Date — Supervisor's Job Title

Source: Adapted from Raia, A. P. (1974). *Managing by objectives.* Glenview, IL: Scott, Foresman, © 1974, p. 60. Reprinted by permission.

EXHIBIT 7.8
A simple format for recording objectives in an MBO program.

ALTERNATIVE WORKING SCHEDULES AS MOTIVATORS FOR A DIVERSE WORK FORCE

Most North Americans work a five-day week of approximately 40 hours—the "nine-to-five grind." However, many organizations have begun to experiment with modifying these traditional working schedules. The purpose of these modifications isn't to motivate people to work harder and thus produce direct performance benefits. Rather, the purpose is to meet diverse workforce needs and promote job satisfaction. In turn, this should facilitate recruiting the best personnel and reduce costly absenteeism and turnover.

Flex-time

One alternative to traditional working schedules is **flex-time**, which was first introduced on a large scale in Europe. In its most simple and common form, management requires employees to report for work on each working day and work a given number of hours. However, the times at which they arrive and leave are flexible, as long as they are present during certain core times. For example, companies might permit employees to begin their day anytime after 7 A.M. and work until 6 P.M., as long as they put in eight hours and are present during the core times of 9:15 until noon and 2 until 4:15 (Exhibit 7.9).

Flex-time. An alternative work schedule in which arrival and quitting times are flexible.

Other systems permit employees to tally hours on a weekly or monthly basis, although they are still usually required to be present during the core time of each working day.[51]

Flex-time is obviously well suited to meeting the needs of a diverse work force, since it allows employees to tailor arrival and departure time to their own transportation and childcare situation. It should reduce absenteeism, since employees can handle personal matters during conventional business hours.[52] Also, flexible working hours connote a degree of prestige and trust that is usually reserved for executives and professionals.

When jobs are highly interdependent, such as on an assembly line, flex-time becomes an unlikely strategy. To cite an even more extreme example, we simply can't have members of a hospital operating room team showing up for work whenever it suits them! In addition, flex-time might lead to problems in achieving adequate supervisory coverage. For these reasons, not surprisingly, flex-time is most frequently implemented in office environments. For instance, in a bank, the core hours might be when the bank is open to the public.

Although flex-time has generally been limited to white-collar personnel, it has been applied in a variety of organizations, including insurance companies (Metropolitan Life), financial institutions (Canada Trust, Boston's State Street Bank), and government offices (many U.S. states, Canadian and U.S. civil service).

Although the quality of the research on flex-time varies, we can draw a number of conclusions.[53] First, employees who work under flex-time almost always prefer the system to fixed hours. In addition, work attitudes generally

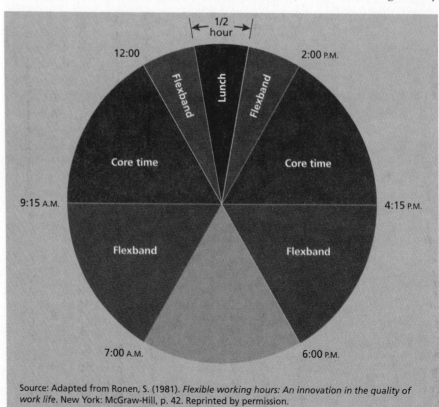

EXHIBIT 7.9
An example of a flex-time schedule.

Source: Adapted from Ronen, S. (1981). *Flexible working hours: An innovation in the quality of work life.* New York: McGraw-Hill, p. 42. Reprinted by permission.

become more positive, and employers report minimal abuse of the arrangement. When measured, absenteeism and tardiness have often shown decreases following the introduction of flex-time, and first-line supervisors and managers are usually positively inclined toward the system. Interestingly, slight productivity gains are often reported under flex-time, probably due to better use of scarce resources or equipment rather than to increased motivation.

Compressed Workweek

A second alternative to traditional working schedules is the **compressed workweek**. This system compresses the hours worked each week into fewer days. The most common compressed workweek is the 4–40 system, in which employees work four ten-hour days each week rather than the traditional five eight-hour days. Thus, the organization or department might operate Monday through Thursday or Tuesday through Friday, although rotation schemes that keep the organization open five days a week are also employed.[54] Printer Quad/Graphics uses a 3–36 system with three 12-hour days a week.

Like flex-time, the shorter workweek might be expected to reduce absenteeism because employees can pursue personal business or family matters in what had been working time. In addition, the 4–40 schedule reduces commuting costs and time by 20 percent and provides an extra day a week for leisure or family pursuits. Although the longer workday could pose a problem for single parents, a working couple with staggered off-days could actually provide their own child care on two of five "working" days.

Technical roadblocks to the implementation of the 4–40 workweek include the possibility of reduced customer service and the negative effects of fatigue that can accompany longer working days. The latter problem is likely to be especially acute when the work is strenuous.

Although research on the effects of the four-day week is less extensive than that for flex-time, a couple of conclusions do stand out.[55] First, people who have experienced the four-day system seem to *like* it. Sometimes this liking is accompanied by increased job satisfaction, but the effect might be short-lived.[56] In many cases, the impact of the compressed workweek might be better for family life than for work life. Second, workers have often reported an increase in fatigue following the introduction of the compressed week. This might be responsible for the uneven impact of the system on absenteeism, sometimes decreasing it and sometimes not. Potential gains in attendance might be nullified as workers take an occasional day off to recuperate from fatigue.[57] Finally, the more sophisticated research studies do not report lasting changes in productivity due to the short workweek.[58]

Job Sharing

Job sharing occurs when two part-time employees divide the work (and perhaps the benefits) of a full-time job.[59] The two can share all aspects of the job equally, or some kind of complementary arrangement can occur in which one party does some tasks and the co-holder does other tasks.

Job sharing is obviously attractive to people who want to spend more time with small children or sick elders than a conventional five-day-a-week routine permits. By the same token, it can enable organizations to attract and/or retain

Compressed workweek. An alternative work schedule in which employees work fewer than the normal five days a week but still put in a normal number of hours per week.

Job sharing. An alternative work schedule in which two part-time employees divide the work of a full-time job.

Job sharing, when two part-time employees divide the work of a full-time job, is an attractive prospect to people who need to spend time out of the office.

Total quality management (TQM). A systematic attempt to achieve continuous improvement in the quality of an organization's products and/or services.

highly capable employees who might otherwise decide against full-time employment.

There is virtually no hard research on job sharing. However, anecdotal reports suggest that the job sharers must make a concerted effort to communicate well with each other as well as with superiors, co-workers, and clients. Such communication is greatly facilitated by contemporary computer technology and voice mail. However, coordination problems are bound to occur if there isn't adequate communication. Also, problems with performance appraisal can occur when two individuals share one job.

TOTAL QUALITY MANAGEMENT AND MOTIVATION

As the earlier sections illustrate, organizations have a lot of options when it comes to using money, job design, goal setting, and work scheduling as motivators. Confused about when to do what? The concepts of *fit* and *balance* can help to resolve this confusion. First, the motivational systems chosen should have a good fit with the strategic goals of the organization. Ultimately, speed, quality, and volume of output involve some tradeoffs, and we won't achieve one of these outcomes if we reward another. Second, balance among the components of a motivational system is critical. Job design and work schedules must allow employees to achieve the goals that are set, and the reward system needs to be directed toward this achievement. Let's examine motivational fit and balance in the context of total quality management.

As we discussed in Chapter 1, **total quality management** (TQM) is a systematic attempt to achieve continuous improvement in the quality of an organization's products and/or services. Quality is defined very broadly to include things such as reliability of performance, ease of use, timely delivery, and value-for-money. A number of characteristics typical of TQM are relevant to our current topic of motivation.[60] These include:

- *An obsession with customer satisfaction.* These customers can be both external customers (e.g., American Express cardholders) and internal customers (e.g., American Express service offices are the customers of the firm's MIS department).

- *A concern for good relations with suppliers.* Suppliers are seen as an integral aspect to achieving high quality, not simply a source of the lowest-priced supply.

- *A search for continuous improvement of processes.* Organizations achieve high quality with meticulous attention to *how* a product or service reaches a customer. Federal Express satisfies customers with fast, reliable delivery. It makes money by understanding *how* to do this at a low cost.

- *The prevention (not just detection) of quality errors.* Rather than fixing things after they go wrong, attention to processes enables organizations to design errors out of the production phase of the product or service.

- *Frequent measurement and assessment.* Customer needs, customer satisfaction, supplier performance, competitor performance, and internal processes are all rigorously tracked and analyzed.

- *Extensive training.* Employee training is seen as an investment and as necessary to support the other TQM initiatives.

- *High employee involvement and teamwork.* The basic philosophy here is that *all* employees at all levels can contribute to delivering high quality products or services by working together.

Now, let's see how the motivation techniques that we have discussed are related to TQM. How, in practice, do they "fit" with this management philosophy? Several of the examples below are from winners of the U.S. government's Malcolm Baldrige National Quality Award.[61]

TQM and Goal Setting

"Continuous improvement" doesn't sound like a very specific goal! However, everything about TQM except its general definition places a high premium on specific goal setting.

Many firms pursuing quality begin at the top using a process called benchmarking to develop quality goals. **Benchmarking** is a systematic process for examining the products, services, and work processes of firms that are recognized as illustrating the best practices for organizational improvement.[62] In other words, it is recognized that quality goals have to be set using information from the organizations that are really *good* at the practice in question. This assures that the goals are challenging but also attainable.

Competitive benchmarking uses firms in the same industry as standards for comparison. Because dealing with competitors is a sensitive issue, this is sometimes done through trade groups that collect and share information anonymously. For example, there is a competitive benchmarking agreement among semiconductor manufacturers (e.g., Intel, DEC, Texas Instruments) and telecommunications competitors (e.g., Bell Atlantic, AT&T, GTE). *Generic benchmarking* looks for the best practices regardless of industry as long as they can be translated into one's own firm. For instance, Xerox visited L.L. Bean (the Maine clothing and outdoors mail order company) to learn about its excellent warehousing, materials handling, and order filling.[63]

Quality-oriented firms often include quality goals as part of the performance appraisal process. For example, at Westinghouse Commercial Nuclear Fuel Division, quality improvement is explicitly included in an MBO program. Since feedback is necessary for goal achievement, these firms are very active in surveying customers, suppliers and their own employees for relevant performance information. Personnel are also trained to collect and interpret quality data in their own domain. Many organizations use goal setting to motivate quality performances from their suppliers, setting explicit standards rather than waiting to see what comes through the door. Ford Motor Company has been a pioneer in this area, especially in assisting its suppliers to achieve its standards by doing things such as giving engineering support.

TQM and Job Design

One aspect of TQM concerns streamlining processes, where possible, so that there are fewer opportunities for things to go wrong in the production of a completed product or service. On the surface, this might look like bad news for interesting jobs. However, many firms with successful TQM programs have accompanied process simplification with the empowerment of the workforce. **Empowerment** entails giving people the authority, opportunity, and motivation to take initiative and solve organizational problems. In TQM, this often

Benchmarking. A systematic process for examining the products, services, and work processes of firms that are recognized as illustrating the best practices for organizational improvement.

Empowerment. Giving people the authority, opportunity, and motivation to take initiative and solve organizational problems.

L.L. Bean, the mail order outdoor store, has long been known for its customer service orientation.

involves the use of job enrichment techniques. For instance, inspection of one's own work (direct feedback) is very common, as is increased autonomy to solve customer service problems expediently. For example, at Motorola, sales representatives have the authority to replace defective products even six years after their purchase. Putting "inside" employees into contact with customers is common in quality-oriented firms, thus enhancing external client relationships for the employee and providing a conduit for information from the customer. For example, employees of Lexus, Toyota's luxury car division, call several purchasers each month to find out how their cars are performing. Things can also work in the other direction. Some firms empower lower-level employees to go to suppliers to sort out quality problems. Finally, many companies have used the problem-solving capabilities inherent in teamwork to foster quality. Baldrige Award winner Cadillac employs semiautonomous work teams. In each of these cases, companies have modified job design to empower employees to prevent or solve quality problems. At Quad/Graphics, the "Spring Fling" holiday for managers is symbolic of the fact that employees are empowered.

TQM and Money

Successful quality-oriented firms go to a lot of trouble to balance individual rewards with team-oriented rewards.[64] This recognizes the fact that individuals can contribute to quality but that job designs often dictate teamwork. Xerox Business Products and Systems uses gainsharing to reward teamwork. At Federal Express and Cadillac, managers can make instant cash awards to recognize special contributions to quality. New Balance, the athletic shoe maker, eliminated piecerate pay and installed a team approach that bases 70 percent of pay on quality and 30 percent on volume. Skill-based pay seems like a natural for TQM, given the system's emphasis on training.

Firms that pursue quality also put a lot of emphasis on nonmonetary recognition, targeting higher order needs such as esteem. For instance, at AMP of Canada, a manufacturer of electric connecting products, teams that have made process improvements showcase them to co-workers in a trade fair-like setting.

Some observers have gone so far as to argue that traditional individually oriented performance appraisal is at odds with the emphasis on processes and teamwork that characterize TQM. Appraisal of teams using customer (internal or external) input is one alternative.[65]

TQM and Alternative Working Schedules

The application of alternative work schedules requires very careful consideration in the context of TQM, especially in the domain of customer satisfaction. For example, the introduction of flex-time means that either internal or external customers might be deprived of the timely advice or attention of a key organizational member who hasn't arrived for work yet or who has left "early." Flex-time can also play havoc with the operation of work teams. The compressed work week can present even greater problems, since key personnel could be unavailable for a whole day. Job sharing can be particularly worrisome in terms of perceptions of service quality. One manager in a computer service company reported that clients sometimes prefer one job sharer more than another or feel that their account is not receiving the full attention of a single service rep.[66]

How to deal with these problems? Balance among the motivational strategies and adherence to other TQM principles often shows the way. For example, organizations can redesign jobs using cross-training so that even with flex-time there is always someone capable present. At Levi Strauss, blue-collar production teams can choose their own schedule as long as all team members agree to abide by it. Finally, again in line with the TQM emphasis on training, organizations can train people to use alternative work schedules appropriately. DuPont and Corning extend this training right down to the employee level (how to design a backup schedule, etc.) rather than simply training managers.

The Manager's Notebook   The Weyerhaeuser Truck Drivers

1. In theory, a monetary incentive could certainly get the drivers' attention and motivate them to haul heavier loads. In practice, however, unions have not shown great enthusiasm for such incentives (especially when they are given individually), and management might balk at paying drivers extra for what they should already be doing. Also, a financial incentive could encourage overloading, and it will require an expensive system to record weights and calculate bonuses.

2. Weyerhaeuser chose goal setting. With the union's cooperation, drivers were assigned a specific, challenging performance goal of loading their trucks to 94 percent of legal weight capacity. Before setting this goal, management simply asked drivers to do their best to maximize their weight. The results? Over the first several weeks, load capacity gradually increased to over 90 percent and remained at this high level for *seven years*! In the first nine months alone, company accountants conservatively estimated the savings at $250,000. These results were achieved without driver participation in setting the goal and without monetary incentives for goal accomplishment. Drivers evidently found the 94 percent goal motivating in and of itself; they frequently recorded their weights in informal competition with other drivers.

EXECUTIVE SUMMARY

◆ Money should be most effective as a motivator when it is made contingent upon performance. Schemes to link pay to performance on production jobs are called wage incentive plans. Piecerate, in which workers are paid a certain amount of money for each item produced, is the prototype of all wage incentive plans. In general, wage incentives increase productivity, but their introduction can be accompanied by a number of problems, one of which is the restriction of production. Attempts to link pay to performance on white-collar jobs are called merit pay plans. Evidence suggests that many merit pay plans are less effective than they could be because merit pay is inadequate, performance ratings are mistrusted, or extreme secrecy about pay levels prevails. Compensation plans to enhance teamwork include profit sharing, gainsharing, and skill based pay.

◆ Recent views advocate increasing the scope (breadth and depth) of jobs to capitalize on their inherent motivational properties, as opposed to the job simplification of the past. The Job Characteristics Model by Hackman and Oldham suggests that jobs have five core characteristics that affect their motivating potential: skill variety, task identity, task significance, autonomy, and feedback. When jobs are high in these characteristics, favorable motivational and attitudinal consequences should occur. Job enrichment involves designing jobs to enhance intrinsic motivation and the quality of working life. Some specific enrichment techniques include combining tasks, establishing client relationships,

reducing supervision and reliance on others, forming work teams, and making feedback more direct.

◆ Goal setting can be an effective motivator when goals are specific, challenging, and acceptable to workers. In some cases, companies can facilitate acceptance of goals through employee participation in goal setting and by financial incentives for goal attainment, but freedom from coercion and punishment seems to be the key factor in achieving goal acceptance. Management by Objectives (MBO) is an elaborate goal-setting and evaluation process that organizations typically use for management jobs.

◆ Some organizations have adopted alternative working schedules such as flex-time, the compressed workweek, or job sharing with expectations of motivational benefits. Although these schemes should have little effect on productivity, they have the potential to reduce absence and turnover and enhance the quality of working life for a diverse work force.

◆ Total quality management is a systematic attempt to achieve continuous improvement in the quality of an organization's products and/or services. It includes great concern with customer satisfaction, supplier relations, continuous process improvement, error prevention, measurement, training, and employee involvement. Effective TQM programs mix and balance the motivation techniques we discussed in this chapter to ensure the implementation of TQM principles.

KEY CONCEPTS

Piecerate
Wage incentive plans
Restriction of productivity
Merit pay plans
Lump sum bonus
Profit sharing
Gainsharing
Skill based pay
Skill variety
Autonomy
Task significance
Task identity

Feedback
Growth need strength
Job enrichment
Goal setting
Management by Objectives (MBO)
Flex-time
Compressed workweek
Job sharing
Total quality management (TQM)
Benchmarking
Empowerment

DISCUSSION QUESTIONS

1. Describe some jobs for which you think it would be difficult to link pay to performance. What is there about these jobs that provokes this difficulty?

2. Imagine two insurance companies that have merit pay plans for salaried white-collar personnel. In one organization the plan truly rewards good performers, while in the other it does not. Both companies decide to make salaries completely public. What will be the consequences of such a change for each company? (Be specific, using concepts such as expectancy, instrumentality, job satisfaction, and turnover.)

3. You are, of course, familiar with the annual lists of the world's ten worst-dressed people or the ten worst movies. Here's a new one: A job enrichment consultant has developed a list of the ten worst jobs, which includes a highway toll collector, pool typist, bank guard, and automatic elevator operator. Use the five core job characteristics to describe each of these jobs. Could you enrich any of these jobs? How? Which should be completely automated? Can you add some jobs to the list?

4. What are the essential distinctions between gainsharing and profit sharing?

5. Some observers have argued that the jobs of the president of the United States and the prime minister of Canada are "too big" for one person to perform adequately. This probably means that the jobs are perceived as having too much scope or being too enriched. Use the Job Characteristics Model to explore the accuracy of this contention.

6. Debate the following statements: Of all the motivational techniques we discussed in this chapter, goal setting is the simplest to implement. Goal setting is no more than doing what a good manager should be doing anyway.

7. Imagine an office setting in which a change to either a four-day week or flex-time would appear to be equally feasible to introduce. What would be the pros and cons of each system? How would factors such as the nature of the business, the age of the workforce, and the average commuting distance affect the choice of systems?

8. Debate the following proposition: The motivational strategies we discussed in this chapter are manipulative and unethical, and they put too much pressure on the workforce.

9. How is the concept of workforce diversity related to the motivational techniques discussed in the chapter?

10. Discuss how organizations can realize the total quality management principle of strong attention to customer satisfaction with the motivational techniques that we have covered.

EXPERIENTIAL EXERCISE
CHOOSE YOUR JOB

People differ in the kinds of jobs they prefer. The following questions give you a chance to consider just what it is about a job that is most important to *you*. For each question, indicate the extent to which you would prefer Job A or Job B if you had to make a choice between them. In answering, assume that everything else about the two jobs is the same except the characteristics being compared. There are no "correct" answers. Just give your personal choice.

SCORING AND INTERPRETATION

These questions make up the Growth Need Strength measure from J. Richard Hackman and Greg Oldham's Job Diagnostic Survey. To determine your own growth need strength, first subtract your responses on items 2, 3, 4, 6, 8, and 9 from six. Then, add up the resulting scores on all twelve items and divide the total by twelve. This is your growth need strength score. It should fall somewhere between 1 and 5.

People with high growth needs have a strong desire to obtain growth satisfaction from their jobs. The average growth score for thousands of individuals employed in a

	JOB A		JOB B

1. A job where the pay is very good.

A job where there is considerable opportunity to be creative and innovative.

1	2	3	4	5
Strongly Prefer A	Slightly Prefer A	Neutral	Slightly Prefer B	Strongly Prefer B

2. A job where you are often required to make important decisions.

A job with many pleasant people to work with.

1	2	3	4	5
Strongly Prefer A	Slightly Prefer A	Neutral	Slightly Prefer B	Strongly Prefer B

3. A job in which greater responsibility is given to those who do the best work.

A job in which greater responsibility is given to loyal employees who have the most seniority.

1	2	3	4	5
Strongly Prefer A	Slightly Prefer A	Neutral	Slightly Prefer B	Strongly Prefer B

4. A job in an organization which is in financial trouble—and might have to close down within the year.

A job in which you are not allowed to have any say whatever in how your work is scheduled, or in the procedures to be used in carrying it out.

1	2	3	4	5
Strongly Prefer A	Slightly Prefer A	Neutral	Slightly Prefer B	Strongly Prefer B

5. A very routine job.

A job where your co-workers are not very friendly.

1	2	3	4	5
Strongly Prefer A	Slightly Prefer A	Neutral	Slightly Prefer B	Strongly Prefer B

6. A job with a supervisor who is often very critical of you and your work in front of other people.

A job which prevents you from using a number of skills that you worked hard to develop.

1	2	3	4	5
Strongly Prefer A	Slightly Prefer A	Neutral	Slightly Prefer B	Strongly Prefer B

7. A job with a supervisor who respects you and treats you fairly.

A job which provides constant opportunities for you to learn new and interesting things.

1	2	3	4	5
Strongly Prefer A	Slightly Prefer A	Neutral	Slightly Prefer B	Strongly Prefer B

8. A job where there is a real chance you could be laid off.

A job with very little chance to do challenging work.

1	2	3	4	5
Strongly Prefer A	Slightly Prefer A	Neutral	Slightly Prefer B	Strongly Prefer B

9. A job in which there is a real chance for you to develop new skills and advance in the organization.

A job which provides lots of vacation time and an excellent fringe benefit package.

1	2	3	4	5
Strongly Prefer A	Slightly Prefer A	Neutral	Slightly Prefer B	Strongly Prefer B

10. A job with little freedom and independence to do your work in the way you think best.

A job where the working conditions are poor.

1	2	3	4	5
Strongly Prefer A	Slightly Prefer A	Neutral	Slightly Prefer B	Strongly Prefer B

11. A job with very satisfying teamwork.

A job which allows you to use your skills and abilities to the fullest extent.

1	2	3	4	5
Strongly Prefer A	Slightly Prefer A	Neutral	Slightly Prefer B	Strongly Prefer B

12. A job which offers little or no challenge.

A job which requires you to be completely isolated from co-workers.

1	2	3	4	5
Strongly Prefer A	Slightly Prefer A	Neutral	Slightly Prefer B	Strongly Prefer B

wide variety of jobs is 4.23. Here are some other growth need norms based on occupation, education, and age.[67]

4.46 White collar	4.92 Sales
4.00 Blue collar	4.13 Machine trades
4.92 Middle managers	4.16 Construction
4.62 First line managers	4.02 High school graduates
4.76 Professional and technical	4.72 University graduates
4.18 Clerical	4.01 Under age 20
	4.25 Ages 20–29

Source: Hackman, J. R., & Oldham, G. R. (1974). *The Job Diagnostic Survey: An instrument for the diagnosis of jobs and the evaluation of job redesign projects.* Yale University Department of Administrative Sciences Technical Report No. 4.

CASE STUDY
THE UNPOPULAR PAY PLAN

Gilbert Porterfield, vice president for compensation at Top Chemical Company, watched nervously as the special committee for compensation redesign gathered to discuss the proposed pay plan. Members from top and middle management, as well as peer group representatives from throughout the company, settled into their seats holding copies of his plan for this 93-year-old, $2 billion company. TopChem CEO Sam Verde opened the meeting.

"Three years ago, when we launched our Quality For All program at TopChem, we expected a great deal of resistance from our troops," Verde began. "People don't like to have their jobs questioned, let alone redesigned. But now they are listening. We're starting to make real changes in the way people work together. And we're making progress in speeding products to market, improving product quality, and routing out inefficiencies.

"But as you all know, change is a process, not an event. That's why we've gathered this committee to investigate how to develop a pay system congruent with the philosophy of QFA. Because employee involvement is critical to everything we do under this new mind-set, all of you have been gleaning information from your peers. Gil's plan reflects your preliminary feedback. Now that it is on the table, I want to move toward implementation. Gil, why don't you give us some background?"

Porterfield stood and addressed the group. "As you know, under QFA we've reorganized employees into product-oriented teams. We had a solid business reason for that: to allow and encourage employees at all levels to develop products quicker, better, and cheaper. As Sam said, the company's organization is starting to reflect that philosophy. "But," he said, pausing for effect, "our compensation hasn't. Our old system just doesn't work any-

more. It pays by the old values of hierarchy, rank, seniority, hours worked, and a lot of other standards that don't mean much in the new organization. We have moved to an all salaried work force, which caused grumblings, sure. It's time to go way beyond that."

Porterfield flicked off the lights and pointed to figures on the overhead screen. The screen read:

"QFA PAY PLAN 92"
BASE PAY = 75% of former pay - determined by internal equity
FLEXIBLE PAY = 25% of former pay - determined by:

- Team's ability to show 5% annual improvement in 4 areas:
  - Quality: 30%
  - Unit Cost to Market: 25%
  - Speed to Market: 20%
  - Safety and Environmental Compliance: 10%
  - Divisional financial performance: 15%

"Very simply," Porterfield explained, "the plan is designed to give employees working on teams real incentives for constant improvement and overall excellence. It's meant to recognize the real changes that have taken place in the company. New products and new processes are now the results of teams that work together solving their own problems. This system supports that philosophy.

"The premise is fundamentally very simple. Pay is divided into two parts: one fixed share of individual salary is based on internal equity—roughly, what others in and out of the company make for similar jobs. The variable aspect of the system pays employees for the performance of their group. Are they showing incremental improvements as a team in quality, unit cost, speed to market? Are they working with other divisions to raise profits for their entire division? The metrics of the equation, such as how many defects per product constitute high quality, will be determined by the ways each group works. But whatever the specifics, this new pay plan lines up squarely with the new company managerial philosophy: it's about accountability, excellence, and results. Any questions?"

Sid Noble, head of research and development, broke the silence. "I don't like it," he said flatly. "And I'll tell you why. I think we've gone far enough on this teamwork kick. Frankly, a lot of this is fiction—a motivational happy land that doesn't square with how my people really work. The people I hire and develop in this company are primarily scientists. With scientific degrees and scientific backgrounds. They're damn good at what they do, and what they do is apply their chemical expertise to a business strategy.

"They already spend too much time explaining chem 101 to their other team members, time they could better spend in a lab. I want to free them up to work. To do what they do best and what we need them to do most.

"Most of all, I want to be able to attract and motivate the best and the brightest. But I can't recruit them if their pay depends on the performance of other members of a team. If we go this way, we're going to lose our good people and our whole R&D base. This new plan wants to make them team members first and scientists second. I consider that backwards."

"Of course you do," shot back Ruth Gibson, who worked as a chemical mixer on a packaging team and served as a team representative in the meeting. "You science guys believe your role of inventing products is much more important than those of the people out there actually mixing the chemicals, pouring them into drums, shipping them out, and selling them.

"But you don't represent the thinking of other product developers, especially those who are out there on the factory floor. My industrial packaging team now includes Tim O'Brien, who used to work all alone with the other scientists in the research laboratory. Now he works as part of our 25-person product packaging team, and he likes it. He likes knowing how customers use the materials he designs. He likes knowing what people pay for the product wholesale. He feels he does his job better because he knows how we build the products and he actually has a stake in how we—this packaging team—make the products together. Why not tie his pay to how we improve as a team? His skills are valuable only to the degree that our team succeeds in serving our customers."

"Ruth, perhaps you would like . . . " Noble began.

"Just wait Sid," Gibson continued. "Because I do have a problem with another part of this plan. It ties the performance of my group to that of everyone in the factory by bringing in plant performance. Now I'll tell all of you here that we know there's still a lot of people who haven't caught on yet. My group is going gangbusters. We're shipping products in three weeks that used to take us three months. We've cut defects to one-fifth of what they used to be. We've brought the costs down, and we're developing innovations that other teams are picking up on.

"But these improvements didn't come easily. I worked weekends for close to a year. So did everyone else on my team. Why? Because we bought into the new idea of how this company should work. We like making our own decisions, and, frankly, most of us thought that if we had the power to make choices we could do it as well as upper management—maybe better. And I think we have. But there's something missing here.

"We haven't seen a raise or payout from all our hard work. Sure, our plant manager is down there every month or so telling everyone in the plant about our successes. But the fact is, we're hardly making any more money than we did two years ago.

"This pay plan will make those conditions worse. It's going to punish teams like mine for the failings of others instead of rewarding us for the work we do and have already done. What bonus will my team receive for the progress it's made or will make?" Gibson folded her arms and rested back in her chair.

"If I may?" began Miles Haddock, TopChem's CFO. "I take exception to Ruth's argument. What she may see as a penalty, I see as a natural fact of doing business. We are going to face problems. And those problems are eventually going to show up on the company's bottom line. The real question is who should pay for them? Ruth may be frustrated about having her pay tied to areas beyond her control, but so what? Why should her team be any different from the others? Who is TopChem if not the employees of the entire company?

"Let's imagine that a rise in oil prices drives up the cost of our ethylene, which drives up the cost of our products. The company takes an across-the-board hit. When this happened six years ago, TopChem protected its employees because we saw pay as a fixed cost. We still do. Under this plan, less than 4 percent of an employee's pay is tied up to overall company performance. I don't consider that too onerous. After all, upper management has far more of their pay tied to overall performance—up to 60 percent. Why shouldn't everybody share both the up and the downside? If you ask me, I think we should dramatically increase that aspect."

Gus Teller, corporate head of training, cleared his throat loudly and spoke. "I agree with Miles about tying pay to the performance of the company, but for different reasons. The benefit of tying a large group's performance to the pay of its members is that it encourages everybody to excel. And it ensures excellence through conflict. You see, productive groups have members who tell each other what works and what doesn't: they teach each other how to work better. The same should hold true for teams. Good teams need to raise the level of teams that haven't caught on.

"Why can't a member of Ruth's team invite somebody from plastics out for a beer after work and discuss what plastics could do better? This plan has that built into it. You won't have people working together unless there's an incentive for them to do so: I see that built into this plan. In fact, I would make more pay dependent on how well teams teach other teams useful skills."

Bill Purcell, a team leader from polymers, cut in. "Please, Gus, let's be real. Do you really think any one of us has the time, let alone the *desire*, to take people out for beers and tell them how to do their jobs? Oh sure: 'Hey Al, how's your wife? Heard you traveled to Yosemite last month. And, oh yeah, I wanted to tell your team how you should start thinking about purchasing your materials.' I don't think so.

"Look, I don't have any problems with the plan put forward. But TopChem still has too many people who can't and won't get on board, and we're spending too much time and money trying to train them. You talk about cutting down on bureaucracy but we still have almost as many employees as we did four years ago. I say the alternative to a plan like this is to reduce the entire work force by 15 percent through voluntary severance. Those people who won't change will leave. Then maybe we can think about a pay plan like this."

"Okay, Bill, thanks." Verde said. "Thank you all for your input. Now let me share just a few thoughts in closing. Gil, I know you've spent an enormous amount of time talking to employees and peer groups throughout the company and testing out ideas before sharing this plan with us. And in principle, I like this system. It lines up with our new quality philosophy pretty squarely. It ties the payout to a source. It assumes the good work of empowered employees.

"We never thought we'd design a perfect quality program. I don't believe a perfect pay plan exists either. But I think we've come up with some great suggestions here. I

am going to take Gilbert's plan, think about your input, and roll out our new system next month."

Source: Enrenfeld, T. (1992, January-February). The case of the unpopular pay plan. *Harvard Business Review*, 14–17.

1. Is TopChem correct to be revising its compensation system in light of the Quality For All program?
2. The proposed QFA Pay Plan 92 effectively reduces base pay by 25 percent and puts it "at risk" based on team performance. What are the general conditions that should exist before putting people's pay at risk like this?
3. What are some of the underlying themes that emerge in the voiced resistance to the plan?
4. The QFA program is obviously meant to be a total quality management program. Does the way that this plan is being designed square with TQM principles?
5. What should Sam Verde do now?

SOCIAL BEHAVIOR

AND

ORGANIZATIONAL

PROCESSES

LEARNING OBJECTIVES

AFTER READING CHAPTER 8 YOU SHOULD BE ABLE TO:

1 DEFINE GROUPS, DISTINGUISH BETWEEN FORMAL AND INFORMAL GROUPS, AND DISCUSS THE FACTORS THAT LEAD TO GROUP FORMATION.

2 DISCUSS GROUP DEVELOPMENT.

3 EXPLAIN HOW GROUP SIZE AND MEMBER DIVERSITY INFLUENCE WHAT OCCURS IN GROUPS.

4 REVIEW HOW NORMS, ROLES, AND STATUS AFFECT GROUP INTERACTION.

5 DISCUSS THE CAUSES AND CONSEQUENCES OF GROUP COHESIVENESS.

6 EXPLAIN THE DYNAMICS OF SOCIAL LOAFING.

7 DISCUSS HOW TO DESIGN AND SUPPORT SELF-MANAGED TEAMS.

8 EXPLAIN THE LOGIC BEHIND CROSS-FUNCTIONAL TEAMS AND DESCRIBE HOW THEY CAN OPERATE EFFECTIVELY.

XEL DRAMATICALLY INCREASED ITS PERFORMANCE LEVEL BY USING INNOVATIVE TEAM-BASED MANAGEMENT.

CHAPTER 8

GROUPS AND
TEAMWORK

In the mid-1980s, not long after Bill Sanko and his partners

had engineered the buyout, they could see that their fledgling

telecommunications-equipment company was struggling. Granted.... it was making

money. But Sanko.... knew that he needed to sell more to the Baby Bells and to big

industrial customers that operated their own phone systems.

XEL's only hope was agility. Lightning turnaround of orders, quicker than any big

company could manage. Speedy response to customer needs. All done with close atten-

tion to cost. Fleetness of foot, unhappily, was just what XEL lacked. Costs weren't

rock-bottom, either.

On the shop floor, for example, cycle time—the period from start of production

to finished goods—was about eight weeks. That. . . tied up money in inventory. The

company's chain of command had scarcely changed since GTE days. Line workers reported to supervisors, who reported to unit or departmental managers, who reported on up the ladder to Sanko and a crew of top executives. Every rung added time and expense.

"We needed everybody. . . thinking about how we could better satisfy our customers, how we could improve quality, how we could reduce costs," says the chief executive. Finally, Sanko and [Manufacturing VP John] Puckett decided to set up self-managing teams, then a hot new concept, and brought [in a] consultant to help them get started. By 1988 the teams had been established—and the supervisory and support staff reduced by 30%.

Today, five years later, XEL has rebuilt itself around those teams so thoroughly that the Association for Manufacturing Excellence recently chose the company as one of four to be featured in a video on team-based management. Dozens of visitors, from companies such as Hewlett-Packard, have trooped through XEL's Aurora, Colo., factory.

What they see is striking. Snappily colored banners hang from the plant's high ceiling to mark each team's work area. Charts on the wall track attendance, on-time deliveries, and the other variables by which the teams gauge their performance. Diagrams indicate who on a team is responsible for tasks such as scheduling.

Every week, the schedulers meet with Puckett to review what needs to be built. The teams meet daily, nearly always without a boss, to plan their part in that agenda. Longer meetings, called as necessary, take up topics such as vacation planning or recurring production problems. Once a quarter each team makes a formal presentation to management on what it has and hasn't accomplished. Overheads, with fancy charts, are de rigueur.

And the numbers are right where Sanko had hoped they would be. Since the advent of teams, XEL's cost of assembly has dropped 25%. Inventory has been cut by half; quality levels have risen 30%. The company's all-important cycle time has plummeted from eight weeks to four days and is still falling.[1]

This excerpt from *Inc.* magazine shows how critical groups or teams are in determining organizational success. In this chapter, we will define the term group and discuss the nature of formal groups and informal groups in organizations. After this, we'll present the details of group formation and development. Then, we will consider how groups differ from one another structurally and explore the consequences of these differences. We'll also cover the problem of social loafing. Finally, we will examine how to design effective work teams.

WHAT IS A GROUP?

Group. Two or more people interacting interdependently to achieve a common goal.

We use the word group rather casually in everyday discourse—special-interest group, ethnic group, and others. However, for behavioral scientists, a **group** consists of two or more people interacting interdependently to achieve a common goal.

Interaction is the most basic aspect of a group—it suggests who is in the group and who is not. The interaction of group members need not be face-to-face, and it need not be verbal. For example, employees who "telecommute" can be part of their workgroup at the office even though they live miles away and communicate with a modem. Also, the impromptu group that forms to pass water buckets to fight a fire need not speak to meet the requirement of interaction. Interdependence simply means that group members rely to some degree upon each other to accomplish goals. Ten individuals who independently throw buckets of water on a fire do not constitute a true group. Finally, all groups have one or more goals that their members seek to achieve. These goals can range from having fun to marketing a new product to achieving world peace.

Group memberships are very important for two reasons. First, groups exert a tremendous influence *upon us*. They are the social mechanisms by which we acquire many beliefs, values, attitudes, and behaviors. Group membership is also important because groups provide a context in which *we* are able to exert influence upon *others*.

Formal work groups are groups that organizations establish to facilitate the achievement of organizational goals. They are intentionally designed to channel individual effort in an appropriate direction. The most common formal group consists of a superior and the subordinates who report to that superior. In a manufacturing company, one such group might consist of a production manager and the six shift supervisors who report to him. In turn, the shift supervisors head work groups composed of themselves and their respective subordinates. Thus, the hierarchy of most organizations is a series of formal interlocked work groups. As the XEL case shows, all this direct supervision is not always necessary. Nevertheless, XEL's self-managed teams are still formal work groups.

Other types of formal work groups include task forces and committees. *Task forces* are temporary groups that meet to achieve particular goals or to solve particular problems, such as suggesting productivity improvements. *Committees* are usually permanent groups that handle recurrent assignments outside of the usual work group structures. For example, a firm might have a standing committee on equal employment opportunity.

It is safe to say that early writers about management and organization felt that their work was done when they had described an organization's formal groups. After all, such groups had management's seal of approval and could be illustrated in black and white on an organizational chart. What more was there to say about grouping? In fact, you probably recognize how incomplete this view is. In addition to formal groups sanctioned by management to achieve organizational goals, informal grouping occurs in all organizations. **Informal groups** are groups that emerge naturally in response to the common interests of organizational members. They are seldom sanctioned by the organization, and their membership often cuts across formal groups. Informal groups can either help or hurt an organization, depending on their norms for behavior. We will consider this in detail later.

Formal work groups. Groups that are established by organizations to facilitate the achievement of organizational goals.

Informal groups. Groups that emerge naturally in response to the common interests of organizational members.

GROUP FORMATION

To orient ourselves to the role of groups, it is useful to consider the factors that lead to group formation. In the case of informal groups, we are concerned with the factors that prompt their emergence in the formal work setting. In the case of formal groups, we are interested in the factors that lead organizations to form such groups and the ease with which the groups can be maintained and managed. The formation of both types of groups is affected by opportunity for interaction, potential for goal accomplishment, and the personal characteristics of group members.

Opportunity for Interaction

One obvious prerequisite for group formation is opportunity for interaction. When people are able to interact with one another, they are able to recognize that they might have common goals that they can achieve through dependence on each other.[2] For example, "inside" employees (such as headquarters technical advisors) often develop more informal solidarity than "outside" employees (such as technicians who visit clients) because they are in more constant interaction. Similarly, organizations are adept at using open-plan offices, face-to-face meetings, and electronic networks to bolster formal work groups.

Potential for Goal Accomplishment

Potential for goal accomplishment is another factor that contributes to group formation and maintenance. Physical goals (such as building a bridge) or intellectual goals (such as designing a bridge) are often accomplished most efficiently by the careful division of labor among groups. Groups can also achieve social-emotional goals such as esteem and security. Informally, strangers might band together during a natural disaster, or employees might band together to protest the firing of a co-worker. Formally, organizations might use decision-making groups to spread the risk associated with a tough decision.

Members' Personal Characteristics

Finally, personal characteristics can influence group formation and maintenance. When it comes to attitudes, there is plenty of evidence that "birds of a feather flock together." That is, people with similar attitudes (such as satisfaction with their job) tend to gravitate together.[3] When it comes to personality characteristics, similar people are often attracted to each other, but opposites sometimes attract.[4] For example, dominant people might seek the company of submissive people. We are speaking here mainly of informal attraction and grouping. When organizations staff formal working groups, they often assign people with different but complementary skills, attitudes, or personalities to the group. A tight-fisted, practical accountant might be included to offset an impulsive, creative marketer.

GROUP DEVELOPMENT

Even relatively simple groups are actually complex social devices that require a fair amount of negotiation and trial-and-error before individual members begin to function like a true group. This happened at XEL Communications even though many employees knew each other before the new teams were formed—simple familiarity didn't replace the necessity for team development.

Typical Stages of Group Development

Leaders and trainers have observed that many groups develop through a series of stages over time.[5] Each stage presents the members with a series of challenges they must master in order to achieve the next stage. These stages (forming, storming, norming, performing, and adjourning) are presented in Exhibit 8.1.

Forming. At this early stage, group members try to orient themselves by "testing the waters." What are we doing here? What are the others like? What is our purpose? The situation is often ambiguous, and members are aware of their dependency on each other.

Storming. At this second stage, conflict often emerges. Confrontation and criticism occur as members determine whether they will go along with the way the group is developing. Sorting out roles and responsibilities is often at issue here. At XEL Communications, conflict arose in the stockroom team when the team's attendance taker chose to write up a fellow member who arrived late for work. Problems like this are more likely to happen earlier, rather than later, in group development.

Norming. At this stage, members resolve the issues that provoked the storming, and they develop social consensus. Compromise is often necessary. Interdependence is recognized, norms are agreed to, and the group becomes more cohesive (we'll study these processes later). Information and opinions flow freely.

Performing. With its social structure sorted out, the group devotes its energies toward task accomplishment. Achievement, creativity, and mutual assistance are prominent themes of this stage.

Adjourning. Some groups, such as task forces and design project teams, have a definite life span and disperse after achieving their goals. Also, some groups disperse when corporate layoffs and downsizing occur. At this adjourning

EXHIBIT 8.1
Stages of group development.

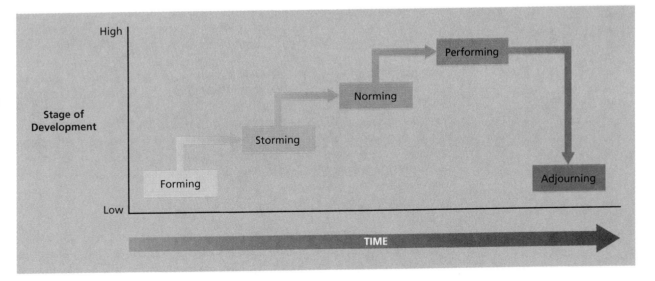

stage, rites and rituals that affirm the group's previous successful development are common (such as ceremonies and parties). Members often exhibit emotional support for each other.[6]

The stages model is a good tool for monitoring and troubleshooting how groups are developing. For example, at XEL Communications, management thought that the stockroom team had backslid when the conflict occurred. More likely, it had never resolved the storming stage.

The "In Focus: *Simulation Aids Team Development*" shows how to use a simulation based on the stages model to provide skills training in group development. It is very important to understand that not all groups go through these stages of development. The process applies mainly to new groups that have never met before. Well-acquainted task forces and committees can short-circuit these stages when they have a new problem to work out.[7] Also, some organizational settings are so structured that storming and norming are unnecessary for even strangers to coalesce into a team. For example, most commercial airline cockpit crews perform effectively even though they can be made up of virtual strangers who meet just before takeoff.[8]

Punctuated Equilibrium

Punctuated equilibrium model.
A model of group development that describes how groups with deadlines are affected by their first meetings and crucial midpoint transitions.

When groups have a specific deadline by which to complete some problem solving task, we can often observe a very different development sequence from that described above. Connie Gersick, whose research uncovered this sequence, describes it as a **punctuated equilibrium model** of group development.[9] Equilibrium means stability, and the research revealed apparent stretches of group stability punctuated by a critical first meeting, a midpoint change in group activity, and a rush to task completion. Along with many real-world work groups, Gersick studied student groups doing class projects, to see if this sequence of events sounds familiar.

Phase 1.   Phase 1 begins with the first meeting and continues until the midpoint in the group's existence. The very first meeting is critical in setting the agenda for what will happen in the remainder of this phase. Assumptions, approaches, and precedents that members develop in the first meeting end up dominating the first half of the group's life. Although it gathers information and holds meetings, the group makes little visible progress toward the goal.

Midpoint Transition.   The midpoint transition occurs at almost exactly the halfway point in time toward the group's deadline. For instance, if the group has a two-month deadline, the transition will occur at about one month. The transition marks a change in the group's approach, and how the group manages it is critical for the group to show progress. The need to move forward is apparent, and the group may seek outside advice. This transition may consolidate previously acquired information or even mark a completely new approach, but it crystallizes the group's activities for Phase 2 just like the first meeting did for Phase 1.

Phase 2.   For better or worse, decisions and approaches adopted at the midpoint get played out in Phase 2. It concludes with a final meeting that reveals a burst of activity and a concern for how outsiders will evaluate the product.

IN FOCUS　Simulation Aids Team Development

"People and the service and quality they can build are your competitive advantage today," says Duffy Smith, vice president of operations for Hostess Frito-Lay Co. in Mississauga, Ontario.

He uses a game called *Self-managed Work Teams: A Business Simulation*, which is produced by People Tech Products in Toronto, Ontario. Smith helped develop the board game when he was at Campbell Soup Co. The one-day workshop includes an elaborate scenario that puts participants into the roles of the members of newly formed teams in a fictitious organization.

The name of the company is One World Energy Systems. One World has commercialized a futuristic technology that converts food waste into electrical energy. The product, *Transformer*, supplies enough energy to power a household or small business. The company has determined that self-managed work teams are the most effective way to sell the new technology. These self-managed teams are responsible for all production, service, installation and billing of their customers. They're responsible for all administrative needs. As the game progresses, each round puts more pressure on the teams. They have more orders to process but not enough capacity for the orders.

"We developed the Self-Managed Work Team game because we believe it's a critical tool for on-the-job training," says Lorne Hartman, managing vice president at People Tech Products. He says that the game gives teams first-hand experience in a low-risk environment. Hartman joined with others at Campbell Soup and at IBM Canada to develop the simulation. It clearly parallels the stages of team development: forming, storming, norming, performing.

During each phase, there are structured exercises that draw the team members' attention to specific behavioral values. For example, at the beginning of the forming round, there's a team meeting, during which the participants commit to a set of shared values and define them behaviorally. Then, after each game round, members review how they worked together as a team—both as a team that's learning to play a new game and one that's working as a team in the simulated world of One World Energy Systems.

Participants at Campbell Soup, Skill Dynamics Canada and Hostess Frito-Lay, among others, have played the game. According to Smith, the game was so helpful for two companies that it became a developmental component of a plan using teams to redesign a factory. "The companies actually [placed] the people who [had played] this game onto a work

The Self-Managed Work Team game, developed in Canada, has become a critical tool for on-the-job training, providing first-hand experience in an unthreatening setting. The game parallels the stages of team development: forming, storming, norming, and performing.

team and used the simulated experience as part of the creative process in redesigning a factory. It's an automatic transfer into the workplace."

Source: Excerpted from Solomon, C. M. (1993, June). Simulation training builds teams through experience. *Personnel Journal*, 100–108.

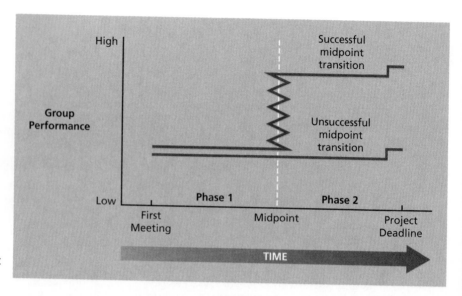

EXHIBIT 8.2
The punctuated equilibrium model of group development for two groups.

Exhibit 8.2 shows how the punctuated equilibrium model works for groups that successfully or unsuccessfully manage the midpoint transition.

What advice does the punctuated equilibrium model offer for managing product development teams, advertising groups, or class project groups?[10]

- Prepare carefully for the first meeting. What is decided here will strongly determine what happens in the rest of Phase 1.

- As long as people are working, don't look for radical progress during Phase 1.

- Manage the midpoint transition carefully. Evaluate the strengths and weaknesses of the ideas that people generate in Phase 1. Clarify any questions with whomever is commissioning your work. Recognize that a fundamental change in approach must occur here for progress to occur. Essential issues are not likely to "work themselves out" during Phase 2.

- Be sure adequate resources are available to actually execute the Phase 2 plan.

- Resist deadline changes. These could damage the midpoint transition.

GROUP STRUCTURE AND ITS CONSEQUENCES

You are no doubt aware that groups frequently seem to differ from one another. The differences that are most obvious might include the way members interact with one another, how members feel about the group, and how the group performs. It is often possible to trace these differences in interaction, feelings, and performance back to how the group is organized.

Group structure refers to the characteristics of the stable social organization of a group, the way a group is "put together." The most basic structural characteristics along which groups vary are size and member diversity. Other structural characteristics are the expectations that members have about each other's behavior (norms), agreements about "who does what" in the group (roles), the rewards and prestige allocated to various group members (status), and how attractive the group is to its members (cohesiveness).

Group Size

Of one thing we can be certain—the smallest possible group consists of two people, such as a superior and a particular subordinate. It is possible to engage in much theoretical nit-picking about just what constitutes an upper limit on group size. However, given the definition of *group* that we presented earlier, it would seem that congressional or parliamentary size (300 to 400 members) is somewhere close to this limit. In practice, most work groups, including task forces and committees, usually have between three and 20 members.

Size and Satisfaction.   The more the merrier? In theory, yes. On an informal level, larger groups provide more opportunities for members to encounter friends who share their attitudes or meet their social needs. For example, in a three-person work group, each member has two friendship possibilities, while in a seven-person work group, six such possibilities exist. In fact, however, members of larger groups rather consistently report less satisfaction with group membership than those who find themselves in smaller groups.[11] What accounts for this apparent contradiction?

For one thing, as opportunities for friendship increase, the chance to work on and develop these opportunities might decrease owing to the sheer time and energy required. In addition, larger groups, in incorporating more members with different viewpoints, might prompt conflict and dissension, which work against member satisfaction. As group size increases, the time available for verbal participation by each member decreases. Also, many people are inhibited about participating in larger groups.[12] To the extent that individuals value such participation, dissatisfaction will again be the outcome. Finally, in larger groups, individual members identify less easily with the success and accomplishments of the group. For example, a particular member of a four-person cancer research team should be able to identify his or her personal contributions to a research breakthrough more easily than can a member of a 20-person team.

Size and Performance.   Satisfaction aside, do large groups perform tasks better than small groups? This question has great relevance to practical organizational decisions: How many people should a bank assign to evaluate loan applications? How many carpenters should a construction company assign to build a garage? If a school system decides to implement team teaching, how big should the teams be? The answers to these and similar questions depend upon the exact task that the group needs to accomplish and on what we mean by good performance.[13]

Some tasks are **additive tasks.** This means that we can predict potential performance by adding the performances of individual group members together. For example, moving a heavy stone is an additive task, and it's possible to estimate the potential productivity of a group of laborers by summing the forces that they are able to exert. Similarly, building a garage is an additive task, and we can estimate potential speed of construction by adding the efforts of individual carpenters. Thus, for additive tasks, the potential performance of the group increases with group size.

Additive tasks. Tasks in which group performance is dependent upon the sum of the performance of individual group members.

Disjunctive tasks. Tasks in which group performance is dependent upon the performance of the best group member.

Some tasks are **disjunctive**. This means that the potential performance of the group depends on the performance of its *best member*. For example, suppose that a research team is looking for a single error in a complicated computer program. In this case, the performance of the team might hinge upon its containing at least one bright, attentive, logical individual. Obviously, the potential performance of groups doing disjunctive tasks also increases with group size because the probability that the group includes a superior performer is greater.

We use the term "potential performance" consistently in the preceding two paragraphs for the following reason: As groups performing tasks get bigger, they tend to suffer from process losses.[14] **Process losses** are performance difficulties that stem from the problems of motivating and coordinating larger groups. Even with good intentions, problems of communication and decision making increase with size—imagine 50 carpenters trying to build a house. Thus, actual performance = potential performance − process losses.

Process losses. Group performance difficulties stemming from the problems of motivating and coordinating larger groups.

These points are summarized in Exhibit 8.3. As you can see in part (a), both potential performance and process losses increase with group size for additive and disjunctive tasks. The net effect is shown in part (b), which demonstrates that actual performance increases with size up to a point and then falls off. Part (c) shows that the *average* performance of group members decreases as size gets bigger. Thus, up to a point, larger groups might perform better as groups, but their individual members should be less efficient.

Conjunctive tasks. Tasks in which group performance is limited by the performance of the poorest group member.

We should note one other kind of task. **Conjunctive tasks** are those in which the performance of the group is limited by its *poorest performer*. For example, an assembly line operation is limited by its weakest link. Also, if team teaching is the technique used to train workers how to perform a complicated, sequential job, one poor teacher in the sequence will severely damage the effectiveness of the team. Both the potential and actual performance of conjunctive tasks should decrease as group size increases because the probability of including a weak link in the group goes up.

In summary, for additive and disjunctive tasks, larger groups might perform better up to a point, but at increasing costs to the efficiency of individual members. By any standard, performance on purely conjunctive tasks should decrease as group size increases.

Diversity of Group Membership

Imagine an eight member product development task force composed exclusively of 30-something white males of basically Western European heritage. Then imagine another task force made up of half men and half women with eight different ethnic or racial backgrounds and an age range from 25 to 55. The first group is obviously homogeneous in its membership, while the latter is heterogeneous, or diverse. Which task force do you think would develop more quickly as a group? Which would be most creative?

There is a very large body of research, most of it conducted in the laboratory, on the impact of group composition. We know much less about this impact (especially cultural mix) in functioning work groups. Nevertheless, the state of the art looks something like this.[15] Group diversity has a strong impact on interaction patterns—more diverse groups have a more difficult time communicating effectively and becoming cohesive (we'll study cohesiveness in more detail shortly). This means that diverse groups might tend to take longer

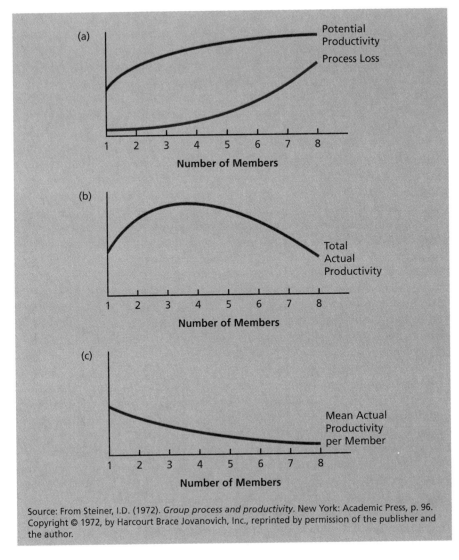

(a)

Potential Productivity

Process Loss

Number of Members

(b)

Total Actual Productivity

Number of Members

(c)

Mean Actual Productivity per Member

Number of Members

Source: From Steiner, I.D. (1972). *Group process and productivity*. New York: Academic Press, p. 96. Copyright © 1972, by Harcourt Brace Jovanovich, Inc., reprinted by permission of the publisher and the author.

EXHIBIT 8.3
Relationships among group size, productivity, and process losses.

to do their forming, storming, and norming.[16] Once they do develop, more and less diverse groups are equally productive. However, diverse groups sometimes perform better when the task requires creativity and problem solving rather than more routine work, because members consider a broader array of ideas.

All of this speaks well for the concepts of valuing and managing diversity, which we discussed in Chapter 4. When management values and manages diversity, it offsets some of the initial process loss costs of diversity and capitalizes on its benefits for team performance.

Group Norms

Social **norms** are collective expectations that members of social units have regarding the behavior of each other. As such, they are codes of conduct that specify what individuals ought and ought not do or standards against which we evaluate the appropriateness of behavior.

Norms. Collective expectations that members of social units have regarding the behavior of each other.

Much normative influence is unconscious, and we are often aware of such influence only in special circumstances, such as when we see children struggling to master adult norms or foreigners sparring with the norms of our culture. We also become conscious of norms when we encounter ones that seem to conflict ("Get ahead," but "Don't step on others") or when we enter new social situations. For instance, the first day on a new job, workers frequently search for cues about what is considered proper office etiquette: Should I call the boss "mister"? Can I personalize my work space?

Norm Development.   *Why* do norms develop? The most important function that norms serve is to provide regularity and predictability to behavior. This consistency provides important psychological security and permits us to carry out our daily business with minimal disruption.

What do norms develop *about?* Norms develop to regulate behaviors that are considered at least marginally important to their supporters. For example, managers are more likely to adopt norms regarding the performance and attendance of subordinates than norms concerning how workers personalize and decorate their offices. In general, less deviation is accepted from norms that concern more important behaviors. Stealing from a co-worker's desk will probably result in ostracism, while failing to assist her on the job might not. Groups frequently develop norms that correspond to their goals to aid in goal attainment.

How do norms develop? As we discussed in Chapter 5, individuals develop attitudes as a function of a related belief and value. In many cases, their attitudes affect their behavior. When the members of a group *share* related beliefs and values, we can expect them to share consequent attitudes. These shared attitudes then form the basis for norms.[17] Notice that it really doesn't make sense to talk about "my personal norm." Norms are *collectively* held expectations, depending upon two or more people for their existence. However, norms can be targeted at a single individual. For example, work groups frequently develop shared expectations about how their bosses should behave.

Why do individuals tend to comply with norms? Much compliance occurs simply because the norm corresponds to privately held attitudes. This is the case with true supporters of the norm. In addition, even when norms support trivial social niceties (such as when to shake hands or when to look serious), they often save time and prevent social confusion. Most interesting, however, is the case in which individuals comply with norms that *go against* their privately held attitudes and opinions. For example, couples without religious convictions frequently get married in religious services, and people who hate neckties often wear them to work. In short, groups have an extraordinary range of rewards and punishments available to induce conformity to norms. In the next chapter, we will examine this process in detail.

Some Typical Norms.   There are some classes of norms that seem to crop up in most organizations and affect the behavior of members. They include the following:

- *Loyalty norms.* Groups and organizations frequently attempt to exact a strong degree of commitment and loyalty from their members. In the military, these norms are formalized with specific sanctions to be applied to traitors and deserters. In most other cases, loyalty norms tend to be informal. Managers frequently perceive that they must work late, come in on weekends, and accept transfers to other cities in order to prove their loyalty to the company and to their peers.

- *Dress norms.* Social norms frequently dictate the kind of clothing people wear to work.[18] Again, military and quasi-military organizations tend to invoke formal norms that support polished buttons and razor-edged creases. Of course, sometimes normative expectations from above confront informal counternorms from below. A certain pub that is popular with university students required its waiters to wear ties. They did so—usually with jeans and hunting shirts! Even in organizations that have adopted casual dress policies, employees often express considerable concern about what they wear at work. Such is the power of social norms.

- *Reward allocation norms.* There are at least four norms that might dictate how rewards such as pay, promotions, and informal favors could be allocated in organizations:

  a. Equity—reward according to inputs such as effort, performance, or seniority.

  b. Equality—reward everyone equally.

  c. Reciprocity—reward people the way they reward you.

  d. Social responsibility—reward those who truly need the reward.[19]

  Officially, of course, most organizations tend to stress allocation according to some combination of equity and equality norms—give employees what they deserve, but no favoritism. However, further normative forces may come into play in reward allocation. In the preceding chapter we mentioned that managers often equalize pay increases awarded to subordinates under merit pay plans. In this case, equality subverts equity. If supervisors award overtime according to seniority (equity) or randomly (equality), a work group might invoke a social responsibility norm to insist that supervisors give a financially needy co-worker special consideration. Finally, the reciprocity norm is frequently invoked, especially among managers. Those who rise in rank might feel that they owe special favors to those who sponsored their progress.

- *Performance norms.* The performance of organizational members might be as much a function of social expectations as it is of inherent ability, personal motivation, or technology.[20] Work groups provide their members with potent cues about what is an appropriate level of performance. New group members are alert for these cues: Is it OK to take a break now? Under what circumstances can I be absent from work without being punished? (See the "In Focus: *Absence Cultures—Norms in Action*.") Of course, the official organizational norms that managers send to subordinates usually favor high performance. However, work groups often establish their own informal performance norms, such as those that restrict productivity under a piecerate pay system.

IN FOCUS   Absence Cultures—Norms in Action

On first thought, you might assume that absenteeism from work is a pretty individualized behavior, a product of random sickness, or personal job dissatisfaction. Although these factors contribute to absenteeism, there is growing evidence that group norms also have a strong impact on how much work people miss.

We can see cross-national differences in absenteeism. Traditionally, absence has been rather high in Italy and England, lower in the United States and Canada, and lower yet in Japan and Switzerland. Clearly, these differences are not due to sickness, but rather to differences in cultural values about the legitimacy of taking time off work. These differences get reflected in work group norms.

Within the same country and company, we can still see group differences in absenteeism. A company I studied had four plants that made the same products and had identical personnel policies. Despite this, one plant had a 12 percent absence rate while another had a rate of 5 percent. Within one plant, some departments had virtually no absence while others approached 25 percent!

Moving to the small group level, I also studied small customer service groups in a utility company. Despite all doing the same work in the same firm, there were again striking cross-group differences in absenteeism, ranging from 1 to 13 percent.

I and others call these normative differences in absenteeism across groups *absence cultures*. How do they develop? People tend to adjust their own absence behavior to what they see as typical of their group. Then, other factors come into play. In the utility company study, I found groups that monitored each others' behavior more closely had lower absence. A Canadian study found that air traffic controllers traded off calling in sick so that their colleagues could replace them at double overtime. An English study found that industrial workers actually posted "absence schedules" so that they could take time off without things getting out of hand! All of these are examples of norms in action.

Source: Johns, G. (1994, July). *Medical, ethical, and cultural constraints on work absence and attendance.* Presentation made at the 23rd International Congress of Applied Psychology, Madrid, Spain.

Roles

Roles. Positions in groups that have a set of expected behaviors attached to them.

Roles are positions in a group that have a set of expected behaviors attached to them. Thus, in a sense, roles represent "packages" of norms that apply to particular group members. As we implied in the previous section, many norms apply to all group members in order to be sure that they engage in *similar* behaviors (such as restricting productivity or dressing a certain way). However, the development of roles is indicative of the fact that group members might also be required to act *differently* from one another. For example, in a committee meeting, not every member is required to function as a secretary or a chairperson, and these become specific roles that are fulfilled by particular people.

In organizations, we find two basic kinds of roles. First, we can identify designated or assigned roles. These are roles that are formally prescribed by an organization as a means of dividing labor and responsibility to facilitate task achievement. In general, assigned roles indicate "who does what" and "who can tell others what to do." In a manufacturing organization, labels that we might apply to formal roles include president, engineer, machinist, manager, and subordinate. In addition to assigned roles, we invariably see the development of emergent roles. These are roles that develop naturally to meet the social-emotional needs of group members or to assist in formal job accomplishment. The class clown and the office gossip fulfill emergent social-emotional roles, while an "old pro" might emerge to assist new group members learn their jobs. Other emergent roles might be assumed by informal leaders or by scapegoats who are the targets of group hostility.

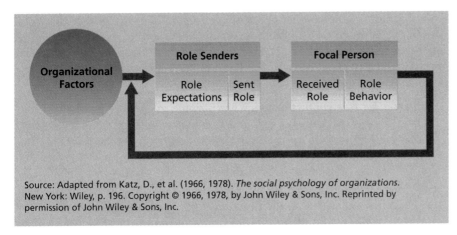

Source: Adapted from Katz, D., et al. (1966, 1978). *The social psychology of organizations.* New York: Wiley, p. 196. Copyright © 1966, 1978, by John Wiley & Sons, Inc. Reprinted by permission of John Wiley & Sons, Inc.

EXHIBIT 8.4
A model of the role assumption process.

Role Ambiguity.   **Role ambiguity** exists when the goals of one's job or the methods of performing it are unclear. Ambiguity might be characterized by confusion about how performance is evaluated, how good performance can be achieved, or what the limits of one's authority and responsibility are.

Exhibit 8.4 shows a model of the process that is involved in assuming an organizational role. As you can see, certain organizational factors lead role senders (such as managers) to develop role expectations and "send" roles to focal people (such as subordinates). The focal person "receives" the role and then tries to engage in behavior to fulfill the role. This model reveals a variety of elements that can lead to ambiguity.

- *Organizational factors.* Some roles seem inherently ambiguous because of their function in the organization. For example, middle management roles might fail to provide the "big picture" that upper management roles do. Also middle management roles do not require the attention to supervision necessary in lower management roles. Thus, two factors that can contribute to role clarity are absent.

- *The role sender.* Role senders might have unclear expectations of a focal person. A sales manager might be unsure about how sales representatives assigned to do business in another culture should entertain a customer. Even when the sender has specific role expectations, they might be ineffectively sent to the focal person. A weak orientation session, vague performance reviews, or inconsistent feedback and discipline may send ambiguous role messages to subordinates.

- *The focal person.* Even role expectations that are clearly developed and sent might not be fully digested by the focal person. This is especially true when he or she is new to the role. Ambiguity tends to decrease as length of time in the job role increases.[21]

What are the practical consequences of role ambiguity? The most frequent outcomes appear to be job stress, dissatisfaction, reduced organizational commitment, and intentions to quit.[22] Managers can do much to reduce unnecessary role ambiguity by providing clear performance expectations and performance feedback, especially for new employees and for those in more intrinsically ambiguous jobs.

Role ambiguity. Lack of clarity of job goals or methods.

Role conflict. A condition of being faced with incompatible role expectations.

Intrasender role conflict. A single role sender provides incompatible expectations to a role occupant.

Intersender role conflict. Two or more role senders provide a role occupant with incompatible expectations.

Interrole conflict. Several roles held by a role occupant involve incompatible expectations.

Person-role conflict. Role demands call for behavior that is incompatible with the personality or skills of a role occupant.

Role Conflict.   **Role conflict** exists when an individual is faced with incompatible role expectations. Conflict can be distinguished from ambiguity in that role expectations might be crystal clear but incompatible in the sense that they are mutually exclusive, can't be fulfilled simultaneously, or don't suit the role occupant.

- **Intrasender role conflict** occurs when a single role sender provides incompatible role expectations to the role occupant. For example, a manager might tell a subordinate to take it easy and not work so hard while delivering yet another batch of reports that requires immediate attention. This form of role conflict seems especially likely to also provoke ambiguity.

- If two or more role senders differ in their expectations for a role occupant, **intersender role conflict** can develop. Boundary role occupants who straddle the boundary between the organization and its clients or customers are especially likely to encounter this form of conflict. Salespeople, police officers, and teachers may face very different sets of demands from those inside and those outside of the organization. For example, the National Association of Securities Dealers has penalized brokerage houses for pressuring brokers to sell clients company mutual funds over superior competing products.[23] Intersender conflict can also stem exclusively from within the organization. The classic example here is the first-level supervisor, who serves as the interface between "management" and "the workers." From above, the supervisor might be pressured to get the work out and keep the troops in line. From below, he or she might be encouraged to behave in a considerate and friendly manner.

- Organizational members necessarily play several roles at one time, especially if we include roles external to the organization. Often, the expectations inherent in these several roles are incompatible, and **interrole conflict** results.[24] One person, for example, might fulfill the roles of a functional expert in marketing, head of the market research group, subordinate to the vice-president of marketing, and member of a product development task force. As a member of the task force, this individual might have to contribute to plans that go against the best interests of her research group. To complicate matters, she also fulfills a number of roles outside of the organization, including wife, mother, daughter, and daughter-in-law. This is obviously a busy person, and competing demands for her time are a frequent symptom of interrole conflict.

- Even when role demands are clear and otherwise congruent, they might be incompatible with the personality or skills of the role occupant—thus, **person-role conflict** results.[25] At XEL Communications, some employees found that the shift to self-managed teams put a strain on their social skills of cooperation and compromise. Many examples of "whistle-blowing" are signals of person-role conflict. The organization has demanded some role behavior that the occupant considers unethical.

As with role ambiguity, the most consistent consequences of role conflict are job dissatisfaction, stress reactions, lowered organizational commitment, and turnover intentions.[26] Managers can help prevent subordinate role conflict by avoiding self-contradictory messages, conferring with other role senders, being sensitive to multiple role demands, and fitting the right person to the right role.

Status

Status is the rank, or social position, or prestige accorded to group members. Put another way, it represents the group's *evaluation* of a member. Just *what* is evaluated depends on the status system in question. However, when a status system works smoothly, the group will exhibit clear norms about who should be awarded more or less status.

Status. The rank, social position, or prestige accorded to group members.

Formal Status Systems. All organizations have both formal and informal status systems. Since formal systems are most obvious to observers, let's begin there. The formal status system represents management's attempt to publicly identify those people who have more status than others. It is so obvious because this identification is implemented by the application of *status symbols* that are tangible indicators of status. Status symbols might include titles, particular working relationships, the pay package, the work schedule, and the physical working environment. Just what are the criteria for achieving formal organizational status? One criterion is often seniority in one's work group. Employees who have been with the group longer might acquire the privilege of choosing day shift work or a more favorable office location. Even more important than seniority, however, is one's assigned role in the organization, one's job. Because they perform different jobs, secretaries, laborers, supervisors, and executives acquire different statuses. Organizations often go to great pains to tie status symbols to assigned roles, as this description of past telephone allocation policies at Western Electric indicates:

> As the junior manager moves up through the ranks, he will usually first have a Touch-Tone desk set. He will then progressively move up to a colored Touch-Tone desk set, a Touch-Tone set with a "hands free" device, a Touch-Tone telephone with a set of programmed cards to insert that dial the desired number; an electronic preset dialing system requiring only the touch of one button to dial a specific number; and—for the president and executive vice-presidents—a Picturephone.[27]

Why do organizations go to all this trouble to differentiate status? For one thing, status and the symbols connected to it serve as powerful magnets to induce members to aspire to higher organizational positions (recall Maslow's need for esteem). Second, status differentiation reinforces the authority hierarchy in workgroups and in the organization as a whole, since people *pay attention* to high-status individuals.

The differences in formal status that exist within organizations usually carry over to the evaluation of the status of occupations by the public at large. Thus, doctors have more prestige than nurses in the community, just as they do in the hospital. Exhibit 8.5 summarizes ratings of occupational prestige from a number of cross-national surveys. In general, surveys of this nature show remarkable stability over time and good agreement across cultures. In addition, people who themselves differ in status tend to agree very closely in their ratings of the prestige of various occupations.[28] Thus, status judgments of the public at large are influenced by some of the same factors that indirectly lead to formal status differences in organizations—the skill, training, and education of the people being judged.

Informal Status Systems. In addition to formal status systems, one can detect informal status systems in organizations. Such systems are not well advertised,

78	College and university teachers; physicians
72	Architects; lawyers
70	Dentists
69	Chemists
67	Bank officers and financial managers
66	Psychologists; airplane pilots; chemical and mechanical engineers
63	Controllers and treasurers
62	Accountants
60	Clergymen; economists
57	Elementary school teachers
56	Stock and bond salesmen; painters and sculptors
55	Office managers; draftsmen
54	Librarians; registered nurses
52	Sales managers (non-retail); actors
51	Computer programmers
50	Radio and television announcers; airline stewardesses
49	Real estate agents and brokers
48	Bank tellers
45	Musicians and composers
44	Insurance agents, brokers, and underwriters
43	Automobile mechanics
40	Farmers; policemen and detectives
39	Foremen
38	Receptionists
37	Air traffic controllers
34	Funeral directors
33	Mail carriers; truck drivers
31	File clerks
23	Bartenders; waiters
22	Garage workers and gas station attendants
14	Newsboys
13	Garbage collectors

Note: Scores can range from 92 to –2. They are derived from studies of occupational prestige carried out in many countries around the world and applied to the 1970 U.S. Census Detailed Occupational Classifications. This is why some labels are sex-typed.

Source: From Donald J. Treiman, *Occupational prestige in comparative perspective*, pp. 306–315. Copyright © 1977 by Academic Press, Inc. Reprinted by permission of the author and the publisher.

EXHIBIT 8.5
Standard prestige scores for various occupations.

and they might lack the conspicuous symbols and systematic support that people usually accord the formal system. Nevertheless, they can operate just as effectively. Sometimes, job performance is a basis for the acquisition of informal status. The "power hitters" on a baseball team or the "cool heads" in a hospital emergency unit might be highly evaluated by co-workers for their ability to assist in task accomplishment. Some managers who perform well early in their careers are identified as "fast trackers" and given special job assignments that correspond to their elevated status. Just as frequently, though, informal status is linked to factors other than job performance, such as gender or race. For example, the man who takes a day off work to care for a sick child may be praised as a model father. The woman who does the same may be questioned about her work commitment.

Consequences of Status Differences.   Status differences have a paradoxical effect on communication patterns. Most people like to communicate with others at their own status or higher, rather than with people who are below

Adopting a casual dress policy at work can reduce status barriers.

them.[29] The result should be a tendency for communication to move up the status hierarchy. However, if status differences are large, people can be inhibited from communicating upward. These opposing effects mean that much communication gets stalled.

Status also affects the amount of various group members' communication and their influence in group affairs. As you might guess, higher-status members do more talking and have more influence.[30] Some of the most convincing evidence comes from studies of jury deliberations, in which jurors with higher-social status (such as managers and professionals) participate more and have more effect on the verdict.[31] Thus, if the plant superintendent, the production manager, and a production supervisor make the rounds on an assembly line, we can offer a pretty good guess about who will do the most talking. Unfortunately, there is no guarantee that the highest-status person is most knowledgeable about the problem at hand!

Reducing Status Barriers.   Although status differences can be powerful motivators, their tendency to inhibit the free flow of communication has led many organizations to downplay status differentiation by doing away with questionable status symbols. The goal is to foster a culture of teamwork and cooperation across the ranks. The high-tech culture of Silicon Valley has always been pretty egalitarian and lacking in conspicuous status symbols, but even old-line industries are getting on the bandwagon. For example, Union Carbide's Connecticut headquarters has equal-sized offices and no executive dining rooms or parking lots. At GM's Saturn plant, the big boss wears the same gear as the line workers, and the executive team at Levi Strauss & Co. wears examples of its own informal clothing line.

Some organizations employ phony or misguided attempts to bridge the status barrier. Some examples of "casual Friday" policies (wearing casual clothes on Fridays) only underline status differences the rest of the week if no other cultural changes are made.

Many observers note that e-mail networks have leveled status barriers.[32] High-speed transmission, direct access, and the opportunity to avoid live confrontation often encourage lower-status parties to communicate directly with organizational VIPs. This has even been seen in the rank-conscious military.

GROUP COHESIVENESS

Group cohesiveness. The degree to which a group is especially attractive to its members.

Group cohesiveness is a critical property of groups. Cohesive groups are those that are especially attractive to their members. Because of this attractiveness, members are especially desirous of staying in the group and tend to describe the group in favorable terms.[33]

The arch-stereotype of a cohesive group is the major league baseball team that begins September looking like a good bet to win its division and get into the World Series. On the field we see well-oiled, precision teamwork. In the clubhouse, all is sweetness and joviality, and interviewed players tell the world how fine it is to be playing with "a great bunch of guys."

Cohesiveness is a relative, rather than absolute, property of groups. While some groups are more cohesive than others, there is no objective line between cohesive and noncohesive groups. Thus, we will use the adjective *cohesive* to refer to groups that are more attractive than average for their members.

Factors Influencing Cohesiveness

What makes some groups more cohesive than others? Important factors include threat, competition, success, member diversity, group size, and toughness of initiation.

Threat and Competition. External threat to the survival of the group increases cohesiveness in a wide variety of situations.[34] As an example, consider the wrangling, uncoordinated corporate board of directors that quickly forms a united front in the face of a takeover bid. Honest competition with another group can also promote cohesiveness.[35] This is the case with the World Series contenders.

Why do groups often become more cohesive in response to threat or competition? They probably feel a need to improve communication and coordination so that they can better cope with the situation at hand. Members now perceive the group as more attractive because it is seen as capable of doing what has to be done to ward off threat or to win. There are, of course, limits to this. Under *extreme* threat or very *unbalanced* competition, increased cohesiveness will serve little purpose. For example, the partners in a firm faced with certain financial disaster would be unlikely to exhibit cohesiveness because it would do nothing to combat the severe threat.

Success. It should come as no surprise that a group becomes more attractive to its members when it has successfully accomplished some important goal,

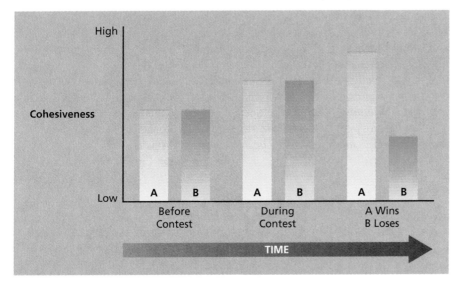

EXHIBIT 8.6
Competition, success, and cohesiveness.

such as defending itself against threat or winning a prize.[36] By the same token, cohesiveness will decrease after failure, although there may be "misery loves company" exceptions. The situation for competition is shown graphically in Exhibit 8.6. Fit-Rite Jeans owns two small clothing stores (A and B) in a large city. To boost sales, it holds a contest between the two stores, offering $150 worth of merchandise to each employee of the store that achieves the highest sales during the next business quarter. Before the competition begins, the staff of each store is equally cohesive. As we suggested above, when competition begins, both groups become more cohesive. The members become more cooperative with each other, and in each store there is much talk about "we" versus "they." At the end of the quarter, store A wins the prize and becomes yet more cohesive. The group is especially attractive to its members because it has succeeded in the attainment of a desired goal. On the other hand, cohesiveness plummets in losing store B—the group has become less attractive to its members.

Member Diversity.   Earlier, we pointed out that groups that are diverse in terms of gender, age, and race can have a harder time developing cohesiveness than more homogeneous groups. However, if the group is especially interested in accomplishing some particular task, its success in performing the task will often outweigh member similarity in determining cohesiveness.[37] For example, one study found no relationship between cohesiveness and similarity of age or education for industrial work groups.[38] Another found that the cohesiveness of groups composed of Black and White southern soldiers was dependent upon successful task accomplishment rather than racial composition.[39]

Size.   Other things being equal, bigger groups should have a more difficult time becoming and staying cohesive. In general, such groups should have a more difficult time agreeing on goals and more problems communicating and coordinating effort to achieve these goals. Earlier, we pointed out that large groups frequently divide into subgroups. Clearly, such subgrouping is contrary to the cohesiveness of the larger group.

Toughness of Initiation.   Despite its rigorous admissions policies, the Harvard Business School doesn't lack applicants. Similarly, exclusive yacht and golf clubs might have waiting lists for membership extending several years into the future. All of this suggests that groups that are tough to get into should be more attractive than those that are easy to join.[40] This is well known in the military, where rigorous physical training and stressful "survival schools" precede entry into elite units, such as the Special Forces or the Rangers.

Sun Microsystems is a firm with extremely rigorous selection procedures, often exposing job applicants to between four and seven interviews with up to 20 questioners.[41] Catalytica, Inc., a Mountain View, California, high-tech up-and-comer that specializes in pollution control also uses tough selection to foster cohesiveness:

> Convinced that in a small company everyone can make a difference, CEO Levy and Chairman Cusumano put most of Catalytica's 120 employees through some of the toughest preemployment testing anywhere. They only go after stars and subject them to grilling for days at a time. No prima donnas need apply, since the founders believe selfless teamwork is the secret of success. . . . The team spirit extends to play too—Catalytica families often go camping together.[42]

Consequences of Cohesiveness

From the previous section, it should be clear that managers or group members might be able to influence the level of cohesiveness of work groups by using competition or threat, varying group size or composition, or manipulating membership requirements. The question remains, however, as to whether *more* or *less* cohesiveness is a desirable group property. This, of course, depends on the consequences of group cohesiveness and who is doing the judging.

More Participation in Group Activities.   Because cohesive groups are attractive to their membership, members should be especially motivated to participate (in several senses of the word) in group activities. For one thing, because members wish to remain in the group, voluntary turnover from cohesive groups should be low. For another, members like being with each other; therefore, absence should be lower than that exhibited by less cohesive groups. During the Fit-Rite sales contest, for example, we might expect casual absence in both stores to drop as the sales staff members become more reliant on each other to achieve their goal. In a third sense, participation should be reflected in a high degree of communication within the group as members strive to cooperate with and assist each other. In addition, this communication might well be of a more friendly and supportive nature, depending on the key goals of the group.[43]

More Conformity.   Because they are so attractive and coordinated, cohesive groups are well equipped to supply information, rewards, and punishment to individual members. These factors take on special significance when they are administered by those who hold a special interest for us. Thus, highly cohesive groups are in a superb position to induce conformity to group norms.

Members of cohesive groups are especially motivated to engage in activities that will *keep* the group cohesive. Chief among these activities is applying pressure to deviants to get them to comply with group norms. Cohesive groups react to deviants by increasing the amount of communication directed at these individuals.[44] Such communication contains information to help the deviant "see the light," as well as veiled threats about what might happen if he or she doesn't. Over time, if such communication is ineffective in inducing conformity, it tends to decrease. This is a signal that the group has isolated the deviant member to maintain cohesiveness among the majority.

More Success. Above, we pointed out that successful goal accomplishment contributes to group cohesiveness. However, it is also true that cohesiveness contributes to group success—in general, cohesive groups are good at achieving their goals. Thus, there is a reciprocal relationship between success and cohesiveness.

Why are cohesive groups effective at goal accomplishment? Probably because of the other consequences of cohesiveness we discussed above. A high degree of participation and communication, coupled with active conformity to group norms, should ensure a high degree of agreement about the goals the group is pursuing and the methods it is using to achieve these goals. Thus, coordinated effort pays dividends to the group.

Since cohesiveness contributes to goal accomplishment, should managers attempt to increase the cohesiveness of work groups by juggling the factors that influence cohesiveness? To answer this question, we must emphasize that cohesive groups are especially effective at accomplishing *their own* goals. If these goals happen to correspond with those of the organization, increased cohesiveness should have substantial benefits for group performance. If not, organizational effectiveness might be threatened. One large-scale study of industrial workgroups reached the following conclusions:

- In highly cohesive groups, the productivity of individual group members tends to be fairly similar to that of other members. In less cohesive groups there is more variation in productivity.

- Highly cohesive groups tend to be *more* or *less* productive than less cohesive groups.[45]

These two facts are shown graphically in Exhibit 8.7. The lower variability of productivity in more cohesive groups stems from the power of such groups to induce conformity. To the extent that work groups have productivity norms, more cohesive groups should be better able to enforce them. Furthermore, if cohesive groups accept organizational norms regarding productivity, they should be highly productive. If cohesive groups reject such norms, they are especially effective in limiting productivity.

One other factor that influences the impact of cohesiveness on productivity is the extent to which the task really requires interdependence and cooperation among group members (e.g., a football team versus a golf team). Cohesiveness is more likely to pay off when the task requires more interdependence.[46]

In summary, cohesive groups tend to be successful in accomplishing what they wish to accomplish. In a good labor relations climate, group cohesiveness on interdependent tasks should contribute to high productivity. If the climate is marked by tension and disagreement, cohesive groups might pursue goals that result in low productivity.

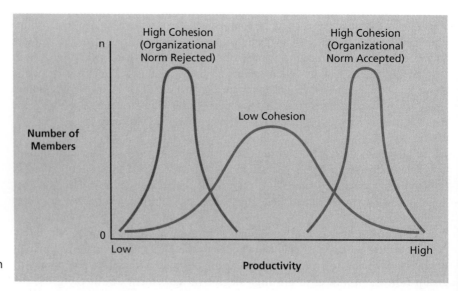

EXHIBIT 8.7
Hypothetical productivity curves for groups varying in cohesiveness.

SOCIAL LOAFING

Have you ever participated in a group project at work or school in which you didn't contribute as much as you could have because other people were there to take up the slack? Or have you ever reduced your effort in a group project because you felt that others weren't pulling their weight? If so, you have been guilty of social loafing. **Social loafing** is the tendency that people have to withhold physical or intellectual effort when they are performing in a group task.[47] The implication is that they would work harder if they were alone rather than part of the group. Earlier we said that process losses in groups could be due to coordination problems or to motivation problems. Social loafing is a motivation problem.

Social loafing. The tendency to withhold physical or intellectual effort when performing a group task.

People working in groups often feel trapped in a social dilemma, in that something that might benefit them individually—slacking off in the group—will result in poor group performance if everybody behaves the same way. Social loafers resolve the dilemma in a way that hurts organizational goal accomplishment. Notice that the tendency for social loafing is probably more pronounced in individualistic North America that in more collective and group-oriented cultures.

As the questions above suggest, social loafing has two different forms. In the *free rider effect*, people lower their effort to get a free ride at the expense of their fellow group members. In the *sucker effect*, people lower their effort because of the feeling that others are free riding; that is, they are trying to restore equity in the group. You can probably imagine a scenario in which the free riders start slacking off and then the suckers follow suit. Group performance suffers badly.

What are some ways to counteract social loafing?[48]

- *Make individual performance more visible.* Where appropriate, the most simple way to do this is to keep the group small in size. Then, individual contributions are less likely to be hidden. Posting performance levels and making presentations of one's accomplishments can also facilitate visibility.

YOU BE THE Manager

SAN DIEGO ZOO

California's San Diego Zoo is considered to be one of the world's premier zoological parks, long noted for its innovative exhibition techniques. In line with its goals of educating the public about conservation and providing an enjoyable experience for visitors, the zoo started to develop a series of bioclimatic zones that immersed visitors in a native habitat of animals and plants rather than having them view them from a distance. For example, in the Tiger River zone, plants, animals, birds, and visitors comingle much more than in a traditional exhibit.

The development of the bioclimatic zones presented zoo management with a problem. In the old days, when plants, animals, and visitors were more separated, it was easy to figure out who was responsible for what; gardeners, animal keepers, maintenance people, and construction

> **THE BIOCLIMATIC ZONES OF THE SAN DIEGO ZOO POSE A UNIQUE CHALLENGE FOR THE ZOO'S MANAGERS.**

people all had their own "territories," but they were professional, not geographic. Under the new zone system, all of these functions became much more interdependent. For example, now some of the plants are there to be eaten by animals, not just admired! Zoo management wondered if jobs and work could be reorganized to better correspond to the new system of bioclimatic zones.

1. How can extreme separation between jobs sometimes hurt organizational effectiveness, including customer service?
2. What should zoo management do to better align its human resources with the new zone system?

To find out what San Diego Zoo did, see *The Manager's Notebook* at the chapter's end.

Source: Adapted from Caudron, S. (1993, December). Are self-directed teams right for your company? *Personnel Journal*, 76–84.

- *Make sure that the work in interesting.* If the work is involving, intrinsic motivation should counteract social loafing.

- *Increase feelings of indispensability.* Group members might slack off because they feel that their inputs are unnecessary for group success. This can be counteracted by using training and the status system to provide group members with unique inputs (e.g., having one person master computer graphics programs).

- *Increase performance feedback.* Some social loafing happens because groups or individual members simply aren't aware of their performance. Increased feedback, as appropriate, from the boss, peers, and customers (internal or external) should encourage self-correction. Group members might require assertiveness training to provide each other with authentic feedback.

- *Reward group performance.* Members are more likely to monitor and maximize their own performance (and attend to that of their colleagues) when the group receives rewards for effectiveness.

Before our discussion of work teams, pause and consider *You Be the Manager.*

DESIGNING EFFECTIVE WORK TEAMS

The double-edged nature of group cohesiveness suggests that a delicate balance of factors dictates whether a work group is effective or ineffective. In turn, this raises the idea that organizations should pay considerable attention to how work groups are designed and managed. At first, the notion of designing a work group might seem strange. After all, don't work groups just "happen" in response to the demands of the organization's goals or technology? While these factors surely set some limits on how groups are organized and managed, organizations are finding that there is still plenty of scope for creativity in work-group design.

A good model for thinking about the design of effective work groups is to consider a successful sports team, whether professional or amateur. In most cases, such teams are small groups made up of highly skilled individuals who are able to meld these skills into a cohesive effort. The task they are performing is intrinsically motivating and provides very direct feedback. If there are status differences on the team, the basis for these differences is contribution to the team, not some extraneous factor. The team shows an obsessive concern with obtaining the right personnel, relying on tryouts or player drafts, and the team is "coached," not supervised. With this informal model in mind, let's examine the concept of group effectiveness more closely.

J. Richard Hackman of Harvard University (co-developer of the Job Characteristics Model, Chapter 7) has written extensively about workgroup effectiveness.[49] According to Hackman, a work group is effective when (1) its physical or intellectual output is acceptable to management and to the other parts of the organization that use this output, (2) group members' needs are satisfied rather than frustrated by the group, and (3) the group experience enables members to *continue* to work together.

What leads to group effectiveness? In colloquial language, we might say "sweat, smarts, and style." More formally, Hackman notes that group effectiveness occurs when high effort is directed toward the group's task, when great knowledge and skill are directed toward the task, and when the group adopts sensible strategies for accomplishing its goals. And just how does an organization achieve this? As with XEL Communications, there is growing awareness in many organizations that the answer is **self-managed work teams.** Although the exact details vary tremendously, such teams generally provide their members with the opportunity to do challenging work under reduced supervision. Other labels that we often apply to such groups are autonomous, semiautonomous, and self-regulated. The general idea, which is more important than the label, is that the groups tend to regulate much of their own members' behavior. Much interest in such teams has been spurred by the success of teams in Japanese industry.

Critical to the success of self-managed teams are the nature of the task, the composition of the group, and various support mechanisms.[50] Notice that many of the suggestions that follow should improve coordination and discourage social loafing.

Self-managed work teams.
Work groups that have the opportunity to do challenging work under reduced supervision.

Tasks for Self-Managed Teams

Experts agree that tasks assigned to self-managed work teams should be complex and challenging, requiring high interdependence among team members for accomplishment. In general, these tasks should have the qualities of enriched jobs, which we described in Chapter 7. Thus, teams should see the task as significant, they should perform the task from beginning to end, and they should use a variety of skills. The point here is that self-managed teams have to have something useful to self-manage, and it is fairly complex tasks that capitalize on the diverse knowledge and skills of a group. Taking a bunch of olive stuffers on a food-processing assembly line, putting them in distinctive jumpsuits, calling them the Olive Squad, and telling them to self-manage will be unlikely to yield dividends in terms of effort expended or brainpower employed. The basic task will still be boring!

Outside of the complexity requirement, the actual range of tasks for which organizations have used self-managed teams is great, spanning both blue- and white-collar jobs. In the white-collar domain, complex service and design jobs seem especially conducive to self-management. Organizations such as 3M, Aetna Life & Casualty, and Federal Express make extensive use of teams. At Federal Express, for example, self-managed back-office clerical teams are credited with improving billing accuracy and reducing lost packages for a savings of millions of dollars.[51]

In the blue-collar domain, Kodak, General Mills, GM's Saturn plant, and Chaparral Steel of Midlothian, Texas, make extensive use of self-managed work groups. In general, these groups are responsible for dividing labor among various subtasks as they see fit and making a variety of decisions about matters that impinge on the group. When a work site is formed from scratch and lacks an existing culture, the range of these activities can be very broad. Consider the self-managed teams formed in a new English confectionery plant.

> Production employees worked in groups of 8 to 12 people, all of whom were expected to carry out each of eight types of jobs involved in the production process. Group members were collectively responsible for allocating jobs among themselves, reaching production targets and meeting quality and hygiene standards, solving local production problems, recording production data for information systems, organizing breaks, ordering and collecting raw materials and delivering finished goods to stores, calling for engineering support, and training new recruits. They also participated in selecting new employees. Within each group, individuals had considerable control over the amount of variety they experienced by rotating their tasks, and each production group was responsible for one product line. Group members interacted informally throughout the working day but made the most important decisions—for example, regarding job allocation—at formal weekly group meetings where performance was also discussed.[52]

Corning, Inc. opened a ceramic filter plant in Blacksburg, Virginia that is organized along similar principles. Autonomous, flexible teams resulted in outstanding profitability.

If a theme runs through this discussion of tasks for self-managed teams, it is the breakdown of traditional, conventional, specialized *roles* in the group. Group members adopt roles that will make the group effective, not ones that are simply related to a narrow specialty. Exhibit 8.8 shows the results of a survey of U.S. firms indicating the extent of tasks performed by self-managing teams.

The Composition of Self-Managed Teams

How should organizations assemble self-managed teams to ensure effectiveness? "Stable, small, and smart" might be a fast answer.[53]

		Number of Employees				
	All Sizes*	100–499	500–999	1,000–2,499	2,500–9,999	10,000 or More
Set Work Schedules	69%	69%	63%	74%	64%	66%
Deal Directly With External Customers	59%	60%	63%	47%	43%	49%
Set Production Quotas/Performance Targets	57%	57%	70%	49%	59%	57%
Training	55%	55%	48%	63%	53%	64%
Purchase Equipment or Services	47%	48%	52%	35%	32%	41%
Deal With Vendors/Suppliers	46%	45%	56%	47%	47%	44%
Performance Appraisals	37%	36%	37%	44%	42%	33%
Budgeting	35%	33%	52%	42%	34%	33%
Hiring	29%	28%	41%	30%	25%	26%
Firing	21%	21%	26%	19%	13%	10%

*Refers to U.S. organizations with 100 or more employees.
Source: Gordon, J. (1992, October). Work teams: How far have they come? *Training*, 59-65.

EXHIBIT 8.8
Functions performed by self-managed teams.

Stability. Self-managed teams require considerable interaction and high cohesiveness among their members. This in turn requires understanding and trust. To achieve this, group membership must be fairly stable. Rotating members into and out of the group will cause it to fail to develop a true group identity.[54]

Size. In keeping with the demands of the task, self-managed teams should be as small as is feasible. The goal here is to keep coordination problems and social loafing to a minimum. These negative factors can be a problem for all groups, but they can be especially difficult for self-managed groups. This is because reduced supervision means that there is no boss to coordinate the group's activities and search out social loafers who don't do their share.

Expertise. It goes without saying that group members should have a high level of expertise about the task at hand. Everybody doesn't have to know everything, but the group as a *whole* should be very knowledgeable about the task. Again, reduced supervision discourages "running to the boss" when problems arise, but the group must have the resources to successfully solve these problems. One set of skills that all members should probably possess to some degree is *social skills*. Understanding how to talk things out, communicate effectively, and resolve conflict is especially important for self-managed groups.

Diversity. Put simply, a team should have members who are similar enough to work well together and diverse enough to bring a variety of perspectives and skills to the task at hand. A product planning group consisting exclusively of new, male M.B.A.s might work well together but lack the different perspectives that are necessary for creativity.

One way of maintaining appropriate group composition might be to let the group choose its own members, as occurred at the confectionery plant we discussed above. In the GM Saturn start-up, a panel of union and management members evaluated applications for all blue- and white-collar jobs, paying particular attention to social skills.[55] A potential problem with having a group choose its own members is that the group might use some irrelevant criterion (such as race or gender) to unfairly exclude others. Thus, human resources department oversight is necessary, as are very clear selection criteria (in terms of behaviors, skills, and credentials). The selection stage is critical, since some studies (including the one in the confectionary plant) have shown elevated turnover in self-managed teams.[56] "Fit" is important, and well worth expending the extra effort to find the right people.

The theme running through this discussion of team composition favors *high cohesiveness* and the development of group *norms* that stress group effectiveness.

Supporting Self-Managed Teams

A number of support factors can assist self-managed teams in becoming and staying effective. Reports of problems with teams can usually be traced back to inadequate support.

Training. In almost every conceivable instance, members of self-managed teams will require extensive training. At Saturn, for example, new workers receive five full days of training, a figure unheard of in the traditional U.S. auto industry. The kind of training depends on the exact job design and on the needs of the workforce. However some common areas include:

- *Technical training.* This might include math, computer use, or any tasks that a supervisor formerly handled. Cross-training in the specialties of other teammates is common.
- *Social skills.* Assertiveness, problem solving, and routine dispute resolution are skills that help the team operate smoothly.
- *Language skills.* This can be important for ethnically diverse teams. Good communication is critical on self-managed teams.
- *Business training.* Some firms provide basic elements of finance, accounting, and production, so that employees can better grasp how their team's work fits into the larger picture.

At XEL Communications, training spanned all of these areas, some of it done in-house, and some done in cooperation with Community College of Aurora.

Rewards. The general rule here is to try to tie rewards to team accomplishment rather than to individual accomplishment while still providing team members with some individual performance feedback. At Levi Strauss & Co., for example, the company moved clothing fabricators from piecerate pay to team-based pay. Gainsharing, profit sharing, and skill based pay (Chapter 7) all seem to be compatible reward systems for a team environment. Skill based pay is especially attractive because it rewards the acquisition of multiple skills that can support the team. XEL combines this strategy with team-based merit pay and profit sharing.

To provide individual performance feedback, some firms have experimented with peer (e.g., team member) performance appraisal. Many have also done away with status symbols that are unrelated to group effectiveness (such as reserved parking and dining areas).

Management.   Self-management will not receive the best support when managers feel threatened and see it as reducing their own power or promotion opportunities. Some, schooled in the traditional role of manager, may simply not adapt. Those who do can serve important functions by mediating relations *between* teams and by dealing with union concerns, since unions are often worried about the cross-functional job sharing in self-management.

A study found that the most effective managers in a self-management environment encouraged groups to observe, evaluate, and reinforce their own task behavior.[57] This suggests that coaching teams to be independent enhances their effectiveness.[58]

Exhibit 8.9 summarizes the factors that influence work-group effectiveness.

Cross-Functional Teams

To close the chapter, let's look at another kind of team that contemporary organizations are using with increasing frequency. **Cross-functional teams** bring people with different functional specialties together to better invent, design, or deliver a product or service.

A cross-functional team might be self-managed and permanent if it is doing a recurrent task that is not too complex. For example, UPS and Times Mirror have multiskilled-sales teams that sell and deliver products and services. If the task is complex and unique (such as designing a car) cross-functional teams require formal leadership, and their lives will generally be limited to the life of the specific project. In both cases, the "cross-functional" label means such diverse specialties are necessary so that cross-training isn't feasible. People have to be experts in their own area but able to cooperate with others.

Cross-functional teams, which have been used in service industries such as banking and hospitals, are probably best known for their successes in product development.[59]

Cross-functional teams. Work groups that bring people with different functional specialities together to better invent, design, or deliver a product or service.

EXHIBIT 8.9
Factors influencing work-group effectiveness.

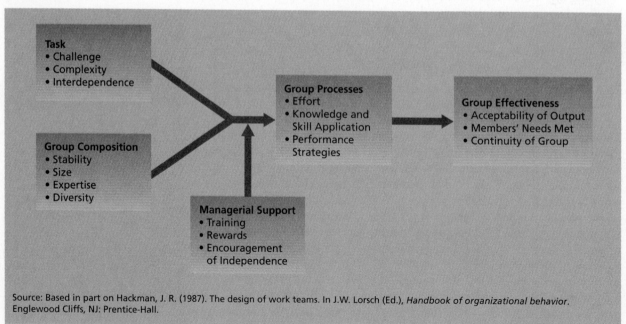

Source: Based in part on Hackman, J. R. (1987). The design of work teams. In J.W. Lorsch (Ed.), *Handbook of organizational behavior.* Englewood Cliffs, NJ: Prentice-Hall.

- Rubbermaid, recently named by *Fortune* as America's Most Admired Company, uses teams to invent and design a remarkable variety of innovative household products. They introduce more than 365 products a year!

- Thermos used a team to invent a very successful ecologically friendly electric barbecue grill. It sped to the market in record time.

- The auto industry has embraced cross-functional teams to reduce the cycle time needed to design new cars. Particular beneficiaries have been the Dodge Viper sports car, Chrysler's LH series (e.g., Dodge Intrepid), and Ford's newest Mustang. Even venerable Rolls-Royce is using such teams.

The general goals of using cross-functional teams include some combination of innovation, speed, and quality that come from early coordination among the various specialties. We can see their value by looking at the traditional way auto manufacturers have designed cars in North America.[60] First, stylists determine what the car will look like and then pass their design on to engineering, which develops mechanical specifications and blueprints. In turn, manufacturing must then consider how to construct what stylists and engineers have designed. Somewhere on down the line, marketing and accounting get their say. This process leads to problems. One link in the chain might have a difficult time understanding what the previous link meant. Worse, one department might resist the ideas of another simply because they "weren't invented here." The result of all of this is slow, expensive development and early quality problems. In contrast, the cross-functional approach gets all the specialties working together from day one. A complex project such as a car design might have over 30 cross-functional teams working at the same time.

The speed factor can be dramatic. Manufacturers have reduced the development of a new car model from five years to around three. Boeing used a cross-functional team to reduce certain design analyses from two weeks to only a few minutes.

Principles for Effectiveness.   Recent research has discovered a number of factors that contribute to the effectiveness of cross-functional teams.[61]

- *Composition.* All relevant specialties are obviously necessary, and effective teams are sure not to overlook anyone. Auto companies put labor representatives on car design teams to warn of assembly problems. On the Mustang, Chrysler LH, and Thermos projects, the companies included outside suppliers.

- *Superordinate goals.* **Superordinate goals** are attractive outcomes that can only be achieved by collaboration. They override detailed functional objectives that might be in conflict (e.g., finance versus design). On the Mustang project, the superordinate goal was to keep the legendary name alive in the face of corporate cost cutters.

- *Physical proximity.* Team members have to be relocated close to each other to facilitate informal contact. Mustang used a former furniture warehouse in Allen Park, Michigan, to house its teams.

- *Autonomy.* Cross-functional teams need some autonomy from the larger organization, and functional specialists need some authority to commit

Superordinate goals. Attractive outcomes that can only be achieved by collaboration.

their function to project decisions. This prevents meddling or "micro-managing" by upper level or functional managers. Chrysler has gone so far as to assign most of its functional specialists to semipermanent "platform" teams (e.g., minivan).

- *Rules and procedures.* Although petty rules and procedures are to be avoided, some basic decision procedures must be laid down to prevent anarchy. On the Mustang project, it was agreed that a single manufacturing person would have a veto over radical body changes.

- *Leadership.* Because of the potential for conflict, cross-functional team leaders need especially strong people skills in addition to task expertise. The "tough engineer" who headed the Mustang project succeeded in developing his people skills for that task.

We'll consider other material relevant to cross-functional teams when we cover conflict management and organizational design.

The Manager's Notebook   San Diego Zoo

The San Diego Zoo experience shows that self-managed teams are appropriate for service jobs as well as in manufacturing environments.

1. Extreme separation between job duties and functions (the zoo has 97 job classifications) can lead to a lack of cooperation and gaps in performance. The gardener who fails to pick up a piece of trash ("let the groundskeeper do it") or the maintenance worker who ignores a bird in distress ("that's the keeper's job") are not performing opti-

mally. Unfortunately, the extreme separation of job functions often leads to this isolation.

2. The Zoo formed self-managed work teams to oversee the various zones. The one for Tiger River has seven people, including specialists in birds, animals, gardening, construction, and maintenance. They are cross-trained to assist each other, have their own budget, and jointly maintain the zone. Both job satisfaction and visitor service have improved under the system.

EXECUTIVE SUMMARY

◆ A group consists of two or more people interacting interdependently to achieve a common goal. The formation and maintenance of groups depend upon opportunity for interaction, potential for goal accomplishment, and the personal characteristics of members.

◆ Some groups go through a series of developmental stages: Forming, storming, norming, performing and adjourning. However, the punctuated equilibrium model stresses an important first meeting, a period of little apparent progress, a critical midpoint transition, and a phase of goal-directed activity.

◆ As groups get bigger, they provide less opportunity for member satisfaction. When tasks are additive

(performance depends upon the addition of individual effort) or disjunctive (performance depends upon that of the best member), larger groups should perform better than smaller groups if the group can avoid process losses due to poor communication and motivation. When tasks are conjunctive (performance is limited by the weakest member), performance decreases as the group gets bigger because the chance of adding a weak member increases.

◆ Norms are expectations that group members have about each other's behavior. They provide consistency to behavior and develop as a function of shared attitudes. In organizations, both formal and informal norms often develop to control loyalty, dress, reward allocation, and performance.

◆ Roles are positions in a group that have associated with them a set of expected behaviors. Role ambiguity refers to a lack of clarity of job goals or methods. Role conflict exists when an individual is faced with incompatible role expectations, and it can take four forms: intrasender, intersender, interrole, and person-role. Both ambiguity and conflict have been shown to provoke job dissatisfaction, stress, and lowered commitment.

◆ Status is the rank or prestige that a group accords its members. Formal status systems use status symbols to reinforce the authority hierarchy and reward progression up the hierarchy. Informal status systems also operate in organizations, though they might lack conspicuous status symbols. Although status differences are motivational, they also lead to communication barriers.

◆ Cohesive groups are especially attractive to their members. Threat, competition, success, and small size contribute to cohesiveness, as does a tough initiation into the group. The consequences of cohesiveness include increased participation in group affairs, improved communication, and increased conformity. Cohesive groups are especially effective in accomplishing their own goals, which might or might not be those of the organization.

◆ Social loafing occurs when people withhold effort when performing a group task. This is less likely when individual performance is visible, the task is interesting, there is good performance feedback, and the organization rewards group achievement.

◆ Members of self-managed work teams do challenging work under reduced supervision. For greatest effectiveness, such teams should be stable, small, well trained, and moderately diverse in membership. Group-oriented rewards are most appropriate.

◆ Cross-functional teams bring people with different functional specialties together to better invent, design, or deliver a product or service. They should have diverse membership, a superordinate goal, some basic decision rules, and a fair degree of autonomy. Members should work in the same physical location and leaders require people skills as well as task skills.

KEY CONCEPTS

Group
Formal work groups
Informal groups
Punctuated equilibrium model
Additive tasks
Disjunctive tasks
Process losses
Conjunctive tasks
Norms
Roles
Role ambiguity

Role conflict
Intrasender conflict
Intersender conflict
Interrole conflict
Person-role conflict
Status
Group cohesiveness
Social loafing
Self-managed work teams
Cross-functional teams

DISCUSSION QUESTIONS

1. Describe the kind of skills that you would look for in members of self-managed teams. Explain your choices.

2. Debate: Effective teamwork is more difficult for individualistic Americans, Canadians, and Australians than for more collectivist Japanese.

3. Consider a large office in an insurance firm that consists of clerks, secretaries, and claims processors. Suppose that several informal friendship groups have formed on the basis of proximity and attitude similarity. Discuss the potential pros and cons of these groups for the organization. Does the existence of such informal groups make special

demands upon office managers? Should organizations try to prevent the development of such groups?

4. Suppose that a group of United Nations representatives from various countries forms to draft a resolution regarding world hunger. Is this an additive, disjunctive, or conjunctive task? What kinds of process losses would such a group be likely to suffer? Can you offer a prediction about the size of this group and its performance?

5. State several norms that exist in your classroom or in your work group. What functions do these norms serve? What are the shared attitudes that underlie these norms? How are the norms enforced?

6. Explain how a cross-functional team could contribute to product or service quality. Explain how one could contribute to speeding up product design.

7. Mark Allen, a representative for an international engineering company, is a very religious person and an elder in his church. Mark's direct superior has instructed him to use "any legal means" to sell a large construction project to a foreign government. The vice-president of international operations had informed Mark that he could offer a generous "kickback" to government officials to clinch the deal, although such practices are illegal. Discuss the three kinds of role conflict that Mark is experiencing.

8. Some organizations have made concerted efforts to do away with many of the status symbols associated with differences in organizational rank. All employees park in the same lot, eat in the same dining room, and have similar offices and privileges. Discuss the pros and cons of such a strategy. How might such a change affect organizational communications?

9. You are an executive in a consumer products corporation. The president assigns you to form a task force to develop new marketing strategies for the organization. You are permitted to choose its members. What things would you do to make this group as cohesive as possible?

10. Discuss the dangers of group cohesiveness for the group itself and for the organization of which the group is a part.

EXPERIENTIAL EXERCISE
THE SUBARCTIC SURVIVAL SITUATION

The purpose of this exercise is to compare individual and group problem solving and to explore the group dynamics that occur in a problem-solving session. It can also be used in conjunction with Chapter 12. The instructor will begin by forming groups of four to seven members.

The situation described in this problem is based on actual cases in which men and women lived or died depending upon the survival decisions they made. Your "life" or "death" will depend upon how well your group can share its present knowledge of a relatively unfamiliar problem, so that the group can make decisions which will lead to your survival.

THE SITUATION

It is approximately 2:30 p.m., October 5th and you have just crash-landed in a float plane on the east shore of Laura Lake in the subarctic region of the northern Quebec-Newfoundland border. The pilot was killed in the crash, but the rest of you are uninjured. Each of you are wet up to the waist and have perspired heavily. Shortly after the crash, the plane drifted into deep water and sank with the pilot's body pinned inside.

The pilot was unable to contact anyone before the crash. However, ground sightings indicated that you are 30 miles south of your intended course and approximately 22 air miles east of Schefferville, your original destination, and the nearest known habitation. (The mining camp on Hollinger Lake was abandoned years ago when a fire destroyed the buildings.) Schefferville (pop. 5,000) is an iron ore mining town approximately 300 air miles north of the St. Lawrence, 450 miles east of the James Bay/Hudson Bay area, 800 miles south of the Arctic Circle, and 300 miles west of the Atlantic Coast. It is reachable only by air or rail; all roads ending a few miles from town. Your party was expected to return from northwestern Labrador to Schefferville no later than October 19th and filed a Flight Notification Form with the Department of Transportation via Schefferville radio to that effect.

The immediate area is covered with small evergreen trees (1½ to 4 inches in diameter). Scattered in the area are a number of hills having rocky and barren tops. Tundra (arctic swamps) make up the valleys between the hills and consist only of small scrubs. Approximately 25 percent of the area in the region is covered by long, narrow lakes which run northwest to southeast. Innumerable streams and rivers flow into and connect the lakes.

Temperatures during October vary between 25°F and 36°F, although it will occasionally go as high as 50°F and as low as 0°F. Heavy clouds cover the sky three-quarters of the time, with only one day in ten being fairly clear. Five to seven inches of snow are on the ground, however, the actual depth varies enormously because the wind sweeps the exposed area clear and builds drifts 3 feet to 5 feet deep in other areas. The wind speed averages 13–15 miles per hour and is mostly out of the west-northwest.

You are all dressed in insulated underwear, socks, heavy wool shirts, pants, knit gloves, sheepskin jackets, knitted wool caps and heavy leather hunting boots. Collectively, your personal possessions include: $153 in bills and 2 half-dollars, 4 quarters, 2 dimes, 1 nickel and 3 new pennies; 1 pocket knife (2 blades and an awl that resembles an ice pick); one stub lead pencil; and an air map.

THE PROBLEM

Before the plane drifted away and sank, you were able to salvage the 15 items listed in Exercie 8.1. Your task is to rank these items according to their importance to your survival, starting with "1" the most important, to "15" the least important.

You may assume:

1. the number of survivors is the same as the number on your team;
2. you are the actual people in the situation;
3. the team has agreed to stick together;
4. all items are dry and in good condition.

Step 1: *Working individually,* each group member should rank order the 15 items in terms of their survival value, giving a 1 to the most useful item, a 2 to the next most useful item, and so on. The least useful item will be ranked 15. List your answers in Column 1 of the grid. (10 minutes)

Step 2: The group will discuss the value of the 15 items as a group and develop a consensus ranking. In doing this, be open to the diverse ideas of others. Do *not* vote or average your answers. Try to reach consensus on the ranking by talking it out. Put your group's ranking in Column 2 of the grid. (30 minutes)

Step 3: Your instructor will provide you with the expert ranking of the items provided by the troops and officers of the Canadian Forces Para Rescue Specialists. Write the expert ranking in Column 3 of the grid.

Step 4: Take the absolute difference between your individual ranking (Column 1) and the experts' ranking (Column 3) for each item and write this difference in Column 4 of the grid. ("Absolute differences" ignore plus or minus signs.)

Step 5: Take the absolute difference between the group ranking (Column 2) and the experts' ranking (Column 3) for each item and write this difference in Column 5 of the grid.

Items	Step 1 Your Individual Ranking	Step 2 The Group's Ranking	Step 3 Survival Experts' Ranking	Step 4 Difference Between Steps 1 and 3	Step 5 Difference Between Steps 2 and 3
A magnetic compass					
A gallon can of maple syrup					
A sleeping bag per person (arctic type down filled with liner)					
A bottle of water purification tablets					
A 20' × 20' piece of heavy duty canvas					
13 wood matches in a metal screwtop, waterproof container					
250 ft. of 1/4 inch braided nylon rope, 50 lb. test					
An operating 4 battery flashlight					
3 pairs of snowshoes					
A fifth Bacardi rum (151 proof)					
Safety razor shaving kit with mirror					
A wind-up alarm clock					
A hand axe					
One aircraft inner tube for a 14 inch wheel (punctured)					
A book entitled *Northern Star Navigation*					
Totals (the lower the score the better)				Individual Accuracy	Group Accuracy

EXERCISE 8.1
The Subarctic survival situation.

Step 6: Calculate your individual accuracy score by totaling the numbers in Column 4 of the grid. The lower the score, the better.

Step 7: Calculate the group's accuracy score by totaling the numbers in Column 5 of the grid. The lower the score, the better.

Step 8: Calculate the *average* individual score for your group by adding up the individual accuracy scores (Step 6) and dividing by the number of members in your group.

DISCUSSION

The instructor will summarize the results on the board for each group, including (a) average individual accuracy score, (b) group accuracy score, (c) gain or loss between the average individual score and the group score, and (d) the lowest individual score (i.e., the best score) in each group.

The following questions will help to guide the discussion:

1. As a group task, is The Subarctic Survival Situation exercise an additive, disjunctive, or conjunctive task?
2. What would be the impact of group size on performance in this task?
3. Did any norms develop in your group that guided how information was exchanged or how the decision was reached?
4. Did any special roles emerge in your group? These could include a leader, a secretary, an "expert," a critic, or a humorist. How did these roles contribute to or hinder group performance?

5. Consider the factors that contribute to effective self-managed teams. How do they pertain to a group's performance on this exercise?

6. How would group diversity help or hinder performance on the exercise?

CASE STUDY
FAIRFIELD COORDINATING GROUP

It was 1:00 P.M. and the meeting of the Fairfield Coordinating Group (FCG) should have been starting. The FCG was the plant operating committee for an air conditioner components plant built by the Ashland Corporation in Fairfield, Iowa. The group consisted of the plant manager and the directors of the functional areas in the plant. I already had spent a few weeks collecting data at the Fairfield Components Plant (FCP) and had been told that the plant manager and his staff placed great importance on punctuality. I arrived ten minutes early, yet at 1:00 the room was still empty. At 1:10, I glanced at my appointment book to make sure that I was in the right place on the right day. At 1:20, I checked with the plant manager's secretary and found out that he and the members of his staff were not yet back from lunch.

The meeting finally began at 2:30. Al Rasky, the plant manager, began by laying out a tentative agenda, but most of the early part of the meeting was spent discussing an item not on the agenda—rumors from corporate headquarters about the future of the plant. Although the plant was still in its start-up phase, the Ashland Corporation recently had experienced a major decrease in business and there were rumors that the plant might be closed. At 2:45, one of the key members of the plant operating staff, the director of manufacturing, arrived and took a seat next to the plant manager. No one seemed to notice that he was late. The group met that afternoon until 5:00 and again the next morning from 8:45 until noon.

HISTORY OF THE FCG

Group Formation: Summer 1980. The roots of the Fairfield Coordinating Group extend back to the summer of 1980 when Peter Michaels, Ashland's vice president for domestic operations, chose Barry Mackay to be the plant manager of a new manufacturing facility in Fairfield, Iowa. Mackay formerly had been the head of a planning team coordinating the financial, marketing, engineering, manufacturing, and purchasing work necessary to bring a new line of energy-efficient air conditioners, code name Q-15, into worldwide production. An empty plant was purchased to provide the floor space for production of components for these air conditioners.

Mackay selected the management staff for the FCG from two very different parts of Ashland: from the Q-15 planning team and from two of Ashland's outlying plants-Ridgeway, Pennsylvania, and Jacksonville, Florida. The members of the Q-15 planning team had spent their years with Ashland working primarily in and around the company's corporate headquarters in Joplin, Missouri. The bulk of Ashland's manufacturing also took place in the Joplin area in large, unionized facilities. Work was organized traditionally in these factories, with hourly employees working within defined job classifications, supervised by a multilayered management hierarchy.

In contrast, Ridgeway and Jacksonville were smaller, non-union facilities. These plants organized employees into teams and emphasized the importance of employee participation and communication across teams and functions. Employees were trained to perform multiple jobs, and status differences were kept to a minimum.

FCG members from Joplin were primarily responsible for the technical areas of the plant, including facilities, manufacturing, computer systems, and the first manufacturing team. Members from the Ridgeway and Jacksonville plants principally managed plant administration, including organizational development and training, finance, and materials.

Two sets of corporate expectations guided the FCG during these early months. First, Ashland's top management expected the Fairfield Components Plant to meet the cost and production standards set for the overall Q–15 project as it produced compressors, gear assemblies, and fans for the new air conditioners. And second, management expected Fairfield to be an "innovative work system" in the tradition of Ashland's Jacksonville and Ridgeway plants.

The FCG Splits: Fall 1980. In the early fall, most of the Fairfield Coordinating Group's meetings were in Joplin. This meant that the personnel from the outlying plants, Ridgeway and Jacksonville, became virtually weekly long-distance commuters to Joplin. To minimize these commutes, most of the personnel from the outlying plants moved their families to Fairfield by the end of the year, and they began to argue that all meetings should be held in the new plant. This created tension with those from Joplin who had an interest in a more extended transition to Fairfield: many of these mangers had lived near Joplin all their lives and were trying to convince their families to move to a new part of the country for the first time.

This geographical conflict exacerbated other differences between the two groups—differences in their priorities for the new plant and in their relative understanding of organizational design issues. Because of their technical responsibilities, those from Joplin were most concerned with seeing that the production systems in Fairfield were completed satisfactorily and on time. Many of their jobs also required them to spend a substantial portion of their time away from the plant working with the manufacturers of the plant's machinery. This created tension with those from Ridgeway and Jacksonville, who placed a higher priority on completing the organizational design work in Fairfield. Even when the whole FCG was able to meet to work on design issues, things did not always go smoothly. Because of their greater previous exposure to participative work systems, those from Ridgeway and Jacksonville tended to be frustrated by the naiveté of the Joplin group about organizational design issues. Conversely, FCG members from Joplin tended to view those from the outlying plants as intolerant.

The Start-Up Falters: Spring 1981. The FCG's work during the first half of 1981 was complicated by difficulties in permanently filling key positions in the Fairfield organization. As of May, the plant still had not hired directors of personnel and product quality. In addition, Alan Goldin, who had been serving as director of manufacturing announced in March that for personal reasons he had decided not to move to Fairfield.

The problems created by these unfilled management positions became particularly acute as the FCG prepared for the anticipated summer hiring of the nonexempt personnel who would run the machine lines. Nonexempt hiring could occur only after the necessary personnel and pay systems were in place—and they were not. Further, the FCG began receiving criticism from headquarters that team members "weren't putting things together quickly enough and in a quality manner." By May, the FCG had roughed out a consensus on a range of issues—from plant philosophy to compensation objectives to team job design. However, none of these systems was completely finalized or approved. During this period, the group began to vacillate between trying to create a unique organizational design for the FCP and trying to make up for lost time by adapting policies and procedures from other Ashland plants.

FCG members reported increased stress levels and decreased satisfaction during this period. The person placed under the most strain was the plant manager, Barry Mackay. Even though Barry was still nominally living in Joplin, he was working ninety-hour weeks in Fairfield. On July 1, stating that he was acting because of concerns about Barry's health, Peter Michaels announced that he was changing Barry's position from plant manager to director of technical services. The new plant manager would be Alan Rasky, previously director of manufacturing for the Jacksonville plant.

The Second Year: July 1981 to August 1982. During the second half of 1981, the FCG devoted its attention primarily to developing the plant systems and policies necessary to allow production to begin in 1982. The group concentrated its work in four major areas: developing a compensation plan, creating a plant orientation and training program, developing a system to manage the delegation of authority from central functional groups to manufacturing teams, and finalizing the architectural plans for a major facilities upgrade. The first three of these projects were completed primarily by subgroups of the FCG and then reviewed, modified, and approved by the group as a whole. The one exception was the facilities upgrade, which followed a highly structured group process led by an architectural design firm.

The continuing split between the members of the group from Joplin and those from the outlying plants complicated the FCG's work on these tasks. This split was exacerbated by another decision made during this period. Because of increases in the size of the work force, the technical functions—manufacturing, engineering and systems—were moved to the back of the plant, or, as it quickly became known, the "outback." In contrast, the administrative functions—finance, personnel, and training—remained "up front." In practice, this meant that informal communication was greatly limited between those FCG members—primarily from Joplin—who were located in the back of the plant and those—primarily from Ridgeway and Jacksonville—who remained in the front. As one FCG member whose office was moved to the outback explained, "There is a certain paranoia of not being able to see people all the time. I think it works better [for those up front] because they are able to see each other every day. They are in closer proximity."

By the end of 1981, the FCG was finally able to complete the plant's organizational design. A number of its elements, including the compensation system and the facilities development plan, were presented to Ashland's top management and enthusiastically approved.

Two themes dominated the first eight months of 1982: first, a shift in focus from the development of plant systems to the development of manufacturing teams and, second, the increasingly serious impact of the national economic recession on Ashland as a corporation and on Fairfield as a plant. Both of these factors had substantial effects on the FCG's activities.

While the rest of the plant worked through the spring and summer to prepare the compressor team for production, the FCG increasingly was forced to deal with the consequences of the drastic reduction in demand for air conditioners. Group meetings were spent discussing ways to cut the plant budget as well as the ramifications of other corporate decisions. The FCG's major effort over the summer was a make-buy study to show that manufacturing certain components at the Fairfield plant would be less expensive than buying them from outside Ashland.

Unfortunately, Ashland's business did not improve soon enough to benefit the Fairfield Components Plant. In

October 1982, a corporate decision was made to move the Q–15 fan line to Ridgeway and to operate the Fairfield plant with two lines, one producing compressors and the other producing Q–15 gear assemblies. Then, in May 1983, Ashland announced the permanent closure of the Fairfield Components Plant.

_____

Source: Excerpted from Eisenstat, R. A. (1990). Fairfield coordinating group. In J. R. Hackman (Ed.), *Groups that work (and those that don't)*. San Francisco: Jossey-Bass.

1. Discuss the stages of development of the FCG.
2. Discuss some of the norms that emerged in the FCG. What was their function?
3. Discuss the role dynamics that emerged in the FCG. Is there any evidence of role ambiguity or role conflict?
4. How cohesive was the FCG? What factors contribute to this level of cohesiveness?
5. Analyze and evaluate the effectiveness of the FCG using the concepts summarized in Exhibit 8.9.
6. The FCG was a cross-functional team. Critique it in terms of the principles for effectiveness for such teams given in the text.
7. Suppose you were Barry Mackay, the manager who formed the FCG. With your knowledge of groups, what might you do differently if you had to do this again?

AFTER READING CHAPTER 9 YOU SHOULD BE ABLE TO:

1 UNDERSTAND THE DIFFERENCE BETWEEN INFORMATION DEPENDENCE AND EFFECT DEPENDENCE.

2 DIFFERENTIATE COMPLIANCE, IDENTIFICATION, AND INTERNALIZATION AS MOTIVES FOR SOCIAL CONFORMITY.

3 DESCRIBE THE FACTORS THAT INFLUENCE CONFORMITY TO SOCIAL NORMS.

4 DESCRIBE THE STAGES OF ORGANIZATIONAL SOCIALIZATION AND SOME METHODS OF SOCIALIZATION.

5 DIFFERENTIATE AFFECTIVE, CONTINUANCE, AND NORMATIVE COMMITMENT AND EXPLAIN HOW ORGANIZATIONS CAN FOSTER COMMITMENT.

6 DEFINE ORGANIZATIONAL CULTURE AND DISCUSS THE CONTRIBUTORS TO A CULTURE.

7 DISCUSS THE ASSETS AND LIABILITIES OF STRONG ORGANIZATIONAL CULTURES.

8 REVIEW HOW WE CAN DIAGNOSE AN ORGANIZATIONAL CULTURE.

HOW DOES THE DISNEY COMPANY ATTRACT AND RETAIN SERVICE EMPLOYEES DESPITE MODEST PAY, RIGOROUS RULES, AND ROUTINE WORK?

CHAPTER 9

SOCIAL INFLUENCE, SOCIALIZATION, AND CULTURE

THE WALT DISNEY COMPANY

The Walt Disney Company empire includes the Disney Studios, Disneyland Park in California, Walt Disney World in Florida, and a lucrative licensing arrangement for products based on Disney characters. There's universal agreement that Disney has been successful, especially in its theme parks and associated resorts, by virtue of an unwavering dedication to excellent customer service. In fact, firms such as General Motors and DuPont have sent executives to Disney-sponsored seminars to understand how Disney has managed to provide guests with such a clean, pleasant, friendly environment for all of these years.

By all appearances, the task doesn't seem easy. The work force is mostly young and not especially well paid. They are particularly likely to be scheduled to work on busy holidays and vacation periods, just when they would like to spend time with friends and family. Much of the work itself is basically routine and boring (try uttering "Welcome Voyager" with conviction thousands of times a day to the hordes who visit Space Mountain!). Also, Disney has some of the most rigid grooming standards in the industry, forbidding beards, mustaches, and dangling jewelry. The company even provides samples of which basic black shoes are acceptable. The image here is cleancut and conservative.

If individuality is discouraged, all-American friendliness is encouraged. Elaborate group selection interviews stress attitudes and personality over academic credentials, and a film is shown to warn job candidates about expected standards of grooming and behavior. If they are accepted, new employees attend "Disney University" and take the courses Traditions I and II, which expose them to the lingo and lore of Disney. In the Disney vocabulary, they are hosts or cast members, not employees, and customers are guests. Similarly, their uniforms are costumes, and they are "on stage" when they are in the public part of the park. There are group tests ("Name the Seven Dwarfs in Snow White") to foster teamwork. Cast members learn that their role in creating happiness includes picking up any stray trash and being able to answer any conceivable question a guest asks. When everyone does this, employees serve as role models for each other. After the group training at Disney U., employees are assigned to experienced peers who train them in the techniques of their specific job assignment. This "paired training," along with the Traditions classes, is much more extensive than is typical in most service organizations. Thus, guests have little reason to expect poor performance from a new cast member, who has been well versed in Walt Disney's values regarding family entertainment.

Disney relies heavily on promotion from within, even in its management ranks. Its white-collar turnover is low by any standard, and its turnover rate is well below average for hourly service employees. Part of this might be due to a system of decidedly social rewards and perks that appeal to younger employees. These include merchandise discounts, company sports leagues, employee nights at the park, and company picnics and beach parties.

In the old days, the cry "Walt's in the park" would motivate cast members to do their very best. Today, Disney U. trainers often exhort students with "Walt's *always* in the park now." The spirit lives.[1]

This description of a successful service organization raises a number of interesting questions. How does Disney attract and retain employees despite low pay, curtailed individuality, and fairly routine work? Do employees actually accept the ideals and values that they encounter in their training? What has maintained the Disney obsession with excellent service over the years? These are the kinds of questions that we will probe in this chapter.

First, we will examine the general issue of social influence in organizations, how members have an impact on each other's behavior and attitudes. Social norms hold an organization together, and conformity to such norms is a product of social influence. Thus, the next section discusses conformity. Following this, we consider the elaborate process of socialization, the learning of the organization's norms and roles. Socialization both contributes to and results from the organizational culture, the final area that we will explore.

SOCIAL INFLUENCE IN ORGANIZATIONS

In the previous chapter, we pointed out that groups exert influence over the attitudes and behavior of their individual members. As a result of social influence, people often feel or act differently than they would as independent operators. What accounts for such influence? In short, in many social settings, and especially in groups, people are highly *dependent* upon others. This dependence sets the stage for influence to occur.

Information Dependence and Effect Dependence

We are frequently dependent upon others for information about the adequacy and appropriateness of our behavior, thoughts, and feelings. How satisfying is this job of mine? How nice is our boss? How much work should I take home to do over the weekend? Should we protest the bad design at the meeting? Objective, concrete answers to such questions might be hard to come by. Thus, we must often rely upon information that others provide.[2] In turn, this **information dependence** gives others the opportunity to influence our thoughts, feelings, and actions via the signals they send to us.[3]

> **Information dependence.** Reliance on others for information about how to think, feel, and act.

Individuals are often motivated to compare their own thoughts, feelings, and actions with those of others as a means of acquiring information about their adequacy. The effects of social information can be very strong, often exerting as much or more influence over others as objective reality.[4]

As if group members were not busy enough tuning in to information provided by the group, they must also be sensitive to the rewards and punishments the group has at its disposal. Thus, individuals are dependent upon the *effects* of their behavior as determined by the rewards and punishments provided by others. **Effect dependence** actually involves two complementary processes. First, the group frequently has a vested interest in how individual members think and act because such matters can affect the goal attainment of the group. Second, the member frequently desires the approval of the group. In combination, these circumstances promote effect dependence.

> **Effect dependence.** Reliance on others due to their capacity to provide rewards and punishment.

In organizations, plenty of effects are available to keep individual members "under the influence." Superiors typically have a fair array of rewards and punishments available, including promotions, raises, and the assignment of more or less favorable tasks. At the informal level, the variety of such effects available to co-workers is staggering. They might reward cooperative behavior with praise, friendship, and a helping hand on the job. Lack of cooperation might result in nagging, harassment, name calling, or social isolation.

SOCIAL INFLUENCE IN ACTION

One of the most obvious consequences of information and effect dependence is the tendency for group members to conform to the social norms that have been established by the group. In the last chapter we discussed the development and function of such norms, but we have postponed until now the discussion of why norms are supported. Put simply, much of the information and many of the effects upon which group members are dependent are oriented toward enforcing group norms.

Motives for Social Conformity

The fact that Roman Catholic priests conform to the norms of the Church hierarchy seems rather different from the case in which convicts conform to norms that prison officials establish. Clearly, the motives for conformity differ in these two cases. What is needed, then, is some system to classify different motives for conformity.[5]

Compliance. Conformity to a social norm prompted by the desire to acquire rewards or avoid punishment.

Compliance.   **Compliance** is the simplest, most direct motive for conformity to group norms. It occurs because a member wishes to acquire rewards from the group and avoid punishment. As such, it primarily involves effect dependence. Although the complying individual adjusts his or her behavior to the norm, he or she does not really subscribe to the beliefs, values, and attitudes that underlie the norm. Most convicts conform to formal prison norms out of compliance. Similarly, very young children behave themselves only because of external forces.

Identification.   Some individuals conform because they find other supporters of the norm attractive. In this case, the individual identifies with these supporters and sees himself or herself as similar to them. Although there are elements of effect dependence here, information dependence is especially important—if someone is basically similar to you, then you will be motivated to rely on them for information about how to think and act. **Identification** as a motive for conformity is often revealed by an imitation process in which established members serve as models for the behavior of others. For example, a newly promoted executive might attempt to dress and talk like her successful, admired boss. Similarly, as children get older, they might be motivated to behave themselves because such behavior corresponds to that of an admired parent with whom they are beginning to identify.

Identification. Conformity to a social norm prompted by perceptions that those who promote the norm are attractive or similar to oneself.

Internalization. Conformity to a social norm prompted by true acceptance of the beliefs, values, and attitudes that underlie the norm.

Internalization.   Some conformity to norms occurs because individuals have truly and wholly accepted the beliefs, values, and attitudes that underlie the norm. As such, **internalization** of the norm has happened, and conformity occurs because it is seen as *right,* not because it achieves rewards, avoids punishment, or pleases others. That is, conformity is due to internal, rather than external, forces. In general, we expect that most religious leaders conform to the norms of their religion for this reason. Similarly, the career army officer might come to support the strict discipline of the military because it seems right and proper, not simply because colleagues support such discipline. In certain organizational settings, some of these motives for conformity are more likely than others. For example, it is highly unlikely that many Disneyland recruits fully internalize the material covered in Traditions I and II. Rather, they appear to *identify* with the company and its experienced members:

> Like employees everywhere, there is a limit to which such overt company propaganda can be effective. Students and trainers alike seem to agree on where the line is drawn, for there is much satirical banter, mischievous winkings, and playful exaggeration in the classroom. All are aware that the label "Disneyland" has both an unserious and artificial connotation and that a full embrace of the Disneyland role would be as deviant as its full rejection. It does seem, however, because of the corporate imagery, the recruiting and selection proce-

dures, the goodwill trainees hold toward the organization at entry, the peer-based employment context, and the smooth fit with real student calendars, the job is considered by most to be a good one. The University of Disneyland, it appears, graduates students with a modest amount of pride and a considerable amount of fact and faith firmly ingrained as important things to know (and accept).[6]

Experiments in Social Influence

The various motives for conformity are illustrated in two well-known studies of social influence.

The Asch Study.   In his research Solomon Asch told subjects that they were participating in an experiment on visual perception.[7] Subjects sat in rows with seven to nine other people, and the experimenter exposed them to lines of the type shown in Exhibit 9.1. The subjects had to indicate which of the three comparison lines was equal in length to the standard line. Judgments were given successively, and the subject was the last to respond.

On the first two trials, things went smoothly, and all of the people agreed as to which line matched the standard. On the third trial an amazing thing happened. The first person to respond gave a clearly inaccurate answer, and others then also gave this response. Quickly, it was the subject's turn to respond. What would you do? As you might have guessed, the other people in the row were confederates of the experimenter, and this was a study in conformity rather than perception. Over a number of trials, the confederates communicated a "false norm" several times. Subjects, who had remarkably varied degrees of independence, conformed to this false norm about one-third of the time.

This study, raises the question: why was there so much conformity to the false norm? Clearly, the perceptual task was very easy; control subjects who performed the task alone made few errors in judgment. When asked why they had yielded, most subjects said something to the effect that "I knew they were wrong, but I gave in anyway." The majority of the subjects did not believe that the false norm was correct, but they doubted both the majority's perceptions

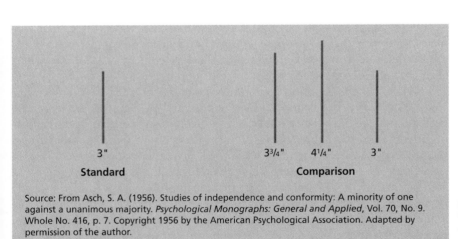

| 3" | | 3³/₄" | 4¹/₄" | 3" |
| **Standard** | | | **Comparison** | |

Source: From Asch, S. A. (1956). Studies of independence and conformity: A minority of one against a unanimous majority. *Psychological Monographs: General and Applied*, Vol. 70, No. 9. Whole No. 416, p. 7. Copyright 1956 by the American Psychological Association. Adapted by permission of the author.

EXHIBIT 9.1
Which comparison line matches the standard? The Asch conformity study task.

The Asch study, in which participants agreed with a false norm, exhibits the strength of social influence.

and their own capacities to judge and were torn in conflicting directions. Evidently, they were in a state of effect dependence, anticipating rejection or other punishment if they disagreed.

The Sherif Study.   Muzafer Sherif also explained his research to the participants as an exercise in visual perception. He asked subjects to estimate the amount of movement of a point of light in a darkened room. In fact, the light was absolutely stationary. However, in this situation, observers invariably report some movement. This phenomenon is called the autokinetic (self-movement) effect, and it is due to certain physiological processes. Because there is no frame of reference in a completely dark environment, individuals usually give widely differing estimates of the distance the light has "moved."

First, Sherif tested subjects individually to determine their estimates without social influence. Then, he assembled subjects into groups of two or three and asked them to judge the movement over a series of trials. On each trial, they made simultaneous judgments. The results were clear-cut. Over the series of trials, group members' estimates of the movement tended to *converge*. Gradually, those who initially reported large movements decreased their estimates, and vice versa—in other words, they reached a compromise. Sherif argued that this convergence represented the development of a norm to which group members conformed.[8]

Notice that the situation here is very different from that in the Asch line study. This is clearly an ambiguous situation, and the subjects are in certain need of information. Thus, minimally, it would appear that identification occurred among group members. The case here is not so much that they found each other attractive as that they recognized each other as equally bemused. In such cases, we often rely upon others for information about how to think or act. In fact, it would appear that the compromise norm was frequently *internalized* as representing correct information. When subjects were tested alone after the group experience, they tended to respond with the group-established norm. Amazingly, researchers found this effect to persist a whole year after the group interaction.[9]

Many decision tasks facing existing groups have elements in common with the Asch and Sherif experimental situations. For example, imagine the negotiating committee of a trade union that is trying to decide whether to accept a company contract offer. Each member offers a successive opinion about the course of action the union should take. If the first three unionists all favor acceptance, will the fourth be willing to offer a contrary view? (Asch situation). Similarly, consider three partners who own a restaurant and are trying to decide whether they should expand their premises during an uncertain economic climate. Initially, one favors no expansion, one favors a large expansion, and one falls in the middle (Sherif situation). Will they compromise on a medium-sized expansion? To answer questions of this nature, we must explore the variables that influence degree of conformity.

Factors Influencing Conformity to Norms

What determines the extent to which a particular group member will be likely to conform to group norms? Put simply, factors that increase or decrease information and effect dependence should influence the extent of conformity of individual group members.

Publicity.   In the Asch setting, one obvious way to reduce the conformity of the naive subject to the false norm is to permit the subject to render opinions about line length in secret. Such a condition reduces effect dependence. For example, suppose an executive group has two equally strong informal norms—not cheating on expense accounts and not leaving the office before six o'clock. Other things being equal, an executive who disagrees with both norms would be more likely to comply with the leaving-time norm than the cheating norm because violation of the former would be more obvious. In some piecerate pay situations in which groups have developed norms to restrict productivity, workers will lie about their own output to prevent pressure from their co-workers.

Size of the Opposition.   Any tendency to "go along with the crowd" is enhanced when the "crowd" is bigger, because a large opposition contains more sources of information and more sources of reward and punishment. In the Asch setting, subjects are less likely to conform to the false norm when confronting only one or two others than when there are seven or eight.[10] Research on jury size shows that small juries tend to render less consistent verdicts than large juries.[11] This might stem in part from the fact that dissenters in small juries feel freer to stand their ground.

Dissension.   Imagine that, in the Asch setting, the naive subject finds that he or she has a "partner in crime" somewhere earlier in the lineup, that is, someone who also rejects the false norm and gives correct responses. As you might guess, such a condition strongly reduces the subject's tendency to conform. Dissenters provide alternative sources of information to the group consensus and change potential reward and punishment patterns.

The Issue at Hand.   In the Asch routine, it is possible to increase the naive subject's tendency to conform to the false norm by making the stimulus lines more nearly equal in length. In general, difficult, ambiguous issues increase the tendency toward conformity to group norms. For example, suppose four sales managers are asked to nominate one of their subordinates for promotion to manager. The subordinates are usually on the road, and there has been little opportunity to observe their managerial abilities. If, for some reason, three of the managers favor a particular candidate, it should be difficult for the fourth to dissent, since the choice is difficult and ambiguous.

Status.   The relationship between status in the group and conformity is complex but easy to understand. If nonconformity occurs, it should usually occur among two classes of people—high-status members or low-status members who have been actively rejected by the group (the latter have often been socially isolated or serve as scapegoats). High-status members have often *achieved* their high status because they have generally conformed to group norms. Thus, on an issue chosen at random, it is often safe to predict conformity from such a person. However, high-status members also receive **idiosyncrasy credits** from the group because of their history of conformity. This means that having paid their dues to the group, they are permitted to occasionally deviate without fear of censure.[12] On the other hand, low-status isolates and scapegoats have already rejected the group as a source of information and suffered the negative effects of doing so. Thus, they have little to gain by conforming in a particular case. Finally, low-status members who are striving to become fully integrated into the group (usually *new* members) should reveal a strong tendency to conform, since they are both effect and information dependent (Exhibit 9.2).

For an example of nonconformity in the form of "whistleblowing," see the "Ethical Focus: *Whistleblowing at Carolina Power & Light.*"

The Subtle Power of Compliance

In many of the examples given in the previous section, especially those dealing with effect dependence, it is obvious that the doubting group member is motivated to conform only in the *compliance* mode. That is, he or she really doesn't support the belief, value, and attitude structure underlying the norm but conforms simply to avoid trouble or obtain rewards. Of course, this happens all

Idiosyncrasy credits. Social credits earned from regular conformity to group norms that allow occasional deviance from the norms.

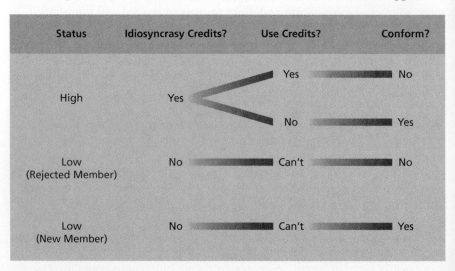

Status	Idiosyncrasy Credits?	Use Credits?	Conform?
High	Yes	Yes	No
		No	Yes
Low (Rejected Member)	No	Can't	No
Low (New Member)	No	Can't	Yes

EXHIBIT 9.2
Status, idiosyncrasy credits, and conformity.

ETHICAL FOCUS   Whistleblowing at Carolina Power & Light

Federal officials ordered Carolina Power & Light Co. to reinstate an employee after an investigation found he was unfairly demoted for complaining about safety problems at the Brunswick nuclear plant.

James B. DeBose filed a complaint with the U.S. Labor Department after he was demoted October 18 from a relay technician to a substation maintenance crew worker.

The department notified CP&L in a letter dated Dec. 16 that the demotion violated the federal whistleblowers act, which protects nuclear industry workers who complain about safety problems.

The department ordered the company to reinstate DeBose and give him his annual salary increase, which amounts to $152 per month.

CP&L officials said they will appeal the decision and declined further comment.

DeBose said he filed the complaint because he was moved from his technician's job after he spoke out about a foreman who he says frequently violated maintenance procedures at the Unit 1 reactor.

DeBose said he once spoke with the foreman when he noticed brittle wires in a piece of backup-power equipment.

"What you have here is an accident waiting to happen," he said, comparing the brittle wires to an exposed wire.

"I was told that this was not my job and none of my business," he wrote in his complaint.

The incidents happened in January, February and March, DeBose said. He was demoted in October.

"They took me out of my technical position," he said. Now, "I wipe oil out of breakers and dig dirt."

As this Associated Press story illustrates, whistleblowing is an act of nonconformity by an organizational member who calls attention to some serious wrongdoing. Myron and Penina Glazer conducted an in-depth study of fifty-five whistleblowers in both the public and private sectors. Far from being perennial malcontents, virtually all of them were dedicated, long-service employees who were finally unable to reconcile unethical organizational practices with their strong sense of individual responsibility. Long service was no protection from retaliation. Many whistleblowers were fired, transferred, blackballed, demoted, or personally intimidated and harassed for their lack of conformity.

Of course, not all whistleblowers face retaliation. Janet Near and Marcia Miceli studied the severity of retaliation against whistleblowers who were U.S. federal employees. Retaliation was more likely when the whistleblowers lacked managerial support, when the wrongdoing was particularly serious, and when the person went outside the organization to blow the whistle. Interestingly, retaliation was not related to position in the organization.

Sources: Associated Press. (1991, December 27). CP&L ordered to reinstate worker who made complaints about safety. *Greensboro News & Record*, p. B3; Glazer, M. P., & Glazer, P. M. (1986, August). Whistleblowing. *Psychology Today*, 36–43; Near, J. P., & Miceli, M. P. (1986). Retaliation against whistleblowers: Predictors and effects. *Journal of Applied Psychology, 71*, 137–145.

the time. Individuals without religious beliefs or values might agree to be married in a church service to please others. Similarly, a store cashier might verify a credit card purchase by a familiar customer even though he feels that the whole process is a waste of time. These examples of compliance seem trivial enough, but a little compliance can go a long way.

A compliant individual is necessarily *doing* something that is contrary to the way he or she *thinks* or *feels*. As we pointed out in our discussion of attitudes in Chapter 5, such a situation is highly dissonant and arouses a certain tension in the individual. Now one way to reduce this dissonance is to cease conformity. This is especially likely if the required behavior is at great variance with one's values or moral standards. However, this might require the person to adopt an isolate or scapegoat role, equally unpleasant prospects. The other method of reducing dissonance is to gradually accept the beliefs, values, and attitudes that support the norm in question. This is more likely when the required behavior is not so discrepant with one's current value system.

Consider Mark, an idealistic graduate of a college social work program who acquires a job with a social services agency. Mark loves helping people but hates the bureaucratic red tape and reams of paperwork that are necessary to accomplish this goal. However, to acquire the approval of his boss and co-workers, and to avoid trouble, he follows the rules to the letter of the law. This is pure compliance. Over time, however, Mark begins to *identify* with his boss and more experienced co-workers because they are in the enviable position of controlling those very rewards and punishments that are so important to him. Obviously, if he is to *be* one of them, he must begin to think and feel like them. Finally, Mark is promoted to a supervisory position partly because he is so cooperative. Breaking in a new social worker, Mark is heard to say, "Our rules and forms are very important. You don't understand now, but you will." The metamorphosis is complete—Mark has *internalized* the beliefs and values that support the bureaucratic norms of his agency.

Although this story is slightly dramatized, the point that it makes is accurate—simple compliance can set the stage for more complete involvement with organizational norms and roles.

SOCIALIZATION: GETTING (SOME) CONFORMITY FROM MEMBERS

Socialization. The process by which people learn the norms and roles that are necessary to function in a group or organization.

The story of Mark, the social worker, in the previous section describes how one individual was socialized into a particular organization. **Socialization** is the process by which people learn the norms and roles that are necessary to function in a group or organization. As we shall see, some of this process might occur before membership formally begins. Furthermore, socialization is an ongoing process by virtue of continuous interaction with others in the workplace. However, there is good reason to believe that socialization is most potent during certain periods of membership transition, such as when one is promoted or assigned to a new work group, and especially when one joins a new organization.[13]

Stages of Socialization

Since organizational socialization is an ongoing process, it is useful to divide this process into three stages.[14] One of these stages occurs before entry, another immediately follows entry, and the last occurs after one has been a member for some period of time. In a sense, the first two stages represent hurdles for achieving passage into the third stage (see Exhibit 9.3).

Anticipatory Socialization.   A considerable amount of socialization might occur even before a person becomes a member of a particular organization. This process is called anticipatory socialization. Some anticipatory socialization includes a formal process of skill and attitude acquisition, such as that which might occur by attending university. Other anticipatory socialization might be informal, such as that acquired through a series of summer jobs or even by watching the portrayal of organizational life in television shows and movies. As we shall see shortly, organizations vary in the extent to which they encourage anticipatory socialization in advance of entry. Also, we shall see that not all anticipatory socialization is accurate and useful for the new member.

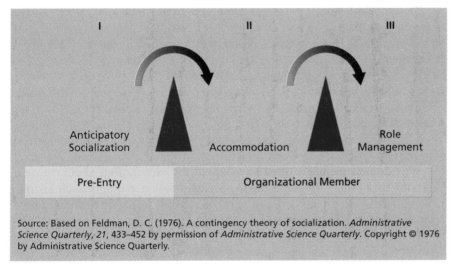

Source: Based on Feldman, D. C. (1976). A contingency theory of socialization. *Administrative Science Quarterly, 21*, 433–452 by permission of *Administrative Science Quarterly.* Copyright © 1976 by Administrative Science Quarterly.

EXHIBIT 9.3
Stages of organizational socialization.

Accommodation.   In the accommodation stage, the new recruit, armed with some expectations about organizational life, encounters the day-to-day reality of this life. Formal aspects of this stage might include orientation programs, training programs (such as that at Disney), and rotation through various parts of the organization. Informal aspects include getting to know and understand the style and personality of one's boss and co-workers. At this stage, the organization and its experienced members are looking for an acceptable degree of conformity to organizational norms and the gradual acquisition of appropriate role behavior. Recruits, on the other hand, are interested in having their personal needs and expectations fulfilled. If accommodation is reached, the recruit will have complied with critical organizational norms and should begin to identify with experienced organizational members.

Role Management.   Having survived the accommodation process and acquired basic role behaviors, the member's attention shifts to fine-tuning and actively managing his or her role in the organization. He or she might be expected to exercise some idiosyncrasy credits and modify the role to better serve the organization. This might require forming connections outside the immediate work group. And the organizational member must confront balancing the now-familiar organizational role with nonwork roles and family demands. Each of these experiences provides additional socialization to the role occupant, who might begin to internalize the norms and values that are prominent in the organization.

     Now that we have seen a basic sketch of how socialization proceeds, let's look in greater detail at some of the key issues in the process.

The Naive New Member

People seldom join organizations without expectations about what membership will be like. In fact, it is just such expectations that lead them to choose one career or job over another. Management majors have some expectations about what they will be doing when they become management trainees at Citicorp. Similarly, even 18-year-old army recruits have notions about what military life will be like.

Research indicates that people entering organizations hold many expectations that are inaccurate and often unrealistically high.[15] In one study of telephone operators, for example, researchers obtained people's expectations about the nature of the job *before* they started work. They also looked at these employees' perceptions of the actual job shortly *after* they started work. The results indicated that many perceptions were less favorable than expectations. A similar result occurred for students entering a Master of Business Administration program.[16] Such changes, which are fairly common, support the notion that socialization has an important impact on new organizational members.

Why do new members often have unrealistic expectations about the organizations they join?[17] To some extent, occupational stereotypes such as those we discussed in Chapter 4 could be responsible. The media often communicate such stereotypes. For example, a person entering nurses' training might have gained some expectations about hospital life from watching *General Hospital*. Those of us who teach might also be guilty of communicating stereotypes. After four years of study, the new management trainee at Citicorp might be dismayed to find that the emphasis is on *trainee* rather than *management*! Finally, unrealistic expectations may also stem from overzealous recruiters who paint rosy pictures in order to attract job candidates to the organization. Taken together, these factors demonstrate the need for socialization.

The Dilemmas of Socialization

Individuals enter organizations with a unique set of skills, interests, and attitudes. This fact of life poses interesting dilemmas for both the individual and the organization.

On one hand, new members wish to maintain their individual identity and self-respect by retaining their unique qualities and building upon them. On the other hand, they are also anxious to learn the ropes of the organization and use these unique qualities in a manner acceptable to peers and superiors. The organization and its experienced members also face a similar dilemma. On one hand, new members need some encouragement to support the norms and role requirements of the organization. Without this support, organizational goals will be impossible to achieve because the firm or institution simply won't be *organized*. On the other hand, complete and total allegiance to existing norms and role requirements will render the organization dinosaurlike, unable to adapt to a changing environment. In this case, creative and innovative behaviors on the part of individual members are stifled, and existing norms and roles take on a life of their own.

These, then, are the dilemmas of socialization: How should individuals react to socialization practices? And how can organizations socialize members to an adequate extent without frustrating them or stifling their uniqueness?

From the individual's viewpoint, many people simply avoid joining organizations whose socialization practices are incompatible with their needs. Of course, this can be tricky business given the inaccurate perceptions of organizational practices that many outsiders hold. Finding themselves at the mercy of socialization that doesn't meet their needs, individuals might effect a compromise or decide to seek employment elsewhere.

Organizations attempt to solve *their* socialization dilemmas by tailoring socialization methods to their particular needs. Intuitively, this seems reasonable. Somehow, the making of a priest seems different from the making of a stockbroker!

Methods of Socialization

For various jobs, organizations differ in terms of *who* does the socializing, *how* it is done, and *how much* is done.

Reliance on External Agents.   Organizations differ in the extent to which they make use of other organizations to help socialize their members. For example, hospitals do not develop experienced cardiologists from scratch. Rather, they depend on medical schools to socialize potential doctors in the basic role requirements of being a physician. Similarly, business firms rely upon university business schools to send them recruits who think and act in a businesslike manner. In this way, a fair degree of anticipatory socialization may exist before a person joins an organization. On the other hand, organizations such as police forces, the military, and religious institutions are less likely to rely upon external socializers. Police academies, boot camps, and seminaries are set up as extensions of these organizations to aid in socialization.

Organizations that handle their own socialization are especially interested in maintaining the continuity and stability of job behaviors over a period of time. Conversely, those that rely on external agencies to perform anticipatory socialization are oriented toward maintaining the potential for creative, innovative behavior on the part of members—there is less "inbreeding." Of course, reliance on external agents might present problems. The engineer who is socialized in university courses to respect design elegance might find it difficult to accept cost restrictions when he or she is employed by an engineering firm. For this reason, organizations that rely heavily upon external socialization always supplement it with formal training and orientation or informal on-the-job training.

At Disney, hiring young employees and promoting from within suggest relatively little reliance on external agents. Perhaps the company is trying to avoid "bad habits" that could be picked up in less meticulous service organizations!

Collective Versus Individual.   Organizations may employ a collective socialization strategy or an individual strategy.[18] In the collective case, a number of new or aspiring members are socialized as a group, going through the same experiences and facing the same challenges. Army boot camps, fraternity pledge classes, and training classes for salespeople and airline attendants are examples. Under an individual system, socialization is tailor-made for each new member. Simple on-the-job training and apprenticeship to develop skilled craftspeople constitute individual socialization.

Collective socialization is often the way to promote organizational loyalty, esprit de corps, and uniformity of behavior among those being socialized. This last characteristic is often very important. No matter where they are in the world, soldiers know whom to salute and how to do it. Similarly, air passengers need not expect any surprises from cabin attendants, thanks to the attendants' collective socialization. Collective socialization is especially effective in inducing uniform behavior because there are so many models present who are undergoing the same experience. In addition, the individuals being socialized might pressure each other to toe the line and "do things right." Thus, in collective socialization, one's peers prove to be especially potent sources of information. This follows from our earlier discussion of conformity.

Under individual socialization, new members are more likely to take on the particular characteristics and style of their socializers. Thus, two newly hired real estate agents who receive on-the-job training from their bosses might soon think and act more like their bosses than like each other. As you can see, uniformity is less likely under individual socialization.

Collective socialization is always followed up by individual socialization as the member joins his or her regular work unit. For example, rookie police officers are routinely partnered with more experienced officers. At this point, they will begin to develop some individuality in the style with which they perform their jobs. At Disney, collective socialization in Traditions I and II is followed up with the more individualized paired training.

Debasement and Hazing. Organizations sometimes put new members through a series of experiences that are designed to humble them and strip away some of their initial self-confidence. These experiences are called **debasement** (or, informally, hazing). Debasement is a way of testing the commitment of new members and correcting for faulty anticipatory socialization. Having been humbled and stripped of preconceptions, members are then ready to learn the norms of the organization. Some debasement experiences are formal and planned. An extreme example is the rough treatment and shaved heads of Marine Corps recruits. A little less extreme are Disney's strict grooming standards. Even new college graduates are not immune to debasement:

Debasement. A series of socialization experiences designed to humble people and remove some self-confidence.

> This may sound like brainwashing or boot camp, but it usually just takes the form of pouring on more work than the newcomer can possibly do. IBM and Morgan Guaranty socialize with training programs in which, to quote one participant, "You work every night until 2 A.M. on your own material, and then help others." Procter & Gamble achieves the same result with what might be called upending experiences—requiring a recent college graduate to color in a map of sales territories, for example. The message is clear: while you may be accomplished in many respects, you are in kindergarten as far as what you know about this organization.[19]

Not all debasement experiences are formal. The immediate work group might take it upon itself to test the new member through informal hazing. For example, the group might ask a newly hired engineer to explain the plans for an impossible or "nonsense" electrical circuit. Similarly, fellow officers might send the rookie cop in alone to shake down a bar that is frequented by unfriendly bikers. Often, such experiences are designed to illustrate how group members must depend upon each other.

Debasement experiences most commonly occur in entry-level jobs, whether blue-collar or white-collar. A new executive vice-president would be unlikely to suffer debasement unless he or she was entering a hostile environment.

Extent of Socialization. Under some circumstances, organizations are pretty much willing to make do with what they get in terms of recruits. That is, they attempt to build upon the characteristics that the person brings into the setting rather than attempting radical socialization. Many volunteer organizations such as charities and community groups are like this, since they have little power over recruits. At the other extreme, some organizations have as their goal the radical socialization of members, hoping to strip them of old beliefs, values, and attitudes and get them to internalize new ones. Whether they are successful or not, prisons, mental hospitals, and religious orders have this orientation toward inmates, patients, and novitiates.[20]

Most business organizations tend to fall between these extremes. However, there has been a growing trend toward more extensive and rigorous socialization, especially in firms that are very concerned with quality and customer service. We'll explore this later in the context of strong organizational cultures.

Realistic Job Previews

We noted earlier that new organizational members often harbor unrealistically inflated expectations about what their jobs will be like. When the job is actually begun, it fails to live up to these expectations, individuals experience "reality shock" and job dissatisfaction results. As a consequence, costly turnover is most likely to occur among newer employees who are unable to survive the discrepancy between expectations and reality. For the organization, this sequence of events represents a failure of socialization.

Obviously, organizations cannot control all sources of unrealistic job expectations, such as those provided by television shows and glorified occupational stereotypes. However, they *can* control those generated during the recruiting process by providing job applicants with realistic job previews. **Realistic job previews** provide a balanced, realistic picture of the positive and negative aspects of the job to job applicants.[21] Thus, they provide "corrective action" to expectations at the anticipatory socialization stage. Exhibit 9.4 compares the realistic job preview process with the traditional preview process that often sets expectations too high by ignoring the negative aspects of the job.

Realistic job previews. The provision of a balanced, realistic picture of the positive and negative aspects of a job to job applicants.

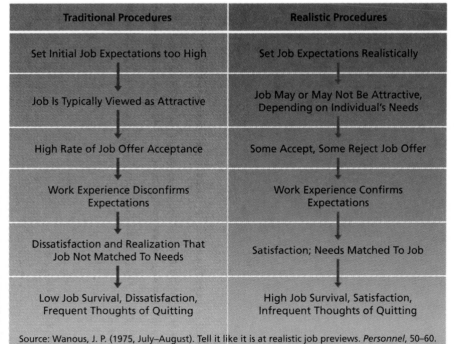

Traditional Procedures	Realistic Procedures
Set Initial Job Expectations too High	Set Job Expectations Realistically
Job Is Typically Viewed as Attractive	Job May or May Not Be Attractive, Depending on Individual's Needs
High Rate of Job Offer Acceptance	Some Accept, Some Reject Job Offer
Work Experience Disconfirms Expectations	Work Experience Confirms Expectations
Dissatisfaction and Realization That Job Not Matched To Needs	Satisfaction; Needs Matched To Job
Low Job Survival, Dissatisfaction, Frequent Thoughts of Quitting	High Job Survival, Satisfaction, Infrequent Thoughts of Quitting

Source: Wanous, J. P. (1975, July–August). Tell it like it is at realistic job previews. *Personnel*, 50–60. © 1975 American Management Association, New York. All rights reserved.

EXHIBIT 9.4
Traditional and realistic job previews compared.

How do organizations design and conduct realistic job previews? Generally, they obtain the views of experienced employees and personnel officers about the positive and negative aspects of the job. Then, they incorporate these views into booklets or videotape presentations for applicants.[22] For example, a video presentation might involve interviews with job incumbents discussing the pros and cons of their jobs. In its video, Disney stresses grooming standards. Realistic previews have been designed for jobs as diverse as telephone operator, life insurance salesperson, Marine Corps recruit, and supermarket worker. Exhibit 9.5 shows the elements of a realistic preview for bank tellers that a bank conducted using booklets.

Sometimes realistic previews use simulations to permit applicants to actually sample the work. One at Toyota USA's Georgetown, Kentucky, plant stresses the repetitive nature of the work and the need to be a team player. Applicants to Nissan's Smyrna, Tennessee, plant work many hours without pay to see what the work is really like.

Evidence shows that realistic job previews are effective in reducing turnover. What is less clear is exactly why this reduction occurs. Reduced expectations and increased job satisfaction are part of the answer. Less clear is whether realistic previews cause those not cut out for the job to withdraw from the application process.[23] Although the turnover reductions from realistic previews are small, they can result in substantial financial savings for organizations.[24]

Topic	Job Preview Coverage
Training	Training described Final exam at the end of training mentioned Failure rate during training reported
Work	Banking transactions described Accuracy important and it is checked daily Working under pressure, e.g., Mondays & Fridays Manager schedules work 1 week in advance Working on your feet Working may become routine and repetitive
Customers	Coutesy is always required Rude customers encountered
Career opportunities	Promotion criteria specified Average promotion rates for each job given How to move into branch management (college degree needed)
Compensation	Pay rates specified Employee benefits described How pay increases are determined
Summary of major points	Summary included—1/2 page long, titled "It's not for everyone"

EXHIBIT 9.5
Elements covered in a realistic job preview for bank tellers.

Source: Adapted from Dean, R. A., & Wanous, J. P. (1984). Effects of realistic preview on hiring bank tellers. *Journal of Applied Psychology, 69,* 61–68. Copyright © 1984 by American Psychological Association. Reprinted by permission.

Gaining Organizational Commitment

In an era of layoffs, downsizing, restructuring, and reengineering, there is evidence that employees are losing commitment to their organizations.[25] People often view their careers as a series of jobs with a variety of potential employers, or they even see themselves as free-lancers rather than having a series of jobs in one organization.

Three Types of Commitment.   Speaking generally, **organizational commitment** is an attitude that reflects the strength of the linkage between an employee and an organization. This linkage has implications for whether someone tends to remain in an organization. Researchers John Meyer and Natalie Allen have identified three very different types of organizational commitment:[26]

- **Affective commitment** is commitment based on a person's identification and involvement with an organization. People with high affective commitment stay with an organization because they *want* to.
- **Continuance commitment** is commitment based on the costs that would be incurred in leaving an organization. People with high continuance commitment stay with an organization because they *have* to.
- **Normative commitment** is commitment based on ideology or a feeling of obligation to an organization. People with high normative commitment stay with an organization because they think that they *should* do so.

We might note that these forms of commitment could also apply to one's work team, union, or profession.

Causes of Commitment.   As you might expect, the causes of these three forms of commitment tend to differ. Far and away the best predictor of affective commitment is interesting, satisfying work of the type found in enriched jobs (Chapter 7).[27] One mistake that organizations sometimes make is starting employees out in unchallenging jobs so that they don't make any serious errors. This can have a negative impact on affective commitment. Role clarity and having one's expectations met after hiring (as fostered by realistic job previews) also contribute to affective commitment.[28]

Continuance commitment occurs when people feel that leaving the organization will result in personal sacrifice, and they perceive that good alternative employment is lacking. Building up "side bets" in pension funds, obtaining rapid promotion, or being well integrated into the community where the firm is located can lock employees into organizations even though they would rather go elsewhere. Not surprisingly, continuance commitment increases with the time a person is employed by his or her organization.[29]

Normative commitment ("I *should* stay here") can be fostered by benefits that build a sense of obligation to the organization. These might include tuition reimbursements or special training that enhances one's skills. Strong identification with an organization's product or service ("I should stay here because the Sierra Club is doing important work") can also foster normative commitment. Finally, certain socialization practices that emphasize loyalty to the organization can stimulate normative commitment. For example, sports coaches often haze players who miss practice to stress the importance of loyalty to the team.

Organizational commitment. An attitude that reflects the strength of the linkage between an employee and an organization.

Affective commitment. Commitment based on identification and involvement with an organization.

Continuance commitment. Commitment based on the costs that would be incurred in leaving an organization.

Normative commitment. Commitment based on ideology or a feeling of obligation to an organization.

Consequences of Commitment.   There is good evidence that all forms of commitment reduce turnover intentions and actual turnover.[30] Organizations plagued with turnover problems among key employees should look carefully at tactics that foster commitment. This would seem to be especially sensible when turnover gets so bad that it threatens customer service. Many service organizations (e.g., restaurants and hotels), however, have traditionally accepted high turnover rates.

Organizations should take care, though, in their targeting of the kind of commitment to boost. Research shows that affective commitment is positively related to performance. However, continuance commitment is *negatively* related to performance, something you might have observed in dealing with burned-out bureaucrats.[31] An especially bad combination for both the employee and the organization is high continuance commitment coupled with low affective commitment—people locked into organizations that they detest. This happened very frequently during the most recent recession.

The Disney Company has been very skilled at building affective and even some normative commitment to keep turnover well below theme park standards and thus enhance customer service. Cross-training (including the opportunity to teach Traditions) provides for job enrichment, and the realistic job preview ensures that new hires have realistic expectations about the work.

Is there a downside to organizational commitment? Very high levels of commitment can cause conflicts between family life and work life. Also, very high levels of commitment have often been implicated in unethical and illegal behavior, including a General Electric price-fixing conspiracy and illegal payoffs made by Lockheed. Finally, high levels of commitment to a particular *form or style* of organization can cause a lack of innovation and lead to resistance when a change in the culture is necessary.[32] With this in mind, let's look at organizational culture.

ORGANIZATIONAL CULTURE

The last several pages have been concerned with socialization into an organization. To a large degree, the course of that socialization both depends on and shapes the culture of the organization. Let's examine culture, a concept that has gained the attention of both researchers and practicing managers.

What Is Organizational Culture?

At the outset, we can say that organizational culture is not the easiest concept to define. Informally, culture might be thought of as an organization's style, atmosphere, or personality. This style, atmosphere, or personality is most obvious when we contrast what it must be like to work in various organizations such as IBM, Sears, the U.S. Marine Corps, or the Toronto Blue Jays. Even from their mention in the popular press, we can imagine that these organizations provide very different work environments. Thus, culture provides uniqueness and social identity to organizations.

More formally, **organizational culture** consists of the shared beliefs, values, and assumptions that exist in an organization.[33] In turn, these shared beliefs, values, and assumptions determine the norms that develop and the pat-

Organizational culture. Shared beliefs, values, and assumptions that exist in an organization.

The culture of the entertainment company Dreamworks SKG will reflect the values of founders Jeffrey Katzenberg, Steven Spielberg, and David Geffen.

terns of behavior that emerge from these norms. The term *shared* does not necessarily mean that members are in close agreement on these matters, although they might well be. Rather, it means that they have had uniform exposure to them and have some minimum common understanding of them. Several other characteristics of culture are important.

- Culture represents a true "way of life" for organizational members, who often take its influence for granted. Frequently, an organization's culture becomes obvious only when it is contrasted with that of other organizations or when it undergoes changes.

- Because culture involves basic assumptions, values, and beliefs, it tends to be fairly stable over time. In addition, once a culture is well established, it can persist despite turnover among organizational personnel, providing social continuity.

- The content of a culture can involve matters that are internal to the organization or external. Internally, a culture might support innovation, risk taking, or secrecy of information. Externally, a culture might support "putting the customer first" or behaving unethically toward competitors.

- Culture can have a strong impact on both organizational performance and member satisfaction.

Culture is truly a social variable, reflecting yet another aspect of the kind of social influence that we have been discussing in this chapter. Thus, culture is not simply an automatic consequence of an organization's technology, products, or size. For example, there is some tendency for organizations to become more bureaucratic as they get larger. However, the culture of a particular large organization might support an informal, nonbureaucratic atmosphere.

Subcultures. Smaller cultures that develop within a larger organizational culture that are based on differences in training, occupation, or departmental goals.

Can an organization have several cultures? The answer is yes. Often unique **subcultures** develop that reflect departmental differences or differences in occupation or training.[34] A researcher who studied Silicon Valley computer companies found that technical and professional employees divided into "hardware types" and "software types." In turn, hardware types subdivided into engineers and technicians, and software types subdivided into software engineers and computer scientists. Each group had its own values, beliefs, and assumptions about how to design computer systems.[35] Effective organizations will develop an overarching culture that manages such divisions. For instance, a widely shared norm might exist that in effect says, "We fight like hell until a final design is chosen, and then we all pull together."

The "Strong Culture" Concept

Strong culture. An organizational culture with intense and pervasive beliefs, values, and assumptions.

Some cultures have more impact on the behavior of organizational members than others. In a **strong culture,** the beliefs, values, and assumptions that make up the culture are both intense and pervasive across the organization.[36] In other words, the beliefs, values, and assumptions are strongly supported by the majority of members, even cutting across any subcultures that might exist. Thus, the strong culture provides great consensus concerning "what the organization is about" or what it stands for. In weak cultures, on the other hand, beliefs, values, and assumptions are less strongly ingrained and/or less widely shared across the organization. Weak cultures are thus fragmented and have less impact on organizational members. All organizations have a culture, although it might be hard to detect the details of weak cultures.

To firm up your understanding of strong cultures, let's consider thumbnail sketches of three organizations that are generally agreed to have strong cultures.

- *General Electric.* Under the leadership of CEO Jack Welch, this industrial giant, based in Fairfield, Connecticut, was transformed from a lethargic and inward-looking company to a fleet-of-foot global competitor with an openness to new ideas. GE became known for extremely high performance standards and its goal to be first or second in the world in all of its businesses (see *You Be the Manager*).
- *Southwest Airlines.* This Dallas-based company has turned a consistent profit in the turbulent airline industry by focusing on low-cost, short distance flights. Southwest is known for fostering a family atmosphere that has inspired extremely high employee motivation and commitment.
- *3M.* This Minneapolis-based company produces tape, adhesives, abrasives, and building materials. The firm is known for its extreme dedication to product innovation. 3M rewards its employees for creativity and risk taking to this end, and accepts failure as part of the game.

Three points are worth emphasizing about these examples of strong cultures. First, an organization need not be big to have a strong culture. If its members agree strongly about certain beliefs, values, and assumptions, a small business, school, or social service agency can have a strong culture. Second, strong cultures do not necessarily result in blind conformity. For example, the strong culture at 3M supports and rewards *non*conformity in the form of innovation and creativity. Finally, General Electric, Southwest Airlines, and 3M are obviously successful organizations. Do strong cultures always result in organizational success?

CULTURAL CHANGE AT GENERAL ELECTRIC

YOU BE THE Manager

When John F. (Jack) Welch, Jr. became CEO of General Electric, he inherited a good balance sheet, but he also inherited a lethargic, inward-looking bureaucracy with modest technology and few global capabilities. Decision making was slow, turf struggles were common, and innovation was lacking. The company's slow-growing electrical equipment business was dominant, and GE had many business units that were not profitable. Low productivity was a particular problem. With increasing global competition, Welch knew that GE needed radical change if it were to survive and prosper.

Early in his tenure, Welch moved on two fronts. One involved radical downsizing and buying and selling dozens of companies to develop a portfolio of 13 major businesses in which GE could excel. The other involved instilling in his top executive team the changes in values

> GENERAL ELECTRIC ATTEMPTED TO INSTILL A CULTURE CHANGE WITHIN THE COMPANY TO INCREASE PRODUCTIVITY AND BOOST PROFITS.

that Welch knew were necessary. Still, Welch was frustrated by repeated evidence that middle- and lower-level managers had not embraced the new values and were resisting cultural change. Also, he was troubled by GE's continued preoccupation with the "not invented here syndrome," its tendency to reject ideas and innovations from outside the company. If you were Welch, what would *you* do?

1. How can the new cultural message be impressed upon middle- and lower-level managers?

2. What can GE do to specifically combat the "not invented here syndrome"?

To find out what the company did, consult *The Manager's Notebook* at the end of the chapter.

Sources: Tichy, N. M., & Sherman, S. (1993, June). Walking the talk at GE. *Training & Development*, 26–35; Tichy, N. M. (1993, December 13). Revolutionize your company. *Fortune*, 114–118; Larson, P. (1993, March 20). There are powerful lessons to be learned from GE's success. *Ottawa Citizen*, p. L1.

Assets of Strong Cultures

Organizations with strong cultures have several potential advantages over those lacking such a culture.

Coordination.   In effective organizations, the right hand (e.g., finance) knows what the left hand (e.g., production) is doing. The overarching values and assumptions of strong cultures can facilitate such communication. In turn, different parts of the organization can learn from each other and can coordinate their efforts. This is especially important in decentralized, team-oriented organizations.

Comparing the General Motors Saturn organization to established GM divisions provides a good contrast in cultural strength and coordination. Saturn, which has a strong culture oriented toward customer service, received praise from the automotive press for its communication with customers and dealers when inevitable early model quality problems cropped up. When quality problems arose with the new Chevy Camaro and Pontiac Firebird, GM received praise for not shipping defective cars, but it was criticized for not communicating well with customers and dealers.[37] Ironically, GM developed Saturn in part to serve as a cultural model for the established GM divisions that have long had rather fragmented cultures.

Conflict Resolution.   You might be tempted to think that a strong culture would produce strong conflicts within an organization. That is, you might expect the intensity associated with strongly held assumptions and values to lead to friction among organizational members. There might be some truth to this. Nevertheless, sharing core values can be a powerful mechanism that helps to ultimately resolve conflicts, a light in a storm as it were. For example, in a firm with a core value of fanatical customer service, it is still possible for managers to differ about how to handle a particular customer problem. However, the core value will often suggest an appropriate dispute resolution mechanism—"Let's have the person who is closest to the customer make the final decision."

Financial Success.   Does a strong culture pay off in dollars and cents terms? That is, do the assets we discussed above get translated into bottom-line financial success? The answer seems to be yes, as long as the liabilities discussed below can be avoided.

One study of insurance companies found that firms whose managers responded more consistently to a culture survey (thus indicating agreement about the firm's culture) had greater asset and premium growth than those with disagreement.[38] Another study had members of six international accounting firms complete a value survey, the results of which you see in Exhibit 9.6. Because all firms were in the same business, there is some similarity to their value profiles (e.g., attention to detail is valued over innovation). However, close inspection shows that the six firms actually differ a good bit in

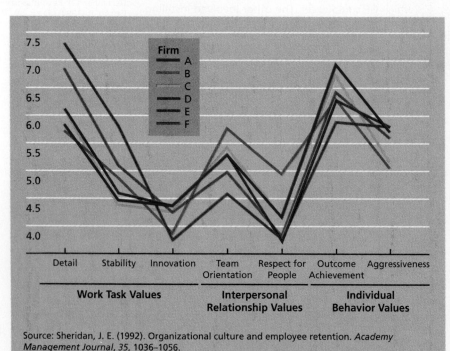

EXHIBIT 9.6
Scores on organizational culture values across six accounting firms.

Source: Sheridan, J. E. (1992). Organizational culture and employee retention. *Academy Management Journal, 35,* 1036–1056.

their value profiles. Firms E and F tended to emphasize the work task values of detail and stability and to deemphasize a team orientation and respect for people. Comparatively, firms A, B, and C tended to emphasize these interpersonal relationship values. The author determined that firms E and F had much higher employee turnover rates, a fact that was estimated to cost each between $6 and $9 million a year compared with firms A, B, and C.[39]

There is growing consensus that strong cultures contribute to financial success and other indicators of organizational effectiveness *when the culture supports the mission, strategy, and goals of the organization.*[40]

Liabilities of Strong Cultures

On the other side of the coin, strong cultures can be a liability under some circumstances.

Resistance to Change.   The mission, strategy, or specific goals of an organization can change in response to external pressures, and a strong culture that was appropriate for past success might not support the new order. That is, the strong consensus about common values and appropriate behavior that makes for a strong culture can prove to be very resistant to change. This means that a strong culture can damage a firm's ability to innovate.

An excellent example is the case of IBM. A strong culture dedicated to selling and providing excellent service for mainframe computers contributed to the firm's remarkable success. However, this strong culture also bred strong complacency that damaged the company's ability to compete effectively with smaller, more innovative firms. IBM's strong mainframe culture limited its competitiveness in desktop computing, software development, and systems compatibility.

Culture Clash.   Strong cultures can mix as badly as oil and water when a merger or acquisition pushes two of them together under the same corporate banner.[41] Both General Electric and Xerox, large organizations with strong cultures of their own, had less than perfect experiences when they acquired small high-technology Silicon Valley companies with unique cultures. The merger of BankAmerica and Security Pacific resulted in a particularly strong culture clash. In each of these cases, the typical scenario concerns a freewheeling smaller unit confronting a more bureaucratic larger unit (see the "In Focus: 'Mega-Merger' Can't Stand Culture Clash").

Pathology.   Some strong cultures can threaten organizational effectiveness simply because the cultures are in some sense pathological.[42] Such cultures may be based on beliefs, values, and assumptions that support infighting, secrecy, and paranoia, pursuits that hardly leave time for doing business. Here's an example of an unsuccessful semiconductor firm whose culture exhibited considerable paranoia.

> The two founders took all kinds of precautions to prevent their ideas from being stolen. They fragmented jobs and processes so that only a few key people in the company really understood the products. They rarely subcontracted work. And they paid employees very high salaries to give them an incentive to stay with the firm. These three precautions combined to make Paratech's costs among the highest in the industry.[43]

IN FOCUS   "Mega-Merger" Can't Stand Culture Clash

The planned merger between Bell Atlantic and Tele-Communications Inc., according to *The Wall Street Journal,* was a mega-merger. It would have been a defining move in the scramble for alliances among the various companies in the information industry. TCI, the giant, aggressive cable company would ally its skills with those of Bell Atlantic, one of the more forward-looking regional telephone companies. The goal? A truly interactive system in which the distinctions between telephone and cable were broken down. At-home shopping and video-on-demand are examples of this trend.

Right from the announcement of talks between the two companies, observers questioned the extent to which the culture mix would work. Although innovative by telephone company standards, Bell Atlantic was still a phone company. This meant that it was fairly bureaucratic, slow to react, and risk averse. Recently, top management had been attempting to move it from a bureaucratic culture to a more team-oriented culture. In contrast, the TCI culture was entrepreneurial and individual-

istic. Fast, aggressive acquisition of smaller cable companies and an obsession with keeping costs down were key strategic elements.

Bell Atlantic, like most phone companies, was oriented toward good customer service, paying a yearly dividend to please institutional investors, and keeping the regulators happy. The cable industry, on the other hand, has never been known for good customer service or good relationships with regulators. Bell worried about TCI's cash flow. TCI worried that Bell did not have the fortitude to pursue a high-growth strategy or to forego paying a dividend to fund this strategy.

The strain between cultures was too much. Within four months of announcing their plans to merge, the deal was off. Despite many complementary business strengths, basic value differences scuttled the mega-merger.

Source: Adapted from Kneale, D., Roberts, J. L., & Cauley, L. (1994, February 25). Why the mega-merger collapsed: Strong wills and big culture gap. *The Wall Street Journal,* pp. B1, B10.

Contributors to the Culture

How are cultures built and maintained? In this section we consider two key factors that contribute to the foundation and continuation of organizational cultures.

The Founder's Role. It is certainly possible for cultures to emerge over time without the guidance of a key individual. However, it is remarkable how many cultures, especially strong cultures, reflect the values of an organization's founder.[44] The imprint of Walt Disney on the Disney Company, Sam Walton on Wal-Mart, Ray Kroc on McDonald's, T. J. Watson on IBM, and Bill Gates on Microsoft is obvious. As we shall see shortly, such imprint is often kept alive through a series of stories about the founder passed on to successive generations of new employees. This provides continuing reinforcement for the firm's core values. In a similar vein, most experts agree that top management strongly shapes the organization's culture. The culture will usually begin to emulate what top management "pays attention to." Sometimes, the culture begun by the founder can cause conflict when top management wishes to see an organization change directions. At Apple Computer, Steven Jobs nurtured a culture based on new technology and new products—innovation was everything. When top management perceived this strategy to be damaging profits, it introduced a series of controls and changes that led to Jobs's resignation as chairman.[45]

The meticulous attention to detail that Roger Penske demands of his Indy car team is also reflected in his other businesses—Detroit Diesel, car dealerships, and Penske truck leasing.

Socialization.   The precise nature of the socialization process is a key to the culture that emerges in an organization, because socialization is the means by which individuals can learn the culture's beliefs, values, and assumptions. Weak or fragmented cultures often feature haphazard selection and a nearly random series of job assignments that fail to present the new hire with a coherent set of experiences. On the other hand, Richard Pascale of Stanford University notes that organizations with strong cultures go to great pains to expose employees to a careful step-by-step socialization process (Exhibit 9.7).[46]

- *Step 1—Selecting Employees.* New employees are carefully selected to obtain those who will be able to adapt to the existing culture, and realistic job previews are provided to allow candidates to deselect themselves. As an example, Pascale cites Procter & Gamble's series of individual interviews, group interviews, and tests for brand management positions.

- *Step 2—Debasement and Hazing.* Debasement and hazing provoke humility in new hires so that they are open to the norms of the organization.

- *Step 3—Training "in the Trenches."* Training begins "in the trenches" so that employees begin to master one of the core areas of the organization. For example, even experienced M.B.A.s will start on the bottom of the professional ladder to ensure that they understand how *this* organization works. At Lincoln Electric, an extremely successful producer of industrial products, new M.B.A.s literally spend eight weeks on the welding line so that they truly come to understand and appreciate Lincoln's unique shopfloor culture.

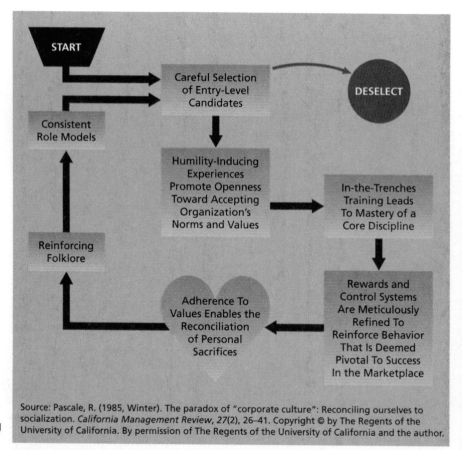

EXHIBIT 9.7
Socialization steps in strong cultures.

Source: Pascale, R. (1985, Winter). The paradox of "corporate culture": Reconciling ourselves to socialization. *California Management Review, 27*(2), 26–41. Copyright © by The Regents of the University of California. By permission of The Regents of the University of California and the author.

- *Step 4—Reward and Promotion.* The reward and promotion system is carefully used to reinforce those employees who perform well in areas that support the goals of the organization.

- *Step 5—Exposure to Core Culture.* Again and again, the culture's core beliefs, values, and assumptions are asserted to provide guidance for member behavior. This is done to emphasize that the personal sacrifices required by the socialization process have a true purpose.

- *Step 6—Organizational Folklore.* Members are exposed to folklore about the organization, stories that reinforce the nature of the culture. We examine this in more detail below.

- *Step 7—Role Models.* Identifying people as "fast-trackers" provides new members with role models whose actions and views are consistent with the culture. These role models serve as tangible examples for new members to imitate.

Pascale is careful to note that it is the *consistency* among these steps and their mutually reinforcing properties that make for a strong culture. Given that they are socializing theme park employees rather than rocket scientists, it is remarkable how many of these tactics Disney uses. Selection is rigorous, and grooming standards serve as mild debasement. Everyone begins at the bottom of the hierarchy. Pay is low, but promotion is tied to performance. Folklore stresses core values ("Walt's in the park."). Better performers serve as role models at Disney U. or in paired training.

Diagnosing a Culture

Earlier, we noted that culture represents a "way of life" for organizational members. Even when the culture is strong, this way of life might be difficult for uninitiated outsiders to read and understand. One way to grasp a culture is to examine the symbols, rituals, and stories that characterize the organization's way of life. For insiders, these symbols, rituals, and stories are mechanisms that teach and reinforce the culture.

Symbols.   At the innovative Chaparral Steel Company in Texas, employees have to walk through the human resources department to get to their lockers. Although this facilitates communication, it also serves as a powerful symbol of the importance that the company places on its human resources. For years, IBM's "respect for the individual" held strong symbolic value that was somewhat shaken with its first-ever layoffs. Such symbolism is a strong indicator of corporate culture.[47]

Some executives are particularly skilled at using symbols consciously to reinforce cultural values. CEO Carl Reichardt of Wells Fargo is known as a fanatic cost cutter. According to one story, Reichardt received managers requesting capital budget increases while sitting in a tatty chair. As managers made their cases, Reichardt picked at the chair's exposed stuffing, sending a strong symbolic message of fiscal austerity. This was in case they had missed the message conveyed by having to pay for their own coffee and their own office Christmas decorations![48]

Rituals.   Observers have noted how rites, rituals, and ceremonies can convey the essence of a culture.[49] For example, at Tandem, a California computer company, Friday afternoon "popcorn parties" are a regular ritual. (For years, these parties were called "beer busts." I'll leave it up to you to decide whether this change of names is symbolic of a major cultural shift!) The parties reinforce a "work hard, play hard" atmosphere and reaffirm the idea that weekly conflicts can be forgotten. The Disney picnics, beach parties, and employee nights are indicative of a peer-oriented, youth-oriented culture. At Mary Kay Cosmetics, elaborate "seminars" with the flavor of a Hollywood premiere combined with a revival meeting are used to make the sales force feel good about themselves and the company. Pink Cadillacs and other extravagant sales awards reinforce the cultural imperative that any Mary Kay woman can be successful. Rituals need not be so exotic to send a cultural message. In some companies, the annual performance review is an act of feedback and development. In others, it might be viewed as an exercise in punishment and debasement.

Stories.   As we noted above, the folklore of organizations—stories about past organizational events—is a common aspect of culture. These stories, told repeatedly to successive generations of new employees, are evidently meant to communicate "how things work," whether they are true, false, or a bit of both. Anyone who has spent much time in a particular organization is familiar

The torch-lighting ritual symbolizes the values of the Olympic Games.

with such stories, and they often appear to reflect the uniqueness of organizational cultures. However, research indicates that a few common themes underlie many organizational stories.

- Is the big boss human?
- Can the little person rise to the top?
- Will I get fired?
- Will the organization help me when I have to move?
- How will the boss react to mistakes?
- How will the organization deal with obstacles?[50]

Issues of equality, security, and control underlie the stories that pursue these themes. Also, such stories often have a "good" version, in which things turn out well, and a "bad" version, in which things go sour. For example, there is a story that Ray Kroc, McDonald's founder, canceled a franchise after finding a single fly in the restaurant.[51] This is an example of a sour ending to a "how will the boss react to mistakes?" story. Whether the story is true or not, its retelling is indicative of one of the core values of the McDonald's culture—a fanatical dedication to clean premises.

AT&T—A Successful Cultural Transition

To conclude our discussion of culture, let's examine an organization that has undergone a radical cultural transition in recent years.[52] On January 1, 1984, a U.S. Justice Department Consent Decree required AT&T to divest itself of its local telephone company operations. This was one of a long series of deregulation changes that forced the former monopoly to confront a new competitive marketplace. The physical consequences of the consent decree were impressive in themselves, as it reduced the workforce considerably and resulted in the sale of millions of dollars in assets. Equally important, however, was the change required in AT&T's culture.

Prior to the years leading up to the divestiture, AT&T had a strong corporate culture based on providing universal telephone service at a reasonable price. The core values were oriented toward excellent service, and stories are told with pride about the dedication of Bell System staff to keeping the lines open. To support this mission, there was a cultural emphasis on loyalty, lifetime careers, and promotion from within. Since it was a monopoly, product development could proceed slowly, and aggressive sales tactics were not necessary.

With deregulation, AT&T had to change its mission to include the development and sale of innovative communications products and services. A new culture that was supportive of this mission had to be grounded on entrepreneurship, fast decision making, and creative risk taking. To accomplish this, the company gave increased power to the marketing function and took increased pains to tie rewards to individual performance. It placed sales personnel on commission and gave service personnel more autonomy in doing their jobs. Information campaigns in which top management regularly asserted the need for a new culture at AT&T provided the support for this change.

Although the AT&T culture is still in transition, observers feel that the change has so far been successful. Resistance was a serious problem for the first several years, and turnover among newly hired MBAs was high. It took a new CEO, Robert Allen, to really galvanize the need for a new way of doing things. Allen brought in a number of executives from outside the firm and gave them the autonomy to run their own units. He has spent a tremendous amount of time communicating AT&T's core values, which include innovation, integrity, teamwork, and customer support.

The Manager's Notebook   Cultural Change at General Electric

The cultural changes that Jack Welch put into place at General Electric are some of the most sweeping in corporate America.

1. GE instituted Work-Out, a program requiring *all* company employees to participate. Groups of employees met at an off-site conference center in workshops run by outside consultants. In part of the workshop, employees met in small groups without their bosses present to define work problems and develop proposals for their solutions. Later, bosses had to make on-the-spot decisions about each proposal in front of the groups. The goal here was to build employee responsibility for continuous improvement, show company responsiveness, and stress the need for managerial decisiveness.

2. To combat the "not invented here syndrome" GE started a Best Practices program in which a team visited companies known for excellent productivity in their respective industries. Teams prepared reports about these successes, which were the basis for a course at GE's management development center. In turn, the Work-Out teams disseminated the Best Practices throughout the company.

EXECUTIVE SUMMARY

◆ There are two basic forms of social dependence. Information dependence means that we rely upon others for information about how we should think, feel, and act. Effect dependence means that we rely on rewards and punishments provided by others. Both contribute to conformity to norms.

◆ There are several motives for conformity to social norms. One is compliance, in which conformity occurs mainly to achieve rewards and avoid punishment. It is mostly indicative of effect dependence. Another motive for conformity is identification with other group members. Here, the person sees himself or herself as similar to them and relies upon them for information. Finally, conformity may be motivated by the internalization of norms, and the person is no longer conforming simply because of social dependence.

◆ Conformity to norms is most likely when others will be aware of deviance, when the opposition is large and unanimous, and when the issue at hand is ambiguous. High-status group members have generally achieved their status by conformity to group norms. However, they may deviate on a particular issue by exercising idiosyncrasy credits that they have built up by previous conformity. Low-status members who are new to the group are especially likely to exhibit conformity, while those rejected by the group have nothing to gain by conformity.

◆ Organizational members learn norm and role requirements through stages of socialization. Some organizations rely on other organizations to do a certain amount of anticipatory socialization, while others handle the process themselves. Some rely on collective socialization, in which new members learn the ropes as a group, while others socialize new members on an individual basis. Debasement and hazing are a way to test the stuff of new members. Also, realistic job previews can help cope with initial unrealistic expectations.

◆ Organizational commitment is an attitude that reflects the strength of the linkage between an employee and an organization. Affective commitment is based on a person's identification with an organization. Continuance commitment is based on the costs of leaving an organization. Normative commitment is based on ideology or feelings of obligation.

◆ Organizational culture consists of the shared beliefs, values, and assumptions that exist in an orga-

nization. Subcultures can develop that reflect departmental or occupational differences. In strong cultures, beliefs, values, and assumptions are intense, pervasive, and supported by consensus.

◆ Potential assets of a strong culture include good coordination, appropriate conflict resolution, and financial success.

◆ Potential liabilities of a strong culture include inherent pathology, resistance to change, and culture clash when mergers or acquisitions occur.

◆ An organization's founder and its socialization practices can strongly shape a culture. Symbols, rituals, and stories are often useful in diagnosing a culture.

KEY CONCEPTS

Information dependence
Effect dependence
Compliance
Identification
Internalization
Idiosyncrasy credits
Socialization
Debasement

Realistic job previews
Organizational commitment
Affective commitment
Continuance commitment
Normative commitment
Organizational culture
Subcultures
Strong culture

DISCUSSION QUESTIONS

1. Compare and contrast information dependence with effect dependence. Under which conditions should people be especially information dependent? Under which conditions should people be especially effect dependent?

2. Describe an instance of social conformity that you have observed in an organizational setting. Did compliance, identification, or internalization motivate this incident? Were the results beneficial for the organization? Were they beneficial to the individual involved?

3. Imagine that a large organization is charged with making illegal financial contributions to a political campaign. What are the situational factors that might prompt executives to conform to such organizational norms at the expense of societal norms that stand against such behavior?

4. Consider how you were socialized into the college or university where you are taking your organizational behavior course. Did you have some unrealistic expectations? Where did your expectations come from? What outside experiences pre-

pared you for college or university? Are you experiencing collective or individual socialization? What is the extent of socialization required by most colleges and universities?

5. Contrast the army's socialization process with that of the typical business firm. Why do they differ?

6. What are the pros and cons of providing realistic job previews for a job that is objectively pretty bad?

7. Imagine that you are starting a new business in the retail trade. You are strongly oriented toward providing excellent customer service. What could you do to nurture a strong organizational culture that would support such a mission?

8. Discuss the advantages and disadvantages of developing a strong organizational culture.

9. Discuss some socialization practices that build a strong organizational culture.

10. Give an example of someone with high normative commitment but low affective and continuance commitment.

EXPERIENTIAL EXERCISE
A DEBATE: AT&T'S PROJECT MIRACLES

More and more North American organizations are exposing their managers to intense outdoor experiences as a management development technique. The purpose of this exercise is for you to critically evaluate the pros and cons of one such program, AT&T's Project Miracles. Speaking generally, intense outdoor programs have been touted as a way to increase morale, motivation, trust, teamwork, and communication. They have also been described as methods to mold organizational culture. Let's debate the issue!

OPTION 1: INFORMAL DEBATE

The instructor will divide the class into small learning groups that will informally debate the pros and cons of Project Miracles. Each group should be prepared to present its conclusions to the class.

OPTION 2: FORMAL DEBATE

The instructor will assign a pro-Miracles position to one small learning group and an anti-Miracles position to another. While the groups meet to plan their presentations, other learning groups will debate informally as above. Each of the formal groups should plan for a seven-minute opening statement, a three-minute rebuttal, and a three-minute closing. The class will vote on the winner.

In debating, use your intuition and experience, but also try to use the theories and concepts that we have been studying. Here are some questions to guide your arguments.

1. Is it plausible that intense outdoor experiences increase job satisfaction? (Chapter 5)
2. Exactly how would outdoor experiences stimulate motivation? (Chapter 6)
3. Can outdoor experiences stimulate group effectiveness and teamwork? (Chapter 8)
4. Do outdoor experiences contribute to socialization and shape the culture? (Chapter 9)
5. Are people truly free to decline participation in outdoor exercises? Are such exercises ethical? (Chapter 9)

PROJECT MIRACLES

"I was feeling victimized," said Jeff McCollum of the period in his career after American Telephone and Telegraph abruptly ended his stint as an acting vice president. "I was very bitter."

McCollum's experience is not unusual among long-time AT&T employees. In 1984, when the federal government forced the company to divest its local telephone companies,

an enormous wave of restructuring and layoffs ensued. The consumer products division, where McCollum is currently the education director, went from 17,000 employees to 8,500 in two years, he said.

To deal with the sagging morale of employees who survived the divestiture, the company spent more than a year researching and developing a motivational training program, known as Project Miracles, that uses intense outdoor experiences. McCollum, one of the earliest participants, said that the program helped him to rethink his career goals and priorities, and get beyond his feeling that "being a vice president was the be-all and end-all of why I was at work." He said he is now quite happy in his current position. Small groups of employees participate in a week-long retreat at an outdoor camp, led by staff from one of several outside agencies that carry out the program for AT&T.

The actual course of the retreat varies somewhat from one agency to another. SportsMind, the Seattle-based firm that helped AT&T develop its program, tailors the length and activities of its programs to fit different clients. Typically, employees do 15 hours each day of aerobic exercise, teamwork experiences, and discussions of the role of individual integrity, honesty and choice in the work place.

AT&T and SportsMind officials, as well as many past participants, believe that the highlight of the program is the afternoon of physically and psychologically intense outdoor experiences.

The activities often are challenges to the participants' fear of heights. "Trust falls," where a participant stands on a five- to six-foot high platform and falls backward into the arms of fellow employees, are a frequent feature. Ropes courses, where participants teeter across ropes strung in trees 20 or even 40 feet off the ground, are also common. For safety, parachute harnesses are used in the ropes courses and other dangerous activities to ensure participants' safety.

According to Bentz, the outdoor work challenges participants to "do more than they thought they could, and after that they're exhilarated." People say to themselves, "maybe there are lots of areas where I'm saying 'I can't' when I can," he said.

Bentz attributes the popularity of SportsMind and similar programs to changes in the workplace. "Companies are looking for ways to increase the level of trust, honesty and openness in communication, and improve the ability of people to work together and solve problems under pressure," he said.

But both AT&T and SportsMind officials acknowledge the potential for employees to be pressured to undergo physical and psychological stress against their will.

Bentz said SportsMind addresses the coercion issue by making discussions of choice a major part of the programs. "At every point, we give people the opportunity to choose" to sit out of activities, he said. "If somebody's got a bad back or a bad knee, we ask them to choose to sit out." He acknowledged, however, that in teamwork building situations such as a group scramble over a high wall, "there's a lot of pressure" to participate. "Any kind of challenge involves some stress," he added.

AT&T employees often return from Project Miracles feeling refreshed and "dewy eyed," said Stinson of AT&T. But, he added, "if after 30 or 60 days, people are back in their normal frame of mind and normal way of doing business, then you've wasted your time."

McCollum, the former AT&T vice president, recalled the first time that he participated in Project Miracles.

"I was scared" of the tree-top and mountainside coursework, he said. But he found that acknowledging and verbalizing his fear made it "much more manageable" than pretending he wasn't afraid. "A very difficult thing for me across my adult life was to ask for support," he added. Project Miracles' emphasis on teamwork helped him address that issue personally, and has also spurred attitude change across his division, he said. "One of the organizational changes that we see is that we regard a request for support as a sign of strength," he said.

AT&T has put several thousand employees through Project Miracles since 1987. The cost per employee varies, depending on which agency carries out the program; SportsMind charges corporations about $1,500 for each participant.

When the first managers returned from a pilot run of the program, they offered overwhelming support for it on employee attitude surveys.

"Eighty percent related the personal value of the program to be extraordinary or very high," McCollum said. "And more than 90 percent recommended that we offer it to other managers as well as to non-management personnel in the organization."

In one department, research showed that measurable output as well as attitudes improved after employees participated in Project Miracles. Sales rates increased, levels of cooperation increased and backlogs fell, McCollum said.

That is the kind of news that corporate management likes to hear. AT&T will continue to evaluate the attitudes and performance of employees to determine whether the company should forge ahead or scale back its efforts, according to Stinson.

But virtually no data have been collected at AT&T or through independent research that would indicate whether specifically challenging employees physically and psychologically in outdoor coursework really pays off back at the office. How the outdoor programs measure up against more conventional motivational training, how long the effects last, and what factors help or hinder the retention of training are all questions thus far unanswered.

Source: Story abridged from Moses, S. (1990, January). Morale programs face effectiveness questions. *APA Monitor*, p. 20. Copyright 1990 by The American Psychological Association. Reprinted by permission.

CASE STUDY
GUY ROBERTS

Guy Roberts joined Millard Construction Ltd, on 7th January, 1985. He had worked for eight years as a quantity surveyor with Fry Bros (Builders) Ltd, but in November, 1984, he had lost his job when Fry Bros went bankrupt. The company had never really recovered from the recession of the early 1980s.

Guy was twenty-eight years old and qualified to AIOB level. He had always been considered good at his job, an efficient and accurate assessor of building materials, and his duties at Fry Bros had incorporated control of the Purchasing Department. He had received a basic salary, and an annual bonus.

Married, with a two-month old son, Guy was extremely worried when faced with unemployment. His young wife was unable to work, because of the baby, and the family had moved into a new, detached house some six months prior to his layoff, incurring a high mortgage.

He was therefore greatly relieved when his wife's brother, Neville, who was the senior quantity surveyor at Millard Construction Ltd, informed him of a vacancy in the company and had recommended him for the job. Millard Construction was a much larger building company than Fry Bros and Guy was offered a higher basic salary. However, he would no longer receive an annual bonus, but instead he was entitled to a gasoline allowance. This he welcomed, since getting to work would now entail a forty-mile round trip.

Before getting down to the task of preparing his first Bill of Quantities, he made a brief study of some past assessments and the jobs to which they related. He was puzzled. In each case, he estimated that an excess of sand and cement had been ordered. Making a mental note to query this with Neville, he proceeded to make his first assessment.

Some time later, his Bill of Quantities was returned by Neville, who told him that he had underestimated the quantities of sand and cement. Guy challenged this, and raised the matter of the past assessments. He was told that it was the usual practice to add on a percentage, to be "on the safe side" and to allow for any accidental loss or damage to materials in transit and on site. While disagreeing with this practice, Guy realized that he was not in any position to argue. He therefore made the necessary amendments, and signed the Bill of Quantities.

The following week, Guy glanced out of his office window, and observed the materials being delivered. Later that day, he was surprised to see the yard foreman loading up a small truck with sand and cement, taken from this delivery, and driving away. The next morning, Guy observed the Millard Construction trucks being loaded with the rest of the material, for delivery to the building site.

Guy could not settle to his work. He kept remembering the incident of the previous day, and at lunch time, unable to contain his inquisitiveness any longer, he found occasion to see the foreman. He asked him to explain his actions, pointing out that the truck used by the foreman was not one of Millard's fleet. The foreman refused to give him any answer, stating quite bluntly that it was none of Guy's business. As he walked angrily away down the yard, he called back over his shoulder, "Take it up with your boss."

On his return from lunch, Guy went immediately to see Neville and raised the issue with him. To his complete amazement, he was told that the foreman's brother owned a do-it-yourself shop nearby, and that for the past two years "an arrangement" had existed between them. Neville had ensured that sand and cement on all Bills of Quantities was overestimated by a few percent, and that this "excess" material was then delivered to the foreman's brother. Payment was always in cash, and was split between the foreman, the senior quantity surveyor and his two assistant surveyors. One of these assistants had recently left Millard's employment, and Guy had taken his place.

Guy listened in stunned silence, as his brother-in-law calmly proposed "cutting him in on the deal." He pointed out to Guy that he knew of his financial circumstances, and that he could well do with some extra money. Moreover, if he agreed to go along with them, and say nothing to anyone else at Millard about their little arrangement, his gasoline claims would be sanctioned "without question." It was apparently common practice for the quantity surveyors to get their local garage to give them blank receipt forms, on the pretext that they had lost some of their original receipts. They would then fill in false receipts and submit them, together with genuine ones, receiving monthly reimbursement. As the senior quantity surveyor sanctioned all claims, no questions were ever asked.

When Guy recovered from the shock of this revelation, his immediate reaction was one of anger. He absolutely refused to have any part of these dishonest practices. Neville leaned back in his chair, smiled slowly, and suggested that he had better think twice before reporting the matter to senior management. After all, his name was already on a falsified Bill of Quantities. In the event of an enquiry, it would not be difficult to contend that Guy had taken a part in the fraudulent practices, and his signature on the Bill would add weight to this statement. Guy realized that he could take the matter no further. He coldly informed Neville that while he had no intention of reporting the matter to senior management, he would, in future, insist on preparing Bills of Quantities for the correct amount of materials.

Almost immediately, Guy noticed the change of atmosphere at work. Neither his brother-in-law nor fellow quantity surveyors would speak to him unless they had to, and he received the same treatment from the yard foreman. This was noticed by others, who started to behave towards him in the same way. The atmosphere became very uncomfortable and Guy's pleasure in his new job quickly disappeared.

At the end of the month, he found that he had not received the correct reimbursement for his gasoline claim. When he took this up with Neville, he was told that he had sanctioned all the receipts that Guy had given to him, and that if this did not tally with Guy's estimated figure, then some of the receipts must have been "lost." Guy was quite certain that he had given him all the receipts, and that if any loss had occurred, then it had occurred in Neville's office.

Early the next week, Guy was summoned to the yard, where he was told that his car had suffered an accident. Apparently, the foreman had been driving the dump truck, and had inadvertently reversed it into Guy's car. As a result, Guy was without a car for a week while the damage was repaired, and had to rely on public transport to get him to work. He was also unable to make any visits for his company.

In the following week, Guy was summoned to the manager's office. He was told that the men, working on a job for which he had prepared the Bill of Quantities, had run out of sand and cement. He was accused of underestimating and to prove his point, the manager produced past estimates for similar jobs, all of which exceeded Guy's estimates by up to 10 per cent. Guy was unable to comment.

Later the same month, Guy was once again summoned to the manager's office. This time, some material he had ordered had failed to arrive on time for an urgent job. The manager once more accused him of failing to do his job properly, saying, "You should be aware of the contingency of late delivery. If you occasionally over-assess on a job, then we will always have a reserve stock to draw on in times of emergency."

That evening, Guy found his wife in tears. She told him that she had been to visit her sister-in-law, and during the course of their conversation, she had learned that Millard was far from happy with Guy's performance. She reminded him that he was still working through his three-month trial period, and begged him to take care. He decided to tell his wife the truth. When he had told her the whole story, she pleaded with him that, for the sake of family unity, he must say nothing to senior management about Neville's dishonesty. However, she strongly urged him to have another word with him, to see if they could come to a better working arrangement.

The next morning, he approached Neville, saying that he had changed his mind. He would henceforth add 10 per cent to his Bills of Quantities for sand and cement, and while he still wanted no part in the fraud, he would never report the matter. However, he was desperately short of money, and for that reason alone, he was willing to submit false gasoline claims. Neville assured him that from that time onward, he would do his best to ensure that Guy's claims were secured against "loss."

Guy completed his three-month trial period, without further mishap. The manager informed him that he had been taken on to the permanent staff, and said how pleased they were with his progress. There had been no further incidence of materials running out on jobs for which he had estimated the Bills of Quantities. The atmosphere at work was no longer estranged, and Guy was grateful for the extra money he made on gasoline claims.

Source: Case prepared by Ron Ludlow. From Tyson, S., & Kakabadse, A. P. (Eds.) (1987). *Cases in human resources management*. London: Heinemann.

1. How information dependent was Guy Roberts in his new job at Millard Construction? How effect dependent was he?

2. What are some of the norms that form the culture at Millard Construction? How strong is the culture, and what is your evidence for your answer?

3. What factors contribute to Guy's eventual conformity to several of the Millard norms? Is this conformity due to compliance, identification, or internalization?

4. Discuss Guy's level of commitment to Millard Construction. Be very explicit in terms of affective, continuance, and normative commitment.

5. Would a realistic job preview have helped resolve the problems Guy encountered?

6. Did Guy behave ethically in this case?

7. Suppose that you, as an entrepreneur, bought out the owner of Millard Construction and then found out about the unusual practices described in the case. What would you do as head of the company?

AFTER READING CHAPTER 10 YOU SHOULD BE ABLE TO:

1 DEFINE AND DISCUSS THE ROLE OF BOTH FORMAL AND EMERGENT LEADERSHIP.

2 EXPLAIN AND CRITICALLY EVALUATE THE TRAIT APPROACH TO LEADERSHIP.

3 EXPLAIN THE CONCEPTS OF CONSIDERATION AND INITIATING STRUCTURE AND THEIR CONSEQUENCES.

4 EVALUATE THE USE OF LEADER REWARD VERSUS LEADER PUNISHMENT BEHAVIORS.

5 DESCRIBE AND EVALUATE FIEDLER'S CONTINGENCY THEORY.

6 DESCRIBE AND EVALUATE HOUSE'S PATH-GOAL THEORY.

7 EXPLAIN HOW AND WHEN TO USE PARTICIPATIVE LEADERSHIP.

8 DISCUSS THE MERITS OF TRANSFORMATIONAL LEADERSHIP AND CHARISMA.

9 EXPLAIN THE CONCEPTS OF LEADERSHIP NEUTRALIZERS AND SUBSTITUTES.

SOUTHWEST AIRLINES EMPLOYEES CREDIT MUCH OF THE COMPANY'S SUCCESS TO THE LEADERSHIP OF CEO HERB KELLEHER, WHO SUPPORTS A CORPORATE CULTURE BASED ON CUSTOMER SERVICE, INNOVATION, AND "FAMILY ORIENTATION" AMONG EMPLOYEES.

CHAPTER 10

LEADERSHIP

SOUTHWEST
AIRLINES'
HERB
KELLEHER

Southwest Airlines began operations in Dallas in 1971. Within two years, it was turning a profit, and it has done so every year since in a turbulent industry where even its strongest competitors have had many unprofitable years. Part of Southwest's success formula has been its ability to exploit profitable market niches. Although it flies to Los Angeles, Chicago, and Detroit, the airline has specialized in short-hop, low-fare flights in the southwest states. In exchange for the low fares, loyal passengers have been willing to forego onboard food, assigned seating, and baggage forwarding. In turn, this lack of complication allows Southwest to turn flights around at the gate quickly and fly more segments per day. This efficient use of its Boeing 737 aircraft makes Southwest the most efficient, lowest-cost carrier in the industry.

Although intelligent operations are part of Southwest's key to success, they would not work without loyalty, commitment, and a corporate culture that stresses customer service, innovation, and "family orientation" among employees. Industry observers are in strong agreement that these competitive advantages are due in large part to the leadership of Southwest founder and CEO Herb Kelleher. Kelleher, a bawdy, fun-loving man with a ready smile, knows many of the company's 16,000 employees personally. Southwest does not scrimp on the salaries and benefits of its highly productive employees. Salaries are roughly comparable to other carriers, there is a lucrative profit-sharing program, and training is state-of-the-art. The company, according to the authors of *The 100 Best Companies to Work for in America,* is one of the 10 best employers.

Under Kelleher's vision, Southwest hires people for their positive attitudes and cooperative values. Then, it empowers them to do what they have to do to continue to top the Department of Transportation's list for on-time flights and customer satisfaction. For example, check-in personnel can permit customers with restricted-date tickets to fly immediately in the case of family emergencies. Innovative personnel developed a series of amusing games to entertain customers during delays for bad weather. The fun-loving Kelleher serves as a strong role model for such actions. At the same time, he clarifies what's important in more serious matters by personally approving all expenses over $1,000 and personally reviewing all pilot performance evaluations, emphasizing the joint importance of low costs and flight safety. The teamwork at Southwest is illustrated by pilots' willingness to load baggage, shuttle wheelchairs, and tidy up planes on layovers.

Some have likened the Southwest employee loyalty to a cult, a comparison that doesn't bother Kelleher. In a video prepared to rally his troops against a competitive threat from United Airlines to its California shuttle routes, Kelleher combined the style of an evangelist with that of General George Patton.

Recently, Southwest employees paid $60,000 for a humorous full-page ad in *USA Today* to honor Kelleher on Boss's Day. Among other things, they thanked him for singing at their holiday party, but for singing only once a year![1]

Herb Kelleher is a case study in successful leadership. But exactly what is leadership, and what makes a leader successful? Would Kelleher be successful in some other leadership situation? These are the kinds of issues that this chapter tackles.

First, we will define leadership and find out if we can identify special leadership traits. After this, we will explore how leaders emerge in groups. Next, we will examine the consequences of various leadership behaviors and examine theories contending that effective leadership depends upon the nature of the work situation. Following this are discussions of participation, transformational leadership, and charisma. We will conclude by critically evaluating the importance of leadership in organizations.

WHAT IS LEADERSHIP?

A recent issue of *Fortune* magazine illustrates the perceived importance of leadership in business and public affairs. The cover story profiles America's toughest bosses and debates the merits of their tyrannical leadership styles. Another story, about total quality management, stresses the absolute necessity for CEOs to be visibly involved if such programs are to be successful. A third story stresses the role of White House and Congressional leadership in a battle over health care legislation. An accompanying piece polls *Fortune* 500 CEOs to find out how these leaders feel about a health care proposal.

    Leadership occurs when particular individuals exert influence upon the goal achievement of others in an organizational context. Thus, *Fortune* debates the merits of "tough" influence and highlights the necessity of CEO influence in steering TQM efforts. Effective leadership exerts influence in a way that achieves organizational goals by enhancing the productivity, innovation, satisfaction, and commitment of the workforce.

    In theory, *any* organizational member can exert influence on other members, thus engaging in leadership. In practice, though, some members are in a better position to be leaders than others. Individuals with titles such as manager, executive, supervisor, and department head occupy formal or assigned leadership roles. As part of these roles they are *expected* to influence others, and they are given specific authority to direct subordinates. Of course, the presence of a formal leadership role is no guarantee that there is leadership. Some managers and supervisors fail to exert any influence on others. These people will usually be judged ineffective leaders. Thus, leadership involves going beyond formal role requirements to influence others.

    Individuals might also emerge to occupy informal leadership roles. Since informal leaders do not have formal authority, they must rely on being well liked or being perceived as highly skilled in order to exert influence. In this chapter we will concentrate on formal leadership, although we will consider informal leadership as well.

Leadership. The influence that particular individuals exert upon the goal achievement of others in an organizational context.

THE (SOMEWHAT ELUSIVE) SEARCH FOR LEADERSHIP TRAITS

Throughout history, social observers have been fascinated by obvious examples of successful interpersonal influence, whether the consequences of this influence were good, bad, or mixed. Individuals such as Henry Ford, Martin Luther King, Jr., Barbara Jordan, Ralph Nader, and Joan of Arc have been

Tootsie Roll president Ellen Gordon and consumer advocate Ralph Nader are examples of effective leaders.

analyzed and reanalyzed to discover what made them leaders and what set them apart from less successful leaders. The implicit assumption here is that those who become leaders and do a good job of it possess a special set of traits that distinguish them from the masses of followers. While philosophers and the popular media have advocated such a position for centuries, trait theories of leadership did not receive serious scientific attention until the 1900s.

Research on Leadership Traits

During World War I the U.S. military recognized that it had a leadership problem. Never before had the country mounted such a massive war effort, and able officers were in short supply. Thus, the search for leadership traits that might be useful in identifying potential officers began. Following the war, and continuing through World War II, this interest expanded to include searching for leadership traits in populations as diverse as school children and business executives. Some studies tried to differentiate traits of leaders and followers, while others were a search for traits that predicted leader effectiveness or distinguished lower-level leaders from higher-level leaders.[2]

Traits. Individual characteristics such as physical attributes, intellectual ability, and personality.

Just what is a trait, anyway? **Traits** are personal characteristics of the individual, including physical characteristics, intellectual ability, and personality. Research has shown that many, many traits are not associated with whether people become leaders or how effective they are. However, research also shows some traits are associated with leadership. There is a list of these traits in Exhibit 10.1.[3] As you might expect, leaders (or more successful leaders) tend to be higher than average on these dimensions, although the connections are not very strong. Notice that the list portrays a high energy person who really wants to have an impact on others but at the same time is smart and stable enough not to abuse his or her power. Interestingly, this is a pretty accurate summary description of Southwest Airlines' Herb Kelleher.

Many prominent firms use personality tests and assessment centers to measure leadership traits when making hiring and promotion decisions. However, there are some aspects to the trait approach that limit its ultimate usefulness.

Limitations of the Trait Approach

Even though some traits appear to be related to leadership, there are several reasons why the trait approach isn't the best means of understanding and improving leadership.

In many cases, it is difficult to determine whether traits make the leader or the opportunity for leadership produces the traits. For example, do dominant individuals tend to become leaders, or do employees become more dominant *after* they successfully occupy leadership roles? This distinction is important. If the former is true, we might wish to seek out dominant people and appoint them to leadership roles. If the latter is true, this strategy will not work.

Even if we know that dominance, intelligence, or tallness is associated with effective leadership, we have few clues about what dominant or intelligent or tall people *do* to influence others successfully. As a result, we have little information about how to train and develop leaders and no way to diagnose failures of leadership.

Intelligence

Energy

Self-confidence

Dominance

Motivation to lead

Emotional stability

Honesty and integrity

Need for achievement

EXHIBIT 10.1
Traits associated with leadership effectiveness.

The most crucial problem of the trait approach to leadership is its failure to take into account the *situation* in which leadership occurs. Intuitively, it seems reasonable that top executives and first-level supervisors might require different traits to be successful. Similarly, physical prowess might be useful in directing a logging crew but irrelevant to managing a team of scientists.

LESSONS FROM EMERGENT LEADERSHIP

The trait approach is mainly concerned with what leaders *bring* to a group setting. The limitations of this approach gradually promoted an interest in what leaders *do* in group settings. Of particular interest were the behaviors of certain group members that caused them to *become* leaders. As we shall see, this study of emergent leadership gives us some good clues about what formally assigned or appointed leaders must do to be effective.

Imagine that a grass-roots organization has assembled to support the election of a local politician to the state legislature. In response to a newspaper ad, 30 individuals show up, all of whom admire Jonathan Greed, the aspiring candidate. The self-appointed chairperson begins the meeting and asks for volunteers for various subcommittees. The publicity subcommittee sounds interesting, so you volunteer and find yourself with six other volunteers, none of whom knows each other. Your assigned goal is to develop an effective public relations campaign for Greed. From experience, you are aware that someone will emerge to become the leader of this group. Who will it be?

Without even seeing your group interact, we can make a pretty good guess as to who will become the leader. Quite simply, it will be the person who *talks* the most, as long as he or she is perceived as having relevant expertise.[4] Remember, leadership is a form of influence, and one important way to influence the group is speaking a lot. What would the "big talker" talk about? Probably about planning strategy, getting organized, dividing labor, and so on—things to get the task at hand accomplished. We often call such a leader a **task leader** because he or she is most concerned with accomplishing the task at hand.

Suppose I also ask the group members who they *liked* the most in the group. Usually, there will be a fair amount of agreement, and the nominated person might be called the **social-emotional leader**. Social-emotional influence is more subtle than task influence, and it involves reducing tension, patching up disagreements, settling arguments, and maintaining morale.

In many cases, the task and social-emotional leadership roles are performed by the same group member.[5] In some instances, though, two separate leaders emerge to fill these roles. When this happens, these two leaders usually get along well with each other and respect each other's complementary skills.[6]

The emergence of two leadership roles has been noted again and again in a wide variety of groups. This suggests that task and social-emotional leadership are two important functions that must occur in groups. On one hand, the group must be structured and organized to accomplish its tasks. On the other hand, the group must stick together and function well as a social unit, or the best structure and organization will be useless. Thus, in general, leaders must be concerned with both the social-emotional and task functions. Furthermore, organizations almost never appoint *two* formal leaders to a work group. Thus,

Task leader. A leader who is concerned with accomplishing a task by organizing others, planning strategy, and dividing labor.

Social-emotional leader. A leader who is concerned with reducing tension, patching up disagreements, settling arguments, and maintaining morale.

the formal appointed leader must often be concerned with juggling the demands of two distinct roles.

There is an important qualifier to the preceding paragraph. It should be obvious that task and social-emotional functions are both especially important in the case of newly developing groups. However, for mature, ongoing groups, one leadership role might be more important than the other. For example, if group members have learned to get along well with each other, the social-emotional role might decrease in importance. Also, the two leadership roles may have different significance in different situations. Suppose a team of geologists is doing a routine series of mineral prospecting studies in a humid, bug-infested jungle. In this case, its leader might be most concerned with monitoring morale and reducing tensions provoked by the uncomfortable conditions. If the team becomes lost, task leadership should become more important—a logical plan for finding the way must be developed.

THE BEHAVIOR OF ASSIGNED LEADERS

We turn now to the behavior of assigned or appointed leaders, as opposed to emergent leaders. What are the crucial behaviors such leaders engage in, and how do these behaviors influence subordinate performance and satisfaction? In other words, is there a particular *leadership style* that is more effective than other possible styles?

Consideration and Initiating Structure

The most involved, systematic study of leadership to date was begun at Ohio State University. The Ohio State researchers began by having subordinates describe their superiors along a number of behavioral dimensions. Statistical analyses of these descriptions revealed that they boiled down to two basic kinds of behavior—consideration and initiating structure.

Consideration is the extent to which a leader is approachable and shows personal concern for subordinates. The considerate leader is seen as friendly, egalitarian, and protective of group welfare. Obviously, consideration is related to the social-emotional function discovered in studies of emergent leadership.

Initiating structure is the degree to which a leader concentrates on group goal attainment. The structuring leader stresses standard procedures, schedules the work to be done, and assigns subordinates to particular tasks. Clearly, initiating structure is related to the task function revealed in studies of emergent leadership.

Theoretically, consideration and initiating structure are not incompatible. Presumably, a leader could be high, low, or average on one or both dimensions. Given our earlier discussion of emergent leadership functions, you might assume that a leader who is high on both dimensions would be the most effective. In the next section we shall consider this possibility.

The Consequences of Consideration and Structure

The association between leader consideration, leader initiating structure, and subordinate responses has been the subject of hundreds of research studies. At first glance, the results of these studies seem confusing and often contradic-

Consideration. The extent to which a leader is approachable and shows personal concern for subordinates.

Initiating structure. The degree to which a leader concentrates on group goal attainment.

tory.[7] Sometimes consideration seems to promote satisfaction or high performance, and sometimes it does not. Sometimes structure prompts satisfaction or performance, and sometimes it does not. However, when we consider the particular *situation* in which the leader finds himself or herself, a clearer picture emerges.

- When subordinates are under a high degree of pressure due to deadlines, unclear tasks, or external threat, initiating structure increases satisfaction and performance. (Soldiers stranded behind enemy lines should perform better under directive leadership.)

- When the task itself is intrinsically satisfying, the need for high consideration and high structure is generally reduced. (The teacher who really enjoys teaching should be able to function with less social-emotional support and less direction from the principal.)

- When the goals and methods of performing the job are very clear and certain, consideration should promote subordinate satisfaction, while structure should promote dissatisfaction. (The job of refuse collection is clear in goals and methods. Here, subordinates should appreciate social support but view excessive structure as redundant and unnecessary.)

- When subordinates lack knowledge as to how to perform a job, or the job itself has vague goals or methods, consideration becomes less important, while initiating structure takes on additional importance. (The new astronaut recruit should appreciate direction in learning a complex, unfamiliar job.)[8]

As you can see, the effects of consideration and initiating structure depend upon characteristics of the task, the subordinate, and the setting in which work is performed. Thus, the leader who is high in both consideration and structure will not always perform better than other types of leaders.[9] In some cases, one type of behavior or the other might be unhelpful or even damaging to subordinate performance or satisfaction.

Leader Reward and Punishment Behaviors

Assigned leaders can do other things besides initiate structure and be considerate. For example, a leader might set goals for subordinate performance, redesign jobs to better suit subordinate needs, or assign subordinates to particular tasks in which they are likely to be effective.[10] From previous chapters, it should be clear that these behaviors will prove effective when leaders pursue them in an intelligent and systematic way.

Two additional leader behaviors that have been the focus of research are leader reward behavior and leader punishment behavior. **Leader reward behavior** provides subordinates with compliments, tangible benefits, and deserved special treatment. When such rewards *are made contingent on performance,* subordinates perform at a high level and experience job satisfaction.[11] Under such leadership, subordinates have a clear picture of what is expected of them, and they understand that positive outcomes will occur if they achieve these expectations.

Leader punishment behavior involves the use of reprimands or unfavorable task assignments and the active withholding of raises, promotions, and other rewards. Compared with reward behavior, the consequences of leader

Leader reward behavior. The leader's provision of subordinates with compliments, tangible benefits, and deserved special treatment.

Leader punishment behavior. The leader's use of reprimands or unfavorable task assignments and the active withholding of rewards.

punishment are much less favorable.[12] At best, punishment seems to have little impact on satisfaction or productivity. At worst, when punishment is perceived as random and not contingent on subordinate behavior, subordinates react with great dissatisfaction. You will recall from Chapter 3 that punishment is extremely difficult to use effectively, and these results prove the point.

Leaders vary considerably in their access to reward opportunities, and this in turn can affect their tendency to resort to punishment. At lower-organizational levels, leaders often exert little control over promotion opportunities or salary decisions. Also, they might have so many subordinates that individualized rewards are difficult to administer. Finally, rigid technologies at lower-organizational levels (such as assembly lines) might prohibit leaders from redesigning jobs or giving subordinates favorable task assignments. Limited by time, technology, or an absence of tangible rewards, supervisors might resort to searching for negative behavior and punishing it.[13] Organizations that want supervisors to be effective leaders must ensure that they have the tools to do so!

Leader punishment behavior is not restricted to the lower-supervisory ranks. *Fortune* magazine's periodic list of the country's toughest CEOs attests to the existence of this style in the upper ranks.[14] As you might guess, it is not a style that inspires much follower loyalty.

SITUATIONAL THEORIES OF LEADERSHIP

We have referred to the potential impact of the situation on leadership effectiveness several times. Specifically, *situation* refers to the *setting* in which influence attempts occur. This setting includes the nature of the subordinates, the nature of the task they are performing, and characteristics of the organization. The two leadership theories below consider situational variables that seem especially likely to influence leadership effectiveness.

Fiedler's Contingency Theory

Contingency Theory. Fred Fiedler's theory that states that the association between leadership orientation and group effectiveness is contingent upon how favorable the situation is for exerting influence.

Fred Fiedler of the University of Washington has spent over three decades developing and refining a situational theory of leadership called **Contingency Theory.**[15] This name stems from the notion that the association between *leadership orientation* and *group effectiveness* is contingent upon (depends upon) the extent to which the *situation is favorable* for the exertion of influence. In other words, some situations are more favorable for leadership than others, and these situations require different orientations on the part of the leader.

Least Preferred Co-Worker. A current or past co-worker with whom a leader has had a difficult time accomplishing a task.

Leadership Orientation. Fiedler has measured leadership orientation by having leaders describe their **Least Preferred Co-Worker (LPC)**. This person may be a current or past co-worker. In either case, it is someone with whom the leader has had a difficult time getting the job done. To obtain an LPC score, the troublesome co-worker is described on eighteen scales of the following nature:

PLEASANT :_ :_ :_ :_ :_ :_ :_ :_ :UNPLEASANT
          8 7 6 5 4 3 2 1

FRIENDLY :_ :_ :_ :_ :_ :_ :_ :_ :UNFRIENDLY
         8 7 6 5 4 3 2 1

The leader who describes the LPC relatively favorably (a high LPC score) can be considered *relationship* oriented. That is, despite the fact that the LPC is or was difficult to work with, the leader can still find positive qualities in him or her. On the other hand, the leader who describes the LPC unfavorably (a low LPC score) can be considered *task* oriented. This person allows the low-task competence of the LPC to color his or her views of the personal qualities of the LPC ("If he's no good at the job, then he's not good, period.").

Fiedler has argued that the LPC score reveals a personality trait that reflects the leader's motivational structure. High LPC leaders are motivated to maintain interpersonal relations, while low LPC leaders are motivated to accomplish the task. Despite the apparent similarity, the LPC score is *not* a measure of consideration or initiating structure. These are observed *behaviors,* while the LPC score is evidently an *attitude* of the leader toward work relationships.

LPC's are attitudes not behaviours

Situational Favorableness. Situational favorableness is the "contingency" part of Contingency Theory. That is, it specifies when a particular LPC orientation should contribute most to group effectiveness. According to Fiedler, a favorable leadership situation exists when the leader has a high degree of control and when the results of this control are very predictable. Factors that affect situational favorableness, in order of importance, are the following:

- *Leader-member relations.* When the relationship between the leader and the group members is good, the leader is in a favorable situation to exert influence. Loyal, supportive subordinates should trust the leader and follow his or her directives with little complaint. A poor relationship should damage the leader's influence and even lead to insubordination or sabotage.

Situational theories of leadership explain how leadership style must be tailored to the demands of the task and the qualities of subordinates.

- *Task structure.* When the task at hand is highly structured, the leader should be able to exert considerable influence on the group. Clear goals, clear procedures to achieve these goals, and straightforward performance measures enable the leader to set performance standards and hold subordinates responsible ("Fill ten of these crates an hour."). When the task is unstructured ("Devise a plan to improve the quality of life in our city."), the leader might be in a poor position to evaluate subordinate work or to prove that her approach is superior to that of the group.

- *Position power.* Position power is formal authority to tell others what to do that is granted by the organization. The more position power the leader holds, the more favorable the leadership situation. In general, committee chairpersons and leaders in volunteer organizations have weak position power. Managers, supervisors, and military officers have strong position power.

In summary, the situation is most favorable for leadership when leader-member relations are good, the task is structured, and the leader has strong position power—for example, a well-liked army sergeant who is in charge of servicing jeeps in the base motor pool. The situation is least favorable when leader-member relations are poor, the task is unstructured, and the leader has weak position power—for instance, the disliked chairperson of a voluntary homeowner's association who is trying to get agreement on a list of community improvement projects.

The Contingency Model.   Under what conditions is one leadership orientation more effective than another? As shown in Exhibit 10.2, we can arrange the possible combinations of situational factors into eight octants, which form a continuum of favorability. The model indicates that a task orientation (low LPC) is most effective when the leadership situation is very favorable (octants I, II, and III) *or* when it is very unfavorable (octant VIII). On the other hand, a relationship orientation (high LPC) is most effective in conditions of medium favorability (octants IV, V, VI, and VII). Why is this so? In essence, Fiedler argues that leaders can "get away" with a task orientation when the situation is favorable—subordinates are "ready" to be influenced. Conversely, when the situation is very unfavorable for leadership, task orientation is necessary to get anything accomplished. In conditions of medium favorability, the boss is faced with some combination of an unclear task or a poor relationship with subor-

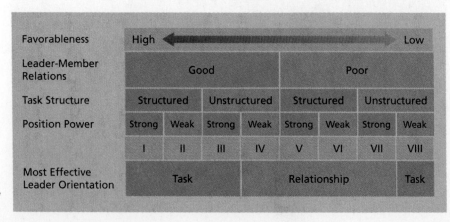

EXHIBIT 10.2
Predictions of leader effectiveness from Fiedler's Contingency Theory of leadership.

Favorableness	High							Low
Leader-Member Relations	Good				Poor			
Task Structure	Structured		Unstructured		Structured		Unstructured	
Position Power	Strong	Weak	Strong	Weak	Strong	Weak	Strong	Weak
	I	II	III	IV	V	VI	VII	VIII
Most Effective Leader Orientation	Task				Relationship			Task

dinates. Here, a relationship orientation will help to make the best of a situation that is stress-provoking but not impossibly bad.

Evidence and Criticism.   The conclusions about leadership effectiveness in Exhibit 10.2 are derived from many studies that Fiedler summarizes.[16] However, the Contingency Theory has been the subject of as much debate as any theory in organizational behavior.[17] Fiedler's explanation for the superior performance of high LPC leaders in the middle octants is not especially convincing, and the exact meaning of the LPC score is one of the great mysteries of organizational behavior. It does not seem to be correlated with other personality measures or predictive of specific leader behavior. It now appears that a major source of the many inconsistent findings regarding Contingency Theory is the small sample sizes that researchers used in many of the studies. Advances in correcting for this problem statistically have led recent reviewers to conclude that there is reasonable support for the theory.[18] However, Fiedler's prescription for task leadership in octant II (good relations, structured task, weak position power) seems contradicted by the evidence, suggesting that his theory needs some adjustment.

House's Path-Goal Theory

Robert House, building on the work of Martin Evans, has proposed a situational theory of leadership—Path-Goal Theory.[19] Unlike Fiedler's Contingency Theory, which relies on the somewhat ambiguous LPC trait, **Path-Goal Theory** is concerned with the situations under which various leader *behaviors* are most effective.

Path-Goal Theory. Robert House's theory concerned with the situations under which various leader behaviors (directive, supportive, participative, achievement-oriented) are most effective.

The Theory.   Why did House choose the name Path-Goal for his theory? According to House, the most important activities of leaders are those that clarify the paths to various goals of interest to subordinates. Such goals might include a promotion, a sense of accomplishment, or a pleasant work climate. In turn, the opportunity to achieve such goals should promote job satisfaction, leader acceptance, and high effort. Thus, *the effective leader forms a connection between subordinate goals and organizational goals.*

House argues that, to provide *job satisfaction* and *leader acceptance,* leader behavior must be perceived as immediately satisfying or as leading to future satisfaction. Leader behavior that subordinates see as unnecessary or unhelpful will be resented. House contends that, to promote subordinate *effort,* leaders must make rewards dependent on performance and ensure that subordinates have a clear picture of how they can achieve these rewards. To do this, the leader might have to provide support through direction, guidance, and coaching. For example, the bank teller who wishes to be promoted to supervisor should exhibit superior effort when his boss promises a recommendation contingent on good work and explains carefully how the teller can do better on his current job.

Leader Behavior.   Path-Goal Theory is concerned with four specific kinds of leader behavior. These include:

- *Directive behavior.* Directive leaders schedule work, maintain performance standards, and let subordinates know what is expected of them. This behavior is essentially identical to initiating structure.

- *Supportive behavior.* Supportive leaders are friendly, approachable, and concerned with pleasant interpersonal relationships. This behavior is essentially identical to consideration.
- *Participative behavior.* Participative leaders consult with subordinates about work-related matters and consider their opinions.
- *Achievement-oriented behavior.* Achievement-oriented leaders encourage subordinates to exert high effort and strive for a high level of goal accomplishment. They express confidence that subordinates can reach these goals.

According to Path-Goal Theory, the effectiveness of each set of behaviors depends upon the situation which the leader encounters.

Situational Factors.   Path-Goal Theory has concerned itself with two primary classes of situational factors—subordinate characteristics and environmental factors. Exhibit 10.3 illustrates the role of these situational factors in the theory. Put simply, the impact of leader behavior on subordinate satisfaction, effort, and acceptance of the leader depends upon the nature of the subordinates and the work environment. Let's consider these two situational factors in turn, along with some of the theory's predictions.

According to the theory, different types of subordinates need or prefer different forms of leadership. For example:

- Subordinates who are high need achievers (Chapter 6) should work well under achievement-oriented leadership.
- Subordinates who prefer being told what to do should respond best to a directive leadership style.
- When subordinates feel that they have rather low task abilities, they should appreciate directive leadership and coaching behavior. When they feel quite capable of performing the task, they'll view such behaviors as unnecessary and irritating.

As you can observe from these examples, leaders might have to tailor their behavior to the needs, abilities, and personalities of individual employees.

Also, according to the theory, the effectiveness of leadership behavior depends upon the particular work environment. For example:

- When tasks are clear and routine, subordinates should perceive directive leadership as a redundant and unnecessary imposition. This should

EXHIBIT 10.3
The Path-Goal Theory of leadership.

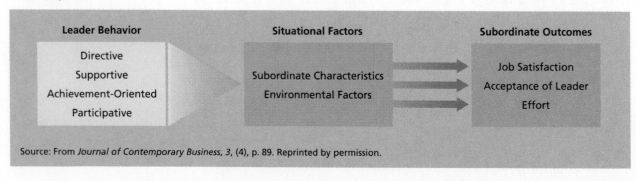

Source: From *Journal of Contemporary Business, 3,* (4), p. 89. Reprinted by permission.

reduce satisfaction and acceptance of the leader. Similarly, participative leadership would not seem to be useful when tasks are clear, since there is little in which to participate. Obviously, such tasks are most common at lower organizational levels.

- When tasks are challenging but ambiguous, subordinates should appreciate both directive and participative leadership. Such styles should clarify the path to good performance and demonstrate that the leader is concerned with helping subordinates to do a good job. Obviously, such tasks are most common at higher organizational levels.

- Frustrating, dissatisfying jobs should increase subordinate appreciation of supportive behavior. To some degree, such support should compensate for a disliked job, although it should probably do little to increase effort.

As you can see from these examples of environmental factors, effective leadership should *take advantage of* the motivating and satisfying aspects of jobs while *offsetting or compensating for* those job aspects that demotivate or dissatisfy. At Southwest Airlines, Herb Kelleher has managed to develop an appropriate mix of supportive, achievement-oriented, and participative leadership.

Evidence and Criticism.   In general, there is some research support for most of the situational propositions discussed above. In particular, there is substantial evidence that supportive or considerate leader behavior is most beneficial in supervising routine, frustrating, or dissatisfying jobs and some evidence that directive or structuring leader behavior is most effective on ambiguous, less-structured jobs.[20] The theory appears to work better in predicting subordinate job satisfaction and acceptance of the leader than in predicting subordinate performance.[21]

PARTICIPATIVE LEADERSHIP: INVOLVING SUBORDINATES IN DECISIONS

In the discussion of Path-Goal Theory, we raised the issue of participative leadership. Because this is such an important topic, let's devote further attention to participation.

What Is Participation?

At a very general level, **participative leadership** means involving subordinates in making work-related decisions. The term *involving* is intentionally broad. Participation is not a fixed or absolute property, but a relative concept. This is illustrated in Exhibit 10.4. Here, we see that leaders can vary in the extent to which they involve subordinates in decision making. Minimally, participation involves obtaining subordinate opinions before making a decision oneself. Maximally, it allows subordinates to make their own decisions within agreed-upon limits. As the "area of freedom" on the part of subordinates increases, the leader is behaving in a more participative manner. There is, however, an upper limit to the area of subordinate freedom available under participation. Participative leadership should not be confused with the *abdication* of leadership, which is almost always ineffective.

Participative leadership. Involving subordinates in making work-related decisions.

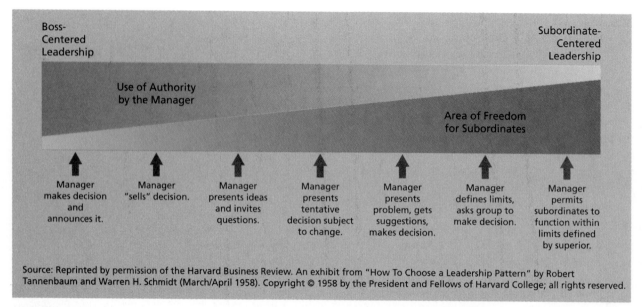

EXHIBIT 10.4
Subordinate participation in decision making can vary.

Participation can involve individual subordinates or the entire group of subordinates that reports to the leader. For example, participation on an individual basis might work best when setting performance goals for particular subordinates, planning subordinate development, or dealing with problem employees. On the other hand, the leader might involve the entire work group in decision making when determining vacation schedules, arranging for telephone coverage during lunch hour, or deciding how to allocate scarce resources such as travel money or secretarial help. As these examples suggest, the choice of an individual or group participation strategy should be tailored to specific situations. The "In Focus: *Imedia's Jo-Anne Dressendofer Fosters Participation*" selection highlights one manager's conversion to participation.

Potential Advantages of Participative Leadership

Just why might participation be a useful leadership technique? What are its potential advantages?

Motivation.   Participation can increase the motivation of subordinates.[22] In some cases, participation permits them to contribute to the establishment of work goals and to decide how they can accomplish these goals. For example, suppose that, early in the spring quarter, a university department chairperson projects that she will have some budget money remaining at the end of the academic year. She informs her department members, and they decide to use the money to fund a trip to a professional conference in New Orleans for the three professors who have the best student evaluations at the end of the quarter. Here, participation has clarified the path toward a valued goal, and the professors should be motivated to perform well in the classroom.

It might also occur to you that participation can increase intrinsic motivation by enriching subordinates' jobs. In Chapter 7 you learned that enriched jobs include high-task variety and increased subordinate autonomy. Participation adds some variety to the job and promotes autonomy by increasing the "area of freedom" (see Exhibit 10.4).

IN FOCUS   Imedia's Jo-Anne Dressendofer Fosters Participation

Jo-Anne Dressendofer is CEO of Imedia, a Morristown, New Jersey, marketing firm. The company is featured in Inc. *magazine's list of 500 successful small companies.*

"I don't think there's ever such a thing as a *flat* 'flat organization,'" says Jo-Anne Dressendofer ... "They have little bumps in them; there still need to be people managing the work and people doing the work. What smooths it out, though, is that managers *also* do the work, and people who usually are just considered workers are brought into the managing arena."

In some cases, it is "the new worker" who forces the issue. Anxious for autonomy yet looking to be part of a team, the bright people who staff growing companies today are too independent and creative to tolerate either bureaucracy or autocracy. They won't bear frustrating structures.

Jo-Anne Dressendofer learned that firsthand. Back in early 1992 she had what she thought was a non-hierarchical company, considering that after three years in business, her company didn't have any bosses.

What it did have was an inordinate CEO supremacy. "One day six or seven people marched into my office and told me that if I didn't let go,

they were all going to quit," she says. "These were the people that if they had walked, the company would have collapsed." One woman was blunt. "Jo-Anne," she said, "it's not going to work if we have to get your permission for everything." Over the next several months the company met in groups to try to figure out a better way to run the business—keeping it as title-free as it already was but distributing accountability as well. What developed was a team-management approach, in which groups of employees have real responsibility for most operational issues and client services—without having to get Dressendofer's sign-off all the time.

With the company a year into the new system, Dressendofer says that decisions get made slowly, that several key employees left because they didn't like the forced participation, and that there are times she sits in on team meetings with her fists clenched under the table, watching novice leaders "go through the experience of making poor decisions." But business is up by $1 million—with profits shared by everyone—and the team decisions are getting better.

Source: Excerpted from Brokaw, L. (1993, October). Thinking flat. *Inc.*, 86–88.

Quality.   Participation can enhance quality in at least two ways. First, an old saying argues that "two heads are better than one." While this is not always true, there do seem to be many cases in which "two heads" (participation) lead to higher-quality decisions than the leader could make alone.[23] In particular, this is most likely when subordinates have special knowledge to contribute to the decision. In many research and engineering departments, it is common for the professional subordinates to have technical knowledge that is superior to that of their boss. This occurs either because the boss is not a professional or because the boss's knowledge has become outdated. Under these conditions, participation in technical matters should enhance the quality of decisions.

2 heads better than 1

Participation can also enhance quality because high levels of participation often empower employees to take direct action to solve problems without checking every detail with the boss. You will recall from Chapter 7 that empowerment gives employees the authority, opportunity, and motivation to take initiative and solve problems. Southwest Airlines empowers employees, and so does Georgia-Pacific:

At the chemical division of Georgia-Pacific Corporation, a quality-and-environmental-assurance supervisor and a plant operator thought of a more effective way to prepare test samples of a certain chemical. They had been trained in collaboration skills, so they felt comfortable sharing their idea. Instead of simply writing down the new procedure, they produced a demonstration video. After seeing the video, managers asked the two employees to share the tape with quality-assurance supervisors at other Georgia-Pacific plants. In turn, the supervisor and operator encouraged employees at other sites to provide feedback and to share their own ideas. [24]

Acceptance. Even when participation does not promote motivation or increase the quality of decisions, it can increase the subordinates' acceptance of decisions. This is especially likely when issues of *fairness* are involved.[25] For example, consider the problems of scheduling vacations or scheduling telephone coverage during lunch hours. Here, the leader could probably make high-quality decisions without involving subordinates. However, the decisions might be totally unacceptable to the employees because they perceive them as unfair. Involving subordinates in decision making could result in solutions of equal quality that do not provoke dissatisfaction. Public commitment and ego involvement probably contribute to the acceptance of such decisions.

Potential Problems of Participative Leadership

You have no doubt learned that every issue in organizational behavior has two sides. Consider the potential difficulties of participation.

Time and Energy.   Participation isn't a state of mind. It involves specific behaviors on the part of the leader (soliciting ideas, calling meetings), and these behaviors use time and energy. When a quick decision is needed, participation isn't an appropriate leadership strategy. The hospital emergency room isn't the place to implement participation on a continuous basis!

Loss of Power.   Some leaders feel that a participative style will reduce their power and influence. Sometimes, they respond by asking subordinates to make trivial decisions of the "what color shall we paint the lounge" type. Clearly, the consequences of such decisions (for motivation, quality, and acceptance) are near zero. A lack of trust in subordinates and a fear that they will make mistakes is often the hallmark of an insecure manager. On the other hand, the contemporary call for flatter hierarchies and increased teamwork make such sharing of power inevitable.

Lack of Receptivity or Knowledge.   Subordinates might not be receptive to participation. When the leader is distrusted, or when a poor labor climate exists, they might resent "having to do management's work." Even when receptive, subordinates might lack the knowledge to contribute effectively to decisions. Usually, this occurs because they are unaware of *external constraints* on their decisions. For example, consider the case of the toy factory with the following production process:

PARTS MADE → PARTS PAINTED → PARTS ASSEMBLED

In this factory, participation among the paint crew led them to establish elevated production levels that led to problems for the parts makers and toy assemblers. Management was forced to take control of production levels, and most of the painters quit.[26]

A Situational Model of Participation

How can leaders capitalize upon the potential advantages of participation while avoiding its pitfalls? Victor Vroom and Arthur Jago have presented a model that attempts to specify in a practical manner when leaders should use participation and to what extent they should use it (the model was originally developed by Vroom and Philip Yetton).[27]

Vroom and Jago begin with the recognition that there are various degrees of participation that a leader can exhibit. For issues involving the entire work group, the following range of behaviors is plausible (A stands for autocratic, C for consultative, and G for group):

AI. You solve the problem or make the decision yourself, using information available to you at the time.

AII. You obtain the necessary information from your subordinates, then decide the solution to the problem yourself. You may or may not tell your subordinates what the problem is in getting the information from them. The role played by your subordinates in making the decision is clearly one of providing the necessary information to you, rather than generating or evaluating alternative solutions.

CI. You share the problem with the relevant subordinates individually, getting their ideas and suggestions without bringing them together as a group. Then you make the decision, which may or may not reflect your subordinates' influence.

CII. You share the problem with your subordinates as a group, obtaining their collective ideas and suggestions. Then you make the decision, which may or may not reflect your subordinates' influence.

GII. You share the problem with your subordinates as a group. Together you generate and evaluate alternatives and attempt to reach agreement (consensus) on a solution. Your role is much like that of chairman. You do not try to influence the group to adopt "your" solution, and you are willing to accept and implement any solution which has the support of the entire group.[28]

Which of these strategies is most effective? According to Vroom and Jago, this depends on the situation or problem at hand. In general, the leader's goal should be to make high-quality decisions to which subordinates will be adequately committed without undue delay. To do this, he or she must consider the questions in Exhibit 10.5. The quality requirement (QR) for a problem might be low if it is very unlikely that a technically bad decision could be made or all feasible alternatives are equal in quality. Otherwise, QR is probably high. The commitment requirement (CR) is likely to be high if subordinates are very concerned about which alternative is chosen or if they will have to actually implement the decision. The problem is structured (ST) when the leader understands the current situation, the desired situation, and how to get from one to the other. Unfamiliarity, uncertainty, and novelty in any of these matters reduces problem structure. The other questions in Exhibit 10.5 are fairly self-explanatory. Notice, however, that all are oriented toward preserving either decision quality or commitment to the decision.

By tracing a problem through the decision tree, the leader encounters the prescribed degree of participation for that problem. In every case, the tree shows the fastest approach possible (i.e., the most autocratic) that still maintains decision quality and commitment. In many cases, if the leader is willing to sacrifice some speed, a more participative approach could stimulate

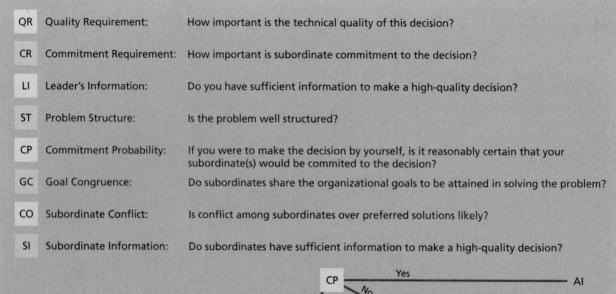

QR	Quality Requirement:	How important is the technical quality of this decision?
CR	Commitment Requirement:	How important is subordinate commitment to the decision?
LI	Leader's Information:	Do you have sufficient information to make a high-quality decision?
ST	Problem Structure:	Is the problem well structured?
CP	Commitment Probability:	If you were to make the decision by yourself, is it reasonably certain that your subordinate(s) would be commited to the decision?
GC	Goal Congruence:	Do subordinates share the organizational goals to be attained in solving the problem?
CO	Subordinate Conflict:	Is conflict among subordinates over preferred solutions likely?
SI	Subordinate Information:	Do subordinates have sufficient information to make a high-quality decision?

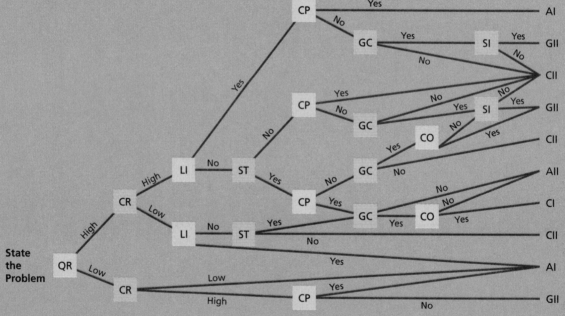

Source: Reprinted from Vroom, V. H., & Jago, A. G. (1988). *The new leadership: Managing participation in organizations.* Englewood Cliffs, NJ: Prentice-Hall. Copyright © 1987 by Vroom, V. H., & Jago, A. G.

EXHIBIT 10.5
The Vroom and Jago decision tree for participative leadership.

subordinate development (as long as quality or commitment is not threatened). The "In Focus: *How the Vroom and Jago Model of Participation Works*" illustrates how the model is applied to a problem.

The original decision model developed by Vroom and Yetton, upon which the Vroom and Jago model is based, has substantial research support.[29] Following the model's prescriptions is more likely to lead to successful managerial decisions than unsuccessful decisions. The model has been used frequently in management development seminars.

IN FOCUS   How the Vroom and Jago Model of Participation Works

Here is a case that illustrates how the Vroom and Jago model works. Read the case and trace the analysis through the decision tree. Vroom and Jago have used such cases to train leaders in decision-making skills.

You are the head of a research and development laboratory in the nuclear reactor division of a large corporation. Often it is not clear whether a particular piece of research is potentially of commercial interest or merely of "academic" interest to the researchers. In your judgment, one major area of research has advanced well beyond the level at which operating divisions pertinent to the area could possibly assimilate or make use of the data being generated.

Recently, two new areas with potentially high returns for commercial development have been proposed by one of the operating divisions. The team working in the area referred to in the previous paragraph is ideally qualified to research these new areas. Unfortunately, both the new areas are relatively devoid of scientific interest, while the project on which the team is currently engaged is of great scientific interest to all members.

At the moment, this is, or is close to being, your best research team. The team is very cohesive, has a high level of morale, and has been very productive. You are concerned not only that they would not want to switch their effort to these new areas,

but also that forcing them to concentrate on these two new projects could adversely affect their morale, their good intragroup working relations, and their future productivity both as individuals and as a team.

You have to respond to the operating division within the next two weeks indicating what resources, if any, can be devoted to working on these projects. It would be possible for the team to work on more than one project but each project would need the combined skills of all the members of the team, so no fragmentation of the team is technically feasible. This fact, coupled with the fact that the team is very cohesive, means that a solution that satisfies any team member would very probably go a long way to satisfying everyone on the team.

Analysis

Quality Requirement	High Importance
Commitment Requirement	High Importance
Leader Information	Probably Yes
Problem Structure	Yes
Commitment Probability	No
Goal Congruence	Probably No
Subordinate Conflict	Probably No
Subordinate Information	No
Highest Overall Effectiveness:	CII

Source: Vroom, V. H., & Jago, A. G. (1988). *The new leadership: Managing participation in organizations.* Englewood Cliffs, NJ: Prentice-Hall, pp. 164–165. Reprinted by permission.

Does Participation Work?

Now we come to the bottom line—does participative leadership result in beneficial outcomes? There is substantial evidence that employees who have the opportunity to participate in work-related decisions report more job satisfaction than those who do not. Thus, most workers seem to *prefer* a participative work environment. However, the positive effects of participation on productivity are open to some question. For participation to be translated into higher productivity, it would appear that certain facilitating conditions must exist. Specifically, participation should work best when subordinates feel favorable toward it, when they are intelligent and knowledgeable about the issue at hand, and when the task is complex enough to make participation useful.[30] In general, these conditions are incorporated into the Vroom and Jago model. Like any other leadership strategy, the usefulness of participation depends upon the constraints of the situation.

TRANSFORMATIONAL LEADERSHIP AND CHARISMA

Thus far in the chapter we have been studying various aspects of what we can call transactional leadership. Transactional leadership is leadership that is based on a fairly straightforward exchange between the leader and the followers—subordinates perform well, and the leader rewards them; the leader uses a participatory style, and the subordinates come up with good ideas. Although it might be difficult to do well, such leadership is routine, in the sense that it is directed mainly toward bringing subordinate behavior in line with organizational goals. However, you might have some more dramatic examples of leadership in mind, examples in which leaders have had a more profound effect on followers by giving them a new vision that instilled true commitment to a project, a department, or an organization. Such leadership is called **transformational leadership** because the leader decisively changes the beliefs and attitudes of followers to correspond to this new vision.[31]

Transformational leadership. Providing followers with a new vision that instills true commitment.

Popular examples of transformational leadership are easy to find—consider Herb Kelleher's founding of Southwest Airlines, Disney CEO Michael Eisner's role in improving Disney's performance, Steven Jobs's vision in bringing the Apple Macintosh to fruition, Mary Ann Lawlor's turnaround of Drake Business Schools, or CEO Jack Welch's ongoing revision of General Electric's strategy. Each of these leaders went beyond a mere institutional figurehead role and even beyond a transactional leadership role to truly transform subordinates' thinking about the nature of their businesses. However, these prominent examples should not obscure the fact that transformational leadership can occur in less visible settings. For example, a new coach might revitalize a sorry peewee soccer team or an energetic new director might turn around a moribund community association using the same types of skills.

But what *are* the skills of these exceptional transformational leaders who encourage considerable effort and dedication on the part of followers? Professor Bernard Bass of the State University of New York at Binghamton has conducted extensive research on transformational leaders.[32] Bass notes that transformational leaders are usually good at the transactional aspects of clarifying paths to goals and rewarding good performance. But he also notes three qualities that set transformational leaders apart from their transactional colleagues: intellectual stimulation, individualized consideration, and charisma.

Intellectual Stimulation

Intellectual stimulation contributes in part to the "new vision" aspect of transformational leadership. People are stimulated to think about problems, issues, and strategies in new ways. Often, creativity and novelty are at work here. For example, Steve Jobs was convinced that the Apple Macintosh had to be extremely user friendly. As you might imagine, many of the technical types who wanted to sign on to the Mac project needed to be convinced of the importance of this quality, and Jobs was just the person to do it, raising their consciousness about what it felt like to be a new computer user.

Individualized Consideration

Individualized consideration involves treating subordinates as distinct individuals, indicating concern for their personal development, and serving as a mentor when appropriate. The emphasis is a one-on-one attempt to meet the needs of the individual in question in the context of the overall goal or mission. Bass implies that individualized consideration is particularly striking when military leaders exhibit it because the military culture generally stresses impersonality and "equal" treatment. General Stormin' Norman Schwartzkopf, commander of U.S. troops during the Gulf war, was noted for this. Herb Kelleher's personal knowledge of many Southwest employees illustrates individualized consideration.

Charisma

Charisma is the third, and by far the most important, aspect of transformational leadership. In fact, many authors simply talk about charismatic leadership, although a good case can be made that a person could have charisma without being a leader. **Charisma** is a term stemming from a Greek word meaning *favored* or *gifted*. Charismatic individuals have been portrayed throughout history as having personal qualities that give them the potential to have extraordinary influence over others. They tend to command strong loyalty and devotion, and this in turn inspires enthusiastic dedication and effort directed toward the leader's chosen mission. In terms of the concepts we developed in Chapter 9, followers come to trust and *identify* with charismatic leaders and to *internalize* the values and goals they hold. Charisma provides the *emotional* aspect of transformational leadership.

> **Charisma.** The ability to command strong loyalty and devotion from followers and thus have the potential for strong influence among them.

It appears that the emergence of charisma is a complex function of traits, behaviors, and being in the right place at the right time.[33] Prominent traits include self-confidence, dominance, and a strong conviction in one's beliefs. Charismatics often act to create an impression of personal success and accomplishment. They hold high expectations for follower performance while at the same time expressing confidence in followers' capabilities. This enhances the self-esteem of the followers. The goals set by charismatic leaders often have a moral or ideological flavor to them. In addition, charismatic leaders often emerge to articulate the feelings of followers in times of stress or discord. If these feelings go against an existing power structure, the leader might be perceived as especially courageous.

Kelleher's video challenging his employees to meet the threat posed by United Airlines had moral and ideological overtones. The loyalty and devotion of Southwest Airlines employees to Herb Kelleher is illustrated by the ad of thanks they took out in *USA Today*.

Charismatic Stages. One interesting view of the emergence of charisma portrays it as a stagelike process.[34] Although such stages probably do not occur in all instances of charisma, this portrayal does clarify how charisma contributes to transformational leadership.

Charisma is an important aspect of transformational leadership. Dave Thomas of Wendy's restaurants is a charismatic leader who commands strong loyalty and devotion from his employees.

- In the first stage, the leader carefully evaluates the status quo for opportunities for change. He or she devotes particular attention to assessing subordinate needs and organizational constraints. At the same time, the leader seeks out or even causes deficiencies in the status quo. For example, he or she might commission market research to show a strong demand for a product or service that the organization does not offer.

- In the second stage, the leader formulates a vision or mission that challenges the status quo but that somehow corresponds to the followers' needs and aspirations. For example, he or she might envision a product

Nelson Mandela is the highly regarded political leader of South Africa. His charisma and his vision for a free South Africa were important factors in his election campaign.

that will return the firm to its former eminence as a respected innovator in engineering. At this stage, impression management is important to articulate the vision to followers. Here is where rhetoric, self-confidence, and showing confidence in others come into play. The new mission's ability to change the unsatisfactory status quo is emphasized.

- In the final stage of charismatic emergence, the leader actually gets subordinates to achieve the new vision or mission, often by setting an example of self-sacrifice and flaunting unconventional expertise to build subordinate trust. For example, the leader might work extensive hours, make risky challenges to other organizational members who threaten the mission, and suggest unusual but workable technical solutions.

Charisma has been studied most intensively among political leaders and the leaders of social movements. Winston Churchill, Martin Luther King, Nelson Mandela, and Gandhi appear charismatic. Among U.S. Presidents, one study concludes that Jefferson, Jackson, Lincoln, Kennedy, and Reagan were charismatic, while Coolidge, Harding, and Buchanan were not.[35] Among business leaders, Mary Kay Ash and Lee Iacocca are often cited as charismatic.

In passing, we must also mention that charisma has a dark side, a side that is revealed when charismatics abuse their strong influence over others for purely personal reasons.[36] Such people often exploit the needs of followers to pursue a reckless goal or mission. Adolf Hitler and cult leader David Koresh personify extreme examples of charismatic abuse. We will explore the abuse of power further in Chapter 13.

To summarize, transformational leaders provide intellectual stimulation and individualized consideration to followers. Most important, though, they exhibit charisma. The recent research evidence suggests that subordinates

LEADERSHIP DEVELOPMENT AT LEVI STRAUSS & CO.

YOU BE THE Manager

During the 1970s Levi Strauss & Co. enjoyed phenomenal success, as jeans became a global fashion statement. Senior management realized that growth in jeans sales could not continue indefinitely and attempted unsuccessful diversification. During the 1980s the crunch came with the falling market for jeans, and the company was forced to close many plants, an action that violated its implicit goals of caring and longterm employment. To put the company back on track, senior management developed a Mission and Aspiration Statement that was meant to clarify company goals and the leadership behaviors necessary to achieve these goals. These included valuing diversity, managing ethically, communicating clearly, and empowering the workforce. Management soon found out that producing such a statement did not guar-

> TOMMY JO DAVES, A 58-YEAR-OLD GRANDMOTHER, IS RESPONSIBLE FOR A LEVIS PLANT IN MURPHY, NORTH CAROLINA, WHICH EMPLOYS 385 WORKERS AND TURNS OUT SOME THREE MILLION PAIRS OF LEVIS PER YEAR.

antee a change in behavior. Thus, it established Leadership Week, a week-long training program to back up the statement with concrete assistance for managers. A survey revealed that employees generally supported the Aspirations but felt that they still weren't being acted on in practice. What would *you* do to translate the Leadership Week training into concrete behavior on the job?

1. What are some of the general factors that constrain the transfer of any leadership training to the job?

2. What can Levi Strauss do to ensure that its managers serve as leaders for the company Aspirations?

To find out what the company did, turn to *The Manager's Notebook* at the end of the chapter.

Sources: Conger, J. A. (1992). *Learning to lead*. San Francisco: Jossey-Bass; Laabs, J. J. (1992, December). HR's vital role at Levi Strauss. *Personnel Journal*, 34–46; Howard, R. (1990, September–October). Values make the company: An interview with Robert Haas. *Harvard Business Review*, 139–141.

perceive such leaders as especially effective in stimulating both satisfaction and effort.[37]

Before continuing, pause and consider the *You Be the Manager* feature about leadership development.

GENDER, CULTURE, AND LEADERSHIP STYLE

Do men and women tend to adopt different leadership styles? Recently, a number of popular books have argued that women leaders tend to be more intuitive, less hierarchically oriented, and more collaborative than their male counterparts. Is this true? Notice that two opposing logics could be at work here. On one hand, different socialization experiences could lead men and women to learn different ways of exerting influence on others. On the other hand, men and women should be equally capable of gravitating toward the style that is most appropriate in a given setting. This would result in no general difference in style.

A very careful review of the evidence by researchers Alice Eagly and Blair Johnson concludes that there are few differences in leadership style between men and women in organizational settings, with one exception—women have a tendency to be more participative or democratic than men.[38] Why is this so? One theory holds that women have better social skills that enable them to successfully manage the give-and-take that participation requires. Another theory holds that women avoid more autocratic styles because they violate gender stereotypes and lead to negative reactions. In fact, there is strong evidence that people negatively evaluate women who adopt stereotypically male (i.e., directive and autocratic) leadership styles.[39] Men have more freedom in choosing a style than women.

Are various leadership styles equally effective across cultures? Some universality is to be expected. For example, anywhere in the world, it seems to be reasonable to be somewhat more directive with inexperienced and untrained subordinates and to be participative when you are uninformed but your subordinates have expert knowledge.

Still, preferences for style will vary with cultural values. For instance, more directive leadership styles will be more acceptable in cultures that favor rather large power differences, such as those characteristic of some South American countries. On the other hand, more participative approaches seem to have flourished in cultures that are removed from the extremes of both power distance and individualism, such as Japan and some Scandinavian countries.

DOES LEADERSHIP MATTER?

Does leadership really *matter*? That is, does it have a strong influence on the effectiveness of organizations? This might seem like an incredible question after we have devoted so many pages to consideration, initiating structure, situational influence, participation, and transformation. However, as you have seen, the study of leadership, despite its great volume, has not produced perfect agreement about what constitutes effective leadership. Perhaps we are tilting at windmills. Maybe leadership just isn't important to organizations. Let's examine the pros and cons of this issue.

Pros and Cons of Leader Influence

The notion that leadership is important rests mainly on the premise that special influence is necessary to get things done because we can't design organizations perfectly and completely. You have probably experienced this phenomenon. The university financial office can't give you a refund until it is okayed by the registrar. The registrar can't okay the refund until it is approved by the professor. And the professor just went on sabbatical to Tasmania! *Here's* a case in which leadership is necessary! In other words, schools, hospitals, and business firms exhibit many loose ends or gaps that can be dealt with only by effective leadership. More specifically:

- Organizations do not have a rule or policy for every contingency. (The boss decides whether a particular absence is legitimate or illegitimate.)

- Organizational environments change, and someone must be responsive to this change. (Leadership is needed to spearhead major changes such as total quality programs and workforce diversity efforts.)
- Organizational members differ in their needs and goals. (A sensitive manager might be able to motivate one employee with challenging work assignments and another with the promise of a raise in pay.)[40]

Conditions of this nature suggest that there is considerable *latitude* for leadership actions that can help or hinder the organization in achieving its goals.[41]

The notion that leadership isn't so important rests mainly on the premise that a number of factors conspire to constrain the influence that individuals in leadership roles might have. In other words, the potential for influence is inhibited, and the leader's latitude is more apparent than real. One author has argued that the following factors limit leader impact:[42]

- In most organizations, rigid selection and promotion policies dictate that those who achieve leadership positions have very similar leadership styles. (If all the managers in a government office behave similarly, they should have similar influence—one manager is easily replaceable by another who should be equally effective.)
- The leader's performance can be strongly affected by external factors beyond his or her control. (The best boss in the company might not be able to overcome subordinates' resentment of the dirty, boring work required by a particular technology.)

Obviously, the argument that leadership matters and the position that leadership doesn't matter both sound pretty rational. This suggests that both positions may be true under certain circumstances. Let's examine what these circumstances might be.

Leadership Neutralizers and Substitutes

Experts have proposed some interesting ideas in response to the dilemma of whether leadership matters.[43] First, they argue that certain subordinate, task, and organizational characteristics can serve as **neutralizers of leadership.** When these factors are present in the work setting, they reduce the leader's opportunities to exercise influence. In this case, then, leadership might not "matter" because the leader's influence attempts are stymied. When such factors are not present, the leader might have an important effect on subordinate satisfaction and performance. For example, consider the following situations:

Neutralizers of leadership.
Factors in the work setting that reduce a leader's opportunity to exercise influence.

- Martin is a petroleum engineer for a major oil company. He is a troubleshooter who deals with company problems around the world, and he is constantly "on the go." He sees his boss about every two months. Martin is very interested in his job, and he doesn't care about what performance rating or merit raise he receives.
- Shawn is a management trainee in a large insurance company. Her office is beside that of her boss, and she consults with him about ten times a day. Shawn hopes to obtain a good performance rating so that she can receive a lucrative promotion.

Substitutes for leadership.
Factors in the work setting that can take the place of active leadership, making it unnecessary or redundant.

Obviously, Shawn's boss is in a better position to exercise influence than Martin's boss. The latter's leadership potential is to some extent neutralized by the fact that he seldom sees Martin and because Martin is unresponsive to the rewards he can provide.

Going a step further, some neutralizers of leadership can actually serve as **substitutes for leadership.** In other words, some subordinate, task, and organizational characteristics might operate to make leadership unnecessary or redundant. While simple neutralizers reduce the *effectiveness* of leadership attempts, substitutes reduce the *necessity* for leadership. For example, consider these situations:

- A group of 10 welders and riveters is assembling a large natural gas pipeline. All of them are highly experienced, and they work well together as a friendly, cohesive unit. Their task is clear and unambiguous—assemble 50 yards of pipe each day.

- A group of computer experts has decided to start a new company to design and market software packages. Although they are all technical experts, they know nothing about financing their venture or marketing their proposed products. There is much disagreement about how to establish the new enterprise and how to choose which software to develop.

In which of these situations does leadership seem more necessary? For the pipe crew, the straightforwardness of the task at hand and the friendly, cooperative working relationships could well serve as substitutes for active, formal leadership. We would not be surprised to see the crew work well if the boss called in sick for several days. On the other hand, the proposed computer firm is begging for leadership. Its goals are unclear, and its founders are unlikely to reach an easy agreement. There are no substitutes for leadership here.

Exhibit 10.6 summarizes a number of potential neutralizers of leadership. In some cases, these neutralizers can also serve as substitutes. In the first

Neutralizing Characteristics	Will Neutralize Considerate or Social-Emotional Leadership	Will Neutralize Initiating Structure or Task Leadership
Of Subordinate		
Ability, experience, knowledge		X
Professional orientation	X	X
Indifference toward rewards	X	X
Of Task		
Routine and clear		X
Provides its own feedback		X
Intrinsically satisfying	X	
Of Organization		
Inflexible rules and procedures		X
Cohesive work groups	X	X
Spatial distance between leader and subordinate	X	X

Source: From Kerr, S., & Jermier, J. M. (1978). Substitutes for leadership: Their meaning and measurement. *Organizational Behavior and Human Performance, 22,* p. 378. Copyright © 1978 by Academic Press. Reprinted by permission.

EXHIBIT 10.6
Neutralizers of leadership.

example discussed above (Martin versus Shawn), indifference toward rewards and spatial distance were presented as simple neutralizers. These factors reduce the impact of leadership, but they do not reduce the need for leadership. In the second example, a clear task, experienced workers, and a cohesive work group served as substitutes for formal leadership for the pipe crew. The computer group did not have the advantages of these substitutes. Notice that some factors neutralize social-emotional influence, some neutralize task influence, and some neutralize both. For example, highly experienced, knowledgeable subordinates might need little task leadership, but they still require social-emotional support from the leader.

In summary, leadership should "matter" most when neutralizers and substitutes are not present in subordinates' skills and attitudes, task design, or the organizational design. The presence of neutralizers and substitutes should reduce the impact of formal leadership.[44]

The Manager's Notebook — Leadership Development at Levi Strauss & Co.

Levi Strauss takes Leadership Week seriously. Senior management sponsors it, and hundreds of managers have experienced the training.

1. Factors that can inhibit leadership training from being transferred back to the job include a) one's boss isn't receptive to the training, b) employees are suspicious about the manager's new behavior, c) the ultimate purpose of the training is unclear to the manager or the employees, d) no rewards are available for successful change on the job.

2. Levi Strauss put in place a system to support its Leadership Week training that avoided or overcame many of these neutralizers of leadership. This included better communication with employees through company newsletters and providing training for employees so that they better understand the firm's mission and aspirations. Task forces studied issues such as empowerment and minority concerns. Such task forces generate information that enable managers to *act out* their training. Performance appraisal and rewards concentrate heavily on the leadership dimension of management jobs.

EXECUTIVE SUMMARY

◆ Leadership occurs when an individual exerts influence upon others' goal achievement in an organizational context. Early studies of leadership were concerned with identifying physical, psychological, and intellectual traits that might predict leader effectiveness. While some traits appear weakly related to leadership capacity, there are no traits that guarantee leadership across various situations.

◆ Studies of emergent leadership have identified two important leadership functions—the task function and the social-emotional function. The former involves helping the group achieve its goals through planning and organizing, while the latter involves resolving disputes and maintaining a pleasant group environment. Explorations of the behavior of assigned leaders have concentrated on initiating structure and consideration, which are similar to task behavior and social-emotional behavior. The effectiveness of consideration and structure depends upon the nature of the task and the subordinates. Leader reward behavior is probably a more foolproof strategy than leader punishment behavior.

◆ We discussed two situational theories of leadership. Fiedler's Contingency Theory suggests that different leadership orientations are necessary depending upon the favorableness of the situation for the leader.

Favorableness depends upon the structure of the task, the position power of the leader, and the satisfactoriness of the relationship between the leader and the group. Fiedler argues that task-oriented leaders perform best in situations that are either very favorable or very unfavorable. Relationship-oriented leaders are said to perform best in situations of medium favorability. House's Path-Goal Theory suggests that leaders will be most effective when they are able to clarify the paths to various subordinate goals that are also of interest to the organization. According to House, the effectiveness of directive, supportive, participative, and achievement-oriented behavior depends upon the nature of the subordinates and the characteristics of the work environment.

◆ Participative leader behavior involves subordinates in work decisions. Participation can increase subordinate motivation and lead to higher-quality and more acceptable decisions. The Vroom and Jago model specifies how much participation is best for various kinds of decisions. Participation works best when subordinates are desirous of participation, when they are intelligent and knowledgeable, and when the task is reasonably complex.

◆ Transformational leaders modify the beliefs and attitudes of followers to correspond to a new vision. They provide intellectual stimulation and individualized consideration. They also have charisma, the ability to command extraordinary loyalty, dedication, and effort from followers.

◆ Leadership is most important when few neutralizers or substitutes for leadership exist. Neutralizers are factors that make leadership attempts less effective, and substitutes are factors that can act in place of leader influence.

KEY CONCEPTS

Leadership
Traits
Task leader
Social-emotional leader
Consideration
Initiating structure
Leader reward behavior
Leader punishment behavior

Contingency Theory
Least Preferred Co-Worker (LPC)
Path-Goal Theory
Participative leadership
Transformational leadership
Charisma
Neutralizers of leadership
Substitutes for leadership

DISCUSSION QUESTIONS

1. Name a physical, intellectual, or personality trait that might be associated with effective leadership and defend your position. Then discuss a situation in which this trait might *not* be associated with effective leadership.

2. Discuss a case of emergent leadership that you have observed. Why did the person in question emerge as a leader? Did he or she fulfill the task role, the social-emotional role, or both?

3. Contrast the relative merits of consideration and initiating structure in the following leadership situations: running the daily operations of a branch bank; commanding an army unit under enemy fire; supervising a group of college students who are performing a hot, dirty, boring summer job. Use House's Path-Goal Theory to support your arguments.

4. Fred Fiedler argues that leader LPC is difficult to change and that situations should be "engineered" to fit the leader's LPC orientation. Suppose that a relationship-oriented (high LPC) person finds herself assigned to a situation with poor leader-member relations, an unstructured task, and weak

position power. What could she do to make the situation more favorable for her relationship-oriented leadership?

5. Describe a situation that would be ideal for having subordinates participate in a work-related decision. Discuss the subordinates, the problem, and the setting. Describe a situation in which participative decision making would be an especially unwise leadership strategy. Why is this so?

6. Discuss the pros and cons of the following statement: Even when a manager can make an adequate decision on his or her own, the manager should attempt to involve subordinates in the decision.

7. Distinguish between neutralizers of leadership and substitutes for leadership. Give an example of each.

8. Julio is an extremely experienced salesperson of sophisticated electronic equipment. He has an M.Sc. in electrical engineering and is on the road 11 months a year. He really enjoys his job, and he is extremely interested in the high commissions the job offers. Discuss Julio's situation from the perspective of neutralizers of and substitutes for the leadership of his sales manager.

9. What are charismatic individuals skilled at doing that gives them extraordinary influence over others?

10. Describe a leadership situation in which a highly charismatic transformational leader would probably *not* be the right person for the job.

EXPERIENTIAL EXERCISE
LEADERSHIP STYLE

Below are three cases in which a leader confronts a problem that requires him or her to make a decision. After reading each case, use your intuition to decide which of Vroom and Jago's five decision strategies (AI, AII, CI, CII, GII) the leader should use. Then reread each case and trace its characteristics through the decision tree shown in Exhibit 10.5. Did your intuitive answers differ from those that the decision tree analysis provides? If so, what factors led to the difference?

CASE I

You are general foreman in charge of a large gang laying an oil pipeline. It is now necessary to estimate your expected rate of progress in order to schedule material deliveries to the next field site.

You know the nature of the terrain you will be travelling and have the historical data needed to compute the mean and variance in the rate of speed over that type of terrain. Given these two variables it is a simple matter to calculate the earliest and latest times at which materials and support facilities will be needed at the next site. It is important that your estimate be reasonably accurate. Underestimates result in idle foremen and workers, and an overestimate results in tying up materials for a period of time before they are to be used.

Progress has been good and your five foremen and other members of the gang stand to receive substantial bonuses if the project is completed ahead of schedule.

CASE II

You are on the division manager's staff and work on a wide variety of problems of both administrative and technical nature. You have been given the assignment of developing a universal method to be used in each of the five plants in the division for manually reading equipment registers, recording the readings, and transmitting the scorings to a centralized information system. All plants are located in a relatively small geographical region.

Until now there has been a high error rate in the reading and/or transmittal of the data. Some locations have considerably higher error rates than others, and the methods used to record and transmit the data vary between plants. It is probable, therefore, that part of the error variance is a function of specific local conditions rather than anything else, and this will complicate the establishment of any system common to all plants. You have the information on error rates but no information on the local practices that generate these errors or on the local conditions that necessitate the different practices.

Everyone would benefit from an improvement in the quality of the data, as it is used in a number of important decisions. Your contacts with the plants are through the quality-control supervisors who are responsible for collecting the data. They are a conscientious group committed to doing their jobs well, but they are highly sensitive to interference on the part of higher management in their own operations. Any solution that does not receive the active support of the various plant supervisors is unlikely to reduce the error rate significantly.

CASE III

You are the head of a staff unit reporting to the vice-president of finance. He has asked you to provide a report on the firm's current portfolio including recommendations for changes in the selection criteria currently employed. Doubts have been raised about the efficiency of the existing system in the current market conditions, and there is considerable dissatisfaction with prevailing rates of return.

You plan to write the report, but at the moment you are quite perplexed about the approach to take. Your own specialty is the bond market, and it is clear to you that a detailed knowledge of the equity market, which you lack, would greatly enhance the value of the report. Fortunately, four members of your staff are specialists in different segments of the equity market. Together they possess a vast amount of knowledge about the intricacies of investment. However, they seldom agree on the best way to achieve anything when it comes to the stock market. While they are obviously conscientious as well as knowledgeable, they have major differences when it comes to investment philosophy and strategy.

You have six weeks before the report is due. You have already begun to familiarize yourself with the firm's current portfolio and have been provided by management with a specific set of constraints that any portfolio must satisfy. Your immediate problem is to come up with some alternatives to the firm's present practices and select the most promising for detailed analysis in your report.

Source of Cases: Vroom, V. H., & Yetton, P. W. (1973). *Leadership and decision-making*. Pittsburgh: University of Pittsburgh Press. © 1973 by University of Pittsburgh Press. Reprinted by permission.

CASE STUDY
CLEARVIEW INSTITUTE OF SCIENCE

Jonathan Leigh, a case writer from the Columbia Business School, met Professor Sam Morris of the Clearview Institute of Science on a flight from New York to Geneva. Morris was on his way to report to a special United

Nations committee on the development of alternative energy sources. In speaking to Leigh about Clearview, Morris seemed frustrated.

> We always had such a great reputation—we did excellent research and published in the most prestigious scientific journals. We are always invited to major scientific conferences and always chair some of the sessions. Last year our department was awarded a United Nations grant for solar energy development. We are using solar energy to grow algae as a cheap source of protein and carbohydrates. We began working on this project several months ago, but somehow nothing has worked out. I'm on my way to Geneva now to report to the committee, but what can I tell them?
>
> We have talented graduate students—we only accept the best. We also have an extremely skilled technical staff; and unlike other research institutes, each professor in our department has his or her own technician. Take my technician Saul Gardner. Even when I was working on the most complicated problems, I could count on him to carry out the daily experiments, and he learned to operate the equipment and report to me the next day. But now, everything is different. The technicians seem to have suddenly become incompetent, and the project is barely progressing.

The flight arrived before Leigh and Morris could discuss the problem; however, Leigh decided to spend more time at Clearview when he returned to New York.

BACKGROUND

Clearview is a world-famous institute of scientific research founded by James D. Clearview in 1948. He strongly believed in the promotion of scientific research for the benefit of mankind. It was his specific wish that each professor be granted the utmost academic freedom and that individual research be facilitated in every way.

A relatively small number of scientists and technicians were employed at Clearview in the early 1950s. The institute was organized as a single unit with a very informal structure.

Milt Irving was one of the first Ph.D. students to graduate from Clearview. Charming and brilliant, his advance was unprecedented. His frequent trips and personal contacts with outstanding members of the scientific community increased the institute's prestige. His name attracted many scientists, several of whom joined Clearview solely to collaborate with him. As time went by the institute expanded, ultimately requiring its division into departments. Irving was appointed head of biophysics.

Among those who joined Clearview because of Irving were Sam Morris and Jack Burton. Both proved to be excellent scientists and teachers who devoted most of their time to teaching in the graduate program. This activity did not interfere with their personal research because most of the laboratory work was performed by their technicians.

Impressed by Burton's and Morris's success, Irving decided to delegate to them full authority to manage and supervise their subordinates. Irving maintained his position as active head of the department but limited other responsibilities to his own graduate students and technicians.

In time, Clearview gained international fame. A national survey of scientific research topics revealed that Clearview's competitors had diversified by undertaking numerous applied research projects. A limited number of researchers at Clearview considered similarly diversifying their personal research interests but refrained from doing so mainly because it demanded a change in institutional policy and the restructuring of most existing departments.

The recent snowballing effect of the energy crisis made Irving reevaluate his approach. About one year ago, although initially hesitant, Irving decided to deviate from institutional policy; he applied for and was awarded the solar energy development grant.

The funds made available in the first year were impressive, although the terms of the grant were rigid. While the United Nations committee did not insist on controlling the spending and allocation of its grant, it did require payback of all funds not spent during the first year. Extension of the grant was subject to a review of the initial success of the project.

DEPARTMENT OF BIOPHYSICS

Walking into Irving's lab at 8:30 one morning, Jonathan Leigh was surprised to meet Ms. Smith, Irving's technician, preparing for an experiment.

> Leigh: Are all of you such early birds?
>
> Smith: No, only me! I come in around 7:00 and leave as soon as I finish. I've known Professor Irving since his first day as a graduate student here, twenty-five years ago! I work only for him. My hours are up to me, as long as I get the day's work done.

Ms. Smith's attitude reflects the strong position technicians enjoy at Clearview. Their union is very active, and firing a technician is unheard of. They receive tenure easily, and promotion is based on a seniority system. They are well paid, and many fringe benefits are provided by the local union. However, they do not receive rewards from their direct supervisors.

The scientific staff is comprised of graduate students, junior and senior scientists, and professors. Most graduate students leave the institute upon receiving their degrees.

The junior and senior scientists are promoted according to ability and performance. There are always a large number of applicants for junior staff positions even though their tenure rate is only 1 in 15. Because of this rate, the technicians are reluctant to work for the junior staff, since not only do they consider themselves superior but also they consider the juniors "temporary workers."

When Professor Irving arrived soon after 8:30, he told Leigh that he was very proud to have been awarded the grant. Despite his administrative load and his recent appointment as chairman of the board of directors, he was able to find sufficient time to spend in the laboratory. He loved the atmosphere and sometimes would work together with Ms. Smith. He relied fully upon Morris and Burton to carry out their share of the project. He did not believe in excessive interaction with those who were not his direct subordinates in the department; they were to report to Morris and Burton. The phone rang in Irving's office. When Irving hung up, he smiled and excused himself, explaining that an unexpected meeting of the board was to begin shortly.

Leigh's next stop was Morris's laboratory. Morris was still in Geneva, and Leigh found Gardner in Morris's recliner, reading the daily sports column. Leigh was not surprised by what he saw. He knew that the 10:00 A.M. coffee break was a well-established tradition at Clearview. The local union maintained a subsidized cafeteria that served mainly coffee and snacks. Each morning around 10:00 many of the technicians met in the relatively small lounge to exchange gossip and first-hand information on their research projects. A favorite topic for some time had been that some technicians had recently received a special bonus for their diligence during a recent project in the chemistry department.

The good news had raised the level of expectation among those employed in biophysics. They knew that working on the solar energy project would disrupt their established routine of the 10:00 o'clock break because they were expected to spend all day on the roof. However, they had confidence in their ability to perform well, and they had expected to receive a generous bonus in appreciation of their efforts. Their expectations had been disappointed, and technicians became hostile and lost all enthusiasm. Burton's and Morris's frequent absences from the laboratory only encouraged the technicians' indifference. Lacking supervision, they showed up and left whenever they pleased. Gardner spoke:

Ms. Smith told me you would be coming here. Let me show you our algae. We're growing them in containers on the roof. I find the whole thing rather stupid—last year our work was supposed to be free of traces of contamination, and now Morris is growing beasts on the roof! He must be out of his mind! I am really supposed to work all day on the roof, taking samples, etc., but it is actually Green who should be doing all this. He was appointed as my helper, but refuses to accept any orders from me. So for the time being he is doing nothing, and between you and me, neither am I. Morris never told us the real purpose of the whole project and never

explained to us our specific tasks. A few days ago I found Ms. Smith taking samples from our containers. She seemed to be doing similar work to what we think we are supposed to be doing. If so, let her at least help us. She always refuses, and I know for a fact that she is hiding and locking all her equipment when she goes home. She belongs to Irving, so to whom can we complain?

Morris never even shows up during the day. He has ordered me to leave the experimental results in his office, and in the morning I always find messages from him on my desk. Actually, even when Morris is in the lab he is hardly to be seen. If he thinks that I will be bullied around by the "baby" graduate students, he is in for a surprise. So, I am enjoying life, not working too hard, I am receiving my salary anyhow—I have tenure—who can fire me?

Gardner's monologue was interrupted by the entrance of Ms. White, Burton's technician.

White: Saul, please help us with the vacuum pump. It's just come back from the workshop but something went wrong again!

Gardner: Tell Burton to help you, we don't work for Burton's group. If you think that you can get away with monopolizing the lab you're mistaken. We all know that you double order from the warehouse, and nothing is left in stock when we get there. If you guys are so smart, you can surely fix a simple pump!

White: So that's the way you see things. OK, there's nothing left for me to say!

Later in the cafeteria Leigh found himself seated next to Sue Cooper, one of Morris's graduate students. She told Leigh:

It's not my business to interfere, but I know something is very wrong. I'm not personally involved with this project and all I know is what I see and hear day in and day out. This department has not had a routine staff meeting for months, everyone seems to be busy with the solar energy project, the way Irving wants to carry it out. One or another of the professors seems always to be out of town or even out of the country. None of the technicians seems to be motivated, and I don't blame them. Working on the roof, they have turned into the laughing stock of the whole building! They demand incentives and rewards for "hard labor." I tried to talk to them and to explain the importance of this project to the department and to the institute, but they will not pay attention to a female graduate student. When I discussed the matter with Morris, he told me not to interfere and stick to my own work. Personally, I feel that it would benefit both the department and the project if the whole department became equally involved. We should exchange information and help one another. The truth is that Burton and Morris have independently decided that the project was their baby. As for the graduate students, our work seems good enough for the professors to put their names on the papers we write, but our advice is never taken seriously.

Some weeks later Jonathan Leigh was talking to Morris, who had returned from Geneva. Morris said, "I'm very worried about the fate of this whole project. If we don't start coming up with results soon, our grant will not be extended. Something drastic has to be done immediately."

Source: Nadler, D. A., Tushman, M. L., & Hatvany, N. G. (1982). *Managing organizations: Readings and cases*. Boston: Little, Brown.

1. Does "leadership matter" on the solar energy project? Discuss any substitutes and neutralizers for leadership that currently face Irving, Morris, and Burton.

2. Use House's Path-Goal Theory to analyze the leadership situation confronting Irving, the head of the project. What leadership style does the theory suggest?

3. Use Fiedler's Contingency Theory to analyze the leadership situation confronting Irving. What leadership style does the theory suggest?

4. Run the solar energy project through the Vroom and Jago decision tree (Exhibit 10.5). What level of participation is indicated?

5. Discuss the merits of transformational or charismatic leadership in this setting.

6. Suppose that you are case writer Jonathan Leigh. What advice would you give to Dr. Irving?

AFTER READING CHAPTER 11 YOU SHOULD BE ABLE TO:

1 DEFINE COMMUNICATION AND EXPLAIN WHY COMMUNICATION BY THE STRICT CHAIN OF COMMAND IS OFTEN INEFFECTIVE.

2 DISCUSS BARRIERS TO EFFECTIVE SUPERIOR-SUBORDINATE COMMUNICATION.

3 EXPLAIN THE ORGANIZATIONAL GRAPEVINE AND DISCUSS ITS MAIN FEATURES.

4 REVIEW THE ROLE OF BOTH VERBAL AND NONVERBAL COMMUNICATION AT WORK.

5 DISCUSS HOW COMMUNICATION DIFFERS ACROSS CULTURES AND HOW IT IS INFLUENCED BY CULTURAL CONTEXT.

6 GENERATE SOME PERSONAL APPROACHES TO IMPROVING COMMUNICATION.

7 DISCUSS SOME ORGANIZATIONAL APPROACHES TO IMPROVING COMMUNICATION.

GROUPWARE ALLOWS MTV'S SALES FORCE TO KEEP ABREAST OF THE CHANGES IN THE FIELD AND REACT ACCORDINGLY.

CHAPTER 11

COMMUNICATION

GROUPWARE
AT MTV

Electronic mail is probably the simplest and most familiar form of groupware, in which notes are zapped across a network between two or more desktop PCs. More sophisticated groupware programs connect many people together at the same time, often functioning like a suite of electronic conference rooms where many conversations can take place at the same time. The programs can also collect these silent conversations and create an electronic transcript.

At MTV Networks, groupware became a new weapon for the affiliate sales force. When the Viacom Inc. unit was battling last summer against rival Turner Broadcasting System Inc.'s Cartoon Channel, trying to get cable operators to carry MTV's new Comedy Central network instead, salesmen in some areas were meeting unexpected resistance. Then a saleswoman in Chicago discovered that a cable system in her territory had been offered a special two-year, rock-bottom price by Cartoon Channel.

She typed this intelligence into a groupware network that tracks most day-to-day activity of the sales force. Others noticed that another salesman in Florida had also heard something about a new, more aggressive deal from the competition. "Suddenly it clicked; we'd figured out their game," says Kris Bagwell, the young MTV salesman who helped design the new network. Top MTV executives were told of the tactic and were able to counterattack by changing their own pricing and terms, saving several pending deals, according to Mr. Bagwell.

He says groupware gives management a better tool to follow what's going on in the field. "Let's say we need to know about every sales call last month on a Cox system where Nickelodeon was discussed," he says. "Or we need to know what people were hearing about Comedy Central's local ad sales in the Southeast last quarter. With a couple of mouse clicks, you can drill in and find what you need."

But some employees are leery of the idea that everyone knows what everyone else is doing. "It's a double-edged sword," says Mr. Bagwell, the MTV salesman. "It helps you do your job, and everyone can see if you're working hard and making sales. But if you aren't, that becomes obvious too. Your manager can see right away whether you're making three calls a day or eight."[1]

This excerpt from the *Wall Street Journal* illustrates the importance of good communication for organizational competitiveness. It also illustrates that the free flow of information has costs as well as opportunities!

In this chapter we shall explore these and other aspects of communication in organizations. First, we will define communication and present a model of the communication process and then illustrate the importance of communication. We will investigate superior-subordinate communication, the "grapevine," the verbal and nonverbal language of work, and cross-cultural communication. Finally, we will discuss personal and organizational means of improving communication.

WHAT IS COMMUNICATION?

Communication. The process by which information is exchanged between a sender and a receiver.

Communication is the process by which information is exchanged between a sender and a receiver. This seductively simple definition is broad enough to cover a wide variety of information exchanges. For example, the wall thermostat and the furnace in your house are constantly engaged in communication. The thermostat (sender) tells the furnace (receiver) how hot it should run. In turn, the furnace (sender) gives the thermostat (receiver) feedback about how hot it is running via the room temperature. This ongoing exchange of information contributes to your comfort.

The kind of communication we are concerned with in this chapter is *interpersonal* communication—the exchange of information between people. The most simple prototype for interpersonal communication is a one-on-one exchange between two individuals. Exhibit 11.1 presents a model of the interpersonal communication process and an example of a communication episode between a purchasing manager and her assistant. As you can see, the sender must *encode* his or her thoughts into some form that can be *transmitted* to the receiver. In this case, the manager has chosen to encode her

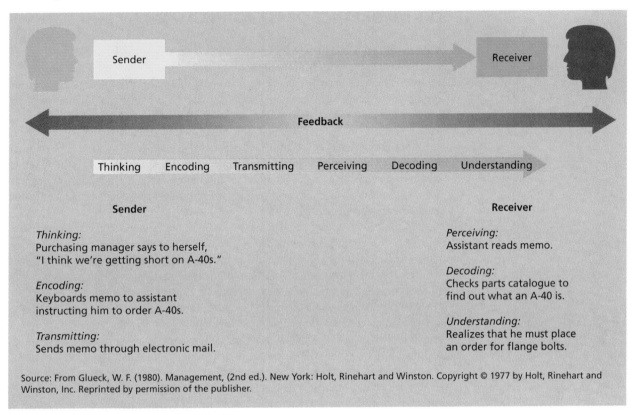

Sender

Receiver

Feedback

Thinking   Encoding   Transmitting   Perceiving   Decoding   Understanding

Sender

Thinking:
Purchasing manager says to herself,
"I think we're getting short on A-40s."

Encoding:
Keyboards memo to assistant
instructing him to order A-40s.

Transmitting:
Sends memo through electronic mail.

Receiver

Perceiving:
Assistant reads memo.

Decoding:
Checks parts catalogue to
find out what an A-40 is.

Understanding:
Realizes that he must place
an order for flange bolts.

Source: From Glueck, W. F. (1980). Management, (2nd ed.). New York: Holt, Rinehart and Winston. Copyright © 1977 by Holt, Rinehart and Winston, Inc. Reprinted by permission of the publisher.

EXHIBIT 11.1
A model of the communication process and an example.

thoughts in writing and transmit them via electronic mail. Alternatively, the manager could have encoded her thoughts in speech and transmitted them via a tape recording or face-to-face. The assistant, as a receiver, must *perceive* the message and accurately decode it to achieve accurate understanding. In this case, the assistant uses a parts catalog to decode the meaning of an "A–40." To provide *feedback*, the assistant might send the manager a copy of the order form for the flange bolts. Such feedback involves yet another communication episode that tells the original sender that her assistant received and understood the message.

This simple communication model is valuable because it points out the complexity of the communication process and demonstrates a number of points at which errors can occur. Such errors lead to a lack of correspondence between the sender's initial thoughts and the receiver's understanding of the intended message. A slip of the finger on the keyboard can lead to improper encoding. A poor electronic mail system can lead to ineffective transmission. An outdated parts catalog can result in inaccurate decoding. As you might imagine, encoding and decoding may be prone to even more error when the message is inherently ambiguous or emotional. This is because the two parties may have very different perceptions of the "facts" at hand.

Effective communication occurs when the right people receive the right information in a timely manner. Violating any of these three conditions results in a communication episode that is ineffective. The MTV story that began the chapter illustrated effective communication.

Effective communication. The right people receive the right information in a timely manner.

THE IMPORTANCE OF COMMUNICATION

A recent large-scale survey by the Families and Work Institute found that the number one factor in influencing respondents' decision to take a job with their current employer was open communication.[2] Global competition, downsizing, and an increased pace of organizational change have all placed a premium on good organizational communication, and this is no doubt reflected in the survey results.

The importance of communication is also revealed by analyses of how organizational members spend their time at work. Careful studies of production workers indicate that they participate in between 16 and 46 communication episodes per hour.[3] Even the low figure of 16 episodes works out to one episode every four minutes.

As we move up the organization's hierarchy, it is evident that more and more time is spent communicating. For first-level supervisors of production jobs, various studies show that 20 to 50 percent of the boss's time at work is spent in verbal communication. When communication through paperwork is added, these figures increase to between 29 and 64 percent.[4]

Moving to the levels of middle and upper management, we find that from 66 to 89 percent of managers' time is spent in verbal (face-to-face meetings and telephone) communication.[5] Since these figures exclude other forms of communication (such as reading and writing letters, memos, and reports), it is obvious that the content of many managerial jobs is composed almost exclusively of communication tasks. For example, Honda's president gave 99 speeches to employees in one year emphasizing the company's need to excel in the race for lower auto exhaust emissions![6]

Now that we have established the critical importance of organizational communication, let's examine some of its basic characteristics.

BASICS OF ORGANIZATIONAL COMMUNICATION

Let's consider a few basic issues about organization communication.

Communication by Strict Chain of Command

Chain of command. Lines of authority and formal reporting relationships.

The lines on an organizational chart represent lines of authority and reporting relationships. For example, a vice-president has authority over the plant manager, who has authority over the production supervisors. Conversely, production workers report to their supervisors, who report to the plant manager, and so on. In theory, organizational communication could stick to this strict **chain of command.** Under this system, three necessary forms of communication can be accomplished.

Downward communication. Information that flows from the top of the organization toward the bottom.

Downward communication flows from the top of the organization toward the bottom. For example, a vice-president of production might instruct a plant manager to gear up for manufacturing a new product. In turn, the plant manager would provide specifics to supervisors, who would instruct the production workers accordingly.

Upward communication. Information that flows from the bottom of the organization toward the top.

Upward communication flows from the bottom of the organization toward the top. For instance, a research engineer might conceive a new plastic formula with unique properties. She might then pass this on to the research and development manager, who would then inform the relevant vice-president.

Horizontal communication occurs between departments or functional units, usually as a means of coordinating effort. Within a strict chain of command, such communication would flow up to and then down from a *common superior*. For example, suppose a salesperson gets an idea for a new product from a customer. To get this idea to the research staff, it would have to be transmitted up to and down from the vice-presidents of marketing and research, the common superiors for these departments.

Clearly, a lot of organizational communication does follow the formal lines of authority shown on organizational charts. This is especially true for the examples of upward and downward communication given above—directives and instructions usually pass downward through the chain of command, and ideas and suggestions pass upward. However, the reality of organizational communication shows that the formal chain of command is an incomplete and sometimes ineffective path of communication.

Deficiencies in the Chain of Command

Managers recognize that sticking strictly to the chain of command is often ineffective.

Informal Communication.   The chain of command obviously fails to consider *informal* communication between members. In previous chapters we discussed how informal interaction helps people accomplish their jobs more effectively. In the vignette that began the chapter, the intelligence that the MTV saleswoman typed into the groupware system was clearly informal communication. Of course, not all informal communication benefits the organization. An informal grapevine might spread unsavory, inaccurate rumors across the organization.

Filtering.   Getting the right information to the right people is often inhibited by filtering. **Filtering** is the tendency for a message to be watered down or stopped altogether at some point during transmission, and it is something of a double-edged sword. On one hand, employees are *supposed* to filter information. For example, production workers are not expected to inform their bosses of every trivial event that occurs on the job. Similarly, vice-presidents are not expected to communicate every detail of the management of the company clear to the shop floor. On the other side of the coin, overzealous filtering will preclude the right people from getting the right information, and the organization will suffer accordingly. Upward filtering often occurs because subordinates are afraid that their boss will use the information against them. Downward filtering is often due to time pressures or simple lack of attention to detail, but more sinister motives may be at work. As the old saying goes, "information is power," and some managers filter downward communications to maintain an edge on their subordinates. For example, a manager who feels that an up-and-coming subordinate could be promoted over her might filter crucial information to make the subordinate look bad at a staff meeting.

Obviously, the potential for filtering increases with the number of links in the communication chain. For this reason, organizations establish channels in addition to those revealed in the formal chain of command. For instance, many managers establish an **open door policy** in which any organizational member below them can communicate directly without going through the chain.[7] Such

Horizontal communication. Information that flows between departments or functional units, usually as a means of coordinating effort.

Filtering. The tendency for a message to be watered down or stopped during transmission.

Open door policy. The opportunity for employees to communicate directly with a manager without going through the chain of command.

a policy should decrease the upward filtering of sensitive information if subordinates trust the system. To prevent downward filtering, many organizations attempt to communicate directly with potential receivers, bypassing the chain of command. For example, the president of a company might use the public address system to accurately inform employees about intended layoffs. Research has shown that certain types of information are more likely to be filtered than are others, thus indicating the selective need for alternative channels of communication. For example, information that is concerned directly with production might pass down through the hierarchy relatively intact, while that concerned with nonproduction matters (such as a change in the parking regulations) might be subjected to considerable filtering.[8]

Slowness.   Even when the chain of command transmits information faithfully, it can be painfully slow. Imagine if the observant MTV salesperson had sent her intelligence up to her sales manager for consideration. There is simply no guarantee that the manager would have acted quickly to distribute the information to her peers. The chain of command can be even slower for horizontal communication between departments, and it is not a good mechanism for reacting quickly to customer problems. Cross-functional teams and employee empowerment, concepts we introduced earlier in the text, have been used to improve communication in these areas by short-circuiting the chain of command.

In summary, informal communication and the recognition of filtering and time constraints guarantee that organizations will develop channels of communication beyond the strict chain of command.

SUPERIOR-SUBORDINATE COMMUNICATION

Superior-subordinate communication consists of the one-to-one exchange of information between a boss and a subordinate. As such, it represents a key element in upward and downward communication in organizations. Ideally, such exchange should enable the boss to instruct the subordinate in proper task performance, clarify reward contingencies, and provide social-emotional support. In addition, it should permit the subordinate to ask questions about his or her work role and make suggestions that might further the goals of the company or institution.

A survey of 32,000 employees in the United States and Canada asked them to rank their preferred and current sources of organizational information. As Exhibit 11.2 illustrates, the immediate supervisor was the actual source *and* the preferred source of most information.[9] In addition, perceptions that supervisors are good communicators tend to be correlated positively with organizational performance.[10] Thus, any organization would wish to establish good superior-subordinate communication.

How Good Is Superior-Subordinate Communication?

The extent to which superiors and subordinates agree about work-related matters and are sensitive to each other's point of view is one index of good communication. Although the parties might "agree to disagree" about certain

Preferred Ranking	Sources of Information	Current Ranking
1	My immediate supervisor	1
2	Small group meetings	4
3	Top executives	11
4	Employee handbook/other brochures	3
5	Local employee publication	8
6	Orientation program	12
7	Organization-wide employee publication	6
8	Annual state-of-the-business report	7
9	Bulletin boards	5
10	Upward communication program	14
11	The union	9
12	Mass meetings	10
13	Audiovisual programs	15
14	Mass media	13
15	The grapevine	2

Source: Foltz, R. G. (1985). Communication in contemporary organizations. In Reuss, C. & Silvis, D. (Eds), *Inside organizational communication* (2nd ed.). New York: Longman, p. 10. Copyright © 1985 by Longman Publishing Group. Reprinted with permission of Longman Publishing Group.

EXHIBIT 11.2
Preferred and current sources of information about organizational issues.

matters, extreme and persistent perceptual differences are problematic. Research indicates that superiors and subordinates often differ in their perceptions of the following issues:

- how subordinates should and do allocate time;
- how long it takes to learn a job;
- the importance subordinates attach to pay;
- the amount of authority the subordinate has;
- the subordinate's skills and abilities;
- the subordinate's performance and obstacles to good performance;
- the superior's leadership style.[11]

Perceptual differences like this suggest a lack of openness in communication, which might contribute to much role conflict and ambiguity, especially on the part of subordinates. In addition, a lack of openness in communication reduces subordinate job satisfaction.[12]

Barriers to Effective Superior-Subordinate Communication

What causes communication problems between superiors and subordinates? In addition to basic differences in personality (Chapter 3) and perception (Chapter 4), the following factors have been implicated.

Conflicting Role Demands. In the previous chapter we noted that the leadership role requires superiors to attend to both task and social-emotional functions. That is, the boss must simultaneously direct and control the subordinate's work *and* be attentive to the emotional needs and desires of the subordinate. Many superiors have difficulties balancing these two role demands. For example, consider the following memo from a sales manager to one of the company's younger sales representatives:

> I would like to congratulate you on being named Sales Rep of the Month for March. You can be very proud of this achievement. I now look forward to your increased contribution to our sales efforts, and I hope you can begin to bring some new accounts into the company. After all, new accounts are the key to our success.

In congratulating the young sales rep and in suggesting that he increase his performance in the future, the manager tries to take care of social-emotional business and task business in one memo. Unfortunately, the sales rep might be greatly offended by this communication episode, feeling that it slights his achievement and implies that he has not been pulling his weight in the company. In this case, two separate communiques, one dealing with congratulations and the other with the performance directive, would probably be more effective.

Mum effect. The tendency to avoid communicating unfavorable news to others.

The Mum Effect.   Another factor inhibiting effective superior-subordinate communication is the **mum effect.** This distinctive term refers to the tendency to avoid communicating unfavorable news to others.[13] Often, people would rather "keep mum" than convey bad news that might provoke negative reactions on the part of the receiver. For example, physicians are often reluctant to inform patients or their families of the existence of terminal illness.

As the example involving the physician illustrates, the sender need not be *responsible* for the bad news in order for the mum effect to occur. For instance, a structural engineer might be reluctant to tell her boss that there are cracks in the foundation of a building, even though a subcontractor was responsible for the faulty work. It should be obvious, though, that the mum effect is probably even more likely when the sender *is* responsible for the bad news. For example, the nurse who mistakenly administers an incorrect drug dosage might be very reluctant to inform the head nurse of her error. Subordinates with strong aspirations for upward mobility are especially likely to encounter communication difficulties with their bosses.[14] This might be due in part to the mum effect—employees who desire to impress their bosses to achieve a promotion have strong motives to withhold bad news.[15]

The mum effect does not apply only to subordinates. The boss might be reluctant to transmit bad news downward. In my research in one organization, I found that subordinates who had good performance ratings were more likely to be informed of those ratings than subordinates who had bad ratings. Managers evidently avoided communicating bad news for which they were partly responsible, since they themselves had done the performance ratings. Given this, it is not surprising that managers and their subordinates often differ in their perceptions of subordinate performance.[16]

Status Effects.   A third factor that might inhibit superior-subordinate communication is the tendency for superiors to *devalue* communication with their subordinates. In Chapter 8 we pointed out that the status of group members affects communication patterns—people reveal a clear desire to communicate with people of a similar or higher status, rather than those of a lower status. From this, it follows that necessary communications with people of lower status, such as one's subordinates, might be viewed negatively. In an interesting study designed to test this proposal, managers were asked to record every communication episode that they engaged in during a week at work.[17] In addition to specifying the method of communication and identifying the other party, they were asked to report their attitude toward each episode. The results indicated a clear tendency for the managers to react more favorably to episodes with higher-status organizational members than to those involving their subordinates. Subordinates doubtless catch on to such negative reactions and begin to withhold information, a situation that contributes to poor communication.

As we also noted in Chapter 8, many contemporary organizations have downplayed status differences, in part to foster better communication among managers and employees.

Time.   A final factor that might lead to poor superior-subordinate communication is the simple constraint of time. This is especially true at lower organizational levels. You will recall that we concluded that first-level supervisors spend between 20 and 50 percent of their working time in verbal communication. Furthermore, these studies reveal that most of this time is spent communicating with subordinates. Now, on the face of it, this seems pretty generous—subordinates may receive up to 50 percent of the boss's time on the job. However, there is a catch here. Remember that many first-level supervisors have more than 20 subordinates reporting to them. Thus, simple division indicates that *each* subordinate might receive less than one percent of the boss's total time on the job each day. Indeed, studies have indicated that superior-subordinate communication on production jobs averages only *four minutes* a day![18] Given this whole string of logic, it's no wonder that managers perceive conversations with subordinates to be more frequent than the subordinates do.[19]

Before continuing, pause and consider the impact of telecommuting on informal communication and superior-subordinate communication. See the *You Be the Manager* feature.

THE GRAPEVINE

Just inside the gate of a steel mill where I used to work there was a large sign that read "X days without a major accident." The sign was revised each day to impress upon the work force the importance of safe working practices. A zero posted on the sign caught one's attention immediately, since this meant that a serious accident or fatality had just occurred. Seeing a zero upon entering the mill, workers seldom took more than five minutes to find someone who knew the details. While the victim's name might be unknown, the location and nature of the accident were always accurate, even though the mill was very large and the accident had often occurred on the previous shift. How did this information get around so quickly? It traveled through the "grapevine."

Characteristics of the Grapevine

The **grapevine** is the informal communication network that exists in any organization. As such, the grapevine often cuts across formal lines of communication that are recognized by management. Observation suggests several distinguishing features of grapevine systems:

- We generally think of the grapevine as communicating information by word of mouth. However, written notes, electronic mail, and fax

Grapevine. An organization's informal communication network.

TELECOMMUTING AT PACIFIC BELL

YOU BE THE Manager

The large telecommunications company Pacific Bell is based in California. In recent years, the company has gradually become increasingly interested in the concept of telecommuting. By telecommuting, employees are able to work at home but stay in touch with their offices via the computer network, voice mail, and electronic messages.

The possibilities of telecommuting were first called to Pacific Bell's attention during the Los Angeles Olympics, when it was adopted as a temporary measure to avoid the horrendous automotive gridlock that was expected when games visitors were added to the city's already clogged freeways. Shortly thereafter, Pacific Bell implemented a pilot project to examine telecommuting, using 100 volunteer managers. On hearing about the project, 400 other managers developed informal arrangements with their bosses to begin telecommuting. Necessity was added to popularity when a large earthquake struck the San Francisco area in fall of 1989. With the Bay Bridge damaged, leading to impossibly long commutes, the value of telecommuting in times of emergency was obvious.

During this period, Pacific Bell realized that it had to get a clear fix on the consequences of telecommuting. Thus, it conducted a survey of managers' opinions. Also, it realized that it had to develop a company policy concerning telecommuting.

Considering its implications for organization communication, what are *your* views about telecommuting?

1. What are the pros and cons of telecommuting?
2. What are some policies you would put in place concerning telecommuting?

To find out what Pacific Bell's survey showed and some details of its telecommuting policy, see *The Manager's Notebook* at the end of the chapter.

> THERE ARE BOTH POSITIVE AND NEGATIVE ASPECTS TO TELECOMMUTING, AS PACIFIC BELL HAS LEARNED.

Source: Adapted from Bailey, D. S., & Foley, J. (1990, August). Pacific Bell works long distance. *HRMagazine*, 50–52.

---

massages can contribute to the transmission of information (see the cartoon). For example, a fax operator in the New York office might tell the Zurich office that the chairman's wife just had a baby.

- Organizations often have several grapevine systems, some of which may be loosely coordinated. For instance, a secretary who is part of the "office grapevine" might communicate information to a mail carrier, who passes it on to the "warehouse grapevine."

- The grapevine may transmit information relevant to the performance of the organization as well as personal gossip.[20] Many times, it is difficult to distinguish between the two: "You won't *believe* who just got fired!"

How accurate is the grapevine? One expert concludes that at least 75 percent of the noncontroversial organizationally related information carried by the grapevine is correct.[21] Personal information and emotionally charged information are most likely to be distorted.

"YOU WOULDN'T WANT TO PUT ANY CLASSIFIED MATERIAL INTO THIS MODEL — IT HAS A GOSSIPING PROGRAM BUILT INTO IT."

Source: *Current Contents*, July 13, 1992, Vol. 24, No. 28, p. 6.

Grapevine information does not run through organizations in a neat chain in which person A tells only person B who tells only person C. Neither does it sweep across the organization like a tidal wave, with each sender telling six or seven others, who each in turn transmit the information to six or seven *other* members. Rather, only a proportion of those who receive grapevine news pass it on, with the net effect that more "know" than "tell."[22]

Who Participates in the Grapevine?

Just who is likely to tell? That is, who is likely to be a transmitter of grapevine information? Personality characteristics may play a role. For instance, extroverts might be more likely to pass on information than introverts. Similarly, those who lack self-esteem might pass on information that gives them a personal advantage.

The nature of the information might also influence who chooses to pass it on. In a hospital, the news that a doctor has obtained a substantial cancer research grant might follow a very different path from news involving his affair with a nurse!

Finally, it is obvious that the *physical* location of organizational members is related to their opportunity to both receive and transmit news via the "vine." Occupants of work stations that receive a lot of traffic are good candidates to be grapevine transmitters. A warm control room in a cold plant or an air-conditioned computer room in a sweltering factory might provide their occupants with a steady stream of potential receivers for juicy information. On the other side of the coin, jobs that require movement throughout the organization also give their holders much opportunity to serve as grapevine transmitters. Mail carriers and maintenance personnel are good examples.

Pros and Cons of the Grapevine

Is the grapevine desirable from the organization's point of view or not? For one thing, it can keep employees informed about important organizational matters such as job security. In some organizations, management is so notoriously lax at this that the grapevine is a regular substitute for formal communication. (As shown in Exhibit 11.2, the grapevine is perceived as the second most common but least preferred source of information!) The grapevine can also provide a test of employee reactions to proposed changes without making formal commitments. Managers have been known to "leak" ideas (such as a change to a four-day workweek) to the grapevine in order to probe their potential acceptance. Finally, participation in the grapevine can add a little interest and diversion to the work setting.

Rumor. An unverified belief that is in general circulation.

The grapevine can become a real problem for the organization when it becomes a constant pipeline for rumors. A **rumor** is an unverified belief that is in general circulation.[23] The key word here is *unverified*—although it is possible for a rumor to be true, it is not likely to *remain* true as it runs through the grapevine. Because people can't verify the information as accurate, rumors are susceptible to severe distortion as they are passed from person to person.

The distortion of rumors can take two forms. Some rumors seem to get longer and more complex as each sender adds his or her "two cents' worth." Other rumors are simplified through retelling, enhancing ease of communication. When this occurs, unfamiliar, difficult-to-remember details will usually be omitted, while interesting, dynamic details will be embellished. For example, a rumor that begins as: "Paul Jones was laid off because of the installation of that new automated casting machine. They think he'll be back on another job soon," may end up as: "Word is that automation will cost a lot of jobs around here. Some guys are already gone."

Rumors seem to spread fastest and farthest when the information is especially ambiguous, when the content of the rumor is important to those involved, when the rumor seems credible, and when the recipient is anxious.[24] Thus, the rumor about Paul Jones would probably circulate most widely among production workers rather than office personnel, and it would probably be more potent if the economic climate of the community was bad.

Increasingly difficult global competition, staff reductions, and restructuring have placed a premium on rumor control. At the same time, organizations should avoid the tendency to be mum about giving bad news. Federal Express used its own TV network to assure U.S. employees that their jobs were secure when it curtailed its European package delivery operations.

THE VERBAL LANGUAGE OF WORK

A friend of mine just moved into a new neighborhood. In casual conversation with a neighbor, he mentioned that he was "writing a book on OB." She replied with some enthusiasm, "Oh, that's great. My husband's in obstetrics too!" My friend, of course, is a management professor who was writing an organizational behavior book. The neighbor's husband was a physician who specialized in delivering babies.

Every student knows what it means to do a little "cramming" in the "caf" before an exam. Although this phrase might sound vaguely obscene to the uninitiated listener, it reveals how circumstances shape our language and how we often take this shaping for granted. In many jobs, occupations, and organizations we see the development of a specialized language or **jargon** that associates use to communicate with each other. Thus, OB means organizational behavior to management professors and obstetrics to physicians.

Jargon. Specialized language used by job holders or members of particular occupations or organizations.

Dr. Rosabeth Moss Kanter, in studying a large corporation, discovered its attempt to foster COMVOC, or "common vocabulary," among its managers.[25] Here, the goal was to facilitate communication among employees who were often geographically separated, unknown to each other, and "meeting" impersonally through telex or memo. COMVOC provided a common basis for interaction among virtual strangers. In addition, managers developed their own informal supplements to COMVOC. Upward mobility, an especially important topic in the corporation, was reflected in multiple labels for the same concept:

Fast trackers	One performers
High fliers	Boy (girl) wonders
Superstars	Water walkers

While jargon is an efficient means of communicating with peers and provides a touch of status to those who have mastered it, it can also serve as a *barrier* to communicating with others. For example, local jargon might serve as a barrier to clear communication between departments such as sales and engineering. New organizational members often find the use of jargon especially intimidating and confusing. For instance, consider the fledgling computer scientist who found himself assigned to a project group to develop a new computer:

> A *canard* was anything false, usually a wrongheaded notion entertained by some other group or company; things could be done in ways that created *no muss, no fuss,* that were *quick and dirty,* that were *clean. Fundamentals* were the source of all right thinking, and weighty sentences often began with the adverb *fundamentally,* while *realistically* prefaced many flights of fancy. There was talk of *wars, shootouts, hired guns* and people who *shot from the hip.* The *win* was the object of all this sport and the *big win* was something that could be achieved by *maximizing* the smaller one.[26]

A second serious problem with the use of jargon is the communication barrier that it presents to those *outside* of the organization or profession. Consider the language of the corporate takeover, with its greenmail, poison pills, and white knights! Kanter, the researcher who studied COMVOC in a large corporation, found that wives of male executives could generate a total of 103 unfamiliar terms and phrases that their husbands used in relation to work! Such a situation might contribute to a poor understanding of what the spouse does at work and how work can make such heavy demands on family life.

THE NONVERBAL LANGUAGE OF WORK

Have you ever come away from a conversation having heard one thing yet believing the opposite of what was said? Professors frequently hear students say that they understand a concept but somehow know that they don't.

Nonverbal communication.
The transmission of messages by some medium other than speech or writing.

Students often hear professors say, "Come up to my office any time," but somehow know that they don't mean it. How can we account for these messages that we receive in spite of the words we hear? The answer is often nonverbal communication.

Nonverbal communication refers to the transmission of messages by some medium other than speech or writing. As indicated above, nonverbal messages can be very powerful in that they often convey "the real stuff" while words serve as a smoke screen. Raised eyebrows, an emphatic shrug, or an abrupt departure can communicate a lot of information with great economy. The minutes of dramatic meetings (or even verbatim transcripts) can make for extremely boring reading because they are stripped of nonverbal cues. These examples involve the transmission of information by so-called body language. Below we consider body language and the manipulation of objects as major forms of nonverbal communication.

Body Language

Body language. Nonverbal communication by means of a sender's bodily motions, facial expressions, or physical location.

Body language is nonverbal communication that occurs by means of the sender's bodily motions and facial expressions or the sender's physical location in relation to the receiver.[27] Although we can communicate a variety of information via body language, two important messages are the extent to which the sender likes and is interested in the receiver and the sender's views concerning the relative status of the sender and the receiver.

In general, senders communicate liking and interest in the receiver when they

- position themselves physically close to the receiver;
- touch the receiver during the interaction;
- maintain eye contact with the receiver;
- lean forward during the interaction;
- direct the torso toward the receiver.[28]

As you can see, each of these behaviors demonstrates that the sender has genuine consideration for the receiver's point of view.

Senders who feel themselves to be of higher status than the receiver act more *relaxed* than those who perceive themselves to be of lower status. Relaxation is demonstrated by

- the casual, asymmetrical placement of arms and legs;
- a reclining, nonerect seating position;
- a lack of fidgeting and nervous activity.[29]

In other words, the greater the difference in relaxation between two parties, the more they communicate a status differential to each other.

People often attempt to use nonverbal behavior to communicate with others, just like they use verbal behavior. This use could include showing our true feelings, "editing" our feelings, or trying to actively deceive others. It is difficult to regulate nonverbal behavior when we are feeling very strong emotions. However, people are otherwise pretty good at nonverbal "posing," such as looking relaxed when they are not. On the other hand, observers also show some capacity to detect such posing.[30]

As we indicated earlier, when a contradiction exists between verbal behavior and body language, we tend to rely more heavily upon the information transmitted via body language. For example, the boss who claims to be interested in a subordinate's problem while positioning herself across the room, failing to maintain eye contact, and orienting her body away from the subordinate will doubtless signal a true lack of interest.

One area in which research shows that body language has an impact is on the outcome of employment interview decisions. Employment interviewers are usually faced with applicants who are motivated to make a good verbal impression. Thus, in accord with the idea that "the body doesn't lie," interviewers might consciously or unconsciously turn their attention to nonverbal cues on the assumption that they are less likely to be censored than verbal cues. Nonverbal behaviors such as smiling, gesturing, and maintaining eye contact have a favorable impact on interviewers when they are not overdone.[31] However, it is unlikely that such body language can overcome bad credentials or poor verbal performance.[32] Rather, increased body language might give the edge to applicants who are otherwise equally well qualified. Remember, in an employment interview, it's not just what you say, but also what you do!

Props, Artifacts, and Costumes

In addition to the use of body language, nonverbal communication can also occur through the use of various objects such as props, artifacts, and costumes.

Office Decor.   Consider the manner in which people decorate and arrange their offices. Does this tell visitors anything about the occupant? Does it communicate any useful information? One observer thinks so.

The decor and arrangement of furniture in a professor's office convey nonverbal information to students.

The more a person does influence his own surroundings, however, through decoration, personal artifacts, rearrangement, bringing in his own furniture, and the like, the more data he provides about who he is. A visitor can then get information fairly quickly about similarities and differences between himself and the occupant of the place. This can help in establishing a new relationship, since it provides more data about what realistic expectations the visitor may have of the occupant, and it may stimulate the visitor to disclose more information about himself than he would if they were in some anonymous place, starting from zero information.[33]

Does careful research confirm these observations that the decor and arrangement of offices transmit nonverbal information? The answer is yes. One typical study found that students would feel more welcome and comfortable in professors' offices when the office was (1) tidy, (2) decorated with posters and plants, and (3) the desk was against the wall instead of between the student and the professor.[34] A neat office evidently signaled that the prof was well organized and had time to talk to them. Perhaps personal decoration signaled, "I'm human." When the desk was against the wall, there wasn't a tangible barrier between the parties. Other research has shown that people who are more outgoing and internally controlled arrange their desks and visitors' chairs in an open and inviting manner.[35] Thus, it appears that visitor responses to variations in office decor have some validity.

Does Clothing Communicate?   "Wardrobe engineer" John T. Molloy is convinced that the clothing organizational members wear sends clear signals about their competence, seriousness, and promotability. That is, receivers unconsciously attach certain stereotyped meanings to various clothing and then treat the wearer accordingly. For example, Molloy insists that a black raincoat is the kiss of death for an aspiring male executive. He claims that black raincoats signal "lower-middle class," while beige raincoats lead to "executive" treatment both inside and outside of the firm. For the same reason, Molloy strongly vetoes sweaters for women executives. Molloy stresses that proper clothing will not make up for a lack of ambition, intelligence, and savvy. Rather, he argues that the wrong clothing will prevent others from detecting these qualities. To this end, he prescribes detailed "business uniforms," the men's built around a conservative suit and the women's around a skirted suit and blouse.[36] The rise in the number of image consultants who help aspiring executives "dress for success" testifies to the popularity of such thinking.

Research reveals that clothing does indeed communicate.[37] Even at the ages of 10 to 12, children associate various brand names of jeans with different personality characteristics of the wearer! Such effects persist in adulthood. Researchers' simulations have shown that more masculinely dressed and groomed women are more likely to be selected for executive jobs. However, one study shows that there might be a point at which women's dress becomes "too masculine" and thus damages their prospects.[38] Observers note that women's clothing styles have been of special research interest because there is less of a consensus about just how female executives should dress.

If clothing does indeed communicate, it might do so in part because of the impact it has on the wearer's own self-image. Proper clothing might enhance self-esteem and self-confidence to a noticeable degree. One study contrived to have some student job applicants appear for an interview in street clothes, while others had time to dress in more appropriate formal interview gear. Those who wore more formal clothes felt that they had made a better impression on the interviewer. They also asked for a starting salary that was $4,000 higher than the job seekers who wore street clothes![39]

CROSS-CULTURAL COMMUNICATION

Consider a commonplace exchange in the world of international business:

> A Japanese businessman wants to tell his Norwegian client that he is uninterested in a particular sale. To be polite, the Japanese says, "That will be very difficult." The Norwegian interprets the statement to mean that there are still unresolved problems, not that the deal is off. He responds by asking how his company can help solve the problems. The Japanese, believing he has sent the message that there will be no sale, is mystified by the response.[40]

Obviously, ineffective communication has occurred between our international businesspeople, since the Norwegian has not received the right information about the (non)sale. From the Norwegian's point of view, the Japanese has not encoded his message in a clear manner. The Japanese, on the other hand, might criticize the weak decoding skills of his Scandinavian client. Thus, we see that problems in communication across cultures go right to the heart of the communication model that we studied at the beginning of the chapter.

In Chapter 5 we learned that various societies differ in their underlying value systems. In turn, these differences lead to divergent attitudes about a whole host of matters ranging from what it means to be on time for a meeting to how to say "no" to a business deal (as illustrated above). In Chapter 5 we also noted that a surprising number of managers do not work out well in international assignments. Many of these failures stem from problems in cross-cultural communication. Let's examine some important dimensions of such communication.

Language Differences

Communication is generally better between individuals or groups that share similar cultural values. This is all the more so when they share a common language. Thus, despite acknowledged differences in terminology ("lift" versus "elevator," "petrol" versus "gasoline"), language should not be a communication barrier for the American executive who is posted to a British subsidiary. Despite this generality, the role of language in communication involves some subtle ironies. For example, a common language can sometimes cause visitors to misunderstand or be surprised by legitimate cultural differences because they get lulled into complacency. Boarding a Qantas Airlines flight in Australia, I was attempting to pick up a magazine from a rack in the 747 when I was admonished by a male steward with the sharp words "First class, mate." I grinned sheepishly and headed back to my tourist class seat without the magazine. Wise to the ways of Australia, I was not offended by this display of brash informality. However, a less familiar North American, assuming that "They speak English, they're just like us," might have been less forgiving, attributing the steward's behavior to a rude personality rather than national style. By the same token, the steward would be surprised to learn that someone might be offended by his words.

As the Qantas example indicates, speaking the same language is no guarantee of perfect communication. In fact, the Norwegian and Japanese businesspeople described above might have negotiated in a common language, such as English. Even then, the Norwegian didn't get the message. Speaking generally, however, learning a second language should facilitate cross-cultural communication. This is especially true when the second-language facility provides extra insight into the "communication style" of the other culture. Thus, the Norwegian would profit from understanding that the Japanese have sixteen subtle ways to say no, even if he couldn't understand the language perfectly.[41] Even though Americans are notoriously adverse to second-language learning, many executives seem to be getting the message in the face of the increasing globalization of business. Although the language of international business is surely gravitating toward English, learning the second language should provide better insight into the nuances of a business partner's culture.

Nonverbal Communication Across Cultures

From our earlier discussion of nonverbal communication, you might be tempted to assume that it would hold up better than verbal communication across cultures. While there are some similarities across cultures in nonverbal communication, there are also many differences. Here are a few examples.

- *Facial expressions.* People are very good at decoding basic, simple emotions in facial expressions, even across cultures. Americans, Japanese, and members of primitive New Guinea tribes can accurately detect anger, surprise, fear, and sadness in the same set of facial photographs.[42] Thus, paying particular attention to the face in cross-cultural encounters will often yield communication dividends. However, this doesn't always work because some cultures (such as that of Japan) frown upon the display of negative facial expressions, no doubt prompting the "inscrutable" label.

- *Gestures.* Except for literal mimicry ("I need food," "Sign here"), gestures do not translate well across cultures. This is because they involve symbolism that isn't shared. Most amusing are those cases in which the same gesture has different meanings across cultures:

  In the United States a raised thumb is used as a signal of approval or approbation, the "thumbs up" signal, but in Greece it is employed as an insult, often being associated with the expression "katsa pano" or "sit on this." Another example is the ring sign, performed by bringing the tips of the thumb and finger together so that they form a circle. For most English-speaking people it means O.K. and is in fact known as the "O.K. gesture." But in some sections of France the ring means zero or worthless. In English-speaking countries disagreement is signaled by shaking the head, but in Greece and southern Italy the head-toss is employed to signify "no."[43]

- *Gaze.* There are considerable cross-cultural differences in the extent to which it is considered suitable to look others directly in the eye. Latin Americans and Arabs favor an extended gaze, while Europeans do not.

In many parts of the Orient, avoiding eye contact is a means of showing respect. In North America it often connotes disrespect.

- *Touch.* In some cultures, people tend to stand close to one another when meeting and often touch each other as an adjunct to conversation. This is common in Arab, Latin American, and South European countries. On the other hand, North Europeans and North Americans prefer to "keep their distance."[44]

In an interesting experiment on nonverbal cross-cultural communication, English people received training in social skills that were appropriate to the Arab world. These included standing or sitting close to others and looking into their eyes, coupled with extensive touching, smiling, and handshaking. Experimenters then introduced Arabs to a trained subject and to a control subject who had only been exposed to general information about the Middle East. When asked whom they liked better, the Arabs preferred the people who had received training in their own nonverbal communication style.[45] We can well imagine a business meeting between English and Saudi bankers, both true to their cultures. The Saudis, gazing and touching, finish the meeting wondering why the English are so inattentive and aloof. The English, avoiding eye contact and shrinking from touch, wonder why the Saudis are so aggressive and threatening!

Etiquette and Politeness Across Cultures

Cultures differ considerably in how etiquette and politeness are expressed.[46] Very often, this involves saying things that one doesn't literally mean. The problem is that the exact form that this takes varies across cultures, and careful decoding is necessary to avoid confusion and embarrassment. Literal decoding will almost always lead to trouble. Consider the North American manager who says to a subordinate, "Would you like to calculate those figures for me?" This is really a mild order, not an opportunity to say no to the boss's "invitation." However, put yourself in the place of a foreign subordinate who has learned that Americans generally speak directly and expect directness in return. Should she say no to the boss?

In some cultures, politeness is expressed with modesty that seems excessive to North Americans. Consider, for example, the Chinese visitor's response to a Canadian who told him that his wife was very attractive. The Chinese modestly responded, "No, no, my wife is ugly." Needless to say, what was said wasn't what was meant. For another example of high modesty, see "Global Focus: *Chinese Display Modesty Bias in Performance Ratings.*"

In social situations the Japanese are particularly interested in maintaining feelings of interdependence and harmony. To do this, they use a large number of set phrases or "lubricant expressions" to express sympathy and understanding, soften rejection, say no indirectly, or facilitate apology. To North Europeans and North Americans who do not understand the purpose of these ritual expressions, they seem at best to be small talk and at worst to be insincere.

Learning to use lubricant expressions may be as difficult and painful as it is important, particularly in cases where Japanese norms and values are in conflict with those commonly held by Americans. For instance, an American executive who attributes his success in the

Social conventions differ across cultures. Knowledge of other customs and conventions makes it easier to conduct business.

GLOBAL FOCUS   Chinese Display Modesty Bias in Performance Ratings

One method of attempting to improve communication between managers and employees is to have both parties independently complete a performance appraisal of the employee and then sit down together to try to resolve any discrepancies. Although this common practice is a sensible strategy, studies in North America reveal some tendency for employees to rate their own performance higher than the boss rates it. This is probably a function of self-serving tendencies on the part of the subordinate (Chapter 4), and it can certainly contribute to superior-subordinate conflict.

Would such self-inflated ratings occur in all cultures? Jiing-Lih Farh, Gregory Dobbins, and Bor-Shiuan Cheng reasoned that in the collectivist Chinese culture of Taiwan, inflating one's own individual performance rating would be unlikely. Thus, they compared self- and supervisory ratings of performance for 982 subordinate-supervisor pairs in

the Republic of China (Taiwan). Here, subordinates showed a distinct modesty bias—a tendency to underevaluate their own performance compared to the boss's rating. Consider the communication problems this could pose when a manager from either culture has both Chinese and North American subordinates. Interpreting the meaning of the self-ratings would require true cultural sensitivity.

A related problem is the tendency for Chinese job applicants to minimize their skills and abilities in employment interviews. A careful examination of the applicant's credentials will often show that he or she is being far too modest about past accomplishments.

Source: Adapted from Farh, J. L., Dobbins, G. H., & Cheng, B. S. (1991). Cultural relativity in action: A comparison of self-ratings made by Chinese and U.S. Workers. *Personnel Psychology, 44,* 129–147.

American business world to his being articulate, assertive, and decisive is likely to feel strong resistance to using softening lubricant expressions such as, "Well, I'm not really sure about this but . . ." or "It's difficult to say exactly but . . ." in English *or* in Japanese. The area of apologizing also often raises vehement negative reactions from Americans: "I'm not going to say 'I'm sorry' if I didn't do anything wrong"; "They're the ones who are at fault, so why should I apologize?"; "It seems almost dishonest to say we're sorry when we aren't." Japanese, however, are more concerned with smoothing relationships and maintaining harmony than with "objective" determination of who is at fault. Thus, there are a number of rhetorical lubricant expressions of apology that are used regardless of whether one is "truly sorry" or "really at fault."[47]

Social Conventions Across Cultures

Over and above the issue of politeness and etiquette, there are a number of social conventions that vary across cultures and can lead to communication problems.[48] We have already alluded to the issue of directness. Especially in business dealings, North Americans tend to favor "getting down to brass tacks" and being specific about the issue at hand. Thus, the uninitiated businessperson might be quite surprised at the rather long period of informal chat that will begin business meetings in the Arab world or the indirectness and vagueness of many Japanese negotiators.

What individuals consider a proper degree of loudness for speech varies across cultures, and people from "quieter" societies (such as the United

Kingdom) might unfairly view those from "louder" societies (such as the Middle East) as pushy or intimidating.

What people consider proper punctuality also varies greatly around the world. In North America and Japan, punctuality at meetings and social engagements is expected and esteemed. In the Arab world and Latin America, being late for a meeting is not viewed negatively. In fact, one study found that being on time for an appointment connoted success in the United States and being *late* connoted success in Brazil.[49] Notice how an American businessperson might decode a Brazilian's lateness as disrespect, while the Brazilian was just trying to make a proper impression.

Exhibit 11.3 shows the results of a study of differences in the pace of life across cultures. It illustrates the accuracy of clocks, the time to walk 100 feet, and the time to get served in a post office. As you can see, Japan is the most time-conscious, while Indonesia is quite leisurely. Such differences are especially likely to provoke communication problems when we attribute them to a *person* and ignore the overall influence of the culture.

Finally, nepotism, favoring one's relatives in spite of their qualifications, is generally frowned upon in more individualistic societies such as North America and North Europe. However, in more collective cultures, such as those found in Africa and Latin America, people are expected to help their relatives. Hence, an American manager might view his Nigerian colleague's hiring his own son as irresponsible. The Nigerian might see it as irresponsible *not* to hire his own flesh and blood.

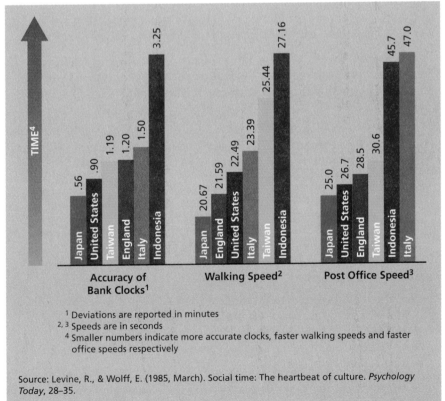

TIME[4]

Accuracy of Bank Clocks[1]	Walking Speed[2]	Post Office Speed[3]

Accuracy of Bank Clocks: Japan .56, United States .90, Taiwan 1.19, England 1.20, Italy 1.50, Indonesia 3.25

Walking Speed: Japan 20.67, England 21.59, United States 22.49, Italy 23.39, Taiwan 25.44, Indonesia 27.16

Post Office Speed: Japan 25.0, United States 26.7, England 28.5, Taiwan 30.6, Indonesia 45.7, Italy 47.0

[1] Deviations are reported in minutes
[2, 3] Speeds are in seconds
[4] Smaller numbers indicate more accurate clocks, faster walking speeds and faster office speeds respectively

Source: Levine, R., & Wolff, E. (1985, March). Social time: The heartbeat of culture. *Psychology Today*, 28–35.

EXHIBIT 11.3
Pace of life in six countries.

Cultural Context

Cultural context. The cultural information that surrounds a communication episode.

In the previous sections, we provided many examples of communication differences across cultures. Is there some organizing principle underlying these differences, something that helps to summarize them? The concept of cultural context provides a partial answer. **Cultural context** is the cultural information that surrounds a communication episode. It is safe to say that context is always important in accurately decoding a message. Still, as Exhibit 11.4 shows, cultures tend to differ in the importance to which context influences the meaning to be put upon communications.[50]

Some cultures, including many Oriental, Latin American, African, and Arab cultures, are high-context cultures. This means that the message contained in communication is strongly influenced by the context in which the message is sent. In high-context cultures, literal interpretations are often incorrect. Examples include those mentioned earlier—the Japanese really meant that the business deal was dead, and the Chinese didn't really mean that his wife was unattractive.

Low-context cultures include North America, Australia, Northern Europe (excluding France), and Scandinavia. Here, messages can be interpreted more literally because more meaning resides in the message than in the context in which the communication occurs. The "straight talk" that Americans favor is such an example. However, such straight talk is not any straighter in meaning than that heard in high-context cultures if one also learns to attend to the context when decoding messages.

Differences in the importance of context across cultures have some interesting implications for organizational communication, especially when we consider what might occur during business negotiations. Consider the following:[51]

- People from high-context cultures want to know about you and the company that you represent in great detail. This personal and organizational information provides a context for understanding your messages to them.

- Getting to the point quickly is not a style of communication that people in high-context cultures favor. Longer presentations and meetings allow people to get to know one another and to consider a proposal in a series of stages.

- When communicating with people from a high-context culture, give careful consideration to the age and rank of the communicator. Age and seniority tend to be valued in high-context cultures, and the status of the communicator is an important contextual factor that gives credibility to a message. Younger fast trackers will do fine in low-context cultures where "it's the message that counts."

- Because they tend to devalue cultural context, people from low-context cultures tend to favor very detailed business contracts. For them, the meaning is in the message itself. High-context cultures place less emphasis on lengthy contracts because the context in which the deal is sealed is critical.

Some more general advice for good cross-cultural communication is presented on the next page.

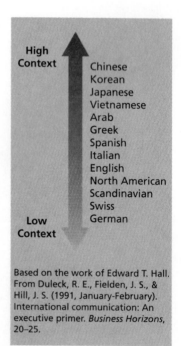

High
Context

Chinese
Korean
Japanese
Vietnamese
Arab
Greek
Spanish
Italian
English
North American
Scandinavian
Swiss
German

Low
Context

Based on the work of Edward T. Hall. From Duleck, R. E., Fielden, J. S., & Hill, J. S. (1991, January-February). International communication: An executive primer. *Business Horizons*, 20–25.

EXHIBIT 11.4
High- versus low-context cultures.

PERSONAL APPROACHES TO IMPROVING COMMUNICATION

What can you do to improve your own ability to communicate better with your boss, your subordinates, your peers, as well as customers, clients, or suppliers? Good question. More and more people are learning that developing their communication skills is just as sensible as developing their accounting skills, their computer skills, or anything else that will give them an edge in the job market.

Improvements in communication skills are very reinforcing. When you communicate well, people generally respond to you in a positive way, even if they aren't totally happy with your message. Poor communication can provoke a negative response that is self-perpetuating, in that it leads to even *poorer* communication. This happens when the other party becomes resistant, defensive, deceptive, or hostile.

Basic Principles of Effective Communication

Let's consider some basic principles of effective face-to-face communication.[52] These principles are basic in that they apply to upward, downward, horizontal, and outside communication. They generally apply to cross-cultural encounters as long as they are applied in conjunction with the advice in the following section, "When in Rome. . . "

Take the Time. Good communication takes time. Managers, in particular, should be aware that status differences, cultural differences, the mum effect, and other barriers mean that they need to devote extra effort to developing good rapport with subordinates. Not taking adequate time often leads to the selection of the wrong communication medium. I have seen a "don't do this" memo sent to 130 subordinates because two of them committed some offense. Of course, the memo irritated 128 people and the two offenders really didn't grasp the problem. The boss should have taken the time to meet face-to-face with the two people in question.

Be Accepting of the Other Person. Try to be accepting of the other person as an individual who has the right to have feelings and perceptions that may differ from your own. You can accept the person even if you are unhappy with something that he or she has done. Having empathy with others (trying to put yourself in their place and see things from their perspective) will increase your acceptance of them. Acting superior or arrogant works against acceptance.

Don't Confuse the Person With the Problem. Although you should be accepting of others, it is generally useful to be problem oriented rather than person oriented. For example, suppose a subordinate does something that you think might have offended a client. It is probably better to focus on this view of the problem than to impute motives to the subordinate ("Don't you care about the client's needs?"). The focus should be on what the person did, not who the person is. Along these same lines, try to be more descriptive rather than evaluative. Again, focus on what exactly the subordinate did to the client, not how bad the consequences are.

Congruence. A condition in which a person's words, thoughts, feelings, and actions all contain the same message.

Say What You Feel. More specifically, be sure that your words, thoughts, feelings, and actions exhibit **congruence**—that they all contain the same message. A common problem is soft-pedaling bad news, such as saying someone's job is probably secure when you feel that it probably isn't. However, congruence can also be a problem with positive messages. Some managers find it notoriously difficult to praise excellent work or even to reinforce routine good performance. Congruence can be thought of as honesty or authenticity, but you should not confuse it with brutal frankness or cruelty. Also, remember that in some high-context cultures, "saying what you feel" is done very indirectly. Still, the words and feelings are congruent in their own context.

Listen Actively. Effective communication requires good listening. People who are preoccupied with themselves or who simply hear what they expect to hear are not good listeners. Good listening improves the accuracy of your reception, but it also shows acceptance of the speaker and encourages self-reflection on his or her part. Developing good listening skills can be harder than acquiring good speaking skills. Good listening isn't a passive process. Rather, good communicators employ active listening to get the most out of an interaction. Techniques of **active listening** include the following:

Active listening. A technique for improving the accuracy of information reception by paying close attention to the sender.

- *Watch your body language.* Sit up, lean forward, and maintain eye contact with the speaker. This shows that you are paying attention and are interested in what the speaker is saying (this is another aspect of congruence).
- *Paraphrase what the speaker means.* Reflecting back what the speaker has said shows interest and ensures that you have gotten the correct message.
- *Show empathy.* When appropriate, show that you understand the feelings that the speaker is trying to convey. A phrase such as "Yes, that client has irritated me, too" might fill the bill.
- *Ask questions.* Have people repeat, clarify, or elaborate what they are saying. Avoid asking leading questions that are designed to pursue some agenda that *you* have.
- *Wait out pauses.* Don't feel pressured to talk when the speaker goes silent. This discourages him or her from elaborating.

Give Timely and Specific Feedback. When you initiate communication to provide others with feedback about their behavior, do it soon and be explicit. Speed maximizes the reinforcement potential of the message, and explicitness maximizes its usefulness to the recipient. Say *what* was good about the person's presentation to the client, and say it soon.

When in Rome . . . Do as the Romans

Frankly, you are off to a pretty good start in cross-cultural communication if you can do a careful job of applying the basic communication principles we discussed above. However, people's basic skills sometimes actually *deteriorate* when they get nervous about a cross-cultural encounter. Let's cover a few more principles for those situations.

Assume Differences Until You Know Otherwise. The material we presented earlier on cross-cultural communication and that in Chapter 4 on workforce diversity should sensitize you to the general tendency for cross-cultural differences. In a cross-cultural situation, caution dictates assuming that such differences exist until we are proven wrong. Remember, we have a tendency to project our own feelings and beliefs onto ambiguous targets (Chapter 4), leading us to ignore differences. Be particularly alert when dealing with good English speakers from cultures that emphasize harmony and avoidance of conflict (e.g., Japan). Their good English will tempt you to think that they think like you do, and their good manners will inhibit them from telling you otherwise.

Recognize Differences *Within* Cultures. Appreciating differences between cultures can sometimes blind us to the differences among people within a culture. This, of course, is what stereotypes do (Chapter 4). Remember, your German subordinates will have as many different personalities, skills, and problems as your North American subordinates. Remember that there are occupational and social class differences in other countries just like there are at home, although they can be harder to decipher (this is why I once shook hands with the chef at a French business school, mistaking him for the dean!).

Watch Your Language (and Theirs). Unless the person with whom you are communicating is very fluent in English, speak particularly clearly, slowly, and simply. Avoid cliches, jargon, and slang. Consider how mystifying phrases such as "I'm all ears," "let's get rolling," and "so long" must be.[53] By the same token, do not assume that those who are facile in your language are smarter, more skilled, or more honest than those who are not.

ORGANIZATIONAL APPROACHES TO IMPROVING COMMUNICATION

In this section we shall discuss some organizational techniques that can improve communication (for some particularly innovative ones, see "Ethical Focus: *Firms Use Innovative Communication Techniques to Foster Ethics*"). We consider other techniques in Chapter 14 (with regard to conflict reduction) and Chapter 17 (with regard to organizational development).

Choosing the Correct Medium

To communicate effectively, it is important to choose the correct medium to properly convey your intended message. Of particular importance is choosing a medium that can transmit information of appropriate richness. **Information richness** is the potential information-carrying capacity of a communication medium.[54] As you can see in Exhibit 11.5, we can rank order various media in terms of their information richness. A face-to-face transmission of information is very high in richness because the sender is personally present, audio and visual channels are used, body language and verbal language are occurring, and feedback to the sender is immediate and ongoing. A telephone conversation is also fairly rich, but it is limited to the audio channel, and it doesn't permit the observation of body language. At the other extreme, communicating via numeric computer output lacks richness because it is impersonal and uses only numeric language. Feedback to such communication might also be very slow.

Information richness. The potential information-carrying capacity of a communication medium.

ETHICAL FOCUS   Firms Use Innovative Communication Techniques to Foster Ethics

Citicorp has developed an ethics board game, which teams of employees use to solve hypothetical quandaries. General Electric employees can tap into specially designed interactive software on their personal computers to get answers to ethical questions. At Texas Instruments, employees are treated to a weekly column on ethics over an international electronic news service. One popular feature: a kind of Dear Abby mailbag, answers provided by the company's ethics officer, Carl Skoogland, that deals with the troublesome issues employees face most often. Managers at Northrop are rated on their ethical behavior by peers and subordinates through anonymous questionnaires.

More and more companies are appointing full-time ethics officers, generally on the corporate vice-presidential level, who report directly to the chairman or an ethics committee of top officers. One of the most effective tools these ethics special-

ists employ is a hotline through which workers on all levels can register complaints or ask about questionable behavior. At Raytheon Corp., Paul Pullen receives some 100 calls a month. Around 80 percent involve minor issues that he can resolve on the spot or refer to the human resources department. Another 10 percent of callers are simply looking for a bit of advice. But about 10 times a month, a caller reports some serious ethical lapse that Pullen must address with senior management. Says he: "Most people have high standards, and they want to work in an atmosphere that is ethical. The complaints come from all levels, and they are typical of what you would find in any business: possible conflicts of interest, cheating on timecards, cheating on expense reports."

Source: Excerpted from Labich, K. (1992, April 20). The new crisis in business ethics. *Fortune*, 167–176, p. 176.

At first thought, always using a rich medium might seem attractive. However, reflection indicates that this is not a good idea. Rich information media can be expensive and time consuming to use, and the messages that they convey can be difficult to send to a large number of receivers. Also, very rich media can inhibit some aspects of communication. For example, research shows that strangers working in face-to-face groups tend to use more inhibited speech than those interacting via computer screens.[55] Also, participation tends to be more equal across group members when they interact via computer, a medium that is richer than a letter (because of fast feedback) but not as rich as the telephone (because of the lack of audio cues). Evidently, people (especially quiet types) are less likely to censor themselves when they are protected by the distance afforded by the computer.

A good rule to follow is that less routine messages require richer communication media.[56] Memos and written reports are fine for recurrent, noncontroversial, impersonal communication. New news, intended changes, controversial messages, and emotional issues generally call for richer (i.e., face-to-face or video) media.

Hallmark Cards shattered whatever complacency resulted from its cosseting culture and seemingly unassailable market position by making a series of videotapes to show to its top 40 executives. Chiefly at issue was the company's pokey process for bringing new products to market. First, small retailers talked about slowly falling store traffic. Then a senior vice-president of Wal-Mart, a not-insignificant customer, delivered the not-subtle message that he hoped their companies could continue to do business. Says Steve Stanton, the CSC Index consultant who had the videos made: "By the time the lights went up, the temperature in the room had fallen 20 degrees."[57]

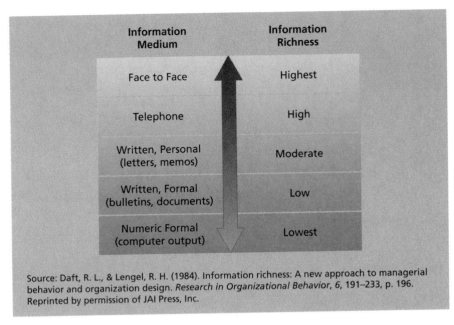

Information
Medium

Information
Richness

Face to Face	Highest
Telephone	High
Written, Personal (letters, memos)	Moderate
Written, Formal (bulletins, documents)	Low
Numeric Formal (computer output)	Lowest

Source: Daft, R. L., & Lengel, R. H. (1984). Information richness: A new approach to managerial behavior and organization design. *Research in Organizational Behavior, 6*, 191–233, p. 196. Reprinted by permission of JAI Press, Inc.

EXHIBIT 11.5
Communication media and information richness.

360 Degree Feedback

Traditionally, employee performance appraisal has been viewed as an exercise in downward communication in which the boss tells the subordinate how he or she is doing. More recently, performance appraisal has become a two-way communication process in which subordinates are also able to have upward impact concerning their appraisal. Most recently, some firms have expanded the communication channels in performance appraisal to include not only superior and self-ratings but also ratings by subordinates, peers, and clients or customers. This so-called **360 degree feedback** is often part of a total quality management system. Firms that have tried it include Honeywell, Sprint, Amoco, and Burger King. At Nebraska's Midlands Community Hospital, patients are incorporated into the process when nurses receive feedback.[58]

The 360 degree system usually focuses on required behavioral competencies rather than bottom line performance. It is usually used for employee development rather than salary determination. It is possible that the various sources of feedback could contradict each other, and ratees may need some assistance in putting all of this input together. However, in a well-designed 360 degree system, the various information sources ideally provide unique data about a person's performance.

360 degree feedback. Performance appraisal that uses the input of superiors, subordinates, peers, and clients or customers of the appraised individual.

Employee Surveys and Survey Feedback

Surveys of the attitudes and opinions of current employees can provide a useful means of upward communication. Since surveys are usually conducted with questionnaires that provide for anonymous responses, employees should feel free to voice their genuine views. A good **employee survey** contains questions that reliably tap employee concerns and also provide information that is useful for practical purposes. Survey specialists must summarize (encode) results in a manner that is easily decoded by management. Surveys are especially useful when they are administered periodically. In this case, managers can detect changes in employee feelings that might deserve attention. For

Employee survey. Anonymous questionnaire that enables employees to state their candid opinions and attitudes about an organization and its practices.

example, a radical decrease in satisfaction with pay might be a precursor of labor troubles and signal needed revision of the compensation package.

When survey results are fed back to employees, along with management responses and any plans for changes, this feedback should enhance downward communication. Survey feedback shows employees that management has heard and considered their comments. Plans for changes in response to survey concerns indicate a commitment to two-way communication.[59]

Suggestion Systems and Query Systems

Suggestion systems. Programs designed to enhance upward communication by soliciting ideas for improved work operations from employees.

Suggestion systems are designed to enhance upward communication by soliciting ideas for improved work operations from employees. They represent a formal attempt to encourage useful ideas and prevent their filtering through the chain of command. The simplest example of a suggestion system involves the use of a suggestion box into which employees put written ideas for improvements (usually anonymously). This simple system is usually not very effective, since there is no tangible incentive for making a submission and no clear mechanism to show that management considered a submission.

Much better are programs that *reward* employees for suggestions that are actually adopted and provide feedback as to how management evaluated each suggestion. For simple suggestions a flat fee is usually paid (perhaps $100). For complex suggestions of a technical nature that might result in substantial savings to the firm, a percentage of the anticipated savings is often awarded (perhaps several thousand dollars). An example of such a suggestion might be how to perform machinery maintenance without costly long-term shutdowns. When strong publicity follows the adopted suggestions (such as explaining them in the organization's employee newsletter), downward communication is also enhanced, since employees receive information about the kind of innovations desired.

Related to suggestion systems are *query systems* that provide a formal means of answering questions that employees may have about the organization. These systems foster two-way communication and are most effective when questions and answers are widely disseminated. Many organizations have a column of questions and answers in their employee newsletters, the content ranging from questions about benefits to the firm's stock performance.

Telephone Hotlines and TV Networks

Many organizations have adopted *telephone hotlines* to further communication. Some are actually query systems in that employees can call in for answers to their questions. For example, C&P Telephone Companies has an interactive system to handle queries about equal employment opportunity and affirmative action. More common are hotlines that use a news format to present company information. (See the "Ethical Focus" presented earlier.) News may be presented live at prearranged times or recorded for 24-hour availability. Such hotlines prove especially valuable at times of crisis such as storms or strikes.[60]

One fast growing technique for promoting good communication is a company-owned television network, such as the one at Ford Motor Company.

More than 90 major companies in North America have their own TV satellites or cable networks, according to a survey from KJH Communications, an Atlanta consulting firm. The companies use TV for rumor control, to boost workers' involvement, to smooth opera-

Many firms have developed their own TV networks to facilitate communication with employees.

tions in emergencies and to cut millions of dollars in travel costs for training and new product briefings.

Ford began with just one monthly news program, but by 1989 it was broadcasting daily. Today, the daily Ford news program—which is broadcast each day at 10 A.M. and repeated throughout the day— is watched by 60% of blue-collar employees and 40% to 45% of white-collar employees, according to internal surveys.[61]

Other prominent firms with their own TV networks include IBM, Federal Express, J.C. Penney, and Chrysler. Chrysler uses its system to train mechanics right at their own dealerships.

Management Training

Is good communication a mysterious inherited art, or can bosses be trained to communicate more effectively with subordinates? The evidence suggests that proper training can improve the communication skills of managers. Notice the specific use of the word *skills* here. Vague lectures about the importance of good communication simply don't tell managers *how* to communicate better. However, isolating specific communication skills and giving the boss an opportunity to practice these skills should have positive effects. The manager who has confidence in how to handle delicate matters should be better able to handle the balance between social-emotional and task demands.

Effective training programs often present videotaped models correctly handling a typical communication problem. Managers then role-play the problem and are reinforced by the trainers when they exhibit effective skills. At General Electric, for example, typical communication problems that this kind of training addresses have included discussing undesirable work habits, reviewing work performance, discussing salary changes, and dealing with subordinate-initiated discussions.[62] North Carolina's Center for Creative Leadership incorporates 360 degree feedback data from peers, superiors, and subordinates into its training.

It might seem that training of this nature is essentially focused on downward communication. However, there is much evidence that the disclosure of one's attitudes and feelings promotes reciprocity on the part of the receiver.[63] Thus, the manager who can communicate effectively downward can expect increased upward communication in return.

The Manager's Notebook   Telecommuting at Pacific Bell

1. Over 3,000 managers responded to Pacific Bell's survey about telecommuting. Expected advantages of the practice included increased job satisfaction and productivity and decreased stress. Many felt that telecommuting would enhance productivity because of fewer interruptions (i.e., less unscheduled informal communication). Managers linked stress reduction to the opportunity to avoid grinding commutes in urban areas. Negative aspects of telecommuting, although not strongly endorsed, centered on its potential damage to informal communication. These included decreased visibility when promotions were considered, problems in handling rush projects, and workload spillover for nontelecommuters.

2. Pacific Bell's telecommuting policy is designed to clarify the telecommuter's role so that superior-subordinate communication problems about the practice do not develop. Both parties sign an agreement, and either can terminate the telecommuting arrangement at any time. Telecommuting is generally done only on a part-time basis and for jobs in which productivity can be measured objectively. Telecommuters are required to be accessible during standard business hours and have a dedicated work space in their homes.

EXECUTIVE SUMMARY

◆ Communication is the process by which information is exchanged between a sender and a receiver. Organizational members (especially managers) spend a considerable portion of their time communicating. Effective communication involves getting the right information to the right people in a timely manner.

◆ Although much routine communication can occur via the chain of command, the chain tends to be slow and prone to filtering. It also ignores informal communication.

◆ Superior-subordinate communication is frequently ineffective. The superior might have difficulty balancing task and social-emotional demands, and both superiors and subordinates might be reluctant to inform each other of bad news (the mum effect). Also, superiors might devalue communicating with subordinates or simply not have enough time to spend interacting with them.

◆ The grapevine is the organization's informal communication network. Only a portion of people who receive grapevine information pass it on. Key physical locations or jobs that require movement around the organization encourage certain members to pass on information. The grapevine can be useful to the organization, and it often transmits information accurately. However, it becomes problematic when rumors (unverified beliefs) circulate.

◆ Verbal language that is tailored to the needs of a particular occupation or organization is known as jargon. While jargon aids communication between experienced associates, it can often prove confusing for new organizational members and people outside the organization.

◆ Nonverbal communication is the transmission of messages by a medium other than speech or writing. One major form is body language, which involves body movement or the placement of the body in relation to the receiver. Much body language is subtle and automatic, communicating factors such as liking, interest, and status differences. Other forms of nonverbal communication involve office decoration, office arrangement, and the clothing worn at work.

◆ Communication across cultures can be difficult owing to obvious language differences but also to less obvious differences in nonverbal style, social conventions, and matters of etiquette.

◆ In low-context cultures, individuals can interpret messages more literally than in high-context cultures, where issues surrounding a message are more critical to understanding it.

◆ Personal approaches to improving communication include taking the time, being accepting of others, concentrating on the problem, saying what you feel, listening actively, and giving timely and specific feedback.

◆ When communicating cross-culturally, assume cultural differences until you know otherwise, recognize differences within cultures, and use simple language.

◆ Organizational approaches to improving communication include 360 degree feedback, employee surveys, suggestion and query systems, hotlines and TV networks, and management training. Communicators should select richer media for less routine messages.

KEY CONCEPTS

Communication
Effective communication
Chain of command
Downward communication
Upward communication
Horizontal communication
Filtering
Open door policy
Mum effect
Grapevine
Rumor

Jargon
Nonverbal communication
Body language
Cultural context
Congruence
Active listening
Information richness
360 degree feedback
Employee survey
Suggestion systems

DISCUSSION QUESTIONS

1. Using Exhibit 11.1 as a guide, describe a communication episode that you have observed in an organization. Who were the sender and receiver? Was the episode effective? Why or why not?

2. Debate: Since more and more global business is being conducted in English, North Americans will not have cross-cultural communication problems in the future.

3. Why does the proportion of working time devoted to communication increase as we move up the hierarchy of the organization?

4. Describe or invent a situation in which communicating strictly by the chain of command would be very ineffective.

5. "It is very difficult to establish good superior-subordinate communication." What evidence would support this position?

6. Discuss the pros and cons of the existence of the grapevine in organizations. Suppose an organization wanted to "kill" the grapevine. How easy do you think this would be?

7. Interview someone who performs a job with which you are unfamiliar. Make a list of the unusual language or jargon that individuals use on this job and define the terminology. Why was this jargon developed?

8. Discuss a case in which you heard one message communicated verbally and "saw" another transmitted nonverbally. What was the content of each message? Which one did you believe?

9. Under what conditions might body language or clothing have a strong communicative effect? When might the effect be weaker?

10. Communication is more subtle in high-context cultures than in low-context cultures. Explain.

EXPERIENTIAL EXERCISE
CROSS-CULTURAL CONFUSION

The purpose of this exercise is to find out whether you can diagnose the reasons for the apparent work-related "cross-cultural confusion" illustrated in the three incidents below. In thinking through your diagnosis, you must consider the relative impact of differences in cultural values versus other factors that might have caused the problem.

Working alone, read each incident and rank order the potential explanations given for the problem in terms of their likelihood. Give a rank of 1 to the most likely, 2 to the next most likely, and so on. Also, jot down a brief rationale for your ranking that considers the cultural difference and other factors. Why or why not is a particular explanation correct? Following this, one of two procedures can be used:

1. The instructor can discuss the rankings with the class as a whole.
2. The class can break into small learning groups, discuss each incident, and develop a group ranking for each incident. Following this, the instructor can compare the group rankings and discuss them with the class as a whole.

Your instructor will give you the expert opinion about the explanations for the events given the cultures involved and the situational factors mentioned in the incidents. Of course, individuals are unique. The correctness of these explanations is based on a "typical" cultural response in the absence of other information.

INCIDENT 1: WHO'S IN CHARGE?

The president of Janice Tani's firm asked her, as chief executive of the marketing division, and her staff (three male MBAs) to set up and close an important contract with a Japanese firm. He thought his choice especially good as Janice (a Japanese American from California) knew the industry well and could also speak Japanese.

As she and her staff were being introduced, Janice noticed a quizzical look on Mr. Yamamoto's face and heard him repeat "chief executive" to his assistant in an unsure manner. After Janice had presented the merits of the strategy in Japanese, referring to notes provided by her staff, she asked Mr. Yamamoto what he thought. He responded by saying that he needed to discuss some things further with the head of her department. Janice explained that was why she was there. Smiling, Mr. Yamamoto replied that she had done an especially good job of explaining, but that he wanted to talk things over with the person in charge. Beginning to be frustrated, Janice stated that she had authority for her company. Mr. Yamamoto glanced at his assistant, still smiling, and he arranged to meet with Janice at another time.

Why did Mr. Yamamoto keep asking Janice about the executive in charge?

1. He did not really believe that she was actually telling the truth about who she was.
2. He had never heard the term "executive" before and did not understand the meaning of "chief executive."
3. He had never personally dealt with a woman in Janice's position, and her language ability caused him to think of her in another capacity.
4. He really did not like her presentation and did not want to deal with her firm.
5. He was attracted to her and wanted to meet with her alone.

INCIDENT 2: SHAPING UP THE OFFICE

Ronald, an ambitious young executive, had been sent to take over the Sales branch of his American company in São Paulo, Brazil. He spent a few weeks learning routines with the departing manager and was somewhat disturbed by the informality and lack of discipline that seemed to characterize the office. People seemed to indulge in excessive socializing, conversations seemed to deal more with personal than business matters and no one seemed to keep to their set schedules. Once he had formally taken over, he resolved to do something about this general slackness and called the staff together for a general meeting. He told them bluntly that work rates and schedules would have to be adhered to and hoped that a more businesslike atmosphere would prevail. Over the next few months he concentrated on improving office efficiency, offering higher bonuses and incentives to those who worked well and private warnings to those who didn't. By the end of the first quarter he felt he had considerably improved the situation and was therefore somewhat surprised to find sales figures had significantly dropped since his takeover.

What reason would you give to Ronald for this drop in sales?

1. He has probably lowered the office morale.
2. The salesmen probably resent his management style and are deliberately trying to make him look bad.
3. The salesmen would probably have responded better to a more participative approach to the problems.
4. Key Brazilian workers lost face through Ronald's actions.

INCIDENT 3: TRANSMITTING INFORMATION ON TRANSMISSION SYSTEMS

"Adjustment to Japan has been much easier than I thought," Ted Owens told his wife about a year after their move from the United States. Ted had been sent by an automobile company in Detroit to see if he could establish production facilities for transmission systems that would be built in Japan and imported to the United States. Having been told that negotiations take a long time in Japan, he was not disappointed that it had taken a year for a major meeting to be set up with the key Japanese counterparts. But the Japanese had studied the proposal and were ready to discuss it this morning, and Ted was excited as he left for work. At the meeting people discussed matters that were already in the written proposal that had been circulated beforehand. Suddenly it occurred to Ted that there was an aspect of quality control inspection that he had left out of the proposal. He knew that the Japanese should know of this concern since it was important to the long-range success of the project. Ted asked the senior person at the meeting if he could speak, apologized for not having already introduced the quality control concern he was about to raise, and then went into his addition to the proposal. His presentation was met with silence, and the meeting was later adjourned without a decision having been made on the whole manufacture-importation program. Since Ted thought that a decision would be made that day, he was puzzled.

What was the reason for Ted's difficulty?

1. Ted had brought up quality control, an issue about which the Japanese are very proud. The Japanese thought that Ted was questioning their commitment to quality control.
2. Ted had brought up an issue on which there had not been prior discussion among the people somehow involved in that specific issue.
3. Ted had asked the senior person about speaking; in actuality, there was a younger person present who was in charge and Ted should have deferred to this person.
4. Expecting a decision in a year is still unrealistic. Ted should be more patient.

Source: Incidents from Brislin, R. W., Cushner, K., Cherrie, C., & Yong, M. (1986). *Intercultural interactions: A practical guide.* Pp. 157–158, 164–165, 172. Copyright © 1986 by Sage Publications, Inc. Reprinted by permission of Sage Publications, Inc.

CASE STUDY
PEDRO'S CULTURAL MAZE

THE PHILIPPINES

The Philippines, located between Australia and the Southeast Asian countries of Singapore, Malaysia and Indonesia, is a group of islands. It is predominantly Christian; about 90 percent of the population is Christian. The country was under Spanish domination for over 350 years. The Americans dominated for 40 years while the Japanese occupied it for five years. All these dominations exerted influences on the people. Even today, these influences are reflected in the Filipino society. Yet, Filipinos still maintain some values of their own.

In Tagalog (a major Filipino language) *Hiya* means shame. In any social interaction, Filipinos are always careful not to "lose face." They tend to be tactful, diplomatic and careful not to offend anyone. Thus, confrontations are rare because "you do not tell one's faults straight to his face."

The literal translation for *Utang Naloob* is gratitude. The sense of gratitude or the feeling that one has to return a good deed or favor done for one, is an important cultural value. It makes people feel obliged to repay any good done for them. Failure to do so makes them an outcast and such people are regarded as someone who does not have *Utang Naloob*.

The Filipinos' faith in God is reflected in their cultural value of *Bahala Na*, which means "leave it to God (*Bahala* is God)." In the western view, this may be considered a fatalistic attitude. People adopt this attitude especially in times of crisis. When confronted with a problem, some Filipinos tend to avoid or ignore the seriousness of it by saying, *Bahala Na*, God will take care of it somehow.

Kagon is a kind of grass commonly found during summer months in Philippines. This grass covers vast fields and when it burns, a bright and brick-colored flame is emitted. The fire spreads quickly. However, it lasts only a short while. The cultural value of *Ningas Kagon (Kagon-fire)* reflects this. The Filipinos have a tendency to be enthusiastic about anything (a cause, fashion, etc.) with a burning passion which lasts only for a short while. Many social scientists say that this tendency has a negative impact on development, especially economic development, because the interest of people cannot be sustained and maintained in long-term industrial projects. Projects are started enthusiastically and when the interest is lost, they are either abandoned or simply terminated.

BATIK

Mr. Renkins, a Dutch entrepreneur, visited some Asian countries with the aim of exploring business venture opportunities. While visiting Indonesia, Malaysia and the Philippines, he was very much attracted to the *batik* cloth products in these countries. He thought that such material would have a good market potential not only in Holland but also in other European countries. He carried out a brief survey in his home country to determine the design, color and the quality preferences of consumers. Meanwhile, he conducted feasibility studies in Indonesia, Malaysia and the Philippines to set up a small factory to manufacture dyes necessary for the *batik* textiles, printing, and making a few clothing items initially.

The feasibility studies indicated that the Philippines might be a better place for this business venture, given the availability of manpower, labor costs and natural dyes. During his previous trips to the Philippines, Renkins had established good relations with some government officials and small businessmen. He thought that such contacts would be handy if he decided to set up a business venture in the Philippines. Further, since most of the Filipinos spoke or understood English, Renkins thought that communication would not be a problem. He was also impressed by the pleasant manners and temperaments of the Filipinos. All these strengthened his decision to set up a factory in the Philippines. Although he had visited the Philippines on three or four occasions, he was not very familiar with the cultural values of Filipinos. He had only superficial knowledge of the country and its people.

Given his busy schedule and other business commitments elsewhere, Renkins could not work permanently in the Philippines. So, after interviewing several candidates for the job of factory manager, Renkins offered the job to Pedro, who was in his mid-forties and had a Bachelor's degree in Science and some business experience in the manufacturing industry. The factory started to function with an employee strength of about 50. Pedro was in charge of all aspects of factory operations including personnel, finance and general administration. He was well-versed with local conditions and problems. The factory started to function smoothly after the initial teething problems were taken care of.

Renkins was present for the factory opening but returned to Holland once the teething problems were solved. However, he kept in close touch with Pedro through telephone, telex and fax services. Initially, it appeared that everything was moving according to expectation. Employees were cooperative and enthusiastic about their work. Soon, however, the *Ningas Kagon* effect crept in among the employees. Employees slowly started to demonstrate a careless attitude, resulting in quality, delay and other problems.

On one occasion an employee accidentally made a mistake in the mixing of raw materials for the preparation of dyes for the *batik* material. Instead of reporting the matter to his supervisor, he just prayed that the mistake would not cause much difficulty. This type of attitude made it difficult for supervisors to implement stricter quality control measures, which are critical for exporting a product, especially to European countries.

Pedro was concerned about these problems although they were rectified from time to time. He thought that time was needed to bring these problems under control. Therefore, he decided not to convey these incidents to Renkins who was under the impression that everything was moving smoothly under the able leadership of Pedro.

Renkins slowly learned that shipments from the Philippines lagged behind schedule. But he did not press Pedro on the reasons for delay. He thought that he would give them some time to shape up. Anyhow, he sent a mild reminder to Pedro. Upon receiving the message, Pedro was worried and feared that if he failed to meet schedules, he might lose his newly-found job. If he were sacked from this job, getting another job might prove difficult.

After analyzing the situation, Pedro found that much of the delay was caused by a particular supervisor, Ilano, in the dye-mixing department. Ilano was having problems with his own workers. Since the initial enthusiasm was slowly fading among the workers, he found it difficult to motivate them to keep up with deadlines and quality standards. While Pedro felt uncomfortable about communicating this message to Ilano, it was difficult for Ilano to pass on the message to his workers. The Filipino cultural value of *Hiya* ("Face") stood as a barrier and no immediate action could be taken to remedy the situation. In situations of this sort, most often than not, the supervisor or manager would not directly reprimand a particular subordinate for his short-comings and failures. Instead they would tell another subordinate who happens to be a friend of that subordinate about the problem so that he or she could pass on the message. The manager then waits to see if some action follows. Thus the peer-level communication is preferred to supervisor-subordinate communication when it comes to passing on the unpleasant messages in work situations. Direct confrontation is avoided because the subordinate should not "lose face." If the faults are not that serious and can be remedied or if the offenses are just first-time ones, then supervisors can communicate these messages in a more positive tone, saying, "Next time, please try to improve." When peer-level communication takes place, people tend to receive the suggestion without "loss of face" and may even make a better attempt to change or improve.

Pedro's predicament was getting greater and greater as the pressure of time was building on him. He was accountable to Renkins and soon might have to report the situation to him. Renkins might not understand and appreciate this particular cultural value of Filipinos. If he did not inform and seek advice from Renkins, he might prolong the problem, aggravating it and causing more damage. That would lead him to lose his job. But, if he did convey news about the state of affairs—the delays in meeting deadlines and the cultural problems he was facing—it would indicate his inefficiency and poor leadership qualities. He almost came close to making a phone call to Renkins but abandoned the idea and asked the secretary to cancel the call. He gathered enough courage to face up to the situation and decided to talk to Ilano about his shortcomings. Pedro could not afford to take a *Bahala Na* attitude.

Pedro had to think very carefully about how to deal with this situation without really offending Ilano, yet at the same time getting the message across to him. In fact Pedro had a cordial, friendly relationship to Ilano. Once he was invited to Ilano's house for a special celebration. He was treated very well by the family and was given a few gifts to take home. While contemplating his course of action, Pedro was reminded of all these past incidents and the cultural value of *Utang Na Loob*, (showing gratitude for one's kindness). If he were to reprimand Ilano, that might be construed as an unkind act by Ilano and other employees in the factory. During his visit to Ilano's house, Ilano's parents requested Pedro to take good care of their son.

Pedro was under severe cultural constraints. He had to respond to a series of questions in formulating a solution which would enhance his image, help to maintain good relations with his employees and enable him to keep his job. The questions in his mind were: How can I sustain the enthusiasm of the employees and prevent them from succumbing to the cultural value of *Ningas Kagon (Kagon-Fire)*? How can I enforce quality standards so vital to export business and not leaving everything to God (*Bahala Na*)? How can I overcome the cultural value of *Hiya* (shame) and yet take prompt actions when necessary?

Specifically, how can I give the message directly to Ilano to shape up or leave the company? How can I help Ilano to pass on the same message to his subordinates?

Pedro left his office on Friday evening, planning to find answers to these questions during the weekend.

Source: Putti, J. M., & Chia, A. (1990). *Culture and management: A casebook*. Singapore: McGraw-Hill.

1. How effective is the communication in this company? Cite specific examples in which effective or ineffective communication occurred.
2. Is there evidence of the mum effect in the case?
3. Discuss how the cultural values of the Philippines affect the events in the case.
4. What is the specific role of *cultural context* in this case?
5. How effective is Pedro as a manager?
6. What should Pedro do now?
7. Could Mr. Renkins do anything to improve the situation at the company?

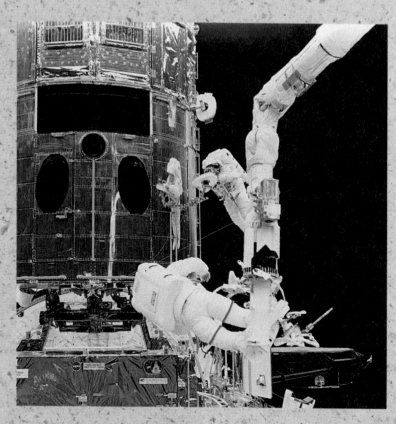

DESPITE EARLY WARNINGS THAT THE LENS OF THE HUBBLE SPACE TELESCOPE WAS FLAWED, NASA LAUNCHED IT ANYWAY, WHICH COST THE AGENCY MILLIONS OF DOLLARS IN REPAIRS.

CHAPTER 12

DECISION MAKING

NASA's
HUBBLE
SPACE
TELESCOPE

In December of 1993, NASA astronauts successfully completed what was surely the most complicated and difficult space flight ever. The flight, which included two lengthy space walks, was made to repair the near-sighted Hubble space telescope. Hubble, which had been launched into position three years earlier, had greatly disappointed the scientific community when the images that it sent back to earth were immediately recognized to be badly flawed. Although fine tuning did improve some of the data being generated, the $1.6 billion telescope in no way lived up to its promise as the most complicated and expensive scientific instrument ever launched into space. The repair improved NASA's image, which was certainly in need of repair after the original Hubble launch and the earlier fatal explosion of the Challenger space shuttle.

The Hubble problem stemmed from an abberation in the telescope's primary mirror. The mirror, the largest ever constructed, was supplied to NASA by Perkin-Elmer Corporation of Danbury, Connecticut. The firm had radically underbid competitor

Kodak to win the $70 million contract, and this low bid put the company under extreme pressure to complete the job without a hitch. The complexity and delicacy of the task were amazing, requiring a wide range of technicians, engineers, and optical designers. The mirror had to be remarkably smooth and precisely curved.

The final product *was* remarkably smooth, but it was incorrectly curved. Subsequent investigation showed that the problem started when technicians improperly shimmed the $1 million device that guided the polishing of the mirror with three metal washers worth about 20 cents. There was evidence of the problem when preliminary grinding of the mirror was completed, but it was discounted because of the still-rough state of the surface. In subsequent internal tests, as the company did more and more work on the mirror, the abberation was again apparent, but each time it was explained away. The engineer who oversaw the tests was said to be leery of outsiders and rejected pleas for external, independent tests "just to be sure." He claimed that pleas for external testing were rejected due to costs.

A retired Perkin-Elmer optical designer who had been hired as a quality trouble shooter was routinely rebuffed by the lens team for intruding on their turf. When he suggested that arch-competitor Kodak be contracted to make independent tests of the lens, he was branded a traitor. NASA's own quality assurance was minimal due to cash problems.

The flawed lens was launched without a NASA quality signoff. A subsequent federal investigation led to an agreement in which Perkin-Elmer agreed to pay $25 million in exchange for a Justice Department deal to drop potential lawsuits. It is estimated that the problem could have been repaired before the launch for $1.7 million. The complicated NASA repair job was pegged at over $600 million.[1]

How could so many smart people make such a bad series of decisions? We'll find out in this chapter. First, we will define decision making and present a model of a rational decision-making process. As we work through this model, we shall be especially concerned with the practical limitations of rationality. After this, we'll investigate the use of groups to make decisions. Finally, the chapter closes with a description of some techniques to improve decision making.

WHAT IS DECISION MAKING?

Consider the following questions that might arise in a variety of organizational settings:

- How much inventory should our store carry?
- Where should we locate the proposed community mental health center?
- Should I remain on this job or accept another?
- How many classes of Philosophy 200 should our department offer next semester?
- Should our diplomats attend the summit conference?

Common sense tells us that someone is going to have to do some decision making to answer such questions.

Decision making is the process of developing a commitment to some course of action.[2] Three things are noteworthy about this definition. First, decision making involves making a *choice* among several action alternatives—the store can carry more or less inventory, and the mental health center can be located on the north or south end of town. Second, decision making is a *process* that involves more than simply the final choice among alternatives—if you decide to accept the offer of a new job, we want to know *how* this decision was reached. Finally, the "commitment" mentioned in the definition usually involves some commitment of *resources* such as time, money, or personnel—if the store carries a large inventory, it will tie up cash; if the chairperson of Philosophy offers too many introductory classes, he might have no one available to teach a graduate seminar. The Hubble telescope project required a substantial resource commitment.

In addition to conceiving of decision making as the commitment of resources, we can also describe it as a process of problem solving.[3] A **problem** exists when a gap is perceived between some existing state and some desired state. For example, the chairperson of the Philosophy department might observe that there is a projected increase in university enrollment for the upcoming year and that his course schedule is not completed (existing state). In addition, he might wish to adequately service the new students with Philosophy 200 classes and at the same time satisfy his Dean with a timely, sensible schedule (desired state). In this case, the decision-making process involves the perception of the existing state, the conception of the desired state, and the steps that the chairperson takes to move from one state to the other.

Well-Structured Problems

For a **well-structured problem,** the existing state is clear, the desired state is clear, and how to get from one state to the other is fairly obvious. Intuitively, these problems are simple, and their solutions arouse little controversy. This is because such problems are repetitive and familiar.

- Assistant bank manager—which of these 10 car loan applications should I approve?
- Welfare officer—how much assistance should this client receive?
- Truck driver—how much weight should I carry?

Because decision making takes time and is prone to error, organizations (and individuals), attempt to program the decision making for well-structured problems. A **program** is simply a standardized way of solving a problem. As such, programs short-circuit the decision-making process by enabling the decision maker to go directly from problem identification to solution.

Programs usually go under labels such as *rules, routines, standard operating procedures, or rules of thumb.* Sometimes, they come from experience and exist only "in the head." Other programs are more formal. You are probably aware that routine loan applications are "scored" by banks according to a fixed formula that takes into account income, debt, previous credit, and so on. Some programs exist in the form of straightforward rules—"Truck drivers will always carry between 85 and 95 percent of legal weight."

Decision making. The process of developing commitment to some course of action.

Problem. A perceived gap between an existing state and a desired state.

Well-structured problem. A problem for which the existing state is clear, the desired state is clear and how to get from one state to another is fairly obvious.

Program. A standardized way of solving a problem.

Many of the problems encountered in organizations are well-structured, and programmed decision making provides a useful means of solving these problems. However, programs are only as good as the decision-making process that led to the adoption of the program in the first place. In computer terminology, "garbage in" will result in "garbage out." Another difficulty with decision programs is their tendency to persist even when problem conditions change.

These difficulties of programmed decision making are seen in the ineffective hiring procedures that some firms use. To solve the recurrent problem of choosing employees for lower-level jobs, almost all companies use application forms. These forms are part of a decision program. However, some firms have persisted in asking for information (such as age or marital status) that violates equal employment and human rights legislation or is not job-related. Costly lawsuits have resulted. Furthermore, there is seldom evidence that this information is a valid predictor of job performance (garbage in-garbage out).

Ill-Structured Problems

Ill-structured problem. A problem for which the existing and desired states are unclear and the method of getting to the desired state is unknown.

The extreme example of an **ill-structured problem** is one in which the existing and desired states are unclear, and the method of getting to the desired state (even if clarified) is unknown. For example, a vice-president of marketing might have a vague feeling that the sales of a particular product are too low. However, she might lack precise information about the product's market share (existing state) and the market share of its most successful competitor (ideal state). In addition, she might be unaware of exactly how to increase the sales of this particular product.

Ill-structured problems are generally unique. That is, they are unusual and have not been encountered before. In addition, they tend to be complex and involve a high degree of uncertainty. As a result, they frequently arouse controversy and conflict among the people who are interested in the decision. For example, consider the following:

- Should we vaccinate the population against a new flu strain when the vaccination might have some bad side effects?
- Should we implement a risky attempt to rescue political hostages?
- In which part of the country should we build a new plant?

It should be obvious that ill-structured problems such as these cannot be solved with programmed decisions. Rather, the decision makers must resort to nonprogrammed decision making. This simply means that they are likely to try to gather more information and be more self-consciously analytical in their approach. Ill-structured problems can entail high risk and stimulate strong political considerations. We will concentrate on them in this chapter.

THE COMPLEAT DECISION MAKER—A RATIONAL DECISION-MAKING MODEL

Exhibit 12.1 presents a model of the decision process that a rational decision maker might use. When a problem is identified, a search for information is begun. This information clarifies the nature of the problem and suggests alter-

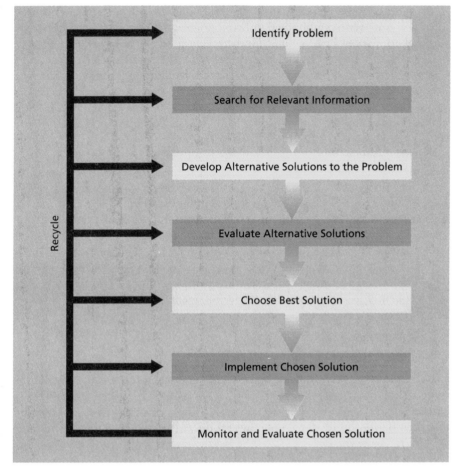

EXHIBIT 12.1
The rational decision-making process.

native solutions. These are carefully evaluated, and the best is chosen for implementation. The implemented solution is then monitored over time to ensure its immediate and continued effectiveness. If difficulties occur at any point in the process, repetition or recycling may be effected.

It might occur to you that we have not yet determined exactly what a "rational" decision maker is. Before we discuss the specific steps of the model in detail, let's contrast two forms of rationality.

Perfect Versus Bounded Rationality

The prototype for **perfect rationality** is the familiar Economic Person (formerly Economic Man), whom we meet in the first chapter of most introductory textbooks in economics. Economic Person is the perfect cool, calculating decision maker. More specifically, he or she:

- can gather information about problems and solutions without cost and is thus completely informed;
- is perfectly logical—if solution A is preferred over solution B, and B is preferred over C, then A is necessarily preferable to C;
- has only one criterion for decision making—economic gain.

Perfect rationality. A decision strategy that is completely informed, perfectly logical, and oriented toward economic gain.

Bounded rationality. A decision strategy that relies on limited information and that reflects time constraints and political considerations.

Framing. Aspects of the presentation of information about a problem that are assumed by decision makers.

Cognitive biases. Tendencies to acquire and process information in an error-prone way.

While Economic Person is useful for theoretical purposes, the perfectly rational characteristics embodied in Economic Person do not exist in real decision makers. Nobel Prize winner Herbert Simon recognizes this and suggests that administrators use **bounded rationality** rather than perfect rationality.[4] That is, while they try to act rationally, they are limited in their capacity to acquire and process information. In addition, time constraints and political considerations (such as the need to please others in the organization) act as bounds to rationality.

Framing and cognitive biases both illustrate the operation of bounded rationality. **Framing** refers to the (sometimes subtle) aspects of the presentation of information about a problem that are assumed by decision makers.[5] A frame could include assumptions about the boundaries of a problem, the possible outcomes of a decision, or the reference points used to decide if a decision is successful.[6] As we shall see, how problems and decision alternatives are framed can have a powerful impact on resulting decisions.

Cognitive biases are tendencies to acquire and process information in a particular way that is prone to error (see the cartoon). These biases constitute assumptions and shortcuts that can improve decision-making efficiency, but they frequently lead to serious errors in judgment. We'll see them at work in the following pages.

Problem Identification and Framing

You will recall that a problem exists when a gap occurs between existing and desired conditions. Such gaps might be signaled by dissatisfied customers or vigilant superiors or subordinates. Similarly, the press might contain articles about legislation or ads for competing products that signal difficulties for the

"IT'S BEGINNING TO SHOW SOME HUMAN CHARACTERISTICS — FAULTY REASONING, FORGETFULNESS AND REPETITION."

Source: *Current Contents,* July 17, 1989.

organization. The perfectly rational decision maker, infinitely sensitive and completely informed, should be a great problem identifier. Bounded rationality, however, can lead to the following difficulties in problem identification:[7]

- *Perceptual defense.* In Chapter 4 we pointed out that the perceptual system may act to defend the perceiver against unpleasant perceptions. For example, the documentation on the Hubble mirror fiasco suggests that some Perkin-Elmer employees simply couldn't see what they didn't want to see—that the mirror had a serious abberation.

- *Problem defined in terms of functional specialty.* Selective perception can cause decision makers to view a problem as being in the domain of their own specialty (e.g., marketing) even when some other perspective might be warranted.

- *Problem defined in terms of solution.* This form of jumping to conclusions effectively short-circuits the rational decision-making process. When Coca-Cola changed its time-honored formula to produce a "new" Coke, it appears that its market share problem was prematurely defined in terms of a particular solution—we need to change our existing product.

- *Problem diagnosed in terms of symptoms.* "What we have here is a morale problem." While this might be true, a concentration on surface symptoms will provide the decision maker with few clues about an adequate solution. The real problem here involves the cause of the morale problem. Low morale due to poor pay suggests different solutions than does low morale due to boring work.

When a problem is identified, it is necessarily framed in some way. Consider how different it is to frame a $10,000 expenditure as a cost (something to be avoided) versus as an investment (something to be pursued). Or, consider how different it is to frame a new product introduction as a military campaign against competitors versus a crusade to help customers. Or, consider how a firm might view a new piece of technology as a threat to its business or an opportunity to be exploited. In each case, the facts of the matter might be the same, but the different decision frames might lead to very different decisions.

Rational decision makers should try to be very self-conscious about how they have framed problems ("We have assumed that this is a product innovation problem"). Also, they should try out alternative frames ("Let's imagine that we don't need a new product here."). Finally, decision makers should avoid overarching, universal frames (corporate culture gone wild). While it's a good idea to "put customers first," we don't want to frame every problem as a customer service problem.[8] For an example of how Pizza Hut reframed a problem please consult *You Be the Manager*.

Information Search

As you can see in Exhibit 12.1, once a problem is identified, a search for information is instigated. This information search may clarify the nature or extent of the problem and begin to suggest alternative solutions. Again, our perfectly rational Economic Person is in good shape at this second stage of the decision-making process. He or she has free and instantaneous access to all information necessary to clarify the problem and develop alternative solutions. Bounded

REFRAMING PIZZA HUT'S PROBLEM

M YOU BE THE anager

PepsiCo is one of the most growth-oriented companies in North America. Despite the recession, the firm's sales grew at a yearly compound rate of 17 percent over the past decade. This growth hasn't been accidental. Under CEO Wayne Calloway, PepsiCo, which includes the soft drink, Frito-Lay products, and Pizza Hut, has established a strong growth-oriented culture. The culture hasn't been pursued just for financial success. Rather, Calloway is a firm believer that growth is the best mechanism to attract and motivate good managerial talent. Without it, he says, companies become inward-looking, bureaucratic, and uncompetitive.

PepsiCo executives feel that growth can occur when managers are open to entirely rethinking their businesses. A good example concerned the Pizza Hut restaurant chain. Over the years, growth had been good. However

> WHEN DOMINO'S CAPTURED THE MAJORITY OF GROWTH IN CHAIN PIZZA, PIZZA HUT MANAGERS RECONCEPTUALIZED THEIR BUSINESS STRATEGY.

when competitor Domino's began its aggressive delivery campaign, it captured 90 percent of the growth in chain pizza. Pizza Hut would obviously have to counter Domino's. But the events also stimulated the company's growth-oriented managers to consider just what business they were in. Was Pizza Hut simply a restaurant chain? You be the manager.

1. Suppose Pizza Hut managers had committed the error of defining their problem in terms of its solution. What would they do, and how would this be limited in terms of PepsiCo's growth culture?

2. Reframe Pizza Hut's problem in a way that suggests growth potential. What business are they in?

To find out what Pizza Hut did, check out *The Manager's Notebook* at the end of the chapter.

Source: Adapted from Magnet, M. (1994, March 7). Let's go for growth. *Fortune,* 60–72.

rationality, however, presents a different picture. Information search might be slow and costly.

Too Little Information.   Sometimes, decision makers don't acquire enough information to make a good decision. Several cognitive biases contribute to this. For one thing, people tend to be mentally lazy and use whatever information is most readily available to them. Often, this resides in the memory, and we tend to remember *vivid, recent* events.[9] Although such events might prove irrelevant in the context of the current problem, we curtail information search and rely on familiar experience. The manager who remembers that "the last time we went to an outside supplier for parts, we got burned" may be ignoring the wisdom of contracting out a current order.

Another cognitive bias that contributes to incomplete information search is the well-documented tendency for people to be overconfident in their decision making.[10] This difficulty is exacerbated by **confirmation bias,** the tendency to seek out only information that conforms to one's own definition of or solution to a problem. Both of these biases can lead people to shirk the

Confirmation bias. The tendency to seek out information that conforms to one's own definition of or solution to a problem.

Information overload can lead to errors, omissions, delays, and stress.

acquisition of additional information. The Hubble mirror decision makers avoided outside tests that would have revealed that the early signals of a problem were, in fact, correct. Similarly, in the fatal *Challenger* space launch, only a limited range of data about the impact of temperature on mechanical failure was examined.

Too Much Information. While the bounds of rationality often force us to make decisions with incomplete or imperfect information, *too much* information can also damage the quality of decisions. Consider the example of former General Electric CEO Reginald Jones.

> Translated and amplified by his subordinates, Jones's thirst for data led to ridiculous excess. Dennis Dammerman, 43, now GE's chief financial officer, says that he had to stop computers in one GE business from spitting out seven daily reports. Just one made a stack of paper 12 feet high, containing product-by-product sales information—accurate to the penny—on hundreds of thousands of items. The bureaucracy routinely emasculated top executives by overwhelming them with useless information and enslaved middle managers with the need to gather it. Old-timers say that as mastery of the facts became impossible, illusion sufficed. Briefing books had grown to such dense impenetrability that managers simply skipped reading them. Instead, they relied on staffers to feed them tough questions—"gotchas" in GE lingo—with which to intimidate subordinates at meetings.[11]

And you think your course assignments are heavy! This **information overload** is the reception of more information than is necessary to make effective decisions.

As you might guess, information overload can lead to errors, omissions, delays, and cutting corners.[12] In addition, decision makers facing overload

Information overload. The reception of more information than is necessary to make effective decisions.

IN FOCUS   E-Mail Overload

At most companies and government agencies, e-mail stops short of the executive suite. Even though many chief executive officers are formally on the network, most of them handle e-mail the way they do post-office mail—they tell their secretaries to sort it, file it, forward it, delegate it or print it out for them to look at. If they want to send e-mail, they dictate to the secretary, who then sends it out.

But in most personal computer and networking companies, e-mail access to the president is part of the culture. Last week at the Networld show in Boston, CEOs described a love-hate relationship with the stuff. "As a CEO, time is always a problem. You're getting bombarded on all sides. You get copied on a lot of stuff you don't want to see, and when you go on the road, it stacks up," says King Lee, president of XTree Co., a network software company based in San Luis Obispo, California. "But it saves a lot of walking and a lot of talking, and everything is condensed. I use it every day."

One reason people get so many messages is that sending copies involves merely adding another name to the distribution list. Because it's so easy, CEOs get copies of weekly status reports for projects they don't need to know about.

At 3Com Corp., a Santa Clara, California, networking company with 2,000 employees around the world, Eric Benhamou, president, says he can handle his 200 daily e-mail messages in half an hour by reading fully only the last message in a series and scanning others. While some people postpone reading their e-mail until lunch time, Mr. Benhamou says he reads it all first thing.

Subordinates' access to CEOs can pay off, Mr. Benhamou says. One software project was completed on time because the engineer in charge sent him a note asking that heat and lights be left on in his building during Christmas shutdown. "If he tried to make an appointment to ask me, he wouldn't have gotten in until February," he says.

While a new generation of e-mail software helps screen out junk e-mail, "necessary" messages pile up fast. There's even "a macho thing about how much e-mail you get," says Jim Manzi, president of Lotus Development Corp., whose cc: Mail software is the industry leader.

Source: Excerpted from Bulkeley, W. M. (1993, January 18). Attention Clinton: Avoid e-mail overload. *The Wall Street Journal*, p. B5.

often attempt to use all of the information at hand, then get confused and permit low-quality information or irrelevant information to influence their decisions.[13] Perhaps you have experienced this when writing a term paper—trying to incorporate too many references and too many viewpoints into a short paper can lead to a confusing, low-quality end product. More isn't necessarily better (see the "In Focus: *E-Mail Overload*").

However, decision makers seem to *think* that more is better. In one study, even though information overload resulted in lower-quality decisions, overloaded decision makers were more *satisfied* than those who did not experience overload.[14] Why is this so? For one thing, even if decisions do not improve with additional information, confidence in the decisions may increase ("I did the best I could"). Second, decision makers may fear being "kept in the dark" and associate the possession of information with power. One research review draws these conclusions about information gathering and use.[15] Managers

- gather much information that has little decision relevance;
- use information that they collected and gathered after a decision in order to justify that decision;
- request information that they don't use;
- request more information, regardless of what's already available;
- complain that there's not enough information to make a decision even though they ignore available information.

In conclusion, although good information improves decisions, organizational members often obtain more or less information than is necessary for adequate decisions.

Alternative Development, Evaluation, and Choice

Perfectly informed or not, the decision maker can now list alternative solutions to the problem, examine the solutions, and choose the best one. For the perfectly rational, totally informed, ideal decision maker, this is easy. He or she conceives of all alternatives, knows the ultimate value of each alternative, and knows the probability that each alternative will work. In this case, the decision maker can exhibit **maximization**—that is, he or she can choose the alternative with the greatest expected value. Consider a simple example:

Maximization. The choice of the decision alternative with the greatest expected value.

	Ultimate Value	Probability	Expected Value
Alternative 1	$100,000 Profit	.4	$40,000 Profit
Alternative 2	$ 60,000 Profit	.8	$48,000 Profit

Here, the expected value of each alternative is calculated by multiplying its ultimate value by its probability. In this case, the perfectly rational decision maker would choose to implement the second alternative.

Unfortunately, things do not go so smoothly for the decision maker working under bounded rationality. He may not know all alternative solutions, and he might be ignorant of the ultimate values and probabilities of success of those solutions that he knows.

Again, cognitive biases come into play. In particular, people are especially weak intuitive statisticians, and they frequently violate standard statistical principles. For example:[16]

- People avoid incorporating known existing data about the likelihood of events ("base rates") into their decisions. For instance, firms continue to launch novelty food products (e.g., foods squeezed from tubes or foods developed by celebrities) even though they have a very high failure rate in the market.

- Large samples warrant more confidence than small samples. Despite this, data from a couple of (vivid) focus groups might be given more weight than data from a large (but anonymous) national survey.

- Decision makers often overestimate the odds of complex chains of events occurring—the scenario sounds sensible despite being less likely with every added link in the chain. "This product will be successful because the price of oil will fall *and* our competitors won't master the technology *and* free trade laws will be enacted."

- People are poor at revising estimates of probabilities and values as they acquire additional information. A good example is the **anchoring effect**, which illustrates that decision makers do not adjust their estimates enough from some initial estimate that serves as an anchor. For example, in one study real estate agents allowed the *asking price* of a house to unduly influence their *professional evaluation* of the house.[17]

Anchoring effect. The inadequate adjustment of subsequent estimates from an initial estimate that serves as an anchor.

Making decisions makers more accountable can sometimes improve decision making. However, these basic statistical cognitive biases are not generally reduced by accountability.[18]

Satisficing. Establishing an adequate level of acceptability for a solution to a problem and then screening solutions until one that exceeds this level is found.

The perfectly rational decision maker can evaluate alternative solutions against a single criterion—economic gain. The decision maker who is bounded by reality might have to factor in other criteria as well, such as the political acceptability of the solution to other organizational members—will the boss like it? Since these additional criteria have their own values and probabilities, the decision-making task increases in complexity.

The bottom line here is that the decision maker working under bounded rationality frequently "satisfices" rather than maximizes.[19] **Satisficing** means that the decision maker establishes an adequate level of acceptability for a solution and then screens solutions until he or she finds one that exceeds this level. When this occurs, evaluation of alternatives ceases, and the solution is chosen for implementation. For instance, the human resources manager who feels that absenteeism has become too high might choose a somewhat arbitrary acceptable level (e.g., the rate one year earlier), then accept the first solution that seems likely to achieve this level. Few organizations seek to *maximize* attendance.

Risky Business

Choosing between decision alternatives often involves an element of risk, and the research evidence on how people handle such risks is fascinating. Consider this scenario that decision researcher Max Bazerman developed. Which alternative solution would you choose?

> Robert Davis, head of the legal staff of a Fortune 500 company, has delayed making one of the most critical recommendations in the organization's history. The company is faced with a class action suit from a hostile group of consumers. While the organization believes that it is innocent, it realizes that a court may not have the same perspective. The organization is expected to lose $50 million if the suit is lost in court. Davis predicts a 50 percent chance of losing the case. The organization has the option of settling out of court by paying $25 million to the "injured" parties. Davis's senior staff has been collecting information and organizing the case for over six months. It is time for action. What should Davis recommend?

> **Alternative A** Settle out of court and accept a sure *loss* of $25,000,000, or

> **Alternative B** Go to court expecting a 50 percent probability of a $50,000,000 loss.[20]

Notice that these two solutions are functionally equivalent in terms of dollars and cents (50 percent of $50 million = $25 million). Nonetheless, you probably tended to choose alternative B—about 80 percent of students do. Notice also that alternative B is the riskier of the two alternatives, in that it exposes the firm to a *potential* for greater loss.

Now, consider two further descriptions of the alternatives. Which solution would you choose?

> **Alternative C** Settle out of court and *save* $25,000,000 that could be lost in court, or

> **Alternative D** Go to court expecting a 50 percent probability of *saving* $50,000,000.

Again, these two solutions are functionally equivalent in monetary terms (and equivalent to options A and B). Yet, you probably chose solution C—80 percent of students do. Notice that this is the *less* risky alternative, in that the firm is not exposed to a potential $50 million loss.

This is a graphic example of the power of framing. Alternatives A and B frame the problem as a choice between losses, while card C and D frame it as a choice between gains or savings. Research by Daniel Kahneman and Amos Tversky shows that when people view a problem as a choice between losses they tend to make risky decisions, rolling the dice in the face of a sure loss. When people frame the alternatives as a choice between gains they tend to make conservative decisions, protecting the sure win.[21]

It is very important to be aware of what reference point you are using when you frame decision alternatives. It is not necessarily wrong to frame a problem as a choice between losses, but this can contribute to a foolish level of risk taking. The (rescinded) decision to alter Coke's formula, the Iran-Contra affair, and the fatal launch of the space shuttle *Challenger* have all been attributed to perceived choices between losses.[22] In the *Challenger* example, the weather conditions were far from ideal for a launch, but a delay would have led to further technical and political problems for NASA. At least this is the way the decision makers framed the available alternatives. If the Hubble mirror contractors went so far as to frame the problem, we can bet that they were considering a $1.7 million expenditure to fix the mirror, not saving $25 million in settlement fees.

We should emphasize that learning history can modify these general preferences for or against risk.[23] For example, suppose that a firm has become very successful by virtue of a series of risky decisions and is now faced with sitting on a handsome market share or investing in a product that could boost its share even higher. This win-win scenario would normally provoke conservatism, but the firm's historical success may tempt managers to choose the risky course of action and invest in the new product.

A major study of the risk-taking propensity of senior U.S. and Canadian business executives reached the following interesting conclusions:[24]

- The executives perceived themselves as being riskier than they actually were.
- The executives were more risk-averse when dealing with their own money than with their firms' money.
- There is no such thing as a "risky personality." People who take great risks in one domain may be very risk-averse in another domain.
- Comparatively, bankers, older managers, and those who had been with the same firm for a long time were risk-averse. Higher-level executives and those from smaller firms took more risks.
- The most successful executives took the most risks.

Solution Implementation

When a decision is made to choose a particular solution to a problem, the solution must be implemented. The perfectly rational decision maker will have factored any possible implementation problems into his or her choice of solutions. Of course, the bounded decision maker will attempt to do the same when estimating probabilities of success. However, in organizations, decision makers are often dependent upon others to implement their decisions, and it might be difficult to anticipate their ability or motivation to do so.

A good example of implementation problems occurs when products such as cars are designed, engineered, and produced in a lengthy series of stages. For example, engineering might have to implement decisions made by designers, and production planning might have to implement decisions made by engineering. As we noted in Chapter 8, this sequential process frequently leads to confusion, conflict, and delay unless cross-functional teams are used during the decision-making process. When they work well, such teams are sensitive to implementation problems.

Solution Evaluation

When the time comes to evaluate the implemented solution, the decision maker is effectively examining the possibility that a new problem has occurred: Does the (new) existing state match the desired state? Has the decision been effective? For all the reasons we stated previously, the perfectly rational decision maker should be able to evaluate the effectiveness of the decision with calm, objective detachment. Again, however, the bounded decision maker might encounter problems at this stage of the process.

Justification.   As we said earlier, people tend to be overconfident about the adequacy of their decisions. Thus, substantial dissonance can be aroused when a decision turns out to be faulty. One way to prevent such dissonance is to avoid careful tests of the adequacy of the decision. As a result, many organizations are notoriously lax when it comes to evaluating the effectiveness of expensive training programs or advertising campaigns. If the bad news cannot be avoided, the erring decision maker might devote his or her energy to trying to justify the faulty decision.

Sunk costs. Permanent losses of resources incurred as the result of a decision.

The justification of faulty decisions is best seen in the irrational treatment of sunk costs. **Sunk costs** are permanent losses of resources incurred as the result of a decision.[25] The key word here is "permanent." Since these resources have been lost (sunk) due to a past decision, they should not enter into future decisions. Despite this, psychologist Barry Staw has studied how people often "throw good resources after bad," acting as if they can recoup sunk costs. This

Escalation of commitment. The tendency to invest additional resources in an apparently failing course of action.

process is **escalation of commitment** to an apparently failing course of action, in which the escalation involves devoting more and more resources to actions implied by the decision.[26] For example, suppose an executive authorizes the purchase of several new computers to improve office productivity. The machines turn out to be very unreliable, and they are frequently out of commission for repair. Perfect rationality suggests admitting to a mistake here. However, the executive might authorize an order for more machines from the same manufacturer to "prove" that he was right all along, hoping to recoup sunk costs with improved productivity from an even greater number of machines.

Dissonance reduction is not the only reason that escalation of commitment to a faulty decision may occur. In addition, a social norm that favors *consistent* behavior by administrators might be at work.[27] Changing one's mind and reversing previous decisions might be perceived as a sign of weakness, a fate to be avoided at all costs.

Escalation of commitment sometimes happens even when the current decision maker is not responsible for previous sunk costs. For example, politicians might continue an expensive unnecessary public works project even though it was begun by a previous political administration. Here, dissonance reduction and the appearance of consistency are irrelevant, suggesting some other causes of escalation. For one thing, decision makers might be motivated not to appear wasteful.[28] ("Even though the airport construction is way over budget and flight traffic doesn't justify a new airport, let's finish the thing. Otherwise, the taxpayers will think we've squandered their money.") Also, escalation of commitment might be due to the way in which decision makers frame the problem once some resources have been sunk. Rather than seeing the savings involved in reversing the decision, the problem might be framed as a decision between a sure loss of x dollars (which have been sunk) and an uncertain loss of $x + y$ dollars (maybe the additional investment will succeed). As we noted earlier, when problems are framed this way, people tend to avoid the certain loss and go with the riskier choice, which in this case is escalation.[29]

Escalation can occur in both competitive and noncompetitive situations. Some Wall Street analysts felt that Viacom Inc. paid too much for entertainment giant Paramount in its five month bidding war with QVC Network. Escalation is frequently seen in competitive bidding. As a noncompetitive example, many respected Wall Street securities analysts advised the purchase of IBM stock even as it was falling lower and lower in response to the firm's difficulties in the early 1990s.

There are elements of escalation in the Hubble mirror fiasco. Perkin-Elmer continued to pour money into smoothing the flawed shape of the mirror despite early warnings of the flaw. The company expended effort justifying the questionable test results.

Are there any ways to prevent the tendency to escalate commitment to a failing course of action? Logic and research suggest the following:[30]

- Encourage continuous experimentation with reframing the problem to avoid the decision trap of feeling that more resources *have* to be invested. Shift the frame to saving rather than spending.

- Set specific goals for the project in advance that must be met if more resources are to be invested. This prevents escalation when early results are "unclear."

- Place more emphasis in evaluating managers on *how* they made decisions and less on decision outcomes. This kind of accountability is the sensible way to teach managers not to fear failure.

It may be tempting to think that using groups to make decisions will reduce the tendency toward escalation. However, research shows that groups are *more* prone than individuals to escalate.[31] Certainly, many of the prominent escalation fiascoes have been group decisions.

Hindsight. The careful evaluation of decisions is also inhibited by faulty hindsight. **Hindsight** refers to the tendency to review the decision-making process that we used in order to find out what we did right (in the case of success) or wrong (in the case of failure). While hindsight can prove useful, it often functions as a cognitive bias.

The classic example of hindsight involves the armchair quarterback who "knew" that a chancy intercepted pass in the first quarter was unnecessary

Hindsight. The tendency to review a decision-making process to find what was done right or wrong.

because the team won the game anyway! The armchair critic is exhibiting the knew-it-all-along effect. This is the tendency to assume after the fact that we knew all along what the outcome of a decision would be. In effect, our faulty memory adjusts the probabilities that we estimated before making the decision to correspond to what actually happened.[32] This can prove quite dangerous. The money manager who consciously makes a very risky investment that turns out to be successful might revise her memory to assume that the decision was a sure thing. The next time, the now-confident investor might not be so lucky!

Another form of faulty hindsight is the tendency to take personal responsibility for successful decision outcomes while denying responsibility for unsuccessful outcomes.[33] Thus, when things work out well, it is because *we* made a careful, logical decision. When things go poorly, some unexpected *external* factor messed up our sensible decision! For example, students are very willing to take responsibility for good grades, while they attribute bad grades to poor teaching or a heavy course load. Similarly, the marketing manager who approves an advertising campaign resulting in increased sales will assume that she planned the campaign properly. She might attribute a downturn in sales to the poor economy or the unanticipated actions of a competitor. Sometimes this tendency reflects conscious excuse making. Usually, however, it probably reflects an unconscious search for additional information when poor decision outcomes occur.

Rational Decision Making—A Summary

The rational decision-making model in Exhibit 12.1 provides a good guide for how many decisions *should* be made but only a partially accurate view of how they *are* made. For complex, unfamiliar decisions, such as choosing an occupation, the rational model provides a pretty good picture of how people actually make decisions.[34] Also, organizational decision makers often follow the

Stage	Perfect Rationality	Bounded Rationality
Problem Identification	Easy, accurate perception of gaps that constitute problems	Perceptual defense; jump to solutions; attention to symptoms rather than problems
Information Search	Free; fast; right amount obtained	Slow; costly; reliance on flawed memory; obtain too little or too much
Development of Alternative Solutions	Can conceive of all	Not all known
Evaluation of Alternative Solutions	Ultimate value of each known; probability of each known; only criterion is economic gain	Potential ignorance of or miscalculation of values and probabilities; criteria include political factors
Solution Choice	Maximizes	Satisfices
Solution Implementation	Considered in evaluation of alternatives	May be difficult owing to reliance on others
Solution Evaluation	Objective, according to previous steps	May involve justification, escalation to recover sunk costs, faulty hindsight

EXHIBIT 12.2
Perfectly rational decision making contrasted with bounded rationality.

rational model when they agree about the goals they are pursuing.[35] On the other hand, there is plenty of case study evidence of short-circuiting the rational model in organizational decisions, in part because of the biases we discussed above.[36] Also, true experts in a field often short-circuit the rational model, using their knowledge base stored in memory to skip steps logically.[37] Exhibit 12.2 summarizes the operation of perfect and bounded rationality at each stage of the decision process. Exhibit 12.3 summarizes the various cognitive biases that we have covered.

GROUP DECISION MAKING

Many, many organizational decisions are made by groups rather than individuals, especially when problems are ill-structured. In this section we shall consider the advantages and problems of group decision making.

Why Use Groups?

There are a number of reasons for employing groups to make organizational decisions.

Decision Quality.   Experts often argue that groups or teams can make higher-quality decisions than individuals. This argument is based on the following three assumptions:

- Groups are *more vigilant* than individuals—more people are scanning the environment.
- Groups can *generate more ideas* than individuals.
- Groups can *evaluate ideas better* than individuals.

At the problem identification and information search stages, vigilance is especially advantageous. A problem that some group members miss might be

- Decision makers tend to be overconfident about the decisions that they make.
- Decision makers tend to seek out information that confirms their own problem definitions and solutions. (Confirmation bias)
- Decision makers tend to remember and incorporate vivid, recent events into their decisions.
- Decision makers fail to incorporate known existing data about the liklihood of events into their decisions.
- Decision makers ignore sample sizes when evaluating samples of information.
- Decision makers overestimate the odds of complex chains of events occurring.
- Decision makers do not adjust estimates enough from some initial estimate that serves as an anchor as they acquire more information. (Anchoring effect)
- Decision makers have difficulty ignoring sunk costs when making subsequent decisions.
- Decision makers overestimate their ability to have predicted events after-the-fact, take responsibility for successful decision outcomes, and deny responsibility for unsuccessful outcomes. (Hindsight)

EXHIBIT 12.3
Summary of cognitive biases in decision making.

identified by others. For example, a member of the board of directors might notice a short article in an obscure business publication that has great relevance for the firm. In searching for information to clarify the problem suggested in the article, other members of the board might possess unique information that proves useful.

When it comes to developing alternative solutions, more people should literally have more ideas, if only because someone remembers something that others have forgotten. In addition, members with different backgrounds and experiences may bring different perspectives to the problem. This is why undergraduate students, graduate students, faculty, and administrators are often included on university task forces to improve the library or develop a course evaluation system.

When it comes to evaluating solutions and choosing the best one, groups have the advantage of checks and balances. That is, an extreme position or incorrect notion held by one member should be offset by the pooled judgments of the rest of the group.

These characteristics suggest that groups *should* make higher-quality decisions than individuals. Shortly, we will find out whether they actually do so.

Decision Acceptance and Commitment.   As we pointed out in our discussion of participative leadership in Chapter 10, groups are often used to make decisions on the premise that a decision made in this way will be more acceptable to those involved. Again, there are several assumptions underlying this premise:

- People wish to be involved in decisions that will affect them.
- People will better understand a decision in which they participated.
- People will be more committed to a decision in which they invested personal time and energy.

The acceptability of group decisions is especially useful in dealing with a problem described earlier—getting the decision implemented. If decision makers truly understand the decision and feel committed to it, they should be willing to follow through and see that it is carried out.

Diffusion of responsibility. The ability of group members to share the burden of the negative consequences of a poor decision.

Diffusion of Responsibility.   High quality and acceptance are sensible reasons for using groups to make decisions. As you may recall from Chapter 10, a somewhat less admirable reason to employ groups is to allow for **diffusion of responsibility** across the members in case the decision turns out poorly. In this case, each member of the group will share part of the burden of the negative consequences, and no one person will be singled out for punishment. Of course, when this happens, individual group members often "abandon ship" and exhibit biased hindsight—"I knew all along that the bid was too high to be accepted, but they made me go along with them."

Do Groups Actually Make Higher-Quality Decisions Than Individuals?

The discussion in the first part of the previous section suggested that groups *should* make higher-quality decisions than individuals. But *do* they? Is the frequent use of groups to make decisions warranted by evidence? The answer is yes. One review concludes that "groups usually produce more and better solutions to problems than do individuals working alone."[38] Another concludes that group performance is superior to that of the average individual in the group.[39] More specifically, groups should perform better than individuals when:

- the group members differ in relevant skills and abilities, as long as they don't differ so much that conflict occurs;
- some division of labor can occur;
- memory for facts is an important issue;
- individual judgments can be combined by weighting them to reflect the expertise of the various members.[40]

To consolidate your understanding of these conditions, consider a situation that should favor group decision making: A small construction company wishes to bid on a contract to build an apartment complex. The president, the controller, a construction boss, and an engineer work together to formulate the bid. Since they have diverse backgrounds and skills, they divide the task initially. The president reviews recent bids on similar projects in the community; the controller gets estimates on materials costs; the engineer and boss review the blueprints. During this process, each racks his or her brain to recall lessons learned from making previous bids. Finally, they put their information together, and each member voices an opinion about what the bid should be. The president decides to average these opinions to arrive at the actual bid, since each person is equally expert in his or her own area.

Disadvantages of Group Decision Making

Although groups have the ability to develop high-quality, acceptable decisions, there are a number of potential disadvantages to group decision making.

Time.   Groups seldom work quickly or efficiently when compared to individuals. This is because of the process losses (Chapter 8) involved in discussion, debate, and coordination. The time problem increases with group size. When the speed of arriving at a solution to a problem is a prime factor, organizations should avoid using groups.

Conflict.   Many times, participants in group decisions have their own personal axes to grind or their own resources to protect. When this occurs, decision quality may take a back seat to political wrangling and infighting. In the example about the construction company we presented earlier, the construction boss might see it to his advantage to overestimate the size of the crew required to build the apartments. On the other hand, the controller might make it her personal crusade to pare labor costs. A simple compromise between these two extreme points of view might not result in the highest-quality or most creative decision (see the "In Focus: *Group Decision Making Damages TV Quality*").

Domination.   The advantages of group decision making will seldom be realized if meetings are dominated by a single individual or a small coalition. Even if a dominant person has good information, this style is not likely to lead to group acceptance and commitment. If the dominant person is particularly misinformed, the group decision is very likely to be ineffective.

IN FOCUS   Group Decision Making Damages TV Quality

Arnold Shapiro, an Emmy and Oscar winning television and film producer, explains the questionable quality of much contemporary television programming:

Most critics and TV reviewers complain about how few good programs there are on television. But I am amazed that there are as many good programs as there are, knowing, as I do, what it takes to get any program on the air.

Those producers who actually wind up with a successful prime-time network series, TV movie or special have usually weathered an ordeal as difficult as trying to become the next President.

What makes the process of getting a show on TV so difficult—and keeping it on if it's a series—is that every project is made by committee. The committee consists of an array of executives, producers, writers, stars, lawyers, business affairs and financial watchdogs, agents, managers, technicians and editors. Some business and financial members of the committee have mandates that restrict or alter the creative process. Some committee members don't understand or support the vision of the creator or writers. And some committee members are less creative or talented, but don't know it.

The most difficult challenge is trying to produce the best program possible within the financial constraints of what the network or other money sources will pay. But even after satisfying all the network requests and requirements, there are still continuous creative differences to be resolved between various opinionated, outspoken and often excitable members of the production team.

Making television programs by committee may not be the best way creatively, but that's the way it's done in television. I often admire the lone artist who sits before a canvas and creates a painting guided only by imagination and talent, with no interference from anyone else.

The executive producer and producer of a series work with more than 100 creative and technical people, plus studio and network executives, to produce and deliver each episode on budget and on schedule—episodes that need to satisfy the network brass, sales people, advertisers, publicity and promotion people, and those who make the show.

I believe that quite a few television producers want to elevate the quality of commercial television with thought-provoking, uplifting, meaningful programs—exploring the human condition through drama, comedy or nonfiction to inspire viewers toward positive actions and choices. But many of these producers find that they are psychologically defeated or are forced by prolonged economic deprivation to sell or produce any program that will finally be bought by a network—however shallow or insignificant compared to their original goals.

Source: Excerpted from Shapiro, A. (1992, August 19). The uphill struggle to bring quality to TV programming. *Los Angeles Times*, pp. F1, F5.

Groupthink. In retrospect, have you ever been involved in a group decision that you knew was a "loser" but that you felt unable to protest? Perhaps you thought you were the only one who had doubts about the chosen course of action. Perhaps you tried to speak up, but others criticized you for not being on the team. Maybe you found yourself searching for information to confirm that the decision was correct and ignoring evidence that the decision was bad. What was happening? Were you suffering from some strange form of possession? Mind control?

In Chapter 9 we discussed the process of conformity in social settings. As you might expect, conformity can have a strong influence on the decisions that groups make. The most extreme influence is seen when **groupthink** occurs. This happens when group pressures lead to reduced mental efficiency, poor testing of reality, and lax moral judgment.[41] In effect, unanimous acceptance of decisions is stressed over quality of decisions.

Psychologist Irving Janis, who developed the groupthink concept, felt that high group cohesiveness was at its root. It now appears that other factors

Groupthink. The capacity for group pressure to damage the mental efficiency, reality testing, and moral judgment of decision-making groups.

might be equally important or more important. These include concern for approval from the group and the isolation of the group from other sources of information. However, the promotion of a particular decision by the group leader appears to be the strongest cause.[42] In any event, Janis provides a detailed list of groupthink symptoms:

- *Illusion of invulnerability.* Members are overconfident and willing to assume great risks. They ignore obvious danger signals.

- *Rationalization.* Problems and counterarguments that members can't ignore are "rationalized away."

- *Illusion of morality.* The decisions the group adopts are not only perceived as sensible, they are also perceived as *morally* correct.

- *Stereotypes of outsiders.* The group constructs unfavorable stereotypes of those outside the group who are the targets of their decisions.

- *Pressure for conformity.* Members pressure each other to fall into line and conform with the group's views.

- *Self-censorship.* Members convince themselves to avoid voicing opinions contrary to the group.

- *Illusion of unanimity.* Members perceive that unanimous support exists for their chosen course of action.

- *Mindguards.* Some group members may adopt the role of "protecting" the group from information that goes against its decisions.[43]

Obviously, victims of groupthink are operating in an atmosphere of unreality that should lead to low-quality decisions. Groupthink has been implicated in the decision process that led to NASA's fatal launch of the *Challenger*.[44] We can also see it in the Hubble mirror decision process.[45] To begin with, a dominant leader in charge of the internal tests appears to have isolated the mirror project team from outside sources of information. Symptoms of groupthink followed: At least three sets of danger signals that the mirror was flawed were ignored or explained away (illusion of invulnerability and rationalization); Kodak was dismissed as too incompetent to test the mirror (stereotype of outsiders); the consultant who suggested that Kodak test the mirror received bitter criticism but still felt he didn't protest enough in the end (mindguarding and self-censorship); the defense of the isolated working methods was viewed as more "theological" than technical (illusion of morality).

What can prevent groupthink? Leaders must be careful to avoid exerting undue pressure for a particular decision outcome and concentrate on good decision processes. Also, leaders should establish norms that encourage and even reward responsible dissent. Some of the decision-making techniques we discuss later in the chapter should help prevent the tendency as well.

How Do Groups Handle Risk?

Almost by definition, problems that are suitable for group decision making involve some degree of risk and uncertainty. This raises a very important question: Do groups make decisions that are more or less risky than those of individuals? Or will the degree of risk assumed by the group simply equal the average risk preferred by its individual members? The answer here is obviously important. Consider the following scenario:

> An accident has just occurred at a nuclear power plant. Several corrections exist, ranging from expensive and safe to low-cost but risky. On the way to an emergency meeting, each nuclear engineer formulates an opinion about what should be done. But what will the group decide?

Conventional wisdom provides few clear predictions about what the group of engineers will decide to do. On one hand, it is sometimes argued that groups will make riskier decisions than individuals because there is security in numbers. That is, diffusion of responsibility for a bad decision encourages the group to take greater chances. On the other hand, it is often argued that groups are cautious, with the members checking and balancing each other so much that a conservative outcome is sure to occur. Just contrast the committee-laden civil service with the swashbuckling style of independent operators such as Ted Turner and Donald Trump!

Risky shift. The tendency for groups to make riskier decisions than the average risk initially advocated by their individual members.

Given this contradiction of common sense, the history of research into group decision making and risk is both interesting and instructive. A Massachusetts Institute of Technology student, J.A.F. Stoner, reported in a Master's thesis that he had discovered clear evidence of a **risky shift** in decision making.[46] Participants in the research reviewed hypothetical cases involving risk, such as those involving career choices or investment decisions. As individuals, they recommended a course of action. Then they were formed into groups, and the groups discussed each case and came to a joint decision. In general, the groups tended to advise riskier courses of action than the average risk initially advocated by their members. This is the risky shift. As studies were conducted by others to explore the reasons for its causes, things got more complicated. For some groups and some decisions, **conservative shifts** were observed. In other words, groups came to decisions that were *less* risky than those of the individual members before interaction.

Conservative shift. The tendency for groups to make less risky decisions than the average risk initially advocated by their individual members.

It is now clear that both risky and conservative shifts are possible, and they occur in a wide variety of real settings, including investment and purchasing decisions. But what determines which kind of shift occurs? A key factor appears to be the initial positions of the group members before they discuss the problem. This is illustrated in Exhibit 12.4. As you can see, when group members are somewhat conservative before interaction (the X's), they tend to exhibit a conservative shift when they discuss the problem. When group members are somewhat risky initially (the ●'s), they exhibit a risky shift after discussion. In other words, *group discussion seems to polarize or exaggerate the initial position of the group.*[47] Returning to the nuclear accident, if the engineers initially prefer a somewhat conservative solution, they should adopt an even more conservative strategy during the meeting.

Why do risky and conservative shifts occur when groups make decisions? Evidence seems to indicate two main factors:[48]

- Group discussion generates ideas and arguments that individual members haven't considered before. This information naturally favors the members' initial tendency toward risk or toward conservatism. Since discussion provides "more" and "better" reasons for the initial tendency, the tendency ends up being exaggerated.

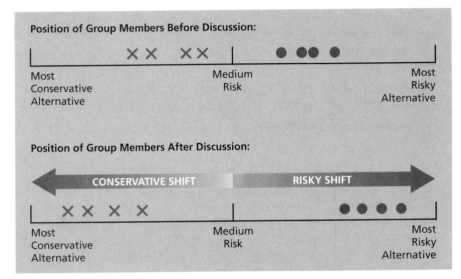

Position of Group Members Before Discussion:

Most
Conservative
Alternative

Medium
Risk

Most
Risky
Alternative

Position of Group Members After Discussion:

CONSERVATIVE SHIFT   RISKY SHIFT

Most
Conservative
Alternative

Medium
Risk

Most
Risky
Alternative

EXHIBIT 12.4
The dynamics of risky
and conservative shifts
for two groups.

- Group members try to present themselves as basically similar to other members but "even better." Thus, they try to one-up others in discussion by adopting a slightly more extreme version of the group's initial stance.

In summary, administrators should be aware of the tendency for group interaction to polarize initial risk levels. If this polarization results from the sensible exchange of information, it might actually improve the group's decision. However, if it results from one-upmanship it might lead to low-quality decisions.

IMPROVING DECISION MAKING IN ORGANIZATIONS

It stands to reason that organizational decision making can improve if decision makers receive encouragement to follow more closely the rational decision-making model shown in Exhibit 12.1. This should help to preclude the various biases and errors that we have alluded to throughout the chapter. Each of the following techniques has this goal.

Training Discussion Leaders

When organizations utilize group decision making, an appointed leader often convenes the group and guides the discussion. The actions of this leader can "make or break" the decision. On one hand, if the leader behaves autocratically, trying to "sell" a preconceived decision, the advantages of using a group are obliterated, and decision acceptance can suffer. If the leader fails to exert *any* influence, however, the group might develop a low-quality solution that does not meet the needs of the organization. The use of role-playing training to develop these leadership skills has increased the quality and acceptance of group decisions. The following are examples of the skills that people learn in discussion leader training.[49]

- State the problem in a nondefensive, objective manner. Do not suggest solutions or preferences.

- Supply essential facts and clarify any constraints on solutions (e.g., "We can't spend more than $5000").
- Draw out all group members. Prevent domination by one person, and protect members from being attacked or severely criticized.
- Wait out pauses. Don't make suggestions or ask leading questions.
- Ask stimulating questions that move the discussion forward.
- Summarize and clarify at several points to mark progress.

Stimulating and Managing Controversy

Full-blown conflict among organizational members is hardly conducive to good decision making. Individuals will withhold information, and personal or group goals will take precedence over developing a decision that solves organizational problems. On the other hand, a complete lack of controversy can be equally damaging, since alternative points of view that may be very relevant to the issue at hand will never surface. Such a lack of controversy is partially responsible for the groupthink effect, and it also contributes to many cases of escalation of commitment to flawed courses of action. For example, stifled controversy played a part in the disastrous launch of the space shuttle *Challenger* and the Hubble fiasco.

Research shows a variety of ways to stimulate controversy in decision-making groups—incorporating members with diverse ideas and backgrounds, forming subgroups to "tear the problem apart," and establishing norms that favor the open sharing of information.[50] However, these tactics must be managed carefully to ensure that open conflict does not result. The discussion skills covered in the previous section can help here.

One interesting method of controversy stimulation is the appointment of a **devil's advocate** to challenge existing plans and strategies. The advocate's role is to challenge the weaknesses of the plan or strategy and state why it should not be adopted. For example, a bank might be considering offering an innovative kind of account. Details to be decided include interest rate, required minimum balance, and so on. A committee might be assigned to develop a position paper. Before a decision is made, someone would be assigned to read the paper and "tear it apart," noting potential weaknesses. Thus, a decision is made in full recognition of the pros and cons of the plan.

Evidence indicates that the controversy promoted by the devil's advocate improves decision quality.[51] However, to be effective, the advocate must present his or her views in an objective, unemotional manner.

Traditional Brainstorming

Brainstorming is the "brain child" of a Madison Avenue advertising executive.[52] Its major purpose is to increase the number of creative solution alternatives to problems. Thus, **brainstorming** focuses on the *generation* of ideas rather than the *evaluation* of ideas. If a group generates a large number of ideas, the chance of obtaining a truly creative solution is increased.

Brainstorming was originally conceived as a group technique. It was assumed that in generating ideas, group members could feed off each other's suggestions and be stimulated to offer more creative solutions. To ensure this, the group is encouraged to operate in a free-wheeling, off-the-wall manner. No

Devil's advocate. A person appointed to identify and challenge the weaknesses of a proposed plan or strategy.

Brainstorming. An attempt to increase the number of creative solution alternatives to problems by focusing on idea generation rather than evaluation.

Stimulating controversy in groups, as depicted here in the Roberts Pharmaceutical annual report, can generate new ideas and challenge existing plans and strategies.

ideas should be considered too extreme or unusual to be voiced. In addition, no criticism of ideas should be offered, since this can inhibit useful lines of thinking. For instance, an advertising agency might convene a group to generate names for a new toothpaste or soft drink. Similarly, a government agency might convene a group to generate possible solutions for welfare fraud.

Traditional brainstorming has not fulfilled its creative promise. Research has shown conclusively that individuals working alone tend to generate more ideas than when in groups.[53] In other words, four people working independently (and encouraged to be creative and nonevaluative) will usually generate more ideas than the same people working as a team. Why is this? Likely explanations include inhibition, domination of the group by an ineffective member, or the sheer physical limitations of people trying to talk simultaneously. Later, we'll consider an electronic alternative to traditional brainstorming that has proven successful.

Nominal Group Technique

The fact that nominal (in name only) brainstorming groups generate more ideas than interacting brainstorming groups gave rise to the **nominal group technique** (NGT) of decision making. Unlike brainstorming, NGT is concerned with both the generation of ideas and the evaluation of these ideas:

Imagine a meeting room in which seven to ten individuals are sitting around a table in full view of each other; however, at the beginning of

Nominal group technique. A structured group decision-making technique in which ideas are generated without group interaction and then systematically evaluated by the group.

the meeting they do not speak to each other. Instead, each individual is writing ideas on a pad of paper in front of him or her. At the end of five to ten minutes, a structured sharing of ideas takes place. Each individual, in round-robin fashion, presents one idea from his or her private list. A recorder writes that idea on a flip chart in full view of other members. There is still no discussion at this point of the meeting—only the recording of privately narrated ideas. Round-robin listing continues until all members indicate they have no further ideas to share. Discussion follows during the next phase of the meeting; however, it is structured so that each idea receives attention before independent voting. This is accomplished by asking for clarification, or stating support or nonsupport of each idea listed on the flip chart. Independent voting then takes place. Each member privately, in writing, selects priorities by rank-ordering (or rating). The group decision is the mathematically pooled outcome of the individual votes.[54]

As you can see, NGT carefully separates the generation of ideas from their evaluation. Ideas are generated nominally (without interaction) to prevent inhibition and conformity. Evaluation permits interaction and discussion, but it occurs in a fairly structured manner to be sure that each idea gets adequate attention. NGT's chief disadvantage would seem to be the time and resources required to assemble the group for face-to-face interaction. The Delphi technique was developed in part to overcome this problem.

The Delphi Technique

Delphi technique. A method of pooling a large number of expert judgments by using a series of increasingly refined questionnaires.

The **Delphi technique** of decision making was developed at the Rand Corporation to forecast changes in technology. Its name derives from the future-telling ability of the famous Greek Delphic Oracle.[55] Unlike NGT, the Delphi process relies solely upon a nominal group—participants do not engage in face-to-face interaction. Thus, it is possible to poll a large number of experts without assembling them in the same place at the same time. We should emphasize that these experts do not actually make a final decision; rather, they provide information for organizational decision makers.

The heart of Delphi is a series of questionnaires sent to respondents. Minimally, there are two waves of questionnaires, but more are not unusual. The first questionnaire is usually general in nature and permits free responses to the problem. For example, suppose the CEO of a large corporation wishes to evaluate and improve the firm's total quality management program. A random sample of managers who have worked closely with TQM would receive an initial questionnaire asking them to list the strengths and weaknesses of the program. Staff would collate the responses and develop a second questionnaire that might share these responses and ask for suggested improvements. A final questionnaire might then be sent asking respondents to rate or rank each improvement. The staff would then merge the ratings or rankings mathematically and present them to the president for consideration.

A chief disadvantage of Delphi is the rather lengthy time frame involved in the questionnaire phases, although fax and e-mail can speed up sending and receiving. In addition, its effectiveness depends upon the writing skills of the respondents and their interest in the problem, since they must work on their own rather than as part of an actual group. Despite these problems, Delphi is an efficient method of pooling a large number of expert judgments while avoiding the problems of conformity and domination that can occur in interacting groups.

The University of Michigan Transportation Research Institute uses a Delphi survey to poll auto executives about future trends in automobile design and marketing. Results show the difficulties of looking too far into the future. The survey of 10 years ago badly overestimated current gas prices and underestimated current car sizes and the extent of Japanese imports.[56]

ELECTRONIC DECISION-MAKING GROUPS—PROMISE AND PROBLEMS

In closing the chapter, let's consider the impact that electronic, computer-mediated information technology has on organizational decision making. You have probably heard of some of the more exotic forms of this technology, such as decision support systems and expert systems. These systems use databases compiled by experts to aid in the diagnosis and solution of problems. Here, we will consider something less exotic but equally interesting, the formation of electronic groups.

Electronic groups are simply decision-making groups whose members are linked together electronically rather than face-to-face. A typical group would interact on an electronic mail network, sending messages with a keyboard and receiving them via a monitor. These messages can be saved in computer memory for future reference.

> **Electronic groups.** Decision-making groups whose members are linked electronically rather than face-to-face.

Contrasting electronic groups with their face-to-face counterparts suggests some of the factors that might influence electronic decisions. For one thing, in electronic groups there is the potential for members to enter information anonymously. And even if contributions are not anonymous, people might *feel* somewhat more anonymous than in a face-to-face group. Second, visual sources of information about how other members feel, expressed in body language and tone of voice, is missing. Finally, in electronic groups, many people can "talk" at the same time. As we'll see, these differences affect the social structure of groups and consequently affect their decision making.

Electronic Brainstorming

Some research on electronic groups has concentrated on the idea generation aspect of decision making. **Electronic brainstorming** uses computer-mediated technology to accomplish the same goals as traditional brainstorming, the generation of novel ideas without evaluation. As we noted above, face-to-face interaction actually reduces individual brainstorming performance. But what happens if people brainstorm as an electronic group?

> **Electronic brainstorming.** The use of computer-mediated technology to improve traditional brainstorming practices.

Once over the size of two members, electronic brainstorming groups perform better than face-to-face groups in terms of both quantity and quality of ideas.[57] Also, as electronic groups get larger, they tend to produce more ideas, but the ideas-per-person measure remains stable. In contrast, as face-to-face groups get bigger, fewer and fewer ideas per person are generated (remember social loafing from Chapter 8). What accounts for the success of electronic brainstorming? Reduced inhibition about participating and the ability for people to enter ideas simultaneously without waiting for others seem to be the main reasons. Notice that these factors become especially critical as the group gets bigger. Some organizations have done electronic brainstorming with up to 30-member groups.

Beyond Brainstorming

Other research on electronic groups has gone beyond brainstorming to look at more complex and complete decision tasks that actually require reaching a solution. The results reveal both promise and problems.[58]

Electronic groups tend to be more egalitarian than face-to-face groups. That is, status barriers tend to be broken down, and participation is more evenly distributed among members. In one study of executives, men were five times more likely than women to make an initial decision proposal in a face-to-face meeting.[59] In an electronic meeting, men and women were equally likely to make the first proposal. This egalitarianism is obviously a good thing. On the other hand, electronic communication has also encouraged impulsive, rude messages and the expression of extreme views ("flaming").

For some well-established groups, electronic meetings seem to speed up the decision process. However, for newly formed groups, electronic interaction invariably slows the decision process and leads to difficulty for the group to reach consensus. "Flaming" might be a partial cause, but the lack of verbal and nonverbal cues also makes it difficult to recognize subtle trends toward consensus. This suggests the need for an electronic version of some of the discussion leader skills we listed earlier.

A final trend is the apparent tendency for electronic groups to make more extreme decisions than face-to-face groups, especially when it comes to risk. This trend, if confirmed, is disturbing, because we have pointed out that face-to-face groups themselves have problems dealing with risk. Perhaps people feel less accountable for electronic decisions.

The impact of electronic groups on organizational decisions is obviously of importance to managers. Such groups provide great potential for crossing the barriers of time and space to improve group decisions. All the same, it is clear that they add some new complexities to the challenging task of making good decisions.

The Manager's Notebook   Reframing Pizza Hut's Problem

1. Defining Pizza Hut's problem in terms of a solution would go something like this: Domino's is our arch-competition. Domino's delivers pizza and we do not. We can solve our problem by offering delivery. This solution is very limited in terms of growth potential because it doesn't expand the pie (pun intended) in any way. It is only oriented toward taking some customers back from the competition.

2. Pizza Hut did institute delivery. However, it also reframed itself as a pizza *distribution* com-pany rather than a pizza *restaurant* chain. Although this distinction seems subtle, its consequences are not. The reframing led the company to pursue deals with concessions that served pizza in schools, hospitals, airports, corporate cafeterias, and even Wal-Mart. Revenues doubled. The firm is currently examining using its distribution system to provide other food products, having recognized with reframing that it is essentially in a service business.

EXECUTIVE SUMMARY

◆ Decision making is the process of developing a commitment to some course of action. Alternatively, it is a problem-solving process. A problem exists when a gap is perceived between some existing state and some desired state.

◆ Some problems are well structured. This means that existing and desired states are clear, as is the means of getting from one state to the other. Well-structured problems are often solved with programs, which simply standardize solutions. Programmed decision making is effective as long as the program is developed rationally and as long as conditions do not change.

◆ Ill-structured problems contain some combination of an unclear existing state, an unclear desired state, or unclear methods of getting from one state to the other. They tend to be unique and nonrecurrent, and they require nonprogrammed decision making, in which the rational model comes into play.

◆ Rational decision making includes (1) problem identification, (2) information search, (3) development of alternative solutions, (4) evaluation of alternatives, (5) choice of best alternative, (6) implementation, and (7) ongoing evaluation of the implemented alternative. The imaginary, perfectly rational decision maker has free and easy access to all relevant information, can process it accurately, and has a single ultimate goal—economic maximization. Real decision makers must suffer with bounded rationality. They do not have free and easy access to information, and the human mind has limited information processing capacity and is susceptible to a variety of cognitive biases. In addition, time constraints and political considerations can outweigh anticipated economic gain. As a result, bounded decision makers usually satisfice (choose a solution that is "good enough") rather than maximize. Perceptual defense, faulty hindsight, attempts to recover sunk costs, inadequate information, and information overload may damage the quality of decisions.

◆ Groups can often make higher-quality decisions than individuals because of their vigilance and their potential capacity to generate and evaluate more ideas. Also, group members might accept more readily a decision in which they have been involved. Given the proper problem, groups will frequently make higher-quality decisions than individuals. However, using groups takes a lot of time and might provoke conflict. In addition, groups might fall prey to groupthink, in which social pressures to conform to a particular decision outweigh rationality. Groups might also make decisions that are more risky or conservative than those of individuals.

◆ Attempts to improve decision making have involved training discussion leaders, stimulating controversy, brainstorming, the nominal group technique, and the Delphi technique.

◆ Electronic groups are decision-making groups that interact electronically rather than face-to-face. Electronic brainstorming is effective in generating ideas, and participation in electronic decision making tends to be egalitarian. However, electronic groups can have a hard time reaching consensus, and they tend to make riskier decisions than face-to-face groups.

KEY CONCEPTS

Decision making
Problem
Well-structured problem
Program
Ill-structured problem
Perfect rationality
Bounded rationality

Framing
Cognitive biases
Confirmation bias
Information overload
Maximization
Anchoring effect
Satisficing

Sunk costs
Escalation of commitment
Hindsight
Diffusion of responsibility
Groupthink
Risky shift
Conservative shift

Devil's advocate
Brainstorming
Nominal group technique
Delphi technique
Electronic groups
Electronic brainstorming

DISCUSSION QUESTIONS

1. The director of an urban hospital feels that there is a turnover problem among the hospital's nurses. About 25 percent of the staff resign each year, leading to high replacement costs and disruption of services. Use the decision model in Exhibit 12.1 to explore how the director might proceed to solve this problem. Discuss probable bounds to the rationality of the director's decision.

2. Give an example of how framing a problem affects the subsequent decision process.

3. Describe a decision-making episode (in school, work, or personal life) in which you experienced information overload. How did you respond to this overload? Did it affect the quality of your decision?

4. Many universities must register thousands of students for courses each semester. Is this a well-structured problem or an ill-structured problem? Does it require programmed decisions or nonprogrammed decisions? Elaborate.

5. An auditing team fails to detect a case of embezzlement that has gone on for several months at a bank. How might the team members use hindsight to justify their faulty decisions?

6. A very cohesive planning group for a major oil company is about to develop a long-range strategic plan. The head of the unit is aware of the groupthink problem and wishes to prevent it. What steps should she take?

7. Discuss the implications of diffusion of responsibility, risky shift, and conservative shift for the members of a parole board.

8. Discuss how the concepts of groupthink and escalation of commitment might be related to some cases of unethical decision making (and its coverup) in business.

9. What are the similarities and differences of the nominal group technique and the Delphi technique? What are the comparative advantages and disadvantages?

10. Discuss the reasons why decision makers might continue to commit resources to a failing course of action.

EXPERIENTIAL EXERCISE
THE NEW TRUCK DILEMMA

PREPARATION FOR ROLE-PLAYING

The instructor will:

1. Read general instructions to class as a whole.
2. Place data regarding name, length of service, and make and age of truck on chalkboard for ready reference by all.
3. Divide class into groups of six. Any remaining members should be asked to join one of the groups and serve as observers.
4. Assign roles to each group by handing out slips with the names Chris Marshall, Terry, Sal, Jan, Sam, and Charlie. Ask each person to read his or her own role only. Instructions should not be consulted once role-playing is begun.
5. Ask the Chris Marshalls to stand up when they have completed reading their instructions.
6. When all Chris Marshalls are standing, ask that each crew member display conspicuously the slip of paper with his or her role name so that Chris can tell who is who.

THE ROLE-PLAYING PROCESS

1. The instructor will start the role-playing with a statement such as the following: "Chris Marshall has asked the crew to wait in the office. Apparently Chris wants to discuss something with the crew. When Chris sits down that will mean he or she has returned. What you say to each other is entirely up to you. Are you ready? All Chris Marshalls please sit down."
2. Role-playing proceeds for twenty-five to thirty minutes. Most groups reach agreement during this interval.

COLLECTION OF RESULTS

1. Each supervisor in turn reports his or her crew's solution. The instructor summarizes on the chalkboard by listing the initials of each repair person and indicating with arrows which truck goes to whom.
2. A tabulation should be made of the number of people getting a different truck, the crew members considering the solution unfair, and the supervisor's evaluation of the solution.

DISCUSSION OF RESULTS

1. Comparison of solutions will reveal differences in the number of people getting a different truck, who gets

the new one, the number dissatisfied, etc. Discuss why the same facts yield different outcomes.
2. The quality of the solution can be measured by the trucks retained. Highest quality would require the poorest truck to be discarded. Evaluate the quality of the solutions achieved.
3. Acceptance is indicated by the low number of dissatisfied repair people. Evaluate solutions achieved on this dimension.
4. List problems that are similar to the new truck problem. See how widely the group will generalize.

GENERAL INSTRUCTIONS

This is a role-playing exercise. *Do not read the roles given below until assigned to do so by your instructor*!

Assume that you are a repair person for a large utility. Each day you drive to various locations in the city to do repair work. Each of you drives a small truck and you take pride in keeping it looking good. You have a possessive feeling about your truck and like to keep it in good running order. Naturally, you'd like to have a new truck too, because a new truck gives you a feeling of pride.

Here are some facts about the trucks and the crew that reports to Chris Marshall, the supervisor of repairs:

Terry—17 years with the company, has a 2-year-old Ford

Sal—11 years with the company, has a 5-year-old Dodge

Jan—10 years with the company, has a 4-year-old Ford

Sam—5 years with the company, has a 3-year-old Ford

Charlie—3 years with the company, has a 5-year-old Chevrolet

Most of you do all of your driving in the city, but Jan and Sam cover the jobs in the suburbs.

You will be one of the people mentioned above and will be given some further individual instructions. In acting your part in role-playing, accept the facts as well as assume the attitude supplied in your specific role. From this point on, let your feelings develop in accordance with the events that transpire in the role-playing process. When facts or events arise that are not covered by the roles, make up things that are consistent with the way it might be in a real-life situation.

When the role-playing begins, assume that Chris Marshall called the crew into the repair office.

Role for Chris Marshall, Supervisor.   You are the supervisor of a repair crew, each of whom drives a small service truck to and from various jobs. Every so often you get a new truck to exchange for an old one, and you have the problem of deciding to which one of your crew you should give the new truck. Often there are hard feelings because each person seems to feel entitled to the new truck, so you have a tough time being fair. As a matter of fact, it usually turns out that whatever you decide, most of the crew consider wrong. You now have to face the issue again because a new truck has just been allocated to you for assignment. The new truck is a Chevrolet.

In order to handle this problem you have decided to put the decision up to the crew themselves. You will tell them about the new truck and will put the problem in terms of what would be the fairest way to assign the truck. *Don't take a position yourself, because you want to do what the crew thinks is most fair.* However, be sure that the group reaches a decision.

Role for Terry.   When a new Chevrolet truck becomes available, you think you should get it because you have most seniority and don't like your present truck. Your own car is a Chevrolet, and you prefer a Chevrolet truck such as you drove before you got the Ford.

Role for Sal.   You feel you deserve a new truck. Your present truck is old, and since the more senior crew member has a fairly new truck, you should get the next one. You have taken excellent care of your present Dodge and have kept it looking like new. People deserve to be rewarded if they treat a company truck like their own.

Role for Jan.   You have to do more driving than most of the other crew because you work in the suburbs. You have a fairly old truck and feel you should have a new one because you do so much driving.

Role for Sam.   The heater in your present truck is inadequate. Since Charlie backed into the door of your truck, it has never been repaired to fit right. The door lets in too much cold air, and you attribute your frequent colds to this. You want a warm truck since you have a good deal of driving to do. As long as it has good tires, brakes, and is comfortable, you don't care about its make.

Role for Charlie.   You have the poorest truck in the crew. It is five years old, and before you got it, it had been in a bad wreck. It has never been good, and you've put up with it for three years. It's about time you got a good truck to drive, and you feel the next one should be yours. You have a good accident record. The only accident you had was when you sprung the door of Sam's truck when he opened it as you backed out of the garage. You hope the new truck is a Ford, since you prefer to drive one.

Source: Adapted from Maier, N. R. F., & Verser, G. C. (1982). *Psychology in industrial organizations* (5th ed.). Copyright 1982 by Houghton Mifflin Company. Adapted with permission.

The board of the Upstage Theatre Company had assembled to hear the Artistic Director's proposals for the following year's season. Mark Buck, the Artistic Director, had built a reputation on his staging of popular comic seasons, and most members of the board expected a similar proposal this year.

Buck entered the boardroom, and after a few general remarks, began to speak about his plans for the season. As he spoke, the board members began to look at each other with astonishment. Buck was proposing a radical departure for the theatre, a season of serious works, starting with a Shakespearian tragedy and working up to a piece by Arthur Miller. At the end of this totally unexpected proposal, he looked round at his audience. "Any questions?" he asked rather blandly, while privately enjoying the obvious bewilderment on the part of the board. He loved surprising people!

Jean Carlisle, the chairman of the board, was the only one not surprised by the proposal, as Buck had approached her several weeks ago and dropped some hints about his idea. Buck, she had a shrewd suspicion, was out primarily to promote his own career. Known as a "comedy man" first and foremost, he was in danger of being typecast within the industry. Only by rounding out his production experience could he hope to progress.

Carlisle, however, could see a lot of possibilities in the proposal for a "serious" season, even though she knew it would be dismissed as foolhardy by a number of the established board members. Her involvement with the Upstage Theatre was based upon a sincere commitment to the cultural development of the community. Lately she had been coming under some fire from her family and friends for not urging that more "culturally significant" work be performed by the theatre. When she had first heard of Buck's proposal, she had decided to support it, and had accordingly begun to consider how best to get the board to support it as well.

Now she turned to Robert Ramsay, a board member who had been brought in for his connections with the business community. "Well, Robert, it's an interesting proposal we have in front of us," she said. "What do you think?"

Ramsay, she happened to know, had been considerably embarrassed in front of the board recently, as a result of his inability to raise money for the theatre. She also knew that much of the resistance to corporate support of the theatre had come from the fact that its plays were not considered serious enough. Thus Ramsay, she reasoned, would support the departure proposed by Buck.

This was indeed the case. "I think it's a marvellous idea. And I'm sure it's the kind of season the financial community would support," said Ramsay.

Several others on the board protested strongly against the proposed season. The most vociferous of these was Olaf Vickers, a local playwright of some repute. Vickers had had several of his comedy works performed by the Upstage Company over the years. The argument presented by Buck, Carlisle, and Ramsay managed to quiet these objections, however, at least to the point where the board voted to examine the marketing and financial implications of the proposal and meet again in two weeks' time.

When the board met again, a month later, the battle lines were more clearly drawn. Olaf Vickers spoke first. "I move that we dismiss the proposal for a 'tragedy' season," he said. "The theatre has always had a reputation for comic works, and this reputation should not be thrown away lightly. I feel that our artistic director should go back and rethink his proposals."

Jean Carlisle, however, was ready with an answer. "I know how you feel," she said. "But I think we have to consider some other factors too. For years now our theatre has been losing money, and how long the various arts councils will go on funding us is an open question. As I told you last year, some of the government people are very concerned that we develop more in the way of box office support and outside funding. Now as I see it, this proposal may give us a chance to do just that. I've asked Mark Buck to do an unofficial survey among the town's theatre community, and I think you'll find the results interesting."

The artistic director now stood up. "We've been able to put together a random sample of theatergoers from the subscription lists of other theatres in town," he said. "I had a couple of people in the administrative office phone these people and do a straw poll survey of their preferences. The results indicate that a majority would patronize a new tragedy season. So I think we can expect some box office support for this proposal."

He sat down amid murmurs from the board members. Carlisle then asked Ramsay to address the meeting. "I've canvassed the business community," he said. "A number of corporations have indicated their interest in supporting a 'serious season' here. I think it's safe to say that we could count on fairly generous corporate support should we decide to go ahead."

A heated debate followed these announcements. While many of the previously uncommitted board members now leaned toward acceptance of the proposed season, a significant minority, lead by Olaf Vickers, opposed it. As the bylaws required a two-thirds majority to approve a policy change, the meeting adjourned without any decision being taken. It was decided to meet again the following week to resolve the crisis if possible.

During that week, Jean Carlisle paid a visit to Olaf Vickers. After some polite discussion of theatre matters, she came to the point. "You know Olaf," she said sadly, "it's rather a pity you don't support the proposal for a 'serious' season."

"Why's that?" inquired the playwright suspiciously.

"Well," explained Carlisle, "it's just that I was talking to Buck the other day, and he wanted to commission you to write a work to wrap up the season. He says he's sure a serious piece by you would be just the thing to cap the year."

"I'm glad that he at least remembers part of the theatre's original mandate," growled Vickers. "After all, the Upstage is supposed to be committed to the development of new local authors."

"And it's a commitment he takes very seriously," replied Carlisle. "And so do I, I can assure you. That's why if we were to go ahead with the season he suggests, I would move that your new play be commissioned immediately. I hope we can come to some agreement when we next meet," she added as she rose to go.

"Maybe," Vickers replied thoughtfully.

At the next meeting, Vickers announced that after some thought he had changed his mind and would now support the new season. Several weeks later, it was announced that, as local playwright, he had been asked to write a serious work to be performed as season finale.

Source: Morgan, G. (1989). *Creative organization theory.* Newbury Park, CA: Sage.

1. In the formal sense of the word, what is the general problem facing the board of directors of the Upstage Theatre Company? Is this a well-structured or an ill-structured problem?

2. How have various members of the board framed the problem that the board is wrestling with? What accounts for the differences?

3. To what extent has the board complied with or deviated from the rational decision-making model shown in Exhibit 12.1?

4. Is there any evidence in the case of escalation to a failing course of action? Of groupthink? If so, account for these tendencies.

5. Discuss the merits and demerits of using this particular group to make this particular decision. In general, is this the kind of problem that warrants using a group?

6. The board appears to be on the way to approving a rather risky foray into serious theatre. Use framing to explain this decision, then use group dynamics.

7. In retrospect, can you suggest any improvements that could have been made to the decision process?

Learning Objectives

After reading Chapter 13 you should be able to:

1. Define power and review the bases of individual power.

2. Explain how people obtain power in organizations.

3. Discuss the concept of empowerment.

4. Review various influence tactics.

5. Provide a profile of power seekers.

6. Explain strategic contingencies and discuss how sub-units obtain power.

7. Define organizational politics and discuss its various forms.

8. Define ethics and review the ethical dilemmas that managers face.

Power, politics, and ethics all played a part in Mark Jorgensen's dismissal and eventual vindication at the Prudential Insurance Company of America.

CHAPTER 13

POWER, POLITICS, AND ETHICS

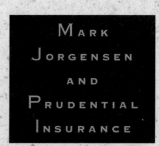

MARK
JORGENSEN
AND
PRUDENTIAL
INSURANCE

Mark Jorgensen thought he was just being an honest guy, exposing fraud in the real-estate funds he managed for the Prudential Insurance Company of America. Then his world fell apart: The boss who had once been his friend abandoned him. His circle of colleagues at work shunned him. Company lawyers accused him of breaking the law. The once powerful and respected executive soon found himself hiding in the local public library, embarrassed that he had been forbidden to return to the office and hoping not to be seen by his neighbors. His long and successful career seemed to be dwindling to a pathetic end.

Finally, in February, came the bitterest moment, the phone call from a middle manager at Prudential telling him he had been dismissed.

How could it have happened? He and his wife, Billie, prayed and consulted the Bible. That night, they lay in bed, unable to sleep. They talked about their finances, and worried what would happen when their health benefits were cut off. They decided the only way to survive financially would be to sell their home.

Overwhelmed, Billie Jorgensen held her husband and cried. It seemed they had been defeated.

"That was the low point," Mr. Jorgensen said in a recent interview. "It was very, very sad. All of our dreams and aspirations had just fallen apart."

Then, last month, salvation—in the form of another phone call. But this time the caller was the most powerful man at the financial-services giant, the chairman, Robert Winters. He wanted a meeting with Mr. Jorgensen to convey some stunning news: Prudential now believed him. Moreover, the company wanted to reinstate him and force out the boss he had accused of falsely inflating the value of properties in the real-estate funds.

The turnabout resulted from the persistence of the man, who, even when he felt the most powerless, impressed some of Prudential's largest institutional investors with his willingness to fight for his convictions. Faced with continuing questions from those investors, Prudential shelved the results of an internal inquiry that found no wrongdoing and commissioned a second investigation. The findings of the second inquiry, filling hundreds of pages, could be summed up in four words: Mark Jorgensen was right.

That realization put Prudential in an unusual position in corporate America—siding with a whistle-blower it had battled for months against one of its own top executives. The decision, which will cost the company as much as $50 million to compensate investors harmed by overvaluations, has transformed Mr. Jorgensen from a soft-spoken man battling for professional survival to an industry hero.

Perhaps the most distressing lesson in Mr. Jorgensen's story is that even when a company's top management encourages its employees to speak up about misdeeds, as Prudential's did, whistle-blowers can be cut down by middle managers who may play down the problem and even accuse the employee himself of improprieties in an attempt at intimidation. Indeed, had Prudential not reversed itself, Mr. Jorgensen's life could well have been destroyed.[1]

··· ■

This excerpt from the *New York Times* illustrates the main themes of this chapter—power, politics, and ethics. First, we shall define power and discuss the bases of individual power. Then we shall examine how people get and use power and who seeks it. After this, we shall explore how organizational subunits, such as particular departments, obtain power; define organizational politics, and explore the relationship of politics to power. Finally, we'll look at ethics in organizations.

At one time, power and politics were not considered polite topics for coverage in organizational behavior textbooks. At best, they were seen as irrational, and at worst, as evil. Now, though, theorists and researchers recognize what managers have known all along—that power and politics are *natural* expressions of life in organizations. They often develop as a rational response to a complex set of needs and goals, and their expression can be beneficial. However, it can also put a strain on ethical standards.

WHAT IS POWER?

Power is the capacity to influence others who are in a state of dependence. Several points about this definition deserve elaboration. First, notice that power is the *capacity* to influence the behavior of others. Power is not always exercised.[2] For example, most professors hold a great degree of potential power over students in terms of grades, assignment load, and the ability to embarrass students in class. Under normal circumstances, professors use only a small amount of this power.

Second, the fact that the target of power is dependent upon the power-holder does not imply that a poor relationship exists between the two. For instance, your best friend has power to influence your behavior and attitudes because you are dependent upon him or her for friendly reactions and social support. Presumably, you can exert reciprocal influence for similar reasons.

Third, power can flow in any direction in an organization. Often, members at higher organizational levels have more power than those at lower levels. However, in specific cases, reversals can occur. For example, the janitor who finds the president in a compromising position with a secretary might find himself in a powerful position if the president wishes to maintain his reputation in the organization!

Finally, power is a broad concept that applies to both individuals and groups. On one hand, an individual production manager might exert considerable influence over the supervisors who report to her. On the other, the marketing department at XYZ Foods might be the most powerful department in the company, able to get its way more often than other departments. But from where do the production manager and the marketing department obtain their power? We explore this issue in the following sections. First, we consider individual bases of power. Then we examine how organizational subunits, such as the marketing department, obtain power.

THE BASES OF INDIVIDUAL POWER

If you wanted to marshal some power to influence others in your organization, where would you get it? As psychologists John French and Bertram Raven explained, power can be found in the *position* that you occupy in the organization or the *resources* that you are able to command.[3] The first base of power, legitimate power, is dependent upon one's position or job. The other bases (reward, coercive, referent, and expert power) involve the control of important resources. If other organizational members do not respect your position or value the resources that you command, they will not be dependent on you, and you will lack power to influence them.

Legitimate Power

Legitimate power derives from a person's position or job in the organization. It constitutes the organization's judgment about who is formally permitted to influence whom, and it is often called authority. As we move up the

Power. The capacity to influence others who are in a state of dependence.

Legitimate power. Power derived from a person's position or job in an organization.

organization's hierarchy, we find that members possess more and more legitimate power. In theory, organizational equals (e.g., all vice-presidents) have equal legitimate power. Of course, some people are more likely than others to *invoke* their legitimate power—"Look, *I'm* the boss around here."

Organizations differ greatly in the extent to which they emphasize and reinforce legitimate power. At one extreme is the U.S. Army, which has many levels of command, differentiating uniforms, and rituals (e.g., salutes), all designed to emphasize legitimate power. On the other hand, the academic hierarchy of universities tends to downplay differences in the legitimate power of lecturers, professors, chairpeople, and deans.

When legitimate power works, it often does so because people have been socialized to accept its influence. Experiences with parents, teachers, and law enforcement officials cause members to enter organizations with a degree of readiness to submit to (and exercise) legitimate power. In fact, studies consistently show that employees cite legitimate power as a major reason for following their boss's directives, even across various cultures.[4]

Reward Power

Reward power. Power derived from the ability to provide positive outcomes and prevent negative outcomes.

Reward power means that the powerholder can exert influence by providing positive outcomes and preventing negative outcomes. In general, it corresponds to the concept of positive reinforcement in Chapter 3. Reward power often backs up legitimate power. That is, managers and supervisors are given the chance to recommend raises, do performance evaluations, and assign preferred tasks to subordinates. Of course, *any* organizational member can attempt to exert influence over others with praise, compliments, and flattery, which also constitute rewards.

Coercive Power

Coercive power. Power derived from the use of punishment and threat.

Coercive power is available when the powerholder can exert influence using punishment and threat. Like reward power, it is often a support for legitimate power. Supervisors and managers might be permitted to dock pay, assign unfavorable tasks, or block promotions. Despite a strong civil service system, even U.S. government agencies provide their executives with plenty of coercive power.

> Some agencies have a Siberia—an unpleasant or professionally unproductive duty station, to which rebellious employees may be reassigned. Faced with Siberia, an employee may, of course, resign, but even if he accepts exile, he is effectively removed from the position in which he caused difficulty. "You'd be surprised how many resignations we had when people discovered they had been reassigned to Anchorage," said one former Federal Aeronautics Administration official.[5]

Of course, coercive power is not perfectly correlated with legitimate power. Lower-level organizational members can also apply their share of coercion. For example, consider work-to-rule campaigns that slow productivity by adhering religiously to organizational procedures. Cohesive work groups are especially skillful at enforcing such campaigns.

In Chapter 3 we pointed out that the use of punishment to control behavior is very problematic because of emotional side effects. Thus, it is not surprising that when managers use coercive power it is generally ineffective and can provoke considerable employee resistance.[6] Mark Jorgensen was the victim of coercive power at Prudential. He was assigned to a remote office, stripped of subordinates, and shunned by his peers.

Referent Power

Referent power exists when the powerholder is *well liked* by others. It is not surprising that people we like readily influence us. We are prone to consider their points of view, ignore their failures, seek their approval, and use them as role models. In fact, it is often highly dissonant to hold a point of view that is discrepant from that held by someone we like.[7]

Referent power is especially potent for two reasons. First, it stems from *identification* with the powerholder. Thus, it represents a truer or deeper base of power than reward or coercion, which may stimulate mere compliance to achieve rewards or avoid punishment. In this sense, charismatic leaders (Chapter 10) have referent power. Second, *anyone* in the organization may be well liked, irrespective of his or her other bases of power. Thus, referent power is available to everyone from the janitor to the president.

Friendly interpersonal relations often permit influence to extend across the organization, outside of the usual channels of legitimate authority, reward, and coercion. For example, a production manager who becomes friendly with the design engineer through participation in a task force might later use this contact to ask for a favor in solving a production problem.

Referent power. Power derived from being well-liked by others.

Expert Power

A person has **expert power** when he or she has special information or expertise that the organization values. In any circumstance, we tend to be influenced by experts or by those who perform their jobs well. However, the more crucial and unusual this expertise, the greater the expert power available. Thus, expert power corresponds to difficulty of replacement. Consider the business school that has one highly published professor who is an internationally known scholar and past presidential cabinet member. Such a person would obviously be difficult to replace and should have much greater expert power than an unpublished lecturer.

One of the most fascinating aspects of expert power occurs when lower-level organizational members accrue it. Many secretaries have acquired expert power through long experience in dealing with clients, keeping records, or sparring with the bureaucracy. Frequently, they have been around longer than those they serve. In this case, it is not unusual for bosses to create special titles and develop new job classifications to reward their expertise and prevent their resignation. FedEx sends a quarterly magazine to 350,000 secretaries in recognition of the power they wield to select a courier.[8]

Expert power is especially common among lower-level members in scientific and technical areas. Consider the solid-state physicist who has just completed her Ph.D. dissertation on a topic of particular interest to her new employer. Although new to the firm, she might have considerable expert

Expert power. Power derived from having special information or expertise that is valued by an organization.

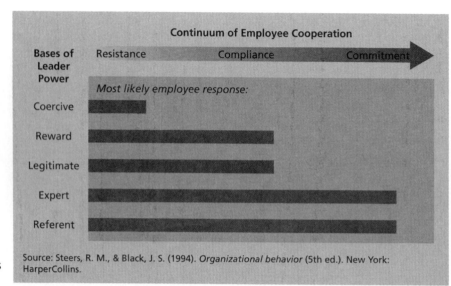

EXHIBIT 13.1
Employee responses to bases of power.

power. Put simply, she *knows* more than her boss, whose scientific knowledge in this area is now outdated.

Expert power is a valuable asset for managers. Of all the bases of power, expertise is most consistently associated with subordinate effectiveness.[9] Also, research shows that subordinates perceive women managers as more likely than male managers to be high on expert power.[10] Women often lack easy access to more organizationally based forms of power, and expertise is free for self-development. Thus, being "better" than their male counterparts is one strategy that women managers have used to gain influence.

Exhibit 13.1 summarizes likely employee responses to various bases of managerial power. As you can see, coercion is likely to produce resistance and lack of cooperation. Legitimate power and reward power are likely to produce compliance with the boss's wishes. Referent and expert power are most likely to generate true commitment and enthusiasm for the manager's agenda.

HOW DO PEOPLE OBTAIN POWER?

Now that we have discussed the individual bases of power, we can turn to the issue of how people *get* power. That is, how do organizational members obtain promotions to positions of legitimate power, demonstrate their expertise, and get others to like them? And how do they acquire the ability to provide others with rewards and punishment? Rosabeth Moss Kanter, an organizational sociologist, has provided some succinct answers—Do the right things, and cultivate the right people.[11]

Doing the Right Things

According to Kanter, some activities are "righter" than others for obtaining power. She argues that activities lead to power when they are extraordinary, highly visible, and especially relevant to the solution of organizational problems.

Deborah Kent of Ford Motor Company motivates high subordinate effectiveness as a result of her expert power.

Extraordinary Activities. Excellent performance of a routine job might not be enough to obtain power. What one needs is excellent performance in *unusual* or *nonroutine* activities. In the large company that Kanter studied, these activities included occupying new positions, managing substantial changes, and taking great risks. For example, consider the manager who establishes and directs a new TQM program. This is a risky major change that involves the occupancy of a new position. If successful, the manager should acquire substantial power.

Visible Activities. Extraordinary activities will fail to generate power if no one knows about them. People who have an interest in power are especially good at identifying visible activities and publicizing them. The successful marketing executive whose philosophy is profiled in *Fortune* will reap the benefits of power. Similarly, the innovative surgeon whose techniques are reported in the *New England Journal of Medicine* will enhance her influence in the hospital.

Relevant Activities. Extraordinary, visible work may fail to generate power if no one cares. If nobody sees the work as relevant to the solution of important organizational problems, it will not add to one's influence. The English professor who wins two Pulitzer prizes will probably not accrue much power if his small college is financially strapped and hurting for students. He would not be seen as contributing to the solution of pressing organizational problems. As we shall see shortly, being in the right place at the right time is crucial to the acquisition of power. In another college, these extraordinary, visible activities might generate considerable influence.

Cultivating the Right People

An old saying advises, "It's not what you know, it's *who* you know." In reference to power in organizations, there is probably more than a grain of truth to the latter part of this statement. Developing informal relationships with the right people (especially when coupled with doing the right things) can prove a useful means of acquiring power. Dr. Kanter suggests that the right people can include organizational subordinates, peers, and superiors. To these we might add certain crucial outsiders.

Outsiders. Establishing good relationships with key people outside of one's organization can lead to increased power within the organization. Sometimes this power is merely a reflection of the status of the outsider, but all the same it may add to one's internal influence. The assistant director of a hospital who is friendly with the president of the American Medical Association might find herself holding power by association. Cultivating outsiders may also contribute to more tangible sources of power. Organizational members who are on the boards of directors of other companies might acquire critical information about business conditions that they can use in their own firms.

Subordinates. At first blush, it might seem unlikely that power can be enhanced by cultivating relationships with subordinates. However, as Kanter notes, an individual can gain influence if she is closely identified with certain up-and-coming subordinates—"I taught her everything she knows." In academics, some professors are better known for the brilliant Ph.D. students they have supervised than for their own published work. Of course, there is also the possibility that an outstanding subordinate will one day become one's boss! Having cultivated the relationship earlier, one might then be rewarded with special influence.

Cultivating subordinate interests can also provide power when a manager can demonstrate that he or she is backed by a cohesive team. The research director who can oppose a policy change by honestly insisting that "My people won't stand for this" knows that there is strength in numbers.

Peers.   Cultivating good relationships with peers is mainly a means of ensuring that nothing gets in the way of one's *future* acquisition of power. As one moves up through the ranks, favors can be asked of former associates, and fears of being "stabbed in the back" for a past misdeed are precluded. Organizations often reward good "team players" with promotions on the assumption that they have demonstrated good interpersonal skills. On the other side of the coin, people often avoid contact with peers whose reputation is seen as questionable. Mark Jorgensen was shunned by his colleagues for this reason.

Superiors.   Liaisons with key superiors probably represent the best way of obtaining power through cultivating others. Such superiors are often called mentors or sponsors because of the special interest they show in a promising subordinate. Mentors can provide power in several ways. Obviously, it is useful to be identified as a protégé of someone higher in the organization. More concretely, mentors can provide special information and useful introductions to other "right people."

EMPOWERMENT—PUTTING POWER WHERE IT'S NEEDED

Empowerment. Giving people the authority, opportunity, and motivation to take initiative and solve organizational problems.

Early organizational theorists used to treat power as something of a fixed quantity: An organization had so much, the people on the top had a lot, and lower-level employees had a little. Our earlier analysis of the more informal sources of power (such as being liked and being an expert) hints at the weakness of this idea. Thus, contemporary views of power treat it less as a fixed-sum phenomenon. This is best seen in the concept of **empowerment,** which means giving people the authority, opportunity, and motivation to take initiative to solve organizational problems.[12] We used this concept earlier in the text when discussing total quality management (Chapter 7) and participative leadership (Chapter 10). Here, we'll examine the idea in a little more detail.

In practice, having the authority to solve an organizational problem means having legitimate power. This might be included in a job description, or a boss might delegate it to a subordinate.

Having opportunity usually means freedom from bureaucratic barriers and other system problems that block initiative. In a service encounter, if you've ever heard "Sorry, the computer won't let me do that" or "that's not my job," you've been the victim of limited opportunity. Opportunity also includes any relevant training and information about the impact of one's actions on other parts of the organization.

The motivation part of the empowerment equation suggests selecting people for positions who will be intrinsically motivated by power and opportunity and aligning extrinsic rewards with successful performance. Also, leaders who express confidence in subordinates' abilities (especially transformational leaders, Chapter 10) can contribute to empowerment. A good example occurred when a nay-saying union shop steward, doubting General Electric's commitment to changing its corporate culture, explained a recurrent problem with a supplier's component. His manager, sensing he was correct, chartered a plane and the subordinate left that same night to visit the supplier and solve the problem.[13] It goes without saying that managers have to be tolerant of occasional mistakes from empowered employees.

People who are empowered have a strong sense of self-efficacy, the feeling that they are capable of doing their jobs well and "making things happen." Empowering lower-level employees can be critical in service organizations, where providing customers with a good initial encounter or correcting any problems that develop can be essential for repeat business. The Nordstrom store chain is one firm that is known for empowering sales personnel to make on-the-spot adjustments or search out merchandise at other stores. Customers have even had enthusiastic store personnel change flat tires. This dedication to customer service enables Nordstrom to spend only a fraction of the industry average on advertising.

We should emphasize that empowerment does not mean providing employees with a maximum amount of unfettered power. Rather, used properly, empowerment puts power where it is *needed* to make the organization effective. This depends on organizational strategy and customer expectations. The average Taco Bell customer does not expect highly empowered counter personnel who offer to make adjustments to the posted menu—a friendly, fast, efficient encounter will do. On the other hand, the unempowered waiter in a fancy restaurant who is fearful of accommodating reasonable adjustments and substitutions can really irritate customers. Speaking generally, service encounters predicated on high volume and low cost need careful engineering. Those predicated on customized personalized service need more empowered personnel.[14] This contrast is illustrated in the comparison between FedEx and UPS in the "In Focus: *Empowerment at FedEx, Rules at UPS*" feature.

Given this discussion, you might wonder whether organizational members could have *too much* power. Exhibit 13.2 nicely illustrates the answer. People

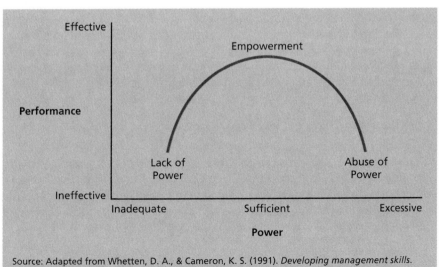

Source: Adapted from Whetten, D. A., & Cameron, K. S. (1991). *Developing management skills.*
New York: HarperCollins.

EXHIBIT 13.2
Relationship between power
and performance.

IN FOCUS   Empowerment at FedEx, Rules at UPS

In 1990, Federal Express (now FedEx) became the first service organization to win the Malcolm Baldrige National Quality Award. The company's motto is "people, service, and profits." Behind its blue, white, and red planes and uniforms are self-managing work teams, gainsharing plans, and empowered employees seemingly consumed with providing flexible and creative service to customers with varying needs.

At UPS, referred to as "Big Brown" by its employees, the philosophy was stated by founder Jim Casey: "Best service at low rates." Here, too, we find turned-on people and profits. But we do not find empowerment. Instead we find control, rules, a detailed union contract, and carefully studied work methods. Nor do we find a promise to do all things for customers, such as handling off-schedule pickups and packages that don't fit size and weight limitations. In fact, rigid operational guidelines help guarantee the customer reliable, low-cost service.

Federal Express and UPS present two different faces to the customer, and behind these faces are different management philosophies and organizational cultures. Federal Express is a high-involvement, horizontally coordinated organization that encourages employees to use their judgment

above and beyond the rulebook. UPS is a top-down, traditionally controlled organization, in which employees are directed by policies and procedures based on industrial engineering studies of how all service delivery aspects should be carried out and how long they should take.

FedEx and UPS, while providing some similar services, have strikingly contrasting management philosophies and organizational cultures.

Source: Excerpted from Bowen, D. E., & Lawler, E. E., III. (1992, Spring). The empowerment of service workers: What, why, how, and when. *Sloan Management Review*, 31–39.

are empowered, and should exhibit effective performance, when they have sufficient power to carry out their jobs. Above, we mainly contrasted empowerment with situations in which people had inadequate power for effective performance. However, as the exhibit shows, excessive power can lead to abuse and ineffective performance. One is reminded of the recurrent and inappropriate use of government aircraft by political bigwigs as an example. As we'll see in the following sections, the fact that people can have too much power doesn't always inhibit them from seeking it anyway!

INFLUENCE TACTICS—PUTTING POWER TO WORK

Influence tactics. Tactics that are used to convert power into actual influence over others.

As we discussed earlier, power is the potential to influence others. But exactly how does power result in influence? Research has shown that various **influence tactics** convert power into actual influence. These are specific behaviors that power holders use to affect others.[15] These tactics include the following:

• Assertiveness—ordering, nagging, setting deadlines, and verbal confrontation;

- Ingratiation—using flattery and acting friendly, polite, or humble;
- Rationality—using logic, reason, planning, and compromise;
- Exchange—doing favors or offering to trade favors;
- Upward appeal—making formal or informal appeals to organizational superiors for intervention;
- Coalition formation—seeking united support from other organizational members.

What determines which influence tactics you might use? For one thing, your bases of power.[16] Other things equal, someone with coercive power might gravitate toward assertiveness, someone with referent power might gravitate toward ingratiation, and someone with expert power might try rationality. Of course, rationality or its appearance is a highly prized quality in organizations and its use is viewed positively by others. Thus, surveys show that people report trying to use rationality very frequently.

As you can guess, the use of influence tactics is also dependent upon just whom you are trying to influence—subordinates, peers, or superiors. Subordinates are more likely to be the recipients of assertiveness than peers or superiors. Despite the general popularity of rationality, it is most likely to be directed toward superiors. Exchange, ingratiation, and upward appeal are favored tactics for influencing both peers and subordinates.[17]

Which influence tactics are most effective? Some of the most interesting research has concerned upward influence attempts directed toward superiors. It shows that, at least for men, using rationality as an influence tactic was associated with receiving better performance evaluations, earning more money, and experiencing less work stress. A particularly ineffective influence style is a "shotgun" style that is high on all tactics with particular emphasis on assertiveness and exchange. In this series of studies, women who used ingratiation as an influence tactic received the highest performance evaluations (from male managers).[18]

WHO WANTS POWER?

Who wants power? At first glance, the answer would seem to be everybody. After all, it is both convenient and rewarding to be able to exert influence over others. Power whisks celebrities to the front of movie lines, gets rock stars the best restaurant tables, and enables executives to shape organizations in their own image. Actually, there are considerable individual differences in the extent to which individuals pursue and enjoy power. On television talk shows, we occasionally see celebrities recount considerable embarrassment over the unwarranted power that public recognition brings.

Earlier we indicated that some people consider power a manifestation of evil. This is due in no small part to the historic image of power seekers that some psychologists and political scientists have portrayed. Several aspects of this image are strikingly similar:

- Power seekers are neurotics who are covering up feelings of inferiority.
- Power seekers are striving to compensate for childhood deprivation.
- Power seekers are substituting power for lack of affection.[19]

There can be little doubt that these characteristics do apply to some power seekers. Underlying this negative image of power seeking is the idea that some power seekers feel weak and resort primarily to coercive power to cover up, compensate for, or substitute for this weakness. Power is sought for its own sake and is used irresponsibly to hurt others. Adolf Hitler comes to mind as an extreme example.

But can one use power responsibly to influence others? Psychologist David McClelland says yes. In Chapter 6 we discussed McClelland's research on need for power (*n* Pow). You will recall that *n* Pow is the need to have strong influence over others. This need is a reliable personality characteristic—some people have more *n* Pow than others.[20] Also, just as many women have high *n* Pow as men.[21] In "pure" form, people who are high in *n* Pow conform to the negative stereotype depicted above—they are rude, sexually exploitive, abusive of alcohol, and show a great concern with status symbols. However, when *n* Pow is responsible and controlled, these negative properties are not observed. Specifically, McClelland argues that the most effective managers:

- have high *n* Pow;
- use their power to achieve organizational goals;
- adopt a participative or "coaching" leadership style;
- are relatively unconcerned with how much others like them.

McClelland calls such managers *institutional managers* because they use their power for the good of the institution rather than for self-aggrandizement. They refrain from coercive leadership but don't play favorites, since they aren't worried about being well liked. His research reveals that institutional managers are more effective than *personal power managers,* who use their power for personal gain, and *affiliative managers,* who are more concerned with being liked than with exercising power. Exhibit 13.3 shows that institutional managers are generally superior in giving subordinates a sense of responsibility, clarifying organizational priorities, and instilling team spirit.[22] We can conclude that the need for power can be a useful asset as long as it is not a neurotic expression of perceived weakness.

Finally, what happens when people want power but can't get it because they are locked in a low-level job or faced with excessive rules and regulations? People react to such powerlessness by trying to gain control, but if they can't succeed, they feel helpless and become alienated from their work.[23] This is something that empowerment is designed to prevent.

CONTROLLING STRATEGIC CONTINGENCIES—HOW SUBUNITS OBTAIN POWER

Thus far we have been concerned with the bases of *individual* power and how individual organizational members obtain influence. In this section we shift our concern to **subunit power.** Most straightforwardly, the term subunit applies to organizational departments. In some cases, subunits could also refer to particular jobs, such as those held by software engineers or environmental lawyers.

How do organizational subunits acquire power? That is, how do they achieve influence that enables them to grow in size, get a bigger share of the

Subunit power. The degree of power held by various organizational subunits, such as departments.

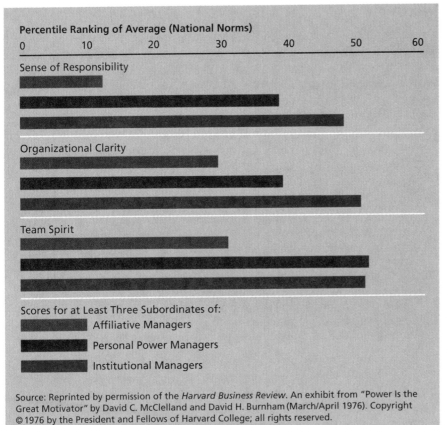

Percentile Ranking of Average (National Norms)

Sense of Responsibility

Organizational Clarity

Team Spirit

Scores for at Least Three Subordinates of:
Affiliative Managers
Personal Power Managers
Institutional Managers

EXHIBIT 13.3
Responses of subordinates of managers with different motive profiles.

budget, obtain better facilities, and have greater impact on decisions? In short, they control **strategic contingencies**, which are critical factors affecting organizational effectiveness. This means that the work *other* subunits perform is contingent upon the activities and performance of a key subunit. Again, we see the critical role of *dependence* in power relationships. If some subunits are dependent upon others for smooth operations (or their very existence), they are susceptible to influence. We turn now to the conditions under which subunits can control strategic contingencies.

Strategic contingencies. Critical factors affecting organizational effectiveness that are controlled by a key subunit.

Scarcity

Differences in subunit power are likely to be magnified when resources become scarce.[24] When there is plenty of budget money or office space or support staff for all subunits, they will seldom waste their energies jockeying for power. If cutbacks occur, however, differences in power will become apparent. For example, well-funded quality of worklife programs or organizational development efforts might disappear when economic setbacks occur because the subunits that control them are not essential to the firm's existence.

Subunits tend to acquire power when they are able to *secure* scarce resources that are important to the organization as a whole. One study of a large state university found that the power of academic departments was associated with their ability to obtain funds through consulting contracts and research grants. This mastery over economic resources was more crucial to their power than was the number of undergraduates taught by the department.[25]

Uncertainty

Organizations detest the unknown. Unanticipated events wreak havoc with financial commitments, long-range plans, and tomorrow's operations. The basic sources of uncertainty exist mainly in the organization's environment—government policies might change, sources of supply and demand might dry up, or the economy might take an unanticipated turn. It stands to reason that the subunits that are most capable of coping with uncertainty will tend to acquire power.[26] In a sense, these subunits are able to protect the others from serious problems. By the same token, uncertainty promotes confusion, which permits *changes* in power priorities as the organizational environment changes.

> The most power goes to those people in those functions that provide greater control over what the organization finds currently problematic: sales and marketing people when markets are competitive; production experts when materials are scarce and demand is high; personnel or labor relations specialists when labor is scarce; lawyers, lobbyists, and external relations specialists when government regulations impinge; finance and accounting types when business is bad and money tight. There is a turning to those elements of the system that seem to have the power to create more certainty in the face of dependency, to generate a more advantageous position for the organization.[27]

A dramatic example of a shift in subunit power has occurred for the personnel or human resource departments of large corporations during the past 20 years. For many years, the personnel function in most organizations had relatively little power. However, beginning in the 1970s, increased government intervention into personnel policies began. This was especially true in the area of employment discrimination, in which legislation provoked considerable uncertainty. In coming to the rescue, personnel departments acquired a long-awaited measure of power. Currently, the uncertainty provoked by downsizing, new technology, and mergers and acquisitions continues the trend.

Centrality

Other things being equal, subunits whose activities are most central to the work flow of the organization should acquire more power than those whose activities are more peripheral.[28] A subunit's activities can be central in at least three senses. First, they may influence the work of most other subunits. The finance or accounting department is a good example here—its authority to approve expenses and make payments affects every other department in the firm.

Centrality also exists when a subunit has an especially crucial impact on the quantity or quality of the organization's key product or service. This is one reason for the former low power of personnel departments—their activities were then seen as fairly remote from the primary goals of the organization. Similarly, a production department should have more power than a research and development department that only "fine-tunes" existing products.

Finally, a subunit's activities are more central when their impact is more immediate. As an example, consider a large city government that includes a fire department, a police department, and a public works department. The impact of a lapse in fire or police services will be felt more immediately than a lapse in street repairs. This gives the former departments more potential for power acquisition.

One prominent trend in large North American organizations has been the reduction in power of corporate headquarters staff units. An example would be a marketing research department that is set up to do studies for several divisional product lines. Many organizations have found that, because of their centrality (literal and figurative) in the decision process, such units slow decision making and damage communication between top management and the field. This is out of step with the increasing global pace of business. One reaction has been to slash corporate staff and push more of its responsibilities down into the divisions.

Substitutability

A subunit will have relatively little power if others inside or outside of the organization can perform its activities. If the subunit's staff is nonsubstitutable, however, it can acquire substantial power.[29] One crucial factor here is the labor market for the specialty performed by the subunit. A change in the labor market can result in a change in the subunit's influence:

> In the 1950s, when there were relatively few engineers to service an expanding American economy, engineers had great prestige and power. They could force employers to provide them with large salaries and benefits, by threatening to withhold their services. By the early 1970s, however, many persons had become engineers and consequently the bargaining power of engineers with employers was practically nil.[30]

In the 1990s there is again a shortage of engineers (and scientists), with a consequent increase in their bargaining power. Precisely in line with the strategic contingencies idea, observers note how this shortage has provided real opportunities for properly trained women and members of minorities to move into positions of power from which they were excluded when there were plenty of white male engineers and scientists to go around.[31]

If the labor market is constant, subunits whose staffs are highly trained in technical areas tend to be less substitutable than those which involve minimal technical expertise. For example, consider the large telephone company that makes extensive use of a computerized management information system. The department in charge of this system might acquire considerable power because its computer analysts perform specialized work that others in the company can't do. On the other hand, if telephone operators go on strike, management personnel can substitute for them by handling the phones.

Finally, if work can be contracted out, the power of the subunit that usually performs these activities is reduced. Typical examples include temporary office help, off-premises data entry, and contracted maintenance, laboratory, and security services. The subunits that control these activities often lack power because the threat of "going outside" can counter their influence attempts.

The Irrational Face of Power

The strategic contingencies theory presents a very rational view of subunit power—power gravitates to where it is needed to solve pressing organizational problems. In the previous chapter, however, we covered in some detail how many organizational decisions are made on less-than-rational terms, and the acquisition of power by subunits is no exception. For example, we have all heard of empire building, the process by which departments expand in size or responsibility beyond what is necessary in terms of strict effectiveness. Similarly, a study in the semiconductor industry showed that the founder's functional background (e.g., engineering, science) influenced which department had the most power in newly founded companies.[32]

When a subunit acquires power, however that happens, it will often attempt to hold onto that power. This goal is aided considerably by the fact that it has power at its disposal to influence other departments and their key members. Thus, power can get institutionalized in a department even though organizational priorities appear to have changed. This is often accomplished by playing organizational politics, a topic to which we now turn.

ORGANIZATIONAL POLITICS—USING AND ABUSING POWER

In previous pages, we have avoided using the terms *politics* or *political* in describing the acquisition and use of power. This is because not all uses of power constitute politics.

The Basics of Organizational Politics

Organizational politics. The pursuit of self-interest in an organization, whether or not this self-interest corresponds to organizational goals.

Organizational politics is the pursuit of self-interest within an organization, whether or not this self-interest corresponds to organizational goals.[33] Frequently, politics involves using means of influence that the organization doesn't sanction and/or pursuing ends or goals that are not sanctioned by the organization.[34]

We should make several preliminary points about organizational politics. First, political activity is self-conscious and intentional. This separates politics from ignorance or lack of experience with approved means and ends. Second, implicit in all but the mildest examples of politics is the idea of resistance, the idea that political influence would be countered if detected by those with different agendas. Third, we can conceive of politics as either individual activity or subunit activity. Either a person or a whole department could act politically. Finally, it is possible for political activity to have beneficial outcomes for the organization, even though these outcomes are achieved by questionable tactics.

We can explore organizational politics using the means/ends matrix in Exhibit 13.4. It is the association between influence means and influence ends that determines whether activities are political and whether these activities benefit the organization.

- *I. Sanctioned means/sanctioned ends.* Here, power is used routinely to pursue agreed-upon goals. Familiar, accepted means of influence are employed to achieve sanctioned outcomes. For example, a manager agrees to recommend a raise for a subordinate if she increases her net sales 30 percent in the next six months. There is nothing political about this.

- *II. Sanctioned means/nonsanctioned ends.* In this case, acceptable means of influence are abused to pursue goals that the organization doesn't

	Influence Ends	
Influence Means	Organizationally Sanctioned	Not Sanctioned by Organization
Organizationally Sanctioned	Nonpolitical Job Behavior I	II Organizationally Dysfunctional Political Behavior
Not Sanctioned by Organization	Political Behavior Potentially Functional to the Organization III	IV Organizationally Dysfunctional Political Behavior

Source: From Mayes, B. T., & Allen, R. T. (1977, October) Conceptual notes—Toward a definition of organizational politics, *The Academy of Management Review*, Vol. 2, No. 4, p. 675. Reprinted by permission.

EXHIBIT 13.4
The dimensions of organizational politics.

approve. For instance, a head nurse agrees to assign a subordinate nurse to a more favorable job if the nurse agrees not to report the superior for stealing medical supplies. While job assignment is often a sanctioned means of influence, covering up theft is not a sanctioned end. This is dysfunctional political behavior.

- *III. Nonsanctioned means/sanctioned ends.* Here, ends that are useful for the organization are pursued through questionable means. For example, a commercial artist is vying with a co-worker to have his proposal accepted for an advertising campaign. Feeling that his proposal is truly better, the artist takes the account executive to dinner, flatters him, and subtly discredits the co-worker's proposal. Currying favor and discrediting others are seldom approved methods of influence. However, if the proposal is really superior, the consequences might be beneficial for the firm. This is obviously a gray area of politics.

- *IV. Nonsanctioned means/nonsanctioned ends.* This quadrant may exemplify the most flagrant abuse of power, since disapproved tactics are used to pursue disapproved outcomes. For example, to increase his personal power, the head of an already overstaffed legal department wishes to increase its size. He intends to hire several of his friends in the process. To do this, he falsifies workload documents and promises special service to the accounting department in exchange for the support of its manager.

We have all seen cases in which politics have been played out publicly in order to "teach someone a lesson." More frequently, though, politicians conceal their activities with a "cover story" or "smoke screen" to make them appear legitimate.[35] Such a tactic will increase the odds of success and avoid punishment from superiors. A common strategy is to cover nonsanctioned means and ends with a cloak of rationality:

The head of a research unit requests permission to review another research group's proposal in case she can add information to improve the project. Her covert intent is to maintain her current power which will be endangered if the other research group carries out the project. Using her informational power base, her covert means are to introduce irrelevant information and pose further questions. If she sufficiently confuses the issues, she can discredit the research group and prevent the project from being carried out. She covers these covert intents and means with the overt ones of improving the project and reviewing its content.[36]

Do political activities occur under particular conditions or in particular locations in organizations? Some tentative conclusions include the following:

- Managers report that most political maneuvering occurs among middle and upper management levels rather than at lower levels.

- Some subunits are more prone to politicking than others. Clear goals and routine tasks (e.g., production) might provoke less political activity than vague goals and complex tasks (e.g., research and development).

- Some issues are more likely than others to stimulate political activity. Budget allocation, reorganization, and personnel changes are likely to be the subjects of politicking. Setting performance standards and purchasing equipment are not.

- In general, scarce resources, uncertainty, and important issues provoke political behavior.[37]

Returning to the story that began the chapter, Mark Jorgensen was obviously exposed to quadrant IV political activity. He was threatened with a lawsuit that accused *him* of improper behavior in an evident move to silence him. To external constituents, such legal maneuverings often have an appearance of rationality. Middle management figured prominently in pressuring Jorgensen to protect the tainted investment funds from close scrutiny.

Machiavellianism—the Harder Side of Politics

Have you ever known people in an organization or another social setting who had the following characteristics?

- Act very much in their own self-interest, even at the expense of others.

- Cool and calculating, especially when others get emotional.

- High self-esteem and self-confidence.

- Form alliances with powerful people to achieve their goals.

Machiavellianism. A set of cynical beliefs about human nature, morality, and the permissibility of using various tactics to achieve one's ends.

These are some of the characteristics of individuals who are high on a personality dimension known as Machiavellianism. **Machiavellianism** is a set of cynical beliefs about human nature, morality, and the permissibility of using various tactics to achieve one's ends. The term derives from the sixteenth-century writings of the Italian civil servant Niccolo Machiavelli, who was concerned with how people achieve social influence and the ability to manipulate others. The degree to which an individual endorses the beliefs of Machiavelli is representative of a stable psychological trait.

Compared with "low Machs," "high Machs" are more likely to advocate the use of lying and deceit to achieve desired goals and to argue that morality can be compromised to fit the situation in question. In addition, high Machs assume that many people are excessively gullible and do not know what is best for themselves. Thus, in interpersonal situations, the high Mach acts in an exceedingly practical manner, assuming that the ends justify the means. Not surprisingly, high Machs tend to be convincing liars and good at "psyching out" competitors by creating diversions. Furthermore, they are quite willing to form coalitions with others to outmaneuvre or defeat people who get in their way.[38] In summary, high Machs are likely to be enthusiastic organizational politicians.

This discussion of the Machiavellian personality trait probably raises two questions on your part. First, you might wonder, do high Machs feel guilty about the social tactics that they utilize? The answer would appear to be no. Since they are cool and calculating, rather than emotional, high Machs seem to be able to insulate themselves from the negative social consequences of their tactics. Second, you might wonder how successful high Machs are at manipulating others and why others would tolerate such manipulation. After all, the characteristics we detail above are hardly likely to win a popularity contest, and you might assume that targets of a high Mach's tactics would vigorously resist manipulation by such a person. Again, the high Mach's rationality seems to provide an answer to this question. Put simply, it appears that high Machs are able to accurately identify situations in which their favored tactics will work. Such situations have the following characteristics:

- The high Mach can deal face-to-face with those he or she is trying to influence.
- The interaction occurs under fairly emotional circumstances.
- The situation is fairly unstructured, with few guidelines for appropriate forms of interaction.[39]

In combination, these characteristics reveal a situation in which the high Mach can use his or her tactics because emotion distracts others. High Machs, by remaining calm and rational, can create a social structure that facilitates their personal goals at the expense of others. Thus, it would appear that high Machs are especially skilled at getting their way when power vacuums or novel situations confront a group, department, or organization. For example, imagine a small family-run manufacturing company whose president dies suddenly without any plans for succession. In this power vacuum, a high Mach vice-president would have an excellent chance of manipulating the choice of a new president. The situation is novel, emotion-provoking, and unstructured, since no guidelines for succession exist. In addition, the decision-making body would be small enough for face-to-face influence and coalition formation.

Networking—the Softer Side of Politics

Only a small proportion of the population has the personality profile characteristic of the hardball Machiavellian politician. Despite this, political influence is often necessary to enable organizational members to achieve their goals, especially if these goals involve some degree of change or innovation. Thus, a more common and more subtle form of political behavior involves networking. **Networking** can be defined as establishing good relations with key organizational members and/or outsiders in order to accomplish one's goals. If these goals are beneficial to the organization, we can describe networking as functional political behavior. In essence, networking involves developing informal social contacts to enlist the cooperation of others when their support is necessary. Upper-level managers often establish very large political networks both inside and outside of the organization (see Exhibit 13.5). Lower-level organizational members might have a more restricted network, but the principle remains the same.

Networking. Establishing good relations with key organizational members and/or outsiders in order to accomplish one's goals.

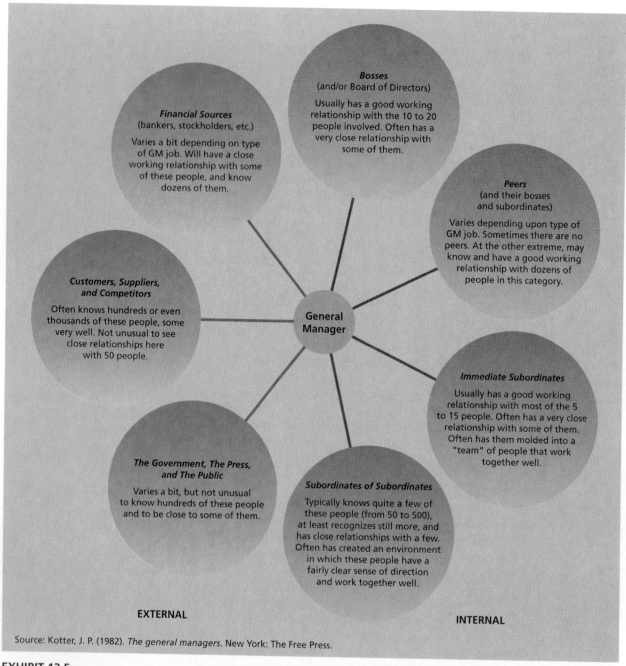

Source: Kotter, J. P. (1982). *The general managers.* New York: The Free Press.

EXHIBIT 13.5
A typical general manager's network.

Some networking is a function of one's location in the organization's work flow and formal communication channels.[40] A key location provides the opportunity to interact with and establish influence over others. However, individuals can also pursue networking more aggressively. One study of general managers found that they used face-to-face encounters and informal small talk to bolster their political networks. They also did favors for others and stressed the obligations of others to them. Personnel were hired, fired, and transferred to bolster a workable network, and the managers forged connections among network members to create a climate conducive to goal accomplishment.[41]

Networking is an effective way to develop informal social contacts.

High-powered executives aren't the only people who are concerned about networking. Many telecommuters who work at home worry about being "cut out of the loop" of office influence because they aren't physically present for informal office interaction. In turn, they fret that this will damage their promotion opportunities. Successful telecommuters report that they go to extra trouble to keep their bosses and co-workers informed about what they're doing at home, keeping their names visible in the communication network. At Bell Atlantic, they showed their bosses videotapes of their home offices.[42]

Defensiveness—Reactive Politics

So far, our discussion of politics has focused mainly on the proactive pursuit of self-interest. Another form of political behavior, however, is more reactive in that it concerns the defense or protection of self-interest. The goal here is to reduce threats to one's own power by avoiding actions that don't suit one's own political agenda or avoiding blame for events that might threaten one's political capital. Blake Ashforth and Ray Lee describe some tactics for doing both.[43]

Avoiding Action. Astute organizational politicians are aware that sometimes the best action to take is no action at all. A number of defensive behaviors can accomplish this mission:

- *Stalling.* Moving slowly when someone asks for your cooperation is the most obvious way of avoiding taking action without actually saying no. With time, the demand for cooperation may disappear. The civil service bureaucracy is infamous for stalling on demands from acting governments.

- *Overconforming.* Sticking to the strict letter of your job description or to organizational regulations is a common way to avoid action. The same dedicated politician may be happy to circumvent his job description or organizational regulations when it suits his agenda.

- *Buck passing.* Having someone else take action is an effective way of avoiding doing it yourself. Buck passing is especially dysfunctional politics when the politician is best equipped to do the job but worries that it might not turn out successfully ("Let's let the design department get stuck with this turkey.").
- *Playing dumb.* Claiming to lack expertise about a particular matter can preclude taking action. Due to role stereotypes, lower-level organizational members are especially well placed to use this tactic.
- *Depersonalizing.* Viewing those making demands as numbers or objects is an easy way to put off taking action. In universities that reward research but not teaching, professors can avoid devoting time to students by depersonalizing them.

Avoiding Blame.   Another set of defensive behaviors is oriented around the motto "If you can't avoid action, avoid blame for its consequences." These behaviors include:

- *Buffing.* Buffing is the tactic of carefully documenting information showing that an appropriate course of action was followed. Getting "sign offs," authorizations, and so on are examples. Buffing can be sensible behavior, but it takes on political overtones when doing the documenting becomes more important than making a good decision. It is clearly dysfunctional politics if it takes the form of fabricating documentation.
- *Scapegoating.* Blaming others when things go wrong is classic political behavior. Scapegoating works best when you have some power behind you. One study found that when organizations performed poorly, more powerful CEOs stayed in office and the scapegoated managers below them were replaced. Less powerful CEOs were dismissed.[44]
- *Justifying.* If buffing or scapegoating aren't possible, we can try to justify our actions after-the-fact. The range of possible mechanisms is wide, including self-serving attributions (Chapter 4), biased hindsight (Chapter 12), and escalating commitment to the actions hoping that they will turn out well (Chapter 12).

The point of discussing these defensive political tactics has not been to teach you how to do them. Rather, it is to ensure that you recognize them as political behavior. Many of the tactics are quite mundane, and it is easy to write them off as isolated cases of laziness or some such thing. However, viewing them in context again illustrates the sometimes subtle ways that individuals pursue political self-interest in organizations. Politics, like power, is natural in all organizations. Whether or not politics is functional for the organization depends on the ends that are pursued and the influence means that are used.

Before continuing, consider the *You Be the Manager* feature.

ETHICS IN ORGANIZATIONS

Several years ago, the Johnson & Johnson subsidiary that was responsible for Tylenol quickly and decisively withdrew the product from the market after poison-laced examples of it were discovered. Subsequent to this, Copley Pharmaceutical was criticized for acting slowly to recall tainted drugs, and Syntex and Upjohn were both charged with obscuring negative side effects in

POWER AND POLITICS AT HONDA

M YOU BE THE anager

Japan's Honda Motor Company is widely regarded as one of the world's most successful organizations. Born out of the devastation of post–World War II Japan, the company has continued to perfect the culture set down by founder Soichiro Honda. That culture stresses technical excellence, the relentless pursuit of quality, and a trusting relationship among employees. Perhaps because of the stereotype that the Japanese value harmony so highly, it is not widely appreciated that Honda has many characteristics that could stimulate intense conflict. For example, to provoke innovation and constant questioning about its products, Honda has structurally separated its various functions (engineering, R&D, manufacturing, and sales) much more than is usually the case in the vehicle industry. This is traditionally a certain recipe for political turf wars and power jockeying. To complicate this extreme decentralization, management has constantly pressed for great increases in productivity and reductions in the cycle time for new product development. On top of this, the company is known for providing great opportunities for youthful managers and engineers, a practice that goes against the strong age-related power hierarchy of most industrial firms, especially in Japan.

Honda's plants at Marysville, Ohio, and Alliston, Ontario, are managed according to Honda corporate principles rather than conventional North American style. Much emphasis is placed on corporate values, team meetings, and employee flexibility to fill in on various jobs. Despite careful selection procedures, people are sometimes hired who do not adapt to the Honda culture. Firings have occurred at both sites. However, both sites have remained firmly nonunionized.

> HONDA HAS A STRUCTURE THAT COULD EASILY LEAD TO POLITICAL TURF WARS.

1. Speculate about how Honda manages political turf wars among its functional units.

2. Speculate as to why firings in the North American plants have not led to unionization.

To learn how Honda manages power and politics, see *The Manager's Notebook*.

Source: Pascale, R. T. (1990). *Managing on the edge.* New York: Simon & Schuster; McCallum, T. (1990, Summer). Democracy at work. *Inside Guide*, 40–44; Shook, R. L. (1988). *Honda: An American success story.* New York: Prentice Hall Press.

---

newly developed medicines. How can we account for the apparent difference in ethics reflected in the decisions that underpinned these actions?

For our purposes, **ethics** can be defined as systematic thinking about the moral consequences of decisions. Moral consequences can be framed in terms of the potential for harm to any stakeholders in the decision. **Stakeholders** are simply people inside or outside of the organization who have a potential to be affected by the decision. This could range from the decision makers themselves to "innocent bystanders."[45] Ethics is a major branch of philosophy, and we won't attempt to describe the various schools of ethical thought. Instead, we will focus on the kinds of ethical issues that organizational decision makers face and some of the factors that stimulate unethical decisions.

Over the years, researchers have conducted a number of surveys to determine managers' views about the ethics of decision making in business.[46] Some

Ethics. Systematic thinking about the moral consequences of decisions.

Stakeholders. People inside or outside of an organization who have the potential to be affected by organizational decisions.

A popular ethical theme for salespeople is how far to go in enticing customers. Although many products are designed to entice young buyers (or their parents), do you think advertising should target people under the age of 18?

striking similarities across studies provide an interesting picture of the popular psychology of business ethics. First, far from being shy about the subject, a large majority agree that unethical practices occur in business. Furthermore, a substantial proportion (between 40 and 90 percent, according to the particular study) report that they have been pressured to compromise their own ethical standards when making organizational decisions. Finally, in line with the concept of self-serving attributions, managers invariably tend to see themselves as having higher ethical standards than their peers and sometimes their superiors.[47] The unpleasant picture emerging here is one where unethical behavior tempts managers who sometimes succumb, but feel that they still do better than others on moral grounds.

In case you think that students are purer than organizational decision makers, think again. Research is fairly consistent in showing that business students have looser ethical standards than practicing managers, at least when responding to written descriptions of ethical issues.[48]

The Nature of Ethical Dilemmas

What are the kinds of ethical dilemmas that most frequently face organizational decision makers? Exhibit 13.6 shows the results of a Conference Board survey of 300 companies around the world. As you can see, conflicts of interest, questionable gift giving, and sexual harassment top the list of ethical concerns (while executive salaries are seen to present fewer problems!). Especially noteworthy is the fact that 77 percent of firms report problems in dealing with foreign business practices that are contrary to their own ethical norms.

Conflict of interest was a particular problem in the Prudential Insurance case in which Mark Jorgensen blew the whistle. The higher the valuation placed on the real estate included in the funds, the higher the fees that Prudential was entitled to collect from investors.

Ethical issues often tend to be peculiar to the specific domain in which we're usually making decisions. As an example, let's consider the ethical dilemmas that the various subspecialties of marketing face.[49] Among market researchers, telling subjects the true sponsor of the research has been an ongoing topic of debate. Among purchasing managers, where to draw the line in accepting favors (e.g., sports tickets) from vendors poses ethical problems. Among product managers, issues of planned obsolescence, unnecessary packaging, and differential pricing (e.g., charging more in the inner city) raise ethical concerns. When it comes to salespeople, how far to go in enticing customers and how to be fair in expense account use have been prominent ethical themes. Finally, in advertising, the range of ethical issues can (and does) fill books. Consider, for example, the decision to use sexual allure to sell a product.

In contrast to these occupationally specific ethical dilemmas, what are the common themes that run through ethical issues that managers face? An in-depth interview study of an occupationally diverse group of managers discovered seven themes that defined their moral standards for decision making.[50] Here are those themes and some typical examples of associated ethical behavior:

- *Honest communication.* Evaluate subordinates candidly; advertise and label honestly; don't slant proposals to senior management.

The Conference Board asked executives at 300 companies worldwide whether the following constituted ethical issues for business. The percentage of affirmative responses is listed next to the issue.

Issue	Percent
Employee conflicts of interest	91
Inappropriate gifts to corporate personnel	91
Sexual harassment	91
Unauthorized payments	85
Affirmative action	84
Employee privacy	84
Environmental issues	82
Employee health screening	79
Conflicts between company's ethics and foreign business practices	77
Security of company records	76
Workplace safety	76
Advertising content	74
Product safety standards	74
Corporate contributions	68
Shareholder interests	68
Corporate due process	65
Whistleblowing	63
Employment at will	62
Disinvestment	59
Government contract issues	59
Financial and cash management procedures	55
Plant/facility closures and downsizing	55
Political action committees	55
Social issues raised by religious organizations	47
Comparable worth	43
Product pricing	42
Executive salaries	37

Source: From *Corporate Ethics*, a Conference Board research report (New York: The Conference Board). Reprinted by permission.

EXHIBIT 13.6
A survey of ethical issues.

- *Fair treatment.* Pay equitably; respect the sealed bid process; don't give preference to suppliers with political connections; don't use lower-level people as scapegoats (see the "Ethical Focus: *Is Integrity Testing Ethical?*").

- *Special consideration.* The "fair treatment" standard can be modified for special cases, such as helping out a long-time employee, giving preference to hiring the disabled, or giving business to a loyal but troubled supplier.

- *Fair competition.* Avoid bribes and kickbacks to obtain business; don't fix prices with competitors.

- *Responsibility to organization.* Act for the good of the organization as a whole, not for self-interest; avoid waste and inefficiency.

- *Corporate social responsibility.* Don't pollute; think about the community impact of plant closures; show concern for employee health and safety.

- *Respect for law.* Legally avoid taxes, don't evade them; don't bribe government inspectors; follow the letter and spirit of labor laws.

ETHICAL FOCUS   Is Integrity Testing Ethical?

How would you like to apply for a job and have the recruiter ask you to take a written test that purports to measure your honesty? This is a more and more common occurrence in North American organizations. Estimates suggest that there are somewhere around 5 million integrity tests administered in the U.S. each year. This testing stems directly from an increasing concern about employee theft and fraud and indirectly from the passage of the Employee Polygraph Protection Act. This act, which effectively prohibits the use of electronic "lie detectors" for selection, prompted increased research into the use of written integrity tests. These tests, much cheaper to administer, have been embraced by many more businesses. There are two basic kinds of integrity tests. Some are straightforward measures of attitudes toward dishonesty that may also ask about past dishonest acts. Surprisingly, faking responses does not seem to be a serious problem. Other integrity tests are less overt in purpose, because they measure personality characteristics such as conscientiousness and reliability. A careful and comprehensive review by Deniz Ones, Chockalingam Viswesvaran, and Frank Schmidt concludes that integrity tests are valid predictors of work behavior. Although the correlations of the tests scores with

theft per se are small, the tests do a pretty good job of predicting a broader class of counterproductive behaviors that include theft, absenteeism, substance abuse, property damage, and so on. But are such tests ethical? Some observers have criticized the tests on the grounds of invasion of privacy. However, Dan Dalton and Michael Metzger take a different viewpoint. They argue that such tests are ethically questionable because they generate many "false positives," labeling people dishonest who are not dishonest. *All* tests make such classification errors, but they contend that integrity tests are especially prone because true dishonesty is fairly uncommon, and rare events are hard to predict. They further argue that the unfairly rejected applicant is unlikely to be told the true reason due to fear of legal problems.

What do you think about the ethics of integrity testing? Remember, they do predict counterproductive behavior despite the classification errors.

Sources: Ones, D. S., Viswesvaran, C., & Schmidt, F. L. (1993). Comprehensive meta-analysis of integrity test validities: Findings and implications for personnel selection and theories of job performance. *Journal of Applied Psychology, 78,* 679–703; Dalton, D. R., & Metzger, M. B. (1993). "Integrity testing" for personnel selection: An unsparing perspective. *Journal of Business Ethics, 12,* 147–156.

Causes of Unethical Behavior

What are the causes of unethical behavior? The answer to this question is important so that you can anticipate the circumstances that warrant special vigilance. Knowing the causes of unethical behavior can aid in its prevention. Because the topic is sensitive, you should appreciate that this is not the easiest area to research. The major evidence comes from surveys of executive opinion, case studies of prominent ethical failures, business game simulations, and responses to written scenarios involving ethical dilemmas (such as the exercise at the end of this chapter).

Gain. Although the point might seem mundane, it is critical to recognize the role of temptation in unethical activity. The anticipation of healthy reinforcement for following an unethical course of action, especially if no punishment is expected, should promote unethical decisions.[51] Consider, for example, Dennis Levine, the Drexel Burnham Lambert investment banker who was convicted of insider trading in Wall Street's biggest scandal.

> It was just so easy. In seven years I built $39,750 into $11.5 million, and all it took was a 20-second phone call to my offshore bank a couple of times a month—maybe 200 calls total. My account was growing at 125% a year, compounded. Believe me, I felt a rush when I would check the price of one of my stocks on the office Quotron and

learn I'd just made several hundred thousand dollars. I was confident that the elaborate veils of secrecy I had created—plus overseas bank-privacy laws—would protect me.[52]

Role Conflict.   Many ethical dilemmas that occur in organizations are actually forms of role conflict (Chapter 8) that get resolved in an unethical way. For example, consider the ethical theme of corporate social responsibility we listed above. Here, an executive's role as custodian of the environment (don't pollute) might be at odds with his or her role as a community employer (don't close the plant that pollutes).

A very common form of role conflict that provokes unethical behavior occurs when our "bureaucratic" role as an organizational employee is at odds with our role as the member of a profession.[53] For example, engineers who in their professional role opposed the fatal launch of the space shuttle *Challenger* due to cold weather were pressured to put on their bureaucratic "manager's hats" and agree to the launch. More recently, both the insurance and brokerage businesses have been rocked by similar ethics problems. Agents and brokers report being pressured as employees to push products that are not in the best interests of their clients. Frequently, reward systems (i.e., the commission structure) heighten the conflict, which then becomes a conflict of interest between self and client.

Competition.   Stiff competition for scarce resources can stimulate unethical behavior. This has been observed in both business game simulations and industry studies of illegal acts, in which trade offenses such as price fixing and monopoly violations have been shown to increase with industry decline.[54] For example, observers cite a crowded and mature market as one factor prompting price fixing violations in the folding-carton packaging industry.[55] We should note one exception to the "competition stresses ethics" thesis. In cases in which essentially *no* competition exists, there is also a strong temptation to make unethical decisions. This is because the opportunity to make large gains is not offset by market checks and balances. Prominent examples have occurred in the defense industry, in which monopoly contracts to produce military hardware have been accompanied by some remarkable examples of overcharging taxpayers.

Personality.   Are there certain types of personalities that are prone to unethical decisions? Perhaps. Business game simulations have shown that people with strong economic value orientations (Chapter 5) are more likely to behave unethically than those with weaker economic values.[56] Also, there are marked individual differences in the degree of sophistication that people use in thinking about moral issues.[57] Other things being equal, it is sensible to expect that people who are more self-conscious about moral matters will be more likely to avoid unethical decisions. Finally, people with a high need for personal power (especially Machiavellians) might be prone to make unethical decisions, using this power to further self-interest rather than for the good of the organization as a whole.

In closing this section, let's recall that we have a tendency to exaggerate the role of dispositional factors, such as personality, in explaining the behavior of others (Chapter 4). Thus, when we see unethical behavior, we should look at situational factors, such as competition and the organization's culture, as well as the personality of the actor.

Organizational and Industry Culture.   Bart Victor and John Cullen found that there were considerable differences in ethical values across the organizations they studied.[58] These differences involved factors such as consideration for employees, respect for the law, and respect for organizational rules. In addition, there were differences across groups within these organizations. This suggests that aspects of an organization's culture (and its subcultures) can influence ethics. This corresponds to the repeated finding in executive surveys that peer and superior conduct are viewed as strongly influencing ethical behavior, for good or for bad. The presence of role models helps to shape the culture (Chapter 9). If these models are actually rewarded for unethical behavior, rather than punished, the development of an unethical culture is likely. In fact, firms convicted of illegal acts often tend to be repeat offenders.[59]

The role of culture is also seen in the tendency for firms in certain industries to be convicted of illegal acts, although competition may also play a part. The food, lumber, oil refining, and automobile industries are more prone than others to such problems.[60]

Observers of the folding-carton price-fixing scandal we mentioned above note how top managers frequently seemed out of touch with the difficulty of selling boxes in a mature, crowded market. They put in place goal setting and reward systems (e.g., commission forming 60 percent of income) that almost guaranteed unethical decisions, systems that are much more appropriate for products on a growth cycle.[61] In fact, research shows that upper-level managers generally tend to be naive about the extent of ethical lapses below them. This can easily contribute to a success-at-any-cost culture.[62]

Finally, a consideration of culture suggests the conditions under which corporate codes of ethics might actually have an impact on decision making. If such codes are specific, tied to the actual business being done, and correspond to the reward system, they should bolster an ethical climate. If vague codes that do not correspond to other cultural elements exist, the negative symbolism might actually damage the ethical climate.

Is Playing Politics Ethical?

Is political activity ethical? It is particularly important to be clear about who the relevant stakeholders are when we decide to act politically. Because politics by definition involves self-interest, it is easy to gloss over others' legitimate interests when playing the game.

Perhaps the most easily identified stakeholders are political opponents, if they exist for the particular political episode in question. For instance, we discussed above several examples of individuals or groups contending for resources or control. Political opponents may invoke very different ethical criteria to justify their actions, and these criteria might be difficult to reconcile.

The larger organization's role as a stakeholder in political activity can itself be ethically complicated. One study found that managers who established a strong political network were most likely to obtain frequent promotions. However, in terms of setting performance standards and developing subordinate satisfaction and commitment, less political managers performed better, using their communication and human resource management skills. In the researchers' words, the political managers were more "successful" but less "effective."[63] However, it would be difficult to question the ethics of the political managers for shortchanging the organization when they were tangibly rewarded for acting politically!

This example raises a third category of stakeholders whose interests we might consider in the political arena—subordinates or co-workers who are affected by political activity. A common instance involves making unreasonable demands on subordinates to curry favor with superiors, as this R&D group leader explains:

> There is no way we can meet all our objectives. Objectives are only added to the list, never taken off. On each project, (_____) wants us to explore every possibility that higher management has suggested, no matter how illogical. Anything they want, he assures them we can do; and if we don't deliver, it's our fault. The situation has become so impossible, people don't care anymore.[64]

Employing Ethical Guidelines

A few simple guidelines, regularly used, should help in the ethical screening of decisions. The point isn't to paralyze your decision making but to get you to think seriously about the moral implications of your decisions before they are made.[65]

- Identify the stakeholders that will be affected by any decision.
- Identify the costs and benefits of various decision alternatives to these stakeholders.
- Consider the relevant moral expectations that surround a particular decision. These might stem from professional norms, laws, organizational ethics codes, and principles such as honest communication and fair treatment.
- Be familiar with the common ethical dilemmas that decision makers face in your specific organizational role or profession.
- Discuss ethical matters with decision stakeholders and others. Don't think ethics without talking about ethics.
- Convert your ethical judgments into appropriate action.

What this advice does is enable you to recognize ethical issues, make ethical judgments, and then convert these judgments into behavior.[66]

Training and education in ethics have become very popular in North American organizations. Boeing has a noteworthy program in an industry (aerospace) that has seen its share of ethical scandals.

> Boeing, which has been singled out for its outstanding internal program for ethics, trains its more than 145,000 employees in ethical values and uses a communication channel that enables employees to report infractions or concerns. A company-created pamphlet entitled "Business Conduct Guidelines" which emphasizes policies on ethics and standards of conduct and compliance is used in the training program. Training includes a video tape customized with an opening message by the general manager of each division. Situations are presented, both dramatic (FBI visits to homes) or routine (exchanges between customers, employees, suppliers, managers, and subordinates). Training is led by a business ethics advisor in each division.[67]

The evidence that exists so far indicates that formal education in ethics does have a positive impact on ethical attitudes.[68]

The Manager's Notebook   Power and Politics at Honda

Very generally, the Honda Motor Company's culture tends to stress good communication and speaking one's mind. Also, core values, such as enhancing product quality, provide a superordinate goal around which disputes can be resolved. However, some more specific management tactics for dealing with power and politics are seen at Honda.

1. Honda uses face-to-face sessions called *waigaya* ("chattering" or "hubbub") both to legitimate the value of conflict for learning purposes and to resolve conflict. In these sessions, traditional concessions to rank and status are put aside, and participants are encouraged to say what is truly on their minds. Anything goes, except direct criticism of one's colleagues or boss. *Waigaga* are used at all

corporate levels, from the shopfloor to the executive suite, Frank discussion and a variety of viewpoints, coupled with a strong overarching culture, turn political conflict into improved decisions.

2. When the North American Honda plants decide to terminate an employee, he or she can choose to appear before a review panel of other employees. If the review panel decides that the dismissal was unwarranted, the employee is reinstated. The existence of the review panel mechanism reminds supervisors to avoid capricious discipline and signals management trust in employee judgment. It provides for a balance of power that increases perceptions of fairness.

EXECUTIVE SUMMARY

◆ Power is the capacity to influence other people who are in a state of dependence. People have power by virtue of their position in the organization (legitimate power) or by virtue of the resources that they command (reward, coercion, friendship, or expertise).

◆ People can obtain power by doing the right things and cultivating the right people. Activities that lead to power acquisition need to be extraordinary, visible, and relevant to the needs of the organization. People to cultivate include outsiders, subordinates, peers, and superiors. Managers with high need for power are effective when they use this power to achieve organizational goals.

◆ Empowerment means giving people the authority, opportunity, and motivation to solve organizational problems. Power is thus located where it is needed to give employees the feeling that they are capable of doing their jobs well.

◆ Influence tactics are interpersonal strategies that convert power into influence. They include assertiveness, ingratiation, rationality, exchange, upward appeal, and coalition formation. Rationality (logic, reason, planning, compromise) is generally the most efficient tactic.

◆ Organizational subunits obtain power by controlling strategic contingencies. This means that they are able to affect events that are critical to *other* subunits. Thus, departments that can obtain resources for the organization will acquire power. Similarly, subunits gain power when they are able to reduce uncertainty for the organization, when their function is central to the work flow, and when other subunits or outside contractors can't perform their tasks.

◆ Organizational politics occurs when influence means that are not sanctioned by the organization are used or when nonsanctioned ends are pursued. The pursuit of nonsanctioned ends is always dysfunctional, but the organization may benefit when nonsanctioned means are used to achieve approved goals.

◆ Several political tactics were discussed: Machiavellianism is a set of cynical beliefs about human nature, morality, and the permissibility of using various means to achieve one's ends. Situational morality, lying, and "psyching out" are common tactics. Networking is establishing good relations with key people to accomplish goals. Defensiveness means avoiding taking actions that don't suit one's political agenda and avoiding blame for negative events.

◆ Ethics is systematic thinking about the moral consequences of decisions. Of particular interest is impact on stakeholders, people who have the potential to be affected by the decision.

◆ Common themes that run through ethical dilemmas that managers face include honest communication, fair treatment, special consideration, fair competition, responsibility to the organization, social responsibility, and respect for law.

◆ Causes of unethical behavior include the potential for great gain, the existence of role conflict, the extremes of business competition (great or none), organizational and industry culture, and certain personality characteristics.

KEY CONCEPTS

Power
Legitimate power
Reward power
Coercive power
Referent power
Expert power
Empowerment
Influence Tactics

Subunit power
Strategic contingencies
Organizational politics
Machiavellianism
Networking
Ethics
Stakeholders

DISCUSSION QUESTIONS

1. Contrast the bases of power available to an army sergeant with those available to the president of a voluntary community association. How would these differences in power bases affect their influence tactics?

2. Are the bases of individual power easily substitutable for each other? Are they equally effective? For example, can coercive power substitute for expert power?

3. Suppose that you are an entrepreneur who has started a new chain of consumer electronic stores. Your competitive edge is to offer excellent customer service. What would you do to empower your employees to help achieve this goal?

4. Imagine that you are on a committee at work or in a group working on a project at school that includes a "high Mach" member. What could you do to neutralize the high Mach's attempts to manipulate the group?

5. Discuss the conditions under which the following subunits of an organization might gain or lose power: Legal department; research and development unit; public relations department. Use the concepts of scarcity, uncertainty, centrality, and substitutability in your answers.

6. Differentiate between power and politics. Give an example of the use of power that is not political.

7. There is a saying that "politics is a way of life in organizations." Do you agree? Is political activity necessary for organizations to function?

8. In what sense can buck passing, stalling, and playing dumb be political? Aren't these just signs of laziness?

9. Give a good example of how role conflict can result in an ethical lapse.

10. Besides role conflict, what are some other factors that can provoke unethical organizational behavior?

EXPERIENTIAL EXERCISE
ETHICAL DECISION MAKING

The purpose of this exercise is to get you to consider some of the ethical aspects of decision making. Imagine that you are a marketing executive. Given below are several decision dilemmas, each of which might have an ethical dimension to it. Working alone, consider each dilemma in turn. For each dilemma, decide and record whether you would agree with the suggested course of action (yes) or disagree with the suggested course of action (no).

Students will then form into small learning groups and discuss each decision dilemma. After each dilemma is discussed, the group should calculate the *percentage* of its members that *agree* with each proposed course of action (some people might have changed their minds after discussion). The instructor will record the percentage of each group favoring each alternative on the board and discuss the results. **Do not read the debriefing until told to do so by the instructor!**

DILEMMAS

1. One of your dealers in an important territory has had family troubles recently and is not producing the sales he used to. He was one of the company's top producers in the past. It is not clear how long it will take before his family trouble straightens out. In the meantime, many sales are being lost. There is a legal way to terminate the dealer's franchise and replace him. What would you do?

2. You have a chance to win a big account that will mean a lot to you and your company. The purchasing agent hinted that he would be influenced by a "gift." Your assistant recommends sending a fine color television set to his home. What would you do?

3. You have heard that a competitor has a new product feature that will make a big difference in sales. She will have a hospitality suite at the annual trade show and unveil this feature at a party thrown for her dealers. You can easily send a snooper to this meeting to learn what the new feature is. What would you do?

4. You are eager to win a big contract, and during sales negotiations you learn that the buyer is looking for a better job. You have no intention of hiring him, but if you hinted that you might, he would probably give you the order. What would you do?

5. You are a marketing vice president working for a beer company, and you have learned that a particularly lucrative state is planning to raise the minimum legal drinking age from 18 to 21. You have been asked to join other breweries in lobbying against this bill and to make contributions. What would you do?

6. You want to interview a sample of customers about their reactions to a competitive product. It has been suggested that you invent an innocuous name like the Marketing Research Institute and interview people. What would you do?

7. You produce an antidandruff shampoo that is effective with one application. Your assistant says that the product would turn over faster if the instructions on the label recommended two applications. What would you do?

DEBRIEFING

George M. Zinkham, Michael Bisesi, and Mary Jane Saxton gave this ethics quiz to M.B.A. students at a major southwestern university over a number of semesters spanning six years. Below are the percentages of the students who agreed with the suggestion posed in each dilemma, including the highest semester, the lowest semester, and the average over twelve semesters:

	High %	Low %	Twelve-semester average
1. Terminate franchise?	65	0	18
2. Bribe agent?	35	16	27
3. Send snooper?	88	48	63
4. Hint at job?	25	4	12
5. Join lobby?	70	53	60
6. Invent name?	78	30	48
7. Recommend double dose?	72	32	49

Were there any trends in these responses over time? The researchers found that there was an increasing trend over time to bribe an agent (2), send a snooper (3), and invent a name of a research institute (6). However, recent responses were more resistant to joining an alcohol lobby (5).

Source: Dilemmas from Kotter, P. (1980). *Marketing management: Analysis, planning and control,* (4th ed.). pp. 706–707. Reprinted by permission of Prentice-Hall, Inc., Englewood Cliffs, NJ. Research results from Zinkham, G. M., Bisesi, M., & Saxton, M. J. (1989). MBAs' changing attitudes toward marketing dilemmas: 1981–1987. *Journal of Business Ethics, 8,* 963–974. Reprinted by permission of Kluwer Academic Publishers.

CASE STUDY
FAKING IT

Byron Smith was fiercely proud of the Capital Consulting Group, an economic and political consultancy that he'd established in Ottawa in 1983 and nurtured through five years of exceptional growth and success. During that time, his company had developed an impeccable reputation for its detailed, perceptive reports and advice and its high ethical standards. So when Smith discovered that one of his key analysts had lied about his education when he'd originally been hired, Smith felt overcome by panic.

Rudy Singh had joined Capital a few months after it started. Smith had met him at a cocktail party thrown by a prominent Ottawa journalist and was impressed by Singh's urbane, relaxed manner. In conversation, Singh told him he had graduated from the University of California–Berkeley with a masters degree in political science—his thesis was on the effectiveness of minority governments in Canadian history—and that he was looking for a more challenging job than his present position with a federal government department. Singh explained that although he was born in Canada, he had moved to Los Angeles with his mother eight years previously, following his parents' divorce. He had returned to Canada a few years after that because of his interest in the Canadian political system. Smith was so impressed with the 26-year-old that he invited him for a job interview the next day.

During the interview, Singh continued to impress Smith with his far-ranging knowledge of politics. Singh also demonstrated that he was well-read in literature, philosophy and economics. The rapport between the two men was such that Smith paid scant attention to Singh's résumé, which listed an undergraduate and masters degree. Smith offered him a job a few days later without checking any of Singh's background or references.

Rudy Singh proved to be an excellent addition to the Capital Group. His insightful reports and sophisticated manner with clients won him rave reviews. Occasionally quoted and interviewed by the media, he quickly established himself as one of Smith's most valuable associates.

In September, 1987, however, Smith learned that the seemingly well-educated Singh was anything but. Smith was at dinner with a close friend one evening when the couple's daughter began talking about her political science studies at the University of Toronto. She was particularly interested in the workings of the parliamentary system. When Smith mentioned Singh's thesis topic, she immediately asked if she could read it.

The next day Smith asked Singh if he minded letting the young woman read his thesis. Singh said he'd be happy to, but unfortunately it was packed away in a box at his mother's home in Los Angeles. Smith had one of his staff telephone Singh's university to see about getting a photocopy of the thesis sent by courier. But there was no record of any such thesis nor of a Rudy Singh ever having been registered at Berkeley.

The news hit Smith like a shock wave. He immediately called Singh into his office and confronted him with the news. Ashen-faced, Singh admitted that he'd falsified his résumé. He explained that although he loved to read and had always been considered of above-average intelligence, he had never done well at school. Sitting in class bored him and he barely managed to graduate from high school in Los Angeles. His marks were too low to gain him entry to university, so he decided to educate himself. He read voraciously and he talked some Berkeley professors into letting him sit in on their classes. Freed from the official strictures at school, he learned at a phenomenal rate. He apologized profusely for faking his résumé but said that he had doubted anyone would have considered hiring him without the appropriate credentials.

Smith felt truly confused. He liked and admired Singh. He respected his intelligence and really didn't care whether Singh had "the right pieces of paper." But Smith was deeply concerned about what might happen if Singh's deception became public. Would Singh, and subsequently The Capital Consulting Group, lose credibility? Should he fire Singh, ask for his resignation or just maintain the status quo and hope nobody ever finds out?

Source: Case by Paul McLaughlin. From McLaughlin, P. (1988, June). Faking it. *Canadian Business*, 273–274.

1. Before the faked résumé was discovered, describe Rudy Singh's bases of power. Explain the process by which Rudy acquired this power.

2. Was faking the résumé an example of organizational politics? Defend your answer.

3. What are some factors that might have contributed to Rudy's decision to pad his résumé? Was it ethical?

4. Is it ethical to fire Singh? Is it ethical to keep Singh on at Capital Consulting?

5. Who are the stakeholders in this episode?

6. What should Byron Smith do?

Learning Objectives

After reading Chapter 14 you should be able to:

1 Define interpersonal conflict and review its causes in organizations.

2 Explain the process by which conflict occurs.

3 Discuss the various modes of managing conflict.

4 Review a range of negotiation techniques.

5 Discuss the merits of stimulating conflict.

6 Distinguish among stressors, stress, and stress reactions.

7 Discuss the role that personality plays in stress.

8 Review the sources of stress encountered by various organizational role occupants.

9 Describe behavioral, psychological, and physiological reactions to stress and discuss techniques for reducing or coping with stress.

The ongoing success of Motorola can be partly credited to a company culture that encourages constructive conflict.

CHAPTER 14

CONFLICT AND STRESS

MOTOROLA— CONFLICT, STRESS, AND SUCCESS

Motorola, based in Schaumburg, Illinois, produces semiconductors, microprocessors, and communications equipment. The company is big, old, and well established. As you probably know, many big, old, established firms have had a very difficult time changing to meet the strong competitive demands of today's global business climate. Not Motorola. The firm has learned how to couple aggressive research and development with a fanatical concern for manufacturing quality. As a result, Motorola is the worldwide market leader in pagers, two-way radios, and cellular phones. It is the recipient of a Malcolm Baldrige National Quality Award, publicly striving for "six sigma quality," only 3.4 defects per million parts produced.

An extremely unusual aspect of Motorola's success is that it is achieved by a culture that encourages conflict. Open dissent and ferocious verbal combat are common in the company. Engineers are encouraged to dispute peers and superiors in meetings and to file minority reports if they think that their good ideas lack support. Members consider it bad form to seek retribution from the dissenters. One of the most famous examples of dissent occurred when the head of the radio group stood up at a self-congratulating social function and derided the group's own product quality. Such incidents galvanized the firm's subsequent quality efforts.

Observers credit the "cult of conflict" at Motorola with identifying errors, killing illogical ideas, preventing groupthink, and keeping management informed. However, it has also led to incorrect decisions when well entrenched but less clever design teams have outshouted upstart teams. Also, coupled with the extremely high quality goals, the conflictful atmosphere has prompted burnout among managers and engineers. Still, Motorola relies on conflict as one approach to motivate people to accept competition and change.[1]

How would you like to work in the shouting match atmosphere of Motorola? Like power and politics, conflict is a natural occurrence in organizations, although not always in this extreme and open form. As the story illustrates, conflict can have its benefits, but it can also lead to problems such as employee stress.

In this chapter we will define interpersonal conflict, discuss its causes, and examine various ways of handling conflict. We place particular emphasis on negotiation. Then, we'll explore organizational stress, noting its causes and the consequences that it can have for both the individual and the organization. Various strategies for reducing or coping with stress will be considered.

WHAT IS CONFLICT?

Interpersonal conflict. A process that occurs when one person, group, or organizational subunit frustrates the goal attainment of another.

Interpersonal conflict is a process that occurs when one person, group, or organizational subunit frustrates the goal attainment of another. Thus, the curator of a museum might be in conflict with the director over the purchase of a particular work of art. Likewise, the entire curatorial staff might be in conflict with the financial staff over cutbacks in acquisition funds.

In its classic form, conflict often involves antagonistic attitudes and behaviors. As for attitudes, the conflicting parties might develop a dislike for each other, see each other as unreasonable, and develop negative stereotypes of their opposites ("Those scientists should get out of the laboratory once in a while."). Antagonistic behaviors might include name calling, sabotage, or even physical aggression. This Motorola-style overt antagonism is not evident in all organizations. In some, the conflict process is managed in a collaborative way that keeps antagonism at a minimum. In others, conflict is hidden or suppressed and not nearly so obvious (e.g., some gender conflict).[2]

CAUSES OF ORGANIZATIONAL CONFLICT

It is possible to isolate a number of factors that contribute to organizational conflict.[3]

Group Identification and Intergroup Bias

An especially fascinating line of research has shown how identification with a particular group or class of people can set the stage for organizational conflict. In this research, people have typically assigned people to groups randomly or on the basis of some trivial characteristic, such as eye color. Even without interaction or cohesion, people have a tendency to develop a more positive view of their own "in-group" (be it a friendship group, a work group, or a department) and a less positive view of the "out-group" of which they are not a member.[4] The ease with which this unwarranted intergroup bias develops is disturbing.

Why does intergroup bias occur? Self-esteem is probably a critical factor. Identifying with the successes of one's own group and disassociating oneself from out-group failures boosts self-esteem and provides comforting feelings of social solidarity. In my own research, for example, I found that people felt that their work group's attendance record was superior to that of their occupation in general (and, by extension, other work groups).[5] Attributing positive behavior to your own work group should contribute to your self-esteem.

In organizations, there are a number of groups or classes with which people might identify. These might be based on personal characteristics (e.g., race or gender), job function (e.g., sales or production), or job level (e.g., manager or nonmanager). Furthermore, far from being random or trivial, differences between groups might be accentuated by real differences in power, opportunity, clients serviced, and so on. The best prognosis is that people who identify with some groups will tend to be leery of out-group members. The likelihood of conflict increases as the factors we cover below enter into the relationship between groups.

The increased emphasis on teams in organizations generally places a high premium on getting employees to identify strongly with their team. The prevalence of intergroup bias suggests that organizations will have to pay special attention to managing relationships *between* these teams.

Interdependence

When individuals or subunits are mutually dependent upon each other to accomplish *their own* goals, the potential for conflict exists. For example, the sales staff is dependent upon the production department for the timely delivery of high-quality products. This is the only way sales can maintain the good will of its customers. On the other hand, production depends upon the sales staff to provide routine orders with adequate lead times. Custom-tailored emergency orders will wreak havoc with production schedules and make the production department look bad. In contrast, the sales staff and the office maintenance staff are not highly interdependent. Salespeople are on the road a lot and should not make great demands on maintenance. Conversely, a dirty office probably won't lose a sale!

Interdependence can set the stage for conflict for two reasons. First, it necessitates interaction between the parties so that they can coordinate their interests. Conflict will not develop if the parties can "go it alone." Second, as we noted in the previous chapter, interdependence implies that each party has some *power* over the other. It is relatively easy for one side or the other to abuse its power and create antagonism.

Interdependence does not *always* lead to conflict. In fact, it often provides a good basis for collaboration through mutual assistance. Whether interdependence prompts conflict depends upon the presence of other conditions, which we will now consider.

Differences in Power, Status, and Culture

Conflict can erupt when parties differ significantly in power, status, or culture.

Power. If dependence is not mutual, but one way, the potential for conflict increases. If party A needs the collaboration of party B to accomplish its goals, but B does not need A's assistance, antagonism may develop. B has power over A, and A has nothing with which to bargain. A good example is the quality control system in many factories. Production workers might be highly dependent upon inspectors to approve their work, but this dependence is not reciprocated. The inspectors might have a separate boss, their own office, and their own circle of friends (other inspectors). In this case, production workers might begin to treat inspectors with hostility, one of the symptoms of conflict.

Status. Status differences provide little impetus for conflict when people of lower status are dependent upon those of higher status. This is the way organizations often work, and most members are socialized to expect it. However, because of the design of the work, there are occasions when employees with technically lower status find themselves giving orders to, or controlling the tasks of, higher-status people. The restaurant business provides a good example. In many restaurants, lower-status waiters and waitresses give orders and initiate queries to higher-status cooks or chefs. The latter might come to resent this reversal of usual lines of influence.[6] The advent of the "electronic office" led to similar kinds of conflict. As secretaries mastered the complexities of electronic mail, they found themselves having to educate senior executives about the capabilities and limitations of such systems. Some executives are defensive about this reversal of roles.

Culture. When two or more very different cultures develop in an organization, the clash in beliefs and values can result in overt conflict. Hospital administrators who develop a strong culture centered on efficiency and cost-effectiveness might find themselves in conflict with physicians who share a strong culture based on providing excellent patient care at any cost. A telling case of cultural conflict occurred when Apple Computer expanded and hired professionals away from several companies with their own strong cultures.

> During the first couple of years Apple recruited heavily from Hewlett-Packard, National Semiconductor, and Intel, and the habits and differences in style among these companies were reflected in Cupertino. There was a general friction between the rough and tough ways of the semiconductor men (there were few women) and the people who made computers, calculators, and instruments at Hewlett-Packard.... Some of the Hewlett-Packard men began to see themselves as civilizing influences and were horrified at the uncouth rough-and-tumble practices of the brutes from the semiconductor industry.... Many of the men from National Semiconductor and other stern backgrounds harbored a similar contempt for the Hewlett-Packard recruits. They came to look on them as prissy fusspots.[7]

Ambiguity

Ambiguous goals, jurisdictions, or performance criteria can lead to conflict. Under such ambiguity the formal and informal rules that govern interaction break down. In addition, it might be difficult to accurately assign praise for good outcomes or blame for bad outcomes when it is hard to see who was responsible for what. For example, if sales drop following the introduction of a "new and improved" product, the design group might blame the marketing department for a poor advertising campaign. In response, the marketers might claim that the "improved" product is actually inferior to the old product.

Ambiguous jurisdictions are often revealed when new programs are introduced. This is a common occurrence in universities. For instance, the division of continuing education might initiate a series of management development seminars that compete with those the business school offers. Likewise, the political science department might wish to establish a master's degree in applied politics that is similar to a degree the school of public administration offers. In both cases, charges of "poaching" are almost certain to occur.

Ambiguous performance criteria are a frequent cause of conflict between superiors and subordinates. The basic scientist who is charged by a chemical company to "discover new knowledge" might react negatively when her boss informs her that her work is inadequate. This rather open-ended assignment is susceptible to a variety of interpretations.

Scarce Resources

In the previous chapter, we pointed out that differences in power are magnified when resources become scarce. This does not occur without a battle, however, and conflict often surfaces in the process of power jockeying. Limited budget money, secretarial support, or computer time can contribute to conflict. Consider the company that installs a new computer for administrative and research purposes. At first, there is plenty of computer time and space for both uses. However, as both factions make more and more use of the computer, access becomes a problem. Conflict may erupt at this point.

Scarcity has a way of turning latent or disguised conflict into overt conflict. Two scientists who don't get along very well may be able to put up a peaceful front until a reduction in laboratory space provokes each to protect his domain.

TYPES OF CONFLICT

Although a variety of causes contribute to the emergence of organizational conflict, most conflicts boil down to several basic types or combinations of these types. These include disputes over goals, facts, and procedures.[8]

Disputes over goals are very common in organizations. Consider this General Mills general manager for fruit snacks as she reflects on the common conflict between marketing and manufacturing:

> "The goal of the people in the plants is to run lots of cases fast," she says. "Our goal is to constantly bring something new to consumers." The manufacturing people do not like the way she changes the colors of the fruit-snack wrapping and places new prizes, such as

glow-in-the-dark sharks, inside the boxes. She argues, "Doing these things is crucial to growing the business."[9]

Disputes over facts very frequently arise in technical situations. Motorola's biggest project, a worldwide cellular phone network, was nearly scuttled by debate over its technical feasibility.

Disputes over procedures generally center around one party's expectations about how the other party should behave. Matters of ethics (Chapter 13), fairness (Chapter 5), and respecting status hierarchies often fuel procedural conflicts. For example, a well-documented source of conflict between employees and managers has to do with the legitimacy of employee absenteeism and the fairness of management response to it.[10]

Being aware of these different types of conflict should sensitize you to the need to be sure that you understand what a conflict episode is really about. For instance, very basic differences in goals (should we expand the business?) are not necessarily resolvable by clearing up disputes over facts (what's our potential market size?). Also, notice that spillover between domains can occur. For instance, a conflict over facts (which project has more technical merit?) can lead to procedural conflict if one party is seen as trying to unethically sabotage the other's work. When this happens, true conflict resolution can occur only when *all* aspects of the conflict (i.e., both facts and procedures) are dealt with. Finally, one party might frame a conflict as a goal conflict while the other might see it as a procedural conflict or a conflict over facts. In seeking resolution, it is important to try to see the conflict from your opponent's frame of reference.

THE CONFLICT PROCESS

A number of events occur when one or more of the causes of conflict we noted above takes effect. We will assume here that the conflict in question occurs between groups, such as organizational departments. However, much of this is also relevant to conflict between individuals. Specifically, when conflict begins, we often see the following events transpire:

- "Winning" the conflict becomes more important than developing a good solution to the problem at hand.
- The parties begin to conceal information from each other or to pass distorted information.
- Each group becomes more cohesive. Deviants who speak of conciliation are punished, and strict conformity is expected.
- Contact with the opposite party is discouraged except under formalized, restricted conditions.
- While the opposite party is negatively stereotyped, the image of one's own position is boosted.
- On each side, more aggressive people who are skilled at engaging in conflict may emerge as leaders.[11]

You can certainly see the difficulty here. What begins as a problem of interdependence, ambiguity, or scarcity quickly escalates to the point that the conflict process *itself* becomes an additional problem. The elements of this process then work against the achievement of a peaceful solution. The conflict continues to cycle "on its own steam."

MODES OF MANAGING CONFLICT

How do you tend to react to conflict situations? Are you aggressive? Do you tend to hide your head in the sand? As conflict expert Kenneth Thomas notes, there are several basic reactions that can be thought of as styles, strategies, or intentions for dealing with conflict. As shown in Exhibit 14.1, these approaches to managing conflict are a function of both how *assertive* you are in trying to satisfy your own or your group's concerns and how *cooperative* you are in trying to satisfy those of the other party or group.[12] It should be emphasized that none of the five styles for dealing with conflict in Exhibit 14.1 is inherently superior. As we'll see, each style might have its place given the situation in which the conflict episode occurs.

Avoiding

The **avoiding** style is characterized by low assertiveness of one's own interests and low cooperation with the other party. This is the "hiding the head in the sand" response. Although avoidance can provide some short-term stress reduction from the rigors of conflict, it doesn't really change the situation. Thus, its effectiveness is often limited. Some press accounts of IBM's difficulties have suggested that its culture avoided the kind of goal conflict that was necessary to shake its outdated reliance on mainframe computers.

Avoiding. A conflict management style characterized by low assertiveness of one's own interests and low cooperation with the other party.

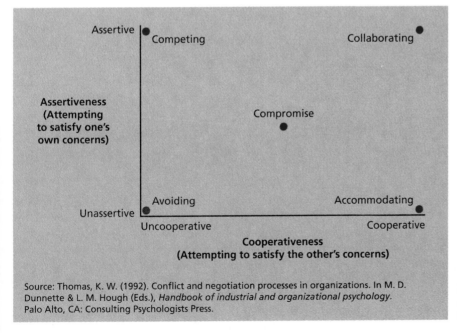

Source: Thomas, K. W. (1992). Conflict and negotiation processes in organizations. In M. D. Dunnette & L. M. Hough (Eds.), *Handbook of industrial and organizational psychology.* Palo Alto, CA: Consulting Psychologists Press.

EXHIBIT 14.1
Approaches to managing organizational conflict.

Of course, avoidance does have its place. If the issue is trivial, information is lacking, people need to cool down, or the opponent is very powerful and very hostile, avoidance might be a sensible response.

Accommodating

Accommodating. A conflict management style in which one cooperates with the other party while not asserting one's own interests.

Cooperating with the other party's wishes while not asserting one's own interests is the hallmark of **accommodating.** The Clinton administration was accused of accommodating the military government of Haiti when it allowed a small band of protestors to turn back a U.S. ship that was acting as an advance guard for the return of the country's deposed president.

If people see accommodation as a sign of weakness it does not bode well for future interactions. However, it can be an effective reaction when you are wrong, the issue is more important to the other party, or you want to build goodwill.

Competing

Competing. A conflict management style that maximizes assertiveness and minimizes cooperation.

A **competing** style tends to maximize assertiveness for your own position and minimize cooperative responses. In doing so, you tend to frame the conflict in strict win-lose terms. Full priority is given to your own goals, facts, or procedures. Bill Gates, the billionaire chairman of Microsoft, tends to pursue the competing style:

> Gates is famously confrontational. If he strongly disagrees with what you're saying, he is in the habit of blurting out, "That's the stupidest . . . thing I've ever heard!" People tell stories of Gates spraying saliva into the face of some hapless employee as he yells, "This stuff isn't hard! I could do this stuff in a weekend!" What you're supposed to do in a situation like this, as in encounters with grizzly bears, is stand your ground: if you flee, the bear will think you're game and will pursue you, and you can't outrun a bear.[13]

The competing style holds promise when you have a lot of power (e.g., Gates), you're sure of your facts, the situation is truly win-lose, or you won't have to interact with the other party in the future.

Compromise

Compromise. A conflict management style that combines intermediate levels of assertiveness and cooperation.

Compromise combines intermediate levels of assertiveness and cooperation. Thus, it is itself a compromise between pure competition and pure accommodation. In a sense, you attempt to satisfice (Chapter 12) rather than maximize your outcomes and hope that the same occurs for the other party. In the law, a plea-bargain is an example of a compromise between the defending lawyer and the prosecutor.

Compromise places a premium on determining rules of exchange between the two parties. As such, it always contains the seeds for procedural conflict in addition to whatever else is being negotiated. Also, compromise doesn't always result in the most creative response to conflict. Compromise isn't so useful for resolving conflicts that stem from power asymmetry, because the weaker party may have little to offer the stronger party. However, it is a sensible reaction to conflict stemming from scarce resources. Also, it is a good fall-back position if other strategies fail.

Collaborating

In the **collaborating** mode, both assertiveness and cooperation are maximized in the hope that an integrative agreement occurs that fully satisfies the interests of both parties. Emphasis is put on a win-win resolution in which there is no assumption that someone must lose something. Rather, it is assumed that the solution to the conflict can leave both parties in a better condition. Ideally, collaboration occurs as a kind of problem solving exercise (Chapter 12). It probably works best when the conflict is not intense and when each party has information that is useful to the other. Although, effective collaboration can take time and practice to develop, it frequently enhances productivity and achievement.[14]

Some of the most remarkable examples of collaboration in contemporary organizations are those between companies and their suppliers. Traditionally, adversarial competition in which buyers try to squeeze the very lowest price out of suppliers, who are frequently played off against each other, has dominated these relationships. This obviously doesn't provide much incentive for the perpetually insecure suppliers to invest in improvements dedicated toward a particular buyer.

Things are changing. Honda provides copious engineering advice to its suppliers. One, Donelly Corporation of Holland, Michigan, was chosen to be Honda's exclusive supplier of mirrors for its U.S.-built cars. Donelly built an entirely new plant to make exterior mirrors based on a handshake deal. As you might guess from the vignette that began the chapter, Motorola does things a little differently with its suppliers, falling somewhere between competing and collaborating. The firm teaches suppliers total quality management practices at its "Motorola University" but then scores the suppliers against each other on frequent report cards that give them feedback for improvement. It also involves them from the beginning of all design projects.[15]

Collaboration also helps to manage conflict within organizations. Our discussion of cross-functional teams in Chapter 8 is a good example. Research shows that collaboration between organizational departments is particularly important for providing good customer service.[16]

Collaborating. A conflict management style that maximizes both assertiveness and cooperation.

Collaboration can provide unions and management with win-win solutions.

MANAGING CONFLICT WITH NEGOTIATION

The stereotype we have of negotiation is that it is a formal process of bargaining between labor and management or buyer and seller. However, job applicants negotiate for starting salaries, employees negotiate for better job assignments, and people with sick kids negotiate to leave work early. To encompass all of these situations, we might define **negotiation** as "a decision-making process among interdependent parties who do not share identical preferences."[17] Negotiation constitutes conflict management in that it is an attempt either to prevent conflict or to resolve existing conflict.

Negotiation is an attempt to reach a satisfactory exchange among or between the parties (See the cartoon). Sometimes, negotiation is very explicit, as in the case of the labor negotiation or the buyer-seller interaction. However, negotiation can also proceed in a very implicit or tacit way.[18] For instance, in trying to get a more interesting job assignment or to take off from work early, the terms of the exchange are not likely to be spelled out very clearly. Still, this is negotiation.

Negotiation. A decision-making process among interdependent parties who do not share identical preferences.

Distributive negotiation.
Win-lose negotiation in which a fixed amount of assets is divided between parties.

Integrative negotiation.
Win-win negotiation that assumes that mutual problem solving can enlarge the assets to be divided between parties.

It has become common to distinguish between distributive and integrative negotiation tactics.[19] **Distributive negotiation** assumes a zero-sum, win-lose situation in which a fixed pie is divided up between the parties. If you reexamine Exhibit 14.1, you can imagine that distributive negotiation occurs on the axis between competition and accommodation. In theory, the parties will more or less tend toward some compromise. On the other hand, **integrative negotiation** assumes that mutual problem solving can result in a win-win situation in which the pie is actually enlarged before distribution. Integrative negotiation occurs on the axis between avoiding and collaborating, ideally tending toward the latter.

Distributive and integrative negotiation can take place simultaneously. We'll discuss them separately for pedagogical purposes.

Distributive Negotiation Tactics

Distributive negotiation is essentially single-issue negotiation. Many potential conflict situations fit this scenario. For example, suppose you find a used car that you really like. Now, things boil down to price. You want to buy the car for the minimum reasonable price, while the seller wants to get the maximum reasonable price.

THE FAR SIDE   By GARY LARSON

"Ok, Johnson — we've got a deal. We'll let your people and my people work out the details."

The essence of the problem is shown in Exhibit 14.2. Party is a consulting firm who would like to win a contract to do an attitude survey in Other's firm. Party would like to make $90,000 for the job (Party's target) but would settle for $70,000, a figure that provides for minimal acceptable profit (Party's resistance point). Other thinks that the survey could be done for as little as $60,000 (Other's target) but would be willing to spend up to $80,000 for a good job (Other's resistance point). Theoretically, an offer in the Settlement range between $70,000 and $80,000 should clinch the deal if the negotiators can get into this range. Notice that every dollar that Party earns is a dollar's worth of cost for Other. How will they reach a settlement?[20]

Threats and Promises.   Threat consists of implying that you will punish the other party if he or she does not concede to your position. For example, the Other firm might imply that it will terminate its other business with the consulting company if it does not lower its price on the attitude survey job. Promises are pledges that concessions will lead to rewards in the future. For example, Other might promise future consulting contracts if Party agrees to do the survey at a lower price. Of course, the difference between a threat and a promise can be subtle, as when the promise implies a threat if no concession is made.

Threat has some merit as a bargaining tactic if one party has power over the other that corresponds to the nature of the threat, especially if no future negotiations are expected or if the threat can be posed in a civil and subtle way.[21] If power is more balanced and the threat is crude, a counterthreat could scuttle the negotiations, despite the fact that both parties could be satisfied in the Settlement range. Promises have merit when your side lacks power and anticipates future negotiations with the other side. Both threat and promises work best when they send interpretable signals to the other side about your true position, what really matters to you. Careful timing is critical.

Firmness versus Concessions.   How about intransigence—sticking to your target position, offering few concessions, and waiting for the other party to

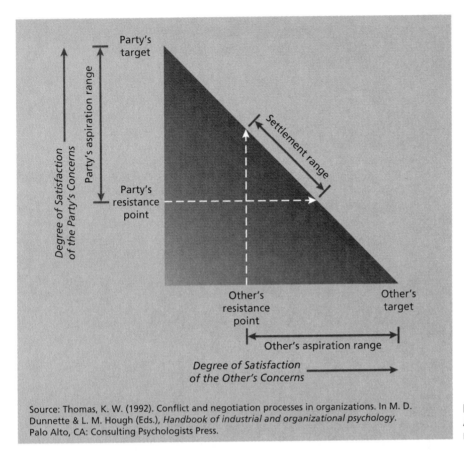

Source: Thomas, K. W. (1992). Conflict and negotiation processes in organizations. In M. D. Dunnette & L. M. Hough (Eds.), *Handbook of industrial and organizational psychology*. Palo Alto, CA: Consulting Psychologists Press.

EXHIBIT 14.2
A model of distributive negotiation.

give in? Research shows that such a tactic is likely to be reciprocated by the other party, thus increasing the chances of a deadlock.[22] On the other hand, a series of small concessions early in the negotiation will often be matched. Good negotiators often use face-saving techniques to explain concessions. For example, the consulting firm might claim that it could reduce the cost of the survey by printing it on cheaper paper.

Persuasion.   Verbal persuasion or debate is common in negotiations. Often, it takes a two-pronged attack. One prong asserts the technical merits of the party's position. For example, the consulting firm might justify its target price by saying "We have the most qualified staff. We do the most reliable surveys." The other prong asserts the fairness of the target position. Here, the negotiator might make a speech about the expenses the company would incur in doing the survey.

Verbal persuasion is an attempt to change the attitudes of the other party toward your target position. You will recall that such persuaders are most effective when they are perceived as expert, likable, and unbiased (Chapter 5). The obvious problem in distributive negotiations is bias—each party knows the other is self-interested. One way to deal with this is to introduce some unbiased parties. For example, the consulting firm might produce testimony from satisfied survey clients. Also, disputants often bring third parties into negotiations (see next page) on the assumption that they will process argumentation in an unbiased manner.

IN FOCUS   Why Do Women Earn Less? Gender Differences in Salary Negotiation

One of the best-documented inequities in the diverse contemporary workplace is the salary gap between men and women. Consistently, studies show that women are paid less, even when sophisticated controls match men and women in terms of education and experience. No single factor is responsible for this salary disparity. Rather, it probably stems from a mixture of biased starting salaries, biased performance evaluations, and the segregation of women into lower-paying jobs.

Cynthia Kay Stevens, Anna Bavetta, and Marilyn Gist were interested in the starting salary part of this equation. First, they reviewed research that suggested men were inclined to use more, or more skillful, tactics in negotiating their starting salaries. In one survey, the men reported receiving an average of $742 more for their negotiation efforts than did women. Stevens, Bavetta, and Gist reasoned that the differential socialization of women and men could result in women either having less tactical understanding of negotiation, being less persistent in negotiation, or being less confident about their ability to negotiate. Thus, they designed three training modules for MBA students.

The first module was oriented toward conveying an understanding of negotiation tactics. After this training, a simulated salary negotiation showed that women negotiated $1,350 less than men! This showed that tactical knowledge wasn't the problem. Next, half of the students were exposed to goal-setting training in which they set specific, challenging goals for salary negotiation (Chapter 7). The other half experienced self-management training in which they also identified obstacles to good negotiation and planned how to overcome them (Chapter 3). A second simulated negotiation revealed that goal setting did not reduce the disparity between men and women, although it helped both groups negotiate higher salaries. The self-management training helped both groups negotiate better salaries, and it erased the difference between men's and women's starting salaries.

Source: Adapted from Stevens, C. K., Bavetta, A. G., & Gist, M. E. (1993). Gender differences in the acquisition of salary negotiation skills: The role of goals, self-efficacy, and perceived control. *Journal of Applied Psychology, 78,* 723–735.

Before continuing, consider the "In Focus: *Why Do Women Earn Less? Gender Differences in Salary Negotiation*" which discusses salary negotiation, a traditional example of distributive bargaining.

Integrative Negotiation Tactics

As we noted earlier, integrative negotiation rejects a fixed-pie assumption and strives for collaborative problem solving that advances the interests of both parties. At the outset, it's useful but sobering to realize that people have a decided bias for fixed-pie thinking. A good example is seen in the North American manufacturing sector, where such thinking by both unions and management badly damaged the global competitiveness of manufacturing firms.[23]

Why the bias for fixed-pie thinking? First, integrative negotiation requires a degree of creativity. Most people are not especially creative, and the stress of typical negotiation does not provide the best climate for creativity in any event. This means that many of the role models that negotiators have (e.g., following labor negotiations on TV) are more likely to use distributive than integrative tactics. To complicate matters, if you are negotiating for constituents, they are also more likely to be exposed to distributive tactics and likely to pressure you to use them. Nevertheless, attempts at integrative negotiation can be well worth the effort.[24]

plenty

Copious Information Exchange.   Most of the information exchanged in distributive bargaining is concerned with attacking the other party's position and trying to persuade them of the correctness of yours. Otherwise, mum's the word. A freer flow of information is critical to finding an integrative settlement. The problem, of course, is that we all tend to be a bit paranoid about information being used against us in bargaining situations. This means that trust must be built slowly. One way to proceed is to give away some noncritical information to the other party to get the ball rolling. As we noted earlier, much negotiation behavior tends to be reciprocated. Also, ask the other party a lot of questions, and *listen* to their responses. This is at odds with the tell-and-sell approach in most distributive negotiations. If all goes well, both parties will begin to reveal their true interests, not just their current positions.

Framing Differences As Opportunities.   Parties in a negotiation often differ in their preferences for everything from the timing of a deal to the degree of risk that each party wants to assume. Traditionally, such differences are framed as barriers to negotiations. However, such differences can often serve as a basis for integrative agreements because again, they contain information that can telegraph each party's real interests. For instance, imagine that two co-workers are negotiating for the finishing date of a project that they have to complete by a certain deadline. Due to competing demands, one wants to finish it early, and the other wants to just make the deadline. In the course of the discussion, they realize that they can divide the labor such that one begins the project while the other finishes it, satisfying both parties fully (notice that this isn't a compromise).

Cutting Costs.   If you can somehow cut the costs that the other party associates with an agreement, the chance of an integrative settlement increases. For example, suppose that you are negotiating with your boss for a new, more interesting job assignment, but she doesn't like the idea because she relies on your excellent skills on your current assignment. Asking good questions (see above) you find out that she is ultimately worried about the job being done properly, not about you leaving it. You take the opportunity to inform her that you have groomed a subordinate to do your current job. This reduces the costs of her letting you assume the new assignment.

Integrative solutions are especially attractive when they reduce costs for *all* parties in a dispute. For example, firms in the computer and acoustics industries have joined together to support basic research on technology of interest to all firms. This reduces costly competition to perfect a technology that all parties need anyway.

Increasing Resources.   Increasing available resources is a very literal way of getting around the fixed-pie syndrome. This isn't as unlikely as it sounds when you realize that two parties, working together, might have access to twice as many resources as one party. I once saw two academic departments squabbling to get the approval to recruit one new faculty member for whom there was a budget line. Seeing this as a fixed pie leads to one department winning all or to the impossible compromise of half a recruit for each department. The chairs of the two departments used their *combined* political clout to get the dean to promise that they could also have exclusive access to one budget line the following year. The chairs then flipped a coin to see who would recruit immediately and who would wait a year. This minor compromise on time was less critical than the firm guarantee of a budget line.

Superordinate goals. Attractive outcomes that can be achieved only by collaboration.

Introducing Superordinate Goals.   As discussed in Chapter 8, **superordinate goals** are attractive outcomes that can be achieved only by collaboration.[25] Neither party can attain the goal on its own. Superordinate goals probably represent the best example of creativity in integrative negotiation because they change the entire landscape of the negotiation episode.

Given its recent success, you might be surprised to know that Chrysler Corporation almost went broke in 1980. With the prospect of bankruptcy and massive unemployment looming large, the United Auto Workers and Chrysler management collaborated on a scheme to renew the company. This collaboration was far removed from the auto industry's traditional fixed-pie, distributive bargaining.

Third Party Involvement

Sometimes, third parties come into play to intervene between negotiating parties. Often, this happens when the parties reach an impasse. For example, a manager might have to step into a conflict between two subordinates or even between two departments. In other cases, third party involvement exists right from the start of the negotiation. For example, real estate agents serve as an interface between home sellers and buyers.

Mediation.   The process of mediation occurs when a neutral third party helps to facilitate a negotiated agreement. Formal mediation has a long history in

Although President Clinton was not directly involved in the negotiations between the Palestinians and the Israelis, his administration played a significant role in mediating the agreement between the two parties.

labor disputes, international relations, and marital counseling. However, by definition, almost any manager might be required to occasionally play an informal mediating role.

What do mediators do?[26] First, almost anything that aids the *process or atmosphere* of negotiation can be helpful. Of course, this depends on the exact situation at hand. If there is tension, the mediator might serve as a lightning rod for anger or try to introduce humor. The mediator might try to help the parties clarify their underlying interests, both to themselves and to each other. Occasionally, imposing a deadline or helping the parties deal with their own constituents might be useful. Introducing a problem-solving orientation to move toward more integrative bargaining might be appropriate.

The mediator might also intervene in the *content* of the negotiation, highlighting points of agreement, pointing out new options, or encouraging concessions.

Research shows that mediation has a fairly successful track record in dispute resolution. However, mediators can't turn water into wine, and the process seems to work best when the conflict is not too intense and the parties are resolved to use negotiation to resolve their conflict. If the mediator is not seen as neutral or if there is dissension in the ranks of each negotiating party, mediation doesn't work so well.[27]

Before continuing, please consult the *You Be the Manager* feature.

Arbitration.   The process of arbitration occurs when a third party is given the authority to dictate the terms of settlement of a conflict (although there is nonbinding arbitration, which we won't consider here). Although disputing parties sometimes agree to arbitration, it can also be mandated formally by law or informally by upper management or parents. The key point is that negotiation has broken down, and the negotiator has to make a final distributive allocation—this isn't the way to integrative solutions.

In *conventional arbitration*, the arbitrator can choose any outcome, such as splitting the difference between the two parties. In *final offer arbitration*, each party makes a final offer, and the arbitrator chooses one of them. This latter invention was devised to motivate the two parties to make sensible offers that have a chance of being upheld. Also, fear of the all-or-nothing aspect of final arbitration seems to motivate more negotiated agreement.[28]

One of the most commonly arbitrated disputes between employers and employees is dismissal for excessive absenteeism. One study found that the arbitrators sided with the company in over half of such cases, especially when the company could show evidence of a fair and consistently applied absentee policy.[29]

Some Final Words on Negotiation

Here are a few additional points to keep in mind when negotiating.

Interests Versus Positions.   In negotiating, it is critically important to try to stay focused on underlying interests, not just on stated positions. What does the other party really need here? What do *I* really need? Really listening to the other party and trying to send credible messages can go a long way in this regard.

MANAGING CONFLICT AND DIVERSITY AT MONSANTO CHEMICAL

YOU BE THE Manager

The management of The Chemical Group, an operating unit of St. Louis-based Monsanto Company, believed that the unit had to make a major shift in its culture in order to attract and retain women and people of color. While the turnover rate for women and minorities was running at about the industry average, management didn't believe this was acceptable for a company that values diversity and places a high priority on the management of its people. When white males did leave, exit interviews indicated that it was mainly to grasp special opportunities offered by other employers. In contrast, women and minorities more often reported that they were leaving because of unsatisfactory working relationships. Many well-qualified people were being lost. An in-depth cultural audit convinced Monsanto management that some fundamental changes were necessary to build a climate

IN ORDER TO CURTAIL HIGH TURNOVER RATES OF WOMEN AND MINORITIES, A UNIT OF MONSANTO CONDUCTED AN IN-DEPTH CULTURAL AUDIT. WHAT FACTORS DO YOU THINK THEY TOOK INTO CONSIDERATION?

that was more nurturing and supportive of a diverse work force. In particular, Monsanto felt that diversity sometimes prompted conflict because of unshared assumptions and expectations between supervisors and employees who differed in gender or race. Monsanto wanted to manage workforce conflict more effectively and stem turnover among its employees. How would you proceed?

1. Are highly trained counselors and psychologists the only people capable of managing conflict? Who else might do the job?

2. When is the best time for supervisors and employees to clarify their assumptions and expectations vis-à-vis each other?

To find out what Monsanto did to manage conflict and diversity, check out *The Manager's Notebook* at the end of the chapter.

Source: Adapted from Laabs, J. J. (1993, December). Employees manage conflict and diversity. *Personnel Journal*, 30–36.

Credibility.   Negotiator credibility is important in all forms of negotiations. In distributive negotiations, credible negotiators are viewed as good persuaders and as being capable of following through on threats and promises. In integrative negotiations, putting high quality information on the table is a key source of credibility. For third parties, perceived neutrality is key. As these examples imply, actual experience with someone is an important way to gain credibility. However, some points can usually be gained up front by assigning high status people as negotiators. Remember, though, that this will vary across cultures. In the West, a technically expert middle manager might be seen as credible. In the East, technical expertise might be less relevant than age and seniority.

Maintaining Face.   Imagine that you are trying to sell your old but beloved car, and a potential buyer makes fun of its appearance and offers you a ridiculously low sum for it. This insult to your car will be perceived as an insult to yourself. Good negotiators avoid personalizing the problem, try to have some empathy for their counterpart, and avoid passing gratuitous insults. Causing the opponent to lose face will damage the chance of a settlement.[30]

Constituency Effects. Negotiators who negotiate for a constituency (such as their department) should be aware that their constituents can stimulate competitive bargaining and an escalation of conflict between the parties.[31] Our earlier discussion of group identification, intergroup bias, and the conflict process provides the rationale for this. Negotiators are especially likely to fall prey to this problem when they feel under very close scrutiny by their constituents and very accountable to them. This is one good reason to use high status negotiators who can resist undue pressure for conflict escalation.

IS ALL CONFLICT BAD?

In everyday life, there has traditionally been an emphasis on the negative, dysfunctional aspects of conflict. This is not difficult to understand. Discord between parents and children, severe labor strife, and international disputes are unpleasant experiences. To some degree, this emphasis on the negative aspects of conflict is also characteristic of thinking in organizational behavior. Recently, though, as at Motorola, there has been growing awareness of the potential *benefits* of organizational conflict.

The argument that conflict can be functional rests mainly on the idea that it promotes necessary organizational change. One advocate of this position puts it this way:

$$\text{CONFLICT} \rightarrow \text{CHANGE} \rightarrow \text{ADAPTATION} \rightarrow \text{SURVIVAL}^{32}$$

In other words, for organizations to survive, they must adapt to their environments. This requires changes in strategy that may be stimulated through conflict. For example, consider the museum that relies heavily upon government funding and consistently mounts exhibits that are appreciated only by "true connoisseurs" of art. Under a severe funding cutback, the museum can survive only if it begins to mount more popular exhibits. Such a change might occur only after much conflict within the board of directors.

Just how does conflict promote change? For one thing, it might bring into consideration new ideas that would not be offered without conflict. In trying to "one up" the opponent, one of the parties might develop a unique idea that the other can't fail to appreciate. In a related way, conflict might promote change because each party begins to monitor the other's performance more carefully. This search for weaknesses means that it is more difficult to hide errors and problems from the rest of the organization. Such errors and problems (e.g., a failure to make deliveries on time) might be a signal that changes are necessary. Finally, conflict may promote useful change by signaling that a redistribution of power is necessary. Consider the personnel department that must battle with managers to get diversity programs implemented. This conflict might be a clue that some change is due in power priorities. All of these outcomes have occurred at Motorola, where conflict is used strategically as a catalyst for change but is not so high that it is completely dysfunctional.

Conflict stimulation. A strategy of increasing conflict in order to motivate change.

All of this suggests that there are times when managers might use a strategy of **conflict stimulation** to cause change. But how does a manager know when some conflict might be a good thing? One signal is the existence of a "friendly rut," in which peaceful relationships take precedence over organizational goals. Another signal is seen when parties that should be interacting closely have chosen to withdraw from each other to avoid overt conflict. A third signal occurs when conflict is suppressed or downplayed by denying differences, ignoring controversy, and exaggerating points of agreement.[33]

Logic suggests that the causes of conflict discussed earlier could be manipulated by managers to achieve change.[34] Consider the following:

- *Scarcity.* The president and the controller of a manufacturing company felt that the budgets allocated to various departments were not a good reflection of changing priorities. They introduced a zero-base budget that required all departments to justify their needs regardless of past allocations. Since the departments were required to compete for a scarce resource, considerable conflict developed. It was agreed that this conflict helped to promote needed changes in funding emphasis.

- *Ambiguity.* The director of a medical research laboratory was very unhappy with the lack of coordination among the lab's research projects. The position of assistant director was opening up because of a retirement, and the director gave contradictory, ambiguous signals about who might be promoted to the job. This led to conflict, which magnified the lack of coordination so much that the researchers held meetings to resolve the problem.

A MODEL OF STRESS IN ORGANIZATIONS

It is easy to imagine situations that must surely prove stressful for organizational members. Baseball players battling for the World Series, the White House staff during the Whitewater affair, and personnel working in nuclear power plants during emergencies have obviously been exposed to elevated levels of tension. However, these dramatic cases should not obscure the fact that stress can be part of the everyday routine of organizations. In fact, many cases of conflict of the kind we have just been discussing can provoke considerable stress. The model of a stress episode in Exhibit 14.3 can guide our introduction to this topic.[35]

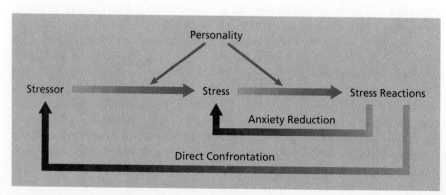

EXHIBIT 14.3
Model of a stress episode.

Stressors

Stressors are environmental events or conditions that have the potential to induce stress. There are some conditions that would prove stressful for just about everyone. These include things like extreme heat, extreme cold, isolation, or hostile people. More interesting is the fact that the individual personality often determines the extent to which a potential stressor becomes a real stressor and actually induces stress.

Stressors. Environmental events or conditions that have the potential to induce stress.

Stress

Stress is a psychological reaction to the demands inherent in a stressor that has the potential to make a person feel tense or anxious because the person does not feel capable of coping with these demands.[36] Stress is not intrinsically bad. All people require a certain level of stimulation from their environment, and moderate levels of stress can serve this function. In fact, one would wonder about the perceptual accuracy of a person who *never* experienced tension. On the other hand, stress does become a problem when it leads to especially high levels of anxiety and tension.

Stress. A psychological reaction to the demands inherent in a stressor that has the potential to make a person feel tense or anxious.

Stress Reactions

Stress reactions are the behavioral, psychological, and physiological consequences of stress. Some of these reactions are essentially passive responses over which the individual has little direct control, such as elevated blood pressure. Other reactions are active attempts to *cope* with some previous aspect of the stress episode. Exhibit 14.3 indicates that stress reactions that involve coping attempts might be directed toward dealing directly with the stressor or simply reducing the anxiety generated by stress. In general, the former strategy has more potential for effectiveness than the latter because the chances of the stress episode being *terminated* are increased.[37]

Stress reactions. Behavioral, psychological, and physiological consequences of stress.

Often, reactions that are useful for the individual in dealing with a stress episode may be very costly to the organization. The individual who is conveniently absent from work on the day of a difficult inventory check might prevent personal stress but leave the organization short-handed (provoking stress in others). Thus, organizations should be interested in the stress that individual employees experience.

Personality and Stress

Personality (Chapter 3) can have an important influence on the stress experience. As shown in Exhibit 14.3, it can affect both the extent to which potential stressors are perceived as stressful and the types of stress reactions that occur. Let's look at two key personality traits.

Locus of Control. You will recall from Chapter 3 that locus of control concerns people's beliefs about the factors that control their behavior. Internals believe that they control their own behavior, while externals believe that their behavior is controlled by luck, fate, or powerful people. Compared with internals, externals are more likely to feel anxious in the face of potential stressors.[38] Most people like to feel in control of what happens to them, and externals feel less in control. Internals are more likely to confront stressors directly because they assume that this response will make a difference. Externals, on the other hand, are anxious but don't feel that they are masters of their own fate. Thus, they are more prone to simple anxiety-reduction strategies that only work in the short run.

Type A Behavior Pattern.   Interest in the Type A behavior pattern began when physicians noticed that many sufferers of coronary heart disease, especially those who developed the disease relatively young, tended to exhibit a distinctive pattern of behaviors and emotions.[39] Individuals who exhibit the **Type A behavior pattern** tend to be aggressive and ambitious. Their hostility is easily aroused, and they feel a great sense of time urgency. They are impatient, competitive, and preoccupied with their work. The Type A individual can be contrasted with the Type B, who does not exhibit these extreme characteristics. Compared to Type B individuals, Type A people report heavier workloads, longer work hours, and more conflicting work demands.[40] Whether or not these reports are accurate, we will see later that such factors turn out to be potent stressors. Thus, either Type A people encounter more stressful situations than Type Bs, or they perceive themselves as doing so. In turn, Type A individuals are likely to exhibit adverse physiological reactions in response to stress. These include elevated blood pressure, elevated heart rate, and modified blood chemistry. Frustrating, difficult, or competitive events are especially likely to prompt these adverse reactions. In addition, Type A people perform better than Type Bs in situations that call for persistence, endurance, or speed. They can ignore fatigue and distraction to accomplish their goals. Type A individuals seem to have a strong need to control their work environment. This is doubtless a full-time task that stimulates their feelings of time urgency and leads them to overextend themselves physically.[41]

As research has accumulated, it has become increasingly clear that the major component of Type A behavior that contributes to adverse physiological reactions is hostility and repressed anger. This may also be accompanied by exaggerated cynicism and distrust of others. When these factors are prominent in a particular Type A individual's personality, stress is most likely to take its toll.[42]

The Type A behavior pattern has some interesting ramifications. For one thing, Type A people do not generally *report* more tension, anxiety, or job dissatisfaction than Type Bs, even though they do report more of the stressors noted earlier.[43] Thus, Type A people might be unaware of the impact that work stress has on them. To complicate matters, many work organizations reward the very behaviors that Type A people favor—achievement orientation, long work hours, and extreme work involvement. Thus, it is not surprising that Type A individuals as a group tend to reach higher organizational levels and achieve higher occupational success than Type Bs. The message here is that organizations might be unintentionally threatening the health and well-being of their best performers.

Type A behavior pattern. A personality pattern that includes aggressiveness, ambitiousness, competitiveness, hostility, impatience, and a sense of time urgency.

STRESSORS IN ORGANIZATIONAL LIFE

In this section we will examine potential stressors in detail. Some stressors can affect almost everyone in any organization, while others seem especially likely to affect people who perform particular roles in organizations.

Executive and Managerial Stressors

Executives and managers make key organizational decisions and direct the work of others. In these capacities, they seem to experience special forms of stress.

Role Overload. **Role overload** occurs when one must perform too many tasks in too short a time period, and it is a common stressor for managers, especially in today's downsized organizations.[44] The open-ended nature of the managerial job is partly responsible for this heavy and protracted workload.[45] Management is an ongoing *process*, and there are few signposts to signify that a task is complete and that rest and relaxation are permitted. Especially when coupled with frequent moves or excessive travel demands, a heavy workload often provokes conflict between the manager's role as an organizational member and his or her role as a spouse or parent. Thus, role overload may provoke stress while at the same time preventing the executive from enjoying the pleasures of life that can reduce stress. Some executives even ignore threats to their health in combating role overload.

> Ray Brant, vice-president for human relations at National Semiconductor, contracted a rare blood disease that had to be treated with intravenous medication twenty-four hours a day. The disease required hospitalization, but Brant talked his way out of that because of his heavy workload. The semiconductor executive carried his intravenous bottle and pump with him to business meetings and arranged his car so the medication pumped as he drove. "If I backed off work for six weeks, I'd be too far offstream when I came back," he said.[46]

Heavy Responsibility. Not only is the workload of the executive heavy, but it can have extremely important consequences for the organization and its members. A vice-president of labor relations might be in charge of a negotiation strategy that could result in either labor peace or a protracted and bitter strike. To complicate matters, the personal consequences of an incorrect decision can be staggering. For example, the courts have fined or even jailed executives who have engaged in illegal activities on behalf of their organizations. Finally, executives are responsible for people as well as things, and this influence over the future of others has the potential to induce stress. The executive who must terminate the operation of an unprofitable plant, putting many out of work, or the manager who must fire a subordinate, putting one out of work, might experience guilt and tension.[47]

Operative-Level Stressors

Operatives are individuals who occupy nonprofessional and nonmanagerial positions in organizations. In a manufacturing organization, operatives perform the work on the shop floor and range from skilled craftspeople to unskilled laborers. As is the case with other organizational roles, the occupants of operative positions are sometimes exposed to a special set of stressors.

Poor Physical Working Conditions. Operative-level employees are more likely than managers and professionals to be exposed to physically unpleasant and even dangerous working conditions. Although social sensibility and union

Role overload. The requirement for too many tasks to be performed in too short of a time period.

activity have improved working conditions over the years, many employees must still face excessive heat, cold, noise, pollution, and the chance of accidents. Speaking about stress and safety, a crane operator reported:

> It's not so much the physical, it's the mental. When you're working on a tunnel and you're down in a hole two hundred feet, you use hand signals. You can't see these. You have to have something else that's your eyes. There has been men dropped and such because some fellow gave the wrong signal. . . . The average crane operator lives to be fifty-five years old. They don't live the best sort of life. There's a lot of tension. We've had an awful lot of people have had heart attacks.[48]

Job demands-job control model. A model that asserts that jobs promote high stress when they make high demands while offering little control over work decisions.

Poor Job Design.   Although bad job design can provoke stress at any organizational level (executive role overload is an example), lower-level blue- and white-collar jobs are particular culprits. It might seem paradoxical that jobs that are too simple or not challenging enough can act as stressors. However, monotony and boredom can prove extremely frustrating to people who feel capable of handling more complex tasks.

According to Robert Karasek's **job demands-job control model,** jobs that make high demands on employees while giving them little control over workplace decisions are especially prone to produce stress and negative stress reactions.[49] High demands might include a hectic work pace, excessive workload, limited time to accomplish tasks, or responsibility for extreme economic loss. Lack of control means limited decision latitude and authority. Jobs that often involve high demand and little control include telephone operators, nurse's aides, assembly line workers, garment stitchers, and bus drivers. As Exhibit 14.4 demonstrates, these jobs fall into a zone of increased risk for heart disease (the area to the right of the dashed curve). Stress might be partially responsible for this elevated risk.

Boundary Role Stressors and Burnout

Boundary roles. Positions in which organizational members are required to interact with members of other organizations or with the public.

Boundary roles are positions in which organizational members are required to interact with members of other organizations or with the public. For example, a vice-president of public relations is responsible for representing his or her company to the public. At the operative level, receptionists, salespeople, and installers often interact with customers or suppliers.

Occupants of boundary role positions are especially likely to experience stress as they straddle the imaginary boundary between the organization and its environment. This is yet another form of role conflict in which one's role as an organizational member might be incompatible with the demands made by the public or other organizations. A classic case of boundary role stress involves salespeople. In extreme cases, buyers desire fast delivery of a large quantity of custom-tailored products. The salesperson might be tempted to "offer the moon" but is at the same time aware that such an order could place a severe strain on his or her organization's production facilities. Thus, the salesperson is faced with the dilemma of doing his or her primary job (selling) while protecting another function (production) from unreasonable demands that could result in a broken delivery contract.

Burnout. Emotional exhaustion, depersonalization, and reduced personal accomplishment among those who work with people.

A particular form of stress experienced by some boundary role occupants is burnout. **Burnout,** as Christina Maslach and Susan Jackson define it, is a combination "of emotional exhaustion, depersonalization, and reduced per-

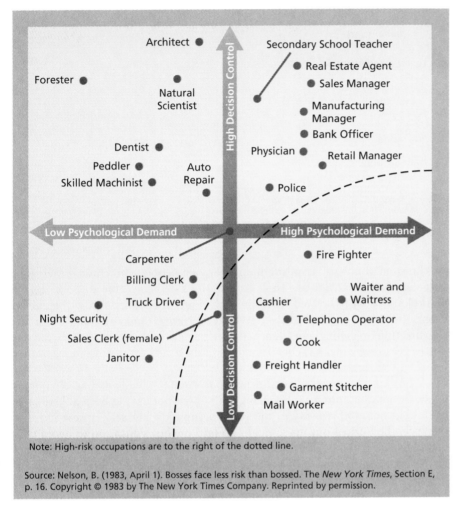

Note: High-risk occupations are to the right of the dotted line.

Source: Nelson, B. (1983, April 1). Bosses face less risk than bossed. The *New York Times*, Section E, p. 16. Copyright © 1983 by The New York Times Company. Reprinted by permission.

EXHIBIT 14.4
Heart disease risk for various occupations.

sonal accomplishment that can occur among individuals who work with people in some capacity."[50] Frequently, these other people are organizational clients who require very special attention or who are experiencing severe problems. Thus, teachers, nurses, paramedics, social workers, and police are especially likely candidates for burnout.

Burnout appears to follow a stagelike process that begins with emotional exhaustion (see Exhibit 14.5). The person feels fatigued in the morning, drained by the work, and frustrated by the day's events. One way to deal with this extreme exhaustion is to distance oneself from one's clients, the "cause" of the exhaustion. In an extreme form, this might involve treating them like objects and lacking concern for what happens to them. The clients might also be seen as blaming the employee for their problems. Finally, the burned-out individual develops feelings of low personal accomplishment—"I can't deal with these people, I'm not helping them, I don't understand them." In fact, because of the exhaustion and depersonalization, there might be more than a grain of truth to those feelings. Although the exact details of this progression are open to some question, these three sets of symptoms paint a reliable picture of burnout.[51]

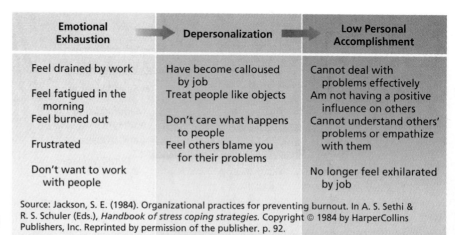

Emotional Exhaustion	Depersonalization	Low Personal Accomplishment
Feel drained by work	Have become calloused by job	Cannot deal with problems effectively
Feel fatigued in the morning	Treat people like objects	Am not having a positive influence on others
Feel burned out	Don't care what happens to people	Cannot understand others' problems or empathize with them
Frustrated	Feel others blame you for their problems	
Don't want to work with people		No longer feel exhilarated by job

Source: Jackson, S. E. (1984). Organizational practices for preventing burnout. In A. S. Sethi & R. S. Schuler (Eds.), *Handbook of stress coping strategies.* Copyright © 1984 by HarperCollins Publishers, Inc. Reprinted by permission of the publisher. p. 92.

EXHIBIT 14.5
The stages of burnout and their symptoms.

Burnout seems to be most common among people who entered their jobs with especially high ideals. Their expectations of being able to "change the world" are badly frustrated when they encounter the reality shock of troubled clients (who are often perceived as unappreciative) and the inability of the organization to help them. Teachers get fed up with being disciplinarians, nurses get upset when patients die, and police officers get depressed when they must constantly deal with the "losers" of society.[52]

What are the consequences of burnout? Some individuals bravely pursue a new occupation, often experiencing guilt about not having been able to cope in the old one. Others stay in the same occupation but seek a new job. For instance, the burned-out nurse might go into nursing education to avoid contact with sick patients. Some people pursue administrative careers in their profession, attempting to "climb above" the source of their difficulties. These people often set cynical examples for idealistic subordinates. Finally, some people stay in their jobs and become part of the legion of "deadwood," collecting their paychecks but doing little to contribute to the mission of the organization. Many "good bureaucrats" seem to choose this route.[53]

Some General Stressors

To conclude our discussion of stressors that people encounter in organizational life, we will consider some that are probably experienced equally by occupants of all roles.

Interpersonal Conflict.   From our earlier discussion of interpersonal conflict, you might correctly guess that it can be a potent stressor, especially for those with strong avoidance tendencies. The entire range of conflict, from personality clashes to intergroup strife, is especially likely to cause stress when it leads to real or perceived attacks on our self-esteem or integrity. Although conflict can lead to stress in many settings, outside of work we often have the option of terminating the relationship, of "choosing our friends," as it were. This option is often not available at work.

Work-Family Conflict.   Two facts of life in contemporary society have increased the stress stemming from the interrole conflict between being a

Police officers must deal with a unique type of on-the-job stress: workplace violence. There has been an upswing in psychological counseling for officers experiencing stress reactions.

member of one's family and the member of an organization. First, the increase in the number of homes in which both parents work and the increase in the number of single parent families has led to a number of stressors centered around child care. Finding adequate daycare and disputes between partners about sharing child care responsibilities can prove to be serious stressors.

Second, increased life spans have meant that many people in the prime of their careers find themselves providing support for elderly parents, some of whom may be seriously ill. This inherently stressful elder-care situation is often compounded by feelings of guilt about the need to tend to matters at work.

There is every reason to believe that women are particularly victimized by stress due to work-family conflict. Much anecdotal evidence suggests that women who take time off work to deal with pressing family matters are more likely than men to be labeled disloyal or undedicated to their work. Also, many managers seem to be insensitive to the demands that these basic demographic shifts are making on their subordinates, again compounding the potential for stress.

Job Insecurity.   Secure employment is an important goal for almost everyone, and stress may be encountered when it is threatened. At the operative level, unionization has provided a degree of employment security for some, but the vagaries of the economy and the threat of technology hang heavy over many workers. Among professionals, a paradox exists. In many cases, the very specialization that enables them to obtain satisfactory jobs becomes a millstone whenever social or economic forces change. For example, aerospace scientists and engineers have long been prey to the boom and bust nature of their industry. When layoffs occur, these people are often perceived as overqualified or too specialized to easily obtain jobs in related industries. Finally, the executive suite does not escape job insecurity. Recent pressures for corporate performance have made cost cutting a top priority for many companies. One of the surest ways to cut costs in the short run is to reduce executive positions and thus reduce the total management payroll. Many top corporations have greatly thinned their executive ranks in recent years.

Role Ambiguity.   We have already noted how role conflict, having to deal with incompatible role expectations, can provoke stress. There is also substantial evidence that role ambiguity can provoke stress.[54] From Chapter 8, you will recall that role ambiguity exists when the goals of one's job or the methods of performing the job are unclear. Such a lack of direction can prove stressful, especially for people who are low in their tolerance for such ambiguity. For example, the president of a manufacturing firm might be instructed by the board of directors to increase profits and cut costs. While this goal seems clear enough, the means by which it can be achieved might be unclear. This ambiguity can be devastating, especially when the organization is doing poorly and no strategy seems to improve things.

Exhibit 14.6 summarizes the sources of stress at various points in the organization. The "Ethical Focus: *Workplace Violence Is a Source of Stress*" selection illustrates a contemporary source of stress.

REACTIONS TO ORGANIZATIONAL STRESS

In this section we shall examine the reactions that people who experience organizational stress might exhibit. These reactions can be divided into behavioral, psychological, and physiological responses.

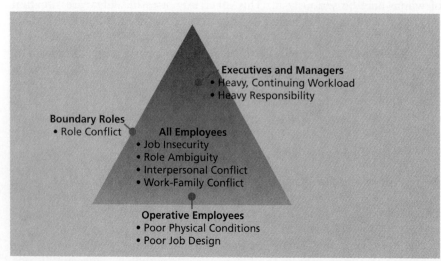

EXHIBIT 14.6
Sources of stress at various points in the organization.

ETHICAL FOCUS   Workplace Violence Is Source of Stress

On-the-job violence has long been a documented source of stress for police officers. Seeing violence being committed by others, having to resort to deadly force, and even accidentally shooting one's own partner are stressors that are unique to police work. The result can be substance abuse, marital problems, and even the use of violence within the family. Trained to control their emotions on the job, officers can find it difficult to discern an appropriate outlet for the feelings provoked by work violence. As a result, there has been a steady rise in the number of police departments offering psychological counseling for officers who are experiencing stress reactions.

In recent years it has become apparent that violence on the job is not confined to police work. A recent U.S. Labor Department study found that one-sixth of job-related fatalities were homicides. Northwestern National Life Insurance determined that in one year 2.2 million people were physically assaulted at work and 6.3 million were threatened with assault. Co-workers, customers, and strangers are all potential sources of violence. Some observers have blamed the stresses of the recession as contributing to workplace violence.

One of the most extreme examples of workplace violence has been a string of mass shootings in U.S. post offices, including those in Royal Oak and Dearborn, Michigan, Dana Point, California, and Edmond, Oklahoma. These shootings (only the visible tip of an iceberg of violent acts in the post office) provoked considerable stress among survivors. At Royal Oak, for example, a team of 100 mental health volunteers provided extensive crisis intervention counseling. This was followed up by sessions on communication and conflict resolution designed to get at the sources of violence.

Violence and crime have become a particular source of stress for delivery people, whether the thing being delivered is mail, pizza, or parcels. Domino's Pizza, FedEx, and United Parcel have all responded to attacks and robbery against delivery people. Domino's devoted a complete issue of its company newsletter to safety issues. In response to the killing of its first courier in 20 years, FedEx issued cellular phones to some employees, double-teamed personnel on some routes, and divided up dangerous routes to lessen chronic stress. Counseling was provided to a number of employees following the slaying.

Sources: Pulley, B. (1994, March 7). Crime becomes occupational hazard of deliverers. *The Wall Street Journal*, p. B1; Braverman, M. (1993, December 12). Violence: the newest worry on the job. *New York Times*, De Angelis, T. (1993, October). Psychologists aid victims of violence in post office. *APA Monitor*, pp. 1, 44, 45.

Behavioral Reactions to Stress

Behavioral reactions to stress are overt activities that the stressed individual uses in an attempt to cope with the stress. They include problem solving, withdrawal, and the use of addictive substances.

Problem Solving.   In general, problem solving is directed toward terminating the stressor or reducing its potency, not toward simply making the person feel better in the short run. Problem solving is reality oriented, and while it is not always effective in combating the stressor, it reveals flexibility and realistic use of feedback. Most examples of a problem-solving response to stress are undramatic because problem solving is generally the routine, sensible, obvious approach that an objective observer might suggest. Consider the following examples of problem solving.

- *Delegation.* A busy executive reduces her stress-provoking workload by delegating some of her many tasks to a capable subordinate.
- *Time management.* A manager who finds the day too short writes a daily schedule, requires his subordinates to make formal appointments to see him, and instructs his secretary to screen phone calls more selectively.

- *Talking it out.* An engineer who is experiencing stress because of poor communication with her nonengineer superior resolves to sit down with the boss and hammer out an agreement concerning the priorities on a project.
- *Asking for help.* A salesperson who is anxious about his company's ability to fill a difficult order asks the production manager to provide a realistic estimate of the probable delivery date.
- *Searching for alternatives.* A machine operator who finds his monotonous job stress-provoking applies for a transfer to a more interesting position for which the pay is identical.

The presence of stress or stressors is implicated in reduced job performance.[55] Notice that these problem-solving responses will often reduce stress and stimulate performance, benefiting both the individual and the organization's bottom line.

Withdrawal. Withdrawal from the stressor is one of the most basic reactions to stress. In organizations, this withdrawal takes the form of absence and turnover. Compared with problem-solving reactions to stress, absenteeism fails to attack the stressor directly. Rather, the absent individual is simply attempting some short-term reduction of the anxiety prompted by the stressor. When the person returns to the job, the stress is still there. From this point of view, absence is a dysfunctional reaction to stress for both the individual and the organization. The same can be said about turnover when a person resigns from a stressful job on the spur of the moment merely to escape stress. However, a good case can be made for a well-planned resignation in which the intent is to assume another job that should be less stressful. This is actually a problem-solving reaction that should benefit both the individual and the organization in the long run. We are as yet unsure just how much absence and turnover represent specific withdrawal from stress. However, there is some evidence that stress-prone operative jobs are likely to prompt absence.[56] In addition, several potential stressors we discussed earlier (role ambiguity and poor job design) are associated with absence.[57] Turnover and turnover intentions have often been linked with stress and its causes.[58]

Use of Addictive Substances. Smoking, drinking, and drug use represent the least satisfactory behavioral responses to stress for both the individual and the organization. These activities fail to terminate stress episodes, and they leave employees less physically and mentally prepared to perform their jobs. We have all heard of hard-drinking newspaper reporters and advertising executives, and it is tempting to infer that the stress of their boundary role positions is responsible for their drinking. Unfortunately, like these, most reports of the relationship between stress and the use of addictive substances are anecdotal. However, there are indications that cigarette use and alcohol abuse are associated with the presence of work-related stress.[59]

Psychological Reactions to Stress

Psychological reactions to stress primarily involve emotions and thought processes, rather than overt behavior, although these reactions are frequently revealed in the individual's speech and actions. The most common psychological reaction to stress is the use of defense mechanisms. **Defense mechanisms** are psychological attempts to reduce the anxiety associated with stress. Notice that, by definition, defense mechanisms concentrate on *anxiety reduction*, rather than actually confronting or dealing with the stressor. Some common defense mechanisms include the following:

- **Rationalization** involves attributing socially acceptable reasons or motives to one's actions so that they will appear reasonable and sensible, at least to oneself. For example, a male nurse who becomes very angry and abusive when learning that he will not be promoted to supervisor might justify his anger by claiming that the head nurse discriminates against men.

- **Projection** involves attributing one's own undesirable ideas and motives to others so that they seem less negative. For example, a sales executive who is undergoing conflict about offering a bribe to an official of a foreign government might reason that the official is corrupt.

- **Displacement** involves directing feelings of anger at a "safe" target rather than expressing them where they may be punished. For example, a construction worker who is severely criticized by the boss for sloppy workmanship might take out his frustrations in an evening hockey league.

- **Reaction formation** involves expressing oneself in a manner that is directly opposite to the way one truly feels, rather than risking negative reactions to one's true position. For example, a low-status member of a committee might vote with the majority on a crucial issue rather than stating his true position and opening himself to attack.

- **Compensation** involves applying one's skills in a particular area to make up for failure in another area. For example, a professor who is unable to get her research published might resolve to become a superb teacher.

- **Repression** involves preventing threatening ideas from becoming conscious, so that the stressor need not be confronted. For example, the assembly line worker who finds his routine but demanding job stressful might honestly forget to set his alarm clock and consequently wake up too late to go to work.

Is the use of defense mechanisms a good or bad reaction to stress? Used occasionally to temporarily reduce anxiety, they appear to be a useful reaction. For example, the construction worker who displaces aggression in an evening hockey league rather than attacking a frustrating boss might calm down, return to work the next day, and "talk it out" with the boss. Thus, the occasional use of defense mechanisms as short-term anxiety reducers probably benefits both the individual and the organization. In fact, people with "weak defenses" can be incapacitated by anxiety and resort to dysfunctional withdrawal or addiction.

When the use of defense mechanisms becomes a chronic reaction to stress, however, the picture changes radically. The problem stems from the very character of defense mechanisms—they simply don't change the objective character of the stressor, and the basic conflict or frustration remains in operation. After some short-term relief from anxiety, the basic problem remains unresolved. In fact, the stress might *increase* with the knowledge that the defense has been essentially ineffective.

Defense mechanisms. Psychological attempts to reduce the anxiety associated with stress.

Rationalization. Attributing socially acceptable motives to one's actions.

Projection. Attributing one's own undesirable ideas and motives to others.

Displacement. Directing feelings of anger at a safe target rather than expressing them where they might be punished.

Reaction formation. Expressing oneself in a manner that is directly opposite to the way one truly feels.

Compensation. Applying one's skills in a particular area to make up for failure in another area.

Repression. The prevention of threatening ideas from becoming conscious.

Physiological Reactions to Stress

Can work-related stress kill you? This is clearly an important question for organizations, and it is even more important for individuals who experience excessive stress at work. Many studies of physiological reactions to stress have concentrated on the cardiovascular system, specifically on the various risk factors that might prompt heart attacks. For example, there is evidence that work stress is associated with electrocardiogram irregularities and elevated levels of blood pressure, cholesterol, and pulse.[60] Although dentists probably cause *you* stress, you might be surprised to learn that *they* also suffer from a fairly high rate of physiological problems that might be due to stress. One study found that the difficulties of building a dental practice, the image of the dentist as an inflictor of pain, and a lack of appreciation from patients were related to various cardiovascular risks.[61] Stress has also been associated with the onset of diseases such as respiratory and bacterial infections.[62]

REDUCING OR COPING WITH STRESS

This chapter would be incomplete without a discussion of personal and organizational strategies that can reduce or cope with stress.

Prepare for Stress

One approach to preparing employees for anticipated stress might be to institute *realistic job previews,* which attempt to clearly specify the nature of the work the person will encounter before he or she is hired (Chapter 9). In their zeal to hire people, many recruiters tend to gloss over negative aspects of a job, including its potential to induce stress. Realistic previews should permit applicants who feel incapable of coping with stress to decline a job offer or to go into a job adequately forewarned. They might prove especially valuable in alerting idealistic candidates for burnout-prone jobs to the demands that difficult clients could pose. Realistic job previews can also inform candidates for promotion or internal transfer about possible stressors in a new job.

One very interesting study used a "realistic merger preview" to inform employees about the way the merger would affect their work life. The preview reduced uncertainty and stress among the workforce.[63]

In a similar vein, many multinational firms have instituted seminars to help employees and their families prepare for the stress that they might encounter in moving to another country and experiencing culture shock. Such programs warn transferees about the difficulties they might confront and provide them with an arsenal of stress-preventing suggestions.

Job Redesign

Organizations can redesign jobs to reduce their stressful characteristics. In theory, it's possible to redesign jobs anywhere in the organization to this end. Thus, an overloaded executive might be given an assistant to reduce the number of tasks he or she must perform. In practice, most formal job redesign efforts have involved enriching operative-level jobs to make them more stimulating and challenging. As we noted in Chapter 7, this is usually accomplished by giving employees more control over the pace of their work and permitting them to use more of their skills and abilities. Although enrichment often increases job satisfaction and reduces withdrawal, there have been almost no studies of the impact of enrichment on stress reduction or physiological indicators of stress. One exception is a study in the production and packing department of a candy producer that showed distinct improvements in employee mental health after job enrichment.[64] Such tests are important because it is conceivable that job enrichment could provoke stress rather than reduce it. In general, job redesign is an important method of dealing with stress because it attempts to *remove* stressors rather than simply helping employees to *cope with* stressors.

Social Support

Everyday experience suggests to us that the support of others can help us deal with stress. We have all seen children who are facing a tense experience run to an adult for support and comfort, and we have all seen on television the victims of natural disasters finding solace in others. Although the dynamics of job stress might be more subtle, there is every reason to believe that social support should work the same way for people who experience job stress.

Speaking generally, social support simply refers to having close ties with other people. In turn, these close ties could affect stress by bolstering self-esteem, providing useful information, offering comfort and humor, or even providing material resources (such as a loan). Research evidence shows that the benefits of social support are double-barreled. First, people with stronger social networks exhibit better psychological and physical well-being. Second, when people encounter stressful events, those with good social networks are likely to cope more positively. Thus, the social network acts as a buffer against stress.[65]

Off the job, individuals might find social support in a spouse, family, or friends. On the job, social support might be available from one's superior or co-workers. Logic and some research evidence suggest that the buffering aspects of social support are most potent when they are directly connected to the source of stress. This means that co-workers and superiors might be the best sources of support for dealing with *work*-related stress. In particular, most managers need better training to recognize subordinate stress symptoms, clarify role requirements, and so on. Unfortunately, some organizational cultures, especially those that are very competitive, do not encourage members to seek support in a direct fashion. In this event, relationships that people develop in professional associations can sometimes serve as an informed source of social support.

"Family Friendly" Personnel Policies

In order to reduce stress associated with dual careers, child care, and elder care, many organizations are beginning to institute "family friendly" personnel policies.[66] These policies generally include some combination of formalized social support, material support, and increased flexibility to adapt to employee needs.

In the domain of social support, some firms (such as Dow Jones, Atlantic Richfield, and Colgate-Palmolive) distribute newsletters such as *Work and Family Life* that deal with work-family issues. Others, such as Lincoln

Companies in the 1990s are striving to be much more "family friendly" than in past years. Some organizations offer daycare for children of employees.

National insurance, have developed company support groups for employees dealing with elder care problems. Some companies have contracted specialized consultants to provide seminars on elder care issues.

A most prominent and welcome form of material support consists of corporate daycare centers. Flexibility (which provides more *control* over family issues) includes flex-time and job sharing (Chapter 7) as well as family leave policies that allow time off for caring for infants, sick children, and aged dependents. Although many firms boast of having such flexible policies, a common problem is encouraging managers to *use* them in an era of downsizing and lean staffing.

Firms that are noted for their family friendly personnel policies include Corning, Xerox, IBM, American Express, and US West, a large regional telecommunications company. Exhibit 14.7 profiles some of US West's policies.

Stress Management Programs

Some organizations have experimented with programs designed to help employees "manage" work-related stress. Such programs are also available from independent off-work sources. Some of these programs help physically and mentally healthy workers prevent problems due to stress. Others are therapeutic in nature, aimed at individuals who are already experiencing stress problems. Although the exact content of the programs varies, most involve

A sampling of "family friendly" programs available to most U S West employees:

INFORMATION AND COUNSELING

Employee assistance: counseling for family problems.

Resource and referral: toll-free referral service for child care, elderly care, adults with disabilities, adoption and other issues.

Workshops: seminars offered at locations with more than 200 employees on more than 60 topics, such as dealing with child's self-esteem and finances of elderly relatives.

Learning centers: five free video courses on topics such as parenting and elder care, available at seven locations.

TIME OFF AND FLEXIBLE SCHEDULES

Personal days: eight paid days and one nonpaid day can be taken in one-hour increments, and at least two of the eight days can be taken on short notice.

Death in family: three paid days for deaths of immediate family members, including grandparents.

Care-of-newborn-child leave: six weeks of paid sickness disability for mothers. Employees can apply for unpaid leave of six months, with company-paid medical and dental coverage, with same job guaranteed upon return; leave may be extended for another six months, with position of "like status and pay" guaranteed, but company doesn't pay medical or dental benefits for this period.

Family-care leave: unpaid leave for care of seriously ill family member for 12 months during a 24-month period, with reinstatement guaranteed at the end of leave; medical and dental coverage continues for six months.

Flexible work: arrangements such as "flextime," 10-hour day/four-day week, work at home, job sharing and excused time. Available "based on the needs of the business."

FINANCIAL ASSISTANCE

Dependent-care spending account: allows employees to use pretax dollars for dependent-care expenses.

Child-care discounts: negotiated discounts with several national child-care centers.

Business expenses: with prior approval, reimbursement for some child-care expenses incurred for travel or for working "out of the ordinary" hours.

Source: Rose, R. L. (1993, June 21). Small steps. *The Wall Street Journal*, p. R10.

EXHIBIT 14.7
Family friendly personnel policies at US West.

one or more of the following techniques: meditation; training in muscle-relaxation exercises; biofeedback training to control physiological processes; training in time management; training to think more positively and realistically about sources of job stress.[67] Although each of these techniques has been useful in reducing anxiety and tension in other contexts, they have only recently been applied in the work setting. Tentative evidence suggests that these applications are useful in reducing physiological arousal, sleep disturbances, and self-reported tension and anxiety.[68]

Many of these programs take job requirements as given and then train workers to cope with the resulting stress. This approach does not try to permanently remove sources of stress, as job redesign might do. Is this ethical?[69] To some degree the answer to this question depends on the situation. If one is dealing with a large number of Type A individuals, who are evidently especially sensitive to stressors, a stress management program seems sensible because the source of much stress is within the employee. On the other hand, if clear and obvious stressors to which almost anyone would object are present (such as extreme overload or horrible working conditions), stress management programs look a lot less ethical.

Fitness Programs

Many people have argued that physical exercise can reduce stress and counteract some of the adverse physiological effects of stress. The basic mechanics involve muscle relaxation, modified blood chemistry, and simple distraction from the daily grind. To this end, some organizations have established fitness programs for their members. These range from simple arrangements with local health clubs or YMCAs to complete in-house facilities with resident trainers. Studies show that fitness training is associated with improved mood, a better self-concept, reduced absenteeism, and reports of better performance. Some of these improvements probably stem from stress reduction.[70]

The Manager's Notebook   Managing Conflict and Diversity at Monsanto Chemical

Monsanto adopted a system called "consulting pairs" to help facilitate conflict management and diversity management. The pairs are two-person teams made up of specially trained volunteer employees who otherwise hold a variety of jobs in the company. They are assigned to "clients" who need help clarifying expectations or resolving conflict. This is essentially a mediation role.

1. Years of training are not necessary to head off interpersonal conflict or to help resolve conflict that is not too intense. The Monsanto volunteers receive 13 days of training in diversity issues (e.g., ethnic and gender dynamics) as well as listening and questioning techniques. They range from secretaries to scientists to senior managers. An attempt is made to match the consulting pair to their "clients" by race, gender, and job type.

2. The consulting pairs teams concentrate on new supervisor-employee relationships, although they also intervene in mature conflicts. Early in the relationship is the best time to create dialog which can clarify expectations. More than 1,000 of these "join ups" have been managed by consulting pairs.

EXECUTIVE SUMMARY

◆ Interpersonal conflict is a process that occurs when one person, group, or organizational unit frustrates the goal attainment of another. Such conflict can revolve around facts, procedures, or the goals themselves.

◆ Causes of conflict include intergroup bias, high interdependence, ambiguous jurisdictions, and scarce resources. Differences in power, status, and culture are also a factor.

◆ The conflict process includes factors such as the need to win the dispute, withholding information,

increased cohesiveness, negative stereotyping of the other party, reduced contact, and emergence of aggressive leaders.

◆ Modes of managing conflict include avoiding, accommodating, competing, compromise, and collaborating.

◆ Negotiation is a decision-making process among parties that do not have the same preferences.

◆ Distributive negotiation essentially attempts to divide up a fixed amount of outcomes. Frequent tactics include threats, promises, firmness, concession making, and persuasion. Integrative negotiation attempts to enlarge the amount of outcomes via collaboration or problem solving. Tactics include exchanging copious information, framing differences as opportunities, cutting costs, increasing resources, and introducing superordinate goals.

◆ Stressors are environmental conditions that have the potential to induce stress. Stress is a psychological reaction that can prompt tension or anxiety because an individual feels incapable of coping with the demands made by a stressor.

◆ Personality characteristics can cause some individuals to perceive more stressors than others, experience more stress, and react more negatively to this stress. In particular, people with external locus of control and the Type A behavior pattern are prone to such reactions. Type A individuals are aggressive, ambitious, and often hostile. They are preoccupied with their work and feel a great sense of time urgency. Hostility is the key factor in physiological risk.

◆ At the managerial or executive level, common stressors include role overload and high responsibility. At the operative level, poor physical working conditions and underutilization of potential due to poor job design are common stressors. Boundary role occupants often experience stress in the form of conflict between demands from inside the employing organization and demands from outside. Burnout may occur when interaction with clients produces emotional exhaustion, depersonalization, and low accomplishment. Job insecurity, role ambiguity, interpersonal conflict, and work-family conflicts have the potential to induce stress in all organizational members.

◆ Behavioral reactions to stress include problem solving, withdrawal, and the use of addictive substances. Problem solving is the most effective reaction because it confronts the stressor directly and thus has the potential to terminate the stress episode. The most common psychological reaction to stress is the use of defense mechanisms to temporarily reduce anxiety. The majority of studies on physiological reactions to stress focus on cardiovascular risk factors.

◆ Strategies that might reduce organizational stress include preparation for anticipated stress, job redesign, social support, family-friendly personnel policies, stress management programs, and exercise programs.

KEY CONCEPTS

Interpersonal conflict
Avoiding
Accommodating
Competing
Compromise
Collaborating
Negotiation
Distributive negotiation
Integrative negotiation
Superordinate goals
Conflict stimulation
Stressors
Stress

Stress reactions
Type A behavior pattern
Role overload
Job demands-job control model
Boundary roles
Burnout
Defense mechanisms
Rationalization
Projection
Displacement
Reaction formation
Compensation
Repression

DISCUSSION QUESTIONS

1. The manager of a fast food restaurant sees that conflict among the staff is damaging service. How might she implement a superordinate goal to reduce this conflict?

2. The same company hires two finance majors right out of college. Being in a new and unfamiliar environment, they begin their relationship cooperatively. However, over time, they develop a case of deep interpersonal conflict. What factors could account for this?

3. What are some of the factors that make it a real challenge for conflicting parties to develop a collaborative relationship and engage in integrative negotiation?

4. What are the negative aspects of using an avoiding mode of managing conflict?

5. Two social workers just out of college join the same county welfare agency. Both find their case loads very heavy and their roles very ambiguous. One exhibits negative stress reactions, including absence and elevated alcohol use. The other seems to cope very well. Use the stress episode model to explain why this might occur.

6. Imagine that a person who greatly dislikes bureaucracy assumes her first job as an investigator in a very bureaucratic government tax office. Describe the stressors that she might encounter in this situation. Give an example of a problem-solving reaction to this stress. Give an example of a defensive reaction to it.

7. The jobs in the previous two questions are boundary role jobs. Explain this, and describe why boundary roles often prove stressful.

8. Give an example of a role conflict that might provoke anxiety. Describe a problem-solving reaction to this anxiety.

9. Compare and contrast the stressors that might be experienced by an assembly line worker and the president of a company.

10. Discuss the advantages and disadvantages of hiring employees with Type A personality characteristics.

EXPERIENTAL EXERCISE
COPING WITH STRESS

To what extent does each of the following fit as a description of you? (Circle one number in each line across:)

	Very true	Quite true	Some-what true	Not very true	Not at all true
1. I "roll with the punches" when problems come up.	1	2	3	4	5
2. I spend almost all of my time thinking about my work.	5	4	3	2	1
3. I treat other people as individuals and care about their feelings and opinions.	1	2	3	4	5
4. I recognize and accept my own limitations and assets.	1	2	3	4	5
5. There are quite a few people I could describe as "good friends."	1	2	3	4	5
6. I enjoy using my skills and abilities both on and off the job.	1	2	3	4	5
7. I get bored easily.	5	4	3	2	1
8. I enjoy meeting and talking with people who have different ways of thinking about the world.	1	2	3	4	5
9. Often in my job I "bite off more than I can chew."	5	4	3	2	1
10. I'm usually very active on weekends with projects or recreation.	1	2	3	4	5
11. I prefer working with people who are very much like myself.	5	4	3	2	1
12. I work primarily because I have to survive, and not necessarily because I enjoy what I do.	5	4	3	2	1
13. I believe I have a realistic picture of my personal strengths and weakness.	1	2	3	4	5
14. Often I get into arguments with people who don't think my way.	5	4	3	2	1
15. Often I have trouble getting much done on my job.	5	4	3	2	1
16. I'm interested in a lot of different topics.	1	2	3	4	5
17. I get upset when things don't go my way.	5	4	3	2	1
18. Often I'm not sure how I stand on a controversial topic.	5	4	3	2	1
19. I'm usually able to find a way around anything which blocks me from an important goal.	1	2	3	4	5
20. I often disagree with my boss or others at work.	5	4	3	2	1

SCORING AND INTERPRETATION

Dr. Alan A. McLean, who developed this checklist, feels that people who cope with stress effectively have five characteristics. First, they know themselves well and accept their own strengths and weaknesses. Second, they have a variety of interests off the job, and they are not total "workaholics." Third, they exhibit a variety of reactions to stress, rather than always getting a headache or always becoming depressed. Fourth, they are accepting of others who have values or styles different from their own. Finally, good copers are active and productive both on and off the job.

Add together the numbers you circled for the four questions contained in each of the five coping scales.

Coping scale	Add together your responses to these questions	Your score (write in)
Knows self	4, 9, 13, 18	_____
Many interests	2, 5, 7, 16	_____
Variety of reactions	1, 11, 17, 19	_____
Accepts other's values	3, 8, 14, 20	_____
Active and productive	6, 10, 12, 15	_____

Then, add the five scores together for your overall total score:

Scores on each of the five areas can vary between 5 and 20. Scores of 12 or above perhaps suggest that it might be useful to direct more attention to the area. The overall total score can range between 20 and 100. Scores of 60 or more may suggest some general difficulty in coping on the dimensions covered.

Source: McLean, A. A. (1979). *Work stress.* Reading, MA: Addison-Wesley, pp. 126–127. Copyright © 1976 by Management Decision Systems, Inc. Reprinted by permission.

CASE STUDY
KATE COOPER

My name is Kate Cooper. I am 31, a registered nurse with a bachelor's degree in nursing and 6 years of supervisory experience. I was charge nurse and then house supervisor in the medical/surgical wing of a large regional medical center and was in-service director in charge of continuing education and staff development in a geriatric nursing setting. In addition, I have been teaching nursing courses in the night program at a local technical school.

Ready for the next step in my career, I obtained the position of Manager of Adult Services for the twenty-bed adult psychiatric wing at Green Meadows Hospital. Green Meadows was a newly constructed forty-room community hospital for the care of acutely ill psychiatric patients. It was the twenty-third facility owned by Southern Hospitals Corporation (SHC), the largest chain of acute-care psychiatric hospitals in the country.

I felt excited about my new position. I saw it as a fine opportunity for career development in nursing, and the possibility of transferring to other facilities in the chain was a definite benefit in my eyes. I had many projects to complete before the planned opening of the hospital in two weeks, and I started my new position with high energy and enthusiasm.

My supervisor, Alan Jones, who hired me, was assistant administrator of the hospital. He had one year of previous experience as director of nursing at a fifty-bed acute-care psychiatric hospital. On my first day he encouraged me to "just dig right in and get started" organizing my department. I asked to see my job description and the hospital policy manual to become familiar with the organization employing me. Alan gave me a job description and explained that I was part of the "start-up" process. At this time there was no personnel handbook for employees.

One condition of employment I stipulated in accepting the job was that I be able to continue my schooling as a part-time graduate student working on my master's degree in nursing education. Alan Jones readily agreed to this condition, stating that he was a strong supporter of continuing education for all managers and staff.

In my opinion the first week I worked for Green Meadows consisted of many wasted hours. I learned on my own that my main task prior to the opening was to hire the patient care staff for my twenty-bed unit. I tried to line up interviews for nurses and mental health workers, since Alan Jones had told me to "go ahead and hire the personnel you need for your unit."

Peter Smith, manager of the eighteen-bed chemical dependency unit, had previously worked with Alan Jones at a psychiatric hospital 50 miles from Green Meadows. Peter had been hired by Alan along with two other managers from that location who had not yet arrived at Green Meadows. Peter was hiring staff for his unit, and he told me he wanted to interview the nurses and mental health workers also, since those employees would be working on his unit as well.

This request surprised me. I tried to find an organization chart and asked the hospital administrator, Doug Anderson, in passing one morning if he had one I could see. He jokingly asked me if I was serious. "After all," he said, "I think it is changing every day." I laughed at first, but my amusement was short-lived when no chart was forthcoming. Eventually, I came to visualize the organization chart as presented in Case Exhibit 14.1.

Doug Anderson had served as office manager in a small hospital in California. His wife, an occupational therapist, was also a part-time employee at Green Meadows. Two of Doug's hires were a personal friend from California, Leonard Snare, and Leonard's wife. Leonard's sole job qualification was certification to be a psychiatric technician, earned by attending workshops. His wife worked in the business office.

Construction work had progressed, and Green Meadows was ready for staff occupancy one week before

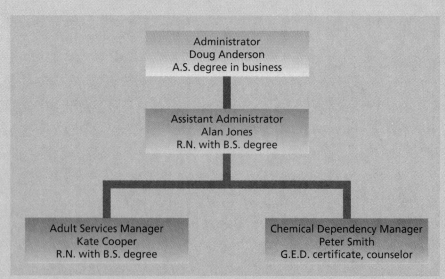

CASE EXHIBIT 14.1
Green Meadows Hospital
management staff—partial
organizational chart.

Administrator
Doug Anderson
A.S. degree in business

Assistant Administrator
Alan Jones
R.N. with B.S. degree

Adult Services Manager
Kate Cooper
R.N. with B.S. degree

Chemical Dependency Manager
Peter Smith
G.E.D. certificate, counselor

the planned hospital opening. Although much remained to be done and things were still confused, I was excited about moving into my new office.

During the previous week Peter and I had hired our initial staff. I was worried my unit would not be ready to receive patients and had written a 5-day orientation program specific to the unit that included information I thought my patient care staff would find beneficial. I shared the orientation outline with Peter, who informed me that he would need 2½ days to teach the new staff members *his* program alone.

I was shocked and angered that he had planned this commitment for my staff. With one week left, both orientation programs could not be completed prior to opening. I asked Peter if his plan had been cleared with Alan Jones. Peter replied with a grin, "Of course. It was his idea." As a result, I sought out Alan and asked if he could meet on some neutral ground with the adult psychiatric and chemical dependency units. I told him that orientation to my department was just as important as orientation to Peter's department. Alan told me that Peter had his program all ready to go and would only need "a couple of days" to present it. All of this left me feeling very frustrated.

I had other problems with Alan. Despite his having told me to go ahead and hire the staff nurses and mental health workers, I later discovered he was hiring those people at the same time I was interviewing prospective employees. In addition, Alan had instructed me to assume the role of inservice director and write the staff orientation program. He told me that I would have to be the unit head nurse for the chemical dependency unit, although I told him that I thought the responsibilities would be too great due to my duties as the adult services unit manager. Alan's response to my doubts was his standard one in such situations: "You are tough, and I know you can handle it."

As a result of these and similar interactions with Alan, I became confused and frustrated by his lack of support and his behavior, which seemed inconsistent with directions he had given me. I was overwhelmed with the amount of work and responsibility. I was most frustrated and angered when additional tasks were "dumped" on me because I felt I had to complete the extra work as soon as possible in addition to doing my own work on the unit.

Alan apparently had difficult relationships with some other employees as well. Other female managers com-

plained almost from the start that Alan needed to be "put in his place" for his sexist remarks and behaviors. Doug Anderson received reports indicating that Alan's behavior had been inappropriate on several occasions. Doug also heard second-hand that Alan was overstepping his responsibilities as assistant administrator and making policy statements contrary to Doug's positions.

This general employee dissatisfaction continued. Three months after the opening of the hospital Alan Jones strongly implied that I would have to quit school. He explained that he expected people to be there, saying that "to be a good manager you should be here all the time." I took issue with this and sought Doug Anderson's assistance. Doug had never been informed about my going to school and was unaware that I was even taking classes. Alan alone had approved my return to school to continue my education. Doug's response was simply to encourage me to speak with Alan again and "communicate better with him."

Feeling pressure on several fronts, I reached the limit of my tolerance with Alan Jones and handed in my notice of resignation. Alan Jones subsequently refused to speak with me. The manager of the chemical dependency unit told me that my timing was lousy, accused me of trying to create waves, and said I should put work as a priority over continuing my education.

Source: Case prepared by William E. Stratton, Idaho State University; David Efraty, University of Houston—Downtown; and Kim Jardine. From *Case Research Journal*, Spring 1993. The manager cooperated in the field research for this case, which was written solely for the purpose of stimulating student discussion. All incidents and individuals are real, but the names of persons and of the organization have been disguised. Copyright © 1993 by the *Case Research Journal* and William E. Stratton.

1. What are the various causes of the conflict that can be observed in this case?
2. What approaches does Kate Cooper take to trying to manage the conflict she is experiencing?
3. Is Kate experiencing stress? If so, what are its causes?
4. What kinds of stress reactions does Kate exhibit?
5. Evaluate the management style of Alan Jones.
6. What evidence of negotiation is seen in the case? What kind of negotiation *should have* occurred?

PART FOUR

THE TOTAL
ORGANIZATION

Learning Objectives

After reading Chapter 15 you should be able to:

1 Define organizational structure and explain how it corresponds to division of labor.

2 Discuss the relative merits of various forms of departmentation.

3 Review the more basic and more elaborate means of achieving organizational coordination.

4 Discuss the nature and consequences of traditional structural characteristics.

5 Explain the distinction between organic and mechanistic structures.

6 Discuss the emergence of network organizations.

7 Review important considerations concerning downsizing.

McDonald's and W.L. Gore have achieved success with very different organizational structures—McDonald's is highly structured while Gore operates with "unmanagement."

CHAPTER 15

ORGANIZATIONAL STRUCTURE

MCDONALD'S
VS.
W.L. GORE
& ASSOCIATES,
INC.

They are two of America's most successful organizations. Wherever in the world you live—from Manhattan to Moscow— you know McDonald's, the firm that perfected the fast food concept. Building on the ideas of California's McDonald

brothers, Ray Kroc built McDonald's first franchise restaurant in 1955. Today, head-quartered in Illinois, McDonald's has become the leading purveyor of the fast-food lifestyle and the premier model for aspiring franchisers.

Unless you are an avid hiker or camper, you may be less familiar with W.L. Gore & Associates, Inc. The firm, based in Newark, Delaware, is best known for Gore-Tex® brand fabric, a breathable, waterproof fabric laminate found in premium outdoor clothing and space suits. However, Gore also produces other high-tech products including electrical cable, vascular grafts and other medical products, and a wide variety of environmental filters and other industrial products. Founded in 1958 by Bill Gore, an ex-DuPont R&D chemist, the firm has 40 plants worldwide. Its annual revenue is around $1 billion, and it has posted good profits for over 30 years straight.

Given the success of both organizations, it is tempting to assume that they might be organized in a similar manner. Guess again! Gore's 5,600 "associates" (not employees) operate under what the company describes as unmanagement. There are no titles, no bosses, and no budgets. By extension, there is no hierarchy and no fixed organizational structure. How does any work get done? The company uses what it calls a lattice system in which an associate assumes responsibility for developing a new product. Then, he or she has to recruit volunteers from other parts of the company to form a team. This team could eventually become a plant, which would be divided into smaller teams that choose their own leaders. Gore intentionally limits plant size to no more than 200 associates to foster good communication.

If Gore has achieved success with unmanagement, McDonald's has achieved success with Management. Nothing is left to chance or voluntarism in a McDonald's restaurant, from layout, to equipment, to the behavior of the staff (who *are* called employees!). All of this is dictated in a detailed operations manual developed at company headquarters. The manual provides instructions for training employees how to present themselves, what to say to customers, and how to do their jobs. Frozen burgers and fries are used to maintain strict product uniformity. Burgers are constructed in precise assembly line fashion, and employees are instructed which row of frying burgers to flip first. Where possible, technology is used to reduce employee variability and to prevent mistakes—bells ring when the food is cooked, drink dispensers shut themselves off, and cash registers are preprogrammed to avoid entry errors. These and many other standards and procedures have contributed to the company's worldwide success.[1]

How can two organizations that are organized or structured so differently both be so successful? And how do these differences affect organizational members and the overall effectiveness of the organization? These are the kinds of questions that we shall attempt to answer in this chapter and the next.

First, we'll define organizational structure and discuss the methods for dividing labor and forming departments. Then we will consider some methods for coordinating labor as well as traditional structural characteristics and the relationship between size and structure. Finally, we will review some signals of structural problems.

A PROLOGUE: THE ROLE OF ORGANIZATIONAL STRUCTURE

In previous chapters we were concerned primarily with the bits and pieces that make up organizations. First, we analyzed organizational behavior from the standpoint of the individual member—how his or her learning, perception, attitudes, and motivation affect behavior. Then we shifted our analysis to groups and to some of the processes that occur in organizations, including communication, leadership, and decision making. In this chapter we adopt yet another level of analysis by looking at the organization as a whole. Our primary interest is the causes and consequences of organizational structure.

Shortly, we will discuss organizational structure in detail. For now, it is enough to know that it broadly refers to how the organization's individuals and groups are *put together* or *organized* to accomplish work. This is an important issue. An organization could have well-motivated individual members and properly led groups and still fail to fulfill its potential because of the way their efforts are divided and coordinated.

We are not used to thinking about the structure of organizations and how it affects us (especially when we are having a Big Mac Attack!). Frequently, we confuse the effects of structure with motivation, leadership, or communication. For example, consider the Master's-level engineering student who must withdraw from a course that is cancelled because its enrollment is too small. She is able to withdraw from the course at the graduate office, but she learns that she must go to the accounts office to obtain a tuition refund. At the accounts office, she finds that she must have a note from the department that cancelled the course. Returning with a note from the electrical engineering department, she discovers that she must also obtain a copy of her registration from the registrar's office before the accounts office can grant a refund. Ready to scream, she proceeds to give the poor accounts clerk a lecture on leadership, motivation, and communication. In fact, each of the subunits described in this example might be doing its own job perfectly well. It is probably the way the university is *structured* that is causing the student problems.

In Chapter 1 we defined organizations as social inventions for accomplishing common goals through group effort. In this chapter and the next, we shall see that organizational structure intervenes between goals and organizational accomplishments and thus influences organizational effectiveness. Among other things, structure affects how effectively and efficiently group effort is coordinated.

WHAT IS ORGANIZATIONAL STRUCTURE?

Organizational structure is not the easiest concept to define precisely because the concept covers so much territory. However, we can get a little more precise than our previous allusion to structure as being how an organization is "put together" or "organized."

Let's begin this way: To achieve its goals, an organization has to do two very basic things—*divide* labor among its members and then *coordinate* what has been divided. The university mentioned above divided its labor—some members taught electrical engineering, some ran the graduate program, some took care of accounts, and some handled registration. It is simply unlikely that anyone could do *all* of these things well. Furthermore, within each of these subunits, labor would be further divided. For example, the registrar's office would include a director, secretaries, clerks, and so on. With all this division, some coordination is obviously necessary. Although the student didn't feel that the coordination was adequate, a good organizational detective would spot

Organizational structure. The manner in which an organization divides its labor into specific tasks and achieves coordination among these tasks.

evidence of its existence—everyone knew whom she should see to solve her refund problem.

We can conclude that **organizational structure** is the manner in which an organization divides its labor into specific tasks and achieves coordination among these tasks.[2]

THE DIVISION AND COORDINATION OF LABOR

Labor must be divided because individuals have physical and intellectual limitations. *Everyone* can't do *everything;* even if this were possible, tremendous confusion and inefficiency would result. There are two basic dimensions to the division of labor, a vertical dimension and a horizontal dimension. Once labor is divided, it must be coordinated to achieve organizational effectiveness.

Vertical Division of Labor

The vertical division of labor is concerned primarily with apportioning authority for planning and decision making—who gets to tell whom what to do? As we see in Exhibit 15.1, in a manufacturing firm the vertical division of labor is usually signified by titles such as president, manager, and supervisor. In a university it might be denoted by titles such as president, dean, and chairperson. Organizations differ greatly in the extent to which labor is divided vertically. For example, the U.S. Army has nine levels of command ranging from four-star generals to sergeants. Wal-Mart has five levels between its CEO and its store managers. On the other hand, an automobile dealership might have only two or three levels, and a university would usually fall between the extremes. Separate departments, units, or functions *within* an organization will also often vary in the extent to which they vertically divide labor. A production unit might have several levels of management, ranging from supervisor to general manager. A research unit in the same company might have only two levels of management. A couple of key themes or issues underlie the vertical division of labor.

Autonomy and Control.   Holding other factors constant, the domain of decision making and authority is reduced as the number of levels in the hierarchy increases. Put another way, managers have less authority over fewer matters. On the other hand, a flatter hierarchy pushes authority lower and involves people further down the hierarchy in more decisions.

Communication.   A second theme underlying the vertical division of labor is communication or coordination between levels. As labor is progressively divided vertically, timely communication and coordination can become harder to achieve. Recall our discussion in Chapter 11 of information filtering as a barrier to communication. As the number of levels in the hierarchy increases, filtering is more likely to occur.

These two themes illustrate that labor must be divided vertically enough to ensure proper control but not so much as to make vertical communication and coordination impossible. The proper degree of such division will vary across organizations and across their functional units.

Horizontal Division of Labor

The horizontal division of labor groups the basic tasks that must be performed into jobs and then into departments so that the organization can achieve its goals. Required work flow is the main basis for this division. The firm schematized in Exhibit 15.1 must produce and sell goods, keep its finances straight, and keep its employees happy. A hospital must admit patients, subject them to lab tests, fix what ails them, and keep them comfortable, all the while staying within its budget. Just as organizations differ in the extent to which they divide labor vertically, they also differ in the extent of horizontal division of labor. In a small business, the owner might be a "jack-of-all-trades," making estimates, delivering the product or service, and keeping the books. As the organization grows, horizontal division of labor is likely, with different groups of employees assigned to perform each of these tasks. Thus, the horizontal division of labor suggests some specialization on the part of the work force. Up to a point, this increased specialization can promote efficiency. A couple of key themes or issues underlie the horizontal division of labor.

Job Design. The horizontal division of labor is closely tied to our earlier consideration of job design (Chapter 7). An example will clarify this. Suppose that an organization offers a product or service that consists of A work, B work, and C work (e.g., fabrication, inspection, and packaging). There are at least three basic ways in which it might structure these tasks:

- Form an ABC Department in which all workers do ABC work.
- Form an ABC Department in which workers specialize in A work, B work, or C work.
- Form a separate A Department, B Department, and C Department.

There is nothing inherently superior about any of these three designs. Notice, however, that each has implications for the jobs involved and how these jobs are coordinated. The first design provides for enriched jobs in which each worker can coordinate his or her own A work, B work, and C work. It also reduces the need for supervision and allows for self-managed teams. However, this design might require highly trained workers, and it

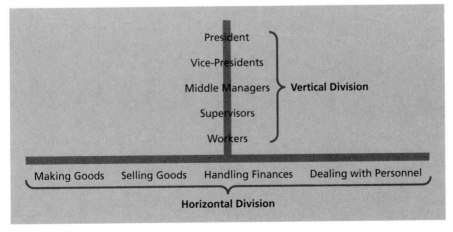

EXHIBIT 15.1
The dimensions of division of labor in a manufacturing firm.

might be impossible if A work, B work, and C work are complex specialties that require (for example) engineering, accounting, and legal skills. The second design involves increased horizontal division of labor in which employees specialize in tasks and in which the coordination of A work, B work, and C work becomes more critical. However, much of this coordination could be handled by properly designing the head of the department's job. Finally, the third design offers the greatest horizontal division of labor in that A work, B work, and C work are actually performed in separate departments. This design provides for great control and accountability for the separate tasks, but it also suggests that someone above the department heads will have to get involved in coordination. There are several lessons here. First, the horizontal division of labor strongly affects job design. Second, it has profound implications for the degree of coordination necessary. Finally, it also has implications for the vertical division of labor and where control over work processes should logically reside.

Differentiation. A second theme occasioned by the horizontal division of labor is related to the first. As organizations engage in increased horizontal division of labor, they usually become more and more differentiated. **Differentiation** is the tendency for managers in separate functions or departments to differ in terms of goals, time spans, and interpersonal styles.[3] In tending to their own domains and problems, managers often develop distinctly different psychological orientations toward the organization and its products or services.

Differentiation. The tendency for managers in separate departments to differ in terms of goals, time spans, and interpersonal styles.

A classic case of differentiation is that which often occurs between marketing managers and those in research and development. The goals of the marketing managers might be external to the organization and oriented toward servicing the marketplace. Those of R&D managers might be oriented more toward excellence in design and state-of-the-art use of materials. While marketing managers want products to sell *now,* R&D managers might feel that "good designs take time." Finally, marketing managers might believe that they can handle dispute resolution with R&D through interpersonal tactics learned when they were on the sales force ("Let's discuss this over lunch"). R&D managers might feel that "the design data speaks for itself" when a conflict occurs. The essential problem here is that the marketing department and the R&D department *need* each other to do their jobs properly![4] Shortly, we will review some tactics to help achieve necessary coordination.

Differentiation is a natural and necessary consequence of the horizontal division of labor, but it again points to the need for coordination, a topic that we will consider in more detail below. For now, let's examine more closely how organizations can allocate work to departments.

Departmentation

As we suggested above, once basic tasks have been combined into jobs, a question still remains as to how to group these jobs so that they can be managed effectively. The assignment of jobs to departments is called departmentation, and it represents one of the core aspects of the horizontal division of labor. It should be recognized that "department" is a generic term; some organizations use an alternative term such as unit, group, or division. There are

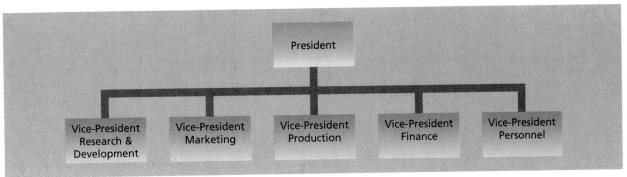

EXHIBIT 15.2
Functional departmentation.

several methods of departmentation, each of which has its strengths and weaknesses.

Functional Departmentation. This form of organization is basic and familiar. Under **functional departmentation,** employees with closely related skills and responsibilities (functions) are located in the same department (see Exhibit 15.2). Thus, those with skills in sales and advertising are assigned to the marketing department, and those with skills in accounting and credit are assigned to the finance department. Under this kind of design, employees are grouped according to the kind of resources they contribute to achieving the overall goals of the organization.[5]

What are the advantages of functional departmentation? The most-cited advantage is that of efficiency. When all of the engineers are located in an engineering department, rather than scattered throughout the organization, it is easier to be sure that they are neither overloaded nor underloaded with work. Also, support factors such as reference books, computer terminals, and laboratory space can be allocated more efficiently with less duplication. Some other advantages of functional departmentation include the following:

- Communication within departments should be enhanced, since everyone "speaks the same language."
- Career ladders and training opportunities within the function are enhanced because all parties will share the same view of career progression.
- It should be easier to measure and evaluate the performance of functional specialists when they are all located in the same department.

What are the disadvantages of functional departmentation? Most of them stem from the specialization within departments that occurs in the functional arrangement. As a result, a high degree of differentiation can occur between functional departments. At best, this can lead to poor coordination and slow response to organizational problems. At worst, it can lead to open conflict between departments in which the needs of clients and customers are ignored. Departmental empires might be built at the expense of pursuing organizational goals.

There is consensus that functional departmentation works best in small to medium-sized firms that offer relatively few product lines or services. It can also be an effective means of organizing the smaller divisions of large corporations.

Functional departmentation.
Employees with closely related skills and responsibilities are assigned to the same department.

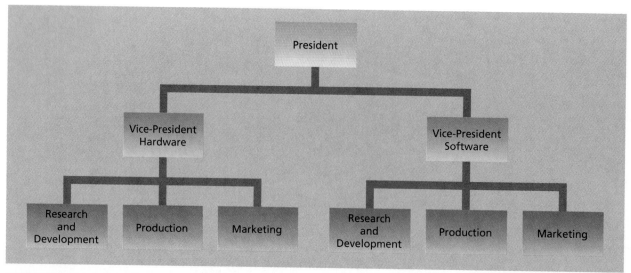

EXHIBIT 15.3
Product departmentation.

When scale gets bigger and the output of the organization gets more complex, most firms gravitate toward product departmentation or its variations.

Product departmentation.
Departments are formed on the basis of a particular product, product line, or service.

Product Departmentation.   Under **product departmentation,** departments are formed on the basis of a particular product, product line, or service. Each of these departments can operate fairly autonomously because it has its own set of functional specialists dedicated to the output of that department. For example, a computer firm might have a hardware division and a software division, each with its own staff of production people, marketers, and research and development personnel (see Exhibit 15.3).

What are the advantages of product departmentation? One key advantage is better coordination among the functional specialists who work on a particular product line. Since their attentions are focused on one product and they have fewer functional peers, fewer barriers to communication should develop. Other advantages include flexibility, since product lines can be added or deleted without great implications for the rest of the organization. Also, product-focused departments can be evaluated as profit centers, since they have independent control over costs and revenues. This is not feasible for most functional departments (e.g., the research and development department doesn't have revenues). Finally, product departmentation often serves the customer or client better, since the client can see more easily who produced the product (the software group, not Ajax Computers). All in all, product structures have more potential than functional structures for responding to customers in a timely way.

Are there any disadvantages to product departmentation? Professional development might suffer without a critical mass of professionals working in the same place at the same time. Also, economies of scale might be threatened and inefficiency might occur if relatively autonomous product-oriented departments are not coordinated. R&D personnel in an industrial products division and a consumer products division might work on a similar problem for months without being aware of each other's efforts. Worse, product-oriented departments might actually work at cross-purposes.

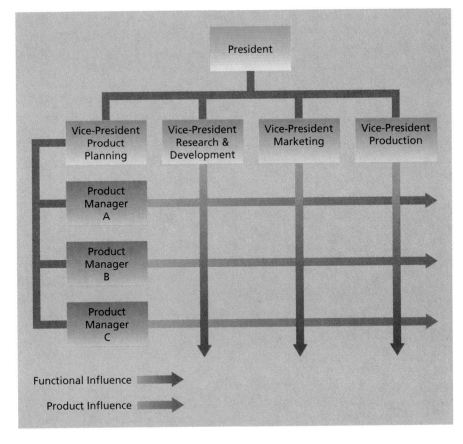

EXHIBIT 15.4
Matrix departmentation.

Matrix Departmentation. The system of **matrix departmentation** is an attempt to capitalize simultaneously on the strengths of both functional and product departmentation.[6] In its most literal form, employees remain tied to a functional department such as marketing or production, but they also report to a product manager who draws upon their services (Exhibit 15.4). For example, in a firm in the chemical industry, a marketing expert might matrix with the household cleaning products group.

There are many variations on matrix design. Most of them boil down to what exactly gets crossed with functional areas to form the matrix and the degree of stability of the matrix relationships. For example, besides products, a matrix could be based on geographical regions or projects. For instance, a mechanical engineer in a global engineering company could report both to the mechanical engineering department at world headquarters and the regional manager for Middle East operations. This would probably be a fairly stable arrangement.

On the other hand, a matrix could be based on shorter-term projects. NASA uses this system, as do many consulting firms and research labs. The cross-functional team that designed the newest Ford Mustang (Chapter 8) drew members from various Ford functions (e.g., styling, marketing, engineering) to support this project. When the design was completed, members went on to other assignments.

The matrix system is quite elegant when it works well. Ideally, it provides a degree of *balance* between the abstract demands of the product or project

Matrix departmentation.
Employees remain members of a functional department while also reporting to a product or project manager.

and the people who actually do the work, resulting in a better outcome. Also, it is very flexible. People can be moved around as project flow dictates, and projects, products, or new regions can be added without total restructuring. Being focused on a particular product or project can also lead to better communication among the representatives from the various functional areas (precisely why Ford used a cross-functional team to design the Mustang).

Two interrelated problems threaten the matrix structure. First, there is no guarantee that product or project managers will see eye-to-eye with various functional managers. This can create conflict that reduces the advantages of the matrix. Next, employees assigned to a product or project team in essence report to two managers, their functional manager and their product or project manager. This violation of a classical management principle (every employee should have only one boss) can result in role conflict and stress, especially at performance review time. The upshot of this is that managers need to be well trained under matrix structures. In your author's opinion, some of the bad press that matrix designs received stems from their early application in technical environments where neither functional mangers nor project managers had very well developed people-management skills.

Other Forms of Departmentation.   Several other forms of departmentation also exist.[7] Two of these are simply variations on product departmentation. One is geographic departmentation. Under **geographic departmentation,** relatively self-contained units deliver the organization's products or services in specific geographic territories (Exhibit 15.5). This form of departmentation shortens communication channels, allows the organization to cater to regional tastes, and gives some appearance of local control to clients and customers. National retailers, insurance companies, and oil companies generally exhibit geographic departmentation.

Another form of departmentation closely related to product departmentation is customer departmentation. Under **customer departmentation,** relatively self-contained units deliver the organization's products or services to specific

Geographic departmentation.
Relatively self-contained units deliver an organization's products or services in a specific geographic territory.

Customer departmentation.
Relatively self-contained units deliver an organization's products or services to specific customer groups.

EXHIBIT 15.5
Geographic departmentation.

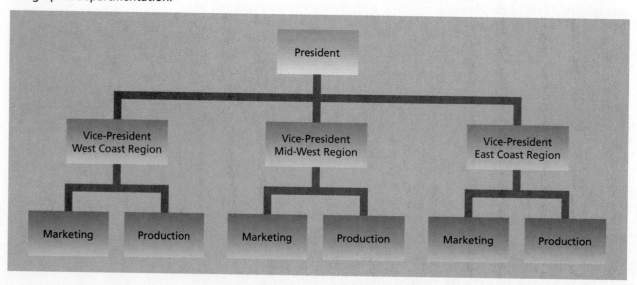

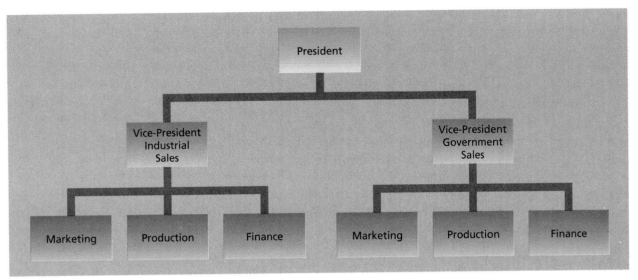

EXHIBIT 15.6
Customer departmentation.

customer groups (Exhibit 15.6). The obvious goal is to provide better service to each customer group through specialization. For example, many banks have commercial lending divisions that are separate from the consumer loan operations. Universities might have separate graduate and undergraduate divisions. An engineering firm might have separate divisions to cater to civilian and military customers. In general, the advantages and disadvantages of geographic and customer departmentation parallel those for product departmentation.

Finally, we should recognize that few organizations represent "pure" examples of functional, product, geographic, or customer departmentation. It is not unusual to see **hybrid departmentation,** which involves some combination of these structures. For example, a manufacturing firm might retain personnel, finance, and legal services in a functional form at headquarters but use product departmentation to organize separate production and sales staffs for each product. Similarly, McDonald's and Wal-Mart centralize many activities at their respective headquarters but also have geographic divisions that cater to regional tastes and make for efficient distribution. The hybrids attempt to capitalize on the strengths of various structures while avoiding the weaknesses of others.

Hybrid departmentation. A structure based on some mixture of functional, product, geographic, or customer departmentation.

Basic Methods of Coordinating Divided Labor

When the tasks that will help the organization achieve its goals have been divided among individuals and departments, they must be coordinated so that goal accomplishment is actually realized. We can identify five basic methods of **coordination,** which is a process of facilitating timing, communication, and feedback.[8]

Coordination. A process of facilitating timing, communication, and feedback among work tasks.

Direct Supervision.   This is a very traditional form of coordination. Working through the chain of command, designated supervisors or managers coordinate the work of their subordinates. For instance, a production supervisor coordinates the work of his or her subordinates. In turn, the production superintendent coordinates the activities of all the supervisors. This method of coordination is closely associated with our discussion of leadership in Chapter 10.

Standardization of Work Processes. Some jobs are so routine that the technology itself provides a means of coordination. Little direct supervision is necessary for these jobs to be coordinated. The automobile assembly line provides a good example. When a car comes by, worker X bolts on the left A-frame assembly, and worker Y bolts on the right assembly. These workers do not have to interact, and they require minimal supervision. Work processes can also be standardized by rules and regulations. McDonald's stringent routine for constructing a burger is such an example.

Standardization of Outputs. Even when direct supervision is minimal and work processes are not standardized, coordination can be achieved through the standardization of work outputs. Concern shifts from how the work is done to ensuring that the work meets certain physical or economic standards. For instance, workers in a machine shop might be required to construct complex valves that require a mixture of drilling, lathe work, and finishing. The physical specifications of the valves will dictate how this work is to be coordinated. Standardization of outputs is often used to coordinate the work of separate product or geographic divisions. Frequently, top management assigns each division a profit target. These standards ensure that each division "pulls its weight" in contributing to overall profit goals. Thus, budgets are a form of standardizing outputs.

Standardization of Skills. Even when work processes and output cannot be standardized, and direct supervision is unfeasible, coordination can be achieved through standardization of skills. This is seen very commonly in the case of technicians and professionals. For example, a large surgery team can often coordinate its work with minimal verbal communication because of its high degree of interlocked training—surgeons, anesthesiologists, and nurses all know what to expect from each other because of their standard training. MBA programs are often designed to provide some standardized skills (e.g., the ability to read a balance sheet) to people with different functional specialties.

Mutual Adjustment. Mutual adjustment relies upon informal communication to coordinate tasks. Paradoxically, it is useful for coordinating the most simple and the most complicated divisions of labor. For example, imagine a small florist shop that consists of the owner-operator, a shop assistant, and a delivery person. It is very likely that these individuals will coordinate their work through informal processes, mutually adjusting to each other's needs. At the other extreme, consider the top executive team of virtually any corporation. Such teams are generally composed of people with a variety of skills and backgrounds (e.g., finance, marketing) and tend to be preoccupied with very nonroutine problems. Again, mutual adjustment would be necessary to coordinate their efforts because standardization would be impossible.

Now that we have reviewed the five basic methods of coordinating divided labor, a few comments are in order. First, as we see in Exhibit 15.7, the methods can be crudely ordered in terms of the degree of *discretion* they permit individual workers in terms of task performance. Applied strictly, direct

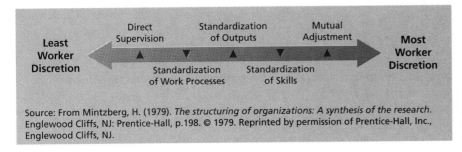

Source: From Mintzberg, H. (1979). *The structuring of organizations: A synthesis of the research.* Englewood Cliffs, NJ: Prentice-Hall, p.198. © 1979. Reprinted by permission of Prentice-Hall, Inc., Englewood Cliffs, NJ.

EXHIBIT 15.7
Methods of coordination as a continuum of worker discretion.

supervision permits little discretion. Standardization of processes and outputs permits successively more discretion. (However, clever workers can "beat" these forms of standardization.) Finally, standardization of skills and mutual adjustment put even more control into the hands of those who are actually doing the work. Obviously, a McDonald's restaurant tends toward the left of the continuum and a W.L. Gore plant leans toward the right.

Notice that just as division of labor affects the design of jobs, so does the method of coordination employed. As we move from the left side to the right side of the continuum of coordination, there is greater potential for jobs to be designed in an enriched manner. By the same token, an improper coordination strategy can destroy the intrinsic motivation of a job. Traditionally, much work performed by professionals (e.g., scientists and engineers) is coordinated by their own skill standardization. If the manager of a research lab decides to coordinate work with a high degree of direct supervision, the motivating potential of the scientists' jobs might be damaged. *The manager* is doing work that *they* should be doing.

The use of the various methods of coordination tends to vary across different parts of the organization. These differences in coordination stem from the way labor has been divided. As we noted, upper management relies heavily upon mutual adjustment for coordination. Where tasks are more routine, such as in the lower part of the production subunit, we tend to see coordination via direct supervision or standardization of work processes or outputs.[9] Advisory subunits staffed by professionals, such as a legal department or a marketing research group, often rely upon a combination of skill standardization and mutual adjustment.

Finally, methods of coordination may change as task demands change. Under peacetime conditions or routine wartime conditions, the army relies heavily on direct supervision through a strict chain of command. However, this method of coordination can prove ineffective for fighting units under heavy fire. Here, we might see a sergeant with a radio instructing a captain where to direct artillery fire. This reversal of the chain of command is indicative of mutual adjustment. Similarly, the trend toward self-managed work teams (Chapter 8) downplays direct supervision and focuses on mutual adjustment among team members.

Other Methods of Coordination

The forms of coordination we discussed above are very basic in that almost every organization uses them. After all, when do we see an organization that *doesn't* exhibit some supervision, some standardization, and some talking things out? Sometimes, however, coordination problems are such that more customized, elaborate mechanisms are necessary to achieve coordination. This is especially true when we are speaking of lateral coordination across highly differentiated departments. Recall that the managers of such departments might vary greatly in goals, time spans, and interpersonal orientation. Figuratively, at least, they often "speak different languages." The process of attaining coordination across differentiated departments usually goes by the special name of **integration**.[10] Good integration achieves coordination without reducing the differences that enable each department to do its own job well.[11] For example, in a high-technology firm, we don't *want* production and engineering to be so cozy that innovative tension is lost.[12]

> **Integration.** The process of attaining coordination across differentiated departments.

In ascending order of elaboration, three methods of achieving integration include the use of liaison roles, task forces, and full-time integrators.[13]

Liaison Roles.   A **liaison role** is occupied by a person in one department who is assigned, as part of his or her job, to achieve coordination with another department. In other words, one person serves as a part-time link between two departments. Sometimes the second department might reciprocate by nominating its own liaison person. For example, in a university library, reference librarians might be required to serve as liaison people for certain academic departments or schools. In turn, an academic department might assign a faculty member to "touch base" with its liaison in the library. Sometimes, liaison people might actually be located physically in the corresponding department. For instance, consider Laura Kozol, a design engineer in GE's Lynn, Massachusetts, jet engine plant:

> **Liaison role.** A person is assigned to help achieve coordination between his or her department and another department.

> She would hear that the workers in Building 69 had difficulty adapting her designs to their machines. "I used to get mad at them," she said, "making these mistakes, requiring me to fix what were their problems." Then she started coming over to Building 69. "Last summer, I came over full time," she said. "I can talk to the guys actually making the parts. That lets me see what they have to do to meet my requirements." Right on the spot now, she can fix a glitch in a design, rather than tie people up in meetings, paperwork and delay.[14]

Task Forces and Teams.   When coordination problems arise that involve several departments simultaneously, liaison roles are not very effective. **Task forces** are temporary groups set up to solve coordination problems across several departments. Representatives from each department are included on a full-time or part-time basis, but when adequate integration is achieved, the task force is disbanded. Citicorp, Xerox, and Ford are firms that have made extensive use of task forces.

> **Task forces.** Temporary groups set up to solve coordination problems across several departments.

Self-managed and cross-functional teams (Chapter 8) are also an effective means of achieving coordination. Such teams require interaction among employees who might otherwise operate in an independent vacuum. Cross-functional teams are especially useful in achieving coordination for new product development and introduction.

Integrators.   **Integrators** are organizational members who are permanently installed between two departments that are in clear need of coordination. In a sense, they are full-time problem solvers. Integrators are especially useful

> **Integrators.** Organizational members permanently assigned to facilitate coordination between departments.

SWEDEN'S KAROLINSKA HOSPITAL

You be the Manager

Sweden's prestigious Karolinska Hospital is located in Stockholm. The hospital faced financial problems due to a 20 percent cutback in government funding. The chief executive at the time, Jan Lindsten, feared that patient care would suffer, since cost cutting measures had already been undertaken. With the help of the Boston Consulting Group, Lindsten came to see that an extreme degree of functional departmentation was contributing to elevated costs. Recently, the hospital had been decentralized into 47 separate departments, each focused on its own specialty. As a result, patients simply spent too much time in too many visits shuffling between separate departments and waiting

> FEARING PATIENT CARE WOULD SUFFER AFTER GOVERNMENT CUTS IN FUNDING, SWEDEN'S KAROLINSKA HOSPITAL RESTRUCTURED TO IMPROVE SERVICE EFFICIENCY.

for appointments. Even when Lindsten reduced the number of departments to 11, coordination problems remained. He was convinced that a more efficient structure could by implemented. What do *you* think?

1. What are some alternative ways of thinking about the hospital's problems other than in terms of medical specialties?

2. What are some design innovations that might improve teamwork and efficiency in the hospital?

To find out what happened at Karolinska Hospital, consult *The Manager's Notebook.*

Source: Adapted from Jacob, R. (1995, April 3). The struggle to create an organization for the 21st century. *Fortune,* 90–99.

for dealing with conflict between (1) highly interdependent departments, (2) which have very diverse goals and orientations, (3) in a very ambiguous environment. Such a situation occurs in many high-technology companies.[15] For example, a solid-state electronics firm might introduce new products almost every month. This is a real strain on the production department, which might need the assistance of the design scientists to implement a production run. The scientists, on the other hand, rely on production to implement last-minute changes due to the rapidly changing technology. This situation badly requires coordination.

Integrators usually report directly to the executive to whom the heads of the two departments report. Ideally, they are rewarded according to the success of both units. A special kind of person is required for this job, since he or she has great responsibility but no direct authority in either department. The integrator must be unbiased, "speak the language" of both departments, and rely heavily on expert power.[16] An engineer with excellent interpersonal skills might be an effective integrator for the electronics firm.

Before continuing, please consider *You Be the Manager* featuring Sweden's Karolinska Hospital.

TRADITIONAL STRUCTURAL CHARACTERISTICS

Every organization is unique in the exact way that it divides and coordinates labor. Few business firms, hospitals, or schools have perfectly identical structures. What is needed, then, is some efficient way to summarize the effects of the vertical and horizontal division of labor and its coordination on the structure of the organization. Over the years, management scholars and practicing managers have agreed upon a number of characteristics that summarize the structure of organizations.[17]

Span of Control

Span of control. The number of subordinates supervised by a superior.

The **span of control** is the number of subordinates supervised by a superior. There is one essential fact about span of control: The larger the span, the less *potential* there is for coordination by direct supervision. As the span increases, the attention that a supervisor can devote to each subordinate decreases. When work tasks are routine, coordination of labor through standardization of work processes or output often substitutes for direct supervision. Thus, at lower levels in production units, it is not unusual to see spans of control ranging to over 20. In the managerial ranks, tasks are less routine, and adequate time is necessary for informal mutual adjustment. As a result, spans at the upper levels tend to be smaller. Also, at lower organizational levels, workers with only one or a few specialties report to a supervisor. For instance, an office supervisor might supervise only clerks. As we climb the hierarchy, workers with radically different specialties might report to the boss. For example, the president might have to deal with vice-presidents of personnel, finance, production, and marketing. Again, the complexity of this task might dictate smaller spans.[18]

Flat Versus Tall

Flat organization. An organization with relatively few levels in its hierarchy of authority.

Tall organization. An organization with relatively many levels in its hierarchy of authority.

Holding size constant, a **flat organization** has relatively few levels in its hierarchy of authority, while a **tall organization** has relatively many levels. Thus, flatness versus tallness is an index of the vertical division of labor. Again, holding size constant, it should be obvious that flatness and tallness are associated with the average span of control. This is shown in Exhibit 15.8. Both schematized organizations have 31 members. However, the taller one has five hierarchical levels and an average span of two, while the flatter one has three levels and an average span of five. Flatter structures tend to push decision-making powers downward in the organization because a given number of decisions are apportioned among fewer levels. Also, flatter structures generally enhance vertical communication and coordination.

Radical differences in organizational height can exist even within industries. For example, at Ford and GM, the number of levels between the chief executive and plant workers varies between 17 and 22. At Toyota, only seven levels intervene.[19] Some analysts have argued that this reduced height is in part responsible for the ability of the Japanese manufacturer to get products to market more quickly. In general, there has been a North American trend toward flatter organizations, especially with downsizing, a topic we'll cover shortly.

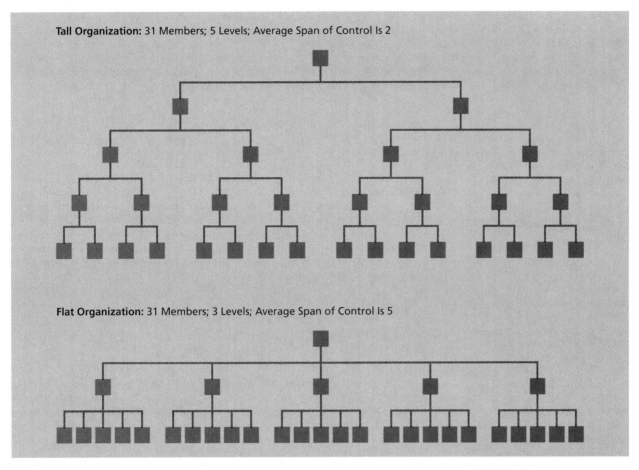

Tall Organization: 31 Members; 5 Levels; Average Span of Control Is 2

Flat Organization: 31 Members; 3 Levels; Average Span of Control Is 5

EXHIBIT 15.8
The relationship between span of control and organizational flatness and tallness.

Formalization

Formalization refers to the extent to which work roles are highly defined by the organization.[20] A very formalized organization tolerates little variability in the way members perform their tasks. Some formalization stems from the nature of the job itself; the work requirements of the assembly line provide a good example of this. More interesting, however, is formalization that stems from rules, regulations, and procedures that the firm or institution chooses to implement. Detailed, written job descriptions, thick procedures manuals, and the requirement to "put everything in writing" are evidence of such formalization. Many government organizations use this method of formalization. So does the fast food chain McDonald's:

> Rules and regulations are the gospel at McDonald's. The company's operating bible has 385 pages describing the most minute activities in each outlet. The manual prescribes that certain equipment—cigarette, candy, and pinball machines—is not permitted in the stores. It also prescribes strict standards for personal grooming. Men must keep their hair short and their shoes black and highly polished. Women are expected to wear hair nets and to use only very light

Formalization. The extent to which work roles are highly defined by an organization.

makeup. The store manager is even provided with a maintenance reminder for each day of the year, such as "Lubricate and adjust potato-peeler belt."[21]

Needless to say, such formalization helps the company to maintain uniform quality standards despite global operations. Sometimes, formalization seems excessive. Perhaps this is why so many fast food employees ignore the hairnet rule. A U.S. Energy Department document detailing how to change a light bulb in a radioactive area is 317 pages long and specifies duties for 43 people.[22]

Centralization

Centralization. The extent to which decision-making power is localized in a particular part of an organization.

Centralization refers to the extent to which decision-making power is localized in a particular part of the organization. In the most centralized organization, the power for all key decisions would rest in a single individual, such as the president. In a more decentralized organization, decision-making power would be dispersed down through the hierarchy and across departments. One observer suggests that limitations to individual brainpower often prompt decentralization:

> How can the Baghdad salesperson explain the nature of his clients to the Birmingham manager? Sometimes the information can be transmitted to one center, but a lack of cognitive capacity (brainpower) precludes it from being comprehended there. How can the president of the conglomerate corporation possibly learn about, say, 100 different product lines? Even if a report could be written on each, he would lack the time to study them all.[23]

Of course, the information-processing capacity of executives is not the only factor that dictates degree of centralization. Some organizations consciously pursue a more participative climate through decentralization. Bill Gore thought this way very explicitly. In others, top management might wish to maintain greater control and opt for stronger centralization. One of Ray Kroc's innovations was not to permit *regional* franchises that could grow powerful and challenge the firm's basic principles.[24] The successful North Carolina-based supermarket chain Food Lion has generally decentralized with growth, giving local managers more autonomy in order to stay close to customers and cater to regional differences. However, the buying function and store design and construction have remained centralized to maintain efficiency and contain costs. Also, the lighting of all 1,041 stores in 14 states is centralized with computer control.[25]

At Food Lion, buying is centralized, but local managers have autonomy to stay close to customers.

Hewlett-Packard, producer of computers, printers, and interactive video, has long relied on the merits of decentralization to foster high tech innovation and creativity:

> H-P executives have an enviable degree of freedom. For one thing, they are authorized to reinvest the capital their businesses generate. They can attack markets in their own ways, rather than slavishly wait for orders that reduce them to just one part of a grand corporate strategy. Says video products general manager [Jim] Olson: "We don't feel an allegiance to any other part of H-P. We feel an allegiance to the customer."[26]

IN FOCUS · · · · **KFC, Levi Strauss Centralize Some Activities**

If decentralized management is increasingly popular among corporations, it also has its dark side. Consider this cautionary tale: KFC envisioned tastier food and happier customers when it kicked off a quality-improvement drive for its 2,000 company-owned restaurants two years ago. Instead, it got a bureaucratic mess—including three different plans to improve service nationwide. The chain's autonomous regional divisions failed to coordinate their efforts. "There was so much redundancy [that] the process became dysfunctional," says Edward A. Meagher III, a vice president of the PepsiCo Inc. unit.

Facing the same problem, a growing number of U.S. companies are now reasserting central authority over a range of corporate activities. To be sure, getting "close to the customer" by shifting power away from headquarters is an idea that continues to gain popularity in many companies, including multinationals that are transferring global business units abroad. But numerous companies find that increased autonomy can create "a different set of problems," says Bill Eaton, a senior vice president and chief information officer of Levi Strauss & Co. Mr. Eaton is now replacing six separate order-processing computer systems with one system under centralized control. The systems resulted from the clothing maker's creation of separate business units around different product lines in the early 1980s. Levi Strauss reversed that move partly because many retailers complained that they had to deal with a plethora of different divisions—each with its own procedures—to buy the company's goods, Mr. Eaton says.

KFC is trying to better orchestrate and control its divisions' joint projects. Division executives began working more closely this past spring and now contribute delegates to teams from several divisions. "Projects are coming to conclusion faster. There's better communication, expectations are more realistic and we're saving money," Mr. Meagher says.

Companies still want to decentralize operations closest to customers—those actually making and

KFC found that the increased centralization of some functions improved coordination and customer service.

marketing products—because they "realize they must be more nimble in the marketplace," says Jim Down, who directs the Boston office of Mercer Management Consulting Inc. But at the same time, companies are consolidating less visible internal functions such as personnel, "where there can be massive economies of scale," says John J. Parkington, who heads organizational research for consultants Wyatt Co. in New York.

Source: Excerpted from Fuchsberg, G. (1992, December 9). Decentralized Management can have its drawbacks. *The Wall Street Journal*, pp. B1, B8.

As you can see in the "In Focus: *KFC, Levi Strauss Centralize Some Activities*," degree of centralization should put decision-making power where the best *knowledge* is located. Often, this means decentralizing functions with direct customer contact, while centralizing functions that have a more internal orientation (e.g., MIS).

Complexity

Complexity refers to the extent to which organizations divide labor vertically, horizontally, and geographically.[27] A fairly simple organization will have few management levels (vertical division) and not many separate job

Complexity. The extent to which an organization divides labor vertically, horizontally, and geographically.

titles (horizontal division). In addition, jobs will be grouped into a small number of departments, and work will be performed in only one physical location (geographic division). At the other extreme, a very complex organization will be tall, will have a large number of job titles and departments, and might be spread around the world. The essential characteristic of complexity is *variety*—as the organization becomes more complex, it has more kinds of people performing more kinds of tasks in more places, whether these places are departments or geographic territories.

EMPLOYEE REACTIONS TO STRUCTURAL CHARACTERISTICS

What are the implications of structural characteristics for the job satisfaction of employees? The research literature provides us with some answers to this important question.[28]

There is no simple association between tallness or flatness and job satisfaction. Managers in organizations with fewer than 5,000 employees seem to exhibit more job satisfaction when they operate under flatter structures. Those in organizations with over 5,000 employees seem happier with taller structures.[29] We have noted that larger organizations tend to be taller. This suggests that exceptions to the general rule (i.e., small, tall organizations and large, flat organizations) prompt dissatisfaction. In the former, managers might have few opportunities for decision making. In the latter, coordination might be so poor that role ambiguity results.

Formalization often prompts job dissatisfaction, except for individuals who have very strong needs for the security that rules provide.[30] Formalization is a particular problem for boundary role occupants who must deal directly with outsiders.[31] Salespeople, welfare officers, and courthouse desk clerks often find themselves held to rules and red tape that damage their relationships with clients and customers and thus provoke considerable disillusionment.

There is no simple, straightforward relationship between job satisfaction and degree of organizational centralization. This might be because different degrees of centralization are appropriate for different subunits and across various kinds of organizations.

There is very little research on individual reactions to varying spans of control. However, one study of sales representatives found that role ambiguity increased as more reps reported to the same manager.[32] Thus, spans that are too large might contribute to communication and coordination problems. On the other hand, very small spans might reduce employee autonomy and provoke dissatisfaction, especially among well-trained and experienced personnel.

One important mechanism by which structural characteristics influence job satisfaction is job design.[33] We saw earlier that job design is affected by the way labor is divided and coordinated. For example, extreme division of labor might reduce the task variety of individual jobs and prompt dissatisfaction. Similarly, coordination of this divided labor by high formalization might reduce autonomy, again stimulating dissatisfaction. Again, the intimate relationship between structure and job design is highlighted.

SUMMARIZING STRUCTURE—ORGANIC VERSUS MECHANISTIC

Do the various structural characteristics that we have been reviewing have any natural relationship to one another? Is there any way to summarize how they tend to go together?

If you think back to the very first chapter of the book, you will recall how early prescriptions about management tended to stress employee specialization, along with a very high degree of control and coordination. These themes were common to the classical management theorists, Taylor's Scientific Management, and Weber's bureaucracy. On the other hand, you will also recall how the human relations movement detected some of the problems that specialization and control can lead to—boredom, resentment, and low motivation. Consequently, these human relations advocates favored more flexible management systems, open communication, employee participation, and so on (See the "Global Focus: *Bureaucracy, Japanese Style: New United Motor Manufacturing, Inc.*").

In general, the classical theorists tended to favor **mechanistic structures**.[34] As Exhibit 15.9 demonstrates, these structures tend toward tallness, narrow spans, specialization, high centralization, and high formalization. The other structural and personnel aspects in the exhibit complement these basic structural prescriptions. By analogy, the organization is structured as a mechanical device, each part serving a separate function, each part closely coordinated

Mechanistic structures. Organizational structures characterized by tallness, specialization, centralization, and formalization.

Organizational Characteristics	Types of Organization Structure	
Index	**Organic**	**Mechanistic**
Span of control	Wide	Narrow
Number of levels of authority	Few	Many
Ratio of administrative to production personnel	High	Low
Range of time span over which an employee can commit resources	Long	Short
Degree of centralization in decision making	Low	High
Proportion of persons in one unit having opportunity to interact with persons in other units	High	Low
Quantity of formal rules	Low	High
Specificity of job goals	Low	High
Specificity of required activities	Low	High
Content of communications	Advice and information	Instructions and decisions
Range of compensation	Narrow	Wide
Range of skill levels	Narrow	Wide
Knowledge-based authority	High	Low
Position-based authority	Low	High

Source: From Seiler, J. A. (1967). *Systems analysis in organizational behavior.* Homewood, IL: Irwin, p. 168. © Richard D. Irwin, Inc. 1967. This exhibit is an adaptation of one prepared by Paul R. Lawrence and Jay W. Lorsch in an unpublished "Working Paper on Scientific Transfer and Organizational Structure," 1963. The latter, in turn, draws heavily on criteria suggested by W. Evans. "Indices of the Hierarchical Structure of Industrial Organizations," *Management Science,* Vol. IX (1963), pp. 468–77, Burns and Stalker, *op. cit.,* and Woodward, *op. cit.,* as well as those suggested by R. H. Hall, "Intraorganizational Structure Variables," *Administrative Science Quarterly,* Vol. IX (1962), pp. 295–308.

EXHIBIT 15.9
Mechanistic and organic structures.

GLOBAL FOCUS   Bureaucracy, Japanese Style: New United Motor Manufacturing, Inc.

Highly bureaucratic, regimented work environments have often been criticized as being alienating and demotivating. Paul Adler set out to study an apparent exception to this assumption, New United Motor Manufacturing, Inc. (NUMMI). NUMMI is a joint venture between Toyota and General Motors. Located in Fremont, California, it started operation in 1984 and currently produces the Chevrolet Geo Prizm, Toyota Corolla, and Toyota Tacoma pickup truck. The design and operation of NUMMI are based on the Toyota Production System, a "Japanese management" style developed at Toyota's Takaoka plant in Japan. The majority of NUMMI's unionized workforce was employed at a former GM plant on the same site. This plant had a terrible record for quality, productivity, and labor relations. When closed in 1982, it often suffered from absenteeism rates of more than 20 percent on Mondays and Fridays and had hundreds of unresolved grievances. Shortly after going on line, NUMMI achieved higher productivity than any GM plant. The quality of its production, measured by independent standards, was also remarkably high. And what about the workforce? Absenteeism has averaged about 3 percent, turnover is low, grievances are few, and employees report high satisfaction on company attitude surveys. About 90 percent of the workforce participates in the company suggestion system.

This record is somewhat surprising given the extremely mechanistic design and tight work discipline at NUMMI. The jobs are very regimented, even by assembly line standards. They are very narrow in scope, and most take less than a minute to complete. Gesture-by-gesture standardization is the rule. Formalized procedures exist for ensuring that these work methods are identical across employees and shifts. Job cycle times are very low, although most employees do rotate through two or three jobs on a given day. Penalties for absenteeism are strict.

Adler notes that some critics of Japanese management techniques have cited ultra-Taylorism and "management by stress." Although the jobs at NUMMI are ultra Tayloristic, Adler found little evidence of management by stress. His research found several reasons for NUMMI's success despite its mostly mechanistic structure. For one thing, the job design at the plant is not handed down by an

Using a Japanese style of management, Toyota and General Motors combined their efforts to produce the new Geo Prism.

industrial engineering department, as is typical in most plants. Rather, workers are taught to time their own jobs with stop watches and to compare various procedures in terms of efficiency. In his terms, this is democratic Taylorism rather than despotic Taylorism. If a more efficient process is discovered, it is formalized. Also, management has been effective in instilling a culture that stresses the efficiencies of bureaucracy for manufacturing standardized products while deemphasizing its use as a method of controlling workers. Adler terms the results a "learning bureaucracy," a system in which both employees and managers see the wisdom of continuous improvement and actually have a standardized procedure for achieving it.

Sources: Adler, P. S. (1993). The 'learning bureaucracy': New United Motor Manufacturing, Inc. *Research in Organizational Behavior, 15*, 111–194; Adler, P. S., & Cole, R. E. (1993, Spring). Designed for learning: A tale of two auto plants. *Sloan Management Review*, 85–94.

Organic structures. Organizational structures characterized by flatness, low specialization, low formalization, and decentralization.

with the others. Speaking generally, functional structures tend to be rather mechanistic.

We can contrast mechanistic structures with organic structures. As shown in Exhibit 15.9, **organic structures** tend to favor wider spans, fewer authority levels, less specialization, less formalization, and decentralization. Flexibility and informal communication are favored over rigidity and the strict chain of command. Thus, organic structures are more in line with the dictates of the human relations movement. Speaking generally, the matrix form is organic.

The labels *mechanistic* and *organic* represent theoretical extremes, and structures can and do fall between these extremes. But is one of these structures superior to the other? To answer this, pause for a moment and consider the structures of the two firms we contrasted in the opening vignette. At the restaurant level, McDonald's is structured very mechanistically. This structure makes perfect sense for the rather routine task of delivering basic convenience food to thousands of people every day and doing it with uniform quality and speed. Of course, McDonald's headquarters, which deals with less routine tasks (e.g., product development, strategic planning), would be more organically structured. W.L. Gore & Associates develops and manufactures products that are highly dependent upon fast-changing high technology. Its founder also despised bureaucracy. An organic structure suits Gore perfectly.

In general, more mechanistic structures are called for when an organization's environment is more stable and its technology is more routine. Organic structures tend to work better when the environment is less stable and the technology is less routine. We'll examine these matters in more detail in the next chapter. For now, it is enough to recognize that there is no "one best way" to organize.

NETWORK ORGANIZATIONS

Recent years have seen the advent of new, more organic organizational structures. Global competition and deregulation as well as advances in technology and communications have motivated these structures. Typically, the removal of unnecessary bureaucracy and the decentralization of decision making result in a more adaptable organization. A more extreme example is the increasing existence of network organizations. In a **network organization,** various functions are coordinated as much by market mechanisms as by managers and formal lines of authority.[35] That is, emphasis is placed on who can do what most effectively and economically rather than on fixed ties dictated by an organizational chart. All of the assets necessary to produce a finished product or service are present in the network as a whole, not held in-house by one firm. Ideally, the network members cooperate, share information, and customize their services to meet the needs of the network.

Network organization. Liaisons between specialist organizations that rely strongly on market mechanisms for coordination.

In stable networks, core firms that are departmentized by function, product, or some other factor contract out some functions to favored partners so that they can concentrate on the things that they do best (see the left of Exhibit 15.10). Chrysler, for instance, has its car seats supplied by an upstream firm that also does all of the research associated with seating. Nike, the sports shoe and apparel firm, works closely with manufacturers in Korea, Thailand, and China while concentrating its own efforts on research and development.

The most interesting networks are dynamic ones such as that illustrated in the right portion of Exhibit 15.10. A "broker" firm with a good idea invents a network in which a large amount of the work is done by other network partners who might change over time or projects. Contemporary book

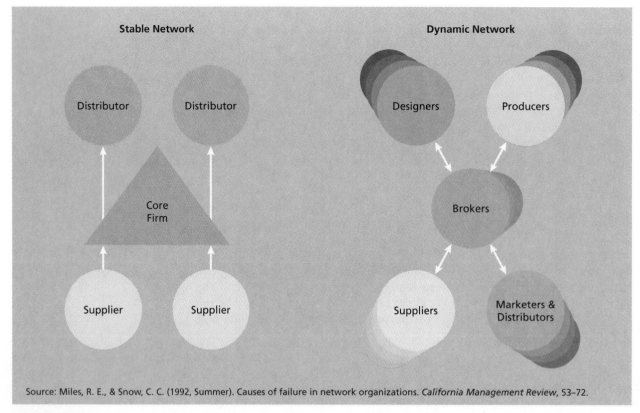

Source: Miles, R. E., & Snow, C. C. (1992, Summer). Causes of failure in network organizations. *California Management Review*, 53–72.

EXHIBIT 15.10
Types of network organizations.

publishers are good examples. These firms do not employ authors, print books, or distribute books. Rather, they specialize in contracting authors for a particular project, providing developmental assistance, and marketing the final product. Printing, distribution, and some editorial and design work are handled by others in the network. Such networks are not new, as they have been used for years in the fashion and film industries. However, more firms in other industries, such as computers and biotechnology, are now adopting network forms.

As indicated, a key advantage of the network form is its flexibility and adaptability. The dynamic network is even more flexible than a matrix. Networks also allow organizations to specialize in what they do best. In its network, Chrysler has intentionally positioned itself as a car manufacturer, not a car seat manufacturer. In turn, its supplier has a strong incentive to specialize in its product because Chrysler is a good, stable customer.

Network organizations face some special problems.[36] Stable networks can deteriorate when the companies dealing with the core firm devote so much of their effort to this firm that they are isolated from normal market demands. This can make them "lazy," resulting in a loss of their technological edge. Dynamic networks lose their organic advantage when they become legalistic, secretive, and too binding of the other partners. The computer industry, including IBM and Apple, is currently experiencing this problem with its network arrangements.

THE IMPACT OF SIZE

It is perhaps trivial to note that the giant General Motors Corporation is structured differently from a small video rental shop. But exactly how does organizational size (measured by number of employees) affect the structure of organizations?[37]

Size and Structure

In general, large organizations are more complex than small organizations.[38] For example, a small organization is unlikely to have its own legal department or market research group, and these tasks will probably be contracted out. Economies of scale enable large organizations to perform these functions themselves but with a consequent increase in the number of departments and job titles. In turn, this horizontal specialization often stimulates the need for additional complexity in the form of appointing integrators or creating planning departments. As horizontal specialization increases, management levels must be added (making the organization taller) so that spans of control do not get out of hand.[39] To repeat, size is associated with increased complexity.

Complexity means coordination problems in spite of integrators, planning departments, and the like. This is where other structural characteristics come into play. In general, bigger organizations are less centralized than smaller organizations.[40] In a small company, the president might be involved in all but the least critical decisions. In a large company, the president would be overloaded with such decisions, and they could not be made in a timely manner. In addition, since the large organization will also be taller, top management is often too far removed from the action to make many operating decisions. How is control retained with decentralization? The answer is formalization—large organizations tend to be more formal than small organizations. Rules, regulations, and standard procedures help to ensure that decentralized decisions fall within accepted bounds. This comparison of a small, independent bank with a larger, more complex bank with several branches illustrates the point nicely:

> Interestingly, the larger bank may be much more decentralized than the small bank. In the small bank, the president may give final approval on all loans simply because time is available to do so. In large banks with many branches no one person can examine all the loan applications, so the decisions are decentralized to officers within the branches. However, this delegation of responsibility is accompanied by *standard procedures* for evaluating loan applications. Decision rules are carefully worked out in advance and communicated downward through policy updates, newsletters, and other formal documents. In this way the large organization can control its lower levels.[41]

Two further points about the relationship between size and structure should be emphasized. First, you will recall that product departmentation is often preferable to functional departmentation as the organization increases in size. Logically, then, organizations with product departmentation should exhibit more complexity and more decentralization than those with functional departmentation. A careful comparison of Exhibits 15.2 and 15.3 will confirm

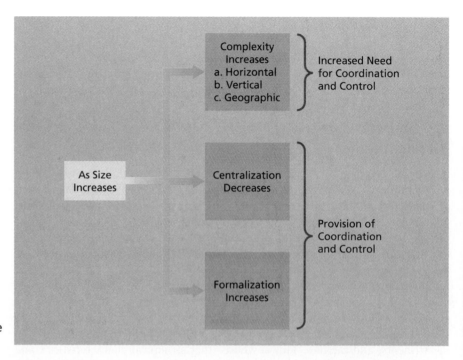

EXHIBIT 15.11
The relationship between size and structure.

this logic. In the firm where the product structure, research, production, and marketing are duplicated, increasing complexity. In addition, since each product line is essentially self-contained, decisions can be made at a lower organizational level.

Finally, we should recognize that size is only one determinant of organizational structure. Even at a given size, organizations might require different structures to be maximally effective. In the next chapter we will examine other determinants of structure, principally environmental pressures and technology.

Exhibit 15.11 summarizes the relationship between size and structural variables.

Downsizing

A reduction in workforce size, popularly called downsizing, has been an organizational trend of the 1980s and 1990s. During this period, millions of jobs have disappeared as organizations seek to bolster efficiency and cut costs in an era of global competition, government deregulation, corporate raiding, changing consumer preferences, and advancing technologies.[42] We have discussed this topic in passing earlier in the book. For example, the "In Focus: *Does Downsizing Decrease Motivation?*" (Chapter 6) considered how poorly-executed downsizing can damage employee motivation. Here, I want to concentrate on some structural aspects of downsizing.

Downsizing. The intentional reduction of workforce size with the goal of improving organizational efficiency or effectiveness.

Downsizing and Structure. **Downsizing** might be formally defined as the intentional reduction in workforce size with the goal of improving organizational efficiency or effectiveness.[43] Notice that this definition does not imply that the organization's fortunes are necessarily in decline, although a shrinking market could motivate downsizing. In fact, Compaq Computer announced substantial downsizing during a year of record revenues and shipments in anticipation of the need to be more competitive in the future.[44]

How should downsizing affect organizational structure? It is tempting to "work backwards" through Exhibit 15.11 and simply say that as size *decreases* the firm should reduce its complexity, centralize, and become less formalized. In the case of a very simple downsizing, this logic might work. However, notice its limitations. First, some of the conditions listed above that often prompt downsizing are *new* conditions, not simply the opposite of the factors that led to organizational growth in the past. For example, deregulation has led to a completely new cast of competitors in the banking and telecommunications industries. Second, the logic of simply working backward through Exhibit 15.11 would assume that downsizing occurs proportionally in all parts of an organization. As you may know, this is not the case recently. White collar managerial and staff jobs have been disproportionately reduced in the most recent downsizing, for reasons varying from high salaries to improvements in information technology. The upshot of all of this is that a new downsized structure should not necessarily look like a mini version of the old structure.

Downsizing can be accomplished in a variety of ways. Although layoffs have been common, some organizations have relied on hiring freezes and natural attrition. In practice, downsizing is often accompanied by reducing horizontal or vertical complexity. Vertically, management levels have been

In the 90s, downsizing has become a popular way of trying to reduce workforce size while improving organizational efficiency. IBM created a downsizing team to achieve these effects.

removed to make organizations flatter. This has sometimes made sense when information technology enables the remaining managers to more effectively monitor the performance of their subordinates. Also, self-managed teams (Chapter 8) can act as substitutes for a level of management. Horizontally, functions can be combined (e.g., inspection and quality) or removed altogether by contracting them out.

Problems with Downsizing. Experience and research indicate that many organizations have not done a good job of anticipating and managing the structural and human consequences of downsizing. For instance, when faced with serious decline, organizations have a decided tendency to become more mechanistic, particularly more formalized and centralized.[45] Rules are closely enforced, and higher levels of management take part in more day-to-day decisions. This can be useful to get the organization back on track, but it can also reduce flexibility just when it is needed. A good rule to follow is to avoid unnecessary formalization or centralization of matters that might have a negative impact on customers or clients. In other words, do not allow internal tightening up to damage external relationships.

One downsizing tactic has been to greatly reduce or even to eliminate whole departments of headquarters advisory staff. For instance, a human resources department might be downsized or the legal department eliminated. Many such staff units have become bloated over the years, and they have been known to isolate top management from divisional concerns and to bureaucratize decision making. Thus, downsizing can provoke decentralization, giving line managers more power and speeding up decisions. On the other hand, some firms have eliminated such positions and then turned around and hired consultants to do the same work. Contracting work out can be a viable strategy, but it is clear that some consulting arrangements have proven more expensive than the original in-house unit.[46] A good rule to follow is to think very carefully about the *work* that needs to be done and *who* should do it before downsizing.

A common structural downsizing error has been to flatten organizations by removing management levels without considering the implications for job design and workload. A glance at Exhibit 15.8 illustrates the crux of the problem: If only the management ranks are thinned, managers have larger spans below them and less support above them. This works well if decentralization is called for and if the people in the lower ranks are ready to assume greater decision-making responsibility. It does not work well if managers are overloaded with work or are incapable of delegating to subordinates. Advanced information technology and training can sometimes assist managers in coping with increased spans of control.

Thinking in advance about the structural aspects of downsizing is not a substitute for involving employees in downsizing plans. Surprising people with workforce cuts is very likely to result in low morale, reduced personal productivity, and continuing distrust of management. Some survivors of downsizing have even reported being guilty because they retained their jobs.[47]

In summary, downsizing has the potential to improve organizational effectiveness in certain circumstances, but its impact on structure and morale must be anticipated and managed.

A FOOTNOTE: SYMPTOMS OF STRUCTURAL PROBLEMS

At the beginning of the chapter, I observed that it is sometimes difficult to appreciate the impact of organizational structure on the behavior that occurs in organizations. Now that you have been through the basics of structure, your appreciation of this impact should be much improved. Let's conclude the chapter by considering some symptoms of structural problems in organizations.

- *Bad job design.* As we noted at several points, there is a reciprocal relationship between job design and organizational structure. Frequently, improper structural arrangements turn good jobs on paper into poor jobs in practice. A tall structure and narrow span of control in a research and development unit can reduce autonomy and turn exciting jobs into drudgery. An extremely large span of control can overload the most dedicated supervisor.

- *The right hand doesn't know what the left is doing.* If repeated examples of duplication of effort occur, or if parts of the organization work at cross-purposes, structure is suspect. One author gives the example of one division of a large organization laying off workers while another division was busy recruiting from the same labor pool![48] The general problem here is one of coordination and integration.

- *Persistent conflict between departments.* Managers are often inclined to attribute such conflicts to personality clashes between key personnel in the warring departments. Just as often, a failure of integration is the problem. One clue here is whether the conflict persists even when personnel changes occur.

- *Slow response times.* Ideally, labor is divided and coordinated to do business quickly. Delayed responses might be due to improper structure. Centralization might speed responses when a few decisions about a few products are required (dictating functional departmentation). Decentralization might speed responses when many decisions about many products are required (dictating product departmentation).

- *Decisions made with incomplete information.* In Chapter 12 we noted that managers generally acquire more than enough information to make decisions. After the fact, if we find that decisions have been made with incomplete information, and the information existed somewhere in the organization, structure could be at fault. It is clear that structural deficiencies were in part responsible for keeping top NASA administrators unaware of the mechanical problems that contributed to the explosion of the space shuttle *Challenger*.[49] This information was known to NASA personnel, but it did not move up the hierarchy properly.

- *A proliferation of committees.* Committees exist in all organizations, and they often serve as one of the more routine kinds of integrating mechanisms. However, when committee is piled upon committee, or when task forces are being formed with great regularity, it is often a sign that the basic structure of the organization is being "patched up" because it doesn't work well.[50] A structural review might be in order if too many people are spending too much time in committee meetings.

The Manager's Notebook   Sweden's Karolinska Hospital

The structural and coordination innovations at Karolinska Hospital were responsible for reducing the waiting time for surgery from seven months to three weeks. Twenty-five percent more operations were performed with fewer active operating theatres.

1. Because of the high degree of required training and education, it is extremely common to view medical work in terms of discrete specializations. However Jan Lindsten reorganized the work at the hospital around patient flow—the process that individual patients required to go from ill health to wellness. This viewpoint adds customer oriented dimensions to a strict functional structure. The point is to avoid costly inefficiencies associated with patients having to make several all-day visits for several tests, for example.

2. To reduce waiting time and enhance coordination, specialists in internal medicine and surgery now meet together with patients rather than in separate consultations. Thus, teams are used as a coordination mechanism. A new position of "nurse coordinator" was established to integrate between functions and minimize the number of visits required of patients.

EXECUTIVE SUMMARY

◆ Organizational structure is the manner in which an organization divides its labor into specific tasks and achieves coordination among these tasks. Labor is divided vertically and horizontally. Vertical division of labor concerns the apportioning of authority. Horizontal division of labor involves designing jobs and grouping them into departments. While functional departmentation locates employees with similar skills in the same department, other forms of departmentation locate employees in accordance with product, geography, or customer requirements.

◆ Basic methods of coordinating divided labor include direct supervision, standardization of work processes, standardization of outputs, standardization of skills, and mutual adjustment. Workers are permitted more discretion as coordination moves from direct supervision through mutual adjustment. More elaborate methods of coordination are aimed specifically at achieving integration across departments. These include liaison roles, task forces, teams, and integrators.

◆ Traditional structural characteristics include span of control, flatness versus tallness, formalization, centralization, and complexity. Larger organizations tend to be more complex, more formal, and less centralized than smaller organizations.

◆ The classical organizational theorists tended to favor mechanistic organizational structures (small spans, tall, formalized, and fairly centralized). The human relations theorists, having noted the flaws of bureaucracy, tended to favor organic structures (larger spans, flat, less formalized, and less centralized). However, there is no one best way to organize, and both mechanistic and organic structures have their places.

◆ As organizations grow in size they tend to become more complex (vertically, horizontally, geographically), more formalized, and less centralized.

◆ Downsizing is the intentional reduction in workforce size with the goals of improving organizational efficiency or effectiveness. Sensible downsizing avoids mechanistic tendencies, retains necessary personnel, and respects good job design principles.

◆ Symptoms of structural problems include poor job design, extreme duplication of effort, conflict between departments, slow responses, too many committees, and decisions made with incomplete information.

KEY CONCEPTS

Organizational structure	Integrators
Differentiation	Span of control
Functional departmentation	Flat organization
Product departmentation	Tall organization
Matrix departmentation	Formalization
Geographic departmentation	Centralization
Customer departmentation	Complexity
Hybrid departmentation	Mechanistic structures
Coordination	Organic structures
Integration	Network organization
Liaison role	Downsizing
Task forces	

DISCUSSION QUESTIONS

1. Discuss the division of labor in a college class-room. What methods are used to coordinate this divided labor? Do differences exist between very small and very large classes?

2. Is the departmentation in a small college essentially functional or product-oriented? Defend your answer. (*Hint:* In what department will the historians find themselves? In what department will the groundskeepers find themselves?)

3. Which basic method(s) of coordination is (are) most likely to be found in a pure research laboratory? On a football team? In a supermarket?

4. What are the relative merits of mechanistic versus organic structures?

5. Discuss the logic behind the following statement: "We don't want to remove the differentiation that exists between sales and production. What we want to do is achieve integration."

6. As Spinelli Construction Company grew in size, its founder and president, Joe Spinelli, found that he was overloaded with decisions. What two basic structural changes should Spinelli make to rectify this situation without losing control of the company?

7. Describe a situation in which a narrow span of control might be appropriate and contrast it with a situation in which a broad span might be appropriate.

8. Make up a list of criteria that would define a good downsizing effort.

EXPERIENTIAL EXERCISE
WATERMARK CARDS

In this activity, class members form miniature organizations, to see whether one or another type of structure works best.

Step 1: Form groups of six to eight; the groups should be of equal size.

Step 2: Half of the groups read the instructions headed "Watermark Cards: Eastern Region" while the other half read the instructions labeled "Watermark Cards: Western Region."

Step 3: The instructor randomly selects one person in each group to be Regional Executive. Regional Executives are charged with carrying out the organizing guidelines given in their instructions. Allow about five minutes for this.

Step 4: There will be at least three ten-minute production periods. The instructor acts as the CEO of Watermark Cards, at its national headquarters, and provides work requirements to Regional Executives as well as keeping track of time.

Step 5: The first ten-minute work round begins. The CEO should make sure that everyone hears the two-minute signal that the round is about to end. When the round is over, the CEO briefly confers with the Regional Executives, meeting first with all Western Region Executives and then, separately, with all Eastern Region Executives.

Step 6: Begin the second work round, repeating the instructions in Step 5.

Step 7: Begin the third work round, repeating the instructions in Step 5.

Step 8: Announce that the activity is over. Each organization is to record on flip chart or newsprint its production record for each round.

Step 9: Everyone moves around the room for a few minutes, to look over the various production records.

Step 10: The entire group reassembles to review the exercise and discuss the results. Some relevant questions include:

• Was one or the other region consistently more productive? If so, why?
• Did the Western and Eastern Regional organizations face different problems? In what ways?
• Which organization—Eastern Region or Western Region—usually had more satisfied employees? Why?

JOB DEFINITIONS AND TASK ACTIVITIES

The raw materials used by the firm are blank sheets of 8½" × 11" paper, and blue-or black-ink pens. *Materials preparation* consists of cutting the raw material (the 8½" × 11" paper) precisely in half, and lightly folding each half to form a standard size greeting card blank.

Creative verse writers prepare the verses that the calligraphers copy onto the card blanks. Verses are always two line, and rhyme. Every verse is different; no duplications are permissible.

Calligraphers transcribe the verses onto the inside right-hand pages of the card blanks. On the outside card blank cover, they print the occasion definition in block letters ("HAPPY BIRTHDAY" for a general purpose birthday card, for instance). Inside lettering may be done in print or script, but must be of highest quality, that is neat and unsmeared, centered, and straight. Cards with defective calligraphy will be rejected.

The final prep task consists of checking the rhyme for rhythm and to make sure it matches the occasion definition, checking the calligraphy for neatness, etc., writing "REJECT" on the cover of cards that do not meet the standards and setting them aside, and folding and sorting by occasion those cards accepted. (If an unacceptable card is not rejected but is identified later by headquarters inspectors, a penalty will be assessed to the region by headquarters.)

QUARTERLY PLAN

The CEO informs Regional Executives of the product mix for each quarter. The first quarter, for example, contains one major occasion—Valentine's Day—and a substantial proportion of cards produced during this quarter will be valentines. The second and subsequent quarters' production plans will be based on information provided by the CEO after the close of the preceding quarter.

WATERMARK CARDS: WESTERN REGION

Watermark Cards, Inc., is one of the world's largest producers of greeting cards of all kinds. Operations are divided into several regions, with each region operating relatively autonomously. Regional Executives are fully responsible for setting up their own organizations, and are accountable to headquarters only with regard to the quarterly plan, specifying the types of cards to be produced in the coming quarter (that is, so many percent will be Father's Day cards in the second quarter, so many percent will be Christmas cards in the fourth quarter, and so on).

The Regional Executive has set up the organization as product teams. That is, each team is responsible for producing one or two types of card, from the preparation of materials, development of verses, and calligraphy to the sorting and folding of products in preparation for shipping.

If organization size is six, there will be two teams of two and a Teams Manager, in addition to the Regional Executive.

If organization size is seven there will be three teams of two or two teams of three (the Regional Executive is to decide) and the Regional Executive.

If the organization size is eight, there will be three teams of two or two teams of three, a Teams Manager, and the Regional Executive (the Regional Executive determines team size).

WATERMARK CARDS: EASTERN REGION

Watermark Cards, Inc., is one of the world's largest producers of greeting cards of all kinds. Operations are divided into several regions, with each region operating relatively autonomously. Regional Executives are fully responsible for setting up their own organizations, and are accountable to headquarters only with regard to the quarterly plan, specifying the types of cards to be produced in the coming quarter (that is, so many percent will be Father's Day cards in the second quarter, so many percent will be Christmas cards in the fourth quarter, and so on).

The Regional Executive has set up the organization in terms of functional departments. There is a materials preparation department, a creative verse department that makes up the verses that go on the cards, a calligraphy department that writes verses onto blank cards, and a final prep/shipping department.

If the organization size is six, two persons will be in the calligraphy department, one in the creative verse department, and one will handle both the materials preparation department and will also receive the products from the calligraphy department for final prep/shipping. One person will be Operations Manager and the remaining person is, of course, the Regional Executive.

If the organization size is seven, two persons will be in the calligraphy department, one in the creative verse department, one in the materials prep department, and one in the final prep/shipping department. One person will be Operations Manager and report to the Regional Executive.

If the organization size is eight, two persons will be in the calligraphy department, two in the creative verse department, one in materials prep, and one final prep/shipping. One person will be Operations Manager and report to the Regional Executive.

CASE STUDY
NATIONAL BUSINESS MACHINES

National Business Machines branch office number 120 is a marketing and service organization consisting of nearly 200 employees. The data-processing division is divided into four sections: two marketing units and two systems engineering units. This arrangement is depicted in Case Exhibit 15.1.

The two marketing units sell new hardware. Each marketing unit has ten salespersons. The two systems engineering (SE) units provide technical assistance to the marketing units. They help in selecting hardware, systems design, computer programming, operator training, installed systems review, computer application development, and many other functions associated with selling and installing computer systems. Each SE unit has ten systems engineers.

The SE units are independent of each other. One unit supports marketing unit A, and the other unit supports marketing unit B.

Systems engineering includes three types of skills and knowledge: those associated with small, medium, and large computer systems. Small systems are usually purchased by the brand-new data-processing user getting first exposure to the world of automation. Systems engineers in this area must of course be skilled systems analysts and programmers, but they must also be educators and psychologists. New data-processing users know only as much about the machines as the marketing representatives have told them. They are often unsure about whether they can deal with the machines. The small-system SE's must expand their knowledge and help them build confidence.

The medium-system SE works with a larger, higher-priced machine that has probably been installed for a few years. Users have their own data-processing staffs. Instead of being concerned with programming and operator training, the medium-system SE spends time looking for more advanced applications, such as installing terminals in different user departments.

The large-system SE deals with sophisticated data-processing installations. Large-system users are data-processing professionals with high standards, internal education programs and staffs of 50 or more.

The small-system SE may be working on five or six accounts per day, while the large-system SE may spend a week at one location.

In NBM branch office number 120, both SE units have systems engineers of all three types. This organizational structure has several advantages, but it also causes several problems.

The first problem occurs because the three data-processing system types—small, medium, and large—represent

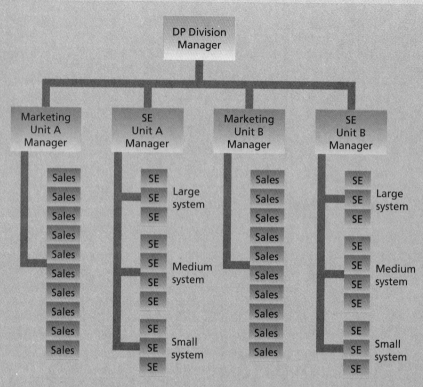

CASE EXHIBIT 15.1
Organization Chart for
National Business Machines.

Source: Ford, R. C., Armandi, B. R., & Heaton, C. P. (1988). *Organization theory: An integrative approach.* Copyright © 1988 by Harper & Row, Publishers, Inc. Reprinted by permission of HarperCollins Inc.

three quite different technologies. The effective SE manager must be well versed in the latest trends of three separate disciplines. Both SE managers do a good job, but communications problems sometimes arise because they do not have experience in working on data-processing systems of all three kinds.

For example, both current SE managers have backgrounds in medium and large systems. The common misconception is that they should thoroughly understand small computer installations because small systems must be easier to install than large systems. However, in addition to designing the system and writing the programs, the small-system SE performs tasks that the SE's working on medium and large systems never perform. The small-system SE has to explain why the new user must spell the customer's name in exactly the same way every time, or why a diskette created on one type of personal computer cannot be compatible with another. Mistakes in these details can cause unbelievable delays in an installation and can be very difficult to locate.

Another problem is the division's sales quota. Since NBM makes more money when installing large machines,

the manager naturally meets the quota faster by installing large machines. Of course, everyone realizes the advantages of selling small machines to many customers in the expectation that they will later graduate to medium and large machines. However, the short-run emphasis always seems to be on the large systems.

This situation causes a morale problem among the small-system SE's. They see the large-system people getting the bonuses and the recognition at branch office meetings. The small-system SE's also think that their compensation is not proportionate to the compensation of the large-system SE's. Actually, most large-system SE's have worked longer for NBM and have developed more skills, so their average compensation is justifiably higher. However, the small-system SE's tend to overlook this fact.

Having two SE managers each control three SE classifications may be inherently inefficient. For instance, imagine this situation. Manager A needs a small-system SE and does not have one available. Manager B has an available SE with the proper talents. Manager A asks to borrow the SE. If manager B allows the borrowing, the borrowed SE may be needed by manager B but unavailable the very next day. On the other hand, NBM is a service organization, so manager B probably allows manager A to borrow the SE.

Consider the borrowed SE. Once assigned to the project, the SE will probably have to stay with it until it is finished, even if an SE from unit A becomes available. Once the borrowed SE gets to know the people and situation at the new installation and begins to design systems and develop programs, manager B will be reluctant to make a change. So the borrowed SE will be working for a manager who does not appraise performance or make salary recommendations. The borrowed SE may work 60 to 80 hours a week on a crash project, and manager B may never hear about it.

Source: Ford, R. C., Armandi, B. R., & Heaton, C. P. (1988). *Organization theory: An integrative approach*. Copyright 1988 by Harper & Row, Publishers, Inc. Reprinted by permission of HarperCollins Inc.

1. Noting that the case involves only the data-processing division of one branch of National Business Machines, speculate about the structure of the firm as a whole. Use concepts such as complexity, centralization, and formalization. What form of departmentation does the firm as a whole likely rely upon?

2. What form of departmentation is seen in NBM branch 120? Discuss the advantages and disadvantages of this form of departmentation with reference to the issues mentioned in the case.

3. Use the concepts of differentiation and integration to analyze the events in branch 120.

4. Suggest at least one structural alternative to that currently seen in branch 120. Explain how this alternative will deal with the problems cited in the case. Does the alternative design have any potential problems?

AFTER READING CHAPTER 16 YOU SHOULD BE ABLE TO:

1 DISCUSS THE COMPONENTS OF AN ORGANIZATION'S EXTERNAL ENVIRONMENT.

2 EXPLAIN HOW ENVIRONMENTAL UNCERTAINTY AND RESOURCE DEPENDENCE AFFECT WHAT HAPPENS IN ORGANIZATIONS.

3 UNDERSTAND HOW ORGANIZATIONAL STRUCTURE CAN SERVE AS A STRATEGIC RESPONSE TO ENVIRONMENTAL DEMANDS.

4 EXPLAIN HOW VERTICAL INTEGRATION, MERGERS, ACQUISITIONS, STRATEGIC ALLIANCES, INTERLOCKING DIRECTORATES, AND THE ESTABLISHMENT OF LEGITIMACY REFLECT STRATEGIC RESPONSES.

5 DESCRIBE THE BASIC DIMENSIONS OF ORGANIZATIONAL TECHNOLOGY.

6 EXPLAIN HOW ORGANIZATIONS MUST MATCH ORGANIZATIONAL STRUCTURE TO TECHNOLOGY.

7 DISCUSS THE IMPACT OF ADVANCED INFORMATION TECHNOLOGY ON JOB DESIGN AND ORGANIZATIONAL STRUCTURE.

GENERAL MOTORS' SUCCESSFUL SATURN LINE WAS CONCEIVED AS A TOTALLY NEW CORPORATION WITH INNOVATIONS IN AUTOMOBILE DESIGN, MANUFACTURING, AND MARKETING.

CHAPTER 16

ENVIRONMENT, STRATEGY, AND TECHNOLOGY

Saturn was conceived as a totally new corporation, a wholly owned General Motors subsidiary that delivered its first cars in fall 1990. The formerly autonomous division, headquartered in Spring Hill, Tennessee, has its own sales and service operations.

At the time, why did GM decide to separate Saturn so decisively from the existing corporate structure, rather than just add yet another product line to its Chevrolet, Oldsmobile, Pontiac, Buick, and Cadillac lines? General Motors insiders and auto industry analysts cited two primary reasons. First, GM badly needed to find ways to cut costs to compete in the small car market, in which estimates suggested that Japanese manufacturers enjoyed a great cost advantage. Second, top GM executives hoped to use the Saturn venture as a testing ground for innovations that could be applied throughout the rest of the organization, especially ones that could get new models to the market more quickly. To accomplish both of these goals, the freedom of a completely "fresh start" and the protection autonomy offered seemed to be essential.

With the exception of the use of plastic for all vertical body parts, Saturn cars do not represent a radical technical departure for GM. Rather, it is the way in which the cars are designed, built, and marketed that is innovative. Even at the early design stages, representatives from engineering, manufacturing, and marketing work together to ensure early coordination of efforts. Extensively trained self-managed work teams assemble the cars, maintain their own equipment, order supplies, set work schedules, and even select new team members. To control quality and reduce transport costs, much subassembly is done by suppliers that are located close to the plant or even within the plant itself, thus fostering a close cooperative arrangement. Parts that do come in from the outside are delivered precisely when they are needed and directly to the location where they are used in assembly. In the marketing domain, dealers are given more exclusive territories than is typical of North American auto manufacturers. As long as they meet stiff requirements in several key areas, they are given substantial autonomy to tailor their operations to local needs.

These changes in design procedure, manufacturing, and marketing are supported by a number of departures from conventional structure, management style, and labor relations practices. Saturn has a flatter management structure than the traditional GM divisions. A computerized "paperless" operation of electronic mail and a single, highly integrated database speed decisions and counter bureaucracy. Finally, GM agreed to a truly ground-breaking labor contract with the United Auto Workers. There are no time clocks, and workers are on salaries, although these salaries average only 80 percent of industry hourly wages. In addition, restrictive work rules were eliminated to support the team assembly concept. In exchange for these concessions, GM devotes 20 percent of the industry hourly wage to performance incentives and a profit-sharing plan for Saturn workers. Also, 80 percent of the workforce is granted what amounts to lifetime employment security. Union representatives sit on all planning and organizing committees.

The Saturn project is not as radical as it was planned to be. The company rejected initial ideas for more extensive use of computers and robotics in assembly on the basis of experiences in some other GM plants. Instead, GM placed even more emphasis on developing a motivated workforce. Also, Saturn's initial marketing scheme called for showrooms in malls, dealers without inventories, computerized ordering, and so on. Some of these plans were downscaled in part because of stringent state regulations about the permitted configuration of car dealerships.

Has Saturn fulfilled the promise of its multibillion dollar investment? Early cars suffered from quality glitches that the company attended to quickly, even replacing some faulty cars for free. As a result of such tactics and extremely cooperative dealers (many of whom organize customer picnics and car clinics), Saturn customer satisfaction ratings are close to those for luxury Japanese and German cars. This intense customer loyalty resulted in Saturn turning a profit three years after the first car rolled off the assembly line.

On the other side of the coin, some observers have been dismayed by the slow pace with which other parts of GM have embraced Saturn innovations. The United Auto Workers have already given notice that they will resist

Saturn-type labor agreements at any other manufacturing sites. Saturn has been slow to develop new models, and competitors are beginning to outpace the company in terms of technical refinement and safety, even copying some of its "buyer friendly" sales techniques. Although Saturn buyers have good demographics in terms of income and education, the company has no larger sedans, minivans, or sports utility vehicles to offer them. Gaining investment funds for such projects from GM has been difficult because the parent firm has been busy recentralizing much vehicle development and engineering. In fall 1994, GM announced its fourth reorganization in 10 years. Saturn lost its distinctive status as an autonomous unit, becoming part of the GM Small Car Group. Industry observers wonder if Saturn can continue to innovate under this structure.[1]

■

The Saturn story illustrates some of the major questions that we will consider in this chapter. How does the external environment influence organizations? How can an organization develop a strategy to cope with this environment? And how can technology and other factors be used to implement strategy? In the previous chapter we concluded that there is no one best way to design an organization. In this chapter we will see that the proper organizational structure is contingent on environmental, strategic, and technological factors.

THE EXTERNAL ENVIRONMENT OF ORGANIZATIONS

In previous chapters we have been concerned primarily with the internal environments of organizations—those events and conditions inside the organization—that affect the attitudes and behaviors of members. In this section we turn our interest to the impact of the **external environment**—those events and conditions surrounding the organization that influence its activities.

There is ample evidence in everyday life that the external environment has tremendous influence on organizations. The OPEC oil embargo of 1973 and subsequent oil price increases shook North American automobile manufacturers to their foundations. Faced with gasoline shortages, increasing gasoline prices, and rising interest rates, consumers postponed automobile purchases or shifted to more economical foreign vehicles. As a consequence, workers were laid off, plants were closed, and dealerships failed, while the manufacturers scrambled to develop more fuel-efficient smaller cars. The emphasis of advertising strategies changed from styling and comfort to economy and value. Significant portions of the manufacturers' environment (Middle East oil suppliers, American consumers, and Japanese competitors) prompted this radical regrouping.

Environmental conditions change, and by the mid-1980s an international oil surplus pushed gasoline prices down. Consumers responded with increased interest in size, styling, and performance. Auto industry analysts noted that some manufacturers responded to this shift faster than others. Chrysler, trimmed of bureaucracy by its near demise several years earlier, responded quickly and scored a number of marketing coups. General Motors responded less quickly, and the Saturn project was an attempt to enable the company to respond more quickly to environmental trends.

External environment. Events and conditions surrounding an organization that influence its activities.

In the 1990s, the auto industry faces accelerated global competition, especially to supply the increasing middle class in developing countries. Joint ventures between companies are common. California's legislation requiring zero exhaust emissions from a portion of each manufacturer's cars has prompted experimentation with electric vehicles. As always, the external environment profoundly shapes organizational behavior.

Organizations as Open Systems

Open systems. Systems that take inputs from the external environment, transform some of them, and send them back into the environment as outputs.

Organizations can be described as open systems. **Open systems** are systems that take inputs from the external environment, transform some of these inputs, and send them back into the external environment as outputs (Exhibit 16.1).[2] Inputs include capital, energy, materials, information, technology, and people; outputs include various products and services. Some inputs are transformed (e.g., raw materials), while other inputs (e.g., skilled craftspeople) assist in the transformation process. Transformation processes may be physical (e.g., manufacturing or surgery), intellectual (e.g., teaching or programming), or even emotional (e.g., psychotherapy). For example, an insurance company imports actuarial experts, information about accidents and mortality, and capital in the form of insurance premiums. Through the application of financial knowledge, it transforms the capital into insurance coverage and investments in areas such as real estate. Universities import seasoned scholars and aspiring students from the environment. Through the teaching process, educated individuals are returned to the community as outputs.

The value of the open systems concept is that it sensitizes us to the need for organizations to cope with the demands of the environment on both the input side and the output side. As we will see, some of this coping involves adaptation to environmental demands. On the other hand, some coping may be oriented toward changing the environment.

First, let's examine the external environment in greater detail.

Components of the External Environment

The external environment of any given organization is obviously a "big" concept. Technically, it involves any person, group, event, or condition outside the direct domain of the organization. For this reason it is useful to divide the environment into a manageable number of components.[3]

The General Economy.   Organizations that survive through selling products or services often suffer from an economic downturn and profit by an upturn. When a downturn occurs, competition for remaining customers increases, and organizations might postpone needed capital improvements. Of course, some organizations thrive under a poor economy, including welfare offices and law firms that deal heavily in bankruptcies. In addition, if a poor economy is accompanied by high unemployment, some organizations might find it opportune to upgrade the quality of their staffs, since they will have an ample selection of candidates.

We see a clear example of the impact of the general economy in the most recent recession. Faced with falling orders (reduced inputs), thousands of organizations engaged in radical downsizing as a means of cutting costs.

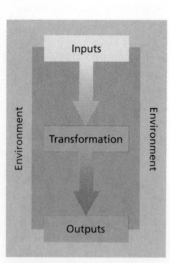

EXHIBIT 16.1
The organization as an open system.

Customers. All organizations have potential customers for their products and services. Piano makers have musicians, and consumer activist associations have disgruntled consumers. The customers of universities include not only students, but also the firms that employ their graduates and seek their research assistance. Organizations must be sensitive to changes in customer demands. For example, the small liberal arts college that resists developing a business school might be faced with declining enrollment.

Successful firms are generally highly sensitive to customer reactions. L'Oréal, the world's largest producer of cosmetics, announced that it would no longer test its products on animals in response to customer demand. Taco Bell moved to a nonsmoking environment in its company-owned restaurants as a result of a year long survey that showed that the majority of both smokers and nonsmokers preferred a smoke-free environment in restaurants.

Suppliers. Organizations are dependent on the environment for supplies that include labor, raw materials, equipment, and component parts. Shortages can cause severe difficulties. For instance, the lack of a local technical school might prove troublesome for an electronics firm that requires skilled labor. Similarly, a strike by a company that supplies component parts might cause the purchaser to shut down its assembly line.

As alluded to earlier in the text, many contemporary firms have changed their strategy for dealing with suppliers. It used to be standard practice to have many of them and to keep them in stiff competition for one's business, mainly by extracting the lowest price. Now, more exclusive relationships with suppliers, based on quality and reliable delivery, are becoming more common. Dell Computer reduced its suppliers from 140 to 80 and its freight carriers from 21 to 3.

Competitors. Environmental competitors vie for resources that include both customers and suppliers.[4] Thus, hospitals compete for patients, and consulting firms compete for clients. Similarly, utility companies compete for coal, and professional baseball teams compete for free agent ballplayers. Successful organizations devote considerable energy to monitoring the activities of competitors.

The computer software industry provides an instructive lesson in how competition can change over time. In the early days of software development (not very long ago!) there were a large number of players in the field, and small companies could find a profitable niche. There was plenty of room for many competitors in what was an essentially technology-driven business. However, the growing domination of Microsoft, which slashed prices and consolidated multiple functions in its programs, has prompted a great number of mergers, acquisitions, and failures among firms dealing in basic consumer software such as word processing and spreadsheets.[5]

For another twist on the impact of competitors, see the "In Focus: *Canada Post Uses Training To Stay Competitive*."

Social/Political Factors. Organizations cannot ignore the social and political events that occur around them. Changes in public attitudes toward ethnic diversity, the proper age for retirement, or the proper role of big business will soon affect them. Frequently, these attitudes find expression in law through

IN FOCUS   Canada Post Uses Training To Stay Competitive

Canada Post won't survive the age of electronic mail if the corporation doesn't get faster and cheaper, president Georges Clermont said yesterday.

And the key to survival is whether 58,000 posties across the country can compete with staff at private couriers and telecommunications companies, he said.

SURVIVAL DEPENDS ON FLEXIBILITY

"The hard reality is that Canada Post's long-term survival depends on our ability to change the way we think, the way we act and the way we treat our customers," Clermont said.

Unlike many other Crown corporations, Canada Post has been making profits almost continually since 1988. Yet Clermont said many employees still believe they're working for a company that has a monopoly on mail service in Canada.

"We're facing huge competition in the mail business right now from couriers, faxes, electronic mail and telecommunications companies," Clermont said.

"One could argue that paper mail will eventually be replaced by electronic mail within the next decade or two. Our job as a postal service is to hold off the inevitable as long as possible by being faster and cheaper."

Toward that end, Canada Post announced yesterday it is tripling its investment in staff develop-ment across the country to pump up its customer-service skills. . . . The permanent in-house education program will cost around $56 million to set up. It will increase training investment per employee to $1,000 annually from the current level of $350.

By comparison, communications companies in the United States spend an estimated $1,600 annually on training each employee, while those in Japan spend $4,000 per employee a year.

Clermont said the learning institute will teach supervisors better management skills and offer cus-tomer-relations courses for all employees.

"Canada Post will become a dinosaur if it doesn't boost the efficiency level of its employees," said Jean Guertin, director of the l'École des Hautes Études Commerciales.

THINK LIKE ENTREPRENEURS

"Over the past decade, the corporation has made huge investments in state-of-the-art technology. But it will be dead in 10 years if its employees don't start to think like entrepreneurs rather than gov-ernment employees."

Source: Excerpted from Davidson, J. (1994, June 8). Canada Post returns to school. *The Gazette* (Montreal). p. E3. (Canadian Press).

the political process. Thus, organizations must cope with a series of legal regulations that prescribe fair employment practices, proper competitive activities, product safety, and clients' rights.

One example of the impact of social trends on organizations is Wal-Mart's move to ban handgun sales in its stores. Another is the increasing public interest in environmentalism. Many firms have been fairly proactive in their responses. For example, Pacific Gas & Electric works closely with environmental groups and has a dedicated environmentalist on its board. And McDonald's has become a visible proponent of recycling and an active educator of the public on environmental issues.[6]

An example of the conversion of a social trend into political and governmental action is the deregulation of the U.S. and Canadian airline industries. Part of a general trend to reduce federal regulation of business, this action spurred a long series of market entries, fare wars, route wars, mergers, acquisitions, and bankruptcies. Many a harried airline executive felt the target of the ancient Chinese curse "May you live in interesting times"! A similar trend took place in deregulation of financial services.

Technology. The environment contains a variety of technologies that are useful for achieving organizational goals. As we shall see, technology refers to ways of doing things, not simply to some form of machinery. The ability to adopt the proper technology should enhance an organization's effectiveness. For a business firm this might involve the choice of a proper computer system or production technique. For a mental health clinic it might involve implementing a particular form of psychotherapy that is effective for the kinds of clients serviced.

An example of the impact of technology on organizational life is the advent of computer-aided design (CAD). With CAD, designers, engineers, and draftspeople can produce quick, accurate drawings via computer. They can store databases and run simulations that produce visual records of the reaction of objects to stress, vibration, and design changes. Some firms have found that CAD reduces design lead times and increases productivity. Others have had a difficult time reorganizing to exploit this technology. In general, CAD has broken down the traditional role differences between designers, engineers, and drawing technicians.

Now that we have outlined the basic components of organizational environments, a few more detailed comments are in order. First, this brief list does not provide a perfect picture of the large number of actual interest groups that can exist in an organization's environment. **Interest groups** are parties or organizations other than direct competitors that have some vested interest in how an organization is managed. For example, Exhibit 16.2 shows the interest groups that surround a small private college. As you can see, our list of six

Interest groups. Parties or organizations other than direct competitors that have some vested interest in how an organization is managed.

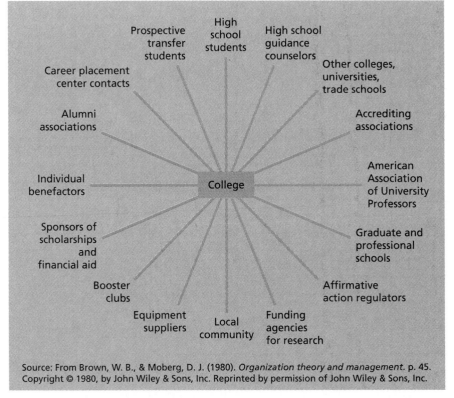

Source: From Brown, W. B., & Moberg, D. J. (1980). *Organization theory and management.* p. 45. Copyright © 1980, by John Wiley & Sons, Inc. Reprinted by permission of John Wiley & Sons, Inc.

EXHIBIT 16.2
Interest groups in the external environment of a small private college.

environmental components actually involves quite an array of individuals and agencies with which the college must contend. To complicate matters, some of these individuals and agencies might make competing or conflicting demands on the college. For instance, booster clubs might press the college to allocate more funds to field a winning football team, while scholarship sponsors might insist that the college match their donations for academic purposes.

Such competition for attention from different segments of the environment is not unusual. While antidrug organizations have sometimes supported the screening of employees for drug use, the American Civil Liberties Union has taken a keen interest in the violation of privacy that such tests can involve. Obviously, different interest groups evaluate organizational effectiveness according to different criteria.[7]

Different parts of the organization will often be concerned with different environmental components. For instance, we can expect a marketing department to be tuned in to customer demands and a legal department to be interested in regulations stemming from the social/political component. As we indicated in the previous chapter, coordination of this natural division of interests is a crucial concern for all organizations. Also, as environmental demands change, it is important that power shifts occur to allow the appropriate functional units to cope with these demands.

Finally, events in various components of the environment provide both constraints and opportunities for organizations. Although environments with many constraints (e.g., high interest rates, strong competition, and so on) appear pretty hostile, an opportunity in one environmental sector might offset a constraint in another. For example, the firm that is faced with a dwindling customer base might find its salvation by exploiting new technologies that give it an edge in costs or new product development.

The Environment of Saturn

Let's return to the story that began the chapter and analyze some of the environmental components that shaped General Motors' plans regarding the Saturn project. A strong impetus for the Saturn venture was the $2,000 cost advantage per small car that Japanese competitors held at the time. However, cost reductions mean little unless the quality of the Saturn automobile is comparable to that of Japanese makes. To enhance quality, GM exercised particular control over parts suppliers, inducing them to locate within or near the plant to facilitate communication with Saturn engineering and manufacturing personnel.

During the recessionary early 1980s, the general economy faltered, and unions lost considerable bargaining power. Union membership fell, and GM capitalized upon changing social attitudes toward unions to forge an innovative contract with the United Auto Workers. However, an interest group, the National Right to Work Legal Defense Foundation, challenged the legality of the contract. This group, which provides legal aid to workers who do not wish to join unions, argued that it was improper for GM to specify the United Auto Workers as a bargaining agent in advance of any workers having been hired.[8] The challenge failed.

Several technological advances were exploited at Saturn, although not as many as GM envisioned at the start of the project. Still, the plastic body parts are innovative, as is a sophisticated paperless database operation.

Finally, GM gambled that it could exploit a segment of customers that would not normally consider a domestic car—dedicated import buyers. It didn't wish to develop a new car only to divert sales from existing GM product lines.

Clearly, Saturn is a product of environmental constraints and opportunities. But exactly how do such constraints and opportunities affect the organization? To answer this question, we turn to the concepts of environmental uncertainty and resource dependence.

Environmental Uncertainty

In our earlier discussion of environmental components we implied that environments have considerable potential for causing confusion among managers. Customers may come and go, suppliers may turn from good to bad, and competitors may make surprising decisions. The resulting uncertainty can be both challenging and frustrating. **Environmental uncertainty** exists when an environment is vague, difficult to diagnose, and unpredictable. We all know that some environments are less certain than others. Your hometown provides you with a fairly certain environment. There, you are familiar with the transportation system, the language, and necessary social conventions. Thrust into the midst of a foreign culture, you encounter a much less certain environment. How to greet a stranger, order a meal, and get around town become significant issues. There is nothing intrinsically bad about this uncertainty. It simply requires you to marshal a particular set of skills in order to be an effective visitor.

Like individuals, organizations can find themselves in more or less certain environments. But just exactly what makes an organizational environment uncertain? Put simply, uncertainty depends upon the environment's *complexity* (simple versus complex) and its *rate of change* (static versus dynamic).[9]

- *Simple environment*. A simple environment involves relatively few factors, and these factors are fairly similar to each other. For example, consider the pottery manufacturer that obtains its raw materials from two small firms and sells its entire output to three small pottery outlets.

- *Complex environment*. A complex environment contains a large number of dissimilar factors that affect the organization. For example, the college in Exhibit 16.2 has a more complex environment than the pottery manufacturer. In turn, the Saturn organization has a more complex environment than the college.

- *Static environment*. The components of this environment remain fairly stable over time. The small-town radio station that plays the same music format, relies on the same advertisers, and works under the same FCC regulations year after year has a stable environment. (Of course, no environment is *completely* static; we are speaking in relative terms here.)

- *Dynamic environment*. The components of a highly dynamic environment are in a constant state of change, which is unpredictable and irregular, not cyclical. For example, consider the firm that designs and manufactures microchips for electronics applications. New scientific and technological advances occur rapidly and unpredictably in this field. In addition, customer demands are highly dynamic as firms devise new uses for microchips. A similar dynamic environment faces Saturn, in part owing to the vagaries of the energy situation and in part owing to the fact that marketing automobiles has become an international rather

Environmental uncertainty. A condition that exists when the external environment is vague, difficult to diagnose, and unpredictable.

than a national business. For example, fluctuations in the relative value of international currencies can radically alter the cost of competing imported cars quite independently of anything Saturn management does.

As we see in Exhibit 16.3, it's possible to arrange rate of change and complexity in a matrix. A simple/static environment (cell 1) should provoke the least uncertainty, while a dynamic/complex environment (cell 4) should provoke the most. Some research suggests that change has more influence than complexity on uncertainty.[10] Thus, we might expect a static/complex environment (cell 2) to be somewhat more certain than a dynamic/simple environment (cell 3).

Earlier, we stated that different portions of the organization are often interested in different components of the environment. To go a step further, it stands to reason that some aspects of the environment are less certain than others. Thus, some subunits might be faced with more uncertainty than others. For example, the research and development department of a microchip company would seem to face a more uncertain environment than the personnel department.

Increasing uncertainty has several predictable effects on organizations and their decision makers.[11] For one thing, as uncertainty increases, cause-and-

Rate of Change	**Complexity** Simple	Complex
Static	CELL 1 *Low Perceived Uncertainty* 1. Small number of factors and components in the environment 2. Factors and components are somewhat similar to one another 3. Factors and components remain basically the same and are not changing	CELL 2 *Moderately Low Perceived Uncertainty* 1. Large number of factors and components in the environment 2. Factors and components are not similar to one another 3. Factors and components remain basically the same
Dynamic	CELL 3 *Moderately High Perceived Uncertainty* 1. Small number of factors and components in the environment 2. Factors and components are somewhat similar to one another 3. Factors and components of the environment are in continual process of change	CELL 4 *High Perceived Uncertainty* 1. Large number of factors and components in the environment 2. Factors and components are not similar to one another 3. Factors and components of environment are in a continual process of change

Source: Duncan, R. B. (1972). Characteristics of organizational environments and perceived environmental uncertainty. Copyright © 1972 by the Administrative Science Quarterly, *17*, 313–327, p. 320. Reprinted by permission.

EXHIBIT 16.3
Environmental uncertainty as a function of complexity and rate of change.

effect relationships become less clear. If we are certain that a key competitor will not match our increased advertising budget, we may be confident that our escalated ad campaign will increase our market share. Uncertainty about the competitor's response reduces confidence in this causal inference. Second, environmental uncertainty tends to make priorities harder to agree upon, and it often stimulates a fair degree of political jockeying within the organization. To continue the example, if the consequences of increased advertising are unclear, other functional units might see the increased budget allocation as being "up for grabs." Finally, as environmental uncertainty increases, more information must be processed by the organization to make adequate decisions. Environmental scanning, boundary spanning, planning, and formal management information systems will become more prominent.[12] This illustrates that organizations will act to cope with or reduce uncertainty because uncertainty increases the difficulty of decision making and thus threatens organizational effectiveness. Shortly, we will examine in greater detail means of managing uncertainty. First we explore another aspect of the impact of the environment on organizations.

Resource Dependence

Earlier, we noted that organizations are open systems that receive inputs from the external environment and transfer outputs into this environment. Many inputs from various components of the environment are valuable resources that are necessary for organizational survival. These include things such as capital, raw materials, and human resources. By the same token, other components of the environment (such as customers) represent valuable resources on the output end of the equation. All of this suggests that organizations are in a state of **resource dependence** with regard to their environments.[13] Carefully managing and coping with this resource dependence is a key to survival and success.

Resource dependence. The dependency of organizations upon environmental inputs such as capital, raw materials, and human resources.

Although all organizations are dependent upon their environments for resources, some organizations are more dependent than others. This is because some environments have a larger amount of readily accessible resources.[14] A classic case of a highly resource dependent organization is a newly formed small business. Cautious bank managers, credit-wary suppliers, and a dearth of customers all teach the aspiring owner the meaning of dependence. Also, many organizations in traditional "smokestack" industries encounter a much less munificent environment. Investors are wary, customers are disappearing, and skilled human resources are attracted to situations with better career prospects. Historically, the computer and software industries were located in munificent environments. Capital was readily available, human resources were trained in relevant fields, and new uses for computers were continually being developed. Although this is still to some extent the case, we have already alluded to the shakeout in the market for basic software. The days are gone when business amateurs can develop a new word-processing package and become multimillionaires, like the founders of WordPerfect. The big firms have consolidated the market.

Resource dependence can be fairly independent of environmental uncertainty, and dealing with one issue will not necessarily have an effect on the other. For example, although the computer industry generally faces a fairly munificent environment, this environment is uncertain, especially with regard to rate of change. On the other hand, many mature small businesses exist in a fairly certain environment but remain highly resource dependent.

Competitors, regulatory agencies, and various interest groups can have a considerable stake in how an organization obtains and transforms its resources.[15] In effect, the organization might be indirectly resource dependent upon these bodies and thus susceptible to a fair degree of social control. For example, Saturn could have begun operations without unionization (the Nissan plant located in Tennessee is not unionized). However, other GM plants are organized by the United Auto Workers. To preclude labor difficulties and ensure the presence of committed human resources, GM agreed to United Auto Workers representation from the outset of the project.

The concept of resource dependence does not mean that organizations are totally at the mercy of their environments. Rather, it means that they must develop strategies for managing both resource dependence and environmental uncertainty.

STRATEGIC RESPONSES TO UNCERTAINTY AND RESOURCE DEPENDENCE

Strategy. The process by which top executives seek to cope with the constraints and opportunities that an organization's environment poses.

Organizations devote considerable effort to developing and implementing strategies to cope with environmental uncertainty and resource dependence. **Strategy** can be defined as the process by which top executives seek to cope with the constraints and opportunities posed by an organization's environment.

Exhibit 16.4 outlines the nature of the relationship between environment and strategy. At the top, the objective organizational environment is portrayed in terms of uncertainty and available resources, as we discussed above. However, much of the impact that the environment has on organizations is indirect rather than direct, filtered through the perceptual system of managers and other organizational members.[16] By means of the perceptual process we discussed in Chapter 4, personality characteristics and experience may color managers' perceptions of the environment. For example, the environment might seem much more complex and unstable for a manager who is new to his job than for one who has years of experience. Similarly, the optimistic manager might perceive more resources than the pessimistic manager.[17] It is the perceived environment that comprises the basis for strategy formulation.

Strategy formulation itself involves determining the mission, goals, and objectives of the organization. At the most basic level, for a business firm, this would even involve consideration of just what business the organization should pursue. Then, the organization's orientation toward the perceived environment must be determined. This might range from being defensive and protective of current interests (such as holding market share) to prospecting vigorously for new interests to exploit (such as developing totally new products).[18] There is no single correct strategy along this continuum. Rather, the chosen strategy must correspond to the constraints and opportunities of the environment. Finally, the strategy must be implemented by selecting appropriate managers for the task and employing appropriate techniques as shown in Exhibit 16.4.

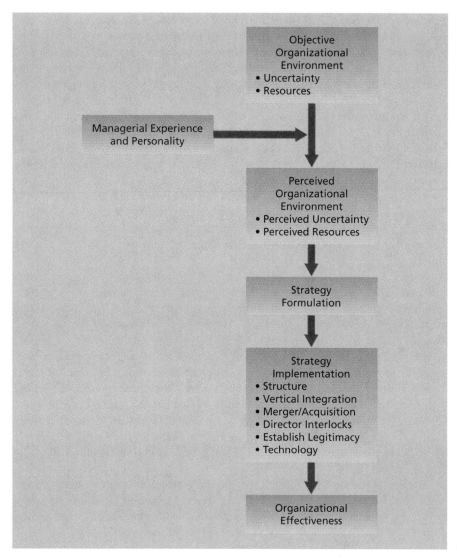

EXHIBIT 16.4
Environment, strategy, and organizational effectiveness.

Organizational Structure as a Strategic Response

How should organizations be structured to cope with environmental uncertainty? Paul Lawrence and Jay Lorsch of Harvard University have studied this problem.[19]

Lawrence and Lorsch chose for their research more and less successful organizations in three industries—plastics, packaged food products, and paper containers. These industries were chosen intentionally because it was assumed that they faced environments that differed in perceived uncertainty. This was subsequently confirmed by questionnaires and interviews. The environment of the plastics firms was perceived as very uncertain because of rapidly changing scientific knowledge, technology, and customer demands. Decisions had to be made even though feedback about their accuracy often involved considerable delay. At the opposite extreme, the container firms faced an environment that was perceived as much more certain. No major changes in technology had occurred in 20 years, and the name of the game was simply to produce high-quality standardized containers and get them to the customer quickly. The consequences of decisions could be learned in a short period of time. The perceived uncertainty faced by the producers of packaged foods fell between that experienced by the plastics producers and that faced by container firms.

Going a step further, Lawrence and Lorsch also examined the sectors of the environment that were faced by three departments in each company: sales (market environment), production (technical environment), and research (scientific environment). Their findings are shown in Exhibit 16.5. The crucial factor here is the *range* of uncertainty across the subenvironments faced by the various departments. In the container companies, producing, selling, and research (mostly quality control) were all fairly certain activities. In contrast, the range of uncertainty encountered by the plastics firms was quite broad. Research worked in a scientific environment that was extremely uncertain. On the other hand, production faced a technical environment that was a good bit more routine.

When Lawrence and Lorsch examined the attitudes of organizational managers, the impact of perceived environmental uncertainty became apparent. First of all, because the departments of the plastics firms had to cope with sectors of the environment that differed in certainty, the plastics firms tended to be highly differentiated (Chapter 15). Thus, their managers tended to differ rather greatly in terms of goals, interpersonal relationships, and time spans. For example, production managers were interested in immediate, short-term problems, while managers in the research department were concerned with longer-range scientific development. Conversely, the container firms were not highly differentiated because the environmental sectors with which they dealt were more similar in perceived certainty. The food packaging firms were more differentiated than the container firms but less differentiated than the plastic companies.

Because they faced a fairly certain environment and because they were fairly undifferentiated, the container firms had adopted mechanistic structures. The most successful was organized along strict functional lines and was

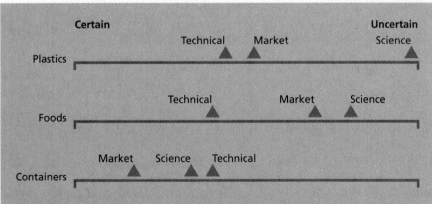

EXHIBIT 16.5
Relative perceived uncertainty of environmental sectors in the Lawrence and Lorsch study.

Source: Modified with permission from Paul R. Lawrence and Jay W. Lorsch, *Organization and Environment: Managing Differentiation and Integration.* Boston: Division of Research, Harvard Business School, 1967, p. 91. (Republished as a Harvard Business School Classic. Boston: Harvard Business School Press, 1986).

highly centralized. Coordination was achieved through direct supervision and formalized written schedules. All in all, this container firm conformed closely to the classical prescriptions for structure. At the other extreme, the most successful plastics companies had adopted organic structures. This was the most sensible way to deal with an uncertain environment and high differentiation. Decision-making power was decentralized to locate it where the appropriate knowledge existed. Coordination was achieved through informal mutual adjustment, ad hoc teams that cut across departments, and special integrators who coordinated between departments (Chapter 15). In addition, the departments themselves were structured somewhat differently, research being the most organic and production the least organic.

The Lawrence and Lorsch study is important because it demonstrates a close connection among environment, structure, and effectiveness. However, follow-up research has not been entirely supportive of their findings, and several contradictory studies exist.[20] Despite these spotty research findings, organizations very commonly tailor structure to strategy in coping with the environment. Consider Union Pacific Railroad, which was, like many American railroads, losing more and more market share to truckers. Why? It showed poor responsiveness to customers' needs. This included late pickups, late deliveries, dirty rail cars, and a host of other sins. Mike Walsh, UP's former chief officer, spearheaded a new strategy based on customer service and quality. To do this, he implemented a revised, flatter structure that was designed to put more decision-making authority down where the customer is located:

> Nine layers of management stood between Walsh and the superintendents, the field officers responsible for the operations of trains in the territories. A super had to get permission from the bureaucracy in Omaha to spend more than a hundred bucks, and nobody outside the executive wing wanted to make a move without getting at least three signatures. Walsh eliminated six of the layers and reduced management ranks in the operating department by 800, or 50%. The superintendents now report to a single assistant vice president in Omaha, who reports to a single executive vice president, who reports to the chief. To get managers in the habit of acting quickly and innovatively, and without prodding from above, he has given superintendents power and a budget to manage; each has authority to spend as much as $25,000. This year a group of managers asked Walsh to approve a plan to forestall a shortage of grain cars. He said, "Look, you guys are at a pretty high level in the organization. If you can't make the decision, who can? I'd rather have to rein you in than kick you in the pants to get you going."[21]

Of course, UP still moved freight, a task that requires much coordination. To provide these superintendents with adequate information, a new computer-controlled dispatching system was put in place.

Union Pacific's decentralization and reduction of bureaucracy correspond to a current trend that has been prompted in part by a more dynamic and/or more complex (e.g., global) business environment and accompanying revisions in strategic thinking. Part of the GM Saturn organization's strategy is to reduce the development time for new models. This helps to counteract uncertainty in the marketplace. To implement the strategy, the company opted for a flatter, more organic, less bureaucratic structure for Saturn.

Union Pacific's decentralization and reduction of bureaucracy correspond to a current trend prompted by a more dynamic and complex business environment.

The argument presented so far suggests that strategy always determines structure, rather than the other way around. This is a reasonable conclusion when considering an organization undergoing great change (such as Union Pacific) or the formation of a new organization (such as Saturn). However, for ongoing organizations, structure sometimes dictates strategy formulation. For instance, highly complex decentralized structures might dictate strategies that are the product of political bargaining between functional units. More centralized simple structures might produce strategies that appear more rational and less political (although not necessarily superior in effectiveness).[22]

Other Forms of Strategic Response

Variations on organizational structure are not the only strategic response that organizations can make. Structural variations often accompany other responses that are oriented toward coping with environmental uncertainty or resource dependence. Some forms of strategy implementation appear extremely routine, yet they might have a strong effect on the performance of the organization. For example, economic forecasting might be used to predict the demand for goods and services. In turn, formal planning might be employed to synchronize the organization's actions with the forecasts. All of this is done to reduce uncertainty and to predict trends in resource availability. Lobbying and public relations are also common strategic responses. Simple negotiating and contracting are other forms of implementing strategy. The innovative agreement between GM and the United Auto Workers regarding

Saturn is one such example. General Motors' strategy involved guaranteeing itself a ready supply of flexible labor at somewhat less than the going wage rate at its other plants.

Some more elaborate forms of strategic response are worth a more detailed look. Notice how many of these concern relationships *between* organizations.

Vertical Integration.　Many managers live in fear of disruption on the input or output end of their organizations. A lack of raw materials to process or a snag in marketing products or services can threaten the very existence of the organization. One basic way to buffer the organization against such uncertainty over resource control is to use an inventory policy of stockpiling both inputs and outputs. For example, an automaker might stockpile needed parts in advance of an anticipated strike at a supplier. At the same time, it might have 30 days' supply of new cars in its distribution system at all times. Both inventories serve as environmental "shock absorbers." A natural extension of this logic is **vertical integration,** the strategy of formally taking control of sources of supply and distribution.[23] Major oil companies, for instance, are highly vertically integrated, handling their own exploration, drilling, transport, refining, retail sales, and credit. Starbucks, the Seattle-based chain of espresso bars, imports, roasts, and packages its own coffee and refuses to franchise its bars in order to maintain high quality.

Vertical integration can reduce risk for an organization in many cases. However, when the environment becomes very turbulent, it can reduce flexibility and actually increase risk.[24]

Vertical integration. The strategy of formally taking control of sources of organizational supply and distribution.

Mergers and Acquisitions.　In recent years, we've seen the headlines again and again: General Electric acquires RCA; desktop publishing founders Adobe and Aldus merge; pharmaceutical giant Merck buys drug discounter Medco; Philip Morris takes over Kraft. Such mergers of two firms or the acquisition of one firm by another are increasingly common strategic responses. Some mergers and acquisitions are stimulated by simple economies of scale. For example, a motel chain with 100 motels might have the same advertising costs as one with 50 motels. Other mergers and acquisitions are pursued for purposes of vertical integration. For instance, a paper manufacturer might purchase a timber company. When mergers and acquisitions occur within the *same* industry, they are being effected partly to reduce the uncertainty prompted by competition. When they occur across *different* industries (a diversification strategy), the goal is often to reduce resource dependence on a particular segment of the environment. A portfolio is created so that if resources become threatened in one part of the environment, the organization can still prosper.[25] This was one motive for Philip Morris to take over food companies such as Kraft. Antismoking sentiments and legislation have provided much uncertainty for the firm's core cigarette business.

One trend in contemporary North America has been mergers between hospitals to avoid duplication and thus cut costs. In the U.S., this has been particularly motivated by "managed care" health providers who have insisted that hospitals become more efficient.

Strategic Alliances.　We've all heard about bad blood following a merger or acquisition, especially after a hostile takeover. This failure of cultures to integrate smoothly (Chapter 9) is only one reason that mergers that look good

Strategic alliances. Actively cooperative relationships between legally separate organizations.

from a financial point of view often end up as operational disasters. Is there any way to have the benefits of matrimony without the attendant risks? Increasingly, the answer seems to be **strategic alliances,** that is, actively cooperative relationships between legally separate organizations. The organizations in question retain their own cultures, but true cooperation replaces distrust, competition, or conflict for the project at hand. Properly designed, such alliances reduce risk and uncertainty for all parties, and resource *interdependence* is recognized. The network organization we discussed in the previous chapter is one form of strategic alliance.

Organizations can engage in strategic alliances with competitors, suppliers, customers, and unions.[26] Among competitors, one common alliance is a research and development consortium in which companies band together to support basic research that is relevant for their products. For example, several Canadian producers of audio speakers formed a consortium under the National Research Council to perfect the technology for "smart speakers" that adjust automatically to room configuration. Another common alliance between competitors is the joint venture, in which organizations combine complementary advantages for economic gain or new experience. The Toyota-General Motors joint venture in a California auto plant gave Toyota manufacturing access to the United States and gave GM experience with Japanese management techniques. This experience heavily influenced GM's subsequent decisions about how to structure and manage Saturn.

Strategic alliances with suppliers and customers have a similar theme of reducing friction and building trust and cooperation. At Union Pacific, for example, customers can place orders and track the progress of their own shipments by accessing UP's own mainframe. In manufacturing, it used to be standard procedure to have a number of suppliers that were chosen on the basis of low cost. If one supplier's quality or delivery was poor, it was dropped, and the slack was made up by another. Now it is becoming common for manufacturers to work closely with a small set of stable suppliers to ensure ongoing excellence in quality, delivery, and service. Hewlett-Packard, Ford, and General Motors are notably progressive in this.[27]

Finally, strategic alliances can occur between companies and unions. The innovative Saturn labor contract is just such an example.

Strategic alliances are most successful and stable when the senior managers of the firms meet frequently and when the firms behave "transparently" toward one another, exchanging information quickly and accurately. A prior history of cooperation and a feeling that the partner is not taking unfair advantage of the alliance are also important.[28]

Strategic alliances between global partners are increasingly common. Examples include the Ford-Mazda connection, the European Airbus consortium, and a Canon-Olivetti joint venture in copiers. These global alliances can be especially difficult to manage due to cross-cultural differences in expectations. For example, North Americans favor shorter time horizons and a rather direct approach to conflicts. Far Eastern cultures favor longer time horizons and "talking around" overt conflict[29] (see the "Global Focus: *Global Strategic Alliance to Develop New Computer Chip Leads to Cross-Cultural Confusion.*")

Interlocking Directorates. If we added up all the positions on boards of directors in the country and then added up all the people who serve as direc-

GLOBAL FOCUS   Global Strategic Alliance to Develop New Computer Chip Leads to Cross-Cultural Confusion

EAST FISHKILL, N.Y. — Three competing companies from three continents—Siemens AG of Germany, Toshiba Corp. of Japan and IBM—are trying to develop a revolutionary computer memory chip together. The Triad, as they call themselves, has been working for a year at the IBM facility in this small Hudson River Valley town on research scheduled to last until at least 1997. The undertaking is cutting-edge, both in technology and in the scope of its cross-cultural cooperation.

Initially, some organizers wondered whether more than 100 scientists from competitive, culturally diverse backgrounds could work together on such a large project. They were right to worry.

At East Fishkill, Siemens scientists were shocked to find Toshiba colleagues closing their eyes and seeming to sleep during meetings (a common practice for overworked Japanese managers when talk doesn't concern them). The Japanese, who normally work in big groups, found it painful to sit in small, individual offices and speak English; some now withdraw when they can into all-Japanese groups. IBMers complained that the Germans plan too much and that the Japanese—who like to review ideas constantly—won't make clear decisions. Suspicions circulate that some researchers are withholding information from the group.

The separation has prevented the hoped-for big creative leaps that researchers call Aha! effects. "I wish I had a good example of breaking through that and coming up with a great new idea, but unfortunately that hasn't happened very much," says [IBM's Matt] Wordeman. He adds, however, that the engineers themselves are extremely talented, and this has permitted them to overcome disappointments and wasted time, keeping the project on track.

Mr. Wordeman and other Triad participants emphasize that, despite the huge extra effort required, the project isn't in trouble. Work is on schedule—even a bit ahead in part—and they are finding ways to overcome communications problems, they say. Members of all three teams say they

Worker cooperation can be a challenge and a reward in cross-cultural projects.

have learned huge amounts, both about technology and about cooperating with outsiders.

Cooperative projects of this kind are likely to proliferate, and the reason is money. In business after business, development costs are ballooning, driving more and more cash-strapped companies to look for ways to cooperate with competitors.

Source: Excerpted from Browning, E. S. (1994, May 3). Computer chip project brings rivals together, but the cultures clash. *The Wall Street Journal*, pp. A1, A8.

tors, the second number would be considerably smaller than the first. This is because of **interlocking directorates,** the condition that is said to exist when one person serves as a director on two or more boards. Such interlocking is legally prohibited when the firms are direct competitors; but as you can imagine, a fine line may exist as to the definition of a direct competitor. Many have recognized that interlocking directorates provide a subtle but effective means of coping with environmental uncertainty and resource dependence. The director's expertise and experience with one organization can provide valuable information for another. Sometimes the value of the interlock is more

Interlocking directorates. A condition existing when one person serves on two or more boards of directors.

direct. This is especially true when it is a "vertical interlock" in which one firm provides inputs to or receives outputs from the other (for instance, a director might serve on the board of a steel company and an auto producer):

> In addition to reducing uncertainty concerning inputs or outputs, a vertical interlock may also create a more efficient method of dealing with the environment. The outside director might be able not only to obtain the critical input, but also to procure favorable treatment such as a better price, better payment terms, or better delivery schedules. In addition, the search costs or the complexity involved in dealing with the environment may be reduced.[30]

Interlocks can also serve as a means of influencing public opinion about the wealth, status, or social conscience of a particular organization. Highly placed university officials, clergy, and union leaders are effectively board members in their own organizations, and they may be sought as board members by business firms to convey an impression of social responsibility to the wider public.[31] Resources are easier to obtain from a friendly environment than from a hostile environment!

Establishing Legitimacy. It is something of a paradox that environmental uncertainty seems to increase the need to make correct organizational responses but at the same time makes it harder to know which response is correct! One strategic response to this dilemma is to do things that make the organization appear *legitimate* to various constituents.[32] Taking actions that conform to prevailing norms and expectations will often be strategically correct, but equally important, it will have the *appearance* of being strategically correct. In turn, management will appear to be rational, and providers of resources will feel comfortable with the organization's actions.

How can legitimacy be achieved? One way is by association with higher status individuals or organizations. For example, an organization without much established status might put a high-status outsider on its board or form a strategic alliance with a more prestigious partner. Another way is to be seen as doing good deeds in the community. Thus, many companies engage in corporate philanthropy and various charity activities. A third way to achieve legitimacy is to make very visible responses to social trends and legal legislation. For example, many firms have appointed directors of workforce diversity or established official units to deal with implementing the ramifications of the Americans with Disabilities Act. Although such highly visible responses are not the only way to proceed with these matters, they do send obvious signals to external constituents that the organization is meeting social expectations. Probably the most common way of achieving legitimacy is to imitate management practices that other firms have institutionalized.

Attempts to achieve legitimacy can backfire. This is especially evident when management practices from other firms are copied without careful thought. Firms that "got on the bandwagon" of total quality management or downsizing without clear rationale have often had unsuccessful experiences despite the appearance of following recognized business trends.

The preceding are just a few examples of the kinds of strategic responses that organizations can implement to cope with the environment. Now, let's examine in greater detail another such response—technological choice.

THE TECHNOLOGIES OF ORGANIZATIONS

The term *technology* brings to mind physical devices such as turret lathes, handsaws, computers, and electron microscopes. However, as we pointed out earlier, this is an overly narrow view of the concept. To broaden this view, we might define **technology** as the activities, equipment, and knowledge necessary to turn organizational inputs into desired outputs. In a hospital, relevant inputs might include sick patients and naive interns, while desired outputs include well people and experienced doctors. In a steel mill, crucial inputs include scrap metal and energy, while desired outputs consist of finished steel. What technologies should the hospital and the steel mill use to facilitate this transformation? More important for our purposes, do different technologies require different organizational structures to be effective?

The concepts of technology and environment are closely related.[33] The inputs that are transformed by the technology come from various segments of the organization's environment. In turn, the outputs that the technology creates are returned to the environment. In addition, the activities, equipment, and knowledge that constitute the technology itself seldom spring to life within the organization. Rather, they are imported from the technological segment of the environment to meet the organization's needs.

Organizations choose their technologies.[34] In general, this choice will be predicated on a desired strategy. For example, the directors of a university mental health center might decide that they wish to deal only with students suffering from transitory anxiety or mild neuroses. Given these inputs, certain short-term psychotherapies would constitute a sensible technology. More disturbed students would be referred to clinics that have different strategies and different technologies.

Different parts of the organization rely on different technologies, just as they respond to different aspects of the environment as a whole. For example, the personnel department uses a different technology than the finance department. However, research has often skirted this problem, concentrating on the "core" technology used by the key operating function (e.g., the production department in manufacturing firms).

Basic Dimensions of Technology

Organizational technology has been defined, conceptualized, and measured in literally dozens of different ways.[35] Some analysts have concentrated on degree of automation; others have focused on the degree of discretion granted to workers. Here we will consider other classifications of technologies, specifically those of Charles Perrow and James D. Thompson. These classification schemes are advantageous because we can apply both to manufacturing firms and to service organizations such as banks and schools.

Perrow's Routineness.   According to Perrow, the key factor that differentiates various technologies is the routineness of the transformation task that confronts the department or organization.[36] **Technological routineness** is a function of two factors:

- *Exceptions.* Is the organization taking in standardized inputs and turning out standardized outputs (few exceptions)? Or is the organization

> **Technology.** The activities, equipment, and knowledge necessary to turn organizational inputs into desired outputs.

> **Technological routineness.** The extent to which exceptions and problems affect the task of converting inputs into outputs.

EXHIBIT 16.6
Perrow's matrix of technologies.

Source: From Perrow, C. (1967, April). Framework for the comparative analysis of organizations, *ASR*, Vol. 32, No. 2, Figures 1 and 2, pp. 196, 198. Copyright © 1967 by the American Sociological Association. Reprinted by permission.

encountering varied inputs or turning out varied outputs (many exceptions)? The technology becomes less routine as exceptions increase.

- *Problems.* When exceptions occur, are the problems easy to analyze or difficult to analyze? That is, can programmed decision making occur, or must workers resort to nonprogrammed decision making? The technology becomes less routine as problems become more difficult to analyze.

As Exhibit 16.6 demonstrates, the exceptions and problems dimensions can be arranged to produce a matrix of technologies. This matrix includes the following technologies:

- *Craft technologies* typically deal with fairly standard inputs and outputs. Cabinetmakers use wood to make cabinets, and public schools attempt to educate "typical" students. However, when exceptions are encountered (a special order or a slow learner), analysis of the correct action might be difficult.

- *Routine technologies* such as assembly line operations and technical schools also deal with standardized inputs and outputs. However, when exceptions do occur (a new product line or a new subject to teach), the correct response is fairly obvious.

- *Nonroutine technologies* must deal frequently with exceptional inputs or outputs, and the analysis of these exceptions is often difficult. By definition, research units are set up to deal with difficult, exceptional problems. Similarly, psychiatric hospitals encounter patients with a wide variety of disturbances. Deciding on a proper course of therapy can be problematic.

- *Engineering technologies* encounter many exceptions of input or required output, but these exceptions can be dealt with by using standardized responses. For example, individuals with a wide variety of physical conditions visit health spas, and each has a particular goal (e.g., weight loss, muscle development). Despite this variety, the recommendation of a training regimen for each individual is a fairly easy decision.

From most routine to least routine, we can order Perrow's four technological classifications in the following manner: routine, engineering, craft, nonroutine. Shortly, we will consider which structures are appropriate for these technologies. First, let's examine Thompson's technological classification.

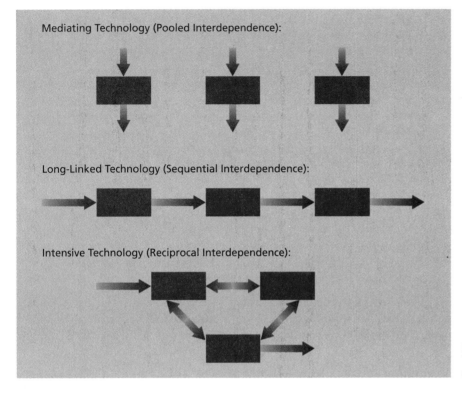

EXHIBIT 16.7
Thompson's technology classification.

Thompson's Interdependence.   In contrast to Perrow, James D. Thompson was interested in the way in which work activities are sequenced or "put together" during the transformation process.[37] A key factor here is **technological interdependence,** the extent to which organizational subunits depend on each other for resources, such as raw materials or information. In order of increasing interdependence, Thompson proposed three classifications of technology (Exhibit 16.7). These classifications are as follows:

- *Mediating technologies* operate under **pooled interdependence.** This means that each unit is to some extent dependent upon the pooled resources generated by the other units but is otherwise fairly independent of those units. Thompson gives rather abstract examples, such as banks, which mediate between depositors and borrowers, and post offices, which mediate between the senders and receivers of letters. However, the same argument can be applied more clearly to the branches of banks or post offices. The health of a bank as a whole might depend on the existence of several branches, but these branches operate almost independently of each other. Each has its own borrowers and depositors. Similarly, post office branches are dependent upon other branches to forward and receive mail, but this is the limit of their required interaction. A taxi company is another good example of pooled interdependence.

- *Long-linked technologies* operate under **sequential interdependence.** This means that each unit in the technology is dependent on the activity of the unit that preceded it in a sequence. The transformed product of each unit becomes a resource or raw material for the next unit. Mass production assembly lines are the classic example of long-linked technology.

Technological interdependence. The extent to which organizational subunits depend on each other for resources, raw materials, or information.

Pooled interdependence. A condition in which organizational subunits are dependent upon the pooled resources generated by other subunits but are otherwise fairly independent.

Sequential interdependence. A condition in which organizational subunits are dependent upon the resources generated by units that precede them in a sequence of work.

Reciprocal interdependence. A condition in which organizational subunits must engage in considerable interplay and mutual feedback to accomplish a task.

However, many "paper-processing" technologies, such as the claims department of an insurance company, are also sequentially interdependent (claims must be verified before they are adjusted and must be adjusted before they are settled).

- *Intensive technologies* operate under **reciprocal interdependence.** This means that considerable interplay and mutual feedback must occur between the units performing the task in order to accomplish it properly. This is necessary because each task is unique, and the intensive technology is thus a customized technology. One example might be the technology employed by a multidisciplinary research team. Thompson cites a general hospital as a prime example of intensive technology:

At any moment an emergency admission may require some combination of dietary, x-ray, laboratory, and housekeeping or hotel services, together with the various medical specialties, pharmaceutical services, occupational therapies, social work services, and spiritual or religious services. Which of these is needed, and when, can be determined only from evidence about the state of the patient.[38]

As technologies become increasingly interdependent, problems of coordination, communication, and decision making increase. To perform effectively, each technology requires a tailored structure to facilitate these tasks.

Structuring to Cope with Technology

How does technology affect organizational structure?

Perrow. According to Perrow, routine technologies should function best under mechanistic structures, while nonroutine technologies call for more organic structures. In the former case, few exceptions to the normal course of events and easily analyzable problems suggest high formalization and centralization. In the latter case, many exceptions and difficult problems suggest that decision-making power should be located "where the action is." The craft and engineering technologies fall between these prescriptions. Research has generally supported his notion that more routine technologies adopt more mechanistic structures.[39]

Thompson. According to Thompson, increasing technological interdependence must be accompanied by increased coordination or integration mechanisms. There is research evidence to support this proposition.[40] Furthermore, the *methods* used to achieve coordination should be reflected in structural differences across the technologies. Mediating technologies, operating only under pooled interdependence, should be able to achieve coordination via standardization of rules, regulations, and procedures. This formalization is indicative of a mechanistic structure (consider banks and the post office). Long-linked technologies must also be structured mechanistically, but the increased demands for coordination prompted by sequential interdependence must be met by planning, scheduling, and meetings. Finally, intensive technologies require intensive coordination, and this is best achieved by mutual adjustment and an organic structure that permits the free and ready flow of information among units.[41]

Woodward.   The most famous study of the relationship between technology and structure is that of Joan Woodward. Woodward examined the technology, structure, and organizational effectiveness of 100 firms in South Essex, England.[42] This study is especially interesting because it began as an attempt to test the classical argument that mechanistic structures will prove most effective in all cases. In brief, this test failed—there was no simple, consistent relationship between organizational structure and effectiveness—and many of the successful firms exhibited organic structures. Woodward then analyzed and classified the technologies of the 80 firms in her sample that had clear-cut, stable production processes. She used the classifications unit, mass and process production. Some examples of these classifications include the following:

- *Unit* (production of single units or small batches)

  Custom-tailored units

  Prototype production

  Fabrication of large equipment in stages (e.g., locomotives)

  Small batches to order

- *Mass* (production of large batches or mass production)

  Large batches on assembly lines

  Mass production (e.g., bakeries)

- *Process* (input transformed as an ongoing process)

  Chemicals processed in batches

  Continuous-flow production (e.g., gasoline, propane)

From top to bottom, this scale of technology reflects both increasing smoothness of production and increasing impersonalization of task requirements.[43] Less and less personal intervention is necessary as machines control more and more of the work. Woodward's mass technology incorporates aspects of Perrow's routine technology and Thompson's long-linked technology. Her unit technology seems to cover Perrow's craft and engineering technologies and some aspects of Thompson's intensive technology. It is difficult to isolate Woodward's process technology in the Perrow or Thompson classifications.

Now for the key questions. Did organizational structures tend to vary with technology? If so, was this variance related to organizational effectiveness? The answer in both cases is yes. Each of the three technologies tended to have distinctive structures, and the most successful firms had structures that closely approximated the average of their technological groups. For instance, Woodward found that as the production process became smoother, more continuous, and more impersonal, the management of the system took on increasing importance. That is, moving from unit to mass to process, there were more managers relative to workers, more hierarchical levels, and lower labor costs. This is not difficult to understand. Unit production involves custom-tailored craftswork in which the workers can essentially manage their own work activity. However, it is very labor intensive. On the other hand, sophisticated continuous-process systems (such as those used to refine gasoline) take a great amount of management skill and technical attention to start up. Once rolling, a handful of workers can monitor and maintain the system.

Successful firms with unit and process technologies relied upon organic structures, while successful firms that engaged in mass production relied upon mechanistic structures. For example, the latter firms had more specialization of labor, more controls, and greater formalization (a reliance on written rather than verbal communication). At first glance, it might strike you as unusual that the firms at the extremes of the technology scale (unit and process) both tended to rely on organic structures. However, close consideration of the actual tasks performed under each technology resolves this apparent contradiction. Unit production generally involves custom-building complete units to customer specifications. As such, it relies upon skilled labor, teamwork, and coordination by mutual adjustment and standardized skills. The work itself is not machine-paced and is far from mechanistic. At the other extreme, process production is almost totally automated. The workers are essentially skilled technicians who monitor and maintain the system, and they again tend to work in teams. While the machinery itself operates according to a rigid schedule, workers can monitor and maintain it at their own pace. Informal relationships with supervisors replace close control.

Woodward's research is a landmark in demonstrating the general proposition that structure must be tailored to the technology the organization adopts to achieve its strategic goals. Her findings have been replicated and extended by others.[44] However, there have been disconfirming studies, and a constant debate has gone on about the relative importance of organizational size versus technology in determining structure.[45]

Saturn.   The design of the Saturn organization shows evidence of an attempt to match structure to technology. In Woodward's terms, the core technology at Saturn is obviously mass production. However, some of its unique features, such as building automatic and manual transmissions on the same line to

Advanced manufacturing technology is renewing North America's productive competitiveness, by allowing service centers to perform more efficiently.

exactly match a car order, mean that the technology is somewhat less routine (in Perrow's terms) than the conventional monolithic assembly line. To take advantage of this, the shopfloor organization, with its work teams and reduced supervision, is more organic than is typical for the North American auto industry. This, then, is also reflected in the managerial and professional ranks, in which the technology for designing cars was modified. Instead of passing designs from department to department (Thompson's sequential interdependence), early involvement of all critical departments was obtained (Thompson's reciprocal interdependence). Again, this points to a more organic structure backed up by sophisticated electronic aids to facilitate coordination and communication. In fact, let's now turn our attention to advanced information technology.

IMPLICATIONS OF ADVANCED INFORMATION TECHNOLOGY

In concluding the chapter, let's consider some of the implications that ongoing advances in information technology are having for organizational behavior. Speaking broadly, **advanced information technology** refers to the generation, aggregation, storage, modification, and speedy transmission of information made possible by the advent of computers and related devices. Information technology is equally applicable in the factory or the office. In the factory, examples include robots, computer numerically-controlled machine tools, and automated inventory management. In the office, it covers everything from word processing to electronic mail to automated filing to expert systems. Between the office and the factory, it includes computer-aided design and engineering.

Advanced information technology. The generation, aggregation, storage, modification, and speedy transmission of information made possible by the advent of computers and related devices.

The Two Faces of Advanced Technology

It is important to recognize that there has been much inaccurate hoopla about advanced information technology. This began even before the first mainframe computers were perfected, and it continues today. To exaggerate only slightly, doomsayers have painted a dark picture of job loss and de-skilling, with technology running wild and stifling the human spirit. Opponents of this view (often vendors of hardware and software) have painted a rosy picture of improved productivity, superior decision making, and upgraded, happy employees. It probably doesn't surprise you that research fails to support either of these extremes as a general state of affairs. In the early days of mainframe batch data processing, de-skilling, job pacing, and loss of routine clerical jobs did occur. However, as we shall see, the consequences of current advanced information technology are much less deterministic.

This discussion of extremes alerts us to a more realistic issue that we might call the "two faces" of technology.[46] This means that a given form of advanced information technology can have exactly *opposite* effects depending upon how it is employed. For example, the same system that is designed to monitor and control employees (say, by counting keystrokes) can also provide feedback and reduce supervision. Additionally, the same technology that can de-skill jobs can build skills *into* jobs. How can these opposite effects occur? They are possible because information technology is so *flexible*. In fact, we are discussing information technology separately from the core technologies discussed earlier because it is so flexible that it can be applied in conjunction with any of them.

IMPROVING CUSTOMER SERVICE AT GTE

Myou be the Manager

Telephone operations account for four-fifths of GTE's $20 billion in annual revenues. With deregulation, the telephone business has become intensely competitive, and GTE was looking for ways to both cut costs and improve customer service. Improved service can reduce service costs in the field, improve existing customers' relationships, and attract new customers. The traditional approach to such improvements has been to try to "fine tune" existing procedures in the repair, billing, and marketing departments. However, GTE saw merit in trying to totally reengineer the way customers interacted with the company to make the process more efficient and satisfying, perhaps using some of its own technology.

GTE was using a traditional system in which a customer needing repair service called an operator who took down basic information and then bounced the customer around various departments until someone could solve his or her problem. This system of passing on customers was both expensive and inefficient. What if a single customer wanted to question a bill, obtain a calling card, and report a dial tone problem? Could technology and job redesign improve GTE service? You be the manager.

1. What would you do to improve customer service at GTE?

2. How does advanced information technology provide opportunities for improved customer service?

To find out what GTE did, consult *The Manager's Notebook* at the end of the chapter.

> **HOW WOULD YOU SUGGEST GTE CUT COSTS AND IMPROVE CUSTOMER SERVICE IN THE INTENSELY COMPETITIVE TELEPHONE INDUSTRY?**

Sources: Sager, I. (1994). The great equalizer. *Business Week* (Special issue: The Information Revolution). 100–107; Stewart, T. A. (1993, August 23). Reengineering: The hot new management tool. *Fortune*, 41–48; Greengard, S. (1993, December). Reengineering: Out of the rubble. *Personnel Journal*, 48A–48O; Brian Blevins, GTE.

The flexibility of information technology means that it is not deterministic of a particular organization structure or job design. Rather, it gives organizations *choices* about how to organize work. The company that wishes to decentralize can use information technology to provide lower-level employees with data to make decisions. The company that wishes to centralize can use the other face of the same technology to gather information from below to retain control. Such choices are a function of organizational culture and management values rather than inherent in the hardware. They should match the strategy the organization is pursuing, as our discussion of advanced manufacturing will show.

For purposes of discussion, we will distinguish between advanced manufacturing technology and advanced office technology. However, as we shall see, this distinction is artificial, since advanced technology has the capability to link the office more closely to the factory or to clients, customers, and suppliers in the outside environment. For an example, please consider the *You Be the Manager* feature.

Advanced Manufacturing Technology

Three major trends underlie advanced manufacturing technology.[47] The first is an obvious capitalization on computer intelligence and memory. The second is flexibility, in that the technology can accomplish a changing variety of tasks. This is usually the product of an organizational strategy that favors adaptiveness, small batch production, and fast response. In turn, this strategy follows from attempting to find and exploit short-term "niches" in the marketplace rather than hoping to produce large volumes of the same product year after year. Consider this textile firm:

> Milliken has reduced its average production run from 20,000 to 4,000 yards and can dye lots as small as 1,000 yards. Apparel makers, textile and fiber firms, and retailers have recently joined to launch the so-called Quick Response program, designed to improve the flow of information among the various groups and speed order times. The program's goal is to cut the 66-week cycle from fiber to retail in the U.S. to 21 weeks.[48]

As a third trend, advanced manufacturing technologies are increasingly being designed to be integrated with *other* advanced technologies that organizations use. For example, the computer-aided design system that is used to design and modify a product can also be used to design, operate, and modify its production process via computer-aided manufacturing programs (the result being a so-called CAD/CAM system). Ultimately, using most of the technologies mentioned here, computer-integrated manufacturing systems (CIM) that integrate and automate all aspects of design, manufacturing, assembly, and inspection can be put in place. In turn, computerized information systems can link these tasks to supply and sales networks. Exhibit 16.8 compares highly flexible manufacturing systems with traditional mass production.[49]

What are the general implications of advanced manufacturing technology for organizational behavior? Such technology tends to automate the more routine information-processing and decision-making tasks. Depending on job design, what might remain for operators are the more complex, nonroutine tasks—those dealing with system problems and exceptions. In addition, task interdependence tends to increase under advanced technologies. For example,

Organizational Characteristic	Flexible Manufacturing	Mass Production
Strategy	• Adapt to environment • Produce small batches • Small inventory, fast turnover • Respond fast	• Buffer against environment • Produce large batches • Large inventory, slow turnover • Respond predictably
Product	• Many variations, variable life cycles	• Few variations, long life cycles
Marketing	• Exploit niche markets	• Cater to mass market
Structure	• Organic, integrated	• Mechanistic, differentiated
Suppliers	• Few, chosen for reliability and responsiveness	• Many, chosen on basis of cost
Jobs	• Flexible jobs; teamwork	• Rigid, specialized jobs; little teamwork

EXHIBIT 16.8
Flexible manufacturing compared with traditional mass production.

design, manufacturing, and marketing become more reciprocally than sequentially interdependent in a flexible manufacturing system. Finally, let's remember that such advanced technologies are adopted in part to cope with a less certain environment. Thus, many advanced technological systems result in nonroutine, highly interdependent tasks that are embedded in an uncertain environment.[50]

Organizational Structure.   What are the implications of this shift in technology? As Exhibit 16.8 shows, one effect is a movement toward flatter, more organic structures to capitalize on the technology's flexibility.[51] This corresponds to Woodward's finding that unit technologies require more organic designs than mass technologies, and the adoption of more flexible, short-term production batches is an example of unit technology. The expectation of flatter structures stems from the fact that more highly automated systems will handle information processing and diagnoses that were formerly performed by middle managers. Implications of advanced technology for centralization are interesting. On one hand, matters such as ordering raw materials and scheduling production should become more highly centralized. This is both required by the flexibility of the system and permitted by its enhanced information-processing capability. On the other hand, when problems or exceptions occur or when new designs are conceived, decentralization might be called for to locate decision making in the hands of lower-level specialists. However, the whole thrust of advanced technology dictates greater integration among specialties such as design, engineering, production, and marketing. This might require a retreat from the rigid functional structures (Chapter 15) that are common in manufacturing firms. Minimally, it suggests the increased use of integrators, task forces, planning committees, and other mechanisms that stimulate coordination. One study of 185 firms that adopted advanced manufacturing technology found a general trend toward decentralization with more formalized rules and procedures to ensure coordination and effective exploitation of the technology.[52]

Job Design.   Advanced manufacturing technology can be expected to affect the design of jobs, and this is where the issue of choice we alluded to earlier clearly comes into play. There is evidence that such technology can reduce worker control over shopfloor jobs and water down existing skills.[53] An example is having skilled machinists operate lathes that have been programmed by a remote technician. However, other choices are possible, including teaching the machinists to program the lathe or at least to edit existing programs for local conditions. The latter approaches have been shown to gain cooperation and commitment to the new technology and to enhance performance.[54] Following this logic, since advanced technology tends to automate routine tasks, operative workers must usually acquire advanced skills (e.g., computer skills). Also, since advanced technology tends to be flexible as well as expensive to operate, workers themselves must be flexible and fast to respond to problems. Extreme division of labor can be counterproductive in advanced technology. For example, operators simply might not be able to wait for someone else to perform routine maintenance and thus might have to have the flexibility to do this themselves. Similarly, traditional distinctions between roles (electrical maintenance versus mechanical maintenance or drafting versus design) begin to blur when the needs for coordination that advanced technology imposes are recognized.

All of this points to the design of jobs for advanced manufacturing technology according to the principles of job enrichment we discussed in Chapter 7. In turn, this suggests that proper training is critical and that pay levels should be revised to fit the additional skills and responsibilities prompted by the technology. Many observers have recommended that self-managed teams (Chapter 8) be made responsible for setting up, running, and maintaining the system.[55] In fact, GM has adopted this scheme for the Saturn plant. Such teams permit cross-transfer of skills and provide the cross-task integration that is necessary to keep things working smoothly. The team concept is also applicable to other forms of advanced technology. For example, one company organized its CAD/CAM users into teams composed of two designers, a draftsperson, and a toolmaker.[56]

Advanced Office Technology

As we noted above, the label advanced office technology can be applied sensibly to everything from word processing to exotic expert decision systems. Advanced office technology illustrates the coming together of some combination of three previously separate technologies—computers, office machines, and telecommunications (for example, a word processor combines a computer and a typewriter). The most common basic functions of the technology are the following:[57]

- text processing
- communication (e.g., electronic mail, fax)
- information storage and retrieval
- analysis and manipulation of information
- administrative support (e.g., electronic calendars).

As with advanced manufacturing technology, we can point to some environmental and strategic concerns that have stimulated the adoption of advanced office technology, although these concerns are more general. One is obviously the potential for *labor saving*. Consider, for example, word processing (revisions are easy), video conferencing (a trip to the Coast is unnecessary), or spreadsheet analysis (many "What if?" scenarios can be probed by one manager). Another major concern stimulating the adoption of advanced technology is *responsiveness*, both within the organization and also to customers and suppliers. Speed and personalization of response are common goals. Finally, *improved decision making* is a goal of various decision support systems, expert systems, and the like.

The implications of advanced office technology are far reaching. What follows is an illustrative sample, again focusing on organizational structure and job design.

Organizational Structure.　At least as it pertains to management jobs, the link between office technology and organizational structure has been dominated by two related issues—the impact of information technology on tallness/flatness and centralization. Regarding tallness and flatness, advanced technology has enabled a reduction in the number of supervisory and middle-management personnel.[58] Fewer supervisors are needed because electronic monitoring and feedback often replaces routine supervision, and existing supervisors can handle larger spans of control. With fewer supervisors, fewer middle managers are required. Also, some advanced technology, such as decision support and expert systems, can make up for analyses performed by middle managers. For its size (over 80,000 employees), FedEx is a flat organization, having only five levels. This is due in part to advanced electronic communication systems.

Actual research evidence on all this is rather scanty and mainly targeted at the middle-management issue. Although there are reports of staff reductions, it is difficult to know how much of this is a direct result of office technology as opposed to the imposition of flatness to make organizations more responsive to the external environment. Some research points to increased demands on middle-management jobs as larger spans require them to be in charge of more diverse areas and as their performance is more monitorable by top management due to the technology.[59]

The impact of advanced office technology on centralization of decision making is variable, precisely as it should be.[60] Again, the key is the extreme flexibility of information technology. The same systems that allow senior managers to meddle in lower-level operations might enable junior staffers to assemble data and make decisions. Notice, though, that advanced technology does imply a freer, more democratic flow of information and general communication. This suggests that advanced technology enables a wider range of people at more levels to be involved in organizational decision making.[61] Exactly how this capacity gets played out in decision-making practice is most likely a function of strategy and prevailing culture.

Job Design. The impact of advanced office technology on job design and related quality of working life differs considerably with job status. Among clerical and secretarial employees, when jobs have not been lost altogether, there is the potential for de-skilling and reduced motivating potential.[62] A good case in point occurred in many organizations when word processing was introduced. Because the equipment was then expensive, secretarial support was often shifted into word processing pools to make efficient use of the hardware.[63] This frequently resulted in task specialization and a reduction in task identity. However, most observers agree that such technology can actually upgrade skills if it is used to optimal capacity and the work is not highly fragmented.[64] Yet again, we see the issue of flexibility and choice.

Turning to quality of working life, word processing and related video display work have been known to provoke eyestrain, muscular strain, and stress symptoms. However, proper work station design and work pacing can cope with these problems. Computer monitoring (such as counting keystrokes or timing the length of phone calls by service workers) has also been linked to stress reactions. However, there are studies that show that such monitoring may be viewed favorably by employees when it is used for job feedback rather than as a basis for punishment.[65]

On the whole, professionals and managers seem to have taken to advanced office technology remarkably well. Routine aspects of such jobs (such as doing tedious calculations) have often been replaced by more cerebral pursuits. One exception may be some semiprofessional jobs, such as drafting, in which de-skilling can occur without thoughtful job redesign.

There are many examples of organizations that have had poor success in introducing advanced technology because they ignored the human dimension. This raises the issue of implementing change in organizations, a concern of the next chapter.

The Manager's Notebook   Improving Customer Service at GTE

1. To improve customer service, GTE instituted "one-step shopping" in which a single call to one number can deal with repair problems as well as enable customers to add new services. Customer advocates, newly recruited from GTE's experienced field technicians and other technical areas to work on the front-line, have access to numerous company databases that enable them to deal directly with problems and requests. For example, many problems with lines and switches can now be diagnosed and fixed while the customer is on the line. By interacting with the customer while conducting the diagnostic procedures, GTE's customer advocate can ask questions that can help to further pinpoint the problem or determine if the customer would benefit by ordering additional types of services. Many of these new services that the customer requests can be implemented by the customer advocate on-the-spot, through software modifications. Such procedures obviously impress customers, and they remove the inevitable inefficiencies and expenses that accrue when aspects of a repair are handed off from one employee to another.

2. Advanced information technology can have a fairly direct impact on customer service in several ways. At GTE, access to company databases gives customer advocates the *knowledge* required to deal with customers directly and on-line. In addition, information technology *empowers* them to conduct diagnoses and correct problems. Having the person who fields the call also fix the service increases the *contact* between the customer and the actual service provider. By listening to the customer and recommending additional products and services to meet their needs, GTE's customer advocates generated *additional revenues* of $1.8 million in 1993 and $6.8 million in 1994. And, needless to say, the information technology increases the speed with which customer problems are solved. Of course, the success of all of this requires that jobs be redesigned to properly exploit the advanced technology.

EXECUTIVE SUMMARY

◆ Organizations are open systems that take inputs from the external environment, transform some of these inputs, and send them back into the environment as outputs. The external environment includes all of the events and conditions surrounding the organization that influence this process. Major components of the environment include the economy, customers, suppliers, competitors, social/political factors, and existing technologies.

◆ One key aspect of the external environment is its uncertainty. More uncertain environments are vague, difficult to diagnose, and unpredictable. Uncertainty is a function of complexity and rate of change. The most uncertain environments are complex and dynamic—they involve a large number of dissimilar components that are changing unpredictably. More certain environments are simple and stable—they involve a few similar components that exhibit little change. As environmental uncertainty increases, cause-effect relationships get harder to diagnose, and agreeing on priorities becomes more difficult because more information must be processed.

◆ Another key aspect of the external environment is the amount of resources it contains. Some environments are richer or more munificent than others, and all organizations are dependent upon their environments for resources.

◆ Strategy is the process that executives use to cope with the constraints and opportunities posed by the organization's environment, including uncertainty and scarce resources. One critical strategic response involves tailoring the organization's structure to suit the environment. In general, as the Lawrence and Lorsch study demonstrates, mechanistic structures are most suitable for more certain environments, and organic structures are better suited to uncertain environments. Other strategic responses include vertical integration, mergers and acquisitions, strategic alliances, interlocking directorates, establishing legitimacy, and technological choice.

◆ Technology includes the activities, equipment, and knowledge necessary to turn organizational inputs into desired outputs. One key aspect of technology is the extent of its routineness. A routine technology involves few exceptions to usual inputs or outputs and readily analyzable problems. A nonroutine technology involves many exceptions that are difficult to analyze. Another key aspect of technology is the degree of interdependence that exists between organizational units. This may range from simple pooling of resources to sequential activities to complex reciprocal interdependence.

◆ The most famous study of the relationship between technology and structure was Joan Woodward's. She determined that unit and process technologies performed best under organic struc-

tures, while mass production functioned best under a mechanistic structure. In general, less routine technologies and more interdependent technologies call for more organic structures.

◆ Advanced information technology generates, aggregates, stores, modifies, and speedily transmits information. In the factory, it permits flexible manufacturing that calls for organic structures, enriched jobs, and increased teamwork. In the office and the organization as a whole, the flexibility of advanced information technology means that its effects are highly dependent upon management values and culture.

KEY CONCEPTS

External environment
Open systems
Interest groups
Environmental uncertainty
Resource dependence
Strategy
Vertical integration
Strategic alliances

Interlocking directorates
Technology
Technological routineness
Technological interdependence
Pooled interdependence
Sequential interdependence
Reciprocal interdependence
Advanced information technology

DISCUSSION QUESTIONS

1. Construct a diagram of the various interest groups in the external environment of CBS Television. Discuss how some of these interest groups may make competing or contradictory demands on CBS.

2. Describe a real or a hypothetical organization with a very uncertain environment. Do the same for an organization with a fairly certain environment. Be sure to cover both the complexity and rate of change dimensions.

3. Give an example of vertical integration. Use the concept of resource dependence to explain why an organization might choose a strategic response of vertical integration.

4. Discuss how interlocking directorates might reduce environmental uncertainty and help manage resource dependence.

5. Explain why organizations operating in more uncertain environments require more organic structures.

6. Locate the technology of a branch bank situated in a shopping center in Perrow's technology matrix (Exhibit 16.6). Defend your answer.

7. Distinguish among pooled interdependence, sequential interdependence, and reciprocal interdependence in terms of the key problem each poses for organizational effectiveness.

8. Give an example of unit technology, mass technology, and process technology. For which type of technology are the prescriptions of the classical organizational theorists best suited?

9. Imagine that a company is converting from conventional mass technology to a highly flexible, computerized, integrated production system. List structural and behavioral problems that the company might have to anticipate in making this conversion.

10. Discuss this statement: The effects of advanced information technology on job design and organizational structure are highly predictable.

EXPERIENTIAL EXERCISE
DIAGNOSING AN ORGANIZATION

The purpose of this exercise is to choose an organization and to diagnose it in terms of the concepts we covered in the chapter. Doing such a diagnosis should enable you to see better how the degree of "fit" among organizational structure, environment, strategy, and technology influences the effectiveness of the organization. The discussion throughout the chapter of the General Motors Saturn organization provides a general model for the nature of the exercise.

This exercise is suitable for an individual or group project completed outside of class or a class discussion guided by the instructor. In the case of the group project completed outside of class, each group might choose and contact a local organization for information. Alternatively, library resources might be consulted to diagnose a prominent national or international organization. Your instructor might suggest one or more organizations for diagnosis.

1. Discuss in detail the external environment of the chosen organization.
   a) How has the general economy affected this organization recently? Is the organization especially sensitive to swings in the economy?
   b) Who are the organization's key customers? What demands do they make on the organization?
   c) Who are the organization's key suppliers? What impact do they have on the organization?
   d) Who are the organization's important competitors? What threats or opportunities do they pose for the organization?
   e) What general social and political factors (e.g., the law, social trends, environmental concerns) affect the organization in critical ways?
2. Drawing on your answers to question 1, discuss both the degree of environmental uncertainty and the nature of resource dependence the organization faces. Be sure to locate the firm or institution in the appropriate cell of Exhibit 16.3 and defend your answer.
3. What broad strategies (excluding structure) has the organization chosen to cope with its environment?
4. Describe in as much detail as possible the structure of the organization and explain how this structure represents a strategic response to the demands of the environment. Is this the proper structure for the environment and broad strategies that you described in response to the earlier questions?
   a) How big is the organization?
   b) What form of departmentation is used?
   c) How big is spans of control?
   d) How tall is the organization?
   e) How much formalization is apparent?
   f) To what extent is the organization centralized?
   g) How complex is the organization?
   h) Where does the organization fall on a continuum from mechanistic to organic?
5. Describe the organization's core technology in terms of routineness (Exhibit 16.6) and interdependence (Exhibit 16.7). Is its structure appropriate for its technology?
6. What impact has advanced information technology had on the organization?

CASE STUDY
LETTERS OF CREDIT

New York's Citibank faced a problem common to many of North America's largest banks, a problem created in part by its own success. The economic upsurge of the 1950s and 1960s, coupled with the advent of high-capacity centralized computers, had resulted in a radical increase in banking volume. This increase in volume was accompanied by a corresponding increase in banking transactions, each of which generated considerable paperwork. To cope with this avalanche of paperwork, more and more clerks were hired. Generally inexperienced and less than extensively trained because of time constraints, these clerks were assigned to routine, repetitive paperhandling jobs. Single tasks with little apparent relationship to an entire banking transaction were performed over and over again. As a result of monotony, processing errors, discrepancies, and confusion became all too common, and on one occasion a backlog of 36,000 customer inquiries existed.

Not surprisingly, an Opinion Research Corporation survey ranked Citibank very low on customer service. Thus, despite its increased staffing and improved computer capacity, the bank was falling behind in the very area it had sought to maintain or improve—accurate, timely service. To add insult to injury, internal operating costs had been increasing at a rate of 15 percent a year.

The initial response of top management to Citibank's problems was a program that lasted for five years. The program involved recruiting a new management team from organizations not traditionally associated with banking—especially from manufacturing industries. The new managers, educated in quantitative methods and production management, examined Citibank from a fresh perspective. In this analysis, they tended to view Citibank as a factory—albeit a paper and data-processing factory—and they concluded that major changes in organizational structure were necessary to improve the bank's position. These changes were implemented to increase management control over a situation that had gotten out of hand.

Prior to the new program, transactions were processed using what might be called a "centralized assembly line." That is, whether a transaction was initiated from a branch bank, a correspondent bank, or the Federal Reserve, it went into a first-come, first-served queue where it was sorted and processed in an assembly-line manner. The same applied whether the transaction involved a stock, bond, loan, or deposit. This meant that if a bottleneck in the processing occurred, the bank's entire operations would be affected. Furthermore, a functional manager (such as one responsible for dealing with loans issued by branch banks) would have a difficult time resolving processing errors, since they occurred outside of his or her line of authority.

In response to these problems, the new management program divided transactions into source (i.e., branch bank, correspondent bank, Federal Reserve) and type (e.g., loan, deposit, stock, bond) and then set up a separate processing unit under each division. Now, managers had control over the processing of transactions relevant to their own function from the time the transaction entered the bank until the customer was advised of its disposition. Quality control systems similar to those used in manufacturing were devised, and increased automation occurred, although the processing jobs remained essentially the same as they had before the transition—work was still fragmented. The centralized assembly line had been replaced by many parallel assembly lines.

By many standards, the program developed was successful. Despite inflation, the costs of processing transactions had stabilized. In addition, another customer survey indicated improvements in accuracy and speed. However, management was still unhappy about the bank's current position, even though it had moved to the middle of the pack of surveyed banks. Also, this survey pointed out a particularly disturbing problem. Evidently, in improving the *efficiency* of its interaction with customers, the bank had acquired the image of being *less personal*. Especially when compared with smaller institutions, Citibank was seen as offering less personalized service in a business that is founded on such service.

To cope with the need to provide unique, personalized service to its customers, Citibank embarked on a second program—services management. Services management consisted of three interrelated components. First, the market was segmented more carefully than it had been with the previous management program. A real attempt was made to tie customers who had particular needs (e.g., a British correspondent bank seeking credit for a chemical producer) to an appropriately specialized Citibank unit. This effectively moved expertise and decision-making power closer to the customer. Secondly, minicomputers were adopted to tailor the processing of transactions to this particular customer segment. Even the parallel assembly lines had relied upon standardized, centralized computing. Finally, and very importantly, processing jobs were redesigned to correspond to the new market segmentation and technology. When possible, the assembly lines were abolished.

The nature of the new services management program is well illustrated by the revision of the bank's letter of credit operation. A letter of credit is a complex financial instrument by which a bank in effect serves as an intermediary between one of its customers and a third party. The letter guarantees that the bank will pay the third party on behalf of its customer when certain conditions of a business transaction have been met. Letters of credit are commonly used in international trade. For example, a customer in Saudi Arabia may request a letter of credit to finance the shipment of oil drilling equipment from a Texas manufacturer. When the bank determines that delivery has been made according to agreed-upon conditions, it makes payment to the Texas firm's bank. The basic process of issuance of the letter and payment to the beneficiary is often complicated by intermediate amendments to the letter as the deal progresses and by inquiries from the customer concerning the status of the letter.

A typical letter of credit required the sequential attention of at least fourteen clerks, managers, and officers. This preparation, checking, verifying, and approving involved over 30 separate processing steps and took several days to accomplish. If the customer then requested an amendment to the letter, the process was repeated by a revised cast of characters. A similar unwieldy, lengthy system was followed when it was time to make the payment guaranteed by the letter. This complex, specialized assembly line was simply too slow and fragmented. Employees who could process an issuance knew nothing about amendment, and customer service was handled separately from issuance, amendment, and payment. It was no wonder that customers questioned the personalization of Citibank's service.

In order to improve the letter of credit operation, a services management team began by taking a long, hard look at the actual work that went into processing a letter of credit. Beginning with the simplest, most straightforward examples, they had an experienced veteran process the letters before their eyes, questioning the need for every step, form, file, and rubber stamp. In addition, comprehensive interviews were conducted with other employees. Gradually, the management team was able to develop a streamlined basic letter of credit process which involved half the steps of its predecessor. This new process then became the foundation for simplifying yet more complex letters. It was concluded that a letter of credit could be processed by a single employee using a specially programmed computer.

Careful planning was necessary to move the letter of credit operation from a fourteen-person assembly line to a one-person process. Clerks who were formerly familiar with only one or two steps in the process were to become full-fledged letter of credit professionals. First, computer work stations were designed. Each included a telephone to answer customer inquiries. In addition, the computers themselves were programmed to provide the operator with complete data about his or her customers, so that the customers would no longer be an anonymous cipher on a form. After-hours training in computer operation was provided, and employees began to cross-train each other in the various aspects of letters of credit. Those who knew issuance trained those who knew amendment and vice versa. At all stages, pains were taken to communicate to employees what was happening, and their participation in decision making was sought. For example, workers were consulted extensively about the design of the new work stations. Employees who did not desire the revised jobs were permitted to transfer to other functions. Those who remained were given pay raises to correspond to their increased responsibility.

Now individual employees who were formerly clerks are responsible for all aspects of "their" letters of credit for "their" personal customers. If the customer has a problem to be solved or an amendment to be processed, it is done by the same person who issued the letter. Employees feel possessive about their work stations and often decorate them with souvenirs of the nations they serve. Less direct supervision is necessary since employees now have the knowledge and perspective to solve many problems on their own. In turn, managers in the letter of credit operation can devote their time to customer development rather than to coordinating a fragmented series of processing steps. Since the workers who process letters of credit now understand an important bank process in full, career paths into other aspects of the organization have opened up. By almost all standards, Citibank considers its services management program a great success.

Source: This case is adapted from Matteis, R. J. (1979, March-April). The new back office focuses on customer service. *Harvard Business Review*.

1. Discuss the environmental components of Citibank that are exerting influence at the time of the case.
2. Apply the concepts of environmental uncertainty, resource dependence, and strategy to the Citibank case.
3. Discuss Citibank's first program to improve its services, considering the interplay among strategy, structure, and technology. Why was this program partially successful? Why was it not more successful?
4. Discuss Citibank's second program (services management) to improve its services, again considering the interplay among strategy, structure, and technology.
5. Discuss how advanced technology shaped the design of the letters of credit jobs. Were the jobs enriched? Support your answer.
6. Not all efforts at organizational change turn out successfully. What factors contributed to the success of the redesign of the letters of credit job at Citibank?

LEARNING OBJECTIVES

AFTER READING CHAPTER 17 YOU SHOULD BE ABLE TO:

1 EXPLAIN THE ENVIRONMENTAL FORCES THAT MOTIVATE ORGANIZATIONAL CHANGE.

2 DESCRIBE THE BASIC CHANGE PROCESS AND THE ISSUES THAT REQUIRE ATTENTION AT VARIOUS STAGES OF CHANGE.

3 EXPLAIN HOW ORGANIZATIONS CAN DEAL WITH RESISTANCE TO CHANGE.

4 DEFINE ORGANIZATIONAL DEVELOPMENT AND DISCUSS ITS GENERAL PHILOSOPHY.

5 DISCUSS TEAM BUILDING, SURVEY FEEDBACK, TOTAL QUALITY MANAGEMENT AND REENGINEERING AS ORGANIZATIONAL DEVELOPMENT EFFORTS.

6 DISCUSS THE PROBLEMS INVOLVED IN EVALUATING ORGANIZATIONAL DEVELOPMENT EFFORTS.

7 DEFINE INNOVATION AND DISCUSS THE FACTORS THAT CONTRIBUTE TO SUCCESSFUL ORGANIZATIONAL INNOVATION.

8 UNDERSTAND THE FACTORS THAT HELP AND HURT THE DIFFUSION OF INNOVATIONS.

HARLEY-DAVIDSON WAS PULLED FROM THE BRINK OF BANKRUPTCY BY INNOVATIVE MANAGEMENT AND A DEDICATED WORKFORCE.

CHAPTER 17

ORGANIZATIONAL CHANGE, DEVELOPMENT, AND INNOVATION

HARLEY-
DAVIDSON
MOTOR
COMPANY

In 1906 Harley-Davidson Motor Company had one full-time employee who had, up to that point, built a total of 50 motorcycles. This compares to today's production of several hundred bikes per day. The problem was that between the company's 1903 inception and the 1970s production had rapidly expanded at the expense of quality. The quality of the bikes was so bad that at one point it was said you could tell where a Harley had been parked by the puddle of oil on the pavement.

By the mid 1970s the situation became more critical when Japanese motorcycle makers, such as Honda and Yamaha, aggressively introduced high quality state-of-the-art heavyweight machines in direct competition to Harley's once exclusive market known as "Hog Heaven." Harley's share of the heavyweight motorcycle market eroded from

78 percent in 1973 to 31 percent in 1980 to 13 percent in 1983. The number of employees went from a peak of 4,000 in 1980 to 2,200 in 1982. The company nearly went bankrupt because of its outdated technology and badly managed manufacturing processes.

In 1981, new management began to examine the management and manufacturing techniques used by the Japanese. A 10 year plan was formulated to improve engines to provide better performance and attract new customers by offering the same quality as the Japanese bikes. To accomplish these goals, Harley adapted three Japanese techniques that were seldom used at the time in North America: 1) Intensive employee involvement in decision making, 2) Just-in-time inventory control to reduce expensive parts inventories and deliver parts to the assembly line when needed, 3) Statistical operator control which enables employees to measure and manage the quality of their own production. In combination, these three techniques formed the Productivity Triad. Initial resistance was overcome by intensive team building and by sending managers to the University of Tennessee's Institute of Productivity and Quality.

In an attempt to become close to its customer, Harley also formed the Harley Owners Group (HOG) in 1983. This two-way medium allows the company to communicate with the over 200,000 members through magazines and newsletters as well as receive feedback from these customers.

Harley is experiencing phenomenal growth. Market share rose to 51 percent by 1990 and to over 60 percent by 1993. The company has 20 percent of Japan's heavyweight motorcycle market. Today, Harley-Davidson has more than $1.2 billion in sales. Its market share and sales continue to increase in the face of a shrinking market.

The vice-president of sales sums up his philosophy and that of the Harley-Davidson Motor Company: "Success is a journey and not a destination. And the journey is never over."[1]

───

This story reflects the themes of our chapter. Harley's environment changed, and it had to change with it to survive and prosper. This change required innovations in both products and management processes.

In this chapter we will discuss the concept of organizational change, including the whys and whats of change. Then, we'll consider the process by which change occurs and examine problems involved in managing change. Following this, we define organizational development and explore several development strategies as well as innovation, a special class of organizational change.

THE CONCEPT OF ORGANIZATIONAL CHANGE

Common experience indicates that organizations are far from static. Our favorite small restaurant experiences success and expands. We return for a visit to our alma mater and observe a variety of new programs and new buildings. The local Chevy dealer also begins to sell Geos. As consumers, we are aware that such changes may have a profound impact on our satisfaction with the product or service offered. By extension, we can also imagine that these changes have a strong impact on the people who work at the restaurant, university, or car dealership. In and of themselves, such changes are neither good nor bad. Rather, it is the way in which the changes are *implemented* and *managed* that is crucial to both customers and members. This is the focus of the present chapter.

Why Organizations Must Change

All organizations face two basic sources of pressure to change—external sources and internal sources.

In Chapter 16 we pointed out that organizations are open systems that take inputs from the environment, transform some of these inputs, and send them back into the environment as outputs. Most organizations work hard to stabilize their inputs and outputs. For example, a manufacturing firm might use a variety of suppliers to avoid a shortage of raw materials and attempt to turn out quality products to ensure demand. However, there are limits on the extent to which such control over the environment can occur. In this case, environmental changes must be matched by organizational changes if the organization is to remain effective. For example, consider the successful producer of record turntables in 1970. In only a few years, the turntable market virtually disappeared with the advent of reasonably priced cassette and CD players. If the firm was unable to anticipate this by developing a new product and a market, it surely ceased to exist.

Probably the best recent example of the impact of the external environment in stimulating organizational change is the increased competitiveness of business. Brought on in part by a more global economy, deregulation, and advanced technology, businesses have had to become, as the cliche goes, leaner and meaner. Companies such as IBM and GM have laid off thousands of employees. Many firms did away with layers of middle managers, developing flatter structures so as to be more responsive to competitive demands. Mergers, acquisitions, and joint ventures with foreign firms have become commonplace, as have less adversarial relationships with unions and suppliers. Harley-Davidson was an early player in this game as it came to grips with the threat that Japanese motorcycle producers posed.

Change can also be provoked by forces in the internal environment of the organization. Low productivity, conflict, strikes, sabotage, and high absenteeism and turnover are some of the factors that signal to management that change is necessary. Very often, internal forces for change occur in response to organizational changes that are designed to deal with the external environment. Thus, many mergers and acquisitions that were to bolster the competitiveness of an organization have been followed by cultural conflict between the merged parties. This conflict often stimulates further changes that were not anticipated at the time of the merger.

The discussion of organizational change is traditional in organizational behavior texts. However, the trends we are discussing here have truly magnified the importance of this topic. In contemporary organizations, much change is led by top management and involves sweeping modifications of a strategy. The entire organization is likely to be affected, and familiar employee values are likely to be challenged.[2]

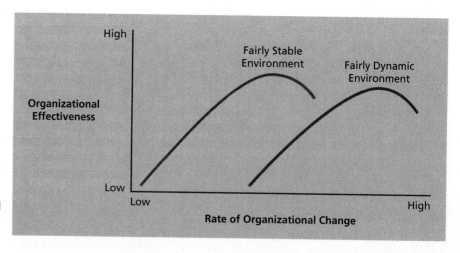

EXHIBIT 17.1
Relationships among environmental change, organizational change, and organizational effectiveness.

In spite of these trends toward change, the internal and external environments of various organizations will be more or less dynamic. In responding to this, organizations should differ in the amount of change they exhibit. Exhibit 17.1 shows that organizations in a dynamic environment must generally exhibit more change to be effective than those operating in a more stable environment. Also, change in and of itself is not a good thing, and organizations can exhibit too much change as well as too little. The company that is in constant flux fails to establish the regular patterns of organizational behavior that are necessary for effectiveness.

What Organizations Can Change

In theory, organizations can change just about any aspect of their operations they wish. Since change is a broad concept, it is useful to identify several specific domains in which modifications can occur. Of course, the choice of *what* to change depends upon a well-informed analysis of the internal and external forces signaling that change is necessary.[3] Factors that can be changed include:

- *Goals and strategies.* Organizations frequently change their goals and the strategies they use to reach these goals. Expansion, the introduction of new products, and the pursuit of new markets represent such changes.

- *Technology.* Technological changes can vary from minor to major. The introduction of on-line computer access for employees is a fairly minor change. Moving from a rigid assembly line to flexible manufacturing is a major change.

- *Job design.* Companies can redesign individual groups of jobs to offer more or less variety, autonomy, identity, significance, and feedback, as we discussed in Chapter 7.

- *Structure.* Organizations can be modified from a functional to a product form or vice versa. Formalization and centralization can be manipulated, as can tallness, spans of control, and networking with other firms. Structural changes also include modifications in rules, policies, and procedures.

- *Processes.* The basic processes by which work is accomplished can be changed. For instance, some stages of a project might be done concurrently rather than sequentially.
- *People.* The membership of an organization can be changed in two senses. First, the actual *content* of the membership can be changed through a revised hiring process. This is often done to introduce "new blood" or to take advantage of the opportunities that a more diverse labor pool offers. Second, the existing membership can be changed in terms of skills and attitudes by various training and development methods.

Two important points should be made about the various areas in which organization can introduce change. First, a change in one area very often calls for changes in others. Failure to recognize this systemic nature of change can lead to severe problems. For example, consider the functionally organized East Coast chemical firm that decides to expand its operations to the West Coast. To be effective, this goal and strategy change might require some major structural changes, including a more geographic form and decentralization of decision-making power.

Second, changes in goals, strategies, technology, structure, process, and job design almost always require that organizations give serious attention to people changes. As much as possible, necessary skills and favorable attitudes should be fostered *before* these changes are introduced. For example, although providing bank employees with a revised computer system is a fairly minor technological change, it might provoke anxiety on the part of those whose jobs are affected. Adequate technical training and clear, open communication about the change can do much to alleviate this anxiety. At Harley-Davidson, the introduction of process changes such as just-in-time inventory wouldn't have worked without the employee involvement program.

The Change Process

By definition, change involves a sequence of organizational events or a psychological process that occurs over time. The distinguished psychologist Kurt Lewin has suggested that this sequence or process involves three basic stages—unfreezing, changing, and refreezing.[4]

Unfreezing. Unfreezing occurs when recognition exists that some current state of affairs is unsatisfactory. This might involve the realization that the present structure, task design, or technology is ineffective or that member skills or attitudes are inappropriate. *Crises* are especially likely to stimulate unfreezing. A dramatic drop in sales, a big lawsuit, or an unexpected strike are examples of such crises. At Ontario Hydro, for example, hundreds of managers had to reapply for their own jobs as part of a massive reorganization and culture-change effort. Talk about getting people's attention! A visit to Honda's U.S. motorcycle plant by Harley-Davidson executives shocked them. The plant's great efficiency was obtained without a computer and with very few support staff. Of course, unfreezing can also occur without crisis. Employee attitude surveys, customer surveys, and accounting data are often used to anticipate problems and initiate change before crises are reached.

Unfreezing. The recognition that some current state of affairs is unsatisfactory.

Change. The implementation of a program or plan to move an organization and/or its members to a more satisfactory state.

Change.   Change occurs when some program or plan is implemented to move the organization and/or its members to a more satisfactory state. The terms *program* and *plan* are used rather loosely here, since some change efforts reveal inadequate planning. Change efforts can range from minor to major. A simple skills training program and a revised hiring procedure constitute fairly minor changes in which few organizational members are involved. Conversely, major changes that involve many members might include extensive job enrichment, radical restructuring, or serious attempts at empowering the workforce.

Refreezing. The condition that exists when newly developed behaviors, attitudes, or structures become an enduring part of the organization.

Refreezing.   When changes occur, the newly developed behaviors, attitudes, or structures must be subjected to **refreezing** that is, they must become an enduring part of the organization. At this point, the effectiveness of the change can be examined, and the desirability of extending the change further can be considered. It should be emphasized that refreezing is a relative and temporary state of affairs. As the "In Focus: *Organizational Learning*" shows, contemporary organizations need to be prepared for continuous learning and frequent change.

ISSUES IN THE CHANGE PROCESS

The simple sketch of the change process presented in the preceding section ignores several important issues that organizations must confront during the process. These issues represent problems that must be overcome if the process is to be effective. Exhibit 17.2 illustrates the relationship between the stages of change and these problems, which include diagnosis, resistance, evaluation, and institutionalization.

Diagnosis

Diagnosis. The systematic collection of information relevant to impending organizational change.

Diagnosis is the systematic collection of information relevant to impending organizational change. Initial diagnosis can provide information that contributes to unfreezing by showing that a problem exists. Once unfreezing occurs, further diagnosis can clarify the problem and suggest just what changes should be implemented. It is one thing to feel that "hospital morale has fallen drastically" but quite another to be sure that this is true and to decide what to do about it.

Relatively routine diagnosis might be handled through existing channels. For example, suppose the director of a hospital laboratory believes that many

EXHIBIT 17.2
The change process and change problems.

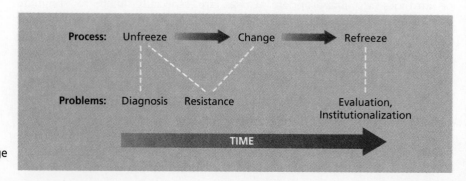

IN FOCUS   Organizational Learning

Dr. Matthew J. Kiernan, chairman of the Innovest Group International, describes the concept of organizational learning:

In the twenty-first century, the case for the "learning organization," with knowledge creation as its primary strategic task, will be overwhelming. Organizational learning will replace control as the dominant responsibility and test of senior management and leadership. It requires, first of all, an organizational culture which exalts above all else continuous improvement and innovation from everybody, and which embraces change rather than fearing and seeking to minimize it.

Successful firms of the next century (and, increasingly, even of this one) will also have to have feedback and data-gathering instruments, such as MIS and performance measurement systems, which are capable of delivering *strategically* relevant information—ie., qualitative as well as quantitative—to the right people, and in real time. Performance measurement is absolutely fundamental to organizational learning. If one has little or no idea how successful one's last marketplace intervention has been, or why, the prospects for learning very much of use to the next project are slim indeed.

One important technique for maximizing organizational learning from the business environment is bench marking best practices; not only those of direct competitors but of *anyone* from whom something useful can be learned or adapted. Yet another potentially useful but grossly under used instrument for gathering strategic intelligence is the training and deployment of the firm's "front-line troops" (delivery, sales, repair, and secretarial staff, bank tellers and the like) as incredibly fertile sources of customer feedback and market information. A third technique is the strategic use of temporary personnel assignments and rotations—not only between departments but even with suppliers, customers, and strategic alliance partners.

Organizational learning also has major implications for strategic human resource management. For starters, the company's attitude to training needs to change substantially to embrace life-long learning for everyone, and to stress group rather than individual learning experiences. The content of the training programs has to change too, placing far greater emphasis on the "soft" process skills of managing change, innovation and learning, and less on seeking to implant hard "factual" knowledge, which has an increasingly short half-life.

Perhaps most difficult of all, organizational learning also means surfacing and re-examining all of those inarticulate assumptions about the firm and its business environment which, while never explicitly scrutinized or even acknowledged, drive much of what the firm actually does. Thus, organizational learning is about more than simply acquiring *new* knowledge and insights; it is also crucial (and arguably more difficult) to un-learn the *old* ones when they have outlived their relevance. Rigorously rooting out these obsolescent assumptions and challenging them can expose critical discrepancies between external reality and the firm's internal mental models, and it is these gaps which provide much of the creative tension and dynamic energy which drives organizational learning.

Source: Excerpted from Kiernan, M. J. (1993, February). The new strategic architecture: Learning to compete in the twenty-first century. *Academy of Management Executive*, 7–21, pp. 9, 10.

of his lab technicians do not possess adequate technical skills. In conjunction with the hospital personnel manager, the director might arrange for a formal test of these skills. The hospital could devise a training program to correct inadequacies and establish a more stringent selection program to hire better personnel.

For more complex, nonroutine problems, there is considerable merit in seeking out the diagnostic skills of a change agent. **Change agents** are experts in the application of behavioral science knowledge to organizational diagnosis and change. Some large firms have in-house change agents who are available for consultation. In other cases, outside consultants might be brought in. In any event, the change agent brings an independent, objective perspective to the diagnosis while working with the people who are about to undergo change.

Change agents. Experts in the application of behavioral science knowledge to organizational diagnosis and change.

It is possible to obtain diagnostic information through a combination of observations, interviews, questionnaires, and the scrutiny of records. Attention to the views of customers or clients is critical. As the next section will show, there is usually considerable merit in using questionnaires and interviews to involve the intended targets of change in the diagnostic process. The next section will also show why the change agent must be perceived as *trustworthy* by his or her clients.

The importance of careful diagnosis cannot be overemphasized. Proper diagnosis clarifies the problem, suggests *what* should be changed and the proper *strategy* for implementing change without resistance.[5] Unfortunately, many firms have a tendency to imitate the change programs of their competitors or other visible firms without doing a careful diagnosis of their own specific needs. Similarly, managers sometimes confuse symptoms with underlying problems. This usually leads to trouble.

Resistance

As the saying goes, people are creatures of habit, and change is frequently resisted by those at whom it is targeted. More precisely, people may resist both unfreezing and change. At the unfreezing stage, defense mechanisms (Chapter 14) might be activated to deny or rationalize the signals that change is needed. Even if there is agreement that change is necessary, any specific plan for change might be resisted. This has been commonplace in recent years in U.S. national politics. Although Congress has recognized the need to enhance federal revenues or reduce spending to reduce the budget deficit, many specific plans to do one or both have encountered strong resistance.

Resistance. Overt or covert failure by organizational members to support a change effort.

Causes of Resistance.   **Resistance** to change occurs when people either overtly or covertly fail to support the change effort. Why does such failure of support occur? Several common reasons include the following:[6]

- *Politics and self-interest.* People might feel that they personally will lose status, power, or even their jobs with the advent of the change.

- *Low individual tolerance for change.* Predispositions in personality might make some people uncomfortable with changes in established routines.

- *Misunderstanding.* The reason for the change or the exact course that the change will take might be misunderstood.

- *Lack of trust.* People might clearly understand the arguments being made for change but not trust the motives of those proposing the change.

- *Different assessments of the situation.* The targets of change might sincerely feel that the situation does not warrant the proposed change and that the advocates of change have misread the situation. (At UPS, managers saw the introduction of scanning bar-coded packages as a way to help customers trace goods. Employees saw it as a way to track them and spy on them.[7])

- *A resistant organizational culture.* Some organizational cultures have especially stressed and rewarded stability and tradition. Advocates of change in such cultures are viewed as misguided deviants or aberrant outsiders. (When deregulation forced massive changes at AT&T, the resistant traditionalists were labeled "bellheads" by the new guard![8])

Underlying these various reasons for resistance are two major themes: 1) Change is unnecessary because there is only a small gap between the organization's current identity and its ideal identity, 2) Change is unobtainable (and threatening) because the gap between the current and ideal identities is too large. Exhibit 17.3 shows that a moderate identity gap is probably most conducive to increased acceptance of change, because it unfreezes people while not provoking maximum resistance.

Dealing With Resistance.[9]   Low tolerance for change is mainly an individual matter, and it can often be overcome with supportive, patient supervision.

If politics and self-interest are at the root of resistance, it might be possible to co-opt the reluctant by giving them a special, desirable role in the change process or by negotiating special incentives for change. For example, consider office computing. Many heads of information services resisted the proliferation of personal computers, feeling that this change would reduce their power as departments moved away from dependence on the mainframe. Some organizations countered this resistance by giving information services control over the purchase, maintenance, and networking of personal computers, providing an incentive for change.

If misunderstanding, lack of trust, or different assessments are provoking resistance, good communication can pay off. Contemporary organizations are learning that obsessive secrecy about strategy and competition can have more internal costs than external benefits. It is particularly critical that lower-level managers understand the diagnosis underlying intended change and the details of the change so that they can convey this information to employees accurately. Springing "secret" changes on employees, especially when these changes involve matters such as workforce reduction, is sure to provoke resistance.

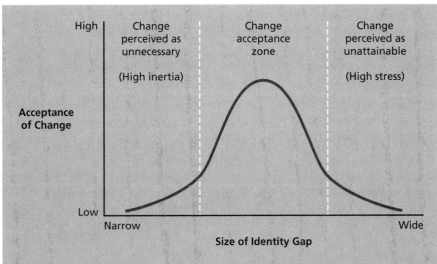

Source: Reger, R. K., Gustafson, L. T., DeMarie, S. M., & Mullane, J. V. (1994). Reframing the organization: Why implementing total quality is easier said than done. *Academy of Management Review, 19*, 565–584.

EXHIBIT 17.3
Probability of acceptance of change.

Involving the people who are the targets of change in the change process often reduces their resistance.[10] This is especially appropriate when there is adequate time for participation, when true commitment ("ownership") to the change is critical, and when the people who will be affected by the change have unique knowledge to offer. Here's how Harley-Davidson dealt with a change to a just-in-time inventory system:

> After a visit to Honda's plant in Marysville, Ohio, and a successful pilot program, they decided to introduce just-in-time inventory control and quality improvement. Some of the workers laughed at the idea of replacing Harley's computerized control system, overhead conveyors, and high-rise parts storage with just-in-time push carts. To deal with the resistance, Harley executives spent months meeting with employees from all departments. The employees were involved in planning the system and working out the details. "No changes were implemented until the people involved understood and accepted them. It took two months before the consensus decision was made to go ahead. That was a Friday—and we started making the changes on Monday." The employees responded with initiative.[11]

Finally, transformational leaders (Chapter 10) are particularly adept at overcoming resistance to change. One way they accomplish this is by "striking while the iron is hot," that is, by being especially sensitive to when followers are *ready* for change. For example, when Lee Iacocca became president of Chrysler, the situation was so bad that employees knew that change would have to occur. The other way is to unfreeze current thinking by installing practices that constantly examine and question the status quo. One research study of CEOs who were transformational leaders noted the following unfreezing practices:[12]

- An atmosphere is established in which dissent is not only tolerated but encouraged. Proposals and ideas are given tough objective reviews, and disagreement is not viewed as disloyalty.

- The environment is scanned for objective information about the organization's true performance. This might involve putting lots of outsiders on the board of directors or sending technical types out to meet customers.

- Organizational members are sent to other organizations and even other countries to see how things are done elsewhere.

- The organization compares itself along a wide range of criteria *against the competition,* rather than simply comparing its performance against last year's. This avoids complacency.

Transformational leaders are skilled at using the new ideas that stem from these practices to create a revised vision for followers about what the organization can do or be. Often, a radically reshaped culture is the result. In the process, as we suggested in Chapter 10, they are good at inspiring trust and encouraging followers to subordinate their individual self-interests for the good of the organization. This combination of tactics keeps followers within the zone of acceptance shown in Exhibit 17.3.

Before continuing, let's see how understanding resistance to change can help in introducing workforce diversity programs. Please consult *You Be the Manager.*

ENCOURAGING WORKFORCE DIVERSITY AT HOECHST CELANESE

YOU BE THE Manager

Hoechst Celanese Corporation is a giant chemical firm based in Somerville, New Jersey. Its former CEO and Chairman, Ernest H. Drew, had several experiences that convinced him that encouraging workforce diversity at all levels could provide the company with an important competitive advantage. In one case, he attended a conference that included the firm's top 125 officers (mostly white males) and a number of lower-ranking women and minorities. Problem-solving teams made up of these individuals were assigned to suggest improvements to the corporate culture. Drew was impressed how the more diverse teams tended to develop broader solutions. At around the same time, a diverse management team in the polyester filament division developed a revised business strategy that resulted in substantial financial improvements.

> FORMER CEO OF HOECHST CELANESE, ERNEST H. DREW, WAS IMPRESSED BY A CONFERENCE THAT ORGANIZED EMPLOYEES INTO TEAMS TO SOLVE A PROBLEM. THE MORE DIVERSE TEAMS TENDED TO DEVELOP BROADER SOLUTIONS.

The record shows that despite corporate rhetoric, many firms have had trouble introducing the kinds of changes that are necessary to increase workforce diversity. Some of this is due to employee resistance, and some of it is due to inadequate change tactics. What can a company do to achieve its goal of encouraging diversity at all levels? You be the manager.

1. What are the sources of resistance to change that diversity programs might encounter?

2. What can a company do to overcome resistance to its diversity efforts?

To find out what Ernest Drew and Hoechst Celanese did, consult *The Manager's Notebook* at the end of the chapter.

Source: Adapted from Rice, F. (1994, August 8). How to make diversity pay. *Fortune*, 78–86.

Evaluation and Institutionalization

It seems only reasonable to evaluate changes to determine whether they accomplished what they were supposed to and whether that accomplishment is now considered adequate. Obviously, objective goals such as return on investment or market share might be easiest and most likely to be evaluated. Of course, organizational politics can intrude to cloud even the most objective evaluation.

Organizations are notorious for doing a weak job of evaluating "soft" change programs that involve skills, attitudes, and values. However, it is possible to do a thorough evaluation by considering a range of variables:

- Reactions—did participants like the change program?
- Learning—what was acquired in the program?
- Behavior—what changes in job behavior occurred?
- Outcomes—what changes in productivity, absence, etc., occurred?[13]

To some extent, reactions measure resistance, learning reflects change, and behavior reflects successful refreezing. Outcomes indicate whether refreezing is useful for the organization. Unfortunately, many evaluations of change efforts never go beyond the measurement of reactions. Again, part of the reason for this may be political. The people who propose the change effort fear reprisal if failure occurs.

If the outcome of change is evaluated favorably, the organization will wish to institutionalize that change. This means that the change becomes a permanent part of the organizational system, a social fact that persists over time despite possible turnover by the members who originally experienced the change.[14]

Logic suggests that it should be fairly easy to institutionalize a change that has been deemed successful. However, we noted that many change efforts go unevaluated or are only weakly evaluated, and without hard proof of success it is very easy for institutionalization to be rejected by disaffected parties. This is a special problem for extensive, broad-based change programs that call for a large amount of commitment from a variety of parties (e.g., extensive participation, job enrichment, or work restructuring). It is one thing to institutionalize a simple training program but quite another to do the same for complex interventions that can be judged from a variety of perspectives.

Studies of more complex change efforts indicate that a number of factors can inhibit institutionalization. For example, promised extrinsic rewards (such as pay bonuses) might not be developed to accompany changes. Similarly, initial changes might provide intrinsic rewards that create higher expectations that cannot be fulfilled. Institutionalization might also be damaged if new hires are not carefully socialized to understand the unique environment of the changed organization. As turnover occurs naturally, the change effort might backslide. In a similar vein, key management supporters of the change effort might resign or be transferred. Finally, environmental pressures such as decreased sales or profits can cause management to regress to more familiar behaviors and abandon change efforts.[15]

It stands to reason that many of the problems of evaluation and institutionalization can be overcome by careful planning and goal setting during the diagnostic stage. In fact, *planning* is a key issue in any change effort. Let's now examine organizational development, a means of effecting planned change.

ORGANIZATIONAL DEVELOPMENT: PLANNED ORGANIZATIONAL CHANGE

Organizational development (OD). A planned, ongoing effort to change organizations to be more effective and more human.

Organizational development (OD) is a planned, ongoing effort to change organizations to be more effective and more human. It uses the knowledge of behavioral science to foster a culture of organizational self-examination and readiness for change. A strong emphasis is placed on interpersonal and group processes.[16]

The fact that OD is *planned* distinguishes it from the haphazard, accidental, or routine changes that occur in all organizations. OD efforts tend to be *ongoing* in at least two senses. First, many OD programs extend over a long period of time, involving several distinct phases of activities. Second, if OD becomes institutionalized, continual reexamination and readiness for further change become permanent parts of the culture. In trying to make organizations more *effective* and more *human,* OD gives recognition to the critical link between personal processes such as leadership, decision making, and communication and organizational outcomes such as productivity and efficiency. The fact that OD uses *behavioral science knowledge* distinguishes it from other change strategies that rely solely upon principles of accounting, finance, or engineering. However, an OD intervention may also incorporate these principles. OD seeks to modify *cultural norms and roles* so that the organization remains self-conscious and prepared for adaptation. Finally, a focus on *interpersonal* and *group* processes recognizes that all organizational change affects members, and their cooperation is necessary to implement change.

To summarize the above, we can say that OD recognizes that systematic attitude change must accompany changes in behavior, whether these behavior changes are required by revisions in tasks, work processes, organizational structure, or business strategies.

Traditionally, the values and assumptions of OD change agents were decidedly humanistic and democratic. Thus, self-actualization, trust, cooperation, and the open expression of feelings among all organizational members have been viewed as desirable.[17] In recent years, OD practitioners have shown a more active concern with organizational effectiveness and with using development practices to further the strategy of the organization. This joint concern with both people and performance has thus become the credo of many contemporary OD change agents. The focus has shifted from simple humanistic advocacy to generating data or alternatives that allow organizational members to make informed choices.[18]

SOME SPECIFIC ORGANIZATIONAL DEVELOPMENT STRATEGIES

The organization that seeks to "develop itself" has recourse to a wide variety of specific techniques, and many have been used in combination. We discussed some of these techniques earlier in the book. For example, job enrichment and management by objectives(Chapter 7) are usually classed as OD efforts, as is diversity training (Chapter 4). In this section we will discuss four additional OD methods that illustrate the diversity of the practice. Team building illustrates how work teams can be fine-tuned to work well together. Survey feedback shows how OD can be conceived of as an ongoing applied research effort. Total quality management shows how organizations can prepare themselves for continuous improvement. Finally, reengineering illustrates the radical redesign of organizational processes. The first two methods are limited in scope and are often a part of other change efforts. The second two methods are broader in scope and lead to more sweeping change.

Team Building

Team building attempts to increase the effectiveness of work teams by improving interpersonal processes, goal clarification, and role clarification.[19] (What is our team trying to accomplish, and who is responsible for what?) As such, it can facilitate communication and coordination. The term *team* can refer to intact work groups, special task forces, new work units, or people from various parts of an organization who must work together to achieve a common goal.

Team building usually begins with a diagnostic session, often held away from the workplace, in which the team explores its current level of functioning. The team might use several sources of data to accomplish its diagnosis. Some data might be generated through sensitivity training, outdoor "survival" exercises, or open-ended discussion sessions. In addition, "hard" data such as

Team building. An effort to increase the effectiveness of work teams by improving interpersonal processes, goal clarification, and role clarification.

attitude survey results and production figures might be used. The goal at this stage is to paint a picture of the current strengths and weaknesses of the team. The ideal outcome of the diagnostic session is a list of needed changes to improve team functioning. Subsequent team-building sessions usually have a decidedly task-oriented slant—How can we actually implement the changes indicated by the diagnosis? Problem solving by subgroups might be used at this stage. Between the diagnostic and follow-up sessions, the change agent might hold confidential interviews with team members to anticipate implementation problems. Throughout, the change agent acts as a catalyst and resource person.

The city government of Tacoma, Washington, assisted by external consultants, has made extensive use of team building to improve communications within and between existing departments.[20] Because the work of the personnel department affected that of all other departments, any errors in personnel had a high degree of impact and visibility. As a result, personnel had become the scapegoat of the system. Initial team-building sessions concentrated on having department members identify and work out internal communication problems. In addition, clients of the personnel department from other city departments were invited to day-long sessions in which they aired their complaints to personnel and worked out solutions. One result of this was a system by which each client department was assigned to a particular member of the personnel department. This member then served as an ongoing "contact person" to expedite requests from clients.

When team building is used to develop *new* work teams, the preliminary diagnostic session might involve attempts to clarify expected role relationships and additional training to build trust among team members. In subsequent sessions the expected task environment might be simulated with role-playing exercises. One company used this integrated approach to develop the management team of a new plant.[21] In the simulation portion of the development, typical problems encountered in opening a new plant were presented to team members via hypothetical in-basket memos and telephone calls. In role-playing the solutions to these problems, they reached agreement about how they would have to work together on the job and gained a clear understanding of each other's competencies. Plant startups were always problem-laden, but this was the smoothest in the history of the company.

Team building can also work to facilitate change. Harley-Davidson used it to introduce resistant middle managers to employee involvement concepts. At Oldsmobile, select dealers who wished to sell the new Aurora had to participate in team building. One goal was to get them to adopt no-haggle pricing policies and not undercut each other's prices. U.S. West Communications used team building to lead a geographically dispersed management group through a stressful downsizing and reorganization.[22]

Ideally, team building is a continuing process that involves regular diagnostic sessions and further development exercises as needed. This permits the team to anticipate new problems and to avoid the tendency to regress to less effective predevelopment habits.

To sell the new Aurora, select Oldsmobile dealers had to participate in team-building exercises.

Survey Feedback

Survey feedback. The collection of data from organizational members and the provision of feedback about the results.

In bare-bones form, **survey feedback** involves collecting data from organizational members and feeding these data back to them in a series of meetings in which members explore and discuss the data.[23] The purpose of the meetings is to suggest or formulate changes that emerge from the data. In some respects, survey feedback is similar to team building. However, survey feedback places more emphasis on the collection of valid data and less emphasis on the interpersonal processes of specific work teams. Rather, it tends to focus on the relationship between organizational members and the larger organization.

As its name implies, survey feedback's basic data generally consists of either interviews or questionnaires completed by organizational members. Before this data is collected, a number of critical decisions must be made by the change agent and organizational management. First, who should participate in the survey? Sometimes, especially in large organizations, the survey could be restricted to particular departments, jobs, or organizational levels where problems exist. However, most survey feedback efforts attempt to cover the entire organization. This approach recognizes the systemic nature of organizations and permits a comparison of survey results across various subunits.

Second, should questionnaires or interviews be used to gather data? The key issues here are coverage and cost. It is generally conceded that *all* members of a target group should be surveyed. This procedure builds trust and confidence in survey results. If the number of members is small, the change agent could conduct structured interviews with each person. Otherwise, cost considerations dictate the use of a questionnaire. In practice, this is the most typical data-gathering approach.

Finally, what questions should the survey ask? Two approaches are available. Some change agents use prepackaged, standardized surveys such as the University of Michigan Survey of Organizations.[24] This questionnaire covers areas such as communication and decision-making practices and employee satisfaction. Such questionnaires are usually carefully constructed and permit comparisons with other organizations in which the survey has been conducted.

There is some danger that prepackaged surveys might neglect critical areas for specific consideration. In and of itself, this is bad enough, but the apparent lack of relevance of a packaged survey can reduce the care that members take in completing it or reduce trust in the final results. For these reasons, many change agents choose to devise their own custom-tailored surveys. They might begin with a series of interviews to determine potential problem areas. In some cases, a task force of organizational members might also be enlisted to help develop the final version of the survey. Again, the goal is to build relevance, trust, and involvement in the people who will be surveyed. This should guarantee valid data. To increase the involvement of managerial personnel, they might be asked to predict the results of the survey.

Feedback seems to be most effective when it is presented to natural working units in face-to-face meetings. This method rules out presenting only written feedback or feedback that covers only the organization as a whole. In a manufacturing firm, a natural working unit might consist of a department such as production or marketing. In a school district, such units might consist of individual schools. Many change agents prefer that the manager of the working unit conduct the feedback meeting. This demonstrates management commitment and acceptance of the data. The change agent attends such meetings and helps facilitate discussion of the data and plans for change.

IBM is one firm that has a very active employee survey program that it administers through its worldwide computerized office information system.[25] Travelling employees can log on and complete the survey wherever they are in the world, and "write in" comments are possible. The computerized format makes it very easy to custom-tailor questions by geographical region or occupational group. Because data collection and processing are part of the same system, analysis and feedback times are very short, sometimes only a matter of days.

Ford Motor Company also has a comprehensive, worldwide employee attitude survey called Ford Pulse.[26] Sixty-five core questions that are linked to strategic issues are always completed by both salaried and hourly employees. Up to 35 supplemental questions are custom-developed to cover local issues. Ford validated the importance of the Pulse results at 147 Ford Credit branches in Canada and the U.S. The results showed that branches with higher Pulse scores had higher customer satisfaction, market share, and business volume and lower loan delinquency and employee turnover. The top part of Exhibit 17.4 shows the association between several Pulse dimensions and customer satisfaction with the branch. The lower part shows the association between Pulse scores and market share. These kind of bottom-line results go a long way toward enhancing the credibility of the survey to managers and underlining the importance of accountability for "people issues."

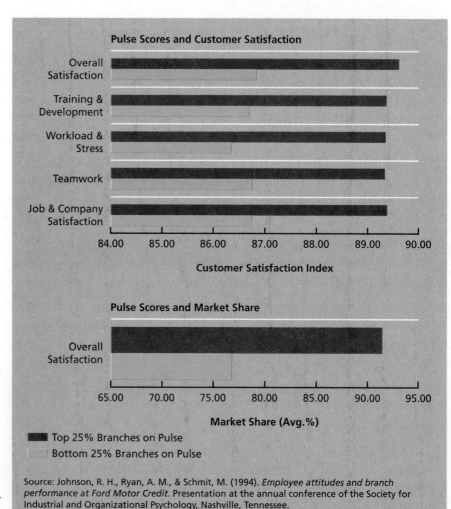

EXHIBIT 17.4
Relationship between Ford Pulse survey scores and customer satisfaction and market share at Ford Motor Credit branches.

Source: Johnson, R. H., Ryan, A. M., & Schmit, M. (1994). *Employee attitudes and branch performance at Ford Motor Credit*. Presentation at the annual conference of the Society for Industrial and Organizational Psychology, Nashville, Tennessee.

Total Quality Management

In Chapters 1 and 7 you will recall that we defined **total quality management** **(TQM)** as a systematic attempt to achieve continuous improvement in the quality of an organization's products and/or services. Typical characteristics of TQM programs include an obsession with customer satisfaction; a concern for good relations with suppliers; continuous improvement of work processes; the prevention of quality errors; frequent measurement and assessment; extensive training; and high employee involvement and teamwork. In Chapter 7 we considered the implication of TQM for employee motivation. Here, we'll focus more on the broad philosophy of TQM and its relationship to organizational change and development.[27]

Prominent names associated with the quality movement include W. Edwards Deming, Joseph Juran, and Philip Crosby.[28] Although each of these "quality gurus" advocates somewhat different paths to quality, all three are concerned with using teamwork to achieve continuous improvement to please customers. Exhibit 17.5 highlights the key principles underlying customer focus, continuous improvement, and teamwork. In turn, each of these principles is associated with certain practices and specific techniques that typify TQM.

The concept of continuous improvement sometimes confuses students of TQM—how can something be more than 100 percent good? To clarify this, it is helpful to view improvement as a continuum ranging from responding to product or service problems (a reactive strategy) to creating new products or services that please customers (a proactive strategy). Exhibit 17.6 illustrates this continuum. Improvement can occur within each stage as well as between stages.[29]

Total quality management (TQM). A systematic attempt to achieve continuous improvement in the quality of an organization's products and/or services.

EXHIBIT 17.5
Principles, practices, and techniques of total quality management.

	Customer Focus	Continuous Improvement	Teamwork
Principles	Paramount importance of providing products and services that fulfill customer needs; requires organizationwide focus on customers	Consistent customer satisfaction can be attained only through relentless improvement of processes that create products and services	Customer focus and continuous improvement are best achieved by collaboration throughout an organization as well as with customers and suppliers
Practices	Direct customer contact Collecting information about customer needs Using information to design and deliver products and services	Process analysis Reengineering Problem solving Plan/do/check/act	Search for arrangements that benefit all units involved in a process Formation of various types of teams Group skills training
Techniques	Customer surveys and focus groups Quality function deployment (translates customer information into product specifications)	Flowcharts Pareto analysis Statistical process control Fishbone diagrams	Organizational development methods such as the nominal group technique Team-building methods (e.g., role clarification and group feedback)

Source: Dean, J. W., Jr., & Bowen, D. E. (1994). Management theory and total quality: Improving research and practice through theory development. *Academy of Management Review, 19*, 392–418.

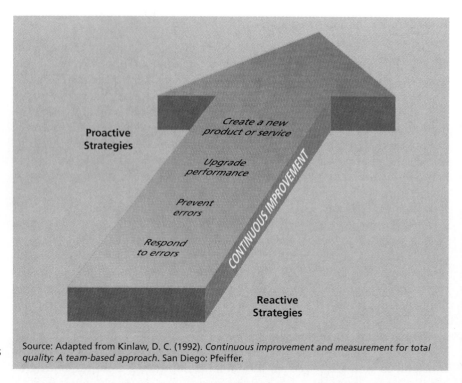

Source: Adapted from Kinlaw, D. C. (1992). *Continuous improvement and measurement for total quality: A team-based approach.* San Diego: Pfeiffer.

EXHIBIT 17.6
A continuum of continuous improvement.

For example, suppose that you check into a hotel and find no towels in your room. Obviously, a fast and friendly correction of this error is better than a slow and surly response, and cutting response time from 15 minutes to 5 minutes would be a great improvement. Better yet, management will try to prevent missing-towel episodes altogether, perhaps using training to move from 96 percent toward 100 percent error-free towel stocking. Although such error *prevention* is a hallmark of TQM, it is also possible to upgrade the service episode. For example, the hotel might work closely with suppliers to provide fluffier towels at the same price or encourage guests to not use too many towels, thus reducing laundry and room costs. Finally, a new service opportunity might be identified and acted on. For example, the Chicago Marriott hotel discovered (after 15 years of operation) that 66 percent of all guests' calls to the housekeeping department were requests for irons or ironing boards. The manager took funds earmarked to replace black-and-white bathroom TVs with color sets and instead equipped each room with an iron and ironing board. No one had ever complained about black-and-white TV in the bathroom.[30]

This chain of hotel examples illustrates several features of the continuous improvement concept and TQM in general.[31] First, continuous improvement can come from small gains over time (e.g., gradually approaching 100 percent error-free room servicing) or from more radical innovation (e.g., offering a new service). In both cases, the goal is long-term improvement, not a short-term "fix." Next, improvement requires knowing where we are in the first place. Thus, TQM is very concerned with measurement and data collection—in our examples, we alluded to speed of service, percent of error-free performance, and frequency of customer requests as examples. Next, TQM stresses teamwork among employees and (in the examples given here) with suppliers and customers. Finally, TQM relies heavily on training to achieve continuous improvement.

Although simple job training can contribute to continuous improvement (as in the towel-stocking example), TQM is particularly known for using specialized training in tools that empower employees to diagnose and solve quality problems on an ongoing basis. Some tools, noted in the bottom row of Exhibit 17.5, include:

- *Flowcharts of work processes.* Flowcharts illustrate graphically the operations and steps in accomplishing some task, noting who does what, and when. For instance, what happens when hotel housekeeping receives a guest request for towels?

- *Pareto analysis.* Pareto analysis collects frequency data on the causes of errors and problems, showing where attention should be directed for maximum improvement. For instance, the Marriott data on reasons for calls to housekeeping corresponds to Pareto data.

- *Fishbone diagrams.* Fishbone (cause-and-effect) diagrams illustrate graphically the factors that could contribute to a particular quality problem. Very specific causes ("small bones") are divided into logical classes or groups ("large bones"). In the hotel example, classes of causes might include people, equipment, methods, and materials.

- *Statistical process control.* Statistical process control gives employees hard data about the quality of their own output that enables them to correct any deviations from standard. TQM places particular emphasis on reducing *variation* in performance over time. Harley-Davidson relied on statistical process control (they called it statistical *operator* control) as part of its Productivity Triad.

These tools to improve the diagnosis and correction of quality problems will not have the desired impact if they fail to improve quality in the eyes of the customer. An essential problem here is that quality has many different and potentially incompatible definitions. For example, ultimate excellence, value for the money, conformance to specifications, or meeting and/or exceeding customer expectations are all potential definitions of quality.[32] Although this last definition would seem to be closest to the TQM principle of customer focus, it is not without its weaknesses. For example, customers might have contradictory expectations. Also, they are more likely to have clear expectations about familiar products and services than new or creative products or services. Nevertheless, organizations with a real commitment to TQM make heavy use of customer surveys, focus groups, mystery shoppers, and customer clinics to stay close to their customers. Harley-Davidson holds customer clinics and sponsors bike rallies to learn from its customers. Also, survey feedback programs allow organizations to obtain information about internal customers (such as how the adjacent department views your department's performance).

TQM programs reveal a large number of successes in firms such as Xerox, L.L. Bean, Motorola, and Ritz-Carlton Hotels. However, they have also had their share of problems, all of which ultimately get expressed as resistance. Despite allowing for radical innovation, TQM is mainly about achieving small gains over a long period of time. This long-term focus can be hard to maintain, especially if managers or employees expect extreme improvements in the short term.

In large, complex organizations, it is possible for real or apparent contradictions to develop among various quality goals. For instance, an intensive study at Northern Telecom discovered that it was pursuing a number of quality initiatives simultaneously, including 1) faster product introduction, 2) cost cutting, 3) enhanced customer satisfaction, 4) certification of the quality of Northern's suppliers, and 5) certification of Northern's quality to its customers. Not surprisingly, this variety of initiatives led to some contradictions both within and between departments as to what was important to focus on. The same study also showed that identifying *internal* customers and providing incentives for satisfying their needs were particular challenges.[33]

Finally, a number of organizations have implemented TQM programs at the same time that they were engaged in radical restructuring or downsizing (e.g., IBM, GM, McDonnell Douglas). Speaking generally, this is not a good recipe for the success of the TQM effort. Employees are likely to be insecure during such periods and unreceptive to calls for initiative and innovation.[34] Cynics may say "the company cares about the customer more than it cares about me."

Despite these problems, the quality movement continues to be one of the most popular of the more elaborate OD efforts.

Reengineering

What does the following mixed bag of companies have in common? Taco Bell, Hallmark Cards, IDS Financial Services, Blue Cross of Washington and Alaska, GTE, Agway, and Bell Atlantic. The answer is that all have experienced reengineering in recent years. Of all the forms of change that we are discussing in this chapter, reengineering is the most fundamental and radical.

Reengineering. The radical redesign of organizational processes to achieve major improvements in factors such as time, cost, quality, or service.

Reengineering is the radical redesign of organizational processes to achieve major improvements in factors such as time, cost, quality, or service.[35] Reengineering does not fine tune existing jobs, structures, technology, or human resources policies. Rather, it uses a "clean slate" approach that asks basic questions such as "What business are we really in?" and "If we were creating this organization today, what would it look like?" Then, jobs, structure, technology, and policy are redesigned around the answers to these questions. Reengineering can be applied to an entire organization, but it can also be applied to a major function such as research and development.

A key word in our definition of reengineering , and one that requires some additional commentary, is *processes*. Processes do not refer to job titles or organizational departments. Rather, **organizational processes** are *activities* or *work* that the organization must accomplish to create outputs that customers (internal or external) value.[36] For example, designing a new product is a process that might involve people holding a variety of jobs in several different departments (R&D, marketing, production, and finance). In theory, the gains from reengineering will be greatest when the process is complex and cuts across a number of jobs and departments.

Organizational processes. Activities or work that have to be accomplished to create outputs that internal or external customers value.

We can contrast reengineering with TQM in that TQM usually seeks incremental improvements in existing processes rather than radical revisions of processes. However, a TQM effort could certainly be part of a reengineering project.

What factors have prompted the current interest in reengineering? One factor is "creeping bureaucracy" that is especially common in large, established firms. With growth, rather than rethinking basic work processes, many firms have simply tacked on more bureaucratic controls to maintain order. This leads to overcomplicated processes and an internal focus on satisfying bureaucratic procedures rather than tending to the customer. Many corporate downsizings have been unsuccessful because they failed to confront bureaucratic controls and basic work processes.

New information technology has also stimulated reengineering. Many firms were disappointed that initial investments in information technology did not result in anticipated reductions in costs or improved productivity. This is because existing processes were simply automated rather that reengineered to correspond to the capabilities of the new technology. Now, it is commonly recognized that advanced technology allows organizations to radically modify (and usually radically simplify) important organizational processes. In other words, work is modified to fit technological capabilities rather than simply fitting the technology to existing jobs. At Ford Motor Company, for example, a look at the entire process for procuring supplies revealed great inefficiencies.[37] Ford employed a large accounts payable staff to issue payments to suppliers when it received invoices. Now, employees at the receiving dock can approve payment when the *goods* are received. Advanced information technology enables them to tap a database to verify that the goods were ordered and issue a check to the supplier. Needless to say, Ford has radically streamlined the payment process, and the accounts payable department now has fewer employees.

How does reengineering actually proceed? In essence, much reengineering is oriented toward one or both of the following goals:[38]

- The number of mediating steps in a process is reduced, making the process more efficient.
- Collaboration among the people involved in the process is enhanced.

Removing the number of mediating steps in a process, if done properly, reduces labor requirements, removes redundancies, decreases chances for errors, and speeds up the production of the final output. All of this happened with Ford's revision of its procurement process. Enhanced collaboration often permits simultaneous, rather than sequential, work on a process and reduces the chances for misunderstanding and conflict.

Some of the nitty gritty aspects of reengineering include the following practices. You'll notice that we've covered many of them in other contexts earlier in the book.[39]

- *Jobs are redesigned, and usually enriched.* Frequently, several jobs are combined into one to reduce mediating steps and provide greater employee control.

- *A strong emphasis is placed on teamwork.* Teamwork (especially cross-functional) is a potent method of enhancing collaboration.

- *Work is performed by the most logical people.* Some firms train customers to do minor maintenance and repairs themselves or turn over the management of some inventory to their suppliers.

- *Unnecessary checks and balances are removed.* When processes are simplified and employees are more collaborative, expensive and redundant controls can sometimes be removed.

- *Advanced technology is exploited.* Computerized technology not only permits combining of jobs, it also enhances collaboration via electronic mail, groupware, and so on.

It is easiest to get a feel for the success of reengineering by considering some of the reductions in mediating steps and improvements in speed that have resulted. CTB Macmillan/McGraw-Hill, a prominent publisher of standardized achievement tests, reduced the steps in its test scoring process from 154 to 68 and its turnaround time for scoring from 21 days to 5. Using software that allows clients to file electronic claims, Blue Cross of Washington and Alaska has handled 17 percent more volume with a 12 percent smaller workforce and halved the time it takes to handle a claim. Using cross-functional teams and advanced technology, Chrysler cut the design time of its successful Jeep Cherokee from 5 years to 39 months.[40] Such "concurrent engineering" is now common in Detroit, enabling North American car manufacturers to approach the short product development cycle time for which the Japanese are noted. At The Limited, fashions now move from design to store in two months rather that the former two *seasons*. Thus, the firm is much more responsive to fickle swings in trends and taste. Computer technology, flatter structures, fewer "signoffs" on new ideas, and a sense of urgency on the part of management often play a role in such transformations.[41]

Reengineering is most extensive in industries where a) much creeping bureaucracy has set in, b) large gains were available with advanced technology and c) deregulation increased the heat of competition. These include the insurance, banking, brokerage, and telecommunications industries.

Because reengineering has the goal of radical change, it requires strong CEO support and transformational leadership qualities. Also, before reengineering begins, it is essential that the organization clarify its overall strategy. What business should we really be in? (Do we want to produce hardware, software, or both?) Given this, who are our customers, and what core processes create value for them? If such strategic clarification is lacking, processes that don't matter to the customer will be reengineered. Strong CEO support and a clear strategy are important for overcoming resistance that simply dismisses people who advocate reengineering as "more efficiency experts." Resistance due to self-interest and organizational politics is likely when radical change may lead to layoffs or major change in work responsibilities.

Recent research shows that reengineering must be both broad and deep to have long-lasting, bottom-line results. That is, it should span a large number of activities that cut costs or add customer value, and it should affect a number of elements including skills, values, roles, incentives, structure, and technology.[42] Half-hearted attempts don't pay off.

DOES ORGANIZATIONAL DEVELOPMENT WORK?

Does it work? That is, do the benefits of OD outweigh the heavy investment of time, effort, and money? At the outset, we should reemphasize that most OD efforts are *not* carefully evaluated. Political factors and budget limitations might be prime culprits, but the situation is not helped by some OD practitioners who argue that certain OD goals (e.g., making the organization more human) are incompatible with impersonal, scientifically rigorous evaluation.

At the very broadest level, two large-scale reviews of a wide variety of OD techniques (including some we discussed in this chapter as well as job redesign, MBO, and goal setting from Chapter 7) reached the following conclusions:[43]

- Most OD techniques have a positive impact on productivity, job satisfaction, or other work attitudes.
- OD seems to work better for supervisors or managers than for blue-collar workers.
- Changes that use more than one technique seem to have more impact.
- There are great differences across sites in the success of OD interventions.

The last finding is probably due to differences in the skill and seriousness with which various organizations have undertaken OD projects.

Exhibit 17.7 summarizes the results of a large number of research studies on the impact of OD change efforts on changes in a variety of outcomes. Organizational arrangements included changes in formal structure and some quality interventions. Social factors included the use of team building and survey feedback. Technology changes mainly involved job redesign. Finally, physical setting interventions (which were rare) included things such as changes to open-plan offices.

As you can see, a healthy percentage of studies reported positive changes following an OD effort. However, many studies also reported no change. This underlines the difficulty of introducing change, and it also suggests that variations in how organizations actually implement change may greatly determine its success. The relative lack of negative change is encouraging, but it is also possible that there is a bias against reporting bad outcomes.[44]

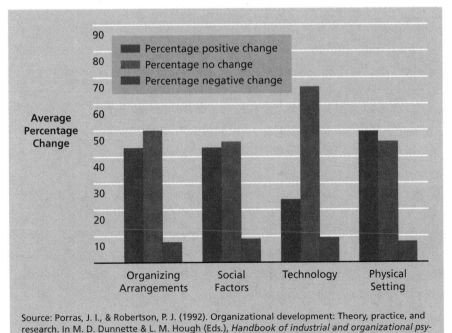

Source: Porras, J. I., & Robertson, P. J. (1992). Organizational development: Theory, practice, and research. In M. D. Dunnette & L. M. Hough (Eds.), *Handbook of industrial and organizational psychology* (2nd ed., Vol. 3). Palo Alto, CA: Consulting Psychologists Press.

EXHIBIT 17.7
Organizational change due to organizational development efforts.

Weak methodology has sometimes plagued research evaluations on the success of OD interventions, although the quality of research seems to be improving over time.[45] Some specific problems include the following:[46]

- OD efforts involve a complex series of changes. There is little evidence of exactly which of these changes produce changes in processes or outcomes.
- Novelty effects or the fact that participants receive special treatment might produce short-term gains that really don't persist over time.
- Self-reports of changes after OD might involve unconscious attempts to please the change agent.
- Organizations may be reluctant to publicize failures.

For these reasons and others, OD continues to be characterized by both problems and promise. Let's hope that promise will overcome problems as organizations try to respond effectively to their increasingly complex and dynamic environments. Speaking of such response, let's turn to innovation.

THE INNOVATION PROCESS

Do you recognize the name Arthur Fry? Probably not. But Arthur Fry is famous in his own way as the inventor of the ubiquitous, sticky Post-its, a top seller among paper office supplies. Fry, a researcher at the innovative 3M Company, developed the product that became Post-its in response to a personal problem—how to keep his place marker from falling out of his church choir hymnal.

To be a successful innovator, an essential ingredient is creativity. Arthur Fry, the inventor of Post-its, used his creativity to establish one of the top sellers in office supplies.

What accounts for the ability of individuals such as Arthur Fry and organizations such as 3M to think up and exploit such innovative ideas? This is the focus of this section of the chapter.

What Is Innovation?

Innovation is the process of developing and implementing new ideas in an organization. The term *developing* is intentionally broad. It covers everything from the genuine invention of a new idea to recognizing an idea in the environment, importing it to the organization, and giving it a unique application.[47] The essential point is a degree of creativity. Arthur Fry didn't invent glue, and he didn't invent paper, but he did develop a creative way to use them together. Then 3M was creative enough to figure out how to market what might have appeared to less probing minds to be a pretty mundane product.

It is possible to roughly classify innovations as product (including service) innovations or process innovations.[48] Product innovations have a direct impact on the cost, quality, style, or availability of a product or service. Thus, they should be very obvious to clients or customers. It is easiest to identify with innovations that result in tangible products, especially everyday consumer products. Thus, we can surely recognize that Polaroid cameras, VCRs, fax machines, and Post-its have been innovative products. Perhaps coming less readily to mind are service innovations such as American Express Travelers Cheques (over 100 years old), FedEx door-to-door courier service, and 24 hour automated banking.

Process innovations are new ways of designing products, making products, or delivering services. In many cases, process changes are invisible to customers or clients, although they help the organization to perform more effectively or efficiently. New technology is a process innovation, whether it be new manufacturing technology or a new management information system. New forms of management and work organization, including job enrichment, participation, reengineering, and quality programs, are also process innovations. Harley-Davidson's Productivity Triad combined three complementary process innovations.

Innovation is often conceived of as a stagelike process that begins with idea generation and proceeds to idea implementation. For some kinds of innovations, it is also hoped that the implemented innovation will diffuse to other sites or locations. This applies especially to process innovations that have begun as pilot or demonstration projects:

$$\text{IDEA GENERATION} \rightarrow \text{IDEA IMPLEMENTATION} \rightarrow \text{IDEA DIFFUSION}$$

In advance of discussing these stages in the following sections, let's note several interesting themes that underlie the process of innovation. First, the beginning of innovation can be pretty haphazard and chaotic, and the conditions necessary to create new ideas might be very different from the conditions necessary to get these ideas implemented. In a related vein, although organizations have to innovate to survive, such innovation might be resisted just like any other organizational change. The result of these tensions is that innovation is frequently a highly political process (Chapter 13).[49] This important point is sometimes overlooked because innovation often involves science and

Innovation. The process of developing and implementing new ideas in an organization.

technology, domains that have a connotation of rationality about them. However, both the champions of innovation and the resisters might behave politically to secure or hold onto critical organizational resources.

Generating and Implementing Innovative Ideas

Innovation requires creative ideas, someone to fight for these ideas, good communication, and the proper application of resources and rewards. Let's examine these factors in detail.

Creativity. The production of novel but potentially useful ideas.

Individual Creativity.   Creative thinking by individuals or small groups is at the core of the innovation process. **Creativity** is usually defined as the production of novel but potentially useful ideas. Thus, creativity is a key aspect of the "developing new ideas" part of our earlier definition of innovation. However, innovation is a broader concept, in that it also involves an attempt to implement new ideas. Not every creative idea gets implemented.

When we see a company such as 3M that is known for its innovations or we see an innovative project completed successfully, we sometimes forget about the role that individual creativity plays in such innovations. However, organizations that have a consistent reputation for innovation have a talent for selecting, cultivating, and motivating creative individuals. Such creativity can come into play at many "locations" during the process of innovation. Thus, the salesperson who discovers a new market for a product might be just as creative as the scientist who developed the product.

What makes a person creative?[50] For one thing, you can pretty much discount the romantic notion of the naive creative genius. Research shows that creative people tend to have an excellent technical understanding of their domain. That is, they understand its basic practices, procedures, and techniques. Thus, creative chemists will emerge from those who are well trained and up-to-date in their field. Similarly, creative money managers will be among those who have a truly excellent grasp of finance and economics. Notice, however, that having good skills in one's specialty doesn't mean that creative people are extraordinarily intelligent. Once we get beyond subnormal intelligence, there is no correlation between level of intelligence and creativity.

Most people with good basic skills in their area are still not creative. What sets the creative people apart are additional *creativity-relevant* skills. These include the ability to tolerate ambiguity, withhold early judgment, see things in new ways, and be open to new and diverse experiences. Some of these skills appear to be a product of certain personality characteristics such as curiosity and persistence. Interestingly, creative people tend to be socially skilled but lower than average in need for social approval. They can often interact well with others to learn and discuss new ideas, but they don't see fit to conform just to get others to like them.

At Harley-Davidson, an important factor in the turnaround was the design creativity of "Willie G." Davidson, grandson of one of the firm's founders. The bearded, leather-garbed motorcyclist has excellent feel for what big bike riders want. In line with our thesis, though, Willie G. isn't a naive genius; he has a degree from Pasadena's respected Art Center College of Design. And of all Harley executives, he is best at establishing rapport with all kinds of customers to learn their views.[51]

Many creativity-related skills can actually be improved by training people to think in divergent ways and withhold early evaluation of ideas.[52] In addition, some of the methods we discussed in Chapter 12 (electronic brainstorming, nominal group, and Delphi techniques) can be used to hone creative skills. Frito-Lay and DuPont are two companies that engage in extensive creativity training.

Finally, people can be experts in their field and have creativity skills but still not be creative if they lack intrinsic motivation for generating new ideas. Such motivation is most likely to occur when there is genuine interest in and fascination with the task at hand. This isn't to say that extrinsic motivation isn't important in innovation, as we shall see shortly. Rather, it means that creativity itself isn't very susceptible to extrinsic rewards.

Having a lot of potentially creative individuals is no guarantee in itself that an organization will innovate. Let's now turn to some other factors that influence innovation.

Idea Champions. Again and again, case studies of successful innovations reveal the presence of one or more **idea champions,** people who see the kernel of an innovative idea and help guide it through to implementation.[53] This role of idea champion is often an informal emergent role, and "guiding" the idea might involve talking it up to peers, selling it to management, garnering resources for its development, or protecting it from political attack by guardians of the status quo. Champions often have a real sense of mission about the innovation. Idea champions have frequently been given other labels, some of which depend on the exact context or content of the innovation. For example, in larger organizations, such champions might be labeled *intrapreneurs* or *corporate entrepreneurs*. In R&D settings, one often hears the term *project champion; product champion* is another familiar moniker. The exact label is less important than the function, which is one of sponsorship and support, often outside of routine job duties.

For a modest innovation whose merits are extremely clear, it is possible for the creative person who thinks up the idea to serve as its sole champion and push the idea into practice. In the case of more complex and radical innovations, especially those that demand heavy resource commitment, it is common to see more than one idea champion emerge during the innovation process. For example, a laser scientist might invent a new twist to laser technology and champion the technical idea within her R&D lab. In turn, a product division line manager might hear of the technical innovation and offer to provide sponsorship to develop it into an actual commercial product. This joint emergence of a technical champion and a management champion is typical. Additional idea champions might also emerge. For example, a sales manager in the medical division might lobby to import the innovation from the optics division.

What kind of people are idea champions, and what are their tactics? One interesting study examined champions who spearheaded the introduction of expensive, visible new information technologies in their firms (e.g., new management information systems).[54] This research compared "project champions" with nonchampions who had also worked on the same project. The champions tended to exhibit more risk taking and innovative behaviors. Also, they exhibited clear signs of transformational leadership (Chapter 10), using charisma, inspiration, and intellectual stimulation to get people to see the potential of the

Idea champions. People who recognize an innovative idea and guide it to implementation.

innovation. They used a wide variety of influence tactics to gain support for the new system. In short, the champions made people truly *want* the innovation despite its disruption of the status quo.

As we noted earlier, championing an innovation is usually an informal role. Would it be possible to actually *assign* people to be champions as part of their regular job duties? Just ask Progressive Corporation, a successful Cleveland-based insurance company. Progressive is known for its innovations in specialty vehicle insurance, including selling to risky drivers and insuring recreational vehicles. Several years ago, Progressive switched from a more centralized structure into several decentralized geographical regions. Management was worried that smaller-volume products (such as mobile homes) might be "lost" in the new decentralized structure and lose their innovative edge. To deal with this, they assigned each product a champion to look out for its interests on a total company basis.[55]

Communication.   Effective communication with the external environment and effective communication within the organization are vital for successful innovation.

The most innovative firms seem to be those that are best at recognizing the relevance of new, external information, importing and assimilating this information, and then applying it.[56] Experience shows that the recognition and assimilation are a lot more chaotic and informal than one might imagine. Rather than relying on a formal network of journal articles, technical reports, and internal memoranda, technical personnel are more likely to be exposed to new ideas via informal oral communication networks. In these networks, key personnel function as **gatekeepers** who span the boundary between the organization and the environment, importing new information, translating it for local use, and disseminating it to project members. These people tend to have well-developed communication networks with other professionals outside the organization and with the professionals on their own team or project. Thus, they are in key positions to both receive and transmit new technical information.[57] Also, they are perceived as highly competent and a good source of new ideas. Furthermore, they have an innovative orientation, they read extensively, and they can tolerate ambiguity.[58] It is important to note that gatekeeping is essentially an informal, emergent role, since many gatekeepers are not in supervisory positions. However, organizations can do several things to enhance the external contact of actual or potential gatekeepers. Generous allowances for subscriptions, telephone use, and database access might be helpful. The same applies to travel allowances for seminars, short courses, and professional meetings.

Technical gatekeepers are not the only means of extracting information from the environment. Many successful innovative firms excel at going directly to users, clients, or customers to obtain ideas for product or service innovation. This works against the development of technically sound ideas that nobody wants, and it also provides some real focus for getting ideas implemented quickly. For example, Sony requires new employees in technical areas to do a stint in retail sales, and Raytheon's New Products Center organizes expeditions by technical types to trade shows, manufacturing facilities, and retail outlets.[59] Notice that we are speaking here about truly getting "close to the customer," not simply doing abstract market research on large samples of people. Such research does not have a great track record in prompting inno-

Gatekeepers. People who span organizational boundaries to import new information, translate it for local use, and disseminate it.

vation; talking directly to users does. Harley-Davidson executives regularly ride in bikers' meets and use the Harley Owners Group to garner direct feedback about their products.

Now that we have covered the importation of information into the organization, what are the requirements of *internal* communication for innovation? At least during the idea generation and early design phase, the more the better. Thus, it is generally true that organic structures (Chapter 15) facilitate innovation.[60] Decentralization, informality, and a lack of bureaucracy all foster the exchange of information that innovation requires. To this mixture, add small project teams or business units and a diversity of member backgrounds to stimulate cross-fertilization of ideas. For example, the early project design team for Mazda's RX–7 had 29 members, 13 from R&D, 6 from production, 7 from sales/marketing, and one each from planning, service, and quality control.[61] There was no room for isolated thinking with that mix! *Fortune* magazine notes a common trend among innovative corporations, including Campbell Soup, 3M, and Apple Computer:

> People in different disciplines are simply not allowed to remain in isolation. Business units are kept small in part to throw engineers, marketers, and finance experts together into the sort of tight groups most often found in start-up companies. Where the interaction fails to arise naturally, it is engineered: all of these companies require their workers to spend a great deal of time at meetings where information is shared and plans are discussed.[62]

In general, internal communication can be stimulated with in-house training, cross-functional transfers, and varied job assignments.[63] One study even found that the actual physical location of gatekeepers was important to their ability to convey new information to co-workers.[64] This suggests the clustering of offices and the use of common lounge areas as a means of facilitating communication. Organizations could also give equal thought to the design of electronic communication media.

One especially interesting line of research suggests just how important communication is to the performance of research and development project groups.[65] This research found that groups with members who had worked together a short time or a long time engaged in less communication (within the group, within the organization, and externally) than groups that had medium longevity. In turn, performance mirrored communication, the high-communicating, medium-longevity groups being the best performers (Exhibit 17.8). Evidently, when groups are new, it takes time for members to decide what information they require and to forge the appropriate communication networks. When groups get "old," they sometimes get comfortable and isolate themselves from critical sources of feedback. It is important to emphasize that the age of the group is at issue here, not the age of the employees or their tenure in the organization.

Although organic structures seem best in the idea generation and design phases of innovation, more mechanistic structures might sometimes be better for actually implementing innovations.[66] Thinking up new computer programs is an organic task. Reproducing these programs in the thousands and marketing them require more bureaucratic procedures. This transition is important. Although audio and video recording innovations were pioneered in the United States, it was the Japanese who successfully implemented recording

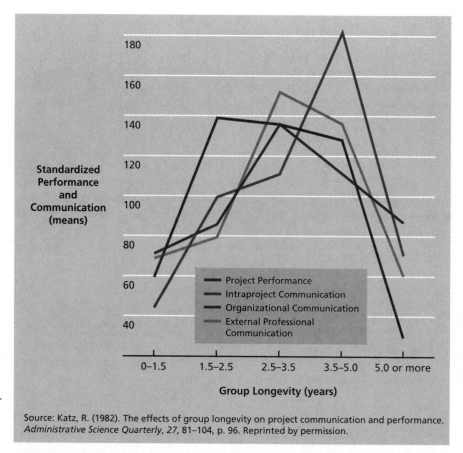

EXHIBIT 17.8
Group longevity, communication, and performance of research and development groups.

Source: Katz, R. (1982). The effects of group longevity on project communication and performance. *Administrative Science Quarterly, 27,* 81–104, p. 96. Reprinted by permission.

products in the marketplace. In part, this stemmed from a recognition of the different organizational requirements for idea generation versus the implementation of ideas.

Resources and Rewards. Despite the romance surrounding the development of innovations on a shoestring using unauthorized "bootlegged" funds, abundant resources greatly enhance the chances of successful innovation.[67] Not only do these resources provide funds in the obvious sense, they also serve as a strong cultural symbol that the organization truly supports innovation. Funds for innovation are seen as an *investment,* not a *cost.* Several observers have noted that such a culture is most likely when the availability of funding is anarchic and multisourced. That is, because innovative ideas often encounter resistance from the status quo under the best of circumstances, innovators should have the opportunity to seek support from more than one source. At 3M, for instance, intrapreneurs can seek support from their own division, from another division, from corporate R&D, or from a new ventures group.[68] (Notice how other idea champions might be cultivated during this process.)

Money is not the only resource that spurs innovation. *Time* can be an even more crucial factor for some innovations. At 3M, tradition dictates that scientists reserve 15 percent of their working time for personal projects. At Chaparral Steel in Midlothian, Texas, supervisors are given "sabbaticals" to work on innovations with customers, suppliers, and universities.[69]

IN FOCUS   FedEx—Innovation par Excellence

Who says college assignments aren't practical? Don't tell that to Frederick W. Smith, founder and head of FedEx. The basic plan for Smith's "fly it anywhere, overnight" company was set down in a Yale University economics term paper he wrote in the mid-1960s. The company was incorporated in 1971 and began operations in 1973. Smith's key innovation, of course, was the provision of door-to-door courier service using the company's own fleet of airplanes and trucks. However, the company has a distinguished history of other innovations:

• The spoke-and-hub system, which originally routed all packages to the company's Memphis superhub for overnight transport to spoke airports.
• One of the first uses of extensive television advertising for what was essentially a business service.
• A grass roots lobbying effort by FedEx employees to have national air transport laws changed.
• Computerized vans and hand-held scanners that enable clients to find out the exact current location of their shipment.
• The establishment of a company weather-forecasting system.

Not all FedEx innovations have been successful. Its foray into the Zapmail electronic mail service lost millions with the faster-than-expected advent of standard fax machines. However, Smith is adamant that some failure is to be expected and that people

need to have the opportunity to fail in order to succeed. Despite the profusion of fax transmission, more than 80 percent of company revenues come from moving packages and freight, and Smith has built a global express transportation network which

A key innovation of FedEx was using the company's own fleet of airplanes and trucks to deliver packages.

uniquely positions the company to maintain its market leadership.

Source: Adapted from Diebold, J. (1990). *The innovators: The discoveries, inventions, and breakthroughs of our time.* Copyright © 1990 by Truman M. Talley, an imprint of Penguin USA. Adapted and reprinted by permission.

Reward systems must match the culture that is seeded by the resource system. Coming up with new ideas is no easy job, so organizations should avoid punishing failure (see the "In Focus: *FedEx—Innovation par Excellence*"). Many false starts with dead ends will be encountered, and innovators need support and constructive criticism, not punishment. In fact, Hallmark puts its executives through a simulation in which they must design a line of greeting cards so that they can better appreciate the frustrations felt by the creative staff.

A survey of research scientists found that freedom and autonomy were the *most* cited organizational factors leading to creativity.[70] Since intrinsic motivation is necessary for creativity, this suggests rewarding good past performance with enhanced freedom to pursue personal ideas. IBM, for example, has a "fellows program" that provides star performers five years of freedom to work on their own projects. In a related vein, many organizations have wised up about extrinsic rewards and innovation. In the past, it was common for creative scientists and engineers to have to move into management ranks to obtain raises and promotions. Many firms now offer dual career ladders that enable these people to be extrinsically rewarded while still doing actual science or engineering.

We have been concerned here mainly with rewarding the people who actually generate innovative ideas. But how about those other champions who sponsor such ideas and push them into the implementation stage? At 3M, bonuses for division managers are contingent on 25 percent of their revenues coming from products that are less than five years old.[71] This stimulates the managers to pay attention when someone drops by with a new idea, and it also stimulates them to turn that new idea into a real product quickly!

Diffusing Innovative Ideas

Many innovations, especially process innovations, begin as limited experiments in one section or division of an organization. This is a cautious and reasonable approach. For example, a company might introduce new automated technology for evaluation in one plant of its multiplant organization. Similarly, an insurance company might begin a limited exploration of job enrichment by concentrating only on clerical jobs at the head office. If such efforts are judged successful, it seems logical to extend them to other parts of the organization. **Diffusion** is the process by which innovations move through an organization. However, this is not always as easy as it might seem!

Richard Walton of Harvard University studied the diffusion of eight major process innovations in firms such as Volvo, Alcan, General Foods, Corning Glass, and Shell U.K. Each effort was rigorous and broad-based, generally including changes in job design, compensation, and supervision.[72]

All of the pilot projects that Walton studied were initially judged successful, and each received substantial publicity, a factor that often contributes to increased commitment to further change. Despite this, substantial diffusion occurred in only one of the observed firms—Volvo. What accounts for this poor record of diffusion? Walton identified these factors:

- Lack of support and commitment by top management.

- Significant differences between the technology or setting of the pilot project and those of other units in the organization, raising arguments that "it won't work here."

- Attempts to diffuse particular *techniques* rather than *goals* that could be tailored to other situations.

- Management reward systems that concentrate on traditional performance measures while ignoring success at implementing innovation.

- Union resistance to extending the negotiated "exceptions" in the pilot project.

- Fears that pilot projects begun in nonunionized locations could not be implemented in unionized portions of the firm.

- Conflict between the pilot project and the bureaucratic structures in the rest of the firm (e.g., pay policies and staffing requirements).

Because of these problems, Walton raises the depressing spectre of a "diffuse or die" principle. That is, if diffusion does not occur, the pilot project and

Diffusion. The process by which innovations move through an organization.

its leaders become more and more isolated from the mainstream of the organization and less and less able to proceed alone. As we noted earlier, innovation can be a highly politicized process. Several of the barriers to diffusion that Walton cites have been implicated in limiting the influence that the Saturn project has had on General Motors, including top management changes, union resistance, and competition for resources from old line GM divisions.

One classic study suggests that the following factors are critical determinants of the rate of diffusion of a wide variety of innovations:[73]

- *Relative advantage.* Diffusion is more likely when the new idea is perceived as truly better than the one it replaces.

- *Compatibility.* Diffusion is easier when the innovation is compatible with the values, beliefs, needs, and current practices of potential new adopters.

- *Complexity.* Complex innovations that are fairly difficult to comprehend and use are less likely to diffuse.

- *Trialability.* If an innovation can be given a limited trial run, its chances of diffusion will be improved.

- *Observability.* When the consequences of an innovation are more visible, diffusion will be more likely to occur.

In combination, these determinants suggest that there is considerable advantage to thinking about how innovations are "packaged" and "sold" so as to increase their chances of more widespread adoption. Also, they suggest the value of finding strong champions to sponsor the innovation at the new site.

The Manager's Notebook   Encouraging Workforce Diversity at Hoechst Celanese

Under the leadership of former CEO Ernest Drew, Hoechst Celanese joined companies such as Xerox, Burger King, Avon, and IBM in following through on planned diversity programs.

1. Change efforts targeted at increasing diversity might be resisted due to simple bigotry. More commonly, however, people probably exhibit resistance due to the feeling that the costs of change will outweigh the benefits, as we noted earlier in the chapter. In fact, it is easy to personalize perceived costs (as a White male, it will be harder for *me* to get promoted) and generalize perceived benefits (maybe the *company* will do better with a more diverse workforce). White males who feel slighted by diversity efforts are a common source of resistance. Sometimes, organizational cultures are predicated on values that run counter to diversity efforts (e.g., a macho engineering culture). Finally, the pressures of downsizing sometimes encourage managers to resist the demands of diversity programs.

2. Probably most important in overcoming resistance, CEO Ernest Drew acted as a visible transformational leader who put his full support behind the diversity program. The company also made diversity a business objective and factored it into managers' salary and bonus decisions. Salary equity reviews were done to look for disparities that were unrelated to seniority or performance. At Hoechst Celanese, senior executives are asked to become members of two organizations in which they have a minority status to sensitize them to this role and provide them with other points of view.

EXECUTIVE SUMMARY

◆ All organizations must change because of forces in the external and internal environments. Although more environmental change usually requires more organizational change, organizations can exhibit too much change as well as too little. Organizations can change goals and strategies, technology, job design, structure, processes, and people. People changes should almost always accompany changes in other factors.

◆ The general change process involves unfreezing current attitudes and behaviors, changing them, and then refreezing the newly acquired attitudes and behaviors. Several key issues or problems must be dealt with during the general change process. One is accurate diagnosis of the current situation. Another is the resistance that might be provoked by unfreezing and change. A third issue is performing an adequate evaluation of the success of the change effort. Many such evaluations are weak or nonexistent.

◆ Organizational development (OD) is a planned, ongoing effort to change organizations to be more effective and more human. It uses the knowledge of behavioral science to foster a culture of organizational self-examination and readiness for change. A strong emphasis is placed on interpersonal and group processes.

◆ Four popular OD techniques are team building, survey feedback, total quality management, and reengineering. Team building attempts to increase the effectiveness of work teams by concentrating on interpersonal processes, goal clarification, and role clarification. Survey feedback requires organizational members to generate data that is fed back to them as a basis for inducing change. Total quality management (TQM) is an attempt to achieve continuous improvement in the quality of products or services. Reengineering is the radical redesign of organizational processes to achieve major improvements in time, cost, quality, or service.

◆ In many OD attempts that received adequate evaluation, positive changes have been observed. Despite this, the careful evaluation of OD programs poses special challenges to researchers.

◆ Innovation is the process of developing and implementing new ideas in an organization. It can include both new products and new processes.

◆ Innovation requires individual creativity and adequate resources and rewards to stimulate and channel that creativity. Also, idea champions who recognize and sponsor creative ideas are critical. Finally, internal and external communication are important for innovation. The role of gatekeepers who import and disseminate technical information is especially noteworthy.

◆ Innovations will diffuse most easily when they are not too complex, can be given a trial run, are compatible with existing practices, and offer a visible advantage over current practices.

KEY CONCEPTS

Unfreezing
Change
Refreezing
Diagnosis
Change agents
Resistance
Organizational development (OD)
Team building
Survey feedback

Total quality management (TQM)
Reengineering
Organizational processes
Innovation
Creativity
Idea champions
Gatekeepers
Diffusion

DISCUSSION QUESTIONS

1. Describe an example of resistance to change that you have observed. Why did it occur?

2. You have been charged with staffing and organizing an R&D group in a new high-technology firm. What will you do to ensure that the group is innovative?

3. What qualities would the ideal gatekeeper possess to facilitate the communication of technical information in his or her firm?

4. Suppose a job enrichment effort in one plant of a manufacturing firm is judged to be very successful. You are the corporate change agent responsible for the project, and you wish to diffuse it to other plants that have a similar technology. How would you sell the project to other plant managers? What kinds of resistance might you encounter?

5. What personal qualities and skills would be useful for an OD change agent to possess? Describe the relative merits of using an internal staff change agent versus an external consultant.

6. Discuss: The best organizational structure to generate innovative ideas might not be the best structure to implement those ideas.

7. Imagine that the U.S. Marine Corps is forming a special hostage rescue unit to aid American hostages around the world. How could team-building principles be used to enhance the formation and functioning of this unit? What are some limitations to using this approach in the military?

8. Debate this statement: Survey feedback can be a problematic OD technique because it permits people who are affected by organizational policies to generate data that speak against those policies.

9. What are the similarities and differences between total quality management and reengineering?

10. What is the role of advanced technology in reengineering?

EXPERIENTIAL EXERCISE
MEASURING TOLERANCE FOR AMBIGUITY

Please read each line of the following statements carefully. Then use the following scale to rate each of them in terms of the extent to which you either agree or disagree with the statement.

Completely disagree			Neither agree nor disagree			Completely agree
1	2	3	4	5	6	7

Place the number that best describes your degree of agreement or disagreement in the blank to the left of each statement.

1. _____ An expert who doesn't come up with a definite answer probably doesn't know too much.

2. _____ I would like to live in a foreign country for a while.

3. _____ The sooner we all acquire similar values and ideals, the better.

4. _____ A good teacher is one who makes you wonder about your way of looking at things.

5. _____ I like parties where I know most of the people more than ones where all or most of the people are complete strangers.

6. _____ Teachers or supervisors who hand out vague assignments give a chance for one to show initiative and originality.

7. _____ A person who leads an even, regular life in which few surprises or unexpected happenings arise really has a lot to be grateful for.

8. _____ Many of our most important decisions are based on insufficient information.

9. _____ There is really no such thing as a problem that can't be solved.

10. _____ People who fit their lives to a schedule probably miss most of the joy of living.

11. _____ A good job is one in which what is to be done and how it is to be done are always clear.

12. _____ It is more fun to tackle a complicated problem than to solve a simple one.

13. _____ In the long run, it is possible to get more done by tackling small, simple problems than large and complicated ones.

14. _____ Often the most interesting and stimulating people are those who don't mind being different and original.

15. _____ What we are used to is always preferable to what is unfamiliar.

16. _____ People who insist upon a yes or no answer just don't know how complicated things really are.

You have just completed the Tolerance for Ambiguity Scale. It was adapted by Paul Nutt from original work by S. Budner. The survey asks about personal and work-oriented situations that involve various degrees of ambiguity. To score your own survey, add 8 to each of your responses to the *odd* numbered items. Then, add up the renumbered odd items. From this total, subtract your score from the sum of the *even* numbered items. Your score should fall between 16 and 112. People with lower scores are tolerant of and even enjoy ambiguous situations. People with high scores are intolerant of ambiguity and prefer more structured situations. In Paul Nutt's research, people typically scored between 20 and 80 with a mean around 45. People with a high tolerance for ambiguity respond better to change. They also tend to be more creative and innovative than those with low tolerance for ambiguity.

Source: Nutt, P. C. (1988). *The tolerance for ambiguity and decision making.* Columbus, Ohio: The Ohio State University College of Business Working Paper Series, WP88–291.

CASE STUDY
CABLECO

Calendarco is a diversified multinational company that has 135 plants in 16 countries throughout the world. It employs some 69,000 employees and, in 1987, had sales of £5.6 billion, its electrical cable business accounting for some 39 percent of total turnover. Cableco, the electrical cable business of Calendarco, was founded in the UK in 1914. It produces a comprehensive range of power and telecommunications cables at four different factories. By 1987 Cableco's turnover had risen to nearly £135 million and the workforce to 2,200 employees. Cableco makes a range of different cables and had been producing building wires, a relatively basic range of "low-tech" electrical cables primarily used for house wiring or domestic appliances at its plant in Southampton. The plant, established in the 1930s, had enjoyed a good relationship with its employees for many years, based upon four important elements:

1. Labor segmentation with employees recruited into various grades with little chance of promotion. Manual staff work for 39 hours per week and non-manual staff work for 35 hours per week. The manual group is made up of process workers (semi-skilled), skilled mechanical trades and skilled elec-

trical trades. The non-manual group is divided between supervisory, clerical, technical and managerial grades.

2. Job-evaluated payment systems graded by skill, with a productivity bonus paid invariably each month and with overtime working on Saturdays.

3. Recognition of six trade unions covering various grades of manual worker and staff.

4. Nationally agreed terms and conditions of employment determined by the Joint Industrial Council (JIC) for cable making, covering all companies in the industry.

BACKGROUND TO THE CASE

Over-capacity within the industry and fierce competition from the UK and abroad meant that the domestic cable division had been making a loss for some time. In 1984 the company was faced with a choice, should it continue in the business or get out completely? If it was to stay in the business, how could it become more competitive?

The technical director argued that an investment of £20 million in a greenfield site, attracting a development grant from the government and utilizing modern process technology, could produce a profitable return on investment within 24 months if, for the same tonnage, the number of employees could be reduced from 350 to 150. He argued that this was possible with the adoption of new technology provided there was full flexibility of labour. Calendarco subsequently decided to build a new plant that would house the latest in computer-integrated manufacturing (CIM) systems. The system would be based upon three fundamental concepts:

1. A CIM system to plan and direct every phase of the business.

2. Flexible manufacturing involving the application of machine technology that allows different areas or zones within the plant to achieve a fast response to varying business needs.

3. Just-in-time (JIT) production techniques with computerized monitoring to schedule and sequence the supply of raw material and work-in-progress, thus eliminating expensive stockholding.

The main board decided that the project would have a greater chance of success if it was developed away from the company's other sites and that the new factory should replace the existing plant in Southampton. Furthermore, the board insisted that, within the environment of advanced technology and the latest techniques of computer integration, it was essential that the personnel policies of the new factory should also reflect "an equivalent degree of advanced thinking in the human resources area."

The site chosen was in South Wales, some distance from Cableco's other plants and in a development area attracting government financial aid. It was also in an area of high unemployment, promising a plentiful supply of labor.

DEVISING APPROPRIATE HUMAN RESOURCE POLICIES

A small project team consisting of two members of Cableco's divisional personnel department and the new plant general and personnel managers, was given the task of developing the new policies in the human resource area. They began with a period of research, visiting companies the team members believed to be innovators in their field and taking part in discussions with the Work Research Unit of the Arbitration, Conciliation and Advisory Services (ACAS).

The new plant personnel manager, recruited from outside the Calendarco organization specifically for the job, had firm views about the way in which employees ought to be managed in the new plant. In particular, he believed that the policies adopted should reflect "best practice" in the UK. He was the driving force behind the company's new philosophy. Instead of the rigid job demarcation, repetitive tasks and traditional supervisory systems in operation at Cableco's other plants, the project team wanted employees in the new factory to work in small, highly adaptable teams. The project team developed plans to create what they called a "model working environment" based upon flexibility and involvement, where all employees would be equal, with no distinction between office and factory.

This model working environment was based upon the principles of single employee status and co-operative teamworking, aimed both at motivating employees and ensuring their commitment to the success of the new plant. All staff would enjoy similar terms and conditions of employment, which would include a salary structure based upon an annual rather than a weekly hours contract, and which would reward adaptability and achievement. However, all senior specialists and managerial staff were to be excluded. They would be treated as a corporate rather than a plant resource liable to be transferred to another part of the Calendarco organization at some time in the future.

The CIM system that had been chosen had certain implications for the type of employee who would be needed to use it. In the first place employees would need to be computer literate. The type of skills they would require were diagnostic rather than motor related, with only a minimal degree of manual skill required. The process was not going to be high speed but it would involve constant operator attention requiring the application of detailed production schedules as shown on the visual display units with little, if any, supervision. Employees were going to be required to work flexibly not only in relation to the performance of tasks but also in relation to skills (for example, operators carrying out day-to-day maintenance tasks) as well as flexibility in relation to hours worked. From this a profile was developed of the characteristics future employees would be required to possess.

The project team saw recruitment as critical to the successful running of the plant. They endeavored to select only those employees who would be suited to the different work requirements and ethos of the plant. They wanted employees who had the "right attitude," people who would be flexible, who were anxious to develop their own potential and who would accept responsibility: they wanted the "best" employees available. The recruitment procedure was time consuming, expensive and sophisticated. It included the assessment of personality profiles and computer aptitude testing as well as conventional interviewing techniques. Interviews were held not only by the potential employee's immediate manager within the plant but also with at least two senior members of the management team.

The various functions within the plant (production, maintenance and administration) were divided up into a number of skill modules, each of which would require a different combination of skills and knowledge. All employees would acquire skill modules across all functions, each skill module requiring between four and eight weeks' training. Employees would be paid a basic salary and an increase of £250 for each skill module they obtained. Calendarco was anxious that pay levels should be kept within reasonable limits and the decision was taken that the level of basic salary should be determined by reference to salaries paid in the local area (a figure that was some £2,000 a year less than at the Southampton plant). Since salaries would increase quite quickly as new skill modules were acquired, Calendarco decided to set levels just below the average for the area.

A key feature of the motivational aspect of the policies was to be comprehensive communication and involvement informally through the free exchange of information, opinions and ideas on operational matters, and formally through joint consultation in the form of the Business Review and Consultative Committee (BRCC). Rather than adopt a non-union position the project team was persuaded to maintain a policy of union recognition well established in the rest of Calendarco. However, copying other forward-thinking organizations opening new ventures on greenfield sites, they decided to withdraw from the JIC and (after holding a 'beauty contest' where a number of unions were invited to make a presentation to the company as to their suitability for recognition), a single union, no-strike agreement was signed with the Managerial,

Administrative, Technical and Supervisory Association (MATSA). Among other things, the agreement stressed the importance of operational objectives and arrangements including complete flexibility and active co-operation in all elements of change and an undertaking to accept training, as well as an obligation on the part of the company to provide training as necessary.

THE PROBLEM: IMPLEMENTING THE HUMAN RESOURCE POLICIES

The original time-scale was for the Southampton plant to close by December 1988. The plant was still open in December 1989. The development and design of Cableco's advanced manufacturing technology were fraught with problems that, in turn, had serious implications for the type of employee policies that Cableco had decided to implement. Many of the suppliers had been asked to make significant advances in the development of their equipment, advances that had not been attempted before. They delivered the machinery to the plant only to discover that it did not perform the tasks Cableco required of it. Attempts by Cableco's technicians to modify or repair the new machinery themselves prior to official acceptance by the company would have led to a breach of the manufacturer's warranty. This meant that Cableco employees (who had not been involved in the original design process) were also excluded from the modification process.

Two major factors affected the operation of the company's reward system. The details of the skill modules could only be drawn up once the plant was operating. This could not be done without machinery that worked. In addition, more and more new plants (also attracted by government financial aid and a ready supply of labor) opened up in South Wales, all requiring skilled maintenance workers. The salaries being paid by Cableco quickly became uncompetitive. This led to the introduction of new hierarchical levels within the maintenance department linked to higher salaries, as attempts were made to recruit and retain staff. Twelve months after the opening of the new plant, the union and management were involved in what the management referred to as "conventional and at times fairly confrontational" negotiations, which led to the nominal award of one skill module, regardless of whether the necessary skills had been acquired. In the mind of employees, skill modules became associated with length of service rather than with skill acquisition and flexibility. This distortion of the payment system and infringement of the single-status principle created much resentment among the production workers.

The plant personnel manager, the driving force behind the new policies, left Cableco in October 1988 to pursue a career elsewhere. With his departure the emphasis on consultation and communication was almost forgotten in the face of the increasing pressures to meet production targets and close down the Southampton factory, and informal communication systems did not develop. The general manager, aware of the substantial difficulties facing the plant, made attempts to keep employees informed but felt that, if they knew how serious the plant's position was, they would revert to "traditional adversarial behavior." The employees argued that they knew things were going badly and they did not believe the information they were being given about the plant's performance was accurate. After the personnel manager's departure the plans for formal communication and information systems were ignored.

_____

Source: Case prepared by Helen Newell. From Gowler, D., Legge, K., & Clegg, C. (Eds.). (1993). *Case studies in organizational behaviour and human resource management* (2nd ed). London, England: Paul Chapman.

1. Describe the environmental changes that prompted the decision to build the new plant, and describe the corresponding internal changes that were proposed. Did these changes constitute reengineering?
2. Evaluate the general concept of the proposed green-field site plant. Did the proposed organization and policies make sense? Why or why not?
3. Defend this statement: The proposed new Cableco plant constituted organizational innovation.
4. List any observed strengths in the way the change at Cableco was implemented.
5. What were the sources of resistance to change that threatened the new plant?
6. List any observed weaknesses in the way change at Cableco was implemented.
7. How could the change process involved in opening the new plant have been improved? Be sure to consider any relevant organizational development techniques.

Learning Objectives

After reading chapter 18 you should be able to:

1. Define the meaning of the terms career, external career, internal career, and occupational identity and explain why the study of careers is important in today's organizations.

2. Explain how people's reactions to a job result from the interaction or fit between career orientation and work environment.

3. Discuss Holland's theory of career types and Schein's theory of career anchors.

4. Define the life stages and career stages adults generally go through during their working lives and discuss key tasks associated with the exploration stage during one's early career.

5. Discuss the career and psychosocial functions often accomplished through a mentoring relationship and identify special problems that women and minorities face in establishing this relationship.

6. Define career resilience and discuss career strategies for developing a resilient career.

7. Explain different initiatives organizations can use to encourage and support employees' efforts to develop resilient careers.

With drive and determination, Sharon Hall carefully crafted her career path and became a successful senior manager with Avon and then with La Petite Academy.

CHAPTER 18

CAREERS*

SHARON
HALL

*Sharon Hall is senior vice-president for Corporate Planning and
Marketing at La Petite Academy, a preschool and child care
facility corporation headquartered in Overland Park, Kansas. She accepted the position
after having risen to general manager of Avon Products' personal-care products group.
Fortune describes Hall's career prior to her current position: Daughter of a salesman, she
grew up on Chicago's South Side and entered Morris Brown College in Atlanta knowing
that she would train for a marketing career. When she graduated in 1978, she made it
her single-minded goal to land a job with Procter & Gamble. It didn't deter her that
P&G was hiring only MBAs. Hall learned everything she could about the company and
dogged the on-campus P&G interviewer to fit her into his packed schedule. "If any
other candidate is six minutes late, call me," she told him. The call came. Dazzling the
recruiter with her energy and her detailed knowledge of P&G's inner workings, she was
offered a job as a brand assistant.*

*This chapter was authored by J. Bruce Prince.

She threw herself into work she loved and soaked up the lessons of product marketing the P&G way. But after two years she concluded that inching up the P&G ladder wouldn't fulfill her ambitions. Hall developed a detailed multi-year plan for her future: First, get an MBA; second, work a few years for Booz Allen & Hamilton, the management consulting outfit she thought would have the most to teach her; third, move to a senior operating position at a big company. "I wouldn't waste a single day," she says.

She had to improvise. She had won a fellowship that paid her way to an MBA at USC, but Booz Allen didn't recruit there. So Hall organized a student management consulting forum and invited all the top consulting outfits—including Booz, of course—to send representatives to meet the students. Impressed with her resourcefulness, Booz hired her.

She arrived with—what else?—three goals; to learn about the marketing practices of Booz's global clients, sharpen her analytical skills, and increase her earning power considerably. "I wanted to get as far as I could as fast as I could so I could devote myself to starting a family while I was still young," she says. After two years she felt she'd accomplished what she set out to do.

Pursued with job offers from headhunters, Hall again went into her planning mode. She decided that it was important she feel passionate about the products she would market, and she wanted to have a big role in her employer's business strategy. Says she: "If a move doesn't serve at least two or more purposes simultaneously, it's not worth making." When Avon called in 1984, looking for an executive to plan its expansion into the Pacific Rim, Hall jumped. "I convinced them that what I wanted was what they needed."

Hall spent the next three years mapping out a new marketing plan and traveling throughout Asia and Latin America. As Avon senior managers came to prize her creativity and initiative, they gave her leeway to define her own jobs. For example, she asked for one at the home office after a budding romance with Kevin Morris, an Avon colleague, blossomed into marriage in 1986. Following the birth of her first child, she worked on improving Avon's system for deciding which new products the company would develop—a job that let her set her own schedule. That led to the next position as senior director for new business development. Self-serving? Of course. But every job also met her crucial, self-imposed guideline: "Always be doing something that contributes significant, positive change to the organization. That's the ultimate job security."[1]

Sharon Hall's career, described here by *Fortune*, illustrates several qualities important to career success. These include self-insight, initiative, a clear plan, competencies valued by employers, and the ability to improvise along the way. This chapter addresses a variety of theory, research, and prescriptive insights that inform our understanding of careers in today's society. To start the chapter, we address the meaning of a career and why it's important. Next, we explore the individual differences and stages of development that influence careers and present various ingredients that contribute to career success. These include organizational career development programs, work-family issues, and the mentor-apprentice relationship. Finally, we discuss career resilience, the ability to adjust and redirect one's career. This includes individual strategies to promote career resilience and organizational initiatives that facilitate workforce resilience.

THE CHANGING CAREER LANDSCAPE

Careers unfold in organizations. In recent years, however, organizations have changed dramatically in the face of severe global competition and increased technological change, particularly advances in information technologies. Downsizing or rightsizing, reengineering, and restructuring have resulted in flatter hierarchies, broader and more complex jobs, and the outsourcing of work to consultants and other firms. The career landscape of organizations has changed accordingly. Promotion opportunities are fewer. Whether it's a lateral transfer to a new job or the continually changing requirements of positions, employees today frequently have to learn new skills and adapt to changing work demands. Academic experts as well as business executives, such as Andy Grove—the top executive at the computer chip manufacturer Intel—agree that employment security is a thing of the past. Employability security, i.e., having skills, knowledge and a reputation that are in high demand, is now the only real form of security.[2] In this context, the best thing organizations can provide employees are the opportunities to continually develop in ways that the larger labor market, including competitors, appreciates.

Increasingly an organization's competitive advantage is in its people.[3] In the global economy of the 1990s, the effective development of human resources—employees' skill, creativity, and commitment—will spell the difference between organizational success and failure.[4] Taken collectively, successful individual careers help create successful organizations and shape the economic prospects of a nation.[5] Careers provide organizations a way to channel people into needed areas and to develop their skills so that they can continue to perform needed organizational functions. When done right, both employers and employees also gain. Careers provide chances to have experiences and jobs that offer valued rewards and develop competencies that lead to more opportunities and a brighter future.

WHAT IS A CAREER?

A **career** is an evolving sequence of work activities and positions that one experiences over time as well as the associated attitudes, knowledge, and competencies that develop throughout one's life.[6] Three elements are important in fully understanding the meaning of a career. First, a career involves moving on a path over time. This path has two sides. One side is the objective sequence of positions, or the **external career**.[7] The pattern of placing new university teachers in an assistant professor position and promoting them to associate professor and eventually full professor is an example. These paths may be planned and orderly, or simply emerge over time and have major discontinuities where the duties in a later position do not naturally build on the skills developed in earlier jobs. The other side of this path is the individual's subjective interpretation of these work experiences, or the **internal career**. For example, being an assistant professor is likely to have a very different subjective meaning to a 29 year-old with a brand new Ph.D. degree than it will ten years later, at 39, without any changes in status. A position that one initially associates with feelings of optimism and a brighter future can later evoke feelings of being "stuck" and a failure.

Career. An evolving sequence of work activities and positions that individuals experience over time as well as the associated attitudes, knowledge, and competencies that develop throughout one's life.

External career. The objective sequence of positions that comprise one's career.

Internal career. The individual's interpretation of objective work experiences known only from a person's own subjective sense of external events.

A second element of a career is the interaction of individual and organizational factors. People's reactions to a job depend on the fit between their occupational self-concepts (i.e., patterns of needs, aptitudes, and preferences) and types of opportunities, constraints, and demands that their roles in the organization provide. One person might find a marketing job interesting and a step to a brighter future. Another might find it stifling. Understanding these differences is critical to effectively managing one's own career, as well as helping others, such as subordinates, manage their careers.

The third important element of a career is that it provides an occupational identity.[8] What people do in our society is very much a key element of their identities. When we are getting acquainted with someone new, the first question is often: "What do you do?" People vary as to how important their occupational identity is to their overall identity, but for many it is the primary factor in how they define who they are.

INDIVIDUAL DIFFERENCES IN CAREER ORIENTATION

Fortunately for everyone concerned, people are not all the same. Each of us differs in terms of skills, values, goals, and preferred activities. However, as different as people are from one another, there are also many similarities between people. Social scientists have developed ways of categorizing people that capture major patterns of similarities and differences in their career orientation. As Exhibit 18.1 demonstrates, **career orientation** is the fairly stable pattern of preferred occupational activities, talents, values, and attitudes.

Different career orientations will be consistent with the particular task demands and rewards that some work environments present. The fit or consistency between one's career orientation and work environment has direct

Career orientation. The fairly stable pattern of preferred occupational activities, talents, values, and attitudes.

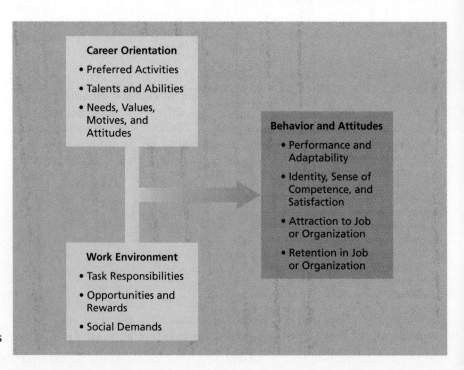

EXHIBIT 18.1
Career orientation and its consequences.

When students choose a major that is consistent with their interests, they experience a sense of competence and satisfaction.

consequences for people's job behavior and attitudes. A student choosing (and changing) a college major can appreciate the consequences of the fit between the individual and the work environment. Often students choose their major without adequate information. As they take courses in their major field, the fit between individual interests and talents and their assignments and class topics becomes clearer. Good fit results in a heightened sense of competence and satisfaction; poor fit leads to the opposite and can motivate students to select a new work environment, i.e., a new major.

Holland's Theory of Career Types

The best-documented theory of career orientation is John Holland's **theory of career types.**[9] Holland and others documented six distinct patterns of career orientation. The hexagonal model in Exhibit 18.2 shows these patterns. The career orientations or types that are opposite each other on the hexagon are least compatible. Those next to one another are more compatible.

Theory of career types. John Holland's theory identifying six distinct patterns of career orientation: conventional, artistic, realistic, social, enterprising, and investigative.

Conventional.   This type of person prefers rule-regulated, orderly activities that generally include organizing written or numerical information or analyzing this information with an unambiguous set of procedures (e.g., computing financial ratios). These people are typically conforming, orderly, efficient, and practical. Less flattering descriptions include unimaginative, inhibited, and inflexible. Accounting and finance jobs, which require the precise organization and evaluation of numerical information in a fairly stable work setting with clear operating procedures, fit people with a conventional orientation.

Artistic.   The artistic career orientation is extremely dissimilar to the conventional type. These people prefer ambiguous and unsystematic activities that entail creating expressive written, verbal, or visual forms. They are often

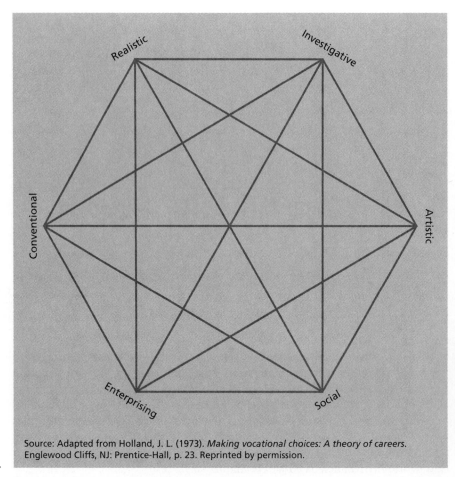

EXHIBIT 18.2
Holland's career types.

Source: Adapted from Holland, J. L. (1973). *Making vocational choices: A theory of careers.* Englewood Cliffs, NJ: Prentice-Hall, p. 23. Reprinted by permission.

imaginative, intuitive, and independent as well as disorderly, emotional, and impractical. The most negative descriptions, like "impractical," are characterizations that the opposite of an artistic type, a conventional career type, is likely to make. Artistic types could be exactly what graphics or advertising departments need.

Realistic.   The realistic career type prefers activities that require the physical manipulation of objects or tools in a well-ordered work environment with few social demands. These people usually have mechanical abilities and are likely to be genuine, stable, and practical as well as possibly shy, uninsightful, and conforming. This type of person will probably be most comfortable in semi-skilled or crafts positions that present consistent task requirements and few social demands, such as negotiating and persuading.

Social.   The social type is practically the opposite of the realistic type. Those with a social orientation prefer activities that involve informing, helping, or developing others and dislike well-ordered and systematic work environments. Social types are often sociable, tactful, friendly, understanding, and helpful. Less positive descriptions (most likely from the opposite of this career type, the realistic type) include dominating and manipulative. Marketing, sales, and training often fit the unique needs of this career type.

Enterprising. The enterprising type also likes to work with people, but focuses his or her energies on leading and controlling others (versus helping or understanding) to reach specific organizational goals or obtain economic gains. Positive characterizations of these people include self-confident, ambitious, energetic, and talkative. Less flattering descriptions include domineering, power-hungry, and impulsive.

Investigative. The investigative person is the near opposite of the person who is an enterprising type. People in this category prefer activities that involve observing and analyzing phenomena in order to develop knowledge and understanding. Many characterize these people as complicated, original, and independent as well as possibly disorderly, impractical, and impulsive; investigative types also have an aversion to repetitive activities and to selling. Within business organizations, these people are attracted to research and development positions and staff positions that require complex analyses with little need to persuade and convince others.

At this point, you might be wondering whether all people neatly fit into one of the six career types. The real world is certainly more complicated than this. How does Sharon Hall from the story at the start of this chapter fit this theory? Clearly she is not artistic or realistic! The best guess is that she is an enterprising-social combination. She seems attracted to understanding people's preferences and leading efforts to capitalize on that knowledge.

Holland's theory recognizes such complexities. Many people are a combination of two, or perhaps three, career types. The combinations that most frequently develop are those next to each other on the hexagon. An example of a consistent combination is the conventional-enterprising combination, which fits many, but certainly not all, managerial positions. The most unlikely combinations are those involving types that are opposite one another on the hexagonal model, such as conventional-artistic or investigative-enterprising.

Career Choice. Holland's theory is primarily concerned with career choice. It identifies types of people and particular types of work environments to which each type is attracted. There is evidence that people in work environments inconsistent with their career orientations tend to be dissatisfied and either gradually shift their orientation (i.e., become more like the career type that is congruent with their work environment) or move to a new work situation. Being in a congruent work environment also increases the likelihood that an individual will be satisfied, achieve a sense of competence, and not quit for another job.

Research finds that people with an inconsistent combination of orientations (i.e., those that are opposite one another on the hexagonal model, such as the artistic-conventional combination) or those with an undifferentiated pattern (i.e., people who see themselves as similar to many types) are the least likely to be strongly attracted to, or satisfied with, a particular work environment. They are also the ones who, if they do stay, are the most likely to adjust their career orientation to an initially inconsistent work environment. Those with a less inconsistent or more differentiated combination of characteristics will have a stronger negative reaction to work demands that don't fit their orientation and will start searching for a better alternative.

Do people use Holland's theory? Yes! It is the basis for much vocational guidance counseling. Many students, attempting to figure out what kinds of occupations or college majors they should select, visit a guidance counselor and complete the Strong Vocational Interest Blank.[10] This instrument compares one's interests to those in a variety of occupations. These occupations are grouped into the six Holland career types. Thus, the test tells you whether you have interests similar to those in occupations in each of the six career type categories. The basic thrust of this counseling is to find out what career type you are and then plan your career strategies to qualify for jobs that are congruent with your orientation. Doing this increases the chances of finding a career that requires you to use your strengths while satisfying your needs.

Schein's Theory of Career Anchors

Theory of career anchors.
Five distinct patterns of self-perceived talents, motives, needs, and values that evolve as one faces early work experiences: technical/functional competence, managerial competence, security, autonomy, and creativity.

Another development in the study of career orientation is Edgar Schein's **theory of career anchors.**[11] Career anchors evolve and develop through the successive new trials and opportunities that one faces in early work experiences. Gradually, as one gains more self-knowledge and a clearer occupational identity, a distinct pattern of self-perceived talents, motives, needs, and values emerges. The five patterns that Schein's early research documents are technical/functional competence, managerial competence, security, autonomy, and creativity. Just as a boat's anchor keeps it from drifting, career anchors keep one centered on certain types of work activities. If people happen to take on inconsistent work assignments, their career anchor acts to pull them back to more consistent activities.

Technical/Functional Competence.   For people with this anchor, the actual content of work is the primary consideration in their career choices and decisions. Their sense of identity is tied to being able to exercise competencies associated with that work. A chance to move to a job that takes them away from their technical or functional area (e.g., engineering, marketing, etc.) is unattractive.

Managerial Competence.   For people with this career anchor, the ultimate goal is to rise to positions of managerial responsibility. A functional area job, such as in marketing or finance, is important not for the content of work, but for what that position leads to. Such a position could be an opportunity to develop analytical and interpersonal competencies and gain valued exposure on the way to the real goal, general management. People with this anchor see their competence tied to three areas: 1) analytical competence with which they can identify and solve problems with incomplete and uncertain information, 2) interpersonal competence through which they can influence others toward the achievement of organizational goals, and 3) emotional competence in dealing with high levels of responsibility and the exercise of power (e.g., firing someone).

Security.   For these people a key career factor is their long-term work life stability and security. A good benefits and retirement package, employment stability (e.g., few cycles of mass layoffs and rehiring), and clear career paths are particularly attractive to a person with this anchor. Opportunities to use certain technical skills or promotion prospects are important if they lead to long-term stability and security.

Autonomy. For the autonomy-anchored person, chances to stay in a technical area, steadily march up a corporate hierarchy, or gain guaranteed-for-life employment are not highly valued. What is important is having freedom and avoiding constraints on one's lifestyle. Autonomy-anchored people are likely to say no to advancement if it means giving up their independence and freedom.

Creativity. While creativity-anchored people may want autonomy or to exercise managerial or technical/functional competence, they are unique in their overarching desire to create something that is entirely of their own making. It might be a product or technical process or a company. Inventing something new is a measure of worth and the key to their sense of competence.

What anchor is guiding Sharon Hall's career? It is easy to eliminate anchors like security and creativity. Her interest in the autonomy of defining her own job at Avon was probably more related to her temporary role of mother to a young child rather than a fundamental direction in her career decisions. Thus far, all of her career choices have kept her involved in marketing; she has avoided being "seasoned" in other functional areas like production. This suggests that she has a technical/functional competence anchor. However, her later positions at Avon and her vice-president position at La Petite involve more managerial duties. This suggests that managerial competence also anchors Sharon's career.

Managerial Implications of Career Orientation

The explicit message of both Holland's and Schein's models of career orientation is that the people who run organizations should consider differences in orientation when managing their human resources. Managerial practices that treat all people the same—which on the surface seems like the fair thing to do—inevitably treat some of those people in ways that are dissatisfying and detract from organizational effectiveness. Thus, appreciating differences in career orientation is one aspect of valuing diversity (Chapter 4).

High-level managers (often having a managerial competence anchor) who create human resource policies and practices sometimes make the mistake of assuming that all reasonable employees basically prefer the same things that they do. As a result, they create reward systems and promotion patterns that conflict with other people's career orientations. Technical/functional competence anchored people might find that they must leave their technical positions and take on managerial roles in order to have higher levels of compensation, status, and influence in the company. The lack of a non-managerial or technical route to greater prestige and rewards puts these technical/functional competence anchored people in a dilemma. If they choose to stay close to the technical work they love, they will feel a sense of inequity (see Chapters 5 and 6) and might decrease their effort (a key input in equity theory terms) or look for another employer who will treat them in what they consider a fair and just manner. The manager with a managerial competence anchor might have a hard time appreciating how an employee who turns down a "good" promotion can feel mistreated! This stems from misunderstanding individual differences and the assumption that "people are either like me or weird." On the other hand, if the technical/functional competence-anchored person takes the temptation to

IN FOCUS   Career Self-Management at Hewlett-Packard

The personal career management course at Hewlett-Packard's Colorado Springs Division focuses first on self-assessment and understanding and then the application of this information by charting a career path for each participant. Senior management's analysis of the program found that this program gave them more flexibility in moving people, reduced turnover, helped meet goals to diversify their workforce through the promotion of minorities and women, and was seen by many participants as being instrumental in helping them get promoted. The self-assessment thrust of the program requires:

• *A written self-interview.* These questions produce an autobiographical life sketch and require participants to think about key past events, transitions in their careers, and future objectives.
• *Strong-Campbell Interest Inventory.* This produces an interest profile using Holland's theory of career types.
• *Allport-Vernon-Lindzey Study of Values.* This assessment instrument measures the relative strength of six basic life values (i.e., theoretical, economic, aesthetic, social, political, and religious).
• *24-hour diaries.* The hour-to-hour activities of one work and non-work day are logged for comparison to other information, such as how values and interests play out in daily choices.
• *Interviews with two "significant others."* Spouses or friends are interviewed to provide points of comparison with how participants see themselves.
• *Life style representations.* This can include the use of pictures (e.g., collages) or drawings as well as words to capture key personal preferences or attributes.

In working through these exercises, participants discover general themes which underpin their past life and career choices and future directions.

How are these self-insights applied back in the workplace? At the conclusion of the self-assessment program, the managers of the participants inter-

view them and provide context specific information, such as describing the background and skills of people in key positions relevant to the participant's career plan. Also, their career plans are related to the strategic direction of the organization and spe-

After Hewlett-Packard began a career management course for its employees, turnover decreased, the workforce diversified, and the company gained more flexibility in promoting and moving people.

cific staffing plans. Through this process the fit or misfit between individual career goals and company plans and requirements should become apparent. The hoped for result is a joint plan with key benchmarks including needed training and development activities and performance objectives. Senior managers monitor these career plans and the employees' progress. Within six months of the first course, 37 percent of the participants had advanced to new jobs in the company. A Canadian Hewlett-Packard division recently formed a task force to investigate how this program applies to their operation.

Sources: Adapted from Cascio, W., & Thacker, J. (1994). *Managing human resources: Productivity, quality of work life, profit.* Toronto: McGraw-Hill Ryerson; and Wilhelm, W. (1983, August). Helping workers to self-manage their careers. *Personnel Administrator*, 83–89.

move to a nontechnical job, the consequence will be dissatisfaction and the potential for poor performance, in spite of the extra rewards. Presenting these types of dilemmas to employees results not only in human costs, but also in organizational costs associated with diminished motivation and a misallocation of human resources.

Treating different people differently is not only satisfying to those involved; it also helps the organization achieve its goals. Doing this requires managers to take some positive steps. These might include the following:

- Understand and identify key individual differences that shape the way employees react to so-called opportunities,
- Identify key job and situational factors that are congruent with each of these characteristics, and
- Develop ways of matching employees to congruent work environment factors.

We've focused on the first two steps in the first part of this chapter, and we'll address approaches for matching individuals and work situations in a later section. See the "In Focus: *Career Self-Management at Hewlett-Packard*" for an example of how organizations use this advice in helping employees manage their careers.

CAREER AND ADULT LIFE STAGES

Both Schein's and Holland's theories of career orientation imply that adults are rather fixed or static. This is clearly not true. Careers, like lives, have a dynamic quality and evolve and change in some predictable ways across adulthood. Behavioral scientists have found evidence of specific patterns of change and development throughout the adult years. While no two people go through a career or life in exactly the same way, the patterns that scientists have discovered are broadly descriptive of many people's careers and adult years. Awareness of these patterns provides a general "road map" of many issues and demands that a young adult will face over his or her adult years.

Adult Life Stages

Patterns of adult development are based on psychological and biological factors and on patterns of social expectations that exist in society. These forces result in **biosocial life stages,** which are alternating periods of stability and transition during which predictable themes are played out. A key social force is **age norms,** which are widely accepted expectations in society about appropriate behavior for a person at a given age.[12] People whose behavior does not fit existing age norms find that they are given cues (such as others asking questions like "How come you're not married?" or "Isn't it time to settle down and think about a career?") that put pressure on them to conform. The timing of Sharon Hall's decision to start a family was no doubt influenced by age norms and related biological and psychological factors.

A number of life-stage theorists have developed theories that, in spite of some differences, are quite consistent with each other. They all generally present the notion that across the adult years there are fairly stable periods that are a time for playing out prior decisions and lifestyle commitments. These stable periods are followed by more dynamic transitional periods during which prior choices are reconsidered and adjustments to various aspects of one's general style of life are explored. Sometimes, but certainly not always, these transitions are fairly traumatic crises that prompt major changes in people's lives.

Biosocial life stages. Alternating periods of stability and transition, with predictable themes that are based in psychological and biological factors and patterns of social expectations.

Age norms. Widely accepted expectations in society about appropriate behavior for a person at a given age.

Approximate Age Range	Life Stage and Major Characteristics
17–22	*Early adult transition.* Leave adolescence, make a preliminary step into the adult world by exploring different lifestyle choices and lessen dependence on parents.
22–28	*Entering adulthood.* Select and test out a specific set of choices of lifestyles and roles.
28–33	*Age 30 transition.* Reassess previous choices, often with a sense of urgency to sort out one's life and make important choices before it is too late; this may be a smooth transition or a painful crisis.
33–40	*Settling down.* Focus on a specific agenda for accomplishing goals and advance, in occupational or nonoccupational terms, to higher levels of status.
40–45	*Mid-life transition.* Reappraise past lifestyle choices and begin to eliminate negative elements and test new choices. Radical changes to major elements (e.g., marriage, occupation) can be the result of a major disillusionment with one's life, called the "mid-life crisis."
45–60	*Middle adulthood era.* Carry out lifestyle changes resulting from the mid-life transition. Often people "shift gears" and direct more time into nonwork, leisure activities.
60+	*Late adult transition & late adult era.* Some evidence of a continued pattern of reassessing prior choices and incorporating new values, interests, and behaviors into an altered lifestyle. Little research has been conducted on the specific qualities of these changes.

Source: Adapted from Levinson, D. J., et al. (1978). *The seasons of a man's life.* These stages were identified through an intensive study of forty adult males in a number of occupations. See the text regarding their applicability to women. Copyright © 1978 by Daniel J. Levinson. Reprinted by permission of Alfred A. Knopf, Inc.

EXHIBIT 18.3
Levinson's adult life stages.

One popular view of adult life stages is summarized in Exhibit 18.3.[13] It starts with the "early adult transition," which involves moving from adolescence and the exploration of various work roles and lifestyle choices to settling into a relatively stable period, called "entering adulthood." In this stage, these preliminary choices about one's lifestyle are more fully tested. Toward the end of the twenties comes a period when those earlier choices are reassessed. This "age 30 transition" can be a traumatic time of disillusionment and change (e.g., divorce, major occupational change), but for many people it is more a time of minor adjustments, not revolution.

After the age 30 transition, the more stable "settling down" period begins. A person in this stage often focuses on establishing a stable and secure niche in society and planning and striving to achieve particular goals, such as owning a house in a particular area, having one's own business, or making vice-president by a certain age. Sometimes "making it" to specific work role goals become a central life focus.

Sometimes the stable settling-down stage comes to a dramatic conclusion with the onset of the "midlife transition." In the study establishing this theory of life stages, 20 percent of the participants went through a period of minor questioning and adjustments. However, for the remaining 80 percent, this transitional period was a traumatic time in which individuals confronted forgotten values, identities, or dreams. The realization of one's biological mortality and a sense of having a limited amount of time are key factors that can be triggered by such events as the death of a friend or parent or a major illness. After the individual resolves the crisis and determines ways of giving forgotten identities more expression, the next stable period, "middle adulthood," begins. The research on life stages after this point is quite limited. No doubt that as people live longer, research will find additional life stages.

Do men and women go through the same life stages? Much of the research in this area focuses on men. However, a recent study focusing on women shows that women's life stage pattern is very similar to the model discussed above.[14] That is, the stable and transitional stages evident in women's lives corresponded closely to those presented in Exhibit 18.3. Two key differences are noteworthy. First, women differ from men in that men have a more uniform and serious career commitment in their early 30s. Women followed two contrasting routes through this age period. One route was finishing their "age 30" transition earlier than men and entering the "settling down" stage by their late 20s or very early 30s. The second route was to postpone serious career commitments until a much later age such as age 40 or beyond. Clearly, Sharon Hall's career fits the first route.

The second difference is that women, compared to men, have a more difficult time adequately incorporating their key preferences and valued goals into career and life roles. One mode of adjustment evident in the lives of the women in the research sample was to lower their career and noncareer expectations and settle for less. This does not seem descriptive of Sharon Hall. While she faced challenges, she seemed able to improvise and get around obstacles rather than drop her expectations.

We should note that the women in this study, like the men investigated in prior studies, were baby boomers and started their adult years in the 1960s and 1970s when life and career choices were more constrained compared to today's life and career options. More research is needed to understand how much these results depend on generational differences or enduring life stage patterns of men and women that continue even for today's post baby-boom generation.

Career Stages

Careers are an important aspect of many people's lives. Thus, they are influenced by the evolving pattern of needs, interests, and concerns associated with adult life stages. There are, however, general patterns of developmental changes in work role activities that are distinct from life stages. These are called **career stages**. While everyone's career contains unique demands that dictate highly specific steps to success, there are issues and key tasks that are of general importance to a wide range of people. Exhibit 18.4 summarizes four career stages: exploration, establishment, advancement and maintenance, and late career.

Career stages. General patterns of developmental issues, key tasks, and changes in work role activities.

Exploration.   This stage is a time of discovery and choice. People often leave adolescence with a wide range of ideas about what they want to do and, generally, what is possible in the world of jobs and occupations. As they move into the adult world, they must leave behind unrealistic views and settle in on a configuration of roles (i.e., student, wife/husband, employee) and develop a lifestyle that fits key elements of their identity. This involves leaving one's family of origin and developing a mix of talents, skills, and complementary interests and values that are in demand. These choices are broader than establishing one's occupational identity, but often one's choice of work role is the major element in this stage.

Approximate Age Range	Career Stage and Characteristics
16–28	*Exploration.* Explore various occupational roles and test out an initial occupational identity. Develop skills, establish a social network and mentor relationship, and cope with the emotional demands of early career.
22–42	*Establishment.* Become an individual contributor with a specific area of expertise. Work through work versus nonwork conflicts and develop a plan for achieving career goals.
32–55	*Advancement and maintenance.* Focus on achieving career goals and maintaining organizational progress. Revise career plan in light of progress. Redetermine the relative importance of work and nonwork roles. For many, the top position in their career becomes evident, and few promotions are likely. Become a mentor.
55– retirement	*Late career.* Usually the highest position has been reached, and people have started to shift more energy into nonwork pursuits. Their main source of contribution is breadth of knowledge and experience. Mentoring can continue throughout this stage.

Source: Adapted from Hall, D. T. (1976). *Careers in organizations.* Glenview, IL: Scott Foresman, and Schein, E. (1977). *Career dynamics.* Reading, MA: Addison-Wesley. Note that the ranges identify the ages within which most people enter and complete each stage. The issues and concerns identified with each stage are based on research on technical, professional, and managerial careers and may have less relevance to craft and blue-collar careers.

EXHIBIT 18.4
Career stages.

During the early part of this stage, several trial runs (such as part-time work or summer jobs during college) in different work roles are explored. These set the stage for more focused explorations during one's first "real" job. For many, this is the first job after graduation from high school or college. This job often has an enduring influence on one's career. Successfully coping with three particular tasks seems to increase the likelihood that this influence will be positive. These tasks include the following:

- establishing a social network of relationships,
- getting a job that challenges one's skills and abilities, and
- coping with the emotional side of work.

A **social network** consists of peers, possibly subordinates, and senior people who provide general information about what is going on in the organization as well as specific advice on how to accomplish job assignments and feedback about the consequences of different career strategies.[15] This network can make up for the limited experiences of a person in this career stage. Additionally, it can also be a source of friendship and emotional support during times of career or personal crisis. Substantial research confirms the importance of finding a mentor early in one's career. A **mentor** is a senior person in the organization who gives a junior person (called an **apprentice** or protégé) special attention. This can include giving advice and creating opportunities. More on the topic of mentoring will be presented later in the chapter.

A challenging first job can have a lasting impact on people's careers.[16] One study followed a group of young managers for a five- to seven-year period and found that performance at the end of the study—as measured by salary level and performance ratings—was directly tied to the level of challenge in the first job assignment. Those who had easy first assignments, even if more chal-

Social network. A group of one's peers, subordinates, and senior people who provide general information about what is going on in the organization, specific advice on how to accomplish job assignments, and feedback about the consequences of different career strategies.

Mentor. An older and more senior person in the organization who gives a junior person special attention, such as giving advice and creating opportunities.

Apprentice. A junior person, sometimes called a protégé, who has a mentor.

lenging assignments were later added, were at a distinct disadvantage. Successfully completing the first job and getting an early first promotion also has a long-term impact on promotion opportunities 10 years later.[17]

Dealing with the emotional side of work is also important. A common phenomenon many young people face when entering the workforce is **reality shock**. This is an unsettling experience caused by the disparity between unrealistic expectations that people often have and the reality that they confront in their first job (see Chapter 9). The consequence can be strong dissatisfaction until the person develops new expectations and more challenging elements are added to the new person's role in the organization. The inherent dependency of being a subordinate can also evoke a negative emotional reaction. This often occurs at a time when the person has recently left his or her family of origin. The dependencies that one has on his or her bosses can often feel like a return to adolescence. Additionally, people who are just starting their careers normally feel a little insecure about their untried and untested skills and abilities. Testing those skills and developing more self-confidence requires people to cope with the emotional challenges of insecurity. Having a social network can go a long way in helping a person through these difficult times.

Reality shock. An unsettling experience caused by the disparity between unrealistic expectations and the reality that people confront in their first job.

Establishment.   The second major career stage involves establishing oneself as an independent contributor in a specific area of expertise. During the earlier period, people tend to try their hand at many tasks. Establishing a career identity involves setting priorities and focusing on key activities that are central to one's goals and plans. It is generally necessary to move away from a close relationship with a mentor at this time. Dealing with the independence of not having someone to closely check their work can provoke feelings of insecurity unless people have developed some sound skills during the earlier stage. Conflict between work and nonwork roles can also be a problem. For example, people with families might find growing children demanding much more of their time (school plays, recreation programs, etc.) at the very time at which their biological vitality has begun to decline. Role conflict (see Chapter 8) can result when meeting one's career goals also demands an extra investment of time and energy.

Advancement and Maintenance.   After people establish themselves in a particular occupational role, they often enter a period in which they focus on advancing toward key career objectives such as making partner in an accounting firm or publishing a respected book. This is then followed by a period in which they are concerned with maintaining their status and position. In the early part of this stage, people often feel a sense of urgency to accomplish certain career goals. Individuals must make final career strategy choices and recognize unrealistic objectives and eliminate them. After this, people enter a phase in which they generally stay close to their proven skills and interests. People's main career assets are likely to be their breadth of experience and a general knowledge of a variety of areas. Some people take on mentoring responsibilities and find satisfaction in training and developing the next generation. All must confront the fact that there is a younger generation of people who see them as old-timers.

Late Career.   For a few, late career is a time for continued growth in status and influence within the organization, but for many it is a time when a person has reached or is close to reaching his or her highest level of responsibility and status. Signs of aging are obvious in this stage, and some people face serious health problems. People make retirement plans and decide on how to spend postretirement years at this point. As one faces pensions and loss of salary, financial considerations can be a source of anxiety. People often withdraw energy and time from career pursuits in this stage and become more concerned with nonwork factors.

People in this stage can be a source of wisdom for the organization. At this point, most people move away from a detailed understanding of their technical area and, perhaps, branch into areas in which others can tap their broad range of experience and general understanding of a variety of issues. Mentoring, which may have begun in the previous stage, can continue throughout this final career stage.

Recycling Through Stages.   What happens to the people who are let go (or fired) in their late forties? Do they continue through the advancement and maintenance stage? If they change jobs and stay in the same career area, then it is likely that they will continue to fit the pattern of this stage. However, if these displaced people start a job in a new career area, they go through a recycling process that is an abbreviated sequence of exploration, establishment, and eventually reenter the advancement and maintenance stage in their new occupational field.[18] Repeating the developmental tasks of each career stage may be necessary for workers in an industry or occupational area with diminishing career prospects. It may even be desirable for someone stuck in a dissatisfying career at midlife. Recycling through these career stages into a new career develops needed skills and establishes a new occupational identity and re-energizes one's motivation. As economic uncertainty and rapid technological change continue, this recycling process will likely increase.[19]

MANAGING A SUCCESSFUL CAREER

Various issues play a role in the creation of a successful career. While the individual has primary responsibility, organizations can play a facilitating role. Also, organizational efforts to help individuals manage their careers can contribute to organizational success. Other individuals in the workplace, notably a mentor, can play critical supporting roles. Nonwork factors also contribute to long-term career success. The interplay of work and family and the demands of a dual career family (i.e., when two people in a relationship are both committed to paid occupational roles) both present issues that individuals must manage carefully.

Organizational Career Management

How can organizations help individuals successfully manage their careers, and how can they do it in ways that contribute to organizational effectiveness? Organizations have many programs and policies for managing human resources. These programs accomplish things like the recruitment and selection of new employees and the training and compensation of the workforce. Traditionally, these programs focus narrowly on the short-term matching of employees to current jobs. If human resource programs focus on the long-term development of "human capital" and anticipate the future job transitions employees should experience, then those efforts will pay off in ways that contribute to both individual and organizational success.[20] Relevant guidelines include the following:

- *Link individual development to business strategy.* Training and developmental assignments should be geared to the strategic direction of the company. Usually, this includes anticipating technological changes and growing important skills before they are needed.[21] For an example, see "Global Focus: *Succession Planning and Career Development at Australia's Westpac Bank*".

- *Connect career development actions to other human resource practices.*[22] Amoco Production Company, the gas and oil exploration and production company, does this by connecting the discussion of career development objectives to the evaluation of performance and continuous improvement practices. Training and selection are two additional human resource practices that organizations should link to career enhancement activities.

- *Get line managers involved and hold them accountable for career development activities.* Boeing, the airplane manufacturer, does this by requiring all managers to attend a course on career development and making employee-development criteria a part of the manager's performance evaluation process.[23]

- *Give career development activities high visibility.* Bechtel, the construction and engineering firm, and AT&T, the telecommunications company, does this through using videos, bulletins, and brochures featuring top management involvement and support for different company actions that advance employee career development.[24]

The Role of the Mentor

Effective supervisor and subordinate relationships obviously influence the career success of individuals within an organization. One element of an effective relationship is the development of an effective mentor-apprentice relationship. While someone other than the junior person's boss can serve as a mentor, often the supervisor is in a unique position to provide mentoring. Many research efforts have documented the importance of having a mentor when starting one's career.[25] Research on business school graduates has shown that having a mentor in early career is associated with increased promotional progress, higher salaries, and more satisfaction with career prospects later in one's career.[26]

Career Functions of Mentoring. A mentor provides many career-enhancing benefits to the young apprentice.[27] These benefits are made possible by the senior person's experience, status, knowledge of how the organization works, and influence with powerful people in the organization. The career functions of mentoring include:

- *Sponsorship.* The mentor might nominate the apprentice for advantageous transfers and promotions.

GLOBAL FOCUS   Succession Planning and Career Development at Australia's Westpac Bank

Until recently, one of Australia's largest banks, Westpac Banking Corporation, managed career development through a number of formal programs. These affected staff across the bank and ranged from pre-management strategies through to senior management. However, following a change in business strategy, succession planning and management development processes have been integrated into an executive review process.

Westpac employs 31,000 people. Every three months, the Chief Executive Officer and twelve Group Executives meet for a day to review critical positions within the organization. This includes assessing ongoing potential as well as the development needs of incumbents. The review allows the Executive Team to be proactive as a group in identifying deployment issues and assessing skill deficiencies arising from business group strategies. In conjunction with human resources advisors the group executives match future business needs with individual development needs of the bank.

Another key aspect of the review is identifying senior managers with potential to move into critical/key positions within the next 2-3 years. As with

incumbents of critical positions, the performance and potential of these managers is reviewed against a set of core management competencies. Broadly

Senior managers meet to review critical positions.

based development plans are then created to provide opportunity or support.

Source: Westpac Media Relations, June 1995.

- *Exposure and visibility.* The mentor might provide opportunities to work with key people and see other parts of the organization.
- *Coaching and feedback.* The mentor might suggest work strategies and identify strengths and weaknesses in the apprentice's performance.
- *Developmental assignments.* Challenging work assignments a mentor can provide will help develop key skills and knowledge that are crucial to career progress.

Peers are infrequently in a position to be able to provide such career functions.

Psychosocial Functions of Mentoring.   Besides helping directly with career progress, mentors can provide certain psychosocial functions that are helpful in developing the apprentice's self-confidence, sense of identity, and ability to cope with emotional traumas that can damage a person's effectiveness. These include:

- *Role-modeling.* This provides a set of attitudes, values, and behaviors for the junior person to imitate.
- *Acceptance and confirmation.* The mentor can also provide encouragement and support, and help the apprentice gain self-confidence.

- *Counseling*. This provides an opportunity to discuss personal concerns and anxieties concerning career prospects, work-family conflicts, and so on.

Can organizations formally assign mentors to apprentices and achieve the career benefits normally associated with more spontaneous informal mentor-apprentice relationships? A number of organizations have implemented what they see as very successful formal mentorship programs.[28] Limited research on such programs concludes that formal programs are nearly as beneficial as informal relationships and are certainly more beneficial than not having a mentor.[29]

While all mentors, by definition, provide some subset of the career functions, mentors don't always provide these psychosocial functions. A network of close peers can go a long way in providing functions that one's mentor isn't. People starting their careers should be aware of the importance of these career and psychosocial functions and attempt to establish a social network that will fulfill them. A mentor relationship is usually a key element in this broader set of relationships. To some extent, a supportive and well-connected social network can substitute for not having an effective mentor.[30]

Benefits to the Mentor.   An effective mentor-apprentice relationship also provides many benefits for the mentor. These benefits come at a cost. So if the benefits are not forthcoming, the mentor is unlikely to be motivated to spend the time and take the risks that mentoring involves. Besides the time investment, one risk of mentoring is that a poor performing apprentice suggests the mentor has poor judgment or other inadequacies. Some benefits are task oriented. A good apprentice will typically do many mundane tasks. These types of tasks (e.g., copying and collating) must be done accurately. Having a reliable apprentice who will handle these details frees the mentor for other concerns. Other benefits relate to the mentor's career and biosocial life stage. Often, mentors are in the stage of their careers in which promotions, transfers, and new work assignments start slowing down. Developing an effective subordinate can contribute to the mentor's sense of competence and self-worth. Life-stage theorists have pointed out that at midlife, people often develop "generativity needs," which can be satisfied only by passing on one's wisdom and experience to the next generation. Effective mentoring will satisfy this need.

Women and Mentors.   One factor that inhibits women's career development, compared with their male counterparts, is the difficulty women have historically faced in establishing an apprentice-mentor relationship with a senior person in the organization.[31] The problem goes well beyond the traditional gender stereotyping we discussed in Chapter 4. It stems from the fact that senior people, who are in the best position to be mentors, are frequently men. A young woman attempting to establish a productive relationship with a senior male associate faces complexities that the male apprentice does not. Part of the problem is the lack of experience many male mentor candidates have in dealing with a woman in roles other than daughter, wife, or lover. Often, a woman's concerns are going to be different from those her male mentor experienced at that stage in his career. As a result, the strategies that he models might have limited relevance to the female apprentice. Perhaps the greatest complexity is associated with fears that their relationship will be perceived as involving sexual intimacy. Concerns about appearances and what others will say can make both people uncomfortable and get in the way of a productive relationship.

Because of these concerns, the prospective female apprentice faces more constraints than her male counterpart. Research has confirmed that cross-gender mentor-apprentice dyads are less likely to get involved in informal after-work social activities. These activities can help apprentices establish relationships with other influential people in a relaxed setting. Research also confirms that apprentices in a cross-gender dyad are less likely to see their mentor as a role model and, thereby, less likely to realize the developmental benefits of an effective model.[32]

How critical is mentoring to a woman's career? The research evidence suggests that mentoring is even more critical to women's career success than it is to men's. Women who make it to executive positions invariably had a mentor along the way. This is true for half to two-thirds of men executives.[33] Thus, for women with these career aspirations, finding a mentor appears to be a difficult but crucial task. The good news here is that there is some evidence that women work harder in an apprentice role and end up being more effective than men apprentices.[34] Also, as time goes on and more women progress into higher organizational levels, more same-gender mentoring relationships will be available for younger women.[35] For women who are unable to find an effective mentor, establishing an informed and supportive social network is a way to obtain some of the career and psychosocial functions we discussed above.

Race, Ethnicity, and Mentoring.   Limited racial and ethnic diversity at higher levels of organizations constrain the mentoring opportunities available to younger minority group employees. Research shows that mentors tend to select apprentices who are similar to them in terms of race and nationality as well as gender.[36] While there are exceptions, research confirms that minority apprentices in cross-ethnic group mentoring relationships tend to report less assistance compared to those with same-race mentors.[37] Cross-race mentoring relationships seem to focus on instrumental or career functions of mentoring (e.g., sponsorship, coaching, and feedback) and provide less psychosocial support functions (e.g., role modeling, counseling) than is generally seen in same-race dyads.[38]Although the increasing diversity of organizations makes this tendency less problematic, it suggests that minority group members should put extra efforts into developing a supportive network of peers who can provide emotional support and role modeling as well as the career functions.

Work-Family Issues and Careers

Career issues extend beyond work. Other life pursuits, notably work-family conflicts and the demands faced by dual career families, influence one's work career and, in turn, are influenced by work demands. Two clear societal patterns make work-family issues increasingly salient to career success in the 1990s. First, female labor force participation continues to increase. The life long stay-at-home wife in a "traditional" family has long ceased to be the norm. Second, the pattern of economic insecurity and increasing work demands for those who survive downsizing and restructuring puts further pressure on family units already juggling the complexities of two careers, leisure pursuits, the marital (or similar nonmarital) relationship, and, often, children.

Work-Family Conflicts. Work-family conflicts have specific sources and change over the life cycle. These role conflicts stem from time shortages and from the psychological discomfort associated with the need to revise priorities and reduce quality standards on lower-priority activities.[39] Demands for long hours and inflexible schedule can leave little time for family responsibilities. Conversely, the roles one takes in a family unit (e.g., marital or nonmarital partner, single parent, care giver for an elderly parent, and so on) and the changing demands of those roles limit the time and flexibility one has to pursue work demands. The parent of small children in a dual career relationship faces more constraints on working long hours and traveling on short notice than does a single employee without children or someone whose children are grown and on their own. At an early life stage, perhaps while in the exploration and advancement career stage, work-family conflicts are likely to be less intense. By midlife, particularly if one has children, both family and work roles have multiplied and these conflicts can become quite intense.

Developing coping strategies to deal with these conflicts is critical for career success as well as overall life satisfaction.[40] Research has identified several coping strategies. The most effective strategy is reducing or modifying the demands and expectations of role senders (e.g., bosses, co-workers, spouse, children, parents) when they create too much strain. Obviously, this requires an effective negotiation strategy and a clear understanding of personal priorities.[41] Research focusing on dual career couples notes the importance of at least one partner having flexibility in his or her work role. Traditional jobs with rigid work schedules create obstacles which are hard to overcome.[42] Spousal support is also key. It helps to counteract role overload and conflict and is positively related to career success, marital adjustment, and mental health.[43] Spousal support includes: emotional support, such as empathy and love; instrumental support, such as time and resources, including financial help; and informational support—such as advice on how to renegotiate an overwhelming work assignment.

Organizational Support for Work-Family Conflicts. Organizations have a stake in helping employees manage these conflicts. Constraints from conflicting nonwork demands distract good employees and can lead to employees turning down assignments or refusing transfers. Using three guidelines can assist organizations to reduce the organizational costs of work-family conflict.[44] First, organizations must give employees accurate information about position demands and career paths available. Clear information can help employees anticipate problems, make informed career decisions, and, if needed, develop a coping strategy. Second, organizations need to look for opportunities to provide flexible work arrangements that can lessen conflicts and may even reduce organizational costs.[45] A reduced work week, job sharing, maternity/paternity leave, and spousal relocation programs are examples. Broadening the array of career paths available, including a less time demanding career route that still draws on needed skills, is an underused alternative.[46] Finally, organizations can provide support services to help employees facing these conflicts. Alternatives include providing on-premise child care facilities, training supervisors to be sensitive to nonwork conflicts, and establishing employee assistance programs that include help with financial planning and marriage counseling.

DEVELOPING A RESILIENT CAREER

People often define careers in terms of their endpoints such as getting a promotion to a high-level position. A deeper understanding of careers places emphasis on the many transition points which occur during a career.[47] In the last few years, the magnitude and frequency of change and redirection that one can expect over a more than 40-year career has increased dramatically. As we described in the introduction of this chapter, changes in the business environment and global economy are driving changes in organizations.[48] The increased rate of mergers and acquisitions, downsizing, restructuring, reduction in hierarchical levels, and use of part-time and contract employees are examples of such change. Globalization enters in a variety of ways. Often mergers or joint ventures involve organizations from different nations. These organizational changes affect the way individual careers evolve. In short, people entering the workforce now should expect to have multiple changes in employers and even in occupational area (e.g., marketing or engineering) over their lifetime.[49] With globalization, the direction of change includes pressure to learn new skills in interacting with partners or customers in different countries and cultures and learning a second language.

These organizational changes present some opportunities, such as a chance to re-energize one's career by pursuing new occupational interests, but they also come at a cost. The major cost is that organizations, in general, are increasingly unable to make long-term commitments to employees.[50] In this new economy, a high commitment to one's own best career interests makes sense, and the ability to be an effective "free agent" is a key to career success.[51] One's career should never be left to the organization to manage. In this new reality, success does not mean never losing a job or being outplaced; it means being able to anticipate problems or quickly bouncing back from career-jarring events and keeping one's career moving forward.[52]

Each employee should manage his or her career like an entrepreneur managing a small business. Thinking of oneself as self-employed, even if employed in a large organization, will help build a resilient career. There are career strategies that can help people anticipate problems, manage the inevitable career twists and turns, and keep their "career business" on track. For example:

- *Know yourself.* What is your occupational identity and career orientation? What are your strengths and weaknesses? What are the ways you can add value to your company's business? These are not easy questions, and the answers will certainly change over time. If people do not understand how their own internal gyroscopes direct their decisions and preferences, then sooner or later they will lose control over career events and be less likely to bounce back from career adversity.

- *Know your business environment.* The career opportunities and constraints people face are directed by economic forces that confront competing companies in a given industry. Knowing what is happening in your company's business environment and your own company's role in its industry can help you anticipate opportunities and avoid career catastrophes. These are always changing and must be monitored continually. Typically, there are clear signals of industry or company performance problems long before layoff notices are issued. If you understand these business realities, you are more likely to develop an effective coping strategy. This could include moving to a new company in a different industry or staying with your current employer and moving to a new specialization or position that is likely to be of increasing strategic importance in the near future.

- *Manage your reputation.* Let others, particularly powerful decision makers inside and outside your company, know about your achievements and unique skills. Make these accomplishments visible by making presentations or getting your name associated with important projects. Maintaining a network of associates can be an important source of information and support as well as a channel to advertise your good works. This network is your invisible résumé, and it is likely to have more influence than your paper résumé.

- *Stay marketable, mobile, and always developing.* Develop and maintain specific skills and abilities that are in high demand in the larger economy. Do not commit yourself to developing company-specific abilities that are not easily transferable to a new employer. Knowing what skills are transferable in a changing economy requires constant homework. If your current job is not making you more attractive to potential employers by adding externally valued skills to your portfolio of career skills, you need to either renegotiate your job requirements or find a new job. Formal training and education should be occurring frequently throughout your life. Maintaining current skills and developing new skills should be a constant focus.

- *Be both specialist and generalist.* Invest in developing a well-defined and deep competency in an area in order to establish yourself as a clear expert; however, also develop general competencies in a broader range of areas to give yourself versatility as well. Think of your skills as analogous to stocks in a stock portfolio. The sum total of your occupational skills, abilities, and knowledge is your **career skills portfolio.** It should not be overinvested in one area; this makes you inflexible and vulnerable. Ideally, it should comprise mature skills that are currently in high demand and developing skills that are likely to be increasingly important in the future.

Career skills portfolio. The sum total of one's occupational skills, abilities, and knowledge.

- *Document your accomplishments.* Look for job and project assignments that will provide objective indicators of your competencies (e.g., dollars saved, sales increased, and so on). Results achieved and identifiable accomplishments sell better than past job titles. Being able

SUN MICROSYSTEMS' CAREER CHALLENGE

You Be The Manager

In the early 1990s Sun Microsystems, the extremely successful manufacturer of network computing solutions located in California's Silicon Valley, was in the midst of rethinking its business strategy. They, like other companies in the computer industry, faced the challenge of needing both constant innovation in response to changing technologies and customer preferences, and stringent management of costs in the face of dropping prices and shrinking profit margins. In this industry, organizations that can adapt quickly to business opportunities and keep their prices competitive are rewarded with survival—and the opportunity to adapt again in response to the next challenge.

Executives at Sun expected overall employment levels to stay constant. However, they knew they required major changes in the composition of their workforce. Like many companies in the industry, Sun needed to drastically reorganize its manufacturing operations. Consequently, hundreds of jobs in that area had to be phased out. Many manufacturing employees would either be terminated and given a severance package or, if possible, be redeployed into different jobs within Sun, such as sales, which expected growth in employment.

Marianne Jackson, human resources director, and other executives became convinced that Sun

> IN RESPONSE TO THE COMPETITIVE MARKETPLACE, SUN MICROSYSTEMS ACTED TO DEVELOP THE CAREER RESILIENCE OF ITS EMPLOYEES.

had a responsibility to put employees in control of their lives and produce a workforce that could better anticipate and adjust to the constant changes inherent in the computer industry. While others faced the challenge of adjusting their workforce composition and forcing employees into career transitions, Ms. Jackson's longer term and more difficult challenge was to create a career resilient workforce which could more easily anticipate and manage future career transitions.

1. How do you create a workforce that naturally adapts itself to the changing realities of this industry and, thus, lessens the likelihood of company-initiated redeployment, which inevitably leaves many employees both alienated and inadequately prepared to find new jobs in a changing industry?

2. Should a company encourage those whose career is better off outside the company to leave? If so, how would you help them leave? How could this benefit the company?

To find out what Sun Microsystems did, see *The Manager's Notebook* at the end of the chapter.

Sources: Adapted from Sun's "Power Pack" listing of the services provided by the Career Management Services; Waterman, R., Waterman, J., & Collard, B. (1994, July-August). Toward a career-resilient workforce. *Harvard Business Review*, 87–95; personal conversation with Lola Gerstenberger, Project Manager at Sun's Career Management Services, August 25, 1994.

to convincingly identify how your performance adds value and satisfies internal or external customers will help you negotiate with your current boss as well as a prospective employer. Being an indistinguishable member of a team on a long-term project where you cannot clearly document your unique accomplishments may weaken your résumé and reputation.

- *Always have a contingency plan and be ready to move.* What if your company merges with another and your function is duplicated in the other company and you are declared surplus? To bounce back, you have to be ready to quickly implement your backup survival plan. Being open to geographical mobility will increase your opportunities. Your backup plan should change as either the environment changes or as you change by developing new competencies and broadening your career skills portfolio.

- *Keep financially and psychologically fit.* Careers in turbulent times can be stressful and involve periods of reduced income. Your stress levels must be explicitly managed (see Chapter 14). Stress management includes establishing a social support system of family and friends as well as staying physically fit. Unreliable employers and the income uncertainties they impose require you to prudently manage your finances and avoid being in a position where a couple of months of no income is a complete disaster.

Did Avon's Sharon Hall have a resilient career strategy? She certainly managed to keep her career moving forward. A close look at her story reveals that she followed several of the above suggestions. For starters, she always had a clear sense of her occupational identity, a specific plan, and the readiness to move to a new employer to realize her career objectives. Besides being mobile, she constantly focused on developing new abilities and broadening her career skills portfolio. Her career transitions also show a nice balancing of specialist versus generalist choices. She started her career with P&G and honed her product marketing skills. Her next move—an MBA—broadened her skills portfolio considerably. Her consulting position with Booz Allen, while specialized in marketing, allowed her to further develop a broad grasp of the marketing function. It may have also provided a chance to document her accomplishments, satisfy key external clients, and develop a broad network of relationships with professionals inside and outside of Booz. This reputation—her invisible résumé—got the attention of an executive search firm that recruited her for Avon. That next move allowed her to develop her expertise in Global and Pacific Rim marketing issues. This specialization, plus her marketing experiences and MBA, seemed to make her a natural choice for senior management positions that followed.

Before continuing, please consider the *You Be the Manager* feature.

PROMOTING CAREER RESILIENCE: THE ORGANIZATION'S ROLE

While individuals have the primary role in managing their careers, organizations should be responsible and supportive partners. Organizations have much to gain by encouraging and facilitating employee efforts to keep their career skills vital and viable. Career resilience enhancing initiatives include:

- *Career planning programs.* These programs help employees identify their needs, goals, values, and other personal characteristics; identify career options either within or outside of the organization; develop a plan that integrates personal preferences and strengths and viable career path alternatives; get started on the implementation of that plan (e.g., getting managers involved, identifying key developmental tasks, etc.).

- *Career counseling.* This is a nonsupervisory external resource to aid employees in exploring career alternatives and making career decisions. Some firms use external consulting firms to provide needed expertise and ensure confidentiality.

- *Career information systems.* These include programs that provide computer-assisted career information searches, resource material in the company library on employment trends, minimum qualifications for key jobs, and so on. Raychem, a maker of specialized industrial products located in California's Silicon Valley, is creating a network of incumbents in key jobs who are available for interviews with people interested in learning more about the nature of their jobs and necessary qualifications.[53] Apple Computer places extensive career information on its "electronic campus" resource facility.

- *Skill benchmarking and assessment.* Employees need to have unambiguous information on their competency levels and how they match up to position requirements. **Skill benchmarking** is the process of identifying required competency levels for key jobs in an industry. Thus, required competencies are clearly defined and linked to jobs in the external labor market as well as within the company. This forces an organization to keep on top of external employment trends. Clear performance assessment and feedback helps employees learn how well their skills meet the requirements of various alternative career paths.

- *Strategic direction and business performance information.* A continuing dialogue about where the company is going and how its performance compares to industry leaders helps employees adapt and adjust career plans based on accurate information. For example, departments in 3Com, the computer networking products company, hold weekly discussion sessions on business performance.[54]

- *Extensive education and training support.* Resilience requires continuous learning. Tuition reimbursement programs and extensive in-house training programs can help here. Motorola expects employees to spend five percent of their time in educational activities. Sun Microsystems and Raychem provide lunchtime and after-hours seminars on topics ranging from job interviewing strategies to managing work and nonwork conflicts to market trends and technical area updates.[55]

- *Workplace flexibility.* Organizations that demand employees to be flexible and adapt to changing demands must reciprocate by being a flexible partner. This requires allowing flexibility in the ways that employees contribute and more voice and choice in the roles that employees take on over their careers.[56]

These efforts attempt to give employees support and complete information. Both are needed to facilitate intelligent strategic career choices—choices that are in the long run good for individuals and their employers. The organizations using these initiatives tend to have pressing strategic demands that necessitate having a workforce with cutting edge skills and the ability to respond quickly to frequent changes in technology or the market trends.

Skill benchmarking. The process of identifying required competency levels for key jobs in an industry.

The Manager's Notebook — Sun Microsystems' Career Challenge

1. Sun Microsystems' solution to the challenge of creating workforce resilience includes most of the career resilience enhancing initiatives we described above. Their Career Self-Reliance program includes:

- Self-assessment processes including one-on-one counseling as well as self-paced career oriented software and workbooks.
- Identification and evaluation of career alternatives based on industry and regional employment trends, Sun's business directions, career paths within the company, and interviews with people in key jobs.
- Helping employees market themselves, e.g., helping them identify and favorably communicate their portfolio of career skills, establishing development plans, writing better résumés, and improving interviewing skills.
- Encouraging reassessment of individual interests, priorities, and career options on a regular basis, e.g., keeping on top of emerging employment trends, expanding one's social network, reevaluating development plans, and adding to one's skills portfolio.

Resources Sun has developed to support the career resilience efforts include: a variety of career related seminars and workshops; lunch hour presentations from career experts; a career library with books, articles, video and audio tapes, and a trained librarian to help target an employee's search; listings of career search related resources outside of the company, e.g., community and university career centers; continually updated postings of job vacancies at Sun, plus over 5,000 listings from other employers in California; and a quarterly career-oriented newsletter and on-line career information through the company's E-mail system.

2. Sun believes that an employee who leaves the company to better develop his or her career may come back in a few years. This is a logical extension of focusing on employability security (versus employment security). This philosophy is most evident in Sun's use of an external organization, the Career Action Center, to further help employees make career decisions. This organization is supported by Sun, as well as other Silicon Valley employers. Sun employees are each given a free day pass to the Career Action Center to use as they please—including lining up a new employer. Additionally, Career Action Center counselors are employed in Sun's own career center. This provides employees with a mix of internal specialists, who know the career options within Sun, and external experts, who are well connected with the larger industry and region, to help them in their efforts to frequently assess their strengths and explore career options.

EXECUTIVE SUMMARY

◆ A career is a sequence of work activities, attitudes, and reactions experienced over a person's lifetime. It involves an objective sequence of positions as well as reactions, attitudes, and an occupational identity that emerges from the fit or interaction between people and their work environments.

◆ Individual differences are a critical factor in determining the fit between people and their work environments. The two major perspectives on career orientation are Holland's theory of career types and Schein's theory of career anchors. These define the job and situational factors that fit each career orientation and increase the likelihood of an individual's attraction, retention, sense of competence, and satisfaction in a given work environment.

◆ People and their careers are dynamic. As we age, we go through a sequence of biosocial life stages. Over the life course, there appears to be a pattern of transitional periods, during which individuals reconsider previous lifestyle choices. Stable periods, during which previous choices are tested out, follow the transition periods. Careers also go through a sequence of stages: exploration, establishment, advancement and maintenance, and late career.

◆ Organizations can facilitate career success. Career management programs can help match individual career needs with developmental opportunities and contribute to both individual success and organizational effectiveness. Research on mentoring identifies key career and psychosocial functions that supervisors and others can provide. Women and racial minorities face unique problems in forming career-enhancing relationships with mentors. The effective management of work-family and dual career couple conflicts contributes to career and organizational success.

◆ Career success requires people to be resilient and bounce back from career threatening events. Being resilient is facilitated by self-insight, understanding one's larger business environment, constant learning, and, among other things, always having a contingency plan and being ready to move.

◆ Organizations can facilitate employee career resilience efforts by developing systematic programs and procedures that provide information that employees need to plan their career development. Additionally, employers interested in a resilient workforce must provide extensive educational opportunities, clear standards for assessing competency levels for key jobs, and increased flexibility in how employee roles are defined over time.

KEY CONCEPTS

Career
External career
Internal career
Career orientation
Theory of career types (Holland)
Theory of career anchors (Schein)
Biosocial life stages
Age norms

Career stages
Social network
Mentor
Apprentice
Reality shock
Career skills portfolio
Skill benchmarking

DISCUSSION QUESTIONS

1. A career has a number of specific elements. What are these elements?

2. Compare and contrast Holland's career types and Schein's career anchors. Identify the career types and anchors that are separate and distinct from one another. Which of these types and anchors have some degree of overlap such that people who fit one category of Holland's also have certain career anchors? What career types and anchors are likely to be negatively related?

3. The father of psychoanalysis, Sigmund Freud, is said to have observed that people are mostly fixed by age six and stay pretty much the same after their early formative years. Is this view consistent or inconsistent with various points presented in this chapter? Identify three different parts of the chapter that back up your answer.

4. Compare and contrast career stages and biosocial life stages. Which life stage is likely to be confronted in which particular career stage?

5. How does having a mentor help one's career? What functions do effective mentors provide to

apprentices? Why would a mentor expend the time and effort involved in mentoring a junior person?

6. What unique obstacles do women and ethnic or racial minorities face in their career development? Why should organizations be concerned with these obstacles?

7. The changes in employment patterns (e.g., downsizing, outsourcing, less traditional job security, and so on) evident in the 1990s suggest discarding traditional definitions of career success. What is a definition of career success that is consistent with the economic and social reality of the 1990s?

8. What does career resilience mean? What are some individual strategies for achieving career resilience?

9. What is the organization's role in promoting career resilience? What are some practices that promote employee career management and increase career resilience? What are the organizational benefits of having a resilient workforce?

EXPERIENTIAL EXERCISE
IDENTIFYING YOUR CAREER ORIENTATION

You have been assigned to create a task force to work on a complex task. Past experience has shown that accomplishing this task requires MAXIMUM skill and personality variety on the team. Interpersonal comfort considerations and the tendency to select people similar to yourself should be MINIMIZED. In order to select this task force, rank order the five people described below. Read over all of these self-descriptions and, first, rank the person who is most dissimilar to you as #1. Then rank the person next most dissimilar to you as number #2, and so on until you have ranked the last person, the one most similar to you, as #6.

Rank	Skill and Personality Self-Descriptions
_____	**A.** "I have always been motivated to seek new and different work settings. The excitement of an endless variety of new challenges is what I look for in my career. I quickly get bored if I have to do the same thing over and over."
_____	**B.** "My long-term security is really key to me. When I investigate a new job opportunity, I always make sure to see how good their retirement program is and whether they can guarantee me a secure job. Good organizations provide life-long employment to their employees."
_____	**C.** "A good job is one that provides me maximum freedom to choose my own approach to getting the job done. I really want to work in an organization that lets me pursue my own lifestyle and doesn't constrain me with a bunch of rules. Freedom and autonomy are key to me."
_____	**D.** "Staying in my area of interest is more desirable than a promotion. I plan to continue to build my career around a specific functional area. Exercising the skills and knowledge in my specialty is crucial to me."
_____	**E.** "Success means supervising, leading and controlling other people. I want to reach a level where my decisions make a difference. Good promotions lead to more responsibility and authority."
_____	**F.** "My main motivation is to create something that is the result of my own effort and ingenuity. I've always wanted to build a new business around an original product or service that is my own creation. I won't be happy until I create something that exists because I thought of it."

1. To what extent do the self-descriptions ranked #5 and #6 represent your overall career orientation? Are there elements of the other descriptions which fit your career orientation? Are there key motives that are not touched by any of these descriptions?
2. What theories of individual career orientation, which we presented early in this chapter, match the self-descriptions you ranked #5 and #6? What motives and preferences in the chapter are least similar to your own? Do they correspond to the self-descriptions you ranked #1 or #2?
3. Do you think that it makes sense to create teams with highly dissimilar people? What are the advantages and disadvantages of this strategy?

Source: Developed by J. Bruce Prince. Used with permission.

CASE STUDY
THE CASE OF THE EXPECTANT EXECUTIVE AND THE ENDANGERED PROMOTION

Jim Serra, vice president of engineering for Hunter Peripherals, sighed heavily as he watched the early morning traffic on Highway 237. Outside his office window, thousands of cars rushed by each day, past the Inter, Acer, and other hightech billboards, symbolizing Silicon Valley's continual fast pace. Jim had always taken Hunter's frenetic environment for granted—had thrived on it, in fact, as had his senior managers. But the competitive pace now left him with a dilemma: Should he promote one of those managers to a crucial new director's position?

Still single, Jim had lived for his job ever since he'd joined Hunter Peripherals five years ago. As one of the founding employees of the $160 million company, he had a lot on the line, including his stock options. Tomorrow morning he had to make a recommendation to his colleagues on the executive management committee [EMC]. However he pitched it, Jim's words would carry a lot of weight with the EMC.

Diane Bryant was the only valid inside candidate for the new opening. Diane, who was Jim's senior engineering group manager in charge of environmental testing, had demonstrated an early knack for leadership and innovation. When she first came on board, she revamped the entire testing procedure. She had credibility with senior executives, was well respected by her staff, and was a sharp thinker. She was also five months pregnant.

"Her timing is just so lousy," Jim thought, staring bleakly at the blinking workstation screen on his crowed desk.

Until recently, director-level openings were virtually nonexistent at the company. But when Mitch Lee, another senior manager, had resigned to join a start-up, Jim had decided to merge Mitch's product compliance group with Diane's environmental testing group. Because these two groups were critical to the upcoming launch of Hunter's next-generation disk drive (code named "Zeuss"), Jim had created a new director's position to oversee these areas and had announced the opening at last week's management meeting.

With his staff of 90 people, including 8 direct reports, Jim needed a strong leader for the job. Zeuss could not be introduced until it met the industry environmental standards for shock, corrosion, and temperature and obtained compliance certification from the international regulatory agencies. Moreover, the first-customer ship deadline (FCS) was only six months away. Already Hunter's existing product orders were declining as customers anticipated the next generation of disk drives. A slip-up in the schedule would give Hunter's competition the edge, and millions of dollars in revenue would be lost.

Jim told himself that Diane's pregnancy was no surprise. She was 36, after all, and he'd known Diane and her husband Brian wanted children. Brian was closer to 40 and had established his own computer consulting business to allow for more flexibility in his schedule. Jim was happy for both of them, but . . .

He swung around in his ergonomic chair, brooding on the empty take-out pizza box on his conference table. For the four years they'd worked together, Diane had been a comrade-in-arms, pounding away on weekends and late at night with the best of them. As a colleague, Jim enjoyed Diane's snappy sense of humor and quick mind. Even now, he knew she could guarantee timely completion of her group's commitments for Zeuss. But when it came to the new director's position, Diane would be on maternity leave two months before the FCS. Given the mess Mitch Lee had left behind in the compliance group, including a staff with chronic high turnover and low morale, Jim wasn't sure how the company could launch Zeuss on schedule without the new director in the office full-time.

At lunch Jim's colleague David Moss only reinforced Jim's worries. David, who was vice president of product engineering and a fellow EMC member, met him in the company cafeteria at noon. David was a gruff, outspoken industry veteran who had been brought in eight months before to help Hunter regain the market share recently lost to its rival, Quality Storage International. David was now responsible for getting Zeuss to market on time. A hard-driving maverick, he started work at 5:00 a.m., jogged six miles every day, and rarely saw his wife and two young sons.

Jim and David managed to avoid talking about the director's opening while they ordered cheeseburgers and fries at the grill. The spacious, modern cafeteria had been redecorated in burgundy and mauve, adorned with neon signs for hot entrées, espresso drinks, and a salad bar—all planned last year when Hunter still had cash to burn, Jim noted wryly. After paying the cashier, he and David headed for the small conference room off the cafeteria. David shut the door firmly before diving into his burger.

"Too bad about Diane," he said with his mouth full. "But this always happens. Remember Rebecca at Datex? She could have been a VP if she hadn't decided to quit and start a family."

Jim didn't answer. He'd always prided himself on being a fair manager, one who evaluated individuals on the basis of accountability and results, never gender. David Moss, however, had made it clear to anyone who would listen his low opinion of Hunter's new parental-leave policy, in which employees could take up to eight weeks off, with pay, and were guaranteed a job when they returned, although it might not be the same position.

David stopped chewing, and his eyes widened. "Are you actually considering Diane for the job?"

"We both know she deserves it," Jim hedged. "Look, I can't penalize Diane for having a baby. If I don't promote her and I bring in a new director, she'll essentially be demoted, and I'm afraid of losing her for good."

David dropped his half-eaten burger. "How do you know she'll even come back to work? She'll be responsible for a family soon, and her priorities will change. The bottom line is, she made the choice." He rubbed at a new grease spot on his shirtsleeve. "And you can't afford a disaster in product compliance."

"I haven't figured that one out yet," Jim admitted.

"The new director has to have the technical know-how to make the right judgment calls at the last minute." David shoved his tray away. "Say it's one month before the Zeuss FCS and testers find that electromagnetic emissions are borderline. This director will have to decide whether to send the drive back to engineering for more work or to push the product through as is. Only someone who's got environmental and compliance specs down cold knows how strict approval agencies are about emissions. Maybe there's a good chance the borderline product will squeak through, or maybe the agencies are watching that particular spec real closely because the electromag interferes with broadcast transmissions. I don't have the expertise to make that call—do you?"

"Diane does," Jim said quietly.

"Sure, Diane's one of the best! But you don't know how reliable she'll be when or if she comes back." David tugged at his tie. "If there's no internal talent available, you've got to look outside. What about Reg Stuart at Vision or Tom Wu at Datex? I hear they're both sniffing around for something new . . . "

Jim stared at the mauve carpeting, his lunch long forgotten. Part of him wanted to wring David's skinny, excitable neck. But his common sense told him he was only angry at the man because he was right—at least from a short-term business point of view.

"Don't tell me you've already informed Diane that you'll be recommending her to the EMC!" David burst out. "We'll have legal problems then!"

"No, I haven't told her anything yet," Jim said.

"Well, good," David said. "Think very seriously about this, Jim, because you've got to do what's right for the company. This is my product, and I simply won't tolerate any more mistakes!"

David picked up his tray and left with a bang of the conference room door. Jim was used to his take-no-prisoners style and tried not to let it bother him. But back in his office, he kept thinking about it and making mental lists of pros and cons.

A knock interrupted his list making. Before Jim's office door opened, he knew it was Diane. He'd been expecting a confrontation with her for days. But when she took a seat at his cluttered conference table, pushing aside a stack of computer magazines, Jim saw that she was even more upset than he'd imagined. Smoothing down her well-tailored maternity dress, Diane didn't bother with greetings, much less her usual wisecracks.

"We both know why I'm here." She smiled stiffly. "I want to make perfectly clear my interest in the director's opening. In fact, I've been waiting for you to say something all week."

"There's absolutely no question that you're qualified for the job, Diane. We need to go through the formal interview process, however." Jim felt uncomfortable adding this last bit since he and Diane had always been honest with each other in the past.

"Let's cut to the chase." she snapped. "I suspect you have some concerns about my pregnancy leave. But I should be back in time for the Zeuss launch. You know me, Jim—I don't want to miss it!"

"Unfortunately, the two months before the launch are the most critical. The new director will have to keep the environmental and compliance groups on track and resolve problems fast before they escalate."

"I know that, but I would have four solid months in the new job before I take my leave. And I'll make damn sure the groups are in good shape before I go. I've been thinking about this a lot, and I'd like to propose that Carl Mullikin assume managerial responsibilities while I'm out. It'll give him some experience and . . ."

"Are you suggesting that Carl be acting director?" Jim shook his head. "Carl's got potential, sure, but he's not up to that. When he ran the engineering test-procedure task force last year, his team didn't make its deadline. Frankly, I don't see anyone in-house who could carry both groups while you're away."

"I still think my group can meet environmental's commitments at 100 percent. Compliance should come in at 85 percent."

"An 85 percent compliance isn't good enough, Diane. You don't want to jeopardize the launch, do you?"

Her gaze remained steady. "No, of course not. But I'm sure you realize that just because I'm starting a family doesn't mean I'm a different person. My commitment to excellence doesn't change. My ability to execute doesn't change. If a man had to go on leave because of a sudden illness, would you deny him the position, if he were the most qualified? Jim, I'm the right person for this job."

He forced himself to meet her eyes. "Would you be willing to take a shorter leave? Say, just four weeks instead of eight?"

Diane looked down, stretching her legs under the table. "I'll be working up to the due date, in any case, but there's no way I can predict exactly when the baby will come. Let's face it, a shorter leave isn't realistic."

"All right, then." Jim tried to smile reassuringly. "You're in the running, but I've got to warn you, this is a tough decision for me."

Diane looked at him for another minute, then left his office without another word. Jim started reading the 17 E-mail messages that had accumulated in the past hour but was too distracted to do them justice. Finally, he turned his back on his workstation and watched traffic as the afternoon rush-hour began.

If only the stakes weren't so high. A successful product launch could take Hunter Peripherals public. Like the other EMC members with stock, Jim could almost taste a big win. If he recommended hiring an outside person with senior credentials, David Moss and the others would easily accept that decision.

Of course, even a senior hire would take at least two months to locate, a month to come on board, and another four months or so to learn the intricacies of Hunter's internal workings. And there was no telling how Diane's staff would react to such a change. Yet that person would be on hand—24 hours a day, if necessary—during the critical two months before the launch. And when Diane returned after eight weeks, would she really be able to handle both a heavy management load and a new baby?

In fact, the stakes were always high at a company like Hunter Peripherals. While long-term performance depended on retaining key employees like Diane, Jim also had short-term goals to meet. With shrinking budgets and slim people resources, he couldn't see an obvious way to deal with her leave.

Source: Mock, C., & Bruno, A. (1994, January-February). The expectant executive and the endangered promotion. *Harvard Business Review*, 16–19.

1. If you were a consultant to Jim Serra, what would you advise him to do? What is the basis for your advice?
2. Is Diane Bryant's confidence about being able to handle the promotion, the Zeuss launch, and the challenges of her new role as mother of an infant reasonable? What would you advise her to do?

GLOSSARY

360 degree feedback. Performance appraisal that uses the input of superiors, subordinates, peers, and clients or customers of the appraised individual. (11)

Accommodating. A conflict management style in which one cooperates with the other party while not asserting one's own interests. (14)

Active listening. A technique for improving the accuracy of information reception by paying close attention to the sender. (11)

Actor-observer effect. The propensity for actors and observers to view the causes of the actor's behavior differently. (4)

Additive tasks. Tasks in which group performance is dependent upon the sum of the performance of individual group members. (8)

Advanced information technology. The generation, aggregation, storage, modification, and speedy transmission of information made possible by the advent of computers and related devices. (16)

Affective commitment. Commitment based on identification and involvement with an organization. (9)

Age norms. Widely accepted expectations in society about appropriate behavior for a person at a given age. (18)

Anchoring effect. The inadequate adjustment of subsequent estimates from an initial estimate that serves as an anchor. (12)

Apprentice. A junior person, sometimes called a protégé, who has a mentor. (18)

Attitude. A fairly stable emotional tendency to respond consistently to some specific object, situation, person, or category of people. (5)

Attribution. The process by which causes or motives are assigned to explain peoples' behavior. (4)

Autonomy. The freedom to schedule one's own work activities and decide work procedures. (7)

Avoiding. A conflict management style characterized by low assertiveness of one's own interests and low cooperation with the other party. (14)

Benchmarking. A systematic process for examining the products, services, and work processes of firms that are recognized as illustrating the best practices for organizational improvement. (7)

Biosocial life stages. Alternating periods of stability and transition, with predictable themes that are based in psychological and biological factors and patterns of social expectations. (18)

Body language. Nonverbal communication by means of a sender's bodily motions, facial expressions, or physical location. (11)

Boundary roles. Positions in which organizational members are required to interact with members of other organizations or with the public. (14)

Bounded rationality. A decision strategy that relies on limited information and that reflects time constraints and political considerations. (12)

Brainstorming. An attempt to increase the number of creative solution alternatives to problems by focusing on idea generation rather than evaluation. (12)

Bureaucracy. Max Weber's ideal type of organization that included a strict chain of command, detailed rules, high specialization, centralized power, and selection and promotion based on technical competence. (1)

Burnout. Emotional exhaustion, depersonalization, and reduced personal accomplishment among those who work with people. (14)

Career. An evolving sequence of work activities and positions that individuals experience over time as well as the associated attitudes, knowledge, and competencies that develop throughout one's life. (18)

Career orientation. The fairly stable pattern of preferred occupational activities, talents, values, and attitudes. (18)

Career skills portfolio. The sum total of one's occupational skills, abilities, and knowledge. (18)

Career stages. General patterns of developmental issues, key tasks, and changes in work role activities. (18)

Central tendency. The tendency to assign most ratees to middle-range job performance categories. (4)

Central traits. Personal characteristics of a target person that are of particular interest to a perceiver. (4)

Centralization. The extent to which decision-making power is localized in a particular part of an organization. (15)

Chain of command. Lines of authority and formal reporting relationship. (11)

Change. The implementation of a program or plan to move an organization and/or its members to a more satisfactory state. (17)

Change agents. Experts in the application of behavioral science knowledge to organizational diagnosis and change. (17)

Charisma. The ability to command strong loyalty and devotion from followers and thus have the potential for strong influence among them. (10)

Classical viewpoint. An early prescription on management that advocated high specialization of labor, intensive coordination, and centralized decision making. (1)

Coercive power. Power derived from the use of punishment and threat. (13)

Cognitive biases. Tendencies to acquire and process information in an error-prone way. (12)

Cognitive dissonance. A feeling of tension experienced when certain cognitions are contradictory or inconsistent with each other. (5)

Collaborating. A conflict management style that maximizes both assertiveness and cooperation. (14)

Communication. The process by which information is exchanged between a sender and a receiver. (11)

Compensation. Applying one's skills in a particular area to make up for failure in another area. (14)

Competing. A conflict management style that maximizes assertiveness and minimizes cooperation. (14)

Complexity. The extent to which an organization divides labor vertically, horizontally, and geographically. (15)

Compliance. Conformity to a social norm prompted by the desire to acquire rewards or avoid punishment. (9)

Compressed workweek. An alternative work schedule in which employees work fewer than the normal five days a week but still put in a normal number of hours per week. (7)

Compromise. A conflict management style that combines intermediate levels of assertiveness and cooperation. (14)

Confirmation bias. The tendency to seek out information that conforms to one's own definition of or solution to a problem. (12)

Conflict stimulation. A strategy of increasing conflict in order to motivate change. (14)

Congruence. A condition in which a person's words, thoughts, feelings, and actions all contain the same message. (11)

Conjunctive tasks. Tasks in which group performance is limited by the performance of the poorest group member. (8)

Consensus cues. Attribution cues that reflect how a person's behavior compares with that of others. (4)

Conservative shift. The tendency for groups to make less risky decisions than the average risk initially advocated by their individual members. (12)

Consideration. The extent to which a leader is approachable and shows personal concern for subordinates. (10)

Consistency cues. Attribution cues that reflect how consistently a person engages in some behavior over time. (4)

Contingency approach. An approach to management that recognizes that there is no one best way to manage, and that an appropriate management style depends on the demands of the situation. (1)

Contingency Theory. Fred Fiedler's theory that states that the association between leadership orientation and group effectiveness is contingent upon how favorable the situation is for exerting influence. (10)

Continuance commitment. Commitment based on the costs that would be incurred in leaving an organization. (9)

Contrast effects. Previously interviewed job applicants affect an interviewer's perception of a current applicant, leading to an exaggeration of differences between applicants. (4)

Control group. A group of research subjects who have not been exposed to the experimental treatment. (2)

Coordination. A process of facilitating timing, communication, and feedback among work tasks. (15)

Correlational research. Research that attempts to measure variables precisely and examine relationships among these variables without introducing change into the research setting. (2)

Creativity. The production of novel but potentially useful ideas. (17)

Cross-functional teams. Work groups that bring people with different functional specialities together to better invent, design, or deliver a product or service. (8)

Cultural context. The cultural information that surrounds a communication episode. (11)

Customer departmentation. Relatively self-contained units deliver an organization's products or services to specific customer groups. (15)

Debasement. A series of socialization experiences designed to humble people and remove some self-confidence. (9)

Decision making. The process of developing commitment to some course of action. (12)

Defense mechanisms. Psychological attempts to reduce the anxiety associated with stress. (14)

Delphi technique. A method of pooling a large number of expert judgments through a series of increasingly refined questionnaires. (12)

Dependent variable. In an experiment, the variable that is expected to vary as a result of the manipulation of the independent variable. (2)

Devil's advocate. A person appointed to identify and challenge the weaknesses of a proposed plan or strategy. (12)

Diagnosis. The systematic collection of information relevant to impending organizational change. (17)

Differentiation. The tendency for managers in separate departments to differ in terms of goals, time spans, and interpersonal styles. (15)

Diffusion. The process by which innovations move through an organization. (17)

Diffusion of responsibility. The ability of group members to share the burden of the negative consequences of a poor decision. (12)

Direct observation. Observational research in which the researcher observes organizational behavior without taking part in the studied activity. (2)

Discrepancy theory. A theory that job satisfaction stems from the discrepancy between the job outcomes wanted and the outcomes that are perceived to be obtained. (5)

Disjunctive tasks. Tasks in which group performance is dependent upon the performance of the best group member. (8)

Displacement. Directing feelings of anger at a safe target rather than expressing them where they might be punished. (14)

Dispositional attributions. Explanations for behavior based on an actor's personality or intellect. (4)

Distinctiveness cues. Attribution cues that reflect the extent to which a person engages in some behavior across a variety of situations. (4)

Distributive fairness. Fairness that occurs when people receive what they think they deserve from their jobs. (5)

Distributive negotiation. Win-lose negotiation in which a fixed amount of assets is divided between parties. (14)

Downsizing. The intentional reduction of workforce size with the goal of improving organizational efficiency or effectiveness. (15)

Downward communication. Information that flows from the top of the organization toward the bottom. (11)

Effect dependence. Reliance on others due to their capacity to provide rewards and punishment. (9)

Effective communication. The right people receive the right information in a timely manner. (11)

Electronic brainstorming. The use of computer-mediated technology to improve traditional brainstorming practices. (12)

Electronic groups. Decision-making groups whose members are linked electronically rather than face-to-face. (12)

Employee survey. Anonymous questionnaire that enables employees to state their candid opinions and attitudes about an organization and its practices. (11)

Empowerment. Giving people the authority, opportunity, and motivation to take initiative and solve organizational problems. (7, 13)

Environmental uncertainty. A condition that exists when the external environment is vague, difficult to diagnose, and unpredictable. (16)

Equity theory. A process theory that job satisfaction and motivation stems from a comparison of the inputs one invests in a job and the outcomes one receives in comparison with the inputs and outcomes of another person or group. (5, 6)

ERG theory. A three-level hierarchical need theory of motivation (existence, relatedness, growth) that allows for movement up and down the hierarchy. (6)

Escalation of commitment. The tendency to invest additional resources in an apparently failing course of action. (12)

Ethics. Systematic thinking about the moral consequences of decisions. (13)

Expectancy theory. A process theory that states that motivation is determind by the outcomes that people expect to occur as a result of their actions on the job. (6)

Expectancy. The probability that a particular first-level outcome can be achieved. (6)

Experimental research. Research which changes or manipulates a variable under controlled conditions and examines the consequences of this manipulation for some other variable. (2)

Expert power. Power derived from having special information or expertise that is valued by an organization. (13)

External career. The objective sequence of positions that comprise one's career. (18)

External environment. Events and conditions surrounding an organization that influence its activities. (16)

Extinction. The gradual dissipation of behavior following the termination of reinforcement. (3)

Extrinsic motivation. Motivation that stems from the work environment external to the task; it is usually applied by others. (6)

Feedback. Information about the effectiveness of one's work performance. (7)

Filtering. The tendency for a message to be watered down or stopped during transmission. (11)

Fixed interval schedule. A partial reinforcement schedule in which some fixed time period occurs between a reinforced response and the availability of the next reinforcement. (3)

Fixed ratio schedule. A partial reinforcement schedule in which some fixed number of responses must be made between a reinforced response and the availability of the next reinforcement. (3)

Flat organization. An organization with relatively few levels in its hierarchy of authority. (15)

Flex-time. An alternative work schedule in which arrival and quitting times are flexible. (7)

Force. The effort directed toward a first-level outcome. (6)

Formal work groups. Groups that are established by organizations to facilitate the achievement of organizational goals. (8)

Formalization. The extent to which work roles are highly defined by an organization. (15)

Framing. Aspects of the presentation of information about a problem that are assumed by decision makers. (12)

Functional departmentation. Employees with closely related skills and responsibilities are assigned to the same department. (15)

Fundamental attribution error. The tendency to overemphasize dispositional explanations for behavior at the expense of situational explanations. (4)

Gainsharing. A group pay incentive plan based on productivity or performance improvements over which the workforce has some control. (7)

Gatekeepers. People who span organizational boundaries to import new information, translate it for local use, and disseminate it. (17)

Geographic deparmentation. Relatively self-contained units deliver an organization's products or services in a specific geographic territory. (15)

Goal setting. A motivational technique that uses specific, challenging, and acceptable goals and provides feedback to enhance performance. (7)

Grapevine. An organization's informal communication network. (11)

Group. Two or more people interacting interdependently to achieve a common goal. (8)

Group cohesiveness. The degree to which a group is especially attractive to its members. (8)

Groupthink. The capacity for group pressure to damage the mental efficiency, reality testing, and moral judgment of decision-making groups. (12)

Growth need strength. The extent to which people desire to achieve higher-order need satisfaction by performing their jobs. (7)

Halo effect. The rating of an individual on one trait or characteristic tends to color ratings on other traits or characteristics. (4)

Harshness. The tendency to perceive the job performance of ratees as especially ineffective. (4)

Hawthorne effect. A favorable response by subjects in an organizational experiment that is the result of a factor other than the independent variable that is formally being manipulated. (2)

Hawthorne studies. Research conducted at the Hawthorne plant of Western Electric in the 1920s and 1930s that illustrated how psychological and social processes affect productivity and work adjustment. (1)

Hindsight. The tendency to review a decision-making process to find what was done right or wrong. (12)

Horizontal communication. Information that flows between departments or functional units, usually as a means of coordinating effort. (11)

Human relations movement. A critique of classical management and bureaucracy that advocated management styles that were more participative and oriented toward employee needs. (1)

Hybrid departmentation. A structure based on some mixture of functional, product, geographic, or customer departmentation. (15)

Hypothesis. A formal statement of the expected relationship between two variables. (2)

Idea champions. People who recognize an innovative idea and guide it to implementation. (17)

Identification. Conformity to a social norm prompted by perceptions that those who promote the norm are attractive or similar to oneself. (9)

Idiosyncrasy credits. Social credits earned from regular conformity to group norms that allow occasional deviance from the norms. (9)

Ill-structured problem. A problem for which the existing and desired states are unclear and the method of getting to the desired state is unknown. (12)

Implicit personality theories. Personal theories that people have about which personality characteristics go together. (4)

Independent variable. The variable that is manipulated or changed in an experiment. (2)

Individualistic vs. collective. Individualistic societies stress independence, individual initiative, and privacy. Collective cultures favor interdependence and loyalty to family or clan. (5)

Influence tactics. Tactics that are used to convert power into actual influence over others. (13)

Informal groups. Groups that emerge naturally in response to the common interests of organizational members. (8)

Information dependence. Reliance on others for information about how to think, feel, and act. (9)

Information overload. The reception of more information than is necessary to make effective decisions. (12)

Information richness. The potential information-carrying capacity of a communication medium. (11)

Initiating structure. The degree to which a leader concentrates on group goal attainment. (10)

Innovation. The process of developing and implementing new ideas in an organization. (17)

Inputs. Anything that people give up, offer, or trade to their organization in exchange for outcomes. (5)

Instrumentality. The probability that a particular first-level outcome will be followed by a particular second-level outcome. (6)

Integration. The process of attaining coordination across differentiated departments. (15)

Integrative negotiation. Win-win negotiation that assumes that mutual problem solving can enlarge the assets to be divided between parties. (14)

Integrators. Organizational members permanently assigned to facilitate coordination between departments. (15)

Interest groups. Parties or organizations other than direct competitors that have some vested interest in how an organization is managed. (16)

Interlocking directorates. A condition existing when one person serves on two or more boards of directors. (16)

Internal career. The individual's interpretation of objective work experiences known only from a person's own subjective sense of external events. (18)

Internalization. Conformity to a social norm prompted by true acceptance of the beliefs, values, and attitudes that underlie the norm. (9)

Interpersonal conflict. A process that occurs when one person, group, or organizational subunit frustrates the goal attainment of another. (14)

Interrole conflict. Several roles held by a role occupant involve incompatible expectations. (8)

Intersender role conflict. Two or more role senders provide a role occupant with incompatible expectations. (8)

Intrasender role conflict. A single role sender provides incompatible expectations to a role occupant. (8)

Intrinsic motivation. Motivation that stems from the direct relationship between the worker and the task; it is usually self-applied. (6)

Intuition. Problem identification and solving based on systematic education and experiences that locate problems within a network of previously acquired information. (1)

Jargon. Specialized language used by job holders or members of particular occupations or organizations. (11)

Job demands-job control model. A model that asserts that jobs promote high stress when they make high demands while offering little control over work decisions. (14)

Job enrichment. The design of jobs to enhance intrinsic motivation and the quality of working life. (7)

Job satisfaction. A collection of attitudes that workers have about their jobs. (5)

Job sharing. An alternative work schedule in which two part-time employees divide the work of a full-time job. (7)

Leader punishment behavior. The leader's use of reprimands or unfavorable task assignments and the active withholding of rewards. (10)

Leader reward behavior. The leader's provision of subordinates with compliments, tangible benefits, and deserved special treatment. (10)

Leadership. The influence that particular individuals exert upon the goal achievement of others in an organizational context. (10)

Learning. A relatively permanent change in behavior potential that occurs due to practice or experience. (3)

Least Preferred Co-Worker (LPC). A current or past co-worker with whom a leader has had a difficult time accomplishing a task. (10)

Legitimate power. Power derived from a person's position or job in an organization. (13)

Leniency. The tendency to perceive the job performance of ratees as especially good. (4)

Liaison role. The assignment of a person to help achieve coordination between his or her department and another department. (15)

Locus of control. A set of beliefs about whether one's behavior is controlled mainly by internal or external forces. (3)

Lump sum bonus. Merit pay that is awarded in a single payment and not built into base pay. (7)

Machiavellianism. A set of cynical beliefs about human nature, morality, and the permissibility of using various tactics to achieve one's ends. (13)

Management by Objectives (MBO). An elaborate, systematic, ongoing program to facilitate goal establishment, goal accomplishment, and employee development. (7)

Management. The art of getting things accomplished in organizations through others. (1)

Maslow's hierarchy of needs. A five-level hierarchical need theory of motivation that specifies that the lowest-level unsatisfied need has the greatest motivating potential. (6)

Matrix departmentation. Employees remain members of a functional department while also reporting to a product or project manager. (15)

Maximization. The choice of the decision alternative with the greatest expected value. (12)

McClelland's theory of needs. A nonhierarchical need theory of motivation that outlines the conditions under which certain needs result in particular patterns of motivation. (6)

Mechanistic structures. Organizational structures characterized by tallness, specialization, centralization, and formalization. (15)

Mentor. An older and more senior person in the organization who gives a junior person special attention, such as giving advice and creating opportunities. (18)

Merit pay plans. Systems that attempt to link pay to performance on white-collar jobs. (7)

Modeling. The process of imitating the behavior of others. (3)

Motivation. The extent to which persistent effort is directed toward a goal. (6)

Mum effect. The tendency to avoid communicating unfavorable news to others. (11)

Need for achievement. A strong desire to perform challenging tasks well. (6)

Need for affiliation. A strong desire to establish and maintain friendly, compatible interpersonal relationships. (6)

Need for power. A strong desire to influence others, making a significant impact or impression. (6)

Need theories. Motivation theories that specify the kinds of needs people have and the conditions under which they will be motivated to satisfy these needs in a way that contributes to performance. (6)

Negative reinforcement. The removal of a stimulus that in turn increases or maintains the probability of some behavior. (3)

Negotiation. A decision-making process among interdependent parties who do not share identical preferences. (14)

Network organization. Liaisons between specialist organizations that rely strongly on market mechanisms for coordination. (15)

Networking. Establishing good relations with key organizational members and/or outsiders in order to accomplish one's goals. (13)

Neutralizers of leadership. Factors in the work setting that reduce a leader's opportunity to exercise influence. (10)

Nominal group technique. A structured group decision-making technique in which ideas are generated without group interaction and then systematically evaluated by the group. (12)

Nonverbal communication. The transmission of messages by some medium other than speech or writing. (11)

Normative commitment. Commitment based on ideology or a feeling of obligation to an organization. (9)

Norms. Collective expectations that members of social units have regarding the behavior of each other. (8)

Observational research. Research that examines the natural activities of people in an organizational setting by listening to what they say and watching what they do. (2)

Open door policy. The opportunity for employees to communicate directly with a manager without going through the chain of command. (11)

Open systems. Systems that take inputs from the external environment, transform some of them, and send them back into the environment as outputs. (16)

Organic structures. Organizational structures characterized by flatness, low specialization, low formalization, and decentralization. (15)

Organizational behavior modification. The systematic use of learning principles to influence organizational behavior. (3)

Organizational behavior. The attitudes and behaviors of individuals and groups in organizations. (1)

Organizational citizenship behavior. Voluntary, informal behavior that contributes to organizational effectiveness. (5)

Organizational commitment. An attitude that reflects the strength of the linkage between an employee and an organization. (9)

Organizational culture. Shared beliefs, values, and assumptions that exist in an organization. (9)

Organizational development (OD). A planned, ongoing effort to change organizations to be more effective and more human. (17)

Organizational politics. The pursuit of self-interest in an organization, whether or not this self-interest corresponds to organizational goals. (13)

Organizational processes. Activities or work that have to be accomplished to create outputs that internal or external customers value. (17)

Organizational structure. The manner in which an organization divides its labor into specific tasks and achieves coordination among these tasks. (15)

Organizations. Social inventions for accomplishing common goals through group effort. (1)

Outcomes. Consequences that follow work behavior and factors that an organization distributes to employees in exchange for their inputs. (5,6)

Participant observation. Observational research in which the researcher becomes a functioning member of the organizational unit being studied. (2)

Participative leadership. Involving subordinates in making work-related decisions. (10)

Path-Goal Theory. Robert House's theory concerned with the situations under which various leader behaviors (directive, supportive, participative, achievement-oriented) are most effective. (10)

Perception. The process of interpreting our senses to provide order and meaning to the environment. (4)

Perceptual defense. The tendency for the perceptual system to defend the perceiver against unpleasant emotions. (4)

Perfect rationality. A decision strategy that is completely informed, perfectly logical, and oriented toward economic gain. (12)

Performance. The extent to which an organizational member contributes to achieving the objectives of the organization. (6)

"Performance causes satisfaction" hypothesis. An assumption that high job performance leads to high job satisfaction. (5)

Person-role conflict. Role demands call for behavior that is incompatible with the personality or skills of a role occupant. (8)

Personality. The relatively stable set of psychological characteristics that influences the way an individual interacts with his or her environment. (3)

Piecerate. A pay system in which individual workers are paid a certain sum of money for each unit of production completed. (7)

Pooled interdependence. A condition in which organizational subunits are dependent upon the pooled resources generated by other subunits but are otherwise fairly independent. (16)

Positive reinforcement. The application or addition of a stimulus that increases or maintains the probability of some behavior. (3)

Power. The capacity to influence others who are in a state of dependence. (13)

Power distance. The extent to which an unequal distribution of power is accepted by society members. (5)

Primacy effect. The tendency for a perceiver to rely on early cues or first impressions. (4)

Problem. A perceived gap between an existing state and a desired state. (12)

Procedural fairness. Fairness that occurs when the process used to determine work outcomes is seen as reasonable. (5)

Process losses. Group performance difficulties stemming from the problems of motivating and coordinating larger groups. (8)

Process theories. Motivation theories that specify the details of how motivation occurs. (6)

Product departmentation. Departments are formed on the basis of a particular product, product line, or service. (15)

Profit sharing. The return of some company profit to employees in the form of a cash bonus or a retirement supplement. (7)

Program. A standardized way of solving a problem. (12)

Projection. The tendency for perceivers to attribute their own undesirable ideas, feelings and motives to others. (4, 14)

Punctuated equilibrium model. A model of group development that describes how groups with deadlines are affected by their first meetings and crucial midpoint transitions. (8)

Punishment. The application of an aversive stimulus following some behavior designed to decrease the probability of that behavior. (3)

Rationalization. Attributing socially acceptable motives to one's actions. (14)

Reaction formation. Expressing oneself in a manner that is directly opposite to the way one truly feels. (14)

Realistic job previews. The provision of a balanced, realistic picture of the positive and negative aspects of a job to job applicants. (9)

Reality shock. An unsettling experience caused by the disparity between unrealistic expectations and the reality that people confront in their first job. (18)

Recency effect. The tendency for a perceiver to rely on recent cues or last impressions. (4)

Reciprocal interdependence. A condition in which organizational subunits must engage in considerable interplay and mutual feedback to accomplish a task. (16)

Reengineering. The radical redesign of organizational processes to achieve major improvements in factors such as time, cost, quality, or service. (17)

Referent power. Power derived from being well-liked by others. (13)

Refreezing. The condition that exists when newly developed behaviors, attitudes, or structures become an enduring part of the organization. (17)

Reinforcement. The process by which stimuli strengthen behaviors. (3)

Reliability. An index of the consistency of a research subject's responses. (2)

Repression. The prevention of threatening ideas from becoming conscious. (14)

Resistance.   Overt or covert failure by organizational members to support a change effort. (17)

Resource dependence.   The dependency of organizations upon environmental inputs such as capital, raw materials, and human resources. (16)

Restriction of productivity.   The artificial limitation of work output that can occur under wage incentive plans. (7)

Reward power.   Power derived from the ability to provide positive outcomes and prevent negative outcomes. (13)

Risky shift.   The tendency for groups to make riskier decisions than the average risk initially advocated by their individual members. (12)

Role ambiguity.   Lack of clarity of job goals or methods. (8)

Role conflict.   A condition of being faced with incompatible role expectations. (8)

Role overload.   The requirement for too many tasks to be performed in too short of a time period. (14)

Roles.   Positions in groups that have a set of expected behaviors attached to them. (8)

Rumor.   An unverified belief that is in general circulation. (11)

"Satisfaction causes performance" hypothesis.   An assumption that high job satisfaction leads to high job performance. (5)

Satisficing.   Establishing an adequate level of acceptability for a solution to a problem and then screening solutions until one that exceeds this level is found. (12)

Scientific Management.   Frederick Taylor's system for using research to determine the optimum degree of specialization and standardization of work tasks. (1)

Self-esteem.   The degree to which a person has a positive self-evaluation. (3)

Self-managed work teams.   Work groups that have the opportunity to do challenging work under reduced supervision. (8)

Self-management.   The use of learning principles to manage one's own behavior. (3)

Self-monitoring.   The extent to which people observe and regulate how they appear and behave in social settings and relationships. (3)

Self-serving bias.   The tendency to take credit for successful outcomes and to deny responsibility for failures. (4)

Sequential interdependence.   A condition in which organizational subunits are dependent upon the resources generated by units that precede them in a sequence of work. (16)

Similar-to-me effect.   A rater gives more favorable evaluations to people who are similar to the rater in terms of background or attitudes. (4)

Situational attributions.   Explanations for behavior based on an actor's external situation or environment. (4)

Skill based pay.   A system in which people are paid according to the number of job skills they have acquired. (7)

Skill benchmarking.   The process of identifying required competency levels for key jobs in an industry. (18)

Skill variety.   The opportunity to do a variety of job activities using various skills and talents. (7)

Social loafing.   The tendency of individuals to withhold physical or intellectual effort when performing a group task. (8)

Social network.   A group of one's peers, subordinates, and senior people who provide general information about what is going on in the organization, specific advice on how to accomplish job assignments, and feedback about the consequences of different career strategies. (18)

Social-emotional leader.   A leader who is concerned with reducing tension, patching up disagreements, settling arguments, and maintaining morale. (10)

Socialization.   The process by which people learn the norms and roles that are necessary to function in a group or organization. (9)

Span of control.   The number of subordinates supervised by a superior. (15)

Stakeholders.   People inside or outside of an organization who have the potential to be affected by organizational decisions. (13)

Status. The rank, social position, or prestige accorded to group members. (8)

Stereotyping. The tendency to generalize about people in a social category and ignore variation among them. (4)

Strategic alliances. Actively cooperative relationships between legally separate organizations. (16)

Strategic contingencies. Critical factors affecting organizational effectiveness that are controlled by a key subunit. (13)

Strategy. The process by which top executives seek to cope with the constraints and opportunities that an organization's environment poses. (16)

Stress. A psychological reaction to the demands inherent in a stressor that has the potential to make a person feel tense or anxious. (14)

Stress reactions. Behavioral, psychological, and physiological consequences of stress. (14)

Stressors. Environmental events or conditions that have the potential to induce stress. (14)

Strong culture. An organizational culture with intense and pervasive beliefs, values, and assumptions. (9)

Subcultures. Smaller cultures that develop within a larger organizational culture that are based on differences in training, occupation, or departmental goals. (9)

Substitutes for leadership. Factors in the work setting that can take the place of active leadership, making it unnecessary or redundant. (10)

Subunit power. The degree of power held by various organizational subunits, such as departments. (13)

Suggestion systems. Programs designed to enhance upward communication by soliciting ideas for improved work operations from employees. (11)

Sunk costs. Permanent losses of resources incurred as the result of a decision. (12)

Superordinate goals. Attractive outcomes that can be achieved only by collaboration. (8, 14)

Survey feedback. The collection of data from organizational members and the provision of feedback about the results. (17)

Tall organization. An organization with relatively many levels in its hierarchy of authority. (15)

Task forces. Temporary groups set up to solve coordination problems across several departments. (15)

Task identity. The extent to which a job involves doing a complete piece of work, from beginning to end. (7)

Task leader. A leader who is concerned with accomplishing a task by organizing others, planning strategy, and dividing labor. (10)

Task significance. The impact that a job has on other people. (7)

Team building. An effort to increase the effectiveness of work teams by improving interpersonal processes, goal clarification, and role clarification. (17)

Technological interdependence. The extent to which organizational subunits depend on each other for resources, raw materials, or information. (16)

Technological routineness. The extent to which exceptions and problems affect the task of converting inputs into outputs. (16)

Technology. The activities, equipment, and knowledge necessary to turn organizational inputs into desired outputs. (16)

Theory of career anchors. Five distinct patterns of self-perceived talents, motives, needs, and values that evolve as one faces early work experiences: technical/functional competence, managerial competence, security, autonomy, and creativity. (18)

Theory of career types. John Holland's theory identifying six distinct patterns of career orientation: conventional, artistic, realistic, social, enterprising, and investigative. (18)

Total quality management (TQM). A systematic attempt to achieve continuous improvement in the quality of an organization's products and/or services. (1, 7, 17)

Traits. Individual characteristics such as physical attributes, intellectual ability, and personality. (10)

Transformational leadership. Providing followers with a new vision that instills true commitment. (10)

Type A behavior pattern. A personality pattern that includes aggressiveness, ambitiousness, competitiveness, hostility, impatience, and a sense of time urgency. (14)

Uncertainty avoidance. The extent to which people
are uncomfortable with uncertain and ambiguous situations. (5)

Unfreezing. The recognition that some current state of affairs is unsatisfactory. (17)

Upward communication. Information that flows from the bottom of the organization toward the top. (11)

Valence. The expected value of work outcomes; the extent to which they are attractive or unattractive. (6)

Validity. An index of the extent to which a measure truly reflects what it is supposed to measure. (2)

Values. A broad tendency to prefer certain states of affairs over others. (5)

Variable interval schedule. A partial reinforcement schedule in which some variable time period occurs between a reinforced response and the chance for the next reinforcement. (3)

Variable ratio schedule. A partial reinforcement schedule in which some variable number of responses must be made between a reinforced response and the availability of the next reinforcement. (3)

Vertical integration. The strategy of formally taking control of sources of organizational supply and distribution. (16)

Wage incentive plans. Various systems that link pay to performance on production jobs. (7)

Well-structured problem. A problem for which the existing state is clear, the desired state is clear and how to get from one state to another is fairly obvious. (12)

Workforce diversity. Differences among recruits and employees in characteristics such as gender, race, age, religion, cultural background, physical ability, and sexual orientation. (4)

References

Chapter 1

1. Sources include Lavin, D. (1993, February 9). GM accuses NBC of rigging test crash of pickup truck on 'Dateline' program. *Wall Street Journal*, p. A3 (first quote); Jensen, E., Lavin, D., & Templin, D. (1993, February 11). How GM one-upped an embarrassed NBC on staged news event. *Wall Street Journal*, pp. A1, A7 (second quote); Alter, J. (1993, March 8). On the ropes at NBC News. *Newsweek*, p. 49; Faison, S. (1993, March 20). 3 dismissals reported at NBC News. *New York Times*.
2. Katz, D. (1964). The motivational basis of organizational behavior. *Behavioral Science, 9*, 131–146.
3. Peters, T. (1990, Fall). Get innovative or get dead. *California Management Review*, 9–26.
4. Porter, L. W., & McKibbin, L. E. (1988). *Management education and development: Drift or thrust into the 21st century?* New York: McGraw-Hill, p. 324.
5. Wren, D. (1987). *The evolution of management thought* (3rd ed.). New York: Wiley.
6. For a summary of their work and relevant references, see Wren, 1987.
7. Taylor, F. W. (1967). *The principles of scientific management*. New York: Norton.
8. Weber, M. (1974). *The theory of social and economic organization* (A. M. Henderson & T. Parsons, Transl.). New York: Free Press.
9. See Wren, 1987.
10. Roethlisberger, F. J., & Dickson, W. J. (1939). *Management and the worker*. Cambridge, MA: Harvard University Press; Wrege, C. D., & Greenwood, R. G. (1986). The Hawthorne studies. In D. A. Wren & J. A. Pearce II (Eds.), *Papers dedicated to the development of modern management*. Academy of Management.
11. Argyris, C. (1957). *Personality and organization*. New York: Harper.
12. Likert, R. (1961). *New patterns of management*. New York: McGraw-Hill.
13. Gouldner, A. W. (1954). *Patterns of industrial bureaucracy*. New York: Free Press.
14. Selznick, P. (1949). *TVA and the grass roots: A study in the sociology of formal organizations*. Berkeley: University of California Press.
15. Johns, G. (1993). Constraints on the adoption of psychology-based personnel practices: Lessons from organizational innovation. *Personnel Psychology, 46*, 569–592; Abrahamson, E. (1991). Managerial fads and fashions: The diffusion and rejection of innovations. *Academy of Management Review, 16*, 586–612.
16. Mintzberg, H. (1973). *The nature of managerial work*. New York: Harper & Row. See also Mintzberg, H. (1994, Fall). Rounding out the manager's job. *Sloan Management Review*, 11–26.
17. See Kraut, A. I., Pedigo, P. R., McKenna, D. D., & Dunnette, M. D. (1989, November). The role of the manager: What's really important in different management jobs. *Academy of Management Executive*, 286–293; Gibbs, B. (1994). The effects of environment and technology on managerial roles. *Journal of Management, 20*, 581–604.
18. Luthans, F., Hodgetts, R. M., & Rosenkrantz, S. A. (1988). *Real managers*. Cambridge, MA: Ballinger.
19. Kotter, J. P. (1982). *The general managers*. New York: The Free Press.
20. Simon, H. A. (1987, February). Making management decisions: The role of intuition and emotion. *Academy of Management Executive*, 57–64; Isenberg, D. J. (1984, November–December). How senior managers think. *Harvard Business Review*, 80–90. See also Sims, H. P., Jr., & Gioia, D. A. (Eds.) (1986). *The thinking organization: Dynamics of organizational social cognition*. San Francisco: Jossey-Bass.
21. Hofstede, G. (1993, February). Cultural constraints in management theories. *Academy of Management Executive*, 81–94.
22. Laabs, J. J. (1993, April). Business growth driven by staff development. *Personnel Journal*, 120–135.
23. Crawford, M. (1993, May). The new office etiquette. *Canadian Business*, 22–31.
24. Jackson, S. E., & Alvarez, E. B. (1992). Working through diversity as a strategic imperative. In S. E. Jackson (Ed.), *Diversity in the workplace: Human resources initiatives*. New York: Guilford.
25. Shellenbarger, S. (1993, September 3). Work-force study finds loyalty is weak, divisions of race and gender are deep. *Wall Street Journal*, pp. B1, B2.
26. Fisher, A. B. (1991, November 18). Morale crisis. *Fortune*, 70–80.
27. Rigon, J. E. (1992, November 2). Lack of communication burdens restructurings. *Wall Street Journal*, p. B1.
28. See Bureau of Business Practice. (1992). *Profiles of Malcolm Baldrige Award winners*. Boston: Allyn and Bacon.

Chapter 2

1. Sutton, R. I. (1991). Maintaining norms about expressed emotions: The case of bill collectors. *Administrative Science Quarterly, 36*, 245–268.
2. Lupton, T. (1963). *On the shop floor*. Oxford: Pergamon.
3. Bensman, J., & Gerver, I. (1963). Crime and punishment in the factory: The function of deviancy in maintaining the social system. *American Sociological Review, 28*, 588–598.
4. Mintzberg, H. (1973). *The nature of managerial work*. New York: Harper & Row.
5. Ragins, B. R., & Cotton, J. L. (1993). Gender and willingness to mentor in organizations. *Journal of Management, 19*, 97–111.
6. Ivancevich, J. M., & Lyon, H. L. (1977). The shortened workweek: A field experiment. *Journal of Applied Psychology, 62*, 34–37.
7. Sutton, R. I., & Rafaeli, A. (1988). Untangling the relationship between displayed emotions and organizational sales: The case of convenience stores. *Academy of Management Journal, 31*, 461–487.
8. Roethlisberger, F. J., & Dickson, W. J. (1939). *Management and the worker*. Cambridge, MA: Harvard University Press; Greenwood, R. G., & Wrege, C. D. (1986). The Hawthorne studies. In D. A. Wren & J. A. Pearce II (Eds.), *Papers dedicated to the development of modern management*. The Academy of Management.
9. Adair, J. G. (1984). The Hawthorne effect: A reconsideration of the methodological artifact. *Journal of Applied Psychology, 69*, 334–345.

10. See Academy of Management. (1992). The Academy of Management code of ethical conduct. *Academy of Management Journal, 35,* 1135–1142; Lowman, R. L. (Ed.). (1985) *Casebook on ethics and standards for the practice of psychology in organizations.* College Park, MD: Society for Industrial and Organizational Psychology.

Chapter 3

1. Sources include Foster, P. (1993). *Towers of debt: The rise and fall of the Reichmanns.* Toronto: Key Porter; Hylton, R. D. (1993, May 17). The man who blew $10 billion. *Fortune,* 92–95; Babad, M., & Mulroney, C. (1989). *Campeau: The building of an empire.* Toronto: Doubleday Canada; Loomis, C. J. (1990, June 18). The biggest looniest deal ever. *Fortune,* 48–72.
2. For a presentation of operant learning theory, see Honig, W. K., & Staddon, J. E. R. (Eds.). (1977). *Handbook of operant behavior.* Englewood Cliffs, NJ: Prentice-Hall. For a presentation of social learning theory, see Bandura, A. (1986). *Social foundations of thought and action.* Englewood Cliffs, NJ: Prentice-Hall.
3. Fuchsberg, G. (1990, December 19). Now you know what we know about how most writers write. *Wall Street Journal,* p. B1.
4. (1972). Performance audit, feedback, and positive reinforcement. *Training and Development Journal, 26,* 8–13; (1973, Winter). At Emery Air Freight: Positive reinforcement boosts performance. *Organizational Dynamics,* 41–50.
5. O'Hara, K., Johnson, C. M., & Beehr, T. A. (1985). Organizational behavior management in the private sector: A review of empirical research and recommendations for further investigation. *Academy of Management Review, 10,* 848–864.
6. Pedalino, E., & Gamboa, V. U. (1974). Behavior modification and absenteeism: Intervention in one industrial setting. *Journal of Applied Psychology, 59,* 694–698.
7. Komaki, J., Barwick, K. D., & Scott, L. R. (1978). A behavioral approach to occupational safety: Pinpointing and reinforcing safe performance in a food manufacturing plant. *Journal of Applied Psychology, 63,* 434–445. For a similar study, see Haynes, R. S., Pine, R. C., & Fitch, H. G. (1982). Reducing accident rates with organizational behavior modification. *Academy of Management Journal, 25,* 407–416.
8. Luthans, F., & Kreitner, R. (1985). *Organizational behavior modification and beyond: An operant and social learning approach.* Glenview, IL: Scott, Foresman; Manz, C. C., & Sims, H. P., Jr. (1981). Vicarious learning: The influence of modeling on organizational behavior. *Academy of Management Review, 6,* 105–113.
9. Bandura, 1986; Goldstein, A. P., & Sorcher, M. (1974). *Changing supervisor behavior.* New York: Pergamon.
10. Luthans, F., & Kreitner, R. (1975). *Organizational behavior modification.* Glenview, IL: Scott, Foresman.
11. However, more research is necessary to establish the extent of this in organizations. See Arvey, R. D., & Ivancevich, J. M. (1980). Punishment in organizations: A review, propositions, and research suggestions. *Academy of Management Review, 5,* 123–132.
12. Punishment in front of others can be effective under restricted conditions. See Trevino, L. K. (1992). The social effects of punishment in organizations: A justice perspective. *Academy of Management Review, 17,* 647–676.
13. Organ, D. W., & Hamner, W. C. (1982). *Organizational behavior: An applied psychological approach* (Revised ed.). Plano, TX: Business Publications.
14. See Parmerlee, M. A., Near, J. P., & Jensen, T. C. (1982). Correlates of whistle–blowers' perceptions of organizational retaliation. *Administrative Science Quarterly, 27,* 17–34.
15. Manz, C. C., & Sims, H. P., Jr. (1980). Self-management as a substitute for leadership: A social learning theory perspective. *Academy of Management Review, 5,* 361–367; Hackman, J. R. (1986). The psychology of self-management in organizations. In M. S. Pollack & R. Perloff (Eds.), *Psychology and work.* Washington, DC: American Psychological Association.
16. Kanfer, F. H. (1980). Self-management methods. In F. H. Kanfer & A. P. Goldstein (Eds.), *Helping people change: A textbook of methods* (2nd ed.). New York: Pergamon.
17. Luthans & Kreitner, 1985; Manz & Sims, 1980.
18. Frayne, C., & Latham, G. (1987). Application of social learning theory to employee self-management of attendance. *Journal of Applied Psychology, 72,* 387–392.
19. Moses, S. (1991, November). Personality tests come back in I/O. *APA Monitor,* p. 9.
20. Adler, S., & Weiss, H. M. (1988). Recent developments in the study of personality and organizational behavior. In C. L. Cooper & I. Robertson (Eds.), *International review of industrial and organizational psychology.* New York: Wiley.
21. Digman, J. M. (1990). Personality structure: Emergence of the five-factor model. *Annual Review of Psychology, 41,* 417–440; Hogan, R. T. (1991). Personality and personality measurement. In M. D. Dunette & L. M. Hough (Eds.), *Handbook of industrial and organizational psychology* (2nd ed., Vol. 2). Palo Alto, CA: Consulting Psychologists Press; Barrick, M. R., & Mount, M. K. (1991). The big five personality dimensions and job performance: A meta-analysis. *Personnel Psychology, 44,* 1–26.
22. Tett, R. P., Jackson, D. N., & Rothstein, M. (1991). Personality measures as predictors of job performance: A meta-analytic review. *Personnel Psychology, 44,* 703–742; Hough, L. M. et al. (1990). Criterion-related validities of personality constructs and the effect of response distortion on those validities. Journal of Applied Psychology, 75, 581–595.
23. Barrick & Mount, 1991.
24. Ones, D. S., Viswesvaran, C., & Schmidt, F. L. (1993). Comprehensive meta-analysis of integrity test validities: Findings and implications for personnel selection and theories of job performance. *Journal of Applied Psychology, 78,* 679–703.
25. Barrick, M. R., & Mount, M. K. (1993). Autonomy as a moderator of the relationship between the big five personality dimensions and job performance. *Journal of Applied Psychology, 78,* 111–118.
26. Rotter, J. B. (1966). Generalized expectancies for internal versus external controls of reinforcement. *Psychological Monographs, 80* (Whole no. 609).
27. Szilagyi, A. D., & Sims, H. P., Jr. (1975). Locus of control and expectancies across multiple organizational levels. *Journal of Applied Psychology, 60,* 638–640.
28. Szilagyi, A. D., Sims, H. P., Jr., & Keller, R. T. (1976). Role dynamics, locus of control, and employee attitudes and behavior., *Academy of Management Journal, 19,* 259–276.
29. Miller, D., Kets de Vries, M. F. R., Toulouse, J. M. (1982). Top executive locus of control and its relationship to strategy-making, structure, and environment. *Academy of Management Journal, 25,* 237–253.
30. Andrisani, P. J., & Nestel, G. (1976). Internal-external control as contributor to and outcome of work experience. *Journal of Applied Psychology, 61,* 156–165.
31. For evidence on stress and locus of control see Anderson, C. R. (1977). Locus of control, coping behaviors, and

performance in a stress setting: A longitudinal study. *Journal of Applied Psychology, 62,* 446–451. For evidence on career planning see Thornton, G. C., III. (1978). Differential effects of career planning on internals and externals. *Personnel Psychology, 31,* 471–476.

32. Blau, G. (1993). Testing the relationship of locus of control to different performance dimensions. *Journal of Occupational and Organizational Psychology, 66,* 125–138.

33. Spector, P. E. (1982). Behavior in organizations as a function of employees' locus of control. *Psychological Bulletin, 91,* 482–497.

34. Snyder, M. (1987). *Public appearances/private realities: The psychology of self-monitoring.* New York: W. H. Freeman.

35. Snyder, 1987.

36. Caldwell, D. F., & O'Reilly, C. A., III. (1982). Boundary spanning and individual performance: The impact of self-monitoring. *Journal of Applied Psychology, 67,* 124–127.

37. Ellis, R. J., Adamson, R. S., Deszca, G., & Cawsey, T. F. (1988). Self-monitoring and leader emergence. *Small Group Behavior, 19,* 312–324; Zaccaro, S. J., Foti, R. J., & Kenny, D. A. (1991). Self-monitoring and trait-based variance in leadership: An investigation of leader flexibility across multiple group situations. *Journal of Applied Psychology, 76,* 308–315.

38. Brockner, J. (1988). *Self-esteem at work: Research, theory, and practice.* Lexington, MA: Lexington.

39. Brockner, 1988.

40. Pierce, J. L., Gardner, D. G., Dunham, R. B., & Cummings, L. L. (1993). Moderation by organization-based self-esteem of role condition-employee response relationships. *Academy of Management Journal, 36,* 271–288.

41. Knight, P. A., & Nadel, J. I. (1986). Humility revisited: Self-esteem, information search, and policy consistency. *Organizational Behavior and Human Decision Processes, 38,* 196–206.

42. Brockner, 1988.

43. Tharanou, P. (1979). Employee self-esteem: A review of the literature. *Journal of Vocational Behavior, 15,* 1–29; Pierce, J. L., Gardner, D. G., Cummings, L. L., & Dunham, R. B. (1989). Organization-based self-esteem: Construct definition, measurement, and validation. *Academy of Management Journal, 32,* 622–648.

44. Pierce et al., 1993.

Chapter 4

1. Sources include Kelly, E. P., Young, A. O., & Clark, L. S. (1993, March–April). Sex stereotyping in the workplace: A manager's guide. *Business Horizons,* 23–29; Lewin, T. (1990, May 16). Partnership in firm awarded to victim of sex bias. *New York Times,* pp. A1, A20; Youngstrom, N. (1990, July). Hopkins wins lawsuit against ex-employer. *APA Monitor,* p. 34.

2. Cox, T., Jr. (1993). *Cultural diversity in organizations: Theory, research, & practice.* San Francisco: Berrett-Koehler.

3. Zahra, S. A., & Chaples, S. S. (1993, May). Blind spots in competitive analysis. *Academy of Management Executive,* 7–28.

4. Bruner, J. S. (1957). On perceptual readiness. *Psychological Review, 64,* 123–152.

5. Warr, P. B., & Knapper, C. (1968). *The perception of people and events.* London: Wiley.

6. Eagly, A. H., Ashmore, R. D., Makhijani, M. G., & Longo, L. C. (1991). What is beautiful is good, but . . . : A meta-analytic review of research on the physical attractiveness stereotype. *Psychological Bulletin, 110,* 109–128.

7. Stone, E. F., Stone, D. L., & Dipboye, R. L. (1992). Stigmas in organizations: Race, handicaps, and physical unattractiveness. In K. Kelley (Ed.), *Issues, theory and research in industrial/organizational psychology.* New York: Elsevier.

8. See Krzystofiak, F., Cardy, R., & Newman, J. E. (1988). Implicit personality and performance appraisal: The influence of trait inferences on evaluations of behavior. *Journal of Applied Psychology, 73,* 515–521.

9. Fiske, S. T. (1993). Social cognition and social perception. *Annual Review of Psychology, 44,* 155–194.

10. Secord, P. F., Backman, C. W., & Slavitt, D. R. (1976). *Understanding social life: An introduction to social psychology.* New York: McGraw-Hill. For elaboration, see Wilder, D. A. (1986). Social categorization: Implications for creation and reduction of intergroup bias. *Advances in Experimental Social Psychology, 19,* 291–349.

11. Dion, K. L., & Schuller, R. A. (1991). The Ms. stereotype: Its generality and its relation to managerial and marital status stereotypes. *Canadian Journal of Behavioural Science, 23,* 25–40.

12. For a more complete treatment see Falkenberg, L. (1990). Improving the accuracy of stereotypes within the workplace. *Journal of Management, 16,* 107–118.

13. Kelley, H. H. (1972). Attribution in social interaction. In E. E. Jones et al. (Eds.), *Attribution: Perceiving the causes of behavior.* Morristown, NJ: General Learning Press. For an integrative attribution model, see Medcof, J. W. (1990). PEAT: An integrative model of attribution processes. *Advances in Experimental Social Psychology, 23,* 111–209.

14. Baron, R. A., Byrne, D., & Griffitt, W. (1974). *Social psychology: Understanding human interaction.* Boston: Allyn and Bacon.

15. This discussion of attribution biases draws upon Fiske, S. T., & Taylor, S. E. (1984). *Social cognition.* Reading, MA: Addison-Wesley.

16. Ross, L. (1977). The intuitive psychologist and his shortcomings: Distortions in the attribution process. *Advances in Experimental Social Psychology, 10,* 173–220; Jones, E. E. (1979). The rocky road from acts to dispositions. *American Psychologist, 34,* 107–117.

17. Mitchell, T. R., & Kalb, L. S. (1982). Effects of job experience on supervisor attributions for a subordinate's poor performance. *Journal of Applied Psychology, 67,* 181–188.

18. Watson, D. (1982). The actor and the observer: How are their perceptions of causality divergent? *Psychological Bulletin, 92,* 682–700.

19. Sonnenfeld, J. (1981). Executive apologies for price fixing: Role biased perceptions of causality. *Academy of Management Journal, 24,* 192–198; Waters, J. A. (1978, Spring). Catch 20.5. Corporate morality as an organizational phenomenon. *Organizational Dynamics,* 2–19.

20. Tetlock, P. E. (1985). Accountability: The neglected social context of judgment and choice. *Research in Organizational Behavior, 7,* 297–332; Greenwald, A. G. (1980). The totalitarian ego: Fabrication and revision of personal history. *American Psychologist, 35,* 603–618.

21. Pyszczynski, T., & Greenberg, J. (1987). Toward an integration of cognitive and motivational perspectives on social inference: A biased hypothesis-testing model. *Advances in Experimental Social Psychology, 20,* 197–340.

22. This section relies on Jackson, S. E., & Alvarez, E. B. (1992). Working through diversity as a strategic imperative. In S. E. Jackson (Ed.), *Diversity in the workplace: Human resources initiatives.* New York: Guilford Press.

23. Cox, 1993; Cox, T., Jr. (1991, May). The multicultural organization. *Academy of Management Executive,* 34–47.

24. Hartley, E. L. (1946). *Problems in prejudice*. New York: King's Crown Press.

25. Cox, T., Jr., & Nkomo, S. M. (1990). Invisible men and women: A status report on race as a variable in organization behavior research. *Journal of Organizational Behavior, 11*, 419–431; Alderfer, C. P., & Thomas, D. A. (1988). The significance of race and ethnicity for organizational behavior. In C. L. Cooper & I. Robertson (Eds.), *International review of industrial and organizational psychology*. New York: Wiley.

26. Sharpe, R. (1993, September 14). Losing ground. *Wall Street Journal*, pp. A1, 12, 13.

27. Brenner, O. C., Tomkiewicz, J., & Stevens, G. E. (1991). The relationship between attitudes toward women and attitudes toward blacks in management positions. *Canadian Journal of Administrative Sciences, 8* (2), 80–89.

28. Cox, 1993.

29. Greenhaus, J. H., & Parasuraman, S. (1993). Job performance attributions and career advancement prospects: An examination of gender and race effects. *Organizational Behavior and Human Decision Processes, 55*, 273–297.

30. Powell, G. N. (1992). The good manager: Business students' stereotypes of Japanese managers versus stereotypes of American managers. *Group & Organizational Management, 17*, 44–56.

31. Schein, V. E. (1975). Relationships between sex role stereotypes and requisite management characteristics among female managers. *Journal of Applied Psychology, 60*, 340–344; Brenner, O. C., Tomkiewicz, J., & Schein, V. E. (1989). The relationship between sex role stereotypes and requisite management characteristics revisited. *Academy of Management Journal, 32*, 662–669; Heilman, M. E., Block, C. J., Martell, R. F., & Simon, M. C. (1989). Has anything changed? Current characterizations of men, women, and managers. *Journal of Applied Psychology, 74*, 935–942.

32. Brenner et al., 1989.

33. Rosen, B., & Jerdee, T. H. (1974). Influence of sex role stereotypes on personnel decisions. *Journal of Applied Psychology, 59*, 9–14.

34. Cohen, S. L., & Bunker, K. A. (1975). Subtle effects of sex role stereotypes on recruiters' hiring decisions. *Journal of Applied Psychology, 60*, 566–572. See also Rose, G. L., & Andiappan, P. (1978). Sex effects on managerial hiring decisions. *Academy of Management Journal, 21*, 104–112.

35. Parasuraman, S., & Greenhaus, J. H. (1993). Personal portrait: The life-style of the woman manager. In E. A. Fagenson (Ed.), *Women in management: Trends, issues, and challenge in managerial diversity*. Newbury Park, CA: Sage.

36. Tosi, H. L., & Einbender, S. W. (1985). The effects of the type and amount of information in sex discrimination research: A meta-analysis. *Academy of Management Journal, 28*, 712–723.

37. For a review, see Latham, G. P., Skarlicki, D., Irvine, D., & Siegel, J. P. (1993). The increasing importance of performance appraisals to employee effectiveness in organizational settings in North America. In C. L. Cooper & I. Robertson (Eds.), *International review of industrial and organizational psychology*. New York: Wiley. For a representative study, see Pulakos, E. D., White, L. A., Oppler, S. A., & Borman, W. C. (1989). Examination of race and sex effects on performance ratings. *Journal of Applied Psychology, 74*, 770–780.

38. Fiske, S. T., Beroff, D. N., Borgida, E., Deaux, K., & Heilman, M. E. (1991). Use of sex stereotyping research in Price Waterhouse v. Hopkins. *American Psychologist, 46*, 1049–1060.

39. Sackett, P. R., DuBois, C. L. Z., & Noe, A. W. (1991). Tokenism in performance evaluation: The effects of work group representation on male-female and white-black differences in performance ratings. *Journal of Applied Psychology, 76*, 263–267.

40. Rosen, B., & Jerdee, T. H. (1976). The nature of job-related age stereotypes. *Journal of Applied Psychology, 61*, 180–183. See also Gibson, K. J., Zerbe, W. J., & Franken, R. E. (1992). Job search strategies for older job hunters: Addressing employers' perceptions. *Canadian Journal of Counselling, 26*, 166–176.

41. Gibson et al., 1992.

42. McEvoy, G. M., & Cascio, W. F. (1989). Cumulative evidence of the relationship between employee age and job performance. *Journal of Applied Psychology, 74*, 11–17. For a broader review on age see Rhodes, S. R. (1983). Age related differences in work attitudes and behavior. *Psychological Bulletin, 93*, 328–367.

43. Rosen, B., & Jerdee, T. H. (1976). The influence of age stereotypes on managerial decisions. *Journal of Applied Psychology, 61*, 428–432. Also see Dietrick, E. J., & Dobbins, G. J. (1991). The influence of subordinate age on managerial actions: An attributional analysis. *Journal of Organizational Behavior, 12*, 367–377.

44. Falkenberg, 1990; Fiske et al., 1991.

45. Cox, 1991, p. 40.

46. Shea, G. F. (1992, December). Learn how to treasure differences. *HRMagazine*, 34–37.

47. Caudron, S. (1993, April). Training can damage diversity efforts. *Personnel Journal*, 51–62.

48. Caudron, 1993.

49. McDaniel, M. A., Whetzel, D. L., Schmidt, F. L., & Maurer, S. D. (1994). The validity of employment interviews: A comprehensive review and meta-analysis. *Journal of Applied Psychology, 79*, 599–616; Wiesner, W. H., & Cronshaw, S. F. (1988). A meta-analytic investigation of the impact of interview format and degree of structure on the validity of the employment interview. *Journal of Occupational Psychology, 61*, 275–290.

50. Hakel, M. D. (1982). Employment interviewing. In K. M. Rowland & G. R. Ferris (Eds.), *Personnel management*. Boston: Allyn and Bacon.

51. Hakel, 1982; Dipboye, R. L. (1989). Threats to the incremental validity of interviewer judgments. In R. W. Eder & G. R. Ferris (Eds.), *The employment interview: Theory, research, and practice*. Newbury Park, CA: Sage.

52. Hollmann, T. D. (1972). Employment interviewers' errors in processing positive and negative information. *Journal of Applied Psychology, 56*, 130–134.

53. Rowe, P. M. (1989). Unfavorable information in interview decisions. In R. W. Eder & G. R. Ferris (Eds.), *The employment interview: Theory, research, and practice*. Newbury Park, CA: Sage.

54. Schmitt, N. (1976). Social and situational determinants of interview decisions: Implications for the employment interview. *Personnel Psychology, 29*, 70–101; Maurer, T. J., & Alexander, R. A. (1991). Contrast effects in behavioral measurement: An investigation of alternative process explanations. *Journal of Applied Psychology, 76*, 3–10; Maurer, T. J., Palmer, J. K., & Ashe, D. K. (1993). Diaries, checklists, evaluations, and contrast effects in measurement of behavior. *Journal of Applied Psychology, 78*, 226–231.

55. For other reasons and a review of the interview literature, see Harris, M. M. (1989). Reconsidering the employment interview: A review of recent literature and suggestions for future research. *Personnel Psychology, 42*, 691–726.

56. Cooper, W. H. (1981). Ubiquitous halo. *Psychological Bulletin, 90*, 218–244; Balzer, W. K., & Sulsky, L. M. (1992). Halo and performance appraisal research: A critical examination. *Journal of Applied Psychology, 77*, 975–985;

Murphy, K. R., Jako, R. A., & Anhalt, R. L. (1993). Nature and consequences of halo error: A critical analysis. *Journal of Applied Psychology, 78,* 218–225.

57. Kingstrom, P. D., & Bass, A. R. (1981). A critical analysis of studies comparing behaviorally anchored rating scales (BARS) and other rating formats. *Personnel Psychology, 34,* 263–289; Landy, F. J., & Farr, J. L. (1983). *The measurement of work performance.* New York: Academic Press.

58. Crino, M. D., White, M. C., & De Sanctis, G. L. (1981). A comment on the dimensionality and reliability of the women as managers scale (WAMS). *Academy of Management Journal, 24,* 866–876.

59. Owen, C. L., & Todor, W. D. (1993, March–April). Attitudes toward women as managers: Still the same. *Business Horizons,* 12–16.

60. Brenner et al., 1991.

Chapter 5

1. Sources include Bulkeley, W. M. (1994, June 14). Ben & Jerry's is looking for Ben's successor. *Wall Street Journal,* pp. B1, B9; Laabs, J. J. (1992, November). Ben & Jerry's caring capitalism. *Personnel Journal,* 50–57; Castelli, J. (1990, September). Finding the right fit. *HRMagazine,* 38–41; Seligman, D. (1991, June 3). Ben & Jerry save the world, *Fortune,* 247–248; Hiatt, F. (Date unknown). Spitting out the chunks . . . *Washington Post.*

2. Hofstede, G. (1980). *Culture's Consequences: International differences in work-related values.* Beverly Hills, CA: Sage, p. 19.

3. Spranger, E. (1928). *Types of men.* New York: Stechat.

4. Rokeach, M. (1973). *The nature of human values.* New York: Free Press.

5. Meglino, B. M., Ravlin, E. C., & Adkins, C. L. (1989). A work values approach to corporate culture: A field test of the value congruence process and its relationship to individual outcomes. *Journal of Applied Psychology, 74,* 424–432.

6. Judge, T. A., & Bretz, R. D., Jr. (1992). Effects of work values on job choice decisions. *Journal of Applied Psychology, 77,* 261–271.

7. Black, J. S., & Mendenhall, M. (1990). Cross-cultural training effectiveness: A review and theoretical framework for future research. *Academy of Management Review, 15,* 113–136.

8. MOW International Research Team. (1987). *The meaning of working.* London: Academic Press.

9. Hofstede, 1980. For a critique of this work, see Dorfman, P. W., & Howell, J. P. (1989). Dimensions of national culture and effective leadership patterns: Hofstede revisited. *Advances in International Comparative Management, 3,* 127–150.

10. Hofstede, G. (1991). *Cultures and organizations: Software of the mind.* London: McGraw-Hill; Hofstede, G., & Bond, M. H. (1988). The Confucius connection: From cultural roots to economic growth. *Organizational Dynamics, 16* (4), 4–21.

11. Hofstede, G. (1984). The cultural relativity of the quality of life concept. *Academy of Management Review, 9,* 389–398; Hofstede, G. (1993, February). Cultural constraints in management theories. *Academy of Management Executive,* 81–94.

12. Lazar, E. (1993, February). Values must blend in overseas operations. *Personnel Journal,* 67–70.

13. Young, S. M. (1992). A framework for successful adoption and performance of Japanese manufacturing practices in the United States. *Academy of Management Review, 17,* 677–700.

14. Basadur, M. (1992, May). Managing creativity: A Japanese model. *Academy of Management Executive,* 29–42.

15. Laabs, J. J. (1993, August). How Gillette grooms global talent. *Personnel Journal,* 64–75.

16. Staff reporter. (1992, December 30). Korea's biggest firm teaches junior execs strange foreign ways. *Wall Street Journal,* pp. 1, 4.

17. Jones, E. E., & Gerard, H. B. (1967). *Foundations of social psychology.* New York: Wiley.

18. Accessible summaries of this work can be found in Middlebrook, P. N. (1974). *Social psychology and modern life.* New York: Knopf; Zimbardo, P. G., Ebbesen, E. B., & Maslach, C. (1972). *Influencing attitudes and changing behavior* (2nd ed.). Reading, MA: Addison-Wesley.

19. Festinger, L. (1957). *A theory of cognitive dissonance.* Stanford, CA: Stanford University Press.

20. Janis, I. L., & Mann, L. (1965). Effectiveness of emotional role-playing in modifying smoking habits and attitudes. *Journal of Experimental Research in Personality, 1,* 84–90; Culbertson, F. M. (1957). Modification of an emotionally held attitude through role-playing. *Journal of Abnormal and Social Psychology, 54,* 230–233.

21. Goldstein, A. P., & Sorcher, M. (1974). *Changing supervisor behavior.* New York: Pergamon.

22. For a review and critique, see Mayer, S. J., & Russell, J. S. (1987). Behavior modeling training in organizations: Concerns and conclusions. *Journal of Management, 13,* 21–40. For an example of cross-cultural training see Harrison, J.K. (1992). Individual and combined effects of behavior modeling and the cultural assimilator in cross-cultural management training. *Journal of Applied Psychology, 77,* 952–962.

23. Locke, E. A. (1976). The nature and causes of job satisfaction. In M. D. Dunnette (Ed.), *Handbook of industrial and organizational psychology.* Chicago: Rand McNally. See also Rice, R. W., Gentile, D. A., & McFarlin, D. B. (1991). Facet importance and job satisfaction. *Journal of Applied Psychology, 76,* 31–39.

24. Smith, P. C. (1992). In pursuit of happiness: Why study general job satisfaction? In C. J. Cranny, P. C. Smith, & E. F. Stone (Eds.), *Job satisfaction.* New York: Lexington.

25. Smith, P. C., Kendall, L. M., & Hulin, C. L. (1969). *The measurement of satisfaction in work and retirement.* Chicago: Rand McNally; Smith, P. C., Kendall, L. M., & Hulin, C. L. (1985). *The job descriptive index* (Rev. ed.). Bowling Green, OH: Department of Psychology, Bowling Green State University.

26. Weiss, D. J., Dawis, R. V., England, G. W., & Lofquist, L. H. (1967). *Manual for the Minnesota satisfaction questionnaire: Minnesota studies in vocational rehabilitation.* Minneapolis: Vocational Psychology Research, University of Minnesota.

27. Locke, E. A. (1969). What is job satisfaction? *Organizational Behavior and Human Performance, 4,* 309–336; Rice, R. W., McFarlin, D. B., & Bennett, D. E. (1989). Standards of comparison and job satisfaction. *Journal of Applied Psychology, 74,* 591–598.

28. Adams, J. S. (1963). Toward an understanding of inequity. *Journal of Abnormal and Social Psychology, 67,* 422–436. For a review, see Greenberg, J., & Cohen, R. L. (Eds.) (1982). *Equity and justice in social behavior.* New York: Academic Press.

29. See Kulik, C. T., & Ambrose, M. L. (1992). Personal and situational determinants of referent choice. *Academy of Management Review, 17,* 212–237.

30. Greenberg, J. (1987). A taxonomy of organizational justice theories. *Academy of Management Review, 12,* 9–22.

31. McFarlin, D. B., & Sweeney, P. D. (1992). Distributive and procedural justice as predictors of satisfaction with personal and organizational outcomes. *Academy of Management Journal, 35,* 626–637; Greenberg, J. (1987). Reactions to procedural injustice in payment distributions: Do the means justify the ends? *Journal of Applied Psychology, 72,* 55–61.

32. Cropanzano, R., & Folger, R. (1989). Referent cognitions and task decision autonomy: Beyond equity theory. *Journal of Applied Psychology, 74,* 293–299, p. 293. See also Folger, R. (1987). Reformulating the preconditions of resentment: A referent cognitions model. In J. C. Masters & W. P. Smith (Eds.), *Social comparison, justice, and relative deprivation: Theoretical, empirical, and policy perspectives.* Hillsdale, NJ: Erlbaum.

33. Judge, T. A. (1992). The dispositional perspective in human resources research. *Research in Personnel and Human Resources Management, 10,* 31–72.

34. Judge, T. A., & Hulin, C. L. (1993). Job satisfaction as a reflection of disposition: A multiple source causal analysis. *Organizational Behavior and Human Decision Processes, 56,* 388–421; Judge, T. A., & Locke, E. A. (1993). Effect of dysfunctional thought processes on subjective well-being and job satisfaction. *Journal of Applied Psychology, 78,* 475–490.

35. Staw, B. M., & Barsade, S. G. (1993). Affect and managerial performance: A test of the sadder-but-wiser vs. happier-and-smarter hypotheses. *Administrative Science Quarterly, 38,* 304–331.

36. This material draws upon Locke, 1976.

37. Warr, P. B. (1987). *Work, unemployment, and mental health.* Oxford: Oxford University Press; Jamal, M., & Mitchell, V. F. (1980). Work, nonwork, and mental health: A model and a test. *Industrial Relations, 19,* 88–93.

38. Tait, M., Padgett, M. Y., & Baldwin, T. T. (1989). Job and life satisfaction: A reevaluation of the strength of the relationship and gender effects as a function of the date of the study. *Journal of Applied Psychology, 74,* 502–507; Judge, T. A., & Watanabe, S. (1993). Another look at the job satisfaction-life satisfaction relationship. *Journal of Applied Psychology, 78,* 939–948.

39. Rhodes, S. R., & Steers, R. M. (1990). *Managing employee absenteeism.* Reading, MA: Addison-Wesley.

40. Hackett, R. D., & Guion, R. M. (1985). A reevaluation of the absenteeism-job satisfaction relationship. *Organizational Behavior and Human Decision Processes, 35,* 340–381; Scott, D. D., & Taylor, G. S. (1985). An examination of conflicting findings on the relationship between job satisfaction and absenteeism: A meta-analysis. *Academy of Management Journal, 28,* 599–612; McShane, S. L. (1984). Job satisfaction and absenteeism: A meta-analytic re-examination. *Canadian Journal of Administrative Sciences, 1* (1), 61–77.

41. Nicholson, N., & Johns, G. (1985). The absence culture and the psychological contract—Who's in control of absence? *Academy of Management Review, 10,* 397–407.

42. Farris, G. F. (1971). A predictive study of turnover. *Personnel Psychology, 24,* 311–328. However, the more general relationship between performance and voluntary turnover is negative, as shown by Bycio, P., Hackett, R. D., & Alvares, K. M. (1990). Job performance and turnover: A review and meta-analysis. *Applied Psychology: An International Review, 39,* 47–76 and Williams, C. R., & Livingstone, L. P. (1994). Another look at the relationship between performance and voluntary turnover. *Academy of Management Journal, 37,* 269–298.

43. Steel, R. P., & Ovalle, N. K., 2d. (1984). A review and meta-analysis of research on the relationship between behavioral intentions and employee turnover. *Journal of Applied Psychology, 69,* 673–686.

44. In general, tests of aspects of the Mobley turnover model have been very supportive. However, not all of the steps in the model can be separated empirically. See Hom, P. W., & Griffeth, R. W. (1991). Structural equations modeling test of a turnover theory: Cross-sectional and longitudinal analyses. *Journal of Applied Psychology, 76,* 350–366.

45. Carsten, J. M., & Spector, P. E. (1987). Unemployment, job satisfaction, and employee turnover: A meta-analytic test of the Muchinsky model. *Journal of Applied Psychology, 72,* 374–381.

46. Steel & Ovalle, 1984.

47. Iaffaldano, M. T., & Muchinsky, P. M. (1985). Job satisfaction and job performance: A meta-analysis. *Psychological Bulletin, 97,* 251–273.

48. Lawler, E. E., III (1973). *Motivation in organizations.* Monterey, CA: Brooks/Cole.

49. Organ, D. W. (1988). *Organizational citizenship behavior: The good soldier syndrome.* Lexington, MA: Lexington. See also Schnake, M. (1991). Organizational citizenship: A review, proposed model, and research agenda. *Human Relations, 44,* 735–759.

50. Organ, 1988.

51. Organ, 1988; Organ, D. W., & Konovsky, M. (1989). Cognitive versus affective determinants of organizational citizenship behavior. *Journal of Applied Psychology, 74,* 157–164.

52. Moorman, R. H. (1991). Relationship betwen justice and organizational citizenship behaviors: Do fairness perceptions influence employee citizenship? *Journal of Applied Psychology, 76,* 845–855.

53. George, J. M. (1991). State or trait: Effects of positive mood on prosocial behaviors at work. *Journal of Applied Psychology, 76,* 299–307.

Chapter 6

1. Sources include the CBS Television show *60 Minutes,* Lincoln Electric Company, 1993; Epstein, G. (1989, October). Inspire your team. *Success,* p. 12; Perry, N.J. (1988, December 19). Here come richer, riskier pay plans. *Fortune,* 50–58; Sharplin, A. D. (1990). Lincoln Electric Company, 1989. In A. A. Thompson, Jr., & A. J. Strickland, III. *Strategic management: Concepts and cases.* Homewood, IL: BPI/Irwin.

2. Campbell, J. P., Dunnette, M. D., Lawler, E. E., III, & Weick, K. E., Jr. (1970). *Managerial behavior, performance, and effectiveness.* New York: McGraw-Hill. Also see Blau, G. (1993). Operationalizing direction and level of effort and testing their relationship to job performance. *Organizational Behavior and Human Decision Processes, 55,* 152–170.

3. Dyer, L., & Parker, D. F. (1975). Classifying outcomes in work motivation research: An examination of the intrinsic-extrinsic dichotomy. *Journal of Applied Psychology, 60,* 455–458; Kanungo, R. N., & Hartwick, J. (1987). An alternative to the intrinsic-extrinsic dichotomy of work rewards. *Journal of Management, 13,* 751–766. Also see Brief, A. P., & Aldag, R. J. (1977). The intrinsic-extrinsic dichotomy: Toward conceptual clarity. *Academy of Management Review, 2,* 496–500.

4. Based on Campbell, J. P., & Pritchard, R. D. (1976). Motivation theory in industrial and organizational psychology. In M. D. Dunnette (Ed.), *Handbook of industrial and organizational psychology.* Chicago: Rand McNally.

5. See Henkoff, R. (1993, March 22). Companies that train best. *Fortune,* 62–75.

6. The distinction between need (content) and process theories was first made by Campbell et al., 1970.

7. Maslow, A. H. (1970). *Motivation and personality* (2nd ed.). New York: Harper & Row.

8. Alderfer, C. P. (1969). An empirical test of a new theory of human needs. *Organizational Behavior and Human Performance, 4,* 142–175. Also see Alderfer, C. P. (1972). *Existence, relatedness, and growth: Human needs in organizational settings.* New York: The Free Press.

9. McClelland, D. C. (1985). *Human motivation.* Glenview, IL: Scott, Foresman.

10. McClelland, D. C., & Winter, D. G. (1969). *Motivating economic achievement.* New York: The Free Press, pp. 50–52.

11. McClelland, D. C., & Boyatzis, R. E. (1982). Leadership motive pattern and long-term success in management. *Journal of Applied Psychology, 67,* 737–743; McClelland, D. C., & Burnham, D. (1976, March–April). Power is the great motivator. *Harvard Business Review,* 159–166. However, need for power might not be the best motive pattern for managers of technical and professional people. See Cornelius, E. T., III, & Lane, F. B. (1984). The power motive and managerial success in a professionally oriented service industry organization. *Journal of Applied Psychology, 69,* 32–39.

12. Wahba, M. A., & Bridwell, L. G. (1976). Maslow reconsidered: A review of research on the need hierarchy theory. *Organizational Behavior and Human Performance, 15,* 212–240.

13. Schneider, B., & Alderfer, C. P. (1973). Three studies of measures of need satisfaction in organizations. *Administrative Science Quarterly, 18,* 498–505. Also see Alderfer, C. P., Kaplan, R. E., & Smith, K. K. (1974). The effect of relatedness need satisfaction on relatedness desires. *Administrative Science Quarterly, 19,* 507–532. For a disconfirming test, see Rauschenberger, J., Schmitt, N., & Hunter, J. E. (1980). A test of the need hierarchy concept by a Markov model of change in need strength. *Administrative Science Quarterly, 25,* 654–670.

14. McClelland, 1985; Spangler, W. D. (1992). Validity of questionnaire and TAT measures of need for achievement: Two meta-analyses. *Psychological Bulletin, 112,* 140–154.

15. Herzberg, F. (1966). *Work and the nature of man.* Cleveland: World Publishing.

16. Lawler, E. E., III. (1973). *Motivation in work organizations.* Monterey, CA: Brooks/Cole.

17. Vroom, V. H. (1964). *Work and motivation.* New York: Wiley.

18. Mitchell, T. R. (1974). Expectancy models of job satisfaction, occupational preference, and effort: A theoretical, methodological, and empirical appraisal. *Psychological Bulletin, 81,* 1053–1077. Also see Pinder, C. C. (1984). *Work motivation: Theory, issues, and applications.* Glenview, IL: Scott, Foresman; Kanfer, R. (1990). Motivation theory in industrial and organizational psychology. In M. D. Dunnette & L. M. Hough (Eds.), *Handbook of industrial and organizational psychology* (2nd ed., Vol. 1). Palo Alto, CA: Consulting Psychologists Press.

19. A good discussion of how managers can strengthen expectancy and instrumentality relationships is presented by Strauss, G. (1977). Managerial practices. In J. R. Hackman & J. L. Suttle (Eds.), *Improving life at work: Behavioral science approaches to organizational change.* Glenview, IL: Scott, Foresman.

20. Adams, J. S. (1965). Injustice in social exchange. *Advances in Experimental Social Psychology, 2,* 267–299.

21. Kulik, C. T., & Ambrose, M. L. (1992). Personal and situational determinants of referent choice. *Academy of Management Review, 17,* 212–237.

22. Mowday, R. T. (1987). Equity theory predictions of behavior in organizations. In R. M. Steers & L. W. Porter (Eds.), *Motivation and work behavior* (4th ed.). New York:

McGraw-Hill; Carrell, M. R., & Dittrich, J. E. (1978). Equity theory: The recent literature, methodological considerations, and new directions. *Academy of Management Review, 3,* 202–210.

23. Mowday, 1987; Carrell & Dittrich, 1978.

24. See Kulik & Ambrose, 1992.

25. Kagitcibasi, C., & Berry, J. W. (1989). Cross-cultural psychology: Current research and trends. *Annual Review of Psychology, 40,* 493–531.

26. Hofstede, G. (1980). *Culture's consequences: International differences in work-related values.* Beverly Hills, CA: Sage.

27. For a review, see Kagitcibasi & Berry, 1989.

28. Adler, N. J. (1992). *International dimensions of organizational behavior* (2nd ed.). Belmont, CA: Wadsworth.

29. Adler, 1992, p. 159.

30. Porter, L. W., & Lawler, E. E., III. (1968). *Managerial attitudes and performance.* Homewood, IL: Dorsey.

31. Deci, E. L., & Ryan, R. M. (1985). *Intrinsic motivation and self-determination in human behavior.* New York: Plenum.

32. Deci & Ryan, 1985.

33. Wiersma, U. J. (1992). The effects of extrinsic rewards in intrinsic motivation: A meta-analysis. *Journal of Occupational and Organizational Psychology, 65,* 101–114; Guzzo, R. A. (1979). Types of rewards, cognitions, and work motivation. *Academy of Management Review, 4,* 75–86.

Chapter 7

1. Sources: Quoted from Rosen, C., Klein, K. J., & Young, K. M. (1986, January). When employees share the profits. *Psychology Today,* 30–36, p. 34; Updated with material from Kehrer, D. M. (1989, May). The P. T. Barnum of printing. *Across the Board,* 53–54, and Lefkoe, M. (1992, June). Unhealthy business. *Across the Board,* 26–31.

2. For reviews, see Lawler, E. E., III. (1971). *Pay and organizational effectiveness: A psychological view.* New York: McGraw-Hill; Chung, K. H. (1977). *Motivational theories and practices.* Columbus, OH: Grid. For a careful study, see Wagner, J. A., III, Rubin, P. A., & Callahan, T. J. (1988). Incentive payment and nonmanagerial productivity: An interrupted time series analysis of magnitude and trend. *Organizational Behavior and Human Decision Processes, 42,* 47–74.

3. Locke, E. A., Feren, D. B., McCaleb, V. M., Shaw, K. N., & Denny, A. T. (1980). The relative effectiveness of four methods of motivating employee performance. In K. D. Duncan, M. M. Gruneberg, & D. Wallis (Eds.), *Changes in working life.* London: Wiley.

4. Fein, M. (1973, September). Work measurement and wage incentives. *Industrial Engineering,* 49–51.

5. For a general treatment of why firms fail to adopt state-of-the-art personnel practices see Johns, G. (1993).Constraints on the adoption of psychology-based personnel practices: Lessons from organizational innovation. *Personnel Psychology, 46,* 569–592.

6. Posner, B. G. (1989, May). If at first you don't succeed. *Inc.,* 132–134, p. 132.

7. Lawler, 1971.

8. Lawler, 1971; Nash, A., & Carrol, S. (1975). *The management of compensation.* Monterey, CA: Brooks/Cole.

9. Heneman, R. L. (1990). Merit pay research. *Research in Personnel and Human Resources Management, 8,* 203–263; Ungson, G. R., & Steers, R. M. (1984). Motivation and politics in executive compensation. *Academy of Management Review, 9,* 313–323; Tosi, H. L., & Gomez-Mejia, L. R. (1989). The decoupling of CEO pay and performance: An

agency theory perspective. *Administrative Science Quarterly,* 34, 169–189.

10. Haire, M., Ghiselli, E. E., & Gordon, M. E. (1967). A psychological study of pay. *Journal of Applied Psychology Monograph,* 51, (Whole No. 636).

11. Meyer, H. H. (1991, February). A solution to the performance appraisal feedback enigma. *Academy of Management Executive,* 68–76.

12. See Zenga, T. R. (1992). Why do employers only reward extreme performance? Examining the relationships among pay, performance, and turnover. *Administrative Science Quarterly,* 37, 198–219.

13. Lawler, E. E., III, (1972). Secrecy and the need to know. In H. L. Tosi, R. J. House, & M. D. Dunnette (Eds.), *Managerial motivation and compensation.* East Lansing, MI: Michigan State University Press.

14. Futrell, C. M., & Jenkins, O. C. (1978). Pay secrecy versus pay disclosure for salesmen: A longitudinal study. *Journal of Marketing Research,* 15, 214–219, p. 215.

15. For a study of the prevalence of these plans see Lawler, E. E. III, Mohrman, S. A., & Ledford, G. E. (1992). *Employee involvement and total quality management: Practices and results in Fortune 1000 companies.* San Francisco: Jossey-Bass.

16. Graham-Moore, B., & Ross, T. L. (1990). *Gainsharing: Plans for improving performance.* Washington, DC: Bureau of National Affairs; Markham, S. E., Scott, K. D., & Little, B. L. (1992, January–February). National gainsharing study: The importance of industry differences. *Compensation & Benefits Review,* 34–45; Miller, C. S., & Shuster, M. H. (1987, Summer). Gainsharing plans: A comparative analysis. *Organizational Dynamics,* 44–67.

17. Davis, V. (1989, April). Eyes on the prize. *Canadian Business,* 93–106.

18. Graham-Moore & Ross, 1990; Moore, B. E, & Ross, T. L. (1978). *The Scanlon way to improved productivity: A practical guide.* New York: Wiley.

19. Perry, N. J. (1988, December 19). Here come richer, riskier pay plans. *Fortune,* 50–58; Lawler, E. E. (1984). Whatever happened to incentive pay? *New Management,* 1(4), 37–41.

20. Hammer, T. H. (1988). New developments in profit sharing, gainsharing, and employee ownership. In J. P. Campbell & R. J. Campbell (Eds.), *Productivity in organizations.* San Francisco: Jossey-Bass.

21. Cooper, C. L., Dyck, B., & Frohlich, N. (1992). Improving the effectiveness of gainsharing: The role of fairness and participation. *Administrative Science Quarterly,* 37, 471–490.

22. Lawler, E. E., III, & Jenkins, G. D., Jr. (1992). Strategic reward systems. In M. D. Dunette & L. M. Hough (Eds.), *Handbook of industrial and organizational psychology* (2nd ed., Vol. 3). Palo Alto, CA: Consulting Psychologists Press.

23. Taylor, F. W. (1967). *The principles of scientific management.* New York: Norton.

24. This discussion draws upon Gibson, J. L., Ivancevich, J. M., & Donnelly, J. H., Jr. (1991). *Organizations* (7th ed.). Homewood, IL: Irwin.

25. Hackman, J. R., & Oldham, G. R. (1980). *Work redesign.* Reading, MA: Addison-Wesley.

26. Oldham, G. R., Hackman, J. R., & Stepina, L. P. (1979). Norms for the job diagnostic survey. *JSAS Catalog of Selected Documents in Psychology,* 9, 14. (Ms. No. 1819).

27. See, for example, Johns, G., Xie, J. L., & Fang, Y. (1992). Mediating and moderating effects in job design. *Journal of Management,* 18, 657–676.

28. Tiegs, R. B., Tetrick, L. E., & Fried, Y. (1992). Growth need strength and context satisfactions as moderators of the relations of the Job Characteristics Model. *Journal of Management,* 18, 575–593; Johns et al., 1992.

29. This section draws in part on Hackman & Oldham, 1980.

30. Dumaine, B. (1989, November 6). P&G rewrites the marketing rules. *Fortune,* 34–48, p. 46.

31. Ford, R. N. (1969). *Motivation through the work itself.* New York: American Management Association. Other description in this section also relies upon Ford. For a recent study of similar jobs see Campion, M. A., & McClelland, C. L. (1993). Follow-up and extension of the interdisciplinary costs and benefits of enlarged jobs. *Journal of Applied Psychology,* 78, 339–351.

32. Job enrichment has proven fairly effective in reducing turnover. See McEvoy, G., & Cascio, W. F. (1985). Strategies for reducing employee turnover: A meta-analysis. *Journal of Applied Psychology,* 70, 342–353.

33. Dowling, W. F. (1973). Job redesign on the assembly line: Farewell to the blue collar blues? *Organizational Dynamics,* 51–67.

34. Locke, E. A., Sirota, D., & Wolfson, A. D. (1976). An experimental case study of the successes and failure of job enrichment in a government agency. *Journal of Applied Psychology,* 61, 701–711.

35. Stonewalling plant democracy (1977, March 28). *Business Week.*

36. The best-developed theoretical position is that of Locke, E. A., & Latham, G. P. (1990). *A theory of goal setting and task performance.* Englewood Cliffs, NJ: Prentice-Hall.

37. Mento, A. J., Steel, R. P., & Kasser, R. J. (1987). A meta-analytic study of the effects of goal setting on task performance: 1966–1984. *Organizational Behavior and Human Decision Processes,* 39, 52–83; Tubbs, M. E. (1986). Goal setting: A meta-analytic examination of the empirical evidence. *Journal of Applied Psychology,* 71, 474–483.

38. See Tubbs, M. E., Boehne, D. M., & Dahl, J. G. (1993). Expectancy, valence, and motivational force functions in goal-setting research: An empirical test. *Journal of Applied Psychology,* 78, 361–373.

39. Mento et al., 1987; Locke, E. A., Latham, G. P., & Erez, M. (1988). The determinants of goal commitment. *Academy of Management Review,* 13, 23–39.

40. See Erez, M., Earley, P. C., & Hulin, C. L. (1985). The impact of participation on goal acceptance and performance: A two-step model. *Academy of Management Journal,* 28, 50–66.

41. Latham, G. P., Erez, M., & Locke, E. A. (1988). Resolving scientific disputes by the joint design of crucial experiments by the antagonists: Application to the Erez-Latham dispute regarding participation in goal setting. *Journal of Applied Psychology,* 73, 753–772.

42. Latham, G. P., Mitchell, T. R., & Dosset, D. L. (1978). The importance of participative goal setting and anticipated rewards on goal difficulty and job performance. *Journal of Applied Psychology,* 63, 163–171; Saari, L. M., & Latham, G. P. (1979). The effects of holding goal difficulty constant on assigned and participatively set goals. *Academy of Management Journal,* 22, 163–168.

43. For a discussion of this issue, see Saari & Latham, 1979.

44. Locke, E. A., & Latham, G. P. (1984). *Goal setting—A motivational technique that works.* Englewood Cliffs, NJ: Prentice-Hall.

45. Wood, R. E., Mento, A. J., & Locke, E. A. (1987). Task complexity as a moderator of goal effects: A meta-analysis. *Journal of Applied Psychology,* 72, 416–425. See also Earley, P. C., Connolly, T., & Ekegren, G. (1989). Goals, strategy development, and task performance: Some limits on the efficacy of goal setting. *Journal of Applied Psychology,* 74, 24–33.

46. Good descriptions of MBO programs can be found in Mali, P. (1986). MBO *updated: A handbook of practices and techniques for managing by objectives.* New York: Wiley; Raia, A. P. (1974). *Managing by objectives.* Glenview, IL: Scott, Foresman; Odiorne, G. S. (1965). *Management by objectives.* New York: Pitman;

47. Rodgers, R., & Hunter, J. E. (1991) Impact of management by objectives on organization productivity. *Journal of Applied Psychology, 76,* 322–336.

48. Rodgers & Hunter, 1991.

49. See Rodgers, R., Huner, J. E., & Rogers, D. L. (1993). Influence of top management commitment on management program success. *Journal of Applied Psychology, 78,* 151–155.

50. For discussions of these and other problems with MBO, see Pringle, C. D., & Longenecker, J. G. (1982). The ethics of MBO. *Academy of Management Review, 7,* 305–312; Levinson, H. (1979, July–August). Management by whose objectives. *Harvard Business Review,* 125–134; McConkey, D. D. (1972, October). 20 ways to kill management by objectives. *Management Review,* 4–13.

51. See Ronen, S. (1984). *Alternative work schedules: Selecting, implementing, and evaluating.* Homewood, IL: Dow Jones-Irwin; Ronen, S. (1981). *Flexible working hours: An innovation in the quality of work life.* New York: McGraw-Hill; Nollen, S. D. (1982). *New work schedules in practice: Managing time in a changing society.* New York: Van Nostrand Reinhold.

52. For a good study showing absence reduction see Dalton, D. R., & Mesch, D. J. (1990). The impact of flexible scheduling on employee attendance and turnover. *Administrative Science Quarterly, 35,* 370–387.

53. Pierce, J. L., Newstrom, J. W., Dunham, R. B., & Barber, A. E. (1989). *Alternative work schedules.* Boston: Allyn and Bacon; Ronen, 1981 and 1984; Golembiewski, R. T., & Proehl, C. W. (1978). A survey of the empirical literature on flexible workhours: Character and consequences of a major innovation. *Academy of Management Review, 3,* 837–853.

54. Ronen, 1984; Nollen, 1982.

55. Pierce et al., 1989; Ronen, 1984; Ronen, S., & Primps, S. B. (1981). The compressed workweek as organizational change: Behavioral and attitudinal outcomes. *Academy of Management Review, 6,* 61–74.

56. Pierce et al., 1989; Ivancevich, J. M., & Lyon, H. L. (1977). The shortened workweek: A field experiment. *Journal of Applied Psychology, 62,* 34–37.

57. Johns, G. (1987). Understanding and managing absence from work. In S. L. Dolan & R. S. Schuler (Eds.), *Canadian readings in personnel and human resource management.* St. Paul, MN: West.

58. Ivancevich & Lyon, 1977; Calvasina, E. J., & Boxx, W. R. (1975). Efficiency of workers on the four-day workweek. *Academy of Management Journal, 18,* 604–610; Goodale, J. G., & Aagaard, A. K. (1975). Factors relating to varying reactions to the 4-day workweek. *Journal of Applied Psychology, 60,* 33–38.

59. This section relies on Pierce et al., 1989.

60. Tenner, A. R., & DeToro, I. J. (1992). *Total quality management: Three steps to continuous improvement.* Reading, MA: Addison-Wesley; Dale, B., & Cooper, C. (1992). *Total quality and human resources: An executive guide.* Oxford: Blackwell; Kinlaw, D. C. (1992). *Continuous improvement and measurement for total quality: A team-based approach.* San Diego: Pfeiffer.

61. Blackburn, R., & Rosen, B. (1993, August). Total quality and human resource management: Lessons learned from Baldrige Award-winning companies. *Academy of Management*

Executive, 49–66; George, S. (1992). *The Baldrige quality system.* New York: Wiley.

62. Spendolini, M. J. (1992). *The benchmarking book.* New York: AMACOM.

63. Spendolini, 1992.

64. Blackburn & Rosen, 1993.

65. Waldman, D. A., Ghali, A., & Rancourt, M. (1983). *Performance appraisal and total quality management: An investigation of user preferences.* Paper presented at the annual meeting of the Academy of Management, Atlanta.

66. Shellenbarger, S. (1992, December 7). Managers navigate uncharted waters trying to resolve work-family conflicts. *Wall Street Journal,* pp. B1, B6.

67. Oldham et al., 1979.

Chapter 8

1. Excerpted with minor editing from Case, J. (1993, September). What the experts forgot to mention. *Inc.* 66–78, pp. 66, 67.

2. For a partial review, see Kahn, A., & McGaughey, T. A. (1977). Distance and liking: When moving close produces increased liking. *Sociometry, 40,* 138–144.

3. Byrne, D. (1969). Attitudes and attraction. In L. Berkowitz (Ed.), *Advances in experimental social psychology* (Vol. 4). New York: Academic Press.

4. Shaw, M. E. (1981). *Group dynamics: The psychology of small group behavior* (3rd ed.). New York: McGraw-Hill; Jones, E. E., & Gerard, H. B. (1967). *Foundations of social psychology.* New York: Wiley.

5. Tuckman, B. W. (1965). Developmental sequence in small groups. *Psychological Bulletin, 63,* 384–399; Tuckman, B. W., & Jensen, M. A. C. (1977). Stages of small-group development revisited. *Group & Organization Studies, 2,* 419–427.

6. Harris, S. G., & Sutton, R. I. (1986). Functions of parting ceremonies in dying organizations. *Academy of Management Journal, 29,* 5–30.

7. Seger, J. A. (1983). No innate phases in group problem solving. *Academy of Management Review, 8,* 683–689.

8. Ginnett, R. C. (1990). Airline cockpit crew. In J. R. Hackman (Ed.), *Groups that work (and those that don't).* San Francisco: Jossey-Bass.

9. Gersick, C. J. G. (1989). Marking time: Predictable transitions in task groups. *Academy of Management Journal, 32,* 274–309; Gersick, C. J. G. (1988). Time and transition in work teams: Toward a new model of group development. *Academy of Management Journal, 31,* 9–41.

10. Gersick, 1989, 1988.

11. Hare, A. P. (1976). *A handbook of small group research.* New York: The Free Press; Shaw, 1981.

12. Hare, 1976; Shaw, 1981.

13. The following discussion relies upon Steiner, I. D. (1972). *Group process and productivity.* New York: Academic Press.

14. Steiner, 1972; Hill, G. W. (1982). Group versus individual performance: Are n+1 heads better than one? *Psychological Bulletin, 91,* 517–539.

15. Jackson, S. E., Stone, V. K., & Alvarez, E. B. (1993). Socialization amidst diversity: The impact of demographics on work team oldtimers and newcomers. *Research in Organizational Behavior, 15,* 45–109; Guzzo, R. A., & Shea, G. P. (1992). Group performance and intergroup relations in organizations. In M. D. Dunnette & L. M. Hough (Eds.), *Handbook of industrial and organizational psychology* (2nd ed., Vol. 3). Palo Alto, CA: Consulting Psychologists Press.

16. Watson, W. E., Kumar, K., & Michaelson, L. K. (1993). Cultural diversity's impact on interaction process and performance: Comparing homogeneous and diverse task groups. *Academy of Management Journal, 36,* 590–602.

17. For an example of the social process by which this sharing may be negotiated in a new group, see Bettenhausen, K., & Murnighan, J. K. (1991). The development of an intragroup norm and the effects of interpersonal and structural challenges. *Administrative Science Quarterly, 36,* 20–35.

18. Kanter, R. M. (1977). *Men and women of the corporation.* New York: Basic Books, p. 37.

19. Leventhal, G. S. (1976). The distribution of rewards and resources in groups and organizations. In L. Berkowitz & E. Walster (Eds.), *Advances in experimental social psychology* (Vol. 9). New York: Academic Press.

20. See Mitchell, T. R., Rothman, M., & Liden, R. C. (1985). Effects of normative information on task performance. *Journal of Applied Psychology, 70,* 48–55.

21. Jackson, S. E., & Schuler, R. S. (1985). A meta-analysis and conceptual critique of research on role ambiguity and role conflict in work settings. *Organizational Behavior and Human Decision Processes, 36,* 16–78. For a methodological critique of this domain, see King, L. A., & King, D. W. (1990). Role conflict and role ambiguity: A critical assessment of construct validity. *Psychological Bulletin, 107,* 48–64.

22. Jackson & Schuler, 1985.

23. Siconolfi, M. (1993, July 27). PaineWebber is penalized for sales pressure on brokers. *Wall Street Journal,* p. C1.

24. O'Driscoll, M. P., Ilgen, D. R., & Hildreth, K. (1992). Time devoted to job and off-job activities, interrole conflict, and affective experiences. *Journal of Applied Psychology, 77,* 272–279.

25. See Latack, J. C. (1981). Person/role conflict: Holland's model extended to role-stress research, stress management, and career development. *Academy of Management Review, 6,* 89–103.

26. Jackson & Schuler, 1985.

27. Robbins, S. P. (1978). *Personnel: The management of human resources.* Englewood Cliffs, NJ: Prentice-Hall, p. 294.

28. Treiman, D. J. (1977). *Occupational prestige in comparative perspective.* New York: Academic Press.

29. Shaw, 1981.

30. Kiesler, S., & Sproull, L. (1992). Group decision making and communication technology. *Organizational Behavior and Human Decision Processes, 52,* 96–123.

31. Strodbeck, F. L., James, R. M., & Hawkins, C. (1957). Social status in jury deliberations. *American Sociological Review, 22,* 713–719.

32. Kiesler & Sproull, 1992.

33. For other definitions and a discussion of their differences, see Mudrack, P. E. (1989). Defining group cohesiveness: A legacy of confusion? *Small Group Behavior, 20,* 37–49.

34. Stein, A. (1976). Conflict and cohesion: A review of the literature. *Journal of Conflict Resolution, 20,* 143–172.

35. Cartwright, D. (1968). The nature of group cohesiveness. In D. Cartwright & A. Zander (Eds.), *Group dynamics* (3rd ed.). New York: Harper & Row.

36. Lott, A., & Lott, B. (1965). Group cohesiveness as interpersonal attraction: A review of relationships with antecedent and consequent variables. *Psychological Bulletin, 64,* 259–309.

37. Anderson, A. B. (1975). Combined effects of interpersonal attraction and goal-path clarity on the cohesiveness of task-oriented groups. *Journal of Personality and Social Psychology, 31,* 68–75. Also see Cartwright, 1968.

38. Seashore, S. (1954). *Group cohesiveness in the industrial workgroup.* Ann Arbor, MI: Institute for Social Research.

39. Blanchard, F. A., Adelman, L., & Cook, S. W. (1975). Effect of group success and failure upon interpersonal attraction in cooperating interracial groups. *Journal of Personality and Social Psychology, 31,* 1020–1030.

40. Aronson, E., & Mills, J. (1959). The effects of severity of initiation on liking for a group. *Journal of Abnormal and Social Psychology, 59,* 177–181.

41. Bowen, D. E., Ledford, G. E., Jr., & Nathan, B. R. (1991, November). Hire for the organization, not the job. *Academy of Management Executive,* 35–51.

42. Bylinski, G. (1993, October 18). How to leapfrog the giants. *Fortune,* p. 80.

43. Cartwright, 1968; Shaw, 1981.

44. Schacter, S. (1951). Deviation, rejection, and communication. *Journal of Abnormal and Social Psychology, 46,* 190–207. See also Barker, J. R. (1993). Tightening the iron cage: Concertive control in self-managing teams. *Administrative Science Quarterly, 38,* 408–437.

45. Seashore, 1954. Also see Stogdill, R. M. (1972). Group productivity, drive, and cohesiveness. *Organizational Behavior and Human Performance, 8,* 26–43. For a critique, see Mudrack, P. E. (1989). Group cohesiveness and productivity: A closer look. *Human Relations, 42,* 771–785.

46. Gulley, S. M., Devine, D. J., & Whitney, D. J. (In press). A meta-analysis of cohesion and performance: Effects of level of analysis and task interdependence. *Small Group Research.*

47. Shepperd, J. A. (1993). Productivity loss in small groups: A motivation analysis. *Psychological Bulletin, 113,* 67–81; Kidwell, R. E., III, & Bennett, N. (1993). Employee propensity to withhold effort: A conceptual model to intersect three avenues of research. *Academy of Management Review, 18,* 429–456.

48. Shepperd, 1993; Kidwell & Bennett, 1993; George, J. M. (1992). Extrinsic and intrinsic origins of perceived social loafing in organizations. *Academy of Management Journal, 35,* 191–202.

49. Hackman, J. R. (1987). The design of work teams. In J. W. Lorsch (Ed.), *Handbook of organizational behavior.* Englewood Cliffs, NJ: Prentice-Hall.

50. Campion, M. A., Medsker, G. J., & Higgs, A. C. (1993). Relations between work group characteristics and effectiveness: Implications for designing effective work groups. *Personnel Psychology, 46,* 823–850.

51. Dumaine, B. (1990, May 7). Who needs a boss? *Fortune,* 52–60.

52. Wall, T. D., Kemp, N. J., Jackson, P. R., & Clegg, C. W. (1986). Outcomes of autonomous workgroups: A field experiment. *Academy of Management Journal, 29,* 280–304, p. 283.

53. Parts of this section rely on Hackman, 1987.

54. See Ashforth, B. E., & Mael, F. (1989). Social identity theory and the organization. *Academy of Management Review, 14,* 20–39.

55. Treece, J. (1990, April 9). Here comes GM's Saturn. *Business Week,* 56–62.

56. Wall et al., 1986; Cordery, J. L., Mueller, W. S., & Smith, L. M. (1991). Attitudinal and behavioral effects of autonomous group working: A longitudinal field study. *Academy of Management Journal, 34,* 264–276.

57. Manz, C. C., & Sims, H. P., Jr. (1987). Leading workers to lead themselves: The external leadership of self-managing work teams. *Administrative Science Quarterly, 32,* 106–128.

58. For reviews of research on self-managed groups, see Chapter 3 of Cummings, T. G., & Molloy, E. S. (1977). *Improving productivity and the quality of working life.* New York: Praeger; Goodman, P. S., Devadas, R., & Hughes, T. L. G. (1988). Groups and productivity: Analyzing the effectiveness of self-managing teams. In J. P. Campbell & R. J. Campbell

(Eds.), *Productivity in organizations*. San Francisco: Jossey-Bass; Pearce, J. A., III, & Ravlin, E. C. (1987). The design and activation of self-regulating work groups. *Human Relations, 40*, 751–782.

59. Farnham, A. (1994, February 7). America's most admired company. *Fortune*, 50–54; Dumaine, B. (1993, December 13). Payoff from the new management. *Fortune*, 103–110.

60. Waterman, R. H., Jr. (1987). *The renewal factor*. New York: Bantam Books; McElroy, J. (1985, April). Ford's new way to build cars. *Road & Track*, 156–158.

61. Pinto, M. B., Pinto, J. K, & Prescott, J. E. (1993). Antecedents and consequences of project team cross-functional cooperation. *Management Science, 39*, 1281–1297; Henke, J. W., Krachenberg, A. R., & Lyons, T. F. (1993). Cross-functional teams: Good concept, poor implementation! *Journal of Product Innovation Management, 10*, 216–229. Mustang examples from White, J. B., & Suris, O. (1993, September 21). How a 'skunk works' kept the Mustang alive—on a tight budget. *Wall Street Journal*, pp. A1, A12.

Chapter 9

1. Sources include Burka, P. (1988, November 8). What they teach you at Disney U. *Fortune*, Special advertising section; Solomon, C. M. (1989, December). How does Disney do it? *Personnel*, 50–57; Van Maanen, J. V., & Kunda, G. (1989). "Real feelings": Emotional expression and organizational culture. *Research in Organizational Behavior, 11*, 43–103.

2. See Morrison, E. W. (1993). Newcomer information seeking: Exploring types, modes, sources, and outcomes. *Academy of Management Journal, 36*, 557–589.

3. The terms information dependence and effect dependence are used by Jones, E. E., & Gerard, H. B. (1967). *Foundations of social psychology*. New York: Wiley.

4. Festinger, L. (1954). A theory of social comparison processes. *Human Relations, 7*, 117–140; Thomas, J., & Griffin, R. (1983). The social information processing model of task design: A review of the literature. *Academy of Management Review, 8*, 672–682.

5. Kelman, H. C. (1961). Processes of opinion change. *Public Opinion Quarterly, 25*, 57–78.

6. Van Maanen & Kunda, 1989, p. 65.

7. Asch, S. E. (1952). *Social psychology*. Englewood Cliffs, NJ: Prentice-Hall.

8. Sherif, M. (1935). A study of some social factors in perception. *Archives of Psychology, 27*, No. 187.

9. Rohrer, J., Baron, S., Hoffman, E., & Swander, D. (1954). The stability of autokinetic judgments. *Journal of Abnormal and Social Psychology, 49*, 595–597.

10. Asch, 1952; Gerard, H., Wilhelmy, R., & Connolley, E. (1968). Conformity and group size. *Journal of Personality and Social Psychology, 8*, 79–82.

11. Saks, M. J. (1977). *Jury verdicts*. Lexington, MA: Heath.

12. Hollander, E. P. (1958). Conformity, status, and idiosyncrasy credit. *Psychological Review, 65*, 117–127; Hollander, E. P. (1964). *Leaders, groups, and influence*. New York: Oxford University Press.

13. Van Maanen, J., & Schein, E. H. (1979). Toward a theory of organizational socialization. *Research in Organizational Behavior, 1*, 209–264.

14. Feldman, D. C. (1976). A contingency theory of socialization. *Administrative Science Quarterly, 21*, 433–452.

15. Wanous, J. P. (1992). *Organizational entry: Recruitment, selection, orientation, and socialization of newcomers*. (2nd ed.). Reading, MA: Addison-Wesley.

16. Wanous, J. P. (1976). Organizational entry: From naive expectations to realistic beliefs. *Journal of Applied Psychology, 61*, 22–29.

17. See Breaugh, J. A. (1992). *Recruitment: Science and practice*. Boston: PWS-Kent.

18. Van Maanen & Schein, 1979.

19. Pascale, R. (1984, May 28). Fitting new employees into the company culture. *Fortune*, 28–43, p. 30.

20. This discussion draws upon Van Maanen & Schein, 1979, but differs in detail.

21. Wanous, 1992; Breaugh, 1992.

22. Wanous, 1992; Breaugh, 1992.

23. Premack, S. L., & Wanous, J. P. (1985). A meta-analysis of realistic job preview experiments. *Journal of Applied Psychology, 70*, 706–719. See also Wanous, J. P., Poland, T. D., Premack, S. L., & Davis, K. S. (1992). The effects of met expectations on newcomer attitudes and behaviors: A review and meta-analysis. *Journal of Applied Psychology, 77*, 288–297.

24. Premack & Wanous, 1985; McEvoy, G. M., & Cascio, W. F. (1985). Strategies for reducing employee turnover: A meta-analysis. *Journal of Applied Psychology, 70*, 342–353.

25. Cascio, W. F. (1993, February). Downsizing: What do we know? What have we learned? *Academy of Management Executive*, 95–104.

26. Meyer, J. P., & Allen, N. J. (1991). A three-component conceptualization of organizational commitment. *Human Resource Management Review, 1*, 61–98; Meyer, J. P., Allen, N. J., & Smith, C. A. (1993). Commitment to organizations and occupations: Extension and test of a three-component conceptualization. *Journal of Applied Psychology, 78*, 538–551.

27. Meyer & Allen, 1991; Mathieu, J. E., & Zajac, D. M. (1990). A review and meta-analysis of the antecedents, correlates, and consequences of organizational commitment. *Psychological Bulletin, 108*, 171–194.

28. Wanous et al., 1992.

29. Mathieu & Zajac, 1990.

30. Mathieu & Zajac, 1990; For a careful study see Jaros, S. J., Jermier, J. M., Koehler, J. W., & Sincich, T. (1993). Effects of continuance, affective, and moral commitment on the withdrawal process: An evaluation of eight structural equation models. *Academy of Management Journal, 36*, 951–995.

31. Meyer, J. P., Paunonen, S. V., Gellatly, I. R., Goffin, R. D., & Jackson, D. N. (1989). Organizational commitment and job performance: It's the nature of the commitment that counts. *Journal of Applied Psychology, 74*, 152–156.

32. Randall, D. M. (1987). Commitment and the organization: The organization man revisited. *Academy of Management Review, 12*, 460–471.

33. For a more complete discussion of various definitions, theories, and concepts of culture, see Schein, E. H. (1992). *Organizational culture and leadership* (2nd ed.). San Francisco: Jossey-Bass; Smircich, L. (1983). Concepts of culture and organizational analysis. *Administrative Science Quarterly, 28*, 339–358; Allaire, Y., & Firsirotu, M. E. (1984). Theories of organizational culture. *Organization Studies, 5*, 193–226; Hatch, M. J. (1993). The dynamics of organizational culture. *Academy of Management Review, 18*, 657–693.

34. Sackmann, S. A. (1992). Culture and subculture: An analysis of organizational knowledge. *Administrative Science Quarterly, 37*, 140–161.

35. Gregory, K. L. (1983). Native-view paradigms: Multiple cultures and culture conflicts in organizations. *Administrative Science Quarterly, 28*, 359–376.

36. Kilmann, R., Saxton, M. J., & Serpa, R. (1986, Winter). Issues in understanding and changing culture. *California Management Review*, 87–94; Deal, T. E., & Kennedy, A. A. (1982). *Corporate cultures: The rites and rituals of corporate life*. Reading, MA: Addison-Wesley. For a critique, see

Saffold, G. S., III. (1988). Culture traits, strength, and organizational performance: Moving beyond "strong" culture. *Academy of Management Review, 13*, 546–558.

37. Raynal, W. (1993, December 20). Down, but not out. *Autoweek*, p. 15.

38. Gordon, G. G., & Di Tomaso, N. (1992). Predicting corporate performance from organizational culture. *Journal of Management Studies, 29*, 783–798. For a critique of such work see Siehl, C., & Martin, J. (1990). Organizational culture: A key to financial performance. In B. Schneider (Ed.), *Organizational climate and culture*. San Francisco: Jossey-Bass.

39. Sheridan, J. E. (1992). Organizational culture and employee retention. *Academy of Management Journal, 35*, 1036–1056.

40. Lorsch, J. W. (1986, Winter). Managing culture: The invisible barrier to strategic change. *California Management Review*, 95–109.

41. Cartwright, S., & Cooper, C. L. (1993, May). The role of culture compatibility in successful organizational marriage. *Academy of Management Executive*, 57–70.

42. Kets de Vries, M. F. R., & Miller, D. (1984). *The neurotic organization: Diagnosing and changing counterproductive styles of management*. San Francisco: Jossey-Bass.

43. Kets de Vries, M. F. R., & Miller, D. (1984, October). Unstable at the top. *Psychology Today*, 26–34, p. 32.

44. See Schein, 1992.

45. Uttal, B. (1985, August 5). Behind the fall of Steve Jobs. *Fortune*, 20–24.

46. Pascale, R. (1985, Winter). The paradox of "corporate-culture": Reconciling ourselves to socialization. *California Management Review*, 26–41; Pascale, 1984; for some research support, see Caldwell, D. F., Chatman, J. A., & O'Reilly, C. A. (1990). Building organizational commitment: A multifirm study. *Journal of Occupational Psychology, 63*, 245–261.

47. Hatch, 1993; Ornstein, S. (1986). Organizational symbols: A study of their meanings and influences on perceived organizational climate. *Organizational Behavior and Human Decision Processes, 38*, 207–229.

48. Nulty, P. (1989, February 27). America's toughest bosses. *Fortune*, 40–54.

49. Trice, H. M., and Beyer, J. M. (1984). Studying organizational cultures through rites and ceremonials. *Academy of Management Review, 9*, 653–669.

50. Martin, J., Feldman, M. S., Hatch, M. J., & Sitkin, S. B. (1983). The uniqueness paradox in organizational stories. *Administrative Science Quarterly, 28*, 438–453.

51. Peters, T., & Austin, N. (1985). *A passion for excellence: The leadership difference*. New York: Random House.

52. The following draws on Kirkpatrick, D. (1993, May 17). Could AT&T rule the world? *Fortune*, 55–66. Tunstall, W. C. (1986, Winter). The breakup of the Bell system: A case study in culture transformation. *California Management Review*, 110–124; Main, J. (1984, December 24). Waking up at AT&T: There's life after culture shock. *Fortune*, 66–74.

Chapter 10

1. Sources include Labick, K. (1994, May 4). Is Herb Kelleher America's best CEO? *Fortune*, 44–52; Veverka, M. (1994, November 21). Blood and guts Kelleher. Southwest Chief rallies troops against United. *Crains's Chicago Business*, p.3; Barrett, C. (1993, November). Giving customers P.O.S. *Sales & Marketing Management*, p. 52; Bovier, C. (1993, June). Teamwork: The heart of an airline. *Training*, 53–58; Maxon, T. (1994, October 14). Hey Herb, have you checked out this morning's USA Today yet? *The Dallas Morning News*, p. 1D.

2. Bass, B. M. (1990). *Bass & Stogdill's handbook of leadership: A survey of research* (3rd ed.). New York: Free Press.

3. This list is derived from Bass, 1990; House, R. J., & Baetz, M. L. (1979). Leadership: Some empirical generalizations and new research directions. *Research in Organizational Behavior, 1*, 341–423; Locke, E. A., et al. (1992). *The essence of leadership: The four keys to leading effectively*. New York: Free Press; Lord, R. G., DeVader, C. L., & Alliger, G. M. (1986). A meta-analysis of the relationship between personality traits and leadership perceptions: An application of validity generalization procedures. *Journal of Applied Psychology, 71*, 402–410.

4. Bottger, P. C. (1984). Expertise and air time as bases of actual and perceived influence in problem-solving groups. *Journal of Applied Psychology, 69*, 214–221.

5. Lewis, G. H. (1972). Role differentiation. *American Sociological Review, 37*, 424–434.

6. Bales, R. F., & Slater, P. E. (1955). Role differentiation in small decision-making groups. In T. Parsons, et al. (Eds.), *Family, socialization, and interaction process*. Glencoe, IL: Free Press; Slater, P. E. (1955). Role differentiation in small groups. *American Sociological Review, 20*, 300–310.

7. For a pessimistic review, see Korman, A. K. (1966). "Consideration," "initiating structure," and organizational criteria—A review. *Personnel Psychology, 19*, 349–361. For an optimistic update, see Kerr, S., & Schriesheim, C. (1974). Consideration, initiating struture, and organizational criteria—An update of Korman's 1966 review. *Personnel Psychology, 27*, 555–568.

8. Kerr, S., Schriesheim, C. A., Murphy, C. J., & Stogdill, R. M. (1974). Toward a contingency theory of leadership based upon the consideration and initiating structure literature. *Organizational Behavior and Human Performance, 12*, 62–82.

9. For a review of the evidence, see Filley, A. C., House, R. J., & Kerr, S. (1976). *Managerial process and organizational behavior* (2nd ed.). Glenview, IL: Scott, Foresman. Also see Larson, L. L., Hunt, J. G., & Osborn, R. N. (1976). The great hi-hi leader behavior myth: A lesson from Occam's razor. *Academy of Management Journal, 19*, 628–641.

10. Oldham, G. R. (1976). The motivational strategies used by supervisors: Relationships to effectiveness indicators. *Organizational Behavior and Human Performance, 15*, 66–86.

11. Ashour, A. S., & Johns, G. (1983). Leader influence through operant principles: A theoretical and methodological framework. *Human Relations, 36*, 603–626; Podsakoff, P. M., & Schriesheim, C. A. (1984). Leader reward and punishment behavior: A review of the literature. In D. F. Ray (Ed.), *Southern Management Association Proceedings*, 12–14.

12. Ashour & Johns, 1983; Podsakoff & Schriesheim, 1984.

13. Ashour & Johns, 1983. Also see Podsakoff, P. M. (1982). Determinants of a supervisor's use of rewards and punishments: A literature review and suggestions for further research. *Organizational Behavior and Human Performance, 29*, 58–83.

14. Dumaine, B. (1993, October 18). America's toughest bosses. *Fortune*, 38–50.

15. Fiedler, F. E. (1967). *A theory of leadership effectiveness*. New York: McGraw-Hill; Fiedler, F. E., & Chemers, M. M. (1974). *Leadership and effective management*. Glenview, IL: Scott, Foresman; Fiedler, F. E. (1978). The contingency model and the dynamics of the leadership process. In L. Berkowitz (Ed.), *Advances in experimental social psychology* (Vol. 11). New York: Academic Press.

16. For a summary, see Fiedler, 1978.

17. See Ashour, A. S. (1973). The contingency model of leader effectiveness: An evaluation. *Organizational Behavior and*

Human Performance, 9, 339–355; Graen, G. B., Alvares, D., Orris, J. B., & Martella, J. A. (1970). The contingency model of leadership effectiveness: Antecedent and evidential results. *Psychological Bulletin, 74,* 285–296.

18. Schriesheim, C. A., Tepper, B. J., & Tetreault, L. A. (1994). Least preferred co-worker score, situational control, and leadership effectiveness: A meta-analysis of contingency and performance predictions. *Journal of Applied Psychology, 79,* 561–573; Peters, L. H., Hartke, D. D., & Pohlmann, J. T. (1985). Fiedler's contingency theory of leadership: An application of the meta-analysis procedures of Schmidt and Hunter. *Psychological Bulletin, 97,* 274–285; Strube, M. J., & Garcia, J. E. (1981). A meta-analytic investigation of Fiedler's contingency model of leadership effectiveness. *Psychological Bulletin, 90,* 307–321.

19. House, R. J., & Dessler, G. (1974). The path-goal theory of leadership: Some post hoc and a priori tests. In J. G. Hunt & L. L. Larson (Eds.), *Contingency approaches to leadership.* Carbondale, IL: Southern Illinois University Press; House, R. J., & Mitchell, T. R. (1974, Autumn). Path-goal theory of leadership. *Journal of Contemporary Business,* 81–97. See also Evans, M. G. (1970). The effects of supervisory behavior on the path-goal relationship. *Organizational Behavior and Human Performance, 5,* 277–298.

20. House & Dessler, 1974; House & Mitchell, 1974; Filley, House, & Kerr, 1976; Wofford, J. C., & Liska, L. Z. (1993). Path-goal theories of leadership: A meta-analysis *Journal of Management, 19,* 857–876.

21. See, for example, Greene, C. N. (1979). Questions of causation in the path-goal theory of leadership. *Academy of Management Journal, 22,* 22–41; Griffin, R. W. (1980). Relationships among individual, task design, and leader behavior variables. *Academy of Management Journal, 23,* 665–683.

22. Mitchell, T. R. (1973). Motivation and participation: An integration. *Academy of Management Journal, 16,* 160–179.

23. Maier, N. R. F. (1973). *Psychology in industrial organizations* (4th ed.). Boston: Houghton Mifflin; Maier, N. R. F. (1970). *Problem solving and creativity in individuals and groups.* Belmont, CA: Brooks/Cole.

24. Dobbs, J. H. (1993, February). The empowerment environment. *Training & Development,* 55–57, p. 56.

25. Maier, 1970, 1973.

26. Strauss, G. (1955). Group dynamics and intergroup relations. In W. F. Whyte, *Money and motivation.* New York: Harper & Row.

27. Vroom, V. H., & Jago, A. G. (1988). *The new leadership: Managing participation in organizations.* Englewood Cliffs, NJ: Prentice-Hall; Vroom, V. H., & Yetton, P. W. (1973). *Leadership and decision-making.* Pittsburgh: University of Pittsburgh Press.

28. Vroom & Yetton, 1973, p. 13.

29. See Vroom & Jago, 1988, for a review. See also Field, R. H. G., Wedley, W. C., & Hayward, M. W. J. (1989). Criteria used in selecting Vroom-Yetton decision styles. *Canadian Journal of Administrative Sciences, 6*(2), 18–24.

30. Reviews on participation reveal a complicated pattern of results. See Miller, K. I., & Monge, P. R. (1986). Participation, satisfaction, and productivity: A meta-analytic review. *Academy of Management Journal, 29,* 727–753; Wagner, J. A., III, & Gooding, R. Z. (1987). Shared influence and organizational behavior: A meta-analysis of situational variables expected to moderate participation-outcome relationships. *Academy of Management Journal, 30,* 524–541; Wagner, J. A., III, & Gooding, R. Z. (1987). Effects of societal trends on participation research. *Administrative Science Quarterly, 32,* 241–262.

31. The transformational/transactional distinction is credited to Burns, J. M. (1978). *Leadership.* New York: Harper & Row.

32. Bass, B. M. (1985). *Leadership and performance beyond expectations.* New York: Free Press; Bass, B. M. (1990, Winter). From transactional to transformational leadership: Learning to share the vision. *Organizational Dynamics,* 19–31.

33. House, R. J. (1977). A 1976 theory of charismatic leadership. In J. G. Hunt & L. L. Larson (Eds.), *Leadership: The cutting edge.* Carbondale, IL: Southern Illinois University Press.

34. Conger, J. A., & Kanungo, R. N. (1988). Behavioral dimensions of charismatic leadership. In J. A. Conger & R. N. Kanungo (Eds.), *Charismatic leadership: The elusive factor in organizational effectiveness.* San Francisco: Jossey-Bass; Conger, J. A., & Kanungo, R. N. (1987). Toward a behavioral theory of charismatic leadership in organizational settings. *Academy of Management Review, 12,* 637–647.

35. House, R. J., Woycke, J., & Fodor, E. M. (1988). Charismatic and noncharismatic leaders: Differences in behavior and effectiveness. In J. A. Conger & R. N. Kanungo (Eds.), *Charismatic leadership: The elusive factor in organizational effectiveness.* San Francisco: Jossey-Bass.

36. Howell, J. M. (1988). Two faces of charisma: Socialized and personalized leadership in organizations. In J. A. Conger & R. N. Kanungo (Eds.), *Charismatic leadership: The elusive factor in organizational effectiveness.* San Francisco: Jossey-Bass; Howell, J. M., & Avolio, B. J. (1992, May). The ethics of charismatic leadership. Submission or liberation? *Academy of Management Executive,* 43–54.

37. Hater, J. J., & Bass, B. M. (1988). Superiors' evaluations and subordinates' perceptions of transformational and transactional leadership. *Journal of Applied Psychology, 73,* 695–702; Avolio, B. J., & Bass, B. M. (1988). Transformational leadership, charisma, and beyond. In J. G. Hunt, B. R. Baglia, H. P. Dachler, & C. A. Schriesheim (Eds.), *Emerging leadership vistas.* Lexington, MA: Lexington Books.

38. Eagley, A. H., & Johnson, B. T. (1990). Gender and leadership style: A meta-analysis. *Psychological Bulletin, 108,* 233–256.

39. Eagley, A. H., Makhijani, M. G., & Klonsky, B. G. (1992). Gender and the evaluation of leaders: A meta-analysis. *Psychological Bulletin, 111,* 3–32.

40. Adapted from Katz, D., & Kahn, R. L. (1978). *The social psychology of organizations* (2nd ed.). New York: Wiley.

41. For a review of the evidence that concludes that leadership matters, see House & Baetz, 1979. See also Thomas, A. B. (1988). Does leadership make a difference in organizational performance? *Administrative Science Quarterly, 33,* 388–400.

42. Pfeffer, J. (1977). The ambiguity of leadership. *Academy of Management Review, 2,* 104–112. Pfeffer also cites evidence that leadership is less important than other organizational factors.

43. Kerr, S. (1977). Substitutes for leadership: Some implications for organizational design. *Organizational and Administrative Sciences, 8,* 135–146; Kerr, S., & Jermier, J. M. (1978). Substitutes for leadership: Their meaning and measurement. *Organizational Behavior and Human Performance, 22,* 375–403.

44. There is some disagreement about how to actually test this theory. In my opinion, the following research provides partial support for the view of neutralizers and substitutes presented in the chapter. Podsakoff, P. M., MacKenzie, S. B., & Fetter, R. (1993) Substitutes for leadership and the management of professionals. *Leadership Quarterly, 4,* 1–44; Podsakoff, P. M., Niehoff, B. P., Mackenzie, S. B., & Williams, M. L. (1993). Do substitutes for leadership really substitute for leadership? An empirical examination of Kerr

and Jermier's situational leadership model. *Organizational Behavior and Human Decision Processes, 54,* 1–44.

Chapter 11

1. Source: Excerpted from Wilke, J. R. (1993, December 9). Computer links erode hierarchical nature of workplace culture. *Wall Street Journal,* pp. A1, A7.
2. Nobel, B. P. (1993, September 19). Dissecting the 90's workplace. *New York Times,* p. F21.
3. Meissner, M. (1976). The language of work. In R. Dubin (Ed.), *Handbook of work, organization, and society.* Chicago: Rand McNally.
4. Meissner, 1976.
5. Mintzberg, H. (1973). *The nature of managerial work.* New York: Harper & Row.
6. Miller, K. L. (1992, August 17). Honda sets its sights on a different checkered flag. *Business Week,* 45–46.
7. Very few organizations formally institute such policies. See Saunders, D. M., & Leck, J. D. (1993). Formal upward communication procedures: Organizational and employee perspectives. *Canadian Journal of Administrative Sciences, 10,* 255–268.
8. Davis, K. (1968). Success of chain-of-command oral communication in a manufacturing management group. *Academy of Management Journal, 11,* 379–387.
9. Foltz, R. G. (1985). Communication in contemporary organizations. In C. Reuss & D. Silvis (Eds.), *Inside organizational communication* (2nd ed.). New York: Longman.
10. Snyder, R. A., & Morris, J. H. (1984). Organizational communication and performance. *Journal of Applied Psychology, 69,* 461–465.
11. From an unpublished review by the author. Some studies are cited in Jablin, F. M. (1979). Superior-subordinate communication: The state of the art. *Psychological Bulletin, 86,* 1201–1222. See also Dansereau, F., & Markham, S. E. (1987). Superior-subordinate communication: Multiple levels of analysis. In F. Jablin, L. Putnam, K. H. Roberts, & L. W. Porter (Eds.), *Handbook of organizational communication.* Newbury Park, CA: Sage; Harris, M. M., & Schaubroeck, J. (1988). A meta-analysis of self-supervisor, self-peer, and peer-supervisor ratings. *Personnel Psychology, 41,* 43–62.
12. Jablin, 1979.
13. Tesser, A., & Rosen, S. (1975). The reluctance to transmit bad news. In L. Berkowitz (Ed.), *Advances in experimental social psychology* (Vol. 8). New York: Academic Press.
14. Read, W. (1962). Upward communication in industrial hierarchies. *Human Relations, 15,* 3–16; For related studies, see Jablin, 1979.
15. Evidence that subordinates tend to suppress communicating negative news to the boss can be found in O'Reilly, C. A., & Roberts, K. H. (1974). Information filtration in organizations: Three experiments. *Organizational Behavior and Human Performance, 11,* 253–265. For evidence that this is probably self-presentational, see Bond, C. F., Jr., & Anderson, E. L. (1987). The reluctance to transmit bad news: Private discomfort or public display? *Journal of Experimental Social Psychology, 23,* 176–187.
16. Ashford, S. J. (1989). Self-assessments in organizations: A literature review and integrated model. *Research in Organizational Behavior, 11,* 133–174; Harris & Schaubroeck, 1988.
17. Lawler, E. E., III, Porter, L. W., & Tennenbaum, A. (1968). Managers' attitudes toward interaction episodes. *Journal of Applied Psychology, 52,* 432–439. For a similar study with similar results, see Whitely, W. (1984). An exploratory study of managers' reactions to properties of verbal communication. *Personnel Psychology, 37,* 41–59.

18. Studies reviewed in Meissner, 1976.
19. Callan, V. J. (1993). Subordinate-manager communication in different sex dyads: Consequences for job satisfaction. *Journal of Occupational and Organizational Psychology, 66,* 13–27.
20. Noon, M., & Delbridge, R. (1993). News from behind my hand: Goosip in organizations. *Organization Studies, 14,* 23–36.
21. Davis, K. (1977). *Human behavior at work* (5th ed.). New York: McGraw-Hill.
22. Davis, K. (1953). Management communication and the grapevine. *Harvard Business Review, 31*(5), 43–49; Sutton, H., & Porter, L. W. (1968). A study of the grapevine in a governmental organization. *Personnel Psychology, 21,* 223–230.
23. Rosnow, R. L. (1980). Psychology of rumor reconsidered. *Psychological Bulletin, 87,* 578–591.
24. Rosnow, R. L. (1991) Inside rumor: A personal journey. *American Psychologist, 46,* 484–496.
25. Kanter, R. M. (1977). *Men and women of the corporation.* New York: Basic Books.
26. Kidder, T. (1981). *The soul of a new machine.* Boston: Little, Brown, p. 46.
27. For reviews, see Heslin, R., & Patterson, M. L. (1982). *Nonverbal behavior and social psychology.* New York: Plenum; Harper, R. G., Wiens, A. N., & Matarazzo, J. D. (1978). *Nonverbal communication: The state of the art.* New York: Wiley.
28. Mehrabian, A. (1972). *Nonverbal communication.* Chicago: Aldine-Atherton.
29. Mehrabian, 1972.
30. DePaulo, B. M. (1992). Nonverbal behavior and self-presentation. *Psychological Bulletin, 111,* 203–243.
31. Edinger, J. A., & Patterson, M. L. (1983). Nonverbal involvement and social control. *Psychological Bulletin, 93,* 30–56.
32. Rasmussen, K. G., Jr. (1984). Nonverbal behavior, verbal behavior, resume credentials, and selection interview outcomes. *Journal of Applied Psychology, 69,* 551–556.
33. Steele, F. I. (1973). *Physical settings and organizational development.* Reading, MA: Addison-Wesley, p. 55.
34. Campbell, D. E. (1979). Interior office design and visitor response. *Journal of Applied Psychology, 64,* 648–653. For a replication, see Morrow, P. C., & McElroy, J. C. (1981). Interior office design and visitor response: A constructive replication. *Journal of Applied Psychology, 66,* 646–650.
35. McElroy, J. C., Morrow, P. C., & Ackerman, R. J. (1983). Personality and interior office design: Exploring the accuracy of visitor attributions. *Journal of Applied Psychology, 68,* 541–544.
36. Molloy, J. T. (1993). *John T. Molloy's new dress for success.* New York: Warner; Molloy, J. T. (1987). *The woman's dress for success book.* New York: Warner.
37. Rafaeli, A., & Pratt, M. G. (1993). Tailored meanings: On the meaning and impact of organizational dress. *Academy of Management Review, 18,* 32–55; Solomon, M. R. (1986, April). Dress for effect. *Psychology Today,* 20–28; Solomon, M. R. (Ed.). (1985). *The psychology of fashion.* New York: Lexington.
38. Forsythe, S., Drake, M. F., & Cox, C. E. (1985). Influence of applicant's dress on interviewer's selection decisions. *Journal of Applied Psychology, 70,* 374–378.
39. Solomon, 1986.
40. Adler, N. J. (1992). *International dimensions of organizational behavior* (2nd ed.). Belmont, CA: Wadsworth, p. 66.
41. Ramsey, S., & Birk, J. (1983). Preparation of North Americans for interaction with Japanese: Considerations of language and communication style. In D. Landis & R. W.

Brislin (Eds.), *Handbook of intercultural training* (Vol. III). New York: Pergamon.

42. Ekman, P. (Ed.). (1982). *Emotion in the human face* (2nd ed.). Cambridge: Cambridge University Press. See also Ekman, P. (1993). Facial expression and emotion. *American Psychologist, 48,* 384–392.

43. Furnham, A., & Bocher, S. (1986). *Culture shock: Psychological reactions to unfamiliar environments.* London: Methuen, pp. 207–208.

44. Examples on gaze and touch draw on Furnham & Bocher, 1986; Argyle, M. (1982). Inter-cultural communication. In S. Bochner (Ed.), *Cultures in contact: Studies in cross-cultural interaction.* Oxford: Pergamon.

45. Collett, P. (1971). Training Englishmen in the non-verbal behaviour of Arabs: An experiment on intercultural communication. *International Journal of Psychology, 6,* 209–215.

46. Furnham & Bochner, 1986; Argyle, 1982.

47. Ramsey & Birk, 1983, p. 235.

48. Furnham & Bochner, 1986; Argyle, 1982.

49. Levine, R., West, L. J., & Reis, H. T. (1980). Perceptions of time and punctuality in the United States and Brazil. *Journal of Personality and Social Psychology, 38,* 541–550.

50. Hall, E. T., & Hall, M. R. (1990). *Understanding cultural differences.* Yarmouth, ME: Intercultural Press.

51. Dulek, R. E., Fielden, J. S., & Hill, J. S. (1991, January–February). International communication: An executive primer. *Business Horizons,* 20–25.

52. The following relies in part on Whetten, D. A., & Cameron, K. S. (1991). *Developing management skills* (2nd ed.). New York: HarperCollins; DeVito, J. A. (1992). *The interpersonal communication book* (6th ed.). New York: HarperCollins; Athos, A. G., & Gabarro, J. J. (1978). *Interpersonal behavior.* Englewood Cliffs, NJ: Prentice-Hall.

53. Duleck et al, 1991.

54. Daft, R. L., & Lengel, R. H. (1984). Information richness: A new approach to managerial behavior and organizational design. *Research in Organizational Behavior, 6,* 191–233.

55. Siegel, J., Dubrovsky, V., Kiesler, S., & McGuire, T. W. (1986). Group processing in computer mediated communication. *Organizational Behavior and Human Decision Processes, 37,* 157–187.

56. Lengel, R. H., & Daft, R. L. (1988, August). The selection of communication media as an executive skill. *Academy of Management Executive,* 225–232.

57. Stewart, T. A. (1993, August 23). Reengineering: The hot new management tool. *Fortune,* 40–48, p. 46.

58. Prince, J. B. (1994, January). Performance appraisal and reward practices for total quality organizations. *Quality Management Journal,* 36–46; Newman, R. J. (1993, November 1). Job reviews go full circle. *U.S. News & World Report*; Cardy, B., & Dobbins, G. (1993, Spring). The changing face of performance appraisal: Customer evaluations and 360 appraisals. *Human Resources Division News,* 17–18.

59. For a good description of how to develop and use organizational surveys, see Dunham, R. B., & Smith, F. J. (1979). *Organizational surveys.* Glenview, IL: Scott, Foresman. See also Rosenfeld, P., Edwards, J. E., & Thomas, M. D. (1993). Improving organizational surveys: New directions and methods (special issue). *American Behavioral Scientist, 36,* 411–550.

60. Taft, W. F. (1985). Bulletin boards, exhibits, hotlines. In C. Reuss & D. Silvis (Eds.), *Inside organizational communication* (2nd ed.). New York: Longman.

61. Templin, N. (1993, December 7). Companies use TV to reach their workers. *Wall Street Journal,* pp. B1, B10.

62. Burnaska, R. (1976). The effects of behavior modeling training upon managers' behaviors and employees' perceptions. *Personnel Psychology, 29,* 329–335.

63. Capella, J. N. (1981). Mutual influence in expressive behavior: Adult-adult and infant-adult dyadic interaction. *Psychological Bulletin, 89,* 101–132.

Chapter 12

1. Sources include Capers, R. S., & Lipton, E. (1993, November). Hubble error: Time, money, and millionths of an inch. *Academy of Management Executive,* 41–57 (originally published in *Hartford Courant*); Broad, W. J. (1993, December 7). Some feared mirror flaws even before Hubble orbit. *New York Times,* pp. C1, C10; Rosewicz, B. (1993, November 29). Shuttle aims to fix Hubble and more. *Wall Street Journal,* p. B6.

2. Mintzberg, H. (1979). *The structuring of organizations.* Englewood Cliffs, NJ: Prentice-Hall.

3. MacCrimmon, K. R., & Taylor, R. N. (1976). Decision making and problem solving. In M. D. Dunnette (Ed.), *Handbook of industrial and organizational psychology.* Chicago: Rand McNally.

4. Simon, H. A. (1957). *Administrative behavior* (2nd ed.). New York: Free Press.

5. Bazerman, M. (1990). *Judgment in managerial decision making* (2nd ed.). New York: Wiley.

6. Whyte, G. (1991, August). Decision failures: Why they occur and how to prevent them. *Academy of Management Executive,* 23–31; Russo, J. E., & Schoemaker, P. J. H. (1989). *Decision traps.* New York: Doubleday.

7. The latter two difficulties are discussed by Huber, G. P. (1980). *Managerial decision making.* Glenview, IL: Scott, Foresman. For further discussion of problem identification, see Kiesler, S., & Sproull, L. (1982). Managerial response to changing environments: Perspectives on problem sensing from social cognition. *Administrative Science Quarterly, 27,* 548–570; Cowan, D. A. (1986). Developing a process model of problem recognition. *Academy of Management Review, 11,* 763–776.

8. Whyte, 1991; Russo & Schoemaker, 1989.

9. Tversky, A., & Kahneman, D. (1973). Availability: A heuristic for judging frequency and probability. *Cognitive Psychology, 5,* 207–232. Also see Taylor, S. E., and Fiske, S. T. (1978). Salience, attention, and attribution: Top of the head phenomena. In L. Berkowitz (Ed.), *Advances in experimental social psychology* (Vol. 11). New York: Academic Press.

10. Lichtenstein, S., Fischhoff, B., & Phillips, L. D. (1982). Calibration of probabilities: The state of the art in 1980. In D. Kahneman, P. Slovic, & A. Tversky (Eds.), *Judgment under uncertainty: Heuristics and biases.* Cambridge: Cambridge University Press.

11. Sherman, S. P. (1989, March 26). The mind of Jack Welch. *Fortune,* 38–50, p. 42.

12. Miller, J. G. (1960). Information input, overload, and psychopathology. *American Journal of Psychiatry, 116,* 695–704.

13. Manis, M., Fichman, M., & Platt, M. (1978). Cognitive integration and referential communication: Effects of information quality and quantity in message decoding. *Organizational Behavior and Human Performance, 22,* 417–430; Troutman, C. M., & Shanteau, J. (1977). Inferences based on nondiagnostic information. *Organizational Behavior and Human Performance, 19,* 43–55.

14. O'Reilly, C. A., III. (1980). Individuals and information overload in organizations: Is more necessarily better? *Academy of Management Journal, 23,* 684–696.

15. Feldman, M. S., & March, J. G. (1981). Information in organizations as signal and symbol. *Administrative Science Quarterly, 26,* 171–186.

16. Kahneman et al, 1982; Tversky, A., & Kahneman, D. (1976). Judgment under uncertainty: Heuristics and biases. *Science, 185,* 1124–1131.

17. Northcraft, G. B., & Neale, M. A. (1987). Experts, amateurs, and real estate: An anchoring-and-adjustment perspective on property pricing decisions. *Organizational Behavior and Human Decision Processes, 39,* 84–97.

18. Simonson, I., & Nye, P. (1992). The effect of accountability on susceptibility to decision errors. *Organizational Behavior and Human Decision Processes, 51,* 416–446.

19. Simon, H. A. (1957). *Models of man.* New York: Wiley; Cyert, R. M., & March, J. G. (1963). *A behavioral theory of the firm.* Englewood Cliffs, NJ: Prentice-Hall. For an example, see Bower, J., & Zi-Lei, Q. (1992). Satisficing when buying information. *Organizational Behavior and Human Decision Processes, 51,* 471–481.

20. Bazerman, 1990, pp. 1–2.

21. Kahneman, D., & Tversky, A. (1979). Prospect theory: An analysis of decision under risk. *Econometrica, 47,* 263–291.

22. Whyte, 1991.

23. Sitkin, S. B., & Pablo, A. L. (1992). Conceptualizing the determinants of risk behavior. *Academy of Management Review, 17,* 9–38.

24. MacCrimmon, K. R., & Wehrung, D. A. (1986). *Taking risks: The management of uncertainty.* New York: The Free Press.

25. For a detailed treatment and other perspectives, see Northcraft, G. B., & Wolf, G. (1984). Dollars, sense, and sunk costs: A life cycle model of resource allocation decisions. *Academy of Management Review, 9,* 225–234.

26. Brockner, J. (1992). The escalation of commitment to a failing course of action: Toward theoretical progress. *Academy of Management Review, 17,* 39–61; Staw, B. M., & Ross, J. (1987). Understanding escalation situations: Antecedents, prototypes, and solutions. *Research on Organizational Behavior, 9,* 39–78.

27. Staw, B. M. (1981). The escalation of commitment to a course of action. *Academy of Management Review, 6,* 577–587. For the limitations on this view, see Knight, P. A. (1984). Heroism versus competence: Competing explanations for the effects of experimenting and consistent management. *Organizational Behavior and Human Performance, 33,* 307–322.

28. Arkes, H. R., & Blumer, C. (1985). The psychology of sunk cost. *Organizational Behavior and Human Decision Processes, 35,* 124–140.

29. Whyte, G. (1986). Escalating commitment to a course of action: A reinterpretation. *Academy of Management Review, 11,* 311–321.

30. Simonson & Nye, 1992; White, 1991; Simonson, I., & Staw, B. M. (1992). Deescalation strategies: A comparison of techniques for reducing commitment to losing courses of action. *Journal of Applied Psychology, 77,* 419–426.

31. Whyte, G. (1993). Escalating commitment in individual and group decision making: A prospect theory approach. *Organizational Behavior and Human Decision Processes, 54,* 430–455.

32. Hawkins, S. A., & Hastie, R. (1990). Hindsight: Biased judgments of past events after outcomes are known. *Psychological Bulletin, 107,* 311–327.

33. Greenwald, A. G. (1980). The totalitarian ego: Fabrication and revision of personal history. *American Psychologist, 35,* 603–618.

34. Mitchell, T. R., & Beach, L. R. (1977). Expectancy theory, decision theory, and occupational preference and choice. M. F. Kaplan & S. Schwartz (Eds.), *Human judgment and decision processes in applied settings.* New York: Academic Press.

35. Pinfield, L. T. (1986). A field evaluation of perspectives on organizational decision making. *Administrative Science Quarterly, 31,* 365–388.

36. Nutt, P. C. (1989). *Making tough decisions.* San Francisco: Jossey-Bass.

37. Lord, R. G., & Maher, K. J. (1990). Alternative information-processing models and their implications for theory, research, and practice. *Academy of Management Review, 15,* 9–28.

38. Shaw, M. E. (1981). *Group dynamics* (3rd ed.). New York: McGraw-Hill, p. 78.

39. Hill, G. W. (1982). Group versus individual performance: Are n+1 heads better than one? *Psychological Bulletin, 91,* 517–539.

40. Shaw, 1981; Davis, J. H. (1969). *Group performance.* Reading, MA: Addison-Wesley; Libby, R., Trotman, K. T., & Zimmer, I. (1987). Member variation, recognition of expertise, and group performance. *Journal of Applied Psychology, 72,* 81–87.

41. Janis, I. L. (1972). *Victims of groupthink.* Boston: Houghton Mifflin.

42. Aldag, R. J., & Fuller, S. R. (1993) Beyond fiasco: A reappraisal of the groupthink phenomenon and a new model of group decision processes. *Psychological Bulletin, 113,* 533–552; McCauley, C. (1989). The nature of social influence in groupthink: Compliance and internalization. *Journal of Personality and Social Psychology, 57,* 250–260. For another view of causes, see Whyte, G. F. (1989). Groupthink reconsidered. *Academy of Management Review, 14,* 40–56.

43. Janis, 1972.

44. Moorhead, G., Ference, R., & Neck, C. P. (1991). Group decision fiascoes continue: Space shuttle Challenger and a revised groupthing framework. *Human Relations,* 539–550.

45. This is my analysis. The data cited is from Capers & Lipton, 1993.

46. Stoner, J. A. F. (1961). *A comparison of individual and group decisions involving risk.* Unpublished Master's thesis. School of Industrial Management, Massachusetts Institute of Technology.

47. Lamm, H., & Myers, D. G. (1978). Group-induced polarization of attitudes and behavior. In L. Berkowitz (Ed.), *Advances in experimental social psychology* (Vol. 11). New York: Academic Press.

48. Isenberg, D. J. (1986). Group polarization: A critical review and meta-analysis. *Journal of Personality and Social Psychology, 50,* 1141–1151.

49. Maier, N. R. F. (1973). *Psychology in industrial organizations* (4th ed.). Boston: Houghton Mifflin; Maier, N. R. F. (1970). *Problem solving and creativity in individuals and groups.* Belmont, CA: Brooks/Cole.

50. Tjosvold, D. (1985). Implications of controversy research for management. *Journal of Management, 11*(3), 21–37.

51. Schwenk, C. R. (1984). Devil's advocacy in managerial decision-making. *Journal of Management Studies, 21,* 153–168. For a study, see Schwenk, C., & Valacich, J. S. (1994). Effects of devil's advocacy and dialectical inquiry on individuals versus groups. *Organizational Behavior and Human Decision Processes, 59,* 210–222.

52. Osborn, A. F. (1957). *Applied imagination.* New York: Scribners.

53. See for example Madsen, D. B., & Finger, J. R., Jr. (1978). Comparison of a written feedback procedure, group brainstorming, and individual brainstorming. *Journal of Applied Psychology, 63,* 120–123.

54. Delbecq, A. L., Van de Ven, A. H., & Gustafson, D. H. (1975). *Group techniques for program planning.* Glenview, IL: Scott, Foresman, p. 8.

55. Delbecq et al., 1975.

56. DeLorenzo, M. (1993, August 9). Delphi survey on autos turns out to be no oracle. *Autoweek*, p. 14.

57. Gallupe, R. B., Dennis, A. R., Cooper, W. H., Valacich, J. S., Bastianutti, L. M., & Nunamaker, J. F., Jr. (1992). Electronic brainstorming and group size. *Academy of Management Journal, 35*, 350–369. See also Dennis, A. R., & Valacich, J. S. (1993). Computer brainstorms: More heads are better than one. *Journal of Applied Psychology, 78*, 531–537.

58. The following relies on Kiesler, S., & Sproull, L. (1992). Group decision making and communication technology. *Organizational Behavior and Human Decision Processes, 52*, 96–123.

59. McGuire, T., Kiesler, S., & Siegel, J. (1987). Group and computer-mediated discussion effects in risk decision making. *Journal of Personality and Social Psychology, 52*, 917–930.

Chapter 13

1. Excerpted from Eichenwald, K. (1994, May 29). He told. He suffered. Now he's a hero. *New York Times*, Section 3, pp. 1,4.

2. Brass, D. J., & Burkhardt, M. E. (1993). Potential power and power use: An investigation of structure and behavior. *Academy of Management Journal, 36*, 441–470.

3. These descriptions of bases of power were developed by French, J. R. P., Jr., & Raven, B. (1959). In D. Cartwright (Ed.), *Studies in social power*. Ann Arbor, MI: Institute for Social Research.

4. Rahim, M. A. (1989). Relationships of leader power to compliance and satisfaction with supervision: Evidence from a national sample of managers. *Journal of Management, 15*, 545–556; Tannenbaum, A. S. (1974). *Hierarchy in organizations*. San Francisco: Jossey-Bass.

5. Vaughn, R. (1975). *The spoiled system*. New York: Charterhouse, p. 19.

6. Podsakoff, P. M., & Schriesheim, C. A. (1985). Field studies of French and Raven's bases of power: Critique, reanalysis, and suggestions for future research. *Psychological Bulletin, 97*, 387–411.

7. Heider, F. (1958). *The psychology of interpersonal relations*. New York: Wiley.

8. Grossman, L. M. (1993, March 10). As secretaries buy more for their firms, marketers regard them with reverence. *Wall Street Journal*, pp. B1, B8.

9. Podsakoff & Schriesheim, 1985.

10. Ragins, B. R., & Sundstrom, E. (1990). Gender and perceived power in manager-subordinate dyads. *Journal of Occupational Psychology, 63*, 273–287.

11. The following is based upon Kanter, R. M. (1977). *Men and women of the corporation*. New York: Basic Books. For additional treatment see Pfeffer, J. (1992). *Managing with power: Politics and influence in organizations*. Boston: Harvard Business School Press.

12. See Thomas, K. W., & Velthouse, B. A. (1990). Cognitive elements of empowerment: An "interpretative" model of intrinsic task motivation. *Academy of Management Review, 15*, 668–681; Conger, J. A., & Kanungo, R. N. (1988). The empowerment process: Integrating theory and practice. *Academy of Management Review, 13*, 471–482.

13. Tichy, N. M., & Sherman, S. (1993, June). Walking the talk at GE. *Training and Development*, 26–35.

14. Bowen, D. E., & Lawler, E. E., III. (1992, Spring). The empowerment of service workers: What, why, how, and when. *Sloan Management Review*, 31–39.

15. Kipnis, D., Schmidt, S. M., & Wilkinson, I. (1980). Intraorganizational influence tactics: Explorations in getting one's way. *Journal of Applied Psychology, 65*, 440–452; Kipnis, D., & Schmidt, S. M. (1988). Upward-influence

styles: Relationship with performance evaluation, salary, and stress. *Administrative Science Quarterly, 33*, 528–542.

16. See Brass & Burkhardt, 1993.

17. Kipnis et al., 1980. See also Keys, B., & Case, T. (1990, November). How to become an influential manager. *Academy of Management Executive*, 38–51.

18. Kipnis & Schmidt, 1988.

19. Kipnis, D. (1976). *The powerholders*. Chicago: University of Chicago Press.

20. McClelland, D. C. (1975). *Power: The inner experience*. New York: Irvington.

21. Winter, D. G. (1988). The power motive in women—and men. *Journal of Personality and Social Psychology, 54*, 510–519.

22. McClelland, D. C., & Burnham, D. H. (1976, March–April). Power is the great motivator. *Harvard Business Review*, 100–110.

23. Ashforth, B. E. (1989). The experience of powerlessness in organizations. *Organizational Behavior and Human Decision Processes, 43*, 207–242.

24. Salancik, G. R., & Pfeffer, J. (1977, Winter). Who gets power—and how they hold on to it: A strategic contingency model of power. *Organizational Dynamics*, 3–21.

25. Salancik, G. R., & Pfeffer, J. (1974). The bases and use of power in organizational decision making: The case of a university. *Administrative Science Quarterly, 19*, 453–473. Also see Pfeffer, J., & Moore, W. L. (1980). Power in university budgeting: A replication and extension. *Administrative Science Quarterly, 25*, 637–653. For conditions under which the power thesis breaks down, see Schick, A. G., Birch, J. B., & Tripp, R. E. (1986). Authority and power in university decision making: The case of a university personnel budget. *Canadian Journal of Administrative Sciences, 3*, 41–64.

26. Hickson, D. J., Hinings, C. R., Lee, C. A., Schneck, R. E., & Pennings, J. M. (1971). A strategic contingency theory of intraorganizational power. *Administrative Science Quarterly, 16*, 216–229; for support of this theory, see Hinings, C. R., Hickson, D. J., Pennings, J. M., & Schneck, R. E. (1974). Structural conditions of intraorganizational power. *Administrative Science Quarterly, 19*, 22–44; Saunders, C. S., & Scamell, R. (1982). Intraorganizational distributions of power: Replication research. *Academy of Management Journal, 25*, 192–200; Hambrick, D. C. (1981). Environment, strategy, and power within top management teams. *Administrative Science Quarterly, 26*, 253–276.

27. Kanter, 1977, pp. 170–171.

28. Hickson et al., 1971; Hinings et al., 1974.

29. Hickson et al., 1971; Hinings et al., 1974; Saunders & Scamell, 1982.

30. Kipnis, 1976, p. 159.

31. Nulty, P. (1989, July 31). The hot demand for new scientists. *Fortune*, 155–163.

32. Boeker, W. (1989). The development and institutionalization of subunit power in organizations. *Administrative Science Quarterly, 34*, 388–410.

33. Nord, W. R., & Tucker, S. (1987). *Implementing routine and radical innovations*. Lexington, MA: Lexington Books.

34. Mayes, B. T., & Allen, R. W. (1977). Toward a definition of organizational politics. *Academy of Management Review, 2*, 672–678.

35. Porter, L. W., Allen, R. W., & Angle, H. L. (1981). The politics of upward influence in organizations. *Research in Organizational Behavior, 3*, 109–149.

36. Schein, V. E., (1977). Individual power and political behaviors in organizations: An inadequately explored reality. *Academy of Management Review, 2*, 64–72, p. 67.

37. Porter et al., 1981; Madison, D. L., Allen, R. W., Porter, L. W., Renwick, P. A., & Mayes, B. T. (1980). Organizational

politics: An exploration of managers' perceptions. *Human Relations, 33,* 79–100.

38. Geis, F., & Christie, R. (1970). Overview of experimental research. In R. Christie & F. Geis (Eds.), *Studies in Machiavellianism.* New York: Academic Press.

39. Geis & Christie, 1970.

40. Brass, D. J. (1984). Being in the right place: A structural analysis of individual influence in an organization. *Administrative Science Quarterly, 29,* 518–539.

41. Kotter, J. P. (1982). *The general managers.* New York: Free Press.

42. Shellenbarger, S. (1993, December 16). I'm still here! Home workers worry they're invisible. *Wall Street Journal,* pp. B1, B4.

43. What follows relies on Ashforth, B. E., & Lee, R. T. (1990). Defensive behavior in organizations: A preliminary model. *Human Relations, 43,* 621–648.

44. Boeker, W. (1992). Power and managerial dismissal: Scapegoating at the top. *Administrative Science Quarterly, 37,* 400–421.

45. This draws loosely on Glenn, J. R., Jr. (1986). *Ethics in decision making.* New York: Wiley.

46. For reviews, see Tsalikis, J., & Fritzsche, D. J. (1989). Business ethics: A literature review with a focus on marketing ethics. *Journal of Business Ethics, 8,* 695–743; Trevino, L. K. (1986). Ethical decision making in organizations: A person-situation interactionist model. *Academy of Management Review, 11,* 601–617.

47. Tyson, T. (1992). Does believing that everyone else is less ethical have an impact on work behavior? *Journal of Business Ethics, 11,* 707–717.

48. Tsalikis & Fritzsche, 1989.

49. Tsalikis & Fritzsche, 1989.

50. Bird, F., & Waters, J. A. (1987). The nature of managerial moral standards. *Journal of Business Ethics, 6,* 1–13.

51. Trevino, L. K., Sutton, C. D., & Woodman, R. W. (1985). *Effects of reinforcement contingencies and cognitive moral development on ethical decision-making behavior: An experiment.* Paper presented at the annual meeting of the Academy of Management, San Diego; Hegarty, W. H., & Sims, H. P., Jr. (1978). Some determinants of unethical behavior: An experiment. *Journal of Applied Psychology, 63,* 451–457.

52. Levine, D. B. (1990, May 21). The inside story of an inside trader. *Fortune,* 80–89, p. 82.

53. Grover, S. L. (1993). Why profesionals lie: The impact of professional role conflict on reporting accuracy. *Organizational Behavior and Human Decision Processes, 55,* 251–272.

54. Staw, B. M., & Szwajkowski, E. W. (1975). The scarcity-munificence component of organizational environments and the commission of illegal acts. *Administrative Science Quarterly, 20,* 345–354.

55. Sonnenfeld, J., & Lawrence, P. R. (1989). Why do companies succumb to price fixing? In K. R. Andrew (Ed.), *Ethics in practice: Managing the moral corporation.* Boston: Harvard Business School Press.

56. Hegarty & Sims, 1978; Hegarty, W. H., & Sims, H. P., Jr. (1979). Organizational philosophy, policies, and objectives related to unethical decision behavior: A laboratory experiment. *Journal of Applied Psychology, 64,* 331–338.

57. Colby, A., & Kohlberg, L. (1987). *The measurement of moral judgment. Volume 1: Theoretical foundations and research validation.* Cambridge: Cambridge University Press; also see Trevino, 1986, and Grover, 1993.

58. Victor, B., & Cullen, J. B. (1988). The organizational bases of ethical work climates. *Administrative Science Quarterly, 33,* 101–125.

59. Baucus, M. S., & Near, J. P. (1991). Can illegal corporate behavior be predicted? An event history analysis. *Academy of Management Journal, 34,* 9–16.

60. Baucus & Near, 1991.

61. Sonnenfeld & Lawrence, 1989. See also Hosmer, L. T. (1987). The institutionalization of unethical behavior. *Journal of Business Ethics, 6,* 439–447.

62. Morgan, R. B. (1993). Self- and co-worker perceptions of ethics and their relationships to leadership and salary. *Academy of Management Journal, 36,* 200–214.

63. Luthans, F., Hodgetts, R. M., & Rosenkrantz, S. A. (1988). *Real managers.* Cambridge, MA: Ballinger.

64. Kelly, C. M. (1987, Summer). The interrelationship of ethics and power in today's organizations. *Organizational Dynamics,* 4–18, p. 14.

65. This draws on Waters, J. A., & Bird, F. (1988). *A note on what a well-educated manager should be able to do with respect to moral issues in management.* Unpublished manuscript.

66. See Jones, T. M. (1991). Ethical decision making by individuals in organizations: An issue-contingent model. *Academy of Management Journal, 16,* 366–395.

67. Harringotn, S. J. (1991, February). What corporate America is teaching about ethics. *Academy of Management Executive,* 21–30, p. 24.

68. Weber, J. (1990). Measuring the impact of teaching ethics to future managers: A review, assessment, and recommendations. *Journal of Business Ethics, 9,* 183–190.

Chapter 14

1. Adapted from Hill, G. C., & Yamada, K. (1992, December 9). Motorola illustrates how an aged giant can remain vibrant. *Wall Street Journal,* pp. A1, A18.

2. Kolb, D. M., & Bartunek, J. M. (Eds.) (1992). *Hidden conflict in organizations: Uncovering behind-the-scenes disputes.* Newbury Park, CA: Sage.

3. This section relies partly on Walton, R. E., & Dutton, J. M. (1969). The management of interdepartmental conflict: A model and review. *Administrative Science Quarterly, 14,* 73–84.

4. Kramer, R. M. (1991). Intergroup relations and organizational dilemmas: The role of categorization processes. *Research in Organizational Behavior, 13,* 191–228; Messick, D. M., & Mackie, D. M. (1989). Intergroup relations. *Annual Review of Psychology, 40,* 45–81; Ashforth, B. E., & Mael, F. (1989). Social identity theory and the organization. *Academy of Management Review, 14,* 20–39.

5. Johns, G. (1994). Absenteeism estimates by employees and managers: Divergent perspectives and self-serving perceptions. *Journal of Applied Psychology, 79,* 229–239.

6. See Whyte, W. F. (1948). *Human relations in the restaurant industry.* New York: McGraw-Hill.

7. Moritz, M. (1984). *The little kingdom: The private story of Apple Computer.* New York: Morrow, pp. 246–247.

8. Thomas, K. W. (1992). Conflict and negotiation in organizations. In M. D. Dunnette & L. M. Hough (Eds.), *Handbook of industrial and organizational psychology* (2nd ed., Vol. 3). Palo Alto, CA: Consulting Psychologists Press.

9. Sellers, P. (1991, November 18). A boring brand can be beautiful. *Fortune,* 169–179, p. 179.

10. Moore, M. L., Nichol, V. W., & McHugh, P. P. (1992). Review of no-fault absenteeism cases taken to arbitration, 1980–1989: A rights and responsibilities analysis. *Employee Rights and Responsibilities Journal, 5,* 29–48; Scott, K. D., & Taylor, G. S. (1983, September). An analysis of absenteeism cases taken to arbitration: 1975–1981. *The Arbitration Journal,* 61–70.

11. See Wilder, D. A. (1986). Social categorization: Implications for creation and reduction of intergroup bias. *Advances in Experimental Social Psychology, 19,* 291–349; Sherif, M. (1966). *In common predicament: Social psychology of intergroup conflict and cooperation.* Boston: Houghton Mifflin; Blake, R. R., Shepard, M. A., & Mouton, J. S. (1964). *Managing intergroup conflict in industry.* Houston: Gulf.

12. Thomas, 1992.

13. Seabrook, J. (1994, January 10). E-mail from Bill. *The New Yorker,* 48–61, p. 52.

14. Johnson, D. W., Maruyama, G., Johnson, R., Nelson, D., & Skon, L. (1981). Effects of cooperative and individualistic goal structures on achievement: A meta-analysis. *Psychological Bulletin, 89,* 47–62. See also Tjosvold, D. (1991). *The conflict-positive organization.* Reading, MA: Addison-Wesley.

15. Magnet, M. (1994, February 21). The new golden rule of business. *Fortune,* 60–64.

16. Tjosvold, D., Dann, V., & Wong, C. (1992). Managing conflict between departments to serve customers. *Human Relations, 45,* 1035–1054.

17. Neale, M. A., & Bazerman, M. H. (1992, August). Negotiating rationally: The power and impact of the negotiator's frame. *Academy of Management Executive,* 42–51, p. 42.

18. Wall, J. A., Jr. (1985). *Negotiation: Theory and practice.* Glenview, IL: Scott, Foresman.

19. Walton, R. E., & McKerzie, R. B. (1991). *A behavioral theory of labor negotiations* (2nd ed.). Ithaca, NY: ILR Press.

20. What follows draws on Pruitt, D. G. (1981). *Negotiation behavior.* New York: Academic Press.

21. Wall, J. A., Jr., & Blum, M. (1991). Negotiations. *Journal of Management, 17,* 273–303.

22. Wall & Blum, 1991.

23. Bazerman, M. H. (1990). *Judgment in managerial decision making* (2nd ed.). New York: Wiley.

24. The following draws on Bazerman, M. H., & Neale, M. A. (1992). *Negotiating rationally.* New York: The Free Press.

25. Sherif, 1966; Hunger, J. D., & Stern, L. W. (1976). An assessment of the functionality of the superordinate goal in reducing conflict. *Academy of Management Journal, 19,* 591–605.

26. Pruitt, 1981; Kressel, K., & Pruitt, D. G. (1989). *Mediation research.* San Francisco: Jossey-Bass.

27. Kressel & Pruitt, 1989.

28. Wall & Blum, 1991; Pruitt, 1981.

29. Scott & Taylor, 1983. See also Moore et al., 1992.

30. Fisher, R., & Ury, W. (1983). *Getting to yes: Negotiating agreement without giving in.* New York: Penguin.

31. Wall & Blum, 1991.

32. Robbins, S. P. (1974). *Managing organizational conflict: A nontraditional approach.* Englewood, Cliffs, NJ: Prentice-Hall, p. 20.

33. Brown, L. D. (1983). *Managing conflict at organizational interfaces.* Reading, MA: Addison-Wesley.

34. Robbins, 1974; also see Brown, 1983.

35. This model has much in common with many contemporary models of work stress. For a comprehensive summary see Kahn, R. L., & Byosiere, P. (1992). Stress in organizations. In M. D. Dunnette & L. M. Hough (Eds.), *Handbook of industrial and organizational psychology* (2nd ed., Vol. 3). Palo Alto, CA: Consulting Psychologists Press.

36. McGrath, J. E. (1970). A conceptual formulation for research on stress. In J. E. McGrath (Ed.), *Social and psychological factors in stress.* New York: Holt, Rinehart, Winston.

37. Roth, S., & Cohen, L. J. (1986). Approach, avoidance, and coping with stress. *American Psychologist, 41,* 813–819.

38. Kahn & Byosiere, 1992. For a recent study see Spector, P. E., & O'Connell, B. J. (1994). The contribution of personality traits, negative affectivity, locus of control, and Type A to the subsequent reports of job stressors and job strains. *Journal of Occupational and Organizational Psychology, 67,* 1–11.

39. Friedman, M., & Rosenman, R. (1974). *Type A Behavior and your heart.* New York: Knopf.

40. Chesney, M. A., & Rosenman, R. (1980). Type A behavior in the work setting. In C. L. Cooper and R. Payne (Eds.), *Current concerns in occupational stress.* Chichester, England: Wiley. For a typical study see Jamal, M., & Baba, V. V. (1991). Type A behavior, its prevalence and consequences among women nurses: An empirical examination. *Human Relations, 44,* 1213–1228.

41. Matthews, K. A. (1982). Psychological perspectives on the Type A behavior pattern. *Psychological Bulletin, 91,* 293–323.

42. Booth-Kewley, S., & Friedman, H. S. (1987). Psychological predictors of heart disease: A quantitative review. *Psychological Bulletin, 101,* 343–362; Williams, R. (1989). *The trusting heart: Great news about Type A behavior.* New York: Random House; Ganster, D. C., Schaubroeck, J., Sime, W. E., & Mayes, B. T. (1991). The nomological validity of the Type A personality among employed adults. *Journal of Applied Psychology, 76,* 143–168.

43. Chesney & Rosenman, 1980.

44. Parasuraman, S., & Alutto, J. A. (1981). An examination of the organizational antecedents of stressors at work. *Academy of Management Journal, 24,* 48–67.

45. Mintzberg, H. (1973). *The nature of managerial work.* New York: Harper & Row.

46. Rogers, E. M., & Larsen, J. K. (1984). *Silicon valley fever: Growth of a high-technology culture.* New York: Basic Books, p. 138.

47. An excellent review of managerial stressors can be found in Marshall, J., & Cooper, C. L. (1979). *Executives under pressure.* New York: Praeger.

48. Terkel, S. (1972). *Working.* New York: Avon, pp. 50–51.

49. Karasek, R. A., Jr. (1979). Job demands, job decision latitude, and mental strain: Implications for job redesign. *Administrative Science Quarterly, 24,* 285–308. Also see Fox, M. L., Dwyer, D. J., & Ganster, D. C. (1993). Effects of stressful job demands and control on physiological and attitudinal outcomes in a hospital setting. *Academy of Management Journal, 36,* 289–318.

50. Maslach, C., & Jackson, S. E. (1984). Burnout in organizational settings. In S. Oskamp (Ed.), *Applied social psychology annual* (Vol. 5). Beverly Hills, CA: Sage, p. 134.

51. Cordes, C. L., & Dougherty, T. W. (1993). A review and integration of research on job burnout. *Academy of Management Review, 18,* 621–656. For a comprehensive study see Lee, R. T., & Ashforth, B. E. (1993). A longitudinal study of burnout among supervisors and managers: Comparisons of the Leiter and Maslach (1988) and Golembiewski et al. (1986) models. *Organizational Behavior and Human Decision Processes, 54,* 369–398.

52. For a study of burnout among police personnel, see Burke, R. J., & Deszca, E. (1986). Correlates of psychological burnout phases among police officers. *Human Relations, 39,* 487–501.

53. See Pines, A. M., & Aronson, E. (1981). *Burnout: From tedium to personal growth.* New York: The Free Press.

54. Jackson, S. E., & Schuler, R. S. (1985). Meta-analysis and conceptual critique of research on role ambiguity and conflict in work settings. *Organizational Behavior and Human Decision Processes, 36,* 16–78. For a critique of some of this research, see Fineman, S., & Payne, R. (1981). Role stress—

A methodological trap? *Journal of Occupational Behaviour,* 2, 51–64.

55. Jamal, M. (1984). Job stress and job performance controversy: An empirical assessment. *Organizational Behavior and Human Performance, 33,* 1–21; Motowidlo, S. J., Packard, J. S., & Manning, M. R. (1986). Occupational stress: Its causes and consequences for job performance. *Journal of Applied Psychology, 71,* 618–629.

56. Katz, D., & Kahn, R. L. (1978). The social psychology of organizations (2nd ed.). New York: Wiley; Farrell, D., & Stamm, L. (1988). Meta-analysis of the correlates of employee absence. *Human Relations, 41,* 211–227.

57. Gupta, N., & Beehr, T. A. (1979). Job stress and employee behavior. *Organizational Behavior and Human Performance, 23,* 373–387; Jackson & Schuler, 1985.

58. See Kemery, E. R., Bedian, A. G., Mossholder, K. W., & Touliatos, J. (1985). Outcomes of role stress: A multisample constructive replication. *Academy of Management Journal, 28,* 363–375; Parasuraman, S., & Alutto, J. A. (1984). Sources and outcomes of stress in organizational settings: Toward the development of a structural model. *Academy of Management Journal, 27,* 330–350.

59. Beehr, T. A., & Newman, J. E. (1978). Job stress, employee health, and organizational effectiveness: A facet analysis, model, and literature review. *Personnel Psychology, 32,* 665–699; Kahn & Byosiere, 1992.

60. Beehr & Newman, 1978. For a later review and a strong critique of this work, see Fried, Y., Rowland, K. M., & Ferris, G. R. (1984). The physiological measurement of work stress: A critique. *Personnel Psychology, 37,* 583–615. See also Fried, Y. (1989). The future of physiological assessments in work situations. In C. L. Cooper & R. Payne (Eds.), *Causes, coping, and consequences of stress at work.* Chichester, England: Wiley & Sons.

61. Cooper, C. L., Mallinger, M., & Kahn, R. (1978). Identifying sources of occupational stress among dentists. *Journal of Occupational Psychology, 61,* 163–174. See also DiMatteo, M. R, Shugars, D. A., & Hays, R. D. (1993). Occupational stress, life stess and mental health among dentists. *Journal of Occupational and Organizational Psychology, 66,* 153–162.

62. Cohen, S., & Williamson, G. M. (1991). Stress and infectious disease in humans. *Psychological Bulletin, 109,* 5–24.

63. Schweiger, D. M., & DeNisi, A. S. (1991). Communication with employees following a merger: A longitudinal field experiment. *Academy of Management Journal, 34,* 110–135.

64. Wall, T. D., & Clegg, C. W. (1981). A longitudinal field study of group work redesign. *Journal of Occupational Behaviour, 2,* 31–49.

65. Cohen, S., & Wills, T. A. (1985). Stress, social support, and the buffering hypothesis. *Psychological Bulletin, 98,* 310–357; Kahn & Byosiere, 1992.

66. This section relies on a *Wall Street Journal* special section on Work & Family (1993, June 21) and Shellenbarger, S. (1993, June 29). Work & family. *Wall Street Journal,* p. B1.

67. Ivancevich, J. M., Matteson, M. T., Freedman, S. M., & Phillips, J. S. (1990). Worksite stress management interventions. *American Psychologist, 45,* 252–261; Murphy, L. R. (1984). Occupational stress management: A review and appraisal. *Journal of Occupational Psychology, 57,* 1–15.

68. Ivancevich et al., 1990; Murphy, 1984.

69. See Johnston, D. C., Mayes, B. T., Sime, W. E., & Tharp, G. D. (1982). Managing occupational stress: A field experiment. *Journal of Applied Psychology, 67,* 533–542.

70. Gebhardt, D. L., & Crump, C. E. (1990). Employee fitness and wellness programs in the workplace. *American Psychologist, 45,* 262–272; Jex, S. M. (1991). The psychological benefits of exercise in work settings: A review,

critique, and dispositional model. *Work and Stress, 5,* 133–147; Falkenberg, L. E. (1987). Employee fitness programs: Their impact on the employee and the organization. *Academy of Management Review, 12,* 511–522.

Chapter 15

1. Sources include Huey, J. (1994, February 21). The new postheroic leadership. *Fortune,* 42–50; Corbett, B. (1989, September). A system of non-management. *Canadian,* 14–20; Ritzer, G. (1993). *The McDonaldization of society.* Thousand Oaks, CA: Pine Forge Press.

2. Mintzberg, H. (1979). *The structuring of organizations.* Englewood Cliffs, NJ: Prentice-Hall.

3. Lawrence, P. R., & Lorsch, J. W. (1969). *Organization and environment: Managing differentiation and integration.* Homewood, IL: Irwin.

4. For an extended treatment of the role of interdependence between departments, see McCann, J., & Galbraith, J. R. (1981). Interdepartmental relations. In P. C. Nystrom & W. H. Starbuck (Eds.), *Handbook of organizational design* (Vol. 2). Oxford, England: Oxford University Press.

5. For a comparison of functional and product departmentation, see McCann & Galbraith, 1981; Walker, A. H., & Lorsch, J. W. (1968, November–December). Organizational choice: Product vs. function. *Harvard Business Review,* 129–138.

6. See Davis, S. M., & Lawrence, P. M. (1977). *Matrix.* Reading, MA: Addison-Wesley.

7. Contemporary treatment of these forms of departmentation can be found in Daft, R. L. (1992). *Organization theory and design* (4th ed.). St. Paul, MN: West; Robey, D. (1991). *Designing organizations* (3rd ed.). Homewood, IL: Irwin.

8. Mintzberg, 1979.

9. See Hall, R. H. (1962). Intraorganizational structural variation: Application of the bureaucratic model. *Administrative Science Quarterly, 7,* 295–308.

10. Lawrence & Lorsch, 1969.

11. Galbraith, J. R. (1977). *Organization design.* Reading, MA: Addison-Wesley.

12. See Birnbaum, P. H. (1981). Integration and specialization in academic research. *Academy of Management Journal, 24,* 487–503.

13. This discussion relies on Galbraith, 1977.

14. Kilborn, P. T. (1993, September 5). The workplace, after the deluge. *New York Times,* pp. 3–1, 3–4.

15. Lawrence & Lorsch, 1969.

16. Galbraith, 1977.

17. These definitions of structural variables are common. However, there is considerable disagreement about how some should be measured. See Walton, E. J. (1981). The comparison of measures of organizational structure. *Academy of Management Review, 6,* 155–160.

18. Research on these hypotheses is sparse and not always in agreement. See Dewar, R. D., & Simet, D. P. (1981). A level specific prediction of spans of control examining effects of size, technology, and specialization. *Academy of Management Journal, 24,* 5–24; Van Fleet, D. D. (1983). Span of management research and issues. *Academy of Management Journal, 26,* 546–552.

19. Treece, J. B. (1990, April 9). Here comes GM's Saturn. *Business Week,* 56–62.

20. For a study, see Hetherington, R. W. (1991). The effects of formalization on departments of a multi-hospital system. *Journal of Management Studies, 28,* 103–141.

21. Daft, R. L. (1989). *Organization theory and design* (3rd ed.). St. Paul, MN: West, p. 179.

22. *60 Minutes*, October 17, 1993.

23. Mintzberg, 1979, p. 182.

24. Ritzer, 1993.

25. Personal communication with Food Lion's Brian Peace, April and May 1995.

26. Deutschman, A. (1994, May 2). How H-P continues to grow and grow. *Fortune*, 90–100, p. 98.

27. Daft, 1992.

28. For comprehensive reviews, see Berger, C. J., & Cummings, L. L. (1979). Organizational structure, attitudes, and behavior. *Research in Organizational Behavior, 1*, 169–208; Porter, L. W., & Lawler, E. E., III. (1965). Properties of organizational structure in relation to job attitudes and job behavior. *Psychological Bulletin, 81*, 23–51.

29. Porter & Lawler, 1965.

30. Crozier, M. (1964). *The bureaucratic phenomenon*. Chicago: University of Chicago Press.

31. Merton, R. K. (1957). *Social theory and social structure* (rev. ed.). New York: Free Press.

32. Chonko, L. B. (1982). The relationship of span of control to sales representatives' experienced role conflict and role ambiguity. *Academy of Management Journal, 25*, 452–456.

33. Oldham, G. R., & Hackman, J. R. (1981). Relationships between organizational structure and employee reactions: Comparing alternative frameworks. *Administrative Science Quarterly, 26*, 66–83.

34. The terms *mechanistic* and *organic* (to follow) were first used by Burns, T., & Stalker, G. M. (1961). *The management of innovation*. London: Tavistock Publications. For a relevant study, see Courtright, J. A., Fairhurst, G. T., & Rogers, L. E. (1989). Interaction patterns in organic and mechanistic systems. *Academy of Management Journal, 32*, 773–802.

35. Snow, C. C., Miles, R. E., & Coleman, H. J., Jr. (1992, Winter). Managing 21st century network organizations. *Organizational Dynamics*, 5–19; Miles, R. E., & Snow, C. C. (1992, Summer). Causes of failure in network organizations. *California Management Review*, 53–72.

36. Miles & Snow, 1992.

37. For a good general review of size research see Bluedorn, A. C. (1993). Pilgrim's progress: Trends and convergence in research on organizational size and environments. *Journal of Management, 19*, 163–191.

38. Much of this research was stimulated by Blau, P. M. (1970). A theory of differentiation in organizations. *American Sociological Review, 35*, 201–218. For a review and test, see Cullen, J. B., Anderson, K. S., & Baker, D. D. (1986). Blau's theory of structural differentiation revisited: A theory of structural change or scale? *Academy of Management Journal, 29*, 203–229.

39. Dewar, R., & Hage, J. (1978). Size, technology, complexity, and structural differentiation: Toward a theoretical synthesis. *Administrative Science Quarterly, 23*, 111–136; Marsh, R. M., & Mannari, H. (1981). Technology and size as determinants of the organizational structure of Japanese factories. *Administrative Science Quarterly, 26*, 33–57.

40. Mansfield, R. (1973). Bureaucracy and centralization: An examination of organizational structure. *Administrative Science Quarterly, 18*, 77–88; Hage, J., & Aiken, M. (1967). Relationship of centralization to other structural properties. *Administrative Science Quarterly, 12*, 79–91.

41. Robey, 1991, p. 103.

42. DeWitt, R. L. (1993). The structural consequences of downsizing. *Organization Science, 4*, 30–40.

43. Freeman, S. J., & Cameron, K. S. (1993). Organizational downsizing: A convergence and reorientation framework. *Organization Science, 4*, 10–29.

44. Cascio, W. F. (1993, February). Downsizing: what do we know? What have we learned? *Academy of Management Executive*, 95–104.

45. DeWitt, 1993; Sutton, R. L., & D'Aunno, T. (1989). Decreasing organizational size: Untangling the effects of money and people. *Academy of Management Review, 14*, 194–212.

46. Cascio, 1993.

47. Brockner, J. (1988). The effects of work layoffs on survivors: Research, theory, and practice. *Research in Organizational Behavior, 10*, 213–255.

48. Child, J. (1984). *Organization: A guide to problems and practice*. London: Harper & Row.

49. Presidential Commission. (1986). *The report on the space shuttle Challenger accident*. Washington, DC: U.S. Government Printing Office.

50. Pugh, D. (1979, Winter). Effective coordination in organizations. *Advanced Management Journal*, 28–35.

Chapter 16

1. Sources include: Staff. (1994, October 17). Will it work this time? *Autoweek*, 4–5; Bennet, J. (1994, March 29). Saturn, GM's big hope, is taking its first lumps. *New York Times*, pp. A1, A12; Woodruff, J. (1992, August 17). Saturn. *Business Week*, 86–91; Treece, J. B. (1990, April 9). Here comes GM's Saturn. *Business Week*, 56–62; Taylor, A., III. (1988, August 1). Back to the future at Saturn. *Fortune*, 63–69; Fisher, A. B. (1985, November 11). Behind the hype at GM's Saturn. *Fortune*, 34–49.

2. Katz, D., & Kahn, R. L. (1978). *The social psychology of organizations* (2nd ed.). New York: Wiley.

3. This list relies upon Duncan, R. (1972). Characteristics of organization environments and perceived environmental uncertainty. *Administrative Science Quarterly, 17*, 313–327.

4. See Khandwalla, P. (1981). Properties of competing organizations. In P. C. Nystrom & W. H. Starbuck (Eds.), *Handbook of organization design* (Vol. 1). Oxford: Oxford University Press.

5. Zachary, G. P. (1994). Consolidation sweeps the software industry; small firms imperiled. *Wall Street Journal*, pp. A1, A6.

6. Kirkpatrick, D. (1990, February 12). Environmentalism: The new crusade. *Fortune*, 44–55.

7. Connolly, T., Conlon, E. J., & Deutsch, S. J. (1980). Organizational effectiveness: A multiple-constituency approach. *Academy of Management Review, 5*, 211–217.

8. Fisher, 1985.

9. Duncan, 1972; Just how to measure uncertainty has provoked controversy. See Milliken, F. J. (1987). Three types of perceived uncertainty about the environment: State, effect, and response uncertainty. *Academy of Management Review, 12*, 133–143; Downey, H. K., & Ireland, R. D. (1979). Quantitative versus qualitative: Environmental assessment in organizational studies. *Administrative Science Quarterly, 24*, 630–637.

10. Duncan, 1972; Tung, R. L. (1979). Dimensions of organizational environments: An exploratory study of their impact on organization structure. *Academy of Management Journal, 22*, 672–693. For contrary evidence, see Downey, H., Hellriegel, D., & Slocum, J. (1975). Environmental uncertainty: The construct and its application. *Administrative Science Quarterly, 20*, 613–629.

11. See also Leblebici, H., & Salancik, G. R. (1981). Effects of environmental uncertainty on information and decision processes in banks. *Administrative Science Quarterly, 26*, 578–596.

12. See At-Twaijri, M. I. A., & Montanari, J. R. (1987). The impact of context and choice on the boundary-spanning process: An empirical extension. *Human Relations, 40,* 783–798.

13. Pfeffer, J., & Salancik, G. R. (1978). *The external control of organizations: A resource dependence perspective.* New York: Harper & Row; Yasai-Ardekani, M. (1989). Effects of environmental scarcity and munificence on the relationship of context to organizational structure. *Academy of Management Journal, 32,* 131–156.

14. Castrogiovanni, G. J., (1991). Environmental munificence: A theoretical assessment. *Academy of Management Review, 16,* 542–565.

15. Pfeffer & Salancik, 1978.

16. Boyd, B. K., Dess, G. G., & Rasheed, A. M. A. (1993). Divergence between archival and perceptual measures of the environment: Causes and consequences. *Academy of Management Review, 18,* 204–226.

17. For an analog, see Miller, D., Dröge, C., & Toulouse, J. M. (1988). Strategic process and content as mediators between organizational context and structure. *Academy of Management Journal, 31,* 544–569.

18. Miles, R. C., & Snow, C. C. (1978). *Organizational strategy, structure, and process.* New York: McGraw-Hill.

19. Lawrence, P. R., & Lorsch, J. W. (1967). *Organization and environment: Managing differentiation and integration.* Homewood, IL: Irwin. For a follow-up study, see Lorsch, J. W., & Morse, J. J. (1974). *Organizations and their members: A contingency approach.* New York: Harper & Row.

20. For a review, see Miner, J. B. (1982). *Theories of organizational structure and process.* Chicago: Dryden.

21. Kupfer, A. (1989, December 18). An outsider fires up a railroad. *Fortune,* 133–146, p. 138.

22. Frederickson, J. W. (1986). The strategic decision process and organizational structure. *Academy of Management Review, 11,* 280–297.

23. Romme, A. G. L. (1990). Vertical integration as organizational strategy formation. *Organization Studies, 11,* 239–260.

24. Chatterjee, S., Lubatkin, M., & Schoenecker, T. (1992). Vertical strategies and market structure: A systematic risk analysis. *Organization Science, 3,* 138–156; D'Aveni, R. A., & Ilinitch, A. Y. (1992). Complex patterns of vertical integration in the forest products industry: Systematic and bankruptcy risks. *Academy of Management Journal, 35,* 596–625.

25. Pfeffer & Salancik, 1978; Hill, C. W. L., & Hoskisson, R. E. (1987). Strategy and structure in the multiproduct firm. *Academy of Management Review, 12,* 331–341; Lubatkin, M., & O'Neill, H. M. (1987). Merger strategies and capital market risk. *Academy of Management Journal, 30,* 665–684.

26. Kanter, R. M. (1989, August). Becoming PALS: Pooling, allying, and linking across companies. *Academy of Management Executive,* 183–193.

27. Burtt, D. N. (1989, July–August). Managing suppliers up to speed. *Harvard Business Review,* 127–135.

28. Parkhe, A. (1993). Strategic alliance structuring: A game theoretic and transaction cost examination of interfirm cooperation. *Academy of Management Journal, 36,* 794–829. See also Ring, P. S., & Van de Ven, A. H. (1994). Developmental processes of cooperative interorganizational relationships. *Academy of Management Review, 19,* 90–118.

29. Parkhe, A. (1993). Partner nationality and the structure-performance relationship in strategic alliances. *Organizational Science, 4,* 301–324.

30. Schoorman, F. D., Bazerman, M. H., & Atkin, R. S. (1981). Interlocking directorates: A strategy for reducing environmental uncertainty. *Academy of Management Review, 6,* 243–251, p. 244. For a recent study, see Haunschild, P. R.,

(1993). Interorganizational imitation: The impact of interlocks on corporate acquisition activity. *Administrative Science Quarterly, 38,* 564–592.

31. Schoorman et al., 1981.

32. See Oliver, C. (1991). Strategic responses to institutional processes. *Academy of Management Review, 16,* 145–179; Davis, G. F., & Powell, W. W. (1992). Organization-environment relations. In M. D. Dunnette & L. M. Hough (Eds.), *Handbook of industrial and organizational psychology* (2nd ed., Vol. 3). Palo Alto, CA: Consulting Psychologists Press.

33. Rousseau, D. M. (1979). Assessment of technology in organizations: Closed versus open systems approaches. *Academy of Management Review, 4,* 531–542.

34. Child, J. (1972). Organizational structure, environment and performance: The role of strategic choice. *Sociology, 6,* 2–22.

35. Rousseau, 1979; Gillsepie, D. F., & Mileti, D. S. (1977). Technology and the study of organizations: An overview and appraisal. *Academy of Management Review, 2,* 7–16.

36. Perrow, C. A. (1967). A framework for the comparative analysis of organizations. *American Sociological Review, 32,* 194–208.

37. Thompson, J. D. (1967). *Organizations in action.* New York: McGraw-Hill.

38. Thompson, 1967, p. 17.

39. Miller, C. C., Glick, W. H., Wang, Y. D., & Huber, G. P. (1991). Understanding technology-structure relationships: Theory development and meta-analystic throery testing. *Academy of Management Journal, 34,* 370–399. For information on measurement, see Withey, M., Daft, R. L., & Cooper, W. H. (1983). Measures of Perrow's work unit technology: An empirical assessment and a new scale. *Academy of Management Journal, 26,* 45–63.

40. Cheng, J. L. C. (1983). Interdependence and coordination in organizations: A role-system analysis. *Academy of Management Journal, 26,* 156–162.

41. Van de Ven, A. H., Delbecq, A. L., & Koenig, R., Jr. (1976). Determinants of coordination modes within organizations. *American Sociological Review, 41,* 322–338.

42. Woodward, J. (1965). *Industrial organization: Theory and practice.* London: Oxford University Press.

43. Mintzberg, H. (1979). *The structuring of organizations.* Englewood Cliffs, NJ: Prentice-Hall.

44. Marsh, R. M., & Mannari, H. (1981). Technology and size as determinants of the organizational structure of Japanese factories. *Administrative Science Quarterly, 26,* 33–57; Keller, R. T., Slocum, J. W., Jr., & Susman, G. J. (1974). Uncertainty and type of management in continuous process organizations. *Academy of Management Journal, 17,* 56–68; Zwerman, W. L. (1970). *New perspectives on organizational theory.* Westport, CT: Greenwood.

45. Singh, J. V. (1986). Technology, size, and organizational structure: A reexamination of the Okayma study data. *Academy of Management Journal, 29,* 800–812.

46. Walton, R. E. (1989). *Up and running: Integrating information technology and the organization.* Boston: Harvard Business School Press.

47. Child, J. (1987). Organizational design for advanced manufacturing technology. In T. D. Wall, C. W. Clegg, & N. J. Kemp (Eds.), *The human side of advanced manufacturing technology.* Sussex, England: Wiley.

48. From the Massachusetts Institute of Technology report *Made in America,* as excerpted in *Fortune,* May 22, 1989, p. 94.

49. This table draws in part on Nemetz, P. L., & Fry, L. W. (1988). Flexible manufacturing organizations: Implications for strategy formulation and organization design. *Academy of Management Review, 13,* 627–638; Main, J. (1990, May 21). Manufacturing the right way. *Fortune,* 54–64;

Jelinek, M., & Goldhar, J. D. (1986). Maximizing strategic opportunities in implementing advanced manufacturing systems. In D. D. Davis (Ed.), *Managing technological innovation*. San Francisco: Jossey-Bass.

50. Cummings, T. G., & Blumberg, M. (1987). Advanced manufacturing technology and work design. In Wall et al.

51. Zammuto, R. F., & O'Connor, E. J. (1992). Gaining advanced manufacturing technologies' benefits: The roles of organizational design and culture. *Academy of Management Review, 17*, 701–728; Nemetz & Fry, 1988; Child, 1987. The following draws upon Child.

52. Dean, J. W., Jr., Yook, S. J., & Susman, G. I. (1992). Advanced manufacturing technology and organizational structure: Empowerment or subordination? *Organization Science, 3*, 203–229.

53. Wall, T. D., & Davids, K. (1992). Shopfloor work organization and advanced manufacturing technology. *International Review of Industrial and Organizational Psychology, 7*, 363–398.

54. Wall, T. D., Jackson, P. R., & Davids, K. (1992). Operator work design and robotics systems performance: A serendipitous field study. *Journal of Applied Psychology, 77*, 353–362; Wall, T. D., Corbett, J. M., Martin, R., Clegg, C. W., & Jackson, P. R. (1990). Advanced manufacturing technology, work design, and performance: A change study. *Journal of Applied Psychology, 75*, 691–697.

55. Cummings & Blumberg, 1987; Blumberg, M., & Gerwin, D. (1984). Coping with advanced manufacturing technology. *Journal of Occupational Behaviour, 5*, 113–130.

56. From an unpublished paper by C. A. Voss, cited in Child, 1987.

57. Long, R. J. (1987). *New office information technology: Human and managerial implications*. London: Croom Helm.

58. Long, 1987.

59. Dopson, S., & Stewart, R. (1990). What is happening to middle management? *British Journal of Management, 1*, 3–16.

60. See Bloomfield, B. P., & Coombs, R. (1992). Information technology, control and power: The centralization and decentralization debate revisited. *Journal of Management Studies, 29*, 459–484.

61. Huber, G. P. (1990). A theory of the effects of advanced information technologies on organizational design, intelligence, and decision making. *Academy of Management Review, 15*, 47–71.

62. Long, 1987; Hughes, K. D. (1989). Office automation: A review of the literature. *Relations Industrielles, 44*, 654–679.

63. Long, 1987.

64. Medcof, J. W. (1989). The effect and extent of use of information technology and job of the user upon task characteristics. *Human Relations, 42*, 23–41.

65. Long, 1987.

Chapter 17

1. Vignette prepared by Ayman Ghali. Sources include Maska, B. S. (1993, August 2). Born to be real. *Industry Week*, 14–18; Slutsker, B. (1993, May 24). Hog wild. *Forbes*, 45–46; Reid, P. C. (1990). *Well made in America*. New York: McGraw-Hill. Quote from Boyd, M. (1993, September). Harley-Davidson Motor Company. *Incentive*, 26–31.

2. Nadler, D. A., & Tushman, M. L. (1989, August). Organizational frame bending: Principles for managing reorientation. *Academy of Management Executive*, 194–203.

3. This list relies mostly on Leavitt, H. (1965). Applied organizational changes in industry: Structural, technological, and humanistic approaches. In J. G. March (Ed.), *Handbook of organizations*. Chicago: Rand McNally.

4. Lewin, K. (1951). *Field theory in social science*. New York: Harper & Row.

5. See Howard, A. (Ed.) (1994). *Diagnosis for organizational change: Methods and models*. New York: Guilford; Levinson, H. (1972). *Organizational diagnosis*. Cambridge, MA: Harvard University Press.

6. The first five reasons are from Kotter, J. P., & Schlesinger, L. A. (1979, March–April). Choosing strategies for change. *Harvard Business Review*, 106–114.

7. Frank, R. (1994, May 23). As UPS tries to deliver more to its customers, labor problems grow. *Wall Street Journal*, pp. A1, A8.

8. Tichy, N. M., & Devanna, M. A. (1986). *The transformational leader*. New York: Wiley.

9. The following relies partly on Kotter & Schlesinger, 1979.

10. For reviews, see Macy, B. A., Peterson, M. F., & Norton, L. W. (1989). A test of participation theory in a work redesign field setting: Degree of participation and comparison site contrasts. *Human Relations, 42*, 1095–1165; Filley, A. C., House, R. J., & Kerr, S. (1976). *Managerial process and organizational behavior* (2nd ed.). Glenview, IL: Scott, Foresman.

11. Strebel, P. (1994, Winter). Choosing the right change path. *California Management Review*, 29–51, pp. 41, 42.

12. Tichy & Devanna, 1986; Yukl, G. A. (1989). *Leadership in organizations* (2nd ed.). Englewood Cliffs, NJ: Prentice-Hall.

13. Catalanello, R. F., & Kirkpatrick, D. L. (1968). Evaluating training programs—The state of the art. *Training and Development Journal, 22*, 2–9.

14. Goodman, P. S., Bazerman, M., & Conlon, E. (1980). Institutionalization of planned organizational change. *Research in Organizational Behavior, 2*, 215–246.

15. Goodman et al., 1980.

16. For a review of various definitions, see Porras, J. I., & Robertson, P. J. (1992). Organizational development: Theory, practice, and research. In M.D. Dunnette & L. M. Hough (Eds.), *Handbook of industrial and organizational psychology* (2nd ed., Vol. 3). Palo Alto, CA: Consulting Psychologists Press.

17. French, W. L., & Bell, C. H., Jr. (1973). *Organization development*. Englewood Cliffs, NJ: Prentice-Hall.

18. Beer, M., & Walton, E. (1990). Developing the competitive organization: Interventions and strategies. *American Psychologist, 45*, 154–161; Beer, M. (1980). Organization change and development: A systems view. Glenview, IL: Scott, Foresman.

19. Beer, M. (1976). The technology of organizational development. In M. D. Dunnette (Ed.) *Handbook of industrial, and organizational psychology*. Chicago: Rand McNally. See also Dyer, W. (1987). *Team building: Issues and alternatives* (2nd ed.). Reading, MA: Addison-Wesley.

20. Bell, C. H., Jr., & Rosenzweig, J. (1978). Highlights of an organizational improvement program in a city government. In W. L. French, C. H. Bell, Jr., & R. A. Zawacki (Eds.), *Organization development: Theory, practice, and research*. Dallas: Business Publications.

21. Wakeley, J. H., & Shaw, M. E. (1965). Management training: An integrated approach. *Training Directors Journal, 19*, 2–13.

22. Bennet, J. (1993, June 23). Team spirit is new message at Olds. *New York Times*, pp. D1, D15; Tarr, S. C., & Juliano, W. J. (1992, October). Leading a team through downsizing. *HRMagazine*, 91–100.

23. This description relies upon Beer, 1980; Huse, E. F., & Cummings, T. G. (1985). *Organization development and change* (3rd ed.). St. Paul, MN: West; Nadler, D. A. (1977). *Feedback and organization development: Using data-based methods*. Reading, MA: Addison-Wesley.

24. Taylor, J., & Bowers, D. (1972). *Survey of organizations: A machine-scored standardized questionnaire instrument.* Ann Arbor, MI: Center for Research on Utilization of Scientific Knowledge, Institute for Social Research, University of Michigan.

25. Read, W. H. (1991, January). Gathering opinion on-line. *HRMagazine,* 51–53.

26. Johnson, R. H., Ryan, A. M., & Schmit, M. (1994). *Employee attitudes and branch performance at Ford Motor Credit.* Presentation at the annual conference of the Society for Industrial and Organizational Psychology, Nashville, Tennessee.

27. For an eclectic view of current TQM concerns, see the Total Quality Special Issue of the July 1994 *Academy of Management Review.*

28. Deming, W. E. (1986). *Out of the crisis.* Cambridge, MA: Massachusetts Institute of Technology Center for Advanced Engineering Study; Crosby, P. B. (1979). *Quality is free.* New York: McGraw-Hill; Juran J. M. (1992). *Juran on quality by design.* New York: Free Press.

29. Kinlaw, D.C. (1992). *Continuous improvement and measurement for total quality: A team-based approach.* San Diego: Pfeiffer.

30. Berry, L. L., Parasuraman, A., & Zeithaml, V. A. (1994, May). Improving service quality in America: Lessons learned. *Academy of Management Executive,* 32–45.

31. Kinlaw, 1992; Bounds, G., Yorks, L., Adams, M., & Ranney, G. (1994). *Beyond total quality management: Toward the emerging paradigm.* New York: McGraw-Hill.

32. Reeves, C. A., & Bednar, D. A. (1994). Defining quality: Alternatives and implications. *Academy of Management Review, 19,* 419-445.

33. Krishnan, R., Shani, A. B., Grant, R. M., & Baer, R. (1993, November). In search of quality improvement: Problems of design and implementation. *Academy of Management Executive,* 7–20.

34. Krishnan et al., 1993.

35. Hammer, M., & Champy, J. (1993). *Reengineering the corporation: A manifesto for business revolution.* New York: HarperBusiness; Stewart, T. A. (1993, August 23). Reengineering: The hot new management tool. *Fortune,* 41–48; Greengard, S. (1993, December). Reengineering: Out of the rubble. *Personnel Journal,* 48B–48O.

36. Hammer & Champy, 1993.

37. Hammer & Champy, 1993.

38. Teng, J. T. C., Grover, V., & Fiedler, K. D. (1994, Spring). Business process reengineering: Charting a strategic path for the information age. *California Management Review,* 9–31.

39. Hammer & Champy, 1993; Teng et al., 1994.

40. Examples from Greengard, 1993 and Teng et al., 1994.

41. See Dumaine, B. (1989, February 14). How managers can succeed through speed. *Fortune,* 54–59.

42. Hall, G., Rosenthal, J., & Wade, J. (1993, November–December). How to make reengineering really work. *Harvard Business Review,* 119–131.

43. Neuman, G. A., Edwards, J. E., & Raju, N. S. (1989). Organizational development interventions: A meta-analysis of their effects on satisfaction and other attitudes. *Personnel Psychology, 42,* 461–489; Guzzo, R. A., Jette, R. D., & Katzell, R. A. (1985). The effects of psychologically based intervention programs on worker productivity: A meta-analysis. *Personnel Psychology, 38,* 275–291.

44. For a meta-analytic summary, see Robertson, P. J., Roberts, D. R., & Porras, J. I. (1993). Dynamics of planned organizational change: Assessing support for a theoretical model. *Academy of Management Journal, 36,* 619–634. See also Macy, B. A., & Izumi, H. (1993). Organizational change, design, and work innovation: A meta-analysis of 131 North American field studies—1961–1991. *Research in Organizational Change and Development, 7,* 235–313.

45. Porras & Robertson, 1992; Nicholas, J. M., & Katz, M. (1985). Research methods and reporting practices in organization development: A review and some guidelines. *Academy of Management Review, 10,* 737–749.

46. White, S. E., & Mitchell, T. R. (1976). Organization development: A review of research content and research design. *Academy of Management Review, 1,* 57–73.

47. For an attempt to provide some order to this subject see Wolfe, R. A. (1994). Organizational innovation: Review, critique and suggested research directions. *Journal of Management Studies, 31,* 405–431.

48. Tushman, M., & Nadler, D. (1986, Spring). Organizing for innovation. *California Management Review,* 74–92.

49. Frost, P. J., & Egri, C. P. (1991). The political process of innovation. *Research in Organizational Behavior, 13,* 229–295.

50. This three-part view of creativity is from Amabile, T. M. (1988). A model of creativity and innovation in organizations. *Research in Organizational Behavior, 10,* 123–167. See also Woodman, R. W., Sawyer, J. E., & Griffin, R. W. (1993). Toward a theory of organizational creativity. *Academy of Management Review, 18,* 293–321.

51. Reid, 1990.

52. Basadur, M. (1994). Managing the creative process in organizations. In M. A. Runco (Ed.), *Problem finding, problem solving, and creativity.* Norwood, NJ: Ablex; Kabanoff, B., & Rossiter, J. R. (1994). Recent developments in applied creativity. *International Review of Industrial and Organizational Psychology, 9,* 283–324.

53. Galbraith, J. R. (1982, Winter). Designing the innovating organization. *Organizational Dynamics,* 4–25.

54. Howell, J. M., & Higgins, C. A. (1990). Champions of technological innovation. *Administrative Science Quarterly, 35,* 317–341.

55. Orlicke, J. (1985). *The Progressive Corporation (B).* Boston: Harvard Business School.

56. Cohen, W. M., & Levinthal, D. A. (1990). Absorptive capacity: A new perspective on learning and innovation. *Administrative Science Quarterly, 35,* 128–152.

57. Tushman, M. L., & Scanlan, T. J. (1981). Characteristics and external orientations of boundary spanning individuals. *Academy of Management Journal, 24,* 83–98; Tushman, M. L., & Scanlan, T. J. (1981). Boundary spanning individuals: Their role in information transfer and their antecedents. *Academy of Management Journal, 24,* 289–305.

58. Keller, R. T., & Holland, W. E. (1983). Communicators and innovators in research and development organizations. *Academy of Management Journal, 26,* 742–749.

59. Kanter, R. M. (1988). When a thousand flowers bloom: Structural, collective, and social conditions for innovation in organization. *Research in Organizational Behavior, 10,* 169–211.

60. Kanter, 1988; Nord, W. R., & Tucker, S. (1987). *Implementing routine and radical innovations.* Lexington, MA: Lexington Books; Damanpour, F. (1991). Organizational innovation: A meta-analysis of effects of determinants and moderators. *Academy of Management Journal, 34,* 555–590.

61. Nonaka, I. (1990, Spring). Redundant, overlapping organization: A Japanese approach to managing the innovation process. *California Management Review,* 27–38.

62. Sherman, S. P. (1984, October 15). Eight big masters of innovation. *Fortune,* 66–84, p. 72.

63. Tushman & Scanlan, 1981, pp. 289–305.

64. Keller & Holland, 1983.
65. Katz, R. (1982). The effects of group longevity on project communication and performance. *Administrative Science Quarterly, 27*, 81–104.
66. For a review, see Nord & Tucker, 1987. However, this prescription is controversial. For other views see Kanter, 1988 and Marcus A. A. (1988). Implementing externally induced innovations: A comparison of rule-bound and autonomous approaches. *Academy of Management Journal, 31*, 235–256.
67. Damanpour, 1991; Kanter, 1988.
68. Galbraith, 1982.
69. Peters, T. (1987). *Thriving on chaos*. New York: Knopf.
70. Amabile, 1988.
71. Galbraith, 1982.
72. Walton, R. E. (1975, Winter). The diffusion of new work structures: Explaining why success didn't take. *Organizational Dynamics*, 3–22.
73. Rogers, E. M. (1983). *Diffusion of innovations* (3rd ed.). New York: Free Press.

Chapter 18

1. Excerpted from Richman, L. S. (1994, May 16) How to get ahead in America. *Fortune*, p. 49.
2. Kanter, R. (1989). *When giants learn to dance: Mastering the challenge of strategy, management, and careers in the 1990s*. New York: Simon and Schuster; Lancaster, H. (1994, November 15). Managing your career: You, and only you, must stay in charge of your employability. *Wall Street Journal*, p. B1.
3. Pfeffer, J. (1994). *Competitive advantage through people*. Cambridge, MA: Harvard University Press; Galbraith, J., & Lawler, E., III. (1993). *Organizing for the future: The new logic for managing complex organizations*. San Francisco: Jossey-Bass; Quinn, J. B. (1992). *Intelligent enterprise: A knowledge and service based paradigm for industry*. New York: Free Press; Peters, T. (1992). *Liberation Management: Necessary disorganization for the nanosecond nineties*. New York: Alfred A. Knopf.
4. Naisbitt, J., & Aburdeen, P. (1990). *Megatrends 2000: Ten new directions for the 1990s*. New York: Morrow.
5. Carnevale, A. P., & Goldstein, H. (1990). Schooling and training for work in America: An overview. In L. Ferman, M. Hoyman, J. Cutcher-Gershenfeld, & E. Savoie (Eds.), *New developments in worker training: A legacy for the 1990s*. Madison, WI: Industrial Relations Research Association; Kanter, R. (1989). Careers and the wealth of nations. In M. Arthur, D. Hall, & B. Lawrence (Eds.), *Handbook of career theory*. Cambridge: Cambridge University Press.
6. Arthur, Hall, & Lawrence, 1989; Bird, A. (1994). Careers as repositories of knowledge: A new perspective on boundaryless careers. *Journal of Organizational Behavior, 15*, 325–344; Hall, D. (1976). *Careers in organizations*. Pacific Palisades, CA: Goodyear.
7. Van Maanen, J., & Schein, E. (1977). Career development. In J. R. Hackman & J.L. Suttle (Eds.), *Improving life at work: Behavioral science approaches to organizational change*. Glenview, IL: Scott, Foresman.
8. Van Maanen, J., & Barley, S. (1984). Occupational communities: Culture and control in organizations. *Research in Organizational Behavior, 6*, 287–365.
9. Holland, J. (1985). *Making vocational choices* (2nd ed.). Englewood Cliffs, NJ: Prentice-Hall; Holland, J., & Gottfredson, G. (1992). Studies of the hexagonal model: An evaluation (or, the perils of stalking the perfect hexagon). *Journal of Vocational Behavior, 40*, 158–170.

10. Strong, E., Jr., & Campbell, D. (1981). *Strong-Campbell interest inventory*. Stanford, CA: Stanford University Press.
11. Schein, E. (1975). How "career anchors" hold executives to their career paths. *Personnel, 52*, 11–24; Schein, E. (1978). *Career dynamics*. Reading, MA: Addison-Wesley.
12. Neugarten, B. (1968). Adult personality: Toward a psychology of the life cycle. In B. Neugarten (Ed.), *Middle age and aging*. Chicago: University of Chicago Press.
13. Levinson, D. J., Darrow, C. N., Klein, E. B., Levinson, M. H., & McKee, B. (1978). *The seasons of a man's life*. New York: Knopf. For research support, see Ornstein, S., Cron, W. L., & Slocum, J. W., Jr. (1989). Life stage versus career stage: A comparative test of the theories of Levinson and Super. *Journal of Organizational Behavior, 10*, 117–133.
14. Gersick, K. (1994). Life structure and maturation across the life span. Presentation at the Careers Division Pre-Conference Workshop, Academy of Management Conference, Dallas, TX; Daniel Levinson's manuscript presenting the women's study that follows up his men's life structure study was completed two weeks before his death. At this time publication plans have not been finalized, but it may be published as *Seasons of a woman's life* in 1995 with Dr. Levinson as the first author.
15. Kram, K. & Isabella, L. (1985). Mentoring alternatives: The role of peer relationships in career development. *Academy of Management Journal, 28*, 110–132.
16. Hall, D. T., & Hall, D. T. (1966). The socialization of managers: Effects of expectations of performance. *Administrative Science Quarterly, 11*, 207–223.
17. Rosenbaum, J. E. (1984). *Career mobility in a corporate hierarchy*. New York: Academic Press.
18. Mivis, P., & Hall, D. (1994). Psychological success and the boundaryless career. *Journal of Organizational Behavior, 15*, 365–380.
19. Boyett, J., & Conn, H. (1991). *Workplace 2000: The revolution reshaping American business*. New York: Penguin Books; Hall, D. (1991). Business restructuring and strategic human resource development. In P. Doeringer (Ed.), *Turbulence in the American workplace*. Oxford: Oxford University Press.
20. Ornstein, S., & Isabella, L. (1993). Making sense of careers: A review 1989–1992. *Journal of Management, 19*, 243–267; Russell, J. (1991). Career development interventions in organizations. *Journal of Vocational Behavior, 38*, 237–287; Hall, 1991.
21. Gutteridge, T., Liebowitz, Z., & Shore, J. (1993). *Organization career development: Benchmarks for building a world-class workforce*. San Francisco: Jossey-Bass Publishers.
22. Von Glinow, M. A., Driver, M., Brousseau, K., & Prince, J. B. (1983). The design of career-oriented human resource systems. *Academy of Management Review, 8*, 23–32.
23. Gutteridge et al., 1993.
24. Gutteridge et al., 1993.
25. Scandura, T. (1992). Mentorship and career mobility: An empirical investigation. *Journal of Organizational Behavior, 13*, 169–174; Fagenson, E. (1989). The mentor advantage: Perceived career/job experiences of protégés versus nonprotégés. *Journal of Organizational Behavior, 10*, 309–320; Fagenson, E. (1988). The power of a mentor: Protégés and nonprotégés' perceptions of their own power in organizations. *Group and Organization Studies, 13*, 182–192; Dalton, G. W., Thompson, P. H., & Price, R. (1977, Summer). The four stages of professional careers—A new look at performance by professionals. *Organizational Dynamics*, 19–42.
26. Dreher, G., & Ash, R. (1990). A comparative study of mentoring among men and women in managerial, professional

and technical positions. *Journal of Applied Psychology, 75,* 539–546; Whitely, W., Dougherty, T., & Dreher, G. (1991). Relationship of career mentoring and socioeconomic origin to managers' and professionals' early career progress. *Academy of Management Journal, 34,* 331–351.

27. Kram, K. (1985). *Mentoring.* Glenview, IL: Scott, Foresman.

28. Murray, M. (1991). *Beyond the myths and magic of mentoring: How to facilitate an effective mentoring program.* San Francisco, CA: Jossey-Bass; Lawrie, J. (1987). How to establish a mentoring program. *Training & Development Journal, 41*(3), 25–27.

29. Chao, G., Walz, P., & Gardner, P. (1992). Formal and informal mentorships: A comparison on mentoring functions and contrast with nonmentored counterparts. *Personnel Psychology, 45,* 619–636; Noe, R. (1988). An investigation of the determinants of successful assigned mentoring relationships. *Personnel Psychology, 41,* 457–479.

30. Kram & Isabella, 1985. Mentoring alternatives: The role of peer relationships in career development. *Academy of Management Journal, 28,* 110–132.

31. Ragins, B. R. (1989). Barriers to mentoring: The female manager's dilemma. *Human Relations, 42,* 1–22; Noe, R. A. (1988). Women and mentoring: A review and research agenda. *Academy of Management Review, 13,* 65–78; Cox, T., Jr. (1993). *Cultural diversity in organizations: Theory, research, & practice.* San Francisco: Berrett-Koehler.

32. Ragins, B., & McFarlin, D. (1990). Perceptions of mentor roles in cross-gender mentoring relationships. *Journal of Vocational Behavior, 37,* 321–339.

33. Morrison, A., White, R., & Van Velsor, E. (1987). *Breaking the glass ceiling: Can women reach the top of America's largest corporations?* Reading, MA: Addison-Wesley; Burke, R., & McKeen, C. (1990). Mentoring in organizations: Implications for women. *Journal of Business Ethics, 9,* 317–322; Dennett, D. (1985, November). Risks, mentoring helps women to the top. *APA Monitor,* p. 26.

34. Noe, R. (1988). An investigation of the determinants of successful assigned mentoring relationships. *Personnel Psychology, 41,* 457–479; Cox, 1993.

35. Morrison et al., 1987.

36. Cox, 1993; Ibarra, H. (1993). Personal networks of women and minorities in management. *Academy of Management Review, 18,* 56–87.

37. Nkomo, S., & Cox, T. (1989). Gender differences in the upward mobility of black managers: Double whammy or double advantage? *Sex Roles, 21,* 825–839.

38. Thomas, D. (1989). Mentoring and irrationality: The role of racial taboos. *Human Resource Management, 28,* 279–290; Thomas, D. (1990). The impact of race on managers' experiences of developmental relationships: An intraorganizational study. *Journal of Organizational Behavior, 11,* 479–492.

39. Greenhaus, J. (1993). *Career Management.* Chicago: Dryden Press; Wiersma, U. (1994). A taxonomy of behavioral strategies for coping with work-home role conflict. *Human Relations, 47,* 211–221; Wiersma, U., & Berg, P. (1991). Work-home role conflict, family climate, and domestic responsibilities among men and women. *Journal of Applied Social Psychology, 21,* 1207–1217; Granrose, C., Parasuraman, S., & Greenhaus, J. (1992). A proposed

model of support provided by two-earner couples. *Human Relations, 45,* 1367–1393.

40. Wiersma, 1994; Hall, D. (1972). A model of coping with role conflict: The role behavior of college-educated women. *Administrative Science Quarterly, 17,* 471–489; Hall, D., & Hall, F. (1972). *The two-career couple.* Reading, MA: Addison-Wesley; Greenhaus, J., & Beutell, N. (1985). Sources of conflict between work and family roles. *Academy of Management Review, 10,* 76–88; Sekran, U. (1986). *Dual-career families.* San Francisco: Jossey-Bass.

41. Werbel, J., & Roberg, A. (1993). A role theory perspective on career decision making. *Research in Personnel and Human Resources Management, 7,* 227–258.

42. Hall et al., 1979; Greenhaus, 1993.

43. Granrose et al., 1993; Aneshensel, C (1986). Marital and employment role strain, social support, and depression among adult women. In S. Hobfoll (Ed.), *Stress, social support and women.* New York: Hemisphere; Bird, G. W., & Bird, G. (1986). Strategies for reducing role strain among dual career couples. *International Journal of Sociology of the Family, 16,* 83–94; Ladewig, B., & McGee, G. (1986). Occupational commitment, a supportive family environment, and marital adjustment. *Journal of Marriage and the Family, 48,* 821–829.

44. Greenhaus, 1993.

45. Greenhaus & Beutell, 1985.

46. Schwartz, F. (1989). Management women and the new facts of life. *Harvard Business Review, 67,* 65–82; Hall, D., & Richter, J. (1990, August). Career gridlock: baby boomers hit the wall. *Academy of Management Executive, 7–22.*

47. Nicholson, N., & West, M. (1988). *Managerial job change: Men and women in transition.* Cambridge: Cambridge University Press; Nicholson, N. (1984). A theory of work role transitions. *Administrative Science Quarterly, 25,* 172–192.

48. Doeringer, (1991); Peters, 1992; Handy, C. (1989). *The age of unreason.* Boston: Harvard University Press; Drucker, P. (1989). *The new realities: In government and politics, in economics and business, in society and work view.* New York: Harper & Row.

49. Waterman, R., Jr., Waterman, J., & Collard, B. (1994, July–August). Toward a career-resilient workforce. *Harvard Business Review,* 87–95.

50. Huey, J. (1994, June 27). Waking up to the new economy. *Fortune,* 36–46; O'Reilly, B. (1994, June 13). The new deal: What companies and employees owe one another. *Fortune,* 44–52.

51. Hirsch, P. (1987). *Pack Your Own Parachute: How to survive mergers, takeovers, and other corporate disasters.* Reading, MA: Addison-Wesley; Henkoff, R. (1993, July 12) Winning the new career game. *Fortune,* 46–49; Kanter, 1989.

52. Labich, K. (1991, November 18). Take control of your career. *Fortune,* 87–96.

53. Waterman et al., 1994.

54. Waterman et al., 1994.

55. Waterman et al., 1994.

56. Galbraith et al., 1993.

CREDITS

Literary Credits

9 From: *The Montreal Gazette*, November 7, 1992, p. 12. Reprinted by permission of The Associated Press.

12 From: D. Ulrich & D. Lake, "Organizational Capability: Creating Competitive Advantage," *Academy of Management Executive*, February 1991, pp. 77–92. Reprinted by permission.

19 Adapted from Hill, L. A., 1992, *Becoming A Manager: Mastery of a New Identity*. Boston: Harvard Business School Press, 1992.

26 Disguised case prepared by Stephen Tax under the direction of Professor Walter Good, University of Manitoba. From D. Stoffman, "Caught in a Bind," *Canadian Business*, November 1987, pp. 173–174. Reprinted by permission of Daniel Stoffman.

33 From: R. J. Wagner, T. T. Baldwin, and C. C. Roland, "Outdoor Training: Revolution or Fad?" Reprinted from (the) *Training and Development* (Journal). Copyright March 1991, the American Society for Training and Development. Reprinted with permission. All rights reserved.

45 From: J. J. Laabs, "Pearle Vision's Managers Think Like Entrepreneurs," *Personnel Journal*, January 1993, pp. 38–46. Reprinted by permission.

63 From: A. Farnham, "Mary Kay's Lessons in Leadership," *Fortune*, September 20, 1993, pp. 68–77. © 1993 Time, Inc. All rights reserved; and *Mary Kay on People Management*, Warner Books. Reprinted by permission of Warner Books, Inc.

66 Adapted from: Dan Todd in "Teaching Machines," by B. F. Skinner, *Scientific American*, November 1961, p. 96 (top). Copyright © 1961 by Scientific American, Inc. All rights reserved.

69 From: D. H. B. Welsh, F. Luthans, and S. M. Sommer, "Managing Russian Factory Workers: The Impact of US Based Behavioral and Participative Techniques," *Academy of Management Journal*, 1993, pp. 36, 58–79. Reprinted by permission.

73 From: S. Shellengbarger, "California Stays Rigid on Scheduling," *The Wall Street Journal*, October 13, 1993, p. B1. Reprinted by permission of The Wall Street Journal, © 1993 Dow Jones & Company, Inc. All Rights Reserved Worldwide.

83 From: P. Spector, "Development of the Work Locus of Control Scale," *Journal of Occupational Psychology*, 1988, Vol. 61, pp. 335–340. Reprinted by permission of the publisher and the author.

83 From: Hilgert/Schoen/Ling, *Cases & Experiential Exercises in Human Resource Management*, © 1990, pp. 65–68. Reprinted by permission of Prentice-Hall, Inc., Englewood Cliffs, NJ.

90 T. Cox, Jr., *Cultural Diversity in Organizations: Theory, Research, and Practice*. Berrett-Koehler, 1993, p. 119. Reprinted by permission.

95 From: E. F. Stone, D. L. and R. L. Dipboye, "Stigmas in Organizations: Race, Handicaps, and Physical Unattractiveness". In K. Kelley (ed.) *Issues, Theory, and Research in Industrial/Organizational Psychology*, pp. 419–420. Copyright Elsevier Science Publishers, B. V. Reprinted by permission.

97 Bank of Montreal Task Force on the Advancement of Women in the Bank, November Advancement of Women in the Bank. 1991 Report to Employees. Reprinted by permission of the Bank of Montreal.

104 From: T. H. Cox and S. Blake, "Managing Cultural Diversity: Implications for Organizational Competitiveness, *Academy of Management Executive*, August 1991, pp. 45–47. Reprinted by permission.

108 From: Staff, "Diversity Training Extends Beyond US," *The Wall Street Journal*, March 12, 1993, p. B1. Reprinted by permission of The Wall Street Journal, © 1993 Dow Jones & Company, Inc. All Rights Reserved Worldwide.

113 From: J. P. Campbell, M. D. Dunnette, E. E. Lawler, III, and K. E. Weick, Jr., *Managerial Behavior, Performance, and Effectiveness*, McGraw-Hill, Inc. 1970, p. 121. Reprinted by permission of McGraw-Hill, Inc.

117 Case prepared by Kathleen Solonika and Blake Ashforth. From J. Kelly, J. B. Prince, and B. Ashforth, *Organizational Behavior: Readings, Cases, and Exercises*, 2/e. Copyright © 1991 Prentice-Hall Canada, Inc. Reprinted by permission.

124 From: MOW International Research Team (1987) *The Meaning of Work*, p. 83. Reprinted by permission of Academic Press, Ltd., London, England.

126 Graph by author. Data from G. Hofstede, *Cultures and Organizations: Software of the Mind*. Copyright 1992 McGraw-Hill, Inc. Reprinted by permission of McGraw-Hill, Inc.

127 From: G. Hofstede, "The Cultural Relativity of the Quality of Life Concept," *Academy of Management Review*, 9, 389–398, p. 391, 1984. Reprinted by permission.

130 From: M. Forsberg, "Cultural Training Improves Relations With Asian Clients," *Personnel Journal*, May, 1993, pp. 79–89. Reprinted with permission.

131 From: N. J. Adler, and S. Bartholomew, "Managing Globally Competent People," *Academy of Management Executive*, August 1992, pp. 52–60. Reprinted by permission.

137 From: A. P. Goldstein and M. Sorcher,

332 From: S. Kerr, and J. M. Jermier, "Substitutes for Leadership: Their Meaning and Measurement," *Organizational Behavior and Human Performance*, 22, p. 378, 1978, Academic Press. Reprinted by permission.

336 From: *Leadership and Decision Making*, by Victor H. Vroom and Philip W. Yetton. © 1973 by University of Pittsburgh Press. Reprinted by permission of the publisher.

336 From: D. A. Nadler, M. L. Tushman, and N. G. Hatvany, *Managing Organizations: Readings and Cases*. Copyright © 1982, HarperCollins College Publishers.

341 From: J. R. Wilkie, "Computer Links Erode Hierarchical Nature of Workplace Culture," *The Wall Street Journal*, December 9, 1993, pp. A1, A7. Reprinted by permission of The Wall Street Journal, © 1993 Dow Jones & Company, Inc. All Rights Reserved Worldwide.

343 Figure from *Management*, Second Edition by William F. Glueck. Copyright © 1980 by The Dryden Press, reproduced by permission of the publisher.

347 From: "Communication in Contemporary Organizations," by R. G. Foltz. In *Inside Organizational Communication*, Second Edition, edited by C. Reuss and D. Silvis. Copyright © 1985 by Longman Publishers USA. Reprinted with permission.

350 From: D. S. Bailey and J. Foley, "Pacific Bell Works Long Distance," *Human Resource Management*, August 1990, pp. 50–52. Reprinted with permission of *HRMagazine* published by the Society for Human Resource Management, Alexandria, VA.

360 J. L. Farh and B. S. Cheng, "Cultural Relativity in Action: A Comparison of Self-Ratings Made by Chinese and US Workers," *Personnel Psychology*, 44, 1991, pp. 129–147. Reprinted by permission.

361 From: R. Levine and E. Wolff, "Social Time: The Heartbeat of Culture," *Psychology Today*, March 1985, pp. 28–25. Reprinted with permission from *Psychology Today* magazine. Copyright 1985 (Sussex Publishers, Inc.).

362 Based on the work of Edward T. Hall. From R. E. Duleck, J. S. Fielden, and J. S. Hill, International Communication: An Executive Primer," Reprinted from *Business Horizons*, January/February 1991, pp. 20–25, by the Foundation for the School of Business at Indiana University. Used with permission.

366 From: K. Labich, "The New Crisis in Business Ethics," *Fortune*, April 20, 1992, pp. 167–176. © 1992 Time, Inc. All rights reserved.

367 From: R. L. Daft and R. H. Lengel, "Business Richness: A New Approach to Managerial Behavior and Organizational Design," *Research on Organizational Behavior*, JAI Press, 1984, pp. 191–233, Vol. 6. Reprinted by permission.

372 From: R. W. Brislin, K. Cushner, C. Cherrie, and M. Yong, *Intercultural Interactions: A Practical Guide*, pp. 157–158, 164–165, 172. Copyright © 1986 by Sage Publications, Inc. Reprinted by permission of Sage Publications, Inc.

373 From: J. M. Putti and A. Chia, *Culture and Management: A Casebook*. Copyright 1990, McGraw-Hill, Inc. Reprinted by permission of McGraw-Hill, Inc.

384 M. Magnet, "Let's Go For Growth," *Fortune*, March 7, 1994, pp. 60–72. Copyright © 1994 Time, Inc.

386 From: W. M. Bulkeley, "Attention Clinton—Avoid E-Mail Overload," *The Wall Street Journal*. January 18, 1993, p. B5. Reprinted by permission of The Wall Street Journal, © 1993 Dow Jones & Company, Inc. All Rights Reserved Worldwide.

396 From: A. Shapiro, "The Uphill Struggle to Bring Quality to TV Programming," *Los Angeles Times*, August 19, 1992, pp. F1, F5. Reprinted by permission of Arnold Shapiro.

408 From: G. Morgan, *Creative Organization Theory*. Copyright © 1989 by Sage Publications, Inc. Reprinted by permission of Sage Publications, Inc.

411 From: K. Eichenwald, "He Told. He Suffered. He's a Hero," the *New York Times*, May 29, 1994, Section 3, pp. 1, 4. Copyright © 1994 by The New York Times Company. Reprinted by permission.

416 From: R. M. Steers and J. S. Black, *Organizational Behavior*, 5/e, HarperCollins, 1994. Reprinted by permission of HarperCollins College Publishers.

419 From: D. Whetton and K. Cameron, *Developing Management Skills*, 1991 HarperCollins Publishers, Inc. Reprinted by permission of HarperCollins College Publishers.

420 Reprinted from "The Empowerment of Service Workers, What, Why, How, and When," by D. E. Bowen and E. E. Lawler, III. *Sloan Management Review*, Spring 1992, pp. 31–39 by permission of publisher. Copyright 1992 by the Sloan Management Review Association. All rights reserved.

423 Reprinted by permission of *Harvard Business Review*. An exhibit from "Power is the Great Motivator," by David C. McClelland and David H. Burnham, March/April 1976. Copyright © 1976 by the President and Fellows of Harvard College. All rights reserved.

427 From: B. T. Mayes and R. T. Allen, "Conceptual Notes—Toward a Definition of Organizational Politics," *The Academy of Management Review*, October 1977, Vol. 2, No. 4, p. 675. Reprinted by permission.

430 Reprinted with the permission of The Free Press, a Division of Simon & Schuster from *The General Managers* by John P. Kotter. Copyright © 1982 by The Free Press.

435 From "Corporate Ethics," a Conference Board research report. Reprinted by permission.

436 From: D. S. Ones, C. Viswesvaran, and F. L. Schmidt, "Comprehensive Meta-Analysis of Integrity Test Validities: Findings and Implications for Personal Selection and Theories of Job Performance," *Journal of Applied Psychology*, 78, 1993, pp. 679–703. Copyright © 1993 by the American Psychological Association, and D. R. Dalton and M. B. Metzger, "Integrity Testing for Personnel Selection: An Unsparing Perspective," *Journal of Business Ethics*, 12, 147–156. Reprinted by permission of Kluwer Academic Publishers.

442 Case by Paul McLaughlin. From P. MacLaughlin, "Faking It," *Canadian Business*, June 1988, pp. 273–274. Reprinted by permission of the author.

445 G. C. Hill and K. Yamada, "Motorola Illustrates How an Aged Giant Can Remain Vibrant." Reprinted by permission of *The Wall Street Journal*, copyright © 1992, Dow Jones & Company, Inc. All Rights Reserved Worldwide.

451 Modified and reproduced by special permission of the Publisher, Consulting Psychologists Press, Inc., Palo Alto, CA 94303 from *Handbook of Industrial and Organizational Psychology*, volume 3 by M. D. Dunnette and L. M. Hough, eds. Copyright 1992 by Consulting Psychologists Press, Inc. All rights reserved. Further reproduction is prohibited without the Publisher's written consent.

455 Modified and reproduced by special permission of the Publisher, Consulting Psychologists Press, Inc., Palo Alto, CA 94303 from *Handbook of Industrial and Organizational Psychology*, volume 3 by M. D. Dunnette and L. M. Hough, eds. Copyright 1992 by Consulting Psychologists Press, Inc. All rights reserved. Further reproduction is prohibited without the Publisher's written consent.

456 From: C. K. Stevens, A. G. Bavetta, and M. E. Gist, "Gender Differences in the Acquisition of Salary Negotiation Skills: The Role of Goals, Self-Efficacy, and Perceived Control," *Journal of Applied Psychology*, 78, 1993, pp. 723–735. Reprinted by permission of the American Psychological Association.

460 "Employees Manage Conflict and Diversity," by Jennifer J. Laabs, copyright December 1993. Reprinted with the permission of *Personnel Journal*, ACC Communications, Inc., Costa Mesa, California. All rights reserved.

467 From: B. Nelson, "Bosses Face Less Risk Than Bossed," *The New York Times*, April 1, 1983, Section E, p. 16. Copyright © 1983 by The New York Times Company. Reprinted by permission.

468 "Organizational Practices for Preventing Burnout" from *Handbook of Organizational Stress Coping Strategies* by Amarjit Singh Sethi and Randall S. Schuler. Copyright © 1984 by Ballinger Publishing Company. Reprinted by permission of HarperCollins Publishers, Inc.

477 R. L. Rose, "Small Steps". Reprinted by permission of *The Wall Street Journal*. Copyright © 1993 Dow Jones & Company, Inc. All Rights Reserved Worldwide.

481 Case prepared by William E. Stratton, Idaho State University; David Efray, University of Houston—Downtown, and Kim Jardine. From: *Case Research Journal*, Spring 1993. Reprinted by permission.

499 From: Henry Mintzberg, *The Structuring of Organizations*, © 1979, p. 198. Adapted by permission of Prentice Hall, Englewood Cliffs, New Jersey.

501 From: R. Jabob, "The Struggle to Create an Organization for the 21st Century," *Fortune*, April 3, 1995, pp. 90–99. Copyright © 1995 Time, Inc. All rights reserved.

505 Excerpted from G. Fuchsburg, "Decentralized Management Can Have Its Drawbacks". Reprinted by permission of *The Wall Street Journal* © 1992 Dow Jones & Company, Inc. All Rights Reserved Worldwide.

508 Reprinted from "Designed for Learning: A Tale of Two Auto Plants," by P. S. Adler and R. E. Cole, *Sloan Management Review* (Spring, 1993) pp. 85–94, by permission of publisher. Copyright 1993 by the Sloan Management Review Association. All rights reserved; and P. S. Adler, "The Learning Bureaucracy: New United Motor Manufacturing, Inc., *Research in Organizational Behavior*, 15, 11–194, 1993.

Reprinted by permission of Jai Press, Inc.

510 From: R. E. Miles and C. C. Snow, "Causes of Failure in Network Organizations," *California Management Review*, Summer, 1992, pp. 53–72. Copyright © 1992 by The Regents of the University of California. Reprinted from the *California Management Review*, Vol. 34, No. 4. By permission of The Regents.

518 From: Marshall Sashkin and William C. Morris, *Experiencing Management* (pp. 82–85). © 1987 by Addison-Wesley Publishing Company, Inc. Reprinted by permission of the publisher.

519 From: R. C. Armandi and C. P. Heaton, "Organization Theory: An Integrative Approach", 1988 HarperCollins Publishers, Inc. Reprinted by permission of the authors.

528 From: J. Davidson, "Canada Post Returns to School," *The Canadian Press*, June 8, 1994, p. E3. Reprinted by permission.

532 From: Robert B. Duncan, "Characteristics of Organizational Environments and Perceived Environmental Uncertainty," *Administrative Science Quarterly*, 17, #3, 1972, p. 320. Reprinted by permission.

536 Reprinted by permission of Harvard Business School Press from *Organization and Environment: Managing Differentiation and Integration*, by Paul Lawrence and Jay W. Lorsch. Boston, 1986, p. 91. Copyright © 1986 by the President and Fellows of Harvard College.

541 From: E. S. Browning, "Computer Chip Project Brings Rivals Together, but The Cultures New Computer Chip Leads to Clash." Reprinted by permission of *The Wall Street Journal*, © 1994 Dow Jones & Company, Inc. All Rights Reserved Worldwide.

557 Reprinted by permission of *Harvard Business Review*. "The New Back Office Focus on Customer Services," by Richard J. Matteis, March/April, 1979. Copyright © 1979 by the President and Fellows of Harvard College. All rights reserved.

567 From: M. J. Kiernan, "The New Strategic Architecture: Learning to Compete in the Twenty-First Century," *Academy of Management Executive*, February 1993, 7–21, pp. 9, 10. Reprinted by permission.

569 From: R. K. Reger, L. T. Gustafson, S. M. DeMarie, and J. V. Mullane, "Reframing the Organization: Why Implementing Total Quality Is Easier Said Than Done," *Academy of Management Review*, 19, 565–584, 1994. Reprinted by permission.

571 From: F. Rice, "How to Make Diversity Pay," *Fortune*, August 8, 1994, pp. 78–86. Hoechst Celanese © 1994 Time, Inc. All rights reserved.

576 From: R. H. Johnson, A. M. Ryan, and M. Schmidt, "Employee Attitudes and Branch Performance at Ford Motor Credit." Presentation at the annual conference of the Society for Industrial and Organizational Psychology, 1994, Nashville, Tennessee. Reprinted by Ford Motors Credit Branches permission of Raymond Johnson.

577 From: J. W. Dean, Jr., and D. E. Bowen, "Management Theory and Total Quality: Improving Research and Practice Through Theory Development," *Academy of Management Review*, 19, 392–418, 1994. Reprinted by permission.

578 Adapted from *Continuous Improvement and Measurement for Total Quality: A Team Based Approach* by D. C. Kinlaw. Copyright © 1992 Pfeiffer & Company, San Diego, CA. Used with permission.

583 Modified and reproduced by special permission of the Publisher, Consulting Psychologists Press, Inc., Palo Alto, CA 94303 from *Handbook of Industrial and Organizational Psychology*, Vol. 3 by M. D. Dunnette and L. M. Hough, eds. Copyright 1992 by Consulting Psychologist Press, Inc. All rights reserved. Further reproduction is prohibited without the publisher's written consent.

590 From: Ralph Katz, "The Effects of Group Longevity on Project Communication and Performance," *Administrative Science Quarterly*, 1982, 27, #1, p. 96.

591 From: J. Diebold, "The Innovators: The Discoveries, Inventions, and Breakthroughs of Our Time," 1990. Truman M. Tally, an imprint of Penguin USA.

596 From: Stanley S. Budner, "Intolerance of Ambiguity as a Personality Variable," *Journal of Personality*, 30:1, (March 1962). Copyright Duke University Press, 1962. Reprinted with permission of Duke University Press and Jossey Bass, Inc. Publishers.

599 Reprinted with permission from D. Gowler, K. Legge, and C. Clegg (eds.), "Case Studies in Organizational Behavior and Human Resource Management," 2/e 1993. Copyright © 1993 Paul Chapman Publishing Ltd., London.

601 From: L. S. Richman, "How to Get Ahead in America," *Fortune*, May 16, 1994, p. 49. © 1994 Time, Inc. All rights reserved.

606 From J. L. Holland, *Making Voca-*

tional Choices: A Theory of Careers. Copyright © 1973. Reprinted by permission from Allyn & Bacon.

610 From: W. Cascio, and J. Thacker, *Managing Human Resources: Productivity, Quality of Work Life, Profit.* Copyright 1994. Reprinted by permission of McGraw-Hill, Inc. and W. Wilhelm, "Helping Workers to Self-Manage Their Careers," *Personnel Administrator.* Reprinted with the permission of *HRMagazine* published by the Society for Human Resource Management, Alexandria, VA.

612 From: *The Seasons of a Man's Life* by Daniel J. Levinson *et al.* Copyright © 1978 by Daniel J. Levinson. Reprinted by permission of Alfred A. Knopf, Inc.

614 From D. T. Hall, *Careers in Organizations.* Reprinted by permission of D. T. Hall; and E. Schein, *Career Dynamics* (adapted from pp.40–46), © 1978 by Addison-Wesley Publishing Company, Inc. Reprinted by permission of the publisher.

618 Reprinted by permission of Westpac Banking Corporation.

629 Reprinted by permission of *Harvard Business Review.* An excerpt from "The Expectant and the Endangered Promotion," by Cindee Mock and Andrea Bruno, January/February 1994. Copyright © 1994 by the President and Fellows of Harvard College. All rights reserved.

Photo Credits

1   Daniel Forster © 1994/Stock Newport
2   AP/Wide World Photos
5   © 1991 Robert Brenni/PhotoEdit
5   © B. Daemmrich/The Image Works
12   Courtesy of Marriott International
18   © Bob Daemmrich/The Image Works
20   ©MCMXCI Charles Gupton/Stock, Boston
28   © Mark Richards/PhotoEdit
33   © Jay Dickman
40   © Jim Pickerell 1982/Stock, Boston
45   Courtesy of Pearle Vision
46   PhotoEdit
48   Courtesy of AT&T Archives
55   © Wells/The Image Works
56   © Mary Kate Denny/PhotoEdit
63   Courtesy of Mary Kay Cosmetics, Inc.
69   © Chucke Nacke/Woodfin Camp & Associates
86   Bruce Young/New York Times Pictures
97   © Mike Dobel/Masterfile
98   © Nicolas Sapieha/Stock, Boston
103 © Jonathan Newton
108 Courtesy of Avon Products, Inc.
109 © Bob Daemmrich/The Image Works
120 Courtesy of Ben & Jerry's
125 Gerd Ludwig/Woodfin Camp & Associates
130 Amy Ettra/PhotoEdit
131 Courtesy of The Dow Chemical Company
144 © Robert Brenner/PhotoEdit
156 Courtesy Lincoln Electric
160 © Michael Newman/PhotoEdit
167 Mitsu Yasukawa/© 1994 New York Newsday
177 Courtesy of Dupont
178 Peter Menzel/Stock, Boston
188 Courtesy of Quad/Photo
191 James Schnepf/Woodfin Camp & Associates
195 © 1992 Lisa Quinones/Black Star
199 Courtesy of Bell Helicopter Textron
213 Courtesy of Weyerhaeuser
218 © John Coletti/Stock, Boston
220 Courtesy of L. L. Bean, Inc., Freeport, ME 04033
229 Reuters/Bettmann
230 Courtesy XEL Communications, Inc.
237 Courtesy of Change Management Products, a Division of People Tech Consulting, Inc.
249 © Michael Newman/PhotoEdit
255 Courtesy of Mike Roche
270 Bettmann
275 William Vandivert
289 © Jean-Marc Giboux/Gamma Liasion
291 Courtesy of General Electric Corporation
295 All Sport USA
297 © Bob Daemmrich/The Image Works
306 Courtesy Southwest Airlines
309 Courtesy of Tootsie Roll Industries, Inc.
309 UPI/Bettmann
315 PhotoEdit
327 Courtesy of Wendy's International, Inc.
328 UPI/Bettmann
329 © 1994 Michael A. Schwarz
340 MTV Online logo used by permission. MTV Networks, a division of Viacom International © 1995 MTV Networks. All Rights Reserved.
350 © Michael Newman/PhotoEdit
355 © Frank Siteman/The Picture Cube, Inc.
359 © John Coletti/The Picture Cube, Inc.
369 © Frank Siteman/The Picture Cube, Inc.
376 NASA
384 Photo courtesy of Pizza Hut
385 © Jim Pickerell 1992/Stock, Boston
401 Courtesy of Roberts Pharmaceutical Corporation
410 Fred R. Conrad/New York Times Pictures
416 Reuters/Bettmann
420 © Michael Newman/PhotoEdit
431 Courtesy of The Interface Group
433 Courtesy of Roberts Pharmaceutical Corporation
434 David Young Wolff/PhotoEdit
444 © Michael L. Abramson
453 © Skjold/The Image Works
458 Reuters/Bettmann
460 Courtesy of Monsanto
469 © John Simon/Gamma Liasion
476 © Sarah Putnam/The Picture Cube, Inc.
485 Stock, Boston
486 Reuters/Bettmann
501 ©John Coletti/The Picture Cube, Inc.
504 Courtesy of Food Lion
505 © Tony Freeman/PhotoEdit
508 GEO Prizm and Prizm body designs are registered trademarks of GM Corporation used by permission
513 © John Abbott
523 Courtesy of the Saturn Corporation
538 Courtesy of Union Pacific Railroad
541 Elena Rooraid/PhotoEdit
548 Courtesy of the General Electric Corporation
550 Courtesy of GTE
560 Rick Browne/Stock, Boston
571 © 1994 Vincent J. Musi
574 Fritz Hoffmann/New York Times Pictures
584 Courtesy of 3M Corporation
591 Courtesy of the Federal Express Corporation
600 © Sharon Hall
605 © F. Pedrick/The Image Works
610 Courtesy of Hewlett Packard
618 © John Coletti/The Picture Cube, Inc.
624 Courtesy of Sun Microsystems

SUBJECT INDEX

Name Index